Organizational Behavior
Online Learning Center*

www.mhhe.com/kreitner

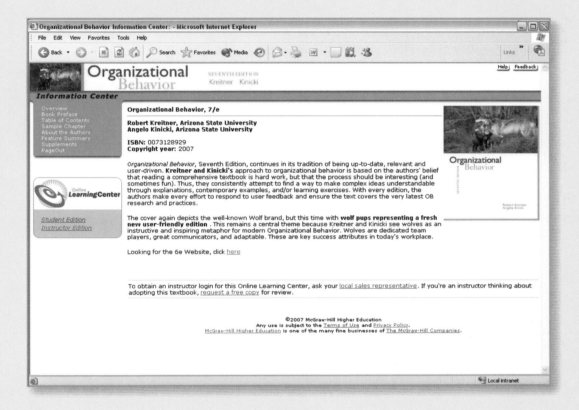

- PowerWeb articles and new updates
- Self-grading quizzes for every chapter
- Chapter reviews, including PowerPoints and Flashcards
- Internet Exercises
- Learning Modules B-E for extended study:
  - B: Self-Management
  - C: Performance Appraisal
  - D: Additional Leadership Models
  - E: Research Methods in OB

*A password-protected portion of the site is also available to instructors, offering downloadable supplements and other teaching resources.

IMPORTANT

HERE IS YOUR REGISTRATION CODE TO ACCESS MCGRAW-HILL PREMIUM CONTENT AND MCGRAW-HILL ONLINE RESOURCES

For key premium online resources you need THIS CODE to gain access. Once the code is entered, you will be able to use the web resources for the length of your course.

Access is provided only if you have purchased a new book.

If the registration code is missing from this book, the registration screen on our website, and within your WebCT or Blackboard course will tell you how to obtain your new code. Your registration code can be used only once to establish access. It is not transferable

To gain access to these online resources

1. **USE** your web browser to go to: **http://www.mhhe.com/kreitner7e**
2. **CLICK** on "First Time User"
3. **ENTER** the Registration Code printed on the tear-off bookmark on the right
4. After you have entered your registration code, click on "Register"
5. **FOLLOW** the instructions to setup your personal UserID and Password
6. **WRITE** your UserID and Password down for future reference. Keep it in a safe place.

If your course is using WebCT or Blackboard, you'll be able to use this code to access the McGraw-Hill content within your instructor's online course.

To gain access to the McGraw-Hill content in your instructor's WebCT or Blackboard course simply log into the course with the user ID and Password provided by your instructor. Enter the registration code exactly as it appears to the right when prompted by the system. You will only need to use this code the first time you click on McGraw-Hill content.

These instructions are specifically for student access. Instructors are not required to register via the above instructions.

The premium content for this book includes:
PowerWeb: articles, weekly update archive, and news feeds, organized by chapter and topic
Build Your Management Skills: Self-Assessments (detailed feedback regarding your personal management style) and Test Your Knowledge (quizzes on key management topics with personalized feedback and scoring)

Thank you, and welcome to your McGraw-Hill/Irwin Online Resources.

Kreitner/Kinicki
Organizational Behavior, 7/e
ISBN-10: 0-07-322299-2
ISBN-13: 978-0-07-322299-8

REGISTRATION CODE

3HCX–VGVC–39EN–E8DX–G9AB

REGISTRATION CODE

The McGraw-Hill Companies
McGraw-Hill Irwin

Organizational Behavior
Seventh Edition

Organizational Behavior

Seventh Edition

Robert Kreitner

Angelo Kinicki

Both of Arizona State University

McGraw-Hill
Irwin

Boston   Burr Ridge, IL   Dubuque, IA   Madison, WI   New York   San Francisco   St. Louis
Bangkok   Bogotá   Caracas   Kuala Lumpur   Lisbon   London   Madrid   Mexico City
Milan   Montreal   New Delhi   Santiago   Seoul   Singapore   Sydney   Taipei   Toronto

The McGraw·Hill Companies

McGraw-Hill
Irwin

ORGANIZATIONAL BEHAVIOR
Published by McGraw-Hill/Irwin, a business unit of The McGraw-Hill Companies, Inc.,
1221 Avenue of the Americas, New York, NY, 10020. Copyright © 2007 by The McGraw-Hill
Companies, Inc. All rights reserved. No part of this publication may be reproduced or
distributed in any form or by any means, or stored in a database or retrieval system, without the
prior written consent of The McGraw-Hill Companies, Inc., including, but not limited to, in any
network or other electronic storage or transmission, or broadcast for distance learning.

Some ancillaries, including electronic and print components, may not be available to customers
outside the United States.

This book is printed on acid-free paper.

1 2 3 4 5 6 7 8 9 0 DOW/DOW 0 9 8 7 6 5

ISBN-13: 978-0-07-312892-4
ISBN-10: 0-07-312892-9

Editorial director: *John E. Biernat*
Executive editor: *John Weimeister*
Managing developmental editor: *Laura Hurst Spell*
Associate marketing manager: *Margaret A. Beamer*
Media producer: *Benjamin Curless*
Project manager: *Dana M. Pauley*
Senior production supervisor: *Rose Hepburn*
Lead designer: *Matthew Baldwin*
Photo research coordinator: *Kathy Shive*
Photo researcher : *Sarah Evertson*
Media project manager: *Betty Hadala*
Typeface: *10/12 Times Roman*
Compositor: *Carlisle Communications, Ltd.*
Printer: *R. R. Donnelley*

Library of Congress Cataloging-in-Publication Data
Kreitner, Robert.
    Organizational behavior / Robert Kreitner, Angelo Kinicki.--7th ed.
        p.cm.
    Includes index.
    ISBN-13: 978-0-07-312892-4 (alk. paper)
    ISBN-10: 0-07-312892-9 (alk. paper)
        1. Organizational behavior. I. Kinicki, Angelo. II. Title.
    HD58.7.K766 2007
    658.3--dc22   2005053128

www.mhhe.com

About the Authors

Robert Kreitner, PhD (pictured left) is a professor emeritus of management at Arizona State University and a member of the WP Carey College of Business Faculty Hall of Fame. Prior to joining ASU in 1975, Bob taught at Western Illinois University. He also taught organizational behavior at Thunderbird. Bob is a popular speaker who has addressed a diverse array of audiences worldwide on management topics. Bob has authored articles for journals such as *Organizational Dynamics, Business Horizons,* and *Journal of Business Ethics.* He also is the co-author (with Fred Luthans) of the award-winning book *Organizational Behavior Modification and Beyond: An Operant and Social Learning Approach,* and the author of *Management,* 10th edition, a best-selling introductory management text.

Among his consulting and executive development clients have been American Express, SABRE Computer Services, Honeywell, Motorola, Amdahl, the Hopi Indian Tribe, State Farm Insurance, Goodyear Aerospace, Doubletree Hotels, Bank One–Arizona, Nazarene School of Large Church Management, US Steel, and Allied-Signal. In 1981–82 he served as chairman of the Academy of Management's Management Education and Development Division. Bob grew up in western New York state. After a four-year enlistment in the US Coast Guard, including service on the icebreaker EASTWIND in Antarctica, Bob attended the University of Nebraska–Omaha on a football scholarship. Bob also holds an MBA from the University of Nebraska–Omaha and a PhD from the University of Nebraska–Lincoln. While working on his PhD in business at Nebraska, he spent six months teaching management courses for the University in Micronesia. In 1996, Bob taught two courses in Albania's first-ever MBA program (funded by the US Agency for International Development and administered by the University of Nebraska–Lincoln). He taught a summer leadership program in Switzerland from 1995 to 1998. Bob and his wife, Margaret, live in Phoenix with a cat and a pet starling. They enjoy travel, hiking, woodcarving, and fishing.

Angelo Kinicki is a professor and Dean's Council of 100 Distinguished Scholars at WP Carey School of Business, Arizona State University. He joined the faculty in 1982, the year he received his doctorate in business administration from Kent State University. His specialty is organizational behavior.

Angelo is recognized for both his research and teaching. He has published more than 50 articles in a variety of leading academic and professional journals and has co-authored five textbooks (13, counting revisions). Angelo's experience as a researcher also resulted in his selection to serve on the editorial review boards for the *Academy of Management Journal,* the *Journal of Vocational Behavior,* and the *Journal of Management.* He received the All-Time Best Reviewer Award from the *Academy of Management Journal* for the period of 1996–99. Angelo's performance in the classroom has earned him several awards. He received the John W Teets Outstanding Graduate Teacher Award (2004–05), the Graduate Teaching Excellence Award (1999–2000), the Continuing Education Teaching Excellence Award (1992–93), and the Undergraduate Teaching Excellence Award (1988–89) from the College of Business at Arizona State University.

One of Angelo's strengths is his ability to teach students at all levels within a university. He uses an interactive environment to enhance undergraduates' understanding about management and organizational behavior. He focuses MBAs on applying management concepts to solve complex problems; PhD students learn the art and science of conducting scholarly research.

Angelo also is a busy consultant and speaker with companies around the world. His clients are many of the *Fortune* 500 companies as well as a variety of entrepreneurial firms. Much of his consulting work focuses on creating organizational change aimed at increasing organizational effectiveness and profitability. One of Angelo's most important and enjoyable pursuits is the practical application of his knowledge about management and organizational behavior.

Angelo and his wife, Joyce, have enjoyed living in the beautiful Arizona desert for 24 years but are natives of Cleveland, Ohio. They enjoy traveling, golfing, and hiking.

With love to my brothers, Clint, Phil, and Pete.

—B.K.

With love and admiration to Joyce, the wind beneath my wings.

—A.K.

Preface

Things move very fast in today's Internet-linked global economy. Competition is intense. Speed, cost, and quality are no longer the trade-offs they once were (meaning improvement in one came at the expense of one or both of the others). Today's customers want immediate access to high-quality products and services at a reasonable price. Thus, managers are challenged to simultaneously speed up the product creation and delivery cycle, cut costs, and improve quality. (And to do so in an ethical manner.) Regardless of the size and purpose of the organization and the technology involved, *people* are the common denominator when facing this immense challenge. Success or failure hinges on the ability to attract, develop, retain, motivate, and lead a diverse array of appropriately skilled people. *The human factor drives everything.* To know more about workplace behavior is to gain a valuable competitive edge. The purpose of this textbook is to help present and future organizational participants better understand and manage people at work.

Although this seventh edition of *Organizational Behavior* is aimed at undergraduate business students in similarly named courses, previous editions have proven highly versatile. *Organizational Behavior* has been used effectively in MBA programs, executive education and management development programs, and industrial and organizational psychology programs around the world. (*Note:* A special European edition is available.) This textbook is the culmination of our combined 60 years of teaching experience and research of organizational behavior and management in the United States, Pacific Rim, and Europe. Thanks to detailed feedback from students, professors, and practicing managers, this seventh edition is shorter, more refined, and better organized. Many new changes have been made in this edition, reflecting new research evidence, new management techniques, and the fruits of our own learning process.

Organizational Behavior, seventh edition, is *user driven* (as a result of carefully listening to our readers). It was developed through close *teamwork* between the authors and the publisher and is the product of *continuous improvement.* This approach has helped us achieve a difficult combination of balances. Among them are balances between theory and practice, solid content and interesting coverage, and instructive detail and readability. Students and instructors say they want an up-to-date, relevant, and interesting textbook that actively involves the reader in the learning process. Our efforts toward this end are evidenced by many new topics and real-life examples, a stimulating art program, timely new cases and boxed inserts, end-of-chapter experiential exercises for both individuals and teams, and 23 exercises integrated into the text. We realize that reading a comprehensive textbook is hard work, but we also firmly believe the process should be interesting (and sometimes fun).

GUIDED TOUR

Structural Improvements in the Seventh Edition

Part One in this seventh edition provides a foundation of understanding as well as a cultural context for the study of organizational behavior. In Parts Two through Four, the material flows from micro (individuals) to macro (groups and organizations) topics. Once again, we have tried to achieve a workable balance between micro and macro topics. As a guide for users of the previous edition, the following structural changes need to be noted:

- This seventh edition is one chapter shorter than the sixth edition and two chapters shorter than the fifth edition.

- Based on reviewer feedback, the material on abilities has been moved from Chapter 6 to Chapter 5 for tighter topical integration.

- Three motivation-related chapters in the sixth edition (8, 9, and 10) have been refined to two in this new edition. Chapter 8 now covers all the major content and process theories of motivation, plus recent developments in the area. Chapter 9 now offers tightly integrated coverage of goal setting, feedback, intrinsic and extrinsic rewards, and positive reinforcement within a performance management framework.

- Group dynamics and teamwork (Chapters 10 and 11) have been moved ahead of individual and group decision making (Chapter 12) to provide needed context.

- Participative management has been moved from the motivation area to the section on empowerment in Chapter 15 for tighter topical integration.

- The social learning model of self-management is now Learning Module B (Web), to provide space for the coverage of intrinsic rewards in Chapter 9.

- Additional leadership concepts and models have been moved to Learning Module D (Web) for on-demand bonus coverage.

- While the very popular Learning Module A (Ethics and Organizational Behavior) remains in the text following Chapter 1, Learning Modules B (Self-Management), C (Performance Appraisal), D (Additional Leadership Models), and E (Research Methods in OB) have been moved to the Web (**www.mhhe.com/kreitner**) for a slimmer book and greater on-demand topical flexibility.

Brief Contents

New and Expanded Coverage

Our readers and reviewers have kindly told us how much they appreciate our efforts to keep this textbook up-to-date and relevant. Toward that end, you will find the following important new and significantly improved coverage in the seventh edition:

Chapter 1
Some FAQs about studying OB; e-leadership; how companies are building human and social capital; Positive organizational behavior

Learning Module A
A decision tree for ethical decisions

Chapter 2
A summary of equal employment opportunity legislation in the United States; updated work force demographics; social categorization theory; surface-level and deep-level dimensions of diversity; process model of the positive and negative effects of diverse work environments

Chapter 3
Examples of embedding organizational culture; onboarding

Chapter 4
Cultural intelligence; new lessons from the GLOBE project; new research data on why US expatriates return home early; nine cross-cultural competencies

Chapter 5
Humility; self-reflection; organization-based self-esteem; Gardner's eight multiple intelligences

Chapter 6
Person–culture fit; amount of time men spend with their families; organizational response to work/family issues; cognitive dissonance; organizational commitment; psychological contracts; costs of absenteeism and turnover

Chapter 7
Galatea effect

Chapter 8
Distinction between content and process theories of motivation

Chapter 9
Performance management model; performance outcome goals and learning goals; feedback for coaching purposes; building blocks of intrinsic rewards and motivation; modern incentive pay plans

Chapter 10
New survey data on sexual harassment

Chapter 11
Developing teamwork competencies

Chapter 12
Intuition in decision making; decision-making blunders; guidelines for developing intuitive awareness; rules for brainstorming

Chapter 13
Why people avoid conflict

Chapter 14
New communication technologies, including handheld devices and blogs; listening styles; formal and informal communication channels; purposeful communication distortion; Internet usage around the world; managing e-mail; group support systems

Chapter 15
Participative management integrated into coverage of empowerment

Chapter 16
Table summarizing various approaches to leadership; characteristics of leaders and managers; expanded coverage of leadership traits; traits of bad leaders; Peter Drucker's tips for improving leadership effectiveness; full-range theory of leadership; behaviors associated with transformational leadership; shared leadership; Level 5 leadership; role of followers in leadership process

Chapter 17
W L Gore's organic organization; new example of a poorly executed merger

Chapter 18
A systems model of change; applying the systems model of change; employee assistance programs

New Feature:
Real World/Real People

While theory and research are important to the study of OB, current examples of real people in real organizational situations are needed to bring OB to life for the reader. New to this seventh edition are 71 Real World/Real People boxed inserts strategically located throughout the text. They are up-to-date (mostly drawn from 2004 or 2005 sources), often provocative, and definitely interesting. The Real World/Real People features tend to be short, for quick reading, and tightly linked to the accompanying textual discussion. They show real people at their best and sometimes at their worst. Fourteen of the Real World/Real People boxes have a diversity theme; 9 have an ethics theme; and 15 have a global theme.

Among the important and interesting topics and insights in the Real World/Real People features are building human and social capital, underemployment, mentoring, the importance of *Guanxi* in China, emotional intelligence, personal values and business, stereotypes and racial bias, feelings of inequity, 360-degree feedback, office architecture and social interaction, trust, intuitive problem solving, rewarding creativity, win–win negotiation, what really goes on during conference calls, electronics gone crazy, an executive who persuaded his kidnappers to release him unharmed, credible leadership, limits of outsourcing, and an American heading up a Japanese company.

An Entrepreneur's Odyssey: Lawyer, Baker, Manager

Four years ago, Warren Brown walked away from a job as a federal litigator to bake cakes. It all started on New Year's 1999 when Brown, an able cook, resolved to become an expert baker as well. After work, he began to whip up cakes. He found that baking provided release from the workaday stress.

[In Washington, DC,] he moved into a 600-square-foot storefront that he christened Cake Love. He funded the business with credit cards and then a $125,000 loan backed by the Small Business Administration....

With about four of his 16 bakery employees present at any one time ... and a steady stream of customers, Cake Love is easily crowded. Brown opened the Love Café across the street in 2002 to provide a little breathing room. The café... serves sandwiches and soups as well as cake....

Though he spends more time managing than frosting cakes these days, he still bakes most mornings.

SOURCE: Excerpted from Cliff, "Because Only in America Will Someone Quit a Secure Job as a Lawyer to Start a Bakery," *Inc.*, April 2005, p 77.

Featured Organizations

Organizations featured in the Real World/Real People boxes include Toyota, JetBlue Airways, Wegmans, Ernst & Young, Williams-Sonoma, Blue Cross Blue Shield of North Carolina, Rodale, Adelphia Communications, Intel, Enron, Lockheed Martin, IndyMac Bank, Wachovia Bank, Apache Corp., Crispin, Porter + Bogusky, Tennessee Bun Company, Motorola, China's Tsinghua University, Dell, Hackensack University Medical Center, Starkey Laboratories, Quest Diagnostics, Harmony, Werner Paddles, Patagonia, Burger King, Time Warner, Kmart, Sears, Hewlett-Packard, Abercrombie & Fitch, Nokia, Xerox, Sony, Mayo Clinic, Switzerland's ABB, Starbucks, Coca-Cola, Britain's GlaxoSmithKline, Marathon Oil, and Wal-Mart.

Blue Cross and Blue Shield of North Carolina (BCBSNC) Effectively Implements a Mentoring Program

Designed to identify high-potential employees, develop talent, enhance cross-functional relationships and create networking opportunities, the program consists of nine-month commitments on the part of the mentor and mentee. Employees who are accepted into the program (anyone can apply) are paired with a mentor who has completed rigorous training and is typically from a different department and/or division than the mentee. . . . Since the program's inauguration in 2000, turnover among mentees has averaged 46% lower than BCBSNC's general employee population. What's more, the BCBSNC's Corporate Leadership Council's formula for calculating the cost of turnover showed that this program, which costs less than $4,500 per year in out-of-pocket expense, generated a cost avoidance of more than $1.4 million. Additionally, 18% of mentees in 2001 and 25% in 2002 received outstanding performance ratings, compared to 10% for the general population for the same periods.

SOURCE: Excerpted from "Best Practices: Mentoring—Blue Cross and Blue Shield of North Carolina," *Training*, March 2004, p 62.

AACSB Coverage

In keeping with the curriculum recommendations from AACSB International (the Association to Advance Collegiate Schools of Business, www.aacsb.edu) for greater attention to managing in a global economy, managing cultural diversity, improving product/service quality, and making ethical decisions, we feature this coverage:

- A full chapter on international organizational behavior and cross-cultural management (Chapter 4). Comprehensive coverage from the landmark GLOBE project. To ensure integrated coverage of international topics, 15 of the Real World/Real People boxed inserts have a global theme.

- Chapter 2 offers comprehensive and up-to-date coverage of managing diversity, and 14 of the Real World/Real People boxed inserts have a diversity theme.

- Principles of total quality management (TQM) and the legacy of W Edwards Deming are discussed in Chapter 1 to establish a quality-improvement context for the entire textbook. Also, many quality-related examples have been integrated into the textual presentation.

- As outlined next, this seventh edition includes comprehensive coverage of ethics-related concepts, cases, and issues. Nine of the Real Work/Real People boxed inserts have an ethics theme.

Chapter 2

Managing Diversity: Releasing Every Employee's Potential

Learning Objectives

When you finish studying the material in this chapter, you should be able to:

1. Define diversity and review the four layers of diversity.
2. Explain the difference between affirmative action and managing diversity.
3. Describe the glass ceiling and the four top strategies used by women to break the glass ceiling.
4. Review the demographic trends pertaining to racial groups, educational mismatches, and an aging workforce.
5. Highlight the managerial implications of increasing diversity in the workforce.
6. Explain the positive and negative effects of diversity by using social categorization theory and information/decision-making theory.
7. Identify the barriers and challenges to managing diversity.
8. Discuss the organizational practices used to effectively manage diversity as identified by Ann Morrison.

By the time Gerstner took the helm in 1993, IBM already had a long history of progressive management when it came to civil rights and equal employment. Indeed, few of the company's executives would have identified workforce diversity as an area of strategic focus. But when Gerstner took a look at his senior executive team, he felt it didn't reflect the diversity of the market for talent or IBM's customers and employees. To rectify the imbalance, in 1995 Gerstner launched a diversity task-force initiative that became a cornerstone of IBM's HR strategy. The effort continued through Gerstner's tenure and remains today under current CEO Sam Palmisano.

Rather than attempt to eliminate discrimination by deliberately ignoring differences among employees, IBM created eight task forces, each focused on a different group such as Asians, gays and lesbians, and women. The goal of the initiative was to uncover and understand differences among the groups and find ways to appeal to a broader set of employees and customers.

The initiative required a lot of work, and it didn't happen overnight—the first task force convened almost two years after Gerstner's arrival.

But the IBM of today looks very different from the IBM of 1995. The number of female executives worldwide has increased by 370%. The number of ethnic minority executives born in the United States has increased by 233%. Fifty-two percent of IBM's Worldwide Management Council (WMC), the top 52 executives who determine corporate strategy, is composed of women, ethnic minorities born in the United States, and non-U.S. citizens. The organization has seen the number of self-identified gay, lesbian, bisexual, and transgender executives increase by 733% and the number of executives with disabilities more than triple.

But diversity at IBM is about more than expanding the talent pool. When I asked Gerstner what had driven the success of the task forces, he said, "We

IBM CEO Sam Palmisano. Palmisano has been CEO since 2002 and became Chairman of the Board in 2003. He started his career at IBM over 30 years ago as a sales representative.

Chapter 4

International OB: Managing across Cultures

Learning Objectives

When you finish studying the material in this chapter, you should be able to:

1. Define the term culture, and explain how societal culture and organizational culture combine to influence on-the-job behavior.
2. Define ethnocentrism, and distinguish between high-context and low-context cultures.
3. Identify and describe the nine cultural dimensions from Project GLOBE.
4. Distinguish between individualist and collectivist cultures, and explain the difference between monochronic and polychronic cultures.
5. Specify the practical lesson from the Hofstede cross-cultural study.
6. Explain what Project GLOBE researchers discovered about leadership.
7. Explain why U.S. managers have a comparatively high failure rate on foreign assignments.
8. Summarize the research findings about North American women on foreign assignments, and tell how to land a foreign assignment.
9. Identify four stages of the foreign assignment cycle and the OB trouble spot associated with each stage.

Carlos Ghosn (rhymes with "bone"), the outsider who successfully turned around Japan's Nissan Motor Co., was born in 1954 in Brazil to Lebanese immigrants and is fluent in English, Portuguese, French, and Arabic (but not Japanese). BusinessWeek recently offered this profile of Ghosn:

He's as smooth as Thai silk in public, and his colleagues marvel at his personal magnetism, his 24/7 work ethic, and his rigorous attachment to benchmarks and targets....

But Nissan insiders will also tell you there is another side to [Ghosn]. If you miss a number or blindside the boss with a nasty development, watch out.[1]

In 2005, Ghosn became the CEO of both Nissan and France's Renault, the owner of a 44% stake in Nissan. Here are some of Ghosn's observations from a recent interview:

In Japan you cannot implement change quickly unless you clearly explain why change is needed, how it will be done, and what is the committed outcome. Once the men and women of Nissan were given a clear vision, a clear strategy, clear priorities, and a framework for action,

they did change. By far the most distinct disadvantage related to the language difference....

I was determined to become assimilated, without sacrificing my individuality or originality . . . Being observant, respectful, and willing to learn helped me overcome most cultural barriers....

Ultimately, my experience has confirmed my belief that nationality is not a determining factor in success. The key is results. In Japan, as in every other country, business results can be quantified. Numbers are universal, having the same value in any market and in any time zone. At the end of the day, the thing that really matters is your performance, not your passport.[2]

FOR DISCUSSION

Why did Ghosn succeed in this difficult cross-cultural situation whereas most others probably would have failed?

Carlos Ghosn (center) greets Nissan Foundation award winners after an award ceremony at Nissan headquarters in Tokyo, March 2005.

Learning Module A
Ethics and Organizational Behavior

The loud message comes from one company after another: Surging health care costs for retired workers are creating a giant burden. So companies have been cutting health benefits for their retirees or requiring them to contribute more of the cost.

Time for a reality check: In fact, no matter how high health care costs go, well over half of large American corporations face only limited impact from the increases when it comes to their retirees. They have established ceilings on how much they will ever spend per retiree for health care. If health costs go above the caps, it's the retiree, not the company, who's responsible.

Yet numerous companies are cutting retirees' health benefits anyway. One possible factor: When companies cut these benefits, they create instant income. This isn't just the savings that come from not spending as much. Rather, thanks to complex accounting rules, the very act of cutting retirees' future health care benefits lets companies reduce a liability and generate an immediate accounting gain.

In some cases it flows straight to the bottom line. More often it sits on the books like a cookie jar, from which a company takes a piece each year that helps it meet earnings estimates. . . .

The fate of retirees can be very different. When Robert Eggleston retired from International Business Machines Corp. 12 years ago, he was paying $40 a month toward health care premiums for himself and his wife, LaRue, with IBM paying the rest. In 1993, IBM set ceilings on its own health care spending for retirees. For those on Medicare, which provides basic hospital and doctor-visit coverage, the cap was $3,000 or $3,500, depending on when they retired. For those younger than 65, the cap was $7,000 or $7,500. Spending hit the caps for the older retirees in 2001, the company says, pushing future health cost increases onto retirees' shoulders.

Mr Eggleston, 66 years old, has seen his premiums jump to $365 a month for the couple. Deductibles and copayments for drugs and doctor visits added $663 a month last year. "It just eats up all the pension," which is $850 a month, Mrs Eggleston says. Her husband has brain cancer. Though he gets free supplies of a tumor-fighting drug through a program for low-income families, he has cashed in his 401(k) account, and he and LaRue have taken out a second mortgage on their Lake Dallas, Texas, home.

IBM retirees as a group saw their health care premiums rise nearly 29% in 2003, on the heels of a 67%-plus increase in 2002. For IBM, with its caps in place, spending on retiree health care declined nearly 5%, after a drop of 18% the year before.

IBM confirms that retirees' spending has risen as its own has fallen.[1]

Comprehensive Ethics Coverage

Ethics is covered early and completely in Learning Module A (following Chapter 1) to set a proper moral tone for managing people at work. Ethical issues are raised throughout the text. Also in this seventh edition are 18 Ethical Dilemmas (one following each chapter). They raise hard-hitting ethical issues and ask tough questions, virtually guaranteeing a lively discussion/debate for cooperative learning. These Ethical Dilemmas, along with the Real World/Real People boxes, are constant reminders of the importance of ethical management.

Ethical Dilemma

Liar! Liar![89]

Calling in with a manufactured cough and a fake, throaty "I'm not feeling well" can seem rather dull compared to some excuses employers hear. . . .

Career-Builder.com, . . . commissioned a nationwide survey of 1,600 people and found that more than one-third of U.S. workers called in sick at least once last year when they felt well. . . .

Among the most unusual excuses that have been heard:

- My bus broke down and was held up by robbers.
- I was arrested as a result of mistaken identity.
- I hurt myself bowling.
- My curlers burned my hair and I had to go to the hairdresser.
- I eloped.
- My cat unplugged my alarm clock.
- I forgot to come back to work after lunch.
- I totaled my wife's Jeep in a collision with a cow.
- I had to be there for my husband's grand jury trial.
- A hit man was looking for me.

If you were a manager, how would you respond to questionable excuses such as these? (what are the ethical implications of your answer?)

1. "I call in sick sometimes when I'm not, so it would be unfair to pick on others who do the same." (So you'll do nothing?)

2. "When someone lies to me it not only insults my intelligence, it destroys any trust I might have in that person. Employees with lame excuses for not being here need to be held accountable." (Explain how.)

3. "It just shows you can't trust people. You give them an inch, they'll take a mile. Flagrant rule-breakers need to be punished as a warning to others." (Explain how.)

4. "Look, people are people. If I cut them a little slack they will return the favor by doing something extra on the job." (What about repeat offenders?)

5. Invent other responses. Discuss.

For the Chapter 1 Internet Exercise featuring The building of human capital at Intel Corp. (www.intel.com), visit our Web site at **www.mhhe.com/kreitner**.

Fresh Cases and Features

Our continuing commitment to a timely and relevant textbook is evidenced by the number of new chapter-opening vignettes and chapter-closing cases. The vignettes and cases highlight male and female role models, public and private organizations, and US and foreign companies such as IBM, General Electric, NASA, Wal-Mart, and Nissan.

Every chapter opens with a real-name, real-world vignette to provide a practical context for the material at hand. All 18 chapter-opening vignettes are new. (Learning Module A on ethics also has an opening vignette.)

Carlos Ghosn (rhymes with "bone"), the outsider who successfully turned around Japan's Nissan Motor Co., was born in 1954 in Brazil to Lebanese immigrants and is fluent in English, Portuguese, French, and Arabic (but not Japanese). *BusinessWeek* recently offered this profile of Ghosn:

> He's as smooth as Thai silk in public, and his colleagues marvel at his personal magnetism, his 24/7 work ethic, and his rigorous attachment to benchmarks and targets. . . .
>
> But Nissan insiders will also tell you there is another side to [Ghosn]. If you miss a number or blindside the boss with a nasty development, watch out.[1]

In 2005, Ghosn became the CEO of both Nissan and France's Renault, the owner of a 44% stake in Nissan. Here are some of Ghosn's observations from a recent interview:

> In Japan you cannot implement change quickly unless you clearly explain why change is needed, how it will be done, and what is the committed outcome. Once the men and women of Nissan were given a clear vision, a clear strategy, clear priorities, and a framework for action, they did change. By far the most distinct disadvantage related to the language difference. . . .
>
> I was determined to become assimilated, without sacrificing my individuality or originality. . . . Being observant, respectful, and willing to learn helped me overcome most cultural barriers. . . .
>
> Ultimately, my experience has confirmed my belief that nationality is not a determining factor in success. The key is results. In Japan, as in every other country, business results can be quantified. Numbers are universal, having the same value in any market and in any time zone. At the end of the day, the thing that really matters is your performance, not your passport.[2]

FOR DISCUSSION
Why did Ghosn succeed in this difficult cross-cultural situation whereas most others probably would have failed?

Carlos Ghosn (center) greets Nissan Foundation award winners after an award ceremony at Nissan headquarters in Tokyo, March 2005.

OB Exercise — What Are the Strategies for Breaking the Glass Ceiling?

Instructions

Read the 13 career strategies shown below that may be used to break the glass ceiling. Next, rank order each strategy in terms of its importance for contributing to the advancement of a woman to a senior management position. Rank the strategies from 1 (most important) to 13 (least important). Once this is completed, compute the gap between your rankings and those provided by the women executives who participated in this research. Their rankings are presented in endnote 23 at the back of the book.[23] In computing the gaps, use the absolute value of the gap. (Absolute values are always positive, so just ignore the sign of your gap.) Finally, compute your total gap score. The larger the gap, the greater the difference in opinion between you and the women executives. What does your total gap score indicate about your recommended strategies?

Strategy	My Rating	Survey Rating	Gap Your Rating − Survey Rating
1. Develop leadership outside office	_____	_____	_____
2. Gain line management experience	_____	_____	_____
3. Network with influential colleagues	_____	_____	_____
4. Change companies	_____	_____	_____
5. Be able to relocate	_____	_____	_____
6. Seek difficult or high visibility assignments	_____	_____	_____
7. Upgrade educational credentials	_____	_____	_____
8. Consistently exceed performance expectations	_____	_____	_____
9. Move from one functional area to another	_____	_____	_____
10. Initiate discussion regarding career aspirations	_____	_____	_____
11. Have an influential mentor	_____	_____	_____
12. Develop style that men are comfortable with	_____	_____	_____
13. Gain international experience	_____	_____	_____

SOURCE: Strategies and data were taken from B R Ragins, B Townsend, and M Mattis. "Gender Gap in the Executive Suite: CEOs and Female Executives Report on Breaking the Glass Ceiling," *Academy of Management Executive*, February 1998, pp. 28–42.

OB Exercises (23) are distributed throughout the text to foster personal involvement and greater self-awareness.

Many Older Employees Now Work for Younger Bosses[78]

For most of his 37-year career, Stephen Schechter reported to bosses older than himself. For six years, he enjoyed the luxury of answering only to himself as owner of a small public-relations agency.

It came as something of a surprise a year ago when Schechter accepted a position as vice president of 5W Public Relations in New York.

His new boss, Chief Executive Ronn Torossian, is young enough to be his son.

"This is dramatic," Schechter said of the role reversal. "It's interesting, exciting and challenging."

"Steve is older than my mom and my dad," Torossian added. "He has a lot of years of experience that I don't have."

Welcome to the 21st-century version of the generation gap. As older Americans delay retirement or return to the labor force, lured by the need for a pay-check or the desire for productive activity, they're increasingly likely to work for someone younger.

A coming shortage of skilled labor will push employers to hire 5.3 million older workers by 2010 and 14 million by 2020, according to the National Commission for Employment Policy. . . .

No one pretends these topsy-turvy arrangements are easy. Younger bosses may harbor stereotypes that older employees resist change. Older workers may regard their younger superiors as arrogant or less loyal to the company.

For Schechter and Torossian, their 30-year age difference became part of the discussion during Schechter's job interview.

"He brought it up," said Torossian, who considers Schechter's age an advantage. "As a young entrepreneur, I need to have smart, successful people around me who can give a variety of insights, regardless of their age."

Schechter says his initial challenges included learning to work within the boundaries Torossian has set for the agency and the staff, and being able to fit in with young colleagues.

"I'm learning a lot from him and from the younger people here," Schechter added. "If anything, it's really energized me and made me feel younger."

Not everyone has such smooth sailing.

"Each generation experienced very different formative years, and as a result brings very different values to the American workplace," said Chuck Underwood; president of Generational Imperative, business consultants in Cincinnati.

The baby-boomer generation, Underwood notes, is a generation that has defined itself by work.

"They made the 60-hour workweek normal," he said. "They took work calls at home and worked on weekends."

In sharp contrast, he continues, Generation X has grown up with a distrust of big business and big government, and older people in general.

"Many Xers in their childhood saw their workaholic parents suffer from fatigue, illness, substance abuse and divorce," Underwood said. "So Xers entered their career years less loyal to the company and more determined to work a reasonable workday and leave the office sharply at 5."

Underwood regards this as an important difference that older workers must recognize in younger bosses.

"It looms as a very significant challenge for younger managers to effectively manage their older subordinates," he said. "From one manager to the next, it might or might not work."

He frames it as an either/or challenge.

"Either be sensitive to each generation's strengths and weaknesses and flourish as a result of them, or don't be sensitive and flounder," he said.

Questions for Discussion

1. What are they key challenges being faced by both Stephen Schechter and Ronn Torossian?

2. If you were Ronn Torossian, what questions would you ask Mr Schechter during the job interview to ensure that he did not have trouble working for a younger boss?

3. If you were Stephen Schechter, what questions would you ask Mr Torossian in the job interview to ensure that he did not have trouble managing an older employee?

4. Do you agree with Chuck Underwood's description of baby boomers and Generation Xers? Explain your rationale.

5. Based on reading this chapter, what advice would you give to a younger manager who is managing an older employee?

Sixteen of the 18 chapter-closing **OB in Action Case Studies** are new. One **Video Case** is provided for each of the 18 chapters plus Learning Module A, each corresponding to a video included in the video package. Each case provides a written overview of the video content as well as additional background information and discussion questions that encourage students to critically examine and apply chapter concepts to analyzing the cases. Video topics and companies feature timely and interesting people, companies, and issues such as Wild Oats Market: A People-Centered Company; Cirque du Soleil: A Truly Global Workforce; Toying with Success: The McFarlane Companies; The Retirement of Jack Welch; Wal-Mart Faces the Biggest Civil Rights Case Ever; and The Columbia Space Shuttle Disaster.

Video Case
Wild Oats

Wild Oats Market is a supermarket with a difference. Since its start in Boulder, Colorado in 1987, Wild Oats has been committed to offering fresh, affordable natural and organic foods and providing knowledgeable customer service that goes beyond selling into consumer education. As it has grown, Wild Oats has reaped a reputation for being environmentally conscious, socially responsible and people-oriented.

Wild Oats sprung up as strong consumer interest in healthy eating developed. Demand for natural foods grew during the 1990s and continues to rise amid concerns about pesticides, fertilizers, artificial ingredients, and genetically-altered food. With sales topping $21 billion in 2004, natural and organic foods are moving from a niche category into the mainstream.1 With more than 100 stores in 25 U.S. states and Canada, Wild Oats is the second largest retailer of natural and organic foods.

Since Perry Odak became CEO in 2001, Wild Oats has undergone massive restructuring to evolve from a company put together by various acquisitions to one with a consistent and profitable store base. Wild Oats planned to open 20 stores in 2005 and 40 the next year.2 To increase profit margins, it has developed a private-label strategy. The company has rolled out hundreds of products under its own brand in its own stores and has tested the brand in a "store within a store" concept at a few outlets operated by other retailers. Wild Oats also has experimented with offering its private-label products online.3

Wild Oats stores are designed to offer a customer friendly shopping experience. A new store in Superior, Colorado, stands as the model outlet. It uses color and attention-getting graphics for a fresh, dynamic feel. The center of the store is open and inviting with low shelves that allow customers an unobstructed view from any area. Educational opportunities abound, including a demonstration kitchen with seating and an information center in the health and beauty aids department.4

Focusing on the customer ranks at the top of Wild Oats' values. The service expectations are higher than at traditional supermarkets, explains Peter Williams. Customers at Wild Oats' stores typically have questions and employees must be able to answer them. The company is careful to hire people who are committed to providing service and to give them the expertise they need. Employee training begins with a full-day orientation centering on the company's mission and values and how to live up to them. Then employees take a month-long course (and written test) in natural foods and receive hands-on training. While some employees were customers first before joining the staff, others were unfamiliar with natural and organic foods but were eager to learn. Once on board, Wild Oats employees share the belief that they make a difference in the health and lives of customers.

Communicating information, ideas, and concerns helps build trust and teamwork at Wild Oats. Experienced employees help new ones learn about the products. The company has an open door policy that extends all the way to the top. Its Ethics Line is an online forum available for employees to give input--anonymously--on what they see as unethical behavior.

A recent Work Life Survey, available to all employees, provided managers with lots of useful feedback and insight into why staffers like or dislike working at Wild Oats. The number one reason employees cited for working there: the company's mission and values, which they share. Among the values is giving back to the community. Each Wild Oats store chooses small, local charities to support, and the company reimburses full-time employees for up to 52 hours of volunteer work a year. Carrying out its mission of service, Wild Oats was named one of "100 Best Corporate Citizens" by Business Ethics magazine and was the highest-ranking food retailer on the list.

1. "Naturally, consumer trends skew to organic foods," DSN Retailing Today, April 11, 2005, 29.
2. Draper, Heather, "Wild Oats Still Awaits Harvest from its Big Turnaround Effort," Wall Street Journal (eastern edition), August 18, 2004, 1.
3. Duff, Mike, "Wild Oats Pushes PL Plan," DSN Retailing Today, November 22, 2004, 5.
4 ."Wild Oats Markets," Chain Store Age, February 2005, 98.

Questions for Discussion

1. What principles of TQM are evident in the management of Wild Oats? How does Wild Oats apply them?

2. In what ways does Wild Oats build human and social capital?

3. Why are "21st century managers" essential to the success of an organization like Wild Oats?

2

Pedagogical and Cooperative Learning Features

The seventh edition of *Organizational Behavior* is designed to be a complete teaching/learning tool that captures the reader's interest and imparts useful knowledge. Some of the most significant pedagogical features of this text are

- **Classic and modern topics** are given balanced treatment in terms of the latest and best available theoretical models, research evidence, and practical applications.

- Several concise **learning objectives** open each chapter to focus the reader's attention and serve as a comprehension check.

- A **colorful and lively art program** includes captioned photographs, figures, and cartoons.

- Hundreds of **real-world examples** involving large and small, public and private organizations have been incorporated into the textual material to make this edition up-to-date, interesting, and relevant.

Chapter 1 — Organizational Behavior: The Quest for People-Centered Organizations

Learning Objectives

When you finish studying the material in this chapter, you should be able to:

1. Define the term *organizational behavior*, and explain why OB is a horizontal discipline.
2. Contrast McGregor's Theory X and Theory Y assumptions about employees.
3. Identify the four principles of total quality management (TQM).
4. Define the term *e-business*, and specify at least three OB-related issues raised by e-leadership.
5. Contrast human and social capital, and explain why we need to build both.
6. Specify the five key dimensions of Luthans's CHOSE model of positive organizational behavior (POB).
7. Define the term *management*, and identify at least five of the eleven managerial skills in Wilson's profile of effective managers.
8. Characterize 21st-century managers.
9. Describe the sources of organizational behavior research evidence.

The plaque outside the ramshackle two-family house at 367 Addison St. in Palo Alto, Calif., identifies the dusty one-car garage out back as the "birthplace of Silicon Valley." But the site, where Dave Packard and Bill Hewlett first set up shop, in 1938, is more than that. It's the birthplace of a new approach to management, a West Coast alternative to the traditional, hierarchical corporation. Sixty-five years later, the methods of Hewlett and Packard remain the dominant DNA for tech companies—and a major reason for U.S. preeminence in the Information Age.

The partnership began when the pair met as students at Stanford University. Packard, an opinionated star athlete from the hardscrabble town of Pueblo, Colo., had a commanding presence to match his 6-ft.-5-in frame. Hewlett, whose technical genius was obscured from teachers by undiagnosed dyslexia, favored dorm-room pranks and bad puns. While different in temperament, the two soon discovered a shared passion for camping and fishing—and for turning engineering theory into breakthrough products.

The result was one of the most influential companies of the 20th century. Hewlett-Packard Co. (they flipped a coin to decide whose name went first) cranked out a blizzard of geeky electronic tools that were crucial to the development of radar, computers, and other digital wonders. Still, the pair's greatest innovation was managerial, not technical. From the first days in the garage, they set out to create a company that would attract like-minded techies. They shunned the rigid hierarchy of companies back East in favor of an egalitarian, decentralized system that came to be known as "the HP Way." The essence of the idea, radical at the time, was that employees' brainpower was the company's most important resource.

To make the idea a reality, the young entrepreneurs instituted a slew of pioneering practices. Starting in 1941, they granted big bonuses to all employees when the company improved

Bill Packard and Bill Hewitt

Let us now begin our exploration of the perceptual process and its associated outcomes. In this chapter we focus on (1) an information processing model of perception, (2) stereotypes, (3) the self-fulfilling prophecy, and (4) how causal attributions are used to interpret behavior.

An Information-Processing Model of Perception

Perception is a cognitive process that enables us to interpret and understand our surroundings. Recognition of objects is one of this process's major functions. For example, both people and animals recognize familiar objects in their environments. You would recognize a picture of your best friend; dogs and cats can recognize their food dishes or a favorite toy. Reading involves recognition of visual patterns representing letters in the alphabet. People must recognize objects to meaningfully interact with their environment. But since OB's principal focus is on people, the following discussion emphasizes *social perception* rather than object perception.

> **Perception**
> Process of interpreting one's environment.

The study of how people perceive one another has been labeled *social cognition* and *social information processing*. In contrast to the perception of objects,

> Social cognition is the study of how people make sense of other people and themselves. It focuses on how ordinary people think about people and how they think they think about people....
> Research on social cognition also goes beyond naive psychology. The study of social cognition entails a fine-grained analysis of how people think about themselves and others, and it leans heavily on the theory and methods of cognitive psychology.[3]

Let us now examine the fundamental processes underlying perception.

Four-Stage Sequence and a Working Example

Perception involves a four-stage information processing sequence (hence, the label "information processing"). Figure 7–1 illustrates a basic information-processing model of perception. Three of the stages in this model—selective attention/comprehension, encoding and simplification, and storage and retention—describe how specific information is observed and stored in memory. The fourth and final stage, retrieval and response, involves turning mental representations into real-world judgments and decisions.

Figure 7–1 *Perception: An Information-Processing Model*

Stage 1 Selective Attention/ Comprehension	Stage 2 Encoding and Simplification	Stage 3 Storage and Retention	Stage 4 Retrieval and Response
Competing environmental stimuli • People • Events • Objects	Interpretation and categorization	Memory	Judgments and decisions

Keep the following everyday example in mind as we look at the four stages of perception. Suppose you were thinking of taking a course in, say, personal finance. Three professors teach the same course, using different types of instruction and testing procedures. Through personal experience, you have come to prefer good professors who rely on the case method of instruction and essay tests. According to the information-processing model of perception, you would likely arrive at a decision regarding which professor to take as follows:

Stage 1: Selective Attention/Comprehension

People are constantly bombarded by physical and social stimuli in the environment. Since they do not have the mental capacity to fully comprehend all this information, they selectively perceive subsets of environmental stimuli. This is where attention plays a role. **Attention** is the process of becoming consciously aware of something or someone. Attention can be focused on information either from the environment or from memory. Regarding the latter situation, if you sometimes find yourself thinking about totally unrelated events or people while reading a textbook, your memory is the focus of your attention. Research has shown that people tend to pay attention to salient stimuli.

> **Attention**
> Being consciously aware of something or someone.

> **Salient Stimuli** Something is *salient* when it stands out from its context. For example, a 250-pound man would certainly be salient in a women's aerobics class but not at a meeting of the National Football League Players' Association. One's needs and goals often dictate which stimuli are salient. For a driver whose gas gauge is on empty, an Exxon or Mobil sign is more salient than a McDonald's or Burger King sign. The reverse would be true for a hungry driver with a full gas tank. Moreover, research shows that people have a tendency to pay more attention to negative than positive information. This leads to a negativ-

During the 2004 summer Olympics, gymnast Paul Hamm helped the United States to achieve its highest gold medal total (5) since 1979. This was a highly salient event during the Olympics.

ity bias.[4] This bias helps explain the gawking factor that slows traffic to a crawl following a car accident.

Back to Our Example You begin your search for the "right" personal finance professor by asking friends who have taken classes from the three professors. You also may interview the various professors who teach the class to gather still more relevant information. Returning to Figure 7–1, all the information you obtain represents competing environmental stimuli labeled A through F. Because you are concerned about the method of instruction (e.g., line A in Figure 7–1), testing procedures (e.g., line C), and past grade distributions (e.g., line F), information in those areas is particularly salient to you. Figure 7–1 shows that these three salient pieces of information are thus perceived, and you then progress to the second stage of information processing. Meanwhile, competing stimuli rep-

Discussion Questions

1. Why do we need people-centered organizations?

2. What reasons do you have for wanting (or not wanting) to study OB?

3. What is your personal experience with Theory X and Theory Y managers (see Table 1–1)? Which did you prefer? Why?

4. How would you respond to someone who said TQM was just a Fad, it's not relevant today?

5. What are your personal experiences with e-leadership? What practical lessons have you learned?

6. What are you doing to build human and social capital?

7. What appeals to you most (or least, or both) about the concept of positive organizational behavior (POB)?

8. Based on either personal experience as a manager or on your observation of managers at work, are the 11 skills in Table 1–4 a realistic portrayal of what managers do?

9. What is your personal experience with 21st-century managers or managers who were stuck in the past? Describe their impact on you and the organization.

10. What "practical" theories have you formulated to achieve the things you want in life (e.g., graduating, keeping fit, getting a good job, meeting that special someone)?

Personal Awareness and Growth Exercise

How Strong Is Your Motivation to Manage?

Objectives

1. To introduce a psychological determinant of managerial success.
2. To assess your readiness to manage.
3. To discuss the implications of motivation to manage, from the standpoint of global competitiveness.

Introduction

By identifying personal traits positively correlated with both rapid movement up the career ladder and managerial effectiveness, John B Miner developed a psychometric test for measuring what he calls motivation to manage. The questionnaire assesses the strength of seven factors relating to the temperament (or psychological makeup) needed to manage others. One word of caution. The following instrument is a shortened and modified version of Miner's original. Our version is for instructional and discussion purposes only. Although we believe it can indicate the *general* strength of your motivation to manage, it is *not* a precise measuring tool.

Instructions

Assess the strength of each of the seven dimensions of *your own* motivation to manage by circling the appropriate numbers on the 1 to 7 scales. Then add the seven circled numbers to get your total motivation to manage score.

Scoring and Interpretation

Arbitrary norms for comparison purposes are as follows: Total score of 7–21 = Relatively low motivation to manage; 22–34 = Moderate; 35–49 = Relatively high. How do you measure up? Remember, though, high motivation to manage is only part of the formula for managerial success. The right combination of ability and opportunity is also necessary.

Years of motivation-to-manage research by Miner and others has serious implications for America's future global competitiveness. Generally, in recent years, college students in the United States have not scored highly on motivation to manage.[85] Indeed, compared with samples of US college students, samples of students from Japan, China, Mexico,

---

Group Exercise

Timeless Advice

Objectives

1. To get to know some of your fellow students.
2. To put the management of people into a lively and interesting historical context.
3. To begin to develop your teamwork skills.

Introduction

Your creative energy, willingness to see familiar things in unfamiliar ways, and ability to have fun while learning are keys to the success of this warm-up exercise. A 20-minute, small-group session will be followed by brief oral presentations and a general class discussion. Total time required is approximately 40 to 45 minutes.

Instructions

Your instructor will divide your class randomly into groups of four to six people each. Acting as a team, with everyone offering ideas and one person serving as official recorder, each group will be responsible for writing a one-page memo to your current class. Subject matter of your group's memo will be "My advice for managing people today is. . . ." The fun part of this exercise (and its creative element) involves writing the memo from the viewpoint of the person assigned to your group by your instructor.

Among the memo viewpoints your instructor may assign are the following:

- Bill Hewlett (chapter-opening vignette).
- An ancient Egyptian slave master (building the great pyramids).

- Mary Parker Follett.
- Douglas McGregor.
- A Theory X supervisor of a construction crew (see McGregor's Theories X and Y in Table 1–1).
- W Edwards Deming.
- A TQM coordinator at 3M Company.
- A contingency management theorist.
- A Japanese auto company executive.
- The chief executive officer of IBM in the year 2030.
- Commander of the Starship Enterprise II in the year 3001.
- Others, as assigned by your instructor.

Use your imagination, make sure everyone participates, and try to be true to any historical facts you've encountered. Attempt to be as specific and realistic as possible. Remember, the idea is to provide advice about managing people from another point in time (or from a particular point of view at the present time).

Make sure you manage your 20-minute time limit carefully. A recommended approach is to spend 2 to 3 minutes putting the exercise into proper perspective. Next, take about 10 to 12 minutes brainstorming ideas for your memo, with your recorder jotting down key ideas and phrases. Have your recorder use the remaining time to write your group's one-page memo, with constructive comments and help from the others. Pick a spokesperson to read your group's memo to the class.

- **Women** play a prominent role throughout this text, as is befitting their large and growing presence in the workplace. Lots of female role models are included. Special effort has been devoted to uncovering research insights about relevant and important gender-related differences.

- **Key terms** are emphasized in bold print where they are first defined and featured in the adjacent margins for review purposes.

- A Summary of **Key Concepts** feature at the end of each chapter restates the chapter learning objectives and concisely answers them.

- Ten **discussion questions** at the end of every chapter challenge the reader to explore the personal and practical implications of what has just been covered. These questions also are useful for classroom discussion and cooperative learning.

- Thirty-six **end-of-chapter exercises** foster hands-on experiential and cooperative learning. Every chapter is concluded with a Personal Awareness and Growth Exercise and a Group Exercise, and Learning Module A ends with a Group Exercise. Each exercise has learning objectives, an introduction, clear instructions, and discussion questions to facilitate interaction and learning.

Comprehensive Supplement Package for Instructors

Videos are available in VHS (ISBN-13: 9780073128931; ISBN-10: 0073128937) or DVD (ISBN-13: 9780073128962; ISBN-10: 0073128961), and one video is provided for each of the 18 chapters plus Learning Module A. Each video has a corresponding written Video Case included at the end of the book, providing a written overview of the video content as well as additional background information and discussion questions that encourage students to critically examine and apply chapter concepts to analyzing the cases. Video topics and companies feature timely and interesting people, companies, and issues, as noted earlier.

The all-in-one **Instructor's Presentation CD-ROM** (ISBN-13: 9780073128955; ISBN-10: 0073128953) includes the Instructor's Manual, Test Bank, EZ Test, and PowerPoint.

- **Instructor's Manual.** Prepared by Kim J Wade of Washington State University, each chapter includes a chapter summary, opening-vignette solution, lecture outline, discussion questions for Real World/Real People boxes, OB in Action Case Solution, Personal Awareness and Growth Exercise notes, Group Exercise notes, list of resources, one or two lecturettes, one or two additional exercises (including an integrative case featuring fictional manager Roberta), and transparency masters and handouts corresponding to lecture materials and exercises. The manual also contains integrative video case teaching notes and transparency masters for highlighting key text concepts.

- **EZ Test.** McGraw-Hill's flexible and easy-to-use electronic testing program allows instructors to create tests from book-specific items. It accommodates a wide range of question types, and instructors may add their own questions. Multiple versions of the test can be created, and any test can be exported for use with course management systems such as WebCT or BlackBoard. EZ Test Online allows

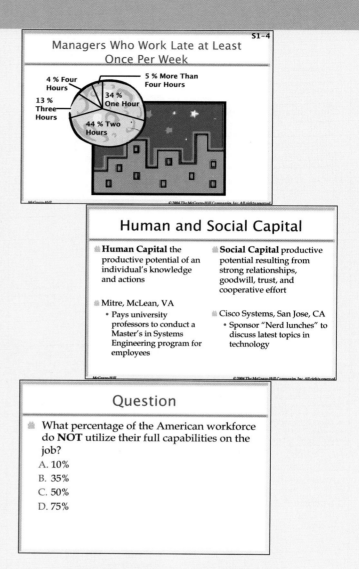

you to administer EZ Test–created exams and quizzes online. The test bank includes approximately 100 test questions per chapter, including true–false, multiple choice, and essay, with answers, page references, and level coding.

- The **improved PowerPoint slides** (prepared by Paige Wolf of George Mason University) are designed to (1) be meaningful lessons for students that encourage active thinking and participation and (2) allow the instructor to have at his or her fingertips the information he or she wants to convey for each slide. Two sets of slides are available for every chapter: one set recaps key concepts, tables, and figures from the text; another provides supplemental examples, charts, and data from outside sources to enhance lecture presentations. eInstruction discussion questions (CPS) are also included in the PowerPoint slides.

The Latest in Technology

The new **Group and Video Resource Manual: An Instructor's Guide to an Active Classroom** (ISBN-13: 9780073044347; ISBN-10: 0073044342) contains everything instructors need to successfully integrate McGraw-Hill technology and additional group activities into the classroom. It includes a menu of items that can be used as teaching tools in class. All of the Build Your Management Skills (self-assessments and Test Your Knowledge) exercises as well as the Hot Seat DVD segments have teaching notes included here, with additional PowerPoint slides (in printed forms) to use in class. In addition, group exercises are included with anything a professor would need to use this exercise in class—handouts, figures, and so forth. The manual is organized into 25 topics such as ethics, decision making, change, and leadership. Each teaching resource is then organized by topic for easy inclusion in a lecture. A matrix at the front of the manual references each resource by topic, and a book-specific matrix is also included on the OLC. PPT files are also included on the individual book OLCs (in the instructor center). All of the actual exercises and assessments are included on the OLC for student access, and the Hot Seat DVD can be packaged with the book.

PageOut is McGraw-Hill's unique point-and-click course Web site tool, enabling you to create a full-featured, professional-quality course Web site without knowing HTML coding. With PageOut you can post your syllabus online, assign McGraw-Hill Online Learning Center or eBook content, add links to important off-site resources, and maintain student results in the online grade book. You can send class announcements, copy your course site to share with colleagues, and upload original files. PageOut is free for every McGraw-Hill/Irwin user.

You can customize this text. **McGraw-Hill/Primis Online's digital database** offers you the flexibility to customize your course, including material from the largest online collection of textbooks, readings, and cases. Primis leads the way in customized eBooks with hundreds of titles available at prices that save your students more than 20% off bookstore prices. Additional information is available at 800-228-0634.

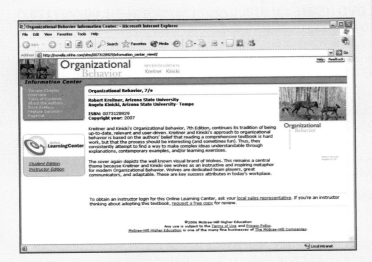

The **Online Learning Center (OLC),** www.mhhe.com/kreitner, is a Web site that follows the text chapter-by-chapter. As students read the book, they can go online to take self-grading quizzes, review material, or work through interactive exercises. Also included are the Build Your Management Skills exercises (e.g., Active Listening Skills, Assessing Your Leader–Member Exchange, Team Roles Preference, etc.), and Learning Modules B–E. OLCs can be delivered multiple ways—professors and students can access them directly through the textbook Web site, through PageOut, or within a course management system.

For Students

Online Learning Center

Visit the book's Web site at www.mhhe.com/kreitner to access self-grading quizzes and chapter review materials, Build Your Management Skills exercises (e.g., Active Listening Skills, Assessing Your Leader–Member Exchange, Team Roles Preference, etc.), Internet Exercises, and additional Learning Modules.

Manager's Hot Seat DVD (ISBN-13: 9780072971767; ISBN-10: 0072971762)

The exercises on this DVD blend real managers with difficult, unscripted situations. This DVD puts students in the hot seat, as they watch the videos, review concepts, and consider other documents before deciding how they would react if they were in the manager's shoes. The Manager's Hot Seat DVD is $5.00 when packaged with any book.

PowerWeb

Harness the assets of the Web to keep your course current with PowerWeb! Now integrated by chapter into the book's online learning center, this resource provides high-quality, peer-reviewed content, including up-to-date articles from leading periodicals and journals, current news, weekly updates with assessment, interactive exercises, Web research guide, study tips, and much more. www.dushkin.com/powerweb.

BusinessWeek Edition

Your students can subscribe to *BusinessWeek* for a specially priced rate of $8.25 in addition to the price of the text when instructors order the *BusinessWeek* Edition. Students will receive a pass code card shrink-wrapped with their new text. The card directs students to a Web site where they enter the code and then gain access to *BusinessWeek*'s registration page to enter address info and set up their print and online subscription as well. To learn more on how to get this package, please contact your sales representative.

Words of Appreciation

This textbook is the fruit of many people's labor. Our colleagues at Arizona State University have been supportive from the start. Through the years, our organizational behavior students at ASU, Thunderbird, and the University of Tirana (Albania) have been enthusiastic and candid academic "customers." We are grateful for their feedback and we hope we have done it justice in this new edition. Sincere appreciation goes to Kim Wade of Washington State University, for her skillful and dedicated work on the *Instructor's Resource Manual* and *Test Bank*. Thank you to Paige Wolf of George Mason University for creating the unique and dynamic PowerPoint presentation. Thank you to Carrie Peters for a very professional job of managing our permissions.

To the manuscript reviewers spanning the prior six editions go our gratitude and thanks. Their feedback was thoughtful, rigorous, constructive, and above all, essential to our goal of *kaizen* (continuous improvement). Our reviewers and focus group participants for this edition were:

Glenda Barrett
University of Maryland University College

Sid Barsuk
Roosevelt University

Beth G Chung-Herrera
San Diego State University

Carmen C Daniels
Columbus State Community College

Ken Dunegan
Cleveland State University

Sandra Edwards
Northeastern State University

Janice S Gates
Western Illinois University

Fred Hughes
Faulkner University

Marvin Loper
Oregon State University

Edward W Miles
Georgia State University

Audrey J Murrell
University of Pittsburgh

Elizabeth C Ravlin
University of South Carolina

Clint Relyea
Arkansas State University

James M Schmidtke
California State University–Fresno

Marjorie Smith
Mountain State University

David Tansik
University of Arizona

Paige P Wolf
George Mason University

Special thanks go to our dedicated "pack" at McGraw-Hill/Irwin: our editors, John Weimeister and Laura Hurst Spell; our marketing team, Meg Beamer and Jared Harless; and our design and production team, Matt Baldwin, Sara Evertson, Dana Pauley, Rose Hepburn, Kathy Shive, Ben Curless, and Betty Hadala.

Finally, we would like to thank our wives, Margaret and Joyce, for being tough and caring "first customers" of our work. This book has been greatly enhanced by their common sense, reality testing, and managerial experience. Thanks in large measure to their love and moral support, this project again was completed on time and it strengthened rather than strained a treasured possession—our friendship.

We hope you enjoy this textbook. Best wishes for success and happiness!

Bob Kreitner
Angelo Kinicki

Brief Contents

Contents

Chapter Nine

Improving Job Performance with Goals, Feedback, Rewards, and Positive Reinforcement 268

Part Three

Group and Social Processes 301

Chapter Ten

Group Dynamics 302

Chapter Eleven
Teams and Teamwork   338

Chapter Twelve
**Individual and Group
Decision Making   370**

The World of Organizational Behavior

Organizational Behavior: The Quest for People-Centered Organizations

Learning Objectives

When you finish studying the material in this chapter, you should be able to:

1 Define the term *organizational behavior,* and explain why OB is a horizontal discipline.

2 Contrast McGregor's Theory X and Theory Y assumptions about employees.

3 Identify the four principles of total quality management (TQM).

4 Define the term *e-business,* and specify at least three OB-related issues raised by e-leadership.

5 Contrast human and social capital, and explain why we need to build both.

6 Specify the five key dimensions of Luthans's CHOSE model of positive organizational behavior (POB).

7 Define the term *management,* and identify at least five of the eleven managerial skills in Wilson's profile of effective managers.

8 Characterize 21st-century managers.

9 Describe the sources of organizational behavior research evidence.

The plaque outside the ramshackle two-family house at 367 Addison St. in Palo Alto, Calif., identifies the dusty one-car garage out back as the "birthplace of Silicon Valley." But the site, where Dave Packard and Bill Hewlett first set up shop, in 1938, is more than that. It's the birthplace of a new approach to management, a West Coast alternative to the traditional, hierarchical corporation. Sixty-five years later, the methods of Hewlett and Packard remain the dominant DNA for tech companies—and a major reason for U.S. preeminence in the Information Age.

The partnership began when the pair met as students at Stanford University. Packard, an opinionated star athlete from the hardscrabble town of Pueblo, Colo., had a commanding presence to match his 6-ft.-5-in frame. Hewlett, whose technical genius was obscured from teachers by undiagnosed dyslexia, favored dorm-room pranks and bad puns. While different in temperament, the two soon discovered a shared passion for camping and fishing—and for turning engineering theory into breakthrough products.

The result was one of the most influential companies of the 20th century. Hewlett-Packard Co. (they flipped a coin to decide whose name went first) cranked out a blizzard of geeky electronic tools that were crucial to the development of radar, computers, and other digital wonders. Still, the pair's greatest innovation was managerial, not technical. From the first days in the garage, they set out to create a company that would attract like-minded techies. They shunned the rigid hierarchy of companies back East in favor of an egalitarian, decentralized system that came to be known as "the HP Way." The essence of the idea, radical at the time, was that employees' brainpower was the company's most important resource.

To make the idea a reality, the young entrepreneurs instituted a slew of pioneering practices. Starting in 1941, they granted big bonuses to all employees when the company improved

Dave Packard and Bill Hewlett.

its productivity. That evolved into one of the first all-company profit-sharing plans. When HP went public in 1957, the founders gave shares to all employees. Later, they were among the first to offer tuition assistance, flex time, and job sharing.

Even HP's offices were unusual. To encourage the free flow of ideas, employees worked in open cubicles. Even supply closets were to be kept open. Once, Hewlett sawed a lock off a closet and left a note:

"HP trusts its employees."

If HP's policies were progressive, there was nothing coddling about either man. Until his death in 1996, Packard was a fearsome paragon of corporate integrity. He was famous for flying to distant branches to make a show of firing managers who skirted ethical lines. Neither man would hesitate to kill a business if it wasn't hitting its profits goals. The result: HP grew nearly 20% a year for 50 years without a loss.

Today, the behavior of the two founders remains a benchmark for business. Hewlett, who died in 2001, and Packard expected employees to donate their time to civic causes. And they gave more than 95% of their fortunes to charity. "My father and Mr. Packard felt they'd made this money almost as a fluke," says Hewlett's son Walter. "If anything, the employees deserved it more than they did." It's an insight that changed Corporate America—and the lives of workers everywhere.[1]

FOR DISCUSSION
Which of HP's employee-friendly practices do you think had the greatest motivational impact?

Hewlett-Packard's founders did more than talk about the importance of their people; they trusted, empowered, and listened to them. They created what Stanford University's Jeffrey Pfeffer calls a "people-centered" organization. Research evidence from companies in both the United States and Germany shows the following seven *people-centered practices* to be strongly associated with much higher profits and significantly lower employee turnover:

1. Job security (to eliminate fear of layoffs).
2. Careful hiring (emphasizing a good fit with the company culture).
3. Power to the people (via decentralization and self-managed teams).
4. Generous pay for performance.
5. Lots of training.
6. Less emphasis on status (to build a "we" feeling).
7. Trust building (through the sharing of critical information).[2]

Importantly, these factors are a *package* deal, meaning they need to be installed in a coordinated and systematic manner—not in bits and pieces.

According to Pfeffer, only 12% of today's organizations have the systematic approaches and persistence to qualify as true people-centered organizations, thus giving them a competitive advantage.[3] Dan Rosensweig, Yahoo's chief operating officer, knows what it takes. He recently told *Fast Company* magazine: "From the outside, my guess is most people think about the incredible technology we have. But what really matters is our people."[4]

To us, an 88% shortfall in the quest for people-centered organizations represents a tragic waste of human and economic potential. There are profound ethical implications as well. Each of us needs to accept the challenge to do better, whatever our role(s) in society—employer/entrepreneur, employee, manager, stockholder, student, teacher, voter, elected official, social/political activist. Toward that end, the mission of this book is to help increase the number of people-centered organizations around the world to improve the general quality of life.[5]

The purpose of this first chapter is to define organizational behavior (OB), examine its contemporary relevance, explore its historical and managerial contexts, and introduce a topical roadmap for the balance of this book.

Welcome to the World of OB

Organizational behavior deals with how people act and react in organizations of all kinds. Think of the many organizations that touch your life on a regular basis; organizations that employ, educate, serve, inform, feed, heal, protect, and entertain you. Cradle to grave, we interface with organizations at every turn. According to Chester I Barnard's classic definition, an **organization** is "a system of consciously coordinated activities or forces of two or more persons."[6] Organizations are a social invention helping us to achieve things collectively that we could not achieve alone. For better or for worse, they extend our reach. Consider the inspiring example of the World Health Organization (WHO):

> In 1967, 10 to 15 million people around the globe were struck annually by smallpox. That year, the World Health Organization set up its smallpox-eradication unit. In 13 years it was able to declare the world free of the disease. In 1988, 350,000 people were afflicted by polio when the WHO set up a similar eradication unit. Since then it has spent $3 billion and received the help of 20 million volunteers from around the world. The result: in 2003 there were only 784 reported cases of polio.[7]

On the other hand, organizations such as *Al Qaeda* kill and terrorize, and others such as Enron squander our resources. Organizations are the chessboard upon which the game of life is played. To know more about *organizational* behavior—life within organizations—is to know more about the nature, possibilities, and rules of that game.

Organization
System of consciously coordinated activities of two or more people.

Organizational Behavior: An Interdisciplinary Field

Organizational behavior, commonly referred to as OB, is an interdisciplinary field dedicated to better understanding and managing people at work. By definition, organizational behavior is both research and application oriented. Three basic levels of analysis in OB are individual, group, and organizational. OB draws upon a diverse array of disciplines, including psychology, management, sociology, organization theory, social psychology, statistics, anthropology, general systems theory, economics, information technology, political science, vocational counseling, human stress management, psychometrics, ergonomics, decision theory, and ethics. This rich heritage has spawned many competing perspectives and theories about human work behavior. By 2003, one researcher had identified 73 distinct theories about behavior within the field of OB.[8]

Organizational behavior
Interdisciplinary field dedicated to better understanding and managing people at work.

Some FAQs about Studying OB

Through the years we (and our colleagues) have fielded some frequently asked questions (FAQs) from our students about our field. Here are the most common ones, along with our answers.

Why Study OB?   If you thoughtfully study this book, you will learn more about yourself, how to interact effectively with others, and how to thrive (not just survive) in organizations. Lots of insights about your own personality, emotions, values, job satisfaction,

Figure 1–1   *OB-Related Skills Are the Ticket to Ride the Virtuous Career Spiral*

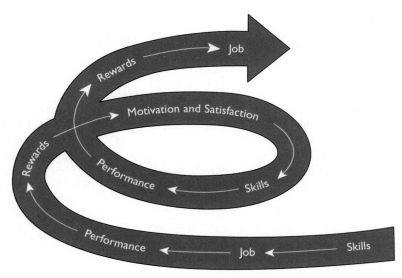

SOURCE: Edward E Lawler III, *Treat People Right! How Organizations and Individuals Can Propel Each Other into a Virtuous Spiral of Success,* © 2003, p 21. Reprinted with permission of John Wiley & Sons, Inc.

perceptions, needs, and goals are available in Part Two. Relative to your interpersonal effectiveness, you will learn about being a team player, building trust, managing conflict, negotiating, communicating, and influencing and leading others. We conclude virtually every major topic with practical how-to-do-it instructions. The idea is to build your skills in areas such as self-management, making decisions, avoiding groupthink, listening, coping with organizational politics, handling change, and managing stress. Respected OB scholar Edward E Lawler III created the "virtuous career spiral" in Figure 1–1 to illustrate how OB-related skills point you toward career success. "It shows that increased skills and performance can lead to better jobs and higher rewards."[9]

If I'm an Accounting (or Other Technical Major), Why Should I Study OB?
Many students in technical fields such as accounting, finance, computer science, and engineering consider OB to be a "soft" discipline with little or no relevance. You may indeed start out in a narrow specialty, but eventually your hard-won success will catch up with you and you will be tapped for some sort of supervisory or leadership position. Your so-called "soft" people skills will make or break your career at that point. Also, in today's team-oriented and globalized workplace, your teamwork, cross-cultural, communication, conflict handling, and negotiation skills and your powers of persuasion will be needed early and often. Our advice: Build a solid base of OB-related skills now to be ready for whatever comes along (see Real World/Real People).

Can I Get a Job in OB?
Organizational behavior is an academic designation. With the exception of teaching/research positions, OB is not an everyday job category such as accounting, marketing, or finance. Students of OB typically do not get jobs in organizational behavior, per se. This reality in no way demeans OB or lessens its importance in ef-

An Entrepreneur's Odyssey: Lawyer, Baker, Manager

Four years ago, Warren Brown walked away from a job as a federal litigator to bake cakes. It all started on New Year's 1999 when Brown, an able cook, resolved to become an expert baker as well. After work, he began to whip up cakes. He found that baking provided release from the workaday stress.

[In Washington, DC,] he moved into a 600-square-foot storefront that he christened Cake Love. He funded the business with credit cards and then a $125,000 loan backed by the Small Business Administration....

With about four of his 16 bakery employees present at any one time ... and a steady stream of customers, Cake Love is easily crowded. Brown opened the Love Café across the street in 2002 to provide a little breathing room. The café ... serves sandwiches and soups as well as cake....

Though he spends more time managing than frosting cakes these days, he still bakes most mornings.

Warren Brown

SOURCE: Excerpted from P Cliff, "Because Only in America Will Someone Quit a Secure Job as a Lawyer to Start a Bakery," *Inc.*, April 2005, p 77.

fective organizational management. OB is a *horizontal* discipline cutting across virtually every job category, business function, and professional specialty. Anyone who plans to make a living in a large or small, public or private, organization needs to study organizational behavior.

A Historical Perspective of OB

A historical perspective of the study of people at work helps in studying organizational behavior. According to a management history expert, this is important because

> Historical perspective is the study of a subject in light of its earliest phases and subsequent evolution. Historical perspective differs from history in that the object of historical perspective is to sharpen one's vision of the present, not the past.[10]

In other words, we can better understand where the field of OB is today and where it appears to be headed by appreciating where it has been and how it is being redirected. Let us examine five significant landmarks in the understanding and management of people in the workplace.

1. The human relations movement.
2. The quality movement.

3. The e-business revolution.
4. The age of human and social capital.
5. The emerging area of positive OB.

The Human Relations Movement

A unique combination of factors during the 1930s fostered the human relations movement. First, following legalization of union–management collective bargaining in the United States in 1935, management began looking for new ways of handling employees. Second, behavioral scientists conducting on-the-job research started calling for more attention to the "human" factor. Managers who had lost the battle to keep unions out of their factories heeded the call for better human relations and improved working conditions. One such study, conducted at Western Electric's Chicago-area Hawthorne plant, was a prime stimulus for the human relations movement. Ironically, many of the Hawthorne findings have turned out to be more myth than fact.

These relay assembly test room employees in the classic Hawthorne Western Electric studies turned in record performance. Why? No one knows for certain, and debate continues to this day. Supportive supervision was long believed to be the key factor. Whatever the reason, Hawthorne gave the budding human relations movement needed research credibility.

The Hawthorne Legacy Interviews conducted decades later with three subjects of the Hawthorne studies and reanalysis of the original data with modern statistical techniques do not support initial conclusions about the positive effect of supportive supervision. Specifically, money, fear of unemployment during the Great Depression, managerial discipline, and high-quality raw materials—not supportive supervision—turned out to be responsible for high output in the relay assembly test room experiments.[11] Nonetheless, the human relations movement gathered momentum through the 1950s, as academics and managers alike made stirring claims about the powerful effect that individual needs, supportive supervision, and group dynamics apparently had on job performance.

The Writings of Mayo and Follett Essential to the human relations movement were the writings of Elton Mayo and Mary Parker Follett. Australian-born Mayo, who headed the Harvard researchers at Hawthorne, advised managers to attend to employees' emotional needs in his 1933 classic, *The Human Problems of an Industrial Civilization.* Follett was a true pioneer, not only as a woman management consultant in the male-dominated industrial world of the 1920s, but also as a writer who saw employees as complex combinations of attitudes, beliefs, and needs. Mary Parker Follett was way ahead of her time in telling managers to motivate job performance instead of merely demanding it, a "pull" rather than "push" strategy. She also built a logical bridge between political democracy and a cooperative spirit in the workplace.[12]

McGregor's Theory Y In 1960, Douglas McGregor wrote a book entitled *The Human Side of Enterprise,* which has become an important philosophical base for the modern view of people at work.[13] Drawing upon his experience as a management consultant, McGregor formulated two sharply contrasting sets of assumptions about human nature (see Table 1–1). His

Table 1–1   *McGregor's Theory X and Theory Y*

Outdated (Theory X) Assumptions about People at Work	Modern (Theory Y) Assumptions about People at Work
1. Most people dislike work; they avoid it when they can.	1. Work is a natural activity, like play or rest.
2. Most people must be coerced and threatened with punishment before they will work. People require close direction when they are working.	2. People are capable of self-direction and self-control if they are committed to objectives.
3. Most people actually prefer to be directed. They tend to avoid responsibility and exhibit little ambition. They are interested only in security.	3. People generally become committed to organizational objectives if they are rewarded for doing so.
	4. The typical employee can learn to accept and seek responsibility.
	5. The typical member of the general population has imagination, ingenuity, and creativity.

SOURCE: Adapted from D McGregor, *The Human Side of Enterprise*, McGraw-Hill, © 1960, Ch 4. Reprinted by permission of The McGraw-Hill Companies, Inc.

Theory X assumptions were pessimistic and negative and, according to McGregor's interpretation, typical of how managers traditionally perceived employees. To help managers break with this negative tradition, McGregor formulated his **Theory Y,** a modern and positive set of assumptions about people. McGregor believed managers could accomplish more through others by viewing them as self-energized, committed, responsible, and creative beings.[14]

According to this recent overview from *HR Magazine,* McGregor's Theory Y is still a distant vision in the American workplace:

> With strikingly similar statistics, several highly respected research and consulting organizations have found that there's a huge population of workers—roughly half of all Americans in the workforce—who show up, do what's expected of them, but don't go that extra mile, don't turn on the creative juices, don't get inspired to create great products or services.
>
> Perhaps the most significant finding: These are people, for the most part, who want to go above and beyond, to be an integral part of the company's success. Something—often a disconnect with an immediate supervisor or a feeling that the organization doesn't care about them—is getting in the way. There is a huge, untapped potential that many executives, managers and employees do not recognize and, therefore, have not addressed. And it's sapping organizations' potential.
>
> "We're running as an economy at 30% efficiency" because so many workers are not contributing as much as they could, says Curt Coffman [from the Gallup Organization].[15]

Theory Y
McGregor's modern and positive assumptions about employees being responsible and creative.

New Assumptions about Human Nature

Unfortunately, unsophisticated behavioral research methods caused the human relationists to embrace some naive and misleading conclusions.[16] For example, human relationists believed in the axiom, "A satisfied employee is a hardworking employee." Subsequent research, as discussed later in this book, shows the satisfaction—performance linkage to be more complex than originally thought.

Despite its shortcomings, the human relations movement opened the door to more progressive thinking about human nature. Rather than continuing to view employees as passive economic beings, managers began to see them as active social beings and took steps to create more humane work environments.

The Quality Movement

In 1980, NBC aired a television documentary titled "If Japan Can . . . Why Can't We?" It was a wake-up call for North American companies to dramatically improve product quality or continue losing market share to Japanese electronics and automobile companies. A full-fledged movement ensued during the 1980s and 1990s. Much was written, said, and done about improving the quality of both goods and services.[17] Thanks to the concept of *total quality management* (TQM) and Six Sigma programs, the quality of the goods and services we purchase today is significantly better than in years past. The underlying principles of TQM are more important than ever given customers' steadily rising expectations:

> Establish a reputation for great value, top quality, or pulling late-night miracles in time for crucial client meetings, and soon enough, the goalposts move. "Greatness" lasts only as long as someone fails to imagine something better. Inevitably, the exceptional becomes the expected.
>
> Call it the performance paradox: If you deliver, you only qualify to deliver more. Great companies and their employees have always endured this treadmill of expectations. But these days, the brewing forces of technology, productivity, and transparency have accelerated the cycle to breakneck speed.[18]

TQM principles have profound practical implications for managing people today.[19]

Total quality management
An organizational culture dedicated to training, continuous improvement, and customer satisfaction.

What Is TQM?   Experts on the subject offered this definition of **total quality management:**

> TQM means that the organization's culture is defined by and supports the constant attainment of customer satisfaction through an integrated system of tools, techniques, and training. This involves the continuous improvement of organizational processes, resulting in high-quality products and services.[20]

Quality consultant Richard J Schonberger sums up TQM as "continuous, customer-centered, employee-driven improvement."[21] TQM is necessarily employee driven because product/service quality cannot be continuously improved without the active learning and participation of *every* employee. Thus, in successful quality improvement programs, TQM principles are embedded in the organization's culture. In fact, according to the results of a field experiment, bank customers had higher satisfaction after interacting with bank employees who had been trained to provide excellent service.[22]

The Deming Legacy   TQM is firmly established today thanks in large part to the pioneering work of W Edwards Deming.[23] Ironically, the mathematician credited with Japan's post–World War II quality revolution rarely talked in terms of quality. He instead preferred to discuss "good management" during the hard-hitting seminars he delivered right up until his death at age 93 in 1993.[24] Although Deming's passion was the statistical measurement and reduction of variations in industrial processes, he had much to say about how employees should be treated. Regarding the human side of quality improvement, Deming called for the following:

Toyota Wrote the Book on Continuous Improvement

The soul of the Toyota production system is a principle called *kaizen*. The word is often translated as "continuous improvement," but its essence is the notion that engineers, managers, and line workers collaborate continually to systematize production tasks and identify incremental changes to make work go more smoothly.

Toyota strives to keep inventories as close to zero as possible, not only to minimize costs but also to ferret out inefficiencies the moment they occur. Toyota deliberately runs production lines at full tilt. And workers are given authority to stop the process and summon assistance at the first sign of trouble.

At the Tsutsumi plant in Toyota City, 6,600 employees working two shifts on two separate production lines can turn out 500,000 vehicles a year in eight model variations at a rate of one per minute. It is a ballet of astonishing precision, enhanced by a myriad of tiny improvements on the factory floor.

It takes local talent
to build
world-class engines.

TOYOTA

SOURCE: C Chandler, "Full Speed Ahead," *Fortune*, February 7, 2005, p 82.

- Formal training in statistical process control techniques and teamwork.
- Helpful leadership, rather than order giving and punishment.
- Elimination of fear so employees will feel free to ask questions.
- Emphasis on continuous process improvements rather than on numerical quotas.
- Teamwork.
- Elimination of barriers to good workmanship.[25]

One of Deming's most enduring lessons for managers is his 85–15 rule.[26] Specifically, when things go wrong, there is roughly an 85% chance the *system* (including management, machinery, and rules) is at fault. Only about 15% of the time is the individual employee at fault. Unfortunately, as Deming observed, the typical manager spends most of his or her time wrongly blaming and punishing individuals for system failures. Statistical analysis is required to uncover system failures.

Principles of TQM   Despite variations in the language and scope of TQM programs, it is possible to identify four common TQM principles:

1. Do it right the first time to eliminate costly rework and product recalls.
2. Listen to and learn from customers and employees.
3. Make continuous improvement an everyday matter (see Real World/Real People).
4. Build teamwork, trust, and mutual respect.[27]

Deming's influence is clearly evident in this list.[28] Once again, as with the human relations movement, we see *people* as the key factor in organizational success.

In summary, TQM advocates have made a valuable contribution to the field of OB by providing a *practical* context for managing people. The case for TQM is strong because, as discovered in two comprehensive studies, *it works!*[29] When people are managed according to TQM principles, more of them are likely to get the employment opportunities and high-quality goods and services they demand.[30] As you will see many times in later chapters, this book is anchored to Deming's philosophy and TQM principles.

The Internet and E-Business Revolution

E-business

Running the *entire* business via the Internet.

Experts on the subject draw an important distinction between *e-commerce* (buying and selling goods and services over the Internet) and **e-business,** using the Internet to facilitate *every* aspect of running a business.[31] Says one industry observer: "Strip away the highfalutin talk, and at bottom, the Internet is a tool that dramatically lowers the cost of communication. That means it can radically alter any industry or activity that depends heavily on the flow of information."[32] Relevant information includes everything from customer needs and product design specifications to prices, schedules, finances, employee performance data, and corporate strategy. Intel has taken this broad view of the Internet to heart. The computer-chip giant is striving to become what it calls an e-corporation, one that relies primarily on the Internet to not only buy and sell things, but to facilitate all business functions, exchange knowledge among its employees, and build partnerships with outsiders as well. Intel is on the right track according to this survey finding: "firms that embraced the Internet averaged a 13.4% jump in productivity . . . compared with 4.9% for those that did not."[33]

E-business has significant implications for OB because it eventually will seep into every corner of life both on and off the job. Thanks to the Internet, we are able to make quicker and better decisions because of speedy access to vital information. The Internet also allows us to seemingly defy the laws of physics by being in more than one place at a time. For example, consider this futuristic situation at Hackensack University Medical Center in New Jersey:

> Doctors can tap an internal Web site to examine X-rays from a PC anywhere. Patients can use 37-inch plasma TVs in their rooms to surf the Net for information about their medical conditions. There's even a life-size robot, Mr Rounder, that doctors can control from their laptops at home. They direct the digital doc, complete with white lab coat and stethoscope, into hospital rooms and use two-way video to discuss patients' conditions.[34]

In short, organizational life will never be the same because of e-mail, e-learning,[35] e-management, e-leadership (see Table 1–2), virtual teams, and virtual organizations.

The Age of Human and Social Capital

Knowledge workers, those who add value by using their brains rather than the sweat off their backs, are more important than ever in today's global economy. What you know and who you know increasingly are the keys to both personal and organizational success[36] (see Figure 1–2). In the United States, the following "perfect storm" of current and emerging trends heightens the importance and urgency of building human and social capital:

- Spread of advanced technology to developing countries with rapidly growing middle classes (e.g., China, India, Russia, and Brazil).
- Offshoring of increasingly sophisticated jobs (e.g., product design, architecture, medical diagnosis).

Table 1–2   *The Brave New World of E-Leadership*

Because it involves electronically mediated interactions, in combination with the traditional face-to-face variety, experts say e-leadership raises these major issues for modern management:

1. Leaders and followers have more access to information and each other, and this is changing the nature and content of their interactions.
2. Leadership is migrating to lower and lower organizational levels and out through the boundaries of the organization to both customers and suppliers.
3. Leadership creates and exists in networks that go across traditional organizational and community boundaries.
4. Followers know more at earlier points in the decision-making process, and this is potentially affecting the credibility and influence of leaders.
5. Unethical leaders with limited resources can now impact negatively a much broader audience of potential followers.
6. The amount of time and contact that even the most senior leaders can have with their followers has increased, although the contact is not in the traditional face-to-face mode.

Making wise hiring and job assignment decisions, nurturing productive relationships, and building trust are more important than ever in the age of e-leadership.

SOURCE: Six implications excerpted from *Organizational Dynamics*, vol. 4, B J Avolio, and S S Kahai, "Adding the 'E' to E-Leadership: How It May Impact Your Leadership," p 333, © 2003, with permission from Elsevier.

- Comparatively poor math and science skills among America's youth.
- Post-9/11 decline in highly skilled immigrants and graduate students.
- Massive brain drain caused by retiring post–World War II baby-boom generation.[37]

What Is Human Capital? (Hint: Think BIG)   A team of human resource management authors recently offered this perspective:

We're living in a time when a new economic paradigm—characterized by speed, innovation, short cycle times, quality, and customer satisfaction—is highlighting the importance of intangible assets, such as brand recognition, knowledge, innovation, and particularly human capital.[38]

Human capital is the productive potential of an individual's knowledge and actions.[39] *Potential* is the operative word in this intentionally broad definition. When you are hungry, money in your pocket is good because it has the potential to buy a meal. Likewise, a present or future employee with the right combination of knowledge, skills, and motivation to excel represents human capital with the potential to give the organization a competitive advantage. Again Intel, a good example, is a high-tech company whose future depends on innovative engineering. It takes years of math and science studies to make world-class engineers. Not wanting to leave the future supply of engineers to chance, Intel annually spends millions of dollars funding education at all levels. The company encourages youngsters to study math and science and sponsors science competitions with generous scholarships for the winners.[40] Additionally, Intel encourages its employees to volunteer at local schools by giving the schools $200 for every 20 hours contributed.[41] Will all of the students end up working for Intel? No. That's not the point. The point is much bigger—namely, to build the *world's* human capital.

Human capital
The productive potential of one's knowledge and actions.

Figure 1–2   *The Strategic Importance and Dimensions of Human and Social Capital*

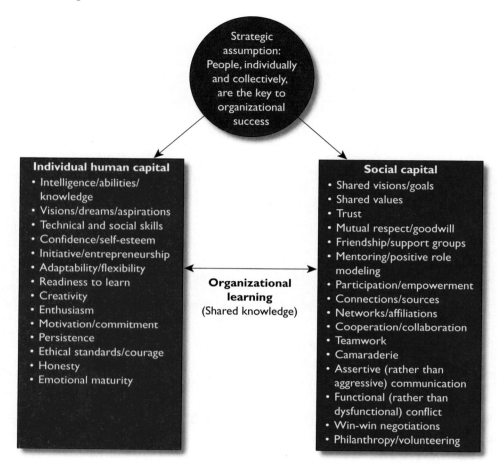

Strategic assumption: People, individually and collectively, are the key to organizational success

Individual human capital
- Intelligence/abilities/knowledge
- Visions/dreams/aspirations
- Technical and social skills
- Confidence/self-esteem
- Initiative/entrepreneurship
- Adaptability/flexibility
- Readiness to learn
- Creativity
- Enthusiasm
- Motivation/commitment
- Persistence
- Ethical standards/courage
- Honesty
- Emotional maturity

Organizational learning
(Shared knowledge)

Social capital
- Shared visions/goals
- Shared values
- Trust
- Mutual respect/goodwill
- Friendship/support groups
- Mentoring/positive role modeling
- Participation/empowerment
- Connections/sources
- Networks/affiliations
- Cooperation/collaboration
- Teamwork
- Camaraderie
- Assertive (rather than aggressive) communication
- Functional (rather than dysfunctional) conflict
- Win-win negotiations
- Philanthropy/volunteering

SOURCES: Based on discussions in P S Adler and S Kwon, "Social Capital: Prospects for a New Concept," *Academy of Management Review*, January 2002, pp 17–40; and C A Bartlett and S Ghoshal, "Building Competitive Advantage through People," *MIT Sloan Management Review*, Winter 2002, pp 34–41.

Social capital
The productive potential of strong, trusting, and cooperative relationships.

What Is Social Capital?

Our focus now shifts from the individual to social units (e.g., friends, family, company, group or club, nation). Think *relationships*. **Social capital** is productive potential resulting from strong relationships, goodwill, trust, and cooperative effort.[42] Again, the word *potential* is key. According to experts on the subject: "It's true: the social capital that used to be a given in organizations is now rare and endangered. But the social capital we can build will allow us to capitalize on the volatile, virtual possibilities of today's business environment."[43] Relationships do matter. In a recent general survey, 77% of the women and 63% of the men rated "Good relationship with boss" extremely important. Other factors—including good equipment, resources, easy commute, and flexible hours—received lower ratings.[44]

What Some Companies Are Doing to Build Human and Social Capital

Company	Human Capital Program or Activity
General Mills Minneapolis, MN 19,019 employees	"This food company makes it easy for employees to get smart. It reimburses tuition at 100% up to $6,000 per year, even for new employees."
MITRE McLean, VA and Bedford, MA 5,383 employees	"This technology consultant to the Pentagon flies a Johns Hopkins professor to Bedford, Mass., every week so employees can earn a master's degree in systems engineering."
Aflac Columbus, GA 3,904 employees	"As long as . . . [employees'] college-age children or grand-children receive a GPA of 2.5 or higher, the company will pay 100% of their tuition, up to $20,000 per year."
	Social Capital Program or Activity
Valero Energy San Antonio, TX 15,882 employees	"This 25-year-old oil refiner and gas retailer has never laid off an employee."
Cisco Systems San Jose, CA 24,433 employees	"Cisco employees surveyed say they love the company's efforts to make the workplace fun, from 'nerd lunches' in which experts lead a discussion of tech topics to movie-themed chow in Cisco's cafés on Oscar night."
TDIndustries Dallas, TX 1,426 employees	"If an employee [at this building supply company] falls ill or a relative dies, an assigned partner helps with household tasks and the like."

SOURCE: Data and excerpts from R Levering and M Moskowitz, "The 100 Best Companies to Work For," *Fortune*, January 24, 2005, pp 72–90.

Building Human and Social Capital Various dimensions of human and social capital are listed in Figure 1–2. They are a preview of what lies ahead in this book, including our discussion of organizational learning in Chapter 17. Formal organizational learning and *knowledge management* programs, as discussed in Chapter 12, need social capital to leverage individual human capital for the greater good. It is a straightforward formula for success. Growth depends on the timely sharing of valuable knowledge. After all, what good are bright employees who do not network, teach, and inspire? Moreover, the rich array of factors in Figure 1–2 can be an agenda for progressive people who want to join our quest for more people-centered organizations (see Real World/Real People).

The Emerging Area of Positive Organizational Behavior (POB)

OB draws heavily on the field of psychology. So major shifts and trends in psychology eventually ripple through to OB. One such shift being felt in OB is the positive psychology movement. This exciting new direction promises to broaden the scope and practical relevance of OB.[45]

President George W. Bush hosts the 2005 Intel Science Talent Search (STS) finalists. The global economy needs this sort of pre-college human capital if the world is to become a better place to live, work, and raise families. The Intel Foundation pumps millions of dollars into sponsoring the STS and funding scholarships for these and other aspiring scientists. Who knows, one of them might be the President some day.

The Positive Psychology Movement

Something curious happened to the field of psychology during the last half of the 20th century. It took a distinctly negative turn. Theory and research became preoccupied with mental and behavioral pathologies; in other words, what was *wrong* with people! Following the traditional medical model, most researchers and practicing psychologists devoted their attention to diagnosing what was wrong with people and trying to make them better. At the turn of the 21st century, bits and pieces of an alternative perspective advocated by pioneering psychologists such as Abraham Maslow and Carl Rogers were pulled together under the label of positive psychology. This approach recommended focusing on human strengths and potential as a way to possibly *prevent* mental and behavioral problems and improve the general quality of life. A pair of positive psychologists described their new multilevel approach as follows:

> The field of positive psychology at the subjective level is about valued subjective experiences: well-being, contentment, and satisfaction (in the past); hope and optimism (for the future); and flow and happiness (in the present). At the individual level, it is about positive individual traits: the capacity for love and vocation, courage, interpersonal skill, aesthetic sensibility, perseverance, forgiveness, originality, future mindedness, spirituality, high talent, and wisdom. At the group level, it is about the civic virtues and the institutions that move individuals toward better citizenship: responsibility, nurturance, altruism, civility, moderation, tolerance, and work ethic.[46]

This is an extremely broad agenda for understanding and improving the human condition. However, we foresee a productive marriage between the concepts of human and social capital and the positive psychology movement, as it evolves into POB.[47]

Positive Organizational Behavior: Definition and Key Dimensions

Positive organizational behavior (POB)
The study and improvement of employees' positive attributes and capabilities.

University of Nebraska OB scholar Fred Luthans defines **positive organizational behavior (POB)** as "the study and application of positively oriented human resource strengths and psychological capacities that can be measured, developed, and effectively managed for performance improvement in today's workplace."[48] His emphasis on study and measurement (meaning a coherent body of theory and research evidence) clearly sets POB apart from the quick-and-easy self-improvement books commonly found on best-seller lists. Also, POB focuses positive psychology more narrowly on the workplace. Luthans created the CHOSE acronym to identify five key dimensions of POB (see Table 1–3). (See Chapter 5 for more on self-efficacy and emotional intelligence.) Progressive managers already know the value of a positive workplace atmosphere, as evidenced by the following situations: At Perkins Coie, in Seattle, " 'Happiness committees' roam the law firm's halls leav-

Table 1–3   *Luthans' CHOSE Model of Key POB Dimensions*

Confidence/self-efficacy: One's belief (confidence) in being able to successfully execute a specific task in a given context.

Hope: One who sets goals, figures out how to achieve them (identify pathways), and is self-motivated to accomplish them, that is, willpower and "waypower."

Optimism: Positive outcome expectancy and/or a positive causal attribution, but is still emotional and linked with happiness, perseverance, and success.

Subjective well-being: Beyond happiness emotion, how people cognitively process and evaluate their lives, the satisfaction with their lives.

Emotional intelligence: Capacity for recognizing and managing one's own and others' emotions—self-awareness, self-motivation, being empathetic, and having social skills.

SOURCE: From F. Luthans, *The Academy of Management Executive: The Thinking Manager's Source*, © 2002. Reprinted by permission of The Academy of Management via The Copyright Clearance Center.

ing baskets of candies and other thank-you treats on employees' desks."[49] In a similar vein, Synovus, a Georgia bank, has developed a "pat-on-the-back culture."[50] Meanwhile, in Atlanta, at Barton Protective Services, " 'Love' appears nine times in this security-guard agency's outline of company values."[51]

POB promises to make helpful contributions to the quest for more people-centered organizations in the years to come.

The Managerial Context: Getting Things Done with and through Others

Like the organizations they run, managers touch our lives in many ways. Schools, hospitals, government agencies, and large and small businesses all require systematic management. Formally defined, **management** is the process of working with and through others to achieve organizational objectives in an efficient and ethical manner. From the standpoint of organizational behavior, the central feature of this definition is "working with and through others." Managers play a constantly evolving role.[52] Today's successful managers are no longer the I've-got-everything-under-control order givers of yesteryear. Rather, they need to creatively envision and actively sell bold new directions in an ethical and people-friendly manner. Effective managers are team players empowered by the willing and active support of others who are driven by conflicting self-interests. Each of us has a huge stake in how well managers carry out their evolving role. Henry Mintzberg, a respected management scholar, observed: "No job is more vital to our society than that of the manager. It is the manager who determines whether our social institutions serve us well or whether they squander our talents and resources."[53]

Let us take a closer look at the skills managers need to perform and the future direction of management.

Management
Process of working with and through others to achieve organizational objectives efficiently and ethically.

What Do Managers Do? A Skills Profile

Observational studies by Mintzberg and others have found the typical manager's day to be a fragmented collection of brief episodes.[54] Interruptions are commonplace, while large blocks of time for planning and reflective thinking are not. In one particular study, four top-level managers spent 63% of their time on activities lasting less than nine minutes each. Only 5% of the managers' time was devoted to activities lasting more than an hour.[55] But what specific skills do effective managers perform during their hectic and fragmented workdays?

Many attempts have been made over the years to paint a realistic picture of what managers do.[56] Diverse and confusing lists of managerial functions and roles have been suggested. Fortunately, a stream of research over the past 20 years by Clark Wilson and others has given us a practical and statistically validated profile of managerial *skills*[57] (see Table 1–4). Wilson's managerial skills profile focuses on 11 observable categories of managerial behavior. This is very much in tune with today's emphasis on managerial competency.[58] Wilson's unique skills-assessment technique goes beyond the usual self-report approach with its natural bias. In addition to surveying a given manager about his or her 11 skills, the Wilson approach also asks those who report directly to the manager to answer questions about their boss's skills. According to Wilson and his colleagues, the result is an assessment of skill *mastery,* not simply skill awareness.[59] The logic behind Wilson's approach is both simple and compelling. Who better to assess a manager's skills than the people who experience those behaviors on a day-to-day basis—those who report directly to the manager?

The Wilson managerial skills research yields four useful lessons:

1. Dealing effectively with *people* is what management is all about. The 11 skills in Table 1–4 constitute a goal creation/commitment/feedback/reward/accomplishment cycle with human interaction at every turn.

2. Managers with high skills mastery tend to have better subunit performance and employee morale than managers with low skills mastery.[60]

3. *Effective* female and male managers *do not* have significantly different skill profiles,[61] contrary to claims in the popular business press in recent years.[62]

Table 1–4   *Skills Exhibited by an Effective Manager*

1. **Clarifies goals and objectives** for everyone involved.
2. **Encourages participation,** upward communication, and suggestions.
3. **Plans and organizes** for an orderly work flow.
4. Has **technical and administrative expertise** to answer organization-related questions.
5. **Facilitates work** through team building, training, coaching, and support.
6. **Provides feedback** honestly and constructively.
7. **Keeps things moving** by relying on schedules, deadlines, and helpful reminders.
8. **Controls details** without being overbearing.
9. Applies reasonable **pressure for goal accomplishment.**
10. **Empowers and delegates** key duties to others while maintaining goal clarity and commitment.
11. **Recognizes good performance** with rewards and positive reinforcement.

SOURCES: Adapted from material in F Shipper, "A Study of the Psychometric Properties of the Managerial Skill Scales of the Survey of Management Practices," *Educational and Psychological Measurement,* June 1995, pp 468–79; and C L Wilson, *How and Why Effective Managers Balance Their Skills: Technical, Teambuilding, Drive* (Columbia, MD: Rockatech Multimedia Publishing, 2003).

Managers' Egos Take a Back Seat at JetBlue Airways

JetBlue's officers don't act aloof and sit at their desks all day. We roll up our sleeves to understand what's going on, because our leaders shouldn't treat others as inferiors. A couple of years ago, we promoted our middle managers without giving them leadership training. They became little dictators, and favoritism started to creep in.

So we had to create a leadership program to reset the expectations of what leaders should do. But we didn't hire a bunch of slick facilitators to talk about principles. Instead, the people who were actually living them at JetBlue were the ones teaching the courses. Now 40 of our top managers spend two days a year leading the group.

In addition, our 23 corporate officers each focus on a different city every year. Once a quarter, they go to the city and listen to the airport staff.

SOURCE: JetBlue CEO David Neeleman, as quoted in B Finn, "How to Turn Managers into Leaders," *Business 2.0*, September 2004, p 70.

4. At all career stages, *derailed* managers (those who failed to achieve their potential) tended to be the ones who *overestimated* their skill mastery (rated themselves higher than their employees did). This prompted the following conclusion from the researcher: "when selecting individuals for promotion to managerial positions, those who are arrogant, aloof, insensitive, and defensive should be avoided."[63]

(See Real World/Real People.)

21st-Century Managers

Today's workplace is indeed undergoing immense and permanent changes.[64] Organizations have been "reengineered" for greater speed, efficiency, and flexibility.[65] Teams are pushing aside the individual as the primary building block of organizations.[66] Command-and-control management is giving way to participative management and empowerment.[67] Ego-centered leaders are being replaced by customer-centered leaders. Employees increasingly are being viewed as internal customers. All this creates a mandate for a new kind of manager in the 21st century. After conducting a Gallup Organization survey of 80,000 managers and doing follow-up studies of the top performers, Marcus Buckingham came to this conclusion:

> I've found that while there are as many styles of management as there are managers, there is one quality that sets truly great managers apart from the rest: They discover what is unique about each person and then capitalize on it. Average managers play checkers, while great managers play chess. The difference? In checkers, all the pieces are uniform and move in the same way; they are interchangeable. You need to plan and coordinate their movements, certainly, but they all move at the same pace, on parallel paths. In chess, each type of piece moves in a different way, and you can't play if you don't know how each piece moves. More important, you won't win if you don't think carefully about how you move the pieces. Great managers know and value the unique abilities and even the eccentricities of their employees, and they learn how best to integrate them into a coordinated plan of attack.[68]

Table 1–5 contrasts the characteristics of past and future managers. As the balance of this book will demonstrate, the managerial shift in Table 1–5 is not just a good idea, it is an absolute necessity in the new workplace.

Table 1–5   *Evolution of the 21st-Century Manager*

	Past Managers	Future Managers
Primary role	Order giver, privileged elite, manipulator, controller	Facilitator, team member, teacher, advocate, sponsor, coach
Learning and knowledge	Periodic learning, narrow specialist	Continuous life-long learning, generalist with multiple specialties
Compensation criteria	Time, effort, rank	Skills, results
Cultural orientation	Monocultural, monolingual	Multicultural, multilingual
Primary source of influence	Formal authority	Knowledge (technical and interpersonal)
View of people	Potential problem	Primary resource; human capital
Primary communication pattern	Vertical	Multidirectional
Decision-making style	Limited input for individual decisions	Broad-based input for joint decisions
Ethical considerations	Afterthought	Forethought
Nature of interpersonal relationships	Competitive (win–lose)	Cooperative (win–win)
Handling of power and key information	Hoard and restrict access	Share and broaden access
Approach to change	Resist	Facilitate

The Contingency Approach: Applying Lessons from Theory, Research, and Practice

Contingency approach
Using management tools and techniques in a situationally appropriate manner; avoiding the one-best-way mentality.

Scholars have wrestled for many years with the problem of how best to apply the diverse and growing collection of management tools and techniques. Their answer is the contingency approach. The **contingency approach** calls for using management techniques in a situationally appropriate manner, instead of trying to rely on "one best way." According to a pair of contingency theorists,

> [Contingency theories] developed and their acceptance grew largely because they responded to criticisms that the classical theories advocated "one best way" of organizing and managing. Contingency theories, on the other hand, proposed that the appropriate organizational structure and management style were dependent upon a set of "contingency" factors, usually the uncertainty and instability of the environment.[69]

The contingency approach encourages managers to view organizational behavior within a situational context. According to this modern perspective, evolving situations, not hard-and-fast rules, determine when and where various management techniques are appropriate. For example, as discussed in Chapter 16, contingency researchers have determined that there is no single best style of leadership. Organizational behavior specialists embrace the contingency approach because it helps them realistically interrelate individuals, groups, and organizations. Moreover, the contingency approach sends a clear message to managers in today's global economy: Carefully read the situation and then be flexible enough to adapt.[70]

As a human being, with years of interpersonal experience to draw upon, you already know a good deal about people at work. This point is underscored by the title of Ann Crittenden's new book: *If You've Raised Kids, You Can Manage Anything: Leadership Begins at Home.*[71] But more systematic and comprehensive understanding is possible and desirable. A working knowledge of current OB theory, research, and practice can help you develop a tightly integrated understanding of why organizational contributors think and act as they do. In order for this to happen, however, prepare yourself for some intellectual surprises from theoretical models, research results, or techniques that may run counter to your current thinking. Research surprises not only make learning fun, they also can improve the quality of our lives both on and off the job. Let us examine the dynamic relationship between OB theory, research, and practice and the value of each.

Figure 1–3 illustrates how theory, research, and practice are related. Throughout the balance of this book, we focus primarily on the central portion, where all three areas overlap. Knowledge of why people behave as they do and what managers can do to improve performance is greatest within this area of maximum overlap. For each major topic, we build a foundation for understanding with generally accepted theory. This theoretical foundation is then tested and expanded by reviewing the latest relevant research findings. After interpreting the research, we discuss the nature and effectiveness of related practical applications.

Sometimes, depending on the subject matter, it is necessary to venture into the areas outside the central portion of Figure 1–3. For example, an insightful theory supported by convincing research evidence might suggest an untried or different way of managing. In other instances, an innovative management technique might call for an explanatory theoretical model and exploratory research. Each area—theory, research, and practice—supports and, in turn, is supported by the other two.[72] Each area makes a valuable contribution to our understanding of, and ability to manage, organizational behavior.

Figure 1–3   *Learning about OB through a Combination of Theory, Research, and Practice*

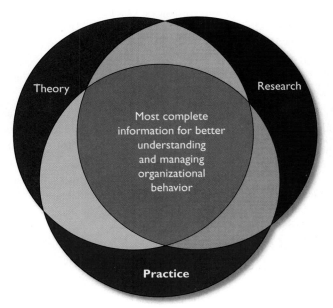

Learning from Theory

Theory

A story defining key terms, providing a conceptual frame-work, and explaining why something occurs.

A respected behavioral scientist, Kurt Lewin, once said there is nothing as practical as a good theory. According to one management researcher, a **theory** is a story that explains "why."[73] Another calls well-constructed theories "disciplined imagination."[74] A good OB theory, then, is a story that effectively explains why individuals and groups behave as they do. Moreover, a good theoretical model

1. *Defines* key terms.
2. Constructs a *conceptual framework* that explains how important factors are interrelated. (Graphic models are often used to achieve this end.)
3. Provides a *departure point* for research and practical application.

Indeed, good theories are a fundamental contributor to improved understanding and management of organizational behavior.[75]

Learning from Research

Because of unfamiliar jargon and complicated statistical procedures, many current and future managers are put off by behavioral research.[76] This is unfortunate because practical lessons can be learned as OB researchers steadily advance the frontier of knowledge. Let us examine the various sources and uses of OB research evidence.

Five Sources of OB Research Insights

Meta-analysis

Pools the results of many studies through statistical procedure.

Field study

Examination of variables in real-life settings.

Laboratory study

Manipulation and measurement of variables in con-trived situations.

Sample survey

Questionnaire responses from a sample of people.

Case study

In-depth study of a single person, group, or organization.

To enhance the instructional value of our coverage of major topics, we systematically cite "hard" evidence from five different categories. Worthwhile evidence was obtained by drawing upon the following *priority* of research methodologies:

- *Meta-analyses.* A **meta-analysis** is a statistical pooling technique that permits behavioral scientists to draw general conclusions about certain variables from many different studies.[77] It typically encompasses a vast number of subjects, often reaching the thousands. Meta-analyses are instructive because they focus on general patterns of research evidence, not fragmented bits and pieces or isolated studies.[78]

- *Field studies.* In OB, a **field study** probes individual or group processes in an organizational setting. Because field studies involve real-life situations, their results often have immediate and practical relevance for managers.

- *Laboratory studies.* In a **laboratory study,** variables are manipulated and measured in contrived situations. College students are commonly used as subjects. The highly controlled nature of laboratory studies enhances research precision. But generalizing the results to organizational management requires caution.[79]

- *Sample surveys.* In a **sample survey,** samples of people from specified populations respond to questionnaires. The researchers then draw conclusions about the relevant population. Generalizability of the results depends on the quality of the sampling and questioning techniques.

- *Case studies.* A **case study** is an in-depth analysis of a single individual, group, or organization. Because of their limited scope, case studies yield realistic but not very generalizable results.[80]

Three Uses of OB Research Findings

Organizational scholars point out that managers can put relevant research findings to use in three different ways:[81]

"THIS IS WHERE WE ADDED HIGH-CAFFEINE CAPPUCCINO TO OUR OFFICE COFFEE MACHINES."

SOURCE: L. Schwadron, *Harvard Business Review*, January 2005, p 72. © 2005 Harley L. Schwadron. Used by permission of the author.

1. *Instrumental use.* This involves directly applying research findings to practical problems. For example, a manager experiencing high stress tries a relaxation technique after reading a research report about its effectiveness.

2. *Conceptual use.* Research is put to conceptual use when managers derive general enlightenment from its findings. The effect here is less specific and more indirect than with instrumental use. For example, after reading a meta-analysis showing a negative correlation between absenteeism and age,[82] a manager might develop a more positive attitude toward hiring older people.

3. *Symbolic use.* Symbolic use occurs when research results are relied on to verify or legitimize already held positions. Negative forms of symbolic use involve self-serving bias, prejudice, selective perception, and distortion. For example, tobacco industry spokespersons routinely deny any link between smoking and lung cancer because researchers are largely, but not 100%, in agreement about the negative effects of smoking. A positive example would be managers maintaining their confidence in setting performance goals after reading a research report about the favorable impact of goal setting on job performance.

By systematically reviewing and interpreting research relevant to key topics, this book provides instructive insights about OB. (For more about OB research methods, see Learning Module E at **www.mhhe.com/kreitner.**)

Learning from Practice

Learning to deal effectively with people and eventually manage them is like learning to ride a bicycle. You watch others do it. Sooner or later, you get up the courage to try it yourself. You fall off and skin your knee. You climb back on the bike a bit smarter, and so on, until wobbly first attempts turn into a smooth ride. Your chances of becoming a successful organizational participant and manager can be enhanced by studying the theory, research, and practical examples in this textbook. Figuratively speaking, however, you eventually must climb aboard the "organizational bicycle" and learn by doing.[83]

The theory→research→practice sequence discussed in this section will help you better understand each major topic addressed later in this book. Attention now turns to a topical model that provides a road map for what lies ahead.

A Topical Model for Understanding and Managing OB

Figure 1–4 is a topical road map for our journey through this book. Our destination is organizational effectiveness through continuous improvement. Four different criteria for determining whether or not an organization is effective are discussed in Chapter 17. The study of OB can be a wandering and pointless trip if we overlook the need to translate OB lessons into effective and efficient organized endeavor.

At the far left side of our topical road map are managers and team leaders, those who are responsible for accomplishing organizational results with and through others. The three circles at the center of our road map correspond to Parts Two, Three, and Four of this text. Logically, the flow of topical coverage in this book (following introductory Part One) goes from individuals, to group processes, to organizational processes. Around the core of our topical road map in Figure 1–4 is the organization. Accordingly, we end our journey with organization-related material in Part Four. Organizational structure and design are covered there in Chapter 17 to establish and develop the *organizational* context of organizational behavior. Rounding out our organizational context is a discussion of organizational change in Chapter 18. Chapters 3 and 4 provide a *cultural* context for OB.

Figure 1–4   *A Topical Model for What Lies Ahead*

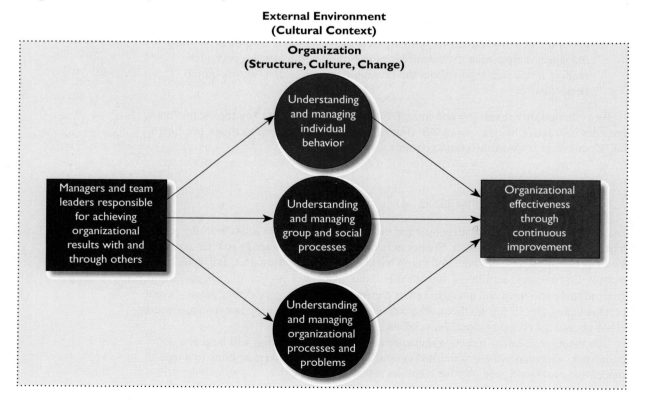

The dotted line represents a permeable boundary between the organization and its environment. Energy and influence flow both ways across this permeable boundary. Truly, no organization is an island in today's highly interactive and interdependent world. Relative to the *external* environment, international cultures are explored in Chapter 4. Organization–environment contingencies are examined in Chapter 17.

Chapter 2 examines the OB implications of significant demographic and social trends, and Module A explores important ethical considerations. These discussions provide a realistic context for studying and managing people at work.

Bon voyage! Enjoy your trip through the challenging, interesting, and often surprising world of OB.

Summary of Key Concepts

1. *Define the term* organizational behavior *and explain why OB is a horizontal discipline.* Organizational behavior (OB) is an interdisciplinary field dedicated to better understanding and managing people at work. It is both research and application oriented. Except for teaching/research positions, one does not normally get a job in OB. Rather, because OB is a horizontal discipline, OB concepts and lessons are applicable to virtually every job category, business function, and professional specialty.

2. *Contrast McGregor's Theory X and Theory Y assumptions about employees.* Theory X employees, according to traditional thinking, dislike work, require close supervision, and are primarily interested in security. According to the modern Theory Y view, employees are capable of self-direction, of seeking responsibility, and of being creative.

3. *Identify the four principles of total quality management (TQM).* (*a*) Do it right the first time to eliminate costly rework. (*b*) Listen to and learn from customers and employees. (*c*) Make continuous improvement an everyday matter. (*d*) Build teamwork, trust, and mutual respect.

4. *Define the term* e-business, *and specify at least three OB-related issues raised by e-leadership.* E-business involves using the Internet to more effectively and efficiently manage every aspect of a business. Six OB-related issues raised by the advent of e-leadership are (*a*) greater access to information for everyone, (*b*) leadership is migrating to lower levels and outside the organization, (*c*) development of nontraditional leadership networks, (*d*) followers have more information earlier in the decision making process,

(*e*) greater influence for unethical leaders with limited resources, and (*f*) more contact between senior leaders and their followers.

5. *Contrast human and social capital, and explain why we need to build both.* The first involves *individual* characteristics, the second involves *social* relationships. Human capital is the productive potential of an individual's knowledge and actions. Dimensions include such things as intelligence, visions, skills, self-esteem, creativity, motivation, ethics, and emotional maturity. Social capital is productive potential resulting from strong relationships, goodwill, trust, and cooperative effort. Dimensions include such things as shared visions and goals, trust, mutual respect, friendships, empowerment, teamwork, win-win negotiations, and volunteering. Social capital is necessary to tap individual human capital for the good of the organization through knowledge sharing and networking.

6. *Specify the five key dimensions of Luthans's CHOSE model of positive organizational behavior (POB).* The CHOSE acronym stands for confidence/self-efficacy, hope, optimism, subjective well-being, and emotional intelligence.

7. *Define the term* management, *and identify at least five of the eleven managerial skills in Wilson's profile of effective managers.* Management is the process of working with and through others to achieve organizational objectives in an efficient and ethical manner. According to the Wilson skills profile, an effective manager (*a*) clarifies goals and objectives, (*b*) encourages participation, (*c*) plans and organizes, (*d*) has technical and administrative expertise, (*e*) facilitates work through team building and coaching, (*f*) provides feedback, (*g*) keeps things moving, (*h*) controls details, (*i*) applies reasonable pressure for goals accomplishment,

(j) empowers and delegates, and (k) recognizes and rewards good performance.

8. *Characterize 21st-century managers.* They will be team players who will get things done cooperatively by relying on joint decision making, their knowledge instead of formal authority, and their multicultural skills. They will engage in life-long learning and be compensated on the basis of their skills and results. They will facilitate rather than resist change, share rather than hoard power and key information, and be multidirectional communicators. Ethics will be a forethought instead of an afterthought. They will be generalists with multiple specialties.

9. *Describe the sources of organizational behavior research evidence.* Five sources of OB research evidence are meta-analyses (statistically pooled evidence from several studies), field studies (evidence from real-life situations), laboratory studies (evidence from contrived situations), sample surveys (questionnaire data), and case studies (observation of a single person, group, or organization).

Discussion Questions

1. Why do we need people-centered organizations?

2. What reasons do you have for wanting (or not wanting) to study OB?

3. What is your personal experience with Theory X and Theory Y managers (see Table 1–1)? Which did you prefer? Why?

4. How would you respond to someone who said TQM was just a fad, it's not relevant today?

5. What are your personal experiences with e-leadership? What practical lessons have you learned?

6. What are you doing to build human and social capital?

7. What appeals to you most (or least, or both) about the concept of positive organizational behavior (POB)?

8. Based on either personal experience as a manager or on your observation of managers at work, are the 11 skills in Table 1–4 a realistic portrayal of what managers do?

9. What is your personal experience with 21st-century managers or managers who were stuck in the past? Describe their impact on you and the organization.

10. What "practical" theories have you formulated to achieve the things you want in life (e.g., graduating, keeping fit, getting a good job, meeting that special someone)?

OB in Action Case Study

IBM's Donna Riley Strives for "Collaborative Influence"[84]

It was at a client meeting in San Francisco in October 2002 that Sam Palmisano, IBM's new CEO, first unveiled the initiative he hoped would transform his company. His idea: The Internet really did change everything (the crash of the New Economy notwithstanding). In a hyperconnected world, IBM's clients needed to become "on-demand" companies, their every business process exquisitely calibrated to respond instantly to whatever got thrown at them. And to help them, IBM would have to do exactly the same thing.

When she heard about the new strategy, Donna Riley, IBM's vice president of global talent, remembers wondering whether the company had the right managers for its new direction. "If leadership is stuck in the past, and the business has changed, we have a problem," she says. By the spring of 2003, Palmisano and his leadership development team realized the strategy would indeed demand a new breed of boss—leaders who were as sensitive to changes in their environment as Indian scouts.

For help, Riley turned to the Hay Group, a consultancy that specializes in executive development. Hay had done work for IBM before, most notably in 1994 when, at former CEO Lou Gerstner's behest, the firm had interviewed a group of the company's top managers. As part of his turnaround strategy for the troubled company, Gerstner wanted to develop a new style of leader who could help transform its failed culture. Ultimately, Hay distilled 11 competencies from the interviews that would guide IBMers' performance as they pulled off one of the most remarkable corporate rebounds in history.

In the summer of 2003, Hay Group returned to conduct another set of interviews with 33 executives who had been identified as outstanding leaders in the new on-demand era—the folks who really got the new strategy and who were on the cutting edge in a high-performance culture. They were drawn from every division of the business, every part of the world, united by their extraordinary ability to get the job done. The plan was to put these top players under a microscope, to divine how they thought about their jobs and the company; how they interacted with clients, peers, and subordinates; how they set goals and went about meeting them—in short, to extract the best practices from the best leaders to see if they could be duplicated.

In a series of three-and-a-half-hour interviews, the managers discussed circumstances in which they had been successful—or not. The interviews were supplemented by surveys of the people they worked with. Researchers then combed through the stories and accompanying data, looking for characteristics and qualities that distinguished these high performers.

The results were stunning. "The experts predicted maybe a third of the competencies would be the same, a third would be slightly different, and a third would be brand new," says Riley. "Much to their surprise—and ours—we found it truly is a new book," requiring all new skills.

To begin with, the best executives no longer thought of the folks to whom they sold stuff as customers; they saw them as clients. The difference? "A customer is transactional," says Harris Ginsberg, IBM's director of global executive and organization capability. "A client is somebody with whom you have a longstanding relationship and a personal investment." It's no longer enough to sell a customer a server. An IBMer should be so focused on becoming a long-term trusted partner that she might even discourage a client from buying some new piece of hardware if it's in the client's best interest to hold off.

The 33 leaders were also adept at a skill IBM calls "collaborative influence." In a highly complex world, where multiple groups might need to unite to solve a client's problems,

old-style siloed thinking just won't cut it, and command-and-control leadership doesn't work. "It's really about winning hearts and minds—and getting people whose pay you don't control to do stuff," says Mary Fontaine, vice president and general manager of Hay's McClelland Center for Research and Innovation.

For example, Frank Squillante, an IBM vice president, has only four direct reports. To do his job—devising the strategy for the company's intranet, and then developing and deploying applications for 325,000 people and 100,000 business partners—he must be a master at cajoling people over whom he has no real power. "I use 'collaborative influence' every minute of every day," he says. "If I tried to pull one of these, 'I'm in charge so you have to do this' maneuvers, the whole thing would break down."

Riley's team is now training IBM's executives in the new competencies. This year, only top management will be assessed against them. The next group—some 4,000 executives—will have a year to study the goals before being held accountable. But the new approach has already spurred some more flexible, collaborative efforts. Cross-functional teams from IBM's global services, software, and systems groups have helped Mobil Travel Guides transform itself from a travel content provider to a real-time, customized travel-planning service; a team of staffers from Big Blue's research, software, and consulting services helped Nextel dramatically improve its customer-care services.

In an interconnected world, such horizontal, collaborative networks of people clearly make more sense than rigid hierarchies. And leading in such a challenging environment is an acquired skill. "Leadership is a personal journey for each person," says Riley, "but I think having a culture that says this stuff matters—particularly when it's linked to your business strategy—is a very powerful combination."

Questions for Discussion

1. What role, if any, does McGregor's Theory Y play in IBM's drive to create a new breed of manager/leader?

2. What evidence of the e-leadership issues presented in Table 1–2 can you detect in this case? Explain.

3. How does the building of human and social capital (Figure 1–2) factor into this case?

4. Which three or four of Wilson's 11 managerial skills (Table 1–4) will be most important for IBM's managers in the years ahead? Explain your choices.

5. What is the linkage between the 21st-century manager, profiled in Table 1–5, and IBM's notion of collaborative influence?

How Strong Is Your Motivation to Manage?

Objectives

1. To introduce a psychological determinant of managerial success.
2. To assess your readiness to manage.
3. To discuss the implications of motivation to manage, from the standpoint of global competitiveness.

Introduction

By identifying personal traits positively correlated with both rapid movement up the career ladder and managerial effectiveness, John B Miner developed a psychometric test for measuring what he calls motivation to manage. The questionnaire assesses the strength of seven factors relating to the temperament (or psychological makeup) needed to manage others. One word of caution. The following instrument is a shortened and modified version of Miner's original. Our version is for instructional and discussion purposes only. Although we believe it can indicate the *general* strength of your motivation to manage, it is *not* a precise measuring tool.

Instructions

Assess the strength of each of the seven dimensions of *your own* motivation to manage by circling the appropriate numbers on the 1 to 7 scales. Then add the seven circled numbers to get your total motivation to manage score.

Scoring and Interpretation

Arbitrary norms for comparison purposes are as follows: Total score of 7–21 = Relatively low motivation to manage; 22–34 = Moderate; 35–49 = Relatively high. How do you measure up? Remember, though, high motivation to manage is only part of the formula for managerial success. The right combination of ability and opportunity is also necessary.

Years of motivation-to-manage research by Miner and others has serious implications for America's future global competitiveness. Generally, in recent years, college students in the United States have not scored highly on motivation to manage.[85] Indeed, compared with samples of US college students, samples of students from Japan, China, Mexico,

Factor	Description	Scale
1. Authority figures	A desire to meet managerial role requirements in terms of positive relationships with superiors.	Weak 1–2–3–4–5–6–7 Strong
2. Competitive games	A desire to engage in competition with peers involving games or sports and thus meet managerial role requirements in this regard.	Weak 1–2–3–4–5–6–7 Strong
3. Competitive situations	A desire to engage in competition with peers involving occupational or work-related activities and thus meet managerial role requirements in this regard.	Weak 1–2–3–4–5–6–7 Strong
4. Assertive role	A desire to behave in an active and assertive manner involving activities that in this society are often viewed as predominantly masculine and thus to meet managerial role requirements.	Weak 1–2–3–4–5–6–7 Strong
5. Imposing wishes	A desire to tell others what to do and to utilize sanctions in influencing others, thus indicating a capacity to fulfill managerial role requirements in relationships with subordinates.	Weak 1–2–3–4–5–6–7 Strong
6. Standing out from group	A desire to assume a distinctive position of a unique and highly visible nature in a manner that is role-congruent for managerial jobs.	Weak 1–2–3–4–5–6–7 Strong
7. Routine administrative functions	A desire to meet managerial role requirements regarding activities often associated with managerial work that are of a day-to-day administrative nature.	Weak 1–2–3–4–5–6–7 Strong
		Total = _____

Korea, and Taiwan consistently scored higher on motivation to manage.[86] Miner believes the United States may consequently lag in developing sufficient managerial talent for a tough global marketplace.[87]

In a study by other researchers, MBA students with higher motivation-to-manage scores tended to earn more money after graduation. But students with a higher motivation to manage did not earn better grades or complete their degree program any sooner than those with a lower motivation to manage.[88]

Questions for Discussion

1. Do you believe our adaptation of Miner's motivation to manage instrument accurately assessed your potential as a manager? Explain.

2. Which of the seven dimensions do you think is probably the best predictor of managerial success? Which is the least predictive? Why?

3. Miner puts heavy emphasis on competitiveness by anchoring two of the seven dimensions of motivation to manage to the desire to compete. Some observers believe the traditional (win–lose) competitive attitude is being pushed aside in favor of a less competitive (win–win) attitude today, thus making Miner's instrument out of date. What is your position on this competitiveness debate? Explain.

4. Do you believe Miner is correct in saying that low motivation to manage hurts the United States's global competitiveness? Explain.

Group Exercise

Timeless Advice

Objectives

1. To get to know some of your fellow students.
2. To put the management of people into a lively and interesting historical context.
3. To begin to develop your teamwork skills.

Introduction

Your creative energy, willingness to see familiar things in unfamiliar ways, and ability to have fun while learning are keys to the success of this warm-up exercise. A 20-minute, small-group session will be followed by brief oral presentations and a general class discussion. Total time required is approximately 40 to 45 minutes.

Instructions

Your instructor will divide your class randomly into groups of four to six people each. Acting as a team, with everyone offering ideas and one person serving as official recorder, each group will be responsible for writing a one-page memo to your current class. Subject matter of your group's memo will be "My advice for managing people today is. . . ." The fun part of this exercise (and its creative element) involves writing the memo from the viewpoint of the person assigned to your group by your instructor.

Among the memo viewpoints your instructor may assign are the following:

- Bill Hewlett (chapter-opening vignette).
- An ancient Egyptian slave master (building the great pyramids).
- Mary Parker Follett.
- Douglas McGregor.
- A Theory X supervisor of a construction crew (see McGregor's Theories X and Y in Table 1–1).
- W Edwards Deming.
- A TQM coordinator at 3M Company.
- A contingency management theorist.
- A Japanese auto company executive.
- The chief executive officer of IBM in the year 2030.
- Commander of the Starship Enterprise II in the year 3001.
- Others, as assigned by your instructor.

Use your imagination, make sure everyone participates, and try to be true to any historical facts you've encountered. Attempt to be as specific and realistic as possible. Remember, the idea is to provide advice about managing people from another point in time (or from a particular point of view at the present time).

Make sure you manage your 20-minute time limit carefully. A recommended approach is to spend 2 to 3 minutes putting the exercise into proper perspective. Next, take about 10 to 12 minutes brainstorming ideas for your memo, with your recorder jotting down key ideas and phrases. Have your recorder use the remaining time to write your group's one-page memo, with constructive comments and help from the others. Pick a spokesperson to read your group's memo to the class.

Questions for Discussion

1. What valuable lessons about managing people have you heard?

2. What have you learned about how *not* to manage people?

3. From the distant past to today, what significant shifts in the management of people seem to have taken place?

4. Where does the management of people appear to be headed?

5. All things considered, what mistakes are today's managers typically making when managing people?

6. How well did your group function as a "team"?

Ethical Dilemma

Liar! Liar![89]

Calling in with a manufactured cough and a fake, throaty "I'm not feeling well" can seem rather dull compared to some excuses employers hear. . . .

CareerBuilder.com, . . . commissioned a nationwide survey of 1,600 people and found that more than one-third of U.S. workers called in sick at least once last year when they felt well. . . .

Among the most unusual excuses that have been heard:

- My bus broke down and was held up by robbers.
- I was arrested as a result of mistaken identity.
- I hurt myself bowling.
- My curlers burned my hair and I had to go to the hairdresser.
- I eloped.
- My cat unplugged my alarm clock.
- I forgot to come back to work after lunch.
- I totaled my wife's Jeep in a collision with a cow.
- I had to be there for my husband's grand jury trial.
- A hit man was looking for me.

If you were a manager, how would you respond to questionable excuses such as these? (what are the ethical implications of your answer?)

1. "I call in sick sometimes when I'm not, so it would be unfair to pick on others who do the same." (So you'll do nothing?)

2. "When someone lies to me it not only insults my intelligence, it destroys any trust I might have in that person. Employees with lame excuses for not being here need to be held accountable." (Explain how.)

3. "It just shows you can't trust people. You give them an inch, they'll take a mile. Flagrant rule-breakers need to be punished as a warning to others." (Explain how.)

4. "Look, people are people. If I cut them a little slack they will return the favor by doing something extra on the job." (What about repeat offenders?)

5. Invent other responses. Discuss.

For the Chapter 1 Internet Exercise featuring the building of human capital at Intel Corp. (www.intel.com), visit our Web site at **www.mhhe.com/kreitner**.

Learning Module A

Ethics and Organizational Behavior

The loud message comes from one company after another: Surging health care costs for retired workers are creating a giant burden. So companies have been cutting health benefits for their retirees or requiring them to contribute more of the cost.

Time for a reality check: In fact, no matter how high health care costs go, well over half of large American corporations face only limited impact from the increases when it comes to their retirees. They have established ceilings on how much they will ever spend per retiree for health care. If health costs go above the caps, it's the retiree, not the company, who's responsible.

Yet numerous companies are cutting retirees' health benefits anyway. One possible factor: When companies cut these benefits, they create instant income. This isn't just the savings that come from not spending as much. Rather, thanks to complex accounting rules, the very act of cutting retirees' future health care benefits lets companies reduce a liability and generate an immediate accounting gain.

In some cases it flows straight to the bottom line. More often it sits on the books like a cookie jar, from which a company takes a piece each year that helps it meet earnings estimates. . . .

The fate of retirees can be very different. When Robert Eggleston retired from International Business Machines Corp. 12 years ago, he was paying $40 a month toward health care premiums for himself and his wife, LaRue, with IBM paying the rest. In 1993, IBM set ceilings on its own health care spending for retirees. For those on Medicare, which provides basic hospital and doctor-visit coverage, the cap was $3,000 or $3,500, depending on when they retired. For those younger than 65, the cap was $7,000 or $7,500. Spending hit the caps for the older retirees in 2001, the company says, pushing future health cost increases onto retirees' shoulders.

Mr Eggleston, 66 years old, has seen his premiums jump to $365 a month for the couple. Deductibles and copayments for drugs and doctor visits added $663 a month last year. "It just eats up all the pension," which is $850 a month, Mrs Eggleston says. Her husband has brain cancer. Though he gets free supplies of a tumor-fighting drug through a program for low-income families, he has cashed in his 401(k) account, and he and LaRue have taken out a second mortgage on their Lake Dallas, Texas, home.

IBM retirees as a group saw their health care premiums rise nearly 29% in 2003, on the heels of a 67%-plus increase in 2002. For IBM, with its caps in place, spending on retiree health care declined nearly 5%, after a drop of 18% the year before.

IBM confirms that retirees' spending has risen as its own has fallen.[1]

> ## FOR DISCUSSION
> Do you think it is ethical for a company like IBM to raise retirees' contributions to health benefits while its own decrease? Explain.

Merck Attacks Critics of Big-Selling Painkiller Vioxx

As academic researchers increasingly raised questions about Vioxx's heart safety, the company struck back hard. It even sued one Spanish pharmacologist, trying unsuccessfully to force a correction of an article he wrote. In another case, it warned that a Stanford University researcher would "flame out" unless he stopped giving "anti-Merck" lectures, according to a letter of complaint written to Merck by a Stanford professor. A company training document listed potential tough questions about Vioxx and said in capital letters, "DODGE!"

The revelations shed new light on the interplay between marketing and science at Merck as bad news piled up about a blockbuster drug used by some 20 million Americans. Amid growing danger signs, Merck fought a rearguard action for four and a half years, clinging to a hope that somehow Vioxx's safety could be confirmed—even though its research chief had already privately acknowledged its risks.

SOURCE: Excerpted from A W Mathews and B Martinez, "Painful Drug: E-Mails Suggest Merck Knew Vioxx's Dangers at Early Stage," *The Wall Street Journal,* November 1, 2004, p A1.

What are the frequency and consequences of unethical behavior? Although it is difficult to obtain precise statistics on the frequency of unethical behavior, a 2005 nationwide survey of 581 human resource professionals revealed that 62% of the respondents occasionally observed unethical behavior at their companies.[2] Unethical behavior occurs from the bottom to the top of organizations. For example, a survey of job applicants for executive positions indicated that 64% had been misinformed about the financial condition of potential employers, and 58% of these individuals were negatively affected by this misinformation.[3] It is very likely that some of these affected individuals moved their families and left their friends only to find out the promise of a great job in a financially stable organization was a lie.

Experts estimated that US companies lose about $600 billion a year from unethical and criminal behavior.[4] Studies in the United States and the United Kingdom further demonstrated that corporate commitment to ethics can be profitable. Evidence suggested that profitability is enhanced by a reputation for honesty and corporate citizenship.[5] Ethics can also impact the quality of people who apply to work in an organization. A recent online survey of 1,020 individuals indicated that 83% rated a company's record of business ethics as "very important" when deciding to accept a job offer. Only 2% rated it as "unimportant."[6]

As you will learn in this module, there are a variety of individual and organizational factors that contribute to unethical behavior. OB is an excellent vantage point for better understanding and improving workplace ethics. If OB can provide insights about managing human work behavior, then it can teach us something about avoiding *misbehavior.*

Ethics involves the study of moral issues and choices. It is concerned with right versus wrong, good versus bad, and the many shades of gray in supposedly black-and-white issues. Moral implications spring from virtually every decision, both on and off the job. Managers are challenged to have more imagination and the courage to do the right thing.

For example, do you think Merck acted ethically when researchers began raising questions about the heart risks associated with its big-selling painkiller Vioxx (see Real World/ Real People on page 32)? Merck responded this way even after its research chief, Edward Scolnick, had e-mailed colleagues in March 2000 that "the cardiovascular events 'are clearly there' and called it a 'shame.' "[7] Vioxx eventually was pulled from the market.

To enhance your understanding about ethics and organizational behavior, we discuss (1) a conceptual framework of ethical behavior, (2) a decision tree for diagnosing ethical decisions, (3) whether moral orientations vary by gender, (4) general moral principles for managers, and (5) how to improve an organization's ethical climate.

> **Ethics**
> Study of moral issues and choices.

A Model of Ethical Behavior

Ethical and unethical conduct is the product of a complex combination of influences (see Figure A–1). At the center of the model in Figure A–1 is the individual decision maker. He or she has a unique combination of personality characteristics, values, and moral principles, leaning toward or away from ethical behavior. Personal experience with being rewarded or reinforced for certain behaviors and punished for others also shapes the individual's tendency to act ethically or unethically. Finally, gender may play an important role in explaining ethical behavior. It it widely believed that men and women have different moral orientations toward organizational behavior.[8] This belief is put to the test later in this module.

Figure A–1   *A Model of Ethical Behavior in the Workplace*

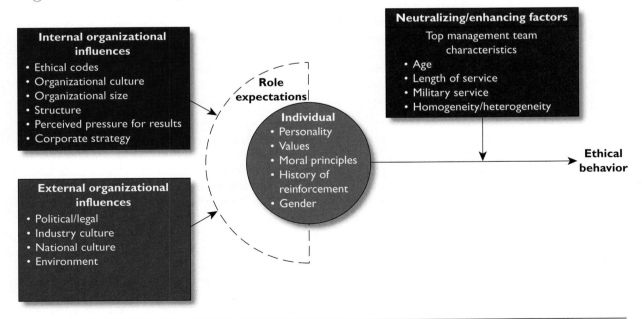

SOURCE: Based in part on A J Daboub, A M A Rasheed, R L Priem, and D A Gray, "Top Management Team Characteristics and Corporate Illegal Activity," *Academy of Management Review,* January 1995, pp 138–70. Reprinted by permission of The Academy of Management via The Copyright Clearance Center.

Next, Figure A–1 illustrates two major sources of influence on one's role expectations. People assume many roles in life, including those of employee or manager. One's expectations for how those roles should be played are shaped by a combination of internal and external organizational factors. Let us now examine how various internal and external organizational influences impact ethical behavior and how these effects are neutralized or enhanced by characteristics possessed by an organization's top management team.

Internal Organizational Influences

Figure A–1 shows six key internal organizational influences on ethical behavior.[9] Corporate ethical codes of conduct and organizational culture, discussed in Chapter 2, clearly contribute to reducing the frequency of unethical behavior. Consider the example of Rudder Finn, the world's largest privately owned public relations agency.

> Rudder Finn established an ethics committee early on in its history because the founders maintain that public relations professionals have a special obligation to believe in what they are doing. David Finn, co-founder and CEO, chairs every ethics committee meeting to demonstrate how seriously he takes this issue. In part, these meetings perform the function of a training program in that all members of staff are invited to participate in an open forum, during which actual ethical problems are freely discussed and an outside adviser provides objectivity. "Employees have to trust that if they go to a line manager to discuss a delicate situation or seek advice, they can do so without fear of repercussions," says Finn.[10]

This example also illustrates the importance of top management support in creating an ethical work environment.

A number of studies have uncovered a positive relationship between organizational size and unethical behavior: Larger firms are more likely to behave illegally. Interestingly, research also reveals that managers are more likely to behave unethically in decentralized organizations. Unethical behavior is suspected to occur in this context because lower-level managers want to "look good" for the corporate office. In support of this conclusion, many studies have found a tendency among middle- and lower-level managers to act unethically in the face of perceived pressure for results. Further, this tendency is particularly pronounced when individuals are rewarded for accomplishing their goals.[11] By fostering a pressure-cooker atmosphere for results, managers can unwittingly set the stage for unethical shortcuts by employees who seek to please and be loyal to the company.

External Organizational Influences

Figure A–1 identifies four key external influences on role expectations and ethical behavior. The political/legal system clearly impacts ethical behavior. As previously mentioned, the United States is currently experiencing an increase in the extent to which its political/legal system is demanding and monitoring corporate ethical behavior. In contrast, other countries such as China do not put as much emphasis on monitoring unethical and potentially illegal actions. Consider the case of counterfeiting. The World Customs Organization estimates counterfeiting cost companies $512 billion in lost revenue in 2004. China is the largest contributor to counterfeiting in the world, accounting for nearly two-thirds of all the fake goods worldwide.[12] Past research also uncovered a tendency for firms in certain industries to commit more illegal acts. Researchers partially explained this finding by speculating that an industry's culture, defined as shared norms, values, and beliefs among firms, predisposes managers to act unethically.

Although China is the largest contributor to counterfeit business around the world, officials like these in Zhejiang Province have been increasing their attempts to confiscate fake products. These officials found 460,000 fake Sony brand batteries and 30,000 fake Sony brand earphones. Would you buy a designer "knock-off" if the price was right?

Moreover, Figure A–1 shows that national culture affects ethical behavior (national cultures are discussed in Chapter 4).[13] This conclusion was supported in a multination study (including the United States, Great Britain, France, Germany, Spain, Switzerland, India, China, and Australia) of management ethics. Managers from each country were asked to judge the ethicality of the 12 behaviors used in the OB Exercise on page 36. Results revealed significant differences across the 10 nations.[14] That is, managers did not agree about the ethicality of the 12 behaviors. What is your attitude toward these behaviors? (You can find out by completing the OB Exercise.) Finally, the external environment influences ethical behavior. For example, unethical behavior is more likely to occur in environments that are characterized by less generosity and when industry profitability is declining.

Neutralizing/Enhancing Factors

In their search for understanding the causes of ethical behavior, OB researchers uncovered several factors that may weaken or strengthen the relationship between the internal and external influencers shown in Figure A–1 and ethical behavior. These factors all revolve around characteristics possessed by an organization's top management team (TMT): A TMT consists of the CEO and his or her direct reports.[15] The relationship between ethical influencers and ethical behavior is weaker with increasing average age and increasing tenure among the TMT. This result suggests that an older and more experienced group of leaders is less likely to allow unethical behavior to occur. Further, the ethical influencers are less likely to lead to unethical behavior as the number of TMT members with military experience increases and when the TMT possesses heterogenous characteristics (e.g., diverse in terms of gender, age, race, religion, etc.). This conclusion has two important implications.

First, it appears that prior military experience favorably influences the ethical behavior of executives. While OB researchers are uncertain about the cause of this relationship, it may be due to the military's practice of indoctrinating recruits to endorse the values of duty, discipline, and honor. Regardless of the cause, military experience within a TMT is positively related to ethical behavior. Organizations thus should consider the merits of including military experience as one of its selection criteria when hiring or promoting

OB Exercise   How Ethical Are These Behaviors?

Instructions

Evaluate the extent to which you believe the following behaviors are ethical. Circle your responses on the rating scales provided. Compute your average score and compare it to the norms.

	Very Unethical	Unethical	Neither Ethical nor Unethical	Ethical	Very Ethical
Accepting gifts/favors in exchange for preferential treatment	1	2	3	4	5
Giving gifts/favors in exchange for preferential treatment	1	2	3	4	5
Divulging confidential information	1	2	3	4	5
Calling in sick to take a day off	1	2	3	4	5
Using the organization's materials and supplies for personal use	1	2	3	4	5
Doing personal business on work time	1	2	3	4	5
Taking extra personal time (breaks, etc.)	1	2	3	4	5
Using organizational services for personal use	1	2	3	4	5
Passing blame for errors to an innocent co-worker	1	2	3	4	5
Claiming credit for someone else's work	1	2	3	4	5
Not reporting others' violations of organizational policies	1	2	3	4	5
Concealing one's errors	1	2	3	4	5

Average score = _____

Norms (average scores by country)

United States = 1.49

Great Britian = 1.70

Australia = 1.44

France = 1.66

China = 1.46

Average of all 10 countries = 1.67

SOURCE: The survey behaviors were taken from T Jackson, "Cultural Values and Management Ethics: A 10-Nation Study," *Human Relations*, October 2001, pp 1287–88.

managers. Second, organizations are encouraged to increase the diversity of its TMT if they want to reduce the chances of unethical decision making. Chapter 2 thoroughly discusses how employee diversity can increase creativity, innovation, group problem solving, and productivity.

A Decision Tree for Ethical Decisions

Ethical decision making frequently involves trade-offs. The opening vignette to this learning module is a good example. IBM's decision to raise their retirees' health benefit contributions saved the company money and thereby created a positive impact on shareholder value. On the other hand, individuals like Robert Eggleston were hurt by this decision. He ultimately had to take out a second mortgage on his home to pay for health-related expenses. This section presents a decision tree that managers can use to help navigate through ethical questions such as the one faced by IBM in the opening vignette.

The decision tree is shown in Figure A–2 and it can be applied to any type of decision or action that an individual manager or corporation is contemplating.[16] Looking at the tree, the first question to ask is whether or not the proposed action is legal. If the action is

Figure A–2   *An Ethical Decision Tree*

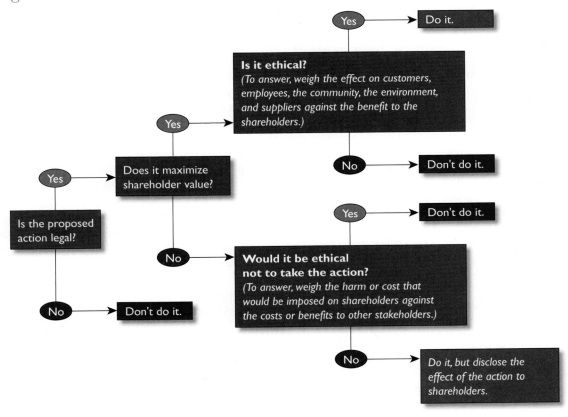

illegal, do not do it. If the action is legal, then consider the impact of the action on shareholder value. A decision maximizes shareholder value when it results in a more favorable financial position (e.g., increased profits) for an organization. Whether or not an action maximizes shareholder value, the decision tree shows that managers still need to consider the ethical implications of the decision or action. For example, if an action maximizes shareholder value, the next question to consider is whether or not the action is ethical. The answer to this question is based on considering the positive effect of the action on an organization's other key constituents (i.e., customers, employees, the community, the environment, and suppliers) against the benefit to the shareholders. According to the decision tree framework, managers should make the decision to engage in an action if the benefits to the shareholders exceed the benefits to the other key constituents. Managers should not engage in the action if the other key constituents would benefit more from the action than shareholders.

Figure A–2 illustrates that managers use a slightly different perspective when their initial conclusion is that an action does not maximize shareholder value. In this case, the question becomes "Would it be ethical not to take action?" This question necessitates that a manager consider the *harm or cost* of an action to shareholders against the *costs or benefits* to other key constituents. If the costs to shareholders from a managerial decision exceed the costs or benefits to other constituents, the manager or company should not engage in the action. Conversely, the manager or company should take action when the perceived costs or benefits to the other constituents are greater than the costs to shareholders. Let us apply this decision tree to the example in the opening vignette on IBM.

Is it legal for a company to decrease its contribution to retiree health care benefits while simultaneously raising retirees' contributions? The answer is yes.[17] Does an organization maximize shareholder value by decreasing its retiree health care expenses? Again, the answer is yes. We now have to consider the overall benefits to shareholders against the overall benefits to other key constituents. The answer to this question is more complex than it appears and is contingent on an organization's corporate values. Consider the following two examples. In company one, the organization is losing money and it needs cash in order to invest in new product development. Management believes that new products will fuel the company's economic growth and ultimate survival. This company's statement of corporate values also reveals that the organization values profits and shareholder return more than employee loyalty. In this case, the company should make the decision to increase retirees' health care contributions. Company two, in contrast, is profitable and has been experiencing increased market share with its products. This company's statement of corporate values also indicates that employees are the most important constituent it has, even more than shareholders: Southwest Airlines is a good example of a company with these corporate values. In this case, the company should not make the decision to decrease its contribution to retirees' benefits.

It is important to keep in mind that the decision tree cannot provide a quick formula that managers and organizations can use to assess every ethical question. It does, however, provide a framework for considering the trade-offs between managerial and corporate actions and managerial and corporate ethics. Try using this decision tree the next time you are faced with a significant ethical question or problem.

Do Moral Orientations Vary by Gender?

It is interesting to note that two women, Sherron Watkins and Maureen Castaneda, played key roles as whistle-blowers (i.e., when an employee informs others about corporate wrongdoing) in the Enron fiasco. "Watkins, Enron's vice president of corporate development, wrote the prescient memo to Enron's chief executive that warned him the company was in deep financial trouble. Castaneda, Enron's director of foreign exchange, is the one who told authorities that Enron was still shredding documents after its officials were ordered to preserve every piece of paper."[18] Does this suggest that women are more likely to be whistle-blowers because they have different moral principles than men?

A study of 300 self-described whistle-blowers revealed that gender was not related to employees' reporting wrongdoing.[19] Still, other research suggests that men and women view moral problems and situations differently. Carol Gilligan, a well-known psychologist, proposed one underlying cause of these gender dif-

Sherron Watkins, former vice president for corporate development at Enron, was one of the whistleblowers who brought the company's unethical practices to light. Former Enron Chief Executive Officer Jeffrey Skilling looks on as she testifies before the Senate Commerce Committee on Enron. Do you think it took a lot of courage for Watkins to testify? What are the consequences of being a whistleblower?

ferences. Her research revealed that men and women differed in terms of how they perceived moral problems. Males perceived moral problems in terms of a **justice perspective,** whereas women relied on a **care perspective.** The two perspectives are described as follows:

> A justice perspective draws attention to problems of inequality and oppression and holds up an ideal of reciprocal rights and equal respect for individuals. A care perspective draws attention to problems of detachment or abandonment and holds up an ideal of attention and response to need. Two moral injunctions, not to treat others unfairly and not to turn away from someone in need, capture these different concerns.[20]

This description underscores the point that men are expected to view moral problems in terms of rights, whereas women are predicted to conceptualize moral problems as an issue of care involving empathy and compassion.

A meta-analysis of 113 studies tested these ideas by examining whether or not the justice and care orientations varied by gender. Results did not support the expectation that the care perspective was used predominantly by females and the justice orientation predominantly by males.[21] The authors concluded that "although distinct moral orientations may exist, these orientations are not strongly associated with gender."[22] This conclusion suggests that future research is needed to identify the source of moral reasoning differences between men and women. Which moral perspective do you prefer: justice or care?

Justice perspective
Based on the ideal of reciprocal rights and driven by rules and regulations.

Care perspective
Involves compassion and an ideal of attention and response to need.

General Moral Principles

Management consultant and writer Kent Hodgson has helpfully taken managers a step closer to ethical decisions by identifying seven general moral principles (see Table A–1).

Hodgson calls them "the magnificent seven" to emphasize their timeless and worldwide relevance. Both the justice and care perspectives are clearly evident in the magnificent seven, which are more detailed and, hence, more practical. Importantly, according to Hodgson, there are no absolute ethical answers for decision makers. The goal for managers should be to rely on moral principles so their decisions are *principled, appropriate,* and *defensible.*[23]

ExxonMobil is a good example of a company trying to follow this recommendation. According to the company's corporate citizenship statement,

> We pledge to be a good corporate citizen in all the places we operate worldwide. We will maintain the highest ethical standards, comply with all applicable laws and regulations, and respect local and national cultures. We are dedicated to running safe and environmentally responsible operations.[24]

Table A–1 *The Magnificent Seven: General Moral Principles for Managers*

1. *Dignity of human life:* The lives of people are to be respected. Human beings, by the fact of their existence, have value and dignity. We may not act in ways that directly intend to harm or kill an innocent person. Human beings have a right to live; we have an obligation to respect that right to life. Human life is to be preserved and treated as sacred.
2. *Autonomy:* All persons are intrinsically valuable and have the right to self-determination. We should act in ways that demonstrate each person's worth, dignity, and right to free choice. We have a right to act in ways that assert our own worth and legitimate needs. We should not use others as mere "things" or only as means to an end. Each person has an equal right to basic human liberty, compatible with a similar liberty for others.
3. *Honesty:* The truth should be told to those who have a right to know it. Honesty is also known as integrity, truth telling, and honor. One should speak and act so as to reflect the reality of the situation. Speaking and acting should mirror the way things really are. There are times when others have the right to hear the truth from us; there are times when they do not.
4. *Loyalty:* Promises, contracts, and commitments should be honored. Loyalty includes fidelity, promise keeping, keeping the public trust, good citizenship, excellence in quality of work, reliability, commitment, and honoring just laws, rules, and policies.
5. *Fairness:* People should be treated justly. One has the right to be treated fairly, impartially, and equitably. One has the obligation to treat others fairly and justly. All have the right to the necessities of life—especially those in deep need and the helpless. Justice includes equal, impartial, unbiased treatment. Fairness tolerates diversity and accepts differences in people and their ideas.
6. *Humaneness.* There are two parts: (1) Our actions ought to accomplish good, and (2) we should avoid doing evil. We should do good to others and to ourselves. We should have concern for the well-being of others; usually, we show this concern in the form of compassion, giving, kindness, serving, and caring.
7. *The common good:* Actions should accomplish the "greatest good for the greatest number" of people. One should act and speak in ways that benefit the welfare of the largest number of people, while trying to protect the rights of individuals.

SOURCE: From Kent Hodgson, *A Rock and a Hard Place: How to Make Ethical Business Decisions When the Choices Are Tough,* © 1992. Used by permission of the author.

How to Improve the Organization's Ethical Climate

A team of management researchers recommended the following actions for improving on-the-job ethics.[25]

- *Behave ethically yourself.* Managers are potent role models whose habits and actual behavior send clear signals about the importance of ethical conduct. Ethical behavior is a top-to-bottom proposition.
- *Screen potential employees.* Surprisingly, employers are generally lax when it comes to checking references, credentials, transcripts, and other information on applicant résumés. More diligent action in this area can screen out those given to fraud and misrepresentation. Integrity testing is fairly valid but is no panacea.[26]
- *Develop a meaningful code of ethics.* Codes of ethics can have a positive impact if they satisfy these four criteria:

  1. They are *distributed* to every employee.
  2. They are firmly *supported* by top management.
  3. They refer to *specific* practices and ethical dilemmas likely to be encountered by target employees (e.g., salespersons paying kickbacks, purchasing agents receiving payoffs, laboratory scientists doctoring data, or accountants "cooking the books").
  4. They are evenly *enforced* with rewards for compliance and strict penalties for noncompliance.

- *Provide ethics training.* Employees can be trained to identify and deal with ethical issues during orientation and through seminar, video, and Internet training sessions.[27]
- *Reinforce ethical behavior.* Behavior that is reinforced tends to be repeated, whereas behavior that is not reinforced tends to disappear. Ethical conduct too often is punished while unethical behavior is rewarded.
- *Create positions, units, and other structural mechanisms to deal with ethics.* Ethics needs to be an everyday affair, not a one-time announcement of a new ethical code that gets filed away and forgotten. Boeing, for example, has hired an outside ethics watchdog in response to several breaches of ethics. Ethics transgressions have cost the company billions of dollars in government contracts and resulted in the firing of several top-level executives. The new external ethics compliance officer will oversee Boeing's new ethics-compliance programs and will report directly to the US Air Force.[28]

Discussion Questions

1. How does Figure A–1 help you to identify the most important influences on IBM's decision to increase retirees' contributions to health benefits while decreasing its contributions (see page 31)?

2. Why do you think there is an increase in the number of indictments against executives in the United States?

3. If you were a professor at a university, what would you do to discourage students from cheating on assignments and exams? Explain your recommendations.

Investigating the Difference in Moral Reasoning between Men and Women

Objectives

1. To determine if men and women resolve moral/ethical problems differently.
2. To determine if males and females use justice and care perspectives, respectively, to solve moral/ethical problems.
3. To improve your understanding about the moral reasoning used by men and women.

Introduction

Men and women may view moral problems and situations dissimilarly. This is one reason men and women sometimes solve identical moral or ethical problems differently. Some researchers believe that men rely on a justice perspective to solve moral problems whereas women are expected to use a care perspective. This exercise presents two scenarios that possess a moral/ethical issue. You will be asked to solve each problem and to discuss the logic behind your decision. The exercise provides you with the opportunity to hear the thought processes used by men and women to solve moral/ethical problems.

Instructions

Your instructor will divide the class into groups of four to six. (An interesting option is to use gender-based groups.) Each group member should first read the scenario alone and then make a decision about what to do. Once this is done, use the space provided to outline the rationale for your decision to this scenario. Next, read the second scenario and follow the same procedure: Make a decision and explain your rationale. Once all group members have completed their analyses for both scenarios, meet as a group to discuss the results. One at a time, each group member should present his or her final decision and the associated reasoning for the first scenario. Someone should keep a running tally of the decisions so that a summary can be turned in to the professor at the end of your discussion. Follow the same procedure for the second scenario.[29]

SCENARIO 1

You are the manager of a local toy store. The hottest Christmas toy of the year is the new "Peter Panda" stuffed animal. The toy is in great demand and almost impossible to find. You have received your one and only shipment of 12, and they are all promised to people who previously stopped in to place a deposit and reserve one. A woman comes by the store and pleads with you, saying that her six-year-old daughter is in the hospital very ill, and that "Peter Panda" is the one toy she has her heart set on. Would you sell her one, knowing that you will have to break your promise and refund the deposit to one of the other customers? (There is no way you will be able to get an extra toy in time.)

Your Decision: _____

	Would Sell	Would Not Sell	Unsure
Men			
Women			

Rationale for your decision:

SCENARIO 2

You sell corporate financial products, such as pension plans and group health insurance. You are currently negotiating with Paul Scott, treasurer of a *Fortune* 500 firm, for a sale that could be in the millions of dollars. You feel you are in a strong position to make the sale, but two competitors are also negotiating with Scott, and it could go either way. You have become friendly with Scott, and over lunch one day he confided in you that he has recently been under treatment for manic depression. It so happens that in your office there is a staff psychologist who does employee counseling. The thought has occurred to you that such a trained professional might be able to coach you on how to act with and relate to a personality such as Scott's, so as to persuade and influence him most effectively. Would you consult the psychologist?

Your Decision: _____

	Would Consult	Would Not Consult	Unsure
Men			
Women			

Rationale for your decision:

Questions for Discussion

1. Did males and females make different decisions in response to both scenarios? (Comparative norms can be found in Note 30.)

2. What was the moral reasoning used by women and men to solve the two scenarios?[31]

3. To what extent did males and females use a justice and care perspectives, respectively?

4. What useful lessons did you learn from this exercise?

Managing Diversity: Releasing Every Employee's Potential

Learning Objectives

When you finish studying the material in this chapter, you should be able to:

1   Define diversity and review the four layers of diversity.

2   Explain the difference between affirmative action and managing diversity.

3   Describe the glass ceiling and the four top strategies used by women to break the glass ceiling.

4   Review the demographic trends pertaining to racial groups, educational mismatches, and an aging workforce.

5   Highlight the managerial implications of increasing diversity in the workforce.

6   Explain the positive and negative effects of diversity by using social categorization theory and information/decision-making theory.

7   Identify the barriers and challenges to managing diversity.

8   Discuss the organizational practices used to effectively manage diversity as identified by Ann Morrison.

By the time Gerstner took the helm in 1993, IBM already had a long history of progressive management when it came to civil rights and equal employment. Indeed, few of the company's executives would have identified workforce diversity as an area of strategic focus. But when Gerstner took a look at his senior executive team, he felt it didn't reflect the diversity of the market for talent or IBM's customers and employees. To rectify the imbalance, in 1995 Gerstner launched a diversity task-force initiative that became a cornerstone of IBM's HR strategy. The effort continued through Gerstner's tenure and remains today under current CEO Sam Palmisano.

Rather than attempt to eliminate discrimination by deliberately ignoring differences among employees, IBM created eight task forces, each focused on a different group such as Asians, gays and lesbians, and women. The goal of the initiative was to uncover and understand differences among the groups and find ways to appeal to a broader set of employees and customers.

The initiative required a lot of work, and it didn't happen overnight—the first task force convened almost two years after Gerstner's arrival.

But the IBM of today looks very different from the IBM of 1995. The number of female executives worldwide has increased by 370%. The number of ethnic minority executives born in the United States has increased by 233%. Fifty-two percent of IBM's Worldwide Management Council (WMC), the top 52 executives who determine corporate strategy, is composed of women, ethnic minorities born in the United States, and non-U.S. citizens. The organization has seen the number of self-identified gay, lesbian, bisexual, and transgender executives increase by 733% and the number of executives with disabilities more than triple.

But diversity at IBM is about more than expanding the talent pool. When I asked Gerstner what had driven the success of the task forces, he said, "We

These recently promoted IBM employees are participating in a training development course that focuses on people management. IBM is noted for promoting diverse employees into its managerial ranks.

made diversity a market-based issue. . . . It's about understanding our markets, which are diverse and multicultural."

By deliberately seeking ways to more effectively reach a broader range of customers, IBM has seen significant bottom-line results. For example, the work of the women's task force and other constituencies led IBM to establish its Market Development organization, a group focused on growing the market of multicultural and women-owned businesses in the United States. One tactic: partnering with vendors to provide much-needed sales and service support to small and midsize businesses, a niche well populated with minority and female buyers. In 2001, the organization's activities accounted for more than $300 million in revenue compared with $10 million in 1998. Based on a recommendation from the people with disabilities task force, in October 2001 IBM launched an initiative focused on making all of its products more broadly accessible to take advantage of new legislation—an amendment to the federal Rehabilitation Act requiring that government agencies make accessibility a criterion for awarding federal contracts. IBM executives estimate this effort will produce more than a billion dollars in revenue during the next five to ten years.

Over the past two years, I have interviewed more than 50 IBM employees—ranging from midlevel managers all the way up to Gerstner and Palmisano—about the task force effort and spent a great deal of time with Ted Childs, IBM's vice president of Global Workforce Diversity and Gerstner's primary partner in guiding this change process. What they described was a significant philosophical shift—from a long tradition of minimizing differences to amplifying them and to seizing on the business opportunities they present.[1]

FOR DISCUSSION
How can the use of task forces help diverse employees succeed in an organization?

The IBM example highlights two key reasons why it is important for managers to effectively manage diversity. Effectively managing diversity is not only a good thing to do in order to attract and retain the most talented employees, but it makes good business sense.[2] Unfortunately, however, some organizations are missing the mark when it comes to managing diversity, and the result can be costly lawsuits. Consider the following examples:

- Seven Afghan Muslim employees at two car dealerships in Solano County, California, said they had been harassed and were called offensive names such as "the bin Laden gang," "sand niggers," "terrorists," and "camel jockeys." Their suit resulted in a $500,000 settlement with the dealerships.

- A major soap manufacturer wound up paying $10 million after it was alleged in a lawsuit that about 100 female employees had been sexually harassed, including being propositioned and groped, for example, at one Illinois facility.

- An 18-year-old male salesclerk for a baby products retailer in New Jersey alleged that he was subjected to a sexually hostile environment—he was called "fag," "faggot," and "happy pants," and he was forcefully stripped of his trousers by co-workers. The retailer settled for $205,000.[3]

It is important to note that these things occurred in these companies despite the existence of laws that prohibit such behaviors. As you will learn in this chapter, managing diversity entails much more than following laws and creating policies and procedures proscribing equal treatment of employees.

Managing diversity is a sensitive, potentially volatile, and sometimes uncomfortable issue. Yet managers are required to deal with it in the name of organizational survival. Accordingly, the purpose of this chapter is to help you get a better understanding of this important context for organizational behavior. We begin by defining diversity. Next, we build the business case for diversity and then discuss the barriers and challenges associated with managing diversity. The chapter concludes by describing the organizational practices used to manage diversity effectively.

Defining Diversity

Diversity represents the multitude of individual differences and similarities that exist among people. This definition underscores a key issue about managing diversity. There are many different dimensions or components of diversity. This implies that diversity pertains to everybody. It is not an issue of age, race, or gender. It is not an issue of being heterosexual, gay, or lesbian or of being Catholic, Jewish, Protestant, or Muslim. Diversity also does not pit white males against all other groups of people. Diversity pertains to the host of individual differences that make all of us unique and different from others.

This section begins our journey into managing diversity by first reviewing the key dimensions of diversity. Because many people associate diversity with affirmative action, this section compares affirmative action with managing diversity. They are not the same.

> **Diversity**
> The host of individual differences that make people different from and similar to each other.

Layers of Diversity

Like seashells on a beach, people come in a variety of shapes, sizes, and colors. This variety represents the essence of diversity. Lee Gardenswartz and Anita Rowe, a team of diversity experts, identified four layers of diversity to help distinguish the important ways in which people differ (see Figure 2–1). Taken together, these layers define your personal identity and influence how each of us sees the world.

Figure 2–1 shows that personality is at the center of the diversity wheel. Personality is at the center because it represents a stable set of characteristics that is responsible for a person's identity. The dimensions of personality are discussed later in Chapter 5. The next layer of diversity consists of a set of internal dimensions that are referred to as surface-level dimensions of diversity.[4] These dimensions, for the most part, are not within our control, but they strongly influence our attitudes and expectations and assumptions about others, which, in turn, influence our behavior. Take the encounter experienced by an African-American woman in middle management while vacationing at a resort:

> While I was sitting by the pool, "a large 50-ish white male approached me and demanded that I get him extra towels. I said, 'Excuse me?' He then said, 'Oh, you don't work here,' with no shred of embarrassment or apology in his voice."[5]

Stereotypes regarding one or more of the surface-level dimensions of diversity most likely influenced this man's behavior toward the woman.

Figure 2–1 reveals that the next layer of diversity is composed of external influences, which are referred to as secondary dimensions of diversity. They represent individual differences that we have a greater ability to influence or control. Examples include where you grew up and live today, your religious affiliation, whether you are married and have children, and your work experiences. These dimensions also exert a significant influence on our perceptions, behavior, and attitudes.

Consider religion as an illustration. Given that Islam is expected to surpass Judaism as the second-most commonly practiced religion in the United States (Christianity is first), organizations need to consider Muslim employees when implementing their policies, procedures, and programs. Ford Motor Company, for example, proactively conducted a series of Islam 101 training sessions in Dearborn, Michigan, after the September 11 terrorist attacks. It did this because the Dearborn area is home to one of the largest Arab-American and Middle Eastern communities in the United States and the company wanted to raise awareness about the Islamic faith.[6]

Figure 2–1   *The Four Layers of Diversity*

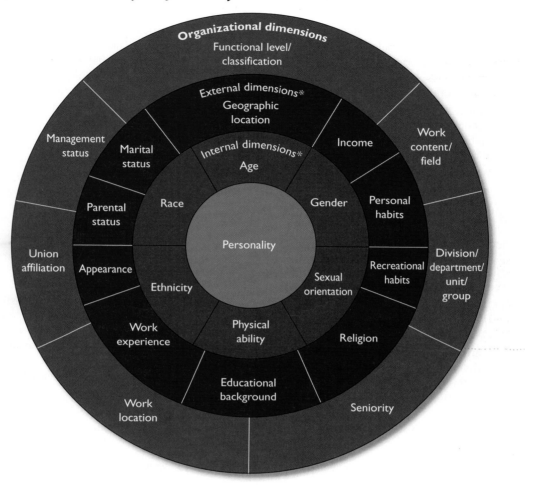

*Internal dimensions and external dimensions are adapted from Loden and Rosener, *Workforce America!* (Homewood, IL: Business One Irwin, 1991).

SOURCE: L Gardenswartz and A Rowe, *Diverse Teams at Work: Capitalizing on the Power of Diversity* (New York: McGraw-Hill, 1994), p. 33. © 1994.

The Ford example illustrates that an organization's level of awareness about the external layer of diversity can foster positive feelings among employees. The final layer of diversity includes organizational dimensions such as seniority, job title and function, and work location.

Affirmative Action and Managing Diversity

Effectively managing diversity requires organizations to adopt a new way of thinking about differences among people. Rather than pitting one group against another, managing diversity entails recognition of the unique contribution every employee can make. As found at Designer

Blinds, a 170-employee company located in Omaha, Nebraska, with a turnover rate of 167%, effectively managing diversity lowered turnover and increased productivity and quality.

> Top managers began by viewing recruiting and retention strategically and quantitatively. An entirely new approach to hiring was launched. One aspect was networking with representatives of various cultures, including the local Sudanese community, which had not been well represented in the workforce. Company supervisors and co-workers studied the culture and embraced it. The firm also identified Hispanics as the fastest-growing group in the area and made a sincere effort to welcome members of the community and to provide English-as-a-second-language classes.
>
> The diversification of the workplace has produced good results for several years, especially the last two. Employee efficiency and productivity is skyrocketing, quality is a benchmark for the industry, and turnover has plunged from stratospheric highs to 8% a year.[7]

The management philosophies used at Designer Blinds earned the company the 2003 Optimas Award for excellence in people management and are much different from the management philosophies associated with affirmative action. This section highlights the differences between affirmative action and managing diversity.

Affirmative Action
Affirmative action is an outgrowth of equal employment opportunity (EEO) legislation. The goal of this legislation is to outlaw discrimination and to encourage organizations to proactively prevent discrimination. **Discrimination** occurs when employment decisions about an individual are due to reasons not associated with performance or are not related to the job. Table 2–1 provides a review of major federal laws pertaining to equal employment opportunity. As you can see from this table, many forms of discrimination are outlawed. For example, organizations cannot discriminate on the basis of race, color, religion, national origin, sex, age, physical and mental disabilities, and pregnancy. Many of these federal laws are enforced by the Equal Employment Opportunity Commission (EEOC), and individuals may sue for back pay and punitive damages when they feel that they have been discriminated against.

In contrast to the proactive perspective of EEO legislation, **affirmative action** is an artificial intervention aimed at giving management a chance to correct an imbalance, an injustice, a mistake, or outright discrimination that occured in the past. Affirmative action does not legitimize quotas. Quotas are illegal. They can only be imposed by judges who conclude that a company has engaged in discriminatory practices. It also is important to note that under no circumstances does affirmative action require companies to hire unqualified people.

Although affirmative action created tremendous opportunities for women and minorities, it does not foster the type of thinking that is needed to effectively manage diversity.[8] For example, affirmative action is resisted more by white males than women and minorities because it is perceived to work against their own self-interest. Affirmative action plans are more successful when employees view them as fair and equitable and when whites are not prejudiced against people of color.[9]

Affirmative action programs also were found to negatively affect the women and minorities expected to benefit from them. Research demonstrated that women and minorities, supposedly hired on the basis of affirmative action, felt negatively stigmatized as unqualified or incompetent. They also experienced lower job satisfaction and more stress than employees supposedly selected on the basis of merit.[10] Another study, however, showed that these negative consequences were reduced for women when a merit criterion was included in hiring decisions. In other words, women hired under affirmative action programs felt better about themselves and exhibited higher performance when they believed they were hired because of their competence rather than their gender.[11]

Discrimination
Occurs when employment decisions are based on factors that are not job related.

Affirmative action
Focuses on achieving equality of opportunity in an organization.

Table 2–1   *Federal Equal Employment Opportunity Legislation*

Year	Law or Regulation	Provisions
1963	Equal Pay Act	Requires men and women be paid equally for performing equal work
1964	Civil Rights Act, Title VII	Prohibits discrimination on basis of race, color, religion, national origin, or sex
1967, amended 1978 and 1986	Age Discrimination in Employment Act (ADEA)	Prohibits discrimination in employees over 40 years old; restricts mandatory retirement
1970	Occupational Safety & Health Act (OSHA)	Establishes minimum health and safety standards in organizations
1974	Employee Retirement Income Security Act (ERISA)	Sets rules for managing pension plans; provides federal insurance to cover bankrupt plans
1978	Pregnancy Discrimination Act	Broadens discrimination to cover pregnancy, childbirth, and related medical conditions; protects job security during maternity leave
1978	Mandatory Retirement Act	Prohibits forced retirement of employees under 70
1986	Consolidated Omnibus Budget Reconciliation Act (COBRA)	Requires an extension of health insurance benefits after termination
1986	Immigration Reform & Control Act	Prohibits unlawful employment of aliens and unfair immigration-related employment practices
1988	Worker Adjustment and Retraining Notification Act	Requires organizations with 100 or more employees to give 60 days notice for mass layoffs or plant closings
1990	Americans with Disabilities Act (ADA)	Prohibits discrimination against qualified employees with physical or mental disabilities or chronic illness; requires "reasonable accommodation" be provided so they can perform duties
1991	Civil Rights Act	Amends and clarifies Title VII, ADA, and other laws; permits suits against employers for punitive damages in cases of intentional discrimination
1993	Family & Medical Leave Act	Requires employers to provide 12 weeks of unpaid leave for medical and family reasons, including for childbirth, adoption, or family emergency
2003	Sarbanes-Oxley Act	Prohibits employers from demoting or firing employees who raise accusations of fraud to a federal agency

SOURCE: A Kinicki and B Williams, *Management: A Practical Introduction,* 2nd ed, McGraw-Hill, © 2006, p 283. Reprinted by permission of McGraw-Hill Companies, Inc.

Managing diversity

Creating organizational changes that enable all people to perform up to their maximum potential.

Managing Diversity

Managing diversity entails enabling people to perform up to their maximum potential. It focuses on changing an organization's culture and infrastructure such that people provide the highest productivity possible. Wegmans, a grocery chain with 67 stores in New York, Pennsylvania, New Jersey, and Virginia that was ranked as the best company to work for in America in 2005 by *Fortune,* is a good example of a company that effectively manages diversity (see Real World/Real People).[12] Ann Morrison, a diversity expert, conducted a study of 16 organizations that successfully managed diversity. Her results uncovered three key strategies for success: education, enforcement, and exposure. She describes them as follows:

Wegmans Effectively Manages Diversity

Wegmans' hourly wages and annual salaries are at the high end of the market. . . . But salaries aren't the whole story. The company has shelled out $54 million for college scholarships to more than 17,500 full- and part-time employees over the past 20 years. It thinks nothing of sending, say, cheese manager Terri Zodarecky on a 10-day sojourn to cheesemakers in London, Paris, and Italy. . . .

A common denominator of passionate customer service sets Wegmans workers apart from those at other retailers. Simply put, no customer is allowed to leave unhappy. To ensure that, employees are encouraged to do just about anything, on the spot, without consulting a higher-up. . . . Empowering employees goes beyond making house calls, though—it also means creating an environment where they can shine, unburdened by hierarchies.

SOURCE: Excerpted from M Boyle, "The Wegman's Way," *Fortune,* January 24, 2005, pp 66, 68.

Buying pastries can be a fun and tasty experience at Wegmans. Ranked as the best American company to work for by *Fortune* in 2005, Wegman's fosters employee effort and commitment by effectively managing diversity.

The education component of the strategy has two thrusts: one is to prepare nontraditional managers for increasingly responsible posts, and the other is to help traditional managers overcome their prejudice in thinking about and interacting with people who are of a different sex or ethnicity. The second component of the strategy, enforcement, puts teeth in diversity goals and encourages behavior change. The third component, exposure to people with different backgrounds and characteristics, adds a more personal approach to diversity by helping managers get to know and respect others who are different.[13]

In summary, both consultants and academics believe that organizations should strive to manage diversity rather than simply using affirmative action. This conclusion was supported by a study of 200 African-American and white males and females employed in retail stores. Results revealed that employees viewed leaders as more accepting of diversity and more desirable to work for when they demonstrated behaviors consistent with managing diversity as opposed to affirmative action.[14] More is said about managing diversity later in this chapter.

Building the Business Case for Managing Diversity

The rationale for managing diversity goes well beyond legal, social, and moral reasons. Quite simply, the primary reason for managing diversity is the ability to grow and maintain a business in an increasingly competitive marketplace. Verizon, the largest telecommunications company in the United States, believes in this proposition. Ivan Seidenberg, Verizon's CEO,

> views diversity as a strategic business imperative. He believes a multifaceted approach to diversity drives Verizon's success and ability to compete. This strategy includes: acknowledging the unique needs of multicultural employees, customers, and other stakeholders; driving value for the customer; enhancing economic development for many types of businesses and communities; increasing shareholder equity; and winning in a global marketplace.[15]

Organizations cannot use diversity as a strategic advantage if employees fail to contribute their full talents, abilities, motivation, and commitment. It is thus essential for an organization to create an environment or culture that allows all employees to reach their full potential. Managing diversity is a critical component of creating such an organization.

This section explores the business need to manage diversity by first reviewing the demographic trends that are creating an increasingly diverse workforce. We then review evidence pertaining to the positive and negative effects associated with diverse work environments.

Increasing Diversity in the Workforce

Workforce demographics
Statistical profiles of adult workers.

Workforce demographics, which are statistical profiles of the characteristics and composition of the adult working population, are an invaluable human-resource planning aid. They enable managers to anticipate and adjust for surpluses or shortages of appropriately skilled individuals. Consider the implications associated with an aging population that will be retiring in record numbers over the next decade, a 2003 US birthrate that is lowest in recorded history, the arrival of 33 million immigrants in the United States during the 1990s, and a population under age 45 that will begin shrinking 6% annually in 2010.[16] Experts suggest that these demographic trends will create a serious shortage of skilled workers in the future.

Moreover, general population demographics give managers a preview of the values and motives of future employees. Demographic changes in the US workforce during the last two or three decades have immense implications for organizational behavior. This section explores four demographic-based characteristics of the workforce that have implications for organizational behavior: (1) women are encountering a glass ceiling, (2) racial groups are encountering a glass ceiling and perceived discrimination, (3) there is a mismatch between workers' educational attainment and occupational requirements, and (4) the workforce is aging.

Glass ceiling
Invisible barrier blocking women and minorities from top management positions.

Women Are Encountering a Glass Ceiling

In spite of the fact that women constituted 46% of the labor force in 1996 and are expected to represent 48% by 2010, they continue to encounter the **glass ceiling.** The glass ceiling represents an invisible barrier that separates women and minorities from advancing into top management positions. Women, therefore, find themselves stuck in lower level jobs, ones that do not have profit-and-loss responsibility, and those with less visibility and influence. In general, these positions result in a lack of power because the job holder does not have control over others, resources, or technology. The end result is that women face legitimate power deficits while trying to climb the corporate ladder.[17]

There are a variety of statistics that support the existence of a glass ceiling. As of March 2004, women were still underpaid relative to men: Women received 76% of men's earnings.[18] Even when women are paid the same as men, they may suffer in other areas of job opportunities. For example, a study of 69 male and female executives from a large multina-

What Are the Strategies for Breaking the Glass Ceiling?

Instructions

Read the 13 career strategies shown below that may be used to break the glass ceiling. Next, rank order each strategy in terms of its importance for contributing to the advancement of a woman to a senior management position. Rank the strategies from 1 (most important) to 13 (least important). Once this is completed, compute the gap between your rankings and those provided by the women executives who participated in this research. Their rankings are presented in endnote 23 at the back of the book.[23] In computing the gaps, use the absolute value of the gap. (Absolute values are always positive, so just ignore the sign of your gap.) Finally, compute your total gap score. The larger the gap, the greater the difference in opinion between you and the women executives. What does your total gap score indicate about your recommended strategies?

Strategy	My Rating	Survey Rating	Gap Your Rating − Survey Rating
1. Develop leadership outside office	_____	_____	_____
2. Gain line management experience	_____	_____	_____
3. Network with influential colleagues	_____	_____	_____
4. Change companies	_____	_____	_____
5. Be able to relocate	_____	_____	_____
6. Seek difficult or high visibility assignments	_____	_____	_____
7. Upgrade educational credentials	_____	_____	_____
8. Consistently exceed performance expectations	_____	_____	_____
9. Move from one functional area to another	_____	_____	_____
10. Initiate discussion regarding career aspirations	_____	_____	_____
11. Have an influential mentor	_____	_____	_____
12. Develop style that men are comfortable with	_____	_____	_____
13. Gain international experience	_____	_____	_____

SOURCE: Strategies and data were taken from B R Ragins, B Townsend, and M Mattis, "Gender Gap in the Executive Suite: CEOs and Female Executives Report on Breaking the Glass Ceiling," *Academy of Management Review*, February 1998, pp. 28–42. Reprinted by permission of The Academy of Management via The Copyright Clearance Center.

tional financial services corporation revealed no differences in base salary or bonus. However, the women in this sample received fewer stock options than the male executives, even after controlling for level of education, performance, and job function, and reported less satisfaction with future career opportunities.[19] A follow-up study of 13,503 female managers and 17,493 male managers from the same organization demonstrated that women at higher levels in the managerial hierarchy received fewer promotions than males at comparable positions.[20] Would you be motivated if you were a woman working in this organization?

Women still have not broken into the highest echelon of corporate America to a significant extent. For example, there were only 8 and 16 female CEOs in the *Fortune* 500 and *Fortune* 1000 as of March 2005, respectively. Women also accounted for only 15.7% of corporate-officer positions and 5.2% of top earners at *Fortune* 500 companies in 2002.[21]

Further, the majority of women in top jobs are working in staff rather than line positions. In general, roles associated with line jobs contain more power and influence than staff positions.

Why does the glass ceiling exist for women? A team of researchers attempted to answer this question by surveying 461 executive women who held titles of vice president or higher in *Fortune* 1000 companies and all of the *Fortune* 1000 CEOs. Respondents were asked to evaluate the extent to which they used 13 different career strategies to break through the glass ceiling. The 13 strategies are shown in the OB Exercise on page 53.[22] Before discussing the results from this study, we would like you to complete the OB Exercise.

Findings indicated that the top nine strategies were central to the advancement of these female executives. Within this set, however, four strategies were identified as critical toward breaking the glass ceiling: consistently exceeding performance expectations, developing a style with which male managers are comfortable, seeking out difficult or challenging assignments, and having influential mentors. These results are consistent with comments made by Sara Lee's new CEO, Brenda Barnes, when asked by a reporter whether she saw any significance in being named CEO the same week Carly Fiorina was forced out at Hewlett-Packard. Barnes said, "The way I see it, CEOs are supposed to drive performance. That comes with the territory, male or female. The fact that we are both female is interesting, but the job is what it is. You have to do the job."[24]

Results from the survey further demonstrated that the CEOs and female executives differed in their assessment of the barriers preventing women from advancing to positions of corporate leadership. CEOs concluded that women do not get promoted because (1) they lack significant general management or line experience and (2) women have not been in the executive talent pool for a long enough period of time to get selected. In contrast, the female executives indicated that (1) male stereotyping and preconceptions and (2) exclusion from informal networks were the biggest inhibitors to their promotability. These findings suggest that it is important to sensitize CEOs to the corporate culture faced by female employees. Breaking the glass ceiling will only occur when senior management has a good understanding of the unique experiences associated with being in the minority.

Racial Groups Are Encountering a Glass Ceiling and Perceived Discrimination

Historically, the United States has been a black-and-white country. The percentage change in U.S. population between 2000 and 2050 by race reveals that this pattern no longer exists (see Figure 2–2). Figure 2–2 shows that Asians and Hispanics are expected to have the largest growth in population between 2000 and 2050. The Asian population will triple to 33 million by 2050, and the Hispanics will increase their ranks by 118% to 102.6 million. Hispanics will account for 25% of the population in 2050. All told, the so-called minority groups will constitute 49.9% of the population in 2050 according to the Census Bureau.[25]

Unfortunately, three additional trends suggest that current day minority groups are experiencing their own glass ceiling. First, minorities are advancing even less in the managerial and professional ranks than women. For example, blacks and Hispanics held 11.3% and 10.9%, respectively, of all managerial and professional jobs in 2001; women held 46.6% of these positions. Second, the number of race-based charges of discrimination that were deemed to show reasonable cause by the US Equal Employment Opportunity Commission increased from 294 in 1995 to 1,189 in 2004. Companies paid a total of $61.1 million to resolve these claims outside of litigation in 2004.[26] Third, minorities also tend to earn less than whites. Median household income in 2003 was $47,800, $29,700, and $33,000 for whites, blacks, and Hispanics, respectively. Interestingly, Asians had the highest median income in the United States—$55,000.[27]

Figure 2-2   *Percentage Change in US Population by Race*

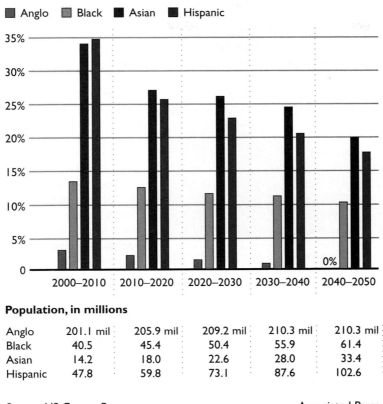

Population, in millions

	2000–2010	2010–2020	2020–2030	2030–2040	2040–2050
Anglo	201.1 mil	205.9 mil	209.2 mil	210.3 mil	210.3 mil
Black	40.5	45.4	50.4	55.9	61.4
Asian	14.2	18.0	22.6	28.0	33.4
Hispanic	47.8	59.8	73.1	87.6	102.6

Source: US Census Bureau   Associated Press

SOURCE: G C Armas, "Almost Half of US Likely to Be Minorities by 2050," *Arizona Republic,* March 18, 2004, p A5. US Census Bureau, Tbl. 1a., "Projected Population of the US by Race and Hispanic Origin: 2000–2050 (www. census.gov/ipc/www/usinterimproj/), March 2004. Used by permission of the Associated Press.

In addition to a racially based glass ceiling, a number of research studies showed that minorities experienced more perceived discrimination than whites. For example, a study of 361 first-year students at an eastern university revealed that whites reported less perceived discrimination than Asians, blacks, and Hispanics.[28] Another study of 44 black managers and 80 white managers revealed that black managers experienced slower rates of promotion and less psychological support than white managers.[29] It thus is not surprising that the turnover rate for black executives is 40% higher than for their white counterparts.[30] Finally, the EEOC noted that the number of workplace complaints from Hispanics has shot up 22% since 1999.[31]

Mismatch between Educational Attainment and Occupational Requirements
Approximately 27% of the labor force has a college degree.[32] Unfortunately, many of these people are working in jobs for which they are overqualified. This creates underemployment. **Underemployment** exists when a job requires less than a person's full potential as determined by his or her formal education, training, or skills. Juliette Katz, who is featured in Real World/Real People on page 57, is a good example of someone who is underemployed. Underemployment is associated with higher arrest rates and the likelihood of becoming an unmarried parent for young adults. It also is negatively correlated

Underemployment
The result of taking a job that requires less education, training, or skills than possessed by a worker.

As was true for women, many people of color encounter the glass ceiling. Rudolpho Lorenzo, who was the recipient of a $5000.00 micro loan to expand his grocery store, escaped the glass ceiling by starting his own business. The number of minority-owned businesses is on the rise, and the number of Hispanic owned businesses partially fueled this growth. Can you recommend other strategies people of color can use to break the glass ceiling?

with job satisfaction, work commitment, job involvement, internal work motivation, life satisfaction, and psychological well-being. Underemployment also is related to higher absenteeism and turnover.[33] Unfortunately, college graduates between 2000–2004 were susceptible to underemployment due to the slow economic growth during this period. A national survey of 2,350 college graduates by CollegeGrad.Com in 2004 revealed that 18% of the respondents were underemployed.[34] On a positive note, however, underemployment is one of the reasons more new college graduates are starting businesses of their own. Moreover, research reveals that over time a college graduate's income ranges from 50% to 100% higher than that obtained by a high-school graduate. Average earnings were $18,900, $25,900, $45,400, and $99,300 for employees who dropped out of high school, graduated high school, graduated college, and with advanced professional degrees (e.g., doctors and lawyers), respectively in 2002.[35] Even though underemployed employees like Juliette Katz are struggling to find jobs commensurate with their skills, don't give up hope. Historical data demonstrates that education pays off over time.

There is another important educational mismatch. The national high-school dropout rate is approximately 16%, and more than 20% of the adult US population reads below the fifth-grade level. Further, it is estimated that 90 million adults are functionally illiterate, and this costs corporate America an estimated $60 billion a year in lost productivity.[36] Literacy is defined as "an individual's ability to read, write, and speak in English, compute and solve problems at levels of proficiency necessary to function on the job and in society, to achieve one's goals, and develop one's knowledge and potential."[37] These statistics are worrisome because 70% of on-the-job reading materials are written for ninth-grade to college levels. Also, 43% of illiterate adults live in poverty; thus organizations are having a hard time finding qualified employees.[38] For example, a survey of 300 executives from manufacturing, technology, and finance firms revealed that a shortage of skilled workers limited sales by as much as 33%.[39] In contrast to underemployment, dropouts and illiterate individuals are unlikely to have the skills organizations need to remain competitive.

The Aging Workforce
America's population and workforce are getting older. Between 1995 and 2020, the number of individuals in the United States over age 65 will increase by 60%, the 45- to 64-year-old population by 34%, and those between ages 18 and 44 by 4%.[40] Life expectancy is increasing as well. The number of people living into their 80s is increasing rapidly, and this group disproportionately suffers from chronic illness. The United States is not the only country with an aging population. Germany, China, Japan, Russia, Brazil, Italy, and other countries in both eastern and western Europe, for example,

Juliette Katz Is Underemployed

Juliette Katz spent the past seven years sharpening her résumé as a marketing manager at America Online, Food.com, and other Internet start-ups. She is versed in programming, account management, and customer acquisition and retention; she has led marketing campaigns for direct mail, trade shows, events, advertising, branding, and positioning.

But the 29-year-old San Francisco resident got laid off from a dot-com in December 2000 and spent a fruitless year prowling for a similar job. Katz, who has a bachelor's degree in business administration from San Diego State University, gave up in October and landed a job shelving moisturizer and shower gels for Bath & Body Works in San Francisco.

"At first I was like, 'Why am I here?'" Katz said. She hadn't worked in retail since folding jeans and hanging shirts at Clothestime when she was 18. "I felt like I was in high school again."

SOURCE: R Konrad, "From High-Tech to Blue Collar," http://news.com, last modified February 4, 2005.

are expected to encounter significant economic, social, and political problems due to an aging population.[41] Figure 2–3 provides a good illustration. It shows the number of retirees per 100 workers across various countries for the years of 2000 and 2025. The key conclusion derived from this data is that the greater the number of retirees that must be supported by a country's workforce, the greater the burden put on current workers to financially support the country's retirees. Relatively speaking, workers in Germany, China, and Japan are more likely to pay increased taxes in 2025 to support retirees than are workers in the United States, Russia, and Brazil based on data presented in Figure 2–3.

An aging population in the United States also underscores a potential skill gap in the future. As those employees in the baby-boom generation retire—the 76 million people born between 1946 and 1964—the US workforce will lose the skills, knowledge, experience, and relationships possessed by the more than a quarter of all Americans. This situation will likely create skill shortages in fast-growing technical fields.[42] One way to combat this problem is to encourage older employees to work longer. Unfortunately, a recent survey of 404 executives revealed that they were concerned about facing age discrimination that would force them to retire before they were ready.[43]

Managerial Implications of Demographic Diversity Regardless of gender, race, or age, all organizations need employees who possess the skills and abilities needed to successfully complete their jobs. To attract the best workers, companies need to adopt policies and procedures that meet the needs of all employees. Programs such as day care, elder care, flexible work schedules, and benefits such as paternal leaves, less rigid relocation policies, concierge services, and mentoring programs are likely to become more popular.[44] Pfizer, for example, offers on-site child care at four locations and elder care.[45] That said, however, special effort is needed to eliminate the glass ceiling that has impacted women and minorities. Ernst & Young, for instance, followed this recommendation after recognizing that the turnover rate among female employees was higher than male peers and that there were very few female partners: The cost of turnover averaged 150% of a departing employee's annual salary. The seven-step program, which is outlined in Real World/Real People on page 59, resulted in significantly reducing the turnover of female employees throughout the organization and tripling the percentage of women partners.[46]

Figure 2–3   *Retirees per 100 Workers around the Globe**

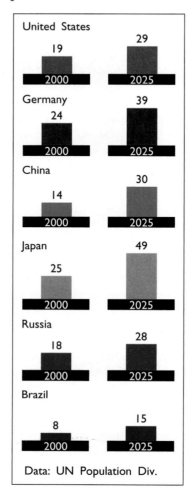

*Retirees over age 65.
SOURCE: P Engardio, C Matlack, G Edmondson, I Rowley, C Barraclough, and G Smith, "Now the Geezer Glut," *Business Week,* January 31, 2005, p 45.

Given the projected increase in the number of Hispanics entering the workforce over the next 25 years, managers should consider progressive methods to recruit, retain, and integrate this segment of the population into their organizations. Consider the examples set by Kmart, the University of North Carolina Health Care System at Chapel Hill, PricewaterhouseCoopers, Chevron, and Pepsi.

Kmart recruits at colleges and universities that have large numbers of Hispanic students. The company also advertises in Hispanic publications and uses online Hispanic job boards. It also has translated employment and benefit information into Spanish. The University of North Carolina Health Care System at Chapel Hill, NC, has brought in Spanish interpreters at its new-employee orientations and printed part of its job application information in Spanish. . . .

Ernst & Young Implements Program to Keep Women on the Path to Partnership

Process Steps	Supportive Tactics
1. Focus	Pilot projects targeted five office locations for improvement on specific issues. For example, Minneapolis focused on mentoring and New Jersey on flexible work arrangements.
2. Committed leadership	E&Y's chairman convened a diversity task force of partners and created an Office of Retention.
3. New roles	Certain individuals are targeted as "career watchers" and are given assignment and projects aimed at improving their leadership skills.
4. Policy changes	All employees were equipped for telework, and it was made policy that flexible work schedules would not affect anyone's opportunity for advancement.
5. Peer networking	Professional women's networks were established in 41 offices, and a three-day women's leadership conference is offered every 18 months.
6. Learning resources	All employees are encouraged to use the company's Achievement Flexibility Web site to learn about flexible work arrangements.
7. Accountability	An annual employee survey is used to assess the extent to which managers foster an inclusive, flexible work environment. Managers are also rated on metrics associated with the number of women on key accounts, in key leadership jobs, and in the partner pipeline.

SOURCE: Excerpted and adapted from S A Hewlett and C Buck Luce, "Off-Ramps and On-Ramps: Keeping Talented Women on the Road to Success," *Harvard Business Review,* March 2005, p 51.

> PricewaterhouseCoopers . . . set up employee support and socialization groups where Hispanic managers act as leaders to Hispanic employees, and the company provides scholarships for Hispanic accounting students. Chevron sponsors a Hispanic employee network. . . . Pepsi works with national Hispanic organizations to help with recruiting and is planning a leadership forum for some Hispanic executives. The program will give the executives access to the CEO and other company leaders.[47]

While the above examples highlight the value of progressively recruiting Hispanics, recruiting is not enough to ensure that minorities advance up the organizational hierarchy. Effective mentoring also is needed.

David Thomas, a researcher from Harvard University, conducted a three-year study of mentoring practices at three US corporations: a manufacturer, an electronics company, and a high-tech firm. His results revealed that successful people of color who advanced the furthest had a strong network of mentors and sponsors who nurtured their professional development. Findings also demonstrated that people of color should be mentored differently than their white counterparts. He recommended that organizations

> should provide a range of career paths, all uncorrelated with race, that lead to the executive suite. . . . Achieving this system, however, would require integrating the principles of opportunity, development, and diversity into the fabric of the organization's management practices and human resource systems. And an important element in the process would be to identify potential mentors, train them, and ensure that they are paired with promising professionals of color.[48]

Mismatches between the amount of education needed to perform current jobs and the amount of education possessed by members of the workforce are growing. Underemployment among college graduates threatens to erode job satisfaction and work motivation. As well-educated workers begin to look for jobs commensurate with their qualifications and expectations, absenteeism and turnover likely will increase. This problem underscores the need for job redesign (see the discussion in Chapter 8). In addition, organizations will need to consider interventions, such as realistic job previews and positive reinforcement programs, to reduce absenteeism and turnover. On-the-job remedial skills and literacy training will be necessary to help the growing number of dropouts and illiterates cope with job demands. For example, US organizations spent $51.4 billion on training in 2004.[49]

Moreover, organizations will continue to be asked to help resolve the educational problems in the United States given that test results show that (1) middle- and high-school students fare poorly on international comparisons of math and science achievement and (2) employers rate the English skills of high-school graduates as poor.[50] Advanced Micro Devices in Sunnyvale, California, for example, devotes more than half its corporate contributions to education programs. Hewlett-Packard (HP) also makes significant contributions aimed at encouraging school reform and equipping school systems with the technology needed for technical education. HP also created the HP Scholar Program to support high-school minority students who are planning to major in computer science and electrical and computer engineering in college. The chosen students receive up to $40,000 in equipment to support their studies.[51] Supporting education is good for business and society at large. A better education system not only contributes to the United States' ability to compete internationally, but it facilitates a better quality of life for all its population.

As the baby-boom generation reaches retirement age after the turn of the century, the workforce will be top-heavy with older employees, creating the problem of career plateauing for younger workers. **Career plateauing** is defined "as that point in a career [at] which future hierarchical mobility seems unlikely."[52] Career plateauing is associated with stress and dissatisfaction.[53] Unfortunately, this problem is intensified by the fact that organizations are flattening—and reducing the number of managerial jobs—in order to save costs and increase efficiency. Managers will thus need to find alternatives other than promotions to help employees satisfy their needs and to feel successful, and employees will need to take a much more active role in managing their careers.

Career plateauing
The end result when the probability of being promoted is very small.

There are three additional recommendations for managing an aging workforce. The first involves the need to help employees deal with personal issues associated with elder care. Elder care is a critical issue for employees that have aging parents, and failing to deal with it can drive up an employer's costs. For example, MetLife estimates that a lack of elder care costs organizations at least $11 billion a year in lost productivity and increased absenteeism, workday interruptions, and turnover.[54] Second, employers need to make a concerted effort to keep older workers engaged and committed and their skills current. The following seven initiatives can help accomplish this objective.[55]

1. Provide challenging work assignments that make a difference to the firm.
2. Give the employee considerable autonomy and latitude in completing a task.
3. Provide equal access to training and learning opportunities when it comes to new technology.
4. Provide frequent recognition for skills, experience, and wisdom gained over the years.
5. Provide mentoring opportunities whereby older workers can pass on accumulated knowledge to younger employees.
6. Ensure that older workers receive sensitive, high-quality supervision.
7. Design a work environment that is both stimulating and fun.

The final recommendation involves the process of managing the cost of health care, which has risen at an average annual rate of 14% and is likely to increase as the population ages.[56] One option used by many companies is to drop different types of coverage or pass the expenses onto employees. Alternatively, other organizations have tried to lower health care costs by offering benefits that encourage employees to adopt a healthier life style. For example, SAS, the Cary, North Carolina, software company, encourages employees to use its 10-lane swimming pool, ping-pong tables, volleyball courts, soccer fields, tennis courts, and putting green. Adobe Systems in San Jose similarly offers its employees a fitness center with trainer and a combination of basketball and bocce courts.[57] Smoking cessation programs are another popular benefit that have been found to lower the cost of health care. Experts esti-

Research shows that exercise such as playing tennis is a good way to stay mentally sharp and improve one's health. In light of this evidence, organizations have found that an investment in health facilities is a good way to increase productivity and reduce health care costs.

mate that smoking causes more than $157 billion in annual heath-related losses. Some organizations, such as Schweitzer Engineering Laboratories in Pullman, Washington, and Weyco Inc., in Okemos, Michigan, have gone so far as to implement a policy of not hiring smokers. This drastic step must be pursued with caution, however, as several states prohibit employers from making nonsmoking a condition of employment. Although the proactive approach of offering lifestyle-related benefits increases costs in the short-run, experience shows that the benefits can exceed the costs over time.[58]

The Positive and Negative Effects of Diverse Work Environments

Earlier in this chapter we stated that effectively managing diversity is not only a good thing to do in order to attract and retain the most talented employees, but it makes good business sense. Although one can easily find testimonials from managers and organizations supporting this conclusion, we need to examine the validity of this claim by considering the evidence provided by OB research. This section reviews the two main theoretical approaches for understanding the effects of diversity and then presents a process model of diversity that integrates them.

Social Categorization Theory A team of OB researchers describe the **social categorization theory** of diversity as follows:

> The social categorization perspective holds that similarities and differences are used as a basis for categorizing self and others into groups, with ensuing categorizations distinguishing between one's own in-group and one or more out-groups. People tend to like and trust in-group members more than out-group members and thus generally tend to favor in-groups over out-groups. . . . [W]ork group members are more positively inclined toward their group and the people within it if fellow group members are similar rather than dissimilar to the self.[59]

Social categorization theory
Similarity leads to linking and attraction.

This perspective further implies that similarity leads to liking and attraction, thereby fostering a host of positive outcome. If this were the case, one would expect that the more homogeneous a work group, the higher the member commitment and group cohesion, and the lower the amount of interpersonal conflicts. There is a large body of research supporting propositions derived from the social categorization model.[60]

For example, past research revealed that people who were different from their work units in racial or ethnic background were less psychologically committed to their organizations, less satisfied with their careers, and perceived less autonomy to make decisions on their jobs.[61] Additional studies showed that demographic diversity was associated with less cooperation among team members and more negative impressions toward people who were demographically different.[62] Finally, recent studies demonstrated that demographic diversity was associated with higher employee turnover and employee deviance (i.e., exhibiting behavior that violates norms and threatens the well-being of the organization) and lower profits.[63] All told then, the social categorization model supports the idea that homogeneity is better than heterogeneity in terms of affecting work-related attitudes, behavior, and performance.

Information/Decision-Making Theory

Information/Decision-Making Theory The second theoretical point of view, referred to as **informational/decision-making theory,** arrives at opposite predictions, proposing that diverse groups should outperform homogenous groups. The logic of this theory was described as follows:

> The idea is that diverse groups are more likely to possess a broader range of task-relevant knowledge, skills, and abilities that are distinct and nonredundant and to have different opinions and perspectives on the task at hand. This not only gives diverse groups a larger pool of resources, but may also have other beneficial effects.[64]

This perspective highlights three positive effects of diverse work groups.[65] First, diverse groups are expected to do a better job in earlier phases of problem solving because they are more likely to use their diverse backgrounds to generate a more comprehensive view of a problem. For example, gender and ethnic diversity can help work teams to better understand the needs and perspectives of a multicultural customer base. Second, the existence of diverse perspectives can help groups to brainstorm or uncover more novel alternatives during problem-solving activities. Finally, diversity can enhance the number of contacts a group or work unit has at its disposal. This broad network enables groups to gain access to new information and expertise, which results in more support for decisions than homogenous groups. Research supports this theory of diversity.

Team performance was positively related to a team's diversity in gender, ethnicity, age, and education.[66] Heterogeneous groups also were found to produce better-quality decisions and demonstrated higher productivity than homogenous groups.[67] Preliminary research also supports the idea that workforce diversity promotes creativity and innovation. This occurs through the sharing of diverse ideas and perspectives. Rosabeth Moss-Kanter, a management expert, was one of the first to investigate this relationship. Her results indicated that innovative companies deliberately used heterogeneous teams to solve problems, and they employed more women and minorities than less innovative companies. She also noted that innovative companies did a better job of eliminating racism, sexism, and classism.[68] A recent summary of 40 years of diversity research supported Moss-Kanter's conclusion that diversity can promote creativity and improve a team's decision making.[69]

Reconciling the Effects of Diverse Work Environments

Reconciling the Effects of Diverse Work Environments   Our previous discussion about social categorization theory and information/decision-making theory revealed that there are both positive and negative effects associated with diversity. The

Information/ decision-making theory
Diversity leads to better task-relevant processes and decision making.

model in Figure 2–4 summarizes the process underlying these effects. Consistent with social categorization theory, there is a negative relationship between the amount of diversity in surface-level and deep-level dimensions of diversity and the quality of interpersonal processes and group dynamics within a work group (path A in Figure 2–4). This negative relationship ultimately results in negative outcomes because of the positive relationship between the quality of interpersonal processes and group dynamics and outcomes (path C). For example, gender and racial diversity in a work group foster more interpersonal conflict, which in turn results in lower job satisfaction, higher turnover, and lower productivity.

In contrast, research regarding the information/decision-making theory tells us that the amount of surface-level and deep-level diversity is positively associated with task-relevant processes and decision making (path B), which in turn fosters positive outcomes (path D). Gender and racial diversity in this case lead to positive outcomes because they lead to improved task-related processes and decision making.

Given that work-group diversity is associated with positive and negative outcomes, we need to consider what management can do to reduce the potential negative effects of diversity. First, organizations can target training to improve the inherent negative relationship between a work group's diversity and its interpersonal processes and group dynamics (path A in Figure 2–4). For example, training can be used to help employees develop interpersonal skills and a greater appreciation for diversity. This training might focus on conflict management, interpersonal influence, giving feedback, communication, and valuing differences. IBM, for instance, uses a program labeled "Shades of Blue" to help employees understand how differences in deep-level dimensions of diversity like values and beliefs influence social interactions at work.[70] Second, managers can seek ways to help employees ease the tensions of working in diverse groups. Such efforts might include the creation of support groups. Finally, steps could be taken to reduce the negative effects of unconscious stereotyping and increase the use of group goals in heterogenous groups.

Figure 2–4   *A Process Model of Diversity*

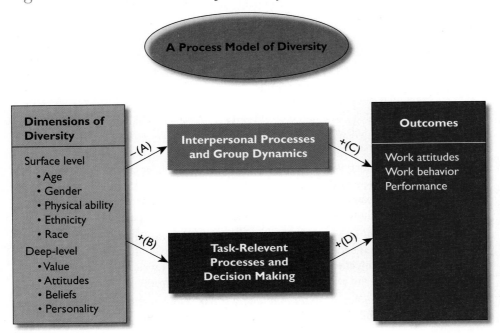

Rewarding groups to accomplish group goals might encourage group members to focus on their common objectives rather than on demographic differences that are unrelated to performance.[71]

Barriers and Challenges to Managing Diversity

We introduced this chapter by noting that diversity is a sensitive, potentially volatile, and sometimes uncomfortable issue. It is therefore not surprising that organizations encounter significant barriers when trying to move forward with managing diversity. The following is a list of the most common barriers to implementing successful diversity programs:[72]

1. *Inaccurate stereotypes and prejudice.* This barrier manifests itself in the belief that differences are viewed as weaknesses. In turn, this promotes the view that diversity hiring will mean sacrificing competence and quality.

2. *Ethnocentrism.* The ethnocentrism barrier represents the feeling that one's cultural rules and norms are superior or more appropriate than the rules and norms of another culture. This barrier is thoroughly discussed in Chapter 4.

3. *Poor career planning.* This barrier is associated with the lack of opportunities for diverse employees to get the type of work assignments that qualify them for senior management positions.

4. *An unsupportive and hostile working environment for diverse employees.* Sexual, racial, and age harassment are common examples of hostile work environments. Whether perpetrated against women, men, or older individuals, hostile environments are demeaning, unethical, and appropriately called "work environment pollution." Moreover, the EEOC holds employers legally accountable for behavior that creates a hostile work environment. An expert on the subject explains:

   > An employer violates Title VII of the Civil Rights of 1964 (see Table 2–1) if it engages in unlawful discrimination by maintaining a hostile work environment. To prove a hostile work environment claim involving co-workers, an employee must show that she was subject to unwelcome harassment based on a protected characteristic [e.g., race, color, religion, national origin, sex, age] and that the harassment was severe or pervasive enough to create a hostile or abusive working environment. In addition, the employee must show that the employer knew or should have known about the environment and failed to act promptly to prevent or end the harassment.[73]

   Sexual harassment, which we discuss in Chapter 11 under the context of men and women working together in groups, is the most frequent type of hostile environment charge filed with the EEOC. Sexual harassment also happens to be an international problem (see Real World/Real People on page 65).

5. *Lack of political savvy on the part of diverse employees.* Diverse employees may not get promoted because they do not know how to "play the game" of getting along and getting ahead in an organization. Research reveals that women and people of color are excluded from organizational networks.[74]

6. *Difficulty in balancing career and family issues.* Women still assume the majority of the responsibilities associated with raising children. This makes it harder for

Sexual Harassment Is a Growing Problem in China

The phrase "sexual harassment" didn't exist in the Chinese language a decade ago. Now lawmakers are hoping to eliminate the action it describes. On March 4, [2005] female Communist Party leaders introduced legislation to make sexual harassment illegal.

The problem has become widespread in China as more women join the workforce. In a recent newspaper survey, 86% of women say they have been hassled by co-workers. In 2003, male officials in Sichuan Province were barred from having female assistants in order to curb incidents.

There is no specific law under which victims can get redress, so most sexual harassment suits in China are dismissed. The only two plaintiffs to win cases—one a man—did so by citing a law protecting their "human dignity." Each got $250 and an apology.

SOURCE: Excerpted from "Gender Watch: Now No Means No in China," *Business Week*, March 28, 2005, p 12.

The increasing number of female employees in the workforce, such as the ones assembling bicycles in Longhua, China, has led to an increase in sexual harassment throughout the country. To what extent will this problem influence China's expanding economic growth?

women to work evenings and weekends or to frequently travel once they have children. Even without children in the picture, household chores take more of a woman's time than a man's time.

7. *Fears of reverse discrimination.* Some employees believe that managing diversity is a smoke screen for reverse discrimination. This belief leads to very strong resistance because people feel that one person's gain is another's loss.

8. *Diversity is not seen as an organizational priority.* This leads to subtle resistance that shows up in the form of complaints and negative attitudes. Employees may complain about the time, energy, and resources devoted to diversity that could have been spent doing "real work."

9. *The need to revamp the organization's performance appraisal and reward system.* Performance appraisals and reward systems must reinforce the need to effectively manage diversity. This means that success will be based on a new set of criteria. Employees are likely to resist changes that adversely affect their promotions and financial rewards.

10. *Resistance to change.* Effectively managing diversity entails significant organizational and personal change. As discussed in Chapter 18, people resist change for many different reasons.

In summary, managing diversity is a critical component of organizational success.

Ann Morrison Identifies Specific Diversity Initiatives

Ann Morrison conducted a landmark study of the diversity practices used by 16 organizations that successfully managed diversity. Her results uncovered 52 different practices, 20 of which were used by the majority of the companies sampled. She classified the 52 practices into three main types: accountability, development, and recruitment.[75] The top 10 practices associated with each type are shown in Table 2–2. They are discussed next in order of relative importance.

Accountability Practices

Accountability practices
Focus on treating diverse employees fairly.

Accountability practices relate to managers' responsibility to treat diverse employees fairly. Table 2–2 reveals that companies predominantly accomplish this objective by creating administrative procedures aimed at integrating diverse employees into the management ranks (practice numbers 3, 4, 5, 6, 8, 9, and 10). In contrast, work and family policies, practice 7, focuses on creating an environment that fosters employee commitment and productivity. Progress Energy, an energy company that serves the Carolinas and Florida, uses a variety of accountability practices in its attempt to manage diversity.

> The chairman of the diversity council is also the chairman and CEO of the company, William Cavanaugh III. The council meets once a quarter and subcouncils throughout the

Table 2–2 *Common Diversity Practices*

Accountability Practices	Development Practices	Recruitment Practices
1. Top management's personal intervention	1. Diversity training programs	1. Targeted recruitment of nonmanagers
2. Internal advocacy groups	2. Networks and support groups	2. Key outside hires
3. Emphasis on EEO statistics, profiles	3. Development programs for all high-potential managers	3. Extensive public exposure on diversity (AA)
4. Inclusion of diversity in performance evaluation goals, ratings	4. Informal networking activities	4. Corporate image as liberal, progressive, or benevolent
5. Inclusion of diversity in promotion decisions, criteria	5. Job rotation	5. Partnerships with educational institutions
6. Inclusion of diversity in management succession planning	6. Formal mentoring program	6. Recruitment incentives such as cash supplements
7. Work and family policies	7. Informal mentoring program	7. Internships (such as INROADS)
8. Policies against racism, sexism	8. Entry development programs for all high-potential new hires	8. Publications or PR products that highlight diversity
9. Internal audit or attitude survey	9. Internal training (such as personal safety or language)	9. Targeted recruitment of managers
10. Active AA/EEO committee, office	10. Recognition events, awards	10. Partnership with nontraditional groups

SOURCE: Abstracted from Tables A.10, A.11, and A.12 in A M Morrison, *The New Leaders: Guidelines on Leadership Diversity in America*, © 1992. Reprinted with permission of John Wiley & Sons, Inc.

company meet monthly. In addition, every manager in the company is accountable for the way diversity is both perceived and practiced within his or her organization. Every year employees fill out a written questionnaire that evaluates employee satisfaction with the work environment. If a particular group provides negative feedback regarding issues (including diversity), the company follows up and addresses the issues.[76]

Development Practices

The use of development practices to manage diversity is relatively new compared with the historical use of accountability and recruitment practices. **Development practices** focus on preparing diverse employees for greater responsibility and advancement. These activities are needed because most nontraditional employees have not been exposed to the type of activities and job assignments that develop effective leadership and social networks. Table 2–2 indicates that diversity training programs, networks and support groups, and mentoring programs are among the most frequently used developmental practices. Consider the networking practices used by Xerox and Fannie Mae.

Development practices
Focus on preparing diverse employees for greater responsibility and advancement.

> Many years ago when Xerox was trying to ensure more participation from blacks in its workforce, a caucus established among black employees had the blessing of then-CEO David Kearns, who encouraged black employees to get together periodically to talk about their challenges in moving through the organization and to get help from other managers. After that, there arose a women's caucus, an Hispanic caucus, and so on. Fannie Mae has taken the idea of employee caucus groups a step further. It has 14 Employee Networking Groups for African-Americans, Hispanics, Native Americans, Catholics, Christians, Muslims, older workers, gays, lesbians, veterans, and so forth. The groups serve as social and networking hubs, and they foster workplace communication about diversity issues among all employees, including senior managers.[77]

Recruitment Practices

Recruitment practices focus on attracting job applicants at all levels who are willing to accept challenging work assignments. This focus is critical because people learn the leadership skills needed for advancement by successfully accomplishing increasingly challenging and responsible work assignments. As shown in Table 2–2, targeted recruitment of nonmanagers (practice 1) and managers (practice 9) are commonly used to identify and recruit women and people of color.

Recruitment practices
Attempts to attract qualified, diverse employees at all levels.

Summary of Key Concepts

1. *Define diversity and review the four layers of diversity.* Diversity represents the individual differences that make people different from and similar to each other. Diversity pertains to everybody. It is not simply an issue of age, race, gender, or sexual orientation. The layers of diversity define an individual's personal identity and constitute a perceptual filter that influences how we interpret the world. Personality is at the center of the diversity wheel. The second layer of diversity consists of a set of internal dimensions that are referred to as surface-level dimensions of diversity. The third layer is composed of external influences and are called secondary dimensions of diversity. The final layer of diversity includes organizational dimensions.

2. *Explain the difference between affirmative action and managing diversity.* Affirmative action is an outgrowth of equal employment opportunity legislation and is an artificial intervention aimed at giving management a

chance to correct past discrimination. Managing diversity entails creating a host of organizational changes that enable all people to perform up to their maximum potential.

3. *Explain the glass ceiling and the four top strategies used by women to break the glass ceiling.* The glass ceiling is an invisible barrier blocking women and minorities from top management positions. The top four strategies used by women included the following: consistently exceed performance expectations, develop a style with which male managers are comfortable, seek out difficult or challenging assignments, and find influential mentors.

4. *Review the demographic trends pertaining to racial groups, educational mismatches, and an aging workforce.* With respect to racial groups, Asians and Hispanics are expected to have the largest growth in the population between 2000 and 2050, and minority groups will constitute 49.9% of the population in 2050. Minority groups also are experiencing a glass ceiling. There is a mismatch between workers' educational attainment and occupational requirements. The workforce is aging.

5. *Highlight the managerial implications of increasing diversity in the workforce.* There are seven broad managerial implications: (*a*) To attract the best workers, companies need to adopt policies and programs that meet the needs of all employees; (*b*) managers should consider progressive methods to recruit, retain, and integrate Hispanic workers into their organizations; (*c*) mentoring programs are needed to help minorities advance within the organizational hierarchy; (*d*) remedial skills training is necessary to help the growing number of dropouts and illiterates cope with job demands; (*e*) organizations will need to tangibly support education if the United States is to remain globally competitive; (*f*) the problem of career plateauing needs to be managed; and (*g*) there are three broad recommendations for managing an aging workforce.

6. *Explain the positive and negative effects of diversity by using social categorization theory and information/decision-making theory.* Social categorization theory implies that similarity leads to liking and attraction, thereby fostering a host of positive outcomes. This theory supports the idea that homogeneity is better than heterogeneity because diversity causes negative interpersonal processes and group dynamics. The information/decision-making theory is based on the notion that diverse groups should outperform homogenous groups because diversity is positively associated with task-relevant processes and decision making.

7. *Identify the barriers and challenges to managing diversity.* There are 10 barriers to successfully implementing diversity initiatives: (*a*) inaccurate stereotypes and prejudice, (*b*) ethnocentrism, (*c*) poor career planning, (*d*) an unsupportive and hostile working environment for diverse employees, (*e*) lack of political savvy on the part of diverse employees, (*f*) difficulty in balancing career and family issues, (*g*) fears of reverse discrimination, (*h*) diversity is not seen as an organizational priority, (*i*) the need to revamp the organization's performance appraisal and reward system, and (*j*) resistance to change.

8. *Discuss the organizational practices used to effectively manage diversity as identified by Ann Morrison.* There are many different practices organizations can use to manage diversity. Ann Morrison's study of diversity practices identified three main types or categories of activities. Accountability practices relate to a manager's responsibility to treat diverse employees fairly. Development practices focus on preparing diverse employees for greater responsibility and advancement. Recruitment practices emphasize attracting job applicants at all levels who are willing to accept challenging work assignments. Table 2–2 presents a list of activities that are used to accomplish each main type.

Discussion Questions

1. Under what conditions are people likely to resist diversity?

2. What role does communication play in effectively managing diversity?

3. Does diversity suggest that managers should follow the rule "Do unto others as you would have them do unto you"?

4. What can be done to break the glass ceiling for women and minorities?

5. What are the biggest challenges associated with an aging workforce?

6. Why is underemployment a serious human resource management problem? If you have ever been underemployed, what were your feelings about it?

7. How can interpersonal conflict be caused by diversity. Explain your rationale.

8. Have you seen any examples that support the proposition that diversity is a competitive advantage?

9. Which of the barriers to managing diversity would be most difficult to reduce? Explain.

10. How can Morrison's specific diversity initiatives be helpful in overcoming the barriers and challenges to managing diversity?

OB in Action Case Study

Many Older Employees Now Work for Younger Bosses[78]

For most of his 37-year career, Stephen Schechter reported to bosses older than himself. For six years, he enjoyed the luxury of answering only to himself as owner of a small public-relations agency.

It came as something of a surprise a year ago when Schechter accepted a position as vice president of 5W Public Relations in New York.

His new boss, Chief Executive Ronn Torossian, is young enough to be his son.

"This is dramatic," Schechter said of the role reversal. "It's interesting, exciting and challenging."

"Steve is older than my mom and my dad," Torossian added. "He has a lot of years of experience that I don't have."

Welcome to the 21st-century version of the generation gap. As older Americans delay retirement or return to the labor force, lured by the need for a paycheck or the desire for productive activity, they're increasingly likely to work for someone younger.

A coming shortage of skilled labor will push employers to hire 5.3 million older workers by 2010 and 14 million by 2020, according to the National Commission for Employment Policy. . . .

No one pretends these topsy-turvy arrangements are easy. Younger bosses may harbor stereotypes that older employees resist change. Older workers may regard their younger superiors as arrogant or less loyal to the company.

For Schechter and Torossian, their 30-year age difference became part of the discussion during Schechter's job interview.

"He brought it up," said Torossian, who considers Schechter's age an advantage. "As a young entrepreneur, I need to have smart, successful people around me who can give a variety of insights, regardless of their age."

Schechter says his initial challenges included learning to work within the boundaries Torossian has set for the agency and the staff, and being able to fit in with young colleagues.

"I'm learning a lot from him and from the younger people here," Schechter added. "If anything, it's really energized me and made me feel younger."

Not everyone has such smooth sailing.

"Each generation experienced very different formative years, and as a result brings very different values to the Amer-ican workplace," said Chuck Underwood, president of Generational Imperative, business consultants in Cincinnati.

The baby-boomer generation, Underwood notes, is a generation that has defined itself by work.

"They made the 60-hour workweek normal," he said. "They took work calls at home and worked on weekends."

In sharp contrast, he continues, Generation X has grown up with a distrust of big business and big government, and older people in general.

"Many Xers in their childhood saw their workaholic parents suffer from fatigue, illness, substance abuse and divorce," Underwood said. "So Xers entered their career years less loyal to the company and more determined to work a reasonable workday and leave the office sharply at 5."

Underwood regards this as an important difference that older workers must recognize in younger bosses.

"It looms as a very significant challenge for younger managers to effectively manage their older subordinates," he said. "From one manager to the next, it might or might not work."

He frames it as an either/or challenge.

"Either be sensitive to each generation's strengths and weaknesses and flourish as a result of them, or don't be sensitive and flounder," he said.

Questions for Discussion

1. What are they key challenges being faced by both Stephen Schechter and Ronn Torossian?

2. If you were Ronn Torossian, what questions would you ask Mr Schechter during the job interview to ensure that he did not have trouble working for a younger boss?

3. If you were Stephen Schechter, what questions would you ask Mr Torossian in the job interview to ensure that he did not have trouble managing an older employee?

4. Do you agree with Chuck Underwood's description of baby boomers and Generation Xers? Explain your rationale.

5. Based on reading this chapter, what advice would you give to a younger manager who is managing an older employee?

How Does Your Diversity Profile Affect Your Relationships with Other People?

Objectives

1. To identify the diversity profile of yourself and others.
2. To consider the implications of similarities and differences across diversity profiles.

Introduction

People vary along four layers of diversity: personality, internal dimensions, external dimensions, and organizational dimensions. Differences across these four layers are likely to influence interpersonal relationships and the ability or willingness to work with others. You will be asked to compare yourself with a group of other people you interact with and then to examine the quality of the relationships between yourself and these individuals. This enables you to gain a better understanding of how similarities and differences among people influence attitudes and behavior.

Instructions

Complete the diversity profile by first selecting five current or past co-workers/work associates or fellow students.[79] Alternatively, you can select five people you interact with in order to accomplish your personal goals (e.g., team members on a class project). Write their names on the diagonal lines at the top of the worksheet. Next, determine whether each person is similar to or different from you with respect to each diversity dimension. Mark an "S" if the person is the same or a "D" if the person is different from yourself. Finally, answer the questions for discussion.

Questions for Discussion

1. To whom are you most similar and different?
2. Which diversity dimensions have the greatest influence with respect to whom you are drawn to and whom you like the best?
3. Which dimensions of diversity seem relatively unimportant with respect to the quality of your interpersonal relationships?
4. Consider the individual that you have the most difficult time working with or getting along with. Which dimensions are similar and different? Which dimensions seem to be the source of your difficulty?
5. If you choose co-workers for this exercise, discuss the management actions, policies, or programs that could be used to increase inclusiveness, reduce turnover, and increase job satisfaction.

Diversity Worksheet

Work Associates

Diversity Dimensions					
Personality					
e.g., Loyalty					
Internal Dimensions					
Age					
Gender					
Sexual orientation					
Physical ability					
Ethnicity					
Race					

Diversity Worksheet

Diversity Dimensions

Work Associates

Diversity Dimensions					
External Dimensions					
Geographic location					
Income					
Personal habits					
Recreational habits					
Religion					
Educational background					
Work experience					
Appearance					
Parental status					
Marital status					
Organizational Dimensions					
Functional level/classification					
Work content/field					
Division/department/unit/group					
Seniority					
Work location					
Union affiliation					
Management status					

Group Exercise

Managing Diversity-Related Interactions

Objectives

1. To improve your ability to manage diversity-related interactions more effectively.
2. To explore different approaches for handling diversity interactions.

Introduction

The interpersonal component of managing diversity can be awkward and uncomfortable. This is partly due to the fact that resolving diversity interactions requires us to deal with situations we may never have encountered before. The purpose of this exercise is to help you manage diversity-related interactions more effectively. To do so, you will be asked to read three scenarios and then decide how you will handle each situation.

Instructions

Presented here are three scenarios depicting diversity-related interactions. Please read the first scenario, and then answer the three questions that follow it. Follow the same procedure for the next two scenarios. Next, divide into groups of three. One at a time, each person should present his or her responses to the three questions for the first scenario. The groups should then discuss the various approaches that were proposed to resolve the diversity interaction and try to arrive at a consensus recommendation. Follow the same procedure for the next two scenarios.

SCENARIO 1

Dave, who is one of your direct reports, comes to you and says that he and Scott are having a special commitment ceremony to celebrate the beginning of their lives together. He has invited you to the ceremony. Normally the department has a party and cake for special occasions. Mary, who is one of Dave's peers, has just walked into your office and asks you whether you intend to have a party for Dave.

A. How would you respond?

_____

_____

B. What is the potential impact of your response?

_____

_____

C. If you choose not to respond, what is the potential impact of your behavior?

_____

_____

_____

SCENARIO 2

You have an open position for a supervisor, and your top two candidates are an African-American female and a white female. Both candidates are equally qualified. The position is responsible for five white team leaders. You hire the white female because the work group likes her. The team leaders said that they felt more comfortable with the white female. The vice president of human resources has just called you on the phone and asks you to explain why you hired the white female.

A. How would you respond?

_____

_____

_____

B. What is the potential impact of not hiring the African-American?

_____

_____

_____

C. What is the potential impact of hiring the African-American

_____

_____

_____

SCENARIO 3

While attending an off-site business meeting, you are waiting in line with a group of team leaders to get your lunch at a buffet. Without any forewarning, one of your peers in the line loudly says, "Thank goodness Terry is at the end of the line. With his size and appetite there wouldn't be any food left for the rest of us." You believe Terry may have heard this comment, and you feel the comment was more of a "weight-related" slur than a joke.

A. How would you respond?

_____

_____

_____

B. What is the potential impact of your response?

_____

_____

_____

C. If you choose not to respond, what is the potential impact of your behavior?

_____

_____

_____

Questions for Discussion

1. What was the recommended response for each scenario?
2. Which scenario generated the most emotion and disagreement? Explain why this occurred.
3. What is the potential impact of a manager's lack of response to Scenarios 1 and 3? Explain.

An Employee Sues Georgia Power for Race Discrimination[80]

In more than a quarter century as an African-American lineman at one of the South's biggest electric companies, Cornelius Cooper says he abided a stream of racial indignities. He says he was passed over for promotions, subjected to racial slurs, and repeatedly spray-painted in his genital area by white employees. Worse, co-workers made light of lynchings, tied hangman's nooses in his presence, and often left such knots displayed in company facilities.

"You didn't do anything but smile, even though it was intimidating to the max," Cooper said in an interview last week.

In July, Cooper and two others filed a lawsuit alleging that managers at Georgia Power Co. and its parent, Southern Co., unfairly denied promotions to African-American workers, gave lower pay to black employees than to similarly qualified whites, and were indifferent to overt harassment of blacks. Attached to the charges, which the companies vigorously deny, was an 8-by-10 color photograph of a noose hanging inside a company building in Cornelia, Ga.

Executives at Georgia Power and its parent company were taken aback. But their surprise wasn't at finding a noose on the premises; it was in discovering that African-Americans could be offended by one.

"I had no earthly idea that anybody today would consider that to be a racial symbol. None whatsoever," testified former Southern chairman and chief executive officer A. W. "Bill" Dahlberg in a deposition given for the case on January 30.

An internal investigation conducted by the company in response to the suit discovered a total of 13 ropes tied as nooses of varying types in eight Georgia Power facilities, according to court filings. The company said it couldn't account for the origins of all the nooses, some of which had been displayed for several years, but insists that only one of the nooses it found appeared to have been an intentional effort to intimidate a black worker.

Cooper's decision to challenge his employer of 27 years came early in 2000, after his ninth try at being promoted to a mid-level management job since becoming a full-fledged lineman in the mid-1970s. Utility linemen repair or install electric power cables running on poles and underground. Cooper, 49 years old and graying at the temples, had long hoped to move into a job training other linemen—which would have boosted his annual earnings to about $60,000 from the approximately $43,000 he makes currently. Every time he was turned down, managers told him he needed another training class or should polish a particular skill. At the suggestion of a supervisor, Cooper, who continues to work at Georgia Power, took a company-organized class on interview techniques. Told by the instructor "you have to sell yourself," he decided to be "more confident" in his next job interview. He still didn't get the job. Cooper says he later was told that one of the managers in the session thought he acted like he "could walk on water."

What would you do if you were the chief executive officer at Georgia Power?

1. Fight the discrimination case and do not implement any special diversity training.

2. Fight the case and implement diversity awareness training and internal network and support groups.

3. Admit wrongdoing, settle the suit, and implement diversity awareness training and internal network and support groups.

4. Invent other options. Discuss.

For the Chapter 2 Internet Exercise featuring your unconscious use of stereotypes (www.tolerance.org), visit our Web site at **www.mhhe.com/kreitner.**

Chapter 3

Organizational Culture, Socialization, and Mentoring

Learning Objectives

When you finish studying the material in this chapter, you should be able to:

1 Define organizational culture and discuss its three layers.

2 Discuss the difference between espoused and enacted values.

3 Describe the manifestations and functions of an organization's culture.

4 Discuss the three general types of organizational culture and their associated normative beliefs.

5 Explain the three perspectives proposed to explain the types of culture that enhance an organization's financial performance.

6 Discuss the process of developing an adaptive culture.

7 Summarize the methods used by organizations to embed their cultures.

8 Describe the three phases in Feldman's model of organizational socialization.

9 Discuss the various socialization tactics used to socialize employees.

10 Explain the four developmental networks associated with mentoring.

The residents of northern California got their first taste of Umpqua Bank last July when the ice-cream trucks rolled in. Only days earlier, the little-known Oregon community bank with the weird name had made headlines when it announced the acquisition of a local 27-branch bank. Now, here came Umpqua's advance guard: trucks filled with free ice-cream sandwiches.

Corny? Maybe. But as Ray Davis, Umpqua's CEO says, "It's the corny things that make the difference" when it comes to providing great customer service. Great service is something every bank claims to offer, of course—and almost never does. Employees helplessly sit on their hands when customers have a simple request, shunting them off to a manager, or worse, the company's 800-number.

The problem, as Davis sees it, is culture. At most banks, a cultural focus on efficiency, process, and controls often stands in the way of doing right by customers. At Umpqua, every element of the culture is focused on serving customers. It's what keeps Umpqua growing in the highly competitive retail banking sector. When

Davis, a onetime CPA who spent years as a banking consultant, took the lead job at Umpqua 11 years ago, the Oregon-based bank had just six branches and $140 million in assets. Now it has 92 branches, stretching from Napa to Seattle, and $5 billion in assets.

Davis knows that establishing a culture starts at the top and demands relentless vigilance. "Maintaining a culture is like raising a teenager," he says. "You're constantly checking in. What are you doing? Where are you going? Who are you hanging out with?" It also means recruiting the right people and training them the right way. One of the driving forces behind Umpqua's unique environment is also one of Davis's most controversial creations: the universal associate program. In a typical bank, employees specialize in certain tasks. "How many times have you walked into a bank where there's someone sitting behind a desk, busy—doing something—and

Umpqua Bank user sits at a computer terminal during bank hours in a plush Portland, Oregon, branch. There are no velvet ropes or marble teller's counters; instead, the interior of Umpqua Bank has the feel of a sleek living room.

you're waiting in line for a half-hour and they won't even look up to make eye contact?" asks Davis. "The reason is because they can't help you. They're doing this job—they don't know that job."

Determined not to let that "it's not my job" philosophy infect their employees, Davis and Steve May, his EVP of "cultural enhancement," decided that every bank staffer should be trained in every task. So a teller, for example, can take a mortgage application, and a loan officer can let you into your safe-deposit box. "Now when a customer walks in, the only people there are people there to serve them," Davis says. After some initial grumbling, the system has made employees a lot happier. Umpqua's staff turnover is just over half the industry average. Customers notice the difference too. Rick Randol has been an Umpqua client for five years. "They've grown, but they still watch out for every customer," he says.[1]

FOR DISCUSSION
How would you describe the culture at Umpqua?

The opening vignette highlights the role of organizational culture in contributing to organizational effectiveness. Umpqua's culture, which highly values employees and customers, significantly contributes to the company's growth and success. CEO Ray Davis also knows that an organization's culture must be nurtured and reinforced. He does this by rewarding employees who provide excellent customer service, one of the bank's core values.[2]

Much has been written and said about organizational culture in recent years. This interest grew from the acknowledgment that an organization's culture could significantly influence an organization's short- and long-term success. Andrew Grove, former CEO of Intel, for example, understood the competitive advantage of having a culture that reinforced entrepreneurialism with discipline. "He gave his colleagues a wide berth to be innovative and to anticipate the future. But he was brutal in demanding that they measure their performance every step of the way. In an era when size is critical to global reach and when speedy adaptability is essential to survival, Intel under Grove demonstrated the way to be big and nimble."[3] Under Grove's leadership from 1987 to 1998, Intel's stock price rose 31.6% a year and revenues grew from $1.9 billion to $25.1 billion.[4]

This chapter will help you better understand how managers can use organizational culture as a competitive advantage. After defining and discussing the context of organizational culture, we examine (1) the dynamics of organizational culture, (2) the development of a high-performance culture, (3) the organization socialization process, and (4) the embedding of organizational culture through mentoring.

Organizational Culture: Definition and Context

Organizational culture

Shared values and beliefs that underlie a company's identity.

Organizational culture is "the set of shared, taken-for-granted implicit assumptions that a group holds and that determines how it perceives, thinks about, and reacts to its various environments."[5] This definition highlights three important characteristics of organizational culture. First, organizational culture is passed on to new employees through the process of socialization, a topic discussed later in this chapter. Second, organizational culture influences our behavior at work. Finally, organizational culture operates at different levels.

Figure 3–1 provides a conceptual framework for reviewing the widespread impact organizational culture has on organizational behavior. It also shows the linkage between this chapter—culture, socialization, and mentoring—and other key topics in this book.

Figure 3–1   *A Conceptual Framework for Understanding Organizational Culture*

Antecedents	Organizational culture	Organizational structure and practices	Group and social processes	Collective attitudes and behavior	Organizational outcomes
• Founder's values • Industry and business environment • National culture (Ch. 4) • Senior leaders' vision and behavior (Ch. 16)	• Observable artifacts ↓ ↑ • Espoused values ↓ ↑ • Basic assumptions	• Reward systems (Ch. 9) • Organizational design (Ch. 17)	• Socialization • Mentoring • Decision making (Ch. 12) • Group dynamics (Ch. 10) • Communication (Ch. 14) • Influence and empowerment (Ch. 15) • Leadership (Ch. 16)	• Work attitudes (Ch. 6) • Job satisfaction (Ch. 6) • Motivation (Chs. 8,9)	• Effectiveness (Ch. 17) • Stress (Ch. 18)

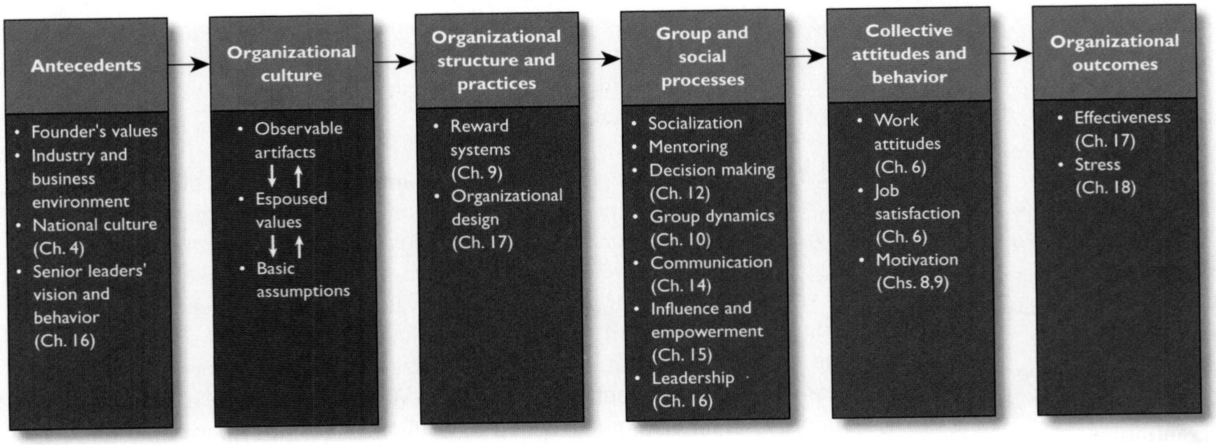

SOURCE: Adapted in part from C Ostroff, A Kinicki, and M Tamkins, "Organizational Culture and Climate," in *Handbook of Psychology,* vol. 12, ed Weiner, p 565–93, © 2003 John Wiley & Sons, Inc. Reprinted with permission of John Wiley & Sons, Inc.

Figure 3–1 reveals organizational culture is shaped by four key components: the founders' values, the industry and business environment, the national culture, and the senior leaders' vision and behavior. In turn, organizational culture influences the type of organizational structure adopted by a company and a host of practices, policies, and procedures implemented in pursuit of organizational goals. These organizational characteristics then affect a variety of group and social processes. This sequence ultimately affects employees' attitudes and behavior and a variety of organizational outcomes. All told, Figure 3–1 reveals that organizational culture is a contextual variable influencing individual, group, and organizational behavior.

Dynamics of Organizational Culture

To gain a better understanding of how organizational culture is formed and used by employees, this section begins by discussing the layers of organizational culture. We then review the manifestation of organizational culture, the four functions of organizational culture, types of organizational culture, and outcomes associated with organizational culture.

Layers of Organizational Culture

Figure 3–1 shows the three fundamental layers of organizational culture: observable artifacts, espoused values, and basic assumptions. Each level varies in terms of outward visibility and resistance to change, and each level influences another level.

Observable Artifacts   At the more visible level, culture represents observable artifacts. Artifacts consist of the physical manifestation of an organization's culture. Organizational examples include acronyms, manner of dress, awards, myths and stories told about the organization, published lists of values, observable rituals and ceremonies, special parking spaces, decorations, and so on. Ensynch, a Tempe, Arizona, information technology services company, for example, wanted to create an artifact to support its stated value of having fun at work. The company did this by naming the company's conference rooms after Seinfeld characters. The largest conference room is called the *Seinfeld* room and its "crazy conference room" is named after *Cosmo Kramer.*[6] This level also includes visible behaviors exhibited by people and groups. Artifacts are easier to change than the less visible aspects of organizational culture.

Values
Enduring belief in a mode of conduct or end-state.

Espoused values
The stated values and norms that are preferred by an organization.

Espoused Values Values possess five key components. "**Values** (1) are concepts or beliefs, (2) pertain to desirable end-states or behaviors, (3) transcend situations, (4) guide selection or evaluation of behavior and events, and (5) are ordered by relative importance."[7] It is important to distinguish between values that are espoused versus those that are enacted.

Espoused values represent the explicitly stated values and norms that are preferred by an organization. They are generally established by the founder of a new or small company and by the top management team in a larger organization. Consider, for example, the espoused values of Williams-Sonoma, Inc. (see Real World/Real People on page 79). This specialty retailer of home furnishings was founded in 1956 and has experienced substantial growth since its inception.

Because espoused values represent aspirations that are explicitly communicated to employees, managers hope that those values will directly influence employee behavior. Unfortunately, aspirations do not automatically produce the desired behaviors because people do not always "walk the talk."

Enacted values
The values and norms that are exhibited by employees.

Enacted values, on the other hand, represent the values and norms that actually are exhibited or converted into employee behavior. They represent the values that employees ascribe to an organization based on their observations of what occurs on a daily basis. The following two examples are excellent representations of the difference between espoused and enacted values.

> A major international corporation hung signs in its hallways proclaiming that "trust" was one of its driving principles. Yet that same company searched employees' belongings each time they entered or exited the building. In another case, a multinational corporation that claimed to be committed to work/life values drew up an excellent plan to help managers incorporate work/life balance into the business. The company gathered its top 80 officers to review the plan—but scheduled the meetings on a weekend.[8]

The first company espoused that it valued trust and then behaved in an untrusting manner by checking employees' belongings. The second company similarly created a mismatch between espoused and enacted values by promoting work/life balance while simultaneously asking managers to attend weekend meetings.

It is important for managers to reduce gaps between espoused and enacted values because they can significantly influence employee attitudes and organizational performance. For example, a study of 312 British rail drivers revealed that employees were more cynical about safety when they believed that senior managers' behavior were inconsistent with the stated values regarding safety.[9] Managers can use a "cultural fit assessment" survey to determine the match between espoused and enacted values. Guidant Corp., an Indianapolis, Indiana–based medical device manufacturer, for instance, implemented its "Vital Signs" survey to assess employees' opinions about the organizational culture, work activities, and total compensation. Results of the survey were used to improve the work environment and to align the organization's espoused and enacted values.[10]

Basic Assumptions Basic underlying assumptions are unobservable and represent the core of organizational culture. They constitute organizational values that have become

Williams-Sonoma's Espoused Values Focus on Employees, Customers, Shareholders, and Ethical Behavior

People First

We believe the potential of our company has no limit and is driven by our associates and their imagination. We are committed to an environment that attracts, motivates and recognizes high performance.

Customers

We are here to please our customers—without them nothing else matters.

Quality

We must take pride in everything we do. From our people, to our products and in our relationships with business partners and our community, quality is our signature.

Shareholders

We must provide a superior return to our shareholders. It's everyone's job.

Ethical Sourcing

Williams-Sonoma, Inc., and all of its brands are committed to maintaining the highest level of integrity and honesty throughout all aspects of our business, and strive to ensure that our business associates, including agents, vendors and suppliers, share our commitment to socially responsible employment conditions.

Environmental Paper Procurement Policy

Williams-Sonoma, Inc., is committed to environmental stewardship, and more specifically, to sound paper procurement practices that ensure the sustainability of forests and other natural resources.

SOURCE: Excerpted from "Corporate Values," www. williams-sonomainc.com/car.car_val.cfm, accessed April 9, 2005.

so taken for granted over time that they become assumptions that guide organizational behavior. They thus are highly resistant to change. When basic assumptions are widely held among employees, people will find behavior based on an inconsistent value inconceivable. Southwest Airlines, for example, is noted for operating according to basic assumptions that value employees' welfare and providing high-quality service. Employees at Southwest Airlines would be shocked to see management act in ways that did not value employees' and customers' needs.

Practical Application of Research on Values Organizations subscribe to a constellation of values rather than to only one and can be profiled according to their values.[11] This enables managers to determine whether or not the organization's values are consistent and supportive of its corporate goals and initiatives. Organizations are less likely to accomplish their corporate goals when employees perceive an inconsistency between espoused values (e.g., honesty) and the behaviors needed to accomplish the goals (e.g., shredding financial documents). Similarly, organizational change is unlikely to succeed if it is based on a set of values highly inconsistent with employees' individual values.[12]

Manifestations of Organizational Culture

When is an organization's culture most apparent? In addition to the physical artifacts of organizational culture that were previously discussed, cultural assumptions assert themselves through socialization of new employees, subculture clashes, and top management behavior. Consider these three situations, for example: A newcomer who shows up late for an important meeting is told a story about someone who was fired for repeated tardiness. Conflict between product design engineers who emphasize a product's function and

Manifestations of Organizational Culture at Setpoint

Instructions

Read the following description and answer the discussion questions. Answers can be found following the Endnotes for this chapter at the end of the book.

Setpoint's CEO, Joe Knight, met them [Steve Petersen and Ted Johnstun, president and chief financial officer at Petersen Inc.] in the lobby and took them on a tour of the facility. . . . Petersen says he was standing there surveying the scene, when he happened to notice a large whiteboard off to one side, on a wall next to a canteen area in a corner of the shop. Scribbled across the board were about 20 rows and 10 columns of numbers forming a table of sort, with a few dollar signs sprinkled here and there.

"What's that?" he asked.

"That's our board," Knight said. "It's how we track our projects and figure out whether or not we're making money.". . .

For one thing, almost half of its [Setpoint] workforce—including its two founders—are dirt-bike fanatics, and they regularly go riding together in the mountains around Ogden, Utah, where Setpoint is located. On the bulletin board in the shop are photographs of various employees flying through the air on their motorcycles. . . .

Somehow it [Setpoint] has built a culture that has everyone involved in the process of controlling cash. The process begins with Setpoint's management system, which allows people throughout the company to track their progress on specific projects with an extraordinarily high degree of accuracy. . . .

Life at Setpoint has changed, everyone agrees, since the introduction of the board and the weekly huddle. "Before that, we had monthly meetings to go over the numbers, but it was too little, too late," says Ken Waudby, the shop manager.

Now there's a huddle every Monday at 11 AM. "[But] we don't just look at the budget and the hours on Monday," says Brad Stryker, a project engineer. "We monitor them throughout the week, and we make decisions based on them." . . .

When it comes to leveraging resources, moreover, the technicians on the shop floor are as focused as the engineers. "I watch GP [gross profit] per hour," says Johnny Lane, a technician. . . . But do people actually talk about their GP per hour while they're working? "Oh, yeah, sure," says Lane. "We discuss it all the time."

That's true, says Waudby, "Like someone will say, 'I worked my butt off, and we only made $50 an hour.' People are always talking about the hours."

That's the most interesting part: the process itself serves as a motivator. "It keeps you involved and lets you understand your impact," says Lyman Houston, a project engineer. "I like to know what condition jobs are in, and why, and what I can do about it. That totally interests and motivates me."

Discussion Questions

1. Identify the shared things, sayings, doings, and feelings at Setpoint.

2. Identify the artifacts, espoused values, and basic assumptions that constitute Setpoint's organizational culture.

3. Does Setpoint's culture attempt to control employees or does it allow them freedom to act as they see fit? Explain.

SOURCE: Excerpted from "What's Your Culture Worth?" *Inc.,* September 2001, pp 126, 128, 130 by Bo Burlingham, Editor-at-Large of Inc. Magazine, and author of *Small Giants: Companies That Choose to Be Great Instead of Big* (Portfolio, 2005).

marketing specialists who demand a more stylish product reveals an underlying clash of subculture values. Top managers, through the behavior they model and the administrative and reward systems they create, prompt a significant improvement in the quality of a company's products. These examples illustrate that an organization's culture can show itself in a variety of ways.

Vijay Sathe, a Harvard researcher, identified four general manifestations or evidence of organizational culture. They are shared things (objects), shared sayings (talk), shared doings (behavior), and shared feelings (emotion).[13] One can begin collecting cultural information within an organization by asking, observing, reading, and feeling.

The OB Exercise on page 80 provides you with the opportunity to practice identifying the manifestations of organizational culture at Setpoint, a custom-manufacturing company with 30 employees and $6 million in sales.

Four Functions of Organizational Culture

As illustrated in Figure 3–2, an organization's culture fulfills four functions. To help bring these four functions to life, let us consider how each of them has taken shape at Southwest Airlines. Southwest is a particularly instructive example because it has grown to become the fourth-largest US airline since its inception in 1971 and has achieved 32 consecutive years of profitability. *Fortune* has ranked Southwest in the top five of the Best Companies to Work For in America from 1997 to 2000; Southwest has chosen not to participate in this ranking process since 2000. Southwest also was ranked as the fifth most admired company in the United States by *Fortune* in 2004, partly due to its strong and distinctive culture.[14]

1. *Give members an organizational identity.* Southwest Airlines is known as a fun place to work that values employee satisfaction and customer loyalty over corporate profits. Herb Kelleher, former CEO and current executive chairman, commented on this issue:

Figure 3–2   *Four Functions of Organizational Culture*

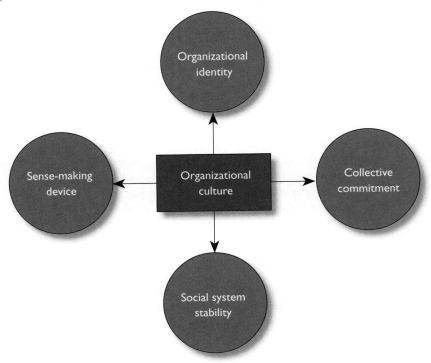

SOURCE: Adapted from discussion in L Smircich, "Concepts of Culture and Organizational Analysis," *Administrative Science Quarterly,* September 1983, pp 339–58. Reproduced by permission of John Wiley & Sons, Inc.

> Who comes first? The employees, customers, or shareholders? That's never been an issue to me. The employees come first. If they're happy, satisfied, dedicated, and energetic, they'll take real good care of the customers. When the customers are happy, they come back. And that makes the shareholders happy.[15]

The company also has a catastrophe fund based on voluntary contributions for distribution to employees who are experiencing serious personal difficulties. Southwest's people-focused identity is reinforced by the fact that it is an employer of choice. For example, Southwest received 225,895 résumés and hired 1,706 new employees in 2004. The company also was noted as an employer of choice among college students by *Fortune,* and a survey of MBA students by consulting firm Universum revealed that Southwest Airlines was among the top 50 most coveted employers.

2. *Facilitate collective commitment.* The mission of Southwest Airlines "is dedication to the highest quality of Customer Service delivered with a sense of warmth, friendliness, individual pride, and Company Spirit."[16] Southwest's more than 32,000 employees are committed to this mission. The Department of Transportation's Air Travel Consumer Report reported Southwest was ranked number one in fewest customer complaints since 1987.

3. *Promote social system stability.* Social system stability reflects the extent to which the work environment is perceived as positive and reinforcing, and the extent to which conflict and change are effectively managed. Southwest is noted for its philosophy of having fun, having parties, and celebrating. For example, each city in which the firm operates is given a budget for parties. Southwest also uses a variety of performance based awards and service awards to reinforce employees. The company's positive and enriching environment is supported by the lowest turnover rates in the airline industry and the employment of 1,039 married couples.

4. *Shape behavior by helping members make sense of their surroundings.* This function of culture helps employees understand why the organization does what it does and how it intends to accomplish its long-term goals. Keeping in mind that Southwest's leadership originally viewed ground transportation as their main competitor in 1971, employees come to understand why the airline's primary vision is to be the best primarily short-haul, low-fare, high-frequency, point-to-point carrier in the United States. Employees understand they must achieve exceptional performance, such as turning a plane in 20 minutes, because they must keep costs down in order to compete against Greyhound and the use of automobiles. In turn, the company reinforces the importance of outstanding customer service and high performance expectations by using performance-based awards and profit sharing. Employees own about 10% of the company stock.

Types of Organizational Culture

Researchers have attempted to identify and measure various types of organizational culture in order to study the relationship between types of culture and organizational effectiveness. This pursuit was motivated by the possibility that certain cultures were more effective than others. Unfortunately, research has not uncovered a universal typology of cultural styles that everyone accepts.[17] Just the same, there is value in providing an example of various types of organizational culture. Table 3–1 is thus presented as an illustration rather than a definitive conclusion about the types of organizational culture that exist. Awareness of these types provides you with greater understanding about the manifestations of culture.

Table 3-1 *Types of Organizational Culture*

General Types of Culture	Normative Beliefs	Organizational Characteristics
Constructive	Achievement	Organizations that do things well and value members who set and accomplish their own goals. Members are expected to set challenging but realistic goals, establish plans to reach these goals, and pursue them with enthusiasm. (Pursuing a standard of excellence)
Constructive	Self-actualizing	Organizations that value creativity, quality over quantity, and both task accomplishment and individual growth. Members are encouraged to gain enjoyment from their work, develop themselves, and take on new and interesting activities. (Thinking in unique and independent ways)
Constructive	Humanistic-encouraging	Organizations that are managed in a participative and person-centered way. Members are expected to be supportive, constructive, and open to influence in their dealings with one another. (Helping others to grow and develop)
Constructive	Affiliative	Organizations that place a high priority on constructive interpersonal relationships. Members are expected to be friendly, open, and sensitive to the satisfaction of their work group. (Dealing with others in a friendly way)
Passive–defensive	Approval	Organizations in which conflicts are avoided and interpersonal relationships are pleasant—at least superficially. Members feel that they should agree with, gain the approval of, and be liked by others. ("Going along" with others)
Passive–defensive	Conventional	Organizations that are conservative, traditional, and bureaucratically controlled. Members are expected to conform, follow the rules, and make a good impression. (Always following policies and practices)
Passive–defensive	Dependent	Organizations that are hierarchically controlled and nonparticipative. Centralized decision making in such organizations leads members to do only what they are told and to clear all decisions with superiors. (Pleasing those in positions of authority)
Passive–defensive	Avoidance	Organizations that fail to reward success but nevertheless punish mistakes. This negative reward system leads members to shift responsibilities to others and avoid any possibility of being blamed for a mistake. (Waiting for others to act first)
Aggressive–defensive	Oppositional	Organizations in which confrontation and negativism are rewarded. Members gain status and influence by being critical and thus are reinforced to oppose the ideas of others. (Pointing out flaws)
Aggressive–defensive	Power	Nonparticipative organizations structured on the basis of the authority inherent in members' positions. Members believe they will be rewarded for taking charge, controlling subordinates and, at the same time, being responsive to the demands of superiors. (Building up one's power base)
Aggressive–defensive	Competitive	Winning is valued and members are rewarded for outperforming one another. Members operate in a "win–lose" framework and believe they must work against (rather than with) their peers to be noticed. (Turning the job into a contest)
Aggressive–defensive	Perfectionistic	Organizations in which perfectionism, persistence, and hard work are valued. Members feel they must avoid any mistake, keep track of everything, and work long hours to attain narrowly defined objectives. (Doing things perfectly)

SOURCE: Reproduced with permission of the authors and publisher from R A Cooke and J L Szumal, "Measuring Normative Beliefs and Shared Behavioral Expectations in Organizations: The Reliability and Validity of the Organizational Culture Inventory," *Psychological Reports*, vol. 72, 1993, pp 1299–330. © *Psychological Reports*, 1993.

Normative beliefs
Thoughts and beliefs about expected behavior and modes of conduct.

Table 3–1 shows that there are three general types of organizational culture—constructive, passive–defensive, and aggressive–defensive—and that each type is associated with a different set of normative beliefs.[18] **Normative beliefs** represent an individual's thoughts and beliefs about how members of a particular group or organization are expected to approach their work and interact with others. A *constructive culture* is one in which employees are encouraged to interact with others and to work on tasks and projects in ways that will assist them in satisfying their needs to grow and develop. This type of culture endorses normative beliefs associated with achievement, self-actualizing, humanistic-encouraging, and affiliative.

The Hartford is a good example of a company that is using its compensation system to reinforce a combination of achievement and self-actualizing beliefs.

> Our compensation philosophy means fair pay based on your role in the company; the market value of your job; your performance in that position; plus the opportunity for additional rewards when we either meet or exceed business objectives....To attract and keep the best people, we offer meaningful rewards when you, your division, and the company achieve specific business goals or when you demonstrate outstanding individual performance.[19]

In contrast, a *passive–defensive culture* is characterized by an overriding belief that employees must interact with others in ways that do not threaten their own job security. This culture reinforces the normative beliefs associated with approval, conventional, dependent, and avoidance (see Table 3–1). Mitsubishi is a good example of a company with a passive–defensive culture. According to *BusinessWeek* reporters,

> This was a company whose managers were so reluctant to relay bad news to higher-ups that they squelched complaints about quality defects for decades to avoid costly product recalls. Many Daimler [DaimlerChrysler spent $2.4 billion to obtain a 37% stake in Mitsubishi] critics also say its culture contributed to the failed turnaround: The push was always on for results, and few wanted to alert Stuttgart to major problems. Later, to help US sales, Mitsubishi resorted to an ultragenerous financing campaign—no money down and no payments for a year. The result was almost half a billion in bad loans.[20]

Finally, companies with an *aggressive–defensive culture* encourage employees to approach tasks in forceful ways in order to protect their status and job security. This type of culture is more characteristic of normative beliefs reflecting oppositional, power, competitive, and perfectionist.

Although an organization may predominately represent one cultural type, it still can manifest normative beliefs and characteristics from the others. Research demonstrates that organizations can have functional subcultures, hierarchical subcultures based on one's level in the organization, geographical subcultures, occupational subcultures based on one's title or position, social subcultures derived from social activities such as a bowling or golf league and a reading club, and countercultures.[21] It is important for managers to be aware of the possibility that conflict between subgroups that form subcultures can undermine an organization's overall performance.

Outcomes Associated with Organizational Culture

Both managers and academic researchers believe that organizational culture can be a driver of employee attitudes and organizational effectiveness and performance. To test this possibility, various measures of organizational culture have been correlated with a variety of individual and organizational outcomes. So what have we learned? First, several studies demonstrated that organizational culture was significantly correlated with employee behavior and attitudes. For example, a constructive culture was positively related with job satisfaction, intentions to stay at the company, and innovation and was negatively associated with work avoidance. In contrast, passive–defensive and aggressive–defensive cultures were negatively correlated with job satisfaction and intentions to stay at the company.[22] These results suggest that employees seem to prefer organizations that encourage people to interact and work with others in ways that assist them in satisfying their needs to grow and develop. Second, results from several studies revealed that the congruence between an individual's values and the organization's values was significantly associated with organizational commitment, job satisfaction, intention to quit, and turnover.[23]

Third, a summary of 10 quantitative studies showed that organizational culture did not predict an organization's financial performance.[24] This means that there is not one type of organizational culture that fuels financial performance. That said, however, a study of 207 companies from 22 industries for an 11-year period demonstrated that financial performance was higher among companies that had adaptive and flexible cultures.[25] Finally, studies of mergers indicated that they frequently failed due to incompatible cultures. Due to the increasing number of corporate mergers around the world, and the conclusion that 7 out of 10 mergers and acquisitions failed to meet their financial promise, managers within merged companies would be well advised to consider the role of organizational culture in creating a new organization.[26]

In summary, these results underscore the significance of organizational culture. They also reinforce the need to learn more about the process of cultivating and changing an organization's culture. An organization's culture is not determined by fate. It is formed and shaped by the combination and integration of everyone who works in the organization. A change-resistant culture, for instance, can undermine the effectiveness of any type of organizational change. Although it is not an easy task to change an organization's culture, the next section provides a preliminary overview of how this might be done.

Developing High-Performance Cultures

An organization's culture may be strong or weak, depending on variables such as cohesiveness, value consensus, and individual commitment to collective goals. Contrary to what one might suspect, a strong culture is not necessarily a good thing. The nature of the culture's central values is more important than its strength. For example, a strong but change-resistant culture may be worse, from the standpoint of profitability and competitiveness, than a weak but innovative culture. This section discusses the types of organizational culture that enhance an organization's financial performance and the process by which cultures are embedded in an organization and learned by employees.

What Types of Culture Enhance an Organization's Financial Performance?

Three perspectives have been proposed to explain the types of culture that enhance an organization's economic performance. They are referred to as the strength, fit, and adaptive perspectives, respectively:

1. The **strength perspective** predicts a significant relationship between strength of corporate culture and long-term financial performance. The idea is that strong

Strength perspective
Assumes that the strength of corporate culture is related to a firm's financial performance.

cultures create goal alignment, employee motivation, and the appropriate structure and controls needed to improve organizational performance.[27] Critics of this perspective believe that companies with a strong culture can become arrogant, inwardly focused, and bureaucratic after they achieve financial success because financial success reinforces the strong culture. This reinforcement can blind senior managers to the need for new strategic plans and may result in a general resistance to change.

Fit perspective
Assumes that culture must align with its business or strategic context.

2. The **fit perspective** is based on the premise that an organization's culture must align with its business or strategic context. A "correct" fit is expected to foster higher financial performance. Hewlett-Packard is a good case study of the fit perspective in action.

When Dave Packard and Bill Hewlett founded the company in 1938, they created a set of six goals—a seventh was added later—and pushed for all employees to work together in accomplishing them. Dave Packard's vision was to instill a culture in which "people work together in unison toward common objectives and avoid working at cross purposes at all levels if the ultimate in efficiency and achievement is to be obtained."[28] The HP culture, which came to be called the HP Way, pushed authority down as far as possible in the organization and created an environment that emphasized integrity, respect for individuals, teamwork, innovation, and an emphasis on customers and community involvement. The fit perspective worked from 1957 through the early 1990s, and the HP Way was a key contributor to the organization's success. The high-technology industry began to change, however, in the late 1990s.[29]

These changes led the board of directors to conclude that the HP Way no longer fit the business or strategic context. The board thus decided to hire Carly Fiorina in 1999 from outside the company to lead a process of cultural and strategic change. As suggested by the fit perspective, the board believed that a change in culture was needed to fit the business and strategic environment. According to a writer from *Business Week,* Fiorina's reforms unfortunately "ended up creating new bureaucracy while fraying the all-important faith of the troops."[30] The cultural and strategic changes pursued under Carly Fiorina's leadership apparently did not work out, and she ultimately left the company in early 2005.

Adaptive perspective
Assumes that adaptive cultures enhance a firm's financial performance.

3. The **adaptive perspective** assumes that the most effective cultures help organizations anticipate and adapt to environmental changes. A team of management experts defined this culture as follows:

> An adaptive culture entails a risk-taking, trusting, and proactive approach to organizational as well as individual life. Members actively support one another's efforts to identify all problems and implement workable solutions. There is a shared feeling of confidence: The members believe, without a doubt, that they can effectively manage whatever new problems and opportunities will come their way. There is widespread enthusiasm, a spirit of doing whatever it takes to achieve organizational success. The members are receptive to change and innovation.[31]

This proactive adaptability is expected to enhance long-term financial performance.

A Test of the Three Perspectives
John Kotter and James Heskett tested the three perspectives on a sample of 207 companies from 22 industries for the period 1977 to 1988. After correlating results from a cultural survey and three different measures of financial performance, results partially supported the strength and fit perspectives. However,

Figure 3–3   *Developing and Preserving an Adaptive Culture*

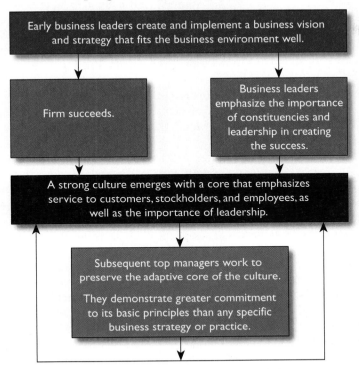

findings were completely consistent with the adaptive culture perspective. Long-term financial performance was highest for organizations with an adaptive culture.[32]

Developing an Adaptive Culture

Figure 3–3 illustrates the process of developing and preserving an adaptive culture. The process begins with leadership; that is, leaders must create and implement a business vision and associated strategies that fit the organizational context. A **vision** represents a long-term goal that describes "what" an organization wants to become. For example, Walt Disney's original vision for Disneyland included the following components.

> Disneyland will be something of a fair, an exhibition, a playground, a community center, a museum of living facts, and a showplace of beauty and magic. It will be filled with the accomplishments, the joys and hopes of the world we live in. And it will remind us and show us how to make those wonders part of our own lives.[33]

Sometimes a vision statement can be short. When Ciba Vision's sales of conventional contacts was threatened by a new, disposable contact lens from Johnson & Johnson in 1987, Ciba president Glenn Bradley reorganized the company into six formal development projects to produce eyewear product breakthroughs. While each unit was free to shape its own organization, processes, and culture, Bradley knew they had to share expertise and resources. Accordingly, he and his team enunciated a new vision statement: "Healthy Eyes

Vision
Long-term goal describing "what" an organization wants to become.

Walt Disney's original vision for Disneyland included the following: "It will be something of a fair, an exhibition, a playground, a community center, a museum of living facts, and a showplace of beauty and magic." To what extent is Walt's vision apparent in the Disneyland parade?

for Life." The statement was not only meaningful to all parts of the business but also underscored the connections between the breakthrough initiatives and the conventional operation. The slogan, Bradley noted, also gave people a social value as well as an economic reason for working together.[34] This example highlights that an adaptive culture is promoted over time by a combination of organizational success and a specific leadership focus.

Figure 3–3 shows that leaders must get employees to buy into a timeless philosophy or set of values that emphasizes service to the organization's key constituents—customers, stockholders, and employees—and also emphasizes the improvement of leadership. An infrastructure must then be created to preserve the organization's adaptiveness. Management does this by consistently reinforcing and supporting the organization's core philosophy or values of satisfying constituency needs and improving leadership. This is precisely what Herb Kelleher, former CEO of Southwest Airlines, did at Southwest Airlines.

> Long before "empowerment" became a management buzzword, Ms Barrett [the number two executive at Southwest] was giving employees freedom from centralized policies. She constantly reinforces the company's message that employees should be treated like customers and continually celebrates workers who go above and beyond the call of duty. And when she sensed the carrier was outgrowing its personality-kid-among-the-impersonal-giants image, she created a "culture committee" of employees charged with preserving Southwest's spirit. . . .
>
> Southwest employees are well-paid compared with counterparts at other airlines. Celebrations are an important part of work, from spontaneous "fun sessions" to Christmas parties beginning in September to a lavish annual awards banquet, where the individual's contribution to the whole is glorified.
>
> At the same time, employees work like crazy between festivities. With that formula, the airline has avoided bureaucracy and mediocrity that infect other companies when they outgrow their entrepreneurial roots.[35]

How Cultures Are Embedded in Organizations

An organization's initial culture is an outgrowth of the founder's values and business philosophy. For example, an achievement culture is likely to develop if the founder is an achievement-oriented individual driven by success. Over time, the original culture is either embedded as is or modified to fit the current environmental situation. Edgar Schein, a well-known OB scholar, notes that embedding a culture involves a teaching process. That is, organizational members teach each other about the organization's preferred values, beliefs, expectations, and behaviors. This is accomplished by using one or more of the following mechanisms:[36]

1. *Formal statements of organizational philosophy, mission, vision, values, and materials used for recruiting, selection, and socialization.* Sam Walton, the founder of Wal-Mart, established three basic beliefs or values that represent the core of the organization's culture. They are (1) respect for the individual, (2) service to our customer, and (3) striving for excellence.[37]

2. *The design of physical space, work environments, and buildings.* Consider how Acordia Inc. attempted to create a more entrepreneurial culture by building a new one-floor facility.

   > The building facilitated interactive workflow procedures. Interactions among new-venture team members and among independent teams became grounded in forming and sharing tacit knowledge. Positive feelings surfacing from these interactions and the knowledge they fostered created positive morale in individuals and between employees and their vice president.[38]

3. *Slogans, language, acronyms, and sayings.* For example, Bank One promotes its desire to provide excellent client service through the slogan "whatever it takes." Employees are encouraged to do whatever it takes to exceed customer expectations.

4. *Deliberate role modeling, training programs, teaching, and coaching by managers and supervisors.* Gary Kelly, the CEO of Southwest Airlines, decided to role-model the corporate value of "having fun" by showing up at a Halloween party dressed as Gene Simmons, the front man for the rock group Kiss.[39]

5. *Explicit rewards, status symbols (e.g., titles), and promotion criteria.* Charles Haldeman, the CEO of Putnam Investments, is trying to change the company's culture by creating a new set of performance criteria and incentives for employees.

   > Now, instead of swinging for the fences as Putnam's leadership did in the go-go days of the 1990s, Haldeman has ordered managers to aim for reliable returns over the long haul. Haldeman wants each of Putnam's 54 funds to rank in the top half of its category every year. . . . In the future, managers will earn bonuses by achieving just that—and not get a penny more for edging their funds into the top 10%, as they once did.[40]

Gary Kelly, CEO of Southwest Airlines, decided to role-model the corporate value of "having fun" by dressing up for Halloween as Kiss's Gene Simmons. Based on the woman dancing with Gary, it looks like he is achieving his goal.

Haldeman is implementing this new approach because the old performance criteria and incentives were partly responsible for serious trading scandals that resulted in investors pulling out $70 billion of their money from Putnam's funds.

6. *Stories, legends, or myths about key people and events.* Imagine how the following story might be used to reinforce PepsiCo's commitment to its employees.

> Four years ago, the then-chairman and chief executive officer of PepsiCo, Roger A Enrico, decided that rather than pocket his $900,000 annual salary, he would ask the company's board to use the money to fund scholarships for children of employees who earn less than $60,000 a year. PepsiCo's foundation already was offering scholarships, but Mr Enrico—who is the son of an iron worker and went to college on a scholarship—wanted to enlarge the fund. "I wanted to do something personal to say thanks to front-line employees who make, sell and move our products," he says.[41]

7. *The organizational activities, processes, or outcomes that leaders pay attention to, measure, and control.* Exxon Mobil Corp makes a concerted effort to measure, control, and reward cost efficiency.

> The company is famous for delivering consistent returns regardless of whether the price of oil is up or down. Exxon's secret: operational efficiency. The company squeezes more money out of each barrel of oil it produces than any other major oil company....The whole credo of our company is efficiency—efficiency in everything we do.[42]

8. *Leader reactions to critical incidents and organizational crises.* Consider the cultural message sent by former Enron leaders as they passed the blame for the financial crises of 2002.

> At a time when former leaders Kenneth L Lay and Jeffrey K Skilling are trying to blame the company's problems on a small group of rogue financial execs, the details of Enron's investment portfolio indicate the company's problems went well beyond the CFO's office—and well beyond its controversial off-balance-sheet partnerships.[43]

Do you think that this leader behavior would instill an accountability-based culture?

9. *The workflow and organizational structure.* Hierarchical structures are more likely to embed an orientation toward control and authority than a flatter organization. Leaders from many organizations are increasingly reducing the number of organizational layers in an attempt to empower employees (see Chapter 17) and increase employee involvement.

10. *Organizational systems and procedures.* Capital One, for example, is using a variety of procedures to reinforce a culture that focuses on self-development.

> And like most development plans, Capital One's program highlights key areas in which associates [employees] might want or need to develop and helps them identify specific ways to reach those goals. But the DAP [development action plan] program goes a step farther and is supported with a performance management process in which an individual's objectives are strategically aligned with company objectives to develop core competencies, maximize individual performance, and provide appropriate rewards for performance. The competency planning and development team accomplishes this through an ongoing cycle of setting objectives, DAPs, ongoing feedback, coaching, mentoring, and, of course, 360-degree performance evaluations at least twice a year.[44]

11. *Organizational goals and the associated criteria used for recruitment, selection, development, promotion, layoffs, and retirement of people.* PepsiCo reinforces a high-performance culture by setting challenging goals.

The Organizational Socialization Process

Organizational socialization is defined as "the process by which a person learns the values, norms, and required behaviors which permit him to participate as a member of the organization."[45] As previously discussed, organization socialization is a key mechanism used by organizations to embed their organizational cultures. In short, organizational socialization turns outsiders into fully functioning insiders by promoting and reinforcing the organization's core values and beliefs. This section introduces a three-phase model of organizational socialization and examines the practical application of socialization research.

Organizational socialization
Process by which employees learn an organization's values, norms, and required behaviors.

A Three-Phase Model of Organizational Socialization

One's first year in a complex organization can be confusing. There is a constant swirl of new faces, strange jargon, conflicting expectations, and apparently unrelated events. Some organizations treat new members in a rather haphazard, sink-or-swim manner. More typically, though, the socialization process is characterized by a sequence of identifiable steps.

Organizational behavior researcher Daniel Feldman has proposed a three-phase model of organizational socialization that promotes deeper understanding of this important process. As illustrated in Figure 3–4, the three phases are (1) anticipatory socialization, (2) encounter, and (3) change and acquisition. Each phase has its associated perceptual and social processes. Feldman's model also specifies behavioral and affective outcomes that can be used to judge how well an individual has been socialized. The entire three-phase sequence may take from a few weeks to a year to complete, depending on individual differences and the complexity of the situation.

© 2003 Ted Goff

"We're in awe of your ability to fit in here, Ms. Stoughton."

Ted Goff. Reprinted by permission.

Phase 1: Anticipatory Socialization

Anticipatory socialization occurs before an individual actually joins an organization. It is represented by the information people have learned about different careers, occupations, professions, and organizations. For example, anticipatory socialization partially explains the different perceptions you might have about working for the US government versus a high-technology company like Intel or Microsoft. Anticipatory socialization information comes from many sources. An organization's current employees are a powerful source of anticipatory socialization. Consider the case of Sedona Center, which includes Amara Creekside Resort, two shopping plazas, and three restaurants in Sedona, Arizona. The organization's 200 employees apparently like to tell others in the labor market about the company's employee-focused organizational culture (see Real World/Real People on page 93). In turn, job openings are filled with

Anticipatory socialization
Occurs before an individual joins an organization, and involves the information people learn about different careers, occupations, professions, and organizations.

Figure 3–4   *A Model of Organizational Socialization*

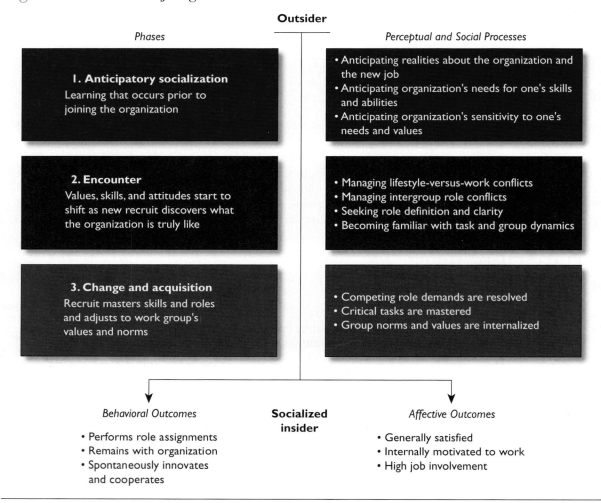

Outsider

Phases

1. Anticipatory socialization
Learning that occurs prior to joining the organization

2. Encounter
Values, skills, and attitudes start to shift as new recruit discovers what the organization is truly like

3. Change and acquisition
Recruit masters skills and roles and adjusts to work group's values and norms

Perceptual and Social Processes

• Anticipating realities about the organization and the new job
• Anticipating organization's needs for one's skills and abilities
• Anticipating organization's sensitivity to one's needs and values

• Managing lifestyle-versus-work conflicts
• Managing intergroup role conflicts
• Seeking role definition and clarity
• Becoming familiar with task and group dynamics

• Competing role demands are resolved
• Critical tasks are mastered
• Group norms and values are internalized

Behavioral Outcomes

• Performs role assignments
• Remains with organization
• Spontaneously innovates and cooperates

Socialized insider

Affective Outcomes

• Generally satisfied
• Internally motivated to work
• High job involvement

SOURCE: Adapted from material in D C Feldman, "The Multiple Socialization of Organization Members," *Academy of Management Review*, April 1981, pp 309–18. Reprinted by permission of The Academy of Management via The Copyright Clearance Center.

employees who better "fit" within Sedona Center's culture and ultimately are more satisfied and less likely to quit. The company's turnover rate—13 to 18%—is less than half the national average for this industry.[46]

Unrealistic expectations about the nature of the work, pay, and promotions are often formulated during phase 1. Because employees with unrealistic expectations are more likely to quit their jobs in the future, organizations may want to use realistic job previews.[47] A **realistic job preview** (RJP) involves giving recruits a realistic idea of what lies ahead by presenting both positive and negative aspects of the job. RJPs may be verbal, in booklet form, audiovisual, or hands-on. Research supports the practical benefits of using RJPs. A meta-analysis of 40 studies revealed that RJPs were related to higher performance and to lower attrition from the recruitment process. Results also demonstrated that RJPs lowered job applicants' initial expectations and led to lower turnover among those applicants who were hired.[48]

Realistic job preview
Presents both positive and negative aspects of a job.

Sedona Center Relies on Current Employees for Anticipatory Socialization

The Sedona company's incentives include higher-than-average pay, scheduling flexibility for family matters, full health benefits at 25 working hours per week, free wiring of paychecks overseas for employees supporting non-US family, and expense-paid vacations for top employees.

Workers have noticed. . . .

The company places profitability sixth on its list of six values, knowing that profits will rise if it adheres to higher ranked values such as a work environment where teamwork is expected and rewarded (No. 1) and encourages employees to seek a work–home balance (No. 2). . . .

Amara employee happiness starts with hiring, general manager Kevin Johnson, said.

He interviews each new hire, looking for the right attitude. In turn, management is willing to listen to employees, he said.

Spector Gomez [chief operating officer] and other employees said word is getting out about working there.

"I'll tell you one thing, our openings don't last," she said.

SOURCE: Excerpted from J Stearns, "Sedona Company Wants Happy Employees," *Arizona Republic*, April 10, 2005, p D2.

Phase 2: Encounter

This second phase begins when the employment contract has been signed. During the **encounter phase** employees come to learn what the organization is really like. It is a time for reconciling unmet expectations and making sense of a new work environment. Many companies use a combination of orientation and training programs to socialize employees during the encounter phase. Onboarding is one such technique. **Onboarding** programs help employees to integrate, assimilate, and transition to new jobs by making them familiar with corporate policies, procedures, and culture and by clarifying work role expectations and responsibilities.[49] Bristol-Myers Squibb's onboarding program, for example, resulted in substantial improvement in the retention rate for managers. The program makes

> new executives the object of a laserlike focus during the first 30 to 60 days of their employment, providing guidelines, clarifying roles, setting up meetings with influential colleagues and fostering each newcomer's understanding of the company's cultural norms. Follow-up meetings are held during the executive's first year to check progress and resolve problems.[50]

Phase 3: Change and Acquisition

The **change and acquisition** phase requires employees to master important tasks and roles and to adjust to their work group's values and norms. Table 3–2 presents a list of socialization processes or tactics used by organizations to help employees through this adjustment process. Trilogy, for example, uses a variety of these tactics in its renowned socialization program. The three-month program takes place at the organization's corporate university, called Trilogy University.

> **Month one.** When you arrive at Trilogy University, you are assigned to a section and to an instruction track. Your section, a group of about 20, is your social group for the duration of TU. . . . Tracks are designed to be microcosms of future work life at Trilogy. . . . The technical challenges in such exercises closely mimic real customer engagements, but the time frames are dramatically compressed. The assignments pile up week after week for the first month, each one successively more challenging than the last. During that time, you're being constantly measured and evaluated, as assignment grades and comments are entered into a database monitoring your progress. . . .

Encounter phase
Employees learn what the organization is really like and reconcile unmet expectations.

Onboarding
Programs aimed at helping employees integrate, assimilate, and transition to new jobs.

Change and acquisition
Requires employees to master tasks and roles and to adjust to work group values and norms.

Table 3-2   *Socialization Tactics*

Tactic	Description
Collective vs. individual	Collective socialization consists of grouping newcomers and exposing them to a common set of experiences rather than treating each newcomer individually and exposing him or her to more or less unique experiences.
Formal vs. informal	Formal socialization is the practice of segregating a newcomer from regular organization members during a defined socialization period versus not clearly distinguishing a newcomer from more experienced members. Army recruits must attend boot camp before they are allowed to work alongside established soldiers.
Sequential vs. random	Sequential socialization refers to a fixed progression of steps that culminate in the new role, compared to an ambiguous or dynamic progression. The socialization of doctors involves a lock-step sequence from medical school, to internship, to residency before they are allowed to practice on their own.
Fixed vs. variable	Fixed socialization provides a timetable for the assumption of the role, whereas a variable process does not. American university students typically spend one year apiece as freshmen, sophomores, juniors, and seniors.
Serial vs. disjunctive	A serial process is one in which the newcomer is socialized by an experienced member, whereas a disjunctive process does not use a role model.
Investiture vs. divestiture	Investiture refers to the affirmation of a newcomer's incoming global and specific role identities and attributes. Divestiture is the denial and stripping away of the newcomer's existing sense of self and the reconstruction of self in the organization's image. During police training, cadets are required to wear uniforms and maintain an immaculate appearance, they are addressed as "officer," told they are no longer ordinary citizens but are representatives of the police force.

SOURCE: Descriptions were taken from B E Ashforth, *Role Transitions in Organizational Life: An Identity-Based Perspective* (Mahwah, NJ: Lawrence Erlbaum Associates, 2001), pp 149–83.

Month two. Month two is TU project month.... In teams of three to five people, they have to come up with an idea, create a business model for it, build the product, and develop the marketing plan. In trying to launch bold new ideas in a hyperaccelerated time frame, they gain a deep appreciation of the need to set priorities, evaluate probabilities, and measure results. Mind you, these projects are not hypothetical—they're the real thing....

Month three. Month three at Trilogy University is all about finding your place and having a broader impact in the larger organization. A few students continue with their TU projects, but most move on to "graduation projects," which generally are assignments within various Trilogy business units. People leave TU on a rolling basis as they find sponsors out in the company who are willing to take them on.[51]

The change and acquisition phase at Trilogy is stressful, exhilarating, and critical for finding one's place within the organization. How would you like to work there? Returning to Table 3–2, can you identify the socialization tactics used by Trilogy?

Practical Application of Socialization Research

Past research suggests five practical guidelines for managing organizational socialization.

1. Managers should avoid a haphazard, sink-or-swim approach to organizational socialization because formalized socialization tactics positively affect new hires.

Formalized or institutionalized socialization tactics were found to positively help employees in both domestic and international organizations.[52]

2. Managers play a key role during the encounter phase. Studies of newly hired accountants demonstrated that the frequency and type of information obtained during their first six months of employment significantly affected their job performance, their role clarity, and the extent to which they were socially integrated.[53] Managers need to help new hires integrate within the organizational culture.

3. Support for stage models is mixed. Although there are different stages of socialization, they are not identical in order, length, or content for all people or jobs.[54] Managers are advised to use a contingency approach toward organizational socialization. In other words, different techniques are appropriate for different people at different times.

4. The organization can benefit by training new employees to use proactive socialization behaviors. A study of 154 entry-level professionals showed that effectively using proactive socialization behaviors reduced the newcomers' general anxiety and stress during the first month of employment and increased their motivation six months later.[55]

5. Managers should pay attention to the socialization of diverse employees. Research demonstrated that diverse employees, particularly those with disabilities, experienced different socialization activities than other newcomers. In turn, these different experiences affected their long-term success and job satisfaction.[56]

Mentoring
Process of forming and maintaining developmental relationships between a mentor and a junior person.

Embedding Organizational Culture through Mentoring

The modern word *mentor* derives from Mentor, the name of a wise and trusted counselor in Greek mythology. Terms typically used in connection with mentoring are *teacher, coach, sponsor,* and *peer.* **Mentoring** is defined as the process of forming and maintaining intensive and lasting developmental relationships between a variety of developers (i.e., people who provide career and psychosocial support) and a junior person (the protégé, if male; or protégée, if female).[57] Mentoring can serve to embed an organization's culture when developers and the protégé/protégée work in the same organization for two reasons. First, mentoring contributes to creating a sense of oneness by promoting the acceptance of the organization's core values throughout the organization. Second, the socialization aspect of mentoring also promotes a sense of membership.

Not only is mentoring important as a tactic for embedding organizational culture, but research suggests it can significantly influence the protégé/protégée's future career. For example, a meta-analysis revealed that mentored employees had higher compensation and more promotions than nonmentored employees. Mentored employees

In today's high-technology work environments, helping or coaching others on the use of computer programs is a key function of mentoring. This type of mentoring is important in embedding an organization's culture because it contributes to a sense of oneness and it enhances employees' feelings of competence.

also reported higher job and career satisfaction and organizational commitment and lower turnover.[58] This section focuses on how people can use mentoring to their advantage. We discuss the functions of mentoring, the developmental networks underlying mentoring, and the personal and organizational implications of mentoring.

Functions of Mentoring

Kathy Kram, a Boston University researcher, conducted in-depth interviews with both members of 18 pairs of senior and junior managers. As a by-product of this study, Kram identified two general functions—career and psychosocial—of the mentoring process. Five *career functions* that enhanced career development were sponsorship, exposure-and-visibility, coaching, protection, and challenging assignments. Four *psychosocial functions* were role modeling, acceptance-and-confirmation, counseling, and friendship. The psychosocial functions clarified the participants' identities and enhanced their feelings of competence.[59]

Developmental Networks Underlying Mentoring

Historically, it was thought that mentoring was primarily provided by one person who was called a mentor. Today, however, the changing nature of technology, organizational structures, and marketplace dynamics requires that people seek career information and support from many sources. Mentoring is currently viewed as a process in which protégés and protégées seek developmental guidance from a network of people, who are referred to as developers. Lori McKee, a project manager with Chubb Group of Insurance Cos., is a good example of someone who used a network of people to advance her career. She started a book club at the company, and 19 Chubb Group women across the country meet via teleconference once a month to discuss career issues associated with books they have read. "As a result of her increased visibility at the company, the 31-year-old Ms McKee says she has been offered bigger assignments, including one to help upgrade the company's financial systems worldwide. 'The way I got it was through these discussions and getting mentoring from other women in the group,' she says."[60] This example implies that the diversity and strength of one's network of relationships is instrumental in obtaining the type of career assistance needed to manage one's career. Figure 3–5 presents a developmental network typology based on integrating the diversity and strength of developmental relationships.[61]

Diversity of developmental relationships
The variety of people in a network used for developmental assistance.

The **diversity of developmental relationships** reflects the variety of people within the network an individual uses for developmental assistance. There are two subcomponents associated with network diversity: (1) the number of different people the person is networked with and (2) the various social systems from which the networked relationships stem (e.g., employer, school, family, community, professional associations, and religious affiliations). As shown in Figure 3–5, developmental relationship diversity ranges from low (few people or social systems) to high (multiple people or social systems).

Developmental relationship strength
The quality of relationships among people in a network.

Developmental relationship strength reflects the quality of relationships among the individual and those involved in his or her developmental network. For example, strong ties are reflective of relationships based on frequent interactions, reciprocity, and positive affect. Weak ties, in contrast, are based more on superficial relationships. Together, the diversity and strength of developmental relationships results in four types of developmental networks (see Figure 3–5): receptive, traditional, entrepreneurial, and opportunistic.

A *receptive* developmental network is composed of a few weak ties from one social system such as an employer or a professional association. The single oval around D1 and D2 in Figure 3–5 is indicative of two developers who come from one social system. In contrast, a *traditional* network contains a few strong ties between an employee and developers that

Figure 3–5   *Developmental Networks Associated with Mentoring*

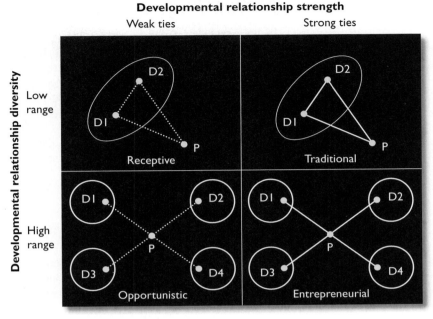

Key: D, developer; P, protégé

SOURCE: M Higgins and K Kram, "Reconceptualizing Mentoring at Work: A Developmental Network Perspective," *Academy of Management Review,* April 2001, p 270. Reprinted by permission of The Academy of Management via The Copyright Clearance Center.

all come from one social system. An entrepreneurial network, which is the strongest type of developmental network, is made up of strong ties among several developers (D1–D4) who come from four different social systems. Finally, an opportunistic network is associated with having weak ties with multiple developers from different social systems.

Personal and Organizational Implications

There are two key personal implications to consider. First, job and career satisfaction are likely to be influenced by the consistency between an individual's career goals and the type of developmental network at his or her disposal. For example, people with an entrepreneurial developmental network are more likely to experience change in their careers and to benefit from personal learning than people with receptive, traditional, and opportunistic networks. If this sounds attractive to you, you should try to increase the diversity and strength of your developmental relationships. In contrast, lower levels of job satisfaction are expected when employees have receptive developmental networks and they desire to experience career advancement in multiple organizations. Receptive developmental networks, however, can be satisfying to someone who does not desire to be promoted up the career ladder.[62] Second, a developer's willingness to provide career and psychosocial assistance is a function of the protégé/protégée's ability, potential, and the quality of the interpersonal relationship.[63] This implies that you must take ownership for enhancing your skills, abilities, and developmental networks if you desire to experience career advancement throughout your life.[64]

Blue Cross and Blue Shield of North Carolina (BCBSNC) Effectively Implements a Mentoring Program

Designed to identify high-potential employees, develop talent, enhance cross-functional relationships and create networking opportunities, the program consists of nine-month commitments on the part of the mentor and mentee. Employees who are accepted into the program (anyone can apply) are paired with a mentor who has completed rigorous training and is typically from a different department and/or division than the mentee. . . . Since the program's inauguration in 2000, turnover among mentees has averaged 46% lower than BCBSNC's general employee population. What's more, the BCBSNC's Corporate Lead-

ership Council's formula for calculating the cost of turnover showed that this program, which costs less than $4,500 per year in out-of-pocket expense, generated a cost avoidance of more than $1.4 million. Additionally, 18% of mentees in 2001 and 25% in 2002 received outstanding performance ratings, compared to 10% for the general population for the same periods.

SOURCE: Excerpted from "Best Practices: Mentoring—Blue Cross and Blue Shield of North Carolina," *Training*, March 2004, p 62.

Research also supports the organizational benefits of mentoring. For example, the Real World/Real People feature shown above illustrates the positive benefits of a mentoring program at Blue Cross and Blue Shield of North Carolina. Mentoring also enhances the effectiveness of organizational communication. Specifically, mentoring increases the amount of vertical communication both up and down an organization, and it provides a mechanism for modifying or reinforcing organizational culture.

Summary of Key Concepts

1. *Define organizational culture and discuss its three layers.* Organizational culture represents the shared assumptions that a group holds. It influences employees' perceptions and behavior at work. The three layers of organizational culture include observable artifacts, espoused values, and basic assumptions. Artifacts are the physical manifestations of an organization's culture. Espoused values represent the explicitly stated values and norms that are preferred by an organization. Basic underlying assumptions are unobservable and represent the core of organizational culture.

2. *Discuss the difference between espoused and enacted values.* Espoused values represent the explicitly stated values and norms that are preferred by an organization. Enacted values, in contrast, reflect the values and norms that actually are exhibited or converted into employee behavior. Employees become cynical when management espouses one set of values and norms and then behaves in an inconsistent fashion.

3. *Describe the manifestations and functions of an organization's culture.* General manifestations of an organization's culture are shared objects, talk, behavior, and emotion. Four functions of organizational culture are organizational identity, collective commitment, social system stability, and sense-making device.

4. *Discuss the three general types of organizational culture and their associated normative beliefs.* The three general types of organizational culture are constructive, passive–defensive, and aggressive–defensive. Each type is grounded in different normative beliefs. Normative beliefs represent an individual's thoughts and beliefs about how members of a particular group or organization are expected to approach their work and interact with others. A constructive culture is associated with the beliefs of achievement, self-actualizing, humanistic-encouraging, and affiliative. Passive–defensive organizations tend to endorse the beliefs of approval, conventional, dependent, and avoidance. Aggressive–defensive cultures tend to endorse the beliefs of oppositional, power, competitive, and perfectionistic.

5. *Explain the three perspectives proposed to explain the types of culture that enhance an organization's financial performance.* The three perspectives are referred to as the strength, fit, and adaptive perspective. The strength perspective assumes that the strength of corporate culture is related to a firm's financial performance. The fit perspective is based on the premise that an organization's culture must align with its business or strategic context. The adaptive perspective assumes that the most effective cultures help organizations anticipate and adapt to environmental changes.

6. *Discuss the process of developing an adaptive culture.* The process begins with charismatic leadership that creates a business vision and strategy. Over time, adaptiveness is created by a combination of organizational success and leaders' ability to get employees to buy into a philosophy or set of values of satisfying constituency needs and improving leadership. Finally, an infrastructure is created to preserve the organization's adaptiveness.

7. *Summarize the methods used by organizations to embed their cultures.* Embedding a culture amounts to teaching employees about the organization's preferred values, beliefs, expectations, and behaviors. This is accomplished by using one or more of the following 11 mechanisms: (*a*) formal statements of organizational philosophy, mission, vision, values, and materials used for recruiting, selection, and socialization; (*b*) the design of physical space, work environments, and buildings; (*c*) slogans, language, acronyms, and sayings; (*d*) deliberate role modeling, training programs, teaching, and coaching by managers and supervisors; (*e*) explicit rewards, status symbols, and promotion criteria; (*f*) stories, legends, and myths about key people and events; (*g*) the organizational activities, processes, or outcomes that leaders pay attention to, measure, and control; (*h*) leader reactions to critical incidents and organizational crises; (*i*) the workflow and organizational structure; (*j*) organizational systems and procedures; and (*k*) organizational goals and associated criteria used for recruitment, selection, development, promotion, layoffs, and retirement of people.

8. *Describe the three phases in Feldman's model of organizational socialization.* The three phases of Feldman's model are anticipatory socialization, encounter, and change and acquisition. Anticipatory socialization begins before an individual actually joins the organization. The encounter phase begins when the employment contract has been signed. Phase 3 involves the period in which employees master important tasks and resolve any role conflicts.

9. *Discuss the various socialization tactics used to socialize employees.* There are six key socialization tactics. They are collective versus individual, formal versus informal, sequential versus random, fixed versus variable, serial versus disjunctive, and investiture versus divestiture (see Table 3–2). Each tactic provides organizations with two opposing options for socializing employees.

10. *Explain the four developmental networks associated with mentoring.* The four developmental networks are based on integrating the diversity and strength of an individual's developmental relationships. The four resulting developmental networks are receptive, traditional, entrepreneurial, and opportunistic. A receptive network is composed of a few weak ties from one social system. Having a few strong ties with developers from one social system is referred to as a traditional network. An entrepreneurial network is made up of strong ties among several developers; and a opportunistic network is associated with having weak ties from different social systems.

Discussion Questions

1. How would you respond to someone who made the following statement? "Organizational cultures are not important as far as managers are concerned."

2. What are the enacted values within your current classroom? Provide examples to support your evaluation.

3. Have you ever worked for a company that endorsed values that were inconsistent with your own? Explain and discuss what you did to reconcile this inconsistency.

4. Based on Table 3–1, what type of organizational culture exists within your current or most recent employer? Explain.

5. Can you think of any organizational heroes who have influenced your work behavior? Describe them, and explain how they affected your behavior.

6. Do you know of any successful companies that do not have a positive adaptive culture? Why do you think they are successful?

7. Why is socialization essential to organizational success?

8. Which of the socialization tactics shown in Table 3–2 have you experienced? Discuss whether or not they were effective in the context you experienced them.

9. How might you find a mentor to assist you in your future career?

10. What will happen if a manager implements an organizational change that is inconsistent with the organization's culture? Explain.

GE's CEO, Jeffrey Immelt, Is Changing the Organization's Culture to Help Grow the Company[65]

Despite his air of easy-going confidence, Jeffrey R Immelt admits to two fears: that General Electric Co. will become boring, and that his top people might act like cowards. That's right: cowards. He worries that GE's famous obsession with bottom-line results—and tendency to get rid of those who don't meet them—will make some execs shy away from taking risks that could revolutionize the company.

Immelt, 49, is clearly pushing for a cultural revolution. For the past 3½ years, the GE chairman and CEO has been on a mission to transform the hard-driving, process-oriented company into one steeped in creativity and wired for growth. He wants to move GE's average organic growth rate—the increase in revenue that comes from existing operations, rather than deals and currency fluctuations—to at least 8% from about 5% over the past decade. Under his former boss, the renowned Jack Welch, the skills GE prized above all others were cost-cutting, efficiency, and deal-making. What mattered was the continual improvement of operations, and that mindset helped make the $152 billion industrial and finance behemoth a marvel of earnings consistency. Immelt hasn't turned his back on the old ways. But in his GE, the new imperatives are risk-taking, sophisticated marketing, and above all, innovation.

This is change borne of necessity. . . .

So how, exactly, do you make a culture as ingrained as GE's sizzle with bold thinking and creative energy? To start, you banish some long-cherished traditions and beliefs. Immelt has welcomed outsiders into the highest ranks, even making one, Sir William M Castell, a vice chairman. That's a serious break with GE's promote-from-within past. He is pushing hard for a more global workforce that reflects the communities in which GE operates. Immelt is also encouraging his home-grown managers to become experts in their industries rather than just experts in managing. Instead of relying on execs who barely had time to position a family photo on their desk before moving on to the next executive assignment, he's diversifying the top ranks and urging his lieutenants to stay put and make a difference where they are.

Most of all, Immelt has made the need to generate blockbuster ideas more than an abstract concept. In true GE fashion, he has engineered a quantifiable and scalable process for coming up with money-making "eureka!" moments. While Welch was best known for the annual Session C meetings during which he personally evaluated the performance of GE's top several hundred managers, Immelt's highest-profile new gathering is the Commercial Council. Immelt leads the group of roughly a dozen top sales and marketing executives, including some unit heads such as GE Consumer Finance CEO David R Nissen. The members hold phone meetings every month and meet each quarter to discuss growth strategies, think up ways to reach customers, and evaluate ideas from the senior ranks that aim to take GE out on a limb. "Jeff has launched us on a journey to become one of the best sales and marketing companies in the world," says Nissen, who describes the meetings as collegial and more experimental than other GE gatherings.

This is no free-for-all, however. Business leaders must submit at least three "Imagination Breakthrough" proposals per year that ultimately go before the council for review and discussion. The projects, which will receive billions in funding in the coming years, have to take GE into a new line of business, geographic area, or customer base. Oh, and each one has to give GE incremental growth of at least $100 million. . . .

To inspire the fresh thinking he's looking for, Immelt is wielding the one thing that speaks loud and clear: money. The GE chief is tying executives' compensation to their ability to come up with ideas, show improved customer service, generate cash growth, and boost sales instead of simply meeting bottom-line targets. As Immelt puts it, "you're not going to stick around this place and not take bets." More concretely, 20% of 2005 bonuses will come from meeting pre-established measures of how well a business is improving its ability to meet customer needs. And while he hasn't exactly repudiated Welch's insistence that managers cull the bottom 10% of their staff, insiders say there's more flexibility, more subjectivity to the process. Risking failure is a badge of honor at GE these days. . . .

The pressure to produce could not be more intense. Many of the company's 307,000 workers weren't exactly hired to be part of a diverse, creative, fleet-footed army of visionaries who are acutely sensitive to customers' needs. "These guys just aren't dreamer types," says one consultant who has worked with the company. "It almost seems painful to them, like a waste of time." Even insiders who are openly euphoric about the changes under Chairman Jeff admit to feeling some fear in the depth of their guts.

"This is a big fundamental structural change, and that can be tough," says Paul T Bossidy, CEO of GE Commercial Equipment Financing, who is reorganizing his sales force so that each person represents all of GE to particular customers. Susan P Peters, GE's vice president for executive development, even talks about the need for employees to "reconceptualize" themselves. "What you have been to date isn't good enough for tomorrow," she says. Ouch. . . .

But there's a limit to how much Immelt can transform his own people. A key strategy—and one that amounts to a gut punch to the culture—involves bringing in more outsiders. In sales and marketing alone, GE has hired more than 1,700 new faces in the past few years, including hundreds of seasoned veterans such as David J Slump, a former ABB Group executive who is the chief marketing officer of GE Energy. "I just didn't think outsiders would do well here," says Slump, who was surprised at the unit's openness to changing its ways, though one of the senior executives did warn him about coming off as "too intense." That said, he was also amazed at the lack of attention to marketing when he arrived—with no marketers among the senior ranks and no real sense of strategy beyond the occasional ad or product push. Slump felt needed.

Immelt is also looking for more leaders who are intensely passionate about their businesses and are experts in the details. "I want to see our people become part of their industries," he says.

Questions for Discussion

1. Using Figure 3–1, explain how Immelt's cultural changes are influencing organizational structure and practices, group and social processes, and collective attitudes and behaviors.

2. Use Table 3–1 to describe the type of organizational culture and normative beliefs that existed before Immelt assumed the role of CEO and the type of culture and normative beliefs he is trying to create.

3. What are the artifacts, espoused values, and basic assumptions that represent GE's new organizational culture?

4. What new behavior is Immelt expecting from GE employees?

5. Which of the techniques for embedding organizational culture are being used by Immelt? What additional techniques would you recommend?

Personal Awareness and Growth Exercise

Have You Been Adequately Socialized?

Objectives

1. To determine whether or not your current employer has properly socialized you.

2. To promote deeper understanding of organizational socialization processes.

Introduction

Organizations use a variety of socialization tactics to help employees learn their new jobs, work roles, and adjust to work group values and norms. The effectiveness of this process has been found to affect employees' job satisfaction, job performance, and role clarity. The questionnaire[66] in this exercise is

designed to help you gauge how well you have been socialized by your current or a past employer.

Instructions

Complete the following survey items by considering either your current job or one you held in the past. If you have never worked, identify a friend who is working and ask that individual to complete the questionnaire for his or her organization. Read each item and circle your response by using the rating scale shown on page 102. Remember, there are no right or wrong answers. Upon completion, compute your total score by adding up your responses and compare it to the scoring norms.

	Strongly Disagree	Disagree	Neutral	Agree	Strongly Agree
1. I have been through a set of training experiences that are specifically designed to give newcomers a thorough knowledge of job-related skills.	1	2	3	4	5
2. This organization puts all newcomers through the same set of learning experiences.	1	2	3	4	5
3. I did not perform any of my normal job responsibilities until I was thoroughly familiar with departmental procedures and work methods.	1	2	3	4	5
4. There is a clear pattern in the way one role leads to another, or one job assignment leads to another, in this organization.	1	2	3	4	5
5. I can predict my future career path in this organization by observing other people's experiences.	1	2	3	4	5
6. Almost all of my colleagues have been supportive of me personally.	1	2	3	4	5
7. My colleagues have gone out of their way to help me adjust to this organization.	1	2	3	4	5
8. I received much guidance from experienced organizational members as to how I should perform my job.	1	2	3	4	5
9. In the last several months, I have been extensively involved with other new recruits in common, job-related activities.	1	2	3	4	5
10. I am gaining a clear understanding of my role in this organization from observing my senior colleagues.	1	2	3	4	5

Total score = _____

Scoring Norms

10–20 = low socialization
21–39 = moderate socialization
40–50 = high socialization

Questions for Discussion

1. How strongly have you been socialized? Do you agree with this assessment?

2. What does your degree of socialization suggest about your job satisfaction and performance? Do you agree with this conclusion? Explain.

3. If your socialization score was low or moderate, what can you do to enhance your socialization within the organization? Discuss.

4. How important is socialization to your success within the organization under consideration? Explain.

Assessing the Organizational Culture at Your School

Objectives

1. To provide you with a framework for assessing organizational culture.

2. To conduct an evaluation of the organizational culture at your school.

3. To consider the relationship between organizational culture and organizational effectiveness.

Introduction

Academics and consultants do not agree about the best way to measure an organization's culture. Some people measure culture with surveys, while others use direct observation or information obtained in interviews/workshops with employees. This exercise uses an informal group-based approach to assess the three levels of organizational culture discussed in this chapter. This approach has successfully been used to measure organizational culture at a variety of organizations.[67]

Instructions

Your instructor will divide the class into groups of four to six people. Each group member should then complete the Cultural Assessment Worksheet by him- or herself. It asks you to identify the artifacts, espoused values, and basic assumptions that are present at your current school: You may find it useful to reread the material on layers of organizational culture discussed earlier. When everyone is done, meet as a group and share the information contained on your individual worksheets. Create a summary worksheet based on a consensus of the cultural characteristics contained at each level of culture. Next, compare the information contained on the summary worksheet with the cultural descriptions contained in Table 3–1 and discuss what type of culture your school possesses. Again, strive to obtain a consensus opinion. Finally, the group should answer the discussion questions that follow the Cultural Assessment Worksheet.

Culture Assessment Worksheet

Artifacts (physical or visible manifestations of culture; they include jargon, heroes, stories, language, ritual, dress, material objects, mascots, physical arrangements, symbols, traditions, and so forth)	Espoused Values (the stated values and norms preferred by the organization)	Basic Assumptions (taken-for-granted beliefs about the organization that exist on an unconscious level)

Questions for Discussion

1. What are the group's consensus artifacts, espoused values, and basic assumptions? Are you surprised by anything on this list? Explain.

2. What type of culture does your school possess? Do you like this organizational culture? Discuss why or why not.

3. Do you think the organizational culture identified in question 2 is best suited for maximizing your learning? Explain your rationale.

4. Is your school in need of any cultural change? If yes, discuss why and recommend how the school's leaders might create this change. The material on embedding organizational culture would help answer this question.

Arthur Andersen's Pursuit of Consulting Income Created Ethical Challenges in Its Auditing Operations[68]

Andersen realized long ago that no one was going to get rich doing just audits. So for partners to share in hundreds of thousands of dollars of firm profits each year, Andersen would have to boost its lucrative consulting business. That quest for revenue is how the firm lost sight of its obligation to cast a critical eye on its clients' accounting practices, some critics say. . . .

The problems with focusing on consulting are evident in Andersen's biggest accounting blowups. Consider Waste Management Inc., which generated millions of dollars in consulting fees for Andersen. Last year, securities regulators alleged that Andersen bent the accounting rules so far the firm committed fraud. Time and again, starting in 1988 up through 1997, when Waste Management announced what at the time was the biggest financial restatement in US history, Andersen auditors knew the company was violating generally accepted accounting principles, the Securities and Exchange Commission said in a settled complaint filed in a Washington, DC, federal court.

Throughout the late 1990s, Andersen proposed hundreds of millions of dollars of accounting adjustments to rectify the situation, the SEC said in its suit. But when Waste Management refused to follow their recommendations, to the auditors' disappointment, they caved in. Those decisions were backed at the highest levels of Andersen's Chicago office, the SEC suit says.

Before taking over Waste Management's audit in 1991, Andersen partner Robert Allgyer had been in charge of coordinating the Chicago office's efforts to cross-sell nonaudit services to Andersen's audit clients. Indeed, for Andersen, nonaudit services were the only potential source of revenue growth from the trash hauler. That year, Waste Management had capped the amount of audit fees it would pay Andersen. The company, however, allowed Andersen to earn additional fees for "special work."

What would you have done if you were auditing Waste Management's financial statements?

1. Vigorously challenge Waste Management employees to correct their accounting practices.
2. Go to your manager when you first realize Waste Management was not following generally accepted accounting principles and tell him or her that you will not work on this account until Waste Management changes its ways.
3. Complete the work as best you can because your efforts contribute to Andersen's financial goals.
4. Invent other options. Discuss.

For the Chapter 3 Internet Exercise featuring what type of organizational culture best suits you (www.monster.com), visit our Web site at **www.mhhe.com/kreitner.**

International OB: Managing across Cultures

Learning Objectives

When you finish studying the material in this chapter, you should be able to:

1 Define the term *culture,* and explain how societal culture and organizational culture combine to influence on-the-job behavior.

2 Define *ethnocentrism,* and distinguish between high-context and low-context cultures.

3 Identify and describe the nine cultural dimensions from Project GLOBE.

4 Distinguish between individualistic and collectivist cultures, and explain the difference between monochronic and polychronic cultures.

5 Specify the practical lesson from the Hofstede cross-cultural study.

6 Explain what Project GLOBE researchers discovered about leadership.

7 Explain why U.S. managers have a comparatively high failure rate on foreign assignments.

8 Summarize the research findings about North American women on foreign assignments, and tell how to land a foreign assignment.

9 Identify four stages of the foreign assignment cycle and the OB trouble spot associated with each stage.

Carlos Ghosn (rhymes with "bone"), the outsider who successfully turned around Japan's Nissan Motor Co., was born in 1954 in Brazil to Lebanese immigrants and is fluent in English, Portuguese, French, and Arabic (but not Japanese). *BusinessWeek* recently offered this profile of Ghosn:

> He's as smooth as Thai silk in public, and his colleagues marvel at his personal magnetism, his 24/7 work ethic, and his rigorous attachment to benchmarks and targets....
>
> But Nissan insiders will also tell you there is another side to [Ghosn]. If you miss a number or blindside the boss with a nasty development, watch out.[1]

In 2005, Ghosn became the CEO of both Nissan and France's Renault, the owner of a 44% stake in Nissan. Here are some of Ghosn's observations from a recent interview:

> In Japan you cannot implement change quickly unless you clearly explain why change is needed, how it will be done, and what is the committed outcome. Once the men and women of Nissan were given a clear vision, a clear strategy, clear priorities, and a framework for action, they did change. By far the most distinct disadvantage related to the language difference....
>
> I was determined to become assimilated, without sacrificing my individuality or originality.... Being observant, respectful, and willing to learn helped me overcome most cultural barriers....
>
> Ultimately, my experience has confirmed my belief that nationality is not a determining factor in success. The key is results. In Japan, as in every other country, business results can be quantified. Numbers are universal, having the same value in any market and in any time zone. At the end of the day, the thing that really matters is your performance, not your passport.[2]

FOR DISCUSSION

Why did Ghosn succeed in this difficult cross-cultural situation whereas most others probably would have failed?

Carlos Ghosn (center) greets Nissan Foundation award winners after an award ceremony at Nissan headquarters in Tokyo, March 2005.

W e hear a lot about the global economy these days. Signs and symptoms of economic globalization making headlines in recent years have been the controversial North American Free Trade Agreement, rapid expansion of the European Union (to 27 nations by 2007), riots at World Trade Organization meetings, and complaints about the offshoring of jobs.[3] Indeed, the evolution of a globalized economy has had some rather stunning results, as evidenced by these realities:

- In 2004, Wal-Mart bought $18 billion worth of goods directly from China.[4]
- Roughly half of eBay's 125 million registered users are outside the United States.[5]
- In 1980, US companies produced 48% of the shoes sold in the American market. Today, that percentage has dwindled to 1.5%.[6]
- About $450 billion of the roughly $700 billion in US currency in circulation is used in foreign countries.[7]
- US oil imports are projected to rise from 60% in 2004 to 68% by the year 2025.[8]

Nissan's Carlos Ghosn is a remarkable manager who has what it takes to thrive in this complex global economy. He moves efficiently from role to role, from organization to organization, and from culture to culture. All the while, he keeps his eye on important targets and business results. He is an inspiring role model for would-be executives. In fact, according to one study, US multinational companies headed by CEOs with international assignments on their résumés tended to outperform the competition.[9] Even managers and employees who stay in their native country will find it hard to escape today's global economy. Many will be thrust into international relationships by working for foreign-owned companies or by dealing with foreign suppliers, customers, and co-workers. *Management Review* offered this helpful perspective:

> It's easy to think that people who have lived abroad or who are multilingual have global brains, while those who still live in their hometowns are parochial. But both notions are fallacies. Managers who have never left their home states can have global brains if they are interested in the greater world around them, make an effort to learn about other people's perspectives, and integrate those perspectives into their own way of thinking.[10]

The global economy is a rich mix of cultures, and the time to prepare to work in it is now. Accordingly, the purpose of this chapter is to help you take a step in that direction by exploring the impacts of culture in today's increasingly internationalized organizations. This chapter draws upon the area of cultural anthropology. We begin with a model that shows how societal culture and organizational culture (covered in Chapter 3) combine to influence work behavior. Next, we examine key dimensions of societal culture with the goal of enhancing cross-cultural awareness. Practical lessons from cross-cultural management research are then reviewed. The chapter concludes by exploring the challenge of accepting a foreign assignment.

Culture and Organizational Behavior

How would you, as a manager, interpret the following situations?

> An Asian executive for a multinational company, transferred from Taiwan to the Midwest, appears aloof and autocratic to his peers.

> A West Coast bank embarks on a "friendly teller" campaign, but its Filipino female tellers won't cooperate.

> A white manager criticizes a black male employee's work. Instead of getting an explanation, the manager is met with silence and a firm stare.[11]

If you attribute the behavior in these situations to personalities, three descriptions come to mind: arrogant, unfriendly, and hostile. These are reasonable conclusions. Unfortunately, they are probably wrong, being based more on prejudice and stereotypes than on actual fact. However, if you attribute the behavioral outcomes to *cultural* differences, you stand a better chance of making the following more valid interpretations: "As it turns out, Asian culture encourages a more distant managing style, Filipinos associate overly friendly behavior in women with prostitution, and blacks as a group act more deliberately, studying visual cues, than most white men."[12] One cannot afford to overlook relevant cultural contexts when trying to understand and manage organizational behavior.

Societal Culture Is Complex and Multilayered

In Chapter 3, we discussed *organizational* culture. Here, the focus is more broadly on *societal* culture. "**Culture** is a set of beliefs and values about what is desirable and undesirable in a community of people, and a set of formal or informal practices to support the values."[13] So culture has both prescriptive (what people should do) and descriptive (what they actually do) elements. Culture is passed from one generation to the next by family, friends, teachers, and relevant others. Most cultural lessons are learned by observing and imitating role models as they go about their daily affairs or as observed in the media.[14]

    Culture is difficult to grasp because it is multilayered. International management experts Fons Trompenaars (from the Netherlands) and Charles Hampden-Turner (from Britain) offered this instructive analogy in their landmark book, *Riding the Waves of Culture*:

> Culture comes in layers, like an onion. To understand it you have to unpeel it layer by layer.
>   On the outer layer are the products of culture, like the soaring skyscrapers of Manhattan, pillars of private power, with congested public streets between them. These are expressions of deeper values and norms in a society that are not directly visible (values such as upward mobility, "the more-the-better," status, material success). The layers of values and norms are deeper within the "onion," and are more difficult to identify.[15]

Consequently, the September 11, 2001, destruction of the New York World Trade Center towers by terrorists was as much an attack on American culture as it was on lives and property.[16] That deepened the hurt and made the anger more profound for Americans and their friends around the world. In both life and business, culture is a serious matter.

Culture
Beliefs and values about how a community of people should and do act.

Culture Is a Subtle but Pervasive Force

Culture generally remains below the threshold of conscious awareness because it involves *taken-for-granted assumptions* about how one should perceive, think, act, and feel. Cultural anthropologist Edward T Hall put it this way:

> Since much of culture operates outside our awareness, frequently we don't even know what we know. We pick . . . [expectations and assumptions] up in the cradle. We unconsciously learn what to notice and what not to notice, how to divide time and space, how to walk and talk and use our bodies, how to behave as men or women, how to relate to other people, how to handle responsibility, whether experience is seen as whole or fragmented. This applies to all people. The Chinese or the Japanese or the Arabs are as unaware of their assumptions as we are of our own. We each assume that they're part of human nature. What we think of as "mind" is really internalized culture.[17]

Intel's Ethnographers Help Tap Foreign Markets

BusinessWeek To target innovations that will resonate in these markets, companies are conducting in-depth studies of peoples' needs. Intel, for instance, has a team of 10 ethnographers traveling the world to find out how to redesign existing products or come up with new ones that fit different cultures or demographic groups. One of its ethnographers, Genevieve Bell, visited 100 homes in Asia over the past three years and noticed that many Chinese families were reluctant to buy PCs, even if they could afford them. Parents were concerned that their children would listen to pop music or surf the Web, distracting them from school work.

Intel turned that insight into a product. At its User-Centered Design Group in Hillsboro, Oregon, industrial designers and other specialists created "personas" of typical Chinese families and pasted pictures that Bell had taken of Chinese households on their walls. They even built sample Chinese kitchens—the room where a computer is most often used. The result: Late this year, Intel expects a leading Chinese PC maker to start selling the China Home Learning PC. It comes with four education applications and a physical lock and key that allows parents to prevent their kids from goofing off when they should be studying.

SOURCE: S Hamm, "Tech's Future," *BusinessWeek*, September 27, 2004. Reprinted by permission of The McGraw-Hill Companies, Inc.

In sum, it has been said: "you are your culture, and your culture is you." As part of the growing sophistication of marketing practices in the global economy, companies are hiring anthropologists to decipher the cultural roots of customer needs and preferences (see Real World/Real People).

Culture Overrides National Boundaries

The term *societal* culture is used here instead of national culture because the boundaries of many nation-states were not drawn along cultural lines. Instead, they evolved through conquest, migration, treaties, and geopolitics. The former Soviet Union, for example, included 15 republics and more than 100 ethnic nationalities, many with their own distinct language.[18] Also, English-speaking Canadians in Vancouver are culturally closer to Americans in Seattle than to their French-speaking compatriots in Quebec.

Nancy McKinstry, the American CEO of Wolters Kluwer, a multinational Dutch publishing company with 20,000 employees, has noticed a blurring of national boundaries. In a recent interview, she made this observation about the United States and Europe:

There's a new kind of multiregional culture which combines the best of both worlds. . . . There are actually more similarities between the US, Germany and Holland than there are between those countries and southern Europe. In southern Europe decision-making is more collaborative, and developing long-term business relationships is essential to success.[19]

If we could redraw the world map along cultural lines instead of along geographical and political lines, we would end up with something very strange and different. That is precisely what researchers at the University of Michigan's Institute for Social Research have done with their World Values Survey, an ongoing study of 65 societies around the world.[20] Their cultural map in Figure 4–1 cross-references two different cultural dimensions: traditional versus secular-rational values and survival versus self-expression values. This odd-looking cultural map includes religious, political, language, and annual income overlays. To a cultural

Figure 4–1   *Redrawing the World Map along Cultural Lines*

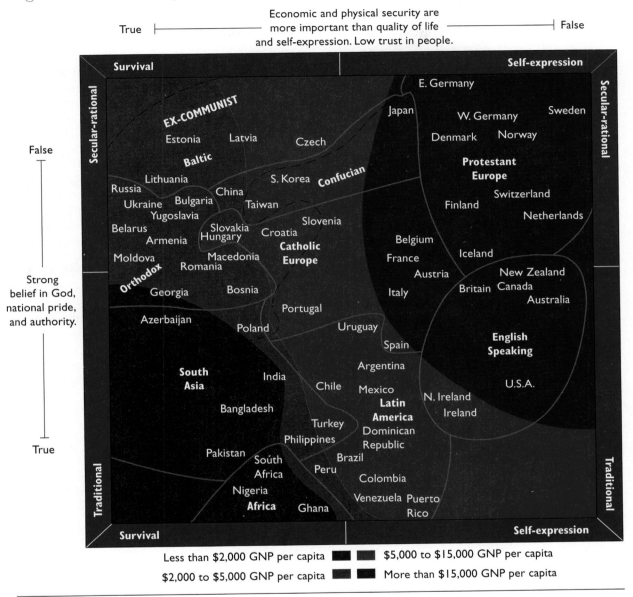

True ├─────────── Economic and physical security are more important than quality of life ───────────┤ False
and self-expression. Low trust in people.

Survival ... Self-expression

Secular-rational

False

E. Germany
Japan   W. Germany   Sweden
Denmark   Norway

EX-COMMUNIST
Estonia   Latvia   Czech
Baltic
Lithuania   S. Korea **Confucian**   **Protestant Europe**
Russia   China   Switzerland
Ukraine   Bulgaria   Taiwan   Finland   Netherlands
Yugoslavia
Belarus   Slovakia   Slovenia   Belgium   Iceland
Armenia   Hungary   Croatia   France
Moldova   Macedonia   **Catholic Europe**   Austria   New Zealand
Orthodox   Romania   Italy   Britain   Canada   Australia
Georgia   Bosnia

Strong belief in God, national pride, and authority.

Azerbaijan   Portugal
Poland   Uruguay   **English Speaking**
Spain
Argentina   U.S.A.
South Asia   India   Chile   Mexico   N. Ireland
Bangladesh   **Latin America**   Ireland
Turkey   Dominican
Philippines   Republic
Pakistan   Brazil
South Africa   Peru
Nigeria   Colombia
Africa   Ghana   Venezuela Puerto Rico

True

Survival   Self-expression

Traditional

Less than $2,000 GNP per capita ▪ ▪ $5,000 to $15,000 GNP per capita
$2,000 to $5,000 GNP per capita ▪ ▪ More than $15,000 GNP per capita

SOURCE: Adapted from R Inglehart and W E Baker, "Modernization's Challenges to Traditional Values: Who's Afraid of Ronald McDonald?" *The Futurist*, March–April 2001, p 19. Used by permission.

anthropologist, the map in Figure 4–1 says a lot more than an ordinary map of the world. For example, notice how Spain and Argentina, although separated by the Atlantic Ocean on a standard map, actually are close neighbors on this cultural map. Meanwhile, physically close Britain and Ireland are distanced from each other by religion on the cultural map. And former East and West Germany may be politically reunited, but a cultural gulf remains.

More than a decade after reunification, Germany remains a nation divided. Many western Germans resent the fact that billions of marks—their future pensions—were transferred

More than a decade after the political reunification of Germany, a cultural gulf lingers between former East and West Germans. Some East Germans have found the transition from Communism to free-market capitalism difficult. As these Berlin school children enjoying an outdoor drawing lesson at the feet of Karl Marx and Friedrich Engels will come to appreciate, history matters when it comes to culture.

to their poorer cousins. Some view the easterners as lazy. Citizens in the east regard their richer counterparts as arrogant know-it-alls who are out to rip them off.[21]

Cultural variables other than the ones in Figure 4–1 would likely produce very different maps. The point is, when preparing to live and work in a different country, be sure to consider more than national boundaries—study the culture.[22]

A Model of Societal and Organizational Cultures

As illustrated in Figure 4–2, culture influences organizational behavior in two ways. Employees bring their societal culture to work with them in the form of customs and language. Organizational culture, a by-product of societal culture, in turn affects the individual's values/ethics, attitudes, assumptions, and expectations. Societal culture is shaped by the various environmental factors listed in the left-hand side of Figure 4–2.

Once inside the organization's sphere of influence, the individual is further affected by the *organization's* culture. Mixing of societal and organizational cultures can produce interesting dynamics in multinational companies. For example, with French and American employees working side by side at General Electric's medical imaging production facility in Waukesha, Wisconsin, unit head Claude Benchimol has witnessed some culture shock:

The French are surprised the American parking lots empty out as early as 5 PM; the Americans are surprised the French don't start work at 8 AM. Benchimol feels the French are more talkative and candid. Americans have more of a sense of hierarchy and are less likely to criticize. But they may be growing closer to the French. Says Benchimol: "It's taken a year to get across the idea that we are all entitled to say what we don't like to become more productive and work better."[23]

Same company, same company culture, yet GE's French and American co-workers have different attitudes about time, hierarchy, and communication. They are the products of different societal cultures.[24]

When managing people at work, the individual's societal culture, the organizational culture, and any interaction between the two need to be taken into consideration. For example, American workers' cultural orientation toward quality improvement differs significantly from the Japanese cultural pattern.

Unlike Japanese workers, Americans aren't interested in making small step-by-step improvements to increase quality. They want to achieve the breakthrough, the impossible dream. The way to motivate them: Ask for the big leap, rather than for tiny steps.[25]

Figure 4–2   *Cultural Influences on Organizational Behavior*

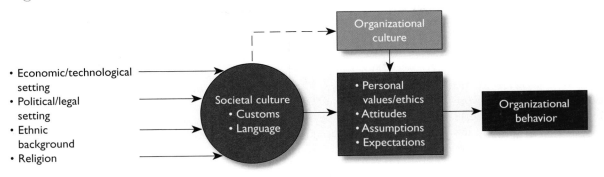

Ethnocentrism: A Cultural Roadblock in the Global Economy

Ethnocentrism, the belief that one's native country, culture, language, and modes of behavior are superior to all others, has its roots in the dawn of civilization. First identified as a behavioral science concept in 1906, involving the tendency of groups to reject outsiders,[26] the term *ethnocentrism* generally has a more encompassing (national or societal) meaning today. Worldwide evidence of ethnocentrism is plentiful. For example, when a congressman said, "It is the English language which unites us,"[27] during a debate on an English-only bill for US federal agencies, charges of ethnocentrism were made by civil rights groups worried about the loss of bilingual ballots for non-English-speaking citizens. Militant ethnocentrism led to deadly "ethnic cleansing" in Bosnia and Kosovo and genocide in the African nations of Rwanda and Burundi.

Less dramatic, but still troublesome, is ethnocentrism within managerial and organizational contexts. Experts on the subject framed the problem this way:

> [Ethnocentric managers have] a preference for putting home-country people in key positions everywhere in the world and rewarding them more handsomely for work, along with a tendency to feel that this group is more intelligent, more capable, or more reliable. . . . Ethnocentrism is often not attributable to prejudice as much as to inexperience or lack of knowledge about foreign persons and situations. This is not too surprising, since most executives know far more about employees in their home environments. As one executive put it, "At least I understand why our own managers make mistakes. With our foreigners, I never know. The foreign managers may be better. But if I can't trust a person, should I hire him or her just to prove we're multinational?"[28]

Research suggests ethnocentrism is bad for business. A survey of 918 companies with home offices in the United States (272 companies), Japan (309), and Europe (337) found ethnocentric staffing and human resource policies to be associated with increased personnel problems. Those problems included recruiting difficulties, high turnover rates, and lawsuits over personnel policies. Among the three regional samples, Japanese companies had the most ethnocentric human resource practices and the most international human resource problems.[29]

Ethnocentrism
Belief that one's native country, culture, language, and behavior are superior.

Big, Wide World 101 for Tim Wright

I spent six months of my junior year in college living, studying, and traveling throughout Argentina. Aside from being a life altering experience rich in adventure, culture, and language, it was a daily exchange of ideas and perceptions with people I met. Good and bad, I learned what it's like to be an ambassador for my country, its views, and its foreign policies. I was able to foster relationships with people of different cultural backgrounds, and political and religious ideologies, because the people I met and the friends I made came from all over the world.

SOURCE: T Wright, "Opening Doors, Crossing Cultures," *Training and Development,* May 2004, p 25.

Current and future managers, and people in general, can effectively deal with ethnocentrism through education, greater cross-cultural awareness, international experience, and a conscious effort to value cultural diversity (see Real World/Real People).

Toward Greater Cross-Cultural Awareness and Competence

This section explores basic ways of describing and comparing cultures. As a foundation, we discuss cultural stereotyping and paradoxes and the need for cultural intelligence. Next we contrast high-context and low-context cultures and introduce nine cultural dimensions identified in the GLOBE project. Then our attention turns to examining cross-cultural differences in terms of individualism, time, space, and religion.

Cultural Paradoxes Require Cultural Intelligence

An important qualification needs to be offered at this juncture. All of the cultural differences in this chapter and elsewhere need to be viewed as *tendencies* and *patterns* rather than as absolutes. As soon as one falls into the trap of assuming *all* Italians are this, and *all* Koreans will do that, and so on, potentially instructive generalizations become mindless stereotypes. A pair of professors with extensive foreign work experience advises: "As teachers, researchers, and managers in cross-cultural contexts, we need to recognize that our original characterizations of other cultures are best guesses that we need to modify as we gain more experience."[30] Consequently, they contend, we will be better prepared to deal with inevitable *cultural paradoxes*. By paradox, they mean there are always exceptions to the rule; individuals who do not fit the expected cultural pattern. A good example is the head of Canon. "By Japanese CEO standards, Canon Inc.'s Fujio Mitarai is something of an anomaly. For starters, he's fast and decisive—a far cry from the consensus builders who typically run Japan Inc."[31] One also encounters lots of cultural paradoxes in large and culturally diverse nations such as the United States and Brazil. This is where the need for cultural intelligence arises.

Cultural intelligence, the ability to accurately interpret ambiguous cross-cultural situations, is an important skill in today's diverse workplaces. Two OB scholars explain:

Cultural intelligence
The ability to interpret ambiguous cross-cultural situations accurately.

A person with high cultural intelligence can somehow tease out of a person's or group's behavior those features that would be true of all people and all groups, those peculiar to this person or this group, and those that are neither universal nor idiosyncratic. The vast realm that lies between those poles is culture.[32]

Those interested in developing their cultural intelligence need to first develop their *emotional intelligence,* discussed in detail in Chapter 5, and then practice in ambiguous cross-cultural situations. Of course, as in all human interaction, there is no adequate substitute for really getting to know, listen to, and care about others.

The career paths for Brian McCann (left) and Jennifer Chang (right) at Price-waterhouseCoopers took a detour recently through this factory in the Central American country of Belize. The pair participated in the accounting and consulting firm's Ulysses Program, whereby up-and-coming leaders are sent to developing countries for eight weeks to do volunteer work on business development projects. For more on this win-win exercise in developing cultural intelligence, see the OB in Action Case Study at the end of this chapter.

High-Context and Low-Context Cultures

This is a broadly applicable and useful cultural distinction[33] (see Figure 4–3). People from **high-context cultures**—including China, Korea, Japan, Vietnam, Mexico, and Arab cultures—rely heavily on situational cues for meaning when perceiving and communicating with others. Nonverbal cues such as one's official position, status, or family connections convey messages more powerfully than do spoken words. In China, for example, one's actions—observed over extended periods of time—do indeed speak louder than words (see Real World/Real People).

High-context cultures
Primary meaning derived from nonverbal situational cues.

Figure 4–3   *Contrasting High-Context and Low-Context Cultures*

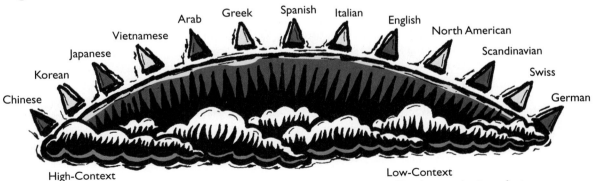

High-Context
- Establish social trust first
- Value personal relations and goodwill
- Agreement by general trust
- Negotiations slow and ritualistic

Low-Context
- Get down to business first
- Value expertise and performance
- Agreement by specific, legalistic contract
- Negotiations as efficient as possible

SOURCE: Reprinted from *Business Horizons,* vol. 36, No. 3, M Munter, "Cross-Cultural Communication for Managers," p 72, © 1993, with permission from Elsevier.

Relationships and *Guanxi* Matter When Doing Business in China

For the Chinese, the concept of *guanxi* plays a large role in successful relationships. While there is no precise English translation, guanxi involves personal connections based on mutually obligated dependency and lifelong commitment— a kind of mutual back scratching, which in the United States might be viewed as a form of nepotism or "a good old boys" network....

As a consequence, you can't simply drop into China, give a series of banquets, and suddenly become a trusted colleague; you must demonstrate a sincere interest and commitment to an individual on an ongoing basis. A particularly important aspect of Chinese networking is that when out for a business meal, it is one person who pays; you don't split the check. The practice is reflective of a mind-set focused on the kind of mutual obligation in which costs will equal out across time.

SOURCE: B Koenig, P Z Tith, and S Ludlum, "Engaging China," *Association Management*, December 2004, p 65.

Low-context cultures

Primary meaning derived from written and spoken words.

Reading the Fine Print in Low-Context Cultures In **low-context cultures,** written and spoken words carry the burden of shared meanings. Low-context cultures include those found in Germany, Switzerland, Scandinavia, North America, and Great Britain. True to form, Germany has precise written rules for even the smallest details of daily life.[34] In *high*-context cultures, agreements tend to be made on the basis of someone's word or a handshake, after a rather prolonged get-acquainted and trust-building period. Low-context Americans and Canadians, at least those with cultural roots in Northern Europe, see the handshake as a signal to get a signature on a detailed, lawyer-approved, iron-clad contract.

Avoiding Cultural Collisions Misunderstanding and miscommunication often are problems in international business dealings when the parties are from high- versus low-context cultures. A Mexican business professor made this instructive observation:

> Over the years, I have noticed that across cultures there are different opinions on what is expected from a business report. US managers, for instance, take a pragmatic, get-to-the-point approach, and expect reports to be concise and action-oriented. They don't have time to read long explanations: "Just the facts, ma'am."
>
> Latin American managers will usually provide long explanations that go beyond the simple facts....
>
> I have a friend who is the Latin America representative for a United States firm and has been asked by his boss to provide regular reports on sales activities. His reports are long, including detailed explanations on the context in which the events he is reporting on occur and the possible interpretations that they might have. His boss regularly answers these reports with very brief messages, telling him to "cut the crap and get to the point!"[35]

Awkward situations such as this can be avoided when those on both sides of the context divide make good-faith attempts to understand and accommodate their counterparts. Here are some practical tips:

• People on both sides of the context barrier must be trained to make adjustments.

• A new employee should be greeted by a group consisting of his or her boss, several colleagues who have similar duties, and an individual located near the newcomer.

- Background information is essential when explaining anything. Include the history and personalities involved.
- Do not assume the newcomer is self-reliant. Give explicit instructions not only about objectives, but also about the process involved.
- High-context workers from abroad need to learn to ask questions outside their department and function.
- Foreign workers must make an effort to become more self-reliant.[36]

Nine Cultural Dimensions from the GLOBE Project

Project GLOBE (Global Leadership and Organizational Behavior Effectiveness) is the brain-child of University of Pennsylvania professor Robert J House.[37] It is a massive and ongoing attempt to "develop an empirically based theory to describe, understand, and predict the impact of specific cultural variables on leadership and organizational processes and the effectiveness of these processes."[38] GLOBE has evolved into a network of more than 150 scholars from 62 societies since the project was launched in Calgary, Canada, in 1994. Most of the researchers are native to the particular cultures they study, thus greatly enhancing the credibility of the project. During the first two phases of the GLOBE project, a list of nine basic cultural dimensions was developed and statistically validated. Translated questionnaires based on the nine dimensions were administered to thousands of managers in the banking, food, and telecommunications industries around the world to build a database. Results are being published on a regular basis. Much work and many years are needed if the project's goal, as stated above, is to be achieved. In the meantime, we have been given a comprehensive, valid, and up-to-date tool for better understanding cross-cultural similarities and differences.

The nine cultural dimensions from the GLOBE project are

- *Power distance.* How much unequal distribution of power should there be in organizations and society?
- *Uncertainty avoidance.* How much should people rely on social norms and rules to avoid uncertainty and limit unpredictability?
- *Institutional collectivism.* How much should leaders encourage and reward loyalty to the social unit, as opposed to the pursuit of individual goals?
- *In-group collectivism.* How much pride and loyalty should individuals have for their family or organization?
- *Gender egalitarianism.* How much effort should be put into minimizing gender discrimination and role inequalities?
- *Assertiveness.* How confrontational and dominant should individuals be in social relationships?
- *Future orientation.* How much should people delay gratification by planning and saving for the future?
- *Performance orientation.* How much should individuals be rewarded for improvement and excellence?
- *Humane orientation.* How much should society encourage and reward people for being kind, fair, friendly, and generous?[39]

What about *Your* Culture?   Take a short break from your reading to complete the OB Exercise on page 118. It will help you better comprehend the nine GLOBE cultural dimensions. Can you trace your cultural profile to family history and country of origin of

What Is Your Cultural Profile?

Instructions

Take two trips through this questionnaire, both times rating your degree of agreement with each statement. In the first round, rate the people in your native culture as you perceive them to be (by putting an X through the appropriate response). In the second round, indicate how *you* think people in general should behave (by circling the appropriate response). There are no right or wrong answers. *Note:* This particular instrument has *not* been validated and is for instructional purposes only.

1. Power Distance
Followers are (should be) expected to obey their leaders without question.

Disagree   Agree
1—2—3—4—5—6—7—8—9—10

2. Uncertainty Avoidance
Most people lead (should lead) highly structured lives with few unexpected events.

Disagree   Agree
1—2—3—4—5—6—7—8—9—10

3. Institutional Collectivism
Leaders encourage (should encourage) group loyalty even if individual goals suffer.

Disagree   Agree
1—2—3—4—5—6—7—8—9—10

4. In-Group Collectivism
Employees feel (should feel) great loyalty toward this organization.

Disagree   Agree
1—2—3—4—5—6—7—8—9—10

5. Gender Egalitarianism
Both women and men have (should have) equal educational and career opportunities.

Disagree   Agree
1—2—3—4—5—6—7—8—9—10

6. Assertiveness
People are (should be) generally dominant in their relationships with each other.

Disagree   Agree
1—2—3—4—5—6—7—8—9—10

7. Future Orientation
People live, plan, and save (should live, plan, and save) for the future.

Disagree   Agree
1—2—3—4—5—6—7—8—9—10

8. Performance Orientation
Students are encouraged (should be encouraged) to strive for continuously improved performance.

Disagree   Agree
1—2—3—4—5—6—7—8—9—10

9. Humane Orientation
People are generally (should be generally) very tolerant of mistakes.

Disagree   Agree
1—2—3—4—5—6—7—8—9—10

Scoring

Draw one vertical line connecting the Xs from your first pass. Draw another vertical line connecting the circles from your second pass. The connected Xs indicate your prescribed cultural values. The connected circles indicate your personal values. The width of the gaps between the two lines indicate how well aligned you are with your native culture.

SOURCE: Adapted from (and nine labels and item descriptions 1–4, 6, 8, and 9 quoted from) M Javidan, R J House, and P W Dorfman, "A Nontechnical Summary of GLOBE Findings," in *Culture, Leadership, and Organizations: The GLOBE Study of 62 Societies*, eds R J House, P J Hanges, M Javidan, P W Dorfman, and V Gupta (Thousand Oaks, CA: Sage, 2004), Table 3.1, p 30.

your ancestors? For example, one of your author's German roots are evident in his cultural profile. What are the personal implications of any cultural "gaps" that surfaced?

Country Profiles and Practical Implications   How do different countries score on the GLOBE cultural dimensions? Data from 18,000 managers yielded the profiles in Table 4–1. A quick overview shows a great deal of cultural diversity around the world. But thanks to the nine GLOBE dimensions, we have more precise understanding of *how* cultures vary. Closer study reveals telling cultural *patterns,* or cultural fingerprints for nations. The US managerial sample, for instance, scored high on assertiveness and performance orientation. Accordingly, Americans are widely perceived as pushy and hardworking. Switzerland's high scores on uncertainty avoidance and future orientation help explain its centuries of political neutrality and world-renowned banking industry. Singapore is known as a great place to do business because it is clean and safe and its people are well educated and hardworking. This is no surprise, considering Singapore's high scores on social collectivism, future orientation, and performance orientation. In contrast, Russia's low scores on future orientation and performance orientation could foreshadow a slower than hoped for transition from a centrally planned economy to free enterprise capitalism. These illustrations bring us to an important practical lesson: *Knowing the cultural tendencies of foreign business partners and competitors can give you a strategic competitive advantage.*

Individualism versus Collectivism

Have you ever been torn between what you personally wanted and what the group, organization, or society expected of you? If so, you have firsthand experience with a fundamental and important cultural distinction: individualism versus collectivism. This source

Table 4–1   *Countries Ranking Highest and Lowest on the GLOBE Cultural Dimensions*

Dimension	Highest	Lowest
Power distance	Morocco, Argentina, Thailand, Spain, Russia	Denmark, Netherlands, South Africa—black sample, Israel, Costa Rica
Uncertainty avoidance	Switzerland, Sweden, Germany—former West, Denmark, Austria	Russia, Hungary, Bolivia, Greece, Venezuela
Institutional collectivism	Sweden, South Korea, Japan, Singapore, Denmark	Greece, Hungary, Germany—former East, Argentina, Italy
In-group collectivism	Iran, India, Morocco, China, Egypt	Denmark, Sweden, New Zealand, Netherlands, Finland
Gender egalitarianism	Hungary, Poland, Slovenia, Denmark, Sweden	South Korea, Egypt, Morocco, India, China
Assertiveness	Germany—former East, Austria, Greece, US, Spain	Sweden, New Zealand, Switzerland, Japan, Kuwait
Future orientation	Singapore, Switzerland, Netherlands, Canada—English speaking, Denmark	Russia, Argentina, Poland, Italy, Kuwait
Performance orientation	Singapore, Hong Kong, New Zealand, Taiwan, US	Russia, Argentina, Greece, Venezuela, Italy
Humane orientation	Philippines, Ireland, Malaysia, Egypt, Indonesia	Germany—former West, Spain, France, Singapore, Brazil

SOURCE: Adapted from M Javidan and R J House, "Cultural Acumen for the Global Manager: Lessons from Project GLOBE," *Organizational Dynamics,* Spring 2001, pp 289–305.

of cultural variation—represented by two of the nine GLOBE dimensions—deserves a closer look. As might be expected with an extensively researched topic, individualism–collectivism has many interpretations.[40] Let us examine the basic concept for greater cultural awareness.

Individualistic culture

Primary emphasis on personal freedom and choice.

Individualistic cultures, characterized as "I" and "me" cultures, give priority to individual freedom and choice. Accordingly, they emphasize *personal* responsibility for one's affairs. This is no small matter in an aging society:

> A strong feeling of "social solidarity," as [Johns Hopkins University professor Gerald F] Anderson sees it, makes Europeans inclined to be generous to older people, more willing to support them. "Their attitude is, we're older and we'll need some help," he says. "The US attitude is, we're all rugged individualists and we're going to take care of ourselves, not others."[41]

This cultural distinction was borne out in a recent survey of the quality-of-life among senior citizens in 16 industrialized nations. The Netherlands was number one and the United States ranked number 13.[42]

Collectivist culture

Personal goals less important than community goals and interests.

Collectivist cultures, oppositely called "we" and "us" cultures, rank shared goals higher than individual desires and goals. People in collectivist cultures are expected to subordinate their own wishes and goals to those of the relevant social unit. A worldwide survey of 30,000 managers by Trompenaars and Hampden-Turner, who prefer the term *communitarianism* to collectivism, found the highest degree of individualism in Israel, Romania, Nigeria, Canada, and the United States. Countries ranking lowest in individualism—thus qualifying as collectivist cultures—were Egypt, Nepal, Mexico, India, and Japan. Brazil, China, and France also ended up toward the collectivist end of the scale.[43]

A Business Success Factor

Of course, one can expect to encounter both individualists and collectivists in culturally diverse countries such as the United States. For example, imagine the frustration of Dave Murphy, a Boston-based mutual fund salesperson, when he tried to get Navajo Indians in Arizona interested in saving money for their retirement. After several fruitless meetings with groups of Navajo employees, he was given this cultural insight by a local official: "If you come to this environment, you have to understand that money is different. It's there to be spent. If you have some, you help your family."[44] (This suggests Navajos would score high on in-group collectivism and low on future orientation on the GLOBE scale.) To traditional Navajos, enculturated as collectivists, saving money is an unworthy act of selfishness. Subsequently, the sales pitch was tailored to emphasize the *family* benefits of individual retirement savings plans.

Allegiance to Whom?

The Navajo example brings up an important point about collectivist cultures. Specifically, which unit of society predominates? For the Navajos, family is the key reference group. But, as Trompenaars and Hampden-Turner observe, important differences exist among collectivist (or communitarian) cultures:

> For each single society, it is necessary to determine the group with which individuals have the closest identification. They could be keen to identify with their trade union, their family, their corporation, their religion, their profession, their nation, or the state apparatus. The French tend to identify with *la France, la famille, le cadre;* the Japanese with the corporation; the former eastern bloc with the Communist Party; and Ireland with the Roman Catholic Church. Communitarian goals may be good or bad for industry depending on the community concerned, its attitude and relevance to business development.[45]

This observation validates GLOBE's distinction between institutional and in-group collectivism.

Cultural Perceptions of Time

In North American and Northern European cultures, time seems to be a simple matter. It is linear, relentlessly marching forward, never backward, in standardized chunks. To the American who received a watch for his or her third birthday, time is like money. It is spent, saved, or wasted.[46] Americans are taught to show up 10 minutes early for appointments. When working across cultures, however, time becomes a very complex matter.[47] Imagine a New Yorker's chagrin when left in a waiting room for 45 minutes, only to find a Latin American government official dealing with three other people at once. The North American resents the lack of prompt and undivided attention. The Latin American official resents the North American's impatience and apparent self-centeredness.[48] This vicious cycle of resentment can be explained by the distinction between **monochronic time** and **polychronic time:**

> The former is revealed in the ordered, precise, schedule-driven use of public time that typifies and even caricatures efficient Northern Europeans and North Americans. The latter is seen in the multiple and cyclical activities and concurrent involvement with different people in Mediterranean, Latin American, and especially Arab cultures.[49]

A Matter of Degree   Monochronic and polychronic are relative rather than absolute concepts. Generally, the more things a person tends to do at once, the more polychronic that person is.[50] Thanks to the Internet and advanced telecommunications systems, highly polychronic managers can engage in "multitasking."[51] For example, it is possible to talk on the telephone, read and respond to e-mail, print a report, check an instant message, *and* eat a stale sandwich all at the same time. Unfortunately, this extreme polychronic behavior too often is not as efficient as hoped and, as discussed in Chapter 18, can be very stressful. Monochronic people prefer to do one thing at a time. What is your attitude toward time?

Practical Implications   Low-context cultures, such as that of the United States, tend to run on monochronic time, while high-context cultures, such as that of Mexico, tend to run on polychronic time. People in polychronic cultures view time as flexible, fluid, and multidimensional. The Germans and Swiss have made an exact science of monochronic time. In fact, a radio-controlled watch made by a German company, Junghans, is "guaranteed to lose no more than one second in 1 million years."[52] Many a visitor has been a minute late for a Swiss train, only to see its taillights leaving the station. Time is more elastic in polychronic cultures. During the Islamic holy month of Ramadan in Middle Eastern nations, for example, the faithful fast during daylight hours, and the general pace of things markedly slows. Managers need to reset their mental clocks when doing business across cultures.

Interpersonal Space

Anthropologist Edward T Hall noticed a connection between culture and preferred interpersonal distance. People from high-context cultures were observed standing close when talking to someone. Low-context cultures appeared to dictate a greater amount of interpersonal space. Hall applied the term **proxemics** to the study of cultural expectations about interpersonal space.[53] He specified four interpersonal distance zones. Some call them space bubbles. They are *intimate* distance, *personal* distance, *social* distance, and *public* distance. Ranges for the four interpersonal distance zones are illustrated in Figure 4–4, along with selected cultural differences.

North American business conversations normally are conducted at about a three- to four-foot range, within the personal zone in Figure 4–4. A range of approximately one foot is com-

Monochronic time
Preference for doing one thing at a time because time is limited, precisely segmented, and schedule driven.

Polychronic time
Preference for doing more than one thing at a time because time is flexible and multidimensional.

Proxemics
Hall's term for the study of cultural expectations about interpersonal space.

Figure 4–4   *Interpersonal Distance Zones for Business Conversations Vary from Culture to Culture*

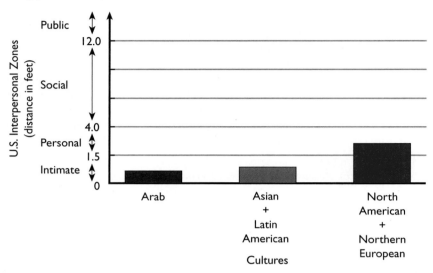

mon in Latin American and Asian cultures, uncomfortably close for Northern Europeans and North Americans. Some Arabs like to get even closer. Mismatches in culturally dictated interpersonal space zones can prove very distracting for the unprepared. Hall explains,

> Arabs tend to get very close and breathe on you. It's part of the high sensory involvement of a high-context culture. . . .
>
> The American on the receiving end can't identify all the sources of his discomfort but feels that the Arab is pushy. The Arab comes close, the American backs up. The Arab follows, because he can only interact at certain distances. Once the American learns that Arabs handle space differently and that breathing on people is a form of communication, the situation can sometimes be redefined so the American relaxes.[54]

Asian and Middle-Eastern hosts grow weary of having to seemingly chase their low-context guests around at social gatherings to maintain what they feel is proper conversational range. Backing up all evening to keep conversational partners at a proper distance is an awkward experience as well. Awareness of cultural differences, along with skillful accommodation, are essential to productive intercultural business dealings.

Religion

Religious beliefs and practices can have a profound effect on cross-cultural relations. A comprehensive treatment of different religions is beyond the scope of our current discussion.[55] However, we can examine the relationship between religious affiliation and work-related values. A study of 484 international students at a midwestern US university uncovered wide variability. The following list gives the most important work-related value for each of five religious affiliations:

Catholic—Consideration ("Concern that employees be taken seriously, be kept informed, and that their judgments be used.")

Protestant—Employer effectiveness ("Desire to work for a company that is efficient, successful, and a technological leader.")

Buddhist—Social responsibility ("Concern that the employer be a responsible part of society.")

Muslim—Continuity ("Desire for stable environment, job longevity, reduction of uncertainty.")

No religious preference—Professional challenge ("Concern with having a job that provides learning opportunities and opportunities to use skills well.")[56]

Thus, there was virtually *no agreement* across religions about the primary work value. This led the researchers to conclude: "Employers might be wise to consider the impact that religious differences (and more broadly, cultural factors) appear to have on the values of employee groups."[57] Of course, in the United States and other selected countries, equal employment opportunity laws forbid managers from basing employment-related decisions on an applicant's religious preference.

Practical Insights from Cross-Cultural Management Research

Nancy Adler, an international OB specialist at Canada's McGill University, has offered the following definition: "**Cross-cultural management** explains the behavior of people in organizations around the world and shows people how to work in organizations with employee and client populations from many different cultures."[58] Historically, cross-cultural management research has focused almost exclusively on cultural differences.[59] But GLOBE researchers Mansour Javidan and Robert J House recommend studying *similarities* as well. They believe tracking cultural similarities will help us judge how applicable specific management practices are in foreign cultures. "For example, leadership theories developed in the US are probably more easily generalizable to UK managers (another member of the Anglo cluster) than to managers in an Arab country."[60] In this section we will examine two different streams of cross-cultural management research. Both offer useful lessons for today's managers.

Cross-cultural management Understanding and teaching behavioral patterns in different cultures.

The Hofstede Study: How Well Do US Management Theories Apply in Other Countries?

The short answer to this important question: *not very well*. This answer derives from a landmark study conducted 30 years ago by Dutch researcher Geert Hofstede. His unique cross-cultural comparison of 116,000 IBM employees from 53 countries worldwide focused on four cultural dimensions:

- *Power distance.* How much inequality does someone expect in social situations?
- *Individualism–collectivism.* How loosely or closely is the person socially bonded?
- *Masculinity–femininity.* Does the person embrace stereotypically competitive, performance-oriented masculine traits or nurturing, relationship-oriented feminine traits?
- *Uncertainty avoidance.* How strongly does the person desire highly structured situations?

The US sample ranked relatively low on power distance, very high on individualism, moderately high on masculinity, and low on uncertainty avoidance.[61]

The high degree of variation among cultures led Hofstede to two major conclusions: (1) Management theories and practices need to be adapted to local cultures. This is particularly true for made-in-America management theories (e.g., Maslow's need hierarchy) and Japanese team management practices. *There is no one best way to manage across cultures.*[62] (2) Cultural arrogance is a luxury individuals, companies, and nations can no longer afford in a global economy.

Leadership Lessons from the GLOBE Project

In phase 2, the GLOBE researchers set out to discover which, if any, attributes of leadership were universally liked or disliked. They surveyed 17,000 middle managers working for 951 organizations across 62 countries. Their results, summarized in Table 4–2, have important implications for trainers and present and future global managers. Visionary and inspirational *charismatic leaders* who are good team builders generally do the best. On the other hand, *self-centered leaders* seen as loners or face-savers generally receive a poor re-

Table 4–2   *Leadership Attributes Universally Liked and Disliked across 62 Nations*

Universally Positive Leader Attributes	Universally Negative Leader Attributes
Trustworthy	Loner
Just	Asocial
Honest	Noncooperative
Foresight	Irritable
Plans ahead	Nonexplicit
Encouraging	Egocentric
Positive	Ruthless
Dynamic	Dictatorial
Motive arouser	
Confidence builder	
Motivational	
Dependable	
Intelligent	
Decisive	
Effective bargainer	
Win–win problem solver	
Administrative skilled	
Communicative	
Informed	
Coordinator	
Team builder	
Excellence oriented	

SOURCE: Excerpted and adapted from P W Dorfman, P J Hanges, and F C Brodbeck, "Leadership and Cultural Variation: The Identification of Culturally Endorsed Leadership Profiles," in *Culture, Leadership, and Organizations: The GLOBE Study of 62 Societies,* eds R J House, P J Hanges, M Javidan, P W Dorfman, and V Gupta (Thousand Oaks, CA: Sage, 2004), Tables 21.2 and 21.3, pp 677–78.

ception worldwide. (See Chapter 16 for a comprehensive treatment of leadership.) Local and foreign managers who heed these results are still advised to use a contingency approach to leadership after using their cultural intelligence to read the local people and culture. David Whitwam, the longtime CEO of appliance maker Whirlpool, recently framed the challenge this way:

> Leading a company today is different from the 1980s and '90s, especially in a global company. It requires a new set of competencies. Bureaucratic structures don't work anymore. You have to take the command-and-control types out of the system. You need to allow and encourage broad-based involvement in the company. Especially in consumer kinds of companies, we need a diverse workforce with diverse leadership. You need strong regional leadership that lives in the culture. We have a North American running the North American business, and a Latin American running the Latin American business.[63]

Preparing Employees for Successful Foreign Assignments

As the reach of global companies continues to grow, many opportunities for living and working in foreign countries will arise. Imagine, for example, the opportunities for foreign duty and cross-cultural experiences at Siemens, the German electronics giant. "While Siemens' corporate headquarters is near Munich, nearly 80% of the firm's business is international. Worldwide the company has 470,000 employees, including 75,000 in the United States and 25,000 in China."[64] Siemens and other global players need a vibrant and growing cadre of employees who are willing and able to do business across cultures. Thus, the purpose of this final section is to help you prepare yourself and others to work successfully in foreign countries.

Why Do US Expatriates Fail On Foreign Assignments?

As we use the term here, **expatriate** refers to anyone living or working outside their home country. Hence, they are said to be *expatriated* when transferred to another country and *repatriated* when transferred back home. US expatriate managers, now at more than 300,000,[65] usually are characterized as culturally inept and prone to failure on international assignments. Research supports this view. A pair of international management experts offered this assessment:

> Over the past decade, we have studied the management of expatriates at about 750 US, European, and Japanese companies. We asked both the expatriates themselves and the executives who sent them abroad to evaluate their experiences. In addition, we looked at what happened after expatriates returned home. . . .
>
> Overall, the results of our research were alarming. We found that between 10% and 20% of all US managers sent abroad returned early because of job dissatisfaction or difficulties in adjusting to a foreign country. Of those who stayed for the duration, nearly one-third did not perform up to the expectations of their superiors. And perhaps most problematic, one-fourth of those who completed an assignment left their company, often to join a competitor, within one year after repatriation. That's a turnover rate double that of managers who did not go abroad.[66]

Expatriate
Anyone living or working in a foreign country.

A more recent study of why expatriate employees returned home early found the situation to be slowly improving. Still, *personal and family adjustment problems* (36.6%) and *homesickness* (31%) were found to be major stumbling blocks for American managers working in foreign countries.[67] A survey asking 72 human resource managers at multinational corporations to identify the most important success factor in a foreign assignment provided this insight: "Nearly 35% said cultural adaptability: patience, flexibility, and tolerance for others' beliefs."[68]

US multinational companies clearly need to do a better job of preparing employees and their families for foreign assignments, particularly in light of the high costs involved:

> The tab for sending an executive who earns $160,000 in the US, plus a spouse and two children, to India for two years is about $900,000, says Jacqui Hauser, vice president of consulting services for Cendant Mobility, a relocation-services firm in Danbury, Conn. This includes housing and cost-of-living allowances, foreign- and hardship-pay premiums, tax-assistance, education and car allowances and paid transportation home each year for the entire family.[69]

A Bright Spot: North American Women on Foreign Assignments

Historically, a woman from the United States or Canada on a foreign assignment was a rarity. Things are changing, albeit slowly. A review of research evidence and anecdotal accounts uncovered these insights:

- The proportion of corporate women from North America on foreign assignments grew from about 3% in the early 1980s to between 11% and 15% in the late 1990s.
- Self-disqualification and management's assumption that women would not be welcome in foreign cultures—not foreign prejudice, itself—are the primary barriers for potential female expatriates.
- Expatriate North American women are viewed first and foremost by their hosts as being foreigners, and only secondarily as being female.
- North American women have a very high success rate on foreign assignments.[70]

Considering the rapidly growing demand for global managers today,[71] self-disqualification by women and management's prejudicial policies are counterproductive. For their part, women and others who desire a foreign assignment need to take affirmative steps[72] (see Table 4–3).

Avoiding OB Trouble Spots in Foreign Assignments

Finding the right person (often along with a supportive and adventurous family) for a foreign position is a complex, time-consuming, and costly process.[73] For our purposes, it is sufficient to narrow the focus to common OB trouble spots in the foreign assignment cycle. As illustrated in Figure 4–5, the first and last stages of the cycle occur at home. The middle two stages occur in the foreign or host country. Each stage hides an OB-related trouble spot that needs to be anticipated and neutralized. Otherwise, the bill for another failed foreign assignment will grow.

Avoiding Unrealistic Expectations with Cross-Cultural Training   Realistic job previews (RJPs) have proven effective at bringing people's unrealistic expectations about a pending job assignment down to earth by providing a realistic balance

Table 4–3   *Tips for Women (and Men) for Landing a Foreign Assignment*

- While still in school, pursue foreign study opportunities and become fluent in one or more foreign languages.
- Starting with the very first job interview, clearly state your desire for a foreign assignment.
- Become very knowledgeable about foreign countries where you would like to work (take vacations there).
- Network with expatriates (both men and women) in your company to uncover foreign assignment opportunities.
- Make sure your family fully supports a foreign assignment.
- Get your boss's support by building trust and a strong working relationship.
- Be visible: make sure upper management knows about your relevant accomplishments and unique strengths.
- Stay informed about your company's international strategies and programs.
- Polish your cross-cultural communication skills daily with foreign-born co-workers.

SOURCES: Based on discussions in A Varma, L K Stroh, and L B Schmitt, "Women and International Assignments: The Impact of Supervisor-Subordinate Relationships," *Journal of World Business*, Winter 2001, pp 380–88; T Wilen, "Women Working Overseas," *Training and Development*, May 2001, pp 120–22; and E Gundling, *Working GlobeSmart: 12 People Skills for Doing Business across Borders* (Palo Alto, CA.: Davies-Black Publishing, 2003).

Figure 4–5   *The Foreign Assignment Cycle (with OB Trouble Spots)*

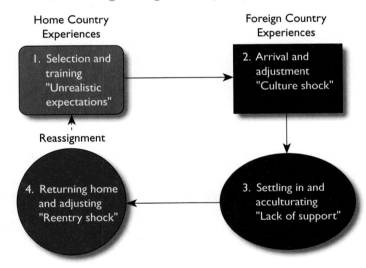

of good and bad news. People with realistic expectations tend to quit less often and be more satisfied than those with unrealistic expectations. RJPs are a must for future expatriates. In addition, cross-cultural training is required.

Cross-cultural training is any type of structured experience designed to help departing employees adjust to a foreign culture. The trend is toward more such training in the United States. But there is a great deal of room for improvement, as indicated by the results of a *Training* magazine survey. Only 12% rated cross-cultural/diversity training as "very important" for preparing employees for international assignments.[74] Experts believe that

Cross-cultural training
Structured experiences to help people adjust to a new culture/country.

A Taste of India in Silicon Valley

[In August 2004], Intel software manager Connie Martin arrived for work and received a new identity. She was handed some fake rupees and a nametag that read "Rekha Gupta," and was told that she now hailed from a northern Indian trading family. For the next eight hours, she hit the books, studying the subtle dietary differences between Jainism and Hinduism, Indian political history, and Bollywood movies. At the end of the day, she was given a test on it all, which she aced. . . .

A North Carolina native, Martin is a graduate of "Working with India," an optional training class that Intel began offering to employees in 2002. With an estimated 400,000 Indian nationals in Silicon Valley—and roughly a third of the 65,000 new H-1B visas issued by the United States in 2004 allocated for Indians—companies such as Adaptec, AMD, Intuit, and Rockwell Automation have also held similar sessions during the past year. "Indian cultural training is at the top of the radar screen right now," says [a cross-cultural trainer].

SOURCE: R Rosmarin, "Mountain View Masala," *Business 2.0*, March 2005, p 54.

cross-cultural training, although costly, is less expensive than failed foreign assignments. Programs vary widely in type and also in rigor. Of course, the greater the difficulty, the greater the time and expense:

- *Easiest.* Predeparture training is limited to informational materials, including books, lectures, films, videos, and Internet searches.

- *Moderately difficult.* Experiential training is conducted through case studies, role playing, assimilators (simulated intercultural incidents), and introductory language instruction (see Real World/Real People).

- *Most difficult.* Departing employees are given some combination of the preceding methods plus comprehensive language instruction and field experience in the target culture. As an example of the latter, PepsiCo Inc. transfers "about 25 young foreign managers a year to the US for one-year assignments in bottling plants."[75]

Which approach is the best? Research to date does not offer a final answer. One study involving US employees in South Korea led the researcher to recommend a *combination* of informational and experiential predeparture training.[76] As a general rule of thumb, the more rigorous the cross-cultural training, the better. Ideally, trainees should walk away with the nine cross-cultural competencies in Table 4–4.

Table 4–4   *Key Cross-Cultural Competencies*

Cross-Cultural Competency Cluster	Knowledge or Skill Required
Building relationships	Ability to gain access to and maintain relationships with members of host culture
Valuing people of different cultures	Empathy for difference; sensitivity to diversity
Listening and observation	Knows cultural history and reasons for certain cultural actions and customs
Coping with ambiguity	Recognizes and interprets implicit behavior, especially nonverbal cues
Translating complex information	Knowledge of local language, symbols or other forms of verbal language, and written language
Taking action and initiative	Understands intended and potentially unintended consequences of actions
Managing others	Ability to manage details of a job including maintaining cohesion in a group
Adaptability and flexibility	Views change from multiple perspectives
Managing stress	Understands own and other's mood, emotions, and personality

SOURCE: Excerpted from Y Yamazaki and D C Kayes, "An Experiential Approach to Cross-Cultural Learning: A Review and Integration of Competencies for Successful Expatriate Adaptation," *Academy of Management Learning and Education,* December 2004, Table 2, p 372.

Avoiding Culture Shock

Have you ever been in a totally unfamiliar situation and felt disoriented and perhaps a bit frightened? If so, you already know something about culture shock. According to anthropologists, **culture shock** involves anxiety and doubt caused by an overload of unfamiliar expectations and social cues.[77] College freshmen often experience a variation of culture shock. An expatriate manager, or family member, may be thrown off balance by an avalanche of strange sights, sounds, and behaviors. Among them may be unreadable road signs, strange-tasting food, inability to use your left hand for social activities (in Islamic countries, the left hand is the toilet hand), or failure to get a laugh with your surefire joke. For the expatriate manager trying to concentrate on the fine details of a business negotiation, culture shock is more than an embarrassing inconvenience. It is a disaster! Like the confused college freshman who quits and goes home, culture-shocked employees often panic and go home early.

Culture shock
Anxiety and doubt caused by an overload of new expectations and cues.

The best defense against culture shock is comprehensive cross-cultural training, including intensive language study. Once again, the best way to pick up subtle—yet important—social cues is via the local language.[78]

Support during the Foreign Assignment

Especially during the first six months, when everything is so new to the expatriate, a support system needs to be in place.[79] *Host-country sponsors,* assigned to individual managers or families, are recommended because they serve as "cultural seeing-eye dogs." In a foreign country, where even the smallest errand can turn into an utterly exhausting production, sponsors can get things done quickly because they know the cultural and geographical territory. Honda's Ohio employees, for example, enjoyed the help of family sponsors when training in Japan:

> Honda smoothed the way with Japanese wives who once lived in the US. They handled emergencies such as when Diana Jett's daughter Ashley needed stitches in her chin. When task force senior manager Kim Smalley's daughter, desperate to fit in at elementary school, had to have a precisely shaped bag for her harmonica, a Japanese volunteer stayed up late to make it.[80]

Avoiding Reentry Shock

Strange as it may seem, many otherwise successful expatriate managers encounter their first major difficulty only after their foreign assignment is over. Why? Returning to one's native culture is taken for granted because it seems so routine and ordinary. But having adjusted to another country's way of doing things for an extended period of time can put one's own culture and surroundings in a strange new light. Three areas for potential reentry shock are work, social activities, and general environment (e.g., politics, climate, transportation, food). Ira Caplan's return to New York City exemplifies reentry shock:

> During the past 12 years, living mostly in Japan, he and his wife had spent their vacations cruising the Nile or trekking in Nepal. They hadn't seen much of the US. They are getting an eyeful now. . . .
>
> Prices astonish him. The obsession with crime unnerves him. What unsettles Mr Caplan more, though, is how much of himself he has left behind.
>
> In a syndrome of return no less stressful than that of departure, he feels displaced, disregarded, and diminished. . . .
>
> In an Italian restaurant, crowded at lunchtime, the waiter sets a bowl of linguine in front of him. Mr Caplan stares at it. "In Asia, we have smaller portions and smaller people," he says.
>
> Asia is on his mind. He has spent years cultivating an expertise in a region of huge importance. So what? This is New York.[81]

Work-related adjustments were found to be a major problem for samples of repatriated Finnish, Japanese, and American employees.[82] Upon being repatriated, a 12-year veteran of one US company said: "Our organizational culture was turned upside down. We now have a different strategic focus, different 'tools' to get the job done, and different buzzwords to make it happen. I had to learn a whole new corporate 'language.' "[83] Reentry shock can be reduced through employee career counseling and home-country sponsors. Simply being aware of the problem of reentry shock is a big step toward effectively dealing with it.[84]

Overall, the key to a successful foreign assignment is making it a well-integrated link in a career chain rather than treating it as an isolated adventure.

Summary of Key Concepts

1. *Define the term* culture, *and explain how societal culture and organizational culture combine to influence on-the-job behavior.* Culture is a set of beliefs and values about what is desirable and undesirable in a community of people, and a set of formal or informal practices to support the values. Culture has both prescriptive and descriptive elements and involves taken-for-granted assumptions about how to think, act, and feel. Culture overrides national boundaries. Key aspects of societal culture, such as customs and language, are brought to work by the individual. Working together, societal and organizational culture influence the person's values, ethics, attitudes, and expectations.

2. *Define* ethnocentrism, *and distinguish between high-context and low-context cultures.* Ethnocentrism is the belief that one's native culture, language, and ways of doing things

are superior to all others. People from low-context cultures infer relatively less from situational cues and extract more meaning from spoken and written words. In high-context cultures such as China and Japan, managers prefer slow negotiations and trust-building meetings, which tends to frustrate low-context Northern Europeans and North Americans who prefer to get right down to business.

3. *Identify and describe the nine cultural dimensions from Project GLOBE.* (1) Power distance—How equally should power be distributed? (2) Uncertainty avoidance—How much should social norms and rules reduce uncertainty and unpredictability? (3) Institutional collectivism—How much should loyalty to the social unit override individual interests? (4) In-group collectivism—How strong should one's loyalty be to family or organization? (5) Gender egalitarianism—How much should gender discrimination and role inequalities be minimized? (6) Assertiveness—

How confrontational and dominant should one be in social relationships? (7) Future orientation—How much should one delay gratification by planning and saving for the future? (8) Performance orientation—How much should individuals be rewarded for improvement and excellence? (9) Humane orientation—How much should individuals be rewarded for being kind, fair, friendly, and generous?

4. *Distinguish between individualistic and collectivist cultures, and explain the difference between monochronic and polychronic cultures.* People in individualistic cultures think primarily in terms of "I" and "me" and place a high value on freedom and personal choice. Collectivist cultures teach people to be "we" and "us" oriented and to subordinate personal wishes and goals to the interests of the relevant social unit (such as family, group, organization, or society). People in monochronic cultures are schedule driven and prefer to do one thing at a time. To them, time is like money; it is spent wisely or wasted. In polychronic cultures, there is a tendency to do many things at once and to perceive time as flexible and multidimensional. Polychronic people view monochronic people as being too preoccupied with time.

5. *Specify the practical lesson from the Hofstede cross-cultural study.* There is no one best way to manage across cultures. Management theories and practices need to be adapted to the local culture.

6. *Explain what Project GLOBE researchers discovered about leadership.* Across 62 cultures, they identified leader attributes that are universally liked and universally disliked. The universally liked leader attributes—including trustworthy, dynamic, motive arouser, decisive, and intelligent—are associated with the charismatic/transformational leadership style that is widely applicable. Universally disliked leader attributes—such as noncooperative, irritable, egocentric, and dictatorial—should be avoided in all cultures.

7. *Explain why US managers have a comparatively high failure rate on foreign assignments.* American expatriates are troubled by personal and family adjustment problems and homesickness. A great deal of money is wasted when expatriates come home early. More extensive cross-cultural training is needed.

8. *Summarize the research findings about North American women on foreign assignments, and tell how to land a foreign assignment.* The number of North American women on foreign assignments is still small, but growing. Self-disqualification and prejudicial home-country supervisors and staffing policies are largely to blame. Foreigners tend to view North American women primarily as foreigners and secondarily as women. North American women have a high success rate on foreign assignments. Foreign language skills, a strong and formally announced desire, foreign experience, networking, family and supervisory support, and visibility with upper management can increase the chances of getting a desired foreign assignment for both women and men.

9. *Identify four stages of the foreign assignment cycle and the OB trouble spot associated with each stage.* Stages of the foreign assignment cycle (with OB trouble spots) are (1) selection and training (unrealistic expectations); (2) arrival and adjustment (culture shock); (3) settling in and acculturating (lack of support); and (4) returning home and adjusting (reentry shock).

Discussion Questions

1. Regarding your cultural awareness, how would you describe the prevailing culture in your country to a stranger from another land?

2. What are your personal experiences with ethnocentrism and cross-cultural dealings? What lessons have you learned?

3. How would you rate your cultural intelligence? What do you need to do to improve it?

4. Why are people from high-context cultures such as China and Japan likely to be misunderstood by low-context Westerners?

5. What are the managerial implications of your GLOBE cultural profile in the OB Exercise?

6. Culturally speaking, are you individualistic or collectivist? How does that cultural orientation affect how you run your personal or business affairs, or both?

7. Do you personally agree with the lists of universally liked and disliked leader attributes in Table 4–2? Explain.

8. What needs to be done to improve the success rate of US managers in foreign assignments?

9. How strong is your desire for a foreign assignment? Why? If it is strong, where would you like to work? Why? How prepared are you for a foreign assignment? What do you need to do to be better prepared?

10. What is your personal experience with culture shock? Which of the OB trouble spots in Figure 4–5 do you believe is the greatest threat to expatriate employee success? Explain.

It Takes a Village—and a Consultant[85]

BusinessWeek [In the summer of 2004], accounting-and-consulting giant Pricewaterhouse-Coopers tapped partner Tahir Ayub for a consulting gig unlike anything he had done before. His job: helping village leaders in the Namibian outback grapple with their community's growing AIDS crisis. Faced with language barriers, cultural differences, and scant access to electricity, Ayub, 39, and two colleagues had to scrap their PowerPoint presentations in favor of a more low-tech approach: face-to-face discussion. The village chiefs learned that they needed to garner community support for programs to combat the disease, and Ayub learned an important lesson as well: Technology isn't always the answer. "You better put your beliefs and biases to one side and figure out new ways to look at things," he said.

Ayub may never encounter as extreme a cultural disconnect at PwC as he did in Namibia. But for the next generation of partners, overcoming barriers and forging a connection with clients the world over will be a crucial part of their jobs. It's those skills that PwC hopes to foster in partners who take part in the Ulysses Program, which sends top mid-career talent to the developing world for eight-week service projects. For a fairly modest investment—$15,000 per person, plus salaries—Ulysses both tests the talent and expands the worldview of the accounting firm's future leaders. Since the company started the program four years ago, it has attracted the attention of Johnson & Johnson, Cisco Systems, and other big companies considering their own programs.

While results are hard to quantify, PwC is convinced that the program works. All two dozen graduates are still working at the company. Half of them have been promoted, and most have new responsibilities. Just as important, all 24 people say they have a stronger commitment to PwC—in part because of the commitment the firm made to them and in part because of their new vision of the firm's values. Says Global Managing Partner Willem Bröcker: "We get better partners from this exercise."

The Ulysses Program is PwC's answer to one of the biggest challenges confronting professional services companies: identifying and training up-and-coming leaders who can find unconventional answers to intractable problems. By tradition and necessity, new PwC leaders are nurtured from within. But with 8,000 partners, identifying those with the necessary business savvy and relationship-building skills isn't easy. Just as the program gives partners a new view of PwC, it also gives PwC a new view of them, particularly their ability to hold up under pressure.

For mid-career partners who were weaned on e-mail and the Blackberry, this was no walk in the park. They had become accustomed to a world of wireless phones, sleek offices, and Chinese take-out—so the rigors of the developing world came as quite a shock. Brain P McCann, 37, a mergers and acquisitions expert from PwC's Boston office, had never been to a Third World country before his stint in Belize, where he encountered dirt-floored houses, sick children, and grinding poverty.

Ayub, having been born in Africa, considered himself worldly. Even so, long days spent among Africa's exploding HIV-positive population took their psychological toll. With his work confined to daylight hours—there was often no electricity—Dinu Bumbacea, a 37-year-old partner in PwC's Romanian office who spent time in Zambia working with an agricultural center, had plenty of time to dwell on the misery all around him. "Africa is poor, and we all know that," says Bumbacea. "But until you go there, you don't understand how poor it is. We take so much for granted."

For more than 15 years, companies have used social-responsibility initiatives to develop leaders. But PwC takes the concept to a new level. Participants spend eight weeks in developing countries lending their business skills to local aid groups—from an ecotourism collective in Belize to small organic farmers in Zambia to AIDS groups in Namibia. Ulysses also presents participants with the challenge of collaborating across cultures with local clients as well as with PwC colleagues from other global regions. Ayub, for example, was paired with partners from Mexico and the Netherlands.

Beyond Accounting

PWC says the program, now in its third cycle, gives participants a broad, international perspective that's crucial for a company that does business around the world. Traditional executive education programs turn out men and women who have specific job skills but little familiarity with issues outside their narrow specialty, according to Douglas Ready, director of the International Consortium for Executive Development Research. PwC says Ulysses helps prepare participants for challenges that go beyond the strict confines of accounting or consulting and instills values such as community involvement that are fundamental to its corporate culture.

Ulysses is also a chance for partners to learn what they can accomplish without their usual resources to lean on. The program forces them to take on projects well outside their expertise. In the summer of 2003, for example, McCann developed a business plan for an ecotourism group in Belize. The experience was an eye-opener. McCann's most lasting memory is a dinner he shared in the home of a Mayan farmer after they spent a day discussing their plan. "He didn't even have electricity," McCann recalls, "but he made do."

PwC partners say they've already adapted their experiences to the task of managing people and clients. Malaysian partner Jennifer Chang says her team noticed a shift in her managerial style after the Belize trip. She listened more and became more flexible. "Once you see how slowly decisions are made in other places, you gain patience for the people you work with," she says. Ayub, who was promoted in June, now manages 20 partners. He says he favors face-to-face conversations over e-mail because the low-tech approach builds trust. "It made the difference in Namibia," he says.

If insights like those ripple out across the firm, Ulysses will be more than a voyage of personal discovery for a handful of partners. It could help build leaders capable of confronting the challenges of an increasingly global business. And that, says PwC, is the whole point.

Questions for Discussion

1. If you were the CEO of PricewaterhouseCoopers, how would you defend the Ulysses Program to shareholders concerned about spending?

2. What benefit would the Ulysses Program be to PwC employees who would not seek or take a foreign assignment?

3. How do the facts of this case confirm the GLOBE project's research findings about leadership? Explain.

4. Using Table 4–4 as a guide, what cross-cultural competencies were developed among the people featured in this case study? Explain.

5. Would you like to participate in this type of leadership development program? Why or why not?

Personal Awareness and Growth Exercise

How Do Your Work Goals Compare Internationally?

Objectives

1. To increase your cross-cultural awareness.
2. To see how your own work goals compare internationally.

Introduction

In today's multicultural global economy, it is a mistake to assume everyone wants the same things from the job as you do. This exercise provides a "window" on the world of work goals.

Instructions

Below is a list of 11 goals potentially attainable in the workplace. In terms of your own personal preferences, rank the goals from 1 to 11 (1 = most important; 11 = least important). After you have ranked all 11 work goals, compare your list with the national samples under the heading *Survey Results*. These national samples represent cross sections of employees from all levels and all major occupational groups. (Please complete your ranking now, before looking at the national samples.) How important are the following in your work life?

Rank Work Goals

_____ A lot of opportunity to *learn* new things
_____ Good *interpersonal relations* (supervisors, co-workers)
_____ Good opportunity for upgrading or *promotion*
_____ *Convenient* work *hours*
_____ A lot of *variety*
_____ *Interesting* work (work that you really like)
_____ Good *job security*
_____ A good *match* between your job requirements and your abilities and experience
_____ Good *pay*
_____ Good physical working *conditions* (such as light, temperature, cleanliness, low noise level)
_____ A lot of *autonomy* (you decide how to do your work)[86]

Questions for Discussion

1. Which national profile of work goals most closely matches your own? Is this what you expected, or not?

2. Are you surprised by any of the rankings in the four national samples? Explain.

3. What sorts of motivational/leadership adjustments would a manager have to make when moving among the four countries?

Survey Results[87]

Ranking of Work Goals by Country

(1 = MOST IMPORTANT; 11 = LEAST IMPORTANT)

Work Goals	United States	Britain	Germany*	Japan
Interesting work	1	1	3	2
Pay	2	2	1	5
Job security	3	3	2	4
Match between person and job	4	6	5	1
Opportunity to learn	5	8	9	7
Variety	6	7	6**	9
Interpersonal relations	7	4	4	6
Autonomy	8	10	8	3
Convenient work hours	9	5	6**	8
Opportunity for promotion	10	11	10	11
Working conditions	11	9	11	10

*Former West Germany.
**Tie.

133

Group Exercise

Looking into a Cultural Mirror

Objectives

1. To generate group discussion about the impact of societal culture on managerial style.
2. To increase your cultural awareness.
3. To discuss the idea of a distinct American style of management.
4. To explore the pros and cons of the American style of management.

Introduction

A time-tested creativity technique involves "taking something familiar and making it strange." This technique can yield useful insights by forcing us to take a close look at things we tend to take for granted. In the case of this group exercise, the focus of your attention will be mainstream cultural tendencies in the United States (or any other country you or your instructor may select) and management. A 15-minute, small-group session will be followed by brief oral presentations and a general class discussion. Total time required is about 35 to 45 minutes.

Instructions

Your instructor will divide your class randomly into small groups of five to eight. Half of the teams will be designated "red" teams, and half will be "green" teams. Each team will assign someone the role of recorder/presenter, examine the cultural traits listed below, and develop a cultural profile of the "American management style." Members of each red team will explain the *positive* implications of each trait in their cultural profile. Green team members will explain the *negative* implications of the traits in their profiles.

During the brief oral presentations by the various teams, the instructor may jot down on the board or flip chart a composite cultural profile of American managers. A general class discussion of positive and negative implications will follow. *Note:* Special effort should be made to solicit comments and observations from foreign students and students who have traveled or worked in other countries. Discussion needs to focus on the appropriateness or inappropriateness of the American cultural style of management in other countries and cultures.

As "seed" for group discussion, here is a list of American cultural traits identified by researchers[88] (feel free to supplement this short list):

- Individualistic
- Independent
- Aggressive/assertive/blunt
- Competitive
- Informal
- Pragmatic/practical
- Impatient
- Materialistic
- Unemotional/rational/objective
- Hard working

Questions for Discussion

1. Are you surprised by anything you have just heard? Explain.
2. Is there a distinct American management style? Explain.
3. Can the American management style be exported easily? If it needs to be modified, how?
4. What do American managers need to do to be more effective at home and in foreign countries?

Ethical Dilemma

3M Tries to Make a Difference in Russia[89]

Russian managers aren't inclined . . . to reward people for improved performance. They spurn making investments for the future in favor of realizing immediate gains. They avoid establishing consistent business practices that can reduce uncertainty. Add in the country's high political risk and level of corruption, and it's no wonder that many multinationals have all but given up on Russia. . . .

The Russian business environment can be corrupt and dangerous; bribes and protection money are facts of life. But unlike many international companies, which try to distance themselves from such practices by simply banning them, 3M Russia actively promotes not only ethical behavior but also the personal security of its employees. . . .

3M Russia also strives to differentiate itself from competitors by being an ethical leader. For example, it holds training courses in business ethics for its customers.

Should 3M export its American ethical standards to Russia?

1. If 3M doesn't like the way things are done in Russia, it shouldn't do business there. Explain your rationale.

2. 3M should do business in Russia but not meddle in Russian culture. "When in Russia, do things the Russian way." Explain your rationale.

3. 3M has a basic moral responsibility to improve the ethical climate in foreign countries where it does business. Explain your rationale.

4. 3M should find a practical middle ground between the American and Russian ways of doing business. How should that happen?

5. Invent other options. Discuss.

For the Chapter 4 Internet Exercise featuring a virtual trip to the global destination of your choice (www.lonelyplanet.com and www.travlang.com), visit our Web site at **www.mhhe.com/kreitner.**

Individual Behavior in Organizations

Part Two

Self-Concept, Personality, Abilities, and Emotions

Learning Objectives

When you finish studying the material in this chapter, you should be able to:

1   Define self-esteem, and explain how it can be improved with Branden's six pillars of self-esteem.

2   Define self-efficacy, and explain its sources.

3   Contrast high and low self-monitoring individuals, and discuss the ethical implications of organizational identification.

4   Identify and describe the Big Five personality dimensions, and specify which one is correlated most strongly with job performance.

5   Describe the proactive personality, and explain the need to balance an internal locus of control with humility.

6   Identify at least five of Gardner's eight multiple intelligences, and explain "practical intelligence."

7   Distinguish between positive and negative emotions, and explain how they can be judged.

8   Identify the four key components of emotional intelligence, and discuss the practical significance of emotional contagion and emotional labor.

BusinessWeek For Peter Tilton, the office revelation came last February. He was sitting in a conference room at company headquarters, meeting with the group he managed, when an "incompetent" colleague began needling him about his own progress on a project. Tilton felt the trip wire go off, the raw rush that made him feel as if he were slipping into a state of adolescent siege.

Within seconds, he was banging his fist on the whiteboard and "yelling his face off." Even at a place like Microsoft Corp., where Tilton says co-workers routinely blast each others' ideas as "stupid," this wasn't exactly behavior becoming a director-level executive. The emotional outburst, Tilton now realizes, was eerily similar to one he had back in seventh grade, when his parents—"chronic misunderstanders"—forbade him to wear his jeans with the holey knees to school. It was 1967, and he was heavy into his hippie protest phase. "And they wanted me to wear slacks," Tilton says....

That . . . highly rational, utterly left-brained executives are delving into their pasts illustrates a new strain of organizational therapy coursing through the inner sanctums of corporate power. The basic concept: that people tend to recreate their family dynamics at the office. The idea is being fanned by organizational experts, who say that corporate strivers can at times behave a bit like thumb-suckers in knee pants, yearning for pats on the back from boss "daddies and mommies" and wishing those scene-stealing co-worker "siblings" would, well, die. Boardroom arguments can parallel spats at the family dinner table....

Buttressed by new research in workplace dynamics, more high-profile coaches and consultants are applying family-systems therapy to business organizations, to grapple with what has come to be seen as a new frontier in productivity: emotional inefficiency, which includes all that bickering, back-stabbing, and ridiculous playing for approval that are a mark of the modern workplace. A two-year study by Seattle psychologist Brian DesRoches found

Cartoon reprinted from *Harvard Business Review*, January 2004. © David Harbaugh. Used by permission.

"...COULD IT BE, AS A CHILD, ...YOU EXPERIENCED A HOSTILE TAKE OVER OF YOUR LEMONADE STAND LEAVING YOU WITH UNRESOLVED RAGE THAT LED TO YOUR HIGHLY AGGRESSIVE MANAGEMENT STYLE ?..."

that such dramas routinely waste 20% to 50% of workers' time. The theory is also gaining more resonance as corporations become ever more cognizant that talented employees quit bosses, not companies, and that CEOs often get hired for their skills—and fired for their personalities.

Looking backward to move forward makes sense, say group dynamic researchers, considering that the first organization people ever belong to is their families, with parents the first bosses and siblings the first colleagues. "Our original notions of an institution, of an authority structure, of power and influence are all forged in the family," says Warren Bennis, management guru and professor of business at the University of Southern California.

. . . by performing psychological X-rays on clients' pasts, coaches have helped executives at companies as diverse as the *Los Angeles Times,* State Farm Insurance, and American Express understand their own and others' dysfunctional behavior. They learn how to recognize the shadowy emotional subtext that drives many encounters, deconstructing how they may be subconsciously sabotaging themselves, shying from authority figures, or engaging in hypercritical judgments of subordinates. Or why they may unwittingly play the role of the hero, scapegoat, or martyr. "I'm not suggesting that our employees are our kids," says Kenneth Sole, a consulting social psychologist who has worked with Apple Computer Inc. and the UN. "But the psychology is parallel.". . .

Personalities, emotions, behavioral tics—all have started to take on a bigger dimension in an era in which businesses increasingly sell the ideas that come from employees' heads, not just the products from their machines. . . .

Of course, plenty of leaders and their consultants object to therapy invading the office. "The workplace is not the place to explore psychological foibles," says Richard A Chaifetz, CEO of ComPsych Corp., a Chicago employee-assistance firm. "It can open up a can of worms." Chaifetz approves of this kind of inquiry only if it's done off-site, one-on-one, and with a trained professional. And many work dynamics can't be analyzed solely through a family filter. More likely, say critics, work teams carry traits that are characteristic of all group dynamics. Pairing off, for example, usually happens any time people gather. So does complaining. . . .

In Tilton's case, the Microsoft exec had disdained therapy "ever since my parents tried to send me to a pipe-smoking guy in seventh grade." But in the months he has been working with an executive coach, he only wishes he could have cracked through his denial sooner. Like many, he realizes that being analytically savvy isn't enough. Being emotionally competent is now part of the job, too.[1]

FOR DISCUSSION
Is there a legitimate linkage between one's family history and on-the-job behavior, or is it just a lame excuse for being out of control? Explain.

As the world's population continues to grow (more than 6.4 billion at the time of this writing),[2] many of us seek a unique identity that sets us apart from the crowd. This makes understanding and managing people and trying to please them increasingly difficult. As a case in point: "Starbucks not only has more than 19,000 ways it can serve a cup of coffee, but it has five kinds of milk to stir into it: whole, nonfat, half and half, organic, and soy."[3] What's your favorite? Likewise, how do you express yourself in the workplace? Are you a loner or highly social? Do you see yourself as master of your own fate, or a victim of circumstances? Are you emotional, like Microsoft's Peter Tilton in the opening vignette, or calm and cool? Is your job satisfaction through the roof or stuck in the basement? Thanks to a vast array of individual differences such as these, modern organizations have a rich and interesting human texture. On the other hand, individual differences make the manager's job endlessly challenging. In fact, according to research, "variability among workers is substantial at all levels but increases dramatically with job complexity. In life insurance sales, for example, variability in performance is around six times as great as in routine clerical jobs."[4]

Growing workforce diversity compels managers to view individual differences in a fresh new way. The case for this new perspective was presented in Britain's *Journal of Managerial Psychology:*

> For many years America's businesses sought homogeneity—a work force that believed in, supported, and presented a particular image. The notion of the company man dressed for success in the banker's blue or corporation's grey flannel suit was *de riguer.* Those able to move into leadership positions succeeded to the extent they behaved and dressed according to a rather narrowly defined standard.
>
> To compete today, and in preparation for the work force of tomorrow, successful businesses and organisations are adapting to both internal and external changes. New operational styles, language, customs, values, and even dress, are a real part of this adaptation. We now hear leaders talking about "valuing differences," and learning to "manage diversity."[5]

So rather than limiting diversity, as in the past, today's managers need to better understand and accommodate employee diversity and individual differences.[6]

Both this chapter and the next explore the key individual differences portrayed in Figure 5–1. The figure is intended to be an instructional road map showing the bridges between self-concept and self-expression. This chapter focuses on self-concept, personality, abilities, and emotions. Personal values, attitudes, and job satisfaction are covered in Chapter 6. Taken as an integrated whole, all these factors provide a foundation for better understanding each organizational contributor as a unique and special individual.

Figure 5–1   *An Instructional Road Map for the Study of Individual Differences in Chapters 5 and 6*

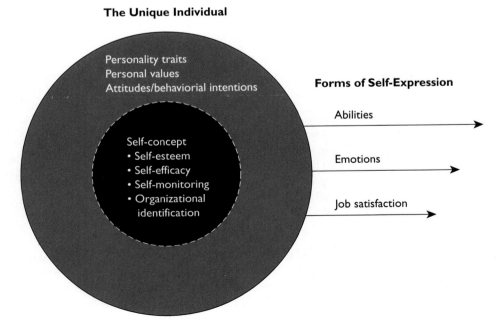

Self-Concept

Self is the core of one's conscious existence. Awareness of self is referred to as one's self-concept. The relevance of this topic surfaced in a broad survey. People ages 16 to 70 were asked what they would do differently if they could live life over again; 48% chose the response category "Get in touch with self."[7] Toward that end, Henry Mintzberg recently reminded us of the value of *self-reflection* when figuring out who we are, how we are doing, and where we are going.

> Reflection is a conversation between yourself as the actor and as an observer of the actions you take. By considering your actions, you get an outsider's view of yourself. So a person who is reflecting is both the subject and the object of reflection, and both the giver and receiver of the reflection.
>
> Reflecting does not mean musing, and it is not casual. It means wondering, probing, analyzing, synthesizing and connecting. And not just about *what* happened, but *why* it happened and *how* it differs from other happenings.[8]

Self-concept

Person's self-perception as a physical, social, spiritual being.

Sociologist Viktor Gecas defines **self-concept** as "the concept the individual has of himself as a physical, social, and spiritual or moral being."[9] In other words, because you have a self-concept, you recognize yourself as a distinct human being. A self-concept would be impossible without the capacity to think. This brings us to the role of cognitions. **Cognitions** represent "any knowledge, opinion, or belief about the environment, about oneself, or about one's behavior."[10] Among many different types of cognitions, those involving anticipation, planning, goal setting, evaluating, and setting personal standards are particularly relevant to OB.

Cognitions

A person's knowledge, opinions, or beliefs.

Our attention now turns to three topics invariably mentioned when behavioral scientists discuss self-concept. They are self-esteem, self-efficacy, and self-monitoring. We also consider the ethical implications of organizational identification, a social aspect of self. A social learning model of self-management can be found in Learning Module B (Learning Module B can be found on our Web site at www.mhhe.com/kreitner) to serve as a practical capstone for this section. Each of these areas deserves a closer look by those who want to better understand and effectively manage themselves and others.

Self-Esteem

Self-esteem

One's overall self-evaluation.

Self-esteem is a belief about one's own self-worth based on an overall self-evaluation.[11] Self-esteem is measured by having survey respondents indicate their agreement or disagreement with both positive and negative statements. A positive statement on one general self-esteem survey is: "I feel I am a person of worth, the equal of other people."[12] Among the negative items is: "I feel I do not have much to be proud of."[13] Those who agree with the positive statements and disagree with the negative statements have high self-esteem. They see themselves as worthwhile, capable, and acceptable. People with low self-esteem view themselves in negative terms. They do not feel good about themselves and are hampered by self-doubts.[14]

Employment and Self-Esteem
What researchers call *organization-based self-esteem* makes paid employment a prime determinant of overall self-esteem in modern life.[15] Consequently, unemployment can have a devastating impact on one's self-esteem. Consider these instructive remarks from Arthur J Fiacco, a 56-year-old executive who was laid off without any warning during the tech downturn in 2001:

> I had never felt so lonely and helpless. I had been working since I was 16 years old. . . .

A job isn't just about working. A job helps define who we are. It is what we talk with our neighbors about. It is the place we go. It is how we are introduced. It is one of the first things people ask about when we meet them. And most important, we measure ourselves from our very first job onward. Without a job, I felt I had lost my identity.[16]

Fiacco eventually turned things around by building a successful consulting business. He says now, "I am making a contribution and feel good. . . . I have learned to listen to what others are trying to tell me."[17]

Self-Esteem across Cultures

What are the cross-cultural implications for self-esteem, a concept that has been called uniquely Western? In a survey of 13,118 students from 31 countries worldwide, a moderate positive correlation was found between self-esteem and life satisfaction. But the relationship was stronger in individualistic cultures (e.g., United States, Canada, New Zealand, Netherlands) than in collectivist cultures (e.g., Korea, Kenya, Japan). The researchers concluded that individualistic cultures socialize people to focus more on themselves, while people in collectivist cultures "are socialized to fit into the community and to do their duty. Thus, how a collectivist feels about him- or herself is less relevant to . . . life satisfaction."[18] Global managers need to remember to deemphasize self-esteem when doing business in collectivist ("we") cultures, as opposed to emphasizing it in individualistic ("me") cultures.

Can General Self-Esteem Be Improved?

The short answer is yes (see Table 5–1). More detailed answers come from research. In one study, youth-league baseball coaches who were trained in supportive teaching techniques had a positive effect on the self-esteem of young boys. A control group of untrained coaches had no such positive effect.[19] Meanwhile, middle-school teachers in the United States reportedly are correcting papers with purple ink rather than the traditional red in an effort to boost self-esteem. "We

Table 5–1   *Branden's Six Pillars of Self-Esteem*

What nurtures and sustains self-esteem in grown-ups is not how others deal with us but how we ourselves operate in the face of life's challenges—the choices we make and the actions we take. This leads us to the six pillars of self-esteem.

1. *Live consciously.* Be actively and fully engaged in what you do and with whom you interact.
2. *Be self-accepting.* Don't be overly judgmental or critical of your thoughts and actions.
3. *Take personal responsibility.* Take full responsibility for your decisions and actions in life's journey.
4. *Be self-assertive.* Be authentic and willing to defend your beliefs when interacting with others, rather than bending to their will to be accepted or liked.
5. *Live purposefully.* Have clear near-term and long-term goals and realistic plans for achieving them to create a sense of control over your life.
6. *Have personal integrity.* Be true to your word and your values.

Between self-esteem and the practices that support it, there is reciprocal causation. This means that the behaviors that generate good self-esteem are also expressions of good self-esteem.

SOURCE: Excerpted and adapted from Nathaniel Branden, *Self-Esteem at Work: How Confident People Make Powerful Companies* (San Francisco: Jossey-Bass, 1998), pp 33–36. Reprinted with permission of John Wiley & Sons, Inc.

cannot keep purple pens in stock," says Robert Silberman, vice president of marketing for Pilot Pen in Connecticut. "It's a major move for teachers, moving away from red and going to a kinder, gentler color."[20] (Hmmm, will the next generation come to hate purple as much as their parents dislike red?) Another study led to this conclusion: "Low self-esteem can be raised more by having the person think of *desirable* characteristics *possessed* rather than of undesirable characteristics from which he or she is free."[21] This approach can help neutralize the self-defeating negative thoughts among those with low self-esteem.

Self-Efficacy

Self-efficacy
Belief in one's ability to do a task.

Have you noticed how those who are confident about their ability tend to succeed, while those who are preoccupied with failing tend to fail? Perhaps that explains the comparative golfing performance of your authors! One consistently stays in the fairways and hits the greens. The other spends the day thrashing through the underbrush, wading in water hazards, and blasting out of sand traps. At the heart of this performance mismatch is self-efficacy, something researchers say is *not* the same as self-esteem.[22] **Self-efficacy** is a person's belief about his or her chances of successfully accomplishing a specific task. According to one OB writer, "Self-efficacy arises from the gradual acquisition of complex cognitive, social, linguistic, and/or physical skills through experience."[23] Childhood experiences have a powerful effect on a person's self-efficacy (see Real World/Real People).

Learned helplessness
Debilitating lack of faith in one's ability to control the situation.

The relationship between self-efficacy and performance is a cyclical one. Efficacy → performance cycles can spiral upward toward success or downward toward failure.[24] Researchers have documented strong linkages between high self-efficacy expectations and success in widely varied physical and mental tasks, anxiety reduction, addiction control, pain tolerance, illness recovery, avoidance of seasickness in naval cadets, and stress avoidance.[25] Oppositely, those with low self-efficacy expectations tend to have low success rates. Chronically low self-efficacy is associated with a condition called **learned helplessness,** the severely debilitating belief that one has no control over one's environment.[26] Although self-efficacy sounds like some sort of mental magic, it operates in a very straightforward manner, as a model will show.

Cheri Blauwet has been paralyzed from the waist down ever since an accident on her family's Iowa farm at the age of 15 months. But for hard-charging Blauwet, learning to get around in a wheelchair wasn't enough. She became a world-class wheelchair racer, winning marathons in Boston and New York, and an inspiring role model for the power of high self-efficacy and a proactive personality. Blauwet is now a Stanford medical student.

How *Hispanic Business* Magazine's 2004 Woman of the Year Developed High Self-Efficacy

Jovita Carranza's first UPS job, as a package handler 29 years ago, gave her a unique reference point as she moved up the corporate ladder.

Now, as vice president of air operations for the $33.5 billion international company, she still maintains the values that enabled her to earn promotion after promotion.

"You perfect each assignment you are given and stay focused on the task at hand," said Carranza, the eldest daughter of a first-generation Mexican-American family from Chicago....

When asked how she moved up the corporate ladder, she cited her decision to keep pursuing her education, eventually earning a master of business administration degree, and learning from many role models.

Not the least of those mentors were her parents, who never learned English. They required her to take a disciplined approach to life and inculcated in her an appreciation for diversity. Carranza herself didn't start speaking English until the first grade.

SOURCE: Excerpted from J J Higuera, "Keep Learning, Hispanic Exec Tells Students," *Arizona Republic,* April 9, 2005, pp D1, D6.

What Are the Mechanisms of Self-Efficacy? A basic model of self-efficacy is displayed in Figure 5–2. It draws upon the work of Stanford psychologist Albert Bandura. Let us explore this model with a simple illustrative task. Imagine you have been told to prepare and deliver a 10-minute talk to an OB class of 50 students on the workings of the self-efficacy model in Figure 5–2. Your self-efficacy calculation would involve cognitive appraisal of the interaction between your perceived capability and situational opportunities and obstacles.

As you begin to prepare for your presentation, the four sources of self-efficacy beliefs would come into play. Because prior experience is the most potent source, according to Bandura, it is listed first and connected to self-efficacy beliefs with a solid line.[27] Past success in public speaking would boost your self-efficacy. But bad experiences with delivering speeches would foster low self-efficacy. Regarding behavior models as a source of self-efficacy beliefs, you would be influenced by the success or failure of your classmates in delivering similar talks. Their successes would tend to bolster you (or perhaps their failure would if you were very competitive and had high self-esteem). Likewise, any supportive persuasion from your classmates that you will do a good job would enhance your self-efficacy. Physical and emotional factors also might affect your self-confidence. A sudden case of laryngitis or a bout of stage fright could cause your self-efficacy expectations to plunge. Your cognitive evaluation of the situation then would yield a self-efficacy belief—ranging from high to low expectations for success. Importantly, self-efficacy beliefs are not merely boastful statements based on bravado; they are deep convictions supported by experience.

Moving to the *behavioral patterns* portion of Figure 5–2, we see how self-efficacy beliefs are acted out. In short, if you have high self-efficacy about giving your 10-minute speech you will work harder, more creatively, and longer when preparing for your talk than will your low-self-efficacy classmates. The results would then take shape accordingly. People program themselves for success or failure by enacting their self-efficacy expectations. Positive or negative results subsequently become feedback for one's base of personal

Figure 5–2   *A Model of How Self-Efficacy Beliefs Can Pave the Way for Success or Failure*

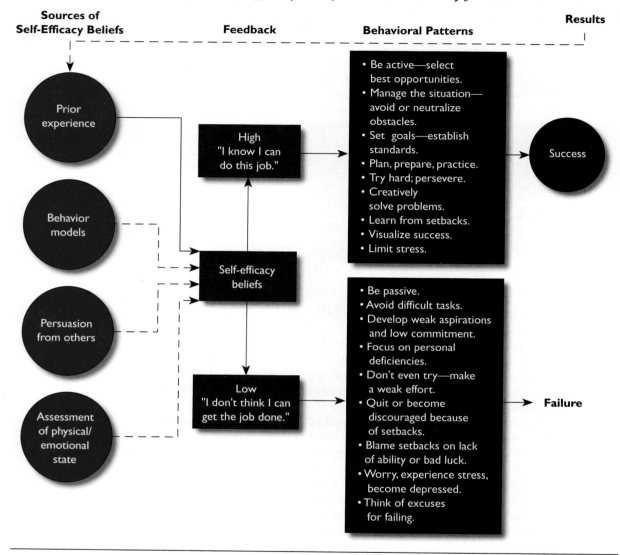

Sources of Self-Efficacy Beliefs

- Prior experience
- Behavior models
- Persuasion from others
- Assessment of physical/ emotional state

Feedback

High "I know I can do this job."

Self-efficacy beliefs

Low "I don't think I can get the job done."

Behavioral Patterns

- Be active—select best opportunities.
- Manage the situation— avoid or neutralize obstacles.
- Set goals—establish standards.
- Plan, prepare, practice.
- Try hard; persevere.
- Creatively solve problems.
- Learn from setbacks.
- Visualize success.
- Limit stress.

- Be passive.
- Avoid difficult tasks.
- Develop weak aspirations and low commitment.
- Focus on personal deficiencies.
- Don't even try—make a weak effort.
- Quit or become discouraged because of setbacks.
- Blame setbacks on lack of ability or bad luck.
- Worry, experience stress, become depressed.
- Think of excuses for failing.

Results

Success

Failure

SOURCES: Adapted from discussion in A Bandura, "Regulation of Cognitive Processes through Perceived Self-Efficacy," *Developmental Psychology*, September 1989, pp 729–35; and R Wood and A Bandura, "Social Cognitive Theory of Organizational Management," *Academy of Management Review*, July 1989, pp 361–84.

experience. Bob Schmonsees, a software entrepreneur, is an inspiring example of the success pathway through Figure 5–2:

> A contender in mixed-doubles tennis and a former football star, Mr Schmonsees was standing near a ski lift when an out-of-control skier rammed him. His legs were paralyzed. He would spend the rest of his life in a wheelchair.
>
> Fortunately, he discovered a formula for his different world: Figure out the new rules for any activity, then take as many small steps as necessary to master those rules. After learning the physics of a tennis swing on wheels and the geometry of playing a second bounce (standard rules), he became the world's top wheelchair player over age 40.[28]

Self-Efficacy Implications for Managers   On-the-job research evidence encourages managers to nurture self-efficacy, both in themselves and in others. In fact, a meta-analysis encompassing 21,616 subjects found a significant positive correlation between self-efficacy and job performance.[29] Self-efficacy requires constructive action in each of the following managerial areas:

1. *Recruiting/selection/job assignments.* Interview questions can be designed to probe job applicants' general self-efficacy as a basis for determining orientation and training needs. Pencil-and-paper tests for self-efficacy are not in an advanced stage of development and validation. Care needs to be taken not to hire solely on the basis of self-efficacy because studies have detected below-average self-esteem and self-efficacy among women and protected minorities.[30]

2. *Job design.* Complex, challenging, and autonomous jobs tend to enhance perceived self-efficacy.[31] Boring, tedious jobs generally do the opposite.

3. *Training and development.* Employees' self-efficacy expectations for key tasks can be improved through guided experiences, mentoring, and role modeling.[32]

4. *Self-management.* Systematic self-management training, as in Learning Module B (found on our Web site at www.mhhe.com/kreitner), involves enhancement of self-efficacy expectations.[33]

5. *Goal setting and quality improvement.* Goal difficulty needs to match the individual's perceived self-efficacy.[34] As self-efficacy and performance improve, goals and quality standards can be made more challenging.

6. *Coaching.* Those with low self-efficacy and employees victimized by learned helplessness need lots of constructive pointers and positive feedback.[35]

7. *Leadership and mentoring.* Needed leadership talent surfaces when top management gives high self-efficacy managers a chance to prove themselves under pressure.[36]

8. *Rewards.* Small successes need to be rewarded as stepping-stones to a stronger self-image and greater achievements.

Self-Monitoring

Consider these contrasting scenarios:

1. You are rushing to an important meeting when a co-worker pulls you aside and starts to discuss a personal problem. You want to break off the conversation, so you glance at your watch. He keeps talking. You say, "I'm late for a big meeting." He continues. You turn and start to walk away. The person keeps talking as if they never received any of your verbal and nonverbal signals that the conversation was over.

2. Same situation. Only this time, when you glance at your watch, the person immediately says, "I know, you've got to go. Sorry. We'll talk later."

In the first all-too-familiar scenario, you are talking to a "low self-monitor." The second scenario involves a "high self-monitor." But more is involved here than an irritating situation. A significant and measurable individual difference in self-expression behavior, called self-monitoring, is highlighted. **Self-monitoring** is the extent to which a person observes their own self-expressive behavior and adapts it to the demands of the situation. Experts on the subject offer this explanation:

> Individuals high in self-monitoring are thought to regulate their expressive self-presentation for the sake of desired public appearances, and thus be highly responsive to social and

Self-monitoring
Observing one's own behavior and adapting it to the situation.

interpersonal cues of situationally appropriate performances. Individuals low in self-monitoring are thought to lack either the ability or the motivation to so regulate their expressive self-presentations. Their expressive behaviors, instead, are thought to functionally reflect their own enduring and momentary inner states, including their attitudes, traits, and feelings.[37]

In organizational life, both high and low monitors are subject to criticism. High self-monitors are sometimes called *chameleons,* who readily adapt their self-presentation to their surroundings. Low self-monitors, on the other hand, often are criticized for being on their own planet and insensitive to others. Former US housing secretary and 1996 vice presidential candidate Jack Kemp frustrated his political handlers with his low self-monitoring ways:

> Bush administration veterans recall windy lectures on US urban policy during cabinet meetings, and friends say Kemp will debate anything with anyone, any time. "We used to laugh at him for going to Iowa, where he'd wind up talking the gold standard with two farmers, three hogs, and two dogs," a former staffer says. "Everyone else had left."[38]

Importantly, within an OB context, self-monitoring is like any other individual difference—not a matter of right or wrong or good versus bad, but rather a source of diversity that needs to be adequately understood by present and future managers.

A Matter of Degree
Self-monitoring is not an either-or proposition. It is a matter of degree; a matter of being relatively high or low in terms of related patterns of self-expression. The OB Exercise is a self-assessment of your self-monitoring tendencies. It can help you better understand your*self.* Take a short break from your reading to complete the 10-item survey. Does your score surprise you in any way? Are you unhappy with the way you present yourself to others? What are the ethical implications of your score (particularly with regard to items 9 and 10)?

Research Findings and Practical Recommendations
A recent meta-analysis encompassing 23,191 subjects in 136 samples found self-monitoring to be relevant and useful when dealing with job performance and emerging leaders.[39] According to field research, there is a positive relationship between high self-monitoring and career success. Among 139 MBA graduates who were tracked for five years, high self-monitors enjoyed more internal and external promotions than did their low self-monitoring classmates.[40] Another study of 147 managers and professionals found that high self-monitors had a better record of acquiring a mentor (someone to act as a personal career coach and professional sponsor).[41] These results mesh well with an earlier study that found managerial success (in terms of speed of promotions) tied to political savvy (knowing how to socialize, network, and engage in organizational politics).[42]

The foregoing evidence and practical experience lead us to make these practical recommendations:

For high, moderate, and low self-monitors: Become more consciously aware of your self-image and how it affects others (the OB Exercise is a good start).

For high self-monitors: Don't overdo it by evolving from a successful chameleon into someone who is widely perceived as insincere, dishonest, phoney, and untrustworthy. You cannot be everything to everyone.

For low self-monitors: You can bend without breaking, so try to be a bit more accommodating while being true to your basic beliefs. Don't wear out your welcome when communicating. Practice reading and adjusting to nonverbal cues in various public situations. If your conversation partner is bored or distracted, stop—because they are not really listening.

What Are Your Self-Monitoring Tendencies?

Instructions

In an honest self-appraisal, mark each of the following statements as true (T) or false (F), and then consult the scoring key.

_____ 1. I guess I put on a show to impress or entertain others.

_____ 2. In a group of people I am rarely the center of attention.

_____ 3. In different situations and with different people, I often act like very different persons.

_____ 4. I would not change my opinions (or the way I do things) in order to please someone or win their favor.

_____ 5. I have considered being an entertainer.

_____ 6. I have trouble changing my behavior to suit different people and different situations.

_____ 7. At a party I let others keep the jokes and stories going.

_____ 8. I feel a bit awkward in public and do not show up quite as well as I should.

_____ 9. I can look anyone in the eye and tell a lie with a straight face (if for a right end).

_____ 10. I may deceive people by being friendly when I really dislike them.

Scoring Key

Score one point for each of the following answers:

1. T; 2. F; 3. T; 4. F; 5. T; 6. F; 7. F; 8. F; 9. T; 10. T

Score: _____

1–3 = Low self-monitoring

4–5 = Moderately low self-monitoring

6–7 = Moderately high self-monitoring

8–10 = High self-monitoring

SOURCE: Excerpted and adapted from M Snyder and S Gangestad, "On the Nature of Self-Monitoring: Matters of Assessment, Matters of Validity," _Journal of Personality and Social Psychology_, July 1986, p 137.

Organizational Identification: A _Social_ Aspect of Self-Concept with Ethical Implications

The dividing line between self and others is not a neat and precise one. A certain amount of blurring occurs, for example, when an employee comes to define him- or herself with a _specific_ organization—a psychological process called _organizational identification_. According to an expert on this emerging OB topic, "**organizational identification** occurs when one comes to integrate beliefs about one's organization into one's identity."[43] Organizational identification goes to the heart of organizational culture and socialization (recall our discussion in Chapter 3).

Organizational identification
Organizational values or beliefs become part of one's self-identity.

Former Enron Employee Paid a Big Price for Her Organizational Identification

What did working at Enron do for [Phyllis] Anzalone? For one thing, it made her a lot of money, so much that the company's failure cost her about $1 million. More important, it made *her*. It took her from being a reasonably successful facilities-management salesperson from rural Louisiana and propelled her into the ranks of sales superstars. It changed her view of herself; it confirmed what she thought she could achieve. "Enron had a profound effect on my life," she says. "As devastating as it was, I'm glad I did it. It was like being on steroids every day."

And what does Anzalone think of the executives who ran Enron—and then ran it into the ground? "They are scum," she says, "They are crooks, and they are traitors. They betrayed many people's trust, including mine. Jeff Skilling [the firm's former CEO now facing federal charges] is lying. Every single employee at Enron knows he's lying."

SOURCE: Excerpted from C Fishman, "What if You'd Worked at Enron?" *Fast Company*, May 2002, pp 104, 106.

Managers put a good deal of emphasis today on organizational mission, philosophy, and values with the express intent of integrating the company into each employee's self-identity. Hopefully, as the logic goes, employees who identify closely with the organization will be more loyal, more committed, and harder working.[44] Some companies, such as consultant McKinsey & Company, go so far as to cultivate organizational identification among *former* employees through corporate alumni networks. Former employees who still identify strongly with the company are potential customers, as well as informal marketers and goodwill ambassadors.[45] As an extreme case in point, organizational identification among employees at Harley-Davidson's motorcycle factories is so strong many have had the company logo tattooed on their bodies.[46] Working at Harley is not just a job, it is a lifestyle. (Somehow, your authors have a hard time imagining an employee with a Pepsi or Burger King tattoo!)

A company tattoo may be a bit extreme, but the ethical implications of identifying too closely with one's employer are profound. Phyllis Anzalone, the former Enron employee profiled in Real World/Real People, is a good case in point. She admitted that Enron *was* her self-identity and she ended up with emotional scars. She seems to have distanced herself from Enron's most unsavory characters during her years with the company. But some of her colleagues, with equally strong organizational identification, evidently turned their backs on their personal ethical standards and values when working on clearly illegal deals. When employees suspend their critical thinking and lose their objectivity, unhealthy groupthink can occur and needed constructive conflict does *not* occur. (Groupthink is covered in Chapter 10 and functional conflict is discussed in Chapter 13.) Company loyalty and dedication are one thing, blind obedience is quite another.

Personality: Concepts and Controversy

Personality
Stable physical and mental characteristics responsible for a person's identity.

Individuals have their own way of thinking and acting, their own unique style or *personality*. **Personality** is defined as the combination of stable physical and mental characteristics that give the individual his or her identity.[47] These characteristics or traits—including how one looks, thinks, acts, and feels—are the product of interacting genetic and environmental influences. In this section, we introduce the Big Five personality dimensions, explore the proactive personality, issue some cautions about workplace personality testing, and examine an important personality factor called locus of control.

The Big Five Personality Dimensions

Decades of research produced cumbersome lists of personality traits. In fact, one recent study identified 1,710 English-language adjectives used to describe aspects of personality.[48] Fortunately, this confusing situation has been statistically distilled in recent years to the Big Five.[49] They are extraversion, agreeableness, conscientiousness, emotional stability, and openness to experience (see Table 5–2 for descriptions). Standardized personality tests determine how positively or negatively a person scores on each of the Big Five. For example, someone scoring negatively on extraversion would be an introverted person prone to shy and withdrawn behavior. Someone scoring negatively on emotional security would be nervous, tense, angry, and worried. Appropriately, the negative end of the emotional stability scale is labeled neuroticism. A person's scores on the Big Five reveal a personality profile as unique as his or her fingerprints.

But one important question lingers: Are personality models ethnocentric or unique to the culture in which they were developed? At least as far as the Big Five model goes, cross-cultural research evidence points in the direction of no. Specifically, the Big Five personality structure held up very well in one study of women and men from Russia, Canada, Hong Kong, Poland, Germany, and Finland and a second study (85% male) of South Korean managers and stockbrokers.[50] A recent comprehensive analysis of Big Five studies led the researchers to this conclusion: "To date, there is no compelling evidence that culture affects personality structure."[51]

Those interested in OB want to know the connection between the Big Five and job performance. Ideally, Big Five personality dimensions that correlate positively and strongly with job performance would be helpful in the selection, training, and appraisal of employees. A meta-analysis of 117 studies involving 23,994 subjects from many professions offers guidance.[52] Among the Big Five, *conscientiousness* had the strongest positive correlation with job performance and training performance. According to the researchers, "those individuals who exhibit traits associated with a strong sense of purpose, obligation, and persistence generally perform better than those who do not."[53] Another recent finding: Extraversion (an outgoing personality) correlated positively with promotions, salary level, and career satisfaction. And, as one might expect, neuroticism (low emotional stability) was associated with low career satisfaction.[54]

Table 5–2   *The Big Five Personality Dimensions*

Personality Dimension	Characteristics of a Person Scoring Positively on the Dimension
1. Extraversion	Outgoing, talkative, sociable, assertive
2. Agreeableness	Trusting, good-natured, cooperative, softhearted
3. Conscientiousness	Dependable, responsible, achievement oriented, persistent
4. Emotional stability	Relaxed, secure, unworried
5. Openness to experience	Intellectual, imaginative, curious, broad-minded

SOURCE: Adapted from M R Barrick and M K Mount, "Autonomy as a Moderator of the Relationships between the Big Five Personality Dimensions and Job Performance," *Journal of Applied Psychology*, February 1993, pp 111–18.

Cashing in on a Proactive Personality

BusinessWeek John Calamos got his first taste of investing as a teenager in the 1950s. His Greek immigrant parents' idea of saving was to squirrel away in a cigar box each silver dollar that passed over the counter of their Chicago grocery store. So it wasn't easy to persuade them to give him $5,000 to try his hand at the market. He bought a few growth stocks, with mixed results: Texas Instruments Inc. tripled in value, while Muntz TV went to zero. His parents, along with a dozen or so other relatives, were among his first clients when he set up shop in 1977. "Not losing your parents' money and not losing money for the people who trust you is paramount to investing," he says. If the firm ever loses sight of that maxim, the Calamos clan will likely have something to say about it.

SOURCE: A Carter, "From Mom and Pop to Megafund," *BusinessWeek*, April 25, 2005, p 102.

The Proactive Personality

Proactive personality
Action-oriented person who shows initiative and perseveres to change things.

As suggested by the above discussion, someone who scores high on the Big Five dimension of conscientiousness is probably a good worker. Thomas S Bateman and J Michael Crant took this important linkage an additional step by formulating the concept of the proactive personality. They define and characterize the **proactive personality** in these terms: "someone who is relatively unconstrained by situational forces and who effects environmental change. Proactive people identify opportunities and act on them, show initiative, take action, and persevere until meaningful change occurs."[55] In short, people with proactive personalities are "hardwired" to change the status quo. In a review of relevant studies, Crant recently found the proactive personality to be positively associated with individual, team, and organizational success.[56]

Successful entrepreneurs exemplify the proactive personality. John P Calamos Sr is an inspiring case in point. His conscientiousness and proactive personality enabled him to turn $5,000 into Calamos Asset Management Inc., a mutual fund company with $38.2 billion in assets (see Real World/Real People). People with proactive personalities truly are valuable *human capital,* as defined in Chapter 1. Those wanting to get ahead would do well to cultivate the initiative, drive, courage, and perseverance of someone with a proactive personality—and managers would do well to hire them.[57]

Issue: What about Personality Testing in the Workplace?

Personality testing as a tool for making decisions about hiring, training, and promotion is commonplace. "According to the Association of Test Publishers, overall employment testing, including personality tests, has been growing at a rate of 10% to 15% in each of the past three years."[58] On-the-job personality testing is questionable for four reasons. First is the issue of *predictive validity.* Can personality tests actually predict job performance? In the Big Five meta-analysis discussed earlier, conscientiousness may have been the best predictor of job performance, but it was *not a strong* predictor. Moreover, the most widely used personality test, the Minnesota Multiphasic Personality Inventory (MMPI), does not directly measure conscientiousness. No surprise that the MMPI and other popular personality tests historically have been poor predictors of job performance.[59]

Second is the issue of *differential validity,* relative to race. Do personality tests measure whites and minority races differently? We still do not have a definitive answer to this important and difficult question. Respected Big Five researchers concluded, "To date, the evidence indicates that differential validity is not typically associated with personality measures. Caution is required in interpreting this conclusion, however, in light of the small number of studies available."[60] Meanwhile, personality testing remains a lightening rod for controversy on the job.[61] In police departments, where psychological testing is routinely used supposedly to weed out racists, critics claim the opposite actually occurs. According to *The Wall Street Journal,* "many black police officers in particular remain skeptical, contending that the psychological evaluations are so subjective that they have been used to discriminate against minorities."[62]

A third issue involves *faking.* Both those who favor and disapprove of personality testing in the workplace generally agree that faking occurs. Faking involves intentionally misrepresenting one's true beliefs on a personality test. For instance, a test taker with knowledge of the proactive personality might want to improve her or his chances of landing a job by pretending to be a proactive person. The crux of the faking issue is this: To what extent does faking alter a personality test's *construct validity* (the degree to which the test actually measures what it is supposed to measure)? Recent research suggests faking is a threat to the construct validity of personality tests.[63]

Finally, there is the issue of *sloppy administration.* Annie Murphy Paul, author of the new book *The Cult of Personality,*[64] explains:

> You hear a lot from psychologists who are supportive of personality testing, and sometimes from testing companies, that there are ideal ways to use these tests. An example would be to bring in a psychologist to do a study of the job itself and design or tailor a test specifically for that position, and then have it administered by a psychologist, and have the results remain confidential. I think the way these tests are actually used is that they're usually bought off the shelf, they're given indiscriminately, often by people who aren't trained or qualified, and then the results aren't kept confidential or private at all. For all the talk about standards on how [these tests] should be used, the way they're used in the real world is more hit-or-miss.[65]

The practical tips in Table 5–3 can help managers avoid abuses and costly discrimination lawsuits when using personality and psychological testing for employment-related decisions. Another alternative for employers is to eliminate personality testing altogether. At Microsoft, where 12,000 résumés stream in every month, recruits are screened with challenging interviews but no psychological tests. When *Fortune* magazine asked David Pritchard, Microsoft's director of recruiting, about the standard practice of screening recruits with psychological tests, Pritchard replied, "It doesn't really interest me much. In the end, you end up with a bunch of people who answer the questions correctly, and that's not always what you want. How can a multiple-choice test tell whether someone is creative or not?"[66] The growing use of job-related skills testing and behavioral interviewing is an alternative to personality testing.

Issue: Why Not Just Forget about Personality?

Personality testing problems and unethical applications do not automatically cancel out the underlying concepts. Present and future managers need to know about personality traits and characteristics, despite the controversy over personality testing. Rightly or wrongly used,

Table 5–3   *Advice and Words of Caution about Personality Testing in the Workplace*

Researchers, test developers, and organizations that administer personality assessments offer the following suggestions for getting started or for evaluating whether tests already in use are appropriate for forecasting job performance:

- Determine what you hope to accomplish. If you are looking to find the best fit of job and applicant, analyze the aspects of the position that are most critical for it.
- Look for outside help to determine if a test exists or can be developed to screen applicants for the traits that best fit the position. Industrial psychologists, professional organizations, and a number of Internet sites provide resources.
- Insist that any test recommended by a consultant or vendor be validated scientifically for the specific purpose that you have defined. Vendors should be able to cite some independent, credible research supporting a test's correlation with job performance.
- Ask the test provider to document the legal basis for any assessment: Is it fair? Is it job-related? Is it biased against any racial or ethnic group? Does it violate an applicant's right to privacy under state or federal laws? Vendors should provide a lawyer's statement that a test does not adversely affect any protected class, and employers may want to get their own lawyer's opinion, as well.
- Make sure that every staff member who will be administering tests or analyzing results is educated about how to do so properly and keeps results confidential. Use the scores on personality tests in tandem with other factors that you believe are essential to the job—such as skills and experience—to create a comprehensive evaluation of the merits of each candidate, and apply those criteria identically to each applicant.

SOURCE: S Bates, "Personality Counts," *HR Magazine*, February 2002, p 34. Reprinted with the permission of HR Magazine, published by the Society for Human Resource Management, Alexandria, VA.

the term *personality* is routinely encountered both on and off the job. Knowledge of the Big Five and the proactive personality encourages more precise understanding of the rich diversity among today's employees. Good management involves taking the time to get to know *each* employee's *unique combination* of personality, abilities, and potential and then creating a productive and satisfying person–job fit.

Let us take a look at locus of control, another important job-related personality factor.

Locus of Control: Self or Environment?

Individuals vary in terms of how much personal responsibility they take for their behavior and its consequences. Julian Rotter, a personality researcher, identified a dimension of personality he labeled *locus of control* to explain these differences. He proposed that people tend to attribute the causes of their behavior primarily to either themselves or environmental factors.[67] This personality trait produces distinctly different behavior patterns.

People who believe they control the events and consequences that affect their lives are said to possess an **internal locus of control.** For example, such a person tends to attribute positive outcomes, such as getting a passing grade on an exam, to her or his own abilities. Similarly, an "internal" tends to blame negative events, such as failing an exam, on personal shortcomings—not studying hard enough, perhaps. Many entrepreneurs eventually succeed because their internal locus of control helps them overcome setbacks and disappointments. They see themselves as masters of their own fate and not simply lucky.[68] But, as

Internal locus of control
Attributing outcomes to one's own actions.

OB Exercise — Where Is Your Locus of Control?

Julian B. Rotter is the developer of a forced-choice 29-item scale for measuring an individual's degree of internal and external control. This I-E test is widely used. The following sample items are from an earlier version of the test and not in the final version. Put an X by your preferred option from each pair of statements and follow the scoring instructions below:

I more strongly believe that:

Or:

1. Promotions are earned through hard work and persistence

Making a lot of money is largely a matter of getting the right breaks.

2. The number of divorces indicates that more and more people are not trying to make their marriages work.

Marriage is largely a gamble.

3. When I am right I can convince others.

It is silly to think that one can really change another person's basic attitudes.

4. In my case the grades I make are the results of my own efforts, luck has little or nothing to do with it.

Sometimes I feel that I have little to do with the grades I get.

5. People like me can change the course of world affairs if we make ourselves heard.

It is only wishful thinking to believe that one can really influence what happens in society at large.

6. I am the master of my fate.

A great deal that happens to me is probably a matter of chance.

7. Getting along with people is a skill that must be practiced.

It is almost impossible to figure out how to please some people.

Scoring: Score 1 point for each X in the left-hand column.

Arbitrary norms for this exercise are: external locus of control = 1–3; balanced internal and external locus of control = 4; internal locus of control = 5–7.

SOURCE: Julian B Rotter, "Internal Control–External Control." Reprinted with permission from *Psychology Today,* Copyright © 1971 www.psychologytoday.com.

Fortune's Jaclyn Fierman humorously noted, luck is a matter of interpretation and not always a bad thing:

> For those of us who believe we are the masters of our fate, the captains of our soul, the notion that a career might hinge on random events is unthinkable. Self-made men and women are especially touchy on this subject. If they get all the breaks, it's because they're smarter and harder working than everyone else. If they know the right people, it's because they network the nights away. Luck? Many successful people think it diminishes them.
>
> Hard workers do get ahead, no doubt about it. . . . But then there are folks like Ringo Starr. One day he was an obscure drummer of limited talent from Liverpool; the next day he was a Beatle.
>
> Nobody demonstrates better than Ringo that true luck is accidental, not inevitable.[69]

On the other side of this personality dimension are those who believe their performance is the product of circumstances beyond their immediate control. These individuals are said to possess an **external locus of control** and tend to attribute outcomes to environmental causes, such as luck or fate. Unlike someone with an internal locus of control, an "external" would attribute a passing grade on an exam to something external (an easy test or a good day) and attribute a failing grade to an unfair test or problems at home. A shortened version of an instrument Rotter developed to measure one's locus of control is presented in the OB Exercise. Where is your locus of control: internal, external, or a combination?

External locus of control
Attributing outcomes to circumstances beyond one's control.

Research Findings on Locus of Control

Researchers have found important behavioral differences between internals and externals:

- Internals display greater work motivation.
- Internals have stronger expectations that effort leads to performance.
- Internals exhibit higher performance on tasks involving learning or problem solving, when performance leads to valued rewards.
- There is a stronger relationship between job satisfaction and performance for internals than externals.
- Internals obtain higher salaries and greater salary increases than externals.
- Externals tend to be more anxious than internals.[70]

Tempering an Internal Locus of Control with *Humility*

Do you have an internal locus of control? Odds are high that you do, judging from the "typical" OB student we have worked with over the years. Good thing, because it should pay off in the workplace with opportunities, raises, and promotions. But before you declare yourself Grade A executive material, here is one more thing to toss into your tool kit: a touch of humility. **Humility** is "a realistic assessment of one's own contribution and the recognition of the contribution of others, along with luck and good fortune that made one's own success possible."[71] Humility has been called the silent virtue. How many truly humble people brag about being humble? Two OB experts recently offered this instructive perspective:

Humility

Considering the contributions of others and good fortune when gauging one's success.

> Humble individuals have a down-to-earth perspective of themselves and of the events and relationships in their lives. Humility involves a capability to evaluate success, failure, work, and life without exaggeration. Furthermore, humility enables leaders to distinguish the delicate line between such characteristics as healthy self-confidence, self-esteem, and self-assessment, and those of over-confidence, narcissism, and stubbornness. Humility is the mid-point between the two negative extremes of arrogance and lack of self-esteem. This depiction allows one to see that a person can be humble and competitive or humble and ambitious at the same time, which contradicts common—but mistaken—views about humility.[72]

We now shift our focus to abilities and intelligence.

Abilities (Intelligence) and Performance

Ability

Stable characteristic responsible for a person's maximum physical or mental performance.

Skill

Specific capacity to manipulate objects.

Individual differences in abilities and accompanying skills are a central concern for managers because nothing can be accomplished without appropriately skilled personnel. An **ability** represents a broad and stable characteristic responsible for a person's maximum—as opposed to typical—performance on mental and physical tasks. A **skill,** on the other hand, is the specific capacity to physically manipulate objects. Consider this difference as you imagine yourself being the only passenger on a small commuter airplane in which the pilot has just passed out. As the plane nose-dives, your effort and abilities will not be enough to save yourself and the pilot if you do not possess flying skills. As shown in Figure 5–3 successful performance (be it landing an airplane or performing any other job) depends on the right combination of effort, ability, and skill.

Figure 5–3 *Performance Depends on the Right Combination of Effort, Ability, and Skill*

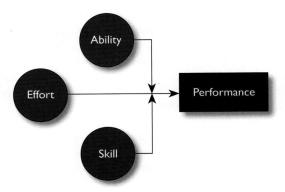

Abilities and skills are getting a good deal of attention in management circles these days. The more encompassing term *competencies* is typically used. According to the head of a New Jersey consulting firm,

> In the past decade, thousands of organizations throughout the world have joined the quest for competencies. Often, they spend a year or more conducting competency studies— identifying "clusters" of knowledge, attitudes, and skills needed to perform various jobs. The competencies turned up by these studies become the basis for decisions about hiring, training, promotions, and other human resource issues.[73]

Among the many desirable competencies are oral communication, initiative, decisiveness, tolerance, problem solving, adaptability, and resilience.[74] Importantly, our cautions about on-the-job personality testing extend to ability, intelligence, and competency testing and certification.

Before moving on, we need to say something about a modern-day threat to abilities, skills, and general competence. That threat, according to public health officials, is *sleep deprivation.*[75]

In a recent survey of 1,506 adults in the United States, only 49% reported getting a "good night's sleep" every night or almost every night.[76] If you are routinely short-changing your basic sleep needs, you are likely to be less effective and more stressed (see Chapter 18) than you should be. Habitually sleep-deprived people need to be aware of this stunning fact: "Staying awake 24 hours impairs cognitive psychomotor performance to the same degree as having a 0.1 percent blood alcohol level. . . . That is above many states' legal driving limits."[77]

The balance of this section explores intelligence, specific cognitive abilities, and the controversial idea of multiple intelligences.

Intelligence and Cognitive Abilities

Although experts do not agree on a specific definition, **intelligence** represents an individual's capacity for constructive thinking, reasoning, and problem solving.[78] Historically, intelligence was believed to be an innate capacity, passed genetically from one generation to the next. Research since has shown, however, that intelligence (like personality) also is a function of environmental influences.[79] Organic factors have more recently been added to the formula as a result of mounting evidence of the connection between alcohol and drug abuse by pregnant women and intellectual development problems in their children.[80]

Intelligence
Capacity for constructive thinking, reasoning, problem solving.

Researchers have produced some interesting findings about abilities and intelligence in recent years. A unique five-year study documented the tendency of people to "gravitate into jobs commensurate with their abilities."[81] This prompts the vision of the labor market acting as a giant sorting or shifting machine, with employees tumbling into various ability bins. Meanwhile, a steady and significant rise in average intelligence among those in developed countries has been observed over the last 70 years. Why? Experts at an American Psychological Association conference concluded, "Some combination of better schooling, improved socioeconomic status, healthier nutrition, and a more technologically complex society might account for the gains in IQ scores."[82] So if you think you're smarter than your parents and your teachers, you're probably right!

Two Types of Abilities   Human intelligence has been studied predominantly through the empirical approach. By examining the relationships between measures of mental abilities and behavior, researchers have statistically isolated major components of intelligence. Using this empirical procedure, pioneering psychologist Charles Spearman proposed in 1927 that all cognitive performance is determined by two types of abilities. The first can be characterized as a general mental ability needed for *all* cognitive tasks. The second is unique to the task at hand.[83] For example, an individual's ability to complete crossword puzzles is a function of his or her broad mental abilities as well as the specific ability to perceive patterns in partially completed words.

Seven Major Mental Abilities   Through the years, much research has been devoted to developing and expanding Spearman's ideas on the relationship between cognitive abilities and intelligence. One research psychologist listed 120 distinct mental abilities. Table 5–4 contains definitions of the seven most frequently cited mental abilities. Of the seven abilities, personnel selection researchers have found verbal ability, numerical ability, spatial ability, and inductive reasoning to be valid predictors of job performance for both minority and majority applicants.[84]

Table 5–4   *Mental Abilities Underlying Performance*

Ability	Description
1. Verbal comprehension	The ability to understand what words mean and to readily comprehend what is read.
2. Word fluency	The ability to produce isolated words that fulfill specific symbolic or structural requirements (such as all words that begin with the letter *b* and have two vowels).
3. Numerical	The ability to make quick and accurate arithmetic computations such as adding and subtracting.
4. Spatial	Being able to perceive spatial patterns and to visualize how geometric shapes would look if transformed in shape or position.
5. Memory	Having good rote memory for paired words, symbols, lists of numbers, or other associated items.
6. Perceptual speed	The ability to perceive figures, identify similarities and differences, and carry out tasks involving visual perception.
7. Inductive reasoning	The ability to reason from specifics to general conclusions.

SOURCE: Adapted from MD Dunnette, "Aptitudes, Abilities, and Skills," in *Handbook of Industrial and Organizational Psychology*, ed MD Dunnette (Skokie, IL: RandMcNally, 1976), pp 478–83. Copyright © 1976. Used with permission of the author.

Do We Have Multiple Intelligences?

Howard Gardner, a professor at Harvard's Graduate School of Education, offered a new paradigm for human intelligence in his 1983 book *Frames of Mind: The Theory of Multiple Intelligences.*[85] He has subsequently identified eight different intelligences that vastly broaden the long-standing concept of intelligence. Gardner's concept of multiple intelligences (MI) includes not only cognitive abilities but social and physical abilities and skills as well:

- *Linguistic intelligence:* potential to learn and use spoken and written languages.
- *Logical-mathematical intelligence:* potential for deductive reasoning, problem analysis, and mathematical calculation.
- *Musical intelligence:* potential to appreciate, compose, and perform music.
- *Bodily-kinesthetic intelligence:* potential to use mind and body to coordinate physical movement.
- *Spatial intelligence:* potential to recognize and use patterns.
- *Intrapersonal intelligence:* potential to understand, connect with, and effectively work with others.
- *Intrapersonal intelligence:* potential to understand and regulate oneself.
- *Naturalist intelligence:* potential to live in harmony with one's environment.[86]

Many educators and parents have embraced MI because it helps explain how a child could score poorly on a standard IQ test yet be obviously gifted in one or more ways (e.g., music, sports, relationship building). Moreover, they believe the concept of MI underscores the need to help each child develop in his or her own unique way and at his or her own pace. They say standard IQ tests deal only with the first two intelligences on Gardner's list. Meanwhile, most academic psychologists and intelligence specialists continue to criticize Gardner's model as too subjective and poorly integrated. They prefer the traditional model of intelligence as a unified variable measured by a single test.

While the academic debate continues, we can draw some practical benefits from Gardner's notion of MI. Already, in Chapter 4, we discussed *cultural intelligence.* In the final section of this chapter, you will encounter the concept of *emotional intelligence.* Yale's Robert J Sternberg recently applied Gardner's "naturalist intelligence" to the domain of leadership under the heading *practical intelligence.* He explains,

> Practical intelligence is the ability to solve everyday problems by utilizing knowledge gained from experience in order to purposefully adapt to, shape, and select environments. It thus involves changing oneself to suit the environment (adaptation), changing the environment to suit

"Enough with the Beethoven, Mom! How about some Usher or Black Eyed Peas?" Some parents strive to develop their baby's multiple intelligences by exposing them to unconventional stimuli. Research tells us the vote is still out on whether or not they are wasting their time. Hmmm. Come to think of it, Tiger Woods' Dad had him playing golf at a very young age.

oneself (shaping), or finding a new environment within which to work (selection). One uses these skills to (a) manage oneself, (b) manage others, and (c) manage tasks.[87]

Others believe MI has important implications for employee selection and training.[88] One-size-fits-all training programs fall short when MI diversity is taken into consideration. We look forward to exciting breakthroughs in this area as MI attracts OB researchers and practicing managers.

Emotions: An Emerging OB Topic

In the ideal world of management theory, employees pursue organizational goals in a logical and rational manner. Emotional behavior seldom is factored into the equation.[89] Yet day-to-day organizational life shows us how prevalent and powerful emotions can be. Anger and jealousy, both potent emotions, often push aside logic and rationality in the workplace. Managers use fear and other emotions to both motivate and intimidate. For example, consider Microsoft CEO Steve Ballmer's management style prior to his recent efforts to become a kinder, gentler leader: "Ballmer shouts when he gets excited or angry—his voice rising so suddenly that it's like an electric shock. . . . By the early 1990s, Ballmer had to have throat surgery to fix problems brought on by shouting."[90]

Less noisy, but still emotion laden, is John Chambers's tightrope act as CEO of Cisco Systems:

> Any company that thinks it's utterly unbeatable is already beaten. So when I begin to think we're getting a little bit too confident, you'll see me emphasizing the paranoia side. And then when I feel that there's a little bit too much fear and apprehension, I'll just jump back to the other side. My job is to keep those scales perfectly balanced.[91]

These admired corporate leaders would not have achieved what they have without the ability to be logical and rational decision makers *and* be emotionally charged. Too much emotion, however, could have spelled career and organizational disaster for either of them.

In this final section, our examination of individual differences turns to defining emotions, reviewing a typology of 10 positive and negative emotions, exploring emotional intelligence and maturity, and focusing on the interesting topics or emotional contagion and emotional labor.

Positive and Negative Emotions

Emotions
Complex human reactions to personal achievements and setbacks that may be felt and displayed.

Richard S Lazarus, a leading authority on the subject, defines **emotions** as "complex, patterned, organismic reactions to how we think we are doing in our lifelong efforts to survive and flourish and to achieve what we wish for ourselves."[92] The word *organismic* is appropriate because emotions involve the *whole* person—biological, psychological, and social. Importantly, psychologists draw a distinction between *felt* and *displayed* emotions.[93] For example, a person might feel angry (felt emotion) at a rude co-worker but not make a nasty remark in return (displayed emotion). As discussed in Chapter 18, emotions play roles in both causing and adapting to stress and its associated biological and psychological problems. The destructive effect of emotional behavior on social relationships is all too obvious in daily life.[94]

Lazarus's definition of emotions centers on a person's goals. Accordingly, his distinction between positive and negative emotions is goal oriented. Some emotions are triggered by frustration and failure when pursuing one's goals. Lazarus calls these *negative* emotions.

They are said to be goal incongruent. For example, which of the six negative emotions in Figure 5–4 are you likely to experience if you fail the final exam in a required course? Failing the exam would be incongruent with your goal of graduating on time. On the other hand, which of the four *positive* emotions in Figure 5–4 would you probably experience if you graduated on time and with honors? The emotions you would experience in this situation are positive because they are congruent (or consistent) with an important lifetime goal. The individual's goals, it is important to note, may or may not be socially acceptable. Thus, a positive emotion, such as love/affection, may be undesirable if associated with sexual harassment. Oppositely, slight pangs of guilt, anxiety, and envy can motivate extra effort. On balance, the constructive or destructive nature of a particular emotion must be judged in terms of both its intensity and the person's relevant goal.[95]

For a dramatic real-life example of the interplay between negative and positive emotions, consider the situation Kenneth I Chenault faced just 10 months after becoming CEO of American Express. The September 11, 2001, terrorist attacks claimed the lives of 11 employees, and the firm's headquarters building, across the street from ground zero in Lower Manhattan, had to be abandoned for what turned out to be eight months of repairs.

> Chenault gathered 5,000 American Express employees at the Paramount Theater in New York on September 20 for a highly emotional "town hall meeting." During the session, Chenault demonstrated the poise, compassion, and decisiveness that vaulted him to the top. He told employees that he had been filled with such despair, sadness, and anger that he had seen a counselor. Twice, he rushed to spontaneously embrace grief-stricken employees. Chenault said he would donate $1 million of the company's profits to the families of the AmEx victims. "I represent the best company and the best people in the world," he concluded. "In fact, you are my strength, and I love you."[96]

Figure 5–4   *Positive and Negative Emotions*

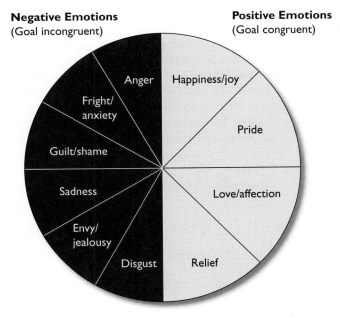

SOURCE: Adapted from discussion in R S Lazarus, *Emotion and Adaptation* (New York: Oxford University Press, 1991), Chs. 6, 7.

Talk about baptism by fire. Just 10 months after being named CEO of American Express, Kenneth I Chenault addressed 5,000 of his co-workers in an emotional meeting to begin the healing process following the September 11, 2001, terrorist attacks. The tragedy claimed the lives of 11 AmEx employees and closed the firm's New York headquarters for eight months of repairs. Chenault, seen here presiding over AmEx's May 13, 2002, headquarters homecoming celebration, reportedly handled the post-9/11 meeting with great skill and compassion.

Emotional intelligence

Ability to manage oneself and interact with others in mature and constructive ways.

Thus, Chenault masterfully used positive emotions to cope with profound negative emotions.

Developing Emotional Intelligence

People cope with powerful emotions in lots of different ways. Take Taryn Rose, for example. She followed in her physician father's footsteps by attending medical school. However, near the end of her residency, she was bitten by the entrepreneurial bug and set her sights on developing and selling stylish shoes that would not ruin women's feet. But she did not want to disappoint her family. "I feared regret more than I feared failure,"[97] she recalled for *Fast Company* magazine, so she followed her dream. Now that she is the CEO of her own $20-million-a-year company, her family understands. For Taryn Rose, it took a good idea and determination to conquer her fears. Another way to deal effectively with fear and other emotions is to become more emotionally mature by developing emotional intelligence.

In 1995, Daniel Goleman, a psychologist turned journalist, created a stir in education and management circles with the publication of his book *Emotional Intelligence*. Hence, an obscure topic among psychologists became mainstream. Building upon Howard Gardner's concept of interpersonal intelligence, Goleman criticizes the traditional model of intelligence (IQ) for being too narrow, thus failing to consider interpersonal competence. Goleman's broader agenda includes "abilities such as being able to motivate oneself and persist in the face of frustrations; to control impulse and delay gratification; to regulate one's moods and keep distress from swamping the ability to think; to empathize and to hope."[98] Thus, **emotional intelligence** is the ability to manage oneself and one's relationships in mature and constructive ways. Referred to by some as EI and others as EQ, emotional intelligence is said to have four key components: self-awareness, self-management, social awareness, and relationship management. The first two constitute *personal competence;* the second two feed into *social competence* (see Table 5–5).

As an integrated package, the proactive personality discussed earlier and the characteristics listed in Table 5–5 constitute a challenging self-development agenda for each of us. Indeed, Goleman and his followers believe greater emotional intelligence can boost individual, team, and organizational effectiveness[99] (see Real World/Real People on p 164).

Practical Research Insights about Emotional Contagion and Emotional Labor

Two streams of OB research on emotions are beginning to yield interesting and instructive insights:

- *Emotional contagion.* Have you ever had someone's bad mood sour your mood? That person could have been a parent, supervisor, co-worker, friend, or someone serving you in a store or restaurant. Appropriately, researchers call this *emotional contagion*. We,

Table 5–5   *Developing Personal and Social Competence through Emotional Intelligence*

Personal Competence: These capabilities determine how we manage ourselves.
Self-Awareness
- *Emotional self-awareness:* Reading one's own emotions and recognizing their impact; using "gut sense" to guide decisions.
- *Accurate self-assessment:* Knowing one's strengths and limits.
- *Self-confidence:* A sound sense of one's self-worth and capabilities.

Self-Management
- *Emotional self-control:* Keeping disruptive emotions and impulses under control.
- *Transparency:* Displaying honesty and integrity; trustworthiness.
- *Adaptability:* Flexibility in adapting to changing situations or overcoming obstacles.
- *Achievement:* The drive to improve performance to meet inner standards of excellence.
- *Initiative:* Readiness to act and seize opportunities.
- *Optimism:* Seeing the upside in events.

Social Competence: These capabilities determine how we manage relationships.
Social Awareness
- *Empathy:* Sensing others' emotions, understanding their perspective, and taking active interest in their concerns.
- *Organizational awareness:* Reading the currents, decision networks, and politics at the organizational level.
- *Service:* Recognizing and meeting follower, client, or customer needs.

Relationship Management
- *Inspirational leadership:* Guiding and motivating with a compelling vision.
- *Influence:* Wielding a range of tactics for persuasion.
- *Developing others:* Bolstering others' abilities through feedback and guidance.
- *Change catalyst:* Initiating, managing, and leading in a new direction.
- *Conflict management:* Resolving disagreements.
- *Building bonds:* Cultivating and maintaining a web of relationships.
- *Teamwork and collaboration:* Cooperation and team building.

SOURCE: D Goleman, R Boyatzis, and A McKee, *Primal Leadership: Realizing the Power of Emotional Intelligence* (Boston: Harvard Business School Press, 2002), p 39. Copyright © 2002 by the Harvard Business School Publishing Corporation; All rights reserved.

quite literally, can catch another person's bad mood or displayed negative emotions. This effect was documented in a recent study of 131 bank tellers (92% female) and 220 exit interviews with their customers. Tellers who expressed positive emotions tended to have more satisfied customers.[100] Two field studies with nurses and accountants as subjects found a strong linkage between the work group's collective mood and the individual's mood.[101] Both foul moods and good moods turned out to be contagious. Perhaps more managers should follow the lead of this German executive:

> After arriving at his Munich office in the morning, Ulrich Schumacher likes to pop a CD into a player on his desk and blast a track by singer James Brown. Nothing like the godfather of soul shouting "I feel good!" to get a manager psyched up for the day ahead, says Schumacher, 43, CEO of German semiconductor maker Infineon Technologies.[102]

- *Emotional labor.* Although they did not have the benefit of a catchy label or a body of sophisticated research, generations of managers have known about the power of emotional contagion in the marketplace. "Smile, look happy for the customers"

Emotional Intelligence Keeps These Executives on an Even Keel

Steve Murphy, president and CEO, Rodale Inc., publisher of magazines such as *Prevention* and *Runner's World:*

> All great executives need to be ambidextrous. They need to have IQ and EQ in equal measure. Creativity and discipline.

Vanessa Wittman, the chief financial officer called in to rescue Adelphia Communications Corp., the scandal-ridden and bankrupt cable company:

> The creditors ... demanded a plan for Adelphia to emerge from bankruptcy as a standalone entity. Wittman didn't let the banks dictate terms for exit financing but instead held an auction. She was able to raise $8.8 billion for Adelphia from four banks without any upfront fees. In meeting after meeting, no matter how heated the discussions, Wittman often disarmed attendees with an ability to keep her cool. "I want to go for the jugular," says one outside lawyer, "and she just keeps a poker face."

SOURCES: P B Brown, "What I Know Now," *Fast Company,* May 2005, p 104; and T Lowry, "The CFO behind Adelphia's Rescue," *BusinessWeek,* April 11, 2005, p 69.

Adelphia CFO Vanessa Wittman

"No, the computers are up. We're down."

employees are told over and over. But what if the employee is having a rotten day? What if they have to mask their true feelings and emotions? What if they have to fake it? Researchers have begun studying the dynamics of what they call *emotional labor.* A pair of authors, one from Australia the other from the United States, recently summarized the research lessons to date:

> Emotional labor can be particularly detrimental to the employee performing the labor and can take its toll both psychologically and physically. Employees ... may bottle up feelings of frustration, resentment, and anger, which are not appropriate to express. These feelings result, in part, from the constant requirement to monitor one's negative emotions and express positive ones. If not given a healthy expressive outlet, this emotional repression can lead to a syndrome of emotional exhaustion and burnout.[103]

Interestingly, a pair of laboratory studies with US college students as subjects found no gender difference in *felt* emotions. But the women were more emotionally *expressive* than the men.[104] This stream of research on emotional labor has major practical implications for productivity and job satisfaction, as well as for workplace anger, aggression, and violence. Clearly, managers need to be attuned to (and responsive to) the emotional states and needs of their people.[105] This requires emotional intelligence.

Summary of Key Concepts

1. *Define self-esteem, and explain how it can be improved with Branden's six pillars of self-esteem.* Self-esteem is how people perceive themselves as physical, social, and spiritual beings. Branden's six pillars of self-esteem are live consciously, be self-accepting, take personal responsibility, be self-assertive, live purposefully, and have personal integrity.

2. *Define self-efficacy, and explain its sources.* Self-efficacy involves one's belief about his or her ability to accomplish specific tasks. Those extremely low in self-efficacy suffer from learned helplessness. Four sources of self-efficacy beliefs are prior experience, behavior models, persuasion from others, and assessment of one's physical and emotional states. High self-efficacy beliefs foster constructive and goal-oriented action, whereas low self-efficacy fosters passive, failure-prone activities and emotions.

3. *Contrast high and low self-monitoring individuals, and discuss the ethical implications of organizational identification.* A high self-monitor strives to make a good public impression by closely monitoring his or her behavior and adapting it to the situation. Very high self-monitoring can create a "chameleon" who is seen as insincere and dishonest. Low self-monitors do the opposite by acting out their momentary feelings, regardless of their surroundings. Very low self-monitoring can lead to a one-way communicator who seems to ignore verbal and nonverbal cues from others. People who supplant their own identity with that of their organization run the risk of blind obedience and groupthink because of a failure to engage in critical thinking and not being objective about what they are asked to do.

4. *Identify and describe the Big Five personality dimensions, and specify which one is correlated most strongly with job performance.* The Big Five personality dimensions are extraversion (social and talkative), agreeableness (trusting and cooperative), conscientiousness (responsible and persistent), emotional stability (relaxed and unworried), and openness to experience (intellectual and curious). Conscientiousness is the best predictor of job performance.

5. *Describe the proactive personality, and explain the need to balance an internal locus of control with humility.* Someone with a proactive personality shows initiative, takes action, and perseveres to bring about change. People with an internal locus of control, such as entrepreneurs, believe they are masters of their own fate. Humility helps "internals" factor the contributions of others and good fortune into their perceived success.

6. *Identify at least five of Gardner's eight multiple intelligences, and explain "practical intelligence."* Harvard's Howard Gardner broadens the traditional cognitive abilities model of intelligence to include social and physical abilities. His eight multiple intelligences include: linguistic, logical-mathematical, musical, bodily-kinesthetic, spatial, interpersonal, intrapersonal, and naturalist. Someone with practical intelligence, according to Sternberg, is good at solving everyday problems and learning from experience by adapting to the environment, reshaping their environment, and selecting new environments in which to work.

7. *Distinguish between positive and negative emotions, and explain how they can be judged.* Positive emotions—happiness/joy, pride, love/affection, and relief—are personal reactions to circumstances congruent with one's goals. Negative emotions—anger, fright/anxiety, guilt/shame, sadness, envy/jealousy, and disgust—are personal reactions to circumstances incongruent with one's goals. Both types of emotions need to be judged in terms of intensity and the appropriateness of the person's relevant goal.

8. *Identify the four key components of emotional intelligence, and discuss the practical significance of emotional contagion and emotional labor.* Goleman's model says the four components are self-awareness, self-management, social awareness, and relationship management. People can, in fact, catch another person's good or bad moods and expressed emotions, much as they would catch a contagious disease. Managers and others in the workplace need to avoid spreading counterproductive emotions. People in service jobs who are asked to suppress their own negative emotions and display positive emotions, regardless of their true feelings at the time, pay a physical and mental price for their emotional labor. Managers who are not mindful of emotional labor may experience lower productivity, reduced job satisfaction, and possibly aggression and even violence.

Discussion Questions

1. How should the reality of a more diverse workforce affect management's approach to dealing with individual differences?

2. What is your personal experience with high and low self-esteem people?

3. How is someone you know with low self-efficacy, relative to a specified task, "programming themselves for failure?" What could be done to help that individual develop high self-efficacy?

4. What are the career implications of your self-monitoring score in the OB Exercise on page 149?

5. Why is organizational identification both a good and bad thing in today's workplace?

6. On scales of low = 1 to high = 10, how would you rate yourself on the Big Five personality dimensions? Is your personality profile suitable for a managerial position?

7. How would you respond to the following statement? "Whenever possible, managers should hire people with an external locus of control."

8. How would you describe someone you know who has "practical" intelligence?

9. What are your personal experiences with negative emotions being positive and positive emotions being negative?

10. How would you rate your emotional intelligence and what steps could you take to improve it?

OB in Action Case Study

What Drives Sherri Heckenast?[106]

As she watched the auction unfold, Sherri Heckenast's heart was racing. She had traveled [in 2004] from Chicago to rural Kentucky with high hopes. Kentucky Lake Motor Speedway, a dirt oval track outside Paducah, was on the block. But once the bidding began, her chances looked slim.

"Going once!" called the auctioneer.

She had persuaded her wary father, a high-school dropout who had built a successful auto-parts company, to put up the money. His limit was $1.4 million. At the auction, he let the other bidders push the price to seven figures without a peep—$1.2 million . . . then $1.4 million.

"Going twice!"

Investing in a track was risky, her father had warned her. The previous owners of Kentucky Lake had gone bankrupt. Still, it was her dream. Thanks to her father, a lifelong driver in racing's minor leagues, she had been throttle-stomping since her teens, leaving boys in her dust. Recently, however, back injuries had forced her to scale back. Her father wanted her to quit, but she couldn't. "Racing's in my blood," she says. Maybe operating a track would be enough, she told him.

"One point four five."

Frank Heckenast's only bid—$1.45 million—came just in time.

True, Sherri Heckenast, who's 30, is younger than other track operators. And true, she's one of the few women running the show in a largely male-dominated sport. But what's equally impressive is her day job: CEO of the family's $30 million company. A-Reliable Auto Parts, located in Blue Island, Illinois, is one of the largest car and truck recyclers in the Midwest. It buys used cars at auction, dismantles them, and sells the parts.

Heckenast's two passions, business and racing, continually fuel each other. On the track, she speeds as fast as 150 miles per hour; off the track, she still operates at full throttle. Before buying Kentucky Lake, she put in 10-hour workdays, then headed to her uncle's race shop to work on her car. Now she drives to Kentucky every other weekend. "I've always been in my dad's shadow," she says. At the company, in the race shop, and on the track. "Kentucky Lake is about finding something that can be mine."

Sherri Heckenast practically grew up at Santa Fe Speedway outside Chicago. When she was just 5, she was using an electric wrench to help change the tires on her father's No. 99 race car. At 16, she bought a cheap 1986 Ford Mustang, stripped off the glass and chrome and painted "99" on the doors. Within a couple of years, she advanced from stock cars to late-model racing. The 800-horsepower engines are not far behind those in the big leagues, NASCAR's Nextel Cup, but the speeds are slower because the tracks are shorter and made of dirt, which has less traction than pavement.

Heckenast was the only woman in the field, but insists she wasn't intimidated. She was just another racer—with long blond hair, fresh lipstick, and a penchant for pink. Her No. 99 car is hot pink with "Bad Ass Barbie" on the hood and "U Go Girl" on the rear spoiler. In 2000, she completed in the Northern Allstars, a top late-model series in the Midwest. Using a semi, she hauled her car to a different race every week for eight months and finished second in the rookie-of-the-year points race. The only thing holding her back from a shot at the big time was her other career. Behind the wheel of No. 99 was the 25-year-old general manager of a growing company. "My dad always taught me that business comes first," she says.

She didn't plan to work at A-Reliable, much less run it. She was studying to become a court reporter when her father had quadruple-bypass surgery in 1995. She took a semester off to help out at the business and never left. To the astonishment of the almost entirely male clientele (and staff, for that matter), she knew cars inside and out. After a year, she was generating $100,000 in monthly sales, nearly double the previous high for one rep. Five days before her 23rd birthday, Frank named her general manager. Five years later, she took the wheel as CEO, freeing her father to oversee auctions and acquire other companies. "It was the same with business and racing. She earned respect," he says.

Just as she's forever tweaking the 99 car, Sherri enjoys finding ways to improve A-Reliable, modernizing a company that was proudly low tech. Employees used to remove as many reusable parts as they could find on a vehicle. Although there was little demand for most of them, they filled the warehouse. Using software, Sherri focused on the best-selling and most-profitable parts, particularly engines and transmissions. Another recent change is bar-coding, so that products are easier to locate. "I'm old school," says Frank, 48, who has yet to use email. "She's new school. She's got computers running computers. I don't know what it all is, but it works." Over the past five years, A-Reliable's annual revenue has doubled.

These days, Heckenast is trying to apply her business savvy to Kentucky Lake Motor Speedway. She longs to re-create the appeal of the old Santa Fe, with bigger purses, crowds, and sponsors. "I want to take the leap I took with A-Reliable," she says. "I've always been the kind of person who wants to do something big, or I don't want to do it." According to

NASCAR, there are about 900 short tracks in North America, and many struggle to make money. Just as not all baseball fans follow the minor leagues, not all 75 million NASCAR fans follow short track.

Heckenast has some advantages, though. Kentucky Lake sits on 600 acres and is considered a miniature NASCAR-caliber speedway. The founders spent more than $5 million to build the track, which is centrally located within three hours of St. Louis, Nashville, and Louisville. Heckenast hopes to put Kentucky Lake back on the map with a race . . . called The 99. The purse, to be divided among the drivers, is $99,000—three times the typical payout. She believes the money will attract the best drivers, who will attract sponsors, fans, and TV cameras. "I'm going out on a limb and putting on a big spectacle," she says.

Chalk it up to some timeless racing advice her father once passed along: Drive your own race, not anybody else's.

Questions for Discussion

1. How would you explain Sherri Heckenast's high self-efficacy?

2. How would you rate Heckenast in terms of conscientiousness, a proactive personality, and locus of control? Explain.

3. Which of Gardner's eight multiple intelligences does Heckenast appear to possess? Explain.

4. Does Heckenast have *practical* intelligence? Explain.

5. How important is *emotional* intelligence in Sherri Heckenast's life? Explain. What advice would you give her to improve it?

6. So, what *does* drive Sherri Heckenast? Explain.

Personal Awareness and Growth Exercise

How Do You Score on the Big Five Personality Factors?

Objectives

1. To learn more about yourself.
2. To learn more about the Big Five personality dimensions, as introduced in this chapter.

Introduction

Personality is an extremely complex subject. There are many ways of measuring personality, as a quick Internet search will reveal. While the Big Five model is not universally accepted

as the best way of understanding personality, it is well established and is accompanied by abundant research. *Note:* The Big Five personality profile presented here is for instructional purposes only; it has not been validated and should not be used for personnel selection or evaluation purposes.

Instructions

Please circle one number on the scale for each pair of adjectives, reflecting your personality. Add the three circled numbers for each Big Five dimension to obtain subscores.

Personality Profile[107]

Introversion–Extraversion

Quiet	I—2—3—4—5—6̃—7—8—9—10	Talkative
Shy	I—2—3—4—⑤—6—7—8—9—10	Outgoing
Retiring	I—2—3—4—5—6—⑦—8—9—10	Sociable

Subscore = __14__

Agreeableness

Critical	I—2—3—4—5—6—⑦—8—9—10	Trusting
Aggressive	I—2—3—4—⑤—6—7—8—9—10	Amiable
Cold	I—2—3—4—5—6—7—⑧—9—10	Affectionate

Subscore = __19__

Conscientiousness

Careless	I—2—3—4—5—6—⑦—8—9—10	Organized
Negligent	I—2—3—4—5—⑥—7—8—9—10	Self-disciplined
Inconsistent	I—2—3—4—⑤—6—7—8—9—10	Reliable

Subscore = __14__

Neuroticism–Emotional Stability

Anxious	I—2—3—4—5—6—⑦—8—9—10	Calm
Insecure	I—2—3—4—5—⑥—7—8—9—10	Self-reliant
Temperamental	I—2—3—4—5—⑥—7—8—9—10	Poised

Subscore = __19__

Openness to Experience

Narrow interests	I—2—3—4—5—6—7—8—⑨—10	Wide interests
Unimaginative	I—2—3—4—5—6—⑦—8—9—10	Imaginative
Imperceptive	I—2—3—4—5—6—7—⑧—9—10	Insightful

Subscore = __24__

Scoring

There are no right or wrong answers on this personality test. There is only an infinite variety of individual differences. You may want to take two passes through this profile. The first indicating how you are now and the second plotting how you would like to be. Any gaps would represent self-improvement challenges. Alternatively, if you have the courage, rate yourself and then have a close acquaintance rate you, for comparison purposes (and probably lively discussion).

Questions for Discussion

1. Any surprises? Explain.

2. What important aspects of personality are overlooked in this particular profile?

3. What other adjective pairings could you use for each of the five dimensions?

4. Why do you have your particular personality traits? Nature (genetics)? Nurture (family traditions, culture, schooling, etc.)? Some combination of nature and nurture (in what proportion)?

5. Why is it supposedly so difficult to alter an individual's personality?

Anger Control Role Play

Objectives

1. To demonstrate that emotions can be managed.
2. To develop your interpersonal skills for managing both your own and someone else's anger.

Introduction

Personal experience and research tell us that anger begets anger. People do not make their best decisions when angry. Angry outbursts often inflict unintentional interpersonal damage by triggering other emotions (e.g., disgust in observers and subsequent guilt and shame in the angry person). Effective managers know how to break the cycle of negative emotions by defusing anger in themselves and others. This is a role-playing exercise for groups of four. You will have a chance to play two different roles. All the roles are generic, so they can be played as either a woman or a man.

Instructions

Your instructor will divide the class into groups of four. Everyone should read all five roles described. Members of each foursome will decide among themselves who will play which roles. All told, you will participate in two rounds of role playing (each round lasting no longer than eight minutes). In round one, one person will play Role 1 and another will play Role 3; the remaining two group members will play Role 5. In round two, those who played Role 5 in the first round will play Roles 2 and 4. The other two will switch to Role 5.

ROLE 1: THE ANGRY (OUT-OF-CONTROL) SHIFT SUPERVISOR

You work for a leading electronics company that makes computer chips and other computer-related equipment. Your factory is responsible for assembling and testing the company's most profitable line of computer microprocessors. Business has been good, so your factory is working three shifts. The day shift, which you are now on, is the most desirable one. The night shift, from 11 PM to 7:30 AM is the least desirable and least productive. In fact, the night shift is such a mess that your boss, the factory manager, wants you to move to the night shift next week. Your boss just broke this bad news as the two of you are having lunch in the company cafeteria. You are shocked and angered because you are one of the most senior and highly rated shift supervisors in the factory. Thanks to your leadership, your shift has broken all production records during the

past year. As the divorced single parent of a 10-year-old child, the radical schedule change would be a major lifestyle burden. Questions swirl through your head. "Why me?" "What kind of reliable child-care will be available when I sleep during the day and work at night?" "Why should I be 'punished' for being a top supervisor?" "Why don't they hire someone for the position?" Your boss asks what you think.

When playing this role, be as realistic as possible without getting so loud that you disrupt the other groups. Also, if anyone in your group would be offended by foul language, please refrain from cursing during your angry outburst.

ROLE 2: THE ANGRY (UNDER-CONTROL) SHIFT SUPERVISOR

Same situation as in Role 1. But this role will require you to read and act according to the tips for reducing chronic anger in the left side of Table 5–6 on p 170. You have plenty of reason to be frustrated and angry, but you realize the importance of maintaining a good working relationship with the factory manager.

ROLE 3: THE (HARD-DRIVING) FACTORY MANAGER

You have a reputation for having a "short fuse." When someone gets angry with you, you attack. When playing this role, be as realistic as possible. Remember, you are responsible for the entire factory with its 1,200 employees and hundreds of millions of dollars of electronics products. A hiring freeze is in place, so you have to move one of your current supervisors. You have chosen your best supervisor because the night shift is your biggest threat to profitable operations. The night-shift supervisor gets a 10% pay premium. Ideally, the move will only be for six months.

ROLE 4: THE (MELLOW) FACTORY MANAGER

Same general situation as in Role 3. However, this role will require you to read and act according to the tips for responding to angry provocation in the right side of Table 5–6 on p 170. You have a reputation for being results-oriented but reasonable. You are good at taking a broad, strategic view of problems and are a good negotiator.

Table 5–6   *How to Manage Anger in Yourself and Others*

Reducing Chronic Anger (in Yourself)	Responding to Angry Provocation
Guides for Action	**Guides for Action**
• Appreciate the potentially valuable lessons from anger.	• Expect angry people to exaggerate.
• Use mistakes and slights to learn.	• Recognize the other's frustrations and pressures.
• Recognize that you and others can do well enough without being perfect.	• Use the provocation to develop your abilities.
• Trust that most people want to be caring, helpful family members and colleagues.	• Allow the other to let off steam.
• Forgive others and yourself.	• Begin to problem solve when the anger is at moderate levels.
• Confront unrealistic, blame-oriented assumptions.	• Congratulate yourself on turning an outburst into an opportunity to find solutions.
• Adopt constructive, learning-oriented assumptions.	• Share successes with partners.
Pitfalls to Avoid	**Pitfalls to Avoid**
• Assume every slight is a painful wound.	• Take every word literally.
• Equate not getting what you want with catastrophe.	• Denounce the most extreme statements and ignore more moderate ones.
• See every mistake and slip as a transgression that must be corrected immediately.	• Doubt yourself because the other does.
• Attack someone for your getting angry.	• Attack because you have been attacked.
• Attack yourself for getting angry.	• Forget the experience without learning from it.
• Try to be and have things perfect.	
• Suspect people's motives unless you have incontestable evidence that people can be trusted.	
• Assume any attempt to change yourself is an admission of failure.	
• Never forgive.	

SOURCE: Reprinted with permission from D Tjosvold, *Learning to Manage Conflict: Getting People to Work Together Productively*, pp 127–29. Copyright © 1993 Dean Tjosvold. First published by Lexington Books. All rights reserved.

ROLE 5: SILENT OBSERVER

Follow the exchange between the shift supervisor and the factory manager without talking or getting actively involved. Jot down some notes (for later class discussion) as you observe whether the factory manager did a good job of managing the supervisor's anger.

Questions for Discussion

1. Why is uncontrolled anger a sure road to failure?

2. Is it possible to express anger without insulting others? Explain.

3. Which is more difficult, controlling anger in yourself or defusing someone else's anger? Why?

4. What useful lessons did you learn from this role-playing exercise?

Hot Heads!

Situation

You are the human resources vice president at a leading overnight express company. After lunch today, one of your top trainers excitedly plopped down in your office and said "Read this short section I marked in a *Business 2.0* article." You took it and read the following:

Thrown any good lamps lately? Of course, you're probably too professional and well-bred to show anger at work. Just be aware: Being restrained may not be doing your career any good.

For some years, Larissa Tiedens, an assistant professor of organizational behavior at Stanford Business School, has been studying the effects of anger in the workplace. Her research has revealed that employers have a bias toward promoting employees who get mad now and again. "I don't think we're cognizant of this," Tiedens says. "We make inferences about people all the time, and we don't always know where the information has come from."

Tiedens began testing her hypothesis at a software firm in Palo Alto. She gave 24 of the employees a list of 10 or so emotions and asked them to rate how often their colleagues expressed each one. At the same time, the group managers filled out a questionnaire about how likely they would be to promote each of the employees. Those who were rated high on the anger scale were more likely to be on the promotion list. In a sep-

arate experiment, Tiedens had MBA students watch video clips of mock job interviews. In one tape the applicant shows visible signs of anger when discussing a presentation that went wrong, and in the other the candidate is fairly restrained. Most of the MBAs said they would have slotted the angry candidate for the higher-paying position.[108]

As you handed the reading back, you remarked "Let me see if I get this. You want to teach our managers *how* to get angry, or get angry *more often?*" An ethical flag went up in your mind.

What would you do?

1. Kill the idea on the spot. Explain how.

2. Take an immediate cue from what you just read and angrily tell the trainer that some research shouldn't be taken so literally. How would you do that?

3. Make an appointment with the trainer to discuss and refine the concept to make it an acceptable part of your management training program. Explain how.

4. Without hurting the trainer's feelings or discouraging creativity, take a few minutes to review the ethical implications of what you just read.

5. Invent other options. Discuss.

For the Chapter 5 Internet Exercise featuring An Emotional Intelligence Test (www.fortune.com), visit our Web site at **www.mhhe.com/kreitner.**

Chapter 6

Values, Attitudes, and Job Satisfaction

Learning Objectives

When you finish studying the material in this chapter, you should be able to:

1 Distinguish between terminal and instrumental values, and describe three types of value conflict.

2 Describe the values model of work/family conflict, and specify at least three practical lessons from work/family conflict research.

3 Identify the three components of attitudes and discuss cognitive dissonance.

4 Explain how attitudes affect behavior in terms of Ajzen's theory of planned behavior.

5 Describe the model of organizational commitment.

6 Define the work attitudes of job involvement and job satisfaction.

7 Identify and briefly describe five alternative causes of job satisfaction.

8 Identify eight important correlates/consequences of job satisfaction, and summarize how each one relates to job satisfaction.

BusinessWeek There has never been a better time to be an auditor. Thanks to congressional demands for more extensive probes, companies and their outside auditors are adding accountants at a record pace. Even the federal government, from the Securities & Exchange Commission to the FBI, is hiring. "We have 1,200 more people today than a year ago, and if we could have another 1,000 people tomorrow, we'd take them," says Allen Thomas, national managing director for human resources for Deloitte & Touche.

The crunch stems largely from auditing reforms passed by Congress in the wake of Enron and other scandals. Those changes have increased the number of hours it takes to do a typical audit by 40% to 60%. Yet even as demand has spiked, the supply of auditors is down. In the 1990s, numbers-savvy students bypassed accounting degrees in favor of finance and technology programs. By 2001 the number of students earning accounting degrees had dropped below 45,000, from more than 60,000 graduates 10 years earlier. . . .

It's not just Big Four firms such as PwC that need to staff up. With CEOs and CFOs of public corporations now required to vouch for their numbers, companies are also scrambling for extra auditors. Giants, including Ford, Motorola, and Johnson & Johnson, have been hiring accountants at a brisk pace, according to university placement officers. Government organizations are also big recruiters. . . .

All of which makes for quite a bonanza in perks and workplace flexibility, particularly for the mid- and senior-level managers most in demand. This summer, Deloitte launched a program that allows top performers to take a leave for up to five years. The firm continues to pay for career education and licensing, and it assigns each leave-taker a personal mentor to keep them involved and up to date. The program is aimed at keeping folks most likely to jump ship—those with enough experience to be attractive to outsiders but who have not yet made partner. Ann Donaghey, 38, had been promoted twice since she joined the firm six years ago, but she was prepared to quit after having twin boys in February. When

Donaghey learned she could apply for a five-year leave, it was a great relief. But it may have been an even bigger relief to Deloitte: Replacing Donaghey would have cost roughly double her annual salary.

Compensation is also on the rise. Most firms say auditors' pay is up 10% to 12% across the board this year. For top people, 20% is probably more like it. Bonuses are more frequent, too. But bigger salaries are just part of the package. Ernst & Young, which boosted hiring of experienced accountants by 36% this year and added 23% more college grads, doles out more vacation time as well. It even offers free concierge service for staff to get personal errands done.

The auditing frenzy won't last forever. Enrollment in accounting classes is climbing, and more students are pursuing a degree. Still, for now, auditing is a great gig.[1]

FOR DISCUSSION

What are the pros and cons of Deloitte & Touche's program of allowing top performers to take a leave for up to five years?

The chapter opening vignette highlights the programs and benefits that Deloitte & Touche used to attract and retain high-quality auditors. Unfortunately, results from a recent nationwide survey of 8,044 people by Monster.com suggest that employee retention might become more of a problem in the future; 93% of the respondents indicated that they planned to job-hop next year even though they were not optimistic about the job market.[2] As discussed later in this chapter, employees quit their jobs for or a variety of reasons. That said, however, research indicates that employees are less likely to quit when their personal values are consistent with the organization's values, when they have positive attitudes about the work environment, and when they are satisfied with their jobs.[3] This is why progressive companies like Goldman Sachs, Pfizer, Booz Allen Hamilton, and MBNA are offering programs and benefits such as day care, flexible work schedules, paternal leaves, generous tuition reimbursement, wellness programs, telecommuting, concierge services, and mentoring to a wider segment of the workforce.[4]

The overall goal of this chapter is to continue our investigation of individual differences from Chapter 5 so that you can get a better idea of how managers and organizations can use knowledge of individual differences to attract, motivate, and retain quality employees. We explore and discuss the impact of personal values and attitudes on important outcomes such as job satisfaction, performance, and turnover.

Personal Values

Value system

The organization of one's beliefs about preferred ways of behaving and desired end-states.

When discussing organizational culture in Chapter 3, we defined *values* as desired ways of behaving or desired end-states. Accordingly, pioneering values researcher Milton Rokeach defined a person's **value system** as an "enduring organization of beliefs concerning preferable modes of conduct or end-states of existence along a continuum of relative importance."[5] Our focus in Chapter 3 was on collective or shared values; here the focus shifts to *personal* values. Consider the value system possessed by David Neeleman, CEO of JetBlue (see Real World/Real People on page 175). His value system contains a mix of values that fostered his motivation for power and success and his desires for an active spiritual life and quality relationships with his family. As true of Neeleman's choice to set rules to be with his family, our behavior patterns are influenced by values that are fairly well set by the time we are in our early teens. However, significant life-altering events—such as having a child, business failure, death of a loved one, going to war, or surviving a serious accident or disease—can reshape an adult's value system.[6]

David Neeleman, CEO of JetBlue, Reconciles His Value System

"I'm a God-fearing guy. And the best advice I ever got came from the head of our [Mormon] church, Gordon B Hinkley. It was when we were going public in 2001, and I was caught up in the money, power, and glory. He cut me right down to size. In a conference where he was speaking, he reminded me, 'It's all about your family, your relationships. You've got to balance that with your work.'

"So I set rules to be with my family and to keep everyone from encroaching on my time. I keep weekends as free as humanly possible. I try to make it home in time for nightly Scripture study and prayer as a family, and I try to make sure to take some good vacations when my kids are out of school. Those rules have had a positive effect on the business."

SOURCE: "The Best Advice I Ever Got," *Fortune*, March 21, 2005, p 112.

David Neeleman poses with a JetBlue flight attendant. Neeleman set rules to keep work from encroaching on his private life and those rules have had a positive effect on both his personal and work life. Why isn't it easier to strike a work/life balance?

Extensive research supports Rokeach's contention that differing value systems go a long way toward explaining individual differences in behavior. Value → behavior connections have been documented for a wide variety of behaviors, ranging from weight loss, shopping selections, and political party affiliation to religious involvement and choice of a college major.[7]

Let us learn more about personal values by distinguishing between instrumental and terminal values, discussing three types of value conflict, and examining the timely value-related topic of work versus family life conflicts.

Instrumental and Terminal Values

Rokeach proposed that personal values can be categorized along two dimensions: terminal and instrumental.[8] **Terminal values,** such as a sense of accomplishment, happiness, pleasure, salvation, and wisdom, are desired end-states or life goals. These values represent the things we want to achieve or accomplish during our lives. For example, if you value family more than career success, you are more likely to work fewer hours and to spend more time with your family than someone who values career success. These values can also change over time depending on what is happening in our lives. Brenda Barnes, for instance, resigned as CEO of Pepsi-Cola's $7.7 billion North America division in 1997 in order to spend more time raising her three children, who were 7, 8, and 10 at the time. She obviously felt that it was more important to be with her children at that time rather than leading a multibillion dollar business. Two years later, however, Brenda returned to an executive position with Starwood Hotels & Resorts, and today she is the CEO of Sara Lee.[9]

Terminal values
Personally preferred end-states of existence.

Instrumental values
Personally preferred ways of behaving.

Instrumental values are alternative behaviors or means by which we achieve our terminal values or desired end-states. Sample instrumental values include ambition, honesty, independence, love, and obedience. The key thing to remember about instrumental values is that they direct us in determining how we should behave in the pursuit of our goals. For example, someone who values the instrumental value of honesty is less likely to lie and cheat in order to accomplish a terminal value associated with a sense of accomplishment than someone who does not value honesty.

Value Conflicts

There are three types of value conflict that are related to an individual's attitudes, job satisfaction, turnover, and potentially performance. They are *intra*personal value conflict, *inter*personal value conflict, and individual–organization value conflict. These sources of conflict are, respectively, from inside the person, between people, and between the person and the organization.

Intrapersonal Value Conflict
Inner conflict and resultant stress typically are experienced when highly ranked instrumental and terminal values pull the individual in different directions. This is somewhat akin to role conflict, as discussed in Chapter 10. The main difference is locus of influence: Role conflict involves *outside* social expectations; intrapersonal value conflict involves *internal* priorities. For employees who want balance in their lives, a stressful conflict arises when one values, for example, "being ambitious" (instrumental value) and "ending up happy" (terminal value). Dan Rosensweig, chief operating officer at Yahoo!, is experiencing intrapersonal value conflict in his current job. He commented about this to a reporter from *Fast Company* by noting that his "biggest challenge is when you're given an opportunity like this, how do you give it everything you have because it deserves it, and also recognize and appreciate that the most important things in your life are your wife and daughters. I'm envious of people who have been able to find better balance."[10] In general, people are happier and less stressed when their personal values are aligned.

Interpersonal Value Conflict
This type of value conflict often is at the core of personality conflicts. Just as people have different styles that may or may not mesh, they also embrace unique combinations of instrumental and terminal values that inevitably spark disagreement. Consider, for example, the situation of Chad Myers, a Peace Corps volunteer who spent his two-year tour of duty building latrines in Bolivia:

> "A lot of my friends were going into high-paying, good jobs," said Chad, a recent graduate of North Carolina State. "They look at me in shock and disgust and ask, 'Why are you working for free when you could be making $50,000 a year?'"
>
> Chad's rationale for joining the Peace Corps was apparent a few minutes later when he explained: "I've set a goal, and this is pretty high. If I can get 20 kids to wash their hands after going to the bathroom, I will have accomplished something that will have changed their lives and someday those of their children."[11]

Chad's goal would seem laughable to classmates acting out more materialistic values. But his unconventional value-driven behavior certainly means a lot to the health of his Bolivian friends.

Individual–Organization Value Conflict
As we saw in Chapter 3, companies actively seek to embed certain values into their corporate cultures. Conflict can occur when values espoused and enacted by the organization collide with employees' personal values. OB researchers refer to this type of conflict as value congruence or person–culture

fit.[12] **Value congruence or person–culture fit** reflects the similarity between an individual's personal values and the cultural value system of an organization. This is an important type of conflict to consider when accepting future jobs because positive outcomes such as satisfaction, commitment, performance, career success, reduced stress, and lower turnover intentions are realized when an individual's personal values are similar or aligned with organizational values.[13]

Value congruence or person–culture fit
The similarity between personal values and organizational values

Handling Value Conflicts through Values Clarification   For intrapersonal conflict, a Toronto management writer and consultant recommends getting out of what she calls "the busyness trap" by asking these questions:

- Is your work really meeting your most important needs?
- Are you defining yourself purely in terms of your accomplishments?
- Why are you working so hard? To what personal ends?
- Are you making significant sacrifices in favor of your work?
- Is your work schedule affecting other people who are important in your life?[14]

Another approach for dealing with all forms of value conflict is a career-counseling and team-building technique called *values clarification*. To gain useful hands-on experience, take a break from your reading and complete the OB Exercise on page 178. Our key learning point is to get you and others to identify and talk about personal values to establish common ground as a basis for teamwork and conflict avoidance/resolution (as discussed in Chapters 10 and 11).

Work versus Family Life Conflict

A complex web of demographic and economic factors makes the balancing act between job and life very challenging for most of us. Demographically, there are more women in the workforce, more dual-income families, more single working parents, and an aging population that gives mid-career employees day care or elder care responsibilities, or both.[15] On the economic front, years of downsizing and corporate cost-cutting have given employees heavier workloads. Meanwhile, an important trend was recently documented in a unique 25-year study of values in the United States: "employees have become less convinced that work should be an important part of one's life or that working hard makes one a better person."[16] Something has to give in this collision of trends. Too often family life suffers. The experience of Debbie Rubenstein and David Flynn is a sign of the times:

Traffic jams rob people of valuable time that could be spent with their families. Some employees are recouping this time by moving to locations that do not have rush hours as depicted here. How can people use dead time in traffic to their benefit?

> Debbie Rubenstein and David Flynn felt like the commuting dead, slogging three hours round-trip from their home in Maplewood, N.J., to day care for the baby, their offices in Manhattan, and then back again. Debbie, 36, made documentaries for PBS. David, 32, worked as a software developer at TIAA-CREFF. Weekdays, they barely saw their 18-month-old daughter; weekends, they barely saw each other. They passed off Samantha like a baton, alternately sprinting through the relay of grocery shopping, dry cleaning drop-offs, and gas tank fill-ups. "We were working all the time just to afford to keep living where we were living," says Debbie. Neither a second child nor an executive MBA for David fit into their

OB Exercise Personal Values Clarification

Instructions for Individuals Working Alone

Review the following list of 30 values and then rank your top 6 values (1 = most important; 6 = least important). What *intra*personal value conflicts can you detect? How can you resolve them? Which, if any, of your cherished values likely conflict with those deemed important by your family, friends, co-workers, and employer? What could be done to reduce this interpersonal and individual-organizational value conflict?

Instructions for Teams

Each team member should begin by ranking their top six personal values, as specified above. Have someone record each team member's top-ranked value on a flip chart or chalkboard (no names attached). Then spend a few minutes discussing both differences and commonalities. Try to find common ground among seemingly different values. If your group is a task team, an additional step could be to derive four or more consensus values to guide the team's work. (Do not short-cut consensus seeking by voting.) How do your personal values align with your teammates' values and the team's consensus values? What needs to be done to reduce actual or threatened value conflict?

_____ Responsibility (joint and/or individual)	_____ Accomplishment
_____ Involvement in decision making	_____ Satisfying relationships
_____ Competence	_____ Creativity
_____ Meaning	_____ Self-worth
_____ Autonomy	_____ Self-expression
_____ Recognition	_____ Leadership opportunities
_____ Personal and professional growth	_____ Financial security
_____ New and different experiences	_____ Diversity
_____ Collaboration on common tasks	_____ Career mobility
_____ Harmony or an absence of conflict	_____ A sense of belonging
_____ Competition	_____ Shared fun and experiences
_____ Meeting deadlines in a timely manner	_____ Peace and serenity
_____ A high standard of excellence	_____ Good health
_____ Status, position	_____ Loyalty
_____ Stimulation from challenge and change	_____ Duty to family
	_____ Other _____

SOURCE: List of values from L Gardenswartz and A Rowe, *Diverse Teams at Work: Capitalizing on the Power of Diversity* (New York: McGraw-Hill, 1994), p 85. © 1994.

5-, 10-, or even 20-year budgets. Thoughts of another terrorist attack plagued them: Trapped in Manhattan, how would they get to Samantha, marooned in day care across the Hudson?[17]

Debbie and David ultimately moved to Charlotte, North Carolina, to resolve their hectic lives and stretched budget.

In this section, we seek to better understand work versus family life conflict by introducing a values-based model and discussing practical research insights. Importantly, our goal here is to get a firmer grasp on this difficult area, not offer quick-and-easy solutions with little chance of success.

A Values-Based Model of Work/Family Conflict   Building upon the work of Rokeach, Pamela L Perrewé and Wayne A Hochwarter constructed the model in Figure 6–1. On the left, we see one's general life values feeding into one's family-related values and work-related values. Family values involve enduring beliefs about the importance of family and who should play key family roles (e.g., child rearing, housekeeping, and income earning). Work values center on the relative importance of work and career goals in one's life. *Value similarity* relates to the degree of consensus among family members about family values. When a housewife launches a business venture despite her husband's desire to be the sole breadwinner, lack of family value similarity causes work/family conflict. *Value congruence,* on the other hand, involves the amount of value agreement between employee and employer. If, for example, refusing to go on a business trip to stay home for a child's birthday is viewed as disloyalty to the company, lack of value congruence can trigger work/family conflict.

In turn, "work-family conflict can take two distinct forms: work interference with family and family interference with work."[18] For example, suppose two managers in the same department have daughters playing on the same soccer team. One manager misses the big soccer game to attend a last-minute department meeting; the other manager skips the meeting to attend the game. Both may experience work/family conflict, but for different reasons.

The last two boxes in the model—value attainment and job and life satisfaction—are a package deal. Satisfaction tends to be higher for those who live according to their values and lower for those who do not. Overall, this model reflects much common sense. How does *your* life track through the model? Sadly, it is a painful trip for many these days.

Figure 6–1   *A Values Model of Work/Family Conflict*

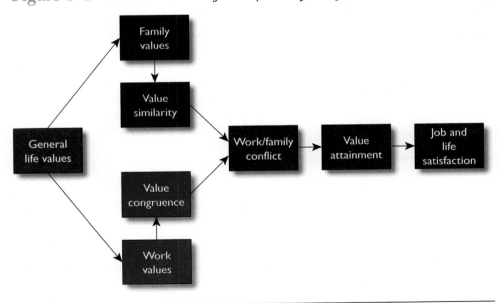

SOURCE: Pamela L Perrewé and Wayne A Hochwarter, "Can We Really Have It All? The Attainment of Work and Family Values," *Current Directions in Psychological Science,* February 2001, p 30. Published by Blackwell Publishers, Inc. © American Psychological Society.

Practical Research Insights about Work/Family Conflict   This is a new but very active area of OB research. Typically, the evidence comes from field surveys of real people in real jobs, rather than from contrived laboratory studies. Recent practical findings include

- *Work/family balance begins at home.* Historically, women shouldered the majority of the standard household chores and child rearing responsibilities. Fortunately, recent data suggest this trend is changing. Table 6–1, which summarizes data collected by the Families & Work Institute, shows that male Gen Xers, those aged 23–37 in 2002, are equally involved with their spouses in taking care of children. In contrast, women still have more responsibility for child care when they are married to male boomers—those aged 38–57 in 2002. Table 6–1 also shows that males are becoming more focused on spending time with family, as evidenced by the percentage of men who want jobs with more responsibility in 2002 versus 1992 and the amount of time that working couples spend with children.

Table 6–1   *Younger Men Spend More Time with Their Families*

Mom used to be the main caregiver ...		
HOURS SPENT WITH CHILDREN ON AVERAGE WORKDAY		
1977		1977
3.3 Mothers		1.8 Fathers
...but now younger dads are equally involved ...		
2002	2002	2002
3.4 Mothers	2.2 Boomer fathers	3.4 Gen X fathers
...doing more household chores ...		
HOURS SPENT ON HOUSEHOLD CHORES ON AVERAGE WORKDAY		
1977		2002
1.2 Married men		1.9 Married men
1977		2002
3.3 Married women		2.7 Married women
...and choosing family time over more career responsibility ...		
COLLEGE-EDUCATED MEN WHO WANT JOBS WITH MORE RESPONSIBILITY		
1992		2002
68%		52%
...so kids are spending more time with their parents than in the past		
HOURS THAT WORKING COUPLE SPENDS WITH CHILDREN ON AVERAGE WORKDAY		
1977		2002
5.1		6.1

SOURCE: This table was presented in D Brady, "Hopping aboard the Daddy Track," *BusinessWeek*, November 8, 2004, p 101.

- *An employer's family-supportive philosophy is more important than specific programs.* Many employers offer family-friendly programs today, including child and elder day care assistance, parental leave, telecommuting, and flexible work schedules. However, if employees are afraid or reluctant to take advantage of those programs because the organization's culture values hard work and long hours above all else, families will inevitably suffer. To be truly family-friendly, the organization needs to provide programs and back them up with a family-supportive philosophy and culture[19] (see the OB Exercise on page 181). Genencor International is a good example of a company that is following this advice.

  > But at Genencor, creativity doesn't start and end on a lab bench or at an office desk. It extends to the company's core human-resources policies. HR director Jim Sjoerdsma designs Genencor's programs by regularly polling employees about which benefits they enjoy and which they would like the company to offer." We found that we had more employees at work doing personal business, and at home doing work," he explains. "We needed creative solutions." And employees embrace being involved in the process of designing their work lives. "There is a philosophy here of supporting an employee's entire lifestyle because it will make for a better employee and facilitate productivity, which it does," says Cynthia Edwards, Genencor's vice president of technology.[20]

- *Work flexibility is more important than time flexibility in promoting work/family balance.* Research suggests management should give a higher priority to job redesign (giving people more control over what they do and how they do it) than to flexible work schedules (such as flextime and job-sharing).[21]

- *Mentors can help.* A field survey of 502 graduates of a US university (63% men), yielded this result: "The results

How Family-Supportive Is Your Employer?

Instructions

Rate the organization where you work by circling one number for each of the following dimensions. Remember, you are rating the *organization's* philosophy or what is really important to the organization as conveyed through its culture and reinforced values. You are *not* rating your personal beliefs. If you are presently unemployed, you can rate a past employer or interview someone who is employed. (*Note:* The higher the score, the more family-supportive the organization.)

	Strongly Disagree	Strongly Agree*
1. Work should be the primary priority in a person's life.	5 —— 4 —— 3 —— 2 —— 1	
2. It is best to keep family matters separate from work.	5 —— 4 —— 3 —— 2 —— 1	
3. Expressing involvement and interest in nonwork matters is viewed as healthy.	1 —— 2 —— 3 —— 4 —— 5	
4. Attending to personal needs, such as taking time off for sick children is frowned upon.	5 —— 4 —— 3 —— 2 —— 1	
5. Employees should keep their personal problems at home.	5 —— 4 —— 3 —— 2 —— 1	
6. Employees are given ample opportunity to perform both their job and their personal responsibilities well.	1 —— 2 —— 3 —— 4 —— 5	
7. Offering employees flexibility in completing their work is viewed as a strategic way of doing business.	1 —— 2 —— 3 —— 4 —— 5	
8. The way to advance is to keep nonwork matters out of the workplace.	5 —— 4 —— 3 —— 2 —— 1	

Arbitrary norms: 8–18 = low family-supportiveness; 19–29 = moderate family-supportiveness; 30–40 = high family supportiveness.
*Items 1, 2, 4, 5, and 8 are reverse weighted.

SOURCE: Adapted from and eight survey items excerpted from T D Allen, "Family-Supportive Work Environments: The Role of Organizational Perceptions," *Journal of Vocational Behavior,* June 2001, p 423, © 2001 with permission from Elsevier.

indicate that having a mentor is significantly related to lower levels of work-family conflict. . . . Such findings suggest another potential benefit of mentoring: a source of social support to reduce employee stress caused by conflicts between the work and family domains."[22]

- *Take a proactive approach to managing work/family conflict.* Research clearly shows that an individual's personal life spills over to his or her work life and vice versa. This means that employees' job satisfaction, organizational commitment, and intentions to quit are significantly related to the amount of work/family conflict that exists in their lives.[23] We thus encourage you to identify and manage the sources of work/family conflict.

Consider the case of Anne Crum Ross:

In the months leading up to her wedding last July, Anne Crum Ross says the line between her work and her personal life dissolved. "For every five work calls I made at the office, I made one wedding-planning call," she says. With just three months to go before the ceremony, she changed jobs in real estate and became director of corporate training at Sussex & Reilly in Chicago. She took the wedding-guest and catering files she had stored on her Palm to her new office. "As long as I was doing my work, my bosses didn't have a problem with me doing wedding planning," she says. "It's all about knowing how to multitask."[24]

Anne resolved the spillover of her personal and work lives by being more organized.

- *Being your own boss is no panacea.* Self-employment turns out to be a good news/bad news proposition, when compared to standard organizational employment. Among the benefits of being self-employed are a stronger sense of autonomy, a higher level of job involvement, and greater job satisfaction. But self-employed people report higher levels of work/family conflict and lower levels of family satisfaction.[25]

Organizational Response to Work/Family Issues Organizations have implemented a variety of family-friendly programs and services aimed at helping employees to balance the interplay between their work and personal lives. Although these programs are positively received by employees, experts now believe that such efforts are partially misguided because they focus on balancing work/family issues rather than integrating them.[26] Balance is needed for opposites, and work and family are not opposites. Rather, our work and personal lives should be a well-integrated whole. A team of researchers arrived at the following conclusion regarding the need to integrate versus balance work/life issues.

> Gendered assumptions and stereotypes based in the separation of [occupational and family] spheres constrain the choices of both women and men. Our vision of gender equity is to relax these social norms about separation so that men and women are free to experience these two parts of their lives as integrated rather than as separate domains that need to be "balanced." Integration would make it possible for both women and men to perform up to their capabilities and find satisfaction in both work and personal life, no matter how they allocate their time commitment between the two. To convey this goal, we speak of integrating work and personal life rather than balancing. This terminology expresses our belief in the need to diminish the separation between these two spheres of life in ways that will *change both*, rather than merely reallocating—or "balancing"—time between them as they currently exist.[27]

Attitudes

Hardly a day goes by without the popular media reporting the results of another attitude survey. The idea is to take the pulse of public opinion. What do we think about candidate X, terrorism, the war on drugs, gun control, or abortion? In the workplace, meanwhile, managers conduct attitude surveys to monitor such things as job and pay satisfaction. All this attention to attitudes is based on the assumption that attitudes somehow influence behavior such as voting for someone, working hard, or quitting one's job. In this section, we discuss the components of attitudes and examine the connection between attitudes and behavior.

The Nature of Attitudes

Attitude
Learned predisposition toward a given object.

An **attitude** is defined as "a learned predisposition to respond in a consistently favorable or unfavorable manner with respect to a given object."[28] Consider your attitude toward chocolate ice cream. You are more likely to purchase a chocolate ice cream cone if you have a positive attitude toward chocolate ice cream. In contrast, you are more likely to purchase some other flavor, say vanilla caramel swirl, if you have a positive attitude toward vanilla and a neutral or negative attitude toward chocolate ice cream. Let us consider a work example. If you have a positive attitude about your job (i.e., you like what you are doing), you would be more willing to extend yourself at work by working longer and harder. These examples illustrate that attitudes propel us to act in a specific way in a specific context. That is, attitudes affect behavior at a different level than do values. While values represent global beliefs that influence behavior across *all* situations, attitudes relate only to behavior directed toward *specific* objects, persons, or situations.[29] Values and attitudes generally, but not always, are in harmony. A manager who strongly values helpful behavior may have a negative attitude toward helping an unethical co-worker. The difference between attitudes and values is clarified by considering the three components of attitudes: affective, cognitive, and behavioral.[30]

Affective Component

The **affective component** of an attitude contains the feelings or emotions one has about a given object or situation. For example, how do you *feel* about people who talk on cell phones in restaurants? If you feel annoyed or angry with such people you are expressing negative affect or feelings toward people who talk on cell phones in restaurants. In contrast, the affective component of your attitude is neutral if you are indifferent about people talking on cell phones in restaurants.

Cognitive Component

What do you *think* about people who talk on cell phones in restaurants? Do you believe this behavior is inconsiderate, productive, completely acceptable, or rude? Your answer represents the cognitive component of your attitude toward people talking on cell phones in restaurants. The **cognitive component** of an attitude reflects the beliefs or ideas one has about an object or situation.

Behavioral Component

The **behavioral component** refers to how one intends or expects to act toward someone or something. For example, how would you intend to respond to someone talking on a cell phone during dinner at a restaurant if this individual were sitting in close proximity to you and your guest? Attitude theory suggests that your ultimate behavior in this situation is a function of all three attitudinal components. You are unlikely to say anything to someone using a cell phone in a restaurant if you are not irritated by this behavior (affective), if you believe cell phone use helps people to manage their lives (cognitive), and you have no intention of confronting this individual (behavioral).

What Happens When Attitudes and Reality Collide? Cognitive Dissonance

What happens when a strongly held attitude is contradicted by reality? Suppose you are extremely concerned about getting AIDS, which you believe is transferred from contact with body fluids, including blood. Then you find yourself in a life-threatening accident in a foreign country and need surgery and blood transfusions—including transfusions of blood (possibly AIDS-infected) from a blood bank with unknown quality control. Would you reject the blood to remain consistent with your beliefs about getting AIDS? According to social psychologist Leon Festinger, this situation would create cognitive dissonance.

Cognitive dissonance represents the psychological discomfort a person experiences when his or her attitudes or beliefs are incompatible with his or her behavior.[31] Festinger proposed that people are motivated to maintain consistency between their attitudes and beliefs and their behavior. He therefore theorized that people will seek to reduce the "dissonance" or psychological tension through one of three main methods.

1. *Change your attitude or behavior, or both.* This is the simplest solution when confronted with cognitive dissonance. Returning to our example about needing a blood transfusion, this would amount to either (1) telling yourself that you can't get AIDS through blood and take the transfusion or (2) simply refusing to take the transfusion.

2. *Belittle the importance of the inconsistent behavior.* This happens all the time. In our example, you could belittle the belief that you can get AIDS from the foreign blood bank. (The doctor said she regularly uses blood from that blood bank.)

3. *Find consonant elements that outweigh dissonant ones.* This approach entails rationalizing away the dissonance. You can tell yourself that you are taking the transfusion because you have no other options. After all, you could die if you don't get the required surgery.

Affective component
The feelings or emotions one has about an object or situation.

Cognitive component
The beliefs or ideas one has about an object or situation.

Behavioral component
How one intends to act or behave toward someone or something.

Cognitive dissonance
Psychological discomfort experienced when attitudes and behavior are inconsistent.

How Stable Are Attitudes?

In one landmark study, researchers found the *job* attitudes of 5,000 middle-aged male employees to be very stable over a five-year period. Positive job attitudes remained positive; negative ones remained negative. Even those who changed jobs or occupations tended to maintain their prior job attitudes.[32] More recent research suggests the foregoing study may have overstated the stability of attitudes because it was restricted to a middle-aged sample. This time, researchers asked: What happens to attitudes over the entire span of adulthood? *General* attitudes were found to be more susceptible to change during early and late adulthood than during middle adulthood. Three factors accounted for middle-age attitude stability: (1) greater personal certainty, (2) perceived abundance of knowledge, and (3) a need for strong attitudes. Thus, the conventional notion that general attitudes become less likely to change as the person ages was rejected. Elderly people, along with young adults, can and do change their general attitudes because they are more open and less self-assured.[33]

Because our cultural backgrounds and experiences vary, our attitudes and behavior vary. Attitudes are translated into behavior via behavioral intentions. Let us examine an established model of this important process.

Attitudes Affect Behavior via Intentions

Building on Leon Festinger's work on cognitive dissonance, Icek Ajzen and Martin Fishbein further delved into understanding the reason for discrepancies between individuals' attitudes and behavior. Ajzen ultimately developed and refined a model focusing on intentions as the key link between attitudes and planned behavior. His theory of planned behavior in Figure 6–2 shows three separate but interacting determinants of one's intention (a person's readiness to perform a given behavior) to exhibit a specific behavior.

Importantly, this model only predicts behavior under an individual's control, not behavior due to circumstances beyond one's control. For example, this model can predict the likelihood of someone skipping work if the person says his intention is to stay in bed tomorrow morning. But it would be a poor model for predicting getting to work on time, because uncontrolled circumstances such as traffic delays or an accident could intervene.

Determinants of Intention   Ajzen has explained the nature and roles of the three determinants of intention as follows:

> The first is the *attitude toward the behavior* and refers to the degree to which a person has a favorable or unfavorable evaluation or appraisal of the behavior in question. The second predictor is a social factor termed *subjective norm;* it refers to the perceived social pressure to perform or not to perform the behavior. The third antecedent of intention is the degree of *perceived behavior control,* which . . . refers to the perceived ease or difficulty of performing the behavior and it is assumed to reflect past experience as well as anticipated impediments and obstacles.[34]

To bring these three determinants of intention to life, let us return to our lazy soul who chose to stay in bed rather than go to work. He feels overworked and underpaid and thus has a favorable attitude about skipping work occasionally. His perceived subjective norm is favorable because he sees his co-workers skipping work with no ill effects (in fact, they collect sick pay). Regarding perceived behavior control, he is completely in charge of acting on his intention to skip work today. So he turns off the alarm clock and pulls the covers over his head. Sweet dreams!

Figure 6–2   *Ajzen's Theory of Planned Behavior*

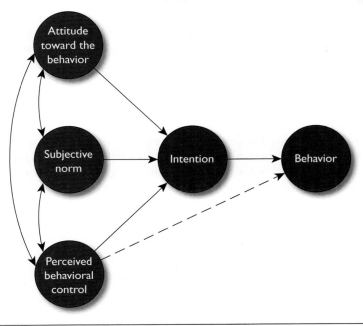

SOURCE: Reprinted from I Aizen, "The Theory of Planned Behavior," *Organizational Behavior and Human Decision Processes*, Figure 1, p 182. Copyright 1991, with permission from Elsevier Science.

Intentions and Behavior Research Lessons and Implications

According to the model of planned behavior, someone's intention to engage in a given behavior is a strong predictor of that behavior. For example, the quickest and possibly most accurate way of determining whether an individual will quit his or her job is to have an objective third party ask if he or she intends to quit. A meta-analysis of 34 studies of employee turnover involving more than 83,000 employees validated this direct approach. The researchers found stated behavioral intentions to be a better predictor of employee turnover than job satisfaction, satisfaction with the work itself, or organizational commitment.[35] A recent study took these findings one step further by considering whether or not job applicants' intention to quit a job before they were hired would predict voluntary turnover six months after being hired. Results demonstrated that intentions to quit significantly predicted turnover.[36]

Research has demonstrated that Ajzen's model accurately predicted intentions to buy consumer products, have children, and choose a career versus becoming a homemaker. Weight loss intentions and behavior, voting for political candidates, attending on-the-job training sessions, managers' use of structured interviews, and reenlisting in the National Guard also have been predicted successfully by the model.[37] In fact, the model correctly identified 82% of the 225 National Guard personnel in the study who actually reenlisted.[38]

From a practical standpoint, the theory of planned behavior has important managerial implications. Managers are encouraged to use prescriptions derived from the model to implement interventions aimed at changing employees' behavior. According to this model, changing behavior starts with the recognition that behavior is modified through intentions, which in turn are influenced by three different determinants (see Figure 6–2). Managers can thus influence behavioral change by doing or saying things that affect the three determinants of employees' intentions to exhibit a specific behavior: attitude toward the behavior, subjective norms, and perceived behavioral control. This is accomplished by modifying the specific beliefs that foster each of these determinants. For example, behavioral beliefs, normative beliefs, and control beliefs directly affect attitude toward the behavior, subjective norms, and perceived behavioral control, respectively. As a case in point, a recent study showed that employees had lower perceptions of job security and more negative attitudes toward temporary workers when they had the behavioral belief that temporaries posed a threat to their jobs.[39] Ultimately, managers change both attitudes and behavior by changing employees' beliefs.

Employee beliefs can be influenced through the information management provides on a day-by-day basis, organizational cultural values, role models, and rewards that are targeted to reinforce certain beliefs. For instance, management can foster the belief that teamwork is valued by setting and rewarding team-based goals instead of individual goals. Beliefs can also be modified through education and training. This conclusion was supported by a study that documented how men's beliefs about gender differences were reduced by taking a women's studies course.[40] Finally, the socialization tactics discussed in Chapter 3 (see Table 3–2) can be used to shape or change employees' beliefs.

Key Work Attitudes

What is your attitude toward work? Is work something meaningful that defines and fulfills you, or is it just a way to pay the bills? Interestingly, attitudes toward work have changed significantly throughout recorded history (see Figure 6–3). Note the difference between the early Greeks' attitude toward work and the current perspective. Having fun at work clearly beats slavery! While everyone does not agree about having fun at work, organizations such as Southwest Airlines have turned it into a strategic competitive advantage. Key employee selection factors at Southwest Airlines are a keen sense of humor and a general positive attitude. Consider how CEO Bob Pike's positive attitude toward work would set the tone for his employees at Creative Training Techniques International, Inc.:

> It is not a choice between fun and work, it is a choice for fun and work. I find it depressing that so many people spend 8 hours a day at work and 16 hours trying to forget that they did! It's time for us to replace the common definition of work: if it is not dull and boring then it can't be work! Work should be about passion, it should have a sense of purpose, it should be about involvement and participation. High-performing teams who do challenging work also know how to have fun. They have an attitude that says they enjoy what they do and that they belong to a diverse group of committed individuals who know the mission, values, and vision of the team. And they look forward to making a contribution.
>
> Understand that there will always be both fun-loving and fun-killing people. Fun-killers don't actually object to the fun; they feel that the fun isn't relevant to the work and therefore not important.[41]

How would you like to work for Bob Pike?

People have a multitude of attitudes about things that happen to them at work, but OB researchers have focused on a limited number of them. This section specifically examines two work attitudes—organizational commitment and job involvement—that have important practical implications. Job satisfaction, the most frequently studied work attitude, is thoroughly discussed in the final section of this chapter.

Figure 6-3 Timeline of Work Values and Attitudes

2000s
Because we spend more time at work than at any other activity, we begin to question whether we live to work or work to live. The beginning of the Fun/Work Fusion.

1990s
Empowerment, Building the Team, and Reengineering begin the decade. Downsizing at the end of the decade completes the near total loss of loyalty as an organizational value.

Ben Franklin
Advocates work as a virtue; not a means to amass wealth but as a contribution of self. America is the land of opportunity. Work becomes the key to wealth.

1980s
Gurus abound. How to make work meaningful. TQM becomes the newest program of the corporate culture.

1970s
Democracy comes to the workplace. Sexes and races begin to assume more equal roles in all aspects of work environments.

Unions
Unions help workers defend their ability to earn a livelihood against managers and owners who see employees as objects.

1950s
The beginning of understanding of the culture of work in terms of Theory X and Theory Y. Loyalty to the organization becomes the expected norm.

Calvin and Luther
Work as a commandment and moral obligation. The evolution of the Protestant Work Ethic.

Industrial Age
The birth of Scientific Management Theory.

The trades
Working with your hands as a skilled artisan is highly prized. Payment provided for work. With the onset of the Renaissance, work and art are merged.

Craftsmen vs Professionals
Separation between people who work with their hands and professionals who work with their heads. The bias is that working with your head is a more esteemed vocation.

Early Greeks
Focus not on work but on personal development. The work was completed by those enslaved. The emergence of the concept of "liberal arts," and the pursuit of knowledge.

SOURCE: Reprinted with permission of the publisher. From *Fun Works: Creating Places Where People Love to Work*, Copyright © 2001 by L. Yerkes, Berrett-Koehler Publishers, Inc., San Francisco, CA. All rights reserved. www.bkconnection.com.

Chuck Carothers and Irene Tse Commit to Their Jobs, Careers, and the Thrill of Achievement

In the realm of extreme sports, Chuck Carothers is a champ. One of the world's leading motocross riders, he has broken 21 bones in his career. Yet he keeps competing, describing the rush he gets from sailing through the air on a motorbike as a "complete addiction." In a weird way, Irene Tse, the 34-year-old head of the government bond-trading desk at Goldman Sachs—Jon Corzine's old job—understands Carothers's passion. "I've done this for 10 years," she says. "And I can count on the fingers of one hand the number of days in my career when I didn't want to come to work. Every day I wake up and I can't wait to get here."

The bond market hasn't exactly been a lot of laughs during that decade. And overseeing a desk that trades billions of dollars daily, with profits and losses in the millions—Wall Street's equivalent of Carothers's famous flying barrel roll—can be hair-raising. "There are days

when you make a lot, and other days where you lose so much you're just stunned by what you've done," Tse admits. But the exhilaration of her work, and the challenge of figuring out what forces are likely to next roil the markets, has kept her motivated through a decade of 80-hour weeks.

Indeed, there's an addictive quality to her work that has rewired her body. There are no broken bones, but Tse says she hasn't slept through the night in years, typically getting up two or three times to check on global market activity. "Through time, your body clock just wakes up when London opens," she says.

SOURCE: Excerpted from L Tischler, "Extreme Jobs," *Fast Company*, April 2005, p 56. © 2005 Gruner & Jahr USA Publishing. First published in *Fast Company* Magazine. Reprinted with permission.

Organizational Commitment

Before discussing a model of organizational commitment, it is important to consider the meaning of the term *commitment*. What does it mean to commit? Common sense suggests that commitment is an agreement to do something for yourself, another individual, group, or organization.[42] Formally, OB researchers define commitment as "a force that binds an individual to a course of action of relevance to one or more targets."[43] This definition highlights that commitment is associated with behavior and that commitment can be aimed at multiple targets or entities. For example, an individual can be committed to his or her job, family, girl- or boyfriend, faith, friends, career, organization, or a variety of professional associations. Chuck Carothers and Irene Tse are good examples of individuals who commit to multiple targets (see Real World/Real People). Let us now consider the application of commitment to a work organization.

Organizational commitment

Extent to which an individual identifies with an organization and its goals.

Organizational commitment reflects the extent to which an individual identifies with an organization and is committed to its goals. It is an important work attitude because committed individuals are expected to display a willingness to work harder to achieve organizational goals and a greater desire to stay employed at an organization. Figure 6–4 presents a model of organizational commitment that identifies its causes and consequences.

A Model of Organizational Commitment
Figure 6–4 shows that organizational commitment is composed of three separate but related components: affective commitment, normative commitment, and continuance commitment. John Meyer and Natalie Allen, a pair of commitment experts, define these components as follows:

Affective commitment refers to the employee's emotional attachment to, identification with, and involvement in the organization. Employees with a strong affective commitment continue employment with an organization because they *want* to do so. *Continuance commit-*

Figure 6–4   *A Model of Organizational Commitment*

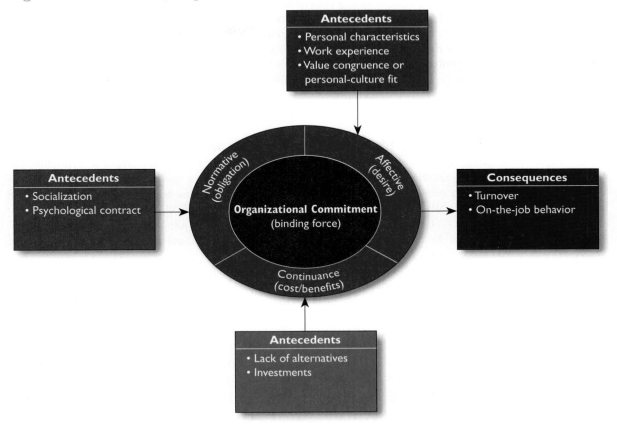

SOURCE: Adapted from J P Meyer and L Herscovitch, "Commitment in the Workplace: Toward a General Model," *Human Resource Management Review,* Autumn 2001, p 317.

ment refers to an awareness of the costs associated with leaving the organization. Employees whose primary link to the organization is based on continuance commitment remain because they *need* to do so. Finally, normative commitment reflects a feeling of obligation to continue employment. Employees with a high level of normative commitment feel that they *ought* to remain with the organization.[44]

Figure 6–4 also reveals that these three components combine to produce a binding force that influences the consequences of employee turnover and on-the-job behavior such as performance, absenteeism, and organizational citizenship, which is discussed later in this chapter.

Each component of commitment is influenced by a separate set of antecedents (see Figure 6–4). In the current context, an antecedent is something that causes the component of commitment to occur. For example, affective commitment is related to a variety of personal characteristics such as personality and locus of control (recall our discussion in Chapter 5), past work experience, and value congruence, which was discussed earlier in this chapter.[45] Because continuance commitment reflects a ratio of the costs and benefits associated with leaving an organization, antecedents are anything that affects the costs and benefits of leaving. Examples are a lack of job/career alternatives and the amount of real and psychological investments a person has in a particular organization or community. Continuance commitment would be high if an individual has no job alternatives, is actively involved in his or her church, has many friends in the community, and needs medical benefits for a family of five. Finally, normative commitment is influenced by the socialization process discussed in Chapter 3 and what is termed the psychological contract. **Psychological contracts** represent an individual's perception about the terms and conditions of a reciprocal exchange between him- or herself and another party.[46] In a work environment, the psychological contract represents an employee's beliefs about what he or she is entitled to receive in return for what he or she provides to the organization.[47]

Psychological contract
An individual's perception about the terms and conditions of a reciprocal exchange with another party.

Research and Practical Applications
Organizational commitment matters. A meta-analysis of 68 studies and 35,282 individuals uncovered a significant and strong relationship between organizational commitment and job satisfaction.[48] This finding encourages managers to increase job satisfaction in order to elicit higher levels of commitment. In turn, a recent meta-analysis involving 26,344 individuals revealed organizational commitment was significantly correlated with job performance.[49] This is an important finding because it implies managers can increase productivity by enhancing employees' organizational commitment.

Finally, a third meta-analysis summarizing results across 67 studies and 27,500 people uncovered a significant, negative relationship between organizational commitment and turnover.[50] This finding underscores the importance of paying attention to employees' organizational commitment because high commitment helps reduce the costs of employee turnover. In summary, managers are encouraged to focus on improving employees' organizational commitment.

Interestingly, companies use a variety of methods to increase employees' organizational commitment. Consider the different approaches used by Jeff Skilling, former Enron CEO, and George David, CEO of United Technologies Corp.

> Skilling hired some 250 bright young MBAs each year, all desperate to prove themselves so they, too, could hit the jackpot. Around Houston, a Porsche was seen as the Enron company car. "Skilling would say all that matters is money: You buy loyalty with money," says an ex-exec.[51]
>
> Six years ago, some of George David's subordinates at United Technologies Corp. thought he was nuts.
>
> But he is the CEO. So they acquiesced to his demand that the big manufacturer turn its undistinguished go-back-to-college program into one of the most generous in corporate America. . . .
>
> UTC pays all tuition and fees upfront for any credit course, no matter what the subject. . . . To lure workers to the classroom, UTC also offers up to three hours off each week—with pay—to study. . . . UTC also gives $5,000 worth of stock to employees who finish an associate's degree and $10,000 worth to those who finish higher degrees. At current market prices, the company has awarded $87 million of stock to 7,457 employees.[52]

While organizations such as Enron might attempt to "buy loyalty," we prefer the long-term, human capital approach used by UTC. UTC builds organizational commitment by investing in its employees. Anecdotal evidence from UTC supports the effectiveness of this method. For example, there is a greater percentage of employees from UTC taking college courses than is typical throughout other US corporations. Further, UTC's employee turnover is lower among employees participating in the educational program (4%) than it is among nonparticipating employees (8–10%).[53]

Managers can also increase the components of employee commitment through the following activities:

- Affective commitment is enhanced by hiring people whose personal values are consistent with the organization's values. A positive, satisfying work environment should also increase employees desire to stay. Harley-Davidson is following this advice. "Employee surveys show 90% strongly identify with the company's riding culture. Some employees get to work at biker rallies at Harley's expense."[54]

- Continuance commitment is enhanced by offering employees a variety of progressive benefits and human resource programs. For instance, Aflac will pay up to $20,000 per year in tuition reimbursement for an employee's college-age children or grandchildren who maintain a GPA of 2.5 or higher. QuikTrip also has a policy of promoting from within, and it provides part-time employees with tuition reimbursement and health coverage.[55]

- Normative commitment can be increased by making sure that management follows up on its commitments and by trying to enhance the level of trust throughout the organization. We provide specific recommendation for building and maintaining trust in Chapter 11.

Job Involvement

Job involvement is defined as "the degree to which one is cognitively preoccupied with, engaged in, and concerned with one's present job."[56] This work attitude manifests itself through the extent to which people are immersed in their job tasks. Take Vinton Studios' animator/directors Sean Burns and Doug Aberle for example. (Vinton Studios trademarked an animation process known as Claymation.® The process has been used in television commercials involving the California Raisins and M&Ms and the television series *The PJs.*) Sean says, "This is a great place to work. We work on truly interesting and cutting-edge stuff. Plus I get to work on things that interest me. Each project is a new situation every time. We suggest interesting twists, new ideas."[57] Doug is involved in his work. "At the end of the day, you've never been so tired—or had so much fun! There's a lot of variety in working on a TV show. There's something different every day."[58] This suggests it is important for managers to understand the causes and consequences of job involvement because of its association with motivation and satisfaction. Let us now consider results from a meta-analytic study involving thousands of people, to learn more about job involvement.[59]

Job involvement was positively associated with job satisfaction, organizational commitment, and intrinsic motivation, and negatively related to intentions to quit. There are three key managerial implications associated with these results. First, managerial

Job involvement
Extent to which an individual is immersed in his or her present job.

Although this little Claymation character seems a bit skeptical, the artists at Vinton Studios exhibit high job involvement. They love working on creative projects that hold their interest and turn hard work into fun. Task variety also is a big plus. An added bonus: their uncooperative subjects can be tossed back into the clay bucket.

attempts to improve either of the two work attitudes discussed in this section are likely to positively affect the other work attitude. Second, managers can increase employees' job involvement by providing work environments that fuel intrinsic motivation. Specific recommendations for doing this are discussed in the section on intrinsic motivation in Chapter 8. Third, improving job involvement can reduce employee turnover.

Past results pertaining to the relationship between job involvement and performance are controversial. While the earlier meta-analysis failed to uncover a significant relationship between job involvement and performance, poor measures of job involvement used in past studies may have biased the results. A more recent study corrected this problem and found a positive relationship between job involvement and performance.[60] Managers thus are encouraged to increase employees' job involvement as a viable strategy for improving job performance.

Job Satisfaction

Job satisfaction

An affective or emotional response to one's job.

Job satisfaction essentially reflects the extent to which an individual likes his or her job. Formally defined, **job satisfaction** is an affective or emotional response toward various facets of one's job. This definition implies job satisfaction is not a unitary concept. Rather, a person can be relatively satisfied with one aspect of his or her job and dissatisfied with one or more other aspects. For example, researchers at Cornell University developed the Job Descriptive Index (JDI) to assess one's satisfaction with the following job dimensions: work, pay, promotions, co-workers, and supervision.[61] Researchers at the University of Minnesota concluded there are 20 different dimensions underlying job satisfaction. Selected Minnesota Satisfaction Questionnaire (MSQ) items measuring satisfaction with recognition, compensation, and supervision are listed in the OB Exercise on page 193. Please take a moment now to determine how satisfied you are with these three aspects of your present or most recent job, and then use the norms to compare your score.[62] How do you feel about your job?

Research revealed that job satisfaction varied across countries. A study of 9,300 adults in 39 countries identified the percentage of workers who said they were "very satisfied with their jobs." The top five countries were Denmark (61%), India (urban middle and upper class only; 55%), Norway (54%), United States (50%), and Ireland (49%). Experts suggest that job satisfaction is highest in Denmark because labor and management have a great working relationship. The bottom five countries were Estonia (11%), China (11%), Czech Republic (10%), Ukraine (10%), and Hungary (9%). Why do Hungarian employees indicate the lowest job satisfaction? An average monthly salary of $302 and poor labor management relations are two possible causes.[63]

Job satisfaction is one of the most frequently studied work attitudes by OB researchers. For example, more than 12,000 job satisfaction studies were published by the early 1990s.[64] We now want to examine this employee attitude in more detail by focusing on the causes and consequences of job satisfaction.

The Causes of Job Satisfaction

Five predominant models of job satisfaction focus on different causes. They are need fulfillment, discrepancy, value attainment, equity, and dispositional/genetic components. A brief review of these models provides insight into the complexity of this seemingly simple concept.[65]

How Satisfied Are You with Your Present Job?

	Very Dissatisfied				Very Satisfied
1. The way I am noticed when I do a good job	1 —	2 —	3 —	4 —	5
2. The recognition I get for the work I do	1 —	2 —	3 —	4 —	5
3. The praise I get for doing a good job	1 —	2 —	3 —	4 —	5
4. How my pay compares with that for similar jobs in other companies	1 —	2 —	3 —	4 —	5
5. My pay and the amount of work I do	1 —	2 —	3 —	4 —	5
6. How my pay compares with that of other workers	1 —	2 —	3 —	4 —	5
7. The way my boss handles employees	1 —	2 —	3 —	4 —	5
8. The way my boss takes care of complaints brought to him/her by employees	1 —	2 —	3 —	4 —	5
9. The personal relationship between my boss and his/her employees	1 —	2 —	3 —	4 —	5

Total score for satisfaction with recognition (add questions 1–3), compensation (add questions 4–6), and supervision (add questions 7–9).

Comparative norms for each dimension of job satisfaction are: total score of 3–6 = low job satisfaction; 7–11 = moderate satisfaction; 12 and above = high satisfaction.

SOURCE: Adapted from D J Weiss, R V Dawis, G W England, and L H Lofquist, *Manual for the Minnesota Satisfaction Questionnaire* (Minneapolis: Industrial Relations Center, University of Minnesota, 1967). Copyright © 1967. Reproduced by permission of Vocational Psychology Research, University of Minnesota.

Need Fulfillment   These models propose that satisfaction is determined by the extent to which the characteristics of a job allow an individual to fulfill his or her needs. For example, a survey of 30 Massachusetts law firms revealed that 35 to 50% of law-firm associates left their employers within three years of starting because the firms did not accommodate family needs. This example illustrates that unmet needs can affect both satisfaction and turnover.[66] Organizations are aware of the premise associated with this model of satisfaction and have responded by providing creative benefits to help satisfy employees' needs. A recent survey of 975 employers, for example, revealed the percentage of companies that provided the following services on the premises to make employees' lives easier: ATM (41%), banking services (24%), dry cleaning/laundry service (21%), credit union (19%), travel services (18%), company store (16%), entertainment discounts and ticket purchase (15%), and mail services (14%).[67] Although need fulfillment models generated a great degree of controversy, it is generally accepted that need fulfillment is correlated with job satisfaction.[68]

Discrepancies   These models propose that satisfaction is a result of met expectations. **Met expectations** represent the difference between what an individual expects to receive from a job, such as good pay and promotional opportunities, and what he or she actually receives. When expectations are greater than what is received, a person will be dissatisfied. In contrast, this model predicts that an individual will be satisfied when he or she attains outcomes above and beyond expectations. A meta-analysis of 31 studies that included 17,241 people demonstrated that met expectations were significantly related to job satisfaction.[69] Many companies use employee attitude or opinion surveys to assess employees' expectations and concerns (see Real World/Real People).

Met expectations
The extent to which one receives what he or she expects from a job.

Lockheed Martin Uses Surveys to Assess Employees' Job Satisfaction and Improve Employee Engagement

Bethesda, Md.-based Lockheed Martin (ranked 9 [in *Fortune's* 100 Best Companies to Work For]) also uses surveys to help measure job retention efforts. The company conducts an all-employee survey biannually to assess satisfaction across 26 job attributes considered critical to recruitment, retention and performance. Survey results in 2001 showed a need for improvement in articulating the corporate mission for objectives and performance management. Lockheed's training organization played a key role in developing programs to meet those needs, including a new performance recognition system, performance management training, a formal mentoring program and training for coaching and mentoring. These carefully targeted programs worked. The results of the 2003 survey showed an 11 to 17% gain on all of Lockheed's targeted indices, including intention to remain and job engagement.

SOURCE: Excerpted from G Johnson, "And the Survey Says . . . ," *Training*, March 2004, p 28.

Value attainment
The extent to which a job allows fulfillment of one's work values.

Value Attainment
The idea underlying **value attainment** is that satisfaction results from the perception that a job allows for fulfillment of an individual's important work values.[70] For example, a recent survey by Salary.com showed that 53% of the respondents valued time off more than a raise of $5,000. These results suggest that organizations should stop measuring productivity in the number of hours people work and that they should encourage employees to take their vacations and turn off the technology while at home.[71] In general, research consistently supports the prediction that value fulfillment is positively related to job satisfaction.[72] Managers can thus enhance employee satisfaction by structuring the work environment and its associated rewards and recognition to reinforce employees' values.

Equity
In this model, satisfaction is a function of how "fairly" an individual is treated at work. Satisfaction results from one's perception that work outcomes, relative to inputs, compare favorably with a significant other's outcomes/inputs. A meta-analysis involving 190 studies and 64,757 people supported this model. Employees' perceptions of being treated fairly at work were highly related to overall job satisfaction.[73] Managers thus are encouraged to monitor employees' fairness perceptions and to interact with employees in such a way that they feel equitably treated. Chapter 8 explores this promising model in more detail.

Dispositional/Genetic Components
Have you ever noticed that some of your co-workers or friends appear to be satisfied across a variety of job circumstances, whereas others always seem dissatisfied? This model of satisfaction attempts to explain this pattern.[74] Specifically, the dispositional/genetic model is based on the belief that job satisfaction is partly a function of both personal traits and genetic factors. As such, this model implies that stable individual differences are just as important in explaining job satisfaction as are characteristics of the work environment. Although only a few studies have tested these propositions, results support a positive, significant relationship between personal traits and job satisfaction over time periods ranging from 2 to 50 years.[75] Genetic factors also were found to significantly predict life satisfaction, well-being, and general job satisfaction.[76] Overall, researchers estimate that 30% of an individual's job satisfaction is associated with

dispositional and genetic components.[77] Pete and Laura Wakeman, founders of Great Harvest Bread Company, have used this model of job satisfaction while running their company for more than 25 years.

> Our hiring ads say clearly that we need people with "strong personal loves as important as their work." This is not a little thing. You can't have a great life unless you have a buffer of like-minded people all around you. If you want to be nice, you can't surround yourself with crabby people and expect it to work. You might stay nice for a while, just because—but it isn't sustainable over years. If you want a happy company, you can do it only by hiring naturally happy people. You'll never build a happy company by "making people happy"—you can't really "make" people any way that they aren't already. Laura and I want to be in love with life, and our business has been a good thing for us in that journey.[78]

Although Pete and Laura's hiring approach is consistent with the dispositional and genetic model of job satisfaction, it is important to note that hiring "like-minded" people can potentially lead to discriminatory decisions. Managers are advised not to discriminate on the basis of race, gender, religion, color, national origin, and age.

Major Correlates and Consequences of Job Satisfaction

This area has significant managerial implications because thousands of studies have examined the relationship between job satisfaction and other organizational variables. Because it is impossible to examine them all, we will consider a subset of the more important variables from the standpoint of managerial relevance.

Table 6–2 summarizes the pattern of results. The relationship between job satisfaction and these other variables is either positive or negative. The strength of the relationship ranges from weak (very little relationship) to strong. Strong relationships imply that managers can significantly influence the variable of interest by increasing job satisfaction. Let us now consider seven key correlates of job satisfaction.

People can be like sunny days and rainy days. Sunny-day people tend to find satisfaction in all aspects of their lives. Rainy-day people generally express dissatisfaction with everything. Pete and Laura Wakeman, founders of Great Harvest Bread Company, have tried to hire people with positive dispositions for the past 25 years. Here, franchisee Dave Scheel, owner of a Great Harvest store in Missoula, Montana, gets down to business. The Wakemans are on the right track because it surely takes an optimist to face mountains of bread dough at 5 AM.

Motivation   A recent meta-analysis of nine studies and 1,739 workers revealed a significant positive relationship between motivation and job satisfaction. Because satisfaction with supervision also was significantly correlated with motivation managers are advised to consider how their behavior affects employee satisfaction.[79] Managers can potentially enhance employees' motivation through various attempts to increase job satisfaction.

Job Involvement   Job involvement represents the extent to which an individual is personally involved with his or her work role. A meta-analysis involving 27,925 individuals from 87 different studies demonstrated that job involvement was moderately related with job satisfaction.[80] Managers are thus encouraged to foster satisfying work environments in order to fuel employees' job involvement.

Table 6–2   *Correlates of Job Satisfaction*

Variables Related with Satisfaction	Direction of Relationship	Strength of Relationship
Motivation	Positive	Moderate
Job involvement	Positive	Moderate
Organizational commitment	Positive	Moderate
Organizational citizenship behavior	Positive	Moderate
Absenteeism	Negative	Weak
Tardiness	Negative	Weak
Withdrawal cognitions	Negative	Strong
Turnover	Negative	Moderate
Heart disease	Negative	Moderate
Perceived stress	Negative	Strong
Pro-union voting	Negative	Moderate
Job performance	Positive	Moderate
Life satisfaction	Positive	Moderate
Mental health	Positive	Moderate

Organizational citizenship behaviors (OCBs)

Employee behaviors that exceed work-role requirements.

Organizational Citizenship Behavior
Organizational citizenship behaviors (OCBs) consist of employee behaviors that are beyond the call of duty. Examples include "such gestures as constructive statements about the department, expression of personal interest in the work of others, suggestions for improvement, training new people, respect for the spirit as well as the letter of housekeeping rules, care for organizational property, and punctuality and attendance well beyond standard or enforceable levels."[81] Managers certainly would like employees to exhibit these behaviors. A meta-analysis covering 7,100 people and 22 separate studies revealed a significant and moderately positive correlation between organizational citizenship behaviors and job satisfaction.[82] Moreover, additional research demonstrated that employees' citizenship behaviors were determined more by leadership and characteristics of the work environment than by an employee's personality.[83] It thus appears that managerial behavior significantly influences an employee's willingness to exhibit citizenship behaviors. This relationship is important to recognize because employees' OCBs were positively correlated with their conscientiousness at work, organizational commitment, and performance ratings.[84] Another recent study demonstrated a broader impact of OCBs on organizational effectiveness. Results revealed that the amount of OCBs exhibited by employees working in 28 regional restaurants was significantly associated with each restaurant's corporate profits one year later.[85] Because employees' perceptions of being treated fairly at work are related to their willingness to engage in OCBs, managers are encouraged to make and implement employee-related decisions in an equitable fashion. More is said about this in Chapter 8.

Absenteeism
Absenteeism is not always what it appears to be, and it can be costly. For example, a recent survey of 700 managers indicated that 20% of them called in sick because they simply did not feel like going to work that day. The top three reasons given for the bogus excuse of being sick were doing personal errands, catching up on sleep, and relaxing.[86] While it is difficult to provide a precise estimate of the cost of absenteeism, a 2002 survey projected it to be $789 per employee.[87] This would suggest that absenteeism costs $236,700 for a company with 300 employees. Imagine the costs for a company with

100,000 employees! Because of these costs, managers are constantly on the lookout for ways to reduce it. One recommendation has been to increase job satisfaction. If this is a valid recommendation, there should be a strong negative relationship (or negative correlation) between satisfaction and absenteeism. In other words, as satisfaction increases, absenteeism should decrease. A researcher tracked this prediction by synthesizing three separate meta-analyses containing a total of 74 studies. Results revealed a weak negative relationship between satisfaction and absenteeism.[88] It is unlikely, therefore, that managers will realize any significant decrease in absenteeism by increasing job satisfaction.

Withdrawal Cognitions
Although some people quit their jobs impulsively or in a fit of anger, most go through a process of thinking about whether or not they should quit.[89] **Withdrawal cognitions** encapsulate this thought process by representing an individual's overall thoughts and feelings about quitting. What causes an individual to think about quitting his or her job? Job satisfaction is believed to be one of the most significant contributors. For example, a study of managers, salespersons, and auto mechanics from a national automotive retail store chain demonstrated that job dissatisfaction caused employees to begin the process of thinking about quitting. In turn, withdrawal cognitions had a greater impact on employee turnover than job satisfaction in this sample.[90] Results from this study imply that managers can indirectly help to reduce employee turnover by enhancing employee job satisfaction.

Withdrawal cognitions
Overall thoughts and feelings about quitting a job.

Turnover
Turnover is important to managers because it both disrupts organizational continuity and is very costly. Costs of turnover fall into two categories: separation costs and replacement costs.

> Separation costs may include severance pay, costs associated with an exit interview, outplacement fees, and possible litigation costs, particularly for involuntary separation. Replacement costs are the well-known costs of a hire, including sourcing expenses, HR processing costs for screening and assessing candidates, the time spent by hiring managers interviewing candidates, travel and relocation expenses, signing bonuses, if applicable, and orientation and training costs.[91]

Experts estimate that the cost of turnover for an hourly employee is roughly 30% of annual salary, whereas the cost can range up to 150% of yearly salary for professional employees.[92]

Although there are various things a manager can do to reduce employee turnover, many of them revolve around attempts to improve employees' job satisfaction.[93] This trend is supported by results from a meta-analysis of 67 studies covering 24,556 people. Job satisfaction obtained a moderate negative relationship with employee turnover.[94] Given the strength of this relationship, managers are advised to try to reduce employee turnover by increasing employee job satisfaction.

Perceived Stress
Stress can have very negative effects on organizational behavior and an individual's health. Stress is positively related to absenteeism, turnover, coronary heart disease, and viral infections.[95] Based on a meta-analysis of seven studies covering 2,659 individuals, Table 6–2 reveals that perceived stress has a strong, negative relationship with job satisfaction.[96] It is hoped that managers would attempt to reduce the negative effects of stress by improving job satisfaction.

Job Performance
One of the biggest controversies within OB research centers on the relationship between job satisfaction and job performance. Although researchers have identified seven different ways in which these variables are related, the dominant beliefs

are either that satisfaction causes performance or performance causes satisfaction.[97] A team of researchers recently attempted to resolve this controversy through a meta-analysis of data from 312 samples involving 54,417 individuals.[98] There were two key findings from this study. First, job satisfaction and performance are moderately related. This is an important finding because it supports the belief that employee job satisfaction is a key work attitude managers should consider when attempting to increase employees' job performance. Second, the relationship between job satisfaction and performance is much more complex than originally thought. It is not as simple as satisfaction causing performance or performance causing satisfaction. Rather, researchers now believe both variables indirectly influence each other through a host of individual differences and work-environment characteristics.[99] There is one additional consideration to keep in mind regarding the relationship between job satisfaction and job performance.

Researchers believe the relationship between satisfaction and performance is understated due to incomplete measures of individual-level performance. For example, if performance ratings used in past research did not reflect the actual interactions and interdependencies at work, inaccurate measures of performance served to lower the reported correlations between satisfaction and performance. Examining the relationship between *aggregate* measures of job satisfaction and organizational performance is one solution to correct this problem.[100] In support of these ideas, a team of researchers conducted a recent meta-analysis of 7,939 business units in 36 companies. Results uncovered significant positive relationships between business-unit-level employee satisfaction and business-unit outcomes of customer satisfaction, productivity, profit, employee turnover, and accidents.[101] It thus appears managers can positively affect a variety of important organizational outcomes, including performance, by increasing employee job satisfaction.

Summary of Key Concepts

1. *Distinguish between terminal and instrumental values, and describe three types of value conflict.* A terminal value is an enduring belief about a desired end-state (e.g., happiness). An instrumental value is an enduring belief about how one should behave. Three types of value conflict are intrapersonal, interpersonal, and individual–organization.

2. *Describe the values model of work/family conflict, and specify at least three practical lessons from work/family conflict research.* General life values determine one's values about family and work. Work/family conflict can occur when there is a lack of value similarity with family members. Likewise, work/family conflict can occur when one's own work values are not congruent with the company's values. When someone does not attain his or her values because of work/family conflicts, job or life satisfaction, or both, can suffer. Six practical lessons from work/family conflict research are (1) work/family balance begins at home, (2) an employer's family-supportive philosophy is more important than specific programs, (3) work flexibility is more important than time flexibility in promoting work/family balance, (4) mentors can help, (5) take a proactive approach to managing work/family conflict, and (6) self-employment has its rewards, but it is associated with higher work/family conflict and lower family satisfaction.

3. *Identify the three components of attitudes and discuss cognitive dissonance.* The three components of attitudes are affective, cognitive, and behavioral. The affective component represents the feelings or emotions one has about a given object or situation. The cognitive component reflects the beliefs or ideas one has about an object or situation. The behavioral component refers to how one intends or expects to act toward someone or something. Cognitive dissonance represents the psychological discomfort an individual experiences when his or her attitudes or beliefs are incompatible with his or her behavior. There are three main methods for reducing cognitive dissonance: change an attitude or behavior, belittle the importance of the inconsistent behavior, and find consonant elements that outweigh dissonant ones.

4. *Explain how attitudes affect behavior in terms of Ajzen's theory of planned behavior.* Intentions are the key link between attitudes and behavior in Ajzen's model. Three determinants of the strength of an intention are one's attitude toward the behavior, subjective norm (social expectations and role models), and the perceived degree of one's control over the behavior. Intentions, in turn, are powerful determinants of behavior.

5. *Describe the model of organizational commitment.* Organizational commitment reflects how strongly a person identifies with an organization and is committed to its goals. Organizational commitment is composed of three related components: affective commitment, continuance commitment, and normative commitment. In turn, each of these components is influenced by a separate set of antecedents: An antecedent is something that causes the component of commitment to occur.

6. *Define the work attitudes of job involvement and job satisfaction.* Job involvement is the extent to which a person is preoccupied with, immersed in, and concerned with their job. Job satisfaction reflects how much people like or dislike their jobs.

7. *Identify and briefly describe five alternative causes of job satisfaction.* They are need fulfillment (the degree to which one's own needs are met), discrepancies (satisfaction depends on the extent to which one's expectations are met), value attainment (satisfaction depends on the degree to which one's work values are fulfilled), equity (perceived fairness of input/outcomes determines one's level of satisfaction), and dispositional/genetic (job satisfaction is dictated by one's personal traits and genetic makeup).

8. *Identify eight important correlates/consequences of job satisfaction, and summarize how each one relates to job satisfaction.* Eight major correlates/consequences of job satisfaction are motivation (moderate positive relationship), job involvement (moderate positive), organizational citizenship behavior (moderate positive), absenteeism (weak negative), withdrawal cognitions (strong negative), turnover (moderate negative), perceived stress (strong negative), and job performance (moderate positive).

Discussion Questions

1. Which type of value—terminal or instrumental—is more powerful in influencing your behavior? Explain.

2. Have you ever encountered a lack of value congruence or person–culture fit? What did you do about this situation?

3. What is your experience with work/family conflict, and what useful lessons did you learn from our discussion of it?

4. Is it easier to change an employee's attitudes or values? Explain.

5. Have you ever experienced cognitive dissonance? Describe the situation and your solution for reconciling the dissonance.

6. How could a specific intention you have at this time be explained with Ajzen's model of planned behavior?

7. Describe a situation in which you had high organizational commitment. What made you feel this way?

8. If you were a manager, which of the three key work attitudes—organizational commitment, job involvement, and job satisfaction—would be most important to cultivate in your employees? Explain your rationale.

9. Do you believe that job satisfaction is partly a function of both personal traits and genetic factors? Explain.

10. Do you think job satisfaction leads directly to better job performance? Provide your rationale.

OB in Action Case Study

Domino's Is Trying to Reduce Employee Turnover[102]

When Rob Cecere became regional manager for eight Domino's Pizza stores in New Jersey four years ago, his boss gave him a mission: slow down turnover.

Store managers in the region were leaving every three to six months. Without a steady boss, workers there who an-swered phones, made pizzas and delivered orders had a turnover rate as high as 300% a year.

Turnover is a chronic and costly headache for fast-food business, which rely on an army of low-paid workers. A harsh boss, a mean colleague, or a boring day can cause workers who earn around the minimum wage—which is $5.15 an hour nationally but slightly higher in some states—to quit for similar pay elsewhere. Average turnover for most large and midsize companies is about 10% to 15%. But at fast-food chains, rates as high as 200% a year for hourly workers aren't unusual.

Some companies are tackling the problem with a higher starting wage. Starbucks Corp. says it pays hourly store workers more than minimum wage, although the rate varies in different markets. The company says its turnover rate for such workers is 80% to 90%. Starbucks says it also focuses on friendly workplaces and good managers, but higher wages make a difference. "If we did all these other things, but we paid minimum wages, I bet our turnover would be higher," says Dave Pace, Starbucks executive vice president for partner resources.

Domino's has a different view. The company is willing to try all sorts of tactics to retain hourly employees—except paying them significantly more. "If we had increased everybody's pay 20%, could we have moved the needle a little bit to buy a little loyalty? Maybe, but that's not a long-term solution," says Domino's chief executive officer David A Brandon.

He says that while pay is a factor, "you can't overcome a bad culture by paying people a few bucks more." He believes the way to attack turnover is by focusing on store managers—hiring more selectively, coaching them on how to create better workplaces, and motivating them with the promise of stock options and promotions.

High turnover hurts the bottom line. It costs money to recruit, hire and train people, and undercuts service when inexperienced employees don't work as efficiently. It costs Domino's about $2,500 each time an hourly store worker leaves and about $20,000 each time a store manager quits, the company estimates.

Domino's turnover crusade started in 1999 when Mr Brandon was named CEO. His first day at Domino's he asked about the company's turnover rate. He was told it was 158%. "Honest to God, I almost fainted," he says.

After doing some math, he realized Domino's was recruiting, hiring and training 180,000 people a year at the time, including those at franchise stores.

Mr Brandon vowed to change things. He renamed the human resources department "People First."

Mr Brandon commissioned research that showed the most important factor in a store's success wasn't neighborhood demographics, packaging or marketing, but the quality of its store manager. "When that position is turning over at a high rate, the ripple effect of that is enormous," he says.

His strategy seems to be working. By last year, the company's overall turnover had declined to 107%.

Domino's has about 15,000 employees; another 135,000 work at its franchisees. Many are part-timers—students or workers with other jobs who need extra income and a flexible schedule.

Store managers oversee people in three entry positions: assistant managers (who earn about $8 to $10 an hour); those who answer phones (and earn an average of $6.15 an hour); and drivers, most of whom make minimum wage. Drivers, who provide their own cars and gas, also get tips and an 82-cent reimbursement for each trip they make.

All the employees make the food, including managers and drivers. . . .

Hoping to pick better managers, Domino's implemented a new test. Those seeking promotion to that job have to take a 30-minute online evaluation of their financial skills and management style. Do they understand terms such as "break even" and "cash flow"? How would they manage a poorly performing employee? Candidates then receive training on their weak points.

To help managers keep track of their best and worst performers, Domino's rolled out a new in-store computer system. The screens, which everyone in the store can see, constantly update statistics such as the average order size for each employee and how long it's taking to get a pizza out the door.

Better financial incentives helped, too. Mr Brandon introduced a program that grants stock options to about 15% of store managers, based on criteria such as sales growth and customer service. This is in addition to profit-linked bonuses that Domino's already had, which traditionally average about 30% of managers' compensation. Today store managers' base salaries start at about $32,000. . . .

Domino's also stresses to store managers that most of its franchise owners came up through the ranks. The company has about 7,603 stores worldwide, with about 10% company-owned. Franchisees must train their workers to meet the same food-making standards and use the same training materials.

When Mr Cecere was promoted to regional manager for eight Domino's stores in New Jersey in 2001, he says his boss told him: "Once you get some stability in the management ranks here, these stores will do much better."

Pep Talk

Mr Cecere, a 14-year Domino's veteran who started as a driver after high school and continued working at the company through college, knew improvements were needed. His stores were averaging $8,500 each in sales a week, about $3,000 less than the chain's current average. He gathered his managers together and gave a pep talk. "How do we get to $15,000? How do we get to $20,000? Where do you start from?" he recalls saying. "It's got to start with people. We've got to hire people and keep people."

Questions for Discussion

1. What are your thoughts about the different approaches taken by Starbucks and Domino's to reduce turnover? Given these strategies, which company will be more effective in the long term? Explain your rationale.

2. Why do you think a store manager has greater impact on employee turnover than neighborhood demographics, packaging, or marketing?

3. How would you describe David Brandon's affective, cognitive, and behavioral components of his attitude toward turnover? Be specific.

4. Use Ajzen's theory of planned behavior (Figure 6–2) to analyze how manager's can reduce voluntary turnover.

Be sure to explain what managers can do to affect each aspect of the theory.

5. Based on what you learned in this chapter, what advice would you give Mr Cecere to increase employees' organizational commitment and job satisfaction? Be specific.

Personal Awareness and Growth Exercise

Are Your Values and Commitments Aligned?[103]

Objectives

1. To discover whether or not your values and commitments are aligned.

2. To determine the cause of any values–commitment gaps and identify ways to close these gaps.

Introduction

We all value different things in our lives. For some it may be spending time with family and friends; for others it is getting the next promotion or going on an exciting vacation. Unfortunately, many of us end up spending time and resources on activities or commitments that we really don't value. As discussed in this chapter, a commitment is an agreement to do something for yourself, another individual, group, or organization. Research tells us that people are unmotivated and unhappy when they spend time, money, and effort on commitments they do not value. It thus is important to reconcile any gaps between what you value and how you spend your time, money, and effort. This exercise was designed to help you identify and reconcile values–commitment gaps.

Instructions

Complete the matrix below.[104] Begin by identifying the five values-based activities that you value most. Be as specific as possible. Avoid using generic terms like *family, friends, money,* or *career.* Instead, start the statement with a verb (e.g., *spending, doing, maintaining, increasing,* etc.) and specifically describe what you value. For example, rather than writing the word *family,* you might state that you value "spending time with them or working hard to support them."

Next, fill in the amount of money you spent in the last year on each of the values-based activities you listed. Now identify how much time you spent on each value over the last week. Remember, there are 168 hours in a week. Again, be as specific as possible. Your time can span several hours or even minutes. For example: You might spend 2 hours getting your children ready for school, 1 hour in the car on the ride home, and 5 hours in the evening for dinner and homework.

Finally fill out the "Energy" column. Energy represents the amount of physical, emotional, and mental effort you put into accomplishing values-based activities. Your energy level can range from (1) very little, (2) little, (3) some, (4) great, and (5) very great. Record a number to indicate the amount of energy you devoted to each values-based activity during the last week. Conclude the exercise by answering the discussion questions.

Values–Commitment Matrix

What Matters to Me	Money	Time	Energy

Questions for Discussion

1. Identify big gaps between what you value and how you spend your money, time, and energy. For example, a gap represents a highly valued activity that receives little or none of your money, time, and energy or a single value that receives a disproportionate amount of your resources.

2. Determine the cause of each big gap. Is it due to a failure to commit resources, a past commitment that no longer is relevant, commitment creep (i.e., the tendency to underestimate the amount of resources needed to get something done), other people's expectations, or changes in your values?

3. Based on your answer to question 2, identify what you can do to close the gaps.

Group Exercise

The Paper Airplane Contest

Objectives

1. To consider how individual abilities influence group performance.

2. To examine the role of attitudes in completing a group-based task.

3. To determine the impact of job satisfaction and job involvement on task performance.

Introduction

In this chapter, we discussed the impact of an individual's values, attitudes, and abilities on a variety of outcomes such as performance and turnover. We did not consider, however, that these same concepts apply in the context of working on a team project. The purpose of this exercise is to examine the role of abilities and attitudes when working on a team project to build a paper airplane. The quality of the team's work will be assessed by measuring three aspects of your team's airplane: (1) how far it flies, (2) how far it flies with a payload, and (3) design characteristics.[105]

Instructions

Your instructor will divide the class into groups of three to six people. Each team should pick a team name. Once formed, begin to plan what type of plane you want to design and actually construct. Keep in mind that the quality of your work will be measured through the three criteria noted above.

You will be provided with one 8.5-by-11-inch sheet of blank paper and adhesive tape. Try not to make mistakes, as you will not be given more than one piece of paper. Use these materials to construct one airplane. Decorate your plane as you see fit. It is recommended that you decorate your plane before actually building it.

Once all groups complete their work, a contest will be held to determine the best overall plane. There will be three rounds to complete this assessment. In the first round, each team will be asked to launch their plane and distance flown will be measured. The second round entails adding a payload—a paperclip—to your plane and then flying it once again. Distance flown will be measured. The final round entails a subjective evaluation by the entire class of the plane's design. Each team's overall performance will be assessed and posted.

Questions for Discussion

1. How did the group decide to design the plane?

2. Did the team consider each member's abilities when designing and flying the plane? Explain.

3. Were all team members equally involved in the task and equally satisfied with the team's final product? Discuss why or why not.

4. How could the team have increased its members' job involvement and task performance? Provide specific recommendations.

Ethical Dilemma

What Is the Impact of the Old College Grind on Personal Values?[106]

BusinessWeek Does an MBA change a person's values? According to a new study, the answer is yes—and perhaps not for the better. The nonprofit Aspen Institute found that students enter B-school with relatively idealistic ambitions, such as creating quality products. By the time they graduate, these goals have taken a backseat to such priorities as boosting share prices.

Sound a lot like MBAs Jeffrey Skilling (Harvard, 1979) and Andrew Fastow (Northwestern, 1987) at Enron? Indeed. The study included 1,978 MBAs who graduated in 2001 from 13 leading B-schools. It asked what a company's priorities should be: 75% said maximizing shareholder value; 71% chose satisfying customers; 33% said producing high-quality goods and services. Only 5% thought environmentalism should be a top goal; just 25% said creating value for their communities.

But two years earlier, when the students started B-school, 68% cited shareholder value; 75%, customer satisfaction; and 43%, quality goods and services.

MBAs also said they would leave companies whose values they can't stomach rather than stay and try to change them. "The Enron fiasco is showing that there are going to be serious cases where an organization's values are disputed, or disregarded," says Jennifer Welsh, Oxford University lecturer and manager of the research project. "We want them to stick up for their values and try to resolve the conflict."

One sure way to get MBAs keen on ethics: Put a number on how much good values add to earnings. Priscilla Wisner, a professor at Thunderbird who links corporate responsibility to profitability, says until that happens, B-schools are unlikely to go beyond the stray ethics course. That means the philosophy MBAs live by is less likely to be "Doing well by doing good" than "Show me the money."

Are your values for sale?

1. Yes, show me the money! What are the broader implications of this approach?

2. No, I have been true to my values through college and will continue to be. Explain.

3. No, I think it's possible to be true to your values and still make a good living. Explain.

4. Maybe, it depends on the situation. Explain.

5. I'm not sure, because I'm not as idealistic as I was when I started college. Explain.

6. Invent other options. Discuss.

For the Chapter 6 Internet Exercise featuring an assessment of your work/life balance and the "Are You Making Time for You?" Quiz at http://tools.monster.com/ quizzes/downtime, visit our Web site at **www.mhhe.com/kreitner.**

7

Chapter

Social Perception and Attributions

Learning Objectives

When you finish studying the material in this chapter, you should be able to:

1. Describe perception in terms of the information-processing model.

2. Identify and briefly explain four managerial implications of social perception.

3. Discuss stereotypes and the process of stereotype formation.

4. Summarize the managerial challenges and recommendations of sex-role, age, racial and ethnic, and disability stereotypes.

5. Describe and contrast the Pygmalion effect, the Galatea effect, and the Golem effect.

6. Discuss how the self-fulfilling prophecy is created and how it can be used to improve individual and group productivity.

7. Explain, according to Kelley's model, how external and internal causal attributions are formulated.

8. Contrast the fundamental attribution bias and the self-serving bias.

We are judged in less than two seconds flat. Studies conducted at Harvard University show that others rate our appearance speedily, for better or worse. More surprising, the first impression is seldom subject to change....

This means that even if appearance is not important to you, it's important to most of the people you'll meet.

"Image architect" Sandy Dumont agrees.

"Studies have shown that people who have learned to present themselves well receive preferential treatment in every area of life." ...

Taking time to educate yourself about image will pay off, she says. Customers respond instinctively to businesses that appear more up to date.

"You wouldn't go to an architect who looked old-fashioned; you'd think you were getting an old-fashioned house, and you'd be right."

Cultivating a "state of the art" appearance doesn't mean breaking the bank.

"It's not the details that give results; it's the overall impression," she said....

According to executive image consultant Pat Newquist of Phoenix, sloppy dressing is out for 2005....

Another trend Newquist is seeing is a lack of image accountability among management.

"If supervisors aren't dressing appropriately themselves; how can they role-model for the employees?" she asks.

"A customer's image of a firm is formed very quickly by the visual image portrayed by employees. A well-kept and professional appearance fosters a sense of trust and well being."

"Proper image says to a customer, 'You can trust me to handle your product, service or needs.'"

Image is not just about clothing, Newquist adds.

"How we dress, groom and conduct ourselves conveys how we feel and what motivates us."

Much of "image management" boils down to common sense. For men, clean fingernails, polished shoes and socks that match trousers are required. Facial hair should be trimmed daily. Women should beware of scuffed shoes or handbags. Overpowering colognes are a no-no for both sexes.

Susan Brooks owns Cookies From Home, a Tempe-based firm that employs 52 employees year-round and close to 200 during peak times like Christmas.

"How a person dresses, especially on a job interview, gives me insight into their spirit," she said. "I'm looking for a crisp, professional look with a splash of individual style."

A professional image also means increased productivity on the job, says Miriam Wagner of Miriam's Designer Clothes in Phoenix.

"If you're dressed as if you're going to accomplish something important, you will," she said "On the other hand, if you're dressed in last year's jeans and T-shirt, you won't feel as motivated or successful."[1]

Perceptions, stereotypes, the self-fulfilling prophecy, and attributions, four topics discussed in this chapter, play a central role in the opening vignette. As suggested by Sandy Dumont, Pat Newquist, and research conducted at Harvard, your appearance is related to the perceptions and attributions that are made about you. The vignette also underscores a key tenant of the self-fulfilling prophecy: Your beliefs and dreams can come true. This proposition explains why Miriam Wagner recommended that you should dress for success.

It is important to remember that our perceptions and associated feelings about others are influenced by information we receive from newspapers, magazines, television, radio, family, and friends. You see, we all use information stored in our memories to interpret and interact with others. As human beings, we constantly strive to make sense of our surroundings. The resulting knowledge influences our behavior and helps us navigate our way through life. Think of the perceptual process that occurs when meeting someone for the first time. Your attention is drawn to the individual's physical appearance, mannerisms, actions, and reactions to what you say and do. You ultimately arrive at conclusions based on your perceptions of this social interaction. The brown-haired, green-eyed individual turns out to be friendly and fond of outdoor activities. You further conclude that you like this person and then ask him or her to go to a concert, calling the person by the name you stored in memory.

This reciprocal process of perception, interpretation, and behavioral response also applies at work. Consider the situation faced by Stephanie Odle and other women employed at Wal-Mart. Stephanie's job perceptions changed after she found a W-2 lying around in the Riverside, California, Sam's Club where she worked as an assistant manager.

> The W-2 belonged to a male assistant manager who turned out to be making $10,000 more a year than she was. She says she was told that her co-worker was paid more because he had "a wife and kids to support." When the single mother protested, she was asked to submit a personal household budget. She did and was granted a $40 a week raise. "It was humiliating," says Odle. And she was still making less than the male manager. Odle claims that she was eventually fired for speaking up. . . .
>
> Other women tell stories of management trips to strip clubs and business meetings at Hooters. One was allegedly advised that if she wanted a better job she needed to "doll up" more and "blow the cobwebs from her makeup."[2]

Stephanie Odle and a host of other women are suing Wal-Mart because they perceive the company is discriminating. In contrast, the company perceives that it fairly compensates women and men and that the organization treats its employees with dignity, a fundamental component of Wal-Mart's organizational culture. This example illustrates the interplay between perceptual processes and managing diverse employees.

Let us now begin our exploration of the perceptual process and its associated outcomes. In this chapter we focus on (1) an information-processing model of perception, (2) stereotypes, (3) the self-fulfilling prophecy, and (4) how causal attributions are used to interpret behavior.

An Information-Processing Model of Perception

Perception is a cognitive process that enables us to interpret and understand our surroundings. Recognition of objects is one of this process's major functions. For example, both people and animals recognize familiar objects in their environments. You would recognize a picture of your best friend; dogs and cats can recognize their food dishes or a favorite toy. Reading involves recognition of visual patterns representing letters in the alphabet. People must recognize objects to meaningfully interact with their environment. But since OB's principal focus is on people, the following discussion emphasizes *social* perception rather than object perception.

The study of how people perceive one another has been labeled *social cognition* and *social information processing.* In contrast to the perception of objects,

> Social cognition is the study of how people make sense of other people and themselves. It focuses on how ordinary people think about people and how they think they think about people. . . .
>
>   Research on social cognition also goes beyond naive psychology. The study of social cognition entails a fine-grained analysis of how people think about themselves and others, and it leans heavily on the theory and methods of cognitive psychology.[3]

Let us now examine the fundamental processes underlying perception.

Perception
Process of interpreting one's environment.

Four-Stage Sequence and a Working Example

Perception involves a four-stage information-processing sequence (hence, the label "information processing"). Figure 7–1 illustrates a basic information-processing model of perception. Three of the stages in this model—selective attention/comprehension, encoding and simplification, and storage and retention—describe how specific information and environmental stimuli are observed and stored in memory. The fourth and final stage, retrieval and response, involves turning mental representations into real-world judgments and decisions.

Figure 7–1   *Perception: An Information-Processing Model*

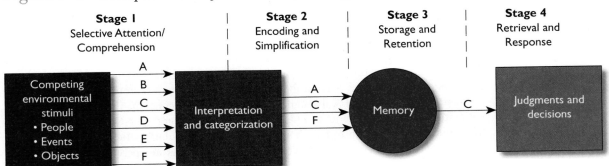

Keep the following everyday example in mind as we look at the four stages of perception. Suppose you were thinking of taking a course in, say, personal finance. Three professors teach the same course, using different types of instruction and testing procedures. Through personal experience, you have come to prefer good professors who rely on the case method of instruction and essay tests. According to the information-processing model of perception, you would likely arrive at a decision regarding which professor to take as follows:

Stage 1: Selective Attention/Comprehension

People are constantly bombarded by physical and social stimuli in the environment. Since they do not have the mental capacity to fully comprehend all this information, they selectively perceive subsets of environmental stimuli. This is where attention plays a role. **Attention** is the process of becoming consciously aware of something or someone. Attention can be focused on information either from the environment or from memory. Regarding the latter situation, if you sometimes find yourself thinking about totally unrelated events or people while reading a textbook, your memory is the focus of your attention. Research has shown that people tend to pay attention to salient stimuli.

Attention
Being consciously aware of something or someone.

Salient Stimuli Something is *salient* when it stands out from its context. For example, a 250-pound man would certainly be salient in a women's aerobics class but not at a meeting of the National Football League Players' Association. One's needs and goals often dictate which stimuli are salient. For a driver whose gas gauge is on empty, an Exxon or Mobil sign is more salient than a McDonald's or Burger King sign. The reverse would be true for a hungry driver with a full gas tank. Moreover, research shows that people have a tendency to pay more attention to negative than positive information. This leads to a negativity bias.[4] This bias helps explain the gawking factor that slows traffic to a crawl following a car accident.

During the 2004 summer Olympics, gymnast Paul Hamm helped the United States to achieve its highest gold medal total (5) since 1979. This was a highly salient event during the Olympics.

Back to Our Example You begin your search for the "right" personal finance professor by asking friends who have taken classes from the three professors. You also may interview the various professors who teach the class to gather still more relevant information. Returning to Figure 7–1, all the information you obtain represents competing environmental stimuli labeled A through F. Because you are concerned about the method of instruction (e.g., line A in Figure 7–1), testing procedures (e.g., line C), and past grade distributions (e.g., line F), information in those areas is particularly salient to you. Figure 7–1 shows that these three salient pieces of information thus are perceived, and you then progress to the second stage of information processing. Meanwhile, competing stimuli represented by lines B, D, and E in Figure 7–1 fail to get your attention and are discarded from further consideration.

Stage 2: Encoding and Simplification

Observed information is not stored in memory in its original form. Encoding is required; raw information is interpreted or translated into mental representations. To accomplish this, perceivers assign pieces of information to **cognitive categories.** "By *category* we mean a number of objects that are considered equivalent. Categories are generally designated by names, e.g., *dog, animal.*"[5] People, events, and objects are interpreted and evaluated by comparing their characteristics with information contained in schemata (or schema in singular form).

Cognitive categories
Mental depositories for storing information.

Schemata   A **schema** represents a person's mental picture or summary of a particular event or type of stimulus. For example, what is your mental picture of the sequence of events that occur when you go out to dinner in a restaurant? Your memory probably is quite similar to the restaurant schema shown in Table 7–1.

Schema
Mental picture of an event or object.

Table 7–1   *Restaurant Schema*

> **Schema: Restaurant.**
> **Characters: Customers, hostess, waiter, chef, cashier.**
> **Scene 1: Entering.**
>   Customer goes into restaurant.
>   Customer finds a place to sit.
>   He may find it himself.
>   He may be seated by a hostess.
>   He asks the hostess for a table.
>   She gives him permission to go to the table.
> **Scene 2: Ordering.**
>   Customer receives a menu.
>   Customer reads it.
>   Customer decides what to order.
>   Waiter takes the order.
>   Waiter sees the customer.
>   Waiter goes to the customer.
>   Customer orders what he wants.
>   Chef cooks the meal.
> **Scene 3: Eating.**
>   After some time the waiter brings the meal from the chef.
>   Customer eats the meal.
> **Scene 4: Exiting.**
>   Customer asks the waiter for the check.
>   Waiter gives the check to the customer.
>   Customer leaves a tip.
>   The size of the tip depends on the goodness of the service.
>   Customer pays the cashier.
>   Customer leaves the restaurant.
>
> SOURCE: From D Rumelhart, *Introduction to Human Information Processing* (New York: John Wiley & Sons, Inc., 1977). Reprinted by permission of John Wiley & Sons, Inc.

Does a Schema Improve the Comprehension of Written Material?

Instructions

The purpose of this exercise is to demonstrate the role of schema in encoding. First read the passage shown below. Once done, rate the comprehensiveness of what you read using the scale provided. Next, examine the schema label presented in note 6 in the Endnotes section at the end of the book. With this label in mind, reread the passage, and rate its comprehensiveness. Now think about the explanation for why your ratings changed. You just experienced the impact of schema in encoding.

Read This Passage

The procedure is actually quite simple. First you arrange things into different groups. Of course, one pile may be sufficient depending on how much there is to do. If you have to go somewhere else due to lack of facilities, that is the next step; otherwise you are pretty well set. It is important not to overdo things. That is, it is better to do too few things at once than too many. In the short run this may not seem important, but complications can easily arise. A mistake can be expensive as well. At first the whole procedure will seem complicated. Soon, however, it will become just another facet of life. It is difficult to foresee any end to the necessity for this task in the immediate future, but then you never can tell. After the procedure is completed, you arrange the materials into different groups again. Then they can be put into their appropriate places. Eventually they will be used once more, and the whole cycle will then have to be repeated. However, that is part of life.

Comprehensive Scale

Very Uncomprehensive		Neither		Very Comprehensive
	1——2——3——4——5			

SOURCE: Reprinted from J D Bransford and M K Johnson, "Contextual Prerequisite for Understanding: Some Investigations of Comprehension & Recall," *Journal of Memory & Language* (formerly *Journal of Verbal Learning & Verbal Behavior*) December 1972, p 722. Copyright © 1972 with permission from Elsevier.

Cognitive-category labels are needed to make schemata meaningful. The OB Exercise above illustrates this by having you rate the comprehensiveness of a schema both without and with its associated category label.[6] Take a moment now to complete this exercise.

Encoding Outcomes We use the encoding process to interpret and evaluate our environment. Interestingly, this process can result in differing interpretations and evaluations of the same person or event. Varying interpretations of what we observe occur due to four key reasons.

First, people possess different information in the schemata used for interpretation. For instance, a recent meta-analysis of 62 studies revealed women and men had different opinions about what type of behaviors constituted sexual harassment. Women defined a broader range of behaviors as harassing.[7] Second, our moods and emotions influence our focus of attention and evaluations of others.[8] Third, people tend to apply recently used cognitive categories during encoding. For example, you are more likely to interpret a neutral behavior exhibited by a professor as positive if you were recently thinking about positive categories and events.[9] Fourth, individual differences influence encoding. Pessimistic or depressed individuals, for instance, tend to interpret their surroundings more negatively than optimistic and happy people.[10] The point is that we should not be surprised when people interpret and evaluate the same situation or event differently. Researchers are currently trying to identify the host of factors that influence the encoding process.

Back to Our Example   Having collected relevant information about the three personal finance professors and their approaches, you compare this information with other details contained in schemata. This leads you to form an impression and evaluation of what it would be like to take a course from each professor. In turn, the relevant information contained on paths A, C, and F in Figure 7–1 are passed along to the third stage of information processing.

Stage 3: Storage and Retention

This phase involves storage of information in long-term memory. Long-term memory is like an apartment complex consisting of separate units connected to one another. Although different people live in each apartment, they sometimes interact. In addition, large apartment complexes have different wings (such as A, B, and C). Long-term memory similarly consists of separate but related categories. Like the individual apartments inhabited by unique residents, the connected categories contain different types of information. Information also passes among these categories. Finally, long-term memory is made up of three compartments (or wings) containing categories of information about events, semantic materials, and people.[11]

Event Memory   This compartment is composed of categories containing information about both specific and general events. These memories describe appropriate sequences of events in well-known situations, such as going to a restaurant (refer back to Table 7–1), going on a job interview, going to a food store, or going to a movie.

Semantic Memory   Semantic memory refers to general knowledge about the world. In so doing, it functions as a mental dictionary of concepts. Each concept contains a definition (e.g., a good leader) and associated traits (outgoing), emotional states (happy), physical characteristics (tall), and behaviors (works hard). Just as there are schemata for general events, concepts in semantic memory are stored as schemata. Given our previous discussion of managing diversity in Chapter 2 and International OB in Chapter 4, it should come as no surprise that there are cultural differences in the type of information stored in semantic memory. The Real World/Real People feature on page 212, for example, is a good illustration of this point. The Chinese did not interpret the ads as expected because the advertisers failed to recognize that the encoding process is influenced by cultural differences in semantic memory.

Person Memory   Categories within this compartment contain information about a single individual (your supervisor) or groups of people (managers).

Back to Our Example   As the time draws near for you to decide which personal finance professor to take, your schemata of them are stored in the three categories of long-term memory. These schemata are available for immediate comparison or retrieval.

Stage 4: Retrieval and Response

People retrieve information from memory when they make judgments and decisions. Our ultimate judgments and decisions are either based on the process of drawing on, interpreting, and integrating categorical information stored in long-term memory or on retrieving a summary judgment that was already made.[12]

Advertising in China Requires Consideration of the Encoding Process

BusinessWeek
The ad campaign left shoemaker Nike Inc. flatfooted. The company's "Chamber of Fear" spot featured LeBron James of the NBA's Cleveland Cavaliers battling—and defeating—a computer-generated Kung Fu master. It might not have raised eyebrows elsewhere, but Chinese consumers found the concept insulting, and Beijing banned the ad last December. . . .

And as Nike's Kung Fu ad shows, campaigns created for China sometimes fall wide of the mark. Toyota had a similar experience with an ad showing a Land Cruiser SUV towing what appeared to be a Chinese military truck and another featuring stone lions, a traditional symbol of power in China, bowing down to Toyota's Prodo GX. Chinese consumers balked at the perceived insult to their armed forces and at the notion of bowing to anything—even a car—representing Japan.

Kung Fu masters. Military trucks. Stone lion. The potential pitfalls are endless.

SOURCE: F Balfour and D Kiley, "Ad Agencies Unchained," *BusinessWeek*, April 25, 2005, pp 50–51.

Concluding our example, it is registration day and you have to choose which professor to take for personal finance. After retrieving from memory your schemata-based impressions of the three professors, you select a good one who uses the case method and gives essay tests (line C in Figure 7–1). In contrast, you may choose your preferred professor by simply recalling the decision you made two weeks ago.

Managerial Implications

Social cognition is the window through which we all observe, interpret, and prepare our responses to people and events. A wide variety of managerial activities, organizational processes, and quality-of-life issues are thus affected by perception. Consider, for example, the following implications.

Hiring Interviewers make hiring decisions based on their impression of how an applicant fits the perceived requirements of a job. Unfortunately, many of these decisions are made within the first 10 minutes of an interview.[13] Inaccurate impressions in either direction produce poor hiring decisions. Moreover, interviewers with racist or sexist schemata can undermine the accuracy and legality of hiring decisions. Those invalid schemata need to be confronted and improved through coaching and training. Failure to do so can lead to poor hiring decisions. For example, a study of 46 male and 66 female financial-institution managers revealed that their hiring decisions were biased by the physical attractiveness of applicants. More attractive men and women were hired over less attractive applicants with equal qualifications.[14] On the positive side, however, another study demonstrated that interviewer training can reduce the use of invalid schema. Training improved interviewers' ability to obtain high-quality, job-related information and to stay focused on the interview task. Trained interviewers provided more balanced judgments about applicants than did nontrained interviewers.[15]

Performance Appraisal Faulty schemata about what constitutes good versus poor performance can lead to inaccurate performance appraisals, which erode work motivation, commitment, and loyalty. For example, a study of 166 production employees indicated that they had greater trust in management when they perceived that the performance appraisal process provided accurate evaluations of their performance.[16] Therefore, it is important for managers to accurately identify the behavioral characteristics and results indicative of good performance at the beginning of a performance review cycle. These characteristics then can serve as the standards for evaluating employee performance. The importance of using objective rather than subjective measures of employee performance was highlighted in a meta-analysis involving 50 studies and 8,341 individuals. Results revealed that objective and subjective measures of employee performance were only moderately related. The researchers concluded that objective and subjective measures of performance are not interchangeable.[17] Managers are thus advised to use more objectively based measures of performance as much as possible because subjective indicators are prone to bias and inaccuracy. In those cases where the job does not possess objective measures of performance, however, managers should still use subjective evaluations. Furthermore, because memory for specific instances of employee performance deteriorates over time, managers need a mechanism for accurately recalling employee behavior.[18] Research reveals that individuals can be trained to be more accurate raters of performance.[19]

Leadership   Research demonstrates that employees' evaluations of leader effectiveness are influenced strongly by their schemata of good and poor leaders.[20] A leader will have a difficult time influencing employees when he or she exhibits behaviors contained in employees' schemata of poor leaders. A team of researchers investigated the behaviors contained in our schemata of good and poor leaders. Good leaders were perceived as exhibiting the following behaviors: (1) assigning specific tasks to group members, (2) telling others that they had done well, (3) setting specific goals for the group, (4) letting other group members make decisions, (5) trying to get the group to work as a team, and (6) maintaining definite standards of performance. In contrast, poor leaders were perceived to exhibit these behaviors: (1) telling others that they had performed poorly, (2) insisting on having their own way, (3) doing things without explaining themselves, (4) expressing worry over the group members' suggestions, (5) frequently changing plans, and (6) letting the details of the task become overwhelming.[21]

Communication   Managers need to remember that social perception is a screening process that can distort communication, both coming and going. Messages are interpreted and categorized according to schemata developed through past experiences and influenced by one's age, gender, and ethnic, geographic, and cultural orientations. Consider how Wal-Mart's German employees perceived and responded to the company's newly translated code of ethics:

> To American eyes, a new ethics manual is standard stuff. But when Wal-Mart Stores, Inc., distributed its newly translated ethics code to German employees a few weeks ago, it created a furor. They read a caution against supervisor–employee romances as a puritanical ban on interoffice relationships, while a call to report improper behavior was seen as an invitation to play the rat. "They have to communicate better," says Ulrich Dalibor, an official at the ver.di service-workers union, which represents German employees of the Bentonville (Arkansas)-based retailer.[22]

Wal-Mart clearly underestimated the German employees' perceptions and response, which was based on local customs. Effective communicators try to tailor their messages to the receiver's perceptual schemata. This requires well-developed listening and observational skills in addition to cross-cultural sensitivity.

Stereotypes: Perceptions about Groups of People

While it is often true that beauty is in the eye of the beholder, perception does result in some predictable outcomes. Managers aware of the perception process and its outcomes enjoy a competitive edge. The Walt Disney Company, for instance, takes full advantage of perceptual tendencies to influence customers' reactions to waiting in long lines at its theme parks:

> In Orlando, at Disney-MGM Studios, visitors waiting to get into a Muppet attraction watch tapes of Kermit the Frog on TV monitors. At the Magic Kingdom, visitors to the Extra Terrestrial Alien Encounter attraction are entertained by a talking robot before the show. At some rides, the company uses simple toys, like blocks, to help parents keep small children busy and happy during the wait.[23]

This example illustrates how the focus of one's attention influences the perception of standing in long lines.

Likewise, managers can use knowledge of perceptual outcomes to help them interact more effectively with employees. For example, Table 7–2 describes five common perceptual errors. Since these perceptual errors often distort the evaluation of job applicants and of employee performance, managers need to guard against them. This section examines one of the most important and potentially harmful perceptual outcomes associated with person perception: stereotypes. After exploring the process of stereotype formation and maintenance, we discuss sex-role stereotypes, age stereotypes, race stereotypes, disability stereotypes, and the managerial challenge to avoid stereotypical biases.

Table 7–2   *Commonly Found Perceptual Errors*

Perceptual Error	Description	Example
Halo	A rater forms an overall impression about an object and then uses that impression to bias ratings about the object.	Rating a professor high on the teaching dimensions of ability to motivate students, knowledge, and communication because we like him or her.
Leniency	A personal characteristic that leads an individual to consistently evaluate other people or objects in an extremely positive fashion.	Rating a professor high on all dimensions of performance regardless of his or her actual performance. The rater that hates to say negative things about others.
Central tendency	The tendency to avoid all extreme judgments and rate people and objects as average or neutral.	Rating a professor average on all dimensions of performance regardless of his or her actual performance.
Recency effects	The tendency to remember recent information. If the recent information is negative, the person or object is evaluated negatively.	Although a professor has given good lectures for 12 to 15 weeks, he or she is evaluated negatively because lectures over the last 3 weeks were done poorly.
Contrast effects	The tendency to evaluate people or objects by comparing them with characteristics of recently observed people or objects.	Rating a good professor as average because you compared his or her performance with three of the best professors you have ever had in college. You are currently taking courses from the three excellent professors.

Stereotype Formation and Maintenance

"A **stereotype** is an individual's set of beliefs about the characteristics or attributes of a group."[24] Stereotypes are not always negative. For example, the belief that engineers are good at math is certainly part of a stereotype. Stereotypes may or may not be accurate. Engineers may in fact be better at math than the general population. In general, stereotypic characteristics are used to differentiate a particular group of people from other groups.[25]

It is important to remember that stereotypes are a fundamental component of the perception process and we use them to help process the large amount of information that bombards us daily. As such, it is not immoral or bad to possess stereotypes. That said, however, inappropriate use of stereotypes can lead to poor decisions; can create barriers for women, older individuals, people of color, and people with disabilities; and can undermine loyalty and job satisfaction. For example, a study of 44 African-American managers and 80 white managers revealed that African-American managers experienced slower rates of promotion and less psychological support than white managers.[26] Another sample of 69 female executives and 69 male executives indicated women reported greater promotional barriers and fewer overseas assignments, and had more assignments with no authority than men.[27]

Stereotyping is a four-step process. It begins by categorizing people into groups according to various criteria, such as gender, age, race, and occupation. Next, we infer that all people within a particular category possess the same traits or characteristics (e.g., all women are nurturing, older people have more job-related accidents, all African-Americans are good athletes, all professors are absentminded). Then, we form expectations of others and interpret their behavior according to our stereotypes. Finally, stereotypes are maintained by (1) overestimating the frequency of stereotypic behaviors exhibited by others, (2) incorrectly explaining expected and unexpected behaviors, and (3) differentiating minority individuals from oneself.[28] It is hard to stop people from using stereotypes because these four steps are self-reinforcing. The good news, however, is that researchers have identified a few ways to break the chain of stereotyping.

Research shows that the use of stereotypes is influenced by the amount and type of information available to an individual and his or her motivation to accurately process information.[29] People are less apt to use stereotypes to judge others when they encounter salient information that is highly inconsistent with a stereotype. For instance, you are unlikely to assign stereotypic "professor" traits to a new professor you have this semester if he or she rides a Harley-Davidson, wears leather pants to class, and has a pierced nose. People also are less likely to rely on stereotypes when they are motivated to avoid using them. That is, accurate information processing requires mental effort. Stereotyping is generally viewed as a less effortful strategy of information processing. Let us now take a look at different types of stereotypes and consider additional methods for reducing their biasing effects.

Sex-Role Stereotypes

A **sex-role stereotype** is the belief that differing traits and abilities make men and women particularly well suited to different roles. A recent Gallup poll sheds light on the sex-role stereotypes held by adults within the United States. Results revealed the majority of respondents viewed women as more emotional, affectionate, talkative, patient, and creative than men. Men, on the other hand, were perceived as more aggressive, courageous, easygoing, and ambitious than women.[30] Although research demonstrates that men and women do not systematically differ in the manner suggested by traditional stereotypes,[31] these stereotypes still persist. Unfortunately, this is true even for some highly educated, influential

Stereotype
Beliefs about the characteristics of a group.

Sex-role stereotype
Beliefs about appropriate roles for men and women.

Stereotypes Still Persist

BusinessWeek Lucie Yueqi Guo and Xianlin Li are proof that girls can love science, too. The two seniors at North Carolina School of Science & Mathematics, a high school in Durham, won the $100,000 grand prize in the team category of the 2004–05 Siemens Westinghouse Competition in Math, Science, & Technology for a project studying the effect of DNA methylation on breast cancer. (Got that?) "Both of us have been interested in science ever since we were very young," says Guo. "Neither of us ever felt our gender was a detriment."

Their perspective is welcome amid the furor over a now-notorious speech by Harvard University President Lawrence H Summers. At a January 14 conference on the paucity of women in the sciences, he suggested there may be "innate differences" between male and female brains that make it harder for women to excel in math and science. He quickly backed down. And in fact most scientists say there's little evidence that men's brains, though different structurally than women's, are better or worse at specific intellectual endeavors. "Intelligence is always the result of an interplay between biology and environment," says Rex E Jung, a University of New Mexico neurologist.

SOURCE: Excerpted from C Arnst, "Getting Girls to the Lab Bench," *BusinessWeek*, February 7, 2005, p 42. Reprinted by permission of The McGraw-Hill Companies, Inc.

individuals (see Real World/Real People). Further, it is important to keep in mind that the use of sex-role stereotypes when making decisions about employees can land an organization in court. For example, in a landmark 1989 Title VII decision, the Supreme Court "ruled in Hopkins v. Price Waterhouse that gender stereotyping in the workplace is illegal. Anne Hopkins had claimed she was terminated from her job at Price Waterhouse because senior partners perceived her dress and behavior as too masculine."[32] The key question now becomes whether these stereotypes influence the hiring, evaluation, and promotion of people at work.

A meta-analysis of 19 studies comprising 1,842 individuals found no significant relationships between applicant gender and hiring recommendations.[33] A second meta-analysis of 24 experimental studies revealed that men and women received similar performance ratings for the same level of task performance. Stated differently, there was no pro-male bias. These experimental results were further supported in a field study of female and male professors.[34] Unfortunately, results pertaining to promotion decisions are not as promising. A field study of 682 employees in a multinational *Fortune* 500 company revealed that gender was significantly related to promotion potential ratings. Men received more favorable evaluations than women in spite of controlling for age, education, organizational tenure, salary grade, and type of job.[35] Another study of 100 male and female US Army commissioned officers at the rank of captain unfortunately produced similar results. Men were consistently judged to be better leaders than women.[36] The existence of sex-role stereotypes may partially explain this finding.[37]

Age Stereotypes

Age stereotypes reinforce age discrimination because of their negative orientation. For example, long-standing age stereotypes depict older workers as less satisfied, not as involved with their work, less motivated, not as committed, less productive than their younger coworkers, and more apt to be absent from work. Older employees are also perceived as being more accident prone. As with sex-role stereotypes, these age stereotypes are based more on fiction than fact.

OB researcher Susan Rhodes sought to determine whether age stereotypes were supported by data from 185 different studies. She discovered that as age increases so do employees' job satisfaction, job involvement, internal work motivation, and organizational commitment. Moreover, older workers were not more accident prone.[38] Consistent results also were found in a more recent study conducted by the National Council on Aging. A survey of 240 employers from 27 states indicated that respondents viewed older workers as thorough and reliable in their work, flexible and willing to change, and interested in learning new tasks.[39]

Results are not as clear-cut regarding job performance. A meta-analysis of 96 studies representing 38,983 people and a cross section of jobs revealed that age and job performance were unrelated.[40] Some OB researchers, however, believe that this finding does not reflect the true relationship between age and performance. They propose that the relationship between age and performance changes as people grow older.[41] This idea was tested on data obtained from 24,219 individuals. In support of this hypothesis, results revealed that age was positively related to performance for younger employees (25 to 30 years of age) and then plateaued: Older employees were not less productive. Age and experience also predicted performance better for more complex jobs than other jobs, and job experience had a stronger relationship with performance than age.[42] Another study examined memory, reasoning, spatial relations, and dual tasking for 1,000 doctors, ages 25 to 92, and 600 other adults. The researchers concluded "that a large proportion of older individuals scored as well or better on aptitude tests as those in the prime of life. We call these intellectually vigorous individuals 'optimal agers.' "[43]

Dr Michael DeBakey is a good example. In 1939, he was one of the first physicians to find a relationship between smoking and cancer and is recognized as one of the greatest surgeons ever. He was interviewed by a reporter from the *Wall Street Journal* to determine his secrets of health: He is still working at the age of 96.

Entering the room, Dr DeBakey looked only slightly older than he did in photographs taken decades ago. . . . Whatever subject I broached, his response reflected a quality that aging experts say is common among the long lived: optimism. Avian flu doesn't worry him: "We're lucky now to pick up those threats early," he says. He sees democracy prevailing over terrorism. . . . But here is what Dr DeBakey sees as the real secret to his longevity: work. He rises at five each morning to write in his study for two hours before driving to the hospital at 7:30 AM, where he stays until 6 PM. He returns to his library after dinner for an additional two to three hours of reading or writing before going to bed after midnight. He sleeps only four to five hours a night, as he always has.[44]

Dr. Michael DeBakey, recognized as one of the greatest surgeons ever, disconfirms many age-related stereotypes. He is very satisfied, committed, and involved with his job despite being 96 years old. Given the choice, would you allow Dr. DeBakey to operate on you?

What about turnover and absenteeism? A meta-analysis containing 45 samples and a total of 21,656 individuals revealed that age and turnover were negatively related.[45] That is older employees quit less often than did younger employees. Similarly, another meta-analysis of 34 studies encompassing 7,772 workers indicated that age was inversely related to both voluntary (a day at the beach) and involuntary (sick day) absenteeism.[46] Contrary to stereotypes, older workers are ready and able to meet their job requirements. Moreover, results from the two meta-analyses suggest managers should focus more attention on the turnover and absenteeism among younger workers than among older workers.

Racial and Ethnic Stereotypes

There are many different racial and ethnic stereotypes that exist. For instance, African-Americans have been viewed as athletic, aggressive, and angry; Asians as quiet, introverted, smarter, and more quantitatively oriented; Hispanics as family oriented and religious; and Arabs as angry.[47] Racial and ethnic stereotypes are particularly problematic because they are automatically triggered and lead to racial bias without our conscious awareness.[48] These stereotypes are often activated by looking at someone's facial features or skin color.[49]

Negative racial and ethnic stereotypes are still apparent in many aspects of life and in many organizations. Consider the experience of Eldrick (Tiger) Woods. Tiger was raised in two different cultures. His mother is from Thailand and his father is African-American. Since becoming a professional golfer in 1996, Tiger has won 59 tournaments and he has more career victories than any other active player on the PGA Tour. He also is the only golfer in history to hold the title for all four major tournaments at the same time.[50] Unfortunately, Tiger has experienced a host of racial stereotypes and biases (see Real World/Real People on page 219). Let us now consider the evidence presented in the following paragraphs about racial and ethnic stereotypes in organizations.

There is not a large percentage of African-American, Hispanic, and Asian managers in the United States. One study examined the relationship of race to employee attitudes across 814 African-American managers and 814 white managers. Results demonstrated that African-Americans, when compared with whites, felt less accepted by peers, perceived lower managerial discretion on their jobs, reached career plateaus more frequently, noted lower levels of career satisfaction, and received lower performance ratings.[51] Negative findings such as these prompted researchers to investigate if race stereotypes actually bias hiring decisions, performance ratings, and promotion decisions.

A meta-analysis of interview decisions from 31 studies with total samples of 4,169 African-Americans and 6,307 whites revealed that whites received higher interviewer evaluations. Another study of 2,805 interviews uncovered a same-race bias for Hispanics and African-Americans but not for whites. That is, Hispanics and African-American interviewers evaluated applicants of their own race more favorably than applicants of other races. White interviewers did not exhibit any such bias.[52] Performance ratings were found to be unbiased in two studies that used large samples of 21,547 and 39,537 rater-ratee pairs of African-American and white employees, respectively, from throughout the United States. These findings revealed that African-American and white managers did not differentially evaluate their employees based on race.[53] Finally, a study of 153 police officers' promotion decisions by panel interviews indicated a same-race rating effect. That is, candidates received higher evaluations when they were racially similar to the interviewers.[54] Given the increasing number of people of color that will enter the workforce over the next 10 years (recall our discussion in Chapter 2), employers should focus on nurturing and developing women and people of color as well as increasing managers' sensitivities to invalid racial stereotypes.

Tiger Woods Experiences Racial Bias

"I became aware of my racial identity on my first day of school, on my first day of kindergarten. A group of sixth graders tied me to a tree, spray-painted the word 'nigger' on me, and threw rocks at me. That was my first day at school. And the teacher really didn't do much of anything. I used to live across the street from school and kind of down the way a little bit. The teacher said, 'Okay, just go home.' So I had to outrun all these kids going home, which I was able to do. It was certainly an eye-opening experience, you know, being five years old. We were the only minority family in all of Cypress, California.

"When my parents moved in, before I was born, they used to have these oranges come through the window all the time. And it could have not been racially initiated or it could have been. We don't know. But it was very interesting, though people don't necessarily know it, that I grew up in the 1980s and still had incidents. I had a racial incident even in the 1990s at my home course where I grew up, the Navy golf course. And right before the 1994 US Amateur, I was 18 years old, I was out practicing, just hitting pitch shots and some guy just yelled over the fence and used the N word numerous times at me. That's in 1994."

SOURCE: C Barkley, *Who's Afraid of a Large Black Man?* (New York: Penguin Press, 2005), p 7.

Phil Mickelson (left) is helping Tiger Woods with the green jacket he received after winning the 2005 Masters golf tournament. Despite his international acclaim and reputation, Tiger Woods has battled racial stereotypes into the mid-90s. What can be done to stop the spread of racism and racial stereotypes?

Disability Stereotypes

People with disabilities not only face negative stereotypes that affect their employability, but they also can be stigmatized by the general population. Consider Paul Stephen Miller's experience after he graduated from Harvard Law School near the top of his class:

> He looked forward to a future full of possibilities, having graduated from arguably the top law school in the country, a virtual guarantee of a high-paying job in an elite law firm. While his classmates snared those prestigious jobs, over 40 firms with whom he interviewed rejected him. Miller is a dwarf. He prefers to call himself "short stature." Most employers simply explained that there were other "more qualified" candidates. A Philadelphia firm explained, however, that while impressed with his credentials, they feared their clients might see Miller in the hallway and "think we were running some sort of circus freak show."[55]

Unfortunately, Miller's experience is not atypical. Although two out of three individuals with disabilities can and want to work, roughly 75% are unemployed.[56] In addition, disabled employees make less money on average than people without disabilities. People with disabilities are more likely to live in poverty than people without disabilities. Moreover, people with disabilities face stereotypes that depict them as more likely to miss work, less capable, needy or helpless, bitter, and antisocial.[57] The American with Disabilities Act (ADA) was created in 1990 in response to these statistics and trends. As mentioned in Chapter 2, this act prohibits discrimination against qualified employees with physical or mental disabilities or chronic illness and requires "reasonable accommodation" of disabled employees.[58] So what do you know about the performance and costs of employing people with disabilities?

Unfortunately, there have not been any rigorous scientific studies comparing the performance of disabled and able-bodied employees performing the same job. There are, however, other data suggesting that disabled employees are highly effective at work. A Harris poll found that almost 90% of disabled workers received "good" or "excellent" performance ratings. They also were found to perform their jobs just as well as employees without disabilities, and they were not more difficult to manage. Another Harris poll indicated that employers supported policies to increase the employment of disabled people because they were so pleased with the performance of their disabled employees. DuPont, for example, found that disabled employees had higher safety ratings than their nondisabled counterparts. The stereotypes about disabled employees being expensive to accommodate also is untrue. Nearly 20% of accommodations cost nothing, and 50% cost less than $500.[59]

Managerial Challenges and Recommendations

The key managerial challenge is to reduce the extent to which stereotypes influence decision-making and interpersonal processes throughout the organization. We recommend that an organization first needs to inform its workforce about the problem of stereotyping through employee education and training. Training also can be used to equip managers with the skills needed to handle situations associated with managing employees with disabilities. The next step entails engaging in a broad effort to reduce stereotypes throughout the organization. Social scientists believe that "quality" interpersonal contact among mixed groups is the best way to reduce stereotypes because it provides people with more accurate data about the characteristics of other groups of people. As such, organizations should create opportunities for diverse employees to meet and work together in cooperative groups of equal status.

Another recommendation is for managers to identify valid individual differences (discussed in Chapter 5) that differentiate between successful and unsuccessful performers. As previously discussed, for instance, research reveals experience is a better predictor of performance than age. Research also shows that managers can be trained to use these valid criteria when hiring applicants and evaluating employee performance.[60]

Removing promotional barriers for men and women, people of color, and persons with disabilities is another viable solution to alleviating the stereotyping problem. This can be accomplished by minimizing the differences in job experience across groups of people. Similar experience, coupled with the accurate evaluation of performance, helps managers to make decisions that are less influenced by stereotypes.

There are several recommendations that can be pursued based on the documented relationship between age and performance:

1. Because performance plateaus with age for noncomplex jobs, organizations may use the variety of job design techniques discussed in Chapter 8 to increase employees' intrinsic motivation.

2. Organizations may need to consider using incentives to motivate employees to upgrade their skills and abilities. This will help avoid unnecessary plateaus.

3. It may be advisable to hire older people in order to acquire their accumulated experience. This is especially useful for highly complex jobs. Moreover, hiring older workers is a good solution for reducing turnover, providing role models for younger employees, and coping with the current shortage of qualified entry-level workers.

It is important to obtain top management's commitment and support to eliminate the organizational practices that support or reinforce stereotyping and discriminatory decisions. Research clearly demonstrates that top management support is essential to successful implementation of the types of organizational changes being recommended.

Self-Fulfilling Prophecy: The Pygmalion Effect

Historical roots of the self-fulfilling prophecy are found in Greek mythology. According to mythology, Pygmalion was a sculptor who hated women yet fell in love with an ivory statue he carved of a beautiful woman. He became so infatuated with the statue that he prayed to the goddess Aphrodite to bring her to life. The goddess heard his prayer, granted his wish, and Pygmalion's statue came to life. The essence of the **self-fulfilling prophecy,** or Pygmalion effect, is that someone's high expectations for another person result in high performance for that person. A related self-fulfilling prophecy effect is referred to as the Galatea effect. The **Galatea effect** occurs when an individual's high self-expectations for him- or herself lead to high performance. The key process underlying both the Pygmalion and Galatea effects is the idea that people's expectations or beliefs determine their behavior and performance, thus serving to make their expectations come true. In other words, we strive to validate our perceptions of reality, no matter how faulty they may be. Thus, the self-fulfilling prophecy is an important perceptual outcome we need to better understand.

Self-fulfilling prophecy
Someone's high expectations for another person result in high performance.

Galatea effect
An individual's high self-expectations lead to high performance.

Research and an Explanatory Model

The self-fulfilling prophecy was first demonstrated in an academic environment. After giving a bogus test of academic potential to students from grades 1 to 6, researchers informed teachers that certain students had high potential for achievement. In reality, students were randomly assigned to the "high potential" and "control" (normal potential) groups. Results showed that children designated as having high potential obtained significantly greater increases in both IQ scores and reading ability than did the control students.[61] The teachers of the supposedly high potential group got better results because their high expectations caused them to give harder assignments, more feedback, and more recognition of achievement. Students in the normal potential group did not excel because their teachers did not expect outstanding results.

THIS ISN'T ONE OF THOSE DUMPS I'VE HEARD ABOUT WHERE THE COOK SPITS ON THE FOOD OF OBNOXIOUS CUSTOMERS, IS IT?

BERT'S SELF-FULFILLING PROPHECY...

WILEY@NON-SEQUITUR.COM   DIST. BY UNIVERSAL PRESS SYNDICATE   WWW.NON-SEQUITUR.COM

SOURCE: NON-SEQUITUR © Wiley Miller. Dist. by Universal Press Syndicate. Reprinted with permission. All rights reserved.

Oprah Winfrey is a great example of the Galatea effect. Born in Kosciusko, Mississippi, where she lived on a farm and was raised by her grandmother, she has evolved into one of the 100 Most Influential People of the 20th Century by Time Magazine.

Research similarly has shown that by raising instructors' and managers' expectations for individuals performing a wide variety of tasks, higher levels of achievement/ productivity can be obtained. Results from a meta-analysis of 17 studies involving 2,874 people working in a variety of industries and occupations demonstrated the Pygmalion effect was quite strong.[62] This finding implies that higher levels of achievement and productivity can be obtained by raising managers' performance expectations of their employees. Further, the performance enhancing Pygmalion effect was stronger in the military, with men, and for people possessing low performance expectations. It is important to note, however, that no study has determined whether or not female leaders can produce the self-fulfilling prophecy among subordinate men. Given the number of women in managerial roles, future research is needed to determine if the Pygmalion effect works in this context.[63]

Figure 7–2 presents a model of the self-fulfilling prophecy that helps explain these results. This model attempts to outline how supervisory expectations affect employee performance. As indicated, high supervisory expectancy produces better leadership (linkage 1), which subsequently leads employees to develop higher self-expectations (linkage 2). Higher expectations motivate workers to exert more effort (linkage 3), ultimately increasing performance (linkage 4) and supervisory expectancies (linkage 5). Successful performance also improves an employee's self-expectancy for achievement (linkage 6). Researchers coined the term *Golem effect* to represent the negative side of the performance enhancing process depicted in Figure 7–2. The **Golem effect** is a loss in performance resulting from low leader expectations.[64] Let us consider how it works.

Golem effect

Loss in performance due to low leader expectations.

Say that an employee makes a mistake such as losing notes during a meeting or exhibits poor performance on a task—turning in a report a day late. A manager then begins to wonder if this person has what it takes to be successful in the organization. This doubt leads the manager to watch this person more carefully. The employee of course notices this doubt and begins to sense a loss of trust. The suspect employee then responds in one of two ways. He or she may doubt his or her own judgment and competence. This in turn leads the individual to become more risk averse and to decrease the amount of ideas and suggestions for the manager's critical review. The manager notices this behavior and interprets it as an example of less initiative. Oppositely, the employee may take on more and more responsibility so that he or she can demonstrate his or her competence and worth. This is likely to cause the employee to screw up on something, which in turn reinforces the manager's suspicions. You can see that this process results in a destructive relationship that is fueled by negative expectations. The point to remember is that the self-fulfilling prophecy works in both directions. The next section discusses ideas for enhancing the Pygmalion effect and reducing the Golem effect.

Figure 7–2   *A Model of the Self-Fulfilling Prophecy*

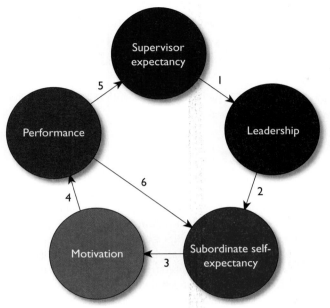

SOURCE: D Eden, "Self-Fulfilling Prophecy as a Management Tool: Harnessing Pygmalion," *Academy of Management Review,* January 1984, p 67. Reprinted by permission of The Academy of Management via The Copyright Clearance Center.

Putting the Self-Fulfilling Prophecy to Work

Largely due to the Pygmalion effect, managerial expectations powerfully influence employee behavior and performance. Consequently, managers need to harness the Pygmalion effect by building a hierarchical framework that reinforces positive performance expectations throughout the organization.

Employees' self-expectations are the foundation of this framework.[65] In turn, positive self-expectations improve interpersonal expectations by encouraging people to work toward common goals. This cooperation enhances group-level productivity and promotes positive performance expectations within the work group. At Microsoft Corporation, for example, employees routinely put in 75-hour weeks, especially when work groups are trying to meet shipment deadlines for new products. Because Microsoft is known for meeting its deadlines, positive group-level expectations help create and reinforce an organizational culture of high expectancy for success. This process then excites people about working for the organization, thereby reducing turnover.[66]

Because positive self-expectations are the foundation for creating an organizationwide Pygmalion effect, let us consider how managers can create positive performance expectations. This task may be accomplished by using various combinations of the following:

1. Recognize that everyone has the potential to increase his or her performance.

2. Instill confidence in your staff.

3. Set high performance goals.

4. Positively reinforce employees for a job well done.

5. Provide constructive feedback when necessary.

6. Help employees advance through the organization.

7. Introduce new employees as if they have outstanding potential.

8. Become aware of your personal prejudices and nonverbal messages that may discourage others.

9. Encourage employees to visualize the successful execution of tasks.

10. Help employees master key skills and tasks.[67]

Causal Attributions

Attribution theory is based on the premise that people attempt to infer causes for observed behavior. Rightly or wrongly, we constantly formulate cause-and-effect explanations for our own and others' behavior. Attributional statements such as the following are common: "Joe drinks too much because he has no willpower; but I need a couple of drinks after work because I'm under a lot of pressure." Formally defined, **causal attributions** are suspected or inferred causes of behavior. Even though our causal attributions tend to be self-serving and are often invalid, it is important to understand how people formulate attributions because they profoundly affect organizational behavior. For example, a supervisor who attributes an employee's poor performance to a lack of effort might reprimand that individual. However, training might be deemed necessary if the supervisor attributes the poor performance to a lack of ability.

Generally speaking, people formulate causal attributions by considering the events preceding an observed behavior. This section explores Harold Kelley's model of attribution, two important attributional tendencies, and related managerial implications.

Kelley's Model of Attribution

Current models of attribution, such as Kelley's, are based on the pioneering work of the late Fritz Heider. Heider, the founder of attribution theory, proposed that behavior can be attributed either to **internal factors** within a person (such as ability and effort) or to **external factors** within the environment (such as task difficulty, help from others, and good/bad luck). This line of thought parallels the idea of an internal versus external locus of control, as discussed in Chapter 5. Building on Heider's work, Kelley attempted to pinpoint major antecedents of internal and external attributions. Kelley hypothesized that people make causal attributions after gathering information about three dimensions of behavior: consensus, distinctiveness, and consistency.[68] These dimensions vary independently, thus forming various combinations and leading to differing attributions.

Figure 7–3 presents performance charts showing low versus high consensus, distinctiveness, and consistency. These charts are now used to help develop a working knowledge of all three dimensions in Kelley's model.

- *Consensus* involves a comparison of an individual's behavior with that of his or her peers. There is high consensus when one acts like the rest of the group and low consensus when one acts differently. As shown in Figure 7–3, high consensus is indicated when persons A, B, C, D, and E obtain similar levels of individual performance. In contrast, person C's performance is low in consensus because it significantly varies from the performance of persons A, B, D, and E.

Causal attributions
Suspected or inferred causes of behavior.

Internal factors
Personal characteristics that cause behavior.

External factors
Environmental characteristics that cause behavior.

Figure 7–3   *Performance Charts Showing Low and High Consensus, Distinctiveness, and Consistency Information*

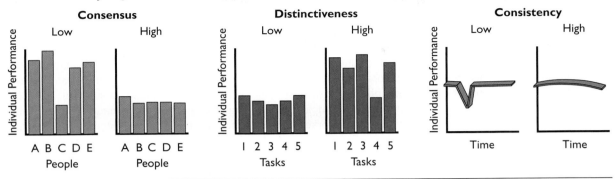

SOURCE: K A Brown, "Explaining Group Poor Performance: An Attributional Analysis," *Academy of Management Review*, January 1984, p 56. Reprinted by permission of The Academy of Management via The Copyright Clearance Center.

- *Distinctiveness* is determined by comparing a person's behavior on one task with his or her behavior on other tasks. High distinctiveness means the individual has performed the task in question in a significantly different manner than he or she has performed other tasks. Low distinctiveness means stable performance or quality from one task to another. Figure 7–3 reveals that the employee's performance on task 4 is highly distinctive because it significantly varies from his or her performance on tasks 1, 2, 3, and 5.

- *Consistency* is determined by judging if the individual's performance on a given task is consistent over time. High consistency implies that a person performs a certain task the same, time after time. Unstable performance of a given task over time would mean low consistency. The downward spike in performance depicted in the consistency graph of Figure 7–3 represents low consistency. In this case, the employee's performance on a given task varied over time.

It is important to remember that consensus relates to other *people,* distinctiveness relates to other *tasks,* and consistency relates to *time.* The question now is: How does information about these three dimensions of behavior lead to internal or external attributions?

Kelley hypothesized that people attribute behavior to *external* causes (environmental factors) when they perceive high consensus, high distinctiveness, and low consistency. *Internal* attributions (personal factors) tend to be made when observed behavior is characterized by low consensus, low distinctiveness, and high consistency. So, for example, when all employees are performing poorly (high consensus), when the poor performance occurs on only one of several tasks (high distinctiveness), and the poor performance occurs during only one time period (low consistency), a supervisor will probably attribute an employee's poor performance to an external source such as peer pressure or an overly difficult task. In contrast, performance will be attributed to an employee's personal characteristics (an internal attribution) when only the individual in question is performing poorly (low consensus), when the inferior performance is found across several tasks (low distinctiveness), and when the low performance has persisted over time (high consistency). Many studies have supported this predicted pattern of attributions in a work setting.[69] Most recently, the attribution process has been extended by marketing researchers to examine consumers' attributions about advertising and consumers' attributions about the behavior of sales associates in various types of stores.[70]

Attributional Tendencies

Researchers have uncovered two attributional tendencies that distort one's interpretation of observed behavior—*fundamental attribution bias* and *self-serving bias.*

Fundamental attribution bias
Ignoring environmental factors that affect behavior.

Fundamental Attribution Bias
The **fundamental attribution bias** reflects one's tendency to attribute another person's behavior to his or her personal characteristics, as opposed to situational factors. This bias causes perceivers to ignore important environmental forces that often significantly affect behavior. For example, a study of 1,420 employees of a large utility company demonstrated that supervisors tended to make more internal attributions about worker accidents than did the workers. Interestingly, research also shows that people from Westernized cultures tend to exhibit the fundamental attribution bias more than individuals from East Asia.[71] A recent study of service encounters similarly showed that consumers attributed a poor service encounter to the service provider and not to situational factors.[72]

Self-serving bias
Taking more personal responsibility for success than failure.

Self-Serving Bias
The **self-serving bias** represents one's tendency to take more personal responsibility for success than for failure. The self-serving bias suggests employees will attribute their success to internal factors (high ability or hard work) and their failures to uncontrollable external factors (tough job, bad luck, unproductive co-workers, or an unsympathetic boss). For example, after losing to the US hockey team in the 2002 winter Olympics, Russian hockey coach Slava Fetisov blamed the referees and the disparity in penalties for his team's loss. He also "leveled charges of conspiracy, saying the tournament was 'designed to have a final with Canada and the US, and you have this final.' "[73]

Much research has investigated the self-serving bias. Two studies, for instance, examined whether or not senior executives fell prey to the self-serving bias when communicating with stockholders in their annual letter to shareholders. Results revealed executives in the United States and Singapore took credit for themselves when their companies did well and blamed negative outcomes on the environment.[74] Overall, however, research on the self-serving bias has produced inconsistent results. Two general patterns of attributions have been observed in past research. The first reveals that individuals make internal attributions for success as predicted by a self-serving bias. In contrast, people make both internal and external attributions for failure.[75] This means people do not automatically blame failure on external factors as originally expected from a self-serving bias. A team of researchers concluded, "When highly self-focused people feel that failure can be rapidly remedied, they will attribute failure to self; when the likelihood of improvement seems low, however, failure will be attributed externally."[76]

Managerial Application and Implications

Attribution models can be used to explain how managers handle poorly performing employees. One study revealed that managers gave employees more immediate, frequent, and negative feedback when they attributed their performance to low effort. This reaction was even more pronounced when the manager's success was dependent on an employee's performance. A second study indicated that managers tended to transfer employees whose poor performance was attributed to a lack of ability. These same managers also decided to take no immediate action when poor performance was attributed to external factors beyond an individual's control.[77]

The preceding situations have several important implications for managers. First, managers tend to disproportionately attribute behavior to *internal* causes.[78] This can result in inaccurate evaluations of performance, leading to reduced employee motivation. No one likes to be blamed because of factors they perceive to be beyond their control. Further, because managers' responses to employee performance vary according to their attributions, attributional biases may lead to inappropriate managerial actions, including promotions, transfers, layoffs, and so forth. This can dampen motivation and performance. Attributional training sessions for managers are in order. Basic attributional processes can be explained, and managers can be taught to detect and avoid attributional biases. Finally, an employee's attributions for his or her own performance have dramatic effects on subsequent motivation, performance, and personal attitudes such as self-esteem. For instance, people tend to give up, develop lower expectations for future success, and experience decreased self-esteem when they attribute failure to a lack of ability. Fortunately, attributional retraining can improve both motivation and performance. Research shows that employees can be taught to attribute their failures to a lack of effort rather than to a lack of ability.[79] This attributional realignment paves the way for improved motivation and performance. It also is important to remember the implications of the self-serving bias. If managers want employees to accept personal responsibility for failure and correspondingly modify their effort and behavior, it is essential for employees to believe that they can improve upon their performance in the future. Otherwise, employees are likely to attribute failure to external causes and they will not change their behavior.

Summary of Key Concepts

1. *Describe perception in terms of the information-processing model.* Perception is a mental and cognitive process that enables us to interpret and understand our surroundings. Social perception, also known as social cognition and social information processing, is a four-stage process. The four stages are selective attention/comprehension, encoding and simplification, storage and retention, and retrieval and response. During social cognition, salient stimuli are matched with schemata, assigned to cognitive categories, and stored in long-term memory for events, semantic materials, or people.

2. *Identify and briefly explain four managerial implications of social perception.* Social perception affects hiring decisions, performance appraisals, leadership perceptions, and communication processes. Inaccurate schemata or racist and sexist schemata may be used to evaluate job applicants. Similarly, faulty schemata about what constitutes good versus poor performance can lead to inaccurate performance appraisals. Invalid schemata need to be identified and replaced with appropriate schemata through coaching and training. Further, managers are advised to use objective rather than subjective measures of performance. With respect to leadership, a leader will have a difficult time

influencing employees when he or she exhibits behaviors contained in employees' schemata of poor leaders. Finally, communication is influenced by schemata used to interpret any message. Effective communicators try to tailor their messages to the receiver's perceptual schemata.

3. *Discuss stereotypes and the process of stereotype formation.* Stereotypes represent grossly oversimplified beliefs or expectations about groups of people. Stereotyping is a four-step process that begins by categorizing people into groups according to various criteria. Next, we infer that all people within a particular group possess the same traits or characteristics. Then, we form expectations of others and interpret their behavior according to our stereotypes. Finally, stereotypes are maintained by (a) overestimating the frequency of stereotypic behaviors exhibited by others, (b) incorrectly explaining expected and unexpected behaviors, and (c) differentiating minority individuals from oneself. The use of stereotypes is influenced by the amount and type of information available to an individual and his or her motivation to accurately process information.

4. *Summarize the managerial challenges and recommendations of sex-role, age, racial and ethnic, and disability stereotypes.* The key managerial challenge is to reduce the extent to which stereotypes influence

decision-making and interpersonal processes throughout the organization. Training can be used to educate employees about the problem of stereotyping and to equip managers with the skills needed to handle situations associated with managing employees with disabilities. Because mixed-group contact reduces stereotyping, organizations should create opportunities for diverse employees to meet and work together in cooperative groups of equal status. Hiring decisions should be based on valid individual differences, and managers can be trained to use valid criteria when evaluating employee performance. Minimizing differences in job opportunities and experiences across groups of people can help alleviate promotional barriers. Job design techniques can be used to reduce performance plateaus associated with age. Organizations also may need to use incentives to motivate employees to upgrade their skills and abilities, and hiring older workers has many potential organizational benefits. It is critical to obtain top management's commitment and support to eliminate stereotyping and discriminatory decisions.

5. *Describe and contrast the Pygmalion effect, Galatea effect, and the Golem effect.* The Pygmalion effect, also known as the self-fulfilling prophecy, describes how someone's high expectations for another person result in high performance for that person. The Galatea effect occurs

when an individual's high self-expectations lead to high self-performance. The Golem effect is a loss of performance resulting from low leader expectations.

6. *Discuss how the self-fulfilling prophecy is created and how it can be used to improve individual and group productivity.* According to the self-fulfilling prophecy, high managerial expectations foster high employee self-expectations. These expectations in turn lead to greater effort and better performance and yet higher expectations.

7. *Explain, according to Kelley's model, how external and internal causal attributions are formulated.* Attribution theory attempts to describe how people infer causes for observed behavior. According to Kelley's model of causal attribution, external attributions tend to be made when consensus and distinctiveness are high and consistency is low. Internal (personal responsibility) attributions tend to be made when consensus and distinctiveness are low and consistency is high.

8. *Contrast the fundamental attribution bias and the self-serving bias.* Fundamental attribution bias involves emphasizing personal factors more than situational factors while formulating causal attributions for the behavior of others. Self-serving bias involves personalizing the causes of one's successes and externalizing the causes of one's failures.

Discussion Questions

1. Why is it important for managers to have a working knowledge of perception and attribution?

2. When you are sitting in class, what stimuli are salient? What is your schema for classroom activity?

3. Have you ever been stereotyped by someone else? Discuss.

4. Which type of stereotype (sex-role, age, racial and ethnic, or disability) do you believe is more pervasive in organizations? Why?

5. What evidence of self-fulfilling prophecies have you seen lately?

6. How might your professor use the process outlined in Figure 7–2 to improve the overall performance of the students in your class?

7. Have you ever experienced the Galatea effect or Golem effect? Describe what happened.

8. How would you formulate an attribution, according to Kelley's model, for the behavior of a classmate who starts arguing in class with your professor?

9. Are poor people victimized by a fundamental attribution bias? Explain.

10. What evidence of the self-serving bias have you observed lately?

OB in Action Case Study

Employees Use Cosmetic Surgery to Improve Their Image[80]

When the executive in the adjacent office returns from a two-week vacation minus any bags under his eyes or deep lines around his mouth, forget what he tells you about a certain Caribbean resort. Chances are, he has been under the knife.

Cosmetic surgery, botox and other de-aging skin treatments are becoming de rigueur for baby-boomer executives of both sexes who fear being judged as over the hill. For many, including some top CEOs who haven't yet gone public, plastic surgery is the next step in their rigorous fitness and beauty regimens that include several hours a week at the gym, expensive personal trainers and diet consultants, and hair treatments. "I can't tell you the number of men I know who no longer are gray or who have covered bald spots with hair transplants," says Pat Cook, president of Cook & Co., a Bronxville, New York, executive-search firm.

In addition to vanity, these executives are driven by job insecurity. They believe that looking older in business now means looking vulnerable, not wise and experienced, as might have been the case in the past. So many 50-something managers have suffered layoffs and early retirement that survivors in this age bracket feel pressured to look and act as young as possible to hang onto their posts. And even 45-year-olds who are unemployed in today's tight market worry that wrinkles will cut them out of the running.

They ignore the financial expense (work on eyelids costs $3,000 to $6,000 and facelifts, $15,000 to $25,000) and the medical risks (novelist Olivia Goldsmith died last month at the age of 54 during a chin-tuck operation).

A recent survey of senior executives by ExecuNet, a networking and job-search service, found that 82% consider age bias a "serious problem," up from 78% three years ago. And 94% of these respondents, who were mostly in their 40s and 50s, said they thought age had cost them a shot at a particular job.

"Ageism is unfortunate but it exists, and if you aren't looking good, you aren't a player, especially now when so many companies are run by younger executives," says Rick Miners, president of FlexCorp Systems, a New York business-process outsourcing company. "It isn't only women waiting for appointments with cosmetic surgeons, it's a lot of men, too, and not just senior executives but middle managers who want to stay competitive." . . .

It isn't something most executives want to discuss publicly, however. A 56-year-old public-relations manager at a New Jersey technology company, who had his lower eyelids done last April, says he was delighted when colleagues told him he looked more rested than they had ever seen him. But he didn't counter their belief that he had just returned from a cruise. "I didn't want to call attention to my age by saying I needed this to look younger," he says. But his new look has given him more confidence at work, prompting him to volunteer for new projects, he adds.

Even more executives are choosing less expensive and less invasive treatments, such as botox injections, which average several hundred dollars per session. Dr Diana Bihova, a New York dermatologist, *says 40% of her patients seeking botox and other cosmetic treatments, including chemical peels and collagen, are now men. . . .*

A major focus for both sexes is removing frown lines between the brows or on the forehead. One woman claimed that losing her worried look helped her land a new job.

Looking younger, however, isn't the most crucial way to counter ageism on the job. Managers who don't repeatedly rejuvenate their thinking—failing to stay informed about current events and popular culture—inevitably date themselves and limit their chances to advance.

Questions for Discussion

1. Would you go under the knife to enhance your career opportunities? Why or why not?

2. What negative stereotypes are fueling the use of cosmetic surgery to change one's appearance?

3. To what extent does the Pygmalion effect, Galatea effect, and Golem effect play a role in this case? Explain.

4. Based on this case and what you learned in this chapter, do the skills that come with age and experience count for less than appearance in today's organizations? Discuss your rationale.

Personal Awareness and Growth Exercise

How Do Diversity Assumptions Influence Team Member Interactions?

Objectives

1. To identify diversity assumptions.

2. To consider how diversity assumptions impact team members' interactions.

Introduction

Assumptions can be so ingrained that we do not even know that we are using them. Negative assumptions can limit our relationships with others because they influence how we perceive and respond to those we encounter in our daily lives. This exercise is designed to help identify the assumptions that you have about groups of people. Although this exercise may make you uncomfortable because it asks you to identify stereotypical assumptions, it is a positive first step at facing and examining the assumptions we make about other people. This awareness can lead to positive behavioral change.

Instructions

Complete the diversity assumptions worksheet.[81] The first column contains various dimensions of diversity. For each dimension, the second column asks you to identify the assumptions held by the general public about people with this characteristic. Use the third column to determine how each assumption might limit team members' ability to effectively interact with each other. Finally, answer the questions for discussion.

Questions for Discussion

1. Where do our assumptions about others come from?

2. Is it possible to eliminate negative assumptions about others? How might this be done?

3. What most surprised you about your answers to the diversity assumption worksheet?

Diversity Assumption Worksheet[82]

Dimension of Diversity	Assumption That Might Be Made	Impact on Team Members' Interactions
Age	Example: You can't teach an old dog new tricks. Older people are closed to new ideas. Example: Younger people haven't had the proper experience to come up with good solutions.	Example: Older people are considered to be resistant to change. Example: Input from younger employee is not solicited.
Ethnicity (e.g., Mexican)		
Gender		
Race		
Physical ability (e.g., hard of hearing)		
Sexual orientation		
Marital/parental status (e.g., single parent with children)		
Religion (e.g., Buddhist)		
Recreational habits (e.g., hikes on weekends)		
Educational background (e.g., college education)		
Work experience (e.g., union)		
Appearance (e.g., overweight)		
Geographic location (e.g., rural)		
Personal habits (e.g., smoking)		
Income (e.g., well-to-do)		

Using Attribution Theory to Resolve Performance Problems

Objectives

1. To gain experience determining the causes of performance.
2. To decide on corrective action for employee performance.

Introduction

Attributions are typically made to internal and external factors. Perceivers arrive at their assessments by using various informational cues or antecedents. To determine the types of antecedents people use, we have developed a case containing various informational cues about an individual's performance. You will be asked to read the case and make attributions about the causes of performance. To assess the impact of attributions on managerial behavior, you will also be asked to recommend corrective action.

Instructions

Presented on the following page is a case that depicts the performance of Mary Martin, a computer programmer. Please read the case to the right and then identify the causes of her behavior by answering the questions following the case. Then determine whether you made an internal or external attribution. After completing this task, decide on the appropriateness of various forms of corrective action. A list of potential recommendations has been developed. The list is divided into four categories. Read each action, and evaluate its appropriateness by using the scale provided. Next, compute a total score for each of the four categories.

Causes of Performance

To what extent was each of the following a cause of Mary's performance? Use the following scale:

Very little			Very much	
1————2————3————4————5				

a. High ability	1	2	3	4	5
b. Low ability	1	2	3	4	5
c. Low effort	1	2	3	4	5
d. Difficult job	1	2	3	4	5
e. Unproductive co-workers	1	2	3	4	5
f. Bad luck	1	2	3	4	5

Internal attribution (total score for causes a, b, and c) _____
External attribution (total score for causes d, e, and f) _____

THE CASE OF MARY MARTIN

Mary Martin, 30, received her baccalaureate degree in computer science from a reputable state school in the Midwest. She also graduated with above-average grades. Mary is currently working in the computer support/analysis department as a programmer for a nationally based firm. During the past year, Mary has missed 10 days of work. She seems unmotivated and rarely has her assignments completed on time. Mary is usually given the harder programs to work on.

Past records indicate Mary, on the average, completes programs classified as "routine" in about 45 hours. Her co-workers, on the other hand, complete "routine" programs in an average time of 32 hours. Further, Mary finishes programs considered "major problems," on the average, in about 115 hours. Her co-workers, however, finish these same "major problem" assignments, on the average, in about 100 hours. When Mary has worked in programming teams, her peer performance reviews are generally average to negative. Her male peers have noted she is not creative in attacking problems and she is difficult to work with.

The computer department recently sent a questionnaire to all users of its services to evaluate the usefulness and accuracy of data received. The results indicate many departments are not using computer output because they cannot understand the reports. It was also determined that the users of output generated from Mary's programs found the output chaotic and not useful for managerial decision making.

Appropriateness of Corrective Action

Evaluate the following courses of action by using the scale below:

Very Inappropriate			Very Appropriate	
1	2	3	4	5

Coercive Actions

	1	2	3	4	5
a. Reprimand Mary for her performance	1	2	3	4	5
b. Threaten to fire Mary if her performance does not improve	1	2	3	4	5

Change Job

	1	2	3	4	5
c. Transfer Mary to another job	1	2	3	4	5
d. Demote Mary to a less demanding job	1	2	3	4	5

Nonpunitive Actions

	1	2	3	4	5
e. Work with Mary to help her do the job better	1	2	3	4	5
f. Offer Mary encouragement to help her improve	1	2	3	4	5

No Immediate Actions

	1	2	3	4	5
g. Do nothing	1	2	3	4	5
h. Promise Mary a pay raise if she improves	1	2	3	4	5

Compute a score for the four categories:
Coercive actions = a + b =
Change job = c + d =
Nonpunitive actions = e + f =
No immediate actions = g + h =

Questions for Discussion

1. How would you evaluate Mary's performance in terms of consensus, distinctiveness, and consistency?

2. Is Mary's performance due to internal or external causes?

3. What did you identify as the top two causes of Mary's performance? Explain why.

4. Which of the four types of corrective action do you think is most appropriate? Explain. Can you identify any negative consequences of this choice?

Enron Employees Try to Alter the Perceptions of Wall Street Analysts[83]

Some current and former employees of Enron's retail-energy unit say the company asked them to pose as busy electricity and natural-gas sales representatives one day in 1998 so the unit could impress Wall Street analysts visiting its Houston headquarters.

Enron rushed 75 employees of Enron Energy Services—including secretaries and actual sales representatives—to an empty trading floor and told them to act as if they were trying to sell energy contracts to businesses over the phone, the current and former employees say.

"When we went down to the sixth floor, I remember we had to take the stairs so the analysts wouldn't see us," said Kim Garcia, who at the time was an administrative assistant for Enron Energy Services and was laid off in December.

"We brought some of our personal stuff, like pictures, to make it look like the area was lived in," Ms Garcia said in an interview. "There were a bunch of trading desks on the sixth floor, but the desks were totally empty. Some of the computers didn't even work, so we worked off of our laptops. When the analysts arrived, we had to make believe we were on the phone buying and selling electricity and natural gas. The whole thing took like 10 minutes."

Penny Marksberry—who also worked as an Enron Energy Services administrative assistant in 1998 and was laid off in December—and two employees who still work at the unit also say they were told to act as if they were trying to sell contracts.

"They actually brought in computers and phones and they told us to act like we were typing or talking on the phone when the analysts were walking through," Ms Marksberry said. "They told us it was very important for us to make a good impression and if the analysts saw that the operation was disorganized, they wouldn't give the company a good rating."

What would you do if you were asked to act busy in front of the analysts?

1. Follow the company's instructions by going to the sixth floor and acting busy in front of the analysts.

2. Explain to your manager that this behavior is inconsistent with your personal values and that you will not participate.

3. Go to the sixth floor in support of the company's request, but do not act busy or bring personal artifacts to create a false impression.

4. Invent other options. Discuss.

For the Chapter 7 Internet Exercise featuring an exploration of stereotypes (www.adl.org), visit our Web site at **www.mhhe.com/kreitner.**

Foundations of Motivation

Learning Objectives

When you finish studying the material in this chapter, you should be able to:

1 Contrast Maslow's, Alderfer's, and McClelland's need theories.

2 Explain the practical significance of Herzberg's distinction between motivators and hygiene factors.

3 Discuss the role of perceived inequity in employee motivation.

4 Explain the differences among distributive, procedural, and interactional justice.

5 Describe the practical lessons derived from equity theory.

6 Explain Vroom's expectancy theory, and review its practical implications.

7 Explain how goal setting motivates an individual, and review the five practical lessons from goal-setting research.

8 Review the mechanistic, motivational, biological, and perceptual-motor approaches to job design.

9 Specify issues that should be addressed before implementing a motivational program.

At Saks Fifth Avenue, the luxury retailer based in New York, executives were looking for ways to boost service to customers in their highly competitive market. Saks officials decided to measure employee engagement and customer engagement at stores, with customer engagement including willingness to make repeat purchases and recommend the store to friends.

"We used both to pinpoint problem spots," says vice president Jay Redman. Saks found that "there absolutely is a correlation between employee engagement and customer engagement" and that customer engagement creates loyal, repeat customers and increased sales.

"We've seen 20 to 25% improvement in stores with great engagement," he says. But it's not just about higher sales figures. "How you get there is important."

There's been a major change in the nature of the dialog between management and the sales force, says Redman. Saks makes a point about asking employees what they need to do their jobs. Every time there is an initiative resulting from such dialog—for example, a flextime program was implemented recently, and many computers were upgraded—managers make sure to remind workers that this resulted from their suggestions.

"We've probably done 100 things over three years" in response to survey results, says Redman. "Some are as simple as opening a stairwell. People said they used to wait five to 10 minutes to go by elevator between floors" in a store.

A key message from Saks management to employees is that the dialog is intended to be a permanent feature. "The first year everyone thinks that it's a program. It's not a program anymore." . . .

At Roche Diagnostics Corp., a diagnostic systems manufacturer based in Indianapolis, high turnover was a troublesome problem. Company officials did some research and concluded that they needed to define and treat the root cause of the too-frequent departures of key workers.

They had what Patty Ayers, vice president for HR, called "a gut feeling" why turnover was high, but employee engagement surveys pinpointed the reasons. The company discovered, for example, that employees had concerns about career development. They needed better computer resources in the field. They wanted to understand the company's business strategy and where they fit in.[1]

FOR DISCUSSION

What are the pros and cons of using surveys to assess employee engagement? Explain.

Motivation
Psychological processes that arouse and direct goal-directed behavior.

Effective employee motivation has long been one of management's most difficult and important duties. Success in this endeavor is becoming more challenging in light of organizational trends to downsize and reengineer and the demands associated with managing a diverse workforce. As revealed in the opening vignette, companies such as Saks Fifth Avenue and Roche Diagnostics consider employee motivation and satisfaction as critical for organizational success.

The term *motivation* derives from the Latin word *movere,* meaning "to move." In the present context, **motivation** represents "those psychological processes that cause the arousal, direction, and persistence of voluntary actions that are goal directed."[2] Researchers have proposed two general categories of motivation theories to explain the psychological processes underlying employee motivation: content theories and process theories. **Content theories of motivation** focus on identifying internal factors such as instincts, needs, satisfaction, and job characteristics that energize employee motivation. These theories do not explain how motivation is influenced by the dynamic interaction between an individual and the environment in which he or she works. This limitation led to the creation of process theories of motivation. **Process theories of motivation** focus on explaining the process by which internal factors and cognitions influence employee motivation.[3] Process theories are more dynamic than content theories.

The purpose of this chapter is to provide you with a foundation for understanding the complexities of employee motivation. After discussing the major content and process theories of motivation, this chapter provides an overview of job design methods used to motivate employees and concludes by focusing on practical recommendations for putting motivational theories to work.

Content theories of motivation
Identify internal factors influencing motivation.

Process theories of motivation
Identify the process by which internal factors and cognitions influence motivation.

Content Theories of Motivation

Needs
Physiological or psychological deficiencies that arouse behavior.

Most content theories of motivation revolve around the notion that an employee's needs influence motivation. **Needs** are physiological or psychological deficiencies that arouse behavior. They can be strong or weak and are influenced by environmental factors. Thus, human needs vary over time and place. The general idea behind need theories of motivation is that unmet needs motivate people to satisfy them. Conversely, people are not motivated to pursue a satisfied need. Let us now consider four popular content theories of motivation: Maslow's need hierarchy theory, Alderfer's ERG theory, McClelland's need theory, and Herzberg's motivator–hygiene model.

Maslow's Need Hierarchy Theory

In 1943, psychologist Abraham Maslow published his now-famous **need hierarchy theory** of motivation. Although the theory was based on his clinical observation of a few neurotic individuals, it has subsequently been used to explain the entire spectrum of human behavior. Maslow proposed that motivation is a function of five basic needs. These needs are

1. *Physiological.* Most basic need. Entails having enough food, air, and water to survive.
2. *Safety.* Consists of the need to be safe from physical and psychological harm.
3. *Love.* The desire to be loved and to love. Contains the needs for affection and belonging.
4. *Esteem.* Need for reputation, prestige, and recognition from others. Also contains need for self-confidence and strength.
5. *Self-actualization.* Desire for self-fulfillment—to become the best one is capable of becoming.

Maslow said these five needs are arranged in the prepotent hierarchy shown in Figure 8–1. In other words, he believed human needs generally emerge in a predictable stair-step fashion. Accordingly, when one's physiological needs are relatively satisfied, one's safety needs emerge, and so on up the need hierarchy, one step at a time. Once a need is satisfied it activates the next higher need in the hierarchy. This process continues until the need for self-actualization is activated.[4]

Although research does not clearly support this theory of motivation, there is one key managerial implication of Maslow's theory worth noting. That is, a satisfied need may lose its motivational potential. Therefore, managers are advised to motivate employees by devising programs or practices aimed at satisfying emerging or unmet needs. Many companies such as IndyMac Bank have responded to this recommendation by using results from employee surveys to develop programs aimed at satisfying employees' needs (see Real World/Real People on page 238). Other companies are beginning to offer specialized benefits aimed at satisfying the needs of unique employees. For example, Wipro, a high-technology company located in India, created a company-sponsored matchmaking service on its company's intranet to help single employees find others to date and marry. Thus far, 621 employees have signed up for the service and several marriages have ensued.[5]

Need hierarchy theory
Five basic needs—physiological, safety, love, esteem, and self-actualization—influence behavior.

Figure 8–1   *Maslow's Need Hierarchy*

IndyMac Bank Uses Surveys to Assess Employees Needs

Last year, to gain better understanding of the drivers of its turnover, IndyMac conducted a statistical analysis of data in hand on many of its 5,000 employees to determine what mattered most to specific segments of its workforce. IndyMac's analysis was based on data from its PeopleSoft system—including job title and compensation—along with survey information from its annual performance review process and some exit interview data....

To better understand the attitudes and preferences of various collections of employees, the bank grouped its more than 100 job titles into job "families" and then grouped the families into seven workforce categories: sales, management, information technology, professional, customer service, operations, and skilled and semi-skilled.

This approach enabled the company to "drill down" into various segments of the employee base in analyzing

patterns of retention and turnover, says Bill Myers, human capital analytics project manager at IndyMac. The patterns were also discerned according to other employee characteristics, such as performance ranking, tenure and previous work experience.

So far, IndyMac's analyses have provided valuable insights.

"Our studies have allowed us to make strategic recommendations regarding compensation and benefits for our existing workforce, and improve our hiring criteria for new employees," says Myers.

SOURCE: Excerpted from P Babcock, "Find What Workers Want," *HR Magazine,* April 2005, pp 53–54. Reprinted with the permission of HR Magazine published by the Society for Human Resource Management, Alexandria, VA.

In conclusion, managers are more likely to fuel employee motivation by offering benefits and rewards that meet individual needs.

Alderfer's ERG Theory

Clayton Alderfer developed an alternative theory of human needs in the late 1960s. Alderfer's theory differs from Maslow's in three major respects. First, a smaller set of core needs is used to explain behavior. From lowest to highest level they are *existence needs* (E)—the desire for physiological and materialistic well-being; *relatedness needs* (R)—the desire to have meaningful relationships with significant others; and *growth needs* (G)—the desire to grow as a human being and to use one's abilities to their fullest potential; hence, the label **ERG theory.** Second, ERG theory does not assume needs are related to each other in a stair-step hierarchy as does Maslow. Alderfer believes that more than one need may be activated at a time. Finally, ERG theory contains a frustration-regression component. That is, frustration of higher-order needs can influence the desire for lower-order needs.[6] For example, employees may demand higher pay or better benefits (existence needs) when they are frustrated or dissatisfied with the quality of their interpersonal relationships (relatedness needs) at work.

> **ERG theory**
> Three basic needs—existence, relatedness, and growth—influence behavior.

Research on ERG theory has provided mixed support for some of the theory's key propositions.[7] That said, however, there are two key managerial implications associated with ERG. The first revolves around the frustration-regression aspect of the theory. Managers should keep in mind that employees may be motivated to pursue lower-level needs because they are frustrated with a higher-order need. For instance, the solution for a stifling work environment may be a request for higher pay or better benefits. Second, ERG theory is consistent with the finding that individual and cultural differences influence our need states.[8] People are motivated by different needs at different times in their lives. This implies that managers should customize their reward and recognition programs to meet employees' varying needs. Consider how Marc Albin, CEO of a $12 million high-tech staffing firm in Sunnyvale, California, handles this recommendation.

> To identify which parts of individual employees' egos need scratching, Albin takes an unconventional approach. "My experience in managing people is, they're all different," says Albin. "Some people want to be recognized for their cheerful attitude and their ability to spread their cheerful attitude. Some want to be recognized for the quality of their work, some for the quantity of their work. Some like to be recognized individually; others want to be recognized in groups." Consequently, at the end of each employee-orientation session Albin e-mails his new hires and asks them how and in what form they prefer their strokes. "It helps me understand what they think of themselves and their abilities, and I make a mental note to pay special attention to them when they're working in that particular arena," he says. "No one has ever said, 'Just recognize me for anything I do well.' "[9]

McClelland's Need Theory

David McClelland, a well-known psychologist, has been studying the relationship between needs and behavior since the late 1940s. Although he is most recognized for his research on the need for achievement, he also investigated the needs for affiliation and power. Let us consider each of these needs.

The Need for Achievement

Need for achievement
Desire to accomplish something difficult.

The **need for achievement** is defined by the following desires:

> To accomplish something difficult. To master, manipulate, or organize physical objects, human beings, or ideas. To do this as rapidly and as independently as possible. To overcome obstacles and attain a high standard. To excel one's self. To rival and surpass others. To increase self-regard by the successful exercise of talent.[10]

Achievement-motivated people share three common characteristics: (1) a preference for working on tasks of moderate difficulty; (2) a preference for situations in which performance is due to their efforts rather than other factors, such as luck; and (3) they desire more feedback on their successes and failures than do low achievers. A review of research on the "entrepreneurial" personality showed that entrepreneurs were found to have a higher need for achievement than nonentrepreneurs.[11]

The Need for Affiliation

Need for affiliation
Desire to spend time in social relationships and activities.

People with a high **need for affiliation** prefer to spend more time maintaining social relationships, joining groups, and wanting to be loved. Individuals high in this need are not the most effective managers or leaders because they have a hard time making difficult decisions without worrying about being disliked.[12]

The Need for Power

Need for power
Desire to influence, coach, teach, or encourage others to achieve.

The **need for power** reflects an individual's desire to influence, coach, teach, or encourage others to achieve. People with a high need for power like to work and are concerned with discipline and self-respect. There is a positive and negative side to this need. The negative face of power is characterized by an "if I win, you lose" mentality. In contrast, people with a positive orientation to power focus on accomplishing group goals and helping employees obtain the feeling of competence. More is said about the two faces of power in Chapter 13. Because effective managers must positively influence others, McClelland proposes that top managers should have a high need for power coupled with a low need for affiliation. He also believes that individuals with high achievement motivation are *not* best suited for top management positions. Several studies support these propositions.[13]

Managerial Implications   Given that adults can be trained to increase their achievement motivation,[14] organizations should consider the benefits of providing achievement training for employees. Moreover, achievement, affiliation, and power needs can be considered during the selection process, for better placement. For example, a study revealed that individuals' need for achievement affected their preference to work in different companies. People with a high need for achievement were more attracted to companies that had a pay-for-performance environment than were those with a low achievement motivation.[15] Finally, managers should create challenging task assignments or goals because the need for achievement is positively correlated with goal commitment, which, in turn, influences performance.[16] Moreover, challenging goals should be accompanied with a more autonomous work environment and employee empowerment to capitalize on the characteristics of high achievers.

Herzberg's Motivator–Hygiene Theory

Motivators

Job characteristics associated with job satisfaction.

Frederick Herzberg's theory is based on a landmark study in which he interviewed 203 accountants and engineers.[17] These interviews sought to determine the factors responsible for job satisfaction and dissatisfaction. Herzberg found separate and distinct clusters of factors associated with job satisfaction and dissatisfaction. Job satisfaction was more frequently associated with achievement, recognition, characteristics of the work, responsibility, and advancement. These factors were all related to outcomes associated with the *content* of the task being performed. Herzberg labeled these factors **motivators** because each was associated with strong effort and good performance. He hypothesized that motivators cause a person to move from a state of no satisfaction to satisfaction (see Figure 8–2). Therefore, Herzberg's theory predicts managers can motivate individuals by incorporating "motivators" into an individual's job.[18]

Figure 8–2   *Herzberg's Motivator–Hygiene Model*

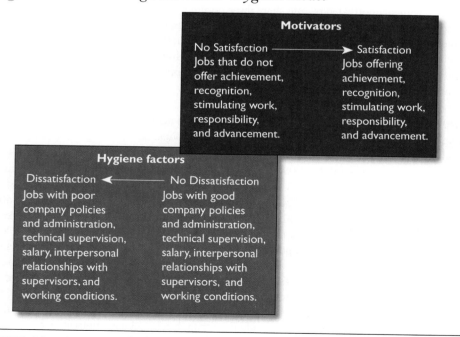

SOURCE: Adapted in part from D A Whitsett and E K Winslow, "An Analysis of Studies Critical of the Motivator–Hygiene Theory," *Personnel Psychology*, Winter 1967, pp 391–415.

Herzberg found job *dissatisfaction* to be associated primarily with factors in the work *context* or environment. Specifically, company policy and administration, technical supervision, salary, interpersonal relations with one's supervisor, and working conditions were most frequently mentioned by employees expressing job dissatisfaction. Herzberg labeled this second cluster of factors **hygiene factors.** He further proposed that they were not motivational. At best, according to Herzberg's interpretation, an individual will experience no job dissatisfaction when he or she has no grievances about hygiene factors (refer to Figure 8–2). In contrast, employees like Katrina Gill are likely to quit when poor hygiene factors lead to job dissatisfaction.

Hygiene factors
Job characteristics associated with job dissatisfaction.

Katrina Gill, a 36-year-old certified nursing aide, worked in one of the premiere long-term care facilities near Portland, Oregon. From 10:30 PM to 7 AM, she was on duty alone, performing three rounds on the dementia ward, where she took care of up to 28 patients a night for $9.32 an hour. She monitored vitals, turned for bedsores, and changed adult diapers. There were the constant vigils over patients like the one who would sneak into other rooms, mistaking female patients for his deceased wife. Worse was the resident she called "the hitter" who once lunged at her, ripping a muscle in her back and laying her flat for four days. Last month, Gill quit and took another job for 68¢ an hour more, bringing her salary to $14,400 a year.[19]

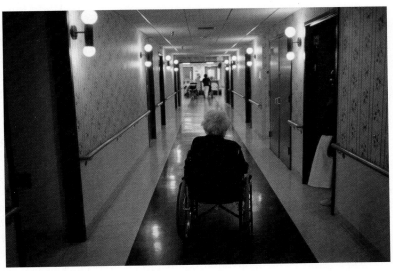

Granted, working in a long-term care facility is not an easy job under any circumstances. But poor working conditions, or hygiene factors, such as long hours and low pay, can only make matters worse by creating job dissatisfaction.

The key to adequately understanding Herzberg's motivator–hygiene theory is recognizing that he believes that satisfaction is not the opposite of dissatisfaction. Herzberg concludes that "the opposite of job satisfaction is not job dissatisfaction, but rather no job satisfaction; and similarly, the opposite of job dissatisfaction is not job satisfaction, but no dissatisfaction."[20] Herzberg thus asserts that the dissatisfaction–satisfaction continuum contains a zero midpoint at which dissatisfaction and satisfaction are absent. Conceivably, an organization member who has good supervision, pay, and working conditions but a tedious and unchallenging task with little chance of advancement would be at the zero midpoint. That person would have no dissatisfaction (because of good hygiene factors) and no satisfaction (because of a lack of motivators).

Herzberg's theory has generated a great deal of research and controversy.[21] Research does not support the two-factor aspect of his theory nor the proposition that hygiene factors are unrelated to job satisfaction. For example, a recent national survey of 600 employees revealed that the five most important job satisfaction factors were all from Herzberg's hygiene category. The five most important factors were benefits, compensation/pay, feeling safe in the work environment, job security, and flexibility to balance work/life issues.[22] On the positive side, however, Herzberg correctly concluded that people are motivated when their needs for achievement, recognition, stimulating work, and advancement are satisfied. As you will learn in a later section of this chapter, Herzberg's theory has important implications for how managers can motivate employees through job design.

Feelings of Inequity Can Lead to Retaliation

A security guard accused of burning down homes at the suburban Washington housing development where he worked told investigators he was upset his employer did not show enough sympathy after his infant son died this year.

Aaron L Speed, 21, who worked for Security Services of America, told police he left his job from August to October because of SSA's "indifference to the death of his infant son," according to court papers released Friday.

When asked by investigators who might have started the fire, Speed said, "Someone who works at the site and recently experienced a great loss." ...

Speed had been hired to protect the Hunters Brooke development, where a string of fires December 6 destroyed 10 houses....

Speed, arrested Thursday on arson charges, failed a polygraph test that included a question as to whether he started the fires, court papers said.

SOURCE: Excerpted from B Witte, "Suspected Arsonist Was Upset: Guard Reportedly Tells Police Why," *Arizona Republic*, December 12, 2004, p A5.

Process Theories of Motivation

Earlier in the chapter we discussed the difference between content theories of motivation, which focus on the impact of internal factors on motivation, and process theories. Process theories go one step further in explaining motivation by identifying the process by which various internal factors influence motivation. These models also are cognitive in nature. That is, they are based on the premise that motivation is a function of employees' perceptions, thoughts, and beliefs. We now explore the three most common process theories of motivation: equity theory, expectancy theory, and goal-setting theory.

Adams's Equity Theory of Motivation

Equity theory
Holds that motivation is a function of fairness in social exchanges.

Defined generally, **equity theory** is a model of motivation that explains how people strive for fairness and justice in social exchanges or give-and-take relationships. As a process theory of motivation, equity theory explains how an individual's motivation to behave in a certain way is fueled by feelings of inequity or a lack of justice. For example, Aaron Speed, a security guard in a Washington housing development, quit his job and allegedly burned several houses in response to feelings of inequity regarding his employer (see Real World/Real People). Psychologist J Stacy Adams pioneered application of the equity principle to the workplace. Central to understanding Adams's equity theory of motivation is an awareness of key components of the individual–organization exchange relationship. This relationship is pivotal in the formation of employees' perceptions of equity and inequity.

The Individual–Organization Exchange Relationship

Adams points out that two primary components are involved in the employee–employer exchange, *inputs* and *outcomes*. An employee's inputs, for which he or she expects a just return, include education/training, skills, creativity, seniority, age, personality traits, effort expended, and personal appearance. On the outcome side of the exchange, the organization provides such things as pay/bonuses, fringe benefits, challenging assignments, job security, promotions, status symbols, and participation in important decisions.

Negative and Positive Inequity

On the job, feelings of inequity revolve around a person's evaluation of whether he or she receives adequate rewards to compensate for his or her contributive inputs. People perform these evaluations by comparing the perceived fairness of their employment exchange to that of relevant others. This comparative process, which is based on an equity norm, was found to generalize across countries.[23] People tend to compare themselves to other individuals with whom they have close interpersonalties—such as friends—or to similar others—such as people performing the same job or individuals of the same gender or educational level—rather than dissimilar others.[24] For example, do you consider the average CEO in the US a relevant comparison person to yourself? If not, then you should not feel inequity because the average CEO pay in 2004 was $9.6 million—a 15% increase—whereas the pay of the average worker increased only 2.9% to $33,176 per year.[25]

Three different equity relationships are illustrated in Figure 8–3: equity, negative inequity, and positive inequity. Assume the two people in each of the equity relationships in Figure 8–3 have equivalent backgrounds (equal education, seniority, and so forth) and perform identical tasks. Only their hourly pay rates differ. Equity exists for an individual when his or her ratio of perceived outcomes to inputs is equal to the ratio of outcomes to inputs for a relevant co-worker (part A in Figure 8–3). Because equity is based on comparing *ratios* of outcomes to inputs, inequity will not necessarily be perceived just because someone

Figure 8–3   *Negative and Positive Inequity*

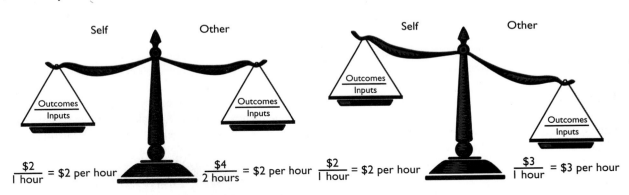

A. An Equitable Situation

Self   Other

$$\frac{\$2}{1 \text{ hour}} = \$2 \text{ per hour} \qquad \frac{\$4}{2 \text{ hours}} = \$2 \text{ per hour}$$

B. Negative Inequity

Self   Other

$$\frac{\$2}{1 \text{ hour}} = \$2 \text{ per hour} \qquad \frac{\$3}{1 \text{ hour}} = \$3 \text{ per hour}$$

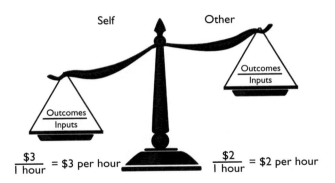

C. Positive Inequity

Self   Other

$$\frac{\$3}{1 \text{ hour}} = \$3 \text{ per hour} \qquad \frac{\$2}{1 \text{ hour}} = \$2 \text{ per hour}$$

Negative inequity
Comparison in which another person receives greater outcomes for similar inputs.

Positive inequity
Comparison in which another person receives lesser outcomes for similar inputs.

Equity sensitivity
An individual's tolerance for negative and positive equity.

else receives greater rewards. If the other person's additional outcomes are due to his or her greater inputs, a sense of equity may still exist. However, if the comparison person enjoys greater outcomes for similar inputs, **negative inequity** will be perceived (part B in Figure 8–3). On the other hand, a person will experience **positive inequity** when his or her outcome to input ratio is greater than that of a relevant co-worker (part C in Figure 8–3).

Dynamics of Perceived Inequity

Managers can derive practical benefits from Adams's equity theory by recognizing that (1) people have varying sensitivities to perceived equity and inequity and (2) inequity can be reduced in a variety of ways.

Thresholds of Equity and Inequity

Have you ever noticed that some people become very upset over the slightest inequity whereas others are not bothered at all? Research has shown that people respond differently to the same level of inequity due to an individual difference called equity sensitivity. **Equity sensitivity** reflects an individual's "different preferences for, tolerances for, and reactions to the level of equity associated with any given situation."[26] Equity sensitivity spans a continuum ranging from benevolents to sensitives to entitled.

Benevolents are people who have a higher tolerance for negative inequity. They are altruistic in the sense that they prefer their outcome/input ratio to be lower than ratios from comparison others. In contrast, equity *sensitives* are described as individuals who adhere to a strict norm of reciprocity and are quickly motivated to resolve both negative and positive inequity. Finally, *entitleds* have no tolerance for negative inequity. They actually expect to obtain greater output/input ratios than comparison others and become upset when this is not the case.[27]

Reducing Inequity

Equity ratios can be changed by attempting to alter one's outcomes or adjusting one's inputs. For example, negative inequity might be resolved by asking for a raise or a promotion (i.e., raising outputs) or by reducing inputs (i.e., working fewer hours or exerting less effort). It also is important to note that equity can be restored by altering one's equity ratios behaviorally or cognitively, or both. A cognitive strategy entails psychologically distorting perceptions of one's own or one's comparison person's outcomes and inputs (e.g., conclude that comparison other has more experience or works harder).

Distributive justice
The perceived fairness of how resources and rewards are distributed.

Procedural justice
The perceived fairness of the process and procedures used to make allocation decisions.

Expanding the Concept of Equity: Organizational Justice

Beginning in the later 1970s, researchers began to expand the role of equity theory in explaining employee attitudes and behavior. This led to a domain of research called *organizational justice*. Organizational justice reflects the extent to which people perceive that they are treated fairly at work. This, in turn, led to the identification of three different components of organizational justice: distributive, procedural, and interactional.[28] **Distributive justice** reflects the perceived fairness of how resources and rewards are distributed or allocated. **Procedural justice** is defined as the perceived fairness of the process and procedures used to make allocation decisions. Research shows that positive perceptions of distributive and procedural justice are enhanced by giving employees a "voice" in decisions that affect them. Voice represents the extent to which employees who are affected by a decision can present relevant information about the decision to others. Voice is analogous to asking employees for their input into the decision-making process.

The last justice component, **interactional justice,** relates to the "quality of the interpersonal treatment people receive when procedures are implemented."[29] This form of justice does not pertain to the outcomes or procedures associated with decision making, but rather it focuses on whether or not people feel they are treated fairly when decisions are implemented. Fair interpersonal treatment necessitates that managers communicate truthfully and treat people with courtesy and respect. Consider the role of interactional justice in how a manager of information-management systems responded to being laid off by a New Jersey chemical company. The man gained access to the company's computer systems from home by using another executive's password and deleted critical inventory and personnel files. The sabotage ultimately caused $20 million in damage and postponed a public stock offering that had been in the works. Why would a former employee do something like this?

> An anonymous note that he wrote to the company president sheds light on his motive. "I have been loyal to the company in good and bad times for over 30 years," he wrote. "I was expecting a member of top management to come down from his ivory tower to face us with the layoff announcement, rather than sending the kitchen supervisor with guards to escort us off the premises like criminals. You will pay for your senseless behavior."[30]

This employee's direct retaliation against the company was caused by the insensitive manner—interactional justice—in which employees were notified about the layoffs.

Many studies of organizational justice have been conducted over the last two decades. Fortunately, two recent meta-analyses of more than 190 studies help summarize what has been learned from this research.[31] The following trends were uncovered: (1) job performance was positively associated with both distributive and procedural justice, but procedural justice was the best predictor of this outcome, (2) all three forms of justice were positively correlated with job satisfaction, organizational commitment, organizational citizenship behaviors, and employees' trust, and negatively with employees' withdrawal cognitions and turnover, and (3) distributive and procedural injustice were negatively related to negative emotions such as anger.[32] All told, these results reinforce the management philosophy of Joe Lee, CEO and chairman of the board of Darden Restaurants, Inc., the largest casual-dining restaurant company in the world.

> I have a lot of thoughts about management, but at the core of my thoughts is to operate with integrity and fairness. Treat people fairly and give them an environment that they can work in and trust. If you do that, you then can take care of your business objectives and your employees' needs and everybody can win.[33]

Practical Lessons from Equity Theory

Equity theory has at least eight important practical implications. First, equity theory provides managers with yet another explanation of how beliefs and attitudes affect job performance. According to this line of thinking, the best way to manage job behavior is to adequately understand underlying cognitive processes. Indeed, we are motivated powerfully to correct the situation when our ideas of fairness and justice are offended.

Second, research on equity theory emphasizes the need for managers to pay attention to employees' perceptions of what is fair and equitable. No matter how fair management thinks the organization's policies, procedures, and reward system are, each employee's *perception* of the equity of those factors is what counts. For example, results contained in the 2000 Global Employee Relationship Report revealed that 25% of the employees surveyed

Interactional justice
Extent to which people feel fairly treated when procedures are implemented.

perceived that their employer treated employees unfairly.[34] Managers thus are encouraged to make hiring and promotion decisions on merit-based, job-related information. Moreover, because justice perceptions are influenced by the extent to which managers explain their decisions, managers are encouraged to explain the rationale behind their decisions.

Third, managers benefit by allowing employees to participate in making decisions about important work outcomes. In general, employees' perceptions of procedural justice are enhanced when they have a voice in the decision-making process.[35] For example, employees were more satisfied with their performance appraisals and resultant outcomes when they had a voice during the appraisal review.[36] Fourth, employees should be given the opportunity to appeal decisions that affect their welfare. Being able to appeal a decision fosters perceptions of distributive and procedural justice. In turn, perceptions of distributive and procedural justice promote job performance, job satisfaction, organizational commitment, and organizational citizenship behavior, and help reduce counterproductive work behavior, psychological distress, absenteeism, and turnover.[37]

Fifth, employees are more likely to accept and support organizational change when they believe it is implemented fairly and when it produces equitable outcomes.

Sixth, managers can promote cooperation and teamwork among group members by treating them equitably. Research reveals that people are just as concerned with fairness in group settings as they are with their own personal interests.[38] Seventh, treating employees inequitably can lead to litigation and costly court settlements. Employees denied justice at work are more likely to turn to arbitration and the courts.

Finally, managers need to pay attention to the organization's climate for justice. For example, an organization's climate for justice was found to significantly influence employees' organizational commitment and job satisfaction.[39] Researchers also believe a climate of justice can significantly influence the type of customer service provided by employees. In turn, this level of service is likely to influence customers' perceptions of "fair service" and their subsequent loyalty and satisfaction.[40]

Managers can attempt to follow these practical implications by monitoring equity and justice perceptions through informal conversations, interviews, or attitude surveys. For example, researchers have developed and validated a host of surveys that can be used for this purpose. Please take a moment now to complete the OB Exercise on page 247. It contains part of a survey that was developed to measure employees' perceptions of fair interpersonal treatment. If you perceive your work organization as interpersonally unfair, you are probably dissatisfied and have contemplated quitting. In contrast, your organizational loyalty and attachment are likely greater if you believe you are treated fairly at work.

Vroom's Expectancy Theory

Expectancy theory

Holds that people are motivated to behave in ways that produce valued outcomes.

Expectancy theory holds that people are motivated to behave in ways that produce desired combinations of expected outcomes. Generally, expectancy theory can be used to predict motivation and behavior in any situation in which a choice between two or more alternatives must be made. For instance, it can be used to predict whether to quit or stay at a job; whether to exert substantial or minimal effort at a task; and whether to major in management, finance, marketing, psychology, or communication.

Victor Vroom formulated a mathematical model of expectancy in his 1964 book *Work and Motivation*.[41] Vroom's theory has been summarized as follows:

> The strength of a tendency to act in a certain way depends on the strength of an expectancy that the act will be followed by a given consequence (or outcome) and on the value or attractiveness of that consequence (or outcome) to the actor.[42]

Measuring Perceived Fair Interpersonal Treatment

Instructions

Indicate the extent to which you agree or disagree with each of the following statements by considering what your organization is like most of the time. Then compare your overall score with the arbitrary norms that are presented.

	Strongly Disagree	Disagree	Neither	Agree	Strongly Agree
1. Employees are praised for good work.	1	2	3	4	5
2. Supervisors do not yell at employees.	1	2	3	4	5
3. Employees are trusted.	1	2	3	4	5
4. Employees' complaints are dealt with effectively.	1	2	3	4	5
5. Employees are treated with respect.	1	2	3	4	5
6. Employees' questions and problems are responded to quickly.	1	2	3	4	5
7. Employees are treated fairly.	1	2	3	4	5
8. Employees' hard work is appreciated.	1	2	3	4	5
9. Employees' suggestions are used.	1	2	3	4	5
10. Employees are told the truth.	1	2	3	4	5

Total score = _____

Arbitrary Norms

Very fair organization = 38–50

Moderately fair organization = 24–37

Unfair organization = 10–23

SOURCE: Adapted in part from M A Donovan, F Drasgow, and L J Munson, "The Perceptions of Fair Interpersonal Treatment Scale: Development and Validation of a Measure of Interpersonal Treatment in the Workplace," *Journal of Applied Psychology,* October 1998, pp 683–92.

Motivation, according to Vroom, boils down to the decision of how much effort to exert in a specific task situation. This choice is based on a two-stage sequence of expectations (effort→performance and performance→outcome). First, motivation is affected by an individual's expectation that a certain level of effort will produce the intended performance goal. For example, if you do not believe increasing the amount of time you spend studying will significantly raise your grade on an exam, you probably will not study any harder than usual. Motivation also is influenced by the employee's perceived chances of getting various outcomes as a result of accomplishing his or her performance goal. Finally, individuals are motivated to the extent that they value the outcomes received.

Vroom used a mathematical equation to integrate the above concepts into a predictive model of motivational force or strength. For our purposes however, it is sufficient to define and explain the three key concepts within Vroom's model—*expectancy, instrumentality,* and *valence.*

Expectancy

An **expectancy,** according to Vroom's terminology, represents an individual's belief that a particular degree of effort will be followed by a particular level of performance. In other words, it is an effort→performance expectation. Expectancies take the form of subjective

Expectancy
Belief that effort leads to a specific level of performance.

probabilities. As you may recall from a course in statistics, probabilities range from 0 to 1. An expectancy of 0 indicates effort has no anticipated impact on performance.

For example, suppose you have not memorized the keys on a keyboard. No matter how much effort you exert, your perceived probability of typing 30 error-free words per minute likely would be 0. An expectancy of 1 suggests that performance is totally dependent on effort. If you decided to memorize the letters on a keyboard as well as practice a couple of hours a day for a few weeks (high effort), you should be able to type 30 words per minute without any errors. In contrast, if you do not memorize the letters on a keyboard and only practice an hour or two per week (low effort), there is a very low probability (say, a 20% chance) of being able to type 30 words per minute without any errors.

The following factors influence an employee's expectancy perceptions:

- Self-esteem.
- Self-efficacy.
- Previous success at the task.
- Help received from a supervisor and subordinates.
- Information necessary to complete the task.
- Good materials and equipment to work with.[43]

Instrumentality

Instrumentality
A performance→
outcome perception.

An **instrumentality** is a performance→outcome perception. It represents a person's belief that a particular outcome is contingent on accomplishing a specific level of performance. Performance is instrumental when it leads to something else. For example, passing exams is instrumental to graduating from college.

Instrumentalities range from −1.0 to 1.0. An instrumentality of 1.0 indicates attainment of a particular outcome is totally dependent on task performance. An instrumentality of 0 indicates there is no relationship between performance and outcome. For example, most companies link the number of vacation days to seniority, not job performance. Finally, an instrumentality of −1.0 reveals that high performance reduces the chance of obtaining an outcome while low performance increases the chance. For example, the more time you spend studying to get an A on an exam (high performance), the less time you will have for enjoying leisure activities. Similarly, as you lower the amount of time spent studying (low performance), you increase the amount of time that may be devoted to leisure activities.

The concept of instrumentality can be seen in practice by considering the national debate regarding pay-for-performance packages for teachers. Arnold Schwarzenegger, governor of California, is leading the charge by pushing for a pay system that makes teacher performance instrumental for receiving pay raises and for retaining one's job (see Real World/Real People).[44]

Farcus

by David Waisglass
Gordon Coulthart

© 1994 Farcus Cartoons   WAISGLASS/COULTHART   www.farcus.com

"Frankly, I didn't think they'd go for this performance incentive stuff."

Governor Schwarzenegger Pushes for Paying Teachers Based on Performance

Today the California governor is taking on the state's powerful teacher's union, only this time his weapon is political clout. His battle plan: to revamp entirely the way teachers in the country's largest educational system are hired, fired, and paid. "The more we tolerate ineffective teachers, the more our teachers will be ineffective," Schwarzenegger declared when he started his offensive in January....

The issues resonate far beyond California. Politicians—most Republicans—are pushing teacher pay-for-performance schemes in other states, including Florida, Kentucky, Minnesota, Texas, and Wisconsin....

Schwarzenegger argues that the only way to improve schools is to reward good teachers and penalize or fire bad ones. He and others point out that right now, teachers get a raise no matter how they perform, giving them no financial incentive to do better. Advocates point to Denver, where 13 school districts instituted a pay-for-performance program four years ago and students scored higher when taught by teachers who met specific objectives set by the district, according to a recent report by Boston's Community Training & Assistance Center.

SOURCE: Excerpted from R Grover and A Bernstein, "Arnold Gets Strict with the Teachers," *BusinessWeek,* May 2, 2005, pp 84–85. Reprinted by permission of The McGraw-Hill Companies, Inc.

Teachers play a critical role in a child's development. Interestingly, California governor Arnold Schwarzenegger wants to positively reward good teachers and punish bad ones. He and others point out that it is counterproductive to give teachers identical raises no matter how they perform. Do you agree with Arnold?

Valence

As Vroom used the term, **valence** refers to the positive or negative value people place on outcomes. Valence mirrors our personal preferences.[45] For example, most employees have a positive valence for receiving additional money or recognition. In contrast, job stress and being laid off would likely result in negative valence for most individuals. In Vroom's expectancy model, *outcomes* refer to different consequences that are contingent on performance, such as pay, promotions, or recognition. An outcome's valence depends on an individual's needs and can be measured for research purposes with scales ranging from a negative value to a positive value. For example, an individual's valence toward more recognition can be assessed on a scale ranging from -2 (very undesirable) to 0 (neutral) to $+2$ (very desirable).

Valence
The value of a reward or outcome.

Vroom's Expectancy Theory in Action

Vroom's expectancy model of motivation can be used to analyze a real-life motivation program. Consider the following performance problem described by Frederick W Smith, founder and chief executive officer of Federal Express Corporation:

[W]e were having a helluva problem keeping things running on time. The airplanes would come in and everything would get backed up. We tried every kind of control mechanism that you could think of, and none of them worked. Finally, it became obvious that the underlying problem was that it was in the interest of the employees at the cargo terminal— they were college kids, mostly—to run late, because it meant that they made more money. So what we did was give them all a minimum guarantee and say, "Look, if you get through before a certain time, just go home, and you will have beat the system." Well, it was unbelievable. I mean, in the space of about 45 days, the place was way ahead of schedule. And I don't even think it was a conscious thing on their part.[46]

How did Federal Express get its college-age cargo handlers to switch from low effort to high effort? According to Vroom's model, the student workers originally exerted low effort because they were paid on the basis of time, not output. It was in their best interest to work slowly and accumulate as many hours as possible. By offering to let the student workers *go home early if and when they completed their assigned duties,* Federal Express prompted high effort. This new arrangement created two positively valued outcomes: guaranteed pay plus the opportunity to leave early. The motivation to exert high effort became greater than the motivation to exert low effort.

Judging from the impressive results, the student workers had both high effort → performance expectancies and positive performance→outcome instrumentalities. Moreover, the guaranteed pay and early departure opportunity evidently had strongly positive valences for the student workers.

Research on Expectancy Theory and Managerial Implications

Many researchers have tested expectancy theory. In support of the theory, a meta-analysis of 77 studies indicated that expectancy theory significantly predicted performance, effort, intentions, preferences, and choice.[47] Another summary of 16 studies revealed that expectancy theory correctly predicted occupational or organizational choice 63.4% of the time; this was significantly better than chance predictions.[48]

Nonetheless, expectancy theory has been criticized for a variety of reasons. For example, the theory is difficult to test, and the measures used to assess expectancy, instrumentality, and valence have questionable validity.[49] In the final analysis, however, expectancy theory has important practical implications for individual managers and organizations as a whole (see Table 8–1).

Managers are advised to enhance effort→performance expectancies by helping employees accomplish their performance goals. Managers can do this by providing support and coaching and by increasing employees' self-efficacy. It also is important for managers to influence employees' instrumentalities and to monitor valences for various rewards. This raises the issue of whether organizations should use monetary rewards as the primary method to reinforce performance. Although money is certainly a positively valent reward for most people, there are many issues to consider when deciding on the relative balance between monetary and nonmonetary rewards. These issues are discussed in Chapter 9.[50]

In summary, there is no one best type of reward. Individual differences and need theories tell us that people are motivated by different rewards. Managers should therefore focus on linking employee performance to valued rewards regardless of the type of reward used to enhance motivation. Managers need to be careful or thoughtful, however, when imple-

Table 8–1   *Managerial and Organizational Implications of Expectancy Theory*

Implications for Managers	Implications for Organizations
Determine the outcomes employees value.	Reward people for desired performance; and do not keep pay decisions secret.
Identify good performance so appropriate behaviors can be rewarded.	Design challenging jobs.
Make sure employees can achieve targeted performance levels.	Tie some rewards to group accomplishments to build teamwork and encourage cooperation.
Link desired outcomes to targeted levels of performance.	Reward managers for creating, monitoring, and maintaining expectancies, instrumentalities, and outcomes that lead to high effort and goal attainment.
Make sure changes in outcomes are large enough to motivate high effort.	Monitor employee motivation through interviews or anonymous questionnaires.
Monitor the reward system for inequities.	Accommodate individual differences by building flexibility into the motivation program.

menting this suggestion. Consider the mistake made by a *Fortune* 500 insurance firm in California when it rewarded its top salespeople with tickets to a Christmas pageant at a local cathedral.

> "The employees were upset and couldn't believe they would give them a gift like that," Davis says. [Helen Davis is president and CEO of Indaba Inc., a management consulting firm.] "What was supposed to be a reward became a disaster for the company." The workers ended up boycotting the firm for six months by bringing in only the minimum amount of sales on the insurance and investment products they sold. They wanted a formal apology from the CEO, but the executive was hoping the matter would just blow over. Although the CEO finally relented, she says, it cost the firm nearly $750,000 in sales over that period and ultimately reached a loss of $1.5 million because many top producers left the firm as a result.[51]

Can you guess what caused the problem? A third of the firm's sales force was Jewish.

Motivation through Goal Setting

Regardless of the nature of their specific achievements, successful people tend to have one thing in common. Their lives are goal oriented. This is as true for politicians seeking votes as it is for world-class athletes. As a process model of motivation, goal-setting theory explains how the simple behavior of setting goals activates a powerful motivational process that leads to sustained, high performance. This section explores the theory and research pertaining to goal setting, and Chapter 9 continues the discussion by focusing on the practical application of goal setting.

Goals: Definition and Background

Goal
What an individual is trying to accomplish.

Edwin Locke, a leading authority on goal setting, and his colleagues define a **goal** as "what an individual is trying to accomplish; it is the object or aim of an action."[52] The motivational effect of performance goals and goal-based reward plans has been recognized for a long time. At the turn of the century, Frederick Taylor attempted to scientifically establish how much work of a specified quality an individual should be assigned each day. He proposed that bonuses be based on accomplishing those output standards: Taylor's theory is discussed in the next section of this chapter. More recently, goal setting has been promoted through a widely used management technique called *management by objectives (MBO)*. The application of MBO is outlined in Chapter 9.

How Does Goal Setting Work?

Despite abundant goal-setting research and practice, goal-setting theories are surprisingly scarce. An instructive model was formulated by Locke and his associates. According to Locke's model, goal setting has four motivational mechanisms.

Goals Direct Attention   Goals direct one's attention and effort toward goal-relevant activities and away from goal-irrelevant activities. If, for example, you have a term project due in a few days, your thoughts and actions tend to revolve around completing that project. Scooter Store, which was included among the list of the 100 best companies to work for in America in 2004 by *Fortune,* uses this motivational function of goal setting on a daily basis. Every morning the company's managers assemble their workers in a 14-minute huddle to discuss the day's goals.[53]

Goals Regulate Effort   Not only do goals make us selectively perceptive, they also motivate us to act. The instructor's deadline for turning in your term project would prompt you to complete it, as opposed to going out with friends, watching television, or studying for another course. Generally, the level of effort expended is proportionate to the difficulty of the goal.

Goals Increase Persistence   Within the context of goal setting, persistence represents the effort expended on a task over an extended period of time: It takes effort to run 100 meters; it takes persistence to run a 26-mile marathon. Persistent people tend to see obstacles as challenges to be overcome rather than as reasons to fail. A difficult goal that is important to an individual is a constant reminder to keep exerting effort in the appropriate direction. Annika Sorenstam is a great example of someone who persisted at her goal of being the best female golfer in the world. She has won 62 tournaments since starting on the LPGA tour in 1994.[54]

> She already has qualified for the LPGA and World Golf Halls of Fame, has won a career Grand Slam, shot the only round of 59 in women's pro golf and has won six Player of the Year titles.
>
> [In 2003] her new challenge was playing in a PGA Tour event, where she made a lasting impression but failed to make the cut. When it was over, she said she didn't care to compete in more men's tournaments but needed to move on.
>
> Moving on meant winning two more LPGA majors. Just like Tiger Woods, major titles and a single-season Grand Slam have become her new focus.
>
> "Nobody else has done it, so I think that says it all," she said. "But I like to set high goals, I like to motivate myself. If you believe it in your mind, I think you can do it."[55]

Goals Foster the Development and Application of Task Strategies and Action Plans

If you are here and your goal is out there somewhere, you face the problem of getting from here to there. For example, the person who has resolved to lose 20 pounds must develop a plan for getting from "here" (his or her present weight) to "there" (20 pounds lighter). Goals can help because they encourage people to develop strategies and action plans that enable them to achieve their goals. By virtue of setting a weight-reduction goal, the dieter may choose a strategy of exercising more, eating less, or some combination of the two.

Practical Lessons from Goal-Setting Research

Research consistently has supported goal setting as a motivational technique. Setting performance goals increases individual, group, and organizational performance. Further, the positive effects of goal setting were found in six other countries or regions: Australia, Canada, the Caribbean, England, West Germany, and Japan. Goal setting works in different cultures. Reviews of the many goal-setting studies conducted over the past few decades have given managers five practical insights:

1. *Difficult goals lead to higher performance.* **Goal difficulty** reflects the amount of effort required to meet a goal. It is more difficult to sell nine cars a month than it is to sell three cars a month. A meta-analysis spanning 4,000 people and 65 separate studies revealed that goal difficulty was positively related to performance.[56]

2. *Specific, difficult goals lead to higher performance for simple rather than complex tasks.* **Goal specificity** pertains to the quantifiability of a goal. For example, a goal of selling nine cars a month is more specific than telling a salesperson to do his or her best. A meta-analysis of 125 studies indicated that goal-setting effects were strongest for easy tasks and weakest for complex tasks.[57]

3. *Feedback enhances the effect of specific, difficult goals.* Feedback plays a key role in all of our lives. Feedback lets people know if they are headed toward their goals or if they are off course and need to redirect their efforts. Goals plus feedback is the recommended approach.[58] Goals inform people about performance standards and expectations so that they can channel their energies accordingly. In turn, feedback provides the information needed to adjust direction, effort, and strategies for goal accomplishment.

4. *Participative goals, assigned goals, and self-set goals are equally effective.* Both managers and researchers are interested in identifying the best way to set goals. Should goals be participatively set, assigned, or set by the employee him- or herself? A summary of goal-setting research indicated that no single approach was consistently more effective than others in increasing performance.[59] Managers are advised to use a contingency approach by picking a method that seems best suited for the individual and situation at hand.

5. *Goal commitment and monetary incentives affect goal-setting outcomes.* **Goal commitment** is the extent to which an individual is personally committed to achieving a goal. In general, an individual is expected to persist in attempts to accomplish a goal when he or she is committed to it. Researchers believe that goal commitment moderates the relationship between the difficulty of a goal and performance. That is, difficult goals lead to higher performance only when employees are committed to their goals. Conversely, difficult goals are hypothesized to lead to lower performance when people are not committed to their

Goal difficulty
The amount of effort required to meet a goal.

Goal specificity
Quantifiability of a goal.

Goal commitment
Amount of commitment to achieving a goal.

goals. A meta-analysis of 21 studies based on 2,360 people supported these predictions.[60] It also is important to note that people are more likely to commit to difficult goals when they have high self-efficacy about successfully accomplishing their goals.[61]

Like goal setting, the use of monetary incentives to motivate employees is seldom questioned. Unfortunately, research uncovered some negative consequences when goal achievement is linked to individual incentives. Empirical studies demonstrated that goal-based bonus incentives produced higher commitment to easy goals and lower commitment to difficult goals. People were reluctant to commit to difficult goals that were tied to monetary incentives. People with high goal commitment also offered less help to their co-workers when they received goal-based bonus incentives to accomplish difficult individual goals. Individuals also neglected aspects of the job that were not covered in the performance goals.[62]

These findings underscore some of the dangers of using goal-based incentives, particularly for employees in complex, interdependent jobs requiring cooperation. Managers need to consider the advantages, disadvantages, and dilemmas of goal-based incentives prior to implementation.

Motivating Employees through Job Design

Job design
Changing the content or process of a specific job to increase job satisfaction and performance.

Job design is used when a manager suspects that the type of work an employee performs or characteristics of the work environment are causing motivational problems. **Job design,** also referred to as *job redesign,* "refers to any set of activities that involve the alteration of specific jobs or interdependent systems of jobs with the intent of improving the quality of employee job experience and their on-the-job productivity."[63] A team of researchers examined the various methods for conducting job design and integrated them into an interdisciplinary framework that contains four major approaches: mechanistic, motivational, biological, and perceptual-motor.[64] As you will learn, each approach to job design emphasizes different outcomes.[65] This section discusses these four approaches to job design and focuses most heavily on the motivational methods.

The Mechanistic Approach

The mechanistic approach draws from research in industrial engineering and scientific management and is most heavily influenced by the work of Frederick Taylor. Taylor, a mechanical engineer, developed the principles of scientific management while working at both Midvale Steel Works and Bethlehem Steel in Pennsylvania. He observed very little cooperation between management and workers and found that employees were underachieving by engaging in output restriction, which Taylor called "systematic soldiering." Taylor's interest in scientific management grew from his desire to improve upon this situation.

Scientific management
Using research and experimentation to find the most efficient way to perform a job.

Scientific management is "that kind of management which conducts a business or affairs by *standards* established by facts or truths gained through *systematic* observation, experiment, or reasoning."[66] Taylor's approach focused on using research and experimentation to determine the most efficient way to perform jobs. The application of scientific management involves the following five steps: (1) develop standard methods for performing jobs by using time and motion studies, (2) carefully select employees with the appropriate abilities, (3) train workers to use the standard methods and procedures, (4) support workers and reduce interruptions, and (5) provide incentives to reinforce performance.[67] Because jobs are highly specialized and standardized when they are designed according to the principles of scientific management, this approach to job design targets efficiency, flexibility, and employee productivity.

Designing jobs according to the principles of scientific management has both positive and negative consequences. Positively, employee efficiency and productivity are increased. On the other hand, research reveals that simplified, repetitive jobs also lead to job dissatisfaction, poor mental health, higher levels of stress, and low sense of accomplishment and personal growth.[68] These negative consequences paved the way for the motivational approach to job design.

Motivational Approaches

The motivational approaches to job design attempt to improve employees' affective and attitudinal reactions such as job satisfaction and intrinsic motivation as well as a host of behavioral outcomes such as absenteeism, turnover, and performance.[69] We discuss four key motivational techniques: job enlargement, job enrichment, job rotation, and a contingency approach called the job characteristics model.

Job Enlargement
This technique was first used in the late 1940s in response to complaints about tedious and overspecialized jobs. **Job enlargement** involves putting more variety into a worker's job by combining specialized tasks of comparable difficulty. Some call this *horizontally loading* the job. Researchers recommend using job enlargement as part of a broader approach that uses multiple motivational methods because it does not have a significant and lasting positive effect on job performance by itself.[70]

Job enlargement
Putting more variety into a job.

Job Rotation
As with job enlargement, job rotation's purpose is to give employees greater variety in their work. **Job rotation** calls for moving employees from one specialized job to another. Rather than performing only one job, workers are trained and given the opportunity to perform two or more separate jobs on a rotating basis. By rotating employees from job to job, managers believe they can stimulate interest and motivation while providing employees with a broader perspective of the organization. Other proposed advantages of job rotation include increased worker flexibility and easier scheduling because employees are cross trained to perform different jobs. General Electric, for example, experienced many of these benefits from its rotation program for human resource (HR) entry-level employees.

Job rotation
Moving employees from one specialized job to another.

The goal of the program is to hire talented people who can become senior HR leaders in the company.... The program offers tremendous

Workers at this Chrysler auto assembly line experience job enlargement because many of their jobs entail completing multiple tasks. What are some possible drawbacks to job enlargement?

opportunities to participants, says Peters [Susan Peters is vice president for executive development]. "The big attraction is the variety they get in the first few years," she says. "They see different businesses and different functions. You might start in labor relations, and then go to compensation, then to staffing, then benefits."

About a decade ago, GE added a cross-functional rotation to the mix, and it has become a key component of the program's success. "You have to go on the audit staff or become a marketing person for one rotation," Peter says. "We've learned that the HR function has to have good connectivity with the business operations and it improves the credibility of the individual later on."[71]

Despite positive experiences from companies like GE, it is not possible to draw firm conclusions about the value of job rotation programs because they have not been adequately researched.

Job Enrichment

Job enrichment
Building achievement, recognition, stimulating work, responsibility, and advancement into a job.

Job Enrichment Job enrichment is the practical application of Frederick Herzberg's motivator–hygiene theory of job satisfaction that we discussed earlier in this chapter. Specifically, **job enrichment** entails modifying a job such that an employee has the opportunity to experience achievement, recognition, stimulating work, responsibility, and advancement. These characteristics are incorporated into a job through vertical loading. Rather than giving employees additional tasks of similar difficulty (horizontal loading), *vertical loading* consists of giving workers more responsibility. In other words, employees take on tasks normally performed by their supervisors.

Intrinsic motivation
Motivation caused by positive internal feelings.

The Job Characteristics Model

Two OB researchers, J Richard Hackman and Greg Oldham, played a central role in developing the job characteristics approach. These researchers tried to determine how work can be structured so that employees are internally or intrinsically motivated. **Intrinsic motivation** occurs when an individual is "turned on to one's work because of the positive internal feelings that are generated by doing well, rather than being dependent on external factors (such as incentive pay or compliments from the boss) for the motivation to work effectively."[72] These positive feelings power a self-perpetuating cycle of motivation. As shown in Figure 8–4, internal work motivation is determined by three psychological states. In turn, these psychological states are fostered by the presence of five core job dimensions. The object of this approach is to promote high intrinsic motivation by designing jobs that possess the five core job characteristics shown in Figure 8–4. Let us examine the core job dimensions.

Core job dimensions
Job characteristics found to various degrees in all jobs.

In general terms, **core job dimensions** are common characteristics found to a varying degree in all jobs. Three of the job characteristics shown in Figure 8–4 combine to determine experienced meaningfulness of work:

- *Skill variety.* The extent to which the job requires an individual to perform a variety of tasks that require him or her to use different skills and abilities.
- *Task identity.* The extent to which the job requires an individual to perform a whole or completely identifiable piece of work. In other words, task identity is high when a person works on a product or project from beginning to end and sees a tangible result.
- *Task significance.* The extent to which the job affects the lives of other people within or outside the organization.

Experienced responsibility is elicited by the job characteristic of autonomy, defined as follows:

- *Autonomy.* The extent to which the job enables an individual to experience freedom, independence, and discretion in both scheduling and determining the procedures used in completing the job.

Figure 8–4   *The Job Characteristics Model*

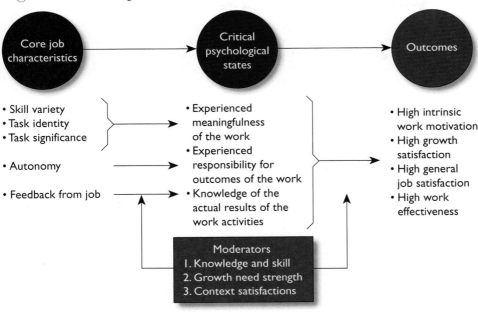

SOURCE: From J R Hackman and G R Oldham, *Work Redesign,* © 1980, p 90. Reprinted by permission of Pearson Education, Inc., Upper Saddle River, NJ.

Finally, knowledge of results is fostered by the job characteristic of feedback, defined as follows:

- *Feedback.* The extent to which an individual receives direct and clear information about how effectively he or she is performing the job.[73]

Hackman and Oldham recognized that everyone does not want a job containing high amounts of the five core job characteristics. They incorporated this conclusion into their model by identifying three attributes that affect how individuals respond to job enrichment. These attributes are concerned with the individual's knowledge and skill, growth need strength (representing the desire to grow and develop as an individual), and context satisfactions (see the box labeled Moderators in Figure 8–4). Context satisfactions represent the extent to which employees are satisfied with various aspects of their job, such as satisfaction with pay, co-workers, and supervision.

There are several practical implications associated with using the job characteristics model to enhance intrinsic motivation: Steps for applying this model are shown in Table 8–2. Managers may want to use this model to increase employee job satisfaction. Research overwhelmingly demonstrates a moderately strong relationship between job characteristics and satisfaction.[74] Consistent with this finding, Booz Allen Hamilton attempted to enhance employee satisfaction by designing more autonomy into employees' jobs. The company focused on increasing employee autonomy and flexibility by investing $10.8 million from 2000 to 2003 on remote access and laptops for its employees.[75] Research supports this investment, as autonomy has been found to be positively associated with job performance.[76]

Unfortunately, job redesign appears to reduce the quantity of output just as often as it has a positive effect. Caution and situational appropriateness are advised. For example, one

Table 8–2   *Steps for Applying the Job Characteristics Model*

1. Diagnose the work environment to determine if a performance problem is due to de-motivating job characteristics. Hackman and Oldham developed a self-report instrument for managers to use called the job diagnostic survey: It is shown and used in the Group Exercise at the end of this chapter. Diagnosis begins by determining whether the core job characteristics are low or high. If the job characteristics are lower than desired, a manager proceeds to step 2. If the performance problem is not due to low job characteristics, then a manager looks to apply another model of motivation or human behavior to solve the performance problem.
2. Determine whether job redesign is appropriate for a given group of employees. Job redesign is most likely to work in a participative environment in which employees have the necessary knowledge and skills to perform the enriched tasks and their job satisfaction is average to high.
3. Determine how to best redesign the job. The focus of this effort is to increase those core job characteristics that are low. Employee input is essential during this step to determine the details of a redesign initiative.

study demonstrated that job redesign works better in less complex organizations (small plants or companies).[77] Nonetheless, managers are likely to find noticeable increases in the quality of performance after a job redesign program. Results from 21 experimental studies revealed that job redesign resulted in a median increase of 28% in the quality of performance.[78] Moreover, two separate meta-analyses support the practice of using the job characteristics model to help managers reduce absenteeism and turnover.[79] Athleta Corp., a sports apparel company in Petaluma, California, for instance, helped reduce employee turnover to less than 1% by using the job characteristic of autonomy to allow employees to set their own schedules and handle personal matters during the workday.[80]

Biological and Perceptual-Motor Approaches

The biological approach to job design is based on research from biomechanics, work physiology, and ergonomics and focuses on designing the work environment to reduce employees' physical strain, fatigue, and health complaints.[81] An attempt is made to redesign jobs so that they eliminate or reduce the amount of repetitive motions from a worker's job. Intel, for example, has implemented the biological approach to job design.

At Intel, the most common types of workplace injuries are musculoskeletal disorders. That's one reason the company has stepped up efforts to prevent and treat repetitive-motion injuries. When employees change offices, Intel will tear down and rebuild their workstations if needed so that they are ergonomically customized. They've created an ergonomics-profile database for their Santa Clara, California, facility which includes information on workers' heights, preferred chairs, mouse arrangement, ideal desk heights, and whether employees are left- or right-handed. A companywide database is under development.[82]

The perceptual-motor approach is derived from research that examines human factors engineering, perceptual and cognitive skills, and information processing. This approach to job design emphasizes the reliability of work outcomes by examining error rates, accidents, and workers' feedback about facilities and equipment.[83] IBM and Steelcase are jointly developing a new interactive office system, labeled BlueSpace, that is based on this method of job design. Its features include[84]

- *BlueScreen.* A touch screen that sits next to a user's computer monitor and puts users in control of their heat or cooling, ventilation, and light.
- *Everywhere Display.* A video projector that displays information on walls, floors, desktops, and other surfaces.
- *Monitor rail.* A moving rail that consists of a work surface that travels the length of a work space and a dual monitor arm that rotates to nearly a complete circle, letting users be positioned almost anywhere.
- *Threshold.* An L-shaped partial ceiling and wall on wheels that provides on-demand visual and territorial privacy to a user.

The frequency of using both the biological and perceptual-motor approaches to job redesign is increasing in light of the number of workers who experience injuries related to overexertion or repetitive motion. A study conducted by the National Research Council and the Institute of Medicine revealed "Musculoskeletal disorders cause about 1 million employees to miss work each year and cost the nation $45 billion to $54 billion in compensation costs, lost wages and decreased productivity."[85] Moreover, the Occupational Safety and Health Administration (OSHA) implemented a new set of guidelines regarding ergonomic standards in the workplace due to this trend. The standards went into effect on October 14, 2001.

Putting Motivational Theories to Work

Successfully designing and implementing motivational programs is not easy. Managers cannot simply take one of the theories discussed in this book and apply it word for word. Dynamics within organizations interfere with applying motivation theories in "pure" form. According to management scholar Terence Mitchell,

> There are situations and settings that make it exceptionally difficult for a motivational system to work. These circumstances may involve the kinds of jobs or people present, the technology, the presence of a union, and so on. The factors that hinder the application of motivational theory have not been articulated either frequently or systematically.[86]

With Mitchell's cautionary statement in mind, this section raises several issues that need to be addressed before implementing a motivational program. Our intent is not to discuss all relevant considerations but rather to highlight a few important ones.

Assuming a motivational program is being considered to improve productivity, quality, or customer satisfaction, the first issue revolves around the difference between motivation and performance. Motivation and performance are not one and the same. Motivation is only one of several factors that influence performance. For example, poor performance may be more a function of outdated or inefficient materials and machinery, not having goals to direct one's attention, a monotonous job, feelings of inequity, a negative work environment characterized by political behavior and conflict, poor supervisory support and coaching, or poor work flow. Motivation cannot make up for a deficient job context. Managers, therefore, need to carefully consider the causes of poor performance and employee misbehavior.

Importantly, managers should not ignore the individual differences discussed in Chapters 5 and 6, which are an important input that influence motivation and motivated behavior.

Pat Summitt loves her job as head coach of Tennessee's women's basketball team. Not only was she the first coach in women's college basketball to win 800 games, she has the highest win percentage (.838) of any current or former men or women's college basketball coach.

Consider the case of Pat Summitt. She has been the head coach of Tennessee's women's basketball team since 1974. "Today she owns six NCAA championships and 24 Southeastern conference regular-season and tournament titles, has made 15 Final Four appearances, has 14 seasons with 30 wins or more and achieved countless other marks." She told a reporter from *USA Today*,

> I love what I do and look forward to going to work. I just love it. One thing that motivates me is the competition. It's greater than it's ever been. So is the desire to help this program stay at the top. It's harder now to stay at the top. That challenge inspires me as a coach. I love practice as much or more than games because teaching is my real passion.[87]

Pat does not need external sources of motivation because she is driven by internal needs and passion.

Managers are advised to develop employees so that they have the ability and job knowledge to effectively perform their jobs.[88] In addition, attempts should be made to nurture positive employee characteristics, such as self-esteem, self-efficacy, positive emotions, and need for achievement.

Because motivation is goal directed, the process of developing and setting goals should be consistent with our previous discussion. Moreover, the method used to evaluate performance also needs to be considered. Without a valid performance appraisal system, it is difficult, if not impossible, to accurately distinguish good and poor performers.[89] Consider the motivational effect of using a performance rating system in which managers are required to rank employees against each other according to some specified distribution:

> At GE, which has used the system for several years, this means that 20% of salaried, managerial, and executive employees are rated outstanding each year, 70% "high-performance middle," and 10% in need of improvement. At Enron, where some have nicknamed the system "rank and yank," employees are put in one of five categories: 5% are identified as superior, 30% excellent, 30% strong, 20% satisfactory, and 15% "needs improvement." And Ford, which began using rating systems last year, dictates that 10% of the auto maker's 18,000 managers will get A grades, 85% Bs, and 5% Cs. (Initially, it asked for 10% Cs.) Those who receive a second consecutive C can be fired.[90]

The problem with ranking systems is that they are based on subjective judgments. Motivation thus is decreased to the extent these judgments are inaccurate. Managers need to keep in mind that both equity theory and expectancy theory suggest that employee motivation is squelched by inaccurate performance ratings. Not only can inaccurate performance rating systems negatively influence motivation, but they can lead to lawsuits: For example, employees and former employees with Microsoft, Ford, and Conoco have filed lawsuits claiming that ranking systems are biased toward some groups over others.[91]

Consistent with expectancy theory, managers should make extrinsic rewards contingent on performance. In doing so, however, it is important to consider two issues. First, managers need to ensure that performance goals are directed to achieve the "right" end-results. For example, health insurers and medical groups wrestle over the relative focus on cost savings versus patient satisfaction. Consider the case of Oakland-based Kaiser Permanente:

> Telephone clerks at California's largest HMO received bonuses for keeping calls with patients brief and limiting the number of doctor visits they set up. . . . The California Nurses Association, the union representing Kaiser's registered nurses, derided the program as deceitful and harmful to patients with serious medical problems.
>
> "Patients don't understand they're talking to a high school graduate with no nursing background," [Jim] Anderson said.
>
> The clerks, who generally have little to no medical training, answer phone calls from customers wanting to set up doctor appointments or asking simple medical questions.
>
> Cash bonuses were paid to those who made appointments for fewer than 35% of callers and spent less than an average of three minutes, 45 seconds on the phone with each patient. Clerks were also encouraged to transfer fewer than 50% of the calls to registered nurses for further evaluation.[92]

Interestingly, incentives based on quality care and patient satisfaction are twice as common as cost-cutting incentives among heath insurers across the United States.[93] Second, the promise of increased rewards will not prompt higher effort and good performance unless those rewards are clearly tied to performance and they are large enough to gain employees' interests or attention.

Moreover, equity theory tells us that motivation is influenced by employee perceptions about the fairness of reward allocations. Motivation is decreased when employees believe rewards are inequitably allocated. Rewards also need to be integrated appropriately into the appraisal system. If performance is measured at the individual level, individual achievements need to be rewarded. On the other hand, when performance is the result of group effort, rewards should be allocated to the group.

Feedback also should be linked with performance. Feedback provides the information and direction needed to keep employees focused on relevant tasks, activities, and goals. Managers should strive to provide specific, timely, and accurate feedback to employees.[94]

Finally, we end this chapter by noting that an organization's culture significantly influences employee motivation and behavior. A positive self-enhancing culture is more likely to engender higher motivation and commitment than a culture dominated by suspicion, faultfinding, and blame.

Summary of Key Concepts

1. *Contrast Maslow's, Alderfer's, and McClelland's need theories.* Maslow proposed that motivation is a function of five basic needs arranged in a prepotent hierarchy. The concept of a stair-step hierarchy has not stood up well under research. Alderfer concluded that three core needs explain behavior—existence, relatedness, and growth. He proposed that more than one need can be activated at a time and frustration of higher-order needs can influence the desire for lower-level needs. McClelland argued that motivation and performance vary according to the strength of an individual's need for achievement. High achievers prefer tasks of moderate difficulty, situations under their control, and a desire for more performance feedback than low achievers. Top managers should have a high need for power coupled with a low need for affiliation.

2. *Explain the practical significance of Herzberg's distinction between motivators and hygiene factors.* Herzberg believes job satisfaction motivates better job performance. His hygiene factors, such as policies, supervision, and salary, erase sources of dissatisfaction. On the other hand, his motivators, such as achievement, responsibility, and recognition, foster job satisfaction. Although Herzberg's motivator–hygiene theory of job satisfaction has been

criticized on methodological grounds, it has practical significance for job enrichment.

3. *Discuss the role of perceived inequity in employee motivation.* Equity theory is a model of motivation that explains how people strive for fairness and justice in social exchanges. On the job, feelings of inequity revolve around a person's evaluation of whether he or she receives adequate rewards to compensate for his or her contributive inputs. People perform these evaluations by comparing the perceived fairness of their employment exchange with that of relevant others. Perceived inequity creates motivation to restore equity.

4. *Explain the differences among distributive, procedural, and interactional justice.* Distributive, procedural, and interactional justice are the three key components underlying organizational justice. Distributive justice reflects the perceived fairness of how resources and rewards are distributed. Procedural justice represents the perceived fairness of the process and procedures used to make allocation decisions. Interactional justice entails the perceived fairness of a decision maker's behavior in the process of decision making.

5. *Describe the practical lessons derived from equity theory.* Equity theory has at least eight practical implications. First, because people are motivated to resolve perceptions of inequity, managers should not discount employees' feelings and perceptions when trying to motivate workers. Second, managers should pay attention to employees' perceptions of what is fair and equitable. It is the employee's view of reality that counts when trying to motivate someone, according to equity theory. Third, employees should be given a voice in decisions that affect them. Fourth, employees should be given the opportunity to appeal decisions that affect their welfare. Fifth, employees are more likely to accept and support organizational change when they believe it is implemented fairly and when it produces equitable outcomes. Sixth, managers can promote cooperation and teamwork among group members by treating them equitably. Seventh, treating employees inequitably can lead to litigation and costly court settlements. Finally, managers need to pay attention to the organization's climate for justice because it influences employee attitudes and behavior.

6. *Explain Vroom's expectancy theory, and review its practical implications.* Expectancy theory assumes motivation is determined by one's perceived chances of achieving valued outcomes. Vroom's expectancy model of motivation reveals how effort→performance expectancies and performance→outcome instrumentalities influence the degree of effort expended to achieve desired (positively valent) outcomes. Managers are advised to enhance effort→performance expectancies by helping employees accomplish their performance goals. With respect to instrumentalities and valences, managers should attempt to link employee performance and valued rewards.

7. *Explain how goal setting motivates an individual, and review the five practical lessons from goal-setting research.* Four motivational mechanisms of goal setting are as follows: act (1) Goals direct one's attention, (2) goals regulate effort, (3) goals increase one's persistence, and (4) goals encourage development of goal-attainment strategies and action plans. Research identifies five practical lessons about goal setting. First, difficult goals lead to higher performance than easy or moderate goals. Second, specific, difficult goals lead to higher performance for simple rather than complex tasks. Third, feedback enhances the effect of specific, difficult goals. Fourth, participative goals, assigned goals, and self-set goals are equally effective. Fifth, goal commitment and monetary incentives affect goal-setting outcomes.

8. *Review the mechanistic, motivation, biological, and perceptual-motor approaches to job design.* The mechanistic approach is based on industrial engineering and scientific management and focuses on increasing efficiency, flexibility, and employee productivity. Motivational approaches aim to improve employees' affective and attitudinal reactions and behavioral outcomes. Job enlargement, job enrichment, job-rotation, and a contingency approach called the job characteristics model are motivational approaches to job design. The biological approach focuses on designing the work environment to reduce employees' physical strain, fatigue, and health complaints. The perceptual-motor approach emphasizes the reliability of work outcomes.

9. *Specify issues that should be addressed before implementing a motivational program.* Managers need to consider the variety of causes of poor performance. Motivation is only one of several factors that influence performance. Managers should not ignore the many individual differences that affect motivation. The method used to evaluate performance as well as the link between performance and rewards must be examined. Performance must be accurately evaluated, and rewards should be equitably distributed. Rewards should also be directly tied to performance. Finally, managers should recognize that employee motivation and behavior are influenced by organizational culture.

Discussion Questions

1. Why should the average manager be well versed in the various motivation theories?

2. From a practical standpoint, what are the major drawbacks of theories of motivation based on internal factors such as needs and satisfaction?

3. How have hygiene factors and motivators influenced your job satisfaction and performance?

4. Have you experienced positive or negative inequity at work? Describe the circumstances in terms of the inputs and outcomes of the comparison person and yourself.

5. What is your definition of studying hard? What is your expectancy for earning an A on the next exam in this course? What is the basis of this expectancy?

6. If someone who reported to you at work had a low expectancy for successful performance, what could you do to increase this person's expectancy?

7. Goal-setting research suggests that people should be given difficult goals. How does this prescription mesh with expectancy theory? Explain.

8. How could a professor use equity, expectancy, and goal-setting theories to motivate students?

9. Which of the four types of job design is most likely to be used in the future? Explain your rationale.

10. What are the three most important lessons about employee motivation that you have learned from this chapter?

OB in Action Case Study

Feelings of Inequity Lead to Lawsuits in the High-Technology Industry[95]

A hallmark of the boom years in high-tech was its work ethic: killer hours, often at modest salaries, without complaint. It was a small price for the excitement and the shot at a bonanza someday.

But as high-tech riches have faded, a different attitude toward employers is popping up: Pay me overtime, or I'll sue.

Hidetomo Morimoto took a job in 2003 at a tech company that translates English software into Japanese. With the tech bubble already burst, he was grateful for the job, even though it paid just $1,800 a month to start. He soon found himself working 60 hours a week, Mr Morimoto says, and during crunch times often didn't leave till 1 AM. Yet he says he never received any overtime pay.

In May, after he complained in an Internet posting that some Japanese employers took advantage of their staff's strong work ethic, Mr Morimoto found himself out of work. Now the 31-year-old is suing his old employer, demanding the overtime pay he says he should have received. The employer, Pacific Software Publishing Inc. in Bellevue, Washington, maintains it wasn't remiss because Mr Morimoto spent all of his extra hours in the office on personal matters, not work. It is countersuing, alleging defamation.

In the past 18 months, labor suits such as this have hit technology outfits ranging from start-ups to established companies. "Wage-and-hour class-action lawsuits have now invaded high-tech in the Valley," says Lynne Hermle, an attorney representing several companies.

Accusations in the spate of suits include denying overtime pay, substituting stock options of little value for cash bonuses, and even not paying promised salaries. In a few cases, notably at videogame publisher Electronic Arts Inc., the ferment is prompting executives to rethink job and compensation policies. . . .

Electronic Arts faces labor litigation despite a robust stock price that can reward employee shareholders just as in the tech boom. An EA employee filed suit in July, accusing the Redwood City, California, company of denying him overtime pay he was due. California labor law says software employees needn't be paid for overtime if they meet certain tests, such as doing "intellectual or creative" work or exercising "discretion and independent judgment." The employee, Jamie Kirschenbaum, said this doesn't mean him. An animator for the game maker, he said in his complaint that as an "image production employee," he follows strict instructions to produce graphics.

Several former EA image workers have joined his suit, which is in California Superior Court in San Mateo County. An EA engineer in Culver City, California, has filed a separate overtime suit in the same court. All of the plaintiffs or their lawyers declined to comment on the suits.

EA "believes it has acted lawfully and appropriately and we dispute the plaintiffs' allegations," said Rusty Rueff, executive vice president for human resources. The company is the largest videogame publisher, with hit franchises such as The Sims and Madden football.

Mr Kirschenbaum's suit set off a firestorm on the Internet. In a posting in November, someone identified as "EA Spouse" wrote a vivid account of how she said the game company was overworking her husband. Joe Straitiff, a former software engineer at EA, wrote that he had worked 70-hour weeks there for months during the frenetic "crunch time" when development milestones are being met.

In an interview, Mr Straitiff said he was fired late last year because of repeated conflicts with his supervisor, mostly over long hours. "At every other company I've worked for, there was no such thing as mandatory overtime, but I was told by my EA manager I was expected to work long hours," he said. EA declines to discuss why Mr Straitiff left.

Need for Change

In December, EA's Mr Rueff acknowledged a need for change. "As much as I don't like what's been said about our company and our industry," he wrote in a memo to employees, "I recognize that at the heart of the matter is a core truth: the work is getting harder, the tasks are more complex and the hours needed to accomplish them have become a burden. We're forced to look at making some changes."

The company recently polled employees on the quality of their working life. In response, Mr Rueff said in an interview, it is developing plans to weed inefficiencies out of the game-creation process to improve the environment for workers. . . .

At start-ups, some lawsuits center on more-basic compensation matters. Dave Benach says he joined Unplugged Inc., a tiny wireless-games maker in Berkeley, two years ago, and was promised a $65,000 annual salary and a 3% equity stake. If the company flourished, he figured, his stake could be worth millions.

In his first months, Mr Benach says, he didn't get paid. He didn't mind at first, figuring Unplugged would pay once its business got off the ground. But he says that even after it published several wireless games in late 2003, his checks didn't materialize.

For living costs, Mr Benach, 32, dug into $30,000 in savings, relied on his wife's income as a restaurant manager and sold some parts from his old BMW on eBay. Mr Benach says that when he complained to the company founder, he was told payments would be coming.

In December 2003, Mr Benach says Unplugged paid him $2,000. He says he got no more until nearly six months later, when he received $1,500. He put out feelers for other jobs, but retracted them when Unplugged landed a gig to develop a game around *Mean Girls,* the teen movie. "It was hard to walk away," he says, because "I'd put my heart and soul into the products for more than a year."

He compared notes with a colleague, Jeff Linam, who also said he wasn't getting his pay. "It was one excuse after another," Mr Linam said in an interview.

By last September, says Mr Benach, he had received just $8,630 for nearly two years of work. Unplugged confirms the number. Mr Benach resigned and asked for $99,700 that he figured he was owed. Not getting it, he sued for the money.

A lawyer for Unplugged, Manuella Hancock, says, "In a start-up, it takes a long time for the money to come in. No one was taking a salary. The plaintiff simply got tired of the frontier, and now he's trying to get some money out of it." The company hasn't gone public.

Ms Hancock also says Mr Benach wasn't a full-time employee but an independent contractor, at $20 an hour, for most of his time there. Mr Benach denies that. His suit, in California's Alameda County Superior Court, is in the discovery phase.

His former colleague Mr Linam filed a wage suit in the same court last month. He says Unplugged paid him only $5,130 after a year and a half of work. The company says he, too, was an independent contractor most of his time there.

Questions for Discussion

1. How does equity theory explain the behavior of Hidetomo Morimoto, Jamie Kirschenbaum, and Dave Benach?

2. How would Maslow's, Alderfer's, or McClelland's need theories explain Dave Benach's motivation and behavior? Explain.

3. To what extent are the hygiene factors and motivators influencing employee behavior at Electronic Arts?

4. To what extent is Dave Benach's motivation and behavior consistent with expectancy theory? Explain.

5. What is your feeling about the ethics of the managers at Electronic Arts? Discuss.

Personal Awareness and Growth Exercise

What Outcomes Motivate Employees?

Objectives

1. To determine how accurately you perceive the outcomes that motivate nonmanagerial employees.

2. To examine the managerial implications of inaccurately assessing employee motivators.

Introduction

One thousand employees were given a list of 10 outcomes people want from their work. They were asked to rank these items from most important to least important. We are going to have you estimate how you think these workers ranked the various outcomes. This will enable you to compare your perceptions with the average rankings documented by a researcher. The survey results are presented in endnote 96 at the end of this book.[96] Please do not read them until indicated.

Instructions

Below is a list of 10 outcomes people want from their work. Read the list, and then rank each item according to how you think the typical nonmanagerial employee would rank them. Rank the outcomes from 1 to 10; 1 = most important and 10 = least important. (Please do this now before reading the rest of these instructions.) After you have completed your ranking, calculate the discrepancy between your perceptions and the actual results. Take the absolute value of the difference between your ranking and the actual ranking for each item, and then add them to get a total discrepancy score. For example, if you gave job security a ranking of 1, your discrepancy score would be 3 because the actual ranking was 4. The lower your discrepancy score, the more accurate your perception of the typical employee's needs. The actual rankings are shown in endnote 96.

How do you believe the typical nonmanagerial employee would rank these outcomes?

_____ Full appreciation of work done
_____ Job security
_____ Good working conditions
_____ Feeling of being in on things
_____ Good wages
_____ Tactful discipline
_____ Personal loyalty to employees
_____ Interesting work
_____ Sympathetic help with personal problems
_____ Promotion and growth in the organization

Questions for Discussion

1. Were your perceptions accurate? Why or why not?

2. What would Vroom's expectancy theory suggest you should do?

3. Based on the size of your discrepancy, what does Herzberg's motivator–hygiene model suggest will happen to satisfaction?

4. Would you generalize the actual survey results to all nonmanagerial employees? Why or why not?

Group Exercise

Applying the Job Characteristics Model

Objectives

1. To assess the motivating potential score (MPS) of several jobs.

2. To determine which core job characteristics need to be changed for each job.

3. To explore how you might redesign one of the jobs.

Introduction

The first step in applying the job characteristics model is to diagnose the work environment to determine if a performance problem is due to de-motivating job characteristics. This can be accomplished by having employees complete the job diagnostic survey (JDS).[97] The JDS is a self-report instrument that assesses the extent to which a specific job possesses the five core job characteristics. With this instrument, it also is possible to calculate a motivating potential score for a job. The motivating potential score (MPS) is a summary index that represents the extent to which the job characteristics foster internal work motivation. Low scores indicate that an individual will not experience high intrinsic motivation from the job. Such a job is a prime candidate for job redesign. High scores reveal that a job is capable of stimulating intrinsic motivation and suggest that a performance problem is not due to de-motivating job characteristics. The MPS is computed as follows:

$$\text{MPS} = \left(\frac{\text{Skill variety} + \text{Task identity} + \text{Task significance}}{3} \right)$$
$$\times \text{Autonomy}$$
$$\times \text{Feedback}$$

Judging from this equation, which core job characteristic do you think is relatively more important in determining the motivational potential of a job? Because autonomy and feedback are not divisible by another number, low amounts of autonomy and feedback have a greater chance of lowering MPS than the job characteristics of skill variety, task identity, and task significance.

Since the JDS is a long questionnaire, we would like you to complete a subset of the instrument. This will enable you to calculate the MPS and to identify deficient job characteristics.

Instructions

Your instructor will divide the class into groups of four to six. Each group member will first assess the MPS of his or her current or former job and then will identify which core job characteristics need to be changed. Once each group member completes these tasks, the group will identify the job with the lowest MPS and devise a plan for redesigning it. The following steps should be used.

You should first complete the 12 items from the JDS. For each item, indicate whether it is an accurate or inaccurate description of your current or most recent job by selecting one number from the scale provided. Write your response in the space provided next to each item. After completing the JDS, use the scoring key to compute a total score for each of the core job characteristics.

1 = very inaccurate   5 = slightly accurate

2 = mostly inaccurate   6 = mostly accurate

3 = slightly inaccurate   7 = very accurate

4 = uncertain

_____ 1. Supervisors often let me know how well they think I am performing the job.

_____ 2. The job requires me to use a number of complex or high-level skills.

_____ 3. The job is arranged so that I have the chance to do an entire piece of work from beginning to end.

_____ 4. Just doing the work required by the job provides many chances for me to figure out how well I am doing.

_____ 5. The job is not simple and repetitive.

_____ 6. This job is one where a lot of other people can be affected by how well the work gets done.

_____ 7. The job does not deny me the chance to use my personal initiative or judgment in carrying out the work.

_____ 8. The job provides me the chance to completely finish the pieces of work I begin.

_____ 9. The job itself provides plenty of clues about whether or not I am performing well.

_____ 10. The job gives me considerable opportunity for independence and freedom in how I do the work.

_____ 11. The job itself is very significant or important in the broader scheme of things.

_____ 12. The supervisors and co-workers on this job almost always give me "feedback" about how well I am doing in my work.

Scoring Key

Compute the *average* of the two items that measure each job characteristic.

Skill variety (2 and 5)   _____

Task identity (3 and 8)   _____

Task significance (6 and 11)   _____

Autonomy (7 and 10)   _____

Feedback from job itself (4 and 9) _____

Feedback from others (1 and 12) _____

Now you are ready to calculate the MPS. First, you need to compute a total score for the feedback job characteristic. This is done by computing the average of the job characteristics entitled "feedback from job itself" and "feedback from others." Second, use the MPS formula presented earlier to compute the MPS. Finally, use the JDS norms provided to interpret the relative status of the MPS and each individual job characteristic.[98]

Once all group members have finished these activities, convene as a group to complete the exercise. Each group member should present his or her results and interpretations of the strengths and deficiencies of the job characteristics. Next, pick the job within the group that has the lowest MPS. Prior to redesigning this job, however, each group member needs more background information. The individual who works in the lowest MPS job should thus provide a thorough description of the job, including its associated tasks, responsibilities, and reporting relationships. A brief overview of the general working environment is also useful. With this information in hand, the group should now devise a detailed plan for how it would redesign the job.

Norms

TYPE OF JOB

	Professional/ Technical	Clerical	Sales	Service
Skill variety	5.4	4.0	4.8	5.0
Task identity	5.1	4.7	4.4	4.7
Task significance	5.6	5.3	5.5	5.7
Autonomy	5.4	4.5	4.8	5.0
Feedback from job itself	5.1	4.6	5.4	5.1
Feedback from others	4.2	4.0	3.6	3.8
MPS	135	90	106	114

Questions for Discussion

1. Using the norms, which job characteristics are high average, or low for the job being redesigned?

2. Which job characteristics did you change? Why?

3. How would you specifically redesign the job under consideration?

4. What would be the difficulties in implementing the job characteristics model in a large organization?

Ethical Dilemma

Should Companies Donate Money to Charities to Help Land Business?[99]

In 2001, two J. P. Morgan Chase & Co. investment bankers were looking for a way to get more work underwriting municipal bonds in Philadelphia. Then the bankers, Charles LeCroy and Anthony Snell, met one of the Philadelphia mayor's top fund-raisers, and their lives got complicated.

The fund-raiser was a folksy lawyer named Ronald A White. According to accounts later introduced in a trial in federal court in Philadelphia, Mr White suggested he could help the bank get bond work and also suggested various ways the bank could compensate him.

J. P. Morgan eventually gave $20,000 to fund a scholarship in Mr White's name. It also donated $70,000 to a charity of which he was co-chairman. And according to accounts later introduced in court, the bankers got J. P. Morgan to pay $50,000 to Mr White's tiny law firm for work that, it turned out, it never did.

Mr Snell, asked later about such events in a J. P. Morgan internal investigation, said that if Mr White "was going to use his contacts to help J. P. Morgan, he expected J. P. Morgan to help his friends." In big cities, Mr Snell added, according to J. P. Morgan lawyers' memo about the debriefing, "99.9% of the time there is a go-to guy" like Mr White.

What would you have done if you were Mr LeCroy or Mr Snell?

1. I would do what they did because Mr White was the go-to guy and this is the way to get the business.

2. I would donate to the scholarship and charity but not pay Mr White's law firm for services it did not provide.

3. I would tell Mr White that he is basically asking for a bribe and then would call the mayor directly.

4. I would sell the positive aspects of doing business with J. P. Morgan Chase and not donate any money.

5. Invent other options. Discuss.

For the Chapter 8 Internet Exercise featuring an examination of motivation programs used by various companies (www.fed.org), which helps managers implement equity-based compensation and employee ownership, visit our Web site at **www.mhhe.com/kreitner.**

Chapter 9

Improving Job Performance with Goals, Feedback, Rewards, and Positive Reinforcement

Learning Objectives

When you finish studying the material in this chapter, you should be able to:

1 Define the term *performance management,* distinguish between learning goals and performance outcome goals, and explain the three-step goal-setting process.

2 Identify the two basic functions of feedback, and specify at least three practical lessons from feedback research.

3 Define upward feedback and 360-degree feedback, and summarize how to give good feedback in a performance management program.

4 Distinguish between extrinsic and intrinsic rewards, and explain the four building blocks of intrinsic rewards and motivation.

5 Summarize the reasons why extrinsic rewards often fail to motivate employees.

6 Discuss how managers can generally improve extrinsic reward and pay-for-performance plans.

7 State Thorndike's law of effect, and explain Skinner's distinction between respondent and operant behavior.

8 Define positive reinforcement, negative reinforcement, punishment, and extinction, and distinguish between continuous and intermittent schedules of reinforcement.

9 Demonstrate your knowledge of behavior shaping.

Leigh Buchanan, senior editor, *Harvard Business Review*:

The genius of Pat McGovern is the way he makes things all about you. That impressed me hugely, because when I first met Pat back in 1989 I wasn't the sort of person *anything* was all about. I was a new copy editor at *CIO* magazine; Pat was (still is) the founder and chairman of *CIO*'s parent, International Data Group, a then $400 million technology publishing and research empire. It hadn't occurred to me that the twain would meet, so I was startled (confused, marginally freaked) when a tall, ruddy man loomed in the entrance to my cubicle a few weeks before Christmas.

Pat thanked me for my contributions. He asked how things were going and looked vaguely disappointed when all I could muster was an unilluminating "Fine." Then he complimented me on a column I had ghostwritten for some technology honcho. The column was my most substantive accomplishment to date and the thing I was proudest of. But my name didn't appear on it anywhere, so how did he know? After three or four minutes, he handed me my bonus and proceeded to the next cubicle.

The formula for Pat's Christmas calls—expression of gratitude/request for feedback/congratulations on specific achievement/delivery of loot—never varied, even as IDG grew into the $2.4 billion global behemoth it is today. To personally thank most every person in every business unit in the US, more than 1,500 employees, takes almost four weeks, he told me years later: Managers provide him with a list of accomplishments for all their reports, and Pat memorizes them the night before his visits. He does this because he wants employees to know that he *sees them*—really sees them—as individuals, and that he considers what they do all day to be meaningful.

Not only does Pat care about his people; he also believes in them. His commitment to decentralization has created a constellation of motivated business units that make their own decisions about everything from how to

Pat McGovern.

reward staff to what new businesses to launch. He also treats his end customers—the readers of such publications as *Computerworld, PC World,* and *Macworld*—with consummate respect. At IDG the quality of content is sacrosanct, a tough ideal to sustain when advertising pays so many of the bills.

Did I mention that he's giving $350 million to MIT to create an institute for brain research? Maybe I shouldn't: I don't want to lay it on too thick.

Another small-company tradition Pat has kept up over the years is taking each employee out for a meal at the Ritz on his or her 10th anniversary with IDG. I left *CIO* after only seven years (to work for *Inc.,* where I could write about people like Pat and not just work for them), so I never got my anniversary dinner. Too bad—it would have been a class act. And I'm not talking about the restaurant.[1]

FOR DISCUSSION

Would you work hard for someone like Pat McGovern? Why?

This final chapter of Part Two serves as a practical capstone for what we have learned so far in Parts One and Two. Our focus here is on improving individual job performance. We need to put to work what we have learned about cultural and individual differences, perception, and motivation. Some managers, such as Pat McGovern in the opening vignette, do a good job in this regard. His personal touch and supportive style triggered fond memories for a former employee. Unfortunately, research shows that most managers fall far short when it comes to carefully nurturing job performance. A consulting firm's ongoing study of more than 500 managers since 1993 led to this recent conclusion:

> Only one out of 100 managers provides every direct report with these five basics every day:
>
> - Performance requirements and standard operating procedures related to tasks and responsibilities.
> - Defined parameters, measurable goals and concrete deadlines for all work assignments for which the direct report will be held accountable.
> - Accurate monitoring, evaluation and documentation of work performance.
> - Specific feedback on work performance with guidance for improvement.
> - Fairly distributed rewards and detriments [penalties].[2]

Performance management
Continuous cycle of improving job performance with goal setting, feedback and coaching, and rewards and positive reinforcement.

The researchers call this situation "under-management." But the popular term these days for doing things the right way is performance management. **Performance management** is an organizationwide system whereby managers integrate the activities of goal setting, monitoring and evaluating, providing feedback and coaching, and rewarding employees on a continuous basis.[3] This contrasts with the haphazard tradition of annual performance appraisals,[4] a largely unsatisfying experience for everyone involved.[5] (See Learning Module C, on the book's Web site, for more on performance appraisal.) OB can shed valuable light on key aspects of performance management. Namely, goal setting, feedback and coaching, and rewards and positive reinforcement.

As indicated in Figure 9–1, job performance needs a life-support system. Like an astronaut drifting in space without the protection and support of a space suit, job performance will not thrive without a support system. First, people with the requisite abilities, skills, and job knowledge need to be hired. Joe Kraus, co-founder and CEO of Jotspot, a Web page hosting service, recently offered this blunt advice:

> **Never compromise on hiring.** Every time I've compromised, I've come to regret it. You have to be tough, even if that means not hiring people who could turn out to be great, because of the damage one person who isn't great can do.

Figure 9–1 *Improving Individual Job Performance: A Continuous Process*

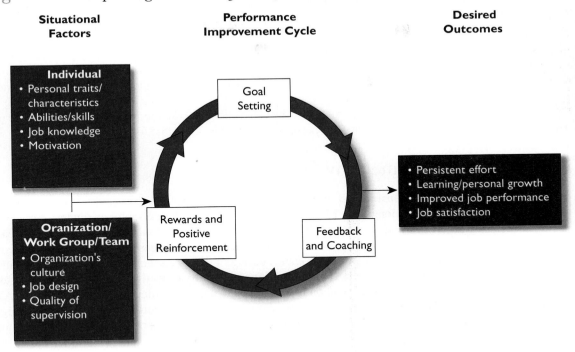

Nothing demotivates people like the equal treatment of unequals. When
you hire a bozo and treat him the same as a rock star, it deflates the rock star.[6]

Next, training is required to correct any job knowledge shortfalls.[7] The organization's structure, culture, and job design and supervisory practices also can facilitate or hinder job performance. At the heart of the model in Figure 9–1 are the key aspects of the performance
improvement cycle that we explore in depth in this chapter. Importantly, it is a dynamic and
continuous *cycle* requiring management's day-to-day attention.

Goal Setting

Goal setting in the workplace could use an extreme makeover. According to a recent
Franklin Covey survey of workers in the United States, 56% don't "clearly understand their
organization's most important goals" and an astounding 81% "don't have clearly defined
goals."[8] These figures could be cut in half and still represent a very unproductive situation.
This section offers corrective advice by distinguishing between two types of goals, discussing management by objectives, and explaining how to manage the goal-setting process.

Two Types of Goals

Goal-setting researchers have drawn an instructive distinction between performance outcome goals and learning goals. A **performance outcome goal** targets a specific end-result.
A **learning goal,** in contrast, strives to improve creativity and develop skills. Managers
typically overemphasize the former and ignore the latter as they try to "motivate" greater

**Performance
outcome goal**
Targets a specific
end-result.

Learning goal
Encourages learning,
creativity, and skill
development.

effort and achieve final results. But for employees who lack the necessary skills, performance outcome goals are more frustrating than motivating. When skills are lacking, a developmental process is needed wherein learning goals precede performance outcome goals. Goal researcher Gerard Seijts and Gary Latham explain with a golfing analogy:

> A performance outcome goal often distracts attention from the discovery of task-relevant strategies. For example, focusing on a golf score of 95 by novices may prevent them from focusing on the mastery of the swing and weight transfer and using the proper clubs necessary for attaining that score. . . .
>
> In short, the novice golfer must learn how to play the game before becoming concerned with attaining a challenging performance outcome (e.g., score equals 95).[9]

Management by Objectives

Management by objectives

Management system incorporating participation in decision making, goal setting, and feedback.

The motivational impact of performance goals and goal-based reward plans has been recognized for a long time. More than a century ago, Frederick Taylor attempted to scientifically establish how much work of a specified quality an individual should be assigned each day. He proposed that bonuses be based on accomplishing those output standards. More recently, goal setting has been promoted through a widely used management technique called management by objectives (MBO). **Management by objectives** is a management system that incorporates participation in decision making, goal setting, and objective feedback.[10] A meta-analysis of MBO programs showed productivity gains in 68 of 70 different organizations. Specifically, results uncovered an average gain in productivity of 56% when top-management commitment was high. The average gain was only 6% when commitment was low. A second meta-analysis of 18 studies further demonstrated that employees' job satisfaction was significantly related to top management's commitment to an MBO implementation.[11] These impressive results are tempered by reports of ethical problems stemming from extreme pressure for results (see Real World/Real People). Ethically sound MBO programs marry learning goals and performance outcome goals.

Managing the Goal-Setting Process

There are three general steps to follow when implementing a goal-setting program. Serious deficiencies in one step cannot make up for strength in the other two. The three steps need to be implemented in a systematic fashion.

Step 1: Set Goals
A number of sources can be used as input during this goal-setting stage. Time and motion studies are one source. Goals also may be based on the average past performance of job holders. Third, the employee and his or her manager may set the goal participatively, through give-and-take negotiation. Fourth, goals can be set by conducting external or internal benchmarking. Benchmarking is used when an organization wants to compare its performance or internal work processes to those of other organizations (external benchmarking) or to other internal units, branches, departments, or divisions within the organization (internal benchmarking). For example, a company might set a goal to surpass the customer service levels or profit of a benchmarked competitor. Finally, the overall strategy of a company (e.g., become the lowest-cost producer) may affect the goals set by employees at various levels in the organization.

In accordance with available research evidence, goals should be "SMART." SMART is an acronym that stands for specific, measurable, attainable, results oriented, and time bound. Table 9–1 contains a set of guidelines for writing SMART goals. There are two

Too Much Emphasis on Short-Term Financial Goals Causes Problems

Such an approach can easily backfire.

For one thing, employee loyalty and teamwork erode quickly, along with innovation and risk taking. So, in some cases, do business ethics. Managers and employees who fear they'll lose their jobs if they don't deliver their assigned numbers are more inclined to fudge results.

And companies that become fixated on hitting quarterly and even daily targets often don't produce sustainable profit growth. "It's hard to capture employees' hearts, and best efforts, with numbers alone," says [organizational psychologist Richard] Hagberg. In a recent study of 31 corporations, his staff found that the highest returns were achieved at companies whose CEOs set challenging financial goals but also articulated a purpose beyond profit making, such as creating a great product, and convinced employees their work mattered.

...[A] manager at a big global bank recently quit his job in Texas after observing how the pressure to hit targets under a new manager had backfired. "The pressure worked at first with increased sales, but now the territory, which used to be the top for our company, is one of the worst in the country," he wrote. "I left because it was tiresome seeing my co-workers getting beat on day in and day out about the number of checking accounts they had opened. When I left it wasn't because of poor performance—my numbers were in the top 1% of all reps in the country.... I was on pace to make over $250,000." But, he added, "the environment they created made it a miserable place to work because teamwork had eroded along with morale."

SOURCES: C Hymowitz, "When Meeting Targets Becomes the Strategy, CEO Is on Wrong Path," *The Wall Street Journal,* March 8, 2005, p B1; and C Hymowitz, "Readers Share Tales of Jobs Where Strategy Became Meeting Targets," *The Wall Street Journal,* March 22, 2005, p B1.

Table 9–1 *Guidelines for Writing SMART Goals*

Specific	Goals should be stated in precise rather than vague terms. For example, a goal that provides for 20 hours of technical training for each employee is more specific than stating that a manager should send as many people as possible to training classes. Goals should be quantified when possible.
Measurable	A measurement device is needed to assess the extent to which a goal is accomplished. Goals thus need to be measurable. It also is critical to consider the quality aspect of the goal when establishing measurement criteria. For example, if the goal is to complete a managerial study of methods to increase productivity, one must consider how to measure the quality of this effort. Goals should not be set without considering the interplay between quantity and quality of output.
Attainable	Goals should be realistic, challenging, and attainable. Impossible goals reduce motivation because people do not like to fail. Remember, people have different levels of ability and skill.
Results oriented	Corporate goals should focus on desired end-results that support the organization's vision. In turn, an individual's goals should directly support the accomplishment of corporate goals. Activities support the achievement of goals and are outlined in action plans. To focus goals on desired end-results, goals should start with the word *to,* followed by verbs such as *complete, acquire, produce, increase,* and *decrease.* Verbs such as *develop, conduct, implement,* or *monitor* imply activities and should not be used in a goal statement.
Time bound	Goals specify target dates for completion.

SOURCE: A J Kinicki, *Performance Management Systems* (Superstition Mt., AZ: Kinicki and Associates Inc., 2005), pp 2–9. Reprinted with permission; all rights reserved.

additional recommendations to consider when setting goals. First, for complex tasks, managers should train employees in problem-solving techniques and encourage them to develop a performance action plan. Action plans specify the strategies or tactics to be used in order to accomplish a goal.

Second, because of individual differences (recall our discussion in Chapter 5), it may be necessary to establish different goals for employees performing the same job. For example, a study of 103 undergraduate business students revealed that individuals high in conscientiousness had higher motivation, had greater goal commitment, and obtained higher grades than students low in conscientiousness.[12] An individual's goal orientation is another important individual difference to consider when setting goals. Parallel to the two types of goals discussed earlier, there are two types of goal orientations: a learning goal orientation and a performance goal orientation. A team of researchers described the differences and implications for goal setting in the following way:

> Individuals with a learning goal orientation are primarily concerned with developing their skills and ability. Given this focus, a difficult goal should be of interest because it provides a challenging opportunity that can lead to personal growth. In contrast, individuals with a performance goal orientation are concerned with obtaining positive evaluations about their ability. Given this focus, a difficult goal should be of lower interest because it provides a greater potential for failure. As goal difficulty increases, the probability of obtaining a positive evaluation through goal attainment decreases.[13]

A series of studies demonstrated that people set higher goals, exerted more effort, engaged in more performance planning, achieved higher performance, and responded more positively to performance feedback when they possessed a learning orientation toward goal setting than a performance orientation.[14] In conclusion, managers should consider individual differences when setting goals.

Step 2: Promote Goal Commitment

Obtaining goal commitment is important because employees are more motivated to pursue goals they view as reasonable, obtainable, and fair. Goal commitment may be increased by using one or more of the following techniques:

1. Provide an explanation for why the organization is implementing a goal-setting program.

2. Present the corporate goals, and explain how and why an individual's personal goals support them.

3. Have employees establish their own goals and action plans. Encourage them to set challenging, stretch goals. Goals should be difficult, but not impossible.[15]

4. Train managers in how to conduct participative goal-setting sessions, and train employees in how to develop effective action plans.

5. Be supportive, and do not use goals to threaten employees.

6. Set goals that are under the employees' control, and provide them with the necessary resources.

7. Provide monetary incentives or other rewards for accomplishing goals.[16]

Step 3: Provide Support and Feedback

Step 3 calls for providing employees with the necessary support elements or resources to get the job done. This includes ensuring that each employee has the necessary abilities and information to reach his or her goals. As a pair of goal-setting experts succinctly stated, "Motivation without knowledge is useless."[17] Training often is required to help employees achieve difficult goals. Moreover, managers should pay attention to employees' perceptions of effort → performance expectancies, self-efficacy, and valence of rewards. Finally, as we discuss next, employees should be provided with timely, specific feedback (knowledge of results) on how they are doing.[18]

Feedback

Numerous surveys tell us that employees' hearty appetite for feedback too often goes unfulfilled. For example, "43% of employees feel they don't get enough guidance to improve their performance, according to the *WorkUSA 2004* survey by Watson Wyatt Worldwide."[19] Achievement-oriented students also want feedback. Following a difficult exam, for instance, students want to know two things: how they did and how their peers did. By letting students know how their work measures up to grading and competitive standards, an instructor's feedback permits the students to adjust their study habits so they can reach their goals. Likewise, managers in well-run organizations follow up goal setting with a feedback program to provide a rational basis for adjustment and improvement. For example, consider the following remarks by Fred Smith, the founder and CEO of Federal Express, the overnight delivery pioneer with $25 billion in annual revenues and nearly 196,000 employees.[20] Smith's experience as a US Marine company commander during the Vietnam War helped shape his leadership style.

> My leadership philosophy is a synthesis of the principles taught by the marines and every organization for the past 200 years.
>
> When people walk in the door, they want to know: What do you expect out of me? What's in this deal for me? What do I have to do to get ahead? Where do I go in this organization to get justice if I'm not treated appropriately? They want to know how they're doing. They want some feedback. And they want to know that what they are doing is important.
>
> If you take the basic principles of leadership and answer those questions over and over again, you can be successful dealing with people.[21]

As the term is used here, **feedback** is objective information about individual or collective performance. Subjective assessments such as, "You're doing a poor job," "You're too lazy," or "We really appreciate your hard work" do not qualify as objective feedback. But hard data such as units sold, days absent, dollars saved, projects completed, customers satisfied, and quality rejects are all candidates for objective feedback programs. Management consultants Chip Bell and Ron Zemke offered this perspective of feedback:

Feedback
Objective information about performance.

> Feedback is, quite simply, any information that answers those "How am I doing?" questions. *Good* feedback answers them truthfully and productively. It's information people can use either to confirm or correct their performance.
>
> Feedback comes in many forms and from a variety of sources. Some is easy to get and requires hardly any effort to understand. The charts and graphs tracking group and individual performance that are fixtures in many workplaces are an example of this variety. Performance

"I'm trying to be less critical. If I say 'good work' what I really mean is 'you're an idiot'."

© Randy Glasbergen. Used by permission.

feedback—the numerical type at least—is at the heart of most approaches to total quality management.

Some feedback is less accessible. It's tucked away in the heads of customers and managers. But no matter how well-hidden the feedback, if people need it to keep their performance on track, we need to get it to them—preferably while it's still fresh enough to make an impact.[22]

Two Functions of Feedback

Experts say feedback serves two functions for those who receive it, one is *instructional* and the other *motivational*. Feedback instructs when it clarifies roles or teaches new behavior. For example, an assistant accountant might be advised to handle a certain entry as a capital item rather than as an expense item. On the other hand, feedback motivates when it serves as a reward or promises a reward.[23] Having the boss tell you that a grueling project you worked on earlier has just been completed can be a rewarding piece of news. As documented by researchers, the motivational function of feedback can be significantly enhanced by pairing *specific,* challenging goals with *specific* feedback about results.[24] With these two functions of feedback in mind, we now explore the vital role of feedback recipients, some practical lessons from feedback research, upward and 360-degree feedback, and how to give feedback for coaching purposes.

Are the Feedback Recipients Ready, Willing, and Able?

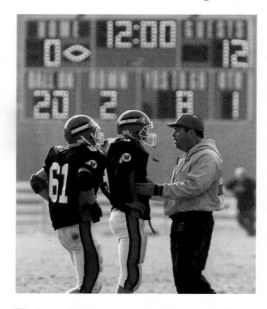

The heat of athletic competition is a great place to experience the power of constructive feedback in the performance improvement cycle (especially when you're behind 12-0)! How do you handle feedback? Do you actively seek it, or fear it because of possible embarrassment?

Conventional wisdom says the more feedback organizational members get, the better. An underlying assumption is that feedback works automatically. Managers simply need to be motivated to give it. According to a meta-analysis of 23,663 feedback incidents, however, feedback is far from automatically effective. While feedback did, in fact, have a generally positive impact on performance, performance actually *declined* in more than 38% of the feedback incidents.[25] Feedback also can be warped by nontask factors, such as race. A laboratory study at Stanford University focused on cross-race feedback on the content (subjective feedback) and writing mechanics (objective feedback) of written essays. White students gave African-American students *less* critical *subjective* feedback than they did to white students. This positive racial bias disappeared with objective feedback.[26] These results are a bright caution light for those interested in improving job performance with feedback. Subjective feedback is easily contaminated by situational factors. Moreover, if objective feedback is to work as intended, managers need to understand the interaction between feedback recipients and their environment.[27]

The Recipient's Characteristics   Personality characteristics such as self-esteem and self-efficacy can help or hinder one's readiness for feedback.[28] Those having low self-esteem and low self-efficacy generally do not actively seek feedback that, unfortunately, would tend to confirm those problems. Needs and goals also influence one's openness to feedback. In a laboratory study, Japanese psychology students who scored high on need for achievement responded more favorably to feedback than did their classmates who had low need for achievement.[29] This particular relationship likely exists in Western cultures as well. For example, 331 employees in the marketing department of a large public utility in the United States were found to seek feedback on important issues or when faced with uncertain situations. Long-tenured employees from this sample also were less likely to seek feedback than employees with little time on the job.[30] High self-monitors, those chameleonlike people we discussed in Chapter 5, are also more open to feedback because it helps them adapt their behavior to the situation. Recall from Chapter 5 that high self-monitoring employees were found to be better at initiating relationships with mentors (who typically provide feedback).[31] Low self-monitoring people, in contrast, are tuned into their own internal feelings more than they are to external cues. For example, someone observed that talking to media kingpin Ted Turner, a very low self-monitor, was like having a conversation with a radio!

Researchers have started to focus more directly on the recipient's actual desire for feedback, as opposed to indirectly on personality characteristics, needs, and goals. Everyday experience tells us that not everyone really wants the performance feedback they supposedly seek. Restaurant servers who ask, "How was everything?" while presenting the bill, typically are not interested in a detailed reply. A study of 498 supervisors yielded an instrument for measuring desire for performance feedback[32] (see the OB Exercise on page 278 for a shortened version). Such desire involves *self-reliance* (items 1–3), *self-assessment ability* (items 4–6), and a *preference for external information* (items 7–10). The general contingency approach to management would require different strategies for giving feedback to employees scoring low versus high on the OB Exercise.

The Recipient's Perception of Feedback

The *sign* of feedback, a term used in feedback research, refers to whether it is positive or negative. Generally, people tend to perceive and recall positive feedback more accurately than they do negative feedback.[33] But feedback with a negative sign (e.g., being told your performance is below average) can have a *positive* motivational impact. In fact, in one study, those who were told they were below average on a creativity test subsequently outperformed those who were led to believe their results were above average. The subjects apparently took the negative feedback as a challenge and set and pursued higher goals. Those receiving positive feedback apparently were less motivated to do better.[34] Nonetheless, feedback with a negative sign or threatening content needs to be administered carefully to avoid creating insecurity and defensiveness. Self-efficacy also can be damaged by negative feedback, as discovered in a pair of experiments with business students. The researchers concluded, "To facilitate the development of strong efficacy beliefs, managers should be careful about the provision of negative feedback. Destructive criticism by managers which attributes the cause of poor performance to internal factors reduces both the beliefs of self-efficacy and the self-set goals of recipients."[35]

The Recipient's Cognitive Evaluation of Feedback

Upon receiving feedback, people cognitively evaluate factors such as its accuracy, the credibility of the source, the fairness of the system (e.g., performance appraisal system), their performance-reward expectancies, and the reasonableness of the standards. Any feedback that fails to clear one or more of these cognitive hurdles will be rejected or downplayed. Personal experience largely dictates how these factors are weighed. For instance, you would probably discount feedback from someone who exaggerates or from someone who performed poorly

How Strong Is Your Desire for Performance Feedback?

Instructions

Circle one number indicating the strength of your agreement or disagreement with each statement. Total your responses, and compare your score with our arbitrary norms.

	Disagree				Agree
1. As long as I think that I have done something well, I am not too concerned about how other people think I have done.	5 — 4 — 3 — 2 — 1
2. How other people view my work is not as important as how I view my own work.	5 — 4 — 3 — 2 — 1
3. It is usually better not to put much faith in what others say about your work, regardless of whether it is complimentary or not.	5 — 4 — 3 — 2 — 1
4. If I have done something well, I know it without other people telling me so.	5 — 4 — 3 — 2 — 1
5. I usually have a clear idea of what I am trying to do and how well I am proceeding toward my goal.	5 — 4 — 3 — 2 — 1
6. I find that I am usually a pretty good judge of my own performance.	5 — 4 — 3 — 2 — 1
7. It is very important to me to know what people think of my work.	1 — 2 — 3 — 4 — 5
8. It is a good idea to get someone to check on your work before it's too late to make changes.	1 — 2 — 3 — 4 — 5
9. Even though I may think I have done a good job, I feel a lot more confident of it after someone else tells me so.	1 — 2 — 3 — 4 — 5
10. Since one cannot be objective about their own performance, it is best to listen to the feedback provided by others.	1 — 2 — 3 — 4 — 5

Total score = _____

Arbitrary Norms

10–23 = low desire for feedback   24–36 = moderate desire for feedback   37–50 = high desire for feedback

SOURCE: Excerpted and adapted from D M Herold, C K Parsons, and R B Rensvold, "Individual Differences in the Generation and Processing of Performance Feedback," *Educational and Psychological Measurement*, February 1996, Table 1, p 9. Copyright © 1996 by Sage Publications. Reprinted by permission of Sage Publications.

on the same task you have just successfully completed. In view of the "trust gap," discussed in Chapter 11, managerial credibility is an ethical matter of central importance today. According to the authors of the book *Credibility: How Leaders Gain and Lose It, Why People Demand It,* "without a solid foundation of personal credibility, leaders can have no hope of enlisting others in a common vision."[36] Managers who have proven untrustworthy and not credible have a hard time improving job performance through feedback.[37]

Feedback from a source who apparently shows favoritism or relies on unreasonable behavior standards would be suspect.[38] Also, as predicted by expectancy motivation theory, feedback must foster high effort→performance expectancies and performance→reward instrumentalities if it is to motivate desired behavior. For example, many growing children have been cheated out of the rewards of athletic competition because they were told by respected adults that they were too small, too short, too slow, too clumsy, and so forth. Feedback can have a profound and lasting impact on behavior.

Practical Lessons from Feedback Research

After reviewing dozens of laboratory and field studies of feedback, a trio of OB researchers cited the following practical implications for managers:

- The acceptance of feedback should not be treated as a given; it is often misperceived or rejected. This is especially true in intercultural situations.
- Managers can enhance their credibility as sources of feedback by developing their expertise and creating a climate of trust.
- Negative feedback is typically misperceived or rejected.
- Although very frequent feedback may erode one's sense of personal control and initiative, feedback is too *infrequent* in most work organizations.
- Feedback needs to be tailored to the recipient.
- While average and below-average performers need extrinsic rewards for performance, high performers respond to feedback that enhances their feelings of competence and personal control.[39]

More recent research insights about feedback include the following:

- Computer-based performance feedback leads to greater improvements in performance when it is received directly from the computer system rather than via an immediate supervisor.[40]
- Recipients of feedback perceive it to be more accurate when they actively participate in the feedback session versus passively receiving feedback.[41]
- Destructive criticism tends to cause conflict and reduce motivation.[42]
- "The higher one rises in an organization the less likely one is to receive quality feedback about job performance."[43]

Managers who act on these research implications and the trouble signs in Table 9–2 can build credible and effective feedback systems.

Our discussion to this point has focused on traditional downward feedback. Let us explore a couple of new and interesting approaches to feedback in the workplace.

Table 9–2   *Six Common Trouble Signs for Organizational Feedback Systems*

1. Feedback is used to punish, embarrass, or put down employees.
2. Those receiving the feedback see it as irrelevant to their work.
3. Feedback information is provided too late to do any good.
4. People receiving feedback believe it relates to matters beyond their control.
5. Employees complain about wasting too much time collecting and recording feedback data.
6. Feedback recipients complain about feedback being too complex or difficult to understand.

SOURCE: Adapted from C Bell and R Zemke, "On-Target Feedback," *Training*, June 1992, pp 36–44.

Nontraditional Feedback: Upward and 360-Degree

Traditional top-down feedback programs have given way to some interesting variations in recent years. Two newer approaches, discussed in this section, are upward feedback and so-called 360-degree feedback. Aside from breaking away from a strict superior-to-subordinate feedback loop, these newer approaches are different because they typically involve *multiple sources* of feedback. Instead of getting feedback from one boss, often during an annual performance appraisal, more and more managers are getting structured feedback from superiors, subordinates, peers, and even outsiders such as customers.

Upward feedback

Subordinates evaluate their boss.

Upward Feedback   Upward feedback stands the traditional approach on its head by having subordinates provide feedback on a manager's style and performance. This type of feedback is generally anonymous. Most students are familiar with upward feedback programs from years of filling out anonymous teacher evaluation surveys. According to *Fortune* magazine, this is how and why upward feedback is being used at computer-maker Dell:

> [Founder and chairman Michael Dell and CEO Kevin Rollins] discovered that their subordinates perceived them as cold technocrats. Now Dell, Rollins, and the rest of management are working hard on the fuzzy stuff. Employees rate their bosses—including Michael and Kevin—every six months in "Tell Dell" surveys. "If you're a manager and you're not addressing [employee] issues, you're not going to get promoted, you're not going to get compensation," says Dell. "And if you consistently score in the bottom rungs of the surveys, we're going to look at you and say, 'Maybe this isn't the right job for you.' "[44]

Managers typically resist upward feedback programs because they believe it erodes their authority.[45] Other critics say anonymous upward feedback can become little more than a personality contest or, worse, be manipulated by managers who make promises or threats. Research findings suggest the practical value of *anonymous* upward feedback used in *combination* with other sources of performance feedback and evaluation.[46] Because of managerial resistance and potential manipulation, using upward feedback as the primary determinant for promotions and pay decisions is *not* recommended. Carefully collected upward feedback is useful for management development programs.

360-degree feedback

Comparison of anonymous feedback from one's superior, subordinates, and peers with self-perceptions.

360-Degree Feedback   The concept of **360-degree feedback** involves letting individuals compare their own perceived performance with behaviorally specific (and usually anonymous) performance information from their manager, subordinates, and peers. Even outsiders may be involved in what is sometimes called full-circle feedback.[47]

A recent meta-analysis of 24 360-degree feedback studies in which the recipients were rated two or more times prompted this helpful conclusion from the researchers:

> improvement is most likely to occur when feedback indicates that change is necessary, recipients have a positive feedback orientation, perceive a need to change their behavior, react positively to the feedback, believe change is feasible, set appropriate goals to regulate their behavior, and take actions that lead to skill and performance improvement.[48]

Our recommendations for upward feedback, *favoring* anonymity and *discouraging* linkage to pay and promotion decisions, apply as well to 360-degree feedback programs. According to one expert, *trust* is the issue:

> Trust is at the core of using 360-degree feedback to enhance productivity. Trust determines how much an individual is willing to contribute for an employer. Using 360 confidentially, for developmental purposes, builds trust; using it to trigger pay and personnel decisions puts trust at risk.[49]

Wachovia Banks on 360-Degree Feedback for Leadership Development

Wachovia's . . . Executive Coaching Practice employs both internal and external coaches using a consistent model and approach to support Wachovia leaders at four levels throughout the corporation. For the past year, coaches have been supporting participants in the company's 360 Assessment Process, which is based on Wachovia's executive leadership competency model. The coaches deliver the 360 feedback, assist participants in understanding the results, support them in developing individual development plans, and provide ongoing coaching and support for a four-month period after the 360 in conjunction with the participant's manager and human resource business partner. Extensive training for the coaches is mandatory and includes substantial reading assignments, self-awareness training, and a two-day, in-depth workshop on the coaching process, the coaching model and how to best support participants.

SOURCE: "Best Practice: Executive Coaching, Wachovia," *Training,* March 2004, p 61.

We agree that 360-degree feedback has a place in the development of managerial skills, especially in today's team-based organizations. Wachovia, the Charlotte, North Carolina, bank and financial services company with more than 96,000 employees,[50] is a good role model in this regard (see Real World/Real People).

How to Give Feedback for Coaching Purposes and Organizational Effectiveness

Managers need to keep the following tips in mind when giving feedback as part of a comprehensive performance management program:

- Focus on *performance,* not personalities.
- Give *specific* feedback linked to learning goals and performance outcome goals.
- Channel feedback toward *key result areas* for the organization.
- Give feedback as *soon* as possible.
- Give feedback for *improvement,* not just final results.
- Base feedback on *accurate* and *credible* information.
- Pair feedback with *clear expectations* for improvement.[51]

Organizational Reward Systems

Rewards are an ever-present and always controversial feature of organizational life.[52] Some employees see their jobs as the source of a paycheck and little else. Others derive great pleasure from their jobs and association with co-workers. In fact, according to a recent Gallup survey, 55% of American workers said "they would continue to work even if they won a lottery jackpot to the tune of $10 million."[53] (How about you?) Even volunteers who donate their time to charitable organizations, such as the Red Cross, walk away with rewards in the form of social recognition and pride of having given unselfishly of their time. Hence, the subject of organizational rewards includes, but goes far beyond, monetary compensation.[54] This section examines key components of organizational reward systems to provide a conceptual background for discussing the timely topics of pay for performance and team-based pay.

Despite the fact that reward systems vary widely, it is possible to identify and interrelate some common components. The model in Figure 9–2 focuses on three important components: (1) types of rewards, (2) distribution criteria, and (3) desired outcomes. Let us examine these components.

Types of Rewards

Extrinsic rewards
Financial, material, or social rewards from the environment.

Intrinsic rewards
Self-granted, psychic rewards.

Financial, material, and social rewards qualify as **extrinsic rewards** because they come from the environment. Psychic rewards, however, are **intrinsic rewards** because they are self-granted. An employee who works to obtain extrinsic rewards, such as money or praise, is said to be extrinsically motivated. One who derives pleasure from the task itself or experiences a sense of competence or self-determination is said to be intrinsically motivated. The relative importance of extrinsic and intrinsic rewards is a matter of culture and personal tastes.[55]

Reward Distribution Criteria

According to one expert on organizational reward systems, three general criteria for the distribution of rewards are as follows:

- *Performance: results.* Tangible outcomes such as individual, group, or organization performance; quantity and quality of performance.
- *Performance: actions and behaviors.* Such as teamwork, cooperation, risk taking, creativity.
- *Nonperformance considerations.* Customary or contractual, where the type of job, nature of the work, equity, tenure, level in hierarchy, and so forth are rewarded.[56]

Figure 9–2   *A General Model of Organizational Reward Systems*

The trend today is toward performance criteria and away from nonperformance criteria such as seniority. For example, CEO Jeffrey Immelt is trying to bolster risk taking and innovation at General Electric by putting more emphasis on the second criterion listed above:

> To inspire the fresh thinking he's looking for, Immelt is wielding the one thing that speaks loud and clear: money. The GE chief is tying executives' compensation to their ability to come up with ideas, show improved customer service, generate cash growth, and boost sales instead of simply meeting bottom-line targets. As Immelt puts it, "you're not going to stick around this place and not take bets."[57]

Desired Outcomes of the Reward System

As listed in Figure 9–2, a good reward system should attract talented people and motivate and satisfy them once they have joined the organization. Further, a good reward system should foster personal growth and development and keep talented people from leaving. A prime example is Worthington Industries, the profitable steel processing firm in Columbus, Ohio, where the usual time clocks are not to be found. "Workers get profit-sharing payouts ranging from 40 to 70% of base pay, and the company pays 100% of health insurance premiums for employees and family members."[58] Worthington enjoys an industry-low turnover rate of 12% and a long line of job applicants.

The Building Blocks of Intrinsic Rewards and Motivation

As defined earlier, intrinsic rewards are self-granted. But this does not leave management out of the picture. Indeed, there is a great deal managers can do to create situations in which employees are more likely to experience intrinsic rewards and be intrinsically motivated.[59] Kenneth Thomas's model of intrinsic motivation provides helpful direction.[60] His model combines the job characteristics model of job design (discussed in Chapter 8), the concept of empowerment (discussed in Chapter 15), and Edward Deci and Richard Ryan's cognitive evaluation theory. Deci and Ryan contend that people must satisfy their needs for autonomy and competence when completing a task for it to be intrinsically motivating.[61] Thomas uses the term *building blocks* to show managers how to construct the right conditions for four basic intrinsic rewards: meaningfulness, choice, competence, and progress (see Figure 9–3). Let us examine management's leadership challenges for each building block.

Leading for Meaningfulness   Managers lead for meaningfulness by *inspiring* their employees and *modeling* desired behaviors. Figure 9–3 reveals managers can accomplish this by helping employees to identify their passions at work and creating an exciting organizational vision employees feel connected to. In support of this recommendation, results from Gallup poll surveys show that employees are more engaged and productive at work when they see the connection between their work and the organization's vision.[62] This connection creates a sense of purpose for employees.

Leading for Choice   Managers lead for choice by *empowering* employees and *delegating* meaningful assignments and tasks. Consider how Gail Evans, an executive vice

Figure 9–3 *Thomas's Building Blocks for Intrinsic Rewards and Motivation*

Choice	Competence
• Delegated authority	• Knowledge
• Trust in workers	• Positive feedback
• Security (no punishment) for honest mistakes	• Skill recognition
• A clear purpose	• Challenge
• Information	• High, noncomparative standards

Meaningfulness	Progress
• A non-cynical climate	• A collaborative climate
• Clearly identified passions	• Milestones
• An exciting vision	• Celebrations
• Relevant task purposes	• Access to customers
• Whole tasks	• Measurement of improvement

SOURCE: Reprinted with permission of the publisher. From K Thomas, *Intrinsic Motivation at Work: Building Energy and Commitment,* copyright © 2000 by K Thomas, Berrett-Koehler Publishers, Inc., San Francisco, CA. All rights reserved. www.bkconnection.com.

president at Atlanta-based CNN, and Judy Lewent, senior vice president and chief financial officer for pharmaceutical giant Merck & Co., feel about leading for choice.

> Gail Evans . . . says delegating is essential. If you refuse to let your staff handle their own projects, you're jeopardizing their advancement—because they aren't learning new skills and adding successes to their resume—and you're wasting your precious hours doing someone else's work. . . . For Lewent, delegating the responsibility of running staff meetings to one of her team members means she can sit back and observe her employees, an activity that helps her make decisions about their career development. It also lets her subordinates hone their leadership skills—a must as they move up the ladder. In fact, when asked for her single definition of a good boss, Lewent says, "someone who understands the true art of teamwork and delegation."[63]

Leading for Competence

Managers lead for competence by *supporting* and *coaching* their employees. Figure 9–3 provides several examples of how this might be done. Managers first need to make sure employees have the knowledge needed to successfully perform their jobs. Deficiencies can be handled through training and mentoring. Providing positive feedback and sincere recognition can also be coupled with the assignment of a challenging task to fuel employees' intrinsic motivation.

Leading for Progress

Managers lead for progress by *monitoring* and *rewarding* others. Julie Stewart, president of the Applebee's division of Applebee's International, a $670 million chain of more than 1,000 restaurants, makes it a point to use some of the building blocks listed in Figure 9–3 to create a sense of progress.

> Every night, Applebee's Stewart uses a trick she learned from a previous boss. After everyone is gone, she leaves a sealed note on the chair of an employee, explaining how critical that person's work is or how much she appreciates the completion of a recent project.

Sometimes she leaves voice mail; other times she might send flowers. "For a lot of people, it means more than any raise," Stewart says. "I do not leave the office without doing this."[64]

We now direct our attention to *extrinsic* rewards—money, opportunities, and recognition granted by others.

Why Do Extrinsic Rewards Too Often Fail to Motivate?

Despite huge investments of time and money for monetary and nonmonetary compensation, the desired motivational impact often is not achieved. A management consultant/writer offers these eight reasons:

1. Too much emphasis on monetary rewards.
2. Rewards lack an "appreciation effect."
3. Extensive benefits become entitlements.
4. Counterproductive behavior is rewarded. (For example, "a pizza delivery company focused its rewards on the on-time performance of its drivers, only to discover that it was inadvertently rewarding reckless driving."[65])
5. Too long a delay between performance and rewards.
6. Too many one-size-fits-all rewards.
7. Use of one-shot rewards with a short-lived motivational impact.
8. Continued use of demotivating practices such as layoffs, across-the-board raises and cuts, and excessive executive compensation.[66]

These stubborn problems have fostered a search for more effective extrinsic reward practices (for example, see Real World/Real People on page 286). While a thorough discussion of modern compensation practices[67] is way beyond our present scope, we can explore two general approaches to boosting the motivational impact of monetary rewards—pay for performance and team-based pay.

Gift cards help overcome the problem of one-size-fits-all extrinsic reward programs.

Pay for Performance

Pay for performance is the popular term for monetary incentives linking at least some portion of the paycheck directly to results or accomplishments. Many refer to it simply as *incentive pay,* while others call it *variable pay.* "Broad-based variable pay programs are offered by 80% of US companies."[68] The general idea behind pay-for-performance schemes—including but not limited to merit pay, bonuses, and profit sharing—is to give employees an incentive for working harder or smarter. Pay for performance is something extra, compensation above and beyond basic wages and salaries. Proponents of incentive compensation say something extra is needed because hourly wages and fixed salaries do little more than motivate people to show up at work and put in the required hours.[69] The most

Pay for performance
Monetary incentives tied to one's results or accomplishments.

Who Says There's No Such Thing as a Free Lunch?

Analytical Graphics Inc. (AGI) of Exton, Pennsylvania, works hard to ease the intense work lives of a staff loaded with the proverbial "rocket scientists." Its aerospace, electrical, and software engineers develop mission-critical software that helps analyze and visualize data from missiles, jets, rockets, and satellites for commercial and military aerospace uses, including NASA's space shuttle. . . .

The company serves daily breakfasts, lunches, and dinners, to which family members are invited. Its kitchen and pantries offer free snack foods and drinks. . . .

The free-flowing food encourages teamwork and camaraderie, employees say, while making their work lives easier and more productive.

Other free family-style perks include a laundry room with free washers, dryers, and supplies; a well-equipped fitness room; and free holiday gift-wrapping. For nominal fees, employees can take advantage of other services, such as dry cleaning, oil changes, car washes, flower delivery, and shoeshines.

SOURCE: L Rubis, "Analytical Graphics Works for Its Workers," *HR Magazine*, July 2004, p 47.

basic form of pay for performance is the traditional piece-rate plan, whereby the employee is paid a specified amount of money for each unit of work. For example, 2,500 artisans at Longaberger's, in Frazeyburg, Ohio, are paid a fixed amount for each handcrafted wooden basket they weave. Together, they produce 40,000 of the prized maple baskets daily.[70] Sales commissions, whereby a salesperson receives a specified amount of money for each unit sold, is another long-standing example of pay for performance. Today's service economy is forcing management to creatively adapt and go beyond piece rate and sales commission plans to accommodate greater emphasis on product and service quality, interdependence, and teamwork.

Current Practices For an indication of current practices, see Table 9–3, which is based on a survey of 156 US executives. The lack of clear patterns in Table 9–3 is indicative of the still experimental nature of incentive compensation today. Much remains to be learned from research and practice.

Research Insights According to available expert opinion and research results, pay for performance too often falls short of its goal of improved job performance. "Experts say that roughly half the incentive plans they see don't work, victims of poor design and administration."[71] In fact, one study documented how incentive pay had a *negative* effect on the performance of 150,000 managers from 500 financially distressed companies.[72] A meta-analysis of 39 studies found only a modest positive correlation between

These folks not only make really cool picnic baskets, they actually work *inside* one! Longaberger's headquarters building in Frazeyburg, Ohio, is a giant replica of the firm's famous maple wood baskets. Each day, 2,500 employees who are paid on a piece-rate basis weave 40,000 hand-crafted baskets. This team of Longaberger employees recently won a prestigious quality award for cutting waste and improving productivity.

Table 9–3   *The Use and Effectiveness of Modern Incentive Pay Plans*

Plan Type	Presently Have	Rated Highly Effective
Annual bonus	74%	20%
Special one-time spot awards (after the fact)	42	38
Individual incentives	39	27
Long-term incentives (executive level)	32	44
Lump-sum merit pay	28	19
Competency-based pay	22	31
Profit-sharing (apart from retirement program)	22	43
Profit-sharing (as part of retirement program)	22	46
ESOP* stock plan	21	33
Suggestion/proposal programs	17	19
Team-based pay	15	29
Long-term incentives (below executive levels)	13	43
Skill-/knowledge-based pay	12	58
Group incentives (not team-based)	11	24
Pay for quality	9	29
Gainsharing	8	38
Special key-contributor programs (before the fact)	7	55

*Employee stock ownership plan.

SOURCE: Adapted from "Incentive Pay Plans: Which Ones Work . . . and Why?" From the April 2001 issue of IOMA's HR Focus newsletter. Used by permission.

financial incentives and performance *quantity* and no impact on performance *quality*.[73] Other researchers have found only a weak statistical link between large executive bonuses paid out in good years and subsequent improvement in corporate profitability.[74] Also, in a survey of small business owners, more than half said their commission plans failed to motivate extra effort from their salespeople.[75] Linking teachers' merit pay to student performance, an exciting school reform idea, turned out to be a big disappointment: "The bottom line is that despite high hopes, none of the 13 districts studied was able to use teacher pay incentives to achieve significant, lasting gains in student performance."[76]

A recent study of variable pay plans by Hewitt Associates, a leading human resources consulting firm, uncovered this instructive pattern:

> [M]ore than one-third (41%) of the companies with single-digit revenue growth said the cost outweighed the benefits for them. Not only have the plans failed to improve business results for a quarter of these organizations, they have actually led to adverse results for 26% of those surveyed.
>
> The situation was reversed, however, for companies experiencing double-digit revenue growth. These companies reported that their programs achieved positive outcomes and contributed to business results. "We've found that companies achieving high-revenue growth have successful programs because they provide the appropriate amount of administrative, communication and monetary support," says Paul Shafer, a business leader for Hewitt. If not implemented well, he says, variable pay "will be seen as an entitlement by employees and a substantial loss to employers."[77]

Clearly, the pay-for-performance area is still very much up in the air.

Team-Based Pay

Team-based pay
Linking pay to
teamwork behavior
and/or team results.

Team-based pay is defined as incentive compensation that rewards individuals for teamwork or rewards teams for collective results, or both. This definition highlights an important distinction between individual *behavior* and team *results*. Stated another way, it takes team players to get team results. Any team-oriented pay plan that ignores this distinction almost certainly will fail.

Problems   The biggest single barrier to effective team-based pay is *cultural,* especially in highly individualistic cultures such as the United States, Canada, Norway, and Australia.[78] Individual competition for pay and pay raises has long been the norm in the United States. Entrenched grading schemes in schools and colleges, focused on individual competition and not group achievement, are a good preview of the traditional American workplace.[79] Team-based pay is a direct assault on the cultural tradition of putting the individual above the group. Indeed, a scientific poll of nearly 1,500 full-time employees across the United States found little support for team-based rewards and a strong preference for permanent pay increases for individual performance. This led the researchers to conclude: "Workers' lack of interest in team pay implies that employers are simply not rewarding teams as effectively as they could."[80]

Another culturally rooted problem is a general *lack of teamwork skills.* Members of high-performance teams are skilled communicators, conflict handlers, and negotiators; they are flexible, adaptable, and open to change. Employees accustomed to being paid for personal achievements tend to resent having their pay dependent upon others' performance and problems.

Research Evidence   Research evidence to date is not encouraging. A comprehensive review of studies that examined team-based rewards in the workplace led to this conclusion: "The field-based empirical evidence is limited and inconclusive."[81]

Recommendations   The state of the art in team-based pay is very primitive today. Given the many different types of teams (as you will see in Chapter 11), we can be certain there is no single best approach. However, based on anecdotal evidence from the general management literature and case studies,[82] we can make these five recommendations:

- *Prepare employees* for team-based systems with as much interpersonal skills training as possible. This ongoing effort should include diversity training and skill training in communication, conflict resolution, trust building, group problem solving, and negotiating.
- *Establish teams* and get them running smoothly before introducing team-based pay incentives to avoid overload and frustration.
- Create a pay plan that *blends* individual achievement and team incentives.
- Begin by rewarding teamwork *behaviors* (such as mutual support, cooperation, and group problem solving), and then phase in pay incentives for team *results.*
- When paying for team results, make sure individual team members see a clear connection between their own work and team results. Compensation specialists call this *a clear line of sight.*

It's Party Time in Houston!

Energy producer Apache has found a generous way to reward workers for $50-a-barrel oil: It's passing out hefty stock awards to its 1,900 employees. After all, the $5.3 billion Houston company's earnings were up 50% last year, to $1.7 billion. And its share price has doubled to $61 in four years.

Ninety percent of the awards are going to the rank and file, with most workers receiving shares worth twice their annual salary. Even mailroom clerks will get shares worth at least as much as their salary. Now that's a gusher.

SOURCE: C Palmeri, "Whooping It Up at Apache," *BusinessWeek*, March 14, 2005, p 12. Reprinted by permission of The McGraw-Hill Companies, Inc.

Getting the Most out of Extrinsic Rewards and Pay for Performance

Based on what we have learned to date,[83] here is a workable plan for maximizing the motivational impact of extrinsic rewards:

- Tie praise, recognition, and noncash awards to *specific* results.
- Make pay for performance an integral part of the organization's basic strategy (e.g., pursuit of best-in-the-industry product or service quality).
- Base incentive determinations on objective performance data.
- Have all employees actively participate in the development, implementation, and revision of the performance-pay formulas.
- Encourage two-way communication so problems with the incentive plan will be detected early.
- Build pay-for-performance plans around participative structures such as suggestion systems or quality circles.
- Reward teamwork and cooperation whenever possible.
- Actively sell the plan to supervisors and middle managers who may view employee participation as a threat to their traditional notion of authority.
- If annual cash bonuses are granted, pay them in a lump sum to maximize their motivational impact.
- Remember that money motivates when it comes in significant amounts, not occasional nickels and dimes (see Real World/Real People).

Positive Reinforcement

Feedback and extrinsic reward programs too often are ineffective because they are administered in haphazard ways. For example, consider these scenarios:

- A young programmer stops e-mailing creative suggestions to his boss because she never responds.
- The office politician gets a great promotion while her more skilled co-workers scratch their heads and gossip about the injustice.

In the first instance, a productive behavior faded away for lack of encouragement. In the second situation, unproductive behavior was unwittingly rewarded. Feedback and rewards need to be handled more precisely. Fortunately, the field of behavioral psychology can help. Thanks to the pioneering work of Edward L Thorndike, B F Skinner, and many others, a behavior modification technique called *positive reinforcement* helps managers achieve needed discipline and desired effect when providing feedback and granting extrinsic rewards.[84]

Thorndike's Law of Effect

During the early 1900s, Edward L Thorndike observed in his psychology laboratory that a cat would behave randomly and wildly when placed in a small box with a secret trip lever that opened a door. However, once the cat accidentally tripped the lever and escaped, the animal would go straight to the lever when placed back in the box. Hence, Thorndike formulated his famous **law of effect,** which says *behavior with favorable consequences tends to be repeated, while behavior with unfavorable consequences tends to disappear.*[85] This was a dramatic departure from the prevailing notion a century ago that behavior was the product of inborn instincts.

Law of effect
Behavior with favorable consequences is repeated; behavior with unfavorable consequences disappears.

Skinner's Operant Conditioning Model

Skinner refined Thorndike's conclusion that behavior is controlled by its consequences. Skinner's work became known as *behaviorism* because he dealt strictly with observable behavior.[86] As a behaviorist, Skinner believed it was pointless to explain behavior in terms of unobservable inner states such as needs, drives, attitudes, or thought processes.[87] He similarly put little stock in the idea of self-determination.

In his 1938 classic, *The Behavior of Organisms,* Skinner drew an important distinction between the two types of behavior: respondent and operant behavior.[88] He labeled unlearned reflexes, or stimulus–response (S–R) connections, **respondent behavior.** This category of behavior was said to describe a very small proportion of adult human behavior. Examples of respondent behavior would include shedding tears while peeling onions and reflexively withdrawing one's hand from a hot stove.[89] Skinner attached the label **operant behavior** to behavior that is learned when one "operates on" the environment to produce desired consequences. Some call this the response–stimulus (R–S) model. Years of controlled experiments with pigeons in "Skinner boxes" helped Skinner develop a sophisticated technology of behavior control, or operant conditioning. For example, he taught pigeons how to pace figure-eights and how to

Respondent behavior
Skinner's term for unlearned stimulus–response reflexes.

Operant behavior
Skinner's term for learned, consequence-shaped behavior.

Renowned behavioral psychologist B F Skinner and your co-author Bob Kreitner met and posed for a snapshot at an Academy of Management meeting in Boston. As a behaviorist, Skinner preferred to deal with observable behavior and its antecedents and consequences in the environment rather than with inner states such as attitudes and cognitive processes. The late professor Skinner was a fascinating man who left a permanent mark on modern psychology.

bowl by reinforcing the underweight (and thus hungry) birds with food whenever they more closely approximated target behaviors. Skinner's work spawned the field of behavior modification and has significant implications for OB because the vast majority of organizational behavior falls into the operant category.[90]

Contingent Consequences

Contingent consequences, according to Skinner's operant theory, control behavior in four ways: positive reinforcement, negative reinforcement, punishment, and extinction. The term *contingent* means there is a systematic if-then linkage between the target behavior and the consequence. Remember Mom (and Pink Floyd) saying something to this effect: "If you don't finish your dinner, you don't get dessert" (see Figure 9–4)? To avoid the all-too-common mislabeling of these consequences, let us review some formal definitions.

Positive Reinforcement Strengthens Behavior
Positive reinforcement is the process of strengthening a behavior by contingently presenting something pleasing. (Importantly, a behavior is strengthened when it increases in frequency and weakened when it decreases in frequency.) A design engineer who works overtime because of praise and recognition from the boss is responding to positive reinforcement.[91]

> **Positive reinforcement**
> Making behavior occur more often by contingently presenting something positive.

Similarly, people tend to return to businesses where they are positively reinforced with high-quality service. For example, Commerce Bank, based in Cherry Hill, New Jersey, owes part of its success and rapid growth to a culture based on positive reinforcement. Commerce tries hard to "wow" its customers with service innovations such as Sunday banking hours.

> Employees are praised for being "wowy." And every March, [CEO Vernon] Hill recognizes top performers at the companywide Wow Awards. "'Wow' is more than a word around here," says John Manning, vice president of—that's right—the Wow Department. "It's a feeling that you give and get."

Figure 9–4   *Contingent Consequences in Operant Conditioning*

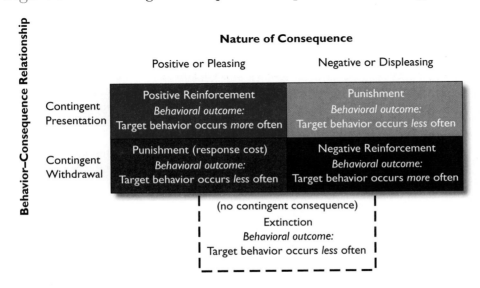

That type of obsessive service culture starts with hiring the right people. "This is not the job for someone who's interested in being cool or indifferent," Manning says. And instead of the usual humdrum orientation class, every new employee attends a one-day course at Commerce University called Traditions. It's part game show, part training session, part common sense. Banks do all sorts of stupid things to customers, Manning tells new hires. That's why the company has a "Kill a Stupid Rule" program. "If you identify a rule that prevents you from wowing customers," Manning says, "we'll pay you 50 bucks."[92]

Negative reinforcement
Making behavior occur more often by contingently withdrawing something negative.

Negative Reinforcement Also Strengthens Behavior
Negative reinforcement is the process of strengthening a behavior by contingently withdrawing something displeasing. For example, an army sergeant who stops yelling when a recruit jumps out of bed has negatively reinforced that particular behavior. Similarly, the behavior of clamping our hands over our ears when watching a jumbo jet take off is negatively reinforced by relief from the noise. Negative reinforcement is often confused with punishment. But the two strategies have opposite effects on behavior. Negative reinforcement, as the word *reinforcement* indicates, strengthens a behavior because it provides relief from an unpleasant situation.

Punishment
Making behavior occur less often by contingently presenting something negative or withdrawing something positive.

Punishment Weakens Behavior
Punishment is the process of weakening behavior through either the contingent presentation of something displeasing or the contingent withdrawal of something positive. A manager assigning a tardy employee to a dirty job exemplifies the first type of punishment. Docking a tardy employee's pay is an example of the second type of punishment, called *response cost punishment*. Legal fines involve response cost punishment. Salespeople who must make up any cash register shortages out of their own pockets are being managed through response cost punishment. Ethical questions can and should be raised about this type of on-the-job punishment.[93]

Extinction
Making behavior occur less often by ignoring or not reinforcing it.

Extinction Also Weakens Behavior
Extinction is the weakening of a behavior by ignoring it or making sure it is not reinforced. Getting rid of a former boyfriend or girlfriend by refusing to answer their phone calls is an extinction strategy. A good analogy for extinction is to imagine what would happen to your houseplants if you stopped watering them. Like a plant without water, a behavior without occasional reinforcement eventually dies. Although very different processes, both punishment and extinction have the same weakening effect on behavior.

Schedules of Reinforcement

As just illustrated, contingent consequences are an important determinant of future behavior. The *timing* of behavioral consequences can be even more important. Based on years of tedious laboratory experiments with pigeons in highly controlled environments, Skinner and his colleagues discovered distinct patterns of responding for various schedules of reinforcement.[94]

Although some of their conclusions can be generalized to negative reinforcement, punishment, and extinction, it is best to think only of positive reinforcement when discussing schedules.

Continuous reinforcement
Reinforcing every instance of a behavior.

Continuous Reinforcement
As indicated in Table 9–4, every instance of a target behavior is reinforced when a **continuous reinforcement** (CRF) schedule is in effect. For instance, when your television set is operating properly, you are reinforced with a picture every time you turn it on (a CRF schedule). But, as with any CRF schedule of reinforcement, the behavior of turning on the television will undergo rapid extinction if the set breaks.

Table 9–4   *Schedules of Reinforcement*

Schedule	Description	Probable Effects on Responding
Continuous (CRF)	Reinforcer follows every response.	Steady high rate of performance as long as reinforcement continues to follow every response. High frequency of reinforcement may lead to early satiation. Behavior weakens rapidly (undergoes extinction) when reinforcers are withheld. Appropriate for newly emitted, unstable, or low-frequency responses.
Intermittent	Reinforcer does not follow every response.	Capable of producing high frequencies of responding. Low frequency of reinforcement precludes early satiation. Appropriate for stable or high-frequency responses.
Fixed ratio (FR)	A fixed number of responses must be emitted before reinforcement occurs.	A fixed ratio of 1:1 (reinforcement occurs after every response); the same as a continuous schedule. Tends to produce a high rate of response, which is vigorous and steady.
Variable ratio (VR)	A varying or random number of responses must be emitted before reinforcement occurs.	Capable of producing a high rate of response, which is vigorous, steady, and resistant to extinction.
Fixed interval (FI)	The first response after a specific period of time has elapsed is reinforced.	Produces an uneven response pattern varying from a very slow, unenergetic response immediately following reinforcement to a very fast, vigorous response immediately preceding reinforcement.
Variable interval (VI)	The first response after varying or random periods of time have elapsed is reinforced.	Tends to produce a high rate of response, which is vigorous, steady, and resistant to extinction.

SOURCE: F Luthans and R Kreitner, *Organizational Behavior Modification and Beyond: An Operant and Social Learning Approach* (Glenview, IL Scott, Foresman, 1985), p 58. Used with authors' permission.

Intermittent Reinforcement

Unlike CRF schedules, **intermittent reinforcement** involves reinforcement of *some* but not all instances of a target behavior. Four subcategories of intermittent schedules, described in Table 9–4, are fixed and variable ratio schedules and fixed and variable interval schedules. Reinforcement in *ratio* schedules is contingent on the number of responses emitted. *Interval* reinforcement is tied to the passage of time. Some common examples of the four types of intermittent reinforcement are as follows:

Intermittent reinforcement
Reinforcing some but not all instances of behavior.

- *Fixed ratio*—piece-rate pay; bonuses tied to the sale of a fixed number of units.
- *Variable ratio*—slot machines that pay off after a variable number of lever pulls; lotteries that pay off after the purchase of a variable number of tickets.
- *Fixed interval*—hourly pay; annual salary paid on a regular basis.
- *Variable interval*—random supervisory praise and pats on the back for employees who have been doing a good job.

Scheduling Is Critical

The schedule of reinforcement can more powerfully influence behavior than the magnitude of reinforcement. Although this proposition grew out of experiments with pigeons, subsequent on-the-job research confirmed it. Consider, for example, a field study of 12 unionized beaver trappers employed by a lumber company to keep the large rodents from eating newly planted tree seedlings.[95]

The beaver trappers were randomly divided into two groups that alternated weekly between two different bonus plans. Under the first schedule, each trapper earned his regular $7 per hour wage plus $1 for each beaver caught. Technically, this bonus was paid on a CRF schedule. The second bonus plan involved the regular $7 per hour wage plus a one-in-four chance (as determined by rolling the dice) of receiving $4 for each beaver trapped. This second bonus plan qualified as a variable ratio (VR-4) schedule. In the long run, both incentive schemes averaged out to a $1-per-beaver bonus. Surprisingly, however, when the trappers were under the VR-4 schedule, they were 58% more productive than under the CRF schedule, despite the fact that the net amount of pay averaged out the same for the two groups during the 12-week trapping season.

Work Organizations Typically Rely on the Weakest Schedule

Generally, variable ratio and variable interval schedules of reinforcement produce the strongest behavior that is most resistant to extinction. As gamblers will attest, variable schedules hold the promise of reinforcement after the next target response. For example, the following drama at a Laughlin, Nevada, gambling casino is one more illustration of the potency of variable ratio reinforcement:

> An elderly woman with a walker had lost her grip on the slot [machine] handle and had collapsed on the floor.
> "Help," she cried weakly.
> The woman at the machine next to her interrupted her play for a few seconds to try to help her to her feet, but all around her the army of slot players continued feeding coins to the machines.
> A security man arrived to soothe the woman and take her away.
> "Thank you," she told him appreciatively.
> "But don't forget my winnings."[96]

Organizations without at least some variable reinforcement are less likely to prompt this type of dedication to task. Consider this approach:

> One global telecommunications firm recently created a rewards bank on its intranet. Managers are given a "points budget" and encouraged to give worthy employees just-in-time compensation for their performance. Employees can redeem these points for time off, cash, and assorted goods.[97]

Despite the trend toward this sort of pay-for-performance, time-based pay schemes such as hourly wages and yearly salaries that rely on the weakest schedule of reinforcement (fixed interval) are still the rule in today's workplaces.

Behavior Shaping

Have you ever wondered how trainers at aquarium parks manage to get bottle-nosed dolphins to do flips, killer whales to carry people on their backs, and seals to juggle balls? The results are seemingly magical. Actually, a mundane learning process called shaping is responsible for the animals' antics.

Two-ton killer whales, for example, have a big appetite, and they find buckets of fish very reinforcing. So if the trainer wants to ride a killer whale, he or she reinforces very basic behaviors that will eventually lead to the whale being ridden. The killer whale is contingently reinforced with a few fish for coming near the trainer, then for being touched, then for putting its nose in a harness, then for being straddled, and eventually for swimming with the trainer on its back. In effect, the trainer systematically raises the behavioral requirement for reinforcement.[98] Thus, **shaping** is defined as the process of reinforcing closer and closer approximations to a target behavior.

Shaping works very well with people, too, especially in training and quality programs involving continuous improvement. Praise, recognition, and instructive and credible feedback cost managers little more than moments of their time. Yet, when used in conjunction with learning goals and a behavior-shaping program, these consequences can efficiently foster significant improvements in job performance. The key to successful behavior shaping lies in reducing a complex target behavior to easily learned steps and then faithfully (and patiently) reinforcing any improvement. For example, Continental Airlines used a cash bonus program to improve its on-time arrival record from one of the worst in the industry to one of the best. Employees originally were promised a $65 bonus each month Continental earned a top-five ranking. Now it takes a second- or third-place ranking to earn the $65 bonus and a $100 bonus awaits employees when they achieve a number one ranking.[99] (Table 9–5 lists practical tips on shaping.)

Shaping
Reinforcing closer and closer approximations to a target behavior.

Table 9–5   *Ten Practical Tips for Shaping Job Behavior*

1. *Accommodate the process of behavioral change.* Behaviors change in gradual stages, not in broad, sweeping motions.
2. *Define new behavior patterns specifically.* State what you wish to accomplish in explicit terms and in small amounts that can be easily grasped.
3. *Give individuals feedback on their performance.* A once-a-year performance appraisal is not sufficient.
4. *Reinforce behavior as quickly as possible.*
5. *Use powerful reinforcement.* To be effective, rewards must be important to the employee— not to the manager.
6. *Use a continuous reinforcement schedule.* New behaviors should be reinforced every time they occur. This reinforcement should continue until these behaviors become habitual.
7. *Use a variable reinforcement schedule for maintenance.* Even after behavior has become habitual, it still needs to be rewarded, though not necessarily every time it occurs.
8. *Reward teamwork—not competition.* Group goals and group rewards are one way to encourage cooperation in situations in which jobs and performance are interdependent.
9. *Make all rewards contingent on performance.*
10. *Never take good performance for granted.* Even superior performance, if left unrewarded, will eventually deteriorate.

SOURCE: Adapted from A T Hollingsworth and D Tanquay Hoyer, "How Supervisors Can Shape Behavior," *Personnel Journal*, May 1985, pp 86, 88.

Summary of Key Concepts

1. *Define the term* performance management, *distinguish between learning goals and performance outcome goals, and explain the three-step goal-setting process.* Performance management is a continuous cycle of improving individual job performance with goal setting, feedback and coaching, and rewards and positive reinforcement. Learning goals encourage learning, creativity, and skill development. Performance outcome goals target specified end-results. The three-step goal-setting process includes (1) set goals that are SMART—specific, measurable, attainable, results oriented, and time bound; (2) promote goal commitment with clear explanations, participation, and supportiveness; (3) provide support and feedback by providing information, needed training, and knowledge of results.

2. *Identify the two basic functions of feedback, and specify at least three practical lessons from feedback research.* Feedback, in the form of objective information about performance, both instructs and motivates. Feedback is not automatically accepted as intended, especially negative feedback. Managerial credibility can be enhanced through expertise and a climate of trust. Feedback must not be too frequent or too scarce and must be tailored to the individual. Feedback directly from computers is effective. Active participation in the feedback session helps people perceive feedback as more accurate. The quality of feedback received decreases as one moves up the organizational hierarchy.

3. *Define upward feedback and 360-degree feedback, and summarize how to give good feedback in a performance management program.* Lower-level employees provide upward feedback (usually anonymous) to their managers. A focal person receives 360-degree feedback from subordinates, the manager, peers, and selected others such as customers or suppliers. Good feedback is tied to performance goals and clear expectations, linked with specific behavior or results, reserved for key result areas, given as soon as possible, provided for improvement as well as for final results, focused on performance rather than on personalities, and based on accurate and credible information.

4. *Distinguish between extrinsic and intrinsic rewards, and explain the four building blocks of intrinsic rewards and motivation.* Extrinsic rewards—including pay, material goods, and social recognition—are granted by others. Intrinsic rewards are psychic rewards, such as a sense of competence or a feeling of accomplishment, that are self-granted and experienced internally. According to Thomas's model, the four basic intrinsic rewards are meaningfulness, choice, competence, and progress. Managers can boost intrinsic motivation by letting employees work on important whole tasks (meaningfulness), delegating and trusting (choice), providing challenge and feedback (competence), and collaboratively celebrating improvement (progress).

5. *Summarize the reasons why extrinsic rewards often fail to motivate employees.* Extrinsic reward systems can fail to motivate employees for these reasons: overemphasis on money, no appreciation effect, benefits become entitlements, wrong behavior is rewarded, rewards are delayed too long, use of one-size-fits-all rewards, one-shot rewards with temporary impact, and demotivating practices such as layoffs.

6. *Discuss how managers can generally improve extrinsic reward and pay-for-performance plans.* They need to be strategically anchored, based on quantified performance data, highly participative, actively sold to supervisors and middle managers, and teamwork oriented. Annual bonuses of significant size are helpful.

7. *State Thorndike's law of effect, and explain Skinner's distinction between respondent and operant behavior.* According to Edward L Thorndike's law of effect, behavior with favorable consequences tends to be repeated, while behavior with unfavorable consequences tends to disappear. B F Skinner called unlearned stimulus–response reflexes respondent behavior. He applied the term *operant behavior* to all behavior learned through experience with environmental consequences.

8. *Define positive reinforcement, negative reinforcement, punishment, and extinction, and distinguish between continuous and intermittent schedules of reinforcement.* Positive and negative reinforcement are consequence management strategies that strengthen behavior, whereas punishment and extinction weaken behavior. These strategies need to be defined objectively in terms of their actual impact on behavior frequency, not subjectively on the basis of intended impact.

   Every instance of a behavior is reinforced with a continuous reinforcement (CRF) schedule. Under intermittent reinforcement schedules—fixed and variable ratio or fixed and variable interval—some, rather than all, instances of a target behavior are reinforced. Variable schedules produce the most extinction-resistant behavior.

9. *Demonstrate your knowledge of behavior shaping.* Behavior shaping occurs when closer and closer approximations of a target behavior are reinforced. In effect, the standard for reinforcement is made more difficult as the individual learns. The process begins with continuous reinforcement, which gives way to intermittent reinforcement when the target behavior becomes strong and habitual.

Discussion Questions

1. Which, if any, factor in the performance improvement cycle portion of Figure 9–1 is more important than the others? Explain.

2. How can the distinction between learning goals and performance outcome goals help you be more effective?

3. Based on what you have read in this chapter, are you good at goal setting, or do you need improvement? Explain.

4. How has feedback instructed or motivated you lately?

5. What is your opinion of 360-degree feedback? Explain.

6. How important are intrinsic rewards to the typical employee today? Explain.

7. How would you respond to a manager who said, "Employees cannot be motivated with money"?

8. What real-life examples of positive reinforcement, negative reinforcement, both forms of punishment, and extinction can you draw from your recent experience? Were these strategies appropriately or inappropriately used?

9. From a schedule of reinforcement perspective, why do people find gambling so addictive?

10. What sort of behavior shaping have you engaged in lately? Explain your success or failure.

OB in Action Case Study

Kill the Commissions[100]

Nate Wolfson could hardly believe his ears. For as long as he had run Thrive Networks, an IT outsourcing company in Concord, Massachusetts, salespeople had been paid almost entirely on a commission basis. The system seemed to be working fine: Revenue at the 35-person firm was up from $2.7 million in 2002 to $3.6 million in 2003.

But Jim Lippie, Wolfson's director of business development, and sales director John Barrows had just presented a radical new idea. Rather than being paid individually, the two men proposed that Thrive's sales staff pool its commissions and be compensated collectively. "I was shocked," says Wolfson, who admits a personal stake in the matter: In addition to wearing the CEO hat, he also is a member of the company's three-person sales department. His own commissions were on the line.

But Lippie and Barrows presented a compelling case. Each of the three salespeople, they emphasized, possessed different strengths. Lippie was a proven lead generator, a master networker who brought in a dozen potential customers a week. Barrow's talent consisted of meeting with prospective clients and generating compelling proposals. And Wolfson was the closer, the guy who could soothe last-minute concerns and make sure the papers were signed. Eliminating the competition between the three and integrating their talents, Lippie and Barrows argued, would result in a kind of three-headed "super-salesman," increasing the likelihood of more deals—and more money—for all concerned.

Wolfson was intrigued, if skeptical. And it's not hard to see why. As long as there have been sales, there have been commissions. It's one of the great themes of American business: the salesman as lone wolf, motivated by competition and driven by self-interest, determined to reap the lion's share and leave everyone else in the dust. For managers, the traditional, commission-driven sales model is simple and easy to implement. What's more, it tends to work.

But Wolfson was aware that his current system had its flaws. Of the nine salespeople hired since Thrive was founded in 2000, only one had lasted more than six months. Between the endless networking, cold-calling, meeting with prospects, and closing transactions, people simply burned out. What's more, because the emphasis was on closing deals rather than developing a pipeline of business, cash-flow problems were not uncommon. Lippie, for example, felt little incentive to hand off leads and lose 50% of a potential commission when he would claim it all if he sealed the deal himself.

In January [2004], Wolfson took the plunge. Now, each team member receives a base salary and shares commissions based on reaching a monthly team goal. They also can earn more for meeting or exceeding individual goals for generating leads, say, or closing deals. In the first three months since implementing the new system, the number of sales meetings increased by 67%. What's more, deals now take 30% less time to complete. "This is the first year that I've been able to take a vacation in the springtime," Barrows says. "I have confidence that the pipeline won't completely dry up while I'm gone."

Wolfson now plans to add similar three-person modules in offices nationwide. It won't be easy. For the system to work, Thrive needs people with the ambition and egos of great salespeople who can still play well with others. The contributions of off-site staff also could prove difficult to monitor. "The company needs to set up a benchmark and detailed accounting within the team to compare the results of their efforts before and after the change is made," says Tom Hopkins, a sales consultant in Scottsdale, Arizona.

But Wolfson is confident. When it works, he says, the new system is like a relay race. Each team member is busy at either the beginning, middle, or end of the sales process. "We're all better off, and the company is too," he says. "None of us could have brought in as much business working individually."

Questions for Discussion

1. If you were Nate Wolfson, would you have stayed with the traditional individual-commission plan or adopted the new sales-team-commission idea? Explain your reasons.

2. How could the salespeople at Thrive Networks benefit from a performance management program?

3. What, if any, role do intrinsic rewards and intrinsic motivation play in this case?

4. Is Thrive Networks' new sales-team-commission program likely to succeed or fail? Explain.

5. What are the odds of success when this sales-team-commission concept is rolled out nationwide? Explain.

What Kind of Feedback Are You Getting?

Objectives

1. To provide actual examples of on-the-job feedback from three primary sources: organization/supervisor, co-workers, and self/task.
2. To provide a handy instrument for evaluating the comparative strength of positive feedback from these three sources.

Introduction

A pair of researchers from Georgia Tech developed and tested a 63-item feedback questionnaire to demonstrate the importance of both the sign and content of feedback messages.[101] Although their instrument contains both positive and negative feedback items, we have extracted 18 positive items for this self-awareness exercise.

Instructions

Thinking of your current job (or your most recent job), circle one number for each of the 18 items. Alternatively, you could ask one or more other employed individuals to complete the questionnaire. Once the questionnaire has been completed, calculate subtotal and total scores by adding the circled numbers. Then try to answer the discussion questions.

Instrument

How frequently do you experience each of the following outcomes in your present (or past) job?

ORGANIZATIONAL/SUPERVISORY FEEDBACK

	Rarely	Occasionally	Very Frequently
1. My supervisor complimenting me on something I have done.	1 — 2 — 3 — 4 — 5		
2. My supervisor increasing my responsibilities.	1 — 2 — 3 — 4 — 5		
3. The company expressing pleasure with my performance.	1 — 2 — 3 — 4 — 5		
4. The company giving me a raise.	1 — 2 — 3 — 4 — 5		
5. My supervisor recommending me for a promotion or raise.	1 — 2 — 3 — 4 — 5		
6. The company providing me with favorable data concerning my performance.	1 — 2 — 3 — 4 — 5		

Subscore = _____

CO-WORKER FEEDBACK

7. My co-workers coming to me for advice.	1 — 2 — 3 — 4 — 5		
8. My co-workers expressing approval of my work.	1 — 2 — 3 — 4 — 5		
9. My co-workers liking to work with me.	1 — 2 — 3 — 4 — 5		
10. My co-workers telling me that I am doing a good job.	1 — 2 — 3 — 4 — 5		
11. My co-workers commenting favorably on something I have done.	1 — 2 — 3 — 4 — 5		
12. Receiving a compliment from my co-workers.	1 — 2 — 3 — 4 — 5		

Subscore = _____

SELF/TASK FEEDBACK

13. Knowing that the way I go about my duties is superior to most others.	1 — 2 — 3 — 4 — 5		
14. Feeling I am accomplishing more than I used to.	1 — 2 — 3 — 4 — 5		
15. Knowing that I can now perform or do things which previously were difficult for me.	1 — 2 — 3 — 4 — 5		
16. Finding that I am satisfying my own standards for "good work."	1 — 2 — 3 — 4 — 5		
17. Knowing that what I am doing "feels right."	1 — 2 — 3 — 4 — 5		
18. Feeling confident of being able to handle all aspects of my job.	1 — 2 — 3 — 4 — 5		

Subscore = _____

Total score = _____

Questions for Discussion

1. Which items on this questionnaire would you rate as primarily instructional in function? Are all of the remaining items primarily motivational? Explain.

2. In terms of your own feedback profile, which of the three types is the strongest (has the highest subscore)? Which is the weakest (has the lowest subscore)? How well does your feedback profile explain your job performance and/or satisfaction?

3. How does your feedback profile measure up against those of your classmates? (Arbitrary norms, for comparative purposes, are as follows: deficient feedback = 18–42; moderate feedback = 43–65; abundant feedback = 66–90.)

4. Which of the three sources of feedback is most critical to your successful job performance or job satisfaction or both? Explain.

Group Exercise

Rewards, Rewards, Rewards

Objectives

1. To tap the class's collective knowledge of organizational rewards.
2. To appreciate the vast array of potential rewards.
3. To contrast individual and group perceptions of rewards.
4. To practice your group creativity skills.

Introduction

Rewards are a centerpiece of organizational life. Both extrinsic and intrinsic rewards motivate us to join and continue contributing to organized effort. But not all rewards have the same impact on work motivation. Individuals have their own personal preferences for rewards. The best way to discover people's reward preferences is to ask them, both individually and collectively. This group brainstorming and class discussion exercise requires about 20 to 30 minutes.

Instructions

Your instructor will divide your class randomly into teams of five to eight people. Each team will go through the following four-step process:

1. Each team will have a six-minute brainstorming session, with one person acting as recorder. The objective of this brainstorming session is to list as many different organizational rewards as the group can think of. Your team might find it helpful to think of rewards by category (such as rewards from the work itself, rewards you can spend, rewards you can eat and drink, rewards you can feel, rewards you can wear, rewards you can share, rewards you cannot see, etc.). Remember, good brainstorming calls for withholding judgments about whether ideas are good or not. Quantity is wanted. Building upon other people's ideas also is encouraged.

2. Next, each individual will take four minutes to write down, in decreasing order of importance, 10 rewards they want from the job. *Note:* These are your *personal* preferences; your "top 10" rewards that will motivate you to do your best.

3. Each team will then take five minutes to generate a list of "today's 10 most powerful rewards." List them in decreasing order of their power to motivate job performance. Voting may be necessary.

4. A general class discussion of the questions listed below will conclude the exercise.

Questions for Discussion

1. How did your personal top 10 list compare with your group's top 10 list? If there is a serious mismatch, how would it affect your motivation? (To promote discussion, the instructor may have several volunteers read their personal top 10 lists to the class.)

2. Which team had the most productive brainstorming session? (The instructor may request each team to read its brainstormed list of potential rewards and top 10 list to the class.)

3. Were you surprised to hear certain rewards getting so much attention? Why?

4. How can managers improve the incentive effect of the rewards most frequently mentioned in class?

5. What is the likely future of organizational reward plans? Which of today's compensation trends will probably thrive, and which are probably passing fads?

CEO Pay: Welcome to the Twilight Zone between Need and Greed

As a matter of basic fairness, Plato posited that no one in a community should earn more than five times the wages of the ordinary worker. Management guru Peter F. Drucker has long warned that the growing pay gap between CEOs and workers could threaten the very credibility of leadership. He argued in the mid-1980s that no leader should earn more than 20 times the company's lowest-paid employee. His reasoning: If the CEO took too large a share of the rewards, it would make a mockery of the contributions of all the other employees in a successful organization.

After massive increases in compensation, Drucker's suggested standard looks quaint. CEOs of large corporations [in 2001] made 411 times as much as the average factory worker. In the past decade, as rank-and-file wages increased 36%, CEO pay climbed 340%, to $11 million.[102]

What is your ethical interpretation of this situation?

1. CEO pay these days is obscene and unethical. Explain why?

2. CEOs deserve whatever they get because of the pressures and demands of their jobs and their many years of dedication and hard work. Explain.

3. CEOs should be paid no more than _____ times the company's lowest-paid employee. Explain your choice. How will this limit be enforced?

4. Like top athletes and Hollywood actors, CEOs should be paid whatever the market dictates. Explain.

5. CEOs should voluntarily cap their compensation at reasonable and fair levels? What's reasonable and fair?

6. Something needs to be done to curb CEO compensation because it is eroding employee trust and loyalty. Suggestions?

7. Invent other options (but not stock options). Discuss.

For the Chapter 9 Internet Exercise featuring a 360-degree feedback exercise (www.panoramicfeedback.com), visit our Web site at **www.mhhe.com/kreitner.**

Group and Social Processes

Group Dynamics

Learning Objectives

When you finish studying the material in this chapter, you should be able to:

1 Identify the four sociological criteria of a group and explain the role of equity in the Workplace Social Exchange Network (WSEN) model.

2 Describe the five stages in Tuckman's theory of group development, and discuss the threat of group decay.

3 Distinguish between role conflict and role ambiguity.

4 Contrast roles and norms, and specify four reasons norms are enforced in organizations.

5 Distinguish between task and maintenance functions in groups.

6 Summarize the practical contingency management implications for group size.

7 Discuss why managers need to carefully handle mixed-gender task groups.

8 Describe groupthink, and identify at least four of its symptoms.

9 Define social loafing, and explain how managers can prevent it.

Penny Baker always considered himself the "huggy, touchy" type. Indeed, the 38-year-old Austin entrepreneur—a former car salesman whose first business consisted of selling "Bad Cop, No Donut" T-shirts in the back of *Rolling Stone* magazine—is the opposite of stuffy. So in 1997, when he founded National Bankcard Systems, he wanted the provider of credit card terminals and Internet payment systems to be as friendly as possible. He hired close friends for key positions and socialized with his staff on a regular basis, going out for happy hour or dinner as often as four nights a week. The company thrived, growing to 75 employees and $5.3 million in sales in just three years.

But Baker began to sense that his huggy, touchy managing style was no longer working. A number of employees, all of them perfectly pleasant as drinking buddies or dinner companions, had grown complacent, behaving as though they had earned some kind of tenure. Even some longtime friends were slacking off. "I figured if I hired my buddies, they'd work their butts off for me," Baker says. Instead, he had to fire two of them. The last straw came one night at happy hour when one of his salespeople—the brother of a college pal—got drunk and proclaimed that he could do a better job than Baker and

was starting a rival business. It was then that Baker realized he had a lot to learn about the difference between being a friend and being a boss.

The fact is, there are no clear-cut rules when it comes to mixing business and buddies. At big corporations, with their often elaborate and rigid hierarchies, this isn't much of a problem. But small companies tend to be far less formal, often behaving more like families. That puts entrepreneurs in a tough spot. Act too chummy and you risk losing employees' respect. But behave too formally and you sacrifice the team spirit and bonhomie on which small companies thrive. "When you show employees that you care about them as people, they may feel an emotional attachment to you and work harder,"

says Glenn Okun, a professor at New York University's Leonard N Stern School of Business who advises CEOs. "But there's also a significant risk involved."

In Baker's case, "hugginess" felt perfectly appropriate when his company was small. But once National Bankcard reached new levels of size and sophistication, he knew it was time to separate the ranks. "It's not that I think I'm better than my employees," he says. "But I don't want people to feel like I owe them anything because we're friends." The happy-hour incident only served to drive that point home. So Baker changed his approach. He still prides himself on being a nice boss who encourages employees to have fun—say, throwing officewide pizza parties to celebrate strong sales. But he says he keeps employees at "arm's length" now, behaving in a more businesslike manner, and avoiding any involvement in their personal affairs.[1]

FOR DISCUSSION
How should a manager properly balance business and friendship?

Because the management of organizational behavior is above all else a social endeavor, as Penny Baker certainly knows, managers need a strong working knowledge of *interpersonal* behavior. Research consistently reveals the importance of social skills for both individual and organizational success. An ongoing study by the Center for Creative Leadership (involving diverse samplings from Belgium, France, Germany, Italy, the United Kingdom, the United States, and Spain) found four stumbling blocks that tend to derail executives' careers. According to the researchers, "A derailed executive is one who, having reached the general manager level, finds that there is little chance of future advancement due to a misfit between job requirements and personal skills."[2] The four stumbling blocks, consistent across the cultures studied, are as follows:

1. Problems with interpersonal relationships.
2. Failure to meet business objectives.
3. Failure to build and lead a team.
4. Inability to change or adapt during a transition.[3]

Notice how both the first and third career stumbling blocks involve social skills—the ability to get along and work effectively with others. Managers with interpersonal problems typically were described as manipulative and insensitive. Interestingly, two-thirds of the derailed European managers studied had problems with interpersonal relationships. That same problem reportedly plagued one-third of the derailed US executives. Management, as defined in Chapter 1, involves getting things done with and through others. Experts say managers need to build social capital with four key social skills: social perception, impression management, persuasion and social influence, and social adaptability (see Table 10–1).[4] How polished are your social skills? Where do you need improvement?

Let us begin by defining the term *group* as a prelude to examining types of groups, functions of group members, social exchanges in the workplace, and the group development process. Our attention then turns to group roles and norms, the basic building blocks of group dynamics. Effects of group structure and member characteristics on group outcomes are explored next. Finally, three serious threats to group effectiveness are discussed. (This chapter serves as a foundation for our discussion of teams and teamwork in the following chapter.)

Groups and Social Exchanges

Groups and teams are inescapable features of modern life.[5] College students are often teamed with their peers for class projects. Parents serve on community advisory boards at their local schools. Managers find themselves on product planning committees and pro-

Table 10–1   *Key Social Skills Managers Need for Building Social Capital*

Social Skill	Description	Topical Linkages in This Text
Social perception	Ability to perceive accurately the emotions, traits, motives, and intentions of others	• Individual differences, Chapters 5 and 6 • Emotional intelligence, Chapter 5 • Social perception, Chapter 7 • Employee motivation, Chapters 8 and 9
Impression management	Tactics designed to induce liking and a favorable first impression by others	• Impression management, Chapter 15
Persuasion and social influence	Ability to change others' attitudes or behavior in desired directions	• Influence tactics and social power, Chapter 15 • Leadership, Chapter 16
Social adaptability	Ability to adapt to, or feel comfortable in, a wide range of social situations	• Emotional intelligence, Chapter 5 • Managing change, Chapter 18

SOURCE: Columns 1 and 2 excerpted from R A Baron and G D Markman, "Beyond Social Capital: How Social Skills Can Enhance Entrepreneurs' Success," *Academy of Management Executive*, February 2000, table 1, p 110.

ductivity task forces. Productive organizations simply cannot function without gathering individuals into groups and teams. But as personal experience shows, group effort can bring out both the best and the worst in people. A marketing department meeting, where several people excitedly brainstorm and refine a creative new advertising campaign, can yield results beyond the capabilities of individual contributors. Conversely, committees have become the butt of jokes (e.g., a committee is a place where they take minutes and waste hours; a camel is a horse designed by a committee) because they all too often are plagued by lack of direction and by conflict. Modern managers need a solid understanding of groups and group processes so as to both avoid their pitfalls and tap their vast potential. Moreover, the huge and growing presence of the Internet—with its own unique network of informal and formal social relationships—is a major challenge for profit-minded business managers.

Although other definitions of groups exist, we draw from the field of sociology and define a **group** as two or more freely interacting individuals who share collective norms and goals and have a common identity.[6] Figure 10–1 illustrates how the four criteria in this definition combine to form a conceptual whole. Organizational psychologist Edgar Schein shed additional light on this concept by drawing instructive distinctions between a group, a crowd, and an organization:

> The size of a group is thus limited by the possibilities of mutual interaction and mutual awareness. Mere aggregates of people do not fit this definition because they do not interact and do not perceive themselves to be a group even if they are aware of each other as, for instance, a crowd on a street corner watching some event. A total department, a union, or a whole organization would not be a group in spite of thinking of themselves as "we," because they generally do not all interact and are not all aware of each other. However, work teams, committees, subparts of departments, cliques, and various other informal associations among organizational members would fit this definition of a group.[7]

Take a moment now to think of various groups of which you are a member. Does each of your groups satisfy the four criteria in Figure 10–1?

Group
Two or more freely interacting people with shared norms and goals and a common identity.

Figure 10–1   *Four Sociological Criteria of a Group*

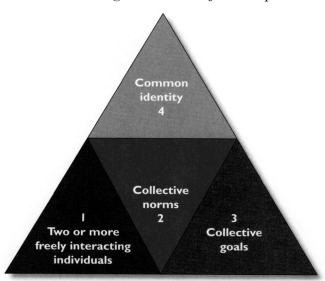

Formal and Informal Groups

Formal group
Formed by the organization.

Informal group
Formed by friends or those with common interests.

Individuals join groups, or are assigned to groups, to accomplish various purposes. If the group is formed by a manager to help the organization accomplish its goals, then it qualifies as a **formal group.** Formal groups typically wear such labels as work group, team, committee, quality circle, or task force. An **informal group** exists when the members' overriding purpose of getting together is friendship or common interests.[8] Although formal and informal groups often overlap, such as a team of corporate auditors heading for the tennis courts after work, some employees are not friends with their co-workers. The desirability of overlapping formal and informal groups is problematic. Some managers firmly believe personal friendship fosters productive teamwork on the job while others view workplace "bull sessions" as a serious threat to productivity. Both situations are common, and it is the manager's job to strike a workable balance, based on the maturity and goals of the people involved.

Functions of Formal Groups

Researchers point out that formal groups fulfill two basic functions: *organizational* and *individual.* The various functions are listed in Table 10–2. Complex combinations of these functions can be found in formal groups at any given time.

For example, consider what Mazda's new American employees experienced when they spent a month working in Japan before the opening of the firm's Flat Rock, Michigan, plant:

> After a month of training in Mazda's factory methods, whipping their new Japanese buddies at softball and sampling local watering holes, the Americans were fired up.... [A maintenance manager] even faintly praised the Japanese practice of holding group calisthenics at the start of each working day: "I didn't think I'd like doing exercises every morning, but I kind of like it."[9]

While Mazda pursued the organizational functions it wanted—interdependent teamwork, creativity, coordination, problem solving, and training—the American workers

Table 10–2   *Formal Groups Fulfill Organizational and Individual Functions*

Organizational Functions	Individual Functions
1. Accomplish complex, interdependent tasks that are beyond the capabilities of individuals.	1. Satisfy the individual's need for affiliation.
2. Generate new or creative ideas and solutions.	2. Develop, enhance, and confirm the individual's self-esteem and sense of identity.
3. Coordinate interdepartmental efforts.	3. Give individuals an opportunity to test and share their perceptions of social reality.
4. Provide a problem-solving mechanism for complex problems requiring varied information and assessments.	4. Reduce the individual's anxieties and feelings of insecurity and powerlessness.
5. Implement complex decisions.	5. Provide a problem-solving mechanism for personal and interpersonal problems.
6. Socialize and train newcomers.	

SOURCE: Adapted from E H Schein, *Organizational Psychology*, 3rd ed (Englewood Cliffs, NJ: Prentice Hall, 1980), pp 149–51.

benefited from the individual functions of formal groups. Among those benefits were affiliation with new friends, enhanced self-esteem, exposure to the Japanese social reality, and reduction of anxieties about working for a foreign-owned company. In short, Mazda created a workable blend of organizational and individual group functions by training its newly hired American employees in Japan.

Social Exchanges in the Workplace

Social relationships are complex, alive, and dynamic. Accordingly, we need dynamic models for realistic understanding. A team of researchers from Auburn University proposed the instructive model shown in Figure 10–2. They call it the Workplace Social Exchange Network (WSEN) because it captures multilevel social *exchanges* within organizations, along with the complex *network* of variables affecting those exchanges.[10]

The Exchange of Currencies   The economic notion of exchange is at the heart of this model. In starkest economic terms, people exchange their time and labor for money when they take a job. But as this model realistically shows, there is much more at stake than just the exchange of time and labor for money. Individuals, organizations, and teams have many "currencies" they can grant or withhold.

Notably, the only social exchange currency that is not self-explanatory is "citizenship." As discussed in Chapter 6, *organizational citizenship* involves going above and beyond what is expected (e.g., voluntarily working late to finish an important project)—in short, being a good citizen.[11]

Three Types of Social Exchange   According to the WSEN model, every employee has social exchanges on three levels: with the organization, with the boss, and with the work team as a whole. From the individual's perspective, exchanges at the various levels can be favorable or unfavorable. They can be motivating or de-motivating, depending on the perceived equity of the exchange. (Recall our discussion of equity motivation theory

Figure 10–2   *The Workplace Social Exchange Network Model*

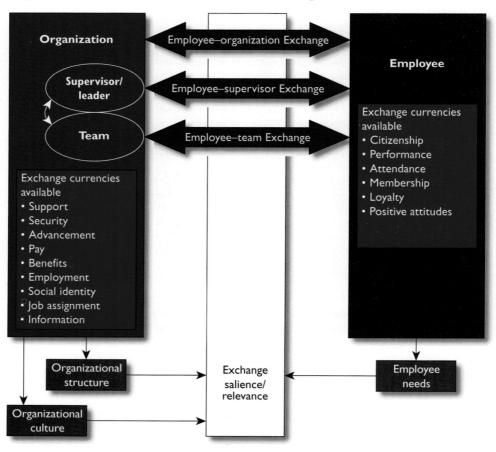

SOURCE: Adapted from M S Cole, W S Schaninger Jr, and S G Harris, "The Workplace Social Exchange Network: A Multilevel, Conceptual Examination," *Group & Organization Management,* March 2002, figure 1, p 148. Copyright © 2002 by Sage Publications. Reprinted by permission of Sage Publications.

in Chapter 8.) For example, someone may have high-quality exchanges with his or her supervisor and work team, and thus want to be around them, be motivated to work hard for them, and be loyal to them. However, because the organization has a reputation for massive layoffs, the employee–organization exchange would be perceived unfavorably, thus fostering dissatisfaction and possibly poor performance and turnover.

Situational Factors   The WSEN model includes three intervening factors: organizational structure, organizational culture, and employee needs. Structure—in the form of reporting relationships, policies, and work rules—shapes the individual's expectations about what is fair and what is unfair. So, too, cultural norms and traditions create a context for judging the fairness of social exchanges. The individual's need profile, as discussed in Chapter 8, will determine which of the organization's exchange currencies are motivating and which are not. People are motivated when they have a realistic chance of having their needs satisfied.

Miami Ad Agency Crispin, Porter + Bogusky Used Architecture to Encourage Social Interaction

"We always assumed that the people who came to work here were just as smart as we were," partner Chuck Porter, 59, explains. "And we never really tried—in any traditional way—to manage people. Because I think that really good people are unmanageable to begin with."

As a guiding philosophy, this sounds close to reckless, and Porter acknowledges that with almost 300 employees, a certain amount of hierarchy is inevitable. Still, he offers examples, large and small, of how this aversion to managing is balanced against the realities of growth. The agency's newish home, a renovated movie theater in Coconut Grove, is a case in point. Porter's instructions for the designer: "Do not design this thing for efficiency. Don't put the printers next to the studio. Don't put the broadcast department right next to the creative department. Put them in all different corners so everyone's got to walk all through the joint every day."

SOURCE: Excerpted from R Walker, "For Verging on Reckless," *Inc.,* April 2005, p 86.

Is the Social Exchange Relevant?   Finally, at the bottom center of the WSEN model is the individual's perceptual filter. Is the particular social exchange salient or relevant? Recall from the discussion of social perception in Chapter 7 that salient stimuli tend to capture and dominate one's attention. An exchange between the employee and his or her organization, leader, or team needs to be salient if it is to influence behavior. If, say, a marketing assistant is indifferent to her teammates on a special project, that particular exchange would not be salient or relevant for her.

Overall, the WSEN model does a good job of building a conceptual bridge between motivation theories and group dynamics. Also, it realistically indicates the multilevel nature of social relationships within organizations (see Real World/Real People).

The Group Development Process

Groups and teams in the workplace go through a maturation process, such as one would find in any life-cycle situation (e.g., humans, organizations, products). While there is general agreement among theorists that the group development process occurs in identifiable stages, they disagree about the exact number, sequence, length, and nature of those stages.[12] One oft-cited model is the one proposed in 1965 by educational psychologist Bruce W Tuckman. His original model involved only four stages (forming, storming, norming, and performing). The five-stage model in Figure 10–3 evolved when Tuckman and a doctoral student added "adjourning" in 1977.[13] A word of caution is in order. Somewhat akin to Maslow's need hierarchy theory, Tuckman's theory has been repeated and taught so often and for so long that many have come to view it as documented fact, not merely a theory. Even today, it is good to remember Tuckman's own caution that his group development model was derived more from group therapy sessions than from natural-life groups. Still, many in the OB field like Tuckman's five-stage model of group development because of its easy-to-remember labels and common-sense appeal.[14]

Figure 10–3   *Tuckman's Five-Stage Theory of Group Development*

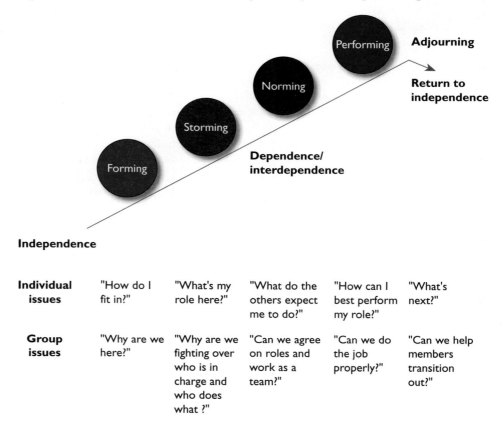

	Forming	Storming	Norming	Performing	Adjourning
Individual issues	"How do I fit in?"	"What's my role here?"	"What do the others expect me to do?"	"How can I best perform my role?"	"What's next?"
Group issues	"Why are we here?"	"Why are we fighting over who is in charge and who does what ?"	"Can we agree on roles and work as a team?"	"Can we do the job properly?"	"Can we help members transition out?"

Five Stages

Let us briefly examine each of the five stages in Tuckman's model. Notice in Figure 10–3 how individuals give up a measure of their independence when they join and participate in a group. Also, the various stages are not necessarily of the same duration or intensity. For instance, the storming stage may be practically nonexistent or painfully long, depending on the goal clarity and the commitment and maturity of the members. You can make this process come to life by relating the various stages to your own experiences with work groups, committees, athletic teams, social or religious groups, or class project teams. Some group happenings that surprised you when they occurred may now make sense or strike you as inevitable when seen as part of a natural development process.

Stage 1: Forming   During this ice-breaking stage, group members tend to be uncertain and anxious about such things as their roles, who is in charge, and the group's goals. Mutual trust is low, and there is a good deal of holding back to see who takes charge and how. If the formal leader (e.g., a supervisor) does not assert his or her authority, an emergent leader will eventually step in to fulfill the group's need for leadership and direction. Leaders typically mistake this honeymoon period as a mandate for permanent control. But later problems may force a leadership change.

Stage 2: Storming

This is a time of testing. Individuals test the leader's policies and assumptions as they try to determine how they fit into the power structure. Subgroups take shape, and subtle forms of rebellion, such as procrastination, occur. Many groups stall in stage 2 because power politics erupts into open rebellion.[15]

Stage 3: Norming

Groups that make it through stage 2 generally do so because a respected member, other than the leader, challenges the group to resolve its power struggles so something can be accomplished. Questions about authority and power are resolved through unemotional, matter-of-fact group discussion. A feeling of team spirit is experienced because members believe they have found their proper roles. **Group cohesiveness,** defined as the "we feeling" that binds members of a group together, is the principal by-product of stage 3.[16] (For a good laugh, see the golfing explanation below the photo).

A *Fortune* article examined the question, Why do people love to mix golf and business? (Hint: It's all about group dynamics.):

> Ask people why they golf with business associates, and the answer is always the same: It's a great way to build relationships. They say this far more about golf than about going to dinner or attending a baseball game, and for good reason. Indeed, this may be the central fact about corporate golf, though it's rarely said: When people golf together, they see one another humiliated. At least 95% of all golfers are terrible, which means that in 18 holes everyone in the foursome will hit a tree, take three strokes in one bunker, or four-putt, with everyone else watching. Bonding is simply a matter of people jointly going through adversity, and a round of golf will furnish plenty of it. Of course it's only a game, but of course it isn't, so the bonds can be surprisingly strong. And what's that worth?

SOURCE: G Colvin, "Why Execs Love Golf," *Fortune,* April 30, 2001, p 46. Photo: (c) George Shelly/Corbis StockMarket

Stage 4: Performing

Activity during this vital stage is focused on solving task problems. As members of a mature group, contributors get their work done without hampering others. (See the Personal Awareness and Growth Exercise at the end of this chapter for a way to measure group maturity.) There is a climate of open communication, strong cooperation, and lots of helping behavior. Conflicts and job boundary disputes are handled constructively and efficiently. Cohesiveness and personal commitment to group goals help the group achieve more than could any one individual acting alone. According to a pair of group development experts,

> the group structure can become flexible and adjust to fit the requirements of the situation without causing problems for the members. Influence can shift depending on who has the particular expertise or skills required for the group task or activity. Subgroups can work on special problems or subproblems without posing threats to the authority or cohesiveness of the rest of the group.[17]

Group Cohesiveness
A "we feeling" binding group members together.

Stage 5: Adjourning

The work is done; it is time to move on to other things. Having worked so hard to get along and get something done, many members feel a compelling sense of loss. The return to independence can be eased by rituals celebrating "the end" and "new beginnings." Parties, award ceremonies, graduations, or mock funerals can provide the needed punctuation at the end of a significant group project. Leaders need to emphasize valuable lessons learned in group dynamics to prepare everyone for future group and team efforts.

Group Development: Research and Practical Implications

A growing body of group development research provides managers with some practical insights.

Extending the Tuckman Model: Group Decay   An interesting study of 10 software development teams, ranging in size from 5 to 16 members, enhanced the practical significance of Tuckman's model.[18] Unlike Tuckman's laboratory groups who worked together only briefly, the teams of software engineers worked on projects lasting *years*. Consequently, the researchers discovered more than simply a five-stage group development process. Groups were observed actually shifting into reverse once Tuckman's "performing" stage was reached, in what the researchers called *group decay*. In keeping with Tuckman's terminology, the three observed stages of group decay were labeled "de-norming," "de-storming," and "de-forming." These additional stages take shape as follows:

- *De-norming.* As the project evolves, there is a natural erosion of standards of conduct. Group members drift in different directions as their interests and expectations change.

- *De-storming.* This stage of group decay is a mirror opposite of the storming stage. Whereas disagreements and conflicts arise rather suddenly during the storming stage, an undercurrent of discontent slowly comes to the surface during the de-storming stage. Individual resistance increases and cohesiveness declines.

- *De-forming.* The work group literally falls apart as subgroups battle for control. Those pieces of the project that are not claimed by individuals or subgroups are abandoned. "Group members begin isolating themselves from each other and from their leaders. Performance declines rapidly because the whole job is no longer being done and group members little care what happens beyond their self-imposed borders."[19]

The primary management lesson from this study is that group leaders should not become complacent upon reaching the performing stage. According to the researchers: "The performing stage is a knife edge or saddle point, not a point of static equilibrium."[20] Awareness is the first line of defense. Beyond that, constructive steps need to be taken to reinforce norms, bolster cohesiveness, and reaffirm the common goal—*even when work groups seem to be doing their best.*

Feedback   Another fruitful study was carried out by a pair of Dutch social psychologists. They hypothesized that interpersonal feedback would vary systematically during the group development process. "The unit of feedback measured was a verbal message directed from one participant to another in which some aspect of behavior was addressed."[21] After collecting and categorizing 1,600 instances of feedback from four different eight-person groups, they concluded the following:

- Interpersonal feedback increases as the group develops through successive stages.

- As the group develops, positive feedback increases and negative feedback decreases.

- Interpersonal feedback becomes more specific as the group develops.

- The credibility of peer feedback increases as the group develops.[22]

These findings hold important lessons for managers. The content and delivery of interpersonal feedback among work group or committee members can be used as a gauge of whether the group is developing properly. For example, the onset of stage 2 (storming) will be signaled by a noticeable increase in *negative* feedback. Effort can then be directed at generating specific, positive feedback among the members so the group's development will not stall. Our discussion of feedback in Chapter 9 is helpful in this regard.

Deadlines   Field and laboratory studies found uncertainty about deadlines to be a major disruptive force in both group development and intergroup relations. The practical implications of this finding were summed up by the researcher as follows:

> Uncertain or shifting deadlines are a fact of life in many organizations. Interdependent organizational units and groups may keep each other waiting, may suddenly move deadlines forward or back, or may create deadlines that are known to be earlier than is necessary in efforts to control erratic workflows. The current research suggests that the consequences of such uncertainty may involve more than stress, wasted time, overtime work, and intergroup conflicts. Synchrony in group members' expectations about deadlines may be critical to groups' abilities to accomplish successful transitions in their work.[23]

Thus, effective group management involves clarifying not only tasks and goals, but schedules and deadlines as well. When group members accurately perceive important deadlines, the pacing of work and timing of interdependent tasks tend to be more efficient.

Leadership Styles   Along a somewhat different line, experts in the area of leadership contend that different leadership styles are needed as work groups develop.

> In general, it has been documented that leadership behavior that is active, aggressive, directive, structured, and task-oriented seems to have favorable results early in the group's history. However, when those behaviors are maintained throughout the life of the group, they seem to have a negative impact on cohesiveness and quality of work. Conversely, leadership behavior that is supportive, democratic, decentralized, and participative seems to be related to poorer functioning in the early group development stages. However, when these behaviors are maintained throughout the life of the group, more productivity, satisfaction, and creativity result.[24]

The practical punch line here is that managers are advised to shift from a directive and structured leadership style to a participative and supportive style as the group develops.[25]

Roles and Norms: Social Building Blocks for Group and Organizational Behavior

Work groups transform individuals into functioning organizational members through subtle yet powerful social forces.[26] These social forces, in effect, turn "I" into "we" and "me" into "us." Group influence weaves individuals into the organization's social fabric by communicating and enforcing both role expectations and norms. We need to understand roles and norms if we are to effectively manage group and organizational behavior.

Roles

Four centuries have passed since William Shakespeare had his character Jaques speak the following memorable lines in Act II of *As You Like It:* "All the world's a stage, And all the men and women merely players; They have their exits and their entrances; And one man in

Roles

Expected behaviors
for a given position.

his time plays many parts." This intriguing notion of all people as actors in a universal play was not lost on 20th-century sociologists who developed a complex theory of human interaction based on roles. According to an OB scholar, "**roles** are sets of behaviors that persons expect of occupants of a position."[27] Role theory attempts to explain how these social expectations influence employee behavior. This section explores role theory by analyzing a role episode and defining the terms *role overload, role conflict,* and *role ambiguity.*

Role Episodes

A role episode, as illustrated in Figure 10–4, consists of a snapshot of the ongoing interaction between two people. In any given role episode, there is a role sender and a focal person who is expected to act out the role. Within a broader context, one may be simultaneously a role sender and a focal person. For the sake of social analysis, however, it is instructive to deal with separate role episodes.

Role episodes begin with the role sender's perception of the relevant organization's or group's behavioral requirements. Those requirements serve as a standard for formulating expectations for the focal person's behavior. The role sender then cognitively evaluates the focal person's actual behavior against those expectations. Appropriate verbal and behavioral messages are then sent to the focal person to pressure him or her into behaving as expected.[28] Consider how Westinghouse used a carrot-and-stick approach to communicate role expectations:

> The carrot is a plan, that . . . rewarded 134 managers with options to buy 764,000 shares of stock for boosting the company's financial performance.
>
> The stick is quarterly meetings that are used to rank managers by how much their operations contribute to earnings per share. The soft-spoken . . . [chairman of the board] doesn't scold. He just charts in green the results of the sectors that have met their goals and charts the laggards in red. Peer pressure does the rest. Shame "is a powerful tool," says one executive.[29]

On the receiving end of the role episode, the focal person accurately or inaccurately perceives the communicated role expectations and modeled behavior. Various combinations of role overload, role conflict, and role ambiguity are then experienced. (These three outcomes are defined and discussed in the following sections.) The focal person then responds constructively by engaging in problem solving, for example, or destructively because of undue tension, stress, and strain.[30]

Figure 10–4   *A Role Episode*

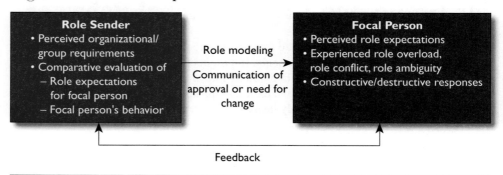

SOURCE: Adapted in part from R L Kohn, D M Wolfe, R P Quinn, and J D Snoek, *Organizational Stress: Studies in Role Conflict and Ambiguity,* 1981 ed. (Malabar, FL: Robert E Krieger Publishing, 1964), p 26.

Plenty of Role Overload and Role Conflict for Son, Husband, and Father Andrew Park

BusinessWeek In the months after my father had a stroke in 2001 at 71, his garbled speech was nearly as useless as his paralyzed right side....

At 34, I'm both a father to two small children and full-time caregiver for my own father. That puts me squarely in the Sandwich Generation—those who care for aging parents while raising their own children. Some 22.4 million US households care for someone over 65. As baby boomers look ahead to old age, with the prospect of remaining there much longer than their parents and grandparents, those numbers are set to soar.

Keeping my father fed, his clothes clean, and his medications filled added complication, as did driving him to doctors and therapists. I came to rely on the Red Cross and other groups that offer free rides for senior citizens, and discovered a nearby senior center where he could exercise and eat lunch. My dad learned to make breakfast and administer his drugs. When my wife and I go out of town, we enlist a nursing service that sends aides to cook his meals.

None of this was rocket science, but adding an adult with special needs to a busy household is arduous. Not surprisingly, caregivers are at higher risks of depression, sickness, and financial instability, and two-thirds have to cut back their hours at work or take unpaid leave to maintain their multiple roles.

Still, I would never trade the past three years. It might be because I spent my adolescence watching my parents care for my grandmother the same way. Maybe it's the bond that has grown between my dad and my 2-year-old son, or that my dad and I have spent more time together in the past year than at any time since I left for college in 1989.

Three generations of Parks in Charlotte, North Carolina.

SOURCE: Excerpted from A Park, "Between a Rocker and a High Chair," *BusinessWeek*, February 21, 2005, pp 86, 88. Reprinted by permission of The McGraw-Hill Companies, Inc.

Role Overload According to organizational psychologist Edgar Schein, **role overload** occurs when "the sum total of what role senders expect of the focal person far exceeds what he or she is able to do."[31] Students who attempt to handle a full course load and maintain a decent social life while working 30 or more hours a week know full well the consequences of role overload. As the individual tries to do more and more in less and less time, stress mounts and personal effectiveness slips.

Role overload
Others' expectations exceed one's ability.

Role Conflict Have you ever felt like you were being torn apart by the conflicting demands of those around you? If so, you were a victim of role conflict. **Role conflict** is experienced when "different members of the role set expect different things of the focal person."[32] Managers often face conflicting demands between work and family, as discussed in Chapter 6. Although women tend to experience greater work-versus-family role conflict than men because they typically shoulder more of the household and child care duties,[33] many men do not get a free pass (see Real World/Real People). Employees in single-person households have their own version of role conflict between work and outside interests.

Role conflict
Others have conflicting or inconsistent expectations.

Role conflict also may be experienced when internalized values, ethics, or personal standards collide with others' expectations. For instance, an otherwise ethical production supervisor may be told by a superior to "fudge a little" on the quality control reports so an important deadline will be met. The resulting role conflict forces the supervisor to choose between being loyal but unethical or ethical but disloyal. Tough ethical choices such as this mean personal turmoil, interpersonal conflict, and even resignation.[34] Consequently, experts say business schools should do a better job of weaving ethics education into their course requirements.

Role ambiguity

Others' expectations are unknown.

Role Ambiguity   Those who experience role conflict may have trouble complying with role demands, but they at least know what is expected of them. Such is not the case with **role ambiguity,** which occurs when "members of the role set fail to communicate to the focal person expectations they have or information needed to perform the role, either because they do not have the information or because they deliberately withhold it."[35] In short, people experience role ambiguity when they do not know what is expected of them. Organizational newcomers often complain about unclear job descriptions and vague promotion criteria. According to role theory, prolonged role ambiguity can foster job dissatisfaction, erode self-confidence, and hamper job performance.

As might be expected, role ambiguity varies across cultures. In a 21-nation study, people in individualistic cultures were found to have higher role ambiguity than people in collectivist cultures.[36] In other words, people in collectivist or "we" cultures had a clearer idea of others' expectations. Collectivist cultures make sure everyone knows their proper place in society. People in individualistic "me" cultures, such as the United States, may enjoy more individual discretion, but comparatively less input from others has its price—namely, greater role ambiguity.

As mentioned earlier, these role outcomes typically are experienced in some combination, usually to the detriment of the individual and the organization. In fact, a study in Israel documented lower job performance when employees experienced a combination of role conflict and role ambiguity.[37]

Take a moment now to complete the self-assessment exercise in the OB Exercise. See if you can distinguish between sources of role conflict and sources of role ambiguity, as they affect your working life.

Norms

Norm

Shared attitudes, opinions, feelings, or actions that guide social behavior.

Norms are more encompassing than roles. While roles involve behavioral expectations for specific positions, norms help organizational members determine right from wrong and good from bad. According to one respected team of management consultants: "A **norm** is an attitude, opinion, feeling, or action—shared by two or more people—that guides their behavior."[38] Although norms are typically unwritten and seldom discussed openly, they have a powerful influence on group and organizational behavior.[39] PepsiCo Inc., for instance, has evolved a norm that equates corporate competitiveness with physical fitness. According to observers,

> Leanness and nimbleness are qualities that pervade the company. When Pepsi's brash young managers take a few minutes away from the office, they often head straight for the company's physical fitness center or for a jog around the museum-quality sculptures outside of PepsiCo's Purchase, New York, headquarters.[40]

At PepsiCo and elsewhere, group members positively reinforce those who adhere to current norms with friendship and acceptance. On the other hand, nonconformists experience

Measuring Role Conflict and Role Ambiguity

Instructions

Step 1. While thinking of your current (or last) job, circle one response for each of the following statements. Please consider each statement carefully because some are worded positively and some negatively.

Step 2. In the space in the far right column, label each statement with either a C for role conflict or an A for role ambiguity. (See endnote 41 for a correct categorization.)[41]

Step 3. Calculate separate totals for role conflict and role ambiguity, and compare them with these arbitrary norms: 5–14 = low; 15–25 = moderate; 26–35 = high.

	Very False	Very True	
1. I feel certain about how much authority I have.	7 — 6 — 5 — 4 — 3 — 2 — 1		_____
2. I have to do things that should be done differently.	1 — 2 — 3 — 4 — 5 — 6 — 7		_____
3. I know that I have divided my time properly.	7 — 6 — 5 — 4 — 3 — 2 — 1		_____
4. I know what my responsibilities are.	7 — 6 — 5 — 4 — 3 — 2 — 1		_____
5. I have to buck a rule or policy in order to carry out an assignment.	1 — 2 — 3 — 4 — 5 — 6 — 7		_____
6. I feel certain how I will be evaluated for a raise or promotion.	7 — 6 — 5 — 4 — 3 — 2 — 1		_____
7. I work with two or more groups who operate quite differently.	1 — 2 — 3 — 4 — 5 — 6 — 7		_____
8. I know exactly what is expected of me.	7 — 6 — 5 — 4 — 3 — 2 — 1		_____
9. I do things that are apt to be accepted by one person and not accepted by others.	1 — 2 — 3 — 4 — 5 — 6 — 7		_____
10. I work on unnecessary things.	1 — 2 — 3 — 4 — 5 — 6 — 7		_____

Role conflict score = _____
Role ambiguity score = _____

SOURCE: Adapted from J R Rizzo, R J House, and S I Lirtzman, "Role Conflict and Ambiguity in Complex Organizations," *Administrative Science Quarterly,* vol. 15 June 1970, p 156. © Johnson Graduate School of Management, Cornell.

---

criticism and even **ostracism,** or rejection by group members. Anyone who has experienced the "silent treatment" from a group of friends knows what a potent social weapon ostracism can be.[42] Norms can be put into proper perspective by understanding how they develop and why they are enforced.

Ostracism
Rejection by other group members.

How Norms Are Developed

Experts say norms evolve in an informal manner as the group or organization determines what it takes to be effective. Generally speaking, norms develop in various combinations of the following four ways:

1. *Explicit statements by supervisors or co-workers.* For instance, a group leader might explicitly set norms about not drinking (alcohol) at lunch.

2. *Critical events in the group's history.* At times there is a critical event in the group's history that establishes an important precedent. (For example, a key recruit may have decided to work elsewhere because a group member said too many negative things about the organization. Hence, a norm against such "sour grapes" behavior might evolve.)

3. *Primacy.* The first behavior pattern that emerges in a group often sets group expectations. If the first group meeting is marked by very formal interaction between supervisors and employees, then the group often expects future meetings to be conducted in the same way.

4. *Carryover behaviors from past situations.* Such carryover of individual behaviors from past situations can increase the predictability of group members' behaviors in new settings and facilitate task accomplishment. For instance, students and professors carry fairly constant sets of expectations from class to class.[43]

We would like you to take a few moments and think about the norms that are currently in effect in your classroom. List the norms on a sheet of paper. Do these norms help or hinder your ability to learn? Norms can affect performance either positively or negatively.[44]

Why Norms Are Enforced   Norms tend to be enforced by group members when they

- Help the group or organization survive.
- Clarify or simplify behavioral expectations.
- Help individuals avoid embarrassing situations.
- Clarify the group's or organization's central values and/or unique identity.[45]

Working examples of each of these four situations are presented in Table 10–3.

Relevant Research Insights and Managerial Implications

Although instruments used to measure role conflict and role ambiguity have questionable validity,[46] two separate meta-analyses indicated that role conflict and role ambiguity negatively affected employees. Specifically, role conflict and role ambiguity were associated with job dissatisfaction, tension and anxiety, lack of organizational commitment, intentions to quit, and, to a lesser extent, poor job performance.[47]

The meta-analyses results hold few surprises for managers. Generally, because of the negative association reported, it makes sense for management to reduce both role conflict and role ambiguity. In this endeavor, managers can use feedback, formal rules and procedures, directive leadership, setting of specific (difficult) goals, and participation. Managers also can use the mentoring process discussed in Chapter 3 to reduce role conflict and ambiguity.

Table 10–3   *Four Reasons Norms Are Enforced*

Norm	Reason for Enforcement	Example
"Make our department look good in top management's eyes."	**Group/organization survival**	After vigorously defending the vital role played by the Human Resources Management Department at a divisional meeting, a staff specialist is complimented by her boss.
"Success comes to those who work hard and don't make waves."	**Clarification of behavioral expectations**	A senior manager takes a young associate aside and cautions him to be a bit more patient with co-workers who see things differently.
"Be a team player, not a star."	**Avoidance of embarrassment**	A project team member is ridiculed by her peers for dominating the discussion during a progress report to top management.
"Customer service is our top priority."	**Clarification of central values/unique identity**	Two sales representatives are given a surprise Friday afternoon party for having received prestigious best-in-the-industry customer service awards from an industry association.

Regarding norms, a recent set of laboratory studies involving a total of 1,504 college students as subjects has important implications for workplace diversity programs. Subjects in groups where the norm was to express prejudices, condone discrimination, and laugh at hostile jokes tended to engage in these undesirable behaviors. Conversely, subjects tended to disapprove of prejudicial and discriminatory conduct when exposed to groups with more socially acceptable norms.[48] So, once again, Mom and our teachers were right when they warned us about the dangers of hanging out with "the wrong crowd." Managers who want to build strong diversity programs need to cultivate favorable role models and group norms. Poor role models and antisocial norms need to be identified and weeded out.

Group Structure and Composition

Work groups of varying size are made up of individuals with varying ability and motivation.[49] Moreover, those individuals perform different roles, on either an assigned or voluntary basis. No wonder some work groups are more productive than others. No wonder some committees are tightly knit while others wallow in conflict. In this section, we examine three important dimensions of group structure and composition: (1) functional roles of group members, (2) group size, and (3) gender composition. Each of these dimensions alternatively can enhance or hinder group effectiveness, depending on how it is managed.

Functional Roles Performed by Group Members

As described in Table 10–4, both task and maintenance roles need to be performed if a work group is to accomplish anything.[50]

Task versus Maintenance Roles   **Task roles** enable the work group to define, clarify, and pursue a common purpose. Meanwhile, **maintenance roles** foster supportive and constructive interpersonal relationships. In short, task roles keep the group *on track* while maintenance roles keep the group *together*. A project team member is performing a task function when he or she stands at an update meeting and says, "What is the real issue here? We don't seem to be getting anywhere." Another individual who says, "Let's hear from those who oppose this plan," is performing a maintenance function. Importantly, each of the various task and maintenance roles may be played in varying combinations and sequences by either the group's leader or any of its members.

Task roles
Task-oriented group behavior.

Maintenance roles
Relationship-building group behavior.

Checklist for Managers   The task and maintenance roles listed in Table 10–4 can serve as a handy checklist for managers and group leaders who wish to ensure proper group development. Roles that are not always performed when needed, such as those of coordinator, evaluator, and gatekeeper, can be performed in a timely manner by the formal leader or assigned to other members. The task roles of initiator, orienter, and energizer are especially important because they are *goal-directed* roles. Research studies on group goal setting confirm the motivational power of challenging goals. As with individual goal setting (in Chapter 9), difficult but achievable goals are associated with better group results.[51] Also in line with individual goal-setting theory and research, group goals are more effective if group members clearly understand them and are both individually and collectively committed to achieving them. Initiators, orienters, and energizers can be very helpful in this regard.

Table 10–4   *Functional Roles Performed by Group Members*

Task Roles	Description
Initiator	Suggests new goals or ideas.
Information seeker/giver	Clarifies key issues.
Opinion seeker/giver	Clarifies pertinent values.
Elaborator	Promotes greater understanding through examples or exploration of implications.
Coordinator	Pulls together ideas and suggestions.
Orienter	Keeps group headed toward its stated goal(s).
Evaluator	Tests group's accomplishments with various criteria such as logic and practicality.
Energizer	Prods group to move along or to accomplish more.
Procedural technician	Performs routine duties (e.g., handing out materials or rearranging seats).
Recorder	Performs a "group memory" function by documenting discussion and outcomes.

Maintenance Roles	Description
Encourager	Fosters group solidarity by accepting and praising various points of view.
Harmonizer	Mediates conflict through reconciliation or humor.
Compromiser	Helps resolve conflict by meeting others half way.
Gatekeeper	Encourages all group members to participate.
Standard setter	Evaluates the quality of group processes.
Commentator	Records and comments on group processes/dynamics.
Follower	Serves as a passive audience.

SOURCE: Adapted from discussion in K D Benne and P Sheats, "Functional Roles of Group Members," *Journal of Social Issues,* Spring 1948, pp 41–49.

International managers need to be sensitive to cultural differences regarding the relative importance of task and maintenance roles. In Japan, for example, cultural tradition calls for more emphasis on maintenance roles, especially the roles of harmonizer and compromiser:

> Courtesy requires that members not be conspicuous or disputatious in a meeting or classroom. If two or more members discover that their views differ—a fact that is tactfully taken to be unfortunate—they adjourn to find more information and to work toward a stance that all can accept. They do not press their personal opinions through strong arguments, neat logic, or rewards and threats. And they do not hesitate to shift their beliefs if doing so will preserve smooth interpersonal relations. (To lose is to win.)[52]

Group Size

How many group members is too many? The answer to this deceptively simple question has intrigued managers and academics for years. Folk wisdom says "two heads are better than one" but that "too many cooks spoil the broth." So where should a manager draw the line when staffing a committee? At 3? At 5 or 6? At 10 or more? Researchers have taken two different approaches to pinpointing optimum group size: mathematical modeling and laboratory simulations. Let us briefly review research evidence from these two approaches.

The Mathematical Modeling Approach

This approach involves building a mathematical model around certain desired outcomes of group action such as decision quality. Due to differing assumptions and statistical techniques, the results of this research are inconclusive. Statistical estimates of optimum group size have ranged from 3 to 13.[53]

The Laboratory Simulation Approach

This stream of research is based on the assumption that group behavior needs to be observed firsthand in controlled laboratory settings. A laboratory study by respected Australian researcher Philip Yetton and his colleague, Preston Bottger, provides useful insights about group size and performance.[54]

A total of 555 subjects (330 managers and 225 graduate management students, of whom 20% were female) were assigned to task teams ranging in size from 2 to 6. The teams worked on the National Aeronautics and Space Administration moon survival exercise. (This exercise involves the rank ordering of 15 pieces of equipment that would enable a spaceship crew on the moon to survive a 200-mile trip between a crash-landing site and home base.)[55] After analyzing the relationships between group size and group performance, Yetton and Bottger concluded the following:

Why is it difficult to get anything through the US Senate or Congress? Two words: giant committees! This committee meeting certainly violates the lessons from research about limiting group size. Making matters worse today are all the electronic gadgets people bring to meetings that focus their attention on everything but the issues at hand.

> It would be difficult, at least with respect to decision quality, to justify groups larger than five members. . . . Of course, to meet needs other than high decision quality, organizations may employ groups significantly larger than four or five.[56]

More recent laboratory studies exploring the brainstorming productivity of various size groups (2 to 12 people), in face-to-face versus computer-mediated situations, proved fruitful. In the usual face-to-face brainstorming sessions, productivity of ideas did not increase as the size of the group increased. But brainstorming productivity increased as the size of the group increased when ideas were typed into networked computers.[57] These results suggest that computer networks are helping to deliver on the promise of productivity improvement through modern information technology.

Managerial Implications   Within a contingency management framework, there is no hard-and-fast rule about group size. It depends on the manager's objective for the group. If a high-quality decision is the main objective, then a three- to five-member group would be appropriate. However, if the objective is to generate creative ideas, encourage participation, socialize new members, engage in training, or communicate policies, then groups much larger than five could be justified. But even in this developmental domain, researchers have found upward limits on group size. According to a meta-analysis, the positive effects of team-building activities diminished as group size increased.[58] Managers also need to be aware of *qualitative* changes that occur when group size increases. A meta-analysis of eight studies found the following relationships: As group size increased, group leaders tended to become more directive, and group member satisfaction tended to decline slightly.[59]

Odd-numbered groups (e.g., three, five, seven members) are recommended if the issue is to be settled by a majority vote. Voting deadlocks (e.g., 2–2, 3–3) too often hamper effectiveness of even-numbered groups. For example, as outlined in this business news clipping, a voting deadlock paved the way for inept government oversight of business:

> Pepsi got the go-ahead for its $13.4 billion acquisition of Quaker Oats after the Federal Trade Commission deadlocked Wednesday on whether to try to block the deal.
>
> In a closed meeting, FTC commissioners split 2–2 on whether to go to court to oppose Pepsi's bid for Quaker and its powerhouse Gatorade sports-drink brand. FTC staff investigating the deal had recommended that the agency try to block it because of the increased clout Pepsi would get in the $56 billion soft-drink industry.
>
> The move to go to court required a majority. After the failed vote, commissioners voted unanimously to close the probe begun after the deal was announced in December. That vote allows Pepsi and Quaker to close the deal without regulatory conditions. Pepsi said it expects to do so before the weekend.[60]

A five-member FTC panel might well have rendered the same outcome, but in a more decisive manner.

Effects of Men and Women Working Together in Groups

As pointed out in Chapter 2, the female portion of the US labor force has grown significantly in recent decades. This demographic shift brought an increase in the number of organizational committees and teams composed of both men and women. Some profound effects on group dynamics might be expected.[61] Let us see what researchers have found in the way of group gender composition effects and what managers can do about them.

One study suggests that females entering male-dominated fields, such as law enforcement, face greater challenges than do males entering female-dominated fields, such as nursing.

Women Face an Uphill Battle in Mixed-Gender Task Groups Laboratory and field studies paint a picture of inequality for women working in mixed-gender groups. Both women and men need to be aware of these often subtle but powerful group dynamics so corrective steps can be taken.

In a laboratory study of six-person task groups, a clear pattern of gender inequality was found in the way group members interrupted each other. Men interrupted women significantly more often than they did other men. Women, who tended to interrupt less frequently and less successfully than men, interrupted men and women equally.[62] A recent laboratory study involving Canadian college students found "both men and women exhibiting higher levels of interruption behavior in male-dominated groups."[63]

A field study of mixed-gender police and nursing teams in the Netherlands found another group dynamics disadvantage for women. These two particular professions—police work and nursing—were fruitful research areas because men dominate the former while women dominate the latter. As women move into male-dominated police forces and men gain employment opportunities in the female-dominated world of nursing, who faces the greatest resistance? The answer from this study was the women police officers. As the representation of the minority gender (either female police officers or male nurses) increased in the work groups, the following changes in attitude were observed:

> The attitude of the male majority changes from neutral to resistant, whereas the attitude of the female majority changes from favorable to neutral. In other words, men increasingly want to keep their domain for themselves, while women remain willing to share their domain with men.[64]

Again, managers are faced with the challenge of countering discriminatory tendencies in group dynamics.

The Issue of Sexual Harassment

According to a recent industry survey by a New York law firm specializing in workplace issues, the problem of sexual harassment refuses to go away:

> 63% of [234] respondents noted that they had handled a sexual harassment complaint at their company. That's up from 2003, when 57% said they had handled one. At least there was some good news here; that's way down from 1995, when 95% of respondents said that they'd handled one.[65]

Another study of social-sexual behavior among 1,232 working men ($n = 405$) and women ($n = 827$) in the Los Angeles area found *nonharassing* sexual behavior to be very common, with 80% of the total sample reporting experience with such behavior. Indeed, according to the researchers, increased social contact between women and men in work groups and organizations has led to increased sexualization (e.g., flirting and romance) in the workplace.[66]

From an OB research standpoint, sexual harassment is a complex and multifaceted problem. For example, a meta-analysis of 62 studies found women perceiving a broader range of behaviors as sexual harassment (see Table 10–5), as opposed to what men perceived. Women and men tended to agree that sexual propositions and coercion qualified as sexual harassment, but there was less agreement about other aspects of a hostile work environment.[67]

Constructive Managerial Action

Male and female employees can and often do work well together in groups. A survey of 387 male US government employees sought to determine how they were affected by the growing number of female co-workers. The researchers concluded, "Under many circumstances, including intergender interaction in work groups, frequent contact leads to cooperative and supportive social relations."[68] Still, managers need to take affirmative steps to ensure that the documented sexualization of work environments does not erode into sexual harassment. Whether perpetrated against women or men, sexual harassment is demeaning, unethical, and appropriately called "work environment pollution." Moreover, the US Equal Employment Opportunity Commission

Table 10–5   *Behavioral Categories of Sexual Harassment*

Category	Description	Behavioral Examples
Derogatory attitudes—impersonal	Behaviors that reflect derogatory attitudes about men or women in general	Obscene gestures not directed at target Sex-stereotyped jokes
Derogatory attitudes—personal	Behaviors that are directed at the target that reflect derogatory attitudes about the target's gender	Obscene phone calls Belittling the target's competence
Unwanted dating pressure	Persistent requests for dates after the target has refused	Repeated requests to go out after work or school
Sexual propositions	Explicit requests for sexual encounters	Proposition for an affair
Physical sexual contact	Behaviors in which the harasser makes physical sexual contact with the target	Embracing the target Kissing the target
Physical nonsexual contact	Behaviors in which the harasser makes physical nonsexual contact with the target	Congratulatory hug
Sexual coercion	Requests for sexual encounters or forced encounters that are made a condition of employment or promotion	Threatening punishment unless sexual favors are given Sexual bribery

SOURCE: M Rotundo, D Nguyen, and P R Sackett, "A Meta-Analytic Review of Gender Differences in Perceptions of Sexual Harassment," *Journal of Applied Psychology,* October 2001, Article 914–922. Copyright © 2001 by the American Psychological Association. Reprinted with permission.

holds employers legally accountable for behavior it considers sexually harassing. An expert on the subject explains:

> What exactly is sexual harassment? The Equal Employment Opportunity Commission (EEOC) says that unwelcome sexual advances, requests for sexual favors, and other verbal or physical conduct of a sexual nature constitute sexual harassment when submission to such conduct is made a condition of employment; when submission to or rejection of sexual advances is used as a basis for employment decisions; or when such conduct creates an intimidating, hostile, or offensive work environment. These EEOC guidelines interpreting Title VII of the Civil Rights Act of 1964 further state that employers are responsible for the actions of their supervisors and agents and that employers are responsible for the actions of other employees if the employer knows or should have known about the sexual harassment.[69]

A *Training* magazine survey of 1,652 US companies with at least 100 employees found 91% conducting some sort of sexual harassment training and 68% doing so at least annually.[70] Given the disagreement between women and men about what constitutes sexual harassment, this type of education is very important.

Beyond avoiding lawsuits by establishing and enforcing antidiscrimination and sexual harassment policies, managers need to take additional steps. Workforce diversity training is a popular approach today. Gender-issue workshops are another option. "Du Pont Co., for example, holds monthly workshops to make managers aware of gender-related attitudes."[71] Phyllis B Davis, a senior vice president at Avon Corporation, has framed the goal of such efforts by saying: "It's a question of consciously creating an environment where everyone has an equal shot at contributing, participating, and most of all advancing."[72]

Importantly, this embracing of organizational and work group diversity goes beyond gender, race, ethnicity, and culture. A laboratory study of US college students found a

An Entrepreneur and Consultant Questions Loyalty

In my experience, when businesspeople talk about loyal employees, they're talking about team players who will implement decisions with little or no challenge. There's nothing inherently wrong with that. But what too often happens is that CEOs surround themselves with sycophants, constructing echo chambers of agreement. Loyalty becomes a code word for intellectual servitude, what I call an "obedience culture."

In obedience cultures, loyalty determines everything: who gets promoted, who gets access to the inner circle, who gets raises, and who wields authority. True, an obedience-based workplace can be extremely efficient—it's a lot easier to get things done when people know their marching orders and debate is kept to a minimum. But obedience cultures suppress ideas. They turn staff meetings into elaborately staged agreement sessions and quash opportunities for improvement.

SOURCE: Excerpted from A Hanft, "The Case against Loyalty," *Inc.*, April 2005, p 144.

stronger positive relationship between group effectiveness and *value* diversity (as opposed to demographic diversity).[73] Once again we see the importance of managers recognizing and accommodating individual differences rather than relying on stereotypes.

Threats to Group Effectiveness

Even when managers carefully staff and organize task groups, group dynamics can still go haywire. Forehand knowledge of three major threats to group effectiveness—the Asch effect, groupthink, and social loafing—can help managers take necessary preventive steps. Because the first two problems relate to blind conformity, some brief background work is in order.

Very little would be accomplished in task groups and organizations without conformity to norms, role expectations, policies, and rules and regulations. After all, deadlines, commitments, and product/service quality standards need to be established and adhered to if the organization is to survive. But conformity is a two-edged sword.[74] Excessive or blind conformity can stifle critical thinking, the last line of defense against unethical conduct (see Real World/Real People). Almost daily accounts in the popular media of executive misdeeds, insider trading scandals, price fixing, illegal dumping of hazardous wastes, and other unethical practices make it imperative that future managers understand the mechanics of blind conformity.

The Asch Effect

More than 50 years ago, social psychologist Solomon Asch conducted a series of laboratory experiments that revealed a negative side of group dynamics.[75] Under the guise of a "perception test," Asch had groups of seven to nine volunteer college students look at 12 pairs of cards such as the ones in Figure 10–5. The object was to identify the line that was the same length as the standard line. Each individual was told to announce his or her choice to the group. Since the differences among the comparison lines were obvious, there should have been unanimous agreement during each of the 12 rounds. But that was not the case.

Figure 10–5   *The Asch Experiment*

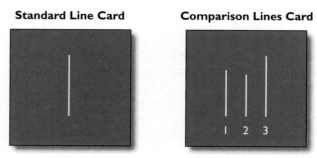

Standard Line Card   **Comparison Lines Card**

A Minority of One   All but one member of each group were Asch's confederates who agreed to systematically select the wrong line during seven of the rounds (the other five rounds were control rounds for comparison purposes). The remaining individual was the naive subject who was being tricked. Group pressure was created by having the naive subject in each group be among the last to announce his or her choice. Thirty-one subjects were tested. Asch's research question was: "How often would the naive subjects conform to a majority opinion that was obviously wrong?"

Only 20% of Asch's subjects remained entirely independent; 80% yielded to the pressures of group opinion at least once! And 58% knuckled under to the "immoral majority" at least twice. Hence, the **Asch effect,** the distortion of individual judgment by a unanimous but incorrect opposition, was documented. (Do you ever turn your back on your better judgment by giving in to group pressure?)

Asch effect
Giving in to a unanimous but wrong opposition.

A Managerial Perspective   Asch's experiment has been widely replicated with mixed results. Both high and low degrees of blind conformity have been observed with various situations and subjects. Replications in Japan and Kuwait have demonstrated that the Asch effect is not unique to the United States.[76] A 1996 meta-analysis of 133 Asch-line experiments from 17 countries found a *decline* in conformity among US subjects since the 1950s. Internationally, collectivist countries, where the group prevails over the individual, produced higher levels of conformity than individualistic countries.[77] The point is not precisely how great the Asch effect is in a given situation or culture, but rather, managers committed to ethical conduct need to be concerned that the Asch effect exists.

For Jeffrey Skilling, the disgraced former CEO of Enron, the Asch effect was something to cultivate and nurture. Consider this organizational climate for blind obedience:

> Skilling was filling headquarters with his own troops. He was not looking for "fuzzy skills," a former employee recalls. His recruits talked about a socialization process called "Enronizing." Family time? Quality of life? Forget it. Anybody who did not embrace the elbows-out culture "didn't get it." They were "damaged goods" and "shipwrecks," likely to be fired by their bosses at blistering annual job reviews known as rank-and-yank sessions. The culture turned paranoid: former CIA and FBI agents were hired to enforce security. Using "sniffer" programs, they would pounce on anyone e-mailing a potential competitor. The "spooks," as the former agents were called, were known to barge into offices and confiscate computers.[78]

Even isolated instances of blind, unthinking conformity seriously threaten the effectiveness and integrity of work groups and organizations. Functional conflict and assertiveness, discussed in Chapters 13 and 14, can help employees respond appropriately when they find themselves facing an immoral majority. Ethical codes mentioning specific practices also can provide support and guidance.

Groupthink

Why did President Lyndon B Johnson and his group of intelligent White House advisers make some very *unintelligent* decisions that escalated the Vietnam War? Those fateful decisions were made despite obvious warning signals, including stronger than expected resistance from the North Vietnamese and withering support at home and abroad. Systematic analysis of the decision-making processes underlying the war in Vietnam and other US foreign policy fiascoes prompted Yale University's Irving Janis to coin the term *groupthink*.[79] Modern managers can all too easily become victims of groupthink, just like President Johnson's staff, if they passively ignore the danger.

"Damn it, Hopkins, didn't you get yesterday's memo?"

Definition and Symptoms of Groupthink   Janis defines **groupthink** as "a mode of thinking that people engage in when they are deeply involved in a cohesive in-group, when members' strivings for unanimity override their motivation to realistically appraise alternative courses of action."[80] He adds, "Groupthink refers to a deterioration of mental efficiency, reality testing, and moral judgment that results from in-group pressures."[81] Unlike Asch's subjects, who were strangers to each other, members of groups victimized by groupthink are friendly, tightly knit, and cohesive.

Groupthink
Janis's term for a cohesive in-group's unwillingness to realistically view alternatives.

The symptoms of groupthink listed in Figure 10–6 thrive in the sort of climate outlined in the following critique of corporate directors in the United States:

> Many directors simply don't rock the boat. "No one likes to be the skunk at the garden party," says [management consultant] Victor H. Palmieri. . . . "One does not make friends and influence people in the boardroom or elsewhere by raising hard questions that create embarrassment or discomfort for management."[82]

Figure 10–6   *Symptoms of Groupthink Lead to Defective Decision Making*

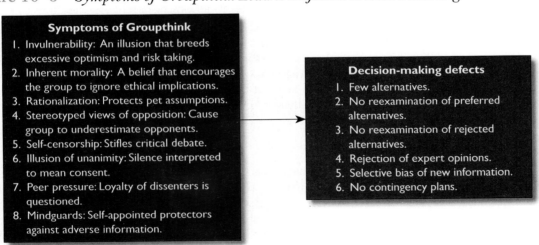

Symptoms of Groupthink

1. Invulnerability: An illusion that breeds excessive optimism and risk taking.
2. Inherent morality: A belief that encourages the group to ignore ethical implications.
3. Rationalization: Protects pet assumptions.
4. Stereotyped views of opposition: Cause group to underestimate opponents.
5. Self-censorship: Stifles critical debate.
6. Illusion of unanimity: Silence interpreted to mean consent.
7. Peer pressure: Loyalty of dissenters is questioned.
8. Mindguards: Self-appointed protectors against adverse information.

Decision-making defects

1. Few alternatives.
2. No reexamination of preferred alternatives.
3. No reexamination of rejected alternatives.
4. Rejection of expert opinions.
5. Selective bias of new information.
6. No contingency plans.

SOURCES: Symptoms adapted from I L Janis, *Groupthink: Psychological Studies of Policy, Decisions and Fiascoes* 2nd ed (Boston: Houghton Mifflin, 1982), pp 174–75. Copyright © 1982 by Houghton Mifflin Company. Used by permission. Defects excerpted from G Moorhead, "Groupthink: Hypothesis in Need of Testing," *Group & Organization Studies*, December 1982, p 434. Copyright © 1982 by Sage Publications. Reprinted by permission of Sage Publications.

In short, policy- and decision-making groups can become so cohesive that strong-willed executives are able to gain unanimous support for poor decisions.

Groupthink Research and Prevention   Laboratory studies using college students as subjects validate portions of Janis's groupthink concept. Specifically, it has been found that

- Groups with a moderate amount of cohesiveness produce better decisions than low- or high-cohesive groups.
- Highly cohesive groups victimized by groupthink make the poorest decisions, despite high confidence in those decisions.[83]

Janis believes prevention is better than cure when dealing with groupthink. He recommends the following preventive measures:

1. Each member of the group should be assigned the role of critical evaluator. This role involves actively voicing objections and doubts.
2. Top-level executives should not use policy committees to rubber-stamp decisions that have already been made.
3. Different groups with different leaders should explore the same policy questions.
4. Subgroup debates and outside experts should be used to introduce fresh perspectives.
5. Someone should be given the role of devil's advocate when discussing major alternatives. This person tries to uncover every conceivable negative factor.
6. Once a consensus has been reached, everyone should be encouraged to rethink their position to check for flaws.[84]

These antigroupthink measures can help cohesive groups produce sound recommendations and decisions. When *BusinessWeek* tackled the issue of corporate governance, this was one of the recommendations:

> The best insurance against crossing the ethical divide is a roomful of skeptics. CEOs must actively encourage dissent among senior managers by creating decision-making processes, reporting relationships, and incentives that encourage opposing viewpoints. At too many companies, the performance review system encourages a "yes-man culture" that subverts the organization's checks and balances. By advocating dissent, top executives can create a climate where wrongdoing will not go unchallenged.[85]

Groupthink also will be less likely.

Avoiding groupthink is a powerful argument in favor of *diversity;* not only racial and gender diversity, but diversity in age, background, religion, education, and world views as well.[86]

The OB in Action Case Study at the end of this chapter explores the possible role of groupthink in the 1986 Challenger Space Shuttle disaster.

Social Loafing

Is group performance less than, equal to, or greater than the sum of its parts? Can three people, for example, working together accomplish less than, the same as, or more than they would working separately? An interesting study conducted more than a half century ago by a French agricultural engineer named Ringelmann found the answer to be "less than."[87] In a rope-pulling exercise, Ringelmann reportedly found that three people pulling together could achieve only two and a half times the average individual rate. Eight pullers achieved less than four times the individual rate. This tendency for individual effort to decline as group size increases has come to be called **social loafing.**[88] Let us briefly analyze this threat to group effectiveness and synergy with an eye toward avoiding it.

Social loafing
Decrease in individual effort as group size increases.

Social Loafing Theory and Research

Among the theoretical explanations for the social loafing effect are (1) equity of effort ("Everyone else is goofing off, so why shouldn't I?"), (2) loss of personal accountability ("I'm lost in the crowd, so who cares?"), (3) motivational loss due to the sharing of rewards ("Why should I work harder than the others when everyone gets the same reward?"), and (4) coordination loss as more people perform the task ("We're getting in each other's way.").

Laboratory studies refined these theories by identifying situational factors that moderated the social loafing effect. Social loafing occurred when

- The task was perceived to be unimportant, simple, or not interesting.[89]
- Group members thought their individual output was not identifiable.[90]
- Group members expected their co-workers to loaf.[91]

But social loafing did *not* occur when group members in two laboratory studies expected to be evaluated.[92] Also, research suggests that self-reliant "individualists" are more prone to social loafing than are group-oriented "collectivists." But individualists can be made more cooperative by keeping the group small and holding each member personally accountable for results.[93]

Practical Implications

These findings demonstrate that social loafing is not an inevitable part of group effort. Management can curb this threat to group effectiveness by making sure the task is challenging and perceived as important. Additionally, it is a good idea to hold group members personally accountable for identifiable portions of the group's task. One way to do this is with the *stepladder technique,* a group decision-making process proven effective by researchers (see Table 10–6). Compared with conventional groups, stepladder groups produced significantly better decisions in the same amount of time. "Furthermore, stepladder groups' decisions surpassed the quality of their best individual members' decisions 56% of the time. In contrast, conventional groups' decisions surpassed the quality of their best members' decisions only 13% of the time."[94] The stepladder technique could be a useful tool for organizations relying on any sort of teams, including self-managed and virtual teams (discussed in the next chapter).

Table 10–6   *How to Avoid Social Loafing in Groups and Teams: The Stepladder Technique*

The stepladder technique is intended to enhance group decision making by structuring the entry of group members into a core group. Increasing or decreasing the number of group members alters the number of steps. In a four-person group, the stepladder technique has three steps. Initially, two group members (the initial core group) work together on the problem at hand. Next, a third member joins the core group and presents his or her preliminary solutions for the same problem. The entering member's presentation is followed by a three-person discussion. Finally, the fourth group member joins the core group and presents his or her preliminary solutions. This is followed by a four-person discussion, which has as its goal the rendering of a final group decision.

The stepladder technique has four requirements. First, each group member must be given the group's task and sufficient time to think about the problem before entering the core group. Second, the entering member must present his or her preliminary solutions before hearing the core group's preliminary solutions. Third, with the entry of each additional member to the core group, sufficient time to discuss the problem is necessary. Fourth, a final decision must be purposely delayed until the group has been formed in its entirety.

SOURCE: Excerpted from S G Rogelberg, J L Barnes-Farrell, and C A Lowe, "The Stepladder Technique: An Alternative Group Structure Facilitating Effective Group Decision Making," *Journal of Applied Psychology* 77 (October 1992), p 731. Copyright © 1992 by the American Psychological Association. Reprinted with permission.

Summary of Key Concepts

1. *Identify the four sociological criteria of a group, and explain the role of equity in the Workplace Social Exchange Network (WSEN) model.* Sociologically, a *group* is defined as two or more freely interacting individuals who share collective norms and goals and have a common identity. The WSEN model identifies three levels of social exchange: employee–organization, employee–supervisor, and employee–team. Individuals judge each type of social exchange in terms of perceived equity or fairness. The greater the perceived fairness, the more loyal, motivated, and hard-working the individual will be. Lack of perceived fairness is demotivating.

2. *Describe the five stages in Tuckman's theory of group development, and discuss the threat of group decay.* The five stages in Tuckman's theory are forming (the group comes together), storming (members test the limits and each other), norming (questions about authority and power are resolved as the group becomes more cohesive), performing (effective communication and cooperation help the group get things done), and adjourning (group members go their own way). According to recent research, group decay occurs when a work group achieves the "performing" stage and then shifts into reverse. Group decay occurs through de-norming (erosion of standards), de-storming (growing discontent and loss of cohesiveness), and de-forming (fragmentation and breakup of the group).

3. *Distinguish between role conflict and role ambiguity.* Organizational roles are sets of behaviors persons expect of occupants of a position. One may experience role overload (too much to do in too little time), role conflict (conflicting role expectations), or role ambiguity (unclear role expectations).

4. *Contrast roles and norms, and specify four reasons norms are enforced in organizations.* While roles are specific to the person's position, norms are shared attitudes that differentiate appropriate from inappropriate behavior in a variety of situations. Norms evolve informally and are enforced because they help the group or organization survive, clarify behavioral expectations, help people avoid embarrassing situations, and clarify the group's or organization's central values.

5. *Distinguish between task and maintenance functions in groups.* Members of formal groups need to perform both task (goal-oriented) and maintenance (relationship-oriented) roles if anything is to be accomplished.

6. *Summarize the practical contingency management implications for group size.* Laboratory simulation studies suggest decision-making groups should be limited to five or fewer members. Larger groups are appropriate when creativity, participation, or socialization are the main objectives. If majority votes are to be taken, odd-numbered groups are recommended to avoid deadlocks.

7. *Discuss why managers need to carefully handle mixed-gender task groups.* Women face special group dynamics challenges in mixed-gender task groups. Steps need to be taken to make sure increased sexualization of work environments does not erode into illegal sexual harassment.

8. *Describe groupthink, and identify at least four of its symptoms.* Groupthink plagues cohesive in-groups that shortchange moral judgment while putting too much emphasis on unanimity. Symptoms of groupthink include invulnerability, inherent morality, rationalization, stereotyped views of opposition, self-censorship, illusion of unanimity, peer pressure, and mindguards. Critical evaluators, outside expertise, and devil's advocates are among the preventive measures recommended by Irving Janis, who coined the term *groupthink*.

9. *Define social loafing, and explain how managers can prevent it.* Social loafing involves the tendency for individual effort to decrease as group size increases. This problem can be contained if the task is challenging and important, individuals are held accountable for results, and group members expect everyone to work hard. The stepladder technique, a structured approach to group decision making, can reduce social loafing by increasing personal effort and accountability.

Discussion Questions

1. Which of the following would qualify as a sociological group? A crowd watching a baseball game? One of the baseball teams? Explain.

2. What is your opinion about employees being friends with their co-workers (overlapping formal and informal groups)?

3. What is your personal experience with groups that failed to achieve stage 4 of group development? At which stage did they stall? Why? Have you observed group decay? Explain.

4. Considering your current lifestyle, how many different roles are you playing? What sorts of role conflict and role ambiguity are you experiencing?

5. What norms do college students usually enforce in class? How are they enforced?

6. Which roles do you prefer to play in work groups: task or maintenance? How could you do a better job in this regard?

7. How would you respond to a manager who made the following statement? "When it comes to the size of work groups, the bigger the better."

8. Are women typically at a disadvantage in mixed-gender work groups? Give your rationale.

9. Have you ever been a victim of either the Asch effect or groupthink? Explain the circumstances.

10. Have you observed any social loafing recently? What were the circumstances and what could be done to correct the problem?

OB in Action Case Study

A 10-Year Retrospective of the Challenger Space Shuttle Disaster: Was It Groupthink?

A Fateful Decision

The debate over whether to launch on January 28, 1986, unfolded as follows, according to the report of the Presidential Commission on the Space Shuttle Challenger Accident:

Shortly after 1 PM ET on January 27, NASA's [the National Aeronautic and Space Administration's] booster rocket manager in Cape Canaveral, Larry Wear, asks officials of rocket maker Morton Thiokol in Utah whether cold weather on the 28th would present a problem for launch.

By 2 PM, NASA's top managers are discussing how temperatures in the 30s at the launch pad might affect the shuttle's performance. In Utah, an hour later, Thiokol engineer Roger Boisjoly learns of the forecast for the first time.

By late afternoon, midlevel NASA managers at the Cape are on the phone with Thiokol managers, who point out that the booster's rubbery O-rings, which seal in hot gases, might be affected by cold.

That concern brings in officials from NASA's Marshall Space Flight Center in Huntsville, Alabama, which buys the rockets from Thiokol and readies them for launch.

Marshall managers decide that a three-way telephone conference call is needed, linking NASA and Thiokol engineers and managers in Alabama, Florida, and Utah.

The first conference call begins about 5:45 PM, and Thiokol tells NASA it believes launch should be delayed until noon or afternoon, when the weather turns warmer. It is decided a second conference call would be needed later that evening.

Marshall deputy project manager Judson Lovingood tells shuttle projects manager Stan Reinartz at the Cape that if Thiokol persists, NASA should not launch. Top NASA managers at Marshall are told of Thiokol's concern.

At 8:45 PM, the second conference call begins, involving 34 engineers and managers from NASA and Thiokol at the three sites.

Thiokol engineers Boisjoly and Arnie Thompson present charts showing a history of leaking O-ring joints from tests and previous flights.

The data show that the O-rings perform worse at lower temperatures and that the worst leak of hot gases came in January 1985, when a shuttle launched with the temperature at 53 degrees. Thiokol managers recommend not flying Challenger at temperatures colder than that.

NASA's George Hardy says he's "appalled" at Thiokol's recommendation. Larry Mulloy, Marshall's booster rocket manager, complains that Thiokol is setting down new launch criteria and exclaims, "My God, Thiokol, when do you want me to launch, next April?"

Thiokol vice president Joe Kilminster asks for five minutes to talk in private. The debate continues for 30 minutes. Boisjoly, Thompson, engineer Bob Ebeling, and others are overruled by Thiokol management, who decide to approve the launch.

At 11 PM, Kilminster tells NASA that Thiokol has changed its mind: Temperature is still a concern but the data are inconclusive. He recommends launch.

Thiokol's concerns that cold weather could hurt the booster joints are not passed up NASA's chain of command beyond officials at the Marshall Space Flight Center.

Challenger is launched at 11:38 AM January 28 in a temperature of 36 degrees.[95]

Shortly after launch on January 28, 1986, Challenger was engulfed in a fiery explosion that led to the deaths of six astronauts and teacher-in-space Christa McAuliffe. As a shocked world watched great billows of smoke trail over the Atlantic, it was clear to those involved that launching Challenger in 36-degree weather was a catastrophic decision.[96]

Ten Years Later

Two who argued the longest and loudest against launch were Thiokol engineers Roger Boisjoly and Arnie Thompson. But their lives took widely differing paths after the accident.

Boisjoly remembers the prelaunch debate this way: "When NASA created the pressure, they all buckled."

He became nationally known as the primary whistle-blower. Thiokol removed Boisjoly from the investigation team and sent him home after he testified before a presidential commission that the company ignored evidence that the booster rocket seals would fail in cold weather.

Boisjoly, 57, says he was blackballed by the industry and run out of town by Thiokol.

For a time, he sought psychiatric help. "It just became unbearable to function," says Boisjoly, who now lives with his wife and daughter in a small mountain town in Utah. He spoke on condition that the town not be named because he fears for his family's safety.

Boisjoly is convinced he is a marked man because some former co-workers believe his testimony contributed to resulting layoffs at Thiokol.

After the accident, he says, drivers would try to run him off the road when he was out on a walk. He got threatening phone calls. Someone tried to break into his house.

"It became so uncomfortable for me that I went out and bought a .38 revolver," he says.

Now retired, Boisjoly earns $1,500 for speeches to universities and business groups. He also runs his own engineering company and teaches Sunday school in the Mormon church, something he says he never would have dreamed of doing before the accident.

Says Thompson, the other voice against launch: "There were the two of us that didn't want to fly and we were defeated. A lot of my top managers were not happy with me."

Yet, with longer ties to Thiokol than Boisjoly, Thompson was promoted to manager and stayed on through the shuttle's redesign.

He retired three years ago at the end of a 25-year-career. Now 66, he spends his time building a small office building in Brigham City, Utah.

"My attitude was, I wanted to stay on and redesign the bird and get back into the air," says Thompson. "I had a personal goal to get flying again." . . .

Thiokol's Bob Ebeling was so sure that Challenger was doomed, he asked his daughter, Leslie, then 33, to his office to watch "a super colossal disaster" unfold on live TV.

When it exploded, "I was in the middle of a prayer for the Lord to do his will and let all these things come to a happy ending and not let this happen," says Ebeling, who managed the rocket ignition system for Thiokol. "We did our level best but it wasn't good enough."

The fact that he foresaw disaster and could not stop it has tortured him since.

Ebeling, 69, says that within a week of the accident he became impotent and suffered high stress and constant headaches, problems he still has today. After 40 years of engineering experience, Thiokol "put me out to pasture on a medical" retirement, he says.

Ebeling still feels "the decision to recommend a launch was pre-ordained by others, by NASA leaning on our upper management. The deck was stacked."

One of those who overruled Ebeling and the others was Jerry Mason, the senior Thiokol manager on the conference call. He took an early retirement from Thiokol five months after the disaster, ending a 25-year career in aerospace.

"I was basically responsible for the operation the day it happened," says Mason, 69. "It was important to the company to put that behind them and get going on the recovery and it would be hard to do that with me sitting there. So I left."

In Mason's case, that meant going abruptly from corporate chieftain to unpaid volunteer. He helped set up a local economic development board and now chairs the Utah Wildlife Federation.

"I had a pretty successful career, and would liked to have gone out with the feeling that I really had done very well all the time instead of having to go out feeling I'd made a mistake at the end."

For Judson Lovingood, the loss was more personal.

Formerly one of NASA's deputy managers for the shuttle project, he wonders still if Challenger contributed to the breakup of his marriage.

"I think (Challenger) had an effect on my personal life," says Lovingood, "a long-term effect."

After the accident, he went to work for Thiokol in Huntsville and retired as director of engineering in 1993. Now remarried, he spends his time puttering in the yard of his Gurley, Alabama, home.

"Sometimes when I think about the seven people (aboard the shuttle), it's pretty painful," says Lovingood.

Besides McAuliffe, on board Challenger were commander Dick Scobee, pilot Mike Smith, and astronauts Ron McNair, Ellison Onizuka, Judy Resnik, and Greg Jarvis.

Their families settled with the government and Thiokol for more than $1.5 billion. Still, "I think people should hold us collectively responsible as a group," Lovingood says. "Every person in that meeting the night before the launch shared in the blame." . . .

Investigations of the Challenger explosion placed much of the blame on NASA's George Hardy, a senior engineering manager.

By saying he was "appalled" by Thiokol's fears of flying in cold weather, critics charged, Hardy pressured Thiokol into approving the launch.

But Hardy refuses to shoulder the blame. "If Thiokol had stuck to their position, there wasn't any way we were going to launch," he says.

Hardy left NASA four months after the accident. Now 65, he runs a small aerospace consulting company in Athens, Alabama.

Whatever else the last decade brought, many of the recollections return to that pressure-packed conference call on the eve of launch.

Questions for Discussion

1. Which task and maintenance roles in Table 10–4 should have been performed or performed better? By whom?

2. Using Figure 10–6 as a guide, which *symptoms* of groupthink are evident in this case?

3. Using Figure 10–6 as a guide, which *decision-making defects* can you identify in this case?

4. Do you think groupthink was a major contributor to the Challenger disaster? Explain.

5. All things considered, who was most to blame for the catastrophic decision to launch? Why?

Personal Awareness and Growth Exercise

Is This a Mature Work Group or Team?

Objectives

1. To increase your knowledge of group processes and dynamics.

2. To give you a tool for assessing the maturity of a work group or task team as well as a diagnostic tool for pinpointing group problems.

3. To help you become a more effective group leader or contributor.

Introduction

Group action is so common today that many of us take it for granted. But are the groups and teams to which we contribute much of our valuable time mature and hence more likely to be effective? Or do they waste our time? How can they be improved? We can and should become tough critical evaluators of group processes.

Instructions

Think of a work group or task team with which you are very familiar (preferably one you worked with in the past or are currently working with). Rate the group's maturity on each of the 20 dimensions.[97] Then add your circled responses to get your total group maturity score. The higher the score, the greater the group's maturity.

	Very False (or Never)				Very True (or Always)
1. Members are clear about group goals.	1	2	3	4	5
2. Members agree with the group's goals.	1	2	3	4	5
3. Members are clear about their roles.	1	2	3	4	5
4. Members accept their roles and status.	1	2	3	4	5
5. Role assignments match member abilities.	1	2	3	4	5
6. The leadership style matches the group's developmental level.	1	2	3	4	5
7. The group has an open communication structure in which all members participate.	1	2	3	4	5
8. The group gets, gives, and uses feedback about its effectiveness and productivity.	1	2	3	4	5
9. The group spends time planning how it will solve problems and make decisions.	1	2	3	4	5
10. Voluntary conformity is high.	1	2	3	4	5
11. The group norms encourage high performance and quality.	1	2	3	4	5
12. The group expects to be successful.	1	2	3	4	5
13. The group pays attention to the details of its work.	1	2	3	4	5
14. The group accepts coalition and subgroup formation.	1	2	3	4	5
15. Subgroups are integrated into the group as a whole.	1	2	3	4	5
16. The group is highly cohesive.	1	2	3	4	5
17. Interpersonal attraction among members is high.	1	2	3	4	5
18. Members are cooperative.	1	2	3	4	5
19. Periods of conflict are frequent but brief.	1	2	3	4	5
20. The group has effective conflict-management strategies.	1	2	3	4	5

Total score = _____

Arbitrary Norms

20–39	When in doubt, run in circles, scream and shout!
40–59	A long way to go
60–79	On the right track
80–100	Ready for group dynamics graduate school

Questions for Discussion

1. Does your evaluation help explain why the group or team was successful or not? Explain.
2. Was (or is) there anything *you* could have done (or can do) to increase the maturity of this group? Explain.
3. How will this evaluation instrument help you be a more effective group member or leader in the future?

Group Exercise

A Committee Decision

Objectives

1. To give you firsthand experience with work group dynamics through a role-playing exercise.
2. To develop your ability to evaluate group effectiveness.

Introduction

Please read the following case before going on.

THE JOHNNY ROCCO CASE[98]

Johnny has a grim personal background. He is the third child in a family of seven. He has not seen his father for several years, and his recollection is that his father used to come home drunk and beat up every member of the family; everyone ran when his father came staggering home.

His mother, according to Johnny, wasn't much better. She was irritable and unhappy, and she always predicted that Johnny would come to no good end. Yet she worked when her health allowed her to do so in order to keep the family in food and clothing. She always decried the fact that she was not able to be the kind of mother she would like to be.

Johnny quit school in the seventh grade. He had great difficulty conforming to the school routine—he misbehaved often, was truant frequently, and fought with schoolmates. On several occasions he was picked up by the police and, along with members of his group, questioned during several investigations into cases of both petty and grand larceny. The police regarded him as "probably a bad one."

The juvenile officer of the court saw in Johnny some good qualities that no one else seemed to sense. Mr O'Brien took it on himself to act as a "big brother" to Johnny. He had several long conversations with Johnny, during which he managed to penetrate to

some degree Johnny's defensive shell. He represented to Johnny the first semblance of personal interest in his life. Through Mr O'Brien's efforts, Johnny returned to school and obtained a high school diploma. Afterwards, Mr O'Brien helped him obtain a job.

Now 20, Johnny is a stockroom clerk in one of the laboratories where you are employed. On the whole Johnny's performance has been acceptable, but there have been glaring exceptions. One involved a clear act of insubordination on a fairly unimportant matter. In another, Johnny was accused, on circumstantial grounds, of destroying some expensive equipment. Though the investigation is still open, it now appears the destruction was accidental.

Johnny's supervisor wants to keep him on for at least a trial period, but he wants "outside" advice as to the best way of helping Johnny grow into greater responsibility. Of course, much depends on how Johnny behaves in the next few months. Naturally, his supervisor must follow personnel policies that are accepted in the company as a whole. It is important to note that Johnny is not an attractive young man. He is rather weak and sickly, and he shows unmistakable signs of long years of social deprivation.

A committee is formed to decide the fate of Johnny Rocco. The chairperson of the meeting is Johnny's supervisor and should begin by assigning roles to the group members. These roles [shop steward (representing the union), head of production, Johnny's co-worker, director of personnel, and social worker who helped Johnny in the past] represent points of view the chairperson believes should be included in this meeting. (Johnny is not to be included.) Two observers should also be assigned. Thus, each group will have eight members.

Instructions

After roles have been assigned, each role player should complete the personal preference part of the work sheet, ranking from 1 to 11 the alternatives according to their appropriateness from the vantage point of his or her role.

Once the individual preferences have been determined, the chairperson should call the meeting to order. The following rules govern the meeting: (1) The group must reach a consensus ranking of the alternatives; (2) the group cannot use a statistical aggregation, or majority vote, decision-making process; (3) members should stay "in character" throughout the discussion. Treat this as a committee meeting consisting of members with different backgrounds, orientation, and interests who share a problem.

After the group has completed the assignment, the observers should conduct a discussion of the group process, using the Group Effectiveness Questions here as a guide. Group members should not look at these questions until after the group task has been completed.

Group Effectiveness Questions

A. Referring to Table 10–4, what task roles were performed? By whom?

B. What maintenance roles were performed? By whom?

C. Were any important task or maintenance roles ignored? Which?

D. Was there any evidence of the Asch effect, groupthink, or social loafing? Explain.

Questions for Discussion

1. Did your committee do a good job? Explain.

2. What, if anything, should have been done differently?

3. How much similarity in rankings is there among the different groups in your class? What group dynamics apparently were responsible for any variations in rankings?

Worksheet

Personal Preference	Group Discussion	
_____	_____	Warn Johnny that at the next sign of trouble he will be fired.
_____	_____	Do nothing, as it is unclear if Johnny did anything wrong.
_____	_____	Create strict controls (dos and don'ts) for Johnny with immediate strong punishment for any misbehavior.
_____	_____	Give Johnny a great deal of warmth and personal attention and affection (overlooking his present behavior) so he can learn to depend on others.
_____	_____	Fire him. It's not worth the time and effort spent for such a low-level position.
_____	_____	Talk over the problem with Johnny in an understanding way so he can learn to ask others for help in solving his problems.
_____	_____	Give Johnny a well-structured schedule of daily activities with immediate and unpleasant consequences for not adhering to the schedule.
_____	_____	Do nothing now, but watch him carefully and provide immediate punishment for any future behavior.
_____	_____	Treat Johnny the same as everyone else, but provide an orderly routine so he can learn to stand on his own two feet.
_____	_____	Call Johnny in and logically discuss the problem with him and ask what you can do to help him.
_____	_____	Do nothing now, but watch him so you can reward him the next time he does something good.

Do Things My Way, or Hit the Highway!

Dr. Kerry J Sulkowicz, a psychiatrist, psychoanalyst, and author of *Fast Company* magazine's "The Corporate Shrink" column, recently fielded this question:

I'm a lawyer, and I have just joined my first corporate board. The chairman, a client of mine, runs meetings as if only his ideas matter; he seems more interested in impressing us rather than in using our counsel. How do I handle this?[99]

What course of action would you recommend?

1. You're too new to "rock the boat." Be quiet and observe the group dynamics of the board until you *really* understand what is going on.

2. Quit the board before you get involved in a bad situation.

3. There is no ethical issue here until an unethical decision is made. Only then will it be time to do something. Do what?

4. The chairman needs to learn something about trust. What would you tell him (or have an influential board member tell him)?

5. This creates a climate for groupthink. Preventive steps should be taken *now*. What steps?

6. Invent other interpretations or options. Discuss.

For the Chapter 10 Internet Exercise featuring social skills and communication self-assessments (www.queendom. com), visit our Web site at **www.mhhe.com/kreitner.**

11

Teams and Teamwork

Learning Objectives

When you finish studying the material in this chapter, you should be able to:

1   Explain how a work group becomes a team.

2   Identify and describe four types of work teams.

3   Explain the model of effective work teams, and specify the two criteria of team effectiveness.

4   Identify five teamwork competencies team members need to possess.

5   Discuss why teams fail.

6   List at least four things managers can do to build trust.

7   Distinguish two types of group cohesiveness, and summarize cohesiveness research findings.

8   Define quality circles, virtual teams, and self-managed teams.

9   Describe high-performance teams.

In Early 2002, the Lally School of Management & Technology at Rensselaer Polytechnic Institute was in a rut. The program was lost in the shadows of bigger, more recognized schools, and enrollment was declining. The bucolic campus had its charms, but being a stone's throw from Albany, in Troy, New York, just didn't have the draw of a big city like New York or Boston. It was time for a change.

That's when administrators at Rensselaer decided to tear apart the traditional MBA curriculum. In its place they began building a new program from scratch—and when the dust settled, what emerged last year was an MBA unlike any other. Rather than relying on conventional texts and case studies in standard courses like marketing and finance, educators, led by Iftekhar Hasan, Rensselaer's acting dean, designed a brand-new program teaming up professors to teach together and guide students through real-world business problems in a holistic way. "This is not your father's MBA," Hasan says.

For starters, the degree is broken down into five "streams of knowledge," rather than traditional majors or concentrations. Each stream delves into a different aspect of business, such as Creating & Managing an Enterprise, and Networks, Innovation & Value Creation. It's not that students don't learn economics, marketing, or strategy. Instead, each of those basics is blended into the larger concepts. A typical class might involve a discussion, led by a finance professor, of a company's change in value after a corporate merger, followed by a look at the case by a management prof from an operations point of view. . . .

To an outsider, a Rensselaer classroom might seem chaotic, with constant discussions and passionate opinions. In the Business Implications of Emerging Technologies stream, for example, students are divided into teams of four, each developing plans for patents on products dreamed up in RPI's Office of Technology Commercialization on another part of campus. The 30-odd students are scattered across the room, huddled around laptops and notebooks. The three professors who make up the

Team teaching and topical integration are central to Rensselaer Polytechnic Institute's recently reorganized MBA curriculum.

teaching team—biology, marketing, and sociology profs in this case—wander around to each group.

It might seem an odd mix, but listen in for a while, and it all comes together. The marketer talks about breakthrough innovation. The biologist covers national policy and the science side of the students' projects. Then the sociologist leads a discussion on consumer trends. Student teams are left to process the information and draw up the best proposals. "The students are getting the functional material, but they're also understanding how that function operates," says Richard Leifer, associate professor and director of executive programs. "When they leave here, they know how to do project management because they've been through it, it's not just something they've heard about." Each stream follows a similar format. . . .

The highly integrated approach requires a lot of cooperation, particularly among professors, who are far more used to competing with each other for status and resources. "Faculty members . . . typically don't play well together," Leifer says. But Rensselaer's professors have to check egos at the door to plan out courses from various points of view so the cross-pollination succeeds. "In working together, we have learned a lot about compromise," [strategy professor Phillip H] Phan says.[1]

FOR DISCUSSION
Will this team approach work? Explain.

Teams and *teamwork* are popular terms in management circles these days. The teamwork movement is even invading the college classroom, as detailed in the opening vignette. Organizational success is increasingly tied to all sorts of teams—and how effectively they perform. Just ask Annette Verschuren, the president of Home Depot Canada, who was a standout basketball player while growing up in Nova Scotia, Canada:

Business is fun—it's a game. I feel like a high-school basketball player. The question is how to get the ball where it needs to be. . . .

Creating the vision, the alignment of the team, developing the plan with that team, and coaching them and motivating them, is what it is all about. And be positive—it's infectious. People are looking for inspiration.[2]

Put us in, we're ready to play! Indeed, the trend toward teams has a receptive audience today. Both women and younger employees, according to recent studies, thrive in team-oriented organizations.[3]

Emphasis in this chapter is on tapping the full and promising potential of work groups and teams. We will (1) identify different types of work teams, (2) look at what makes teams succeed or fail, (3) examine keys to effective teamwork, such as trust, (4) explore modern applications of the team concept, including virtual teams, and (5) discuss team building.

Work Teams: Types, Effectiveness, and Stumbling Blocks

Team

Small group with complementary skills who hold themselves mutually accountable for common purpose, goals, and approach.

Jon R Katzenbach and Douglas K Smith, management consultants at McKinsey & Company, say it is a mistake to use the terms *group* and *team* interchangeably. After studying many different kinds of teams—from athletic to corporate to military—they concluded that successful teams tend to take on a life of their own. Katzenbach and Smith define a **team** as "a small number of people with complementary skills who are committed to a common purpose, performance goals, and approach for which they hold themselves mutually accountable."[4] Relative to Tuckman's theory of group development in Chapter 10—forming,

Table 11–1   *The Evolution of a Team*

A work group becomes a team when
1. *Leadership* becomes a shared activity.
2. *Accountability* shifts from strictly individual to both individual and collective.
3. The group develops its own *purpose* or mission.
4. *Problem solving* becomes a way of life, not a part-time activity.
5. *Effectiveness* is measured by the group's collective outcomes and products.

SOURCE: Condensed and adapted from J R Katzenbach and D K Smith, *The Wisdom of Teams: Creating the High-Performance Organization* (New York: HarperBusiness, 1999), p 214.

storming, norming, performing, and adjourning—teams are task groups that have matured to the *performing* stage (but not slipped into decay). Because of conflicts over power and authority and unstable interpersonal relations, many work groups never qualify as a real team.[5] Katzenbach and Smith clarified the distinction this way: "The essence of a team is common commitment. Without it, groups perform as individuals; with it, they become a powerful unit of collective performance."[6] (See Table 11–1.)

When Katzenbach and Smith refer to "a small number of people" in their definition, they mean between 2 and 25 team members. They found effective teams to typically have fewer than 10 members. This conclusion was echoed in a survey of 400 workplace team members in the United States and Canada: "The average North American team consists of 10 members. Eight is the most common size."[7]

A General Typology of Work Teams

Work teams are created for various purposes and thus face different challenges. Managers can deal more effectively with those challenges when they understand how teams differ. A helpful way of sorting things out is to consider a typology of work teams developed by Eric Sundstrom and his colleagues.[8] Four general types of work teams listed in Table 11–2 are (1) advice, (2) production, (3) project, and (4) action. Each of these labels identifies a basic *purpose*. For instance, advice teams generally make recommendations for managerial decisions. Less commonly do they actually make final decisions. In contrast, production and action teams carry out management's decisions.

Four key variables in Table 11–2 deal with technical specialization, coordination, work cycles, and outputs. Technical specialization is low when the team draws upon members' general experience and problem-solving ability. It is high when team members are required to apply technical skills acquired through higher education or extensive training. The degree of coordination with other work units is determined by the team's relative independence (low coordination) or interdependence (high coordination). Work cycles are the amount of time teams need to discharge their missions. The various outputs listed in Table 11–2 are intended to illustrate real-life impacts. A closer look at each type of work team is in order.[9]

Advice Teams   As their name implies, advice teams are created to broaden the information base for managerial decisions. Quality circles, discussed later, are a prime example because they facilitate suggestions for quality improvement from volunteer

Table 11–2   *Four General Types of Work Teams and Their Outputs*

Types and Examples	Degree of Technical Specialization	Degree of Coordination with Other Work Units	Work Cycles	Typical Outputs
Advice Committees Review panels, boards Quality circles Employee involvement groups Advisory councils	Low	Low	Work cycles can be brief or long; one cycle can be team life span.	Decisions Selections Suggestions Proposals Recommendations
Production Assembly teams Manufacturing crews Mining teams Flight attendant crews Data processing groups Maintenance crews	Low	High	Work cycles typically repeated or continuous process; cycles often briefer than team life span.	Food, chemicals Components Assemblies Retail sales Customer service Equipment repairs
Project Research groups Planning teams Architect teams Engineering teams Development teams Task forces	High	Low (for traditional units) or High (for cross-functional units)	Work cycles typically differ for each new project; one cycle can be team life span.	Plans, designs Investigations Presentations Prototypes Reports, findings
Action Sports teams Entertainment groups Expeditions Negotiating teams Surgery teams Cockpit crews Military platoons and squads Police and fire teams	High	High	Brief performance events, often repeated under new conditions, requiring extended training or preparation.	Combat missions Expeditions Contracts, lawsuits Concerts Surgical operations Competitive events Disaster assistance

SOURCE: Excerpted and adapted from E Sundstrom, K P De Meuse, and D Futrell, "Work Teams," *American Psychologist*, February 1990, p 125. Copyright © 1990 by the American Psychological Association. Reprinted with permission.

production or service workers. Advice teams tend to have a low degree of technical specialization. Coordination also is low because advice teams work pretty much on their own. Ad hoc committees (e.g., the annual picnic committee) have shorter life cycles than standing committees (e.g., the grievance committee).

Production Teams   This second type of team is responsible for performing day-to-day operations. Minimal training for routine tasks accounts for the low degree of technical specialization. But coordination typically is high because work flows from one team to another. For example, railroad maintenance crews require fresh information about needed repairs from train crews, and the train crews, in turn, need to know exactly where maintenance crews are working.

Toss Your Egos Overboard

Dan Lyons, management consultant, Olympian, and 11-time US rowing champion:

Q: Doesn't the winner boil down to the boat with the strongest individual rowers?

A: The race is 2,000 meters, and a lot of crews will be in it for the first half. But an experienced eye will see that they are straining, spending way too much energy. Then there will be a huge opening the last 500 meters. In rowing, as in business, everybody has their own agenda. Some want to pull really hard at the beginning of the stroke, others at the end. The coach's job is to get everyone to apply power at the same time. In business, sports and politics, getting everyone to apply power evenly is really about controlling egos. It's getting everyone to sublimate their own agendas for the company's agenda so that energy is not wasted. For example, there's always dynamic tension between R&D, sales and production because they make different promises to different people.

SOURCE: As quoted in D Jones, "Rowing Teaches Teamwork Lessons," *USA Today,* August 16, 2004, p 3B.

Men's eight, or cox eight, is one of the most grueling and exacting team sports. Trust is essential because the eight rowers who are striving for maximum rhythmic effort can't even see where they're going! It's the job of the coxswain (cox) to call out the rowing cadence and steer the racing shell. A single rower who tries to outdo the others will cause the entire cooperative effort to collapse and fail.

Project Teams Projects require creative problem solving, often involving the application of specialized knowledge. For example, Boeing's 777 jumbo jet was designed by project teams consisting of engineering, manufacturing, marketing, finance, and customer service specialists. State-of-the-art computer modeling programs allowed the teams to assemble three-dimensional computer models of the new aircraft. Design and assembly problems were ironed out in project team meetings before production workers started cutting any metal for the first 777. Boeing's 777 design teams required a high degree of coordination among organizational subunits because they were cross functional.[10] A pharmaceutical research team of biochemists, on the other hand, would interact less with other work units because it is relatively self-contained. Also, project teams can be a useful tool for training and management development programs.

Action Teams This last type of team is best exemplified by a baseball team. High specialization is combined with high coordination. Nine highly trained athletes play specialized defensive positions. But good defensive play is not enough because effective hitting is necessary. Moreover, coordination between the manager, base runners, base coaches, and the bull pen needs to be precise. So it is with airline cockpit crews, firefighters, hospital surgery teams, mountain-climbing expeditions, rock music groups, labor contract negotiating teams, and police SWAT teams, among others. A unique challenge for action teams is to exhibit peak performance on demand[11] (see Real World/Real People).

This four-way typology of work teams is dynamic and changing, not static. Some teams evolve from one type to another. Other teams represent a combination of types. For example, consider the work of a team at General Foods: "The company launched a line of ready-to-eat desserts by setting up a team of nine people with the freedom to operate like entrepreneurs starting their own business. The team even had to oversee construction of a factory with the technology required to manufacture their product."[12] This particular team was a combination advice-project-action team. In short, the General Foods team did everything but manufacture the end product themselves (that was done by production teams).

Effective Work Teams

Team viability
Team members satisfied and willing to contribute.

The effectiveness of athletic teams is a straightforward matter of wins and losses. Things become more complicated, however, when the focus shifts to work teams in today's organizations.[13] Figure 11–1 lists two effectiveness criteria for work teams: performance and viability. Conceptually, the first one is simple: Did the team get the job done? The second criterion is more subtle and easily ignored or overlooked, to the longer-term detriment of the organization. **Team viability** is defined as team members' satisfaction and continued willingness to contribute. Are the team members better or worse off for having contributed to the team effort?[14] A work team is not truly effective if it gets the job done but self-destructs in the process and burns everyone out.

Also, as indicated in Figure 11–1, work teams require a team-friendly organization if they are to be effective. Work teams need a support system. They have a much greater chance of success if they are nurtured and facilitated by the organization. The team's purpose needs to be in concert with the organization's strategy. Similarly, team participation and autonomy require an organizational culture that values those processes. A good role model is Linda Hunt, president of St. Joseph's Hospital and Medical Center in Phoenix, Arizona. She recently noted,

Figure 11–1 *Effective Work Teams*

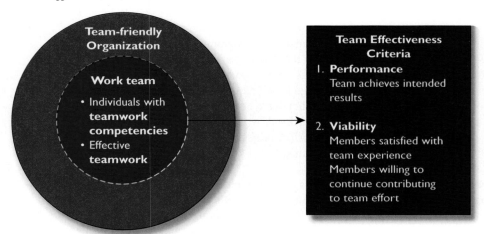

SOURCES: Adapted in part from E Sundstrom, K P DeMeuse, and D Futrell, "Work Teams," *American Psychologist,* February 1990, pp 120–33; and C A Beatty and B A Barker Scott, *Building Smart Teams: A Roadmap to High Performance* (Thousand Oaks, CA: Sage, 2004), pp 5–8.

We live the model of collaboration. We promote it in our centers of excellence and in our teaching programs, and we incorporate teams into quality care wherever possible.[15]

Team members also need appropriate technological tools, *reasonable* schedules, and training. Teamwork needs to be rewarded by the organizational reward system. Such is not the case when pay and bonuses are tied solely to individual output. For a positive example, consider what has taken place at Internet equipment maker Cisco Systems:

[CEO John] Chambers took . . . steps to rein in Cisco's Wild West culture during 2002. Most pointedly, he made teamwork a critical part of top execs' bonus plans. He told them 30% of their bonuses for the 2003 fiscal year would depend on how well they collaborated with others. "It tends to formalize the discussion around how can I help you and how can you help me," says Sue Bostrom, head of Cisco's Internet consulting group.[16]

Contributors Need Teamwork Competencies Forming workplace teams and urging employees to be good team players are good starting points on the road to effective teams.[17] But much more is needed today. Jeff Zucker, president of NBC Universal Television Group, recently framed the issue this way:

My biggest challenge is getting the new team to maximize our potential and combine together into one culture. We have a bunch of people with strong personalities who are extremely good at what they do. I want them to feel they are the best, and yet have us work together as a team.[18]

In short, Zucker has a leadership group that has not yet melded into a true team, as defined earlier. He would do well to make sure his people possess the teamwork competencies in Table 11–3. Teamwork skills and competencies need to be role modeled and taught. Notice in Table 11–3 the importance of group problem solving, mentoring, and conflict management skills.

What Does Effective Teamwork Involve?

Unfortunately, the terms *team* and *teamwork* are tossed around rather casually today. Many work groups are called teams when they are far from it. Real teamwork requires a concerted collective effort (see Table 11–4 on p 347). It requires lots of tolerance, practice, and trial-and-error learning. Using Table 11–4 as a guide, have you ever personally experienced real teamwork?

This Starbucks ad for employee reward gift cards subtly plugs the importance of teamwork and team competencies. For many of us, a fruitful team effort is a big reward in itself.

Why Do Work Teams Fail?

Advocates of the team approach to management paint a very optimistic and bright picture. Yet there is a dark side to teams.[19] While exact statistics are not available, they can and often do fail. Anyone contemplating the use of team structures in the workplace needs a balanced perspective of advantages and limitations.

Table 11–3   *How Strong Are Your Teamwork Competencies?*

Orients Team to Problem-Solving Situation
Assists the team in arriving at a common understanding of the situation or problem.
Determines the important elements of a problem situation. Seeks out relevant data related to
the situation or problem.

Organizes and Manages Team Performance
Helps team establish specific, challenging, and accepted team goals. Monitors, evaluates, and
provides feedback on team performance. Identifies alternative strategies or reallocates
resources to address feedback on team performance.

Promotes a Positive Team Environment
Assists in creating and reinforcing norms of tolerance, respect, and excellence. Recognizes and
praises other team members' efforts. Helps and supports other team members. Models
desirable team member behavior.

Facilitates and Manages Task Conflict
Encourages desirable and discourages undesirable team conflict. Recognizes the type and
source of conflict confronting the team and implements an appropriate resolution strategy.
Employs "win–win" negotiation strategies to resolve team conflicts.

Appropriately Promotes Perspective
Defends stated preferences, argues for a particular point of view, and withstands pressure to
change position for another that is not supported by logical or knowledge-based arguments.
Changes or modifies position if a defensible argument is made by another team member.
Projects courtesy and friendliness to others while arguing position.

SOURCE: G Chen, L M Donahue, and R I Klimoski, "Training Undergraduates to Work in Organizational
Teams," *Academy of Management Learning and Education,* March 2004, App. A, p 40. Copyright © 2004 by
The Academy of Management. Reproduced by permission of The Academy of Management via The
Copyright Clearance Center.

Common Management Mistakes with Teams

The main threats to team effectiveness, according to the center of Figure 11–2 on p 348, are *unrealistic expectations* leading to *frustration*. Frustration, in turn, encourages people to abandon teams. Both managers and team members can be victimized by unrealistic expectations.

On the left side of Figure 11–2 is a list of common management mistakes. These mistakes generally involve doing a poor job of creating a supportive environment for teams and teamwork.

Problems for Team Members

The lower-right portion of Figure 11–2 lists common problems for team members. Contrary to critics' Theory X contention about employees lacking the motivation and creativity for real teamwork, it is common for teams to take on too much too quickly and to drive themselves too hard for fast results. Important group dynamics and team skills get lost in the rush for results. Consequently, team members' expectations need to be given a reality check by management and team members themselves. Also, teams need to be counseled against quitting when they run into an unanticipated obstacle. Failure is part of the learning process with teams, as it is elsewhere in life. Comprehensive training in interpersonal skills can prevent many common teamwork problems.

Table 11–4   *Characteristics of Effective Teamwork*

1. Clear purpose	The vision, mission, goal, or task of the team has been defined and is now accepted by everyone. There is an action plan.
2. Informality	The climate tends to be informal, comfortable, and relaxed. There are no obvious tensions or signs of boredom.
3. Participation	There is much discussion, and everyone is encouraged to participate.
4. Listening	The members use effective listening techniques such as questioning, paraphrasing, and summarizing to get out ideas.
5. Civilized disagreement	There is disagreement, but the team is comfortable with this and shows no signs of avoiding, smoothing over, or suppressing conflict.
6. Consensus decisions	For important decisions, the goal is substantial but not necessarily unanimous agreement through open discussion of everyone's ideas, avoidance of formal voting, or easy compromises.
7. Open communication	Team members feel free to express their feelings on the tasks as well as on the group's operation. There are few hidden agendas. Communication takes place outside of meetings.
8. Clear roles and work assignments	There are clear expectations about the roles played by each team member. When action is taken, clear assignments are made, accepted, and carried out. Work is fairly distributed among team members.
9. Shared leadership	While the team has a formal leader, leadership functions shift from time to time depending on the circumstances, the needs of the group, and the skills of the members. The formal leader models the appropriate behavior and helps establish positive norms.
10. External relations	The team spends time developing key outside relationships, mobilizing resources, and building credibility with important players in other parts of the organization.
11. Style diversity	The team has a broad spectrum of team-player types including members who emphasize attention to task, goal setting, focus on process, and questions about how the team is functioning.
12. Self-assessment	Periodically, the team stops to examine how well it is functioning and what may be interfering with its effectiveness.

SOURCE: G M Parker, *Team Players and Teamwork: The New Competitive Business Strategy* (San Francisco: Jossey-Bass, 1990), table 2, p 33. Copyright © 1990 Jossey-Bass Inc. Reprinted with permission of John Wiley & Sons, Inc.

Effective Teamwork through Cooperation, Trust, and Cohesiveness

As competitive pressures intensify, experts say organizational success increasingly will depend on teamwork rather than individual stars. No where is this more true than in hospitals. Imagine yourself or a loved one being in this terrible situation:

> A 67-year-old woman was admitted to the hospital for treatment of cerebral aneurysms—weakened blood vessels in the brain. Doctors examined her and sent her to her room.
>
> The next day, she was wheeled into cardiology, of all places, where a doctor had threaded a catheter into her heart before someone noticed he had the wrong patient. The procedure was stopped; the patient recovered.[20]

Analysis of this case by researchers revealed the need for better communication and teamwork.

Figure 11–2   *Why Work Teams Fail*

Mistakes typically made by management

- Teams cannot overcome weak strategies and poor business practices.
- Hostile environment for teams (command-and-control culture; competitive/individual reward plans; management resistance).
- Teams adopted as a fad, a quick-fix; no long-term commitment.
- Lessons from one team not transferred to others (limited experimentation with teams).
- Vague or conflicting team assignments.
- Inadequate team skills training.
- Poor staffing of teams.
- Lack of trust.

Unrealistic expectations resulting in frustration

Problems typically experienced by team members

- Team tries to do too much too soon.
- Conflict over differences in personal work styles (and/or personality conflicts).
- Too much emphasis on results, not enough on team processes and group dynamics.
- Unanticipated obstacle causes team to give up.
- Resistance to doing things differently.
- Poor interpersonal skills (aggressive rather than assertive communication, destructive conflict, win-lose negotiation).
- Poor interpersonal chemistry (loners, dominators, self-appointed experts do not fit in).
- Lack of trust.

SOURCES: Adapted from discussion in S R Rayner, "Team Traps: What They Are, How to Avoid Them," *National Productivity Review,* Summer 1996, pp 101–15; L Holpp and R Phillips, "When Is a Team Its Own Worst Enemy?" *Training,* September 1995, pp 71–82; B Richardson, "Why Work Teams Flop—and What Can Be Done about It," *National Productivity Review,* Winter 1994/95, pp 9–13; and C O Longenecker and M Neubert, "Barriers and Gateways to Management Cooperation and Teamwork," *Business Horizons,* September–October 2000, pp 37–44.

Whether in hospitals or the world of business, three components of teamwork receiving the greatest attention are cooperation, trust, and cohesiveness. Let us explore the contributions each can make to effective teamwork.

Cooperation

Individuals are said to be cooperating when their efforts are systematically *integrated* to achieve a collective objective.[21] The greater the integration, the greater the degree of cooperation.

Cooperation versus Competition

A widely held assumption among American managers is that "competition brings out the best in people." From an economic standpoint, business survival depends on staying ahead of the competition. But from an interpersonal standpoint, critics contend competition has been overemphasized, primarily at the expense of cooperation.[22] According to Alfie Kohn, a strong advocate of greater emphasis on cooperation in our classrooms, offices, and factories,

> My review of the evidence has convinced me that there are two ... important reasons for competition's failure. First, success often depends on sharing resources efficiently, and this is nearly impossible when people have to work against one another. Cooperation takes advantage of all the skills represented in a group as well as the mysterious process by which that group becomes more than the sum of its parts. By contrast, competition makes people suspicious and hostile toward one another and actively discourages this process. ...
>
> Second, competition generally does not promote excellence because trying to do well and trying to beat others simply are two different things. Consider a child in class, waving his arm wildly to attract the teacher's attention, crying, "Oooh! Oooh! Pick me!" When he is finally recognized, he seems befuddled. "Um, what was the question again?" he finally asks. His mind is focused on beating his classmates, not on the subject matter.[23]

Research Support for Cooperation

After conducting a meta-analysis of 122 studies encompassing a wide variety of subjects and settings, one team of researchers concluded that

1. Cooperation is superior to competition in promoting achievement and productivity.

2. Cooperation is superior to individualistic efforts in promoting achievement and productivity.

3. Cooperation without intergroup competition promotes higher achievement and productivity than cooperation with intergroup competition.[24]

Given the size and diversity of the research base, these findings strongly endorse cooperation in modern organizations. Cooperation can be encouraged by reward systems that reinforce teamwork, along with individual achievement.

Interestingly, cooperation can be encouraged by quite literally tearing down walls, or not building them in the first place. A recent study of 229 managers and professionals employed by eight small businesses proved insightful:

> The researchers looked at the effects of private offices, shared private offices, cubicles, and team-oriented open offices on productivity, and found to their initial surprise that the small team, open-office configuration (desks scattered about in a small area with no partitions) to be significantly correlated with superior performance. In addition, they found

Farcus

by David Waisglass
Gordon Coulthart

WAISGLASS/COULTHART

© 1995 Farcus Cartoons

www.farcus.com

that the open-office configuration was particularly favored by the youngest employees, who believe open offices provide them greater access to colleagues and the opportunity to learn from their more seasoned senior compatriots.[25]

There is a movement among architects and urban planners to design and build structures that encourage spontaneous interaction, cooperation, and teamwork.[26] Sorry about that private corner office you might have had in mind!

A study involving 84 male US Air Force trainees uncovered an encouraging link between cooperation and favorable race relations. After observing the subjects interact in three-man teams during a management game, the researchers concluded: "[Helpful] teammates, both black and white, attract greater respect and liking than do teammates who have not helped. This is particularly true when the helping occurs voluntarily."[27] These findings suggest that managers can enhance equal employment opportunity and diversity programs by encouraging *voluntary* helping behavior in interracial work teams. Accordingly, it is reasonable to conclude that voluntary helping behavior could build cooperation in mixed-gender teams and groups as well.

Another study involving 72 health care professionals in a US Veterans Affairs Medical Center found a negative correlation between cooperation and team size. In other words, cooperation diminished as the health care team became larger.[28] Managers thus need to restrict the size of work teams if they desire to facilitate cooperation.

Trust

These have not been good times for trust in the corporate world. Years of mergers, downsizings, layoffs, bloated executive bonuses, corporate scandals, and broken promises have left many people justly cynical about trusting what management says and does.[29] In fact, an international survey in 2005 found only 25% of Americans saying information from CEOs is credible. Figures for other regions and countries were Europe, 21%; Japan, 29%; China, 43%; and Brazil, 57%.[30] Those who might be tempted to say "So what?" to these findings need to consider the results of another recent survey: "In a study of 500 business professionals, conducted by MasterWorks, Annandale, Virginia, 95% said the main factor in deciding to stay or leave their job was whether they had a trusting relationship with their manager."[31] Clearly, remedial action is needed to close the huge trust gap.

In this section, we examine the concept of trust and introduce six practical guidelines for building trust.

Trust
Reciprocal faith in others' intentions and behavior.

Reciprocal Faith and a Cognitive Leap

Trust is defined as reciprocal faith in others' intentions and behavior.[32] Experts on the subject explain the reciprocal (give-and-take) aspect of trust as follows:

> When we see others acting in ways that imply that they trust us, we become more disposed to reciprocate by trusting in them more. Conversely, we come to distrust those whose actions appear to violate our trust or to distrust us.[33]

In short, we tend to give what we get: trust begets trust; distrust begets distrust (see Real World/Real People).

Propensity to trust
A personality trait involving one's general willingness to trust others.

A newer model of organizational trust includes a personality trait called **propensity to trust.** The developers of the model explain:

> Propensity might be thought of as the *general willingness to trust others.* Propensity will influence how much trust one has for a trustee prior to data on that particular party being available. People with different developmental experiences, personality types, and

Trust Is Everything for the "Bun Lady"

Ever heard of a high-speed bakery? Neither had we, until we met Cordia Harrington, the self-proclaimed "Bun Lady" and CEO and president of the Tennessee Bun Co....

She began construction in July 1996 on what became the most automated, fastest bakery in the world. Her facility in Dickson, Tennessee, churns out a whopping 60,000 buns an hour.

It took four years and 30 interviews before Harrington persuaded McDonald's to trust her bakery, but today,

McDonald's is her biggest client. TBC supplies hamburger buns and English muffins to about 600 McDonald's restaurants in the southeastern United States and about 20 in the Caribbean. "This relationship is very sacred," says Harrington. "We have no contract, we have a handshake. It's important that my handshake is worthy of their trust."

SOURCE: Excerpted from A Sarma, "Cordia Harrington: The Bun Lady," *Fast Company*, May 2005, p 76.

cultural backgrounds vary in their propensity to trust.... An example of an extreme case of this is what is commonly called blind trust. Some individuals can be observed to repeatedly trust in situations that most people would agree do not warrant trust. Conversely, others are unwilling to trust in most situations, regardless of circumstances that would support doing so.[34]

What is your propensity to trust? How did you develop that personality trait? (See the trust questionnaire in the Personal Awareness and Growth Exercise at the end of this chapter.)

Trust involves "a cognitive 'leap' beyond the expectations that reason and experience alone would warrant"[35] (see Figure 11–3). For example, suppose a member of a newly formed class project team works hard, based on the assumption that her teammates also are working hard. That assumption, on which her trust is based, is a cognitive leap that goes beyond her actual experience with her teammates. When you trust someone, you have *faith* in their good intentions. The act of trusting someone, however, carries with it the inherent risk of betrayal.[36] Progressive managers believe that the benefits of interpersonal trust far outweigh any risks of betrayed trust. For example, Michael Powell, who founded the chain of bookstores bearing his name more than 25 years ago, built his business around the principles of open-book management, empowerment, and trust. Powell's propensity to trust was sorely tested when one of his employees stole more than $60,000 in a used-book purchasing

Figure 11–3 *Interpersonal Trust Involves a Cognitive Leap*

351

scheme. After putting in some accounting safeguards, Powell's propensity to trust remains intact. He observed,

> The incident was a watershed for me and my staff, dispelling any naïveté we may have had about crime. We realized that not only *can* theft happen; it *will* happen. At the same time, dealing with the matter forced us to revisit our basic values and managerial philosophies. We believe that the modern demands of business call for an empowered and fully flexible staff, and we know that such a staff will often have to handle valuable commodities and money. We also believe that most people are not going to abuse our trust if they are put in a position with a reasonable amount of review and responsibility.[37]

How to Build Trust   Management professor/consultant Fernando Bartolomé offers the following six guidelines for building and maintaining trust:

1. *Communication.* Keep team members and employees informed by explaining policies and decisions and providing accurate feedback. Be candid about one's own problems and limitations. Tell the truth.[38]

2. *Support.* Be available and approachable. Provide help, advice, coaching, and support for team members' ideas.

3. *Respect.* Delegation, in the form of real decision-making authority, is the most important expression of managerial respect. Actively listening to the ideas of others is a close second. (Empowerment is not possible without trust.)[39]

4. *Fairness.* Be quick to give credit and recognition to those who deserve it. Make sure all performance appraisals and evaluations are objective and impartial.

5. *Predictability.* As mentioned previously, be consistent and predictable in your daily affairs. Keep both expressed and implied promises.

6. *Competence.* Enhance your credibility by demonstrating good business sense, technical ability, and professionalism.[40]

Trust needs to be earned; it cannot be demanded.

Cohesiveness

Cohesiveness
A sense of "we-ness" helps group stick together.

Socio-emotional cohesiveness
Sense of togetherness based on emotional satisfaction.

Instrumental cohesiveness
Sense of togetherness based on mutual dependency needed to get the job done.

Cohesiveness is a process whereby "a sense of 'we-ness' emerges to transcend individual differences and motives."[41] Members of a cohesive group stick together. They are reluctant to leave the group. Cohesive group members stick together for one or both of the following reasons: (1) because they enjoy each others' company or (2) because they need each other to accomplish a common goal. Accordingly, two types of group cohesiveness, identified by sociologists, are socio-emotional cohesiveness and instrumental cohesiveness.[42]

Socio-Emotional and Instrumental Cohesiveness   **Socio-emotional cohesiveness** is a sense of togetherness that develops when individuals derive emotional satisfaction from group participation. Most general discussions of group cohesiveness are limited to this type. However, from the standpoint of getting things accomplished in task groups and teams, we cannot afford to ignore instrumental cohesiveness. **Instrumental cohesiveness** is a sense of togetherness that develops when group members are mutually dependent on one another because they believe they could not achieve the group's goal by acting separately. A feeling of "we-ness" is *instrumental* in achieving the common goal. Team advocates generally assume both types of cohesiveness are essential to productive teamwork. But is this really true?

Lessons from Group Cohesiveness Research

What is the connection between group cohesiveness and performance? A landmark meta-analysis of 49 studies involving 8,702 subjects provided these insights:

- There is a small but statistically significant cohesiveness→ performance effect.

- The cohesiveness→performance effect was stronger for smaller and real groups (as opposed to contrived groups in laboratory studies).

- The cohesiveness→performance effect becomes stronger as one moves from nonmilitary real groups to military groups to sports teams.

Sergey Brin (left) and Larry Page have a lot to smile about these days. The Moscow and Michigan natives teamed up while pursuing graduate degrees at Stanford University and founded Google in 1998. Who says teamwork doesn't pay? Can you say "billionaire"?

- Commitment to the task at hand (meaning the individual sees the performance standards as legitimate) has the most powerful impact on the cohesiveness→performance linkage.

- The *performance→cohesiveness* linkage is stronger than the cohesiveness→ performance linkage. Thus, success tends to bind group or team members together rather than closely knit groups being more successful.

- Contrary to the popular view, cohesiveness is not "a 'lubricant' that minimizes friction due to the human 'grit' in the system."[43]

- All this evidence led the researchers to this practical conclusion: "Efforts to enhance group performance by fostering interpersonal attraction or 'pumping up' group pride are not likely to be effective."[44]

A second meta-analysis found no significant relationship between cohesiveness and the quality of group decisions. However, support was found for Janis's contention that *groupthink* tends to afflict cohesive in-groups with strong leadership. Groups whose members liked each other a great deal tended to make poorer quality decisions.[45]

Getting Some Positive Impact from Group Cohesiveness

Research tells us that group cohesiveness is no secret weapon in the quest for improved group or team performance. The trick is to keep task groups small, make sure performance standards and goals are clear and accepted, achieve some early successes, and follow the tips in Table 11–5. A good example is Westinghouse's highly automated military radar electronics plant in College Station, Texas. Compared with their counterparts at a traditional factory in Baltimore, each of the Texas plant's 500 employees produces eight times more, at half the per-unit cost:

> The key, says Westinghouse, is not the robots but the people. Employees work in teams of 8 to 12. Members devise their own solutions to problems. Teams measure daily how each person's performance compares with that of other members and how the team's performance compares with the plant's. Joseph L Johnson, 28, a robotics technician, says that is a big change from a previous hourly factory job where he cared only about "picking up my paycheck." Here, peer pressure "makes sure you get the job done."[46]

Table 11–5   *Steps Managers Can Take to Enhance the Two Types of Group Cohesiveness*

Socio-Emotional Cohesiveness
Keep the group relatively small.
Strive for a favorable public image to increase the status and prestige of belonging.
Encourage interaction and cooperation.
Emphasize members' common characteristics and interests.
Point out environmental threats (e.g., competitors' achievements) to rally the group.

Instrumental Cohesiveness
Regularly update and clarify the group's goal(s).
Give every group member a vital "piece of the action."
Channel each group member's special talents toward the common goal(s).
Recognize and equitably reinforce every member's contributions.
Frequently remind group members they need each other to get the job done.

Self-selected work teams (in which people pick their own teammates) and off-the-job social events can stimulate socio-emotional cohesiveness.[47] The fostering of socio-emotional cohesiveness needs to be balanced with instrumental cohesiveness. The latter can be encouraged by making sure everyone in the group recognizes and appreciates each member's vital contribution to the group goal. While balancing the two types of cohesiveness, managers need to remember that groupthink theory and research cautions against too much cohesiveness.

Teams in Action: Quality Circles, Virtual Teams, and Self-Managed Teams

All sorts of interesting approaches to teams and teamwork can be found in the workplace today. A great deal of experimentation is taking place as organizations struggle to be more flexible and responsive. New information technologies also have spurred experimentation with team formats. This section profiles three different approaches to teams: quality circles, virtual teams, and self-managed teams. We have selected these particular types of teams for three reasons: (1) they have recognizable labels, (2) they have at least some research evidence, (3) they range from low to mixed to high degrees of empowerment (refer to Figure 15–2 in Chapter 15).

As indicated in Table 11–6, the three types of teams are distinct but not totally unique. Overlaps exist. For instance, computer-networked virtual teams may or may not have volunteer members and may or may not be self-managed. Another point of overlap involves the fifth variable in Table 11–6: relationship to organization structure. Quality circles are called *parallel* structures because they exist outside normal channels of authority and communication.[48] Self-managed teams, on the other hand, are *integrated* into the basic organizational structure. Virtual teams vary in this regard, although they tend to be parallel because they are made up of functional specialists (engineers, accountants, marketers, etc.) who team up on temporary projects. Keeping these basic distinctions in mind, let us explore quality circles, virtual teams, and self-managed teams.

Table 11–6   *Basic Distinctions among Quality Circles, Virtual Teams, and Self-Managed Teams*

	Quality Circles	Virtual Teams	Self-Managed Teams
Type of team (see Table 11–2)	Advice	Advice or project (usually project)	Production, project, or action
Type of empowerment (see Figure 15–2)	Consultation	Consultation, participation, or delegation	Delegation
Members	Production/service personnel	Managers and technical specialists	Production/service, technical specialists
Basis of membership	Voluntary	Assigned (some voluntary)	Assigned
Relationship to organization structure	Parallel	Parallel or integrated	Integrated
Amount of face-to-face communication	Strictly face to face	Periodic to none	Varies, depending on use of information technology

Quality Circles

Quality circles are small groups of people from the same work area who voluntarily get together to identify, analyze, and recommend solutions for problems related to quality, productivity, and cost reduction. Some prefer the term *quality control circles*. With an ideal size of 10 to 12 members, they typically meet for about 60 to 90 minutes on a regular basis. Some companies allow meetings during work hours, others encourage quality circles to meet after work on employees' time. Once a week or twice a month are common schedules. Management facilitates the quality circle program through skills training and listening to periodic presentations of recommendations. Monetary rewards for suggestions tend to be the exception rather than the rule. Intrinsic motivation, derived from learning new skills and meaningful participation, is the primary payoff for quality circle volunteers.

Quality circles
Small groups of volunteers who strive to solve quality-related problems.

The Quality Circle Movement   American quality control experts helped introduce the basic idea of quality circles to Japanese industry soon after World War II. The idea eventually returned to the United States and reached fad proportions during the 1970s and 1980s. Proponents made zealous claims about how quality circles were the key to higher productivity, lower costs, employee development, and improved job attitudes. At its zenith during the mid-1980s, the quality circle movement claimed millions of employee participants around the world.[49] Hundreds of US companies and government agencies adopted the idea under a variety of labels.[50] Dramatic growth of quality circles in the United States was attributed to (1) a desire to replicate Japan's industrial success, (2) America's penchant for business fads, and (3) the relative ease of installing quality circles without restructuring the organization.[51] All too often, however, early enthusiasm gave way to disappointment, apathy, and abandonment.[52]

But quality circles, if properly administered and supported by management, can be much more than a management fad seemingly past its prime. According to USC researchers Edward E Lawler and Susan A Mohrman, "quality circles can be an important first step toward organizational effectiveness through employee involvement."[53]

Insights from Field Research on Quality Circles
There is a body of objective field research on quality circles. Still, much of what we know comes from testimonials and case histories from managers and consultants who have a vested interest in demonstrating the technique's success. Although documented failures are scarce, one expert concluded that quality circles have failure rates of more than 60%.[54] Poor implementation is probably more at fault than the quality circle concept itself.[55]

To date, field research on quality circles has been inconclusive. Lack of standardized variables is the main problem, as it typically is when comparing the results of field studies.[56] Team participation programs of all sizes and shapes have been called quality circles. Here's what we have learned to date. A case study of military and civilian personnel at a US Air Force base found a positive relationship between quality circle participation and desire to continue working for the organization. The observed effect on job performance was slight. A longitudinal study spanning 24 months revealed that quality circles had only a marginal impact on employee attitudes but had a positive impact on productivity. In a more recent study, utility company employees who participated in quality circles received significantly better job performance ratings and were promoted more frequently than nonparticipants. This suggests that quality circles live up to their billing as a good employee development technique.[57]

Overall, quality circles are a promising participative management tool, *if they are carefully implemented and supported by all levels of management.*

Virtual Teams

Virtual teams are a product of modern times. They take their name from *virtual reality* computer simulations, where "it's almost like the real thing." Thanks to evolving information technologies such as the Internet, e-mail, instant messaging, videoconferencing, groupware, and fax machines, you can be a member of a work team without really being there.[58] Traditional team meetings are location specific. Team members are either physically present or absent. Virtual teams, in contrast, convene electronically with members reporting in from different locations, different organizations, and even different time zones.

Virtual team
Information technology allows group members in different locations to conduct business.

Because virtual teams are relatively new, there is no consensual definition. Our working definition of a **virtual team** is a physically dispersed task group that conducts its business through modern information technology.[59] Advocates say virtual teams are very flexible and efficient because they are driven by information and skills, not by time and location. People with needed information or skills can be team members, regardless of where or when they actually do their work. On the negative side, lack of face-to-face interaction can weaken trust, communication, and accountability.

Research Insights
As one might expect with a new and ill-defined area, research evidence to date is a bit spotty. Here is what we have learned so far from recent studies of computer-mediated groups:

- Virtual groups formed over the Internet follow a group development process similar to that for face-to-face groups.[60] (Recall our discussion of Tuckman's model in Chapter 10.)
- Internet chat rooms create more work and yield poorer decisions than face-to-face meetings and telephone conferences.[61]
- Successful use of groupware (software that facilitates interaction among virtual group members) requires training and hands-on experience.[62]
- Inspirational leadership has a positive impact on creativity in electronic brainstorming groups.[63]

• Conflict management is particularly difficult for *asynchronous* virtual teams (those not interacting in real time) that have no opportunity for face-to-face interaction.[64]

Practical Considerations   Virtual teams may be in fashion, but they are not a cure-all. In fact, they may be a giant step backward for those not well versed in modern information technology. Managers who rely on virtual teams agree on one point: *Meaningful face-to-face contact, especially during early phases of the group development process, is absolutely essential.* Virtual group members need "faces" in their minds to go with names and electronic messages. Periodic face-to-face interaction not only fosters social bonding among virtual team members, it also facilitates conflict resolution. Additionally, virtual teams cannot succeed without some old-fashioned factors such as top-management support, hands-on training, a clear mission and specific objectives, effective leadership, and schedules and deadlines. (See the additional practical tips listed in Table 11–7.)

Self-Managed Teams

Have you ever thought you could do a better job than your boss? Well, if the trend toward self-managed work teams continues to grow as predicted, you just may get your chance. Entrepreneurs and artisans often boast of not having a supervisor. The same generally cannot be said for employees working in offices and factories. But things are changing. In fact, an estimated half of the employees at *Fortune* 500 companies are working on teams.[65] A growing share of those teams are self-managing. For example, "At a General Mills cereal plant in Lodi, California, teams . . . schedule, operate, and maintain machinery so effectively that the factory runs with no managers present during the night shift."[66] More typically, managers are present to serve as trainers and facilitators. Self-managed teams come in every conceivable format today, some more autonomous than others (see the OB Exercise on p 358).

Table 11–7   *How to Manage Virtual Teams*

Establishing trust and commitment, encouraging communication, and assessing team members pose tremendous challenges for virtual team managers. Here are a few tips to make the process easier:

- Establish regular times for group interaction.
- Set up firm rules for communication.
- Use visual forms of communication where possible.
- Emulate the attributes of co-located teams. For example, allow time for informal chitchat and socializing, and celebrate achievements.
- Give and receive feedback and offer assistance on a regular basis. Be persistent with people who aren't communicating with you or each other.
- Agree on standard technology so all team members can work together easily.
- Consider using 360-degree feedback to better understand and evaluate team members.
- Provide a virtual meeting room via intranet, Web site or bulletin board.
- Note which employees effectively use e-mail to build team rapport.
- Smooth the way for an employee's next assignment if membership on the team, or the team itself, is not permanent.
- Be available to employees, but don't wait for them to seek you out.
- Encourage informal, off-line conversation between team members.

SOURCE: C Joinson, "Managing Virtual Teams," *HR Magazine*, June 2002, p 71. Reprinted with the permission of HR Magazine published by the Society for Human Resource Management, Alexandria, VA.

OB Exercise Measuring Work Group Autonomy

Instructions

Think of your current (or past) job and work groups. Characterize the group's situation by choosing one number on the following scale for each statement. Add your responses for a total score:

Strongly Disagree   **Strongly Agree**

1 —— 2 —— 3 —— 4 —— 5 —— 6 —— 7

Work Method Autonomy

1. My work group decides how to get the job done. _____
2. My work group determines what procedures to use. _____
3. My work group is free to choose its own methods when carrying out its work. _____

Work Scheduling Autonomy

4. My work group controls the scheduling of its work. _____
5. My work group determines how its work is sequenced. _____
6. My work group decides when to do certain activities. _____

Work Criteria Autonomy

7. My work group is allowed to modify the normal way it is evaluated so some of our activities are emphasized and some deemphasized. _____
8. My work group is able to modify its objectives (what it is supposed to accomplish). _____
9. My work group has some control over what it is supposed to accomplish. _____

Total score = _____

Norms

9–26 = low autonomy
27–45 = moderate autonomy
46–63 = high autonomy

SOURCE: Adapted from an individual autonomy scale in J A Breaugh, "The Work Autonomy Scales: Additional Validity Evidence," *Human Relations*, November 1989, pp 1033–56.

Self-managed teams
Groups of employees granted administrative oversight for their work.

Self-managed teams are defined as groups of workers who are given administrative oversight for their task domains. Administrative oversight involves delegated activities such as planning, scheduling, monitoring, and staffing. These are chores normally performed by managers. In short, employees in these unique work groups act as their own supervisor. Accountability is maintained *indirectly* by outside managers and leaders. According to a recent study of a company with 300 self-managed teams, 66 "team advisers" relied on these four indirect influence tactics:

- *Relating.* Understanding the organization's power structure, building trust, showing concern for individual team members.
- *Scouting.* Seeking outside information, diagnosing teamwork problems, facilitating group problem solving.
- *Persuading.* Gathering outside support and resources, influencing team to be more effective and pursue organizational goals.
- *Empowering.* Delegating decision-making authority, facilitating team decision-making process, coaching.[67]

Cross-Functional Teamwork Gives Motorola's Cell Phones Pizzazz

Geeks like Jim Wicks, working for a competitor a decade ago, were impressed with the well-engineered products but winced at the industrial look and relentlessly black and gray colors.

"I thought, 'Wow, great products, but why are they so ugly?' " recalled Wick, now Motorola's chief phone designer.

Today, plain is out and sleek and stylish are in as a new focus on design wins back customers and market share at Motorola. . . .

Wicks leads a staff of more than 200 design employees worldwide that reflects a mixture of right- and left-brain thinking, including sociologists, psychologists, musicologists, engineers, graphics designers and software and colors specialists.

"Back then we were saying, 'Here's the features and the technology,' then put a wrapper around it," Wicks said in an interview at Motorola's [Chicago] office overlooking the Lake Michigan shoreline. "Now the starting point is, 'What does the consumer want?' and then apply the technology to that."

SOURCE: Excerpted from D Carpenter, "Motorola Is Winning with Its New Designs," *Arizona Republic*, April 23, 2005, pp D1–D2.

Self-managed teams are variously referred to as semiautonomous work groups, autonomous work groups, and superteams.

Managerial Resistance   Something much more complex is involved than this apparently simple label suggests. The term *self-managed* does not mean simply turning workers loose to do their own thing. Indeed, an organization embracing self-managed teams should be prepared to undergo revolutionary changes in management philosophy, structure, staffing and training practices, and reward systems. Moreover, the traditional notions of managerial authority and control are turned on their heads. Not surprisingly, many managers strongly resist giving up the reins of power to people they view as subordinates. They see self-managed teams as a threat to their job security.

Cross-Functionalism   A common feature of self-managed teams, particularly among those above the shop-floor or clerical level, is **cross-functionalism**.[68] In other words, specialists from different areas are put on the same team (see Real World/Real People). Mark Stefik, a manager at the world-renowned Palo Alto Research Center in California, explains the wisdom of cross-functionalism:

> Something magical happens when you bring together a group of people from different disciplines with a common purpose. It's a middle zone, the breakthrough zone. The idea is to start a team on a problem—a hard problem, to keep people motivated. When there's an obstacle, instead of dodging it, bring in another point of view: an electrical engineer, a user interface expert, a sociologist, whatever spin on the market is needed. Give people new eyeglasses to cross-pollinate ideas.[69]

As described in the opening vignette for this chapter, cross-functionalism is seeping into university programs to help students see the big picture and polish their team skills.

Are Self-Managed Teams Effective? The Research Evidence   Among companies with self-managed teams, the most commonly delegated tasks are work scheduling and dealing directly with outside customers. The least common team chores are hiring and firing.[70] Most of today's self-managed teams remain bunched at the shop-floor level in factory settings. Experts predict growth of the practice in the managerial ranks and in service operations.[71]

Cross-functionalism
Team made up of technical specialists from different areas.

359

Much of what we know about self-managed teams comes from testimonials and case studies. Fortunately, a body of higher quality field research is slowly developing. A review of three meta-analyses covering 70 individual studies concluded that self-managed teams had

- A positive effect on productivity.
- A positive effect on specific attitudes relating to self-management (e.g., responsibility and control).
- No significant effect on general attitudes (e.g., job satisfaction and organizational commitment).
- No significant effect on absenteeism or turnover.[72]

Although encouraging, these results do not qualify as a sweeping endorsement of self-managed teams. Nonetheless, experts say the trend toward self-managed work teams will continue upward in North America because of a strong cultural bias in favor of direct participation (see Table 11–8). Managers need to be prepared for the resulting shift in organizational administration.[73]

Table 11–8   *There Are Many Ways to Empower Self-Managed Teams*

External Leader Behavior
1. Make team members responsible and accountable for the work they do.
2. Ask for and use team suggestions when making decisions.
3. Encourage team members to take control of their work.
4. Create an environment in which team members set their own team goals.
5. Stay out of the way when team members attempt to solve work-related problems.
6. Generate high team expectations.
7. Display trust and confidence in the team's abilities.

Production/Service Responsibilities
1. The team sets its own production/service goals and standards.
2. The team assigns jobs and tasks to its members.
3. Team members develop their own quality standards and measurement techniques.
4. Team members take on production/service learning and development opportunities.
5. Team members handle their own problems with internal and external customers.
6. The team works with a whole product or service, not just a part.

Human Resource Management System
1. The team gets paid, at least in part, as a team.
2. Team members are cross-trained on jobs within their team.
3. Team members are cross-trained on jobs in other teams.
4. Team members are responsible for hiring, training, punishment, and firing.
5. Team members use peer evaluations to formally evaluate each other.

Social Structure
1. The team gets support from other teams and departments when needed.
2. The team has access to and uses important and strategic information.
3. The team has access to and uses the resources of other teams.
4. The team has access to and uses resources inside and outside the organization.
5. The team frequently communicates with other teams.
6. The team makes its own rules and policies.

SOURCE: Reprinted from B L Kirkman and B Rosen, "Powering Up Teams," *Organizational Dynamics,* Winter 2000, ex 3, p 56, © 2000. Used by permission of Elsevier Science.

Executive MBA Team Building at China's Tsinghua University

Executive MBA students pay $30,000 to attend 18 monthly, four-day instruction modules. Many commute thousands of miles to participate. Lin Qin came in search of a strategy for his fast-growing footwear factory in Fujian. "My knowledge is small," he says, "but my company keeps getting bigger." . . .

Tsinghua works hard to encourage bonding. New recruits are bused an hour from Beijing, where they bunk together in spartan dormitories and engage in team-building exercises of the sort that can be found at corporate off-

sites in the US. On a freezing morning in March [2005] a dozen of Lin's classmates clutched the rope attached to his safety harness as he climbed reluctantly to the top of a 30-foot platform. The group shouted encouragement for nearly 20 minutes until he summoned the nerve to lunge for a metal trapeze.

SOURCE: Excerpted from C Chandler, "From Marx to Market," *Fortune*, May 16, 2005, p 112.

Team Building

Team building is a catch-all term for a whole host of techniques aimed at improving the internal functioning of work groups. Whether conducted by company trainers or outside consultants, team-building workshops strive for greater cooperation, better communication, and less dysfunctional conflict. Experiential learning techniques such as interpersonal trust exercises, conflict-handling role-play sessions, and interactive games are common. For example, Germany's Opel uses Lego blocks to teach its autoworkers the tight teamwork necessary for just-in-time production.[74] In the mountains of British Columbia, Canada, DowElanco employees try to overcome fear and build trust as they help each other negotiate a difficult tree-top rope course.[75] Meanwhile, in the United States, the Target department store chain has its salesclerks learn cooperation and teamwork with this exercise: "employees linked in a human chain must each wriggle through two Hula-Hoops moving in opposite directions, without breaking the chain or letting the hoops touch the ground."[76] And in Prescott, Arizona, trainees at Motorola's Advanced Leadership Academy polish their teamwork skills by trying to make music with an odd assortment of percussion instruments[77] (see Real World/Real People).

Rote memorization and lectures/discussions are discouraged by team-building experts who prefer *active* versus passive learning. Greater emphasis is placed on *how* work groups get the job done than on the job itself.

Complete coverage of the many team-building techniques would require a separate book. Consequently, the scope of our current discussion is limited to the goal of team building and the day-to-day development of self-management skills. This foundation is intended to give

Team building
Experiential learning aimed at better internal functioning of groups.

Teamwork and trust are vital in many workplaces today, but perhaps no more so than on an offshore oil-drilling rig. Life and limb are at risk with every move as these workers perform their dangerous ballet. Next time you fill up at the pump, think of the incredible team effort that brought you the product.

you a basis for selecting appropriate team-building techniques from the many you are likely to encounter in the years ahead.[78]

The Goal of Team Building: High-Performance Teams

Team building allows team members to wrestle with simulated or real-life problems. Outcomes are then analyzed by the group to determine what group processes need improvement. Learning stems from recognizing and addressing faulty group dynamics. Perhaps one subgroup withheld key information from another, thereby hampering group progress. With cross-cultural teams becoming commonplace in today's global economy, team building is more important than ever.

A nationwide survey of team members from many organizations, by Wilson Learning Corporation, provides a useful model or benchmark of what we should expect of teams. The researchers' question was simply: "What is a high-performance team?"[79] The respondents were asked to describe their peak experiences in work teams. Analysis of the survey results yielded the following eight attributes of high-performance teams:

1. *Participative leadership.* Creating an interdependency by empowering, freeing up, and serving others.
2. *Shared responsibility.* Establishing an environment in which all team members feel as responsible as the manager for the performance of the work unit.
3. *Aligned on purpose.* Having a sense of common purpose about why the team exists and the function it serves.
4. *High communication.* Creating a climate of trust and open, honest communication.
5. *Future focused.* Seeing change as an opportunity for growth.
6. *Focused on task.* Keeping meetings focused on results.
7. *Creative talents.* Applying individual talents and creativity.
8. *Rapid response.* Identifying and acting on opportunities.[80]

These eight attributes effectively combine many of today's most progressive ideas on management, among them being participation, empowerment, service ethic, individual responsibility and development, self-management, trust, active listening, and envisioning. But patience and diligence are required. According to a manager familiar with work teams, "high-performance teams may take three to five years to build."[81] Let us keep this inspiring model of high-performance teams in mind as we conclude our discussion of team building.

Developing Team Members' Self-Management Skills

Self-management leadership
Process of leading others to lead themselves.

A promising dimension of team building has emerged in recent years. It is an extension of the self-management approach discussed in Learning Module B (on the book's Web site). Proponents call it **self-management leadership,** defined as the process of leading others to lead themselves. An underlying assumption is that self-managed teams likely will fail if team members are not expressly taught to engage in self-management behaviors.[82] This makes sense because it is unreasonable to expect employees who are accustomed to being managed and led to suddenly manage and lead themselves. Transition training is required.

A key transition to self-management involves *current managers* engaging in self-management leadership behaviors. This is team building in the fullest meaning of the term.

Six self-management leadership behaviors were isolated in a field study of a manufacturing company organized around self-managed teams. The observed behaviors were

1. *Encourages self-reinforcement* (e.g., getting team members to praise each other for good work and results).
2. *Encourages self-observation/evaluation* (e.g., teaching team members to judge how well they are doing).
3. *Encourages self-expectation* (e.g., encouraging team members to expect high performance from themselves and the team).
4. *Encourages self-goal-setting* (e.g., having the team set its own performance goals).
5. *Encourages rehearsal* (e.g., getting team members to think about and practice new tasks).
6. *Encourages self-criticism* (e.g., encouraging team members to be critical of their own poor performance).[83]

According to the researchers, Charles Manz and Henry Sims, this type of leadership is a dramatic departure from traditional practices such as giving orders or making sure everyone gets along. Empowerment, not domination, is the overriding goal.

Summary of Key Concepts

1. *Explain how a work group becomes a team.* A team is a mature group where leadership is shared, accountability is both individual and collective, the members have developed their own purpose, problem solving is a way of life, and effectiveness is measured by collective outcomes.

2. *Identify and describe four types of work teams.* Advice teams provide information for managerial decisions. Production teams perform an organization's day-to-day operations. Project teams apply specialized knowledge to solve problems needed to complete a specific project. Action teams are highly skilled and highly coordinated to provide peak performance on demand.

3. *Explain the model of effective work teams, and specify the two criteria of team effectiveness.* Work teams need three things: (a) a team-friendly organization to provide a support system; (b) individuals with teamwork competencies; and (c) effective teamwork. The two team effectiveness criteria are performance (getting the job done) and team viability (satisfied members who are willing to continue contributing to the team).

4. *Identify five teamwork competencies team members need to possess.* They are (a) orients team to problem-solving situation; (b) organizes and manages team performance;

(c) promotes a positive team environment; (d) facilitates and manages task conflict; and (e) appropriately promotes perspective.

5. *Discuss why teams fail.* Teams fail because unrealistic expectations cause frustration and failure. Common management mistakes include weak strategies, creating a hostile environment for teams, faddish use of teams, not learning from team experience, vague team assignments, poor team staffing, inadequate training, and lack of trust. Team members typically try too much too soon, experience conflict over differing work styles and personalities, ignore important group dynamics, resist change, exhibit poor interpersonal skills and chemistry, and display a lack of trust.

6. *List at least four things managers can do to build trust.* Six recommended ways to build trust are through communication, support, respect (especially delegation), fairness, predictability, and competence.

7. *Distinguish two types of group cohesiveness, and summarize cohesiveness research findings.* Cohesive groups have a shared sense of togetherness or a "we" feeling. Socio-emotional cohesiveness involves emotional satisfaction. Instrumental cohesiveness involves goal-directed togetherness. There is a small but significant relationship between cohesiveness and performance. The effect is stronger for smaller groups. Commitment to task

among group members strengthens the cohesiveness→performance linkage. Success can build group cohesiveness. Cohesiveness is not a cure-all for group problems. Too much cohesiveness can lead to groupthink.

8. *Define quality circles, virtual teams, and self-managed teams.* Quality circles are small groups of volunteers who meet regularly to solve quality-related problems in their work area. Virtual teams are physically dispersed work groups that conduct their business via modern information technologies such as the Internet, e-mail, and videoconferences. Self-managed teams are work groups that perform their own administrative chores such as planning, scheduling, and staffing.

9. *Describe high-performance teams.* Eight attributes of high-performance teams are participative leadership, shared responsibility, aligned on purpose, high communication, future focused for growth, focused on task, creative talents applied, and rapid response.

Discussion Questions

1. What evidence have you seen at school or on the job of greater reliance on teams and teamwork?

2. Which of the factors in Table 11–1 is the most crucial to a successful team? Explain.

3. Relative to effective teams, why is team viability important?

4. In your personal friendships, how do you come to trust someone? How fragile is that trust? Explain.

5. Why is delegation so important to building organizational trust?

6. Why should a group leader strive for both socio-emotional and instrumental cohesiveness?

7. Are virtual teams likely to be just a passing fad? Why or why not?

8. Would you like to work on a self-managed team? Explain.

9. How would you respond to a manager who said, "Why should I teach my people to manage themselves and work myself out of a job?"

10. Have you ever been a member of a high-performing team? If so, explain the circumstances and success factors.

OB in Action Case Study

GE's Global Virtual Team Wants to Reap the Wind[84]

BusinessWeek Even before Aeolus controlled the tempestuous winds in Greek mythology, humans have dreamed of harnessing such power for themselves. But as a source of energy, the wind business is in its youth, populated mostly with niche players trying to build markets in a world where policies, cost, and technology still favor traditional forms of energy. General Electric Co. is setting out to change that equation by applying its considerable financial and technological muscle to the field. It launched GE Wind Energy in May, 2002, when it bought Enron's wind businesses after the company's collapse.

What makes GE such a force for innovation in this nascent industry is its ability to harness a vast array of global talent to develop new products and new technology. The $134 billion giant already has people developing sophisticated composites that allow for lighter, stronger blades in jet engines. It has experts in the rail business who know how to make gearing systems operate at peak efficiency, and others who have vastly improved the efficiency of power turbines. And it can bring that talent together at major research centers in Shanghai, Munich, Bangalore, and upstate New York that serve all GE businesses.

While many companies boast a global workforce, few are as skilled at mobilizing experts from diverse disciplines and locales in pursuit of a common goal. The difference stems from culture more than from technology. At GE, executives are encouraged to think beyond the boundaries of their particular business. They come together frequently for training or joint projects. Executives are apt to move among units several times in their careers, letting them build up a rich network of internal contacts. There's also a tradition of plucking people from their day jobs for other projects. At any given time, thousands of GE employees are on so-called bubble assignments—lending their skills to another function or business that pays their salaries for the duration of the project.

Moreover, GE doesn't treat its global outposts as farm teams for US operations. Yes, there's cheaper labor in places like Bangalore and Shanghai. But foreign researchers also handle high-level autonomous research projects that match anything being done at home. GE has set up state-of-the-art training centers to school foreign employees and customers in the GE way. The GE China Learning Center in Shanghai, for example, boasts many of the features of GE's famed training facilities in Crotonville, New York—including classrooms for up to 178 people.

That backdrop has been critical to building up GE's market share in wind energy. It's now a $9 billion global industry that's expected to grow 10% to 15% a year, says Steven Zwolinski, who heads up the wind business, now a part of GE Energy. The unit sold $1.3 billion of energy-generating equipment last year to major utilities and developers. As technical innovations bring the cost of producing wind energy down and governments become more eager to develop renewable resources, growth could accelerate.

Certainly, that's the expectation of James Lyons, a chief engineer at the GE Global Research Center in the leafy residential town of Niskayuna in upstate New York, who is charged with handling the advanced technologies for wind.

Multilingual Mind Meld

Lyons is the fulcrum for the project, charged with marshalling talent from around the world. The 30-year veteran has brought in engineers from other units and navigated cultural hurdles worldwide. Through his extensive internal network, he knew the people and skills he wanted. He has recruited materials experts from down the hall who developed the composites for the fan blades of the GE90 aircraft engine; design teams in Greenville, South Carolina, and Salzbergen, Germany; engineers from Peterborough, Ontario, who are tackling the generators; Bangalore researchers who are crafting analytical models and turbine system design tools; and Shanghai engineers who conduct high-end simulations. Lyons keeps his team focused with e-mails, teleconferences, and clear deadlines.

Still, trying to nurture world-class research outside the US also creates a host of challenges. First was the nervousness of the talent in Niskayuna. They know all too well that their counterparts in Shanghai and Bangalore are making a fraction of their US salaries, although Sanjay M Correa, the global technology leader for energy and propulsion at GE Research insists such tensions dissipate once they realize that the new colleagues are additions rather than replacements. With younger employees at the new centers, there are more questions and less familiarity with the GE way. Still, Bansi Phansalkar, a tech-nology leader at the Bangalore center, says "we all speak the same language of technology."

One way to build team spirit is to foster familiarity. In addition to regular teleconferences, engineers take stints working in other parts of the operation. That has meant trading engineers from Bangalore and Salzbergen, for example, for a week or two at a time. Along with learning about the core design tools being created in Bangalore or the actual products being made in Salzbergen, they establish better lines of communication.

The far-flung team is getting results. Among the innovations so far: a new generation of land-based wind turbines with capacities of more than 2.5 megawatts (at a typical price of $1 million per megawatt) with new blade and advanced control technologies—a boon for customers who want to generate energy on sites where space is limited. GE's 3.6 megawatt unit, which produces enough electricity to power 1,400 average American homes a year, is designed for offshore locations. Its turbine—with blades each longer than a football field—sits 30 stories above the ocean. Current projects range from a wind farm in Inner Mongolia to working on smaller turbines that could help provide clean water to villages in developing countries. "There are a lot of wild and crazy ideas in the wind industry," Lyons says with a laugh. "But there is an incredible amount of pent-up demand as well." And GE staffers around the world are determined to capture as much of that demand as possible.

Questions for Discussion

1. Using Table 11–1 as a reference, is James Lyons turning his multinational group of experts into a *team?* Explain.

2. Using Figure 11–2 as a reference, what could cause Lyons's team to fail? Explain.

3. What evidence of cross-functionalism do you detect in this case? What are the benefits?

4. Are GE's employees likely to have needed teamwork competencies and be ready to work effectively on a virtual team? Explain.

5. In the role of a management consultant, what sort of team-building activities would you recommend to Lyons? Explain.

Personal Awareness and Growth Exercise

How Trusting Are You?

Objectives

1. To introduce you to different dimensions of interpersonal trust.

2. To measure your trust in another person.

3. To discuss the managerial implications of your propensity to trust.

Introduction

The trend toward more open and empowered organizations where teamwork and self-management are vital requires heightened interpersonal trust. Customers need to be able to trust organizations producing the goods and services they buy, managers need to trust nonmanagers to carry out the organization's mission, and team members need to trust each other in order to get the job done. As with any other interpersonal skill, we need to be able to measure and improve our ability to trust others. This exercise is a step in that direction.

Instructions[85]

Think of a specific individual who currently plays an important role in your life (e.g., current or future spouse, friend, supervisor, co-worker, team member, etc.), and rate his or her trustworthiness for each statement according to the following scale. Total your responses, and compare your score with the arbitrary norms provided.

Strongly Disagree   **Strongly Agree**

1 —— 2 —— 3 —— 4 —— 5 —— 6 —— 7 —— 8 —— 9 ——10

Overall Trust   Score

1. I can expect this person to play fair. _____
2. I can confide in this person and know she/he desires to listen. _____
3. I can expect this person to tell me the truth. _____
4. This person takes time to listen to my problems and worries. _____

Emotional Trust

5. This person would never intentionally misrepresent my point of view to other people. _____
6. I can confide in this person and know that he/she will not discuss it with others. _____
7. This person responds constructively and caringly to my problems. _____

Reliableness

8. If this person promised to do me a favor, she/he would carry out that promise. _____
9. If I had an appointment with this person, I could count on him/her showing up. _____
10. I could lend this person money and count on getting it back as soon as possible. _____
11. I do not need a backup plan because I know this person will come through for me. _____

Total score = _____

Trustworthiness Scale

77–110 = high (Trust is a precious thing.)

45– 76 = moderate (Be careful; get a rearview mirror.)

11– 44 = low (Lock up your valuables!)

Questions for Discussion

1. Which particular items in this trust questionnaire are most central to your idea of trust? Why?

2. Does your score accurately depict the degree to which you trust (or distrust) the target person?

3. Why do you trust (or distrust) this individual?

4. If you trust this person to a high degree, how hard was it to build that trust? Explain. What would destroy that trust?

5. Based on your responses to this questionnaire, how would you rate your propensity to trust? Low? Moderate? High?

6. What are the managerial implications of your propensity to trust?

Student Team Development Project

Objectives

1. To help you better understand the components of teamwork.
2. To give you a practical diagnostic tool to assess the need for team building.
3. To give you a chance to evaluate and develop an actual group/team.

Introduction

Student teams are very common in today's college classrooms. They are an important part of the move toward cooperative and experiential learning. In other words, learning by doing. Group dynamics and teamwork are best learned by doing. Unfortunately, many classroom teams wallow in ambiguity, conflict, and ineffectiveness. This team development questionnaire can play an important role in the life cycle of your classroom team or group. All members of your team can complete this evaluation at one or more of the following critical points in your team's life cycle: (1) when the team reaches a crisis point and threatens to break up, (2) about halfway through the life of the team, and (3) at the end of the team's life cycle. Discussion of the results by all team members can enhance the group's learning experience.

Instructions

Either at the prompting of your instructor or by group consensus, decide at what point in your team's life cycle this exercise should be completed. *Tip:* Have each team member write their responses to the 10 items on a sheet of paper with no names attached. This will permit the calculation of a group mean score for each item and for all 10 items. Attention should then turn to the discussion questions provided to help any team development problems surface and to point the way toward solutions.

(An alternative to these instructions is to evaluate a team or work group you are associated with in your current job. You may also draw from a group experience in a past job.)

Questionnaire[86]

1. To what extent do I feel a real part of the team?

5	4	3	2	1
Completely a part all the time.	A part most of the time.	On the edge—sometimes in, sometimes out.	Generally outside except for one or two short periods.	On the outside, not really a part of the team.

2. How safe is it in this team to be at ease, relaxed, and myself?

5	4	3	2	1
I feel perfectly safe to be myself; they won't hold mistakes against me.	I feel most people would accept me if I were completely myself, but there are some I am not sure about.	Generally one has to be careful what one says or does in this team.	I am quite fearful about being completely myself in this team.	I am not a fool; I would never be myself in this team.

3. To what extent do I feel "under wraps," that is, have private thoughts, unspoken reservations, or unexpressed feelings and opinions that I have not felt comfortable bringing out into the open?

1	2	3	4	5
Almost completely under wraps.	Under wraps many times.	Slightly more free and expressive than under wraps.	Quite free and expressive much of the time.	Almost completely free and expressive.

4. How effective are we, in our team, in getting out and using the ideas, opinions, and information of all team members in making decisions?

1	2	3	4	5
We don't really encourage everyone to share their ideas, opinions, and information with the team in making decisions.	Only the ideas, opinions, and information of a few members are really known and used in making decisions.	Sometimes we hear the views of most members before making decisions, and sometimes we disregard most members.	A few are sometimes hesitant about sharing their opinions, but we generally have good participation in making decisions.	Everyone feels his or her ideas, opinions, and information are given a fair hearing before decisions are made.

367

5. To what extent are the goals the team is working toward understood, and to what extent do they have meaning for you?

5	4	3	2	1
I feel extremely good about the goals of our team.	I feel fairly good, but some things are not too clear or meaningful.	A few things we are doing are clear and meaningful.	Much of the activity is not clear or meaningful to me.	I really do not understand or feel involved in the goals of the team.

6. How well does the team work at its tasks?

1	2	3	4	5
Coasts, loafs, makes no progress.	Makes a little progress, but most members loaf.	Progress is slow; spurts of effective work.	Above average in progress and pace of work.	Works well; achieves definite progress.

7. Our planning and the way we operate as a team are largely influenced by:

1	2	3	4	5
One or two team members.	A clique.	Shifts from one person or clique to another.	Shared by most of the members, but some are left out.	Shared by all members of the team.

8. What is the level of responsibility for work in our team?

5	4	3	2	1
Each person assumes personal responsibility for getting work done.	A majority of the members assume responsibility for getting work done.	About half assume responsibility; about half do not.	Only a few assume responsibility for getting work done.	Nobody (except perhaps one) really assumes responsibility for getting work done.

9. How are differences or conflicts handled in our team?

1	2	3	4	5
Differences or conflicts are denied, suppressed, or avoided at all costs.	Differences or conflicts are recognized but remain mostly unresolved.	Differences or conflicts are recognized, and some attempts are made to work them through by some members, often outside the team meetings.	Differences and conflicts are recognized, and some attempts are made to deal with them in our team.	Differences and conflicts are recognized, and the team usually is working them through satisfactorily.

10. How do people relate to the team leader, chairperson, or "boss"?

1	2	3	4	5
The leader dominates the team, and people are often fearful or passive.	The leader tends to control the team, although people generally agree with the leader's direction.	There is some give and take between the leader and the team members.	Team members relate easily to the leader and usually are able to influence leader decisions.	Team members respect the leader, but they work together as a unified team, with everyone participating and no one dominant.

Total score = _____

Questions for Discussion

1. Have any of the items on the questionnaire helped you better understand why your team has had problems? What problems?

2. Based on Table 11–1, are you part of a group or team? Explain.

3. How do your responses to the items compare with the average responses from your group? What insights does this information provide?

4. Refer back to Tuckman's five-stage model of group development in Figure 10–3. Which stage is your team at? How can you tell? Did group decay set in?

5. If you are part way through your team's life cycle, what steps does your team need to take to become more effective?

6. If this is the end of your team's life cycle, what should your team have done differently?

7. What lasting lessons about teamwork have you learned from this exercise?

Ethical Dilemma

Sexy but Sexless Relationships?

Situation

You're the ground crew manager in Chicago for a major commercial airline company. During lunchtime in your office, you run across a curious article while browsing *Fast Company* magazine's Web archives. You begin to read:

"You're intensely together on a project, things are going well, and the adrenaline gets pumping," says David R Eyler. "The chemistry feels right, but you don't want to mess up your personal or professional relationships by having an affair. You recognize that you've got something good here, and you set limits on your behavior."

Can you have a sexy but sexless relationship? Researchers are embracing a new notion that sexual attraction between co-workers may not be bad. It may, in fact, be beneficial.

Eyler and Andrea P Baridon, authors of three books on men and women in the workplace and senior staff members of the National Center for Higher Education in Washington, propose an unconventional alternative to an illicit affair. Instead of giving in to sexual attraction, you manage it. They call the relationship *More than Friends, Less than Lovers*—the title of a book they published in 1991.[87]

The article goes on to say researchers have found men and women using "sexual synergy" to achieve goals in the workplace. Five tips are offered for keeping these close, but not too close, relationships within bounds.

What is your reaction? (Explain the ethical reasoning for your choice.)

1. Hmmm. A little harmless flirting might boost productivity and be good for morale.

2. This is a surefire invitation to sexual harassment abuses and charges. What a stupid idea! (*Tip:* Refer back to Table 10–5, Behavioral Categories of Sexual Harassment.)

3. I should discuss this with our human resource department to check our stance on workplace romances and their relationship to our sexual harassment policy.

4. I could pass a copy of this article around to see if we have a problem with sexual harassment.

5. Invent other options. Discuss.

For the Chapter 11 Internet Exercise featuring a team player quiz (www.fastcompany.com/backissues and http://tools.monster.com/quizzes/teamplayer), visit our Web site at **www.mhhe.com/kreitner.**

Individual and Group Decision Making

Learning Objectives

When you finish studying the material in this chapter, you should be able to:

1 Compare and contrast the rational model of decision making and Simon's normative model.

2 Discuss knowledge management and techniques used by companies to increase knowledge sharing.

3 Explain the model of decision-making styles.

4 Describe the model of escalation of commitment.

5 Explain the model of intuition.

6 Summarize the pros and cons of involving groups in the decision-making process.

7 Contrast brainstorming, the nominal group technique, the Delphi technique, and computer-aided decision making.

8 Describe the stages of the creative process.

9 Explain the model of organizational creativity and innovation.

Many employers are just waking up to the fact that their most experienced and knowledgeable workers will take with them irreplaceable and uncaptured knowledge as they exit.

In 2004, Marilyn Weixel, SPHR, woke up to a looming mass exodus of experienced workers at her organization. She realized that more than 35% of her workforce at Raytheon Vision Systems, a national defense contractor in Goleta, California, would be eligible to retire by 2009. "In many situations, the person [set to retire] was the only one in the whole nation who knew how to do something. They invented it," says Weixel, who is senior manager of HR.

Raytheon was in need of a dynamic solution. So Weixel created a training program called Leave-A-Legacy, which formally pairs employees who have vital knowledge—subject matter experts—with high-potential subordinate employees. Since it began, she has heard anecdotally from management that the program has successfully encouraged near-retirees to share knowledge on a daily basis, and it has also given them a sense of purpose. As one retiring employee said, "This program is the first time I believed I was really valued—after nearly 20 years [at Raytheon]." In addition, the program is securing the commitment of high-potential employees by giving them higher-level work.

Unlike labor market shifts related to economic fluctuations, Weixel stresses, "retirements are predictable. You can see them coming and plan." Raytheon's plan included working with supervisors to identify key people with irreplaceable knowledge who might leave in the next few years and to identify the right people to receive the knowledge. "Mentoring meant things like involving the [protege] in meetings, bringing them along to meet customers, including them in the design or proposal phase, etc.," says Weixel.

Then, Raytheon used third-party coaches to facilitate the knowledge transfer between experts and subordinates. "Most of [the near retirees] are brilliant at what they do, but they don't have great teaching skills," says Weixel. "Very often the people receiving the information don't have the greatest interpersonal skills [either]. The coaches

help develop people's emotional intelligence skills and work with them to ensure that the process isn't haphazard. Each [team] has a plan, and each plan is unique."

But mentoring is not the only way companies are transferring knowledge. HP, for instance, has created online communities of different professional groups, such as sales and software engineering. "They're online knowledge repositories for people who do the same kind of work. They post how they do things, solutions and experience," explains James R Malanson, director of global development and operations, technology solutions group, workforce development, at HP.[1]

FOR DISCUSSION
How important is knowledge transfer to an organization's long-term success? Discuss.

Decision making is one of the primary responsibilities of being a manager. The quality of a manager's decisions is important for two principal reasons. First, the quality of a manager's decisions directly affects his or her career opportunities, rewards, and job satisfaction. Second, managerial decisions contribute to the success or failure of an organization.

The chapter-opening vignette is a good illustration of a concept called *knowledge management*. As you will learn later in this chapter, knowledge management consists of a variety of systems and practices that increase the sharing of knowledge and information throughout an organization. Knowledge management not only improves organizational decision making, but it is a source of competitive advantage for companies like Raytheon.

Decision making
Identifying and choosing solutions that lead to a desired end result.

Decision making entails identifying and choosing alternative solutions that lead to a desired state of affairs. The process begins with a problem and ends when a solution has been chosen. To gain an understanding of how managers can make better decisions, this chapter focuses on (1) models of decision making, (2) the dynamics of decision making, (3) group decision making, and (4) creativity.

Models of Decision Making

There are two fundamental models of decision making. The first, the rational model, identifies the process that *should* be used when making decisions. As we all know, however, decision making does not always follow an orderly plan. This awareness led to the development of a normative model of decision making. The normative model outlines the process *actually* used to make decisions. Each model is based on a different set of assumptions and offers unique insight into the decision-making process. Let us begin our exploration of decision-making models by examining the most orderly or rational explanation of managerial decision making.

The Rational Model

Rational model
Logical four-step approach to decision making.

The **rational model** proposes that managers use a rational, four-step sequence when making decisions: (1) identifying the problem, (2) generating alternative solutions, (3) selecting a solution, and (4) implementing and evaluating the solution. According to this model, managers are completely objective and possess complete information to make a decision. Despite criticism for being unrealistic, the rational model is instructive because it analytically breaks down the decision-making process and serves as a conceptual anchor for newer models.[2] Let us now consider each of these four steps.

Identifying the Problem

A **problem** exists when the actual situation and the desired situation differ. For example, a problem exists when you have to pay rent at the end of the month and don't have enough money. Your problem is not that you have to pay rent. Your problem is obtaining the needed funds. Consider the situation faced by Baptist Health Care in Pensacola, Florida:

> [It] was the largest non-governmental employer in the Florida panhandle, with five hospitals, a nursing home, a mental health agency, and 5,500 employees. It was providing excellent care, but there were problems: low staff morale affected customer satisfaction and customer dissatisfaction was hurting market share. In 1995, flagship Baptist Hospital in Pensacola ranked close to the bottom in national surveys of patient satisfaction.[3]

Baptist Health Care's problem was declining market share. The most immediate cause of this problem was customer dissatisfaction, which in turn was influenced by low staff morale.

How do companies like Baptist Health Care know when a problem exists or is going to occur in the near future? One expert proposed that managers use one of three methods to identify problems: historical cues, planning, and other people's perceptions:

Problem
Gap between an actual and desired situation.

© 2002 Ted Goff

"Our task, then, is to decide how to decide how to decide."

© 2002 Ted Goff. Used by permission.

1. Using historical cues to identify problems assumes that the recent past is the best estimate of the future. Thus, managers rely on past experience to identify discrepancies (problems) from expected trends. For example, a sales manager may conclude that a problem exists because the first-quarter sales are less than they were a year ago. This method is prone to error because it is highly subjective.

2. A planning approach is more systematic and can lead to more accurate results. This method consists of using projections or scenarios to estimate what is expected to occur in the future. A time period of one or more years is generally used. The **scenario technique** is a speculative, conjectural forecast tool used to identify future states, given a certain set of environmental conditions. Once different scenarios are developed, companies devise alternative strategies to survive in the various situations. This process helps to create contingency plans far into the future. For example, the European Commission recently used the scenario technique to develop plans for how best to integrate European nations in the pursuit of economic adaptability in the future.[4] Companies like Royal Dutch/Shell, Fleet Financial Group, IBM, Pfizer, and Deutsche Bank are increasingly using the scenario technique as a planning tool.[5]

Scenario technique
Speculative forecasting method.

3. A final approach to identifying problems is to rely on the perceptions of others. A restaurant manager may realize that his or her restaurant provides poor service when a large number of customers complain about how long it takes to receive food after placing an order. In other words, customers' comments signal that a problem exists. Interestingly, companies frequently compound their problems by ignoring customer complaints or feedback.

Generating Solutions

After identifying a problem, the next logical step is generating alternative solutions. For repetitive and routine decisions such as deciding when to send customers a bill, alternatives are readily available through decision rules. For example, a company might routinely bill customers three days after shipping a product. This is not the case for novel and unstructured decisions. Because there are no cut-and-dried procedures for dealing with novel problems, managers must creatively generate alternative solutions. Unfortunately, a recent study of 400 strategic decisions revealed that this recommendation is easier said than done. Results showed that managers fell prey to three decision-making blunders that restricted the number of solutions they considered when trying to solve a problem. These blunders were (1) rushing to judgment, (2) selecting readily available ideas or solutions, and (3) making poor allocation of resources to study alternative solutions. Decision makers thus are encouraged to slow down when making decisions, to evaluate a broader set of alternatives, and to invest in studying a greater number of potential solutions.[6]

Selecting a Solution

Optimally, decision makers want to choose the alternative with the greatest value. Decision theorists refer to this as maximizing the expected utility of an outcome. This is no easy task. First, assigning values to alternatives is complicated and prone to error. Not only are values subjective, but they also vary according to the preferences of the decision maker. Research demonstrates that people vary in their preferences for safety or risk when making decisions. For example, a meta-analysis summarizing 150 studies revealed that males displayed more risk taking than females.[7] Michael Dell, chairman of Dell, and Kevin Rollins, Dell's CEO, attempt to overcome limitations associated with their personal preferences by extensively collaborating with each other when making decisions (see Real World/Real People on page 375). Their collaborative approach has been very successful. Further, evaluating alternatives assumes they can be judged according to some standards or criteria. This further assumes that (1) valid criteria exist, (2) each alternative can be compared against these criteria, and (3) the decision maker actually uses the criteria. As you know from making your own key life decisions, people frequently violate these assumptions. Finally, the ethics of the solution should be considered.

Implementing and Evaluating the Solution

Once a solution is chosen, it needs to be implemented. After the solution is implemented, the evaluation phase assesses its effectiveness. If the solution is effective, it should reduce the difference between the actual and desired states that created the problem. If the gap is not closed, the implementation was not successful, and one of the following is true: Either the problem was incorrectly identified, or the solution was inappropriate. Assuming the implementation was unsuccessful, management can return to the first step, problem identification. If the problem was correctly identified, management should consider implementing one of the previously identified, but untried, solutions. This process can continue until all feasible solutions have been tried or the problem has changed.[8]

Summarizing the Rational Model

Optimizing
Choosing the best possible solution.

The rational model is based on the premise that managers optimize when they make decisions. **Optimizing** involves solving problems by producing the best possible solution and is based on the fundamental assumptions listed in Figure 12–1. Practical experience, of course, tells us the assumptions outlined in the figure are unrealistic. As noted by Herbert Simon, a decision theorist who in 1978 earned the Nobel prize for his work on decision making, "The assumptions of perfect rationality are contrary to fact. It is not a question of approximation; they do not even remotely describe

Michael Dell and Kevin Rollins Make Decisions Collaboratively

The following comments by Michael Dell and Kevin Rollins were obtained during an interview for the *Harvard Business Review*. The interview questions are shown in bold.

How do your decision-making styles differ?

Dell: We're pretty complementary. We've learned over time that each of us is right about 80% of the time, but if you put us together, our hit rate is much, much higher. We each think about a slightly different set of things, but there's a lot of overlap.

Rollins: We're both opinionated, but we also realize that listening to one another is a good thing. We have a lot of trust in each other's judgment.

You two have been a team for many years. Now Kevin is CEO and Michael is chairman—how does that relationship work?

Dell: We're very collaborative. We share all the issues and opportunities. It's not at all a typical hierarchy, and this transition was not at all a typical CEO-to-chairman transition. . . .

Ultimately, we make much better decisions because each of us comes up with ideas that aren't fully developed, we work through them together, and we end up with better decisions. For example, we both recognized the strategic importance of printers, but we debated the fine points between ourselves, and this led to a better decision process and rollout.

Rollins: From the beginning, Michael was enthusiastic about getting into printers, whereas I was a little risk averse. With regard to our storage partnership with EMC, our positions were reversed. So it's not as though one of us always plays the optimist and one the pessimist. In both cases, we each talked a lot about the issues and our concerns and got the other comfortable. Then we proceeded as a team.

Kevin Rollins (left) and Michael Dell prefer a collaborative approach to decision making. What are the pros and cons of this decision-making style?

the processes that human beings use for making decisions in complex situations."[9] Thus, the rational model is at best an instructional tool. Since decision makers do not follow these rational procedures, Simon proposed a normative model of decision making.

Simon's Normative Model

This model attempts to identify the process that managers actually use when making decisions. The process is guided by a decision maker's bounded rationality. **Bounded rationality** represents the notion that decision makers are "bounded" or restricted by a variety of constraints when making decisions. These constraints include any personal or environmental characteristics that reduce rational decision making. Examples are the limited

Bounded rationality
Constraints that restrict rational decision making.

Figure 12–1   *Assumptions of Rational Decision Making*

SOURCE: S W Williams, *Making Better Business Decisions* (Thousand Oaks, CA: Sage Publications, 2002), p 15. Copyright © 2002, Sage Publications. Reprinted by permission of Sage Publications.

capacity of the human mind, problem complexity and uncertainty, amount and timeliness of information at hand, criticality of the decision, and time demands.[10]

As opposed to the rational model, Simon's normative model suggests that decision making is characterized by (1) limited information processing, (2) the use of judgmental heuristics, and (3) satisficing. Each of these characteristics is now explored.

Limited Information Processing   Managers are limited by how much information they process because of bounded rationality. This results in the tendency to acquire manageable rather than optimal amounts of information. In turn, this practice makes it difficult for managers to identify all possible alternative solutions. In the long run, the constraints of bounded rationality cause decision makers to fail to evaluate all potential alternatives.

Judgmental heuristics

Rules of thumb or shortcuts that people use to reduce information-processing demands.

Judgmental Heuristics   **Judgmental heuristics** represent rules of thumb or shortcuts that people use to reduce information-processing demands.[11] We automatically use them without conscious awareness. The use of heuristics helps decision makers to reduce the uncertainty inherent within the decision-making process. Because these shortcuts represent knowledge gained from past experience, they can help decision makers evaluate current problems. But they also can lead to systematic errors that erode the quality of decisions. Consider the role of judgmental heuristics in how people invest in the stock market.

Behaviorists say investors tend to latch on to extremes. . . . Down or up trends are etched in their minds as certainties, rather than mere probabilities. Take Cisco Systems, Inc. The stock zoomed for years, delivering double-digit returns. Investors got used to it, and expected history to repeat itself. . . . when the stock began to fall as evidence emerged that business was shaky, many investors went into denial, refusing to let go. "Investors have extrapolated Cisco's past performance too far into the future," says Josef Lakonishok, chief investment officer of LSV Asset Management. . . .

Far too often, analysts—and investors who follow them—exhibit "anchoring" behavior. They get attached to inaccurate price targets and ignore evidence that they might be wrong.[12]

There are two common categories of heuristics that are important to consider: the availability heuristic and the representative heuristic.

The **availability heuristic** represents a decision maker's tendency to base decisions on information that is readily available in memory. Information is more accessible in memory when it involves an event that recently occurred, when it is salient (e.g., a plane crash), and when it evokes strong emotions (e.g., a high-school student shooting other students). This heuristic is likely to cause people to overestimate the occurrence of unlikely events such as a plane crash or a high school shooting. This bias also is partially responsible for the recency effect discussed in Chapter 7. For example, a manager is more likely to give an employee a positive performance evaluation if the employee exhibited excellent performance over the last few months.

The **representativeness heuristic** is used when people estimate the probability of an event occurring. It reflects the tendency to assess the likelihood of an event occurring based on one's impressions about similar occurrences. A manager, for example, may hire a graduate from a particular university because the past three people hired from this university turned out to be good performers. In this case, the "school attended" criterion is used to facilitate complex information processing associated with employment interviews. Unfortunately, this shortcut can result in a biased decision. Similarly, an individual may believe that he or she can master a new software package in a short period of time because a different type of software was easy to learn. This estimate may or may not be accurate. For example, it may take the individual a much longer period of time to learn the new software because it involves learning a new programming language.

Satisficing

Satisficing   People satisfice because they do not have the time, information, or ability to handle the complexity associated with following a rational process. This is not necessarily undesirable. **Satisficing** consists of choosing a solution that meets some minimum qualifications, one that is "good enough." Satisficing resolves problems by producing solutions that are satisfactory, as opposed to optimal. Finding a radio station to listen to in your car is a good example of satisficing. You cannot optimize because it is impossible to listen to all stations at the same time. You thus stop searching for a station when you find one playing a song you like or do not mind hearing.

A survey of 479 managers from medium and large companies underscores the existence of satisficing: 77% of the respondents indicated the number of decisions they made had increased over the last three years and 42% revealed the average amount of time to make these decisions had correspondingly decreased.[13] We can generalize from these results that managers are being asked to make more decisions in less and less time.

Dynamics of Decision Making

Decision making is part science and part art. Accordingly, this section examines three dynamics of decision making—knowledge management, decision-making styles, and the problem of escalation of commitment—that affect the "science" component. We also examine the "art" side of the equation by discussing the role of intuition in decision making. An understanding of these dynamics can help managers make better decisions.

Availability heuristic
Tendency to base decisions on information readily available in memory.

Representativeness heuristic
Tendency to assess the likelihood of an event occurring based on impressions about similar occurrences.

Satisficing
Choosing a solution that meets a minimum standard of acceptance.

Improving Decision Making through Effective Knowledge Management

Making good decisions is not easy in today's world. Managers are not only being asked to make faster decisions, but they also must process an overwhelming amount of information during the decision-making process.[14] Furthermore, the orientation toward collaborative decision making and flatter organizational structures necessitates that managers obtain timely information from others dispersed throughout the organization or the world. Have you ever had to make a decision with either too much or too little information? If you have, then you know the quality of a decision is only as good as the information used to make the decision. This realization has spawned a growing interest in the concept of knowledge management. **Knowledge management** (KM) is "the development of tools, processes, systems, structures, and cultures explicitly to improve the creation, sharing, and use of knowledge critical for decision making."[15] The effective use of KM helps organizations improve the quality of their decision making and correspondingly reduce costs and increase productivity.[16] In contrast, ineffective use of knowledge management can be very costly. For example, experts estimate that *Fortune* 500 companies lose at least $31.5 billion a year by failing to share knowledge.[17]

This section explores the fundamentals of KM so that you can use them to improve your decision making.

Knowledge management
Implementing systems and practices that increase the sharing of knowledge and information throughout an organization.

Tacit knowledge
Information gained through experience that is difficult to express and formalize.

Explicit knowledge
Information that can be easily put into words and shared with others.

Knowledge Comes in Different Forms
There are two types of knowledge that impact the quality of decisions: tacit knowledge and explicit knowledge. **Tacit knowledge** "entails information that is difficult to express, formalize, or share. It . . . is unconsciously acquired from the experiences one has while immersed in an environment."[18] Many skills, for example, such as swinging a golf club or writing a speech, are difficult to describe in words because they involve tacit knowledge. Tacit knowledge is intuitive and is acquired by having considerable experience and expertise at some task or job. We more thoroughly discuss the role of intuition in decision making later in this section. In contrast, **explicit knowledge** can easily be put into words and explained to others. This type of knowledge is shared verbally or in written documents or numerical reports. In summary, tacit knowledge represents private information that is difficult to share, whereas explicit knowledge is external or public and is more easily communicated. Although both types of knowledge affect decision making, experts suggest competitive advantages are created when tacit knowledge is shared among employees.[19] Let us now examine how companies foster this type of information sharing.

Knowledge Sharing
Organizations increasingly rely on sophisticated KM software to share explicit knowledge. This software allows companies to amass large amounts of information that can be accessed quickly from around the world. For example, the Real World/Real People feature on page 379 illustrates how KM systems and software are being used by Hackensack University Medical Center to help doctors provide better care and treatment for their patients.[20] In contrast, tacit knowledge is shared most directly by observing, participating, or working with experts or coaches. Mentoring, which was discussed in Chapter 3, is another method for spreading tacit knowledge. Finally, informal networking, periodic meetings, and the design of office space can be used to facilitate KM. Alcoa, for example, designed its headquarters with the aim of increasing information sharing among its executives.

Alcoa, the world's leading producer of aluminum, wanted to improve access between its senior executives. When designing their new headquarters they focused on open offices, family-style kitchens in the center of each floor, and plenty of open spaces. Previously, top

Hackensack University Medical Center Uses Medically Based Knowledge Management Systems to Treat Patients

Peter A Gross has been a doctor for 40 years, rising up the ranks to become the chairman of internal medicine at Hackensack University Medical Center in Hackensack, New Jersey. But one day this winter, a homeless man checked in to the hospital with HIV, and Gross made a decision that could have seriously harmed his patient. He chose to give the patient an HIV drug, tapping a request into a hospital computer and zapping it off to the two-year-old digital drug-order entry system. Moments later he got back a message he never would have received before the system was in place: a warning that the drug could mix dangerously with an antidepressant the patient was already taking. Gross got on the phone to figure out the problem, eventually asking the man's psychiatrist to reduce the dosage of his antidepressant. "There's no way I would have picked that up," Gross says. "It was totally unexpected."

Scenes like this are unfolding across the country, providing a glimpse into the potential of information technology to transform the health-care industry. Hackensack is one of the nation's most aggressive tech adopters. Millions of dollars in investments have paid for projects well beyond the online drug system that tipped off Gross. Doctors can tap an internal Web site to examine X-rays from a PC anywhere. Patients can use 37-inch plasma TVs in their rooms to surf the Net for information about their medical conditions. There's even a life-size robot, Mr Rounder, that doctors can control from their laptops at home. They direct the digital doc, complete with white lab coat and stetho-

scope, into hospital rooms and use two-way video to discuss patients' conditions.

Whimsical? Maybe, but Hackensack's results are perfectly serious. Patient mortality rates are down. Quality of care is up. At the same time, productivity is rising.

Knowledge management systems are helping doctors make better decisions. Doctors at Hackensack University Medical Center, for example, use robots like Mr Rounder to help provide better patient care. Would you like to have Mr Rounder involved with your medical treatment?

SOURCE: Excerpted from T J Mullaney and A Weintraub, "The Digital Hospital," *BusinessWeek,* March 28, 2005, p 77. Reprinted by permission of The McGraw-Hill Companies, Inc.

executives would only interact with a couple of people in the elevator and those they had scheduled meetings with. Now, executives bump into each other more often and are more accessible for serendipitous conversations. This change in space has increased general accessibility as well as narrowed the gap between top executives and employees.[21]

It is important to remember that the best-laid plans for increasing KM are unlikely to succeed without the proper organizational culture. Effective KM requires a knowledge-sharing culture that both encourages and reinforces the spread of tacit knowledge. IBM Global Services has taken this recommendation to heart.

IBM Global Services has incorporated knowledge creation, sharing, and reuse measurements into performance metrics. Performance metrics and incentives, particularly at the executive rank, have driven collaborative behavior into the day-to-day work practices of executive networks. Further, knowledge sharing has been incorporated into personal business commitments, which are required for certification and affect promotion decisions. This encourages employees at all levels to be collaborative with and accessible to each other.[22]

General Decision-Making Styles

It should come as no surprise to learn that personal characteristics influence the manner in which we make decisions. For example, a meta-analysis involving 14 studies and 3,338 individuals revealed that entrepreneurs had higher risk-taking propensities when making decisions than did managers.[23] This finding underscores the value of investigating the relationship between individual differences and decision making. This section therefore focuses on how an individual's decision-making style affects his or her approach to decision making. We believe this awareness can help you make better decisions.

Decision-making style
A combination of how individuals perceive and respond to information.

A **decision-making style** reflects the combination of how an individual perceives and comprehends stimuli and the general manner in which he or she chooses to respond to such information.[24] A team of researchers developed a model of decision-making styles that is based on the idea that styles vary along two different dimensions: value orientation and tolerance for ambiguity.[25] *Value orientation* reflects the extent to which an individual focuses on either task and technical concerns or people and social concerns when making decisions. Some people, for instance, are very task focused at work and do not pay much attention to people issues, whereas others are just the opposite. The second dimension pertains to a person's *tolerance for ambiguity*. This individual difference indicates the extent to which a person has a high need for structure or control in his or her life. Some people desire a lot of structure in their lives (a low tolerance for ambiguity) and find ambiguous situations stressful and psychologically uncomfortable. In contrast, others do not have a high need for structure and can thrive in uncertain situations (a high tolerance for ambiguity). Ambiguous situations can energize people with a high tolerance for ambiguity. When the dimensions of value orientation and tolerance for ambiguity are combined, they form four styles of decision making (see Figure 12–2): directive, analytical, conceptual, and behavioral.

Directive

People with a *directive* style have a low tolerance for ambiguity and are oriented toward task and technical concerns when making decisions. They are efficient, logical, practical, and systematic in their approach to solving problems. People with this style are action oriented and decisive and like to focus on facts. In their pursuit of speed and re-

Figure 12–2   *Decision-Making Styles*

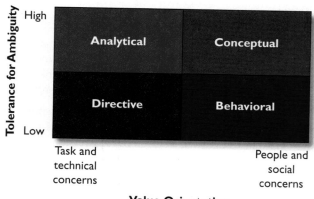

SOURCE: Based on discussion contained in A J Rowe and R O Mason, *Managing with Style: A Guide to Understanding, Assessing, and Improving Decision Making* (San Francisco: Jossey-Bass, 1987), pp 1–17.

sults, however, these individuals tend to be autocratic, exercise power and control, and focus on the short run.

Analytical   This style has a much higher tolerance for ambiguity and is characterized by the tendency to overanalyze a situation. People with this style like to consider more information and alternatives than do directives. Analytic individuals are careful decision makers who take longer to make decisions but who also respond well to new or uncertain situations. They can often be autocratic.

Conceptual   People with a conceptual style have a high tolerance for ambiguity and tend to focus on the people or social aspects of a work situation. They take a broad perspective to problem solving and like to consider many options and future possibilities. Conceptual types adopt a long-term perspective and rely on intuition and discussions with others to acquire information. They also are willing to take risks and are good at finding creative solutions to problems. On the downside, however, a conceptual style can foster an idealistic and indecisive approach to decision making.

Behavioral   This style is the most people oriented of the four styles. People with this style work well with others and enjoy social interactions in which opinions are openly exchanged. Behavioral types are supportive, receptive to suggestions, show warmth, and prefer verbal to written information. Although they like to hold meetings, people with this style have a tendency to avoid conflict and to be too concerned about others. This can lead behavioral types to adopt a wishy-washy approach to decision making and to have a hard time saying no to others and to have difficulty making difficult decisions.

Research and Practical Implications   Research shows that very few people have only one dominant decision-making style. Rather, most managers have characteristics that fall into two or three styles. Studies also show that decision-making styles vary by age, occupations, job level, and countries.[26] You can use knowledge of decision-making styles in three ways. First, knowledge of styles helps you to understand yourself. Awareness of your style assists you in identifying your strengths and weaknesses as a decision maker and facilitates the potential for self-improvement. (You can assess your decision-making style by completing the Personal Awareness and Growth Exercise located at the end of this chapter.) Second, you can increase your ability to influence others by being aware of styles. For example, if you are dealing with an analytical person, you should provide as much information as possible to support your ideas. This same approach is more likely to frustrate a directive type. Finally, knowledge of styles gives you an awareness of how people can take the same information and yet arrive at different decisions by using a variety of decision-making strategies. Different decision-making styles represent one likely source of interpersonal conflict at work (conflict is thoroughly discussed in Chapter 13). It is important to conclude with the caveat that there is not a best decision-making style that applies in all situations.

Escalation of Commitment

Escalation situations involve circumstances in which things have gone wrong but where the situation can possibly be turned around by investing additional time, money, or effort. **Escalation of commitment** refers to the tendency to stick to an ineffective course of action when it is unlikely that the bad situation can be reversed. Personal examples include

Escalation of commitment
Sticking to an ineffective course of action too long.

Figure 12–3   *A Model of Escalation of Commitment*

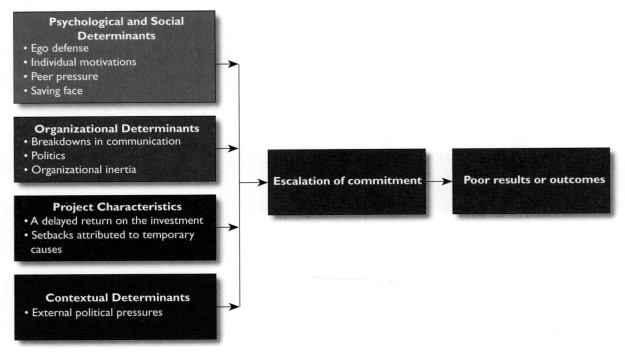

SOURCE: Based on discussion in J Ross and B M Staw, "Organizational Escalation and Exit: Lessons from the Shoreham Nuclear Power Plant," *Academy of Management Journal,* August 1993, pp 701–32.

investing more money into an old or broken car, waiting an extremely long time for a bus to take you somewhere when you could have walked just as easily, or trying to save a disruptive interpersonal relationship that has lasted 10 years. Case studies also indicate that escalation of commitment is partially responsible for some of the worst financial losses experienced by organizations. For example, from 1966 to 1989 the Long Island Lighting Company's investment in the Shoreham nuclear power plant escalated from $65 million to $5 billion, despite a steady flow of negative feedback. The plant was never opened.[27]

OB researchers Jerry Ross and Barry Staw identified four reasons for escalation of commitment (see Figure 12–3). They involve psychological and social determinants, organizational determinants, project characteristics, and contextual determinants.[28]

Psychological and Social Determinants   Ego defense and individual motivations are the key psychological contributors to escalation of commitment. Individuals "throw good money after bad" because they tend to (1) bias facts so that they support previous decisions, (2) take more risks when a decision is stated in negative terms (to recover losses) rather than positive ones (to achieve gains), and (3) get too ego-involved with the project. Because failure threatens an individual's self-esteem or ego, people tend to ignore negative signs and push forward.

Social pressures can make it difficult for a manager to reverse a course of action. For instance, peer pressure makes it difficult for an individual to drop a course of action when he or she publicly supported it in the past. Further, managers may continue to support bad decisions because they don't want their mistakes exposed to others. For example, a study involving 102 students working on a computer-simulated competition revealed that they engaged in less escalation of commitment when their performance was being monitored.[29]

Organizational Determinants
Breakdowns in communication, workplace politics, and organizational inertia cause organizations to maintain bad courses of action.

Project Characteristics
Project characteristics involve the objective features of a project. They have the greatest impact on escalation decisions. For example, because most projects do not reap benefits until some delayed time period, decision makers are motivated to stay with the project until the end.[30] Thus, there is a tendency to attribute setbacks to temporary causes that are correctable with additional expenditures. Moreover, escalation is related to whether the project has clearly defined goals and whether people receive clear feedback about performance. One study, for instance, revealed that escalation was fueled by ambiguous performance feedback and the lack of performance standards.[31]

Contextual Determinants
These causes of escalation are due to forces outside an organization's control. For instance, one study showed that a manager's national culture influenced the amount of escalation in decision making. Samples of decision makers in Mexico and the United States revealed that Mexican managers exhibited more escalation than US managers.[32]

External political forces also represent a contextual determinant. The continuance of the previously discussed Shoreham nuclear power plant, for example, was partially influenced by pressures from other public utilities interested in nuclear power, representatives of the nuclear power industry, and people in the federal government pushing for the development of nuclear power.[33]

Reducing Escalation of Commitment
It is important to reduce escalation of commitment because it leads to poor decision making for both individuals and groups.[34] Researchers recommend the following actions to reduce escalation of commitment:

- Set minimum targets for performance, and have decision makers compare their performance against these targets.
- Stimulate opposing positions by using a devil's advocate approach during project completion. This technique is discussed in Chapter 13.
- Regularly rotate managers in key positions throughout the project.
- Encourage decision makers to become less ego-involved with a project.
- Provide more frequent feedback about project completion and costs.
- Reduce the risk or penalties of failure.
- Make decision makers aware of the costs of persistence.[35]

The Role of Intuition in Decision Making

Have you ever had a hunch or gut feeling about something? If yes, then you have experienced the effects of intuition. **Intuition** "is a capacity for attaining direct knowledge or understanding without the apparent intrusion of rational thought or logical inference."[36] As a process, intuition is automatic and involuntary. It is important to understand the sources of

Intuition
Making a choice without the use of conscious thought or logical inference.

intuition and to develop your intuitive skills because intuition is as important as rational analysis in many decisions.[37] Consider the following examples:

> Ignoring recommendations from advisers, Ray Kroc purchased the McDonald's brand from the McDonald brothers: "I'm not a gambler and I didn't have that kind of money, but my funny bone instinct kept urging me on." Ignoring numerous naysayers and a lack of supporting market research, Bob Lutz, former president of Chrysler, made the Dodge Viper a reality. "It was this subconscious, visceral feeling. And it just felt right." Ignoring the fact that 24 publishing houses had rejected the book and her own publishing house was opposed, Eleanor Friede gambled on a "little nothing book," called *Jonathan Livingston Seagull:* "I felt there were truths in this simple story that would make it an international classic."[38]

Unfortunately, the use of intuition does not always lead to blockbuster decisions such as those by Ray Kroc or Eleanor Friede. To enhance your understanding about the role of intuition in decision making, this section reviews a model of intuition and discusses the pros and cons of using intuition to make decisions.

A Model of Intuition

Figure 12–4 presents a model of intuition. Starting at the far right of the model, you can see that there are two types of intuition: holistic hunches and automated experiences.[39] A *holistic hunch* represents a judgment that is based on a subconscious integration of information stored in memory. People using this form of intuition may not even be able explain or justify why they want to make a certain decision, but they conclude that the choice just "feels right." The previous examples of Ray Kroc and Bob Lutz represent this type of intuition. In contrast, *automated experiences* represent a choice that is based on a familiar situation and a partially subconscious application of previously learned information related to that situation. For example, in writing this book we have developed an intuitive sense for when an example is needed to clarify a concept, like the present situation. We intuitively know this based on our textbook-writing experiences. Driving a car and riding a bicycle are examples of the type of learning that underlies automated experiences.

Figure 12–4   *A Model of Intuition*

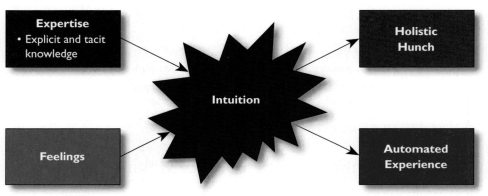

SOURCES: Based in part on E Sadler-Smith and E Shefy, "The Intuitive Executive: Understanding and Applying 'Gut Feel' in Decision-Making," *Academy of Management Executive,* November 2004, pp 76–91; and C C Miller and R D Ireland, "Intuition in Strategic Decision Making: Friend or Foe in the Fast-Paced 21st Century," *Academy of Management Executive,* February 2005, pp 19–30.

John Martin Uses Intuition and Rationality to Solve a Problem

It was 1999, and John C Martin finally had something to show for his decade of leadership at fledgling Gilead Sciences Inc.: Preveon, a promising new drug to combat human immunodeficiency virus (HIV). But late in clinical trials, patients started dying from kidney failure, and the drug had to be scrapped. That was doubly worrying because Gilead's next drug in the pipeline, Viread, was a close cousin to Preveon. With little revenue and big expenses, Martin quickly had to decide whether to pull the plug on Viread. So the former researcher spent months delving into the science to figure out what went wrong. He decided to stick with Viread—and even predicted that it would be 10 times safer.

Martin was right. Just six years later, Viread is Gilead's top-selling drug, with $780 million in revenues. Even Preveon was salvaged, renamed Hepsera, and sold at a lower dosage to treat hepatitis B. It contributed $112 million to Gilead's top line last year. "He turned a defeat into two wins," says Gilead chief financial officer John F Milligan.

SOURCE: Excerpted from S Lacy, "A Small Biotech's Big Growth Spurt," *Business Week*, April 25, 2005, p 82. Reprinted by permission of The McGraw-Hill Companies, Inc.

Returning to Figure 12–4, you can see that there are two sources of intuition: expertise and feelings. *Expertise* represents an individual's combined explicit and tacit knowledge regarding an object, person, situation, or decision opportunity. This source of intuition increases with age and experience. The *feelings* component of intuition simply reflects the automatic, underlying affect one experiences in response to an object, person, situation, or decision opportunity. Ultimately, an intuitive response is based on the interaction between one's expertise and feelings in a given situation. Consider the example of being cut off by another driver on the freeway. You may automatically get mad (intuitive feelings) but decide not to make any obscene hand gestures or tailgate because it may lead to road rage from the other individual (intuitive expertise).

Pros and Cons of Using Intuition When Making Decisions

On the positive side, intuition can speed up the decision-making process.[40] Intuition thus can be valuable in the complex and ever-changing world we live in. Intuition also is a good approach to use when managers are faced with limited resources and tight deadlines. In contrast, intuition is subject to the same type of biases associated with rational decision making. For example, intuition is particularly susceptible to the availability and representativeness heuristics, which were previously discussed, as well as the overconfidence effect (my hunches have been accurate in the past) and the hindsight bias (the I "knew-it-all-along" syndrome).[41] A final limitation involves the difficulty in convincing others that a hunch makes sense. In the end, a good intuitive idea may be ignored because people do not understand the idea's underlying logic.

Where does that leave us with respect to using intuition? We believe that intuition and rationality are complementary and that managers should attempt to use both when making decisions. For example, rational analysis can be used to verify or validate a hunch. John Martin used this approach when trying to decide what to do about a promising new drug called Preveon (see Real World/Real People). Conversely, managers can use intuition to evaluate a rational choice by asking questions such as What does my experience suggest about this decision? You can develop your intuitive awareness by using the guidelines shown in Table 12–1.

385

Table 12–1   *Guidelines for Developing Intuitive Awareness*

Recommendation	Description
1. Open up the closet	To what extent do you experience intuition; trust your feelings; count on intuitive judgments; suppress hunches; covertly rely upon gut feel?
2. Don't mix up your I's	Instinct, insight, and intuition are not synonymous; practice distinguishing between your instincts, your insights, and your intuitions.
3. Elicit good feedback	Seek feedback on your intuitive judgments; build confidence in your gut feel; create a learning environment in which you can develop better intuitive awareness.
4. Get a feel for your batting average	Benchmark your intuitions; get a sense for how reliable your hunches are; ask yourself how your intuitive judgment might be improved.
5. Use imagery	Use imagery rather than words; literally visualize potential future scenarios that take your gut feelings into account.
6. Play devil's advocate	Test out intuitive judgments; raise objections to them; generate counter-arguments; probe how robust gut feel is when challenged.
7. Capture and validate your intuitions	Create the inner state to give your intuitive mind the freedom to roam; capture your creative intuitions; log them before they are censored by rational analysis.

SOURCE: E Sadler-Smith and E Shefy, "The Intuitive Executive: Understanding and Applying 'Gut Feel' in Decision-Making," *Academy of Management Executive*, November 2004, p 88. Reprinted with permission of The Academy of Management via The Copyright Clearance Center.

Group Decision Making

Groups such as committees, task forces, project teams, or review panels often play a key role in the decision-making process. Are two or more heads always better than one? Do all employees desire to have a say in the decision-making process? To what extent are managers involving employees in the decision-making process? What techniques do groups use to improve their decision making? Are face-to-face meetings more effective than computer-aided decision making? This section provides the background for answering these questions. We discuss (1) group involvement in decision making, (2) advantages and disadvantages of group-aided decision making, and (3) group problem-solving techniques.

Group Involvement in Decision Making

Whether groups assemble in face-to-face meetings or rely on other technologically based methods to communicate, they can contribute to each stage of the decision-making process. In order to maximize the value of group-aided decision making, however, it is important to create an environment in which group members feel free to participate and express their opinions. Research sheds light on how managers can create such an environment.

A team of researchers conducted two studies to determine whether a group's innovativeness was related to *minority dissent,* defined as the extent to which group members feel comfortable disagreeing with other group members, and a group's level of participation in decision making. Results showed that the most innovative groups possessed high levels of both minority dissent and participation in decision making.[42] These findings encourage managers to seek divergent views from group members during decision making. They also support the practice of not seeking compliance from group members or punishing group

Assessing Participation in Group Decision Making

Instructions

The following survey measures minority dissent, participation in group decision making, and satisfaction with a group. For each of the items, use the rating scale shown below to circle the answer that best represents your feelings based on a group project you were or currently are involved in. Next, use the scoring key to compute scores for the levels of minority dissent, participation in decision making, and satisfaction with the group.

1 = strongly disagree
2 = disagree
3 = neither agree nor disagree
4 = agree
5 = strongly agree

1. Within my team, individuals disagree with one another.	1	2	3	4	5
2. Within my team, individuals do not go along with majority opinion.	1	2	3	4	5
3. Within my team, individuals voice their disagreement of majority opinion.	1	2	3	4	5
4. Within my team, I am comfortable voicing my disagreement of the majority opinion.	1	2	3	4	5
5. Within my team, individuals do not immediately agree with one another.	1	2	3	4	5
6. As a team member, I have a real say in how work is carried out.	1	2	3	4	5
7. Within my team, most members have a chance to participate in decisions.	1	2	3	4	5
8. My team is designed so that everyone has the opportunity to participate in decisions.	1	2	3	4	5
9. I am satisfied with my group.	1	2	3	4	5
10. I would like to work with this group on another project.	1	2	3	4	5

Scoring Key

Minority dissent (add scores for items 1, 2, 3, 4, 5): _____
Participation in decision making (add scores for items 6, 7, 8): _____
Satisfaction (add scores for items 9, 10): _____

Arbitrary Norms

Low minority dissent = 5–15
High minority dissent = 16–25
Low participation in decision making = 3–9
High participation in decision making = 10–15
Low satisfaction = 2–6
High satisfaction = 7–10

SOURCE: The items in the survey were developed from C K W De Dreu and M A West "Minority Dissent and Team Innovation: The Importance of Participation in Decision Making," *Journal of Applied Psychology,* December 2001, pp 1191–201.

members who disagree with majority opinion. Take a moment now to complete the OB Exercise shown above. It assesses the amount of minority dissent and participation in group decision making for a group project you have completed or are currently working on in school or on the job. Is your satisfaction with the group related to minority dissent and participation in decision making? If not, what might explain this surprising result?

The above study reinforces the notion that the quality of group decision making varies across groups. This in turn raises the issue of how to best assess a group's decision-making effectiveness. Although experts do not agree on the one "best" criterion, there is agreement that groups need to work through various aspects of decision making in order to be effective.

One expert proposed that decision-making effectiveness in a group is dependent on successfully accomplishing the following:[43]

1. Developing a clear understanding of the decision situation.
2. Developing a clear understanding of the requirements for an effective choice.
3. Thoroughly and accurately assessing the positive qualities of alternative solutions.
4. Thoroughly and accurately assessing the negative qualities of alternative solutions.

To increase the probability of groups making high-quality decisions, managers, team leaders, and individual group members are encouraged to focus on satisfying these four requirements.[44]

Advantages and Disadvantages of Group-Aided Decision Making

Including groups in the decision-making process has both pros and cons (see Table 12–2). On the positive side, groups contain a greater pool of knowledge, provide more varied perspectives, create more comprehension of decisions, increase decision acceptance, and create a training ground for inexperienced employees. These advantages must be balanced, however, with the disadvantages listed in Table 12–2. In doing so, managers need to determine the extent to which the advantages and disadvantages apply to the decision situation. The following three guidelines may then be applied to help decide whether groups should be included in the decision-making process.

1. If additional information would increase the quality of the decision, managers should involve those people who can provide the needed information.

Table 12–2   *Advantages and Disadvantages of Group-Aided Decision Making*

Advantages	Disadvantages
1. **Greater pool of knowledge.** A group can bring much more information and experience to bear on a decision or problem than can an individual acting alone.	1. **Social pressure.** Unwillingness to "rock the boat" and pressure to conform may combine to stifle the creativity of individual contributors.
2. **Different perspectives.** Individuals with varied experience and interests help the group see decision situations and problems from different angles.	2. **Domination by a vocal few.** Sometimes the quality of group action is reduced when the group gives in to those who talk the loudest and longest.
3. **Greater comprehension.** Those who personally experience the give-and-take of group discussion about alternative courses of action tend to understand the rationale behind the final decision.	3. **Logrolling.** Political wheeling and dealing can displace sound thinking when an individual's pet project or vested interest is at stake.
4. **Increased acceptance.** Those who play an active role in group decision making and problem solving tend to view the outcome as "ours" rather than "theirs."	4. **Goal displacement.** Sometimes secondary considerations such as winning an argument, making a point, or getting back at a rival displace the primary task of making a sound decision or solving a problem.
5. **Training ground.** Less experienced participants in group action learn how to cope with group dynamics by actually being involved.	5. **Groupthink.** Sometimes cohesive in-groups let the desire for unanimity override sound judgment when generating and evaluating alternative courses of action. (Groupthink was discussed in Chapter 10.)

SOURCE: R Kreitner, *Management*, 8th ed (Boston: Houghton Mifflin, 2001), p 243. Copyright © 2001 by Houghton Mifflin Company. Used with permission.

2. If acceptance is important, managers need to involve those individuals whose acceptance and commitment are important.

3. If people can be developed through their participation, managers may want to involve those whose development is most important.[45]

Group versus Individual Performance

Before recommending that managers involve groups in decision making, it is important to examine whether groups perform better or worse than individuals. After reviewing 61 years of relevant research, a decision-making expert concluded that "Group performance was generally qualitatively and quantitatively superior to the performance of the average individual."[46] Although subsequent research of small-group decision making generally supported this conclusion, there are five important issues to consider when using groups to make decisions:

1. Groups were less efficient than individuals. Consider how long it took a team of Nokia executives to decide whether or not to license its software to other phone makers. "Nokia executives, who prize consensus, debated the issue for nine months from mid-2000 to early 2001. At eight successive monthly meetings of the company's nine-person executive board, members raised questions and stalled the project."[47] This example highlights that time constraints are an important consideration when determining whether to involve groups in decision making.

2. Groups were more confident about their judgments and choices than individuals. Because group confidence is not a surrogate for group decision quality, this overconfidence can fuel groupthink—groupthink was discussed in Chapter 10—and a resistance to consider alternative solutions proposed by individuals outside the group.

3. Group size affected decision outcomes. Decision quality was negatively related to group size.[48]

4. Decision-making accuracy was higher when (a) groups knew a great deal about the issues at hand and (b) group leaders possessed the ability to effectively evaluate the group members' opinions and judgments. Groups need to give more weight to relevant and accurate judgments while downplaying irrelevant or inaccurate judgments made by its members.[49]

5. The composition of a group affects its decision-making processes and ultimately performance. For example, groups of familiar people are more likely to make better decisions when members share a lot of unique information. In contrast, unacquainted group members should outperform groups of friends when most group members possess common knowledge.[50]

Additional research suggests that managers should use a contingency approach when determining whether to include others in the decision-making process. Let us now consider these contingency recommendations.

Practical Contingency Recommendations

If the decision occurs frequently, such as deciding on promotions or who qualifies for a loan, use groups because they tend to produce more consistent decisions than do individuals. Given time constraints, let the most competent individual, rather than a group, make the decision. In the face of environmental threats such as time pressure and potential serious effects of a decision, groups use less information and fewer communication channels. This increases the probability of a bad decision. This conclusion underscores a general recommendation that managers should keep in mind: Because the quality of communication strongly affects a group's productivity, on complex tasks it is essential to devise mechanisms to enhance communication effectiveness.

Group Problem-Solving Techniques

Consensus

Presenting opinions and gaining agreement to support a decision.

Using groups to make decisions generally requires that they reach a consensus. According to a decision-making expert, a **consensus** "is reached when all members can say they either agree with the decision or have had their 'day in court' and were unable to convince the others of their viewpoint. In the final analysis, everyone agrees to support the outcome."[51] This definition indicates that consensus does not require unanimous agreement because group members may still disagree with the final decision but are willing to work toward its success.

Groups can experience roadblocks when trying to arrive at a consensus decision. For one, groups may not generate all relevant alternatives to a problem because an individual dominates or intimidates other group members. This can be overt or subtle. For instance, group members who possess power and authority, such as a CEO, can be intimidating, regardless of interpersonal style, simply by being present in the room. Moreover, shyness inhibits the generation of alternatives. Shy or socially anxious individuals may withhold their input for fear of embarrassment or lack of confidence. Satisficing is another hurdle to effective group decision making. As previously noted, groups satisfice due to limited time, information, or ability to handle large amounts of information. A management expert offered the following dos and don'ts for successfully achieving consensus: Groups should use active listening skills, involve as many members as possible, seek out the reasons behind arguments, and dig for the facts. At the same time, groups should not horse trade (I'll support you on this decision because you supported me on the last one), vote, or agree just to avoid "rocking the boat."[52] Voting is not encouraged because it can split the group into winners and losers.

Decision-making experts have developed three group problem-solving techniques—brainstorming, the nominal group technique, and the Delphi technique—to reduce the above roadblocks. Knowledge of these techniques can help current and future managers to more effectively use group-aided decision making. Further, the advent of computer-aided decision making enables managers to use these techniques to solve complex problems with large groups of people.

Brainstorming

Process to generate a quantity of ideas.

Brainstorming

Brainstorming was developed by A F Osborn, an advertising executive, to increase creativity.[53] **Brainstorming** is used to help groups generate multiple ideas and alternatives for solving problems. This technique is effective because it helps reduce interference caused by critical and judgmental reactions to one's ideas from other group members.

When brainstorming, a group is convened, and the problem at hand is reviewed. Individual members then are asked to silently generate ideas/alternatives for solving the problem. Silent idea generation is recommended over the practice of having group members randomly shout out their ideas because it leads to a greater number of unique ideas. Next, these ideas/alternatives are solicited and written on a board or flip chart. A recent study suggests that managers or team leaders may want to collect the brainstormed ideas anonymously. Results demonstrated that more controversial ideas and more nonredundant ideas were generated by anonymous than nonanonymous brainstorming groups.[54] Finally, a second session is used to critique and evaluate the alternatives. Managers are advised

These ad agency employees are conducting a brainstorming session. Brainstorming can be fun and is used to generate multiple ideas and solutions for solving problems.

to follow the seven rules for brainstorming used by IDEO, the product design company featured in the OB in Action Case Study at the end of this chapter.[55]

1. *Defer judgment.* Don't criticize during the initial stage of idea generation. Phrases such as "we've never done it that way," "it won't work," "it's too expensive," and "our manager will never agree" should not be used.

2. *Build on the ideas of others.* Encourage participants to extend others' ideas by avoiding "buts" and using "ands."

3. *Encourage wild ideas.* Encourage out-of-the-box thinking. The wilder and more outrageous the ideas, the better.

4. *Go for quantity over quality.* Participants should try to generate and write down as many new ideas as possible. Focusing on quantity encourages people to think beyond their favorite ideas.

5. *Be visual.* Use different colored pens (e.g., red, purple, blue) to write on big sheets of flip chart paper, white boards, or poster board that are put on the wall.

6. *Stay focused on the topic.* A facilitator should be used to keep the discussion on target.

7. *One conversation at a time.* The ground rules are that no one interrupts another person, no dismissing of someone's ideas, no disrespect, and no rudeness.

Brainstorming is an effective technique for generating new ideas/alternatives. It is not appropriate for evaluating alternatives or selecting solutions.

The Nominal Group Technique

The **nominal group technique** (NGT) helps groups generate ideas and evaluate and select solutions. NGT is a structured group meeting that follows this format:[56]

A group is convened to discuss a particular problem or issue. After the problem is understood, individuals silently generate ideas in writing. Each individual, in roundrobin fashion, then offers one idea from his or her list. Ideas are recorded on a blackboard or flip chart; they are not discussed at this stage of the process. Once all ideas are elicited, the group discusses them. Anyone may criticize or defend any item. During this step, clarification is provided as well as general agreement or disagreement with the idea. The "30-second soap box" technique, which entails giving each participant a maximum of 30 seconds to argue for or against any of the ideas under consideration, can be used to facilitate this discussion. Finally, group members anonymously vote for their top choices with a weighted voting procedure (e.g., 1st choice = 3 points; 2nd choice = 2 points; 3rd choice = 1 point). The group leader then adds the votes to determine the group's choice. Prior to making a final decision, the group may decide to discuss the top ranked items and conduct a second round of voting.

The nominal group technique reduces the roadblocks to group decision making by (1) separating brainstorming from evaluation, (2) promoting balanced participation among group members, and (3) incorporating mathematical voting techniques in order to reach consensus. The NGT has been successfully used in many different decision-making situations and has been found to generate more ideas than a standard brainstorming session.[57]

Nominal group technique
Process to generate ideas and evaluate solutions.

The Delphi Technique

This problem-solving method was originally developed by the Rand Corporation for technological forecasting.[58] It now is used as a multipurpose planning tool. The **Delphi technique** is a group process that anonymously generates ideas or judgments from physically dispersed experts. Unlike the NGT, experts' ideas are obtained from questionnaires or via the Internet as opposed to face-to-face group discussions.

Delphi technique
Process to generate ideas from physically dispersed experts.

Engineers at Starkey Laboratories Design Products with Information-Sharing Software

Starkey Laboratories Inc. is known for its high-end hearing aids, but until recently the process that engineers at the Eden Prairie (Minnesota) company used to design them was decidedly low-end. They would cook up a design concept and then e-mail it to colleagues so they could make changes. But because multiple copies of each design were circulating, there was a lot of confusion about which version was the most up-to-date.

Rather than wait for Starkey's tech department to deliver a solution, a group of frustrated engineers took matters into their own hands. They used Microsoft Corp. software to covertly set up an internal Web site for collaboration. They were able to go online to set common goals and deadlines, and to maintain one version of a design for their project that anyone could modify.

SOURCE: Excerpted from J Greene, "Combat over Collaboration," *Business Week,* April 18, 2005, p 64.

A manager begins the Delphi process by identifying the issue(s) he or she wants to investigate. For example, a manager might want to inquire about customer demand, customers' future preferences, or the effect of locating a plant in a certain region of the country. Next, participants are identified and a questionnaire is developed. The questionnaire is sent to participants and returned to the manager. In today's computer-networked environments, this often means that the questionnaires are e-mailed to participants. The manager then summarizes the responses and sends feedback to the participants. At this stage, participants are asked to (1) review the feedback, (2) prioritize the issues being considered, and (3) return the survey within a specified time period. This cycle repeats until the manager obtains the necessary information.

The Delphi technique is useful when face-to-face discussions are impractical, when disagreements and conflict are likely to impair communication, when certain individuals might severely dominate group discussion, and when groupthink is a probable outcome of the group process.[59]

Computer-Aided Decision Making The purpose of computer-aided decision making is to reduce consensus roadblocks while collecting more information in a shorter period of time. There are two types of computer-aided decision-making systems: chauffeur driven and group driven.[60] Chauffeur-driven systems ask participants to answer predetermined questions on electronic keypads or dials. Live television audiences on shows such as *Who Wants to Be a Millionaire* are frequently polled with this system. The computer system tabulates participants' responses in a matter of seconds.

Group-driven electronic meetings are conducted in one of two major ways. First, managers can use e-mail systems, which are discussed in Chapter 14, or the Internet to collect information or brainstorm about a decision that must be made. For example, Starkey Laboratories uses its e-mail system coupled with special information-sharing software to allow its engineers to collaboratively design products (see Real World/Real People). Timothy Trine, Starkey's vice president for hearing research and technology, indicated that the company's computer-aided decision-making software led to significant increases in productivity.[61]

The second method of computer-aided, group-driven meetings is conducted in special facilities equipped with individual workstations that are networked to each other. Instead of talking, participants type their input, ideas, comments, reactions, or evaluations on their keyboards. The input simultaneously appears on a large projector screen at the front of the room, thereby enabling all participants to see all input. This computer-driven process reduces consensus roadblocks because input is anonymous, everyone gets a chance to contribute, and no one can dominate the process. Research demonstrated that computer-aided decision making produced greater quality and quantity of ideas than either traditional brainstorming or the nominal group technique for both small and large groups of people.[62]

Interestingly, however, another recent study suggests caution when determining what forms of computer-aided decision making to use. This meta-analysis of 52 studies compared the effectiveness of face-to-face decision-making groups with "chat" groups. Results revealed that the use of chat groups led to decreased group effectiveness and member satisfaction and increased time to complete tasks compared to face-to-face groups.[63] These findings underscore the need to use a contingency approach for selecting the best method of computer-aided decision making in a given situation. Our discussion of a contingency model for selecting communication media in Chapter 14 can help in this process.

Creativity

In light of today's need for fast-paced decisions, an organization's ability to stimulate the creativity and innovation of its employees is becoming increasingly important. Many organizations believe that creativity and innovation are the seeds of success.[64]

To gain further insight into managing the creative process, we begin by defining creativity and highlighting the stages underlying individual creativity. This section then presents a model of organizational creativity and innovation.

Definition and Stages

Although many definitions have been proposed, **creativity** is defined here as the process of using imagination and skill to develop a new or unique product, object, process, or thought.[65] It can be as simple as locating a new place to hang your car keys or as complex as developing a pocket-size microcomputer. This definition highlights three broad types of creativity. One can create something new (creation), one can combine or synthesize things (synthesis), or one can improve or change things (modification).

Creativity
Process of developing something new or unique.

Researchers are not absolutely certain how creativity takes place. Nonetheless, we do know that creativity involves "making remote associations" between unconnected events, ideas, information stored in memory (recall our discussion in Chapter 7), or physical objects. Consider how biologist Napoleone Ferrara's remote associations led to the creation of a new type of cancer therapy that extends cancer patients' lives:

> Twenty years ago biologist Napoleone Ferrara discovered a mysterious protein in the pituitary gland of cows that seemed to make blood vessels grow. He foresaw a new weapon against cancer—block the protein and tumors may be unable to proliferate—but the finding was so obscure that even his boss was skeptical. Last month the drug that resulted from Ferrara's work began to look like a success: Genentech unveiled trial results that showed it extended colon cancer patients' lives by a median of five months, or 30%, one of the biggest advances in years.[66]

Dr Ferrara obviously associated the characteristics of a cow protein with a solution for stopping the growth of cancerous tumors. Researchers, however, have identified five stages underlying the creative process: preparation, concentration, incubation, illumination, and verification. Let us consider these stages.

The *preparation* stage reflects the notion that creativity starts from a base of knowledge. Experts suggest that creativity involves a convergence between tacit or implied knowledge and explicit knowledge. During the *concentration* stage, an individual focuses on the problem at hand. Research shows that creative ideas at work are often triggered by work-related problems, incongruities, or failures.[67] Eli Lilly & Company, for example, uses this awareness to fuel the development of new drug discoveries:

> Lilly has long had a culture that looks at failure as an inevitable part of discovery and encourages scientists to take risks. If a new drug doesn't work out for its intended use, Lilly scientists are taught to look for new uses for a drug. In the early 1990s, W Leigh Thompson, Lilly's chief scientific officer, initiated "failure parties" to commemorate excellent scientific work, done efficiently, that nevertheless resulted in failure.
>
> Other drug companies are also seeing the importance of tolerating—and learning from—failure, a valuable strategy since about 90% of experimental drugs in the industry fail. For example, Pfizer Inc. originally developed the blockbuster impotence drug Viagra to treat angina, or severe heart pain.[68]

Interestingly, Japanese companies are noted for encouraging this stage as part of a quality improvement process more than American companies. For example, the average number of ideas per employee was 37.4 for Japanese workers versus .12 for US workers.[69]

Incubation is done unconsciously. During this stage, people engage in daily activities while their minds simultaneously mull over information and make remote associations. These associations ultimately are generated in the *illumination* stage. Finally, *verification* entails going through the entire process to verify, modify, or try out the new idea.

Let us examine the stages of creativity to determine why Japanese organizations propose and implement more ideas than do American companies. To address this issue, a creativity expert visited and extensively interviewed employees from five major Japanese companies. He observed that Japanese firms have created a management infrastructure that encourages and reinforces creativity. People were taught to identify problems (discontents) on their first day of employment. In turn, discontents were referred to as "golden eggs" to reinforce the notion that it is good to identify problems.

These organizations also promoted the stages of incubation, illumination, and verification through teamwork and incentives. For example, some companies posted the golden eggs on large wall posters in the work area; employees were then encouraged to interact with each other to execute the final three stages of the creative process. Employees eventually received monetary awards for any suggestions that passed all five phases of this process.[70] This research underscores the conclusion that creativity can be enhanced by effectively managing the creativity process and by fostering a positive and supportive work environment.[71]

A Model of Organizational Creativity and Innovation

Organizational creativity and innovation are relatively new topics within the field of OB despite their importance for organizational success. Rather than focus on group and organizational creativity, researchers historically examined the predictors of individual creativity.[72] This final section examines a process model of organizational creativity. Knowledge of its linkages can help you to facilitate and contribute to organizational creativity.

Figure 12–5   *A Model of Organizational Creativity and Innovation*

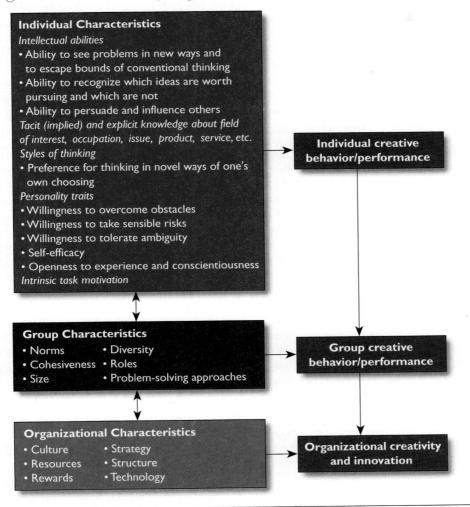

SOURCES: Based on discussion in R J Sternberg and R I Lubart, "Investing in Creativity," *American Psychologist,* July 1996, pp 677–88; and R W Woodman, J E Sawyer, and R W Griffin, "Toward a Theory of Organizational Creativity," *Academy of Management Review,* April 1993, pp 293–321.

Figure 12–5 illustrates the process underlying organizational creativity and innovation. It shows that organizational creativity is directly influenced by organizational characteristics and the amount of creative behavior that occurs within work groups. In turn, a group's creative behavior is influenced by group characteristics and the individual creative behavior/performance of its members.[73] Individual creative behavior is directly affected by a variety of individual characteristics. The double-headed arrows between individual and group and between group and organizational characteristics indicate that the various characteristics all influence each other. Let us now consider the model's major components.

Individual Characteristics   Creativity requires motivation. In other words, people make a decision whether or not they want to apply their knowledge and capabilities to create new ideas, things, or products. Consider the amount of creativity that was unleashed after September 11, 2001, when the Pentagon issued the following plea for help:

> Please, America, send us your ideas for combating terrorism. The request prompted derision from late-night TV comics, while newspapers in Poland and Germany marveled how the world's most powerful military force had been reduced to advertising for advice on how to fight its enemies.
>
> No matter. America's techno-wizards responded with a massive outpouring of ideas. Normally, the Pentagon's Technical Support Working Group (TSWG), which trolls for new technologies to help the military, gets about 900 proposals a year. But the October appeal garnered 12,500 brainstorms in just two months.[74]

In addition to motivation, creative people typically march to the beat of a different drummer. They are highly motivated individuals who spend considerable time developing both tacit and explicit knowledge about their field of interest or occupation. But contrary to stereotypes, creative people are not necessarily geniuses or introverted nerds. In addition, they are not *adaptors*. "Adaptors are those who . . . prefer to resolve difficulties or make decisions in such a way as to have the least impact upon the assumptions, procedures, and values of the organization."[75] In contrast, creative individuals are dissatisfied with the status quo. They look for new and exciting solutions to problems. Because of this, creative organizational members can be perceived as disruptive and hard to get along with.[76] Further, research indicates that male and female managers do not differ in levels of creativity, and there are a host of personality characteristics that are associated with creativity.[77] These characteristics include, but are not limited to, those shown in Figure 12–5. This discussion comes to life by considering the following example.

The Post-it Notes story represents a good illustration of how the individual characteristics shown in Figure 12–5 promote creative behavior/performance. Post-it Notes are a $200 million-a-year product for 3M Corporation:

> The idea originated with Art Fry, a 3M employee who used bits of paper to mark hymns when he sat in his church choir. These markers kept falling out of the hymn books. He decided that he needed an adhesive-backed paper that would stick as long as necessary but could be removed easily. He soon found what he wanted in the 3M laboratory, and the Post-it Note was born.
>
> Fry saw the market potential of his invention, but others did not. Market-survey results were negative; major office-supply distributors were skeptical. So he began giving samples to 3M executives and their secretaries. Once they actually used the little pieces of adhesive paper, they were hooked. Having sold 3M on the project, Fry used the same approach with other executives throughout the United States.[78]

Notice how Fry had to influence others to try out his idea. Figure 12–5 shows that creative people have the ability to persuade and influence others.

Group Characteristics
Figure 12–5 also lists six characteristics that influence the level of creative behavior/performance exhibited by a work group. In general, group creativity is fueled by a cohesive environment that supports open interactions, diverse viewpoints, and playful surroundings.[79] The work environment at E Ink is a good example.

> E Ink CEO Jim Juliano tries to infuse his company's core values into everything it does. When designing the work environment at E Ink, Juliano wanted to encourage a community feeling. He wanted the feeling of sitting at an Italian family's dinner table where "anyone can overhear multiple conversations. When people hear things, cross-fertilization occurs." So E Ink's workplace is without walls, with the exception of several conference rooms.

Quest Diagnostics Measures and Rewards Creativity

In 2003, Quest Diagnostics added innovation to its list of corporate goals, and innovation is now a core company value, says Steinhoff. The company measures its innovation success by quantifying the number of new medical tests developed, the number and acceptance of new electronic products, the number of patents filed, and the number of new strategies implemented.

Steinhoff says they have filed 15% to 20% more patents since the focus on innovation began last year. The number of new medical tests has remained about the same, but the importance of the tests has increased. "Our [increased] sales show that the tests are better targeted now to meet consumer needs," he says.

SOURCE: Excerpted from A Pomeroy, "Cooking Up Innovation," *HR Magazine*, November 2004, p 49.

Juliano also wanted the work environment to resemble an Italian piazza, so the office spaces are built around a central square. This piazza is the company's Chill Center, with toys, games such as Foosball, and free vending machines. Juliano feels the center encourages people to float freely.[80]

Organizational Characteristics Research and corporate examples clearly support the importance of organizational characteristics in generating organizational creativity. Organizations such as Rubbermaid, 3M, Microsoft, The Body Shop, Du Pont, and Quest Diagnostics are all known as innovative companies that encourage creativity via the organizational characteristics shown in Figure 12–5. Quest Diagnostics, for example, has created an organizational culture that measures and rewards creativity (see Real World/Real People).

Summary of Key Concepts

1. *Compare and contrast the rational model of decision making and Simon's normative model.* The rational decision-making model consists of identifying the problem, generating alternative solutions, evaluating and selecting a solution, and implementing and evaluating the solution. Research indicates that decision makers do not follow the series of steps outlined in the rational model.

    Simon's normative model is guided by a decision maker's bounded rationality. Bounded rationality means that decision makers are bounded or restricted by a variety of constraints when making decisions. The normative model suggests that decision making is characterized by (*a*) limited information processing, (*b*) the use of judgmental heuristics, and (*c*) satisficing.

2. *Discuss knowledge management and techniques used by companies to increase knowledge sharing.* Knowledge management involves the implementation of systems and practices that increase the sharing of knowledge and information throughout an organization. There are two types of knowledge that impact the quality of decisions: tacit knowledge and explicit knowledge. Organizations use computer systems to share explicit knowledge. Tacit knowledge is shared by observing, participating, or working with experts or coaches. Mentoring, informal networking, meetings, and design of office space also influence knowledge sharing.

3. *Explain the model of decision-making styles.* The model of decision-making styles is based on the idea that styles vary along two different dimensions: value orientation and tolerance for ambiguity. When these two dimensions are combined, they form four styles of decision making: directive, analytical, conceptual, and behavioral. People with a directive style have a low tolerance for ambiguity and are oriented

toward task and technical concerns. Analytics have a higher tolerance for ambiguity and are characterized by a tendency to overanalyze a situation. People with a conceptual style have a high threshold for ambiguity and tend to focus on people or social aspects of a work situation. This behavioral style is the most people oriented of the four styles.

4. *Describe the model of escalation of commitment.* Escalation of commitment refers to the tendency to stick to an ineffective course of action when it is unlikely that a bad situation can be reversed. Psychological and social determinants, organizational determinants, project characteristics, and contextual determinants cause managers to exhibit this decision-making error.

5. *Explain the model of intuition.* Intuition consists of insight or knowledge that is obtained without the use of rational thought or logical inference. There are two types of intuition: holistic hunches and automated experiences. In turn, there are two sources of intuition: expertise, which consists of an individual's combined explicit and tacit knowledge regarding an object, person, situation, or decision opportunity; and feelings. Intuition is based on the interaction between one's expertise and feelings in a given situation.

6. *Summarize the pros and cons of involving groups in the decision-making process.* There are both pros and cons to involving groups in the decision-making process. Although research shows that groups typically outperform the average individual, there are five important issues to consider when using groups to make decisions. (*a*) Groups are less efficient than individuals. (*b*) A group's overconfidence can fuel groupthink. (*c*) Decision quality is negatively related to group size. (*d*) Groups are more accurate when they know a great deal about the issues at hand and when the leader possesses the ability to effectively evaluate

the group members' opinions and judgments. (*e*) The composition of a group affects its decision-making processes and performance. In the final analysis, managers are encouraged to use a contingency approach when determining whether to include others in the decision-making process.

7. *Contrast brainstorming, the nominal group technique, the Delphi technique, and computer-aided decision making.* Group problem-solving techniques facilitate better decision making within groups. Brainstorming is used to help groups generate multiple ideas and alternatives for solving problems. The nominal group technique assists groups both to generate ideas and to evaluate and select solutions. The Delphi technique is a group process that anonymously generates ideas or judgments from physically dispersed experts. The purpose of computer-aided decision making is to reduce consensus roadblocks while collecting more information in a shorter period of time.

8. *Describe the stages of the creative process.* Creativity is defined as the process of using imagination and skill to develop a new or unique product, object, process, or thought. There are five stages of the creative process: preparation, concentration, incubation, illumination, and verification.

9. *Explain the model of organizational creativity and innovation.* Organizational creativity is directly influenced by organizational characteristics and the creative behavior that occurs within work groups. In turn, a group's creative behavior is influenced by group characteristics and the individual creative behavior/performance of its members. Individual creative behavior is directly affected by a variety of individual characteristics. Finally, individual, group, and organizational characteristics all influence each other within this process.

Discussion Questions

1. What role do emotions play in decision making?

2. Do you think people are rational when they make decisions? Under what circumstances would an individual tend to follow a rational process?

3. Describe a situation in which you satisficed when making a decision. Why did you satisfice instead of optimize?

4. Do you think knowledge management will become more important in the future? Explain your rationale.

5. Why would decision-making styles be a source of interpersonal conflict?

6. Describe a situation in which you exhibited escalation of commitment. Why did you escalate a losing situation?

7. Describe a situation in which you used intuition to make a decision. Was your intuition helpful?

8. Do you prefer to solve problems in groups or by yourself? Why?

9. Do you think you are creative? Why or why not?

10. What advice would you offer a manager who was attempting to improve the creativity of his or her employees? Explain.

IDEO Uses Its Creative Product Design Process to Help Companies Improve Their Products and Customer Service[81]

BusinessWeek From its inception, IDEO has been a force in the world of design. It has designed hundreds of products and won more design awards over the past decade than any other firm. . . . Now, IDEO is transferring its ability to create consumer products into designing consumer experiences in services, from shopping and banking to health care and wireless communication.

Yet by showing global corporations how to change their organizations to focus on the consumer, IDEO is becoming much more than a design company. Indeed, it is now a rival to the traditional purveyors of corporate advice: the management consulting companies such as McKinsey, Boston Consulting, and Bain. . . .

And IDEO works fast. That's because the company requires its clients to participate in virtually all the consumer research, analysis, and decisions that go into developing solutions. When the process is complete, there's no need for a buy-in: Clients already know what to do—and how to do it quickly. Unlike traditional consultants, IDEO shares its innovative process with its customers through projects, workshops, and IDEO U, its customized teaching program. In IDEO-speak, this is "open-source innovation." . . .

Corporate execs probably have the most fun simply participating in the IDEO Way, the design firm's disciplined yet wild-and-woolly five-step process that emphasizes empathy with the consumer, anything-is-possible brainstorming, visualizing solutions by creating actual prototypes, using technology to find creative solutions, and doing it all with incredible speed.

Here's how it works: A company goes to IDEO with a problem. It wants a better product, service, or space—no matter. IDEO puts together an eclectic team composed of members from the client company and its own experts who go out to observe and document the consumer experience. Often, IDEO will have top executives play the roles of their own customers. Execs from food and clothing companies shop for their own stuff in different retail stores and on the Web. Health care managers get care in different hospitals. Wireless providers use their own—and competing—services.

The next stage is brainstorming. IDEO mixes designers, engineers, and social scientists with its clients in a room where they intensely scrutinize a given problem and suggest possible solutions. It is managed chaos: a dozen or so very smart people examining data, throwing out ideas, writing potential solutions on big Post-its that are ripped off and attached to the wall.

IDEO designers then mock up working models of the best concepts that emerge. Rapid prototyping has always been a hallmark of the company. Seeing ideas in working, tangible form is a far more powerful mode of explanation than simply reading about them off a page. IDEO uses inexpensive prototyping tools—Apple-based iMovies to portray consumer experiences and cheap cardboard to mock up examination rooms or fitting rooms. . . .

Like a law firm, IDEO specializes in different practices. The "TEX"—or technology-enabled experiences—aims to take new high-tech products that first appeal only to early adopters and remake them for a mass consumer audience. IDEO's success with the Palm V led AT&T Wireless to call for help on its mMode consumer wireless platform. The company launched mMode in 2002 to allow AT&T Wireless mobile-phone customers to access e-mail and instant messaging, play games, find local restaurants, and connect to sites for news, stocks, weather, and other information. Techies liked mMode, but average consumers were not signing up. "We asked [IDEO] to redesign the interface so someone like my mother who isn't Web savvy can use the phone to navigate how to get the weather or where to shop," says mMode's Hall.

IDEO's Game Plan

It immediately sent AT&T Wireless managers on an actual scavenger hunt in San Francisco to see the world from their customers' perspective. They were told to find a CD by a certain Latin singer that was available at only one small music store, find a Walgreen's that sold its own brand of ibuprofen, and get a Pottery Barn catalog. They discovered that it was simply too difficult to find these kinds of things with their mMode service and wound up using the newspaper or the phone directory instead. IDEO and AT&T Wireless teams also went to AT&T Wireless stores and videotaped people using mMode. They saw that consumers couldn't find the sites they wanted. It took too many steps and clicks. "Even teenagers didn't get it," says Duane Bray, leader of the TEX practice at IDEO.

After dozens of brainstorming sessions and many prototypes, IDEO and AT&T Wireless came up with a new mMode wireless service platform. The opening page starts with "My mMode," which is organized like a Web browser's favorites list and can be managed on a Web site. A consumer can make up an individualized selection of sites, such as ESPN or Sony Pictures Entertainment, and ring tones. Nothing is more than two clicks away.

An mMode Guide on the page allows people to list five places—a restaurant, coffee shop, bank, bar, and retail store— that GPS location finders can identify in various cities around the US. Another feature spotlights the five nearest movie

399

theaters that still have seats available within the next hour. Yet another, My Locker, lets users store a large number of photos and ring tones with AT&T Wireless. The whole design process took only 17 weeks. "We are thrilled with the results," says Hall. "We talked to frog design, Razorfish, and other design firms, and they thought this was a Web project that needed flashy graphics. IDEO knew it was about making the cell phone experience better."

Questions for Discussion

1. Describe IDEO's creative design process.

2. Is IDEO's design process more characteristic of the rational or normative model of decision making? Discuss your rationale.

3. What type of decision-making styles are most and least consistent with IDEO's design process?

4. Is intuition more or less likely to be used during IDEO's design process? Explain.

5. To what extent does IDEO rely on the five stages of the creative process?

Personal Awareness and Growth Exercise

What Is Your Decision-Making Style?

Objectives

1. To assess your decision-making style.
2. To consider the managerial implications of your decision-making style.

Introduction

Earlier in the chapter we discussed a model of decision-making styles that is based on the idea that styles vary along the dimensions of an individual's value orientation and tolerance for ambiguity. In turn, these dimensions combine to form four styles of decision making (see Figure 12–2): directive, analytical, conceptual, and behavioral. Alan Rowe, an OB researcher, developed an instrument called the Decision Style Inventory to measure these four styles. This exercise provides you the opportunity to assess and interpret your decision-making style using this measurement device.

Instructions

The Decision Style Inventory consists of 20 questions, each with four responses.[82] You must consider each possible response for a question and then rank them according to how much you prefer each response. There are no right or wrong answers, so respond with what first comes to mind. Because many of the questions are anchored to how individuals make decisions at work, you can feel free to use your student role as a frame of reference to answer the questions. For each question, use the space on the survey to rank the four responses with either a 1, 2, 4, or 8. Use the number 8 for the responses that are **most** like you, a 4 for those that are **moderately** like

you, a 2 for those that are **slightly** like you, and a 1 for the responses that are **least** like you. For instance, a question could be answered as follows: [8], [4], [2], [1]. Notice that each number was used only once to answer a question. Do not repeat any number when answering a given question. These numbers are placed in the spaces next to each of the answers. Once all of the responses for the 20 questions have been ranked, total the scores in each of the four columns. The total score for column one represents your score for the directive style, column two your analytical style, column three your conceptual style, and column four your behavioral style.

Questions for Discussion

1. In terms of your decision-making profile, which of the four styles best represents your decision-making style (has the highest subscore)? Which is the least reflective of your style (has the lowest subscore)?

2. Do you agree with this assessment? Explain.

3. How do your scores compare with the following norms: directive (75), analytical (90), conceptual (80), and behavioral (55)? What do the differences between your scores and the survey norms suggest about your decision-making style?

4. What are the advantages and disadvantages of your decision-making profile?

5. Which of the other decision-making styles is most inconsistent with your style? How would this difference affect your ability to work with someone who has this style?

1. My prime objective in life is:	to have a position with status	be the best in whatever I do	be recognized for my work	feel secure in my job
2. I enjoy work that:	is clear and well defined	is varied and challenging	lets me act independently	involves people
3. I expect people to be:	productive	capable	committed	responsive
4. My work lets me:	get things done	find workable approaches	apply new ideas	be truly satisfied
5. I communicate best by:	talking with others	putting things in writing	being open with others	having a group meeting
6. My planning focuses on:	current problems	how best to meet goals	future opportunities	needs of people in the organization
7. I prefer to solve problems by:	applying rules	using careful analysis	being creative	relying on my feelings
8. I prefer information:	that is simple and direct	that is complete	that is broad and informative	that is easily understood
9. When I'm not sure what to do:	I rely on my intuition	I search for alternatives	I try to find a compromise	avoid making a decision
10. Whenever possible, I avoid:	long debates	incomplete work	technical problems	conflict with others
11. I am really good at:	remembering details	finding answers	seeing many options	working with people
12. When time is important, I:	decide and act quickly	apply proven approaches	look for what will work	refuse to be pressured
13. In social settings, I:	speak with many people	observe what others are doing	contribute to the conversation	want to be part of the discussion
14. I always remember:	people's names	places I have been	people's faces	people's personalities
15. I prefer jobs where I:	receive high rewards	have challenging assignments	can reach my personal goals	am accepted by the group
16. I work best with people who:	are energetic and ambitious	are very competent	are open minded	are polite and understanding
17. When I am under stress, I:	speak quickly	try to concentrate on the problem	become frustrated	worry about what I should do
18. Others consider me:	aggressive	disciplined	imaginative	supportive
19. My decisions are generally:	realistic and direct	systematic and logical	broad and flexible	sensitive to the other's needs
20. I dislike:	losing control	boring work	following rules	being rejected
Total score				

SOURCE: © Alan J Rowe, Professor Emeritus. Revised December 18, 1998. Reprinted by permission of the author.

Ethical Decision Making

Objectives

1. To apply the rational model of decision making.
2. To examine the ethical implications of a managerial decision.

Introduction

In this chapter we learned there are four steps in the rational model of decision making. The third stage involves evaluating alternatives and selecting a solution. Part of this evaluation entails deciding whether or not a solution is ethical. The purpose of this exercise is to examine the steps in decision making and to consider the issue of ethical decision making. You may want to examine Learning Module A on ethics and organizational behavior.

Instructions

Break into groups of five or six people and read the following case. As a group, discuss the decision made by the company and answer the questions for discussion at the end of the case. Before answering questions 4 and 5, however, brainstorm alternative decisions the managers at TELECOMPROS could have made. Finally, the entire class can reconvene and discuss the alternative solutions that were generated.

THE CASE OF TELECOMPROS

For large cellular service providers, maintaining their own customer service call center can be very expensive. Many have found they can save money by outsourcing their customer service calls to outside companies.

TELECOMPROS is one such company. It specializes in cellular phone customer service. TELECOMPROS saves large cellular companies money by eliminating overhead costs associated with building a call center, installing additional telephone lines, and so forth. Once TELECOMPROS is hired by large cellular service providers, TELECOMPROS employees are trained on the cellular service providers' systems, policies, and procedures. TELECOMPROS' income is derived from charging a per hour fee for each employee.

Six months ago, TELECOMPROS acquired a contract with Cell2u, a large cellular service provider serving the western United States. In the beginning of the contract, Cell2U was very pleased. As a call center, TELECOMPROS has a computer system in place that monitors the number of calls the center receives and how quickly the calls are answered. When Cell2U received its first report, the system showed that TELECOMPROS was a very productive call center and it handled the call volume very well. A month later however, Cell2U launched a nationwide marketing campaign. Suddenly, the call volume increased and TELECOMPROS' customer service reps were unable to keep up. The phone monitoring system showed that some customers were on hold for 45 minutes or longer, and at any given time throughout the day there were as many as 50 customers on hold. It was clear to Cell2U that the original number of customer service reps it had contracted for was not enough. It renegotiated with upper management at TELECOMPROS and hired additional customer service reps. TELECOMPROS was pleased because it was now receiving more money from Cell2U for the extra employees, and Cell2U was happy because the call center volume was no longer overwhelming and its customers were happy with the attentive customer service.

Three months later though, TELECOMPROS' customer service supervisors noticed a decrease in the number of customer service calls. It seemed that the reps had done such a good job that Cell2U customers had fewer problems. There were too many people and not enough calls. With little to do, some reps were playing computer games or surfing the Internet while waiting for calls to come in.

Knowing that if Cell2U analyzed its customer service needs, it would want to decrease the reps to save money, TELECOMPROS' upper management made a decision. Rather than decrease its staff and lose the hourly pay from Cell2U, the upper management told customer service supervisors to call the customer service line. Supervisors called in and spent enough time on the phone with reps to ensure that the computer registered the call and the time it took to "resolve" the call. Then they would hang up and call the call center again. TELECOMPROS did not have to decrease its customer service reps, and Cell2U continued to pay for the allotted reps until the end of the contract.

Questions for Discussion

1. Was the decision made by TELECOMPROS an ethical one? Why or why not?

2. If you were a manager at TELECOMPROS, what would you have done when your manager asked you to call the customer service line? What are the ramifications of your decision? Discuss.

3. Where did the decision-making process at TELECOMPROS break down? Explain.

4. What alternative solutions to the problem at hand can you identify? What is your recommended solution? Explain why you selected this alternative.

5. How would you implement your preferred solution? Describe in detail.

Ethical Dilemma

Are Lawyers at Vinson & Elkins Partly Responsible for Enron's Collapse?[83]

Early in the morning . . . [on] October 23, [2001,] Ronald Astin, a partner at the Houston law firm Vinson & Elkins, joined Enron Corp. executives in a meeting room next to Chairman Kenneth Lay's office. A conference call with analysts was about to begin, and the group needed to script an explanation for Enron's unfolding troubles, which included mysterious partnerships that appeared to be keeping big chunks of debt hidden away.

The tense mood soon grew worse. Mr Astin had drafted a section saying that Enron Chief Financial Officer Andrew Fastow initially presented the idea of the partnerships to the board. According to people at the meeting, Mr Fastow began shouting that he wasn't responsible for forming the partnerships.

It was the climax of a beneath-the-surface struggle between the outside lawyer and the Enron executive. Over five years, as Mr Fastow structured ever-more-complex deals for the big energy and trading company, Mr Astin and other Vinson & Elkins lawyers sometimes objected, saying the deals posed conflicts of interest or weren't in Enron's best interests.

But Vinson & Elkins didn't blow the whistle. Again and again, its lawyers backed down when rebuffed by Mr Fastow or his lieutenants, expressing their unease to Enron's in-house attorneys but not to its most senior executives or to its board. And when asked to assess Enron manager Sherron Watkins' warning to Mr Lay last summer of potential accounting scandals, Vinson & Elkins delivered to Enron a report that largely downplayed the risks.

Now, deals that troubled some Vinson & Elkins lawyers are central to investigations of the collapse of Enron. But while the mantle of heroine has fallen on Ms Watkins, Vinson & Elkins is on the defensive. One of the country's most powerful law firms, with some 850 lawyers in nine cities, Vinson & Elkins now faces lawsuits from Enron shareholders and Enron employees. And a report of a special investigation done for Enron's board has criticized the law firm for an "absence" of "objective and critical professional advice."

The firm's bind casts a stark light on the central issue law firms face when they represent large corporations: Just what are their obligations to the client and the client's shareholders? In terms of legal ethics, outside lawyers have a clear ethical duty to withdraw from transactions in which clients are obviously breaking the law. But many situations are murkier. At what point should the lawyers speak up, and to whom, when the legality of planned corporate moves is merely questionable? And what about when individual executives are planning steps that appear not in the interests of the client company itself?

Vinson & Elkins' managing partner, Joseph Dilg, has told a congressional panel probing Enron that so long as a transaction isn't illegal and has been approved by the client company's management, outside lawyers may advise on the transaction. "In doing so, the lawyers are not approving the business decisions that were made by their clients," he said.

But others, such as Boston University law professor Susan Koniak, say lawyers must do more. They have a duty to make sure a client's managers aren't "breaching their duties to the corporation," says Ms Koniak, who testified before a Senate hearing on Enron and accountability issues in February [2002]. She believes Vinson & Elkins lawyers should have taken their concerns to Enron directors.

What should lawyers at Vinson & Elkins have done in this case?

1. The lawyers are not responsible for the acts of Enron's management. Lawyers are paid to advise their clients, and it is up to the clients to take or ignore this advice.

2. Blow the whistle and let legal authorities know about Enron's mysterious partnerships. Explain your rationale and discuss the ramifications of this choice.

3. Take your concerns to Enron's board of directors. Explain your rationale and discuss the ramifications of this choice.

4. Invent other options. Discuss.

For the Chapter 12 Internet Exercise featuring activities aimed at improving creativity during brainstorming (www.brainstorming.co.uk), visit our Web site at **www.mhhe.com/kreitner.**

13

Managing Conflict and Negotiation

Learning Objectives

When you finish studying the material in this chapter, you should be able to:

1 Define the term *conflict,* and put the three metaphors of conflict into proper perspective for the workplace.

2 Distinguish between functional and dysfunctional conflict, and discuss why people avoid conflict.

3 List six antecedents of conflict, and identify the desired outcomes of conflict.

4 Define *personality conflicts,* and explain how managers should handle them.

5 Discuss the role of in-group thinking in intergroup conflict, and explain what management can do about intergroup conflict.

6 Discuss what can be done about cross-cultural conflict.

7 Explain how managers can stimulate functional conflict, and identify the five conflict-handling styles.

8 Explain the nature and practical significance of conflict triangles and alternative dispute resolution for third-party conflict intervention.

9 Explain the difference between distributive and integrative negotiation, and discuss the concept of added-value negotiation.

Marianne D'Eugenio didn't know what to think. It had been just two weeks since she'd opened Quadrille Quilting, a store in North Haven, Connecticut. Now she was on the phone with the last person she ever expected to talk to—Marty Childs, proprietor of Calico Etc. in nearby Cheshire and her closest competitor.

Childs was calling to ask if she could come by D'Eugenio's new store the next week to have a look and get acquainted—"a friendly welcome to the quilting community," was how she put it. D'Eugenio said yes because she didn't know what else to say. "What does that woman want from me?" she wondered.

At the very least, she assumed, Childs most likely intended to spy on her. As for the possibility that Childs might simply be a nice person looking to make a new friend, it never crossed D'Eugenio's mind. And who could blame her? After all, everyone knows that rivals can't really be pals.

Or can they? New research suggests that not only is it possible to make friends with your competitors—it's advisable. No matter how competitive their industry, rival CEOs who form friendships are at a distinct advantage over those who go it alone, says James D Westphal, professor of management at the University of Texas at Austin, who recently completed a study of CEO friendship in 293 companies in a broad range of sectors. . . .

But before you invite your toughest rival over for tea, there are a few things to consider. Becoming buddies will require you to adjust your attitude about what it means to compete in the first place, says Kaihan Krippendorff, a professor of entrepreneurship at Florida International University. "Our knee-jerk reaction to a competitor's gain is to take it as our loss"—an attitude that is bad for business, he says. Over the past seven years, Krippendorff has analyzed 400 business case studies, the results of which are collected in his 2003 book *The Art of the Advantage*. His key finding: Entrepreneurs who believe they're in business to vanquish the competition are less successful than

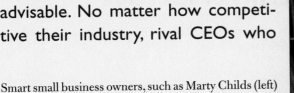

Smart small business owners, such as Marty Childs (left) and Marianne D'Eugenio, realize that selective cooperation is a key component of successful competition.

those who believe their goal is to maximize profits or increase their company's value. . . .

Assuming your psyche is in order and your business boundaries firmly in place, there's no good reason not to pick up the phone, dial the competition, and see if you can't make yourself a new friend. That's what Marty Childs was doing when she first rang Marianne D'Eugenio at her quilt shop. As it happened, the pair developed a friendship that has paid dividends for both of their businesses. D'Eugenio, for example, prefers to work with floral fabrics, while Childs favors bright colors. Rather than stocking up in the other's area of specialty, they refer customers back and forth. "I think customers appreciate the fact that we're friendly with each other," says D'Eugenio. "When you have a friendship rather than a rivalry, it makes your life a lot easier." Indeed, when yet another quilt shop recently opened in the area, D'Eugenio didn't hesitate. She picked up the phone and gave the owner a call. Sure, it was a new competitor—but perhaps it was a new friend, too.[1]

FOR DISCUSSION
Why is it so difficult for many people to reach out to others, especially competitors?

How would you handle this situation?

Your name is Annie and you are a product development manager for Amazon.com. As you were eating lunch today in your cubicle, Laura, a software project manager with an office nearby, asked if she could talk to you for a few minutes. You barely know Laura and you have heard both good and bad things about her work habits. Although your mind was more on how to meet Friday's deadline than on lunch, you waved her in.

She proceeded to pour out her woes about how she is having an impossible time partnering with Hans on a new special project. He is regarded as a top-notch software project manager, but Laura has found him to be ill-tempered and uncooperative. Laura thought you and Hans were friends because she has seen the two of you talking in the cafeteria and parking lot. You told Laura you have a good working relationship with Hans, but he's not really a friend. Still, Laura pressed on. "Would you straighten Hans out for me?" she asked. "We've got to get moving on this special project."

"Why this?" "Why now?" "Why me?!!" you thought as your eyes left Laura and drifted back to your desk.

Write down some ideas about how to handle this all-too-common conflict situation. Set it aside. We'll revisit your recommendation later in the chapter. In the meantime, we need to explore the world of conflict because, as indicated in the opening vignette, the potential for conflict is an ever-present feature of modern life. After discussing a modern view of conflict and four major types of conflict, we learn how to manage conflict both as a participant and as a third party. The related topic of negotiation is examined next. We conclude with a contingency approach to conflict management and negotiation.

Conflict: A Modern Perspective

Make no mistake about it. Conflict is an unavoidable aspect of organizational life. These major trends conspire to make *organizational* conflict inevitable:

- Constant change.
- Greater employee diversity.
- More teams (virtual and self-managed).

- Less face-to-face communication (more electronic interaction).
- A global economy with increased cross-cultural dealings.

Dean Tjosvold, from Canada's Simon Fraser University, notes that "Change begets conflict, conflict begets change"[2] and challenges us to do better with this sobering global perspective:

> Learning to manage conflict is a critical investment in improving how we, our families, and our organizations adapt and take advantage of change. Managing conflicts well does not insulate us from change, nor does it mean that we will always come out on top or get all that we want. However, effective conflict management helps us keep in touch with new developments and create solutions appropriate for new threats and opportunities.
>
> Much evidence shows we have often failed to manage our conflicts and respond to change effectively. High divorce rates, disheartening examples of sexual and physical abuse of children, the expensive failures of international joint ventures, and bloody ethnic violence have convinced many people that we do not have the abilities to cope with our complex interpersonal, organizational, and global conflicts.[3]

But respond we must. As outlined in this chapter, tools and solutions are available, if only we develop the ability and will to use them persistently. The choice is ours: Be active managers of conflict, or be managed by conflict.

A comprehensive review of the conflict literature yielded this consensus definition: "**conflict** is a process in which one party perceives that its interests are being opposed or negatively affected by another party."[4] The word *perceives* reminds us that sources of conflict and issues can be real or imagined. The resulting conflict is the same. Conflict can escalate (strengthen) or deescalate (weaken) over time. "The conflict process unfolds in a context, and whenever conflict, escalated or not, occurs the disputants or third parties can attempt to manage it in some manner."[5] Consequently, current and future managers need to understand the dynamics of conflict and know how to handle it effectively (both as disputants and as third parties).

Conflict
One party perceives its interests are being opposed or set back by another party.

The Language of Conflict: Metaphors and Meaning

Conflict is a complex subject for several reasons. Primary among them is the reality that conflict often carries a lot of emotional luggage.[6] Fear of losing or fear of change quickly raises the emotional stakes in a conflict. Conflicts also vary widely in magnitude. Conflicts have both participants and observers. Some observers may be interested and active, others disinterested and passive. Consequently, the term *conflict* can take on vastly different meanings, depending on the circumstances and one's involvement. For example, consider these three metaphors and accompanying workplace expressions:

- *Conflict as war:* "We shot down that idea."
- *Conflict as opportunity:* "What are all the possibilities for solving this problem?"
- *Conflict as journey:* "Let's search for common ground."[7]

Anyone viewing a conflict as war will try to win at all costs and wipe out the enemy. Alternatively, those seeing a conflict as an opportunity and a journey will tend to be more positive, open-minded, and constructive. In a hostile world, combative and destructive warlike thinking often prevails. But typical daily workplace conflicts are *not* war. So when dealing with organizational conflicts, we are challenged to rely less on the metaphor and language of war and more on the metaphors and language of *opportunity* and *journey*. We need to monitor our choice of words in conflict situations carefully.[8]

While explaining the three metaphors, conflict experts Kenneth Cloke and Joan Goldsmith made this instructive observation that we want to keep in mind for the balance of this chapter:

> Conflict gives you an opportunity to deepen your capacity for empathy and intimacy with your opponent. Your anger transforms the "Other" into a stereotyped demon or villain. Similarly, defensiveness will prevent you from communicating openly with your opponents, or listening carefully to what they are saying. On the other hand, once you engage in dialogue with that person, you will resurrect the human side of their personality—and express your own as well.
>
> Moreover, when you process your conflicts with integrity, they lead to growth, increased awareness, and self-improvement. Uncontrolled anger, defensiveness, and shame defeat these possibilities. Everyone feels better when they overcome their problems and reach resolution, and worse when they succumb and fail to resolve them. It is a bitter truth that victories won in anger lead to long-term defeat. Those defeated turn away, feeling betrayed and lost, and carry this feeling with them into their next conflict.
>
> Conflict can be seen simply as a way of learning more about what is not working and discovering how to fix it. The usefulness of the solution depends on the depth of your understanding of the problem. This depends on your ability to listen to the issue as you would to a teacher, which depends on halting the cycle of escalation and searching for opportunities for improvement.[9]

In short, win–win beats win–lose in both conflict management and negotiation.

A Conflict Continuum

Ideas about managing conflict underwent an interesting evolution during the 20th century. Initially, scientific management experts such as Frederick W Taylor believed all conflict ultimately threatened management's authority and thus had to be avoided or quickly resolved. Later, human relationists recognized the inevitability of conflict and advised managers to learn to live with it. Emphasis remained on resolving conflict whenever possible, however. Beginning in the 1970s, OB specialists realized conflict had both positive and negative outcomes, depending on its nature and intensity. This perspective introduced the revolutionary idea that organizations could suffer from *too little* conflict. Figure 13–1 illustrates the relationship between conflict intensity and outcomes.

Figure 13–1   *The Relationship between Conflict Intensity and Outcomes*

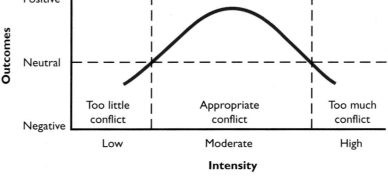

SOURCE: L D Brown, *Managing Conflict at Organizational Interfaces,* 1st edition, © 1983, p 8. Reprinted by permission of Pearson Education, Inc., Upper Saddle River, NJ.

A Friendly Corporate Tug-of-War

BusinessWeek Some business tiffs still get settled the old-fashioned way. Kayak suppliers Harmony and Werner Paddles came to a recent trade show each introducing a new paddle called Cascadia. "People asked: Are you going to fight it out?" says Joe Pulliam, a vice president at Harmony's parent, WaterMark Sports. Not quite. He challenged Werner president Bruce Furrer to a paddle-off. Two kayaks were tied together in a demo pool. After some fierce paddling, Furrer dragged Pulliam to one end. A gracious victor, Furrer says: "It's really nice to talk, instead of the first call being to the lawyer." Harmony renamed its paddle Tortuga, without a court battle.

SOURCE: B Hindo, "Branding Battles: Tug-of-War," *BusinessWeek*, November 8, 2004, p 12. Reprinted by permission of The McGraw-Hill Companies, Inc.

Work groups, departments, or organizations experiencing too little conflict tend to be plagued by apathy, lack of creativity, indecision, and missed deadlines. Excessive conflict, on the other hand, can erode organizational performance because of political infighting, dissatisfaction, lack of teamwork, and turnover. Workplace aggression and violence can be manifestations of excessive conflict.[10] Appropriate types and levels of conflict energize people in constructive directions.[11]

Functional versus Dysfunctional Conflict

The distinction between **functional conflict** and **dysfunctional conflict** pivots on whether the organization's interests are served. According to one conflict expert,

> Some [types of conflict] support the goals of the organization and improve performance; these are functional, constructive forms of conflict. They benefit or support the main purposes of the organization. Additionally, there are those types of conflict that hinder organizational performance; these are dysfunctional or destructive forms. They are undesirable and the manager should seek their eradication.[12]

Functional conflict is commonly referred to in management circles as constructive or cooperative conflict.[13] In terms of what we just discussed about the language of conflict, those engaging in functional conflict apply a win–win attitude to solve problems and find common ground (see Real World/Real People).

Functional conflict
Serves organization's interests.

Dysfunctional conflict
Threatens organization's interests.

Why People Avoid Conflict

Are you uncomfortable in conflict situations? Do you go out of your way to avoid conflict? If so, you're not alone. Many of us avoid conflict for a variety of both good and bad reasons. Tim Ursiny, in his entertaining and instructive book *The Coward's Guide to Conflict,* contends that we avoid conflict because we fear various combinations of the following things: "harm"; "rejection"; "loss of relationship"; "anger"; "being seen as selfish"; "saying the wrong thing"; "failing"; "hurting someone else"; "getting what you want"; and "intimacy."[14] This list is self-explanatory, except for the fear of "getting what you want." By this, Ursiny is referring to those who, for personal reasons, feel undeserving or fear the consequences of success, or both (so they tend to sabotage themselves). For our present purposes, it is sufficient to become consciously aware of our fears and practice overcoming them. Reading, understanding, and acting upon the material in this chapter are steps in a positive direction.

Antecedents of Conflict

Certain situations produce more conflict than others. By knowing the antecedents of conflict, managers are better able to anticipate it and take steps to resolve it if it becomes dysfunctional. Among the situations tending to produce either functional or dysfunctional conflict are

- Incompatible personalities or value systems.
- Overlapping or unclear job boundaries.
- Competition for limited resources.
- Interdepartment/intergroup competition.
- Inadequate communication.
- Interdependent tasks (e.g., one person cannot complete his or her assignment until others have completed their work).
- Organizational complexity (conflict tends to increase as the number of hierarchical layers and specialized tasks increase).
- Unreasonable or unclear policies, standards, or rules.
- Unreasonable deadlines or extreme time pressure.
- Collective decision making (the greater the number of people participating in a decision, the greater the potential for conflict).
- Decision making by consensus.
- Unmet expectations (employees who have unrealistic expectations about job assignments, pay, or promotions are more prone to conflict).
- Unresolved or suppressed conflicts.[15]

Proactive managers carefully read these early warnings and take appropriate action.

Desired Conflict Outcomes

Within organizations, conflict management is more than simply a quest for agreement. If progress is to be made and dysfunctional conflict minimized, a broader agenda is in order. Tjosvold's cooperative conflict model calls for three desired outcomes:

1. *Agreement.* But at what cost? Equitable and fair agreements are best. An agreement that leaves one party feeling exploited or defeated will tend to breed resentment and subsequent conflict.

2. *Stronger relationships.* Good agreements enable conflicting parties to build bridges of goodwill and trust for future use. Moreover, conflicting parties who trust each other are more likely to keep their end of the bargain.

3. *Learning.* Functional conflict can promote greater self-awareness and creative problem solving. Like the practice of management itself, successful conflict handling is learned primarily by doing. Knowledge of the concepts and techniques in this chapter is a necessary first step, but there is no substitute for hands-on practice. In a contentious world, there are plenty of opportunities to practice conflict management.[16]

Types of Conflict

Certain antecedents of conflict, highlighted earlier, deserve a closer look. This section probes the nature and organizational implications of three basic types of conflict: personality conflict, intergroup conflict, and cross-cultural conflict. Our discussion of each type of conflict includes some practical tips and techniques.

Personality Conflict

We visited the topic of personalities in our Chapter 2 discussion of diversity. Also, recall the Big Five personality dimensions introduced in Chapter 5. Once again, your *personality* is the package of stable traits and characteristics creating your unique identity. According to experts on the subject:

> Each of us has a unique way of interacting with others. Whether we are seen as charming, irritating, fascinating, nondescript, approachable, or intimidating depends in part on our personality, or what others might describe as our style.[17]

Given the many possible combinations of personality traits, it is clear why personality conflicts are inevitable. We define a **personality conflict** as interpersonal opposition based on personal dislike, disagreement, or different styles. For example, imagine the potential for a top-level personality conflict at EMC Corp., a leading maker of data storage equipment. Michael C Ruettgers, executive chairman of the Massachusetts-based firm, gave up his CEO position in January 2001 after running the company for nine years.

Personality conflict
Interpersonal opposition driven by personal dislike or disagreement.

> In a January [2002] interview, Ruettgers gave CEO Joseph M Tucci A's in innovation and strategic management, but F's in stock-price performance and financial management because the company lost $508 million in 2001. Ruettgers added that he was disappointed Tucci has attracted so little outside talent during his year at the helm. . . .
>
> At the same time, some former execs say, Tucci has wanted to move faster to cut costs, make acquisitions, and introduce new software but Ruettgers and EMC have slowed the pace of change. And Ruettgers, who had planned to be less active in daily affairs, has continued to attend weekly meetings to review operations. This has analysts and insiders speculating that Tucci could soon take the fall for EMC's poor performance. "In that culture, someone must fail," says a former EMC executive. "There will be a scapegoat." . . .
>
> The personal and management styles of Tucci, a salesman, and Ruettgers, who started at EMC as an operations expert, couldn't be more different. Tucci likes to build one-on-one relationships, while Ruettgers is more aloof. Tucci seems to be more willing than Ruettgers to make tough decisions quickly. Bill Scannell, EMC's senior vice president for global sales, says Tucci gives him an answer immediately when he asks for advice. Ruettgers tends to chew on things awhile. And Tucci praises and thanks his troops regularly, while Ruettgers once told a former executive that saying thank-you is a sign of weakness.[18]

Any way you look at it, Tucci was in a tough spot, and conflicting personalities only made it worse. How did things turn out? By 2005, Tucci's strategy and personal style were vindicated as EMC posted impressive results from hot new products.[19] Good guys don't always finish last!

Workplace Incivility: The Seeds of Personality Conflict
Somewhat akin to physical pain, chronic personality conflicts often begin with seemingly insignificant irritations. A pair of OB researchers recently offered this cautionary overview of the problem and its consequences:

> Incivility, or employees' lack of regard for one another, is costly to organizations in subtle and pervasive ways. Although uncivil behaviors occur commonly, many organizations fail to recognize them, few understand their harmful effects, and most managers and executives are ill-equipped to deal with them. Over the past eight years, as we have learned about this phenomenon through interviews, focus groups, questionnaires, experiments, and executive forums with more than 2,400 people across the US and Canada, we have found that incivility causes its targets, witnesses, and additional stakeholders to act in ways that erode organizational values and deplete organizational resources. Because of their experiences of workplace incivility, employees decrease work effort, time on the job, productivity, and performance. Where incivility is not curtailed, job satisfaction and organizational loyalty diminish as well. Some employees leave their jobs solely because of the impact of this subtle form of deviance.[20]

Vicious cycles of incivility need to be avoided, or broken early, with an organizational culture that places a high value on respect for co-workers. This requires managers and leaders to act as caring and courteous role models. A positive spirit of cooperation, as opposed to one based on negativism and aggression, also helps. Some organizations have resorted to workplace etiquette training.[21] More specifically, constructive feedback or skillful behavior shaping can keep a single irritating behavior from precipitating a full-blown personality conflict (or worse).

Dealing with Personality Conflicts
Personality conflicts are a potential minefield for managers. Let us frame the situation. Personality traits, by definition, are stable and resistant to change. Moreover, according to the American Psychiatric Association's *Diagnostic and Statistical Manual of Mental Disorders,* there are 410 psychological disorders that can and do show up in the workplace.[22] This brings up legal issues. Employees in the United States suffering from psychological disorders such as depression and mood-altering diseases such as alcoholism are protected from discrimination by the Americans with Disabilities Act.[23] (Other nations have similar laws.) Also, sexual harassment and other forms of discrimination can grow out of apparent personality conflicts. Finally, personality conflicts can spawn workplace aggression and violence.

Traditionally, managers dealt with personality conflicts by either ignoring them or transferring one party. In view of the legal implications, just discussed, both of these options may be open invitations to discrimination lawsuits. Table 13–1 presents practical tips for both nonmanagers and managers who are involved in or affected by personality conflicts. Our later discussions of handling dysfunctional conflict and alternative dispute resolution techniques also apply.[24]

Intergroup Conflict

Conflict among work groups, teams, and departments is a common threat to organizational competitiveness. For example, when Michael Volkema became CEO of Herman Miller in the mid-1990s, he found an inward-focused company with divisions fighting over budgets.

Table 13–1   *How to Deal with Personality Conflicts*

Tips for Employees Having a Personality Conflict	Tips for Third-Party Observers of a Personality Conflict	Tips for Managers Whose Employees Are Having a Personality Conflict
• Communicate directly with the other person to resolve the perceived conflict (emphasize problem solving and common objectives, not personalities). • Avoid dragging co-workers into the conflict. • If dysfunctional conflict persists, seek help from direct supervisors or human resource specialists.	• Do not take sides in someone else's personality conflict. • Suggest the parties work things out themselves in a constructive and positive way. • If dysfunctional conflict persists, refer the problem to parties' direct supervisors.	• Investigate and document conflict. • If appropriate, take corrective action (e.g., feedback or behavior shaping). • If necessary, attempt informal dispute resolution. • Refer difficult conflicts to human resource specialists or hired counselors for formal resolution attempts and other interventions.

Note: All employees need to be familiar with and *follow* company policies for diversity, antidiscrimination, and sexual harassment.

He has since curbed intergroup conflict at the Michigan-based furniture maker by emphasizing collaboration and redirecting everyone's attention outward, to the customer.[25] Managers who understand the mechanics of intergroup conflict are better equipped to face this sort of challenge.

In-Group Thinking: The Seeds of Intergroup Conflict

As we discussed in previous chapters, *cohesiveness*—a "we feeling" binding group members together—can be a good or bad thing. A certain amount of cohesiveness can turn a group of individuals into a smooth-running team. Too much cohesiveness, however, can breed groupthink because a desire to get along pushes aside critical thinking. The study of in-groups by small group researchers has revealed a whole package of changes associated with increased group cohesiveness. Specifically,

- Members of in-groups view themselves as a collection of unique individuals, while they stereotype members of other groups as being "all alike."
- In-group members see themselves positively and as morally correct, while they view members of other groups negatively and as immoral.
- In-groups view outsiders as a threat.
- In-group members exaggerate the differences between their group and other groups. This typically involves a distorted perception of reality.[26]

Avid sports fans who simply can't imagine how someone would support the opposing team exemplify one form of in-group thinking. Also, this pattern of behavior is a form of ethnocentrism, discussed as a cross-cultural barrier in Chapter 4. Reflect for a moment on evidence of in-group behavior in your life. Does your circle of friends make fun of others because of their race, gender, nationality, religion, sexual preference, weight, or major in college?[27]

Talk about in-group thinking! Ask any die-hard Chicago Cubs baseball fan about this play that they say cost the Cubs a trip to the 2003 World Series. The umpires failed to call fan interference and, as they say, the rest is history. (Cubs fans would have preferred the response of the guy in back with his hands to his face.)

In-group thinking is one more fact of organizational life that virtually guarantees conflict. Managers cannot eliminate in-group thinking, but they certainly should not ignore it when handling intergroup conflicts.

Research Lessons for Handling Intergroup Conflict

Sociologists have long recommended the contact hypothesis for reducing intergroup conflict. According to the *contact hypothesis,* the more the members of different groups interact, the less intergroup conflict they will experience. Those interested in improving race, international, and union–management relations typically encourage cross-group interaction. The hope is that *any* type of interaction, short of actual conflict, will reduce stereotyping and combat in-group thinking. But recent research has shown this approach to be naive and limited. For example, one study of 83 health center employees (83% female) at a midwest US university probed the specific nature of intergroup relations and concluded

> The number of *negative* relationships was significantly related to higher perceptions of intergroup conflict. Thus, it seems that negative relationships have a salience that overwhelms any possible positive effects from friendship links across groups.[28]

Intergroup friendships are still desirable, as documented in many studies,[29] but they are readily overpowered by negative intergroup interactions. Thus, *priority number one for managers faced with intergroup conflict is to identify and root out specific negative linkages among groups.* A single personality conflict, for instance, may contaminate the entire intergroup experience. The same goes for an employee who voices negative opinions or spreads negative rumors about another group. Our updated contact model in Figure 13–2 is based on

Figure 13–2   *An Updated Contact Model for Minimizing Intergroup Conflict*

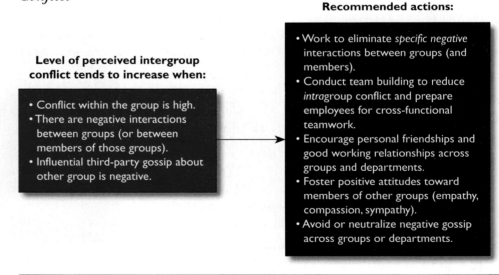

Level of perceived intergroup conflict tends to increase when:

- Conflict within the group is high.
- There are negative interactions between groups (or between members of those groups).
- Influential third-party gossip about other group is negative.

Recommended actions:

- Work to eliminate *specific negative* interactions between groups (and members).
- Conduct team building to reduce *intra*group conflict and prepare employees for cross-functional teamwork.
- Encourage personal friendships and good working relationships across groups and departments.
- Foster positive attitudes toward members of other groups (empathy, compassion, sympathy).
- Avoid or neutralize negative gossip across groups or departments.

SOURCES: Based on research evidence in G Labianca, D J Brass, and B Gray, "Social Networks and Perceptions of Intergroup Conflict: The Role of Negative Relationships and Third Parties." *Academy of Management Journal,* February 1998, pp 55–67; C D Batson et al., "Empathy and Attitudes: Can Feeling for a Member of a Stigmatized Group Improve Feelings toward the Group?" *Journal of Personality and Social Psychology,* January 1997, pp 105–18; and S C Wright et al., "The Extended Contact Effect: Knowledge of Cross-Group Friendships and Prejudice," *Journal of Personality and Social Psychology,* July 1997, pp 73–90.

this and other recent research insights, such as the need to foster positive attitudes toward other groups.[30] Also, notice how conflict within the group and negative gossip from third parties are threats that need to be neutralized if intergroup conflict is to be minimized.[31]

Cross-Cultural Conflict

Doing business with people from different cultures is commonplace in our global economy where cross-border mergers, joint ventures, and alliances are the order of the day.[32] Because of differing assumptions about how to think and act, the potential for cross-cultural conflict is both immediate and huge.[33] Success or failure, when conducting business across cultures, often hinges on avoiding and minimizing actual or perceived conflict. For example, consider this cultural mismatch:

> Mexicans place great importance on saving face, so they tend to expect any conflicts that occur during negotiations to be downplayed or kept private. The prevailing attitude in the [United States], however, is that conflict should be dealt with directly and publicly to prevent hard feelings from developing on a personal level.[34]

This is not a matter of who is right and who is wrong; rather it is a matter of accommodating cultural differences for a successful business transaction. Awareness of the GLOBE project's cross-cultural dimensions, discussed in Chapter 4, is an important first step. Stereotypes also need to be identified and neutralized. Beyond that, cross-cultural conflict can be moderated by using international consultants and building cross-cultural relationships.

International Consultants   In response to broad demand, there is a growing army of management consultants specializing in cross-cultural relations. Competency and fees vary widely, of course. But a carefully selected cross-cultural consultant can be helpful, as this illustration shows:

> [W]hen electronics-maker Canon planned to set up a subsidiary in Dubai through its Netherlands division, it asked consultant Sahid Mirza of Glocom, based in Dubai, to find out how the two cultures would work together.
>
> Mirza sent out the test questionnaires and got a sizeable response. "The findings were somewhat surprising," he recalls. "We found that, at the bedrock level, there were relatively few differences. Many of the Arab businessmen came from former British colonies and viewed business in much the same way as the Dutch."
>
> But at the level of behavior, there was a real conflict. "The Dutch are blunt and honest in expression, and such expression is very offensive to Arab sensibilities." . . . As a result of Mirza's research, Canon did start the subsidiary in Dubai, but it trained both the Dutch and the Arab executives first.[35]

Consultants also can help untangle possible personality and intergroup conflicts from conflicts rooted in differing national cultures. *Note:* Although we have discussed these three basic types of conflict separately, they typically are encountered in complex, messy bundles.

Building Cross-Cultural Relationships to Avoid Dysfunctional Conflict   Rosalie L Tung's study of 409 expatriates from US and Canadian multinational firms is very instructive.[36] Her survey sought to pinpoint success factors for the expatriates (14% female) who were working in 51 different countries worldwide. Nine specific ways to facilitate interaction with host-country nationals, as ranked from most useful to least useful by the respondents, are listed in Table 13–2. Good listening skills topped

Table 13–2   *Ways to Build Cross-Cultural Relationships*

Behavior	Rank
Be a good listener	1
Be sensitive to needs of others	2 > Tie
Be cooperative, rather than overly competitive	2
Advocate inclusive (participative) leadership	3
Compromise rather than dominate	4
Build rapport through conversations	5
Be compassionate and understanding	6
Avoid conflict by emphasizing harmony	7
Nurture others (develop and mentor)	8

SOURCE: Adapted from R L Tung, "American Expatriates Abroad: From Neophytes to Cosmopolitans," *Journal of World Business,* Summer 1998, table 6, p 136. © 1998, with permission from Elsevier.

the list, followed by sensitivity to others and cooperativeness rather than competitiveness. Interestingly, US managers are culturally characterized as just the opposite: poor listeners, blunt to the point of insensitivity, and excessively competitive. Some managers need to add self-management to the list of ways to minimize cross-cultural conflict.

Managing Conflict

As we have seen, conflict has many faces and is a constant challenge for managers who are responsible for reaching organizational goals. Our attention now turns to the active management of both functional and dysfunctional conflict. We discuss how to stimulate functional conflict, how to handle dysfunctional conflict, and how third parties can deal effectively with conflict. Relevant research lessons also are examined.

Stimulating Functional Conflict

Sometimes committees and decision-making groups become so bogged down in details and procedures that nothing substantive is accomplished. Carefully monitored functional conflict can help get the creative juices flowing once again. Managers basically have two options. They can fan the fires of naturally occurring conflict—but this approach can be unreliable and slow. Alternatively, managers can resort to programmed conflict.[37] Experts in the field define **programmed conflict** as "conflict that raises different opinions *regardless of the personal feelings of the managers.*"[38] The trick is to get contributors to either defend or criticize ideas based on relevant facts rather than on the basis of personal preference or political interests. This requires disciplined role playing (see Real World/Real People). Two programmed conflict techniques with proven track records are devil's advocacy and the dialectic method. Let us explore these two ways of stimulating functional conflict.

Programmed conflict
Encourages different opinions without protecting management's personal feelings.

Devil's Advocacy
This technique gets its name from a traditional practice within the Roman Catholic Church. When someone's name came before the College of Cardinals for elevation to sainthood, it was absolutely essential to ensure that he or she had a spotless record. Consequently, one individual was assigned the role of *devil's advocate* to uncover

The Founder of Patagonia Shakes Things Up

Yvon Chouinard, who founded the maker of eco-friendly clothing in 1973:
If you want a company to be around for a while, you have to constantly embrace change and even create an artificial sense of stress or crisis. So you want an entrepreneur at the top and lots of other people running behind picking up

the pieces or saying, "No, this isn't going to work." But somebody has to be responsible for shaking things up.

SOURCE: As quoted in Abrahm Lustgarten, "Warm, Fuzzy, and Highly Profitable," *Fortune,* November 15, 2004, p 194.

and air all possible objections to the person's canonization. In accordance with this practice, **devil's advocacy** in today's organizations involves assigning someone the role of critic.[39] Recall from Chapter 10, Irving Janis recommended the devil's advocate role for preventing groupthink.

In the left half of Figure 13–3 on p 418, note how devil's advocacy alters the usual decision-making process in steps 2 and 3. This approach to programmed conflict is intended to generate critical thinking and reality testing.[40] It is a good idea to rotate the job of devil's advocate so no one person or group develops a strictly negative reputation. Moreover, periodic devil's advocacy role-playing is good training for developing analytical and communication skills and emotional intelligence.

Devil's advocacy
Assigning someone the role of critic.

The Dialectic Method

Like devil's advocacy, the dialectic method is a time-honored practice. This particular approach to programmed conflict traces back to the dialectic school of philosophy in ancient Greece. Plato and his followers attempted to synthesize truths by exploring opposite positions (called *thesis* and *antithesis*). Court systems in the United States and elsewhere rely on directly opposing points of view for determining guilt or innocence. Accordingly, today's **dialectic method** calls for managers to foster a structured debate of opposing viewpoints prior to making a decision.[41] Steps 3 and 4 in the right half of Figure 13–3 set the dialectic approach apart from the normal decision-making process. Here is how Anheuser-Busch's corporate policy committee uses the dialectic method:

Dialectic method
Fostering a debate of opposing viewpoints to better understand an issue.

> When the policy committee . . . considers a major move—getting into or out of a business, or making a big capital expenditure—it sometimes assigns teams to make the case for each side of the question. There may be two teams or even three. Each is knowledgeable about the subject; each has access to the same information. Occasionally someone in favor of the project is chosen to lead the dissent, and an opponent to argue for it. Pat Stokes, who heads the company's beer empire, describes the result: "We end up with decisions and alternatives we hadn't thought of previously," sometimes representing a synthesis of the opposing views. "You become a lot more anticipatory, better able to see what might happen, because you have thought through the process."[42]

A major drawback of the dialectic method is that "winning the debate" may overshadow the issue at hand. Also, the dialectic method requires more skill training than does devil's advocacy. Regarding the comparative effectiveness of these two approaches to stimulating functional conflict, however, a laboratory study ended in a tie. Compared with groups that strived to reach a consensus, decision-making groups using either devil's advocacy or the

Figure 13–3   *Techniques for Stimulating Functional Conflict: Devil's Advocacy and the Dialectic Method*

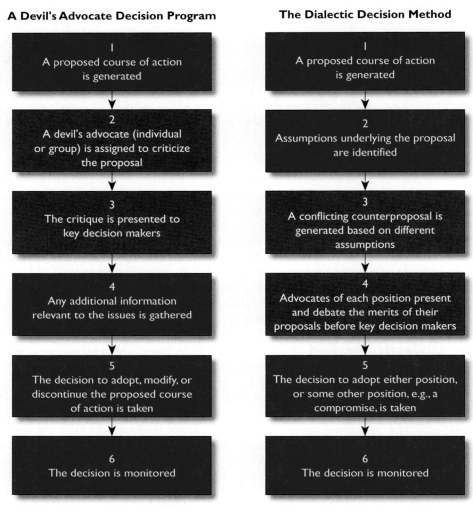

A Devil's Advocate Decision Program

1. A proposed course of action is generated
2. A devil's advocate (individual or group) is assigned to criticize the proposal
3. The critique is presented to key decision makers
4. Any additional information relevant to the issues is gathered
5. The decision to adopt, modify, or discontinue the proposed course of action is taken
6. The decision is monitored

The Dialectic Decision Method

1. A proposed course of action is generated
2. Assumptions underlying the proposal are identified
3. A conflicting counterproposal is generated based on different assumptions
4. Advocates of each position present and debate the merits of their proposals before key decision makers
5. The decision to adopt either position, or some other position, e.g., a compromise, is taken
6. The decision is monitored

SOURCE: R A Cosier and C R Schwenk, "Agreement and Thinking Alike: Ingredients for Poor Decisions," *Academy of Management Executive*, February 1990, pp 72–73. Reprinted with permission of The Academy of Management via The Copyright Clearance Center.

dialectic method yielded equally higher quality decisions.[43] But in a more recent laboratory study, groups using devil's advocacy produced more potential solutions and made better recommendations for a case problem than did groups using the dialectic method.[44]

In light of this mixed evidence, managers have some latitude in using either devil's advocacy or the dialectic method for pumping creative life back into stalled deliberations.[45] Personal preference and the role players' experience may well be the deciding factors in choosing one approach over the other. The important thing is to actively stimulate functional conflict when necessary, such as when the risk of blind conformity or groupthink is high. Joseph M Tucci, the CEO of EMC introduced earlier, fosters functional conflict by creating a supportive climate for dissent:

Good leaders always leave room for debate and different opinions. . . .

The team has to be in harmony. But before you move out, there needs to be a debate. Leadership is not a right. You have to earn it.

. . . [E]very company needs a healthy paranoia. It's the CEO's job to keep it on the edge, to put tension in the system. You have to do the right thing for the right circumstances.[46]

This meshes well with the results of a pair of laboratory studies that found a positive relationship between the degree of minority dissent and team innovation, *but only when participative decision making was used.*[47]

Alternative Styles for Handling Dysfunctional Conflict

People tend to handle negative conflict in patterned ways referred to as *styles*. Several conflict styles have been categorized over the years. According to conflict specialist Afzalur Rahim's model, five different conflict-handling styles can be plotted on a 2 × 2 grid. High to low concern for *self* is found on the horizontal axis of the grid, while low to high concern for *others* forms the vertical axis (see Figure 13–4). Various combinations of these variables produce the five different conflict-handling styles: integrating, obliging, dominating, avoiding, and compromising.[48] There is no single best style; each has strengths and limitations and is subject to situational constraints.

Integrating (Problem Solving)   In this style, interested parties confront the issue and cooperatively identify the problem, generate and weigh alternative solutions, and select a solution. Integrating is appropriate for complex issues plagued by misunderstanding. However, it is inappropriate for resolving conflicts rooted in opposing value systems. Its primary strength is its longer lasting impact because it deals with the underlying problem rather than merely with symptoms. The primary weakness of this style is that it is very time consuming.

Obliging (Smoothing)   "An obliging person neglects his or her own concern to satisfy the concern of the other party."[49] This style, often called *smoothing*, involves playing down differences while emphasizing commonalities. Obliging may be an appropriate conflict-handling strategy when it is possible to eventually get something in return. But it

Figure 13–4   *Five Conflict-Handling Styles*

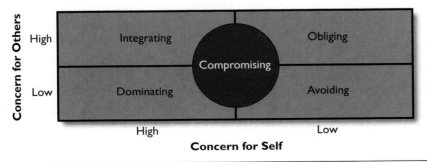

SOURCE: M A Rahim, "A Strategy for Managing Conflict in Complex Organizations," *Human Relations*, January 1985, p 84. Reprinted by permission of Sage Publications Ltd, Copyright (© The Taristock Institute, 1985).

Burger King's CEO Knows When to Use the Hammer

BusinessWeek "Business is a team sport," ... [Gregory Brenneman] says. Each Friday, he broadcasts folksy voice mails about the chain's fortunes to employees and franchisees. He isn't afraid to play tough, though: In [2004], after hearing of nasty e-mails flying be-

tween feuding execs, he told perpetrators to cut it out or they would be fired.

SOURCE: B Grow, "Fat's in the Fire for This Burger King," *BusinessWeek*, November 8, 2004, p 70.

is inappropriate for complex or worsening problems. Its primary strength is that it encourages cooperation. Its main weakness is that it's a temporary fix that fails to confront the underlying problem.

Dominating (Forcing) High concern for self and low concern for others encourages "I win, you lose" tactics. The other party's needs are largely ignored. This style is often called *forcing* because it relies on formal authority to force compliance. Dominating is appropriate when an unpopular solution must be implemented, the issue is minor, a deadline is near, or a crisis looms (see Real World/Real People). It can be awkward in an open and participative climate. Speed is its primary strength. The primary weakness of this domineering style is that it often breeds resentment. Interestingly, the National Center for Women and Policing cites this particular conflict-handling style as a reason for hiring more women.

> Women are 12.7% of the personnel in large police departments but account for 2% of excessive-force cases that are upheld. ... the findings support their contention that women's negotiating and communication skills should prompt police departments to hire more women.[50]

Avoiding This tactic may involve either passive withdrawal from the problem or active suppression of the issue. Avoidance is appropriate for trivial issues or when the costs of confrontation outweigh the benefits of resolving the conflict. It is inappropriate for difficult and worsening problems. The main strength of this style is that it buys time in unfolding or ambiguous situations. The primary weakness is that the tactic provides a temporary fix that sidesteps the underlying problem.

Compromising This is a give-and-take approach involving moderate concern for both self and others. Compromise is appropriate when parties have opposite goals or possess equal power. But compromise is inappropriate when overuse would lead to inconclusive action (e.g., failure to meet important deadlines). The primary strength of this tactic is that the democratic process has no losers, but it's a temporary fix that can stifle creative problem solving.

Third-Party Interventions

In a perfect world, people would creatively avoid conflict and handle actual conflicts directly and positively. Dream on! Organizational politics being what they are, we can find ourselves as unwilling (and often unready) third parties to someone else's conflict. Thus, a working knowledge of conflict triangles and alternative dispute resolution techniques, the focus of this section, is essential to effective management today.

Conflict Triangles
Remember Annie, the Amazon.com manager at the start of this chapter? Her busy day was interrupted by her co-worker Laura's tale of a conflict situation. Laura was recruiting Annie to help settle the situation. This is a classic conflict triangle. A **conflict triangle** "occurs when two people are having a problem and, instead of addressing the problem directly with each other, one of them gets a third person involved."[51] As discussed under the heading of organizational politics, in Chapter 15, employees tend to form political *coalitions* because there is power in numbers. In Annie's case, Laura was engaged in a not-so-subtle attempt to gang up against her adversary, Hans. Moreover, Laura was using Annie to vent her pent-up frustrations. This is a common and often very disruptive situation in today's organizations. The question is, What to do?

Those finding themselves in conflict triangles have a wide range of options, according to experts on the subject. Figure 13–5 shows how responses can promote either functional or dysfunctional conflict. Preferred options 1 and 2, called *detriangling,* involve the third party channeling the disputants' energy in a direct and positive manner, toward each other. Importantly, the third party avoids becoming part of a political coalition in options 1 and 2.[52] Options 3 through 8 can be a slippery slope toward further counterproductive triangling. Also, political and ethical implications multiply as the third party progresses to option 3 and beyond.

Alternative Dispute Resolution (ADR)
Disputes between employees, between employees and their employer, and between companies too often end up in lengthy and costly court battles. A more constructive, less expensive approach called *alternative dispute resolution* has enjoyed enthusiastic growth in recent years.[53] In fact, the widely imitated People's Court–type television shows operating outside the formal judicial system are part of this trend toward what one writer calls "do-it-yourself justice."[54] **Alternative dispute resolution** (ADR), according to a pair of Canadian labor lawyers, "uses faster,

Conflict triangle
Conflicting parties involve a third person rather than dealing directly with each other.

Alternative dispute resolution
Avoiding costly lawsuits by resolving conflicts informally or through mediation or arbitration.

Figure 13–5   *Third-Party Intervention Options for Handling Conflict Triangles*

Detriangling
(least political; low risk of dysfunctional conflict)

More triangling
(most political; high risk of dysfunctional conflict)

1. Reroute complaints by coaching the sender to find ways to constructively bring up the matter with the receiver. Do not carry messages for the sender.
2. Facilitate a meeting with the sender and receiver to coach them to speak directly and constructively with each other.
3. Transmit verbatim messages with the sender's name included and coach the receiver on constructive ways to discuss the message with the sender.
4. Carry the message verbatim but protect the sender's name.
5. Soften the message to protect the sender.
6. Add your spin to the message to protect the sender.
7. Do nothing. The participants will triangle in someone else.
8. Do nothing and spread the gossip. You will triangle in others.

SOURCE: List of options excerpted from P Ruzich, "Triangles: Tools for Untangling Interpersonal Messes," *HR Magazine,* July 1999, p 134.

more user-friendly methods of dispute resolution, instead of traditional, adversarial approaches (such as unilateral decision making or litigation)."[55] The following ADR techniques represent a progression of steps third parties can take to resolve organizational conflicts.[56] They are ranked from easiest and least expensive to most difficult and costly. A growing number of organizations have formal ADR policies involving an established sequence of various combinations of these techniques:

- *Facilitation.* A third party, usually a manager, informally urges disputing parties to deal directly with each other in a positive and constructive manner. This can be a form of detriangling, as discussed earlier.

- *Conciliation.* A neutral third party informally acts as a communication conduit between disputing parties. This is appropriate when conflicting parties refuse to meet face to face. The immediate goal is to establish direct communication, with the broader aim of finding common ground and a constructive solution.

- *Peer review.* A panel of trustworthy co-workers, selected for their ability to remain objective, hears both sides of a dispute in an informal and confidential meeting. Any decision by the review panel may or may not be binding, depending on the company's ADR policy. Membership on the peer review panel often is rotated among employees.

- *Ombudsman.* Someone who works for the organization, and is widely respected and trusted by his or her co-workers, hears grievances on a confidential basis and attempts to arrange a solution. This approach, more common in Europe than North America, permits someone to get help from above without relying on the formal hierarchy chain.

- *Mediation.* "The mediator—a trained, third-party neutral—actively guides the disputing parties in exploring innovative solutions to the conflict. Although some companies have in-house mediators who have received ADR training, most also use external mediators who have no ties to the company."[57] Unlike an arbitrator, a mediator does *not* render a decision. It is up to the disputants to reach a mutually acceptable decision.

- *Arbitration.* Disputing parties agree ahead of time to accept the decision of a neutral arbitrator in a formal courtlike setting, often complete with evidence and witnesses. Participation in this form of ADR can be voluntary or mandatory, depending upon company policy or union contracts.[58] Statements are confidential. Decisions are based on legal merits. Trained arbitrators, typically from outside agencies such as the American Arbitration Association, are versed in relevant laws and case precedents.

Practical Lessons from Conflict Research

Laboratory studies, relying on college students as subjects, uncovered the following insights about organizational conflict:

- People with a high need for affiliation tended to rely on a smoothing (obliging) style while avoiding a forcing (dominating) style.[59] Thus, personality traits affect how people handle conflict.

- Disagreement expressed in an arrogant and demeaning manner produced significantly more negative effects than the same sort of disagreement expressed in a reasonable manner.[60] In other words, *how* you disagree with someone is very important in conflict situations.

- Threats and punishment, by one party in a disagreement, tended to produce intensifying threats and punishment from the other party.[61] In short, aggression breeds aggression.

- As conflict increased, group satisfaction decreased. An integrative style of handling conflict led to higher group satisfaction than did an avoidance style.[62]
- Companies with mandatory or binding arbitration policies were viewed *less* favorably than companies without such policies.[63] Apparently, mandatory or binding arbitration policies are a turn-off for job applicants who dislike the idea of being forced to do something.

Field studies involving managers and real organizations have given us the following insights:

- Both intradepartmental and interdepartmental conflict decreased as goal difficulty and goal clarity increased. Thus, challenging and clear goals can defuse conflict.
- Higher levels of conflict tended to erode job satisfaction and internal work motivation.[64]
- Men and women at the same managerial level tended to handle conflict similarly. In short, there was no gender effect.[65]
- Conflict tended to move around the organization in a case study of a public school system.[66] Thus, managers need to be alerted to the fact that conflict often originates in one area or level and becomes evident somewhere else. Conflict needs to be traced back to its source if there is to be lasting improvement.
- Samples of Japanese, German, and American managers who were presented with the same conflict scenario preferred different resolution techniques. Japanese and German managers did not share the Americans' enthusiasm for integrating the interests of all parties. The Japanese tended to look upward to management for direction, whereas the Germans were more bound by rules and regulations. In cross-cultural conflict resolution, there is no one best approach. Culture-specific preferences need to be taken into consideration prior to beginning the conflict resolution process.[67]

As we transition from conflict to negotiation, take a few minutes to complete the OB Exercise on p 424. What better way to reinforce what you have learned about managing conflict than to apply it to your own life?

Negotiation

Formally defined, **negotiation** is a give-and-take decision-making process involving interdependent parties with different preferences.[68] Common examples include labor–management negotiations over wages, hours, and working conditions and negotiations between supply chain specialists and vendors involving price, delivery schedules, and credit terms. Self-managed work teams with overlapping task boundaries also need to rely on negotiated agreements. Negotiating skills are more important today than ever.[69]

Negotiation
Give-and-take
process between
conflicting interde-
pendent parties.

Two Basic Types of Negotiation

Negotiation experts distinguish between two types of negotiation—*distributive* and *integrative*. Understanding the difference requires a change in traditional fixed-pie thinking:

> A *distributive* negotiation usually involves a single issue—a "fixed-pie"—in which one person gains at the expense of the other. For example, haggling over the price of a rug in a bazaar is a distributive negotiation. In most conflicts, however, more than one issue is at

Instructions

This is a useful tool for understanding the full context of an interpersonal or intergroup conflict. First, identify a conflict situation that has involved and perhaps frustrated you lately (such as a broken friendship, a disagreement at school or work, or a family feud). Next, work your way down the conflict iceberg by writing some brief notes about the apparent issue, the personalities involved, relevant emotions, and so forth. The goal is to achieve "awareness of interconnection." In the spirit of functional or cooperative conflict, see if the other party to the conflict would be willing to complete this exercise from his or her perspective. Use the information gathered from one or both parties to move toward some sort of resolution. Importantly, be very honest with yourself because *you* may be a major obstacle or problem in the conflict situation. How can a similar conflict be avoided in the future?

Awareness of interconnection

(The potential to move above and beyond the conflict,
to have genuine empathy for others.)

SOURCE: Figure from K Cloke and J Goldsmith, *Resolving Conflicts at Work: A Complete Guide for Everyone on the Job* (San Francisco: Jossey-Bass, 2000), p 114. Copyright © 2000, John Wiley & Sons, Inc. Reprinted with permission of John Wiley & Sons, Inc.

stake, and each party values the issues differently. The outcomes available are no longer a fixed-pie divided among all parties. An agreement can be found that is better for both parties than what they would have reached through distributive negotiation. This is an *integrative* negotiation.

However, parties in a negotiation often don't find these beneficial trade-offs because each *assumes* its interests *directly* conflict with those of the other party. "What is good for the other side must be bad for us" is a common and unfortunate perspective that most people have. This is the mind-set we call the *mythical* "fixed-pie."[70]

Distributive negotiation involves traditional win–lose thinking. Integrative negotiation calls for a progressive win–win strategy.[71] (see Real World/Real People). In a laboratory study of joint venture negotiations, teams trained in integrative tactics achieved better outcomes for *both* sides than did untrained teams.[72] North American negotiators generally are too short-term oriented and poor relationship builders when negotiating in Asia, Latin America, and the Middle East.[73] The added-value negotiation technique illustrated in Figure 13–6 on p 426 is an integrative approach that can correct these shortcomings.

Time Warner's CEO, Dick Parsons, Got Some Win–Win Advice

The best business advice I ever received was from Steve Ross, who used to run this company. . . . Steve said to me, "Dick, always remember this is a small business and a long life. You are going to see all these guys come around and around again, so how you treat them on each individual transaction is going to make an impression in the long haul. When you do deals, leave a little something to make everyone happy instead of trying to grab every nickel off the table."

I've used that advice a thousand times since, literally. When I got to this company, for the first seven or eight years I was here I was the principal dealmaker, and I always took that advice with me into a negotiation.

SOURCE: As quoted in "The Best Advice I Ever Got: Dick Parsons," *Fortune*, March 21, 2005, p 103.

Ethical Pitfalls in Negotiation

The success of integrative negotiation, such as added-value negotiation, hinges to a large extent on the *quality* of information exchanged, as researchers have recently documented.[74] Telling lies, hiding key facts, and engaging in the other potentially unethical tactics listed in Table 13–3 on p 427 erode trust and goodwill, both vital in win–win negotiations.[75] An awareness of these dirty tricks can keep good faith bargainers from being unfairly exploited.[76] Unethical negotiating tactics need to be factored into organizational codes of ethics.

Practical Lessons from Negotiation Research

Laboratory and field studies have yielded these insights:

- Negotiators with fixed-pie expectations produced poor joint outcomes because they restricted and mismanaged information.[77]
- A meta-analysis of 62 studies found a *slight* tendency for women to negotiate more cooperatively than men. But when faced with a tit-for-tat bargaining strategy (equivalent countermoves), women were significantly more competitive than men.[78]
- Personality characteristics can affect negotiating success. Negotiators who scored high on the Big Five personality dimensions of extraversion and agreeableness (refer back to Table 5–2) tended to do poorly with distributive (fixed-pie; win–lose) negotiations.[79]

Figure 13–6   *An Integrative Approach: Added-Value Negotiation*

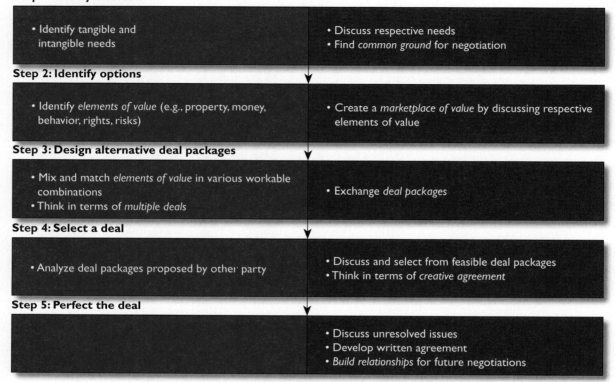

	Separately	**Jointly**
Step 1: Clarify interests	• Identify tangible and intangible needs	• Discuss respective needs • Find *common ground* for negotiation
Step 2: Identify options	• Identify *elements of value* (e.g., property, money, behavior, rights, risks)	• Create a *marketplace of value* by discussing respective elements of value
Step 3: Design alternative deal packages	• Mix and match *elements of value* in various workable combinations • Think in terms of *multiple deals*	• Exchange *deal packages*
Step 4: Select a deal	• Analyze deal packages proposed by other party	• Discuss and select from feasible deal packages • Think in terms of *creative agreement*
Step 5: Perfect the deal		• Discuss unresolved issues • Develop written agreement • *Build relationships* for future negotiations

SOURCE: Adapted from K Albrecht and S Albrecht, "Added Value Negotiating," *Training*, April 1993, pp 26–29. Used by permission of VNU Business Publications via The Copyright Clearance Center.

- Good and bad moods can have positive and negative effects, respectively, on negotiators' plans and outcomes.[80] So wait until both you and your boss are in a good mood before you ask for a raise.

- Studies of negotiations between Japanese, between Americans, and between Japanese and Americans found less productive joint outcomes across cultures than within cultures.[81] Less understanding of the other party makes cross-cultural negotiation more difficult than negotiations at home.

Conflict Management and Negotiation: A Contingency Approach

Three realities dictate how organizational conflict should be managed. First, various types of conflict are inevitable because they are triggered by a wide variety of antecedents. Second, too little conflict may be as counterproductive as too much. Third, there is no single best way of avoiding or resolving conflict. Consequently, conflict specialists recommend a

Table 13–3   *Questionable/Unethical Tactics in Negotiation*

Tactic	Description/Clarification/Range
Lies	Subject matter for lies can include limits, alternatives, the negotiator's intent, authority to bargain, other commitments, acceptability of the opponent's offers, time pressures, and available resources.
Puffery	Among the items that can be puffed up are the value of one's payoffs to the opponent, the negotiator's own alternatives, the costs of what one is giving up or is prepared to yield, importance of issues, and attributes of the products or services.
Deception	Acts and statements may include promises or threats, excessive initial demands, careless misstatements of facts, or asking for concessions not wanted.
Weakening the opponent	The negotiator here may cut off or eliminate some of the opponent's alternatives, blame the opponent for his own actions, use personally abrasive statements to or about the opponent, or undermine the opponent's alliances.
Strengthening one's own position	This tactic includes building one's own resources, including expertise, finances, and alliances. It also includes presentations of persuasive rationales to the opponent or third parties (e.g., the public, the media) or getting mandates for one's position.
Nondisclosure	Includes partial disclosure of facts, failure to disclose a hidden fact, failure to correct the opponents' misperceptions or ignorance, and concealment of the negotiator's own position or circumstances.
Information exploitation	Information provided by the opponent can be used to exploit his weaknesses, close off his alternatives, generate demands against him, or weaken his alliances.
Change of mind	Includes accepting offers one had claimed one would not accept, changing demands, withdrawing promised offers, and making threats one promised would not be made. Also includes the failure to behave as predicted.
Distraction	These acts or statements can be as simple as providing excessive information to the opponent, asking many questions, evading questions, or burying the issue. Or they can be more complex, such as feigning weakness in one area so that the opponent concentrates on it and ignores another.
Maximization	Includes demanding the opponent make concessions that result in the negotiator's gain and the opponent's equal or greater loss. Also entails converting a win–win situation into win–lose.

SOURCE: Reprinted from H J Reitz, J A Wall Jr, and M S Love, "Ethics in Negotiation: Oil and Water or Good Lubrication?" *Business Horizons*, May–June 1998, p 6. © 1998, with permission from Elsevier.

contingency approach to managing conflict. Antecedents of conflict and actual conflict need to be monitored. If signs of too little conflict such as apathy or lack of creativity appear, then functional conflict needs to be stimulated. This can be done by nurturing appropriate antecedents of conflict or programming conflict with techniques such as devil's advocacy and the dialectic method. On the other hand, when conflict becomes dysfunctional, the appropriate conflict-handling style needs to be enacted. Realistic training involving role playing can prepare managers to try alternative conflict styles.

Third-party interventions are necessary when conflicting parties are unwilling or unable to engage in conflict resolution or integrative negotiation. Integrative or added-value negotiation is most appropriate for intergroup and interorganizational conflict. The key is to get the conflicting parties to abandon traditional fixed-pie thinking and their win–lose expectations.

Managers can keep from getting too deeply embroiled in conflict by applying four lessons from recent research: (1) establish challenging and clear goals, (2) disagree in a constructive and reasonable manner, (3) do not get caught up in conflict triangles, and (4) refuse to get caught in the aggression-breeds-aggression spiral.

Summary of Key Concepts

1. *Define the term* conflict, *and put the three metaphors of conflict into proper perspective for the workplace.* Conflict is a process in which one party perceives that its interests are being opposed or negatively affected by another party. Conflict is inevitable but not necessarily destructive. Metaphorically, conflict can be viewed as war (win at all costs), an opportunity (be creative, grow, and improve), or a journey (a search for common ground and a better way). Within organizations, we are challenged to see conflicts as win–win opportunities and journeys rather than as win–lose wars.

2. *Distinguish between functional and dysfunctional conflict, and discuss why people avoid conflict.* Functional conflict enhances organizational interests while dysfunctional conflict is counterproductive. Three desired conflict outcomes are agreement, stronger relationships, and learning. People avoid conflict because of the following fears: harm; rejection; loss of relationship; anger; being seen as selfish; saying the wrong thing; failing; hurting someone else; getting what we want; and intimacy.

3. *List six antecedents of conflict, and identify the desired outcomes of conflict.* Among the many antecedents of conflict are incompatible personalities or value systems; competition for limited resources; inadequate communication; unreasonable or unclear policies, standards, or rules; unreasonable deadlines or extreme time pressure; collective decision making; unmet expectations; and unresolved or suppressed conflicts. The three desired outcomes of conflict are agreement, stronger relationships, and learning.

4. *Define* personality conflicts, *and explain how managers should handle them.* Personality conflicts involve interpersonal opposition based on personal dislike or disagreement (or as an outgrowth of workplace incivility). Care needs to be taken with personality conflicts in the workplace because of the legal implications of diversity, anti-discrimination, and sexual harassment. Managers should investigate and document personality conflict, take corrective actions such as feedback or behavior modification if appropriate, or attempt informal dispute resolution. Difficult or persistent personality conflicts need to be referred to human resource specialists or counselors.

5. *Discuss the role of in-group thinking in intergroup conflict, and explain what management can do about intergroup conflict.* Members of in-groups tend to see themselves as unique individuals who are more moral than outsiders, whom they view as a threat and stereotypically as all alike. In-group thinking is associated with ethnocentric behavior. According to the updated contact model, managers first must strive to eliminate negative relationships between conflicting groups. Beyond that, they need to provide team building, encourage personal friendships across groups, foster positive attitudes about other groups, and minimize negative gossip about groups.

6. *Discuss what can be done about cross-cultural conflict.* International consultants can prepare people from different cultures to work effectively together. Cross-cultural conflict can be minimized by having expatriates build strong cross-cultural relationships with their hosts (primarily by being good listeners, being sensitive to others, and being more cooperative than competitive).

7. *Explain how managers can stimulate functional conflict, and identify the five conflict-handling styles.* There are many antecedents of conflict—including incompatible personalities, competition for limited resources, and unrealized expectations—that need to be monitored. Functional conflict can be stimulated by permitting antecedents of conflict to persist or programming conflict during decision making with devil's advocates or the dialectic method. The five conflict-handling styles are integrating (problem solving), obliging (smoothing), dominating (forcing), avoiding, and compromising. There is no single best style.

8. *Explain the nature and practical significance of conflict triangles and alternative dispute resolution for third-party conflict intervention.* A conflict triangle occurs when one member of a conflict seeks the help of a third party rather than facing the opponent directly. Detriangling is advised, whereby the third-party redirects the disputants' energy toward each other in a positive and constructive manner. Alternative dispute resolution involves avoiding costly court battles with more informal and user-friendly techniques such as facilitation, conciliation, peer review, ombudsman, mediation, and arbitration.

9. *Explain the difference between distributive and integrative negotiation, and discuss the concept of added-value negotiation.* Distributive negotiation involves fixed-pie and win–lose thinking. Integrative negotiation is a win–win approach to better results for both parties. The five steps in added-value negotiation are as follows: step 1, clarify interests; step 2, identify options; step 3, design alternative deal packages; step 4, select a deal; and step 5, perfect the deal. Elements of value, multiple deal packages, and creative agreement are central to this approach.

Discussion Questions

1. What is your experience with people viewing conflict as war, versus seeing it as an opportunity or a journey? How did things turn out?

2. What examples of functional and dysfunctional conflict have you observed lately?

3. Which of the antecedents of conflict do you think are most common (or most troublesome) in today's workplaces?

4. Have you ever been directly involved in a personality conflict? Explain. Was it handled well? Explain. What could have been done differently?

5. How could in-group thinking affect the performance of a manager living and working in a foreign country?

6. Which of the five conflict-handling styles is your strongest? Your weakest? How can you improve your ability to handle conflict?

7. What is your personal experience with conflict triangles? Based on what you have learned in this chapter, do you think you could do a better job of handling conflict triangles in the future? Explain.

8. Which of the six ADR techniques appeals the most to you? Why?

9. Has your concept of negotiation, prior to reading this chapter, been restricted to fixed-pie thinking? Explain.

10. How could added-value negotiation make your life a bit easier? Explain in terms of a specific problem, conflict, or deadlock.

OB in Action Case Study

Pulp Friction at Weyerhaeuser[82]

BusinessWeek Things got ugly in a hurry for Steven R Rogel, CEO of Weyerhaeuser Co. In November 2000, he sent a letter to William Swindells, chairman of Willamette Industries Inc., letting him know that Weyerhaeuser was making a run at his company. This was not the usual takeover attempt, however. Call it a homecoming of sorts: Rogel, 59, had been Swindells' protégé at Willamette in Portland, Oregon—in fact, he had worked there for 25 years, running the place in the final two.

When Rogel left Willamette in 1997 to head up its much hated, far larger, and somewhat troubled rival, it was as if the favorite son had grown up, taken a job at the local bank, and then returned to repossess the family farm. Indeed, one reason Weyerhaeuser board members recruited Rogel was precisely because they believed he could mount a successful hostile takeover if necessary. Weyerhaeuser executives had never formally made an offer, but they knew Swindells' was not likely to be receptive. He had flatly rejected friendly overtures from several other companies. So when Rogel's message arrived, Swindells, 71, had a few choice words for the courier: "You can take this letter back to Steve and tell him where to put it."

It was the first of many angry words in what became one of the most contentious buyouts in recent history. Ultimately, Rogel prevailed. But it took him another year to complete the acquisition of Willamette, and the price was steep—in more ways than one. He had to extend his buyout offer 12 times and paid a final price of $6.2 billion, $825 million more than he originally offered. And he endured a welter of personal attacks. Willamette executives, who considered him a traitor, taped a picture of him to a voodoo doll and jabbed pins into its face. Many of the nearly 15,000 Willamette employees sported "Just Say No Wey" buttons. And [in 2001], Rogel had to walk past Willamette workers picketing their company's annual meeting and carrying signs that read: "Rogue'l: You're looking for love in all the wrong faces."

Rogel knew what he was getting into with the folks at Willamette: The 85-year-old company had a reputation for fierce independence. That was what drew Rogel, a chemical engineer who grew up in a small wheat-farming town in eastern Washington, to Willamette in the first place. It was also a company that prided itself on the loyalty of its employees. When Rogel resigned as chief executive, Swindells insisted he leave the company that very day. The two haven't spoken since: Rogel clinched the deal in conversations with Willamette CEO Duane C McDougall. "I knew [the hostile bid] would be upsetting to them and come back on me personally," Rogel says. What kept him going through those 12 months was his certainty about the benefits of the deal: "I slept well at night. I was doing the right thing not just for Weyerhaeuser but for good friends at Willamette," he says. "Nevertheless, you're human, and it impacts you."

Integrating Weyerhaeuser and Willamette will require considerable finesse. In addition to the usual challenges of merging two companies, Rogel has to overcome the hostilities of his new employees. . . .

Rogel figures the best thing he can do is to get through the integration quickly. So far, he has appointed two Willamette executives to senior positions in Weyerhaeuser's operations and has vowed that those laid off won't all be Willamette employees. He has set up toll-free phone numbers for merger-related questions and promised to post all relevant information on the company intranet. And he is leading forums with Willamette employees to articulate his vision for the new company. "Everyone has to know fairly and honestly what's going on," he says.

Back when he was rising to the top at Willamette, Rogel was respected for his nitty-gritty understanding of the business. Some employees are even welcoming him back. Bob Banister, a Willamette technical analyst who attended one of Rogel's meetings, says: "Steve came across very well and genuine." Putting the bitter fight aside won't be easy for everybody, though. Swindells, who resigned with the rest of the board . . . , declined to comment. And as one senior Willamette executive says: "Were this a friendly, amicable situation, it would probably be different. But it's not." Rogel may be picking voodoo pins out for some time.

Questions for Discussion

1. What evidence of dysfunctional conflict can you find in this case?

2. What antecedents of conflict can you detect in this case? Which one(s) present Rogel with the greatest challenge? Explain.

3. How big a problem was in-group thinking in this case? Explain.

4. Which of the cross-cultural skills in Table 13–2 would serve Rogel well while integrating the two companies? Explain.

5. Which conflict-handling style in Figure 13–4 should Rogel rely most heavily upon during the integration process? Explain.

Personal Awareness and Growth Exercise

What Is Your Primary Conflict-Handling Style?

Objectives

1. To continue building your self-awareness.

2. To assess your approach to conflict.

3. To provide a springboard for handling conflicts more effectively.

Introduction

Professor Afzalur Rahim, developer of the five-style conflict model in Figure 13–4, created an assessment instrument upon which the one in this exercise is based. The original instrument was validated through a factor analysis of responses from 1,219 managers from across the United States.[83]

Instructions

For each of the 15 items, indicate how often you rely on that tactic by circling the appropriate number.

Conflict-Handling Tactics	Rarely Always
1. I argue my case with my co-workers to show the merits of my position.	1 — 2 — 3 — 4 — 5
2. I negotiate with my co-workers so that a compromise can be reached.	1 — 2 — 3 — 4 — 5
3. I try to satisfy the expectations of my co-workers.	1 — 2 — 3 — 4 — 5
4. I try to investigate an issue with my co-workers to find a solution acceptable to us.	1 — 2 — 3 — 4 — 5
5. I am firm in pursuing my side of the issue.	1 — 2 — 3 — 4 — 5
6. I attempt to avoid being "put on the spot" and try to keep my conflict with my co-workers to myself.	1 — 2 — 3 — 4 — 5
7. I hold on to my solution to a problem.	1 — 2 — 3 — 4 — 5
8. I use "give and take" so that a compromise can be made.	1 — 2 — 3 — 4 — 5
9. I exchange accurate information with my co-workers to solve a problem together.	1 — 2 — 3 — 4 — 5
10. I avoid open discussion of my differences with my co-workers.	1 — 2 — 3 — 4 — 5
11. I accommodate the wishes of my co-workers.	1 — 2 — 3 — 4 — 5
12. I try to bring all our concerns out in the open so that the issues can be resolved in the best possible way.	1 — 2 — 3 — 4 — 5
13. I propose a middle ground for breaking deadlocks.	1 — 2 — 3 — 4 — 5
14. I go along with the suggestions of my co-workers.	1 — 2 — 3 — 4 — 5
15. I try to keep my disagreements with my co-workers to myself in order to avoid hard feelings.	1 — 2 — 3 — 4 — 5

Scoring and Interpretation

Enter your responses, item by item, in the five categories below, and then add the three scores for each of the styles. Note: There are no right or wrong answers, because individual differences are involved.

Integrating		Obliging		Dominating	
Item	Score	Item	Score	Item	Score
4.	_____	3.	_____	1.	_____
9.	_____	11.	_____	5.	_____
12.	_____	14.	_____	7.	_____
Total =	_____	Total =	_____	Total =	_____

Avoiding		Compromising	
Item	Score	Item	Score
6.	_____	2.	_____
10.	_____	8.	_____
15.	_____	13.	_____
Total =	_____	Total =	_____

Your primary conflict-handling style is: _____
   (The category with the highest total.)
Your backup conflict-handling style is: _____
   (The category with the second highest total.)

Questions for Discussion

1. Are the results what you expected? Explain.

2. Is there a clear gap between your primary and backup styles, or did they score about the same? If they are about the same, does this suggest indecision about handling conflict on your part? Explain.

3. Will your primary conflict-handling style carry over well to many different situations? Explain.

4. What is your personal learning agenda for becoming a more effective conflict handler?

Group Exercise

Bangkok Blowup—A Role-Playing Exercise

Objectives

1. To further your knowledge of interpersonal conflict and conflict-handling styles.

2. To give you a firsthand opportunity to try the various styles of handling conflict.

Introduction

This is a role-playing exercise intended to develop your ability to handle conflict. There is no single best way to resolve the conflict in this exercise. One style might work for one person, while another gets the job done for someone else.

Instructions

Read the following short case, "Can Larry Fit In?" Pair up with someone else and decide which of you will play the role of Larry and which will play the role of Melissa, the office manager. Pick up the action from where the case leaves off. Try to be realistic and true to the characters in the case. The manager is primarily responsible for resolving this conflict situation. Whoever plays Larry should resist any unreasonable requests or demands and cooperate with any personally workable solution. *Note:* To conserve time, try to resolve this situation in less than 15 minutes.

CAN LARRY FIT IN?[84]

Melissa, Office Manager

You are the manager of an auditing team sent to Bangkok, Thailand, to represent a major international accounting firm headquartered in New York. You and Larry, one of your auditors, were sent to Bangkok to set up an auditing operation. Larry is about seven years older than you and has five more years seniority in the firm. Your relationship has become very strained since you were recently designated as the office manager. You feel you were given the promotion because you have established an excellent working relationship with the Thai staff as well as a broad range of international clients. In contrast, Larry has told other members of the staff that your promotion simply reflects the firm's heavy emphasis on affirmative action. He has tried to isolate

431

you from the all-male accounting staff by focusing discussions on sports, local night spots, and so forth.

You are sitting in your office reading some complicated new reporting procedures that have just arrived from the home office. Your concentration is suddenly interrupted by a loud knock on your door. Without waiting for an invitation to enter, Larry bursts into your office. He is obviously very upset, and it is not difficult for you to surmise why he is in such a nasty mood.

You recently posted the audit assignments for the coming month, and you scheduled Larry for a job you knew he wouldn't like. Larry is one of your senior auditors, and the company norm is that they get the choice assignments. This particular job will require him to spend two weeks away from Bangkok in a remote town, working with a company whose records are notoriously messy.

Unfortunately, you have had to assign several of these less-desirable audits to Larry recently because you are short of personnel. But that's not the only reason. You have received several complaints from the junior staff (all Thais) recently that Larry treats them in a condescending manner. They feel he is always looking for an opportunity to boss them around, as if he were their supervisor instead of an experienced, supportive mentor. As a result, your whole operation works more smoothly when you can send Larry out of town on a solo project for several days. It keeps him from coming into your office and telling you how to do your job, and the morale of the rest of the auditing staff is significantly higher.

Larry slams the door and proceeds to express his anger over this assignment.

Larry, Senior Auditor

You are really ticked off! Melissa is deliberately trying to undermine your status in the office. She knows that the company norm is that senior auditors get the better jobs.

You've paid your dues, and now you expect to be treated with respect. And this isn't the first time this has happened. Since she was made the office manager, she has tried to keep you out of the office as much as possible. It's as if she doesn't want her rival for leadership of the office around. When you were asked to go to Bangkok, you assumed that you would be made the office manager because of your seniority in the firm. You are certain that the decision to pick Melissa is yet another indication of reverse discrimination against white males.

In staff meetings, Melissa has talked about the need to be sensitive to the feelings of the office staff as well as the clients in this multicultural setting. "Where does she come off preaching about sensitivity! What about my feelings, for heaven's sake?" you wonder. This is nothing more than a straightforward power play. She is probably feeling insecure about being the only female accountant in the office and being promoted over someone with more experience. "Sending me out of town," you decide, "is a clear case of 'out of sight, out of mind.' "

Well, it's not going to happen that easily. You are not going to roll over and let her treat you unfairly. It's time for a showdown. If she doesn't agree to change this assignment and apologize for the way she's been treating you, you're going to register a formal complaint with her boss in the New York office. You are prepared to submit your resignation if the situation doesn't improve.

Questions for Discussion

1. What antecedents of conflict appear to be present in this situation? What can be done about them?

2. Having heard how others handled this conflict, did one particular style seem to work better than the others?

3. Did emotions cloud your conflict-handling ability? If so, reread the material on emotional intelligence in Chapter 5.

Fight Night for the Cubicle Dwellers?

Can't stand the sight of that jerkwad in business development? If you work anywhere near Manhattan, you can do more about it than exchange four-letter epithets—you can try to knock him into next week without fear of a pink slip or lawsuit. Assuming that your sworn enemy is similarly inclined, the trick is to sign up for the Grudge Match package at the Trinity Boxing Club (www.trinityboxing.com). For $200, Trinity owner and professional boxing coach Martin Snow offers four weeks of training, the use of protective headgear, some oversize boxing gloves, and a three-round match. Snow hit on the idea two years ago, after getting multiple requests from pairs of co-workers looking to rent the ring. . . . The results, however, tend to be the same: "By the end, these guys are always hugging," Snow says.[85]

Is this idea an ethical low blow?

1. Sign me up. I'd like to put the office wise guy on his butt.
2. It's probably harmless fun that lots of people will talk about but few would actually do. Besides, four weeks of training would get the disputing parties in better physical shape and maybe defuse their anger. Better to have a boxing match now than risk workplace violence later.
3. What employees do on their own time is their own business. Think of it as an exercise class, with an attitude.
4. For legal liability reasons, the organization in no way should condone or reinforce this activity.
5. This is a really dumb idea that only encourages violence as the preferred way to deal with conflict. The organization should proactively discourage any participation by its employees.
6. Invent other options. Discuss.

For the Chapter 13 Internet Exercise featuring practical tips on managing conflict (www.ncpc.org), visit our Web site at **www.mhhe.com/kreitner.**

Organizational Processes

14

Communication in the Internet Age

Learning Objectives

When you finish studying the material in this chapter, you should be able to:

1 Describe the perceptual process model of communication.

2 Describe the process, personal, physical, and semantic barriers to effective communication.

3 Contrast the communication styles of assertiveness, aggressiveness, and nonassertiveness.

4 Discuss the primary sources of nonverbal communication.

5 Review the five dominant listening styles and 10 keys to effective listening.

6 Describe the communication differences between men and women, and explain the source of these differences.

7 Discuss the formal and informal communication channels.

8 Explain the contingency approach to media selection.

9 Demonstrate your familiarity with four antecedents of communication distortion between managers and employees.

10 Explain the information technology of Internet/intranet/extranet, e-mail, handheld devices, blogs, videoconferencing, and group support systems, and explain the related use of telecommuting.

Christopher Frankonis, like many bloggers, first began writing on his Web site about whatever popped into his head—what kind of day he was having, the craziness of Oregon weather. Sometimes, he would comment on a news story that caught his attention, and provide readers with a link to the story.

Then, two years ago, he launched the Portland Communique, a blog that combines firsthand reporting, opinion, and links to articles about Portland news and politics, from mayoral races to neighborhood meetings. In essence, he became a one-man newspaper with about 400 readers a day. Although he had no formal journalism background, he began thinking of himself as a journalist.

Bloggers such as Mr Frankonis are finally moving from the alleys and side streets of the Internet into the mainstream. And as their visibility and clout increases, some are asking: what are the rules of the road? There is no exam to pass or society to join to become a blogger—anybody can set up a "Web log" to publish his or her ideas—and at last count, an estimated eight million people in the US are doing so, writing on everything from pets to porn. Blogs run the gamut from photographs of finished knitting projects to political diatribes to highly personalized attacks on fellow bloggers. Most blogs let readers post their own comments, which inevitably attract still more, which sometimes devolve into name-calling, all in the span of an afternoon.

The audience for such alternative media is growing rapidly. The number of Americans reading blogs jumped 58% in 2004 to an estimated 32 million people, according to a Pew Internet and American Life Project, with about 11 million looking to political blogs for news during the presidential campaign.

And blogs are increasingly having an impact: bloggers first exposed many of the flaws in CBS's *60 Minutes* episode about President Bush's National Guard service. Blogs, among others, widely disseminated premature exit poll results that led many to believe John Kerry was winning the presidential election for much of Election Day.

Bloggers who were paid by people they wrote about have sparked some controversies. In the midst of the fray, bloggers are starting to debate what kinds of ethical responsibilities they have to readers, and standards that might enhance their credibility. . . .

But the nature of the medium also allows rumors and falsehoods and ad hominem attacks to be spread with lightning speed. "Rumors are always more fun than the truth," says Rebecca Blood, author of The Weblog Handbook: Practical Advice on Creating and Maintaining Your Blog. "I think people do scandal monger and deal in rumor, especially the political advocates."

Like reporters, bloggers can be sued for libel or defamation charges, and they are also protected by the First Amendment. In one case, former US Senator James G Abourezk is suing a pair of Web writers in their 20s for libel in US District Court in Sioux Falls, Soath Dakota. The writers, Michael Marino and Ben Marino Jr of Pennsylvania, posted Mr Abourezk's name in a list of traitors on their Pro-Bush.com Web site. A spokesman for the writers said the list is a parody and thus protected by the First Amendement.

In another case, Apple Computer Inc has brought a lawsuit against the owner of a Web site run by a Harvard student, Nicholas Ciarelli, called ThinkSecret. com, for allegedly revealing trade secrets. An attorney for Mr Ciarelli said that holding a Web writer accountable for how his source obtained information would have a chilling effect on free speech.[1]

FOR DISCUSSION

Should organizations encourage or stop employees from blogging about their employers? Explain your rationale.

M anagement is communication. Every managerial function and activity involves some form of direct or indirect communication. Whether planning and organizing or directing and leading, managers find themselves communicating with and through others. Managerial decisions and organizational policies are ineffective unless they are understood by those responsible for enacting them. Consider, for example, how the communication process within Adecco SA, the world's largest temporary help company, negatively affected the company's stock price.

> Eight days ago, the Swiss-based concern announced it wouldn't be able to release its year-end results on schedule in February and warned of "material weaknesses with internal controls" at its North American staffing business. But Adecco officials refused to elaborate on the terse statement, citing legal constraints. At the time, they wouldn't even confirm the identity of an independent counsel that Adecco's board has appointed to conduct its own investigation.
>
> The company's bunker mentalilty stirred anxiety among investors, who quickly dumped Adecco shares. Within a few hours, the company lost 35% of its market capitalization.[2]

Ineffective communication clearly contributed to the drop in Adecco's share price. Effective communication also is critical for employee motivation and job satisfaction. For example, a study of 274 students revealed that student motivation was positively related to the quality of student–faculty communication in the instructor's office. Another study involving 65 savings and loan employees and 110 manufacturing employees revealed that employee satisfaction with organizational communication was positively and significantly correlated with job satisfaction and performance.[3]

Moreover, the chapter-opening vignette highlights how organizational communication has been dramatically affected by the introduction and explosive use of computers and information technology. Who would have guessed that 32 million people would be reading blogs? Managers need more than good interpersonal skills to effectively communicate in today's workplace. They also need to understand the pros and cons of different types of communication media and information technology. More is said about the pros and cons of blogging in the final section of this chapter.

This chapter will help you to better understand how managers can both improve their communication skills and design more effective communication programs. We discuss (1) basic dimensions of the communication process, focusing on a perceptual process model and barriers to effective communication; (2) interpersonal communication; (3) organizational communication; and (4) communicating in the computerized information age.

Basic Dimensions of the Communication Process

Communication is defined as "the exchange of information between a sender and a receiver, and the inference (perception) of meaning between the individuals involved."[4] Analysis of this exchange reveals that communication is a two-way process consisting of consecutively linked elements (see Figure 14–1). Managers who understand this process can analyze their own communication patterns as well as design communication programs that fit organizational needs. This section reviews a perceptual process model of communication and discusses a contingency approach to choosing communication media.

Communication
Interpersonal exchange of information and understanding.

A Perceptual Process Model of Communication

The communication process historically has been described in terms of a *conduit* model. This traditional model depicts communication as a pipeline in which information and meaning are transferred from person to person. Today, communication scholars have criticized the conduit model for being based on unrealistic assumptions. For example, the conduit model assumes communication transfers *intended meanings* from person to person.[5] If this assumption was true, miscommunication would not exist and there would be no need to worry about being misunderstood. We could simply say or write what we want and assume the listener or reader accurately understands our intended meaning.

Figure 14–1   *A Perceptual Model of Communication*

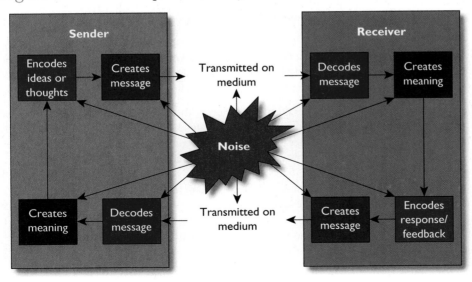

As we all know, communicating is not that simple or clear-cut. Communication is fraught with miscommunication. In recognition of this, researchers have begun to examine communication as a form of social information processing (recall the discussion in Chapter 7) in which receivers interpret messages by cognitively processing information. This view led to development of a **perceptual model of communication** that depicts communication as a process in which receivers create meaning in their own minds. Let us briefly examine the elements of the perceptual process model shown in Figure 14–1.

Perceptual model of communication
Process in which receivers create their own meaning.

Sender
The sender is an individual, group, or organization that desires or attempts to communicate with a particular receiver. Receivers may be individuals, groups, or organizations.

Encoding
Communication begins when a sender encodes an idea or thought. Encoding translates mental thoughts into a code or language that can be understood by others. Managers typically encode using words, numbers, gestures, nonverbal cues such as facial expressions, or pictures. Moreover, different methods of encoding can be used to portray similar ideas. The following short exercise highlights this point.

On a piece of paper, draw a picture of the area currently surrounding you. Now, write a verbal description of the same area. Does the pictorial encoding portray the same basic message as the verbal description? Which mode was harder to use and which more effective? Interestingly, a growing number of companies and management consultants recommend using visual communication, such as drawings, to analyze and improve group interaction and problem solving and to reduce stress.

The Message
The output of encoding is a message. There are two important points to keep in mind about messages. First, they contain more than meets the eye. Messages may contain hidden agendas as well as trigger affective or emotional reactions. For example, comparisons of internal and external documents within the forest products industry over a 10-year period demonstrated that executives' private and public evaluative statements about events and situations were inconsistent. These executives apparently wanted to convey different messages to the public and to internal employees.[6] The second point to consider about messages is that they need to match the medium used to transmit them. How would you evaluate the match between the message of letting someone know he was being let go and the communication medium used in the following example?

> Six months ago [January 2002], Tower Snow was chairman of Brobeck, Phleger & Harrison, one of the nation's premier law firms. Late Friday, as he got off a United Airlines flight in San Francisco, a gate agent handed him an envelope. Inside: notice that Brobeck had fired him.[7]

How would you feel if this happened to you? Surely there is a better way to let someone know he or she is being fired. This example illustrates how thoughtless managers can be when they do not carefully consider the interplay between a message and the medium used to convey it. More is said about this issue later in this chapter.

Selecting a Medium
Managers can communicate through a variety of media. Potential media include face-to-face conversations, telephone calls, electronic mail, voice mail, videoconferencing, written memos or letters, photographs or drawings, meetings, bulletin boards, computer output, and charts or graphs. Choosing the appropriate media depends on many factors, including the nature of the message, its intended purpose, the type of audience, proximity to the audience, time horizon for disseminating the message, and personal preferences.

All media have advantages and disadvantages. Face-to-face conversations, for instance, are useful for communicating about sensitive or important issues and those requiring feedback and intensive interaction. Telephones are convenient, fast, and private, but lack nonverbal information. Although writing memos or letters is time consuming, it is a good medium when it is difficult to meet with the other person, when formality and a written record are important, and when face-to-face interaction is not necessary to enhance understanding. More is said later in this chapter about choosing media.

Decoding   Decoding is the receiver's version of encoding. Decoding consists of translating verbal, oral, or visual aspects of a message into a form that can be interpreted. Receivers rely on social information processing to determine the meaning of a message during decoding. Decoding is a key contributor to misunderstanding in interracial and intercultural communication because decoding by the receiver is subject to social values and cultural values that may not be understood by the sender.[8]

Creating Meaning   In contrast to the conduit model's assumption that meaning is directly transferred from sender to receiver, the perceptual model is based on the belief that a receiver creates the meaning of a message in his or her mind. A receiver's interpretation of a message often will differ from that intended by the sender. In turn, receivers act according to their own interpretations, not the communicator's. Consider how this issue created problems for Arthur Andersen.

> Two Houston employees of Arthur Andersen LLP said they believed they were following the firm's policy when they, and other auditors and personnel, destroyed documents related to the firm's audits of Enron Corp. in the weeks leading up to Andersen's receipt of a subpoena from the Securities and Exchange Commission for Enron-related documents.
>
> Andersen's policy for retaining and destroying documents requires that its auditors retain only those documents "needed to support or defend our work" and "eliminate or destroy" all other documents when they are no longer needed. "Only essential information to support our conclusions should be retained," the policy says.[9]

A spokesperson for the company offered a different interpretation of these policies.

> Andersen spokesman Charlie Leonard said the firm's policy tells firm auditors to "save the documents that support your conclusions" and that the policy doesn't instruct auditors to destroy documents that contradict the firm's audit conclusions.[10]

It appears that Andersen's policies were interpreted differently within the company. Managers are encouraged to rely on *redundancy* of communication to reduce this unintentionality. This can be done by transmitting the message over multiple media. For example, a production manager might follow up a phone conversation about a critical schedule change with a memo or e-mail.

Feedback   Once a receiver decodes a message, he or she encodes a response and then transmits it to the original sender. This new message is then decoded and interpreted. This process repeats itself when further communication is needed. As you can see from this discussion, feedback is used as a comprehension check. It gives senders an idea of how accurately their message is understood.

Noise   Noise represents anything that interferes with the transmission and understanding of a message. It affects all linkages of the communication process. Noise includes factors such as a speech impairment, poor telephone connections, illegible handwriting, inaccurate statistics in a memo or report, poor hearing and eyesight, and physical distance

Noise
Interference with the transmission and understanding of a message.

What Really Goes on during Conference Calls?

Three years ago, engineer Randy Thompson was on a weekly conference call about the design of component parts when another participant was suddenly asked for input. The man dutifully chimed in, and so did the sudden flushing sound of an automatic toilet....

All in all, what you get is little more than meetings with blindfolds—and one whose participants frequently have cause to wonder: What in the Sam Hill is going on out there? That's because conference calls often offer a rhapsody of background noises, including the highly amplified sound of crunched Fritos, paper shuffling, barking dogs, soccer games, traffic, and SpongeBob SquarePants jingles blaring from somebody's home TV. Bursts of text messaging can erupt as participants try to figure out who, for example, is snoring into the telephone....

Without visual clues, conference callers often overanalyze what little input they get, and the process can easily degenerate. A banking department colleague suggested that Peter Larson and his boss surreptitiously sit in on a conference call with a client who was talking about his business. But the client spoke so slowly that Mr Larson's boss whispered, "He sounds like he's playing chess with himself." Clever, sure, but downright hilarious when you consider the two weren't supposed to speak, much less laugh.

The two men quickly unraveled, victims of a bad case of the giggles that, unchecked, soon turned into snorts. "Whenever I try to keep myself from laughing, I exhale completely so there's no air in there to make noise," Mr Larson explains. "But you gasp for breath. If you're not careful it's a snort." ...

Richard Spector, a retired securities attorney, notes that one of the problems with conference calls is that it's so easy to be distracted by other things you'd like to do. He says he used to doodle, draft documents, or watch CNBC while listening in.

SOURCE: Excerpted from J Sandberg, "Funny Things Happen as Conference Callers Attempt to Multitask," *The Wall Street Journal*, January 26, 2005, p B1. Reprinted by permission of Dow Jones & Co. Inc. via The Copyright Clearance Center.

between sender and receiver. Conference calls are particularly subject to many different types of noise, including boredom and the desire to multitask (see Real World/Real People).[11] Managers, and anyone participating in a conference call, can improve communication by reducing noise.

Barriers to Effective Communication

Communication noise is a barrier to effective communication because it interferes with the accurate transmission and reception of a message. Sue Weidemann, director of research for a consulting company, investigated the impact of noise at a large law firm. Her results indicated that "the average number of times that people were interrupted by noise, visual distractions, and chatty visitors prairie-dogging over a cube wall was 16 a day—or 21 a day including work-related distractions." She concluded that it takes 2.9 minutes to recover concentration after these disruptions, "meaning people spend more than an hour a day trying to refocus. And that doesn't even count the time drain of the distraction itself."[12] Management awareness of these barriers is a good starting point to improve the communication process. There are four key barriers to effective communication: (1) process barriers, (2) personal barriers, (3) physical barriers, and (4) semantic barriers.

Process Barriers   Every element of the perceptual model of communication shown in Figure 14–1 is a potential process barrier. Consider the following examples:

1. *Sender barrier.* A customer gets incorrect information from a customer service agent because he or she was recently hired and lacks experience.

2. *Encoding barrier.* An employee for whom English is a second language has difficulty explaining why a delivery was late.

3. *Message barrier.* An employee misses a meeting for which he or she never received a confirmation e-mail.

4. *Medium barrier.* A salesperson gives up trying to make a sales call when the potential customer fails to return three previous phone calls.

5. *Decoding barrier.* An employee does not know how to respond to a manager's request to stop exhibiting passive aggressive behavior.

6. *Receiver barrier.* A student who is talking to his or her friend during a lecture asks the professor the same question that was just answered.

7. *Feedback barrier.* The nonverbal head nodding of an interviewer leads an interviewee to think that he or she is doing a great job answering questions.

Barriers in any of these process elements can distort the transfer of meaning. Reducing these barriers is essential but difficult given the current diversity of the workforce.

Personal Barriers   There are many personal barriers to communication.[13] We highlight eight of the more common ones. The first is our *ability to effectively communicate.* People possess varying levels of communication skills. The *way people process and interpret information* is a second barrier. Chapter 7 highlighted the fact that people use different frames of reference and experiences to interpret the world around them. We also learned that people selectively attend to various stimuli. All told, these differences affect both what we say and what we think we hear. Third, the *level of interpersonal trust between people* can either be a barrier or enabler of effective communication. Communication is more likely to be distorted when people do not trust each other. *Stereotypes and prejudices* are a fourth barrier. They can powerfully distort what we perceive about others. Our *egos* are a fifth barrier. Egos can cause political battles, turf wars, and pursuit of power, credit, and resources. Egos influence how people treat each other as well as our receptiveness to being influenced by others. *Poor listening skills* are a sixth barrier.

Carl Rogers, a renowned psychologist, identified the seventh and eighth barriers that interfere with interpersonal communication.[14] The seventh barrier is a *natural tendency to evaluate or judge a sender's message.* To highlight the natural tendency to evaluate, consider how you might respond to the statement "I like the book you are reading." What would you say? Your likely response is to approve or disapprove the statement. You may say, "I agree," or alternatively, "I disagree, the book is boring." The point is that we all tend to evaluate messages from our own point of view or frame of reference. The tendency to evaluate messages is greatest when one has strong feelings or emotions about the issue being discussed. An *inability to listen with understanding* is the eighth personal barrier to effective communication. Listening with understanding occurs when a receiver can "see the expressed idea and attitude from the other person's point of view, to sense how it feels to him, to achieve his frame of reference in regard to the thing he is talking about."[15] Listening with understanding reduces defensiveness and improves accuracy in perceiving a message.

Physical Barriers   The distance between employees can interfere with effective communication. Communication can be distorted when employees work in close confinement or when they are miles apart. The following example highlights the impact of modern day office design on communication, job satisfaction, and performance.

> Every couple of weeks, Michael McKay, a 33-year-old business analyst with a Santa Clara, California, Internet services company, finds his concentration totally disrupted when three colleagues who sit near his workstation hop onto the same conference call—all on speakerphones.
>
> "You get this stereophonic effect of hearing one person's voice live, and then hearing it coming out of someone else's speakerphone two or three cubes over," fumes Mr McKay.
>
> Incessant phone-ringing, very personal conversations, chitchat about weekend exploits, laughing at bad jokes—day in and day out, office employees hear it all. The modern workplace got so loud in part after the New Economy's forward thinkers surmised that open-office designs would foster creativity, communication, and collaboration among workers. Older-line companies picked up the concept and kicked workers and many managers out of private offices and into cubicles and pods.[16]

Time zone differences around the world represent physical barriers. The quality of telephone lines or crashed computers also represents physical barriers that affect our ability to communicate with information technology.

In spite of the general acceptance of physical barriers, they can be reduced. For example, offices can be redesigned, and employees on the US East Coast can agree to call their West Coast peers prior to leaving for lunch. It is important that managers attempt to manage this barrier by choosing a medium that optimally reduces the physical barrier at hand.

Semantic Barriers   *Semantics* is the study of words. Semantic barriers show up as encoding and decoding errors because these phases of communication involve transmitting and receiving words and symbols. These barriers are partially fueled by the use of jargon and unnecessarily complex words. Consider the following statement: Crime is ubiquitous. Do you understand this message? Even if you do, would it not be simpler to say that "crime is all around us" or "crime is everywhere"? Choosing our words more carefully is the easiest way to reduce semantic barriers. This barrier can also be decreased by attentiveness to mixed messages and cultural diversity. Mixed messages occur when a person's words imply one message while his or her actions or nonverbal cues suggest something different. Obviously, understanding is enhanced when a person's actions and nonverbal cues match the verbal message.

Interpersonal Communication

Communication competence
Ability to effectively use communication behaviors in a given context.

The quality of interpersonal communication within an organization is very important. People with good communication skills helped groups to make more innovative decisions and were promoted more frequently than individuals with less developed abilities.[17] Although there is no universally accepted definition of **communication competence,** it is a performance-based index of an individual's abilities to effectively use communication behaviors in a given context.[18] Business etiquette, for example, is one component of communication competence. At this time we would like you to complete the business etiquette test in the OB Exercise on page 445. How did you score?

OB Exercise What Is Your Business Etiquette?

Instructions

Business etiquette is one component of communication competence. Test your business etiquette by answering the following questions. After circling your response for each item, calculate your score by reviewing the correct answers listed in note 19 in the Endnotes section of the book.[19] Next, use the norms at the end of the test to interpret your results.

1. The following is an example of a proper introduction: "Ms Boss, I'd like you to meet our client, Mr Smith."
   True   False

2. If someone forgets to introduce you, you shouldn't introduce yourself; you should just let the conversation continue.
   True   False

3. If you forget someone's name, you should keep talking and hope no one will notice. This way you don't embarrass yourself or the person you are talking to.
   True   False

4. When shaking hands, a man should wait for a woman to extend her hand.
   True   False

5. Who goes through a revolving door first?
   a. Host   b. Visitor

6. It is all right to hold private conversations, either in person or on a cell phone in office bathrooms, elevators, and other public spaces.
   True   False

7. When two US businesspeople are talking to one another, the space between them should be approximately
   a. 1.5 feet   b. 3 feet   c. 7 feet

8. Business casual attire requires socks for men and hose for women.
   True   False

9. To signal that you do not want a glass of wine, you should turn your wine glass upside down.
   True   False

10. If a call is disconnected, it's the caller's responsibility to redial.
    True   False

11. When using a speakerphone, you should tell the caller if there is anyone else in the room.
    True   False

12. You should change your voicemail message if you are going to be out of the office.
    True   False

Arbitrary Norms

Low business etiquette (0–4 correct): Consider buying an etiquette book or hiring a coach to help you polish your professional image.

Moderate business etiquette (5–8 correct): Look for a role model or mentor, and look for ways you can improve your business etiquette.

High business etiquette (9–12 correct): Good for you. You should continue to practice good etiquette and look for ways to maintain your professional image.

SOURCE: This test was adapted from material contained in M Brody, "Test Your Etiquette," *Training & Development,* February 2002, pp 64–66.

Figure 14–2   *Communication Competence Affects Upward Mobility*

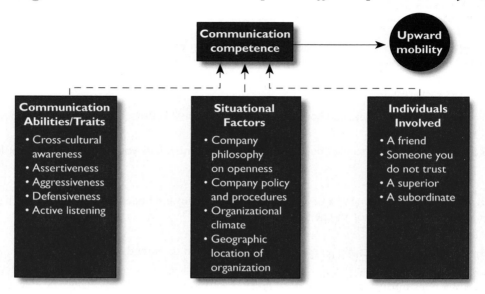

Communication competence is determined by three components: communication abilities and traits, situational factors, and the individuals involved in the interaction (see Figure 14–2). Jorge Blanco, vice president of strategic marketing and portfolio for Avaya, is a good example of someone who understands how to vary his communications based on these three components (see Real World/Real People on page 447). Cross-cultural awareness, for instance, is an important communication ability/trait.[20] Individuals involved in an interaction also affect communication competence. People are likely to withhold information and react emotionally or defensively when interacting with someone they dislike or do not trust. You can improve your communication competence through five communication styles/abilities/traits under your control: assertiveness, aggressiveness, nonassertiveness, nonverbal communication, and active listening. After discussing these styles/traits, we conclude this section by discussing gender differences in communication.

Assertive style
Expressive and self-enhancing, but does not take advantage of others.

Aggressive style
Expressive and self-enhancing, but takes unfair advantage of others.

Nonassertive style
Timid and self-denying behavior.

Assertiveness, Aggressiveness, and Nonassertiveness

The saying "You can attract more flies with honey than with vinegar" captures the difference between using an assertive communication style and an aggressive style. Research studies indicate that assertiveness is more effective than aggressiveness in both work-related and consumer contexts.[21] An **assertive style** is expressive and self-enhancing and is based on the "ethical notion that it is not right or good to violate our own or others' basic human rights, such as the right to self-expression or the right to be treated with dignity and respect."[22] In contrast, an **aggressive style** is expressive and self-enhancing and strives to take unfair advantage of others. A **nonassertive style** is characterized by timid and self-denying behavior. Nonassertiveness is ineffective because it gives the other person an unfair advantage.

Managers may improve their communication competence by trying to be more assertive and less aggressive or nonassertive. This can be achieved by using the appropriate nonverbal and verbal behaviors listed in Table 14–1. For instance, managers should attempt to use

Jorge Blanco Changes His Communication Style for the Situation and Individuals Involved

Jorge Blanco . . . recently gave the same talk to customers in Australia and Japan, but his presentation differed. In English-speaking Australia Mr Blanco says he moved around quite a bit while talking. In Japan, he stood behind a lectern next to a translator and concentrated on each word. "If you use a word like 'pervasiveness' or 'scalability' that can't be easily translated, you start to see people's eyes glaze," he says. He also paused between key points to give the translator time to translate. "You can be a fabulous speaker in Des Moines and not hit it off at all in another country," he says. . . .

He also has learned to simplify his descriptions for non-technical audiences: "If I'm talking to investment bankers or equity researchers, I better not come in with a very geeky speech, because they don't get that," he says.

SOURCE: Excerpted from C Hymowitz, "Unlike Politicians, Business Executives Seek Profit, Not Votes," *The Wall Street Journal*, August 17, 2004, p B1.

Avaya vice president Jorge Blanco has learned to modify his communication style to fit the various audiences he addresses around the world. Such cross-cultural awareness is likely to make Mr Blanco a more effective communicator.

the nonverbal behaviors of good eye contact, a strong, steady, and audible voice, and selective interruptions. They should avoid nonverbal behaviors such as glaring or little eye contact, threatening gestures, slumped posture, and a weak or whiny voice. Appropriate verbal behaviors include direct and unambiguous language and the use of "I" messages instead of "you" statements. For example, when you say, "Mike, I was disappointed with your report because it contained typographical errors," rather than "Mike, your report was poorly done," you reduce defensiveness. "I" statements describe your feelings about someone's performance or behavior instead of laying blame on the person.

Sources of Nonverbal Communication

Nonverbal communication is "Any message, sent or received independent of the written or spoken word . . . [It] includes such factors as use of time and space, distance between persons when conversing, use of color, dress, walking behavior, standing, positioning, seating arrangement, office locations and furnishing."[23]

Communication experts estimate that 65 to 90% of every conversation is partially interpreted through nonverbal communication.[24] It thus is important to ensure that your nonverbal signals are consistent with your intended verbal messages. Inconsistencies create noise and promote miscommunications.[25] Because of the prevalence of nonverbal communication and its significant impact on organizational behavior (including, but not limited to, perceptions of others, hiring decisions, work attitudes, and turnover), it is important that managers become consciously aware of the sources of nonverbal communication.

Nonverbal communication
Messages sent outside of the written or spoken word.

Table 14–1   *Communication Styles*

Communication Style	Description	Nonverbal Behavior Pattern	Verbal Behavior Pattern
Assertive	Pushing hard without attacking; permits others to influence outcome; expressive and self-enhancing without intruding on others	Good eye contact Comfortable but firm posture Strong, steady, and audible voice Facial expressions matched to message Appropriately serious tone Selective interruptions to ensure understanding	Direct and unambiguous language No attributions or evaluations of other's behavior Use of "I" statements and cooperative "we" statements
Aggressive	Taking advantage of others; expressive and self-enhancing at other's expense	Glaring eye contact Moving or leaning too close Threatening gestures (pointed finger; clenched fist) Loud voice Frequent interruptions	Swear words and abusive language Attributions and evaluations of other's behavior Sexist or racist terms Explicit threats or put-downs
Nonassertive	Encouraging others to take advantage of us; inhibited; self-denying	Little eye contact Downward glances Slumped posture Constantly shifting weight Wringing hands Weak or whiny voice	Qualifiers ("maybe"; "kind of") Fillers ("uh," "you know," "well") Negaters ("It's not really that important"; "I'm not sure")

SOURCE: Adapted in part from J A Waters, "Managerial Assertiveness," *Business Horizons,* September–October 1982, pp 24–29.

Body Movements and Gestures   Body movements, such as leaning forward or backward, and gestures, such as pointing, provide additional nonverbal information that can either enhance or detract from the communication process. A study, for example, showed that the use of appropriate hand gestures increased listeners' pragmatic understanding of a message.[26] Open body positions such as leaning forward, communicate *immediacy,* a term used to represent openness, warmth, closeness, and availability for communication. *Defensiveness* is communicated by gestures such as folding arms, crossing hands, and crossing one's legs. Judith Hall, a communication researcher, conducted a meta-analysis of gender differences in body movements and gestures. Results revealed that women nodded their heads and moved their hands more than men. Leaning forward, large body shifts, and foot and leg movements were exhibited more frequently by men than women.[27] Although it is both easy and fun to interpret body movements and gestures, it is important to remember that body-language analysis is subjective, easily misinterpreted, and highly dependent on the context and cross-cultural differences. Thus, managers need to be careful when trying to interpret body movements. Inaccurate interpretations can create additional noise in the communication process.

Touch   Touching is another powerful nonverbal cue. People tend to touch those they like. A meta-analysis of gender differences in touching indicated that women do more touching during conversations than men.[28] Of particular note, however, is the fact that men and women interpret touching differently. Sexual harassment claims might be reduced by keeping this perceptual difference in mind.

Moreover, norms for touching vary significantly around the world. Consider the example of two males walking across campus holding hands. In the Middle East, this behavior would be quite normal for males who are friends or have great respect for each other. In contrast, this behavior is not commonplace in the United States.

Facial Expressions   Facial expressions convey a wealth of information. Smiling, for instance, typically represents warmth, happiness, or friendship, whereas frowning conveys dissatisfaction or anger. Do you think these interpretations apply to different cross-cultural groups? If you said yes, it supports the view that there is a universal recognition of emotions from facial expressions. If you said no, this indicates you believe the relationship between facial expressions and emotions varies across cultures. A summary of relevant research revealed that the association between facial expressions and emotions varies across cultures.[29] A smile, for example, does not convey the same emotion in different countries. Therefore, managers need to be careful in interpreting facial expressions among diverse groups of employees.

Eye Contact   Eye contact is a strong nonverbal cue that serves four functions in communication. First, eye contact regulates the flow of communication by signaling the beginning and end of conversation. There is a tendency to look away from others when beginning to speak and to look at them when done. Second, gazing (as opposed to glaring) facilitates and monitors feedback because it reflects interest and attention. Third, eye contact conveys emotion. People tend to avoid eye contact when discussing bad news or providing negative feedback. Fourth, gazing relates to the type of relationship between communicators.

As is also true for body movements, gestures, and facial expressions, norms for eye contact vary across cultures. Westerners are taught at an early age to look at their parents when spoken to. In contrast, Asians are taught to avoid eye contact with a parent or superior in order to show obedience and subservience.[30] Once again, managers should be sensitive to different orientations toward maintaining eye contact with diverse employees.

Practical Tips   It is important to have good nonverbal communication skills in light of the fact that they are related to the development of positive interpersonal relationships. Communication experts offer the following advice to improve nonverbal communication skills:[31]

Positive Nonverbal Actions That Help Communication
- Maintaining appropriate eye contact.
- Occasionally using affirmative nods to indicate agreement.
- Smiling and showing interest.
- Leaning slightly toward the speaker.
- Keeping your voice low and relaxed.
- Being aware of your facial expressions.

Actions to Avoid
- Licking your lips or playing with your hair or mustache.
- Turning away from the person you are communicating with.
- Closing your eyes and displaying uninterested facial expressions such as yawning.
- Excessively moving in your chair or tapping your feet.
- Using an unpleasant tone and speaking too quickly or too slowly.
- Biting your nails, picking your teeth, and constantly adjusting your glasses.

Active Listening

Some communication experts contend that listening is the keystone communication skill for employees involved in sales, customer service, or management. In support of this conclusion, listening effectiveness was positively associated with customer satisfaction and negatively associated with employee intentions to quit. Poor communication between employees and management also was cited as a primary cause of employee discontent and turnover.[32] Listening skills are particularly important for all of us because we spend a great deal of time listening to others.

Listening involves much more than hearing a message. Hearing is merely the physical component of listening. **Listening** is the process of *actively* decoding and interpreting verbal messages. Listening requires cognitive attention and information processing; hearing does not. With these distinctions in mind, we examine listening styles and offer some practical advice for becoming a more effective listener.

Listening
Actively decoding and interpreting verbal messages.

Listening Styles
Communication experts believe that people listen with a preferred listening style. While people may lean toward one dominant listening style, we tend to use a combination of two or three. There are five dominant listening styles: appreciative, empathetic, comprehensive, discerning, and evaluative.[33] Let us consider each style.

An *appreciative* listener listens in a relaxed manner, preferring to listen for pleasure, entertainment, or inspiration. He or she tends to tune out speakers who provide no amusement or humor in their communications. *Empathetic* listeners interpret messages by focusing on the emotions and body language being displayed by the speaker as well as the presentation media. They also tend to listen without judging. A *comprehensive* listener makes sense of a message by first organizing specific thoughts and actions and then integrates this information by focusing on relationships among ideas. These listeners prefer logical presentations without interruptions. *Discerning* listeners attempt to understand the main message and determine important points. They like to take notes and prefer logical presentations. Finally, *evaluative* listeners listen analytically and continually formulate arguments and challenges to what is being said. They tend to accept or reject messages based on personal beliefs, ask a lot of questions, and can become interruptive.

You can improve your listening skills by first becoming aware of the effectiveness of the different listening styles you use in various situations. This awareness can then help you to modify your style to fit a specific situation. For example, if you are listening to a presidential debate, you may want to focus on using a comprehensive and discerning style. In contrast, an evaluative style may be more appropriate if you are listening to a sales presentation.

Becoming a More Effective Listener
Effective listening is a learned skill that requires effort and motivation. That's right, it takes energy and desire to really listen to others. Unfortunately, it may seem like there are no rewards for listening, but there are negative consequences when we don't. Think of a time, for example, when someone did not pay attention to you by looking at his or her watch or doing some other activity such as typing on a keyboard. How did you feel? You may have felt put down, unimportant, or offended. In turn, such feelings can erode the quality of interpersonal relationships as well as fuel job dissatisfaction, lower productivity, and poor customer service. Listening is an important skill that can be improved by avoiding the 10 habits of bad listeners while cultivating the 10 good listening habits (see Table 14–2).

Table 14–2   *The Keys to Effective Listening*

Keys to Effective Listening	The Bad Listener	The Good Listener
1. Capitalize on thought speed	Tends to daydream	Stays with the speaker, mentally summarizes the speaker, weighs evidence, and listens between the lines
2. Listen for ideas	Listens for facts	Listens for central or overall ideas
3. Find an area of interest	Tunes out dry speakers or subjects	Listens for any useful information
4. Judge content, not delivery	Tunes out dry or monotone speakers	Assesses content by listening to entire message before making judgments
5. Hold your fire	Gets too emotional or worked up by something said by the speaker and enters into an argument	Withholds judgment until comprehension is complete
6. Work at listening	Does not expend energy on listening	Gives the speaker full attention
7. Resist distractions	Is easily distracted	Fights distractions and concentrates on the speaker
8. Hear what is said	Shuts out or denies unfavorable information	Listens to both favorable and unfavorable information
9. Challenge yourself	Resists listening to presentations of difficult subject matter	Treats complex presentations as exercise for the mind
10. Use handouts, overheads, or other visual aids	Does not take notes or pay attention to visual aids	Takes notes as required and uses visual aids to enhance understanding of the presentation

SOURCES: Derived from N Skinner, "Communication Skills," *Selling Power*, July–August 1999, pp 32–34; and G Manning, K Curtis, and S McMillen, *Building the Human Side of Work Community* (Cincinnati: Thomson Executive Press, 1996), pp 127–54.

In addition, a communication expert suggests that we can all improve our listening skills by adhering to the following three fundamental recommendations:[34]

- Attending closely to what's being said, not to what you want to say next.
- Allowing others to finish speaking before taking our turn.
- Repeating back what you've heard to give the speaker the opportunity to clarify the message.

Women and Men Communicate Differently

Women and men have communicated differently since the dawn of time. These differences can create communication problems that undermine productivity and interpersonal communication. Gender-based differences in communication are partly caused by linguistic styles commonly used by women and men. Deborah Tannen, a communication expert, defines **linguistic style** as follows:

> Linguistic style refers to a person's characteristic speaking pattern. It includes such features as directness or indirectness, pacing and pausing, word choice, and the use of such elements as jokes, figures of speech, stories, questions, and apologies. In other words, linguistic style is a set of culturally learned signals by which we not only communicate what we mean but also interpret others' meaning and evaluate one another as people.[35]

Linguistic style
A person's typical speaking pattern.

Men and women possess different communication styles. Do you think that these differences can impede brainstorming sessions like the one shown here? If yes, what can be done to overcome this type of communication roadblock?

Linguistic style not only helps explain communication differences between women and men, but it also influences our perceptions of others' confidence, competence, and abilities. Increased awareness of linguistic styles can thus improve communication accuracy and your communication competence. This section strives to increase your understanding of interpersonal communication between women and men by discussing alternative explanations for differences in linguistic styles, various communication differences between women and men, and recommendations for improving communication between the sexes.

Why Do Linguistic Styles Vary between Women and Men?

Although researchers do not completely agree on the cause of communication differences between women and men, there are two competing explanations that involve the well-worn debate between *nature* and *nurture*. Some researchers believe that interpersonal differences between women and men are due to inherited biological differences between the sexes. More specifically, this perspective, which also is called the *Darwinian perspective* or *evolutionary psychology,* attributes gender differences in communication to drives, needs, and conflicts associated with reproductive strategies used by women and men. For example, proponents would say that males communicate more aggressively, interrupt others more than women, and hide their emotions because they have an inherent desire to possess features attractive to females in order to compete with other males for purposes of mate selection. Although males may not be competing for mate selection during a business meeting, evolutionary psychologists propose that men cannot turn off their biologically based determinants of behavior.[36]

In contrast, social role theory is based on the idea that females and males learn ways of speaking as children growing up. Research shows that girls learn conversational skills and habits that focus on rapport and relationships, whereas boys learn skills and habits that focus on status and hierarchies. Accordingly, women come to view communication as a network of connections in which conversations are negotiations for closeness. This orientation leads women to seek and give confirmation and support more so than men. Men, on the other hand, see conversations as negotiations in which people try to achieve and maintain the upper hand. It thus is important for males to protect themselves from others' attempts to put them down or push them around. This perspective increases a male's need to maintain independence and avoid failure.[37]

Gender Differences in Communication

Research demonstrates that women and men communicate differently in a number of ways.[38] Table 14–3 illustrates 10 different communication patterns that vary between women and men. There are two important issues to keep in mind about the trends identified in Table 14–3. First, the trends identified in the table cannot be generalized to include all women and men. Some men are less likely to boast about their achievements, and some women are less likely to share the credit. The point is that there are always exceptions to the rule. Second, your linguistic style influences perceptions about your confidence, competence, and authority. These judgments may, in turn, affect your future job assignments and subsequent promotability. Consider, for instance, linguistic styles displayed by Greg and Mindy. Greg downplays any uncertainties

Table 14–3   *Communication Differences between Women and Men*

1. Men are less likely to ask for information or directions in a public situation that would reveal their lack of knowledge.
2. In decision making, women are more likely to downplay their certainty; men are more likely to downplay their doubts.
3. Women tend to apologize even when they have done nothing wrong. Men tend to avoid apologies as signs of weakness or concession.
4. Women tend to accept blame as a way of smoothing awkward situations. Men tend to ignore blame and place it elsewhere.
5. Women tend to temper criticism with positive buffers. Men tend to give criticism directly.
6. Women tend to insert unnecessary and unwarranted thank-you's in conversations. Men may avoid thanks altogether as a sign of weakness.
7. Women tend to ask "What do you think?" to build consensus. Men often perceive that question to be a sign of incompetence and lack of confidence.
8. Women tend to give directions in indirect ways, a technique that may be perceived as confusing, less confident, or manipulative by men.
9. Men tend to usurp [take] ideas stated by women and claim them as their own. Women tend to allow this process to take place without protest.
10. Women use softer voice volume to encourage persuasion and approval. Men use louder voice volume to attract attention and maintain control.

SOURCE: Excerpted from D M Smith, *Women at Work: Leadership for the Next Century* (Upper Saddle River, NJ: Prentice Hall, 2000), pp 26–32.

he has about issues and asks very few questions. He does this even when he is unsure about an issue being discussed. In contrast, Mindy is more forthright at admitting when she does not understand something, and she tends to ask a lot of questions. Some people may perceive Greg as more competent than Mindy because he displays confidence and acts as if he understands the issues being discussed.

Improving Communication between the Sexes

Author Judith Tingley suggests that women and men should learn to genderflex. **Genderflex** entails the temporary use of communication behaviors typical of the other gender in order to increase the potential for influence.[39] For example, a female manager might use sports analogies to motivate a group of males. She believes that this approach increases understanding and sensitivity between the sexes. Research has not yet investigated the effectiveness of this approach.

Genderflex
Temporarily using communication behaviors typical of the other gender.

In contrast, Deborah Tannen recommends that everyone needs to become aware of how linguistic styles work and how they influence our perceptions and judgments. She believes that knowledge of linguistic styles helps to ensure that people with valuable insights or ideas get heard. Consider how gender-based linguistic differences affect who gets heard at a meeting:

> Those who are comfortable speaking up in groups, who need little or no silence before raising their hands, or who speak out easily without waiting to be recognized are far more likely to get heard at meetings. Those who refrain from talking until it's clear that the previous speaker is finished, who wait to be recognized, and who are inclined to link their comments to those of others will do fine at a meeting where everyone else is following the same rules but will have a hard time getting heard in a meeting with people whose styles are more like the first pattern. Given the socialization typical of boys and girls, men are more likely to have learned the first style and women the second, making meetings more congenial for men than for women.[40]

Knowledge of these linguistic differences can assist managers in devising methods to ensure that everyone's ideas are heard and given fair credit both in and out of meetings. Furthermore, it is useful to consider the organizational strengths and limitations of your linguistic style. You may want to consider modifying a linguistic characteristic that is a detriment to perceptions of your confidence, competence, and authority. In conclusion, communication between the sexes can be improved by remembering that women and men have different ways of saying the same thing.

Organizational Communication

Examining the broader issue of organizational communication is a good way to identify factors contributing to effective and ineffective management. We structure this discussion by focusing on the "who" and "how" of communication. For example, the first step in any type of communication is deciding who is going to be the recipient of the message. In work settings, you can communicate upward to your boss, downward to direct reports, horizontally with peers, and externally with customers and suppliers. We discuss the who of organizational communication by reviewing the various formal and informal channels used to communicate. We then delve into the how of communication by reviewing a contingency model for selecting medium. You will learn that communication effectiveness is determined by an appropriate match between the content of a message and the medium used to communicate—the how. We conclude this section by discussing the potential problem of communication distortion.

Formal Communication Channels: Up, Down, Horizontal, and External

Formal communication channels
Follow the chain or command or organizational structure.

Formal communication channels follow the chain of command or organizational structure. Messages communicated on formal channels are viewed as official and are transmitted via one or more of three different routes: (1) vertical—either upward or downward, (2) horizontal, and (3) external.

Vertical Communication: Communicating Up and Down the Organization   *Vertical communication* involves the flow of information up and down the organization. As discussed later in this section, communication distortion is more likely to occur when a message passes through multiple levels of an organization.

- *Upward communication* involves sending a message to someone at a higher level in the organization. Employees commonly communicate information upward about themselves, co-workers and their problems, organizational practices and policies, and what needs to be done and how to do it. Organizations and managers are increasingly encouraging employees to communicate upward in the spirit of fostering organizational justice, intrinsic motivation, and empowerment. Upward communication also is a key component of organizational efforts to increase productivity and customer service because frontline employees generally know what it takes to get the job done. Managers encourage upward communication via employee attitude and opinion surveys, suggestion systems (see Real World/Real People on page 455), formal grievance procedures, open-door communication policies, informal meetings, and exit interviews. An exit interview is a chance for managers to get feedback in a brief meeting with a departing employee. The idea is that departing employees are more likely to provide honest feedback.[41]

Effective Employee Suggestion Systems Reap Substantial Benefits

A study of 47 companies with nearly 450,000 employees showed that employee ideas saved the organizations more than $624 million in 2003, according to the Employee Involvement Association (EIA), a Dayton, Ohio–based organization of professional managers of employment involvement programs. In 2003, employees submitted 252,240 suggestions, and 93,034 were adopted. About 32% of the employees submitted at least one idea to their employer.

Moreover, the return on investment can be huge. The average award that companies paid per employee suggestion was $235, the survey report notes, but the value received was about 10 times greater.

"The data show a very big payback—in terms of money and morale," says Jim Spengler, immediate past president of EIA.

SOURCE: Excerpted from S J Wells, "From Ideas to Results," *HR Magazine*, February 2005, p 56.

- *Downward communication* occurs when someone at a higher level in the organization sends information or a message to someone at a lower level (or levels). Managers generally provide five types of information through downward communication: job instructions, job rationale, organizational procedures and practices, feedback about performance, and indoctrination of goals.

Horizontal Communication: Communicating within and between Work Units
Horizontal communication flows within and between employees working in different work units, and its main purpose is coordination. During this sideways communication, employees share information and best practices, coordinate work activities and schedules, solve problems, offer advice and coaching, and resolve conflicts. Horizontal communication is facilitated by project teams, committees, team building (recall our discussion in Chapter 11), social gatherings, and matrix structures, which are discussed in Chapter 17.

External Communication: Communicating with Others outside the Organization
External communication flows between employees inside the organization and a variety of stakeholders outside the organization. External stakeholders include customers, suppliers, shareholder or owners, government officials, community residents, and so on. Many organizations create formal departments, such as public relations, to coordinate their external communications.

Farcus by David Waisglass Gordon Coulthart

© 1992 Farcus Cartoons

WAISGLASS/COULTHART

www.farcus.com

"... and just when I was about to give up on this company."

Informal Communication Channels: The Grapevine

Informal communication channels
Do not follow the chain of command or organizational structure.

Grapevine
Unofficial communication system of the informal organization.

Informal communication channels do not follow the chain of command—information travels in all directions and across all levels. The **grapevine** represents the unofficial communication system of the informal organization. Information traveling along the grapevine supplements official or formal channels of communication. Although the grapevine can be a source of inaccurate rumors, it functions positively as an early warning signal for organizational changes, a medium for creating organizational culture, a mechanism for fostering group cohesiveness, and a way of informally bouncing ideas off others.[42] Evidence indicates that the grapevine is alive and well in today's workplaces.

A national survey of the readers of *Industry Week,* a professional management magazine, revealed that employees used the grapevine as their most frequent source of information.[43] Contrary to general opinion, the grapevine is not necessarily counterproductive. Plugging into the grapevine can help employees, managers, and organizations alike achieve desired results. To enhance your understanding of the grapevine, we will explore grapevine patterns and research and managerial recommendations for monitoring this often-misunderstood system of communication.

Grapevine Patterns Communication along the grapevine follows predictable patterns (see Figure 14–3). The most frequent pattern is not a single strand or gossip chain, but the cluster pattern. Although the probability and cluster patterns look similar, the process by which information is passed is very different between these two grapevine structures. People *randomly* gossip to others in a probability structure. For instance, Figure 14–3 shows that person A tells persons F and D a piece of information but ignores co-workers B and J. Person A may have done this simply because he or she ran into co-workers F and D in the hallway. In turn, persons F and D randomly discuss this information with others in

Figure 14–3   *Grapevine Patterns*

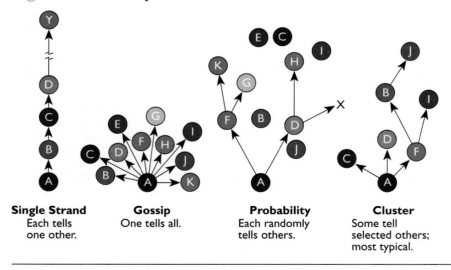

| **Single Strand** | **Gossip** | **Probability** | **Cluster** |
| Each tells one other. | One tells all. | Each randomly tells others. | Some tell selected others; most typical. |

SOURCE: K Davis and J W Newstrom, *Human Behavior at Work: Organizational Behavior,* 7th ed (New York: McGraw-Hill, 1985), p 317. Used with permission. Copyright © 1985. Reprinted by permission of The McGraw-Hill Companies, Inc.

their work environments. In contrast, the cluster pattern is based on the idea that information is *selectively* passed from one person to another. People tend to selectively communicate because they know that certain individuals tend to leak or pass information to others, and they actually want the original piece of information to be spread around. For example, Figure 14–3 shows that person A selectively discusses a piece of information with three people, one of whom—person F—tells two others, and then one of those two—person B—tells one other. Only certain individuals repeat what they hear when the probability or cluster patterns are operating. People who consistently pass along grapevine information to others are called **liaison individuals** or "gossips":

> About 10% of the employees on an average grapevine will be highly active participants. They serve as liaisons with the rest of the staff members who receive information but spread it to only a few other people. Usually these liaisons are friendly, outgoing people who are in positions that allow them to cross departmental lines. For example, secretaries tend to be liaisons because they can communicate with the top executive, the janitor, and everyone in between without raising eyebrows.[44]

Effective managers monitor the pulse of work groups by regularly communicating with known liaisons.

In contrast to liaison individuals, **organizational moles** use the grapevine for a different purpose. They obtain information, often negative, in order to enhance their power and status. They do this by secretly reporting their perceptions and hearsay about the difficulties, conflicts, or failure of other employees to powerful members of management. This enables a mole to divert attention away from him- or herself and to position him- or herself as more competent than others. Management should attempt to create an open, trusting environment that discourages mole behavior because moles can destroy teamwork, create conflict, and impair productivity.

Research and Practical Implications
Although research activity on this topic has slowed in recent years, past research about the grapevine provided the following insights: (1) it is faster than formal channels; (2) it is about 75% accurate; (3) people rely on it when they are insecure, threatened, or faced with organizational changes; and (4) employees use the grapevine to acquire the majority of their on-the-job information.[45]

The key managerial recommendation is to *monitor* and *influence* the grapevine rather than attempt to control it. Effective managers accomplish this by openly sharing relevant information with employees. This is precisely what managers at Shaw's Supermarkets did after acquiring another organization.

> When Shaw's Supermarkets acquired another company rumors ran rampant. How many stores would be closed? How many people would be laid off? Controlling the rumor mill is never easy, especially for a company with 32,000 employees in seven New England states. The solution: Introduction of *The Rumor Buster,* a newsletter published on an as-needed—but at least weekly—basis during the merger, says Ruth Bramson, senior vice president of human resources in East Bridgewater, Massachusetts.
>
> "Communication is the major stumbling block to a successful merger," says Bramson. *The Rumor Buster* "addressed whatever horrendous rumors were going around at the moment. We found it to be an incredibly successful tool."
>
> HR discovered just how useful the newsletter was when employees of the newly acquired company were polled; they indicated that the newsletter had been an important and positive part of the integration.[46]

Liaison individuals
Those who consistently pass along grapevine information to others.

Organizational moles
Those who use the grapevine to enhance their power and status.

Choosing Media: A Contingency Perspective

In this section we turn our attention to discussing the how of the communication process. Specifically, we examine how managers can determine the best method or medium to use when communicating across the various formal and informal channels of communication.

Managers can choose from many different types of communication media (telephone, e-mail, voicemail, cell phone, express mail, memos, video, and so forth). Fortunately, research tells us that managers can help reduce information overload and improve communication effectiveness through their choice of communication media. If an inappropriate medium is used, managerial decisions may be based on inaccurate information, important messages may not reach the intended audience, and employees may become dissatisfied and unproductive. Consider Marnie Puritz Stone's reaction to the inappropriate use of e-mail.

> "All communications regarding hiring and firings were sent via e-mail," Stone explains. Her managers may have felt they were being efficient, but she and her colleagues thought the managers were rude. "I think that callousness with which [some] e-mail delivers news—good or bad—is a poor way to show leadership," she says, "And it creates a lot of resentment."
>
> Stone's manager created even more resentment when it came to providing feedback, which was done mostly through e-mail, "I was reprimanded via e-mail, which was really bad," she recalls, "Criticism via e-mail leaves you very belittled since you can't respond."[47]

This example illustrates that media selection is a key component of communication effectiveness. The following section explores a contingency model designed to help managers select communication media in a systematic and effective manner. Media selection in this model is based on the interaction between information richness and complexity of the problem/situation at hand.

Information Richness

Information richness

Information-carrying capacity of data.

Respected organizational theorists Richard Daft and Robert Lengel define **information richness** in the following manner:

> Richness is defined as the potential information-carrying capacity of data. If the communication of an item of data, such as a wink, provides substantial new understanding, it would be considered rich. If the datum provides little understanding, it would be low in richness.[48]

As this definition implies, alternative media possess levels of information richness that vary from rich to lean.

Information richness is based on four factors: (1) feedback (ranging from fast to very slow), channel (ranging from the combined visual and audio characteristics of a video conference to the limited visual aspects of a computer report), (3) type of communication (ranging from personal to impersonal), and (4) language source (ranging from the natural body language and speech contained in a face-to-face conversation to the numbers contained in a financial statement).

Face-to-face is the richest form of communication. It provides immediate feedback and allows for the observation of multiple language cues such as body language and tone of voice. Although high in richness, the telephone and video conferencing are not as informative as the face-to-face medium. In contrast, newsletters, computer reports, and general e-mail are lean media because feedback is very slow, the channels involve only limited visual information, and the information provided is generic or impersonal.

Complexity of the Managerial Problem/Situation

Managers face problems and situations that range from low to high in complexity. Low-complexity situa-

Figure 14–4   *A Contingency Model for Selecting Communication Media*

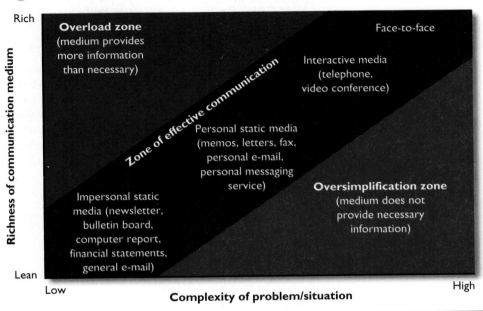

SOURCES: Adapted from R Lengel and R L Daft, "The Selection of Communication Media as an Executive Skill," *Academy of Management Executive,* August 1988, pp 226, and R L Daft and R H Lengel, "Information Richness: A New Approach to Managerial Behavior and Organization Design," *Research in Organizational Behavior,* eds B M Staw and L L Cummings (Greenwich, CT: JAI Press, 1984), p 199.

tions are routine, predictable, and managed by using objective or standard procedures. Calculating an employee's paycheck is an example of low complexity. Highly complex situations, like a corporate reorganization, are ambiguous, unpredictable, hard to analyze, and often emotionally laden. Managers spend considerably more time analyzing these situations because they rely on more sources of information during their deliberations. There are no set solutions to complex problems or situations.

Contingency Recommendations   The contingency model for selecting media is graphically shown in Figure 14–4. As shown, there are three zones of communication effectiveness. Effective communication occurs when the richness of the medium is matched appropriately with the complexity of the problem or situation. Media low in richness—impersonal static and personal static—are better suited for simple problems; media high in richness—interactive media and face-to-face—are appropriate for complex problems or situations. Sun Microsystems, for example, followed this recommendation when communicating with employees about upcoming layoffs. The organization used a series of face-to-face sessions to deliver the bad news and provided managers with a set of slides and speaking points to help disseminate the necessary information.[49]

Conversely, ineffective communication occurs when the richness of the medium is either too high or too low for the complexity of the problem or situation. For example, a district sales manager would fall into the *overload zone* if he or she communicated monthly sales reports through richer media. Conducting face-to-face meetings or telephoning each salesperson would provide excessive information and take more time than necessary to communicate monthly sales data. The *oversimplification zone* represents another ineffective choice of communication medium. In this situation, media with inadequate richness are used to communicate about complicated or emotional issues. An example would be an executive who uses a general e-mail message to communicate about a merger or a major reorganization. This choice of medium is ineffective because employees are likely to be nervous and concerned about how a merger or reorganization will affect their futures.

Research Evidence   The relationship between media richness and problem/situation complexity has not been researched extensively because the underlying theory is relatively new. Available evidence indicates that managers used richer sources when confronted with ambiguous and complicated events, and miscommunication was increased when rich media were used to transmit information that was traditionally communicated through lean media.[50] Moreover, a meta-analysis of more than 40 studies revealed that media usage was significantly different across organizational levels. Upper-level executives/managers spent more time in face-to-face meetings than did lower-level managers.[51] This finding is consistent with recommendations derived from the contingency model just discussed.

Communication Distortion

Communication distortion can be inadvertent or purposeful. Inadvertent distortion is a normal aspect of the communication process. It is caused by the communication barriers discussed earlier in this chapter and frequently occurs when people pass on information with missing or forgotten details. In contrast, **purposeful communication distortion** occurs when an employee purposely modifies the content of a message, thereby reducing the accuracy of communication between managers and employees. Employees tend to engage in this practice because of workplace politics, a desire to manage impressions, or fear of how a manager might respond to a message.[52] Communication experts point out the organizational problems caused by distortion:

Purposeful communication distortion
Purposely modifying the content of a message.

> Distortion is an important problem in organizations because modifications to messages cause misdirectives to be transmitted, nondirectives to be issued, incorrect information to be passed on, and a variety of other problems related to both the quantity and quality of information.[53]

Knowledge of the antecedents or causes of communication distortion can help managers avoid or limit these problems.

Studies have identified four situational antecedents of distortion in upward communication (see Figure 14–5). Distortion tends to increase when supervisors have high upward influence or power. Employees also tend to modify or distort information when they aspire to move upward or when they do not trust their supervisors.[54] Because managers generally do not want to reduce their upward influence or curb their direct reports' desire for upward mobility, they can reduce distortion in several ways:

1. Managers can deemphasize power differences between themselves and their direct reports.

2. They can enhance trust through a meaningful performance review process that rewards actual performance.

3. Managers can encourage staff feedback by conducting smaller, more informal meetings. This is precisely what the Lodge at Vail did to improve upward communication. The company implemented a "lunch with the boss" program in which groups of employees meet with the hotel manager Wolfgang Triebnig for

Figure 14–5   *Sources of Distortion in Upward Communication*

Situational Antecedents			Pattern of Distortion in Upward Communication
1. Supervisor's upward influence	Low ——————→	High	Increased distortion because employees send more favorable information and withhold useful information.
2. Supervisor's power	Low ——————→	High	Increased distortion because employees screen out information detrimental to their welfare.
3. Subordinate's aspiration for upward mobility	Low ——————→	High	Less accuracy because employees tend to pass along information that helps their cause.
4. Subordinate's trust in the supervisor	Low ——————→	High	Considerable distortion because employees do not pass up all information they receive.

SOURCE: Adapted in part from J Fulk and S Mani, "Distortion of Communication in Hierarchical Relationships," in *Communication Yearbook 9*, ed M L McLaughlin (Beverly Hills, CA: Sage Publications, 1986).

lunch in the hotel's five-star restaurant. "The lunch discussion is freewheeling, with no agenda. Triebnig asks participants to introduce themselves and to share any comments or concerns. . . . 'We've learned to let the employees lead,' [Mandy] Wulfe [HR director] says, 'Some come prepared with questions, some come because they were invited and prefer to listen quietly, and some are moved to ask questions because of what they are hearing.' "[55]

4. Managers can establish performance goals that encourage employees to focus on problems rather than personalities.

5. Distortion can be limited by encouraging dialogue between those with opposing viewpoints.

Communication in the Computerized Information Age

As discussed in Chapter 1, the use of computers and information technology is dramatically affecting many aspects of organizational behavior. Consider, for example, how Marty Kotis, CEO of Kotis Properties, a real estate development company in Greensboro, North Carolina is using information technology to change the way in which he works (see Real World/ Real People on page 462). While Marty's behavior may be a bit extreme, a recent study of 2,032 youth by the Kaiser Family Foundation suggests that young people are also multitasking and spending a great deal of time using electronics. Results revealed that "8- to 18-year olds live media-saturated lives, spending 44.5 hours a week with electronics. The 6.5 hours a day compares with 2.25 hours spent with parents, 1.5 hours spent in physical activity and just 50 minutes on homework."[56]

Electronics Gone Crazy!

BusinessWeek
Marty Kotis carries not one but two cell phones: a Bluetooth-enabled Motorola V710 and a Treo 600 (soon to be upgraded to a 650). That's so he can talk on one while simultaneously checking and sending e-mail on the other. His green BMW 740 is equipped with two LCD screens mounted above the front and back seats so he can hold mobile videoconferences. On the beamer's backseat bulges his 50-lb go-bag complete with a laptop, five external drives, an iSight camera, a digital camera, a digital video recorder, and a Bluetooth printer. At stoplights he downloads everything from aerial photographs of new site locations to songs like *Over and Over* by Tim McGraw and Nelly, which he plays wirelessly on his stereo through his iPod. "Sometimes people honk," Kotis says.

The availability of communication technology coupled with the pressure to deliver more results in shorter periods of time leads people to multitask. Do you think the pervasive use of information technology can negatively affect the communication process?

SOURCE: Excerpted from M Conlin, "Take a Vacation from Your Blackberry," *BusinessWeek*, December 20, 2004, p 56.

While you may not want to live your life like Marty Kotis, the computerized information age is radically changing communication patterns in both our personal and work lives. For example, recent statistics reveal that 67% of the population in North America uses the Internet. Cross-culturally, this percentage is higher than the percentage of the population using the Internet in Africa (1.5%), Asia (8.4%), Europe (35.5%), Middle East (7.5%), Latin America/Caribbean (10.3%), and Oceania/Australia (48.6%).[57] Interestingly, some people use the Internet with such frequency that they become dependent on it. For example, a study of 1,300 students at eight colleges revealed that nearly 10% were dependent on the Internet and that their Internet usage affected their academics, ability to meet new people, and sleep patterns.[58] This section explores seven key components of information technology that influence communication patterns and management within a computerized workplace: Internet/intranet/extranet, electronic mail, handheld devices, blogs, videoconferencing, group support systems, and telecommuting.

Internet/Intranet/Extranet

Internet
A global network of computer networks.

Intranet
An organization's private Internet.

The Internet, or more simply, the Net, is more than a computer network. It is a network of computer networks. The **Internet** is a global network of independently operating but interconnected computers. The Internet connects everything from supercomputers, to large mainframes contained in businesses, government, and universities, to the personal computers in our homes and offices. An **intranet** is nothing more than an organization's private Internet. Intranets also have *firewalls* that block outside Internet users from accessing internal information. This is done to protect the privacy and confidentiality of company documents. In contrast to the internal focus of an intranet, an **extranet** is an extended intranet in that it connects internal employees with selected customers, suppliers, and other strategic partners. Ford Motor Company, for instance, has an extranet that connects its dealers worldwide. Ford's extranet was set up to help support the sales and servicing of cars and to enhance customer satisfaction.

The primary benefit of the Internet, intranets, and extranets is that they can enhance the ability of employees to find, create, manage, and distribute information. The effectiveness of these systems, however, depends on how organizations set up and manage their intranet/ extranet and how employees use the acquired information because information by itself cannot solve or do anything; information is knowledge or a thing. For example, communication effectiveness actually can decrease if a corporate intranet becomes a dumping ground of unorganized information. In this case, employees will find themselves flailing in a sea of information. To date, however, no rigorous research studies have been conducted that directly demonstrate productivity increases from using the Internet, intranets, or extranets. But there are case studies that reveal other organizational benefits. For example, the University of Michigan and the University of Louisville saved $200,000 and $90,000 a year, respectively, by asking employees to enroll for employee benefits on their intranets.[59] These costs savings have been realized across corporate America as 77% of US employees used the Internet to enroll for benefits in 2004.[60] United Parcel Service also estimated that productivity increased 35% after the implementation of high-speed wireless Internet access via Wi-Fi.[61] Employee training is another online application that has saved companies millions of dollars. For instance, Hewlett-Packard saved $50 million by using e-learning to help define the new corporate structure after the company merged with Compaq Computer Corp.[62]

In contrast to these positive case studies, a recent study by Harris Interactive revealed that 51% admitted using the Internet at work from one to five hours a week for personal matters. Another survey of 474 human resource professionals indicated that 43% found that employees were viewing pornography while at work.[63] All told, International Data Corp. estimated personal use of the Internet during work hours contributes to a 30 to 40% decrease in productivity.[64] Organizations are taking these statistics to heart and are attempting to root out cyberslackers by tracking employee behavior with electronic monitoring. A survey of more than 700 companies by the Society for Human Resource Management revealed that almost 75% of those companies monitored their employees' use of the Internet and checked their e-mail.[65] Only the future will tell whether the Internet is more useful as a marketing/sales tool, a device to conduct personal transactions such as banking or ordering movies, or a management vehicle that enhances employee motivation and productivity.

Electronic Mail

Electronic mail or e-mail uses the Internet/intranet to send computer-generated text and documents between people. The use of e-mail is on the rise throughout the world. For example, surveys reveal that US employees receive somewhere between 50 to 250 e-mail messages per day.[66] E-mail is becoming a major communication medium because of four key benefits:

1. E-mail reduces the cost of distributing information to a large number of employees.

2. E-mail is a tool for increasing teamwork. It enables employees to quickly send messages to colleagues on the next floor, in another building, or in another country.

Extranet
Connects internal employees with selected customers, suppliers, and strategic partners.

Electronic mail
Uses the Internet/ intranet to send computer-generated text and documents.

3. E-mail reduces the costs and time associated with print duplication and paper distribution. One management expert estimated that these savings can total $9,000 a year per employee.[67]

4. E-mail fosters flexibility. This is particularly true for employees with a portable computer because they can log onto e-mail whenever and wherever they want. Wireless technology and handheld devices enhance the flexibility of e-mail.

In spite of these positive benefits, there are four key drawbacks to consider. First, sending and receiving e-mail can lead to a lot of wasted time and effort, or it can distract employees from completing critical job duties. For example, a national survey of US workers indicated that between 10 and 40% of their e-mail messages were unimportant.[68] Second, the system itself may be cumbersome and ineffective. Consider what happened at AOL Time Warner when the company adopted a new e-mail system.

In a humbling reversal, AOL Time Warner Inc. is retreating from a top-level directive that required the divisions of the old Time Warner to convert to an e-mail system based on AOL software and run by America Online's giant public server computers in Virginia. . . .

Instead, management got months of complaints from both senior and junior executives in the divisions involved, who said the e-mail system, initially designed for consumers, wasn't appropriate for business use. Among the problems cited: The e-mail software frequently crashed, staffers weren't able to send messages with large attachments, they were often kicked offline without warning, and if they tried to send messages to large groups of users they were labeled as spammers and locked out of the system. Sometimes, e-mails were just plain lost in the AOL etherworld and never found. And if there was an out-of-office reply function, most people couldn't find it.[69]

Information overload is the third problem associated with the increased use of e-mail. People tend to send more messages to others, and there is a lot of "spamming" going on: sending junk mail, bad jokes, chain letters, or irrelevant memos (e.g., the "cc" of e-mail). Nucleus Research estimated that 75% of all e-mail traffic in 2004 was spam.[70] Going through junk e-mail clearly wastes a lot of productive time for many employees. Table 14–4 contains suggestions for managing e-mail overload.

Finally, preliminary evidence suggests that people are using electronic mail to communicate when they should be using other media. This practice can result in reduced communication effectiveness. A four-year study of communication patterns within a university demonstrated that the increased use of electronic mail was associated with decreased face-to-face interactions and with a drop in the overall amount of organizational communication. Employees also expressed a feeling of being less connected and less cohesive as a department as the amount of e-mails increased.[71] This interpersonal "disconnection" may be caused by the trend of replacing everyday face-to-face interactions with electronic messages. It is important to remember that employees' social needs are satisfied through the many different interpersonal interactions that occur at work.

There are three additional issues to consider when using e-mail: (1) e-mail only works when the party you desire to communicate with also uses it. E-mail may not be a viable communication medium in all cases. (2) The speed of getting a response to an e-mail message is dependent on how frequently the receiver examines his or her messages. It is important to consider this issue when picking a communication medium. (3) Many companies do not have policies for using e-mail, which can lead to misuse and potential legal liability. For instance, four female employees working at Chevron filed a suit claiming that they were sexually harassed through e-mail. The company settled for $2.2 million, plus legal fees and court costs. Do not assume that your e-mail messages are private and confidential. Organizations are advised to develop policies regarding the use of e-mail.[72]

Table 14–4   *Managing Your E-Mail*

1. Scan first, read second.
2. Learn to delete without reading. Over time, you will get a sense for low-value messages and you should be able to delete messages from unrecognizable addresses.
3. Group messages by topic. Read the first message in a series and then go to the most recent. This enables you to save time by skipping e-mails between the first and last message.
4. Once steps 1–3 are complete, prioritize your inbox and respond in order of a message's importance.
5. Stop the madness by asking people to stop sending you unimportant messages.
6. Rather than continuing to engage in ping-pong e-mailing, determine if a phone call can get to the heart of the matter.
7. Get off cc lists. Ask to be removed from distribution lists.
8. Only respond to a message when it is absolutely required.
9. Keep messages brief and clear. Use clear subject headings and state the purpose of your e-mail in the first sentence or paragraph.
10. Avoid the "reply to all" feature.
11. If the message concerns a volatile or critical matter, e-mail is probably the wrong medium to use. Consider using the phone.

SOURCE: These recommendations were taken from C Cavanagh, *Managing Your E-Mail: Thinking Outside the Inbox.* Copyright © 2003, John Wiley & Sons, Inc. Reprinted with permission of John Wiley & Sons, Inc.

Handheld Devices

Handheld devices, which also are referred to as PDAs (personal digital assistants), offer users the portability to do work from any location. They are used by millions of people and were designed to allow users to multitask from any location. For example, PDAs can be used to make and track appointments, do word processing, crunch numbers on a spreadsheet, check out favorite tunes and video clips, receive and send e-mail, organize photos, play games, and complete a variety of other tasks.[73] Manufactures of these devices claim that the combination of portability and multitasking features enable people to be more efficient and productive. The question from an OB perspective is whether or not these devices actually lead to higher productivity.

Although many people seem addicted to their handheld devices, some academics are skeptical about their real value. Consider the following comments made by several professors to a reporter from *BusinessWeek.*

The idea that gadgets always make us more efficient, "is a scam, and illusion," says David Greenfield director of the Hartford-based Center for Internet Studies. That's because at their heart, gadgets enable multitasking. And a growing body of evidence suggests that multitasking can easily turn into multislacking. It also increases errors, short-circuits attention spans, induces air-traffic-controller-like stress, and elongates the time it takes to accomplish the most basic tasks by up to 50% or more, according to University of Michigan psychology professor David Meyer. . . .

Gadgets also trigger cognitive overload, says Harvard Medical School psychiatry instructor Dr Edward M. Hallowell. . . . All that toggling back and forth "dilutes performance and increases irritability," says Hallowell, causing steady managers to become disorganized and underachievers.[74]

Given these considerations, we wonder why sales of handheld devices continue to explode. Dr Meyer offers one potential explanation. He notes that the use of PDAs activates our dopamine-reward system, which induces a pleasurable state for approximately 6% of the population. Dr Meyer says that this effect is clinically addictive.[75] Alternatively, people may view these devices as one way to cope with increasing pressures to accomplish more in the face of ever increasing informational demands. In the end, time and additional research will determine the actual value of handheld devices.

Blogs

Blog
Online journal in which people comment on any topic.

A **blog** is an online journal in which people write whatever they want about any topic. Blogging is one of the latest Internet trends. Experts estimate that there are around 9 million blogs in existence, and 40,000 new ones pop up every day.[76] Current technology also allows people to blog on cell phones.[77] The benefits of blogs include the opportunity for people to discuss issues in a casual format. These discussions serve much like a chat group and thus provide managers with insights from a wide segment of the employee and customer base as well as the general public. Executives like Jonathan Schwartz, president and COO of Sun Microsystems, and Paul Otellini, the new CEO of Intel, are both using blogs at work to discuss issues of importance.[78] Blogs also give people the opportunity to air their opinions, grievances, and creative ideas. Blogs can also be used to obtain feedback. For example, Robert Scoble, a blogger from Microsoft, reads other people's blogs to see what people are saying about Microsoft's products. Other companies with blogs include Yahoo!, Google, Intuit, Monster.com, and Maytag.[79]

Blogs also have pitfalls. One entails the lack of legal and organizational guidelines regarding what can be posted online. For example, flight attendant Ellen Simonetti and Google employee Mark Jen were both fired for information they included on their blogs. Simonetti posted suggestive pictures of herself in uniform, and Jen commented about his employer's finances.[80] Another involves the potential for employees to say unflattering things about their employer and to leak confidential information. Finally, one can waste a lot of time reading silly and unsubstantiated postings.

We cannot make any overall conclusion regarding blogs because there has not been any research into their effectiveness as a communication, marketing, or managerial tool. Once again, time will tell.

Videoconferencing

Videoconferencing, also known as teleconferencing, uses video and audio links along with computers to enable people in different locations to see, hear, and talk with one another. This enables people from many locations to conduct a meeting without having to travel. Consider the following applications of videoconferencing.

At Harken Energy Corp., an oil and gas exploration company in Houston, engineers use video capabilities to share seismic graphs and other geological displays and data from offices in Latin America. The Department of Labor uses videoconferencing to impart basic computer, financial, and résumé-writing skills to citizens. The potential uses of the technology seem even brighter, particularly in marketing and community outreach efforts....Video also is a critical component of eGetgoing's virtual therapy offering. "Treatment requires the participants to see the reaction of the counselor in order to create an emotional bond," says [Barry] Karlin, who notes that the one-way streaming video eGetgoing uses contains the benefit of maintaining anonymity among the 10 patients in each single-group session.[81]

Videoconferencing can significantly reduce an organization's travel expenses. Many organizations set up special videoconferencing rooms or booths with specially equipped television cameras. More recent equipment enables people to attach small cameras and microphones to their desks or computer monitors. This enables employees to conduct long-distance meetings and training classes without leaving their office or cubicle.

Group Support Systems

Group support systems (GSSs) entail using state-of-the-art computer software and hardware to help people work better together. They enable people to share information without the constraints of time and space. This is accomplished by utilizing computer networks to link people across a room or across the globe. Collaborative applications include messaging and e-mail systems, calendar management, videoconferencing, computer teleconferencing, electronic whiteboards, and the type of computer-aided decision-making systems discussed in Chapter 12.

GSS applications have demonstrated increased productivity and cost savings. A recent meta-analysis of 48 experiments also revealed that groups using GSSs during brainstorming experienced greater participation and influence quality, a greater quantity of ideas generated, and less domination by individual members than did groups meeting face-to-face.[82]

Organizations that use full-fledged GSSs have the ability to create virtual teams or to operate as a virtual organization. Virtual organizations are discussed in Chapter 17. You may recall from Chapter 11 that a virtual team represents a physically dispersed task group that conducts its business by using the types of information technology currently being discussed. Specifically, virtual teams tend to use Internet/intranet systems, GSSs, and videoconferencing systems. These real-time systems enable people to communicate with anyone at anytime.

It is important to keep in mind that modern-day information technology only enables people to interact virtually; it doesn't guarantee effective communications. Interestingly, there are a whole host of unique communication problems associated with using the information technology needed to operate virtually.[83]

Group support systems
Using computer software and hardware to help people work better together.

Telecommuting

Telecommuting is a work practice in which an employee does part of his or her job in a remote location using a variety of information technologies. Examples include "wireless e-mail from Starbucks, videoconferencing from Kinko's and home, and even telework centers in remote villages in India, served by wireless computer links."[84] As you can see from these examples, telecommuting involves receiving and sending work from a remote location via some form of information technology such as wireless devices, fax, or a home computer that is linked via modem to an office computer. Telecommuting is more common for jobs involving computer work, writing, and phone work that require concentration and limited interruptions. The International Telework Association and Council estimated that 44 million US workers telecommuted in 2004.[85] Proposed benefits of telecommuting include

Telecommuting
Doing work that is generally performed in the office away from the office using different information technologies.

1. *Reduction of capital costs.* Sun Microsystems reported saving $50 million in 2002 by letting employees work from home.
2. *Increased flexibility and autonomy for workers.*
3. *Competitive edge in recruitment.* Arthur Andersen, Merrill Lynch, and Cisco used telecommuting to increase their ability to keep and attract qualified personnel.

4. *Increased job satisfaction and lower turnover.* Employees like telecommuting because it helps resolve work family conflicts. AT&T's telecommuters had less absenteeism than traditional employees.

5. *Increased productivity.* Telecommuting resulted in productivity increases of 25 and 35% for FourGen Software and Continental Traffic Services, respectively.

6. *Tapping nontraditional labor pools* (such as prison inmates and homebound disabled persons).[86]

Although telecommuting represents an attempt to accommodate employee needs and desires, it requires adjustments and is not for everybody. Many people thoroughly enjoy the social camaraderie that exists within an office setting. These individuals probably would not like to telecommute. Others lack the self-motivation needed to work at home. Finally, organizations must be careful to implement telecommuting in a nondiscriminatory manner. Organizations can easily and unknowingly violate one of several antidiscrimination laws.

Summary of Key Concepts

1. *Describe the perceptual process model of communication.* Communication is a process of consecutively linked elements. Historically, this process was described in terms of a conduit model. Criticisms of this model led to development of a perceptual process model of communication that depicts receivers as information processors who create the meaning of messages in their own mind. Because receivers' interpretations of messages often differ from those intended by senders, miscommunication is a common occurrence.

2. *Describe the process, personal, physical, and semantic barriers to effective communication.* Every element of the perceptual model of communication is a potential process barrier. There are eight personal barriers that commonly influence communication: (1) the ability to effectively communicate, (2) the way people process and interpret information, (3) the level of interpersonal trust between people, (4) the existence of stereotypes and prejudices, (5) the egos of the people communicating, (6) the ability to listen, (7) the natural tendency to evaluate or judge a sender's message, and (8) the inability to listen with understanding. Physical barriers pertain to distance, physical objects, time, and work and office noise. Semantic barriers show up as encoding and decoding errors because these phases of communication involve transmitting and receiving words and symbols.

3. *Contrast the communication styles of assertiveness, aggressiveness, and nonassertiveness.* An assertive style is expressive and self-enhancing but does not violate others' basic human rights. In contrast, an aggressive style is expressive and self-enhancing but takes unfair advantage of others. A nonassertive style is characterized by timid and self-denying behavior. An assertive communication style is more effective than either an aggressive or nonassertive style.

4. *Discuss the primary sources of nonverbal communication.* There are several identifiable sources of nonverbal communication effectiveness. Body movements and gestures, touch, facial expressions, and eye contact are important nonverbal cues. The interpretation of these nonverbal cues significantly varies across cultures.

5. *Review the five dominant listening styles and 10 keys to effective listening.* The five dominant listening styles are appreciative, empathetic, comprehensive, discerning, and evaluative. Good listeners use the following 10 listening habits: (1) capitalize on thought speed by staying with the speaker and listening between the lines, (2) listen for ideas rather than facts, (3) identify areas of interest between the speaker and listener, (4) judge content and not delivery, (5) do not judge until the speaker has completed his or her message, (6) put energy and effort into listening, (7) resist distractions, (8) listen to both favorable and unfavorable information, (9) read or listen to complex material to exercise the mind, and (10) take notes when necessary and use visual aids to enhance understanding.

6. *Describe the communication differences between men and women, and explain the source of these differences.* Men and women vary in terms of how they ask for information, express certainty, apologize, accept blame, give criticism and praise, say thank you, build consensus, give directions, claim ownership of ideas, and use tone of voice. There are two competing explanations for these differences. The biological perspective attributes gender differences in communication to inherited drives, needs, and conflicts associated with reproductive strategies used by women and men. The second explanation, which is based on social role theory, is based on the idea that females and males learn different ways of speaking as children growing up.

7. *Discuss the formal and informal communication channels.* Formal communication channels follow the chain of command and include vertical, horizontal, and external routes. Vertical communication involves the flow of information up and down the organization. Horizontal communication flows within and between employees working in different work units. External communication flows between employees inside the organization and a variety of stakeholders outside the organization. Informal communication channels do not follow the chain of command. The grapevine represents the unofficial communications system of the informal organization.

8. *Explain the contingency approach to media selection.* Selecting media is a key component of communication effectiveness. Media selection is based on the interaction between the information richness of a medium and the complexity of the problem/situation at hand. Information richness ranges from low to high and is a function of four factors: speed of feedback, characteristics of the channel, type of communication, and language source. Problems/situations range from simple to complex. Effective communication occurs when the richness of the medium matches the complexity of the problem/situation. From a contingency perspective, richer media need to be used as problems/situations become more complex.

9. *Demonstrate your familiarity with four antecedents of communication distortion between managers and employees.* Communication distortion is a common problem that consists of modifying the content of a message. Employees distort upward communication when their supervisor has high upward influence or power. Distortion also increases when employees aspire to move upward or when they do not trust their supervisor.

10. *Explain the information technology of Internet/intranet/extranet, e-mail, handheld devices, blogs, videoconferencing, and group support systems, and explain the related use of telecommuting.* The Internet is a global network of computer networks. An intranet is an organization's private Internet. It contains a firewall that blocks outside Internet users from accessing private internal information. An extranet connects an organization's internal employees with selected customers, suppliers, and strategic partners. The primary benefit of these "nets" is that they can enhance the ability of employees to find, create, manage, and distribute information. E-mail uses the Internet/intranet/extranet to send computer-generated text and documents between people. Handheld devices, also known as PDAs (personal digital assistants), offer users the portability to do work from any location. They serve as minicomputers and communication devices. A blog is an online journal in which people write whatever they want about any topic. Blogging is the latest Internet trend. Videoconferencing uses video and audio links along with computers to enable people located at different locations to see, hear, and talk with one another. GSSs use state-of-the-art computer software and hardware to help people work better together. Information is shared across time and space by linking people with computer networks. Telecommuting involves doing work that is generally performed in the office away from the office using different information technologies.

Discussion Questions

1. Describe a situation where you had trouble decoding a message. What caused the problem?

2. What are some sources of noise that interfere with communication during a class lecture, an encounter with a professor in his or her office, or a movie?

3. Which barrier to effective communication is more difficult to reduce? Explain.

4. Would you describe your prevailing communication style as assertive, aggressive, or nonassertive? How can you tell? Would your style help or hinder you as a manager?

5. Are you good at reading nonverbal communication? Give some examples.

6. Which of the keys to effective listening are most difficult to follow when listening to a class lecture? Explain.

7. Describe a miscommunication that occurred between you and someone of the opposite sex. Now, explain how genderflexing might have been used to improve this interaction.

8. Which of the three zones of communication in Figure 14–4 (overload, effective, oversimplification) do you think is most common in today's large organizations? What is your rationale?

9. What is your personal experience with the grapevine? Do you see it as a positive or negative factor in the workplace? Explain.

10. Have you ever distorted upward communication? What was your reason? Was it related to one of the four antecedents of communication distortion? Explain.

OB in Action Case Study

Is Information Technology More of a Help or Hindrance?[87]

Vickie Farrell had an e-mail account before most people were using desktop computers. Since 1979, when she was a manager at Digital Equipment Corp. in Boston, she has watched e-mail evolve "from an experimental novelty to a significant productivity-improvement tool, to a mainstream work mode enabling people to communicate globally 24/7."

Today, Ms Farrell, now a vice president at Teradata, a unit of NCR Corp., sees e-mail becoming a counterproductive intrusion in the workplace. She, like other managers, are turning off, or ignoring, their e-mail in an effort to get some work accomplished. They've reached the breaking point, where even attempts to put messages in priority or to use filtering systems to delete junk e-mail aren't helping enough.

Managers complain that the relentless flow of computer messages disrupts thought processes and kills creativity. There is no quiet time available during the workday, or even after office hours, to digest information, to ponder fresh ideas, to concentrate wholeheartedly on a difficult problem, or even to daydream. Instead, the expectation that messages from colleagues, bosses, customers and suppliers will be answered promptly requires that employees think only in short bursts, moving quickly from one topic to another.

"The messages keep coming and coming," says Ms Farrell, who recalls how when she first used e-mail she received just three or four messages a day. "Now it has gotten to the point where you can spend your entire day doing nothing but answering e-mail. It's intrusive and disruptive." . . .

As a result, we are losing the ability to initiate work independently and cope with the frustration of not getting answers immediately. The more we are encouraged to remain perpetually logged on, the more we fear separation. We become unable to detach long enough to create a new idea or devise an answer to a complex problem.

Now, Ms Farrell logs off her e-mail for at least two hours a day to grant herself time to write long memos and reports—and think. She also avoids checking her e-mail when she is working away from the office or at a conference. "Some people think that because I have my laptop with me, I should stay connected, but that would prevent me from meeting potential customers, and defeat the purpose of being at the conference," she says.

Even when she is online, she doesn't read or answer every e-mail. Instead, she tells colleagues to phone her when they send an important e-mail, so that she can quickly handle it.

Jeff Phelps, chief operating officer and senior vice president at ABE Services, Sonoma, California, a consulting firm for independent-contractor employment, agrees that the pressure many employees feel to keep up with e-mail traffic undermines their work. "It's like being on a production line and having to plow through the next set of messages, knowing more are coming right behind," he says. "There's no time to think about providing truly thoughtful information."

He understands the value of e-mail when needing to address several people, but he says he is copied on far too many messages. He misses the days when it was acceptable not to respond to an office memo or a letter for at least 24 hours. That interval allowed time to ponder a topic and originate some new ideas.

Mr Phelps also resents the intrusion of e-mail into his personal life, and refuses to get a BlackBerry. "If I had a BlackBerry, I'd be on line all the time and never get a break or a chance to have another form of engagement," he says.

Questions for Discussion

1. How can managers increase their time to think while managing the deluge of e-mail messages? Explain.

2. Which of the four barriers to effective communication is affecting Vickie Farrell and Jeff Phelps? Discuss your rationale.

3. What are the pros and cons of e-mail as a communication tool according to observations by Ms Farrell and Mr Phelps?

4. What advice would you give to Vickie Farrell about managing her e-mail correspondence? Explain.

5. Do you agree with Jeff Phelps's position regarding the use of a BlackBerry? Why or why not?

Assessing Your Listening Skills

Objectives

1. To assess your listening skills.
2. To develop a personal development plan aimed at increasing your listening skills.

Introduction

Listening is a critical component of effective communication. Unfortunately, research and case studies suggest that many of us are not very good at actively listening. This is particularly bad in light of the fact that managers spend more time listening than they do speaking or writing. This exercise provides you the opportunity to assess your listening skills and develop a plan for improvement.

Instructions

The following statements reflect various habits we use when listening to others. For each statement, indicate the extent to which you agree or disagree with it by selecting one number from the scale provided. Circle your response for each statement. Remember, there are no right or wrong answers. After completing the survey, add up your total score for the 17 items, and record it in the space provided.

Listening Skills Survey

1 = strongly disagree
2 = disagree
3 = neither agree nor disagree
4 = agree
5 = strongly agree

1. I daydream or think about other things when listening to others.	1 — 2 — 3 — 4 — 5
2. I do not mentally summarize the ideas being communicated by a speaker.	1 — 2 — 3 — 4 — 5
3. I do not use a speaker's body language or tone of voice to help interpret what he or she is saying.	1 — 2 — 3 — 4 — 5
4. I listen more for facts than overall ideas during classroom lectures.	1 — 2 — 3 — 4 — 5
5. I tune out dry speakers.	1 — 2 — 3 — 4 — 5
6. I have a hard time paying attention to boring people.	1 — 2 — 3 — 4 — 5
7. I can tell whether someone has anything useful to say before he or she finishes communicating a message.	1 — 2 — 3 — 4 — 5
8. I quit listening to a speaker when I think he or she has nothing interesting to say.	1 — 2 — 3 — 4 — 5
9. I get emotional or upset when speakers make jokes about issues or things that are important to me.	1 — 2 — 3 — 4 — 5
10. I get angry or distracted when speakers use offensive words.	1 — 2 — 3 — 4 — 5
11. I do not expend a lot of energy when listening to others.	1 — 2 — 3 — 4 — 5
12. I pretend to pay attention to others even when I'm not really listening.	1 — 2 — 3 — 4 — 5
13. I get distracted when listening to others.	1 — 2 — 3 — 4 — 5
14. I deny or ignore information and comments that go against my thoughts and feelings.	1 — 2 — 3 — 4 — 5
15. I do not seek opportunities to challenge my listening skills.	1 — 2 — 3 — 4 — 5
16. I do not pay attention to the visual aids used during lectures.	1 — 2 — 3 — 4 — 5
17. I do not take notes on handouts when they are provided.	1 — 2 — 3 — 4 — 5

Total score = _____

Preparing a Personal Development Plan

1. Use the following norms to evaluate your listening skills:

   17–34 = good listening skills
   35–53 = moderately good listening skills
   54–85 = poor listening skills

   How would you evaluate your listening skills?

2. Do you agree with the assessment of your listening skills? Why or why not?

3. The 17-item listening skills survey was developed to assess the extent to which you use the keys to effective listening presented in Table 14–2. Use Table 14–2 and the

development plan format shown below to prepare your development plan. First, identify the five statements from the listening skills survey that received your highest ratings—high ratings represent low skills. Record the survey numbers in the space provided in the development plan. Next, compare the content of these survey items to the descriptions of bad and good listeners shown in Table 14–2. This comparison will help you identify the keys to effective listening being measured by each survey item. Write down the keys to effective listening that correspond to each of the five items you want to improve. Finally, write down specific actions or behaviors that you can undertake to improve the listening skill being considered.

Development Plan

Survey Items	Key to Effective Listening I Want to Improve	Action Steps Required (What Do You Need to Do to Build Listening Skills for This Listening Characteristic?)
#		
#		
#		
#		
#		

Group Exercise

Practicing Different Styles of Communication

Objectives

1. To demonstrate the relative effectiveness of communicating assertively, aggressively, and nonassertively.
2. To give you hands-on experience with different styles of communication.

Introduction

Research shows that assertive communication is more effective than either an aggressive or nonassertive style. This *role-playing exercise* is designed to increase your ability to communicate assertively. Your task is to use different communication styles while attempting to resolve the work-related problems of a poor performer.

Instructions

Divide into groups of three, and read the "Poor Performer" and "Store Manager" roles provided here. Then decide who will play the poor performer role, who will play the managerial role, and who will be the observer. The observer will be asked to provide feedback to the manager after each role play. When playing the managerial role, you should first attempt to resolve the problem by using an aggressive communication style. Attempt to achieve your objective by using the nonverbal and verbal behavior patterns associated with the aggressive style shown in Table 14–1. Take about four to six minutes to act out the instructions. The observer should give feedback to the manager after completing the role play. The observer should comment on how the employee responded to the aggressive behaviors displayed by the manager.

After feedback is provided on the first role play, the person playing the manager should then try to resolve the problem with a nonassertive style. Observers once again should provide feedback. Finally, the manager should confront the problem with an assertive style. Once again, rely on the relevant nonverbal and verbal behavior patterns presented in Table 14–1, and take four to six minutes to act out each scenario. Observers should try to provide detailed feedback on how effectively the manager exhibited nonverbal and verbal assertive behaviors. Be sure to provide positive and constructive feedback.

After completing these three role plays, switch roles: manager becomes observer, observer becomes poor performer, and poor performer becomes the manager. When these role plays are completed, switch roles once again.

ROLE: POOR PERFORMER

You sell shoes full-time for a national chain of shoe stores. During the last month you have been absent three times without giving your manager a reason. The quality of your work has been slipping. You have a lot of creative excuses when your boss tries to talk to you about your performance.

When playing this role, feel free to invent a personal problem that you may eventually want to share with your manager. However, make the manager dig for information about this problem. Otherwise, respond to your manager's comments as you normally would.

ROLE: STORE MANAGER

You manage a store for a national chain of shoe stores. In the privacy of your office, you are talking to one of your salespeople who has had three unexcused absences from work during the last month. (This is excessive, according to company guidelines, and must be corrected.) The quality of his or her work has been slipping. Customers have complained that this person is rude, and co-workers have told you this individual isn't carrying his or her fair share of the work. You are fairly sure this person has some sort of personal problem. You want to identify that problem and get him or her back on the right track.

Questions for Discussion

1. What drawbacks of the aggressive and nonassertive styles did you observe?

2. What were major advantages of the assertive style?

3. What were the most difficult aspects of trying to use an assertive style?

4. How important was nonverbal communication during the various role plays? Explain with examples.

Ethical Dilemma

Are Camera Cell Phones Creating Ethical Problems?[88]

Although camera phones have been broadly available for only a few months in the United States, more than 25 million of the devices are out on the streets of Japan. . . .

Now that cell phones with little digital cameras have spread throughout Asia, so have new brands of misbehavior. Some people are secretly taking photos up women's skirts and down into bathroom stalls. Others are avoiding buying books by snapping free shots of desired pages.

"The problem with a new technology is that society has yet to come up with a common understanding about appropriate behavior," said Mizuko Ito, an expert on mobile phone culture at Keio University Tokyo.

Samsung Electronics is banning their use in semiconductor and research facilities, hoping to stave off industrial espionage. Samsung, a leading maker of cell phones, is taking a low-tech approach: requiring employees and visitors to stick tape over the handset's camera lens.

How would you solve this dilemma?

You are the manager of a large bookstore. You have a camera phone as do several of your employees. You have seen customers use their camera phones to take pictures of one another in the store. Yesterday, for the first time, you observed a customer taking photos of 10 pages of material from a cookbook. Although you did not say anything to this customer, you are wondering what should be done in the future. Select one of the following options.

1. Place a sign on the door asking customers to mind their "cell phone manners." This way you don't have to prevent anyone from using their phone; you can rely on common decency.

2. Ask customers to leave their camera phones with an employee at the front of the store. The employee will give the customer a claim check and they can retrieve their phones once they finish shopping.

3. Station an employee at the front of the store who places tape over the lens of camera phones as customers come in.

4. Don't do anything. There is nothing wrong with people taking pictures of materials out of a book.

5. Invent other options. Discuss.

For the Chapter 14 Internet Exercise featuring an assertive communication style assessment (www.queendom.com), visit our Web site at **www.mhhe.com/kreitner.**

Chapter 15

Influence Tactics, Empowerment, and Politics

Learning Objectives

When you finish studying the material in this chapter, you should be able to:

1 Explain the concept of mutuality of interest.

2 Name at least three "soft" and two "hard" influence tactics, and summarize the practical lessons from influence research.

3 Identify and briefly explain Cialdini's six principles of influence and persuasion.

4 Identify and briefly describe French and Raven's five bases of power, and discuss the responsible use of power.

5 Define the term *empowerment*, and explain why it is a matter of degree.

6 Explain why delegation is the highest form of empowerment, and discuss the connections among delegation, trust, and personal initiative.

7 Define *organizational politics*, and explain what triggers it.

8 Distinguish between favorable and unfavorable impression management tactics.

9 Explain how to manage organizational politics.

Meg Whitman is on the last lap of a two-day, if-it's-noon-it-must-be-Rotterdam investor road show. She's pitched eBay's global growth to six rapt audiences in three Dutch cities in eight hours. As we fly into Frankfurt, Whitman is beat, but she gamely engages in a discussion about a topic she professes to dislike: power. "I don't actually think of myself as powerful," she says. When Rajiv Dutta, a native Indian who is eBay's chief financial officer, tosses out a profundity—"To have power, you must be willing to not have any of it"—she agrees. You'd expect Whitman to be glad the talk is over when we touch ground, but as she climbs into the back seat of a black Mercedes, she doesn't let it go: "Ask anyone about me, and they would never think of power. You know, you say, 'sky,' and they say 'blue.' Say 'power,' and no one would say 'Meg Whitman.' "

Well, we would, so here goes: Meg Whitman, 48, is the most powerful woman in American business. . . . Since she arrived as CEO and president almost seven years ago, eBay has grown from $5.7 million to $3.2 billion in estimated 2004 revenues. To put that into perspective, hers is the fastest-growing company in history—faster than Microsoft, Dell, or any other company during the first eight years of its existence. That $3.2 billion in revenues will probably produce more than $1 billion in operating income this year. eBay has such high margins partly because it has no factories or inventory, but also because its customers do the work. Some 48 million active users will select, price, buy, sell, and ship $32 billion worth of merchandise this year. If eBay were a retailer, rather than the world's largest online marketplace, it would be bigger than Best Buy and almost the size of Lowe's. If eBay employed the 430,000 people who earn all or most of their

eBay's CEO Meg Whitman has proven to be a master of influence and understated power.

income selling on its site, it would be the second-largest employer on the Fortune 500, after Wal-Mart.

Despite all that, it's easy to underestimate Whitman's power. As she likes to say, "It's our customers who have built eBay." eBay's business model looks so simple—take an online trading platform, let sellers attract buyers, buyers attract more sellers, and so on—that people say things like, "A monkey could run this thing." Which is exactly what a hotshot MBA, new to eBay, told Whitman to her face. (She laughed; the MBA still has his job.) One of her board members, Scott Cook, the founder of Intuit, jokes that Whitman found "a parade and ran in front of it."

But the idea that anyone with a pulse could run eBay is naive. It's a lot harder than it looks. The fact is, Whitman and her team are building and tuning what many consider to be the company of tomorrow—a model 21st-century organization of minimal staff and maximal profitability. Whitman has steered the company in surprising directions and made counterintuitive strategic choices. Running eBay is an act of imagination; it is the opposite of some straightforward exercise in the caretaker arts.

Her power is unconventional too. Whitman doesn't have the kind of raw, command-and-control power of, say, Exxon Mobil's Lee Raymond. . . . Whitman had to amass a more complex, subtle kind of power. As one of her admirers, A G Lafley, CEO of Procter & Gamble, says of power, "It's not about control, and I don't think it's about size. The measure of a powerful person is that their circle of influence is greater than their circle of control."[1]

FOR DISCUSSION
What responsibilities accompany the kind of power Meg Whitman has?

At the very heart of interpersonal dealings in today's work organizations is a constant struggle between individual and collective interests. For example, Sid wants a raise, but his company doesn't make enough money to both grant raises and buy needed capital equipment. Preoccupation with self-interest is understandable. After all, each of us was born, not as a cooperating organization member, but as an individual with instincts for self-preservation. It took socialization in family, school, religious, sports, recreation, and employment settings to introduce us to the notion of mutuality of interest. Basically, **mutuality of interest** involves win–win situations in which one's self-interest is served by cooperating actively and creatively with potential adversaries. A pair of organization development consultants offered this managerial perspective of mutuality of interest:

Mutuality of interest
Balancing individual and organizational interests through win–win cooperation.

> Nothing is more important than this sense of mutuality to the effectiveness and quality of an organization's products and services. Management must strive to stimulate a strong sense of shared ownership in every employee, because otherwise an organization cannot do its best in the long run. Employees who identify their own personal self-interest with the quality of their organization's output understand mutuality and strive to maintain it in their jobs and work relations.[2]

Figure 15–1 graphically portrays the constant tug-of-war between employees' self-interest and the organization's need for mutuality of interest. It also shows the linkage between this chapter—influence, empowerment, and politics—and other key topics in this book. Managers need a complete tool kit of techniques to guide diverse individuals, who are often powerfully motivated to put their own self-interests first, to pursue common objectives. At stake in this tug-of-war between individual and collective interests is no less than the ultimate survival of organizations such as Meg Whitman's eBay.

Figure 15–1   *The Constant Tug-of-War between Self-Interest and Mutuality of Interest Requires Managerial Action*

Organizational Influence Tactics: Getting One's Way at Work

How do you get others to carry out your wishes? Do you simply tell them what to do? Or do you prefer a less direct approach, such as promising to return the favor? Whatever approach you use, the crux of the issue is *social influence.* A large measure of interpersonal interaction involves attempts to influence others, including parents, bosses, co-workers, spouses, teachers, friends, and children. All of us need to sharpen our influence skills (see the incredible story in Real World/Real People on page 478). A good starting point is familiarity with the following research insights.

Nine Generic Influence Tactics

A particularly fruitful stream of research, initiated by David Kipnis and his colleagues in 1980, reveals how people influence each other in organizations. The Kipnis methodology involved asking employees how they managed to get either their bosses, co-workers, or subordinates to do what they wanted them to do.[3] Statistical refinements and replications by other researchers over a 13-year period eventually yielded nine influence tactics. The nine tactics, ranked in diminishing order of use in the workplace are as follows:

1. *Rational persuasion.* Trying to convince someone with reason, logic, or facts.

2. *Inspirational appeals.* Trying to build enthusiasm by appealing to others' emotions, ideals, or values.

Influence would be easy in a world of programmable robots such as 3-CPO. But legendary film director George Lucas needs a broad repertoire of influence tactics to get the diverse cast of humans wearing *Star Wars* costumes to turn his script into an action-packed hit movie.

Edward S Lampert, the Brains behind the Kmart and Sears Deals, Is a *Very* Persuasive Guy!

BusinessWeek [I]n January, 2003, at the height of the negotiations [to acquire bankrupt Kmart], Lampert was leaving ESL on a Friday night when he was kidnapped in the parking garage. Four hoodlums, led by a 23-year-old ex-Marine, had targeted Lampert after a search for rich people on the Internet. They stuffed him into a Ford Blazer, took him to a cheap motel, and held him bound in the bathtub. They called Lampert's wife, Kinga, playing a tape of his voice. Court documents are sealed, but one person close to the case says the men told Lampert they had been hired to kill him for $5 million but would let him go for $1 million.

Lampert was convinced he was going to be killed, he says in his first public comments on the kidnapping case. "Your imagination goes absolutely wild. I was thinking about my mother and my son and my wife. What would their lives be like? Would it be painful when they shot me?"

In the adjoining room, he recalls, the television was switched on to the news about the search for the body of Laci Peterson. But as the kidnappers became increasingly nervous, Lampert convinced them that if they let him go, he would pay them $40,000 a couple of days later, the source says. The hoodlums let him off on the side of a road in Greenwich early on that Sunday morning and were later arrested and convicted. Lampert arrived home to a house full of friends who had been camping out, waiting for news. "It was very much like going to your own funeral," he says. He was soon back in Kmart negotiations.

SOURCE: Excerpted from R Berner, "The Next Warren Buffett?" *BusinessWeek*, November 22, 2004, p 154. Reprinted by permission of The McGraw-Hill Companies, Inc. Also see P Sellers, "Fast Eddie Roughs up Sears' Staff," *Fortune*, May 2, 2005, p 20.

3. *Consultation.* Getting others to participate in planning, making decisions, and changes.
4. *Ingratiation.* Getting someone in a good mood prior to making a request; being friendly, helpful, and using praise or flattery.
5. *Personal appeals.* Referring to friendship and loyalty when making a request.
6. *Exchange.* Making express or implied promises and trading favors.
7. *Coalition tactics.* Getting others to support your effort to persuade someone.
8. *Pressure.* Demanding compliance or using intimidation or threats.
9. *Legitimating tactics.* Basing a request on one's authority or right, organizational rules or policies, or express or implied support from superiors.[4]

These approaches can be considered *generic* influence tactics because they characterize social influence in all directions and in a wide variety of settings. Researchers have found this ranking to be fairly consistent regardless of whether the direction of influence is downward, upward, or lateral.[5]

Some call the first five influence tactics—rational persuasion, inspirational appeals, consultation, ingratiation, and personal appeals—*soft* tactics because they are friendlier and not as coercive as the last four tactics. Exchange, coalition, pressure, and legitimating tactics accordingly are called *hard* tactics because they involve more overt pressure.

Three Possible Influence Outcomes

Put yourself in this familiar situation. It's Wednesday and a big project you've been working on for your project team is due Friday. You're behind on the preparation of your computer graphics for your final report and presentation. You catch a friend who is great at computer graphics as he heads out of the office at quitting time. You try this *exchange tactic* to get your friend to help you out: "I'm way behind. I need your help. If you could come back in for two to three hours tonight and help me with these graphics, I'll complete those spreadsheets you've been complaining about." According to researchers, your friend will engage in one of three possible influence outcomes:

1. *Commitment.* Your friend enthusiastically agrees and will demonstrate initiative and persistence while completing the assignment.

2. *Compliance.* Your friend grudgingly complies and will need prodding to satisfy minimum requirements.

3. *Resistance.* Your friend will say no, make excuses, stall, or put up an argument.[6]

The best outcome is commitment because the target person's intrinsic motivation will energize good performance. However, managers often have to settle for compliance in today's hectic workplace. Resistance means a failed influence attempt.

Practical Research Insights

Laboratory and field studies have taught us useful lessons about the relative effectiveness of influence tactics along with other instructive insights:

• Commitment is more likely when people rely on consultation, strong rational persuasion, and inspirational appeals and *do not* rely on pressure and coalition tactics.[7] Interestingly, in one study, managers were not very effective at *downward* influence. They relied most heavily on inspiration (an effective tactic), ingratiation (a moderately effective tactic), and pressure (an ineffective tactic).[8]

• A meta-analysis of 69 studies suggests ingratiation (making the boss feel good) can slightly improve your performance appraisal results and make your boss like you significantly more.[9]

• Commitment is more likely when the influence attempt involves something *important* and *enjoyable* and is based on a *friendly* relationship.[10]

• In a survey, 214 employed MBA students (55% female) tended to perceive their superiors' soft influence tactics as fair and hard influence tactics as unfair. *Unfair* influence tactics were associated with greater *resistance* among employees.[11]

• Another study probed male–female differences in influencing work group members. Many studies have found women to be perceived as less competent and less influential in work groups than men. The researchers had male and female work group leaders engage in either task behavior (demonstrating ability and task competence) or dominating behavior (relying on threats). For both women and men, task behavior was associated with perceived competence and effective influence. Dominating behavior was not effective. The following conclusion by the researchers has important practical implications for all current and future managers who desire to successfully influence others: "The display of task cues is an effective means to enhance one's status in groups and . . . the attempt to gain influence in task groups through dominance is an ineffective and poorly received strategy for both men and women."[12]

• Interpersonal influence is culture bound. The foregoing research evidence on influence tactics has a bias in favor of European–North Americans. Much remains to be learned about how to effectively influence others (without unintended insult) in today's diverse labor force and cross-cultural economy.[13]

Finally, Barbara Moses, consultant and author from Toronto, Canada, offers this advice on influencing your boss:

> If your boss doesn't understand the need for change, this might be partly your fault. You can't make change; you have to sell it. And the key to selling anything is to understand where the other person is coming from—rather than to assume that your boss is a complete jerk. But most of us communicate from an egocentric place. We construct an idea or a project mainly in terms of what makes sense to us. Instead, ask yourself: "What's most important to my boss?" "What are his greatest concerns?" Go forward only after you've answered these questions.[14]

How to Do a Better Job of Influencing and Persuading Others

Because of a string of corporate scandals and executive misdeeds at the likes of Enron, Andersen, Tyco, ImClone, and WorldCom, the trust and credibility gap between management and workers remains sizable. According to one survey, "more than 20 percent of American workers say their company's senior managers don't act in a manner consistent with their words."[15] Aside from being a siren call for better ethics,[16] this trend makes managerial attempts at influence and persuasion more challenging than ever. Skill development in this area is essential.

Practical, research-based advice has been offered by Robert B Cialdini, a respected expert at Arizona State University. Based on many years of research by himself and others, Cialdini (pronounced Chal-dee-knee) derived the following six principles of influence and persuasion:[17]

1. *Liking.* People tend to like those who like them. Learning about another person's likes and dislikes through informal conversations builds friendship bonds. So do sincere and timely praise, empathy, and recognition.

2. *Reciprocity.* The belief that both good and bad deeds should be repaid in kind is virtually universal. Managers who act unethically and treat employees with contempt can expect the same in return. Worse, those employees, in turn, are likely to treat each other and their customers unethically and with contempt. Managers need to be positive and constructive role models and fair-minded to benefit from the principle of reciprocity.

3. *Social proof.* People tend to follow the lead of those most like themselves. Role models and peer pressure are powerful cultural forces in social settings. Managers are advised to build support for workplace changes by first gaining the enthusiastic support of informal leaders who will influence their peers.

4. *Consistency.* People tend to do what they are personally committed to do. A manager who can elicit a verbal commitment from an employee has taken an important step toward influence and persuasion. (Recall the importance of attitudes and intentions in our discussion of Ajzen's theory of planned behavior in Chapter 6.)

5. *Authority.* People tend to defer to and respect credible experts. According to Cialdini, too many managers and professionals take their expertise for granted, as in the case of a hospital where he consulted:

> The physical therapy staffers were frustrated because so many of their stroke patients abandoned their exercise routines as soon as they left the hospital. No matter how often the staff emphasized the importance of regular home exercise—it is, in fact, crucial to the process of regaining independent function—the message just didn't sink in.

Interviews with some of the patients helped us pinpoint the problem. They were familiar with the background and training of their physicians, but the patients knew little about the credentials of the physical therapists who were urging them to exercise. It was a simple matter to remedy that lack of information: We merely asked the therapy director to display all the awards, diplomas, and certifications of her staff on the walls of the therapy rooms. The result was startling: Exercise compliance jumped 34% and has never dropped since.[18]

6. *Scarcity.* People want items, information, and opportunities that have limited availability. Special opportunities and privileged information are influence builders for managers.

Importantly, Cialdini recommends using these six principles in combination, rather than separately, for maximum impact. Because of major ethical implications, one's goals need to be worthy and actions need to be sincere and genuine when using these six principles.

By demonstrating the rich texture of social influence, the foregoing research evidence and practical advice whet our appetite for learning more about how today's managers can and do reconcile individual and organizational interests. Let us focus on social power.

Social Power

The term *power* evokes mixed and often passionate reactions. Citing recent instances of government corruption and corporate misconduct, many observers view power as a sinister force. To these skeptics, Lord Acton's time-honored statement that "power corrupts and absolute power corrupts absolutely" is as true as ever.[19] However, OB specialists remind us that, like it or not, power is a fact of life in modern organizations. According to one management writer,

> Power must be used because managers must influence those they depend on. Power also is crucial in the development of managers' self-confidence and willingness to support subordinates. From this perspective, power should be accepted as a natural part of any organization. Managers should recognize and develop their own power to coordinate and support the work of subordinates; it is powerlessness, not power, that undermines organizational effectiveness.[20]

Thus, power is a necessary and generally positive force in organizations. As the term is used here, **social power** is defined as "the ability to marshal the human, informational, and material resources to get something done."[21]

Importantly, the exercise of social power in organizations is not necessarily a downward proposition. Employees can and do exercise power upward and laterally. An example of an upward power play occurred at Alberto-Culver Company, the personal care products firm. Leonard Lavin, founder of the company, was under pressure to revitalize the firm because key employees were departing for more innovative competitors such as Procter & Gamble. Lavin's daughter Carol Bernick, and her husband Howard, both longtime employees, took things into their own hands:

> Even the Bernicks were thinking of jumping ship. Instead, in September 1994, they marched into Lavin's office and presented him with an ultimatum: Either hand over the reins as CEO or run the company without them. It was a huge blow for Lavin, forcing him to face selling his company to outsiders or ceding control to the younger generation. Unwilling to sell, he reluctantly stepped down, though he remains chairman.
>
> How does it feel to push aside your own father and wrest operating control of the company he created? "It isn't an easy thing to do with the founder of any company, whether

Social power
Ability to get things done with human, informational, and material resources.

he's your father or not," says Carol Bernick, 46, now vice chairman and president of Alberto-Culver North America.[22]

Howard Bernick became CEO, the firm's top-down management style was scrapped in favor of a more open culture, and Lavin reportedly is happy with how things have turned out.[23]

Dimensions of Power

While power may be an elusive concept to the casual observer, social scientists view power as having reasonably clear dimensions. Two dimensions of power that deserve our attention are (1) socialized versus personalized power and (2) the five bases of power.

Socialized power
Directed at helping others.

Personalized power
Directed at helping oneself.

Two Types of Power
Behavioral scientists such as David McClelland contend that one of the basic human needs is the need for power (n Pwr), as discussed in Chapter 8. Because this need is learned and not innate, the need for power has been extensively studied. Historically, need for power was said to be high when subjects interpreted TAT pictures in terms of one person attempting to influence, convince, persuade, or control another. More recently, however, researchers have drawn a distinction between **socialized power** and **personalized power.**

> There are two subscales or "faces" in n Pwr. One face is termed "socialized" (s Pwr) and is scored in the Thematic Apperception Test (TAT) as "plans, self-doubts, mixed outcomes and concerns for others, . . ." while the second face is "personalized" power (p Pwr), in which expressions of power for the sake of personal aggrandizement become paramount.[24]

This distinction between socialized and personalized power helps explain why power has a negative connotation for many people.[25] Managers and others who pursue personalized power for their own selfish ends give power a bad name.[26] But a series of interviews with 25 American women elected to public office found a strong preference for socialized power. The following comments illustrate their desire to wield power effectively and ethically:

- "Power in itself means nothing. . . . I think power is the opportunity to really have an impact on your community."
- "My goal is to be a powerful advocate on the part of my constituents."[27]

(See Real World/Real People.)

Reward power
Obtaining compliance with promised or actual rewards.

Coercive power
Obtaining compliance through threatened or actual punishment.

Five Bases of Power
A popular classification scheme for social power traces back more than 45 years ago to the work of John French and Bertram Raven. They proposed that power arises from five different bases: reward power, coercive power, legitimate power, expert power, and referent power.[28] Each involves a different approach to influencing others:

- *Reward power.* A manager has **reward power** to the extent that he or she obtains compliance by promising or granting rewards. On-the-job behavior shaping, for example, relies heavily on reward power.
- *Coercive power.* Threats of punishment and actual punishment give an individual **coercive power.** A sales manager who threatens to fire any salesperson who uses a company car for family vacations is relying on coercive power.[29]

Deposed CEO Carly Fiorina Still Has Power

BusinessWeek [In 2004], James Renick, chancellor of North Carolina Agricultural & Technical State University, invited Hewlett-Packard CEO Carly Fiorina to speak at the historically black university's spring 2005 commencement. Shortly after her February 9 [2005] sacking, Fiorina called Renick and asked: "Do you still want me to come?" Absolutely, Renick said, Fiorina now had something in common with graduates, he reasoned: unemployment.

So on May 7 [2005]—in front of 14,000 people at the Greensboro Coliseum—Fiorina made her first public appearance since being deposed. . . . Implicitly linking the racism the students may face with the male chauvinism she experienced as a woman in tech and telecom, she said she was labeled the "token bimbo" as a young AT&T sales-woman in the late 1970s. Later, she felt the same humiliation when a rival CEO mocked her in front of analysts and reporters. But she refused to let it dampen her spirit. The message resonated with the amped-up crowd, which cheered when Fiorina quoted from the Bible. She later got a standing ovation.

Fiorina didn't give any hint about her future plans, but many speculate she'll make a foray into politics. Judging by her ability to connect with this crowd, that might not be a bad move.

SOURCE: Excerpted from A Park, "Carly: Out, but Not Down," *BusinessWeek*, May 23, 2005, p 14. Reprinted by permission of The McGraw-Hill Companies, Inc.

- *Legitimate power.* This base of power is anchored to one's formal position or authority.[30] Thus, individuals who obtain compliance primarily because of their formal authority to make decisions have **legitimate power.** Legitimate power may express itself in either a positive or negative manner in managing people. Positive legitimate power focuses constructively on job performance. Negative legitimate power tends to be threatening and demeaning to those being influenced. Its main purpose is to build the power holder's ego.

- *Expert power.* Valued knowledge or information gives an individual **expert power** over those who need such knowledge or information. The power of supervisors is enhanced because they know about work schedules and assignments before their employees do. Skillful use of expert power played a key role in the effectiveness of team leaders in a study of three physician medical diagnosis teams.[31] Knowledge *is* power in today's high-tech workplaces.

- *Referent power.* Also called charisma, **referent power** comes into play when one's personality becomes the reason for compliance. Role models have referent power over those who identify closely with them.[32]

To further your understanding of these five bases of power and to assess your self-perceived power, please take a moment to complete the questionnaire in the OB Exercise on page 484. Think of your present job or your most recent job when responding to the various items. What is your power profile?

Legitimate power
Obtaining compliance through formal authority.

Expert power
Obtaining compliance through one's knowledge or information.

Referent power
Obtaining compliance through charisma or personal attraction.

OB Exercise — What Is Your Self-Perceived Power?

Instructions

Score your various bases of power for your current (or former) job, using the following scale:

1 = strongly disagree
2 = disagree
3 = slightly agree

4 = agree
5 = strongly agree

Reward Power Score = _____
1. I can reward persons at lower levels. _____
2. My review actions affect the rewards gained at lower levels. _____
3. Based on my decisions, lower level personnel may receive a bonus. _____

Coercive Power Score = _____
1. I can punish employees at lower levels. _____
2. My work is a check on lower level employees. _____
3. My diligence reduces error. _____

Legitimate Power Score = _____
1. My position gives me a great deal of authority. _____
2. The decisions made at my level are of critical importance. _____
3. Employees look to me for guidance. _____

Expert Power Score = _____
1. I am an expert in this job. _____
2. My ability gives me an advantage in this job. _____
3. Given some time, I could improve the methods used on this job. _____

Referent Power Score = _____
1. I attempt to set a good example for other employees. _____
2. My personality allows me to work well in this job. _____
3. My fellow employees look to me as their informal leader. _____

Arbitrary Norms

3–6 = weak power base
7–11 = moderate power base
12–15 = strong power base

SOURCE: Adapted and excerpted in part from D L Dieterly and B Schneider, "The Effect of Organizational Environment on Perceived Power and Climate: A Laboratory Study," *Organizational Behavior and Human Performance*, June 1974, pp 316–37.

Research Insights about Social Power

In one study, a sample of 94 male and 84 female nonmanagerial and professional employees in Denver, Colorado, completed TAT tests. The researchers found that the male and female employees had similar needs for power (n Pwr) and personalized power (p Pwr). But the women had a significantly higher need for socialized power (s Pwr) than did their male counterparts.[33] This bodes well for today's work organizations where women are playing an ever greater administrative role. Unfortunately, as women gain power in the workplace, greater tension between men and women has been observed. *Training* magazine offered this perspective:

> [O]bservers view the tension between women and men in the workplace as a natural outcome of power inequities between the genders. Their argument is that men still have most of the power and are resisting any change as a way to protect their power base. [Consultant Susan L] Webb asserts that sexual harassment has far more to do with exercising power in an unhealthy way than with sexual attraction. Likewise, the glass ceiling, a metaphor for the barriers women face in climbing the corporate ladder to management and executive positions, is about power and access to power.[34]

Accordingly, "powerful women were described more positively by women than by men" in a study of 140 female and 125 male college students in Sydney, Australia.[35]

A reanalysis of 18 field studies that measured French and Raven's five bases of power uncovered "severe methodological shortcomings."[36] After correcting for these problems, the researchers identified the following relationships between power bases and work outcomes such as job performance, job satisfaction, and turnover:

- Expert and referent power had a generally positive impact.
- Reward and legitimate power had a slightly positive impact.
- Coercive power had a slightly negative impact.

The same researcher, in a follow-up study involving 251 employed business seniors, looked at the relationship between influence styles and bases of power. This was a bottom-up study. In other words, employee perceptions of managerial influence and power were examined. Rational persuasion was found to be a highly acceptable managerial influence tactic. Why? Because employees perceived it to be associated with the three bases of power they viewed positively: legitimate, expert, and referent.[37]

In summary, expert and referent power appear to get the best *combination* of results and favorable reactions from lower-level employees.[38]

Using Power Responsibly and Ethically

As democracy continues to spread around the world, one reality stands clear: Leaders who do not use their power responsibly risk losing it. This holds for corporations and nonprofit organizations as well as for governments. A key to success in this regard is understanding the difference between commitment and mere compliance.

Responsible managers strive for socialized power while avoiding personalized power. In fact, in a survey, organizational commitment was higher among US federal government executives whose superiors exercised socialized power than among colleagues with "power-hungry" bosses. The researchers used the appropriate terms *uplifting power* versus *dominating power*.[39] How does this relate to the five bases of power? As with influence tactics, managerial power has three possible outcomes: commitment, compliance, or resistance. Reward, coercive, and negative legitimate power tend to produce *compliance* (and sometimes, resistance). On the other hand, positive legitimate power, expert power, and referent power tend to foster *commitment*. Once again, commitment is superior to compliance because it is driven by internal or intrinsic motivation.[40] Employees who merely comply require frequent "jolts" of power from the boss to keep them headed in a productive direction. Committed employees tend to be self-starters who do not require close supervision— a key success factor in today's flatter, team-oriented organizations.

Here's a tough question. How would you spend your time if you were a billionaire by birth? If you're Abigail Johnson, granddaughter of the founder of financial services powerhouse Fidelity, you diligently work your way up from the bottom to become president of the company. Even more impressive, Abby wields her considerable power with a light hand. She gives her mutual fund managers a chance to demonstrate their strengths.

Abigail Johnson, president of Fidelity, the financial services giant with $1.4 trillion in mutual funds and other assets under management, is a good example of a manager who responsibly avoids the use of dominating power while building commitment. Abby, as she is known within the company, is the founder's granddaughter and the CEO's daughter. Despite being a billionaire by birth, she worked her way up through the ranks at Fidelity, starting as a customer-service telephone representative after completing high school. She is characterized as self-effacing, committed, and hardworking. Moreover, she does not "share her father's tendency to obsess over details, such as choosing lighting fixtures for a new building. 'It's a mistake for a manager to delve into the details on everything,' she says."[41] Accordingly, she has given her mutual fund managers more flexibility in their stockpicking.

According to research cited earlier, expert and referent power have the greatest potential for improving job performance and satisfaction and reducing turnover. Formal education, training, and self-development can build a manager's expert power. At the same time, one's referent power base can be strengthened by building and maintaining strong internal and external networks.

Empowerment: From Power Sharing to Power Distribution

Empowerment

Sharing varying degrees of power with lower-level employees to tap their full potential.

An exciting trend in today's organizations centers on giving employees a greater say in the workplace. This trend wears various labels, including "high-involvement management," "participative management," and "open-book management." Regardless of the label one prefers, it is all about empowerment. Management consultant and writer W Alan Randolph offers this definition: "**empowerment** is recognizing and releasing into the organization the power that people already have in their wealth of useful knowledge, experience, and internal motivation."[42] A core component of this process is pushing decision-making authority down to progressively lower levels. Steve Kerr, who has served as the "chief learning officer" at General Electric and now Goldman Sachs, adds this important qualification: "We say empowerment is moving decision making down to the lowest level *where a competent decision can be made.*"[43] Of course, it is naive and counterproductive to hand power over to unwilling or unprepared employees.

A Matter of Degree

The concept of empowerment requires some adjustments in traditional thinking. First, power is not a zero-sum situation where one person's gain is another's loss. Social power is unlimited. This requires win–win thinking. Frances Hesselbein, the woman credited with modernizing the Girl Scouts of the USA, put it this way: "The more power you give away, the more you have."[44] Authoritarian managers who view employee empowerment as a threat to their personal power are missing the point because of their win–lose thinking.[45]

Figure 15–2   *The Evolution of Power: From Domination to Delegation*

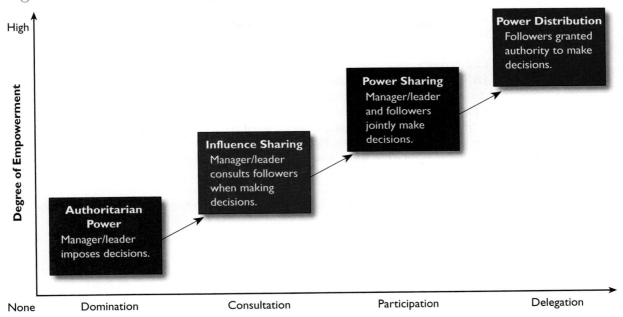

The second adjustment to traditional thinking involves seeing empowerment as *a matter of degree* not as an either–or proposition.[46] Figure 15–2 illustrates how power can be shifted to the hands of nonmanagers step by step. The overriding goal is to increase productivity and competitiveness in leaner organizations. Each step in this evolution increases the power of organizational contributors who traditionally were told what, when, and how to do things. As a case in point, consider how Sumner Redstone, the chairman and CEO of Viacom (the owner of CBS and MTV), empowers his top two executives, Les Moonves and Tom Freston, in a measured fashion:

> "The best thing about Sumner," Moonves says, "is that he's there where I need him—to offer advice or counsel—and at the end of the conversation, it's, 'Do whatever you think is best.' That's very liberating." Freston, who has worked for Redstone since 1987, says, "He has never told me no on anything I've really wanted to do." Of course, Redstone is consulted on key personnel moves, interviewing candidates himself, and he gets deeply involved in any big transaction. "This last NFL deal cost almost $4 billion, so needless to say, that's not a decision I'm going to make by myself," Moonves says.[47]

Participative Management

Confusion exists about the exact meaning of participative management (PM). Management experts have clarified this situation by defining **participative management** as the process whereby employees play a direct role in (1) setting goals, (2) making decisions, (3) solving problems, and (4) making changes in the organization. Participative management includes, but goes beyond, simply asking employees for their ideas or opinions.

Advocates of PM claim employee participation increases employee satisfaction, commitment, and performance. Consistent with both Maslow's need theory and the job characteristics model of job design (see Chapter 8), participative management is predicted to

Participative management
Involving employees in various forms of decision making.

increase motivation because it helps employees fulfill three basic needs: (1) autonomy, (2) meaningfulness of work, and (3) interpersonal contact. Satisfaction of these needs enhances feelings of acceptance and commitment, security, challenge, and satisfaction. In turn, these positive feelings supposedly lead to increased innovation and performance.[48]

Participative management does not work in all situations. The design of work, the level of trust between management and employees, and the employees' competence and readiness to participate represent three factors that influence the effectiveness of PM. With respect to the design of work, individual participation is counterproductive when employees are highly interdependent on each other, as on an assembly line. The problem with individual participation in this case is that interdependent employees generally do not have a broad understanding of the entire production process. Participative management also is less likely to succeed when employees do not trust management. Finally, PM is more effective when employees are competent, prepared, and interested in participating. Northwest Airlines is a good case in point. Employees responded very positively to the company's new employee suggestion system because they were motivated to help the airline reduce operating costs in order to save jobs. The suggestion system resulted in $6 million in annual savings from workers' ideas.

> A flight attendant, for instance, noticed that too many coffeepots were being boarded on planes, so Northwest cut back and now saves $120,000 a year. A customer-service agent suggested that blanket folding and washing be done in-house, for savings of $205,000 annually. A manager in Minneapolis had an idea that resulted in an annual saving of $916,000 on maintenance on DC-10 thrust reversers.[49]

Delegation

Delegation

Granting decision-making authority to people at lower levels

The highest degree of empowerment is **delegation,** the process of granting decision-making authority to lower-level employees.[50] This amounts to *power distribution.* Delegation has long been the recommended way to lighten the busy manager's load while at the same time developing employees' abilities.[51] Importantly, delegation gives nonmanagerial employees more than simply a voice in decisions. It empowers them to make their own decisions. A prime example is the Ritz-Carlton Hotel chain:

> At Ritz-Carlton, every worker is authorized to spend up to $2,000 to fix any problem a guest encounters. Employees do not abuse the privilege. "When you treat people responsibly, they act responsibly," said Patrick Mene, the hotel chain's director of quality.[52]

Not surprising, then, that Ritz-Carlton has won national service quality awards.

Barriers to Delegation
Delegation is easy to talk about, but many managers find it hard to actually do. A concerted effort to overcome the following common barriers to delegation needs to be made:

- Belief in the fallacy, "If you want it done right, do it yourself." (See Real World/Real People.)
- Lack of confidence and trust in lower-level employees.
- Low self-confidence.
- Fear of being called lazy.
- Vague job definition.
- Fear of competition from those below.
- Reluctance to take the risks involved in depending on others.
- Lack of controls that provide early warning of problems with delegated duties.
- Poor example set by bosses who do not delegate.[53]

The CEO of Abercrombie & Fitch Co., Mike Jeffries, Hates to Delegate

[Among his former co-workers at the now-closed New York department store Abraham & Straus, young] Jeffries was known for his ambition. "He worked twice as much as any of us," [one of them] says. Former A&S chairman Alan Gilman remembers something else: Jeffries was so in control that he failed to develop his staff. "A gifted guy who does it himself is different from a gifted guy who helps people help him do it," Gilman says. . . .

None of that prevented Limited CEO Leslie Wexner from hiring Jeffries to reinvent the ailing Abercrombie.

Jeffries' big idea was to make the new A&F sizzle with sex: Bruce Weber photos of scantily clad models dominate the walls of A&F stores and its catalogues. Weber says Jeffries interviews everyone used in his shots. Jeffries' control of the brand goes way beyond imagery, though. To this day, there's no detail that he doesn't approve, from all merchandise at A&F and the three other labels he has developed to how clothes are folded on store tables.

SOURCE: Excerpted from R Berner, "Flip-Flops, Torn Jeans—and Control," *BusinessWeek*, May 30, 2005, p 69.

Delegation Research and Implications for Trust and Personal Initiative

Researchers at the State University of New York at Albany surveyed pairs of managers and employees and did follow-up interviews with the managers concerning their delegation habits. Their results confirmed some important common sense notions about delegation. Greater delegation was associated with the following factors:

1. Competent employee.
2. Employee shared manager's task objectives.
3. Manager had a long-standing and positive relationship with employee.
4. The lower-level person also was a supervisor.[54]

This delegation scenario boils down to one pivotal factor, *trust*.[55]

Managers prefer to delegate important tasks and decisions to the people they trust. As discussed in Chapter 11, it takes time and favorable experience to build trust. Of course, trust is fragile; it can be destroyed by a single remark, act, or omission. Ironically, managers cannot learn to trust someone without, initially at least, running the risk of betrayal. This is where the empowerment evolution in Figure 15–2 represents a three-step ladder to trust: consultation, participation, and delegation. In other words, managers need to start small and work up the empowerment ladder. They need to delegate small tasks and decisions and scale up as competence, confidence, and trust grow. Employees need to work on their side of the trust equation as well. One of the best ways to earn a manager's trust is to show *initiative* (see Figure 15–3). Researchers in the area offer this instructive definition and characterization:

Personal initiative is a behavior syndrome resulting in an individual's taking an active and self-starting approach to work and going beyond what is formally required in a given job. More specifically, personal initiative is characterized by the following aspects: it (1) is consistent with the organization's mission, (2) has a long-term focus, (3) is goal-directed and action-oriented, (4) is persistent in the face of barriers and setbacks, and (5) is self-starting and proactive.[56]

Personal initiative
Going beyond formal job requirements and being an active self-starter.

Recall our discussion of the *proactive personality* in Chapter 5.

Figure 15–3   *Personal Initiative: The Other Side of Delegation*

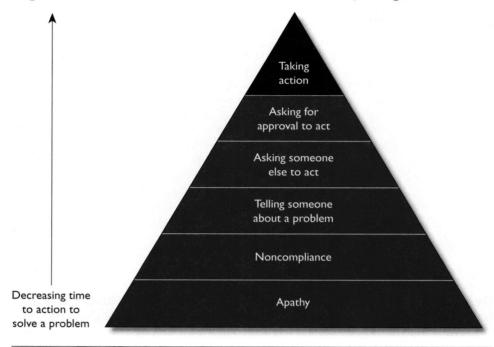

Decreasing time
to action to
solve a problem

SOURCE: Figure from A L Frohman, "Igniting Organizational Change from Below: The Power of Personal Initiative," *Organizational Dynamics*, Winter 1997, p 46. © 1997, with permission from Elsevier.

Empowerment: The Research Record and Practical Advice

Like other widely heralded techniques—such as TQM, 360-degree reviews, teams, and learning organizations—empowerment has its fair share of critics and suffers from unrealistic expectations.[57] Research results to date are mixed, with a recent positive uptrend:

- A meta-analysis encompassing 27 studies and 6,732 individuals revealed that employee participation in the performance appraisal process was positively related to an employee's satisfaction with his or her performance review, perceived value of the appraisal, motivation to improve performance after the review, and perceived fairness of the appraisal process.[58]

- Another meta-analysis of 86 studies involving 18,872 people demonstrated that participation had a small statistically significant positive impact on job performance but only a moderate positive effect on job satisfaction.[59]

- Another study at an insurance company, two textile makers, and a high-tech company in the United States focused on 111 empowered teams. More empowered teams tended to be more productive and render better customer service than less empowered teams. Empowered team members also tended to be more satisfied with (and committed to) their job, team, and employer.[60]

- A study of 164 New Zealand companies employing at least 100 people found a positive correlation between high-involvement management practices and employee retention and company productivity.[61]
- Most recently, a field study with 149 call center employees documented how "high-involvement work processes" more effectively boosted job performance (e.g., customer satisfaction), job satisfaction, and organizational commitment than did self-managed teams.[62]

We believe empowerment has good promise if managers go about it properly. Empowerment is a sweeping concept with many different definitions. Consequently, researchers use inconsistent measurements, and cause-effect relationships are fuzzy. Managers committed to the idea of employee empowerment need to follow the path of continuous improvement, learning from their successes and failures. Eight years of research with 10 "empowered" companies led Randolph to formulate the three-pronged empowerment plan in Figure 15–4. Notice how open-book management and active information sharing are needed to build the necessary foundation of trust. Beyond that, clear goals and lots of relevant training are needed. Noting that the empowerment process can take several years to unfold, Randolph offered this perspective:

> While the keys to empowerment may be easy to understand, they are hard to implement. It takes tremendous courage to start sharing sensitive information. It takes true strength to build more structure just at the point when people want more freedom of action. It takes real growth to allow teams to take over the management decision-making process. And above all, it takes perseverance to complete the empowerment process.[63]

Figure 15–4   *Randolph's Empowerment Model*

The Empowerment Plan

Share Information
- Share company performance information.
- Help people understand the business.
- Build trust through sharing sensitive information.
- Create self-monitoring possibilities.

Create Autonomy through Structure
- Create a clear vision and clarify the little pictures.
- Create new decision-making rules that support empowerment.
- Clarify goals and roles collaboratively.
- Establish new empowering performance management processes.
- Use heavy doses of training.

Let Teams Become The Hierarchy
- Provide direction and training for new skills.
- Provide encouragement and support for change.
- Gradually have managers let go of control.
- Work through the leadership vacuum stage.
- Acknowledge the fear factor.

**Remember: Empowerment is not magic;
it consists of a few simple steps and a lot of persistence.**

SOURCE: W Alan Randolph, "Navigating the Journey to Empowerment," *Organizational Dynamics*, Vol. 24, No. 3, p 46, © 1997, with permission from Elsevier.

Organizational Politics and Impression Management

Some contestants on the reality TV show *The Apprentice* respond to the loom-ing threat of Donald Trump saying "you're fired" by resorting to political antics—blaming, scapegoating, finger pointing, etc. Sure enough, they're fired!

Most students of OB find the study of orga-nizational politics intriguing. Perhaps this topic owes its appeal to the antics of Holly-wood's corporate villains and contestants on *The Apprentice* stepping on each other to avoid Donald Trump's dreaded words, "you're fired!"[64] As we will see, however, organizational politics includes, but is not limited to, dirty dealing. Organizational pol-itics is an ever-present and sometimes annoying feature of modern work life. "Executives say that they spend 19% of their time dealing with political infighting with their staffs, according to a survey by OfficeTeam, a staffing services firm."[65] One expert recently observed, "Many 'new economy' companies use the acronym 'WOMBAT'—or waste of money, brains, and time—to describe office politics."[66] On the other hand, organizational politics can be a positive force in modern work organizations. Skillful and well-timed politics can help you get your point across, neutralize resistance to a key project, or get a choice job assignment.

Roberta Bhasin, a telephone company district manager, put organizational politics into perspective by observing the following:

> Most of us would like to believe that organizations are rationally structured, based on rea-sonable divisions of labor, a clear hierarchical communication flow, and well-defined lines of authority aimed at meeting universally understood goals and objectives.
>
> But organizations are made up of *people* with personal agendas designed to win power and influence. The agenda—the game—is called corporate politics. It is played by avoiding the rational structure, manipulating the communications hierarchy, and ignoring established lines of authority. The rules are never written down and seldom discussed.
>
> For some, corporate politics are second nature. They instinctively know the unspoken rules of the game. Others must learn. Managers who don't understand the politics of their organizations are at a disadvantage, not only in winning raises and promotions, but even in getting things *done.*[67]

We explore this important and interesting area by (1) defining the term *organizational politics,* (2) identifying three levels of political action, (3) discussing eight specific politi-cal tactics, (4) considering a related area called *impression management,* and (5) examin-ing relevant research and practical implications.

Definition and Domain of Organizational Politics

Organizational politics
Intentional enhancement of self-interest.

"**Organizational politics** involves intentional acts of influence to enhance or protect the self-interest of individuals or groups."[68] An emphasis on *self-interest* distinguishes this form of social influence. Managers are constantly challenged to achieve a workable balance between employees' self-interests and organizational interests, as discussed at the beginning of this chapter. When a proper balance exists, the pursuit of self-interest may serve the organization's interests. Political behavior becomes a negative force when self-interests erode or defeat organizational interests. For example, researchers have documented the political tactic of filtering and distorting information flowing up to the boss. This self-serving practice put the reporting employees in the best possible light.[69]

Uncertainty Triggers Political Behavior

Political maneuvering is triggered primarily by *uncertainty*. Five common sources of uncertainty within organizations are

1. Unclear objectives.
2. Vague performance measures.
3. Ill-defined decision processes.
4. Strong individual or group competition.[70]
5. Any type of change.

" Stop whimpering and spin the wheel of blame, Lipton! "

SOURCE: *Harvard Business Review*, November 2003, p 86.
© Scott A Masear. Reprinted by permission of the author.

Regarding this last source of uncertainty, organization development specialist Anthony Raia noted, "Whatever we attempt to change, the political subsystem becomes active. Vested interests are almost always at stake and the distribution of power is challenged."[71]

Thus, we would expect a field sales representative, striving to achieve an assigned quota, to be less political than a management trainee working on a variety of projects. While some management trainees stake their career success on hard work, competence, and a bit of luck, many do not. These people attempt to gain a competitive edge through some combination of the political tactics discussed below. Meanwhile, the salesperson's performance is measured in actual sales, not in terms of being friends with the boss or taking credit for others' work. Thus, the management trainee would tend to be more political than the field salesperson because of greater uncertainty about management's expectations.

Because employees generally experience greater uncertainty during the earlier stages of their careers, are junior employees more political than more senior ones? The answer is yes, according to a survey of 243 employed adults in upstate New York. In fact, one senior employee nearing retirement told the researcher: "I used to play political games when I was younger. Now I just do my job."[72]

Three Levels of Political Action

Although much political maneuvering occurs at the individual level, it also can involve group or collective action. Figure 15–5 illustrates three different levels of political action: the individual level, the coalition level, and the network level.[73] Each level has its distinguishing characteristics. At the individual level, personal self-interests are pursued by the individual. The political aspects of coalitions and networks are not so obvious, however.

People with a common interest can become a political coalition by fitting the following definition. In an organizational context, a **coalition** is an informal group bound together by the *active* pursuit of a *single* issue. Coalitions may or may not coincide with formal group membership. When the target issue is resolved (a sexual-harassing supervisor is fired, for example), the coalition disbands. Experts note that political coalitions have "fuzzy boundaries," meaning they are fluid in membership, flexible in structure, and temporary in duration.[74]

Coalition
Temporary groupings of people who actively pursue a single issue.

Figure 15–5   *Levels of Political Action in Organizations*

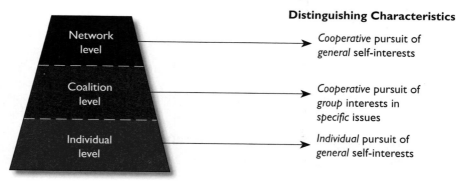

Distinguishing Characteristics

Network level → *Cooperative* pursuit of *general* self-interests

Coalition level → *Cooperative* pursuit of *group* interests in *specific* issues

Individual level → *Individual* pursuit of *general* self-interests

Coalitions are a potent political force in organizations. Consider the situation Charles J Bradshaw faced in a finance committee meeting at Transworld Corporation. Bradshaw, president of the company, opposed the chairman's plan to acquire a $93 million nursing home company:

> [The senior vice president for finance] kicked off the meeting with a battery of facts and figures in support of the deal. "Within two or three minutes, I knew I had lost," Bradshaw concedes. "No one was talking directly to me, but all statements addressed my opposition. I could tell there was a general agreement around the board table." . . .
> Then the vote was taken. Five hands went up. Only Bradshaw voted no.[75]

After the meeting, Bradshaw resigned his $530,000-a-year position, without as much as a handshake or good-bye from the chairman. In Bradshaw's case, the finance committee was a formal group that temporarily became a political coalition aimed at sealing his fate at Transworld. In recent years, coalitions on the corporate boards of Ford, Computer Associates, and Hewlett-Packard ousted the heads of those giant companies.

A third level of political action involves networks.[76] Unlike coalitions, which pivot on specific issues, networks are loose associations of individuals seeking social support for their general self-interests. Politically, networks are people oriented, while coalitions are issue oriented. Networks have broader and longer term agendas than do coalitions. For instance, Avon's Hispanic employees have built a network to enhance the members' career opportunities.

Political Tactics

Anyone who has worked in an organization has firsthand knowledge of blatant politicking. Blaming someone else for your mistake is an obvious political ploy. But other political tactics are more subtle. Researchers have identified a range of political behavior.

One landmark study, involving in-depth interviews with 87 managers from 30 electronics companies in southern California, identified eight political tactics. Top-, middle-, and low-level managers were represented about equally in the sample. According to the researchers: "Respondents were asked to describe organizational political tactics and personal characteristics of effective political actors based upon their accumulated experience in *all* organizations in which they had worked."[77] Listed in descending order of occurrence, the eight political tactics that emerged were

1. Attacking or blaming others.
2. Using information as a political tool.

3. Creating a favorable image. (Also known as *impression management.*)

4. Developing a base of support.

5. Praising others (ingratiation).

6. Forming power coalitions with strong allies.

7. Associating with influential people.

8. Creating obligations (reciprocity).

Table 15–1 describes these political tactics and indicates how often each reportedly was used by the interviewed managers.

The researchers distinguished between reactive and proactive political tactics. Some of the tactics, such as scapegoating, were *reactive* because the intent was to *defend* one's self-interest. Other tactics, such as developing a base of support, were *proactive* because they sought to *promote* the individual's self-interest.

What is your attitude toward organizational politics? How often do you rely on the various tactics in Table 15–1? You can get a general indication of your political tendencies by comparing your behavior with the characteristics in Table 15–2. Would you characterize yourself as politically *naive,* politically *sensible,* or a political *shark?* How do you think others view your political actions? What are the career, friendship, and ethical implications of your political tendencies?[78] (For a more detailed analysis of your political tendencies, see the Personal Awareness and Growth Exercise at the end of this chapter.)

Table 15–1   *Eight Common Political Tactics in Organizations*

Political Tactic	Percentage of Managers Mentioning Tactic	Brief Description of Tactic
1. Attacking or blaming others	54%	Used to avoid or minimize association with failure. Reactive when scapegoating is involved. Proactive when goal is to reduce competition for limited resources.
2. Using information as a political tool	54	Involves the purposeful withholding or distortion of information. Obscuring an unfavorable situation by overwhelming superiors with information.
3. Creating a favorable image (impression management)	53	Dressing/grooming for success. Adhering to organizational norms and drawing attention to one's successes and influence. Taking credit for others' accomplishments.
4. Developing a base of support	37	Getting prior support for a decision. Building others' commitment to a decision through participation.
5. Praising others (ingratiation)	25	Making influential people feel good ("apple polishing").
6. Forming power coalitions with strong allies	25	Teaming up with powerful people who can get results.
7. Associating with influential people	24	Building a support network both inside and outside the organization.
8. Creating obligations (reciprocity)	13	Creating social debts ("I did you a favor, so you owe me a favor").

SOURCE: Adapted from R W Allen, D L Madison, L W Porter, P A Renwick, and B T Mayes, "Organizational Politics: Tactics and Characteristics of Its Actors," *California Management Review,* Fall 1979, pp 77–83.

Table 15–2   *Are You Politically Naïve, Politically Sensible, or a Political Shark?*

Characteristics	Naive	Sensible	Sharks
Underlying attitude	Politics is unpleasant.	Politics is necessary.	Politics is an opportunity.
Intent	Avoid at all costs.	Further departmental goals.	Self-serving and predatory.
Techniques	Tell it like it is.	Network; expand connections; use system to give and receive favors.	Manipulate; use fraud and deceit when necessary.
Favorite tactics	None—the truth will win out.	Negotiate, bargain.	Bully; misuse information; cultivate and use "friends" and other contacts.

SOURCE: Reprinted from J K Pinto and O P Kharbanda, "Lessons for an Accidental Profession," *Business Horizons*, Vol. 38, No. 2, p 45, © 1995, with permission from Elsevier.

Impression Management

Impression management
Getting others to see us in a certain manner.

Impression management is defined as "the process by which people attempt to control or manipulate the reactions of others to images of themselves or their ideas."[79] This encompasses how one talks, behaves, and looks. Most impression management attempts are directed at making a *good* impression on relevant others. But, as we will see, some employees strive to make a *bad* impression. For purposes of conceptual clarity, we will focus on *upward* impression management (trying to impress one's immediate supervisor) because it is most relevant for managers. Still, it is good to remember that *anyone* can be the intended target of impression management. Parents, teachers, peers, employees, and customers are all fair game when it comes to managing the impressions of others.

A Conceptual Crossroads

Impression management is an interesting conceptual crossroads involving self-monitoring, attribution theory, and organizational politics.[80] Perhaps this explains why impression management has gotten active research attention in recent years. High self-monitoring employees ("chameleons" who adjust to their surroundings) are likely to be more inclined to engage in impression management than would low self-monitors. Impression management also involves the systematic manipulation of attributions. For example, a bank president will look good if the board of directors is encouraged to attribute organizational successes to her efforts and attribute problems and failures to factors beyond her control. Impression management definitely fits into the realm of organizational politics because of an overriding focus on furthering one's *self-interests*.

Making a Good Impression

If you "dress for success," project an upbeat attitude at all times, and have polished a 15-second elevator speech for top executives, you are engaging in favorable impression management—particularly so if your motive is to improve your chances of getting what you want in life.[81] There are questionable ways to create a good impression, as well. For instance, Stewart Friedman, director of the University of Pennsylvania's Leadership Program, offered this gem:

> Last year, I was doing some work with a large bank. The people there told me a story that astounded me: After 7 PM, people would open the door to their office, drape a spare jacket on the back of their chair, lay a set of glasses down on some reading material on their

desk—and then go home for the night. The point of this elaborate gesture was to create the illusion that they were just out grabbing dinner and would be returning to burn the midnight oil.[82]

Impression management often strays into unethical territory.

A statistical factor analysis of the influence attempts reported by a sample of 84 bank employees (including 74 women) identified three categories of favorable upward impression management tactics.[83] As labeled in the OB Exercise on page 498, favorable upward impression management tactics can be *job-focused* (manipulating information about one's job performance), *supervisor-focused* (praising and doing favors for one's supervisor), and *self-focused* (presenting oneself as a polite and nice person). Take a short break from your studying to complete the OB Exercise. How did you do? A moderate amount of upward impression management is a necessity for the average employee today. Too little, and busy managers are liable to overlook some of your valuable contributions when they make job assignment, pay, and promotion decisions. Too much, and you run the risk of being branded a "schmoozer," a "phony," and other unflattering things by your co-workers.[84] Excessive flattery and ingratiation can backfire by embarrassing the target person and damaging one's credibility. Also, the risk of unintended insult is very high when impression management tactics cross gender, racial, ethnic, and cultural lines.[85] International management experts warn

> The impression management tactic is only as effective as its correlation to accepted norms about behavioral presentation. In other words, slapping a Japanese subordinate on the back with a rousing "Good work, Hiro!" will not create the desired impression in Hiro's mind that the expatriate intended. In fact, the behavior will likely create the opposite impression.[86]

Making a Poor Impression

At first glance, the idea of consciously trying to make a bad impression in the workplace seems absurd. But an interesting new line of impression management research has uncovered both motives and tactics for making oneself look *bad*. In a survey of the work experiences of business students at a large northwestern US university, more than half "reported witnessing a case of someone intentionally looking bad at work."[87] Why? Four motives came out of the study:

> (1) *Avoidance:* Employee seeks to avoid additional work, stress, burnout, or an unwanted transfer or promotion. (2) *Obtain concrete rewards:* Employee seeks to obtain a pay raise or a desired transfer, promotion, or demotion. (3) *Exit:* Employee seeks to get laid off, fired, or suspended, and perhaps also to collect unemployment or workers' compensation. (4) *Power:* Employee seeks to control, manipulate, or intimidate others, get revenge, or make someone else look bad.[88]

Within the context of these motives, *unfavorable* upward impression management makes sense.

Five unfavorable upward impression management tactics identified by the researchers are as follows:

- *Decreasing performance*—restricting productivity, making more mistakes than usual, lowering quality, neglecting tasks.

- *Not working to potential*—pretending ignorance, having unused capabilities.

- *Withdrawing*—being tardy, taking excessive breaks, faking illness.

- *Displaying a bad attitude*—complaining, getting upset and angry, acting strangely, not getting along with co-workers.

- *Broadcasting limitations*—letting co-workers know about one's physical problems and mistakes, both verbally and nonverbally.[89]

How Much Do You Rely on Upward Impression Management Tactics?

Instructions

Rate yourself on each item according to how you behave on your current (or most recent) job. Add your circled responses to calculate a total score. Compare your score with our arbitrary norms.

	Rarely				Very Often

Job-Focused Tactics

1. I play up the value of my positive work results and make my supervisor aware of them.   1 — 2 — 3 — 4 — 5
2. I try to make my work appear better than it is.   1 — 2 — 3 — 4 — 5
3. I try to take responsibility for positive results, even when I'm not solely responsible for achieving them.   1 — 2 — 3 — 4 — 5
4. I try to make my negative results not as severe as they initially appear to my supervisor.   1 — 2 — 3 — 4 — 5
5. I arrive at work early and/or work late to show my supervisor I am a hard worker.   1 — 2 — 3 — 4 — 5

Supervisor-Focused Tactics

6. I show an interest in my supervisor's personal life.   1 — 2 — 3 — 4 — 5
7. I praise my supervisor on his/her accomplishments.   1 — 2 — 3 — 4 — 5
8. I do personal favors for my supervisor that I'm not required to do.   1 — 2 — 3 — 4 — 5
9. I compliment my supervisor on her/his dress or appearance.   1 — 2 — 3 — 4 — 5
10. I agree with my supervisor's major suggestions and ideas.   1 — 2 — 3 — 4 — 5

Self-Focused Tactics

11. I am very friendly and polite around my supervisor.   1 — 2 — 3 — 4 — 5
12. I try to act as a model employee around my supervisor.   1 — 2 — 3 — 4 — 5
13. I work harder when I know my supervisor will see the results.   1 — 2 — 3 — 4 — 5

Total score = _____

Arbitrary Norms

13–26 = free agent
27–51 = better safe than sorry
52–65 = hello, Hollywood

SOURCE: Adapted from S J Wayne and G R Ferris, "Influence Tactics, Affect, and Exchange Quality in Supervisor-Subordinate Interactions: A Laboratory Experiment and Field Study," *Journal of Applied Psychology*, October 1990, pp 487–99.

Recommended ways to manage employees who try to make a bad impression can be found throughout this book. They include more challenging work, greater autonomy, better feedback, supportive leadership, clear and reasonable goals, and a less stressful work setting.

Research Evidence on Organizational Politics and Impression Management

Field research involving employees in real organizations rather than students in contrived laboratory settings has yielded these useful insights:

- In a study of 514 nonacademic university employees in the southwestern United States, white men had a greater understanding of organizational politics than did racial and ethnic minorities and white women. The researchers endorsed the practice of using mentors to help women and minorities develop their political skills.[90]

- Another study of 68 women and 84 men employed by five different service and industrial companies in the United States uncovered significant gender-based insights about organizational politics. In what might be termed the battle of the sexes,

  > it was found that political behavior was perceived more favorably when it was performed against a target of the opposite gender....Thus subjects of both sexes tend to relate to gender as a meaningful affiliation group. This finding presents a different picture from the one suggesting that women tend to accept male superiority at work and generally agree with sex stereotypes which are commonly discriminatory in nature.[91]

- In a more recent survey of 172 team members in a large company's research and development unit, perceived higher levels of team politics were associated with lower organizational commitment, lower job satisfaction, poorer job performance, and lower unit effectiveness.[92]

The results of a cross-cultural laboratory study are noteworthy. A unique study of 38 Japanese Americans and 39 European Americans at the University of Utah showed how impression management can cause problems across cultures. Consistent with Japanese tradition, the Japanese Americans tended to publicly report their job performance in a self-effacing (or modest) way, *despite confiding in private that they had performed as well as the European Americans.* This Japanese cultural tendency toward understatement created a false impression for third-party European American evaluators (who were kept unaware of any cultural distinctions). According to the researchers, "Japanese American participants were seen as less competent and less likeable than their European American counterparts because of their tendency to downplay their performance."[93] The old American expression "It pays to toot your own horn" appears to be as true as ever. Too much tooting, however, can brand one as arrogant, self-centered, and overbearing. This sort of delicate cultural balancing act makes cross-cultural dealings very challenging.

Managing Organizational Politics

Organizational politics cannot be eliminated. A manager would be naive to expect such an outcome. But political maneuvering can and should be managed to keep it constructive and within reasonable bounds (see Real World/Real People). Harvard's Abraham Zaleznik put the issue this way: "People can focus their attention on only so many things. The more it lands on politics, the less energy—emotional and intellectual—is available to attend to the problems that fall under the heading of real work."[94]

An individual's degree of politicalness is a matter of personal values, ethics, and temperament. People who are either strictly nonpolitical or highly political generally pay a price for their behavior. The former may experience slow promotions and feel left out, while the latter may run the risk of being called self-serving and lose their credibility. People at both ends of the political spectrum may be considered poor team players. A moderate amount of prudent political behavior generally is considered a survival tool in complex organizations. Experts remind us that

> political behavior has earned a bad name only because of its association with politicians. On its own, the use of power and other resources to obtain your objectives is not inherently unethical. It all depends on what the preferred objectives are.[95]

With this perspective in mind, the practical steps in Table 15–3 are recommended. How many of the Enron- and WorldCom–type scandals could have been prevented with this approach? Remember: Measurable objectives are management's first line of defense against negative expressions of organizational politics.[96]

Jorma Ollila, CEO of Finland's Nokia, Hangs Up on Organizational Politics

Ollila has a reputation for being animated and funny—not traditional Finnish traits, say Nokia's Finnish employees. But like many Finns, he is blunt and direct. He gives executives tough assignments, then gives them leeway to get them done or risk his ire. He particularly hates corporate politics.

"It is a plague that has to be weeded out at the first signs," he says. Ollila and his top managers "will tell you what's on their minds—it's very black and white," says

Susan Macke, an American who joined Nokia as a vice president earlier this year. "Everybody has an opinion, and they're not afraid to voice it. But at the end of the day, the leader makes a decision and everybody buys in. There's no posturing."

SOURCE: Excerpted from K Maney, "CEO Ollila Says Nokia's 'Sisu' Will See It Past Tough Times," *USA Today*, July 21, 2004, p 2B.

Table 15-3 *How to Keep Organizational Politics within Reasonable Bounds*

- Screen out overly political individuals at hiring time.
- Create an open-book management system.
- Make sure every employee knows how the business works and has a personal line of sight to key results with corresponding measureable objectives for individual accountability.
- Have nonfinancial people interpret periodic financial and accounting statements for all employees.
- Establish formal conflict resolution and grievance processes.
- As an ethics filter, do only what you would feel comfortable doing on national television.
- Publicy recognize and reward people who get real results without political games.

SOURCE: Adapted in part from discussion in L B MacGregor Server, "The End of Office Politics as Usual" (New York: American Management Association, 2002), pp 184–99.

Summary of Key Concepts

1. *Explain the concept of mutuality of interest.* Managers are constantly challenged to foster mutuality of interest (a win–win situation) between individual and organizational interests. Organization members need to actively cooperate with actual and potential adversaries for the common good.

2. *Name at least three "soft" and two "hard" influence tactics, and summarize the practical lessons from influence research.* Five soft influence tactics are rational persuasion, inspirational appeals, consultation, ingratiation, and personal appeals. They are more friendly and less coercive than the four hard influence

tactics: exchange, coalition tactics, pressure, and legitimating tactics. According to research, soft tactics are better for generating commitment and are perceived as more fair than hard tactics. Ingratiation—making the boss feel good through compliments and being helpful—can slightly improve performance appraisal results and make the boss like you a lot more. Influence through domination is a poor strategy for both men and women. Influence is a complicated and situational process that needs to be undertaken with care, especially across cultures.

3. *Identify and briefly explain Cialdini's six principles of influence and persuasion.* They are liking (people tend to like those who like them), reciprocity (belief that good

and bad deeds should be repaid in kind), social proof (people tend to follow those most like themselves), consistency (people tend to do what they are publicly committed to doing), authority (people tend to defer to and respect credible experts), and scarcity (people tend to want more of what has limited availability).

4. *Identify and briefly describe French and Raven's five bases of power, and discuss the responsible use of power.* French and Raven's five bases of power are reward power (rewarding compliance), coercive power (punishing noncompliance), legitimate power (relying on formal authority), expert power (providing needed information), and referent power (relying on personal attraction). Responsible and ethical managers strive to use socialized power (primary concern is for others) rather than personalized power (primary concern for self). Research found higher organizational commitment among employees with bosses who used uplifting power than among those with power-hungry bosses who relied on dominating power.

5. *Define the term* empowerment, *and explain why it is a matter of degree.* Empowerment involves sharing varying degrees of power and decision-making authority with lower-level employees to tap their full potential. Empowerment is not an either-or, all-or-nothing proposition. It can range from merely consulting with employees, to having them actively participate in making decisions, to granting them decision-making authority through delegation

6. *Explain why delegation is the highest form of empowerment, and discuss the connections among delegation, trust, and personal initiative.* Delegation gives employees more than a participatory role in decision making. It allows them

to make their *own* work-related decisions. Managers tend to delegate to employees they trust. Employees can get managers to trust them by demonstrating personal initiative (going beyond formal job requirements and being self-starters).

7. *Define organizational politics, and explain what triggers it.* Organizational politics is defined as intentional acts of influence to enhance or protect the self-interests of individuals or groups. Uncertainty triggers most politicking in organizations. Political action occurs at individual, coalition, and network levels. Coalitions are informal, temporary, and single-issue alliances.

8. *Distinguish between favorable and unfavorable impression management tactics.* Favorable upward impression management can be job-focused (manipulating information about one's job performance), supervisor-focused (praising or doing favors for the boss), or self-focused (being polite and nice). Unfavorable upward impression management tactics include decreasing performance, not working to potential, withdrawing, displaying a bad attitude, and broadcasting one's limitations.

9. *Explain how to manage organizational politics.* Since organizational politics cannot be eliminated, managers need to keep it within reasonable bounds. Measurable objectives for personal accountability are key. Participative management also helps, especially in the form of open-book management. Formal conflict resolution and grievance programs are helpful. Overly political people should not be hired, and employees who get results without playing political games should be publicly recognized and rewarded. The "how-would-it-look-on-TV" ethics test can limit political maneuvering.

Discussion Questions

1. Of the nine generic influence tactics, which do you use the most when dealing with friends, parents, your boss, or your professors? Would other tactics be more effective?

2. Which of Cialdini's six principles of influence and persuasion have you observed lately? What were the circumstances and was the influence attempt successful?

3. Before reading this chapter, did the term *power* have a negative connotation for you? Do you view it differently now? Explain.

4. What base(s) of power do you rely on in your daily affairs? (Use the OB Exercise on page 484 to assess your power bases at work.) Do you handle power effectively and responsibly?

5. In your opinion, how much empowerment is too much in today's workplaces?

6. What are the main advantages and drawbacks of the trend toward increased delegation?

7. Why do you think organizational politics is triggered primarily by uncertainty?

8. What personal experiences have you had with coalitions? Explain any positive or negative outcomes.

9. According to the OB Exercise on page 498, how heavily do you rely on upward impression management tactics? What are the career implications of your approach to impression management?

10. How much impression management do you see in your classroom or workplace today? Citing specific examples, are those tactics effective?

A Retired US Marine Corps General Wages War on Hunger in Chicago[97]

BusinessWeek When Brigadier General Michael P Mulqueen left the Marine Corps to take command of the Greater Chicago Food Depository, one of the nation's biggest hunger-relief outfits, he ran into a lot of skeptics. Wouldn't someone accustomed to barking out orders clash with the nonprofit world's consensus-oriented culture? And what value could a Vietnam veteran bristling with medals bring to the fight against hunger? "There were a couple of people on the board who were actually offended by the idea," recalls William A Rudnick, a former general counsel at the Chicago depository. "A lot of people in the social-service world don't view the military as a breeding ground for people who want to do good in society."

Now, nearly 14 years after the genial Mulqueen signed on, his operation has emerged as a model of efficiency for the country's food-assistance industry, which helps more than 23 million Americans every year. And Mulqueen, to the surprise of some, never barks out orders and insists on being called Mike. But to no one's surprise, the ex-Marine runs the depository more like a business than a nonprofit. He recruited heavily from the private sector: His chief financial officer is a certified public accountant from Arthur Andersen, the felled accounting giant; the operations director has a PhD in aeronautical engineering and ran logistics for the *Chicago Sun-Times;* and the director of food resources was an engineer at a local utility. Mulqueen also established competitive bids on every purchase over $500 and set performance standards and rewards for his staff, to whom he pays for-profit market salaries ranging up to $150,000 a year (he himself earns about $200,000).

The result is a spit-and-polish operation that attracts food bank officials from around the country eager to learn how the depository does it. Among its successes: a training program in which welfare moms learn restaurant cooking while feeding hungry children through a chain of Kids Cafés; Pantry University, which teaches hundreds of volunteers to run food pantries efficiently; and the depository's new $29 million warehouse in southwest Chicago, built with the guidance of corporate logistics experts to serve some 600 local pantries and soup kitchens. "He's a leader and always willing to share ideas that make us all better," says Lynn Brantley, chief executive of the Capital Area Food Bank of Washington. . . .

No Bully

Mulqueen, who once commanded some 7,000 Marines and sailors in a provisioning group on Okinawa, is as demanding as any no-nonsense CEO. To keep his people in touch with the depository's mission, he insists they spend at least one day a year working at a food pantry or soup kitchen. He did his latest stint in December, helping volunteers repackage and distribute food in a mixed-income suburb near the Indiana border. "When you're in your nice office here, it's easy to forget why you're doing what you're doing," says Mulqueen.

His secret is combining cordiality and efficiency. Even in the military, he says, leaders don't get troops to rally around them by dictating. Leaving room for autonomy works better than simply issuing orders. And recognition matters, whether it's another stripe on a uniform or a simple "attaboy." "He's never intimidating and doesn't use his 'general' status to bully his way around," says Jaynee K Day, CEO of the Second Harvest Food Bank of Middle Tennessee. . . .

Behind the scenes, Mulqueen has also become a powerful voice in the national fight against hunger. He led the search committee that four years ago recruited Robert H Forney, former head of the Chicago Stock Exchange, to become CEO of America's Second Harvest, the national umbrella organization for food banks. The Chicago-based outfit had been hobbled by tensions between it and member food banks, directors say, and Forney worked with board members on a reorganization plan that eased the problems.

Having made his mark in both the military and charitable worlds, Mulqueen, at 67, is still figuring out what to do with the rest of his life. He plans to stay at the depository for another year. Afterward, there will be time for golf, mysteries, historical books, and tending to six grandchildren. Oh, and he'll probably find some time for volunteering.

Questions for Discussion

1. Are you surprised in any way that a former military commander could be so successful in a nonprofit organization that relies heavily on volunteers? Explain.

2. Which, if any, of the nine generic influence tactics are evident in this case? Explain.

3. Does Mulqueen rely on personalized or socialized power? Explain.

4. Which, if any, of the five bases of power are evident in this case? Explain.

5. Has Mulqueen built a supportive climate for empowerment? Explain.

6. Do you think organizational politics is a big problem with Mulqueen in charge? Explain.

How Political Are You?

Objectives

1. To get to know yourself a little bit better.
2. Within an organizational context, to assess your political tendencies.
3. To consider the career implications of your political tendencies.

Introduction

Organizational politics is an unavoidable feature of modern organizational life. Your career success, job performance, and job satisfaction can hinge on your political skills. But it is important to realize that some political tactics can cause ethical problems.

Instructions

For each of the 10 statements below, select the response that best characterizes your behavior. You do not have to engage in the behavior at all times to answer true.[98]

1. You should make others feel important through an open appreciation of their ideas and work.	____ True ____ False
2. Because people tend to judge you when they first meet you, always try to make a good first impression.	____ True ____ False
3. Try to let others do most of the talking, be sympathetic to their problems, and resist telling people that they are totally wrong.	____ True ____ False
4. Praise the good traits of the people you meet and always give people an opportunity to save face if they are wrong or make a mistake.	____ True ____ False
5. Spreading false rumors, planting misleading information, and backstabbing are necessary, if somewhat unpleasant, methods to deal with your enemies.	____ True ____ False
6. Sometimes it is necessary to make promises that you know you will not or cannot keep.	____ True ____ False
7. It is important to get along with everybody, even with those who are generally recognized as windbags, abrasive, or constant complainers.	____ True ____ False
8. It is vital to do favors for others so that you can call in these IOUs at times when they will do you the most good.	____ True ____ False
9. Be willing to compromise, particularly on issues that are minor to you, but important to others.	____ True ____ False
10. On controversial issues, it is important to delay or avoid your involvement if possible.	____ True ____ False

Scoring and Interpretation

The author of this quiz recommends the following scoring system:

A confirmed organizational politician will answer "true" to all 10 questions. Organizational politicians with fundamental ethical standards will answer "false" to questions 5 and 6, which deal with deliberate lies and uncharitable behavior. Individuals who regard manipulation, incomplete disclosure, and self-serving behavior as unacceptable will answer "false" to all or almost all of the questions.[99]

Questions for Discussion

1. Did this instrument accurately assess your tendencies toward organizational politics? Explain.
2. Do you think a confirmed organizational politician would answer this quiz honestly? Explain.
3. Will your political tendencies help or hinder your career? Explain.
4. Are there any potential ethical problems with any of your answers? Which ones?
5. How important is political behavior for career success today? Explain, relative to the industry or organization you have in mind.

You Make Me Feel So Good!

Objectives

1. To introduce a different type of impression management and sharpen your awareness of impression management.
2. To promote self-awareness and diversity awareness by comparing your perceptions and ethics with others.

Introduction

This is a group discussion exercise designed to enhance your understanding of impression management. Personal interpretations are involved, so there are no strictly right or wrong answers.

Researchers recently have explored *beneficial* impression management, the practice of helping friends and significant others look good. This new line of inquiry combines the established OB topics of social support (discussed relative to stress in Chapter 18) and impression management (discussed in this chapter.) In this exercise, we explore the practical and ethical implications of "strategically managing information to make your friends look good." We also consider impression management in general.

Instructions

This is a two-stage exercise: a private note-taking part, followed by a group discussion.

Stage 1 (5 to 7 minutes): Read the two scenarios in the box below and then rate each one according to the following three scales:

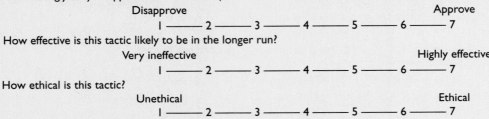

How strongly do you approve of this tactic? (Mark an "X" for scenario 1 and an "O" for scenario 2.)

Disapprove   Approve
1 ——— 2 ——— 3 ——— 4 ——— 5 ——— 6 ——— 7

How effective is this tactic likely to be in the longer run?

Very ineffective   Highly effective
1 ——— 2 ——— 3 ——— 4 ——— 5 ——— 6 ——— 7

How ethical is this tactic?

Unethical   Ethical
1 ——— 2 ——— 3 ——— 4 ——— 5 ——— 6 ——— 7

SCENARIOS[100]

1. A high school ballplayer buoys the spirits of a teammate who struck out at a key moment by emphasizing the latter's game-winning hit last week and noting that even the greatest big-league hitters fail about 7 times out of 10. He may privately suspect his teammate has only mediocre baseball talent, but by putting the best side to his comments and not sharing his doubts, he makes the teammate feel better, builds his confidence so he can face tomorrow's game in a more optimistic frame of mind, and boosts the teammate's image in front of the other players who can hear his reassuring words.

2. At a party, a college student describes her roommate to a potential date she knows her friend finds extremely attractive. She stresses her friend's intelligence, attractiveness, and common interests but fails to mention that her friend can also be quite arrogant.

Stage 2 (10 to 15 minutes): Join two or three others in a discussion group and compare scores for both scenarios. Are there big differences of opinion, or is there a general consensus? Next, briefly discuss these questions: How do *you* create a good first impression in *specific* situations? What goes through your mind when you see someone trying to make a good impression for themselves or for someone else? *Note:* Your instructor may ask you to pick a spokesperson to briefly report the results of your discussion to the class. If so, be sure to keep notes during the discussion.

Questions for Discussion

1. Is the whole practice of impression management a dishonest waste of time, or does it have a proper place in society? Why?

2. In what situations can impression management attempts backfire?

3. How do you know when someone has taken impression management too far?

4. How would you respond to a person who made this statement? "I never engage in impression management."

Your Job: Up in Smoke?[101]

Smokers have been banned from lighting up on airplanes, at work, and in restaurants. Now, a nicotine habit could cost a smoker a job. As of March 25, [2002,] St. Cloud, Florida (population 19,000), requires applicants for city jobs to swear they've been tobacco-free for a year. New hires can't smoke or dip and can be tested to make sure they're not cheating. (Current employees are exempt.)

Other Florida cities have similar laws, but none go as far: North Miami bans smokers from applying for city jobs, too, but relents after they're hired; Coral Gables won't let smokers be cops.

Boosters say the restrictions mean fewer lost workdays, higher productivity, and lower health-insurance costs. Eric Nieves, St. Cloud's human-resources director, says 6 to 12% of the $1.3 million the city spends on health insurance is tobacco-related.

But civil-rights advocates say saving money is not worth the loss of privacy. Smoking is a health risk, "but so is high blood pressure and cholesterol," says Angie Brooks of the American Civil Liberties Union, which is considering whether to file suit. "It's a very slippery slope."

And some say the law will make hiring harder. Says public works director Bob MacKichan: "I could have the most qualified person there is, but now I don't even get to see the application."

What is your position on this ethically charged workplace power play?

1. Smoking is hazardous to all involved and should be discouraged in every possible way. Explain.

2. This is an outrageous abuse of power. Smokers have rights, too. Explain.

3. Current no-smoking policies in most workplaces are strict enough already. Explain.

4. Exempting current employees from a tobacco-free policy for new hires is an unacceptable double standard that could hurt morale and productivity. Explain.

5. Employees in each particular organization should be allowed to vote on tobacco-free hiring. Explain.

6. Invent other options. Discuss.

For the Chapter 15 Internet Exercise featuring a quiz on social influence (www.influenceatwork.com), visit our Web site at **www.mhhe.com/kreitner.**

16

Chapter

Leadership

Learning Objectives

When you finish studying the material in this chapter, you should be able to:

1 Define the term *leadership,* and explain the difference between leading and managing.

2 Review trait theory research and the takeaways from this theoretical perspective.

3 Explain behavioral styles theory and its takeaways.

4 Explain, according to Fiedler's contingency model, how leadership style interacts with situational control.

5 Discuss House's revised path–goal theory.

6 Describe the difference between laissez-faire, transactional, and transformational leadership.

7 Discuss how transformational leadership transforms followers and work groups.

8 Explain the leader–member exchange model of leadership and the concept of shared leadership.

9 Review the Level 5 model of leadership and the principles of servant-leadership.

10 Describe the follower's role in the leadership process.

At a time of great turmoil at the top of many iconic American companies, the job of vetting and selecting CEO candidates has gotten tougher. . . .

The list of criteria boards must weigh is also lengthening. Boeing's [recent] dismissal . . . of CEO Harry Stonecipher, after directors learned about his explicit e-mail to a female employee with whom he was having an affair, is increasing the pressure to scrutinize candidates' private conduct as well as their professional records. That involves not just making certain that CEO choices haven't committed fraud, cheated on expense accounts or performed other dishonest business acts, but also determining if their personal behavior disqualifies them as leaders. Among such behavior: a drinking problem, failing to file personal income-tax returns or a history of making unwanted sexual advances to colleagues or subordinates. . . .

But boards do need to give more weight to a prospective CEO's integrity, and that requires that they understand "the bright line between morality and integrity," says Scott Flanders, the CEO of Columbia House, a New York mail-order marketer of music and videos.

Many people "might be offended by the [four-letter] words that a lot of CEOs use," he notes, but not liking someone's language or their sexual preferences "is a moral judgment, which is very subjective," he says. Integrity, by contrast, is about telling the truth—"and it should always be strike three, you're out, if you lie to your board, your secretary, employees or anyone you do business with," he adds.

While lying to your wife may appear to fall into that category, it's really conduct that compromises your company that matters. After all, there's no Sarbanes-Oxley Act for sex.

Amid the heightened concern about a wide range of candidate traits, boards still have to choose leaders who can actually run the company's businesses. Directors who vet a candidate's character but choose someone who doesn't understand a company's culture, strategy, products and biggest challenges— or simply can't win the trust of subordinates—fail investors.

Former Boeing CEO Harry Stonecipher.

There are all too many examples of CEOs who were named to top jobs after lengthy searches—from Richard Brown at Electronic Data Systems to Carly Fiorina at Hewlett-Packard—who then replaced veteran managers and laid off employees, only to be ousted themselves, with rich severance deals, when they couldn't achieve profit growth. . . .

Standards about what constitutes good personal conduct vary considerably across companies, industries and countries, however. Most European, Latin American and Asian-based companies wouldn't consider booting a CEO over an extramarital romance and can't understand Boeing's decision, says Mr Robert Brudno. "Some overseas companies are still paying for apartments for their top executives' mistresses," he adds.

In the US, most companies no longer prohibit consensual romances between employees, whether they are single or married, as long as neither person reports

to the other. And if Mr Stonecipher "had been CEO at a retail or entertainment company, he might have just gotten a slap on the wrist," especially after acknowledging he had erred in writing explicit e-mail on the company's computers, says Mr Brudno.

But Boeing had little choice but to oust Mr Stonecipher even after he acknowledged his mistake. The former CEO had been brought back from retirement 15 months ago to bolster ethical standards following a string of scandals at Boeing.

"One of the rules of doing business with Boeing's biggest customer—the government—is being discreet," says Mr Brudno.[1]

FOR DISCUSSION
Do you think a CEO should be fired for having an affair? Explain your rationale.

The chapter-opening vignette highlights the variety of characteristics that boards of directors associate with good leaders. Interestingly, the underlying traits preferred by boards are consistent with a number of leadership characteristics uncovered through academic research. For example, research shows that leaders have sound judgment, exhibit integrity, and deliver results.[2] The vignette also reinforces a conclusion we observed in Chapter 4. Specifically, perceptions of acceptable behavior at work are culturally bound. This is why boards in Europe, Latin America, and Asia have very different views of executives' extramarital affairs than boards in the United States. It thus is important to keep in mind the cross-cultural implications of the various theories of leadership discussed in this chapter.

Someone once observed that a leader is a person who finds out which way the parade is going, jumps in front of it, and yells "Follow me!" The plain fact is that this approach to leadership has little chance of working in today's rapidly changing world. In short, successful leaders are those individuals who can step into a difficult situation and make a noticeable difference. But how much of a difference can leaders make in modern organizations?

OB researchers have discovered that leaders can make a difference. One study, for instance, revealed that leadership was positively associated with net profits from 167 companies over a time span of 20 years.[3] Research also showed that a coach's leadership skills affected the success of his or her team. Specifically, teams in both Major League Baseball and college basketball won more games when players perceived the coach to be an effective leader.[4] Rest assured, leadership makes a difference.

After formally defining the term *leadership*, this chapter focuses on the following areas: (1) trait and behavioral approaches to leadership, (2) alternative situational theories of leadership, (3) the full-range theory of leadership, and (4) additional perspectives on leadership. Because there are many different leadership theories within each of these areas, it is impossible to discuss them all. This chapter reviews those theories with the most research support.

What Does Leadership Involve?

Because the topic of leadership has fascinated people for centuries, definitions abound. This section presents a definition of leadership, reviews the different approaches or perspectives used to study leadership, and highlights the similarities and differences between leading and managing.

Leadership Defined

Disagreement about the definition of leadership stems from the fact that it involves a complex interaction among the leader, the followers, and the situation. For example, some researchers define leadership in terms of personality and physical traits, while others believe leadership is represented by a set of prescribed behaviors. In contrast, other researchers define leadership in terms of the power relationship between leaders and followers. According to this perspective, leaders use their power to influence followers' behavior. Leadership also can be seen as an instrument of goal achievement. In other words, leaders are individuals who help others accomplish their goals. Still others view leadership from a skills perspective.

There are four commonalities among the many definitions of **leadership:** (1) leadership is a process between a leader and followers, (2) leadership involves social influence, (3) leadership occurs at multiple levels in an organization (at the individual level, for example, leadership involves mentoring, coaching, inspiring, and motivating; leaders also build teams, generate cohesion, and resolve conflicts at the group level; finally, leaders build culture and generate change at the organizational level),[5] and (4) leadership focuses on goal accomplishment.[6] Based on these commonalities, leadership is defined as "a process whereby an individual influences a group of individuals to achieve a common goal."[7]

Leadership
Process whereby an individual influences others to achieve a common goal.

Approaches to Leadership

Leadership is one of the most frequently investigated topics within the field OB due to its importance to all organizations. As such, there are several different approaches or perspectives that have guided leadership research. While the popularity of these approaches has changed over time, knowledge of each one provides you with a better understanding of how the leadership process unfolds.

This chapter examines the different leadership approaches outlined in Table 16–1. OB researchers began their study of leadership in the early part of the 20th century by focusing on the traits associated with leadership effectiveness. This perspective was followed by attempts in the 1950s and 1960s to examine the behaviors or styles exhibited by effective leaders. This research led to the realization that there is not one best style of leadership, which in turn spawned various contingency approaches to leadership in the 1960s and 70s. Contingency approaches focused on identifying the types of leadership behaviors that are most effective in different settings. The transformational approach is the most popular perspective for studying leadership today. Research based on this approach began in the early 1980s and adheres to the idea that leaders transform employees to pursue organizational goals through a variety of leader behaviors. Finally, there are several emerging perspectives that examine leadership from new or novel points of view.

Table 16–1   *Approaches to Studying Leadership*

1. **Trait Approaches**
   - Stogdill and Mann's five traits—intelligence, dominance, self-confidence, level of energy, and task-relevant knowledge
   - Leadership prototypes—intelligence, masculinity, and dominance
   - Kouzes and Posner's four traits—honesty, forward-looking, inspiring, and competent
   - Goleman—emotional intelligence
   - Judge and colleagues—two meta-analyses: importance of extraversion, conscientiousness, and openness; importance of personality over intelligence
   - Kellerman's bad traits—incompetent, rigid, intemperate, callous, corrupt, insular, and evil
2. **Behavioral Approaches**
   - Ohio State studies—two dimensions: initiating structure behavior and consideration behavior
   - University of Michigan studies—two leadership styles: job-centered and employee centered
3. **Contingency Approaches**
   - Fiedler's contingency model—task-oriented style and relationship-oriented style; and three dimensions of situational control: leader–member relations, task structure, and position power
   - House's path–goal revised theory—eight leadership behaviors clarify paths for followers' goals; and employee characteristics and environmental factors are contingency factors that influence the effectiveness of leadership behaviors
4. **Transformational Approach**
   - Bass and Avolio's four transformational leadership behaviors—inspirational motivation, idealized influence, indivualized consideration, and intellectual stimulation
   - Full-range theory of leadership—leadership varies along a continuum from laissez-faire leadership to transactional leadership to transformational leadership
5. **Emerging Approaches**
   - Leader–member exchange (LMX) model—dyadic relationships between leaders and followers is critical
   - Shared leadership—mutual influence process in which people share responsibility for leading
   - Collins Level 5 leadership—leader has humility plus fearless will to succeed, plus four other capabilities
   - Greenleaf's servant leadership—providing service to others not oneself
   - Role of followers in leadership process—followers manage the leader–follower relationship

SOURCE: Adapted from A Kinicki and B Williams, *Management: A Practical Introduction,* 2nd ed (Burr Ridge, IL: McGraw-Hill/Irwin, 2006), p 449. Reprinted by permission of The McGraw-Hill Companies, Inc.

You would not believe how many different theories exist for each of these perspectives. There are literally a dozen or two. Moreover, the number of leadership theories exponentially increases if we count those proposed by managerial consultants. Rather than overwhelm you with all these theories of leadership, we focus on the historical ones that have received the most research support. We also discuss emerging perspectives that appear to have academic and practical application in the future. That said, we created a special learning module that contains descriptions of several leadership theories that are not covered in this chapter (see Learning Module D on the Web site for this book).

Leading versus Managing

It is important to appreciate the difference between leadership and management to fully understand what leadership is all about. Bernard Bass, a leadership expert, concluded that "leaders manage and managers lead, but the two activities are not synonymous."[8] Bass tells us that although leadership and management overlap, each entails a unique set of activities or functions. Broadly speaking, managers typically perform functions associated with planning, investigating, organizing, and control, and leaders deal with the interpersonal aspects of a manager's job. Leaders inspire others, provide emotional support, and try to get employees to rally around a common goal. Leaders also play a key role in creating a vision and strategic plan for an organization. Managers, in turn, are charged with implementing the vision and strategic plan. Table 16–2 summarizes the key characteristics associated with being a leader and a manager.[9]

There are several conclusions to be drawn from the information presented in Table 16–2. First, good leaders are not necessarily good managers, and good managers are not necessarily good leaders. Second, effective leadership requires effective managerial skills at some level. For example, good managerial skills turn a leader's vision into actionable items and successful implementation. Both Lou Gerstener, former CEO of IBM, and Larry Bossidy, former CEO of Allied Signal, endorsed this conclusion by noting that effective

Table 16–2   *Characteristics of Being a Leader and a Manager*

Being a Leader Means	Being a Manager Means
Motivating, influencing, and changing behavior	Practicing stewardship, directing and being held accountable for resources
Inspiring, setting the tone, and articulating a vision	Executing plans, implementing, and delivering the goods and services
Managing people	Managing resources
Being charismatic	Being conscientious
Being visionary	Planning, organizing, directing, and controlling
Understanding and using power and influence	Understanding and using authority and responsibility
Acting decisively	Acting responsibly
Putting people first; the leader knows, responds to, and acts for his or her followers	Putting customers first; the manager knows, responds to, and acts for his or her customers
Leaders can make mistakes when 1. They choose the wrong goal, direction or inspiration, due to incompetence or bad intentions; or 2. They overlead; or 3. They are unable to deliver on, implement the vision due to incompetence or a lack of follow through commitment	Managers can make mistakes when 1. They fail to grasp the importance of people as the key resource; or 2. They underlead; they treat people like other resources, numbers; or 3. They are eager to direct and to control but are unwilling to accept accountability

SOURCE: Reprinted from P Lorenzi, "Managing for the Common Good: Prosocial Leadership," *Organizational Dynamics*, Vol. 33, No. 3, p 286, © 2004, with permission from Elsevier.

Best Buy Uses Multiple Programs to Develop Its Leaders

Best Buy uses several forums to develop its leaders. At the annual fall leadership meeting, leaders from across the company gather to learn about the needs of the company and its customers, and how key initiatives link to the company strategy. The meeting agenda includes personal storytelling, keynote speakers, video clips, and sessions that allow leaders to articulate a teachable point of view that they can use to engage their workforces.

The accelerated leadership program helps participants address organizational strategies and dilemmas while they develop leadership skills. . . . After identifying strategies and dilemmas, participants form teams of six to nine people and work on subsets of larger goals.

Best Buy CEO Brad Anderson sponsors another leadership initiative. This 15-month emerging leaders program

is designed to ensure that the company has the management talent and breadth of experience it needs. The CEO and other executive sponsors select about 30 participants from a pool of high-performing managers and directors. Participants then take a three-day course and choose real-world business projects to work on. Executives coach participants through the program.

Finally, the company offers a monthly Strategy Leadership Forum. Participants hear from guest speakers and thought leaders.

SOURCE: Excerpted from "Best Practice: Leadership Development," *Training: The Human Side of Business*, March 2005, p 70. Used by permission of VNO Business Publications via The Copyright Clearance Center.

implementation is a key driver of organizational success.[10] All told then, organizational success requires a combination of effective leadership and management. This in turn leads to the realization that today's leaders need to be effective at both leading and managing. While this may seem like a daunting task, the good news is that people can be taught to be more effective leaders and managers (see Real World/Real People).[11]

Trait and Behavioral Theories of Leadership

This section examines the two earliest approaches used to explain leadership. Trait theories focused on identifying the personal traits that differentiated leaders from followers. Behavioral theorists examined leadership from a different perspective. They tried to uncover the different kinds of leader behaviors that resulted in higher work group performance. Both approaches to leadership can teach current and future managers valuable lessons about leading.

Trait Theory

Leader trait
Personal characteristics that differentiate leaders from followers.

Trait theory is the successor to what was called the "great man" theory of leadership. This approach was based on the assumption that leaders such as Abraham Lincoln, Martin Luther King, or Jack Welch were born with some inborn ability to lead. In contrast, trait theorists believed that leadership traits were not innate but could be developed through experience and learning. A **leader trait** is a physical or personality characteristic that can be used to differentiate leaders from followers.

Before World War II, hundreds of studies were conducted to pinpoint the traits of successful leaders. Dozens of leadership traits were identified. During the postwar period, however, enthusiasm was replaced by widespread criticism. This section reviews a series of studies that provide a foundation for understanding leadership traits. We conclude by integrating results across the various studies and summarizing the practical recommendations of trait theory.

Stogdill's and Mann's Findings

Ralph Stogdill in 1948 and Richard Mann in 1959 sought to summarize the impact of traits on leadership. Based on his review, Stogdill concluded that five traits tended to differentiate leaders from average followers: (1) intelligence, (2) dominance, (3) self-confidence, (4) level of energy and activity, and (5) task-relevant knowledge. Among the seven categories of personality traits examined by Mann, intelligence was the best predictor of leadership.[12] Unfortunately, the overall pattern of research findings revealed that both Stogdill's and Mann's key traits did not accurately predict which individuals became leaders in organizations. People with these traits often remained followers.

Leadership Prototypes: Do They Matter?

Yes! A **leadership prototype** is a mental representation of the traits and behaviors that people believe are possessed by leaders. It is important to understand the content of leadership prototypes because we tend to perceive that someone is a leader when he or she exhibits traits or behaviors that are consistent with our prototypes (recall our discussion of encoding and simplification in Chapter 7).[13] Robert Lord and his colleagues attempted to identify employees' leadership prototypes by conducting a meta-analysis of past studies. Results demonstrated that people are perceived as leaders when they exhibit traits and behaviors associated with intelligence, masculinity, and dominance.[14] Another study of 6,052 middle-level managers from 22 European countries revealed that leadership prototypes are culturally based. In other words, leadership prototypes are influenced by national cultural values.[15] Researchers have not yet identified a set of global leadership prototypes.

Leadership prototype
Mental representation of the traits and behaviors possessed by leaders.

Kouzes and Posner's Research: Is Honesty the Most Critical Leadership Trait?

James Kouzes and Barry Posner attempted to identify key leadership traits by asking the following open-ended question to more than 20,000 people around the world: "What values (personal traits or characteristics) do you look for and admire in your superiors?" The top four traits included honesty, forward-looking, inspiring, and competent.[16] The researchers concluded that these four traits constitute a leader's credibility. This research suggests that people want their leaders to be credible and to have a sense of direction. Anne Mulcahy, CEO of Xerox, is a good example of a leader who possesses credibility. She is known for being honest with employees and external constituents (see Real World/Real People on page 514). *BusinessWeek* rated her as one of the best managers around the world in 2004.[17]

Goleman's Research on Emotional Intelligence

We discussed Daniel Goleman's research on emotional intelligence in Chapter 5. Recall that *emotional intelligence* is the ability to manage oneself and one's relationships in mature and constructive ways: The six components of emotional intelligence are shown in Table 5–5. Given that leadership is an influence process between leaders and followers, it should come as no surprise that emotional intelligence is associated with leadership effectiveness. "When I compared star performers with average ones in senior leadership positions," Goleman wrote, "nearly 90% of the difference in their profiles was attributable to emotional intelligence factors rather than cognitive abilities."[18]

Real World Real People

Anne Mulcahy Is a Credible Leader

In October 2000, five months after she took over as president of Xerox, Anne Mulcahy bluntly told Wall Street analysts that the company's business model was unsustainable. Her challenge, she said, was to radically restructure, abandon Xerox's reliance on its aging copier-machine business and stave off bankruptcy. Within hours, Xerox's stock fell 60%. "Some [Xerox] people had warned her that the market would react badly, but she wanted to be candid about the situation we were facing," says Christa Carone, a Xerox spokeswoman.

Ms Mulcahy also traveled to numerous Xerox sites to talk with employees. "She looked people in the eye and said, 'This is going to be one of the most stressful situations of your life, so if your heart isn't in it, please don't stay,'" says Ms Carone.

SOURCE: Excerpted from C Hymowitz, "Should CEOs Tell Truth about Being in Trouble, or Is That Foolhardy?" *The Wall Street Journal*, February 15, 2005, p B1.

Anne Mulcahy began her career with Xerox in 1976 as a field sales representative. Her talents were soon uncovered and she increasingly assumed more responsible positions. When she was named CEO in August 2001, she inherited a company that was experiencing its second consecutive year of losses and rumors of bankruptcy. Since then Xerox has prospered under Mulchahy's leadership. She believes that her success as a leader is driven by her commitment to meeting customers' expectations and developing and nurturing the workforce. Would you like to work for Anne Mulcahy?

Goleman and his colleagues later expanded on the role of emotional intelligence within a leadership context by noting that a leader's mood significantly influences the behavior of followers. "The leader's mood and behaviors drive the moods and behaviors of everyone else," they wrote. "A cranky and ruthless boss creates a toxic organization filled with negative underachievers who ignore opportunities; an inspirational inclusive leader spawns acolytes for whom any challenge is surmountable."[19] Goleman suggests that leaders with high emotional intelligence are more likely to display emotions and moods that are consistent with the situation at hand. For the time being you should interpret the above conclusion with caution. Future research is needed to confirm Goleman's ideas about the link between emotional intelligence and followers moods and performance.

Judge's Research: Is Personality More Important than Intelligence?
Tim Judge and his colleagues completed two meta-analyses that bear on the subject of traits and leadership. The first examined the relationship among the Big Five personality traits (see Table 5–2 for a review of these traits) and leadership emergence and effectiveness in 94 studies. Results revealed that extraversion was most consistently and positively related to both leadership emergence and effectiveness. Conscientiousness and openness to experience also were positively correlated with leadership effectiveness.[20]

Judge's second meta-analysis involved 151 samples and demonstrated that intelligence was modestly related to leadership effectiveness. Judge concluded that personality is more important than intelligence when selecting leaders.[21]

Kellerman's Research: What Traits Are Possessed by Bad Leaders?

Thus far we have been discussing traits associated with "good leadership." Barbara Kellerman believes this approach is limiting because it fails to recognize that "bad leadership" is related to "good leadership." It also ignores the valuable insights that are gained by examining ineffective leaders. Kellerman thus set out to study hundreds of contemporary cases involving bad leadership and bad followers in search of the traits possessed by bad leaders. Her qualitative analysis uncovered seven key traits:[22]

- *Incompetent.* The leader and at least some followers lack the will or skill (or both) to sustain effective action. With regard to at least one important leadership challenge, they do not create positive change.
- *Rigid.* The leader and at least some followers are stiff and unyielding. Although they may be competent, they are unable or unwilling to adapt to new ideas, new information, or changing times.
- *Intemperate.* The leader lacks self-control and is aided and abetted by followers who are unwilling or unable effectively to intervene.
- *Callous.* The leader and at least some followers are uncaring and unkind. Ignored or discounted are the needs, wants, and desires of most members of the group or organization, especially subordinates.
- *Corrupt.* The leader and at least some followers lie, cheat, or steal. To a degree that exceeds the norm, they put self-interest ahead of the public interest.
- *Insular.* The leader and at least some followers minimize or disregard the health and welfare of "the other," that is, those outside the group or organization for which they are directly responsible.
- *Evil.* The leader and at least some followers commit atrocities. They use pain as an instrument of power. The harm done to men, women, and children is severe rather than slight. The harm can be physical, psychological, or both.[23]

Do you know leaders who possess any of these traits? Unfortunately, there are many examples (see Real World/Real People on page 516). Which of these bad traits can you identify in the Real World/Real People example?

Gender and Leadership

The increase of women in the workforce has generated much interest in understanding the similarities and differences in female and male leaders. Three separate meta-analyses and a series of studies conducted by consultants across the country uncovered the following differences: (1) Men and women were seen as displaying more task and social leadership, respectively;[24] (2) women used a more democratic or participative style than men, and men used a more autocratic and directive style than women;[25] (3) men and women were equally assertive;[26] and (4) women executives, when rated by their peers, managers, and direct reports, scored higher than their male counterparts on a variety of effectiveness criteria.[27]

What Are the Takeaways from Trait Theory?

We can no longer afford to ignore the implications of leadership traits. Traits play a central role in how we perceive leaders, and they ultimately impact leadership effectiveness. What can be learned from the

How Would You Like to Work for These Managers?

Graig Stettner was always able to stay in the good graces of his former boss. But that didn't make her vindictiveness or ax-grinding any more appealing to him.

When he e-mailed some friends last week about their former tormentor, "the emotions that the mere mention of her name incited were amazing," he says. One colleague recalled that when she greeted the boss with a "good morning," she was told not to speak unless spoken to. "I don't like to chit-chat," the boss said. Another colleague, who had opposed the woman's promotion openly, was "let go." . . .

High-tech executive Paul Kedrosky also believes "the people who wrong-headedly promote these ragingly incompetent people and don't do anything about it" are the problem. He once had a sales manager who called weekly meetings, asked all the wrong questions, told his subordi-

nates they were idiots, and spent the rest of the week frantically making sales himself to cover for his "incompetent" staff. "We spent a great deal of time golfing," Mr Kedrosky says. "To my knowledge, [the man] was still in the job 10 years later, as bad as ever."

What goes around may come around, "but sometimes it's a very long trip," says Jon Morehouse. He once had a lousy supervisor who managed to keep his post by referring all questions from his staffers to people who knew the answers and by persuading his supervisors that the work his staff was doing was actually his.

SOURCE: Excerpted from J Sandberg, "When Affixing Blame for Inept Managers, Go over Their Heads," *The Wall Street Journal*, April 20, 2005, p B1. Reprinted by permission of Dow Jones & Co. Inc. via The Copyright Clearance Center.

Table 16–3   *Key Positive Leadership Traits*

Positive Traits	
Intelligence	Sociability
Self-confidence	Emotional intelligence
Determination	Extraversion
Honesty/integrity	Conscientiousness

previous research on traits? Integrating across past studies leads to the extended list of positive traits shown in Table 16–3. This list, along with the negative traits identified by Kellerman, provide guidance regarding the leadership traits you should attempt to cultivate if you want to assume a leadership role. Personality tests, which were discussed in Chapter 5, and other trait assessments can be used to evaluate your strengths and weaknesses vis-à-vis these traits. Results can then be used to prepare a personal development plan.[28] We encourage you to use an executive coach in this process.[29]

There are two organizational applications of trait theory. First, organizations may want to include personality and trait assessments into their selection and promotion processes. It is important to remember that this should only be done with valid measures of leadership traits. Second, management development programs can be used to enhance employees' leadership traits. Hasbro Inc., for example, sent a targeted group of managers to a program that included a combination of 360-degree feedback, trait assessments, executive coaching, classroom training, and problem-solving assignments on real-life projects. Hasbro is very excited and pleased with the results of their leadership development program.[30]

Behavioral Styles Theory

This phase of leadership research began during World War II as part of an effort to develop better military leaders. It was an outgrowth of two events: the seeming inability of trait theory to explain leadership effectiveness and the human relations movement, an outgrowth of the Hawthorne Studies. The thrust of early behavioral leadership theory was to focus on leader behavior, instead of on personality traits. It was believed that leader behavior directly affected work group effectiveness. This led researchers to identify patterns of behavior (called *leadership styles*) that enabled leaders to effectively influence others.

The Ohio State Studies

Researchers at Ohio State University began by generating a list of behaviors exhibited by leaders. At one point, the list contained 1,800 statements that described nine categories of leader behavior. Ultimately, the Ohio State researchers concluded there were only two independent dimensions of leader behavior: consideration and initiating structure. **Consideration** involves leader behavior associated with creating mutual respect or trust and focuses on a concern for group members' needs and desires. **Initiating structure** is leader behavior that organizes and defines what group members should be doing to maximize output. These two dimensions of leader behavior were oriented at right angles to yield four behavioral styles of leadership (see Figure 16–1).

It initially was hypothesized that a high-structure, high-consideration style would be the one best style of leadership. Through the years, the effectiveness of the high-high style has been tested many times.[31] Overall, results have been mixed and there has been very little research about these leader behaviors until just recently. Findings from a 2004 meta-analysis of 130 studies and more than 20,000 individuals demonstrated that consideration and initiating structure had a moderately strong, significant relationship with leadership outcomes. Results revealed that followers performed more effectively for structuring leaders even though they preferred considerate leaders.[32] All told, results do not support the idea that there is one best style of leadership, but they do confirm the importance of considerate and structuring leader behaviors. Follower satisfaction, motivation, and performance are

Consideration
Creating mutual respect and trust with followers.

Initiating structure
Organizing and defining what group members should be doing.

Figure 16–1   *Four Leadership Styles Derived from the Ohio State Studies*

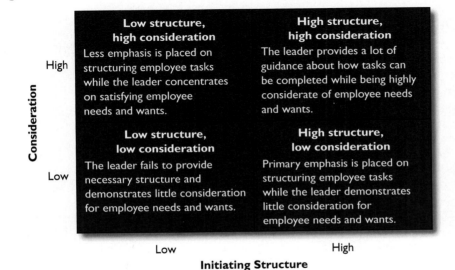

significantly associated with these two leader behaviors. Future research is needed to incorporate them into more contemporary leadership theories.

University of Michigan Studies
As in the Ohio State studies, this research sought to identify behavioral differences between effective and ineffective leaders. Researchers identified two different styles of leadership: one was employee centered, the other was job centered. These behavioral styles parallel the consideration and initiating-structure styles identified by the Ohio State group. In summarizing the results from these studies, one management expert concluded that effective leaders (1) tend to have supportive or employee-centered relationships with employees, (2) use group rather than individual methods of supervision, and (3) set high performance goals.[33]

What Are the Takeaways from Behavioral Styles Theory?
By emphasizing leader behavior, something that is learned, the behavioral style approach makes it clear that leaders are made, not born. This is the opposite of the trait theorists' traditional assumption. Given what we know about behavior shaping and model-based training, leader *behaviors* can be systematically improved and developed.

Behavioral styles research also revealed that there is no one best style of leadership. The effectiveness of a particular leadership style depends on the situation at hand. For instance, employees prefer structure over consideration when faced with role ambiguity.[34] Finally, research also reveals that it is important to consider the difference between how frequently and how effectively managers exhibit various leader behaviors. For example, a manager might ineffectively display a lot of considerate leader behaviors. Such a style is likely to frustrate employees and possibly result in lowered job satisfaction and performance. Because the frequency of exhibiting leadership behaviors is secondary in importance to effectiveness, managers are encouraged to concentrate on improving the effective execution of their leader behaviors.[35]

Finally, Peter Drucker, an internationally renowned management expert and consultant, recommended a set of nine behaviors (see Table 16–4) managers can focus on to improve

Table 16–4   *Peter Drucker's Tips for Improving Leadership Effectiveness*

1. Determine what needs to be done.
2. Determine the right thing to do for the welfare of the entire enterprise or organization.
3. Develop action plans that specify desired results, probable restraints, future revisions, check-in points, and implications for how one should spend his or her time.
4. Take responsibility for decisions.
5. Take responsibility for communicating action plans and give people the information they need to get the job done.
6. Focus on opportunities rather than problems. Do not sweep problems under the rug, and treat change as an opportunity rather than a threat.
7. Run productive meetings. Different types of meetings require different forms of preparation and different results. Prepare accordingly.
8. Think and say "we" rather than "I." Consider the needs and opportunities of the organization before thinking of your own opportunities and needs.
9. Listen first, speak last.

SOURCE: Reprinted by permission of *Harvard Business Review*. These recommendations were derived from P F Drucker, "What Makes an Effective Executive," *Harvard Business Review*, June 2004, pp 58–63. Copyright © 2004 by the Harvard Business School Publishing Corporation; all rights reserved.

their leadership effectiveness. The first two practices provide the knowledge leaders need. The next four help leaders convert knowledge into effective action, and the last two ensure that the whole organization feels responsible and accountable. Drucker refers to the last recommendation as a managerial rule.

Situational Theories

Situational leadership theories grew out of an attempt to explain the inconsistent findings about traits and styles. **Situational theories** propose that the effectiveness of a particular style of leader behavior depends on the situation. As situations change, different styles become appropriate. This directly challenges the idea of one best style of leadership. Let us closely examine two alternative situational theories of leadership that reject the notion of one best leadership style.

Situational theories
Propose that leader styles should match the situation at hand.

Fiedler's Contingency Model

Fred Fiedler, an OB scholar, developed a situational model of leadership. It is the oldest and one of the most widely known models of situational leadership. He labeled the model *contingency theory* because it is based on the premise that a leader's effectiveness is contingent on the extent to which a leader's style fits or matches characteristics of the situation at hand. To understand how this matching process works, we need to consider the key leadership styles identified by Fiedler and the situational variables that constitute what Fiedler labels *situational control*. We then review relevant research and managerial implications.[36]

Leadership Styles   Fiedler believes that leaders have one dominant or natural leadership style that is resistant to change. A leader's style is described as either task-motivated or relationship-motivated. Task-motivated leaders focus on accomplishing goals, whereas relationship-motivated leaders are more interested in developing positive relationships with followers. These basic styles are similar to initiating structure/concern for production and consideration/concern for people that were previously discussed. To determine an individual's leadership style, Fiedler developed the least preferred co-worker (LPC) scale. High scores on the survey (high LPC) indicate that an individual is relationship-motivated, and low scores (low LPC) suggest a task-motivated style.

Situational Control   Situational control refers to the amount of control and influence the leader has in her or his immediate work environment. Situational control ranges from high to low. High control implies that the leader's decisions will produce predictable results because the leader has the ability to influence work outcomes. Low control implies that the leader's decisions may not influence work outcomes because the leader has very little influence. There are three dimensions of situational control: leader–member relations, task structure, and position power. These dimensions vary independently, forming eight combinations of situational control (see Figure 16–2).

The three dimensions of situational control are defined as follows:

- **Leader–member relations** reflect the extent to which the leader has the support, loyalty, and trust of the work group. This dimension is the most important component of situational control. Good leader–member relations suggest that the leader can depend on the group, thus ensuring that the work group will try to meet the leader's goals and objectives.

Leader–member relations
Extent that leader has the support, loyalty, and trust of work group.

Task structure
Amount of structure contained within work tasks.

- **Task structure** is concerned with the amount of structure contained within tasks performed by the work group. For example, a managerial job contains less structure than that of a bank teller. Because structured tasks have guidelines for how the job should be completed, the leader has more control and influence over employees performing such tasks. This dimension is the second most important component of situational control.

Position power
Degree to which leader has formal power.

- **Position power** refers to the degree to which the leader has formal power to reward, punish, or otherwise obtain compliance from employees.[37]

Linking Leadership Motivation and Situational Control

Fiedler suggests that leaders must learn to manipulate or influence the leadership situation in order to create a match between their leadership style and the amount of control within the situation at hand. These contingency relationships are depicted in Figure 16–2. The last row under the Situational Control column shows that there are eight different leadership situations. Each situation represents a unique combination of leader–member relations, task structure, and position power. Situations I, II, and III represent high-control situations. Figure 16–2 shows that task-motivated leaders are hypothesized to be most effective in situations of high control. Under conditions of moderate control (situations IV, V, VI, and VII), relationship-motivated leaders are expected to be more effective. Finally, the results orientation of task-motivated leaders is predicted to be more effective under the condition of very low control (situation VIII).

Figure 16–2 *Representation of Fiedler's Contingency Model*

Situational Control	High-Control Situations			Moderate-Control Situations				Low-Control Situations
Leader-member relations	Good	Good	Good	Good	Poor	Poor	Poor	Poor
Task structure	High	High	Low	Low	High	High	Low	Low
Position power	Strong	Weak	Strong	Weak	Strong	Weak	Strong	Weak
Situation	I	II	III	IV	V	VI	VII	VIII
Optimal Leadership Style		Task-Motivated Leadership			Relationship-Motivated Leadership			Task-Motivated Leadership

SOURCE: Adapted from F E Fiedler, "Situational Control and a Dynamic Theory of Leadership," in *Managerial Control and Organizational Democracy*, eds B King, S Streufert, and F E Fiedler (New York: John Wiley & Sons, 1978), p 114.

Research and Managerial Implications   The first major criticism of contingency theory involves the LPC scale. Research shows that the validity and accuracy of this scale is highly suspect.[38] The second key criticism involves the fact that research does not clearly support predictions derived from the model. Consider findings from a meta-analysis containing 137 leader style–performance relations that were used to test the overall accuracy of Fiedler's contingency theory. According to the researchers' findings, (1) the contingency theory was correctly induced from studies on which it was based; (2) for laboratory studies testing the model, the theory was supported for all leadership situations except situation II; and (3) for field studies testing the model, three of the eight situations (IV, V, and VII) produced completely supportive results, and partial support was obtained for situations I, II, III, VI, and VIII. A more recent meta-analysis of data obtained from 1,282 groups also provided mixed support for the contingency model.[39] These findings suggest that Fiedler's model needs theoretical refinement.[40]

That said, the major contribution of Fiedler's model is that it prompted others to examine the contingency nature of leadership. This research, in turn, reinforced the notion that there is no one best style of leadership. Leaders are advised to alter their task and relationship orientation to fit the demands of the situation at hand. Consider, for example, the different leadership styles of IBM's current CEO—Sam Palmisano—and former CEO—Lou Gerstner:

> His aw-schucks nature, coupled with Palmisano's ability to chat up just about anyone he meets, makes him approachable for customers and employees.... He's constantly on the phone, calling all over the world: "How's your quarter?" "Did we close this deal?".... Software chief Steve Mills calls Palmisano an "execution maniac." ... This single-mindedness about results is a big reason Palmisano was selected by Gerstner to take over IBM two years ago. Says Merrill Lynch security analyst ... Steve Milunovich: "Sam is the right guy to run IBM right now. He's great externally and a hard-charging Marine internally."
>
> Palmisano's style is a big departure from that of the gruff and intimidating Gerstner. But then Gerstner's role wasn't to be nice; it was to keep IBM from disintegrating. He took over just as it was about to split itself up into 13 distinct, loosely affiliated entities.[41]

Sam Palmisano and Lou Gerstner used different leadership styles to successfully lead employees within IBM. As suggested by Fiedler, they both were effective because their respective leadership styles were appropriate for the situation at the time.

Path–Goal Theory

Path–goal theory was originally proposed by Robert House in the 1970s.[42] It was based on the expectancy theory of motivation discussed in Chapter 8. Recall that expectancy theory is based on the idea that motivation to exert effort increases as one's effort→performance→outcome expectations improve. Leader behaviors thus are expected to be acceptable when employees view them as a source of satisfaction or as paving the way to future satisfaction. In addition, leader behavior is predicted to be motivational to the extent it (1) reduces roadblocks that interfere with goal accomplishment, (2) provides the guidance and support needed by employees, and (3) ties meaningful rewards to goal accomplishment.

House proposed a model that describes how leadership effectiveness is influenced by the interaction between four leadership styles (directive, supportive, participative, and achievement-oriented) and a variety of contingency factors. **Contingency factors** are situational variables that cause one style of leadership to be more effective than another. Path–goal theory has two groups of contingency variables. They are employee characteristics and environmental factors. Five important employee characteristics are locus of control,

Contingency factors
Variables that influence the appropriateness of a leadership style.

task ability, need for achievement, experience, and need for clarity. Two relevant environmental factors are task structure (independent versus interdependent tasks) and work group dynamics. In order to gain a better understanding of how these contingency factors influence leadership effectiveness, we illustratively consider locus of control (see Chapter 5), task ability and experience, and task structure.

Employees with an internal locus control are more likely to prefer participative or achievement-oriented leadership because they believe they have control over the work environment. Such individuals are unlikely to be satisfied with directive leader behaviors that exert additional control over their activities. In contrast, employees with an external locus tend to view the environment as uncontrollable, thereby preferring the structure provided by supportive or directive leadership. An employee with high task ability and experience is less apt to need additional direction and thus would respond negatively to directive leadership. This person is more likely to be motivated and satisfied by participative and achievement-oriented leadership. Oppositely, an inexperienced employee would find achievement-oriented leadership overwhelming as he or she confronts challenges associated with learning a new job. Supportive and directive leadership would be helpful in this situation. Finally, directive and supportive leadership should help employees experiencing role ambiguity. However, directive leadership is likely to frustrate employees working on routine and simple tasks. Supportive leadership is most useful in this context.

There have been about 50 studies testing various predictions derived from House's original model. Results have been mixed, with some studies supporting the theory and others not.[43] House thus proposed a new version of path–goal theory in 1996 based on these results and the accumulation of new knowledge about OB.

A Reformulated Theory   The revised theory is presented in Figure 16–3.[44] There are three key changes in the new theory. First, House now believes that leadership is more complex and involves a greater variety of leader behavior. He thus identified eight categories of leadership styles or behavior (see Table 16–5). The need for an expanded list of leader behaviors is supported by current research and descriptions of business leaders.[45]

Figure 16–3   *A General Representation of House's Revised Path–Goal Theory*

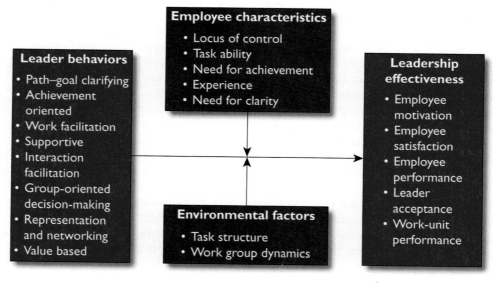

Table 16–5   *Categories of Leader Behavior within the Revised Path–Goal Theory*

Category of Leader Behavior	Description of Leader Behaviors
Path–goal clarifying behaviors	Clarifying employees' performance goals; providing guidance on how employees can complete tasks; clarifying performance standards and expectations; use of positive and negative rewards contingent on performance
Achievement-oriented behaviors	Setting challenging goals; emphasizing excellence; demonstrating confidence in employees' abilities
Work-facilitation behaviors	Planning, scheduling, organizing, and coordinating work; providing mentoring, coaching, counseling, and feedback to assist employees in developing their skills; eliminating roadblocks; providing resources; empowering employees to take actions and make decisions
Supportive behaviors	Showing concern for the well-being and needs of employees; being friendly and approachable; treating employees as equals
Interaction-facilitation behaviors	Resolving disputes; facilitating communication; encouraging the sharing of minority opinions; emphasizing collaboration and teamwork; encouraging close relationships among employees
Group-oriented decision-making behaviors	Posing problems rather than solutions to the work group; encouraging group members to participate in decision making; providing necessary information to the group for analysis; involving knowledgeable employees in decision making
Representation and networking behaviors	Presenting the work group in a positive light to others; maintaining positive relationships with influential others; participating in organizationwide social functions and ceremonies; doing unconditional favors for others
Value-based behaviors	Establishing a vision, displaying passion for it, and supporting its accomplishment; demonstrating self-confidence; communicating high performance expectations and confidence in others' abilities to meet their goals; giving frequent positive feedback

SOURCE: Descriptions were adapted from R J House, "Path–Goal Theory of Leadership: Lessons, Legacy, and a Reformulated Theory," *Leadership Quarterly*, 1996, pp 323–52.

Take a moment to read the Real World/Real People feature on page 524 and consider the different leadership behaviors exhibited by Sony Corp.'s president, Ryoji Chubachi. Mr Chubachi displayed achievement-oriented behaviors, work-facilitation behaviors, supportive behaviors, representation and networking behaviors, and value-based behaviors.

The second key change involves the role of intrinsic motivation (discussed in Chapter 9) and empowerment (discussed in Chapter 15) in influencing leadership effectiveness. House places much more emphasis on the need for leaders to foster intrinsic motivation through empowerment. Shared leadership represents the final change in the revised theory. That is, path–goal theory is based on the premise that an employee does not have to be a supervisor or manager to engage in leader behavior. Rather, House believes that leadership is shared among all employees within an organization. More is said about shared leadership in the final section of this chapter.

Research and Managerial Implications

There are not enough direct tests of House's revised path–goal theory using appropriate research methods and statistical procedures to draw overall conclusions. Future research is clearly needed to assess the accuracy of this model. That said, there are two important managerial implications. First, effective leaders possess and use more than one style of leadership. Managers are encouraged

Real World Real People

Sony's President, Ryoji Chubachi, Uses Multiple Leader Behaviors to Get the Job Done

In one of his first interviews after his appointment was announced earlier this month, Mr Chubachi said Sony must be prepared to take a knife to costs, as well as move more people and engineering resources out of less profitable areas and into high-growth products and promising new businesses. . . .

He said Sony must try to bolster profitability by improving the collaboration between the divisions that plan, manufacture and sell products. And Mr Chubachi wants to "reduce the layers" in the chain of command in Sony's electronics business—a sentiment shared by Mr Stringer.

People who have worked with Mr Chubachi say he's experienced at cutting costs and strict about hitting goals. . . .

Mr Chubachi said his leadership style is soft-spoken. "I'm a consensus-type leader. I'm not top-down," he said. "I believe the ability to communicate is the most important quality for a leader."

Engineers who've worked with Mr Chubachi say he's good at spotting talent and motivating younger workers, something that could be important in helping to build morale in the electronics group. And he can battle fiercely

SOURCE: Excerpted from P Dvorak, "Sony's Chubachi Sets His Sights on Cost Cutting," *The Wall Street Journal,* March 25, 2005, pp B1, B4. Reprinted by permission of Dow Jones & Co. Inc. via The Copyright Clearance Center.

for projects he believes in, said colleague Tatsuya Akashi, head of an online data-storage project Mr Chubachi successfully championed—in the face of opposition—in 2000. "He's excellent at balancing business goals without killing creativity," said Mr Akashi.

New Sony president and COO, Ryoji Chubachi (right) shakes hands with new Sony chairman and CEO Howard Stringer (left) at a news conference in Tokyo. Do you think that cross-cultural differences between Welsh-born Mr. Stringer, the company's first foreign CEO, and Mr. Chubachi will affect their working relationship?

to familiarize themselves with the different categories of leader behavior outlined in path–goal theory and to try new behaviors when the situation calls for them. Second, a small set of employee characteristics (i.e., ability, experience, and need for independence) and environmental factors (task characteristics of autonomy, variety, and significance) are relevant contingency factors.[46] Managers are advised to modify their leadership style to fit these various employee and task characteristics.

The Full-Range Theory of Leadership: From Laissez-Faire to Transformational Leadership

One of the most recent approaches to leadership is referred to as a *full-range theory of leadership.*[47] The authors of this theory, Bernard Bass and Bruce Avolio, proposed that leadership behavior varied along a continuum from laissez-faire leadership (i.e., a general failure to take responsibility for leading) to transactional leadership to transformational leadership.

Of course, laissez-faire leadership is a terrible way for any manager to behave and should be avoided. What gender do you think engages in more laissez-faire leadership? A meta-analysis revealed that men displayed more of this type of leadership than women.[48] It is important for organizations to identify managers who lead with this style and to train and develop them to use behaviors associated with transactional and transformational leadership. Both transactional and transformational are positively related to a variety of employee attitudes and behaviors and represent different aspects of being a good leader. Let us consider these two important dimensions of leadership.

Transactional leadership focuses on clarifying employees' role and task requirements and providing followers with positive and negative rewards contingent on performance. Further, transactional leadership encompasses the fundamental managerial activities of setting goals, monitoring progress toward goal achievement, and rewarding and punishing people for their level of goal accomplishment.[49] You can see from this description that transactional leadership is based on using extrinsic motivation (recall our discussion in Chapter 9) to increase employee productivity. Consider how Jim McNerney, chairman and CEO of 3M, uses transactional leadership to improve organizational performance.

> McNerney's secret to success is elementary. He sets high goals that can be measured, such as business-unit sales or the rate of product introductions, and demands that his managers meet them. Granted, many CEOs do that today. But like a dedicated teacher or coach, McNerney also works with his team day in, day out, to help them make the grade.[50]

In contrast, **transformational leaders** "engender trust, seek to develop leadership in others, exhibit self-sacrifice and serve as moral agents, focusing themselves and followers on objectives that transcend the more immediate needs of the work group."[51] Transformational leaders can produce significant organizational change and results because this form of leadership fosters higher levels of intrinsic motivation, trust, commitment, and loyalty from followers than does transactional leadership. That said, however, it is important to note that transactional leadership is an essential prerequisite to effective leadership and that the best leaders learn to display both transactional and transformational leadership to various degrees. In support of this proposition, research reveals that transformational leadership leads to superior performance when it augments or adds to transactional leadership.[52] Let us return to the example of Jim McNerney, CEO of 3M, to see how he augments transactional leadership with transformational leadership:

> "Some people think you either have a demanding, command-and-control management style or you have a nurturing, encouraging style," he says. "I believe you can't have one without the other." . . . McNerney is praised as an inspirational leader comfortable speaking to big groups or conversing one-on-one. . . . He is quick to attribute 3M's achievement to the entire organization and praises 3Mers for their work ethic. "My experience is that if people are convinced they're growing as they pursue company goals, that's when you get ignition," he says."[53]

We now turn our attention to examining the process by which transformational leadership influences followers.

How Does Transformational Leadership Transform Followers?

Transformational leaders transform followers by creating changes in their goals, values, needs, beliefs, and aspirations. They accomplish this transformation by appealing to followers' self-concepts—namely their values and personal identity. Figure 16–4 presents a model of how leaders accomplish this transformation process.

Transactional leadership
Focuses on clarifying employees' roles and providing rewards contingent on performance.

Transformational leadership
Transforms employees to pursue organizational goals over self-interests.

Figure 16–4 *A Transformational Model of Leadership*

SOURCE: Based in part on D A Waldman and F J Yammarino, "CEO Charismatic Leadership: Levels-of-Management and Levels-of-Analysis Effects," *Academy of Management Review*, April 1999, pp 266–85; and B Shamir, R J House, and M B Arthur, "The Motivational Effects of Charismatic Leadership: A Self-Concept Based Theory," *Organization Science*, November 1993, pp 577–94.

Figure 16–4 shows that transformational leader behavior is first influenced by various individual and organizational characteristics. For example, research reveals that transformational leaders tend to have personalities that are more extraverted, agreeable, and proactive and less neurotic than nontransformational leaders.[54] Female leaders also were found to use transformational leadership more than male leaders.[55] It is important to note, however, that the relationship between personality traits and transformational leadership is relatively weak. This suggests that transformational leadership is less traitlike and more susceptible to managerial influence. This conclusion reinforces the notion that an individual's life experiences play a role in developing transformational leadership and that transformational leadership can be learned.[56] Finally, Figure 16–4 shows that organizational culture influences the extent to which leaders are transformational. Cultures that are adaptive and flexible rather than rigid and bureaucratic are more likely to create environments that foster the opportunity for transformational leadership to be exhibited.

Transformational leaders engage in four key sets of leader behavior (see Figure 16–4).[57] The first set, referred to as *inspirational motivation*, involves establishing an attractive vision of the future, the use of emotional arguments, and exhibition of optimism and enthusiasm. A vision is "a realistic, credible, attractive future for your organization."[58] According to Burt Nanus, a leadership expert, the "right" vision unleashes human potential because it serves as a beacon of hope and common purpose. It does this by attracting commitment, energizing workers, creating meaning in employees' lives, establishing a standard of excellence, promoting high ideals, and bridging the gap between an organization's present problems and its future goals and aspirations. Ed Zander, Motorola's CEO, understands the importance of using a vision to energize his workforce. He has been talking to employees, customers, and suppliers in pursuit of information to create a vision for Motorola. He feels this is necessary because customers and employees told him that the company "does too many things—and not enough of them well."[59] A good vision will enable Zander to marshal the company's efforts and resources toward a common long-term goal.

The importance of inspirational motivation was highlighted in a recent survey of executives attending strategy and leadership courses at Columbia Business School's Executive Education Division: 61% of the respondents indicated that establishing an attractive vision was one of the three most important skills needed by today's executives. Unfortunately, 31% of these same respondents also stated that their organizations' did not have an effective vision.[60]

Idealized influence, the second set of leader behaviors, includes behaviors such as sacrificing for the good of the group, being a role model, and displaying high ethical standards. Through their actions, transformational leaders model the desired values, traits, beliefs, and behaviors needed to realize the vision. The third set, *individualized consideration,* entails behaviors associated with providing support, encouragement, empowerment, and coaching to employees. *Intellectual stimulation,* the fourth set of leadership behaviors, involves behaviors that encourage employees to question the status quo and to seek innovative and creative solutions to organizational problems.

Research and Managerial Implications

Components of the transformational model of leadership have been the most widely researched leadership topic over the last decade. Overall, the relationships outlined in Figure 16–4 generally were supported by previous research. For example, transformational leader behaviors were positively associated with the extent to which employees identified with both their leaders and immediate work groups.[61] Followers of transformational leaders also were found to set goals that were consistent with those of the leader, to be more engaged in their work, to have higher levels of intrinsic motivation, and to have higher levels of group cohesion.[62] With respect to the direct relationship between transformational leadership and work outcomes, a recent meta-analysis showed that transformational leadership was positively associated with followers' job satisfaction, satisfaction with the leader, and motivation. Transformational leadership also was positively related to group and organizational performance and measures of a leader's effectiveness.[63]

These results have four important managerial implications. First, the best leaders are not just transformational; they are both transactional and transformational, and they avoid a laissez-faire or "wait-and-see" style. This conclusion was reinforced by results from a recent meta-analysis. Findings demonstrated that transactional leadership was positively correlated with followers' job satisfaction, satisfaction with the leader, and motivation as well as group and organizational performance and measures of a leader's effectiveness. The opposite pattern was found for laissez-faire leadership.[64]

Second, transformational leadership not only affects individual-level outcomes like job satisfaction, organizational commitment, and performance, but it also influences group dynamics and group-level outcomes. Managers can thus use the four types of transformational leadership shown in Figure 16–4 as a vehicle to improve group dynamics and work-unit outcomes. This is important in today's organizations because most employees do not work in isolation. Rather, people tend to rely on the input and collaboration of others, and many organizations are structured around teams. The key point to remember is that transformational leadership transforms individuals as well as teams and work groups. We encourage you to use this to your advantage.

Third, employees at any level in an organization can be trained to be more transactional and transformational.[65] This reinforces the organizational value of developing and rolling out a combination of transactional and transformational leadership training for all employees. These programs, however, should be based on an overall corporate philosophy that constitutes the foundation of leadership development.

Fourth, transformational leaders can be ethical or unethical. Whereas ethical transformational leaders enable employees to enhance their self-concepts, unethical ones select or produce obedient, dependent, and compliant followers. Top management can create and maintain ethical transformational leadership by

1. Creating and enforcing a clearly stated code of ethics.
2. Recruiting, selecting, and promoting people who display ethical behavior.
3. Developing performance expectations around the treatment of employees—these expectations can then be assessed in the performance appraisal process.
4. Training employees to value diversity.
5. Identifying, rewarding, and publicly praising employees who exemplify high moral conduct.[66]

Additional Perspectives on Leadership

This section examines five additional perspectives on leadership: leader–member exchange theory, shared leadership, Level 5 leadership, servant-leadership, and a follower perspective.

The Leader–Member Exchange (LMX) Model of Leadership

The leader–member exchange model of leadership revolves around the development of dyadic relationships between managers and their direct reports. This model is quite different from those previously discussed in that it focuses on the quality of relationships between managers and subordinates as opposed to the behaviors or traits of either leaders or followers. It also is different in that it does not assume that leader behavior is characterized by a stable or average leadership style as do the previously discussed models. In other words, most models of leadership assume a leader treats all employees in about the same way. In contrast, the LMX model is based on the assumption that leaders develop unique one-to-one relationships with each of the people reporting to them. Behavioral scientists call this sort of relationship a *vertical dyad*. The forming of vertical dyads is said to be a naturally occurring process, resulting from the leader's attempt to delegate and assign work roles. As a result of this process, two distinct types of leader–member exchange relationships are expected to evolve.[67]

One type of leader–member exchange is called the **in-group exchange.** In this relationship, leaders and followers develop a partnership characterized by reciprocal influence, mutual trust, respect and liking, and a sense of common fates. In the second type of exchange, referred to as an **out-group exchange,** leaders are characterized as overseers who fail to create a sense of mutual trust, respect, or common fate.[68]

Research Findings   If the leader–member exchange model is correct, there should be a significant relationship between the type of leader–member exchange and job-related outcomes. Research supports this prediction. For example, a positive leader–member exchange was positively associated with job satisfaction, job performance, goal commitment, trust between managers and employees, work climate, and satisfaction with leadership.[69] The type of leader–member exchange also was found to predict not only turnover among

In-group exchange
A partnership characterized by mutual trust, respect, and liking.

Out-group exchange
A partnership characterized by a lack of mutual trust, respect, and liking.

OB Exercise — Assessing Your Leader–Member Exchange

Instructions

For each of the items shown below, use the following scale and circle the answer that best represents how you feel about the relationship between you and your current manager/supervisor. If you are not currently working, complete the survey by thinking about a previous manager. Remember, there are no right or wrong answers. After circling a response for each of the 12 items, use the scoring key to compute scores for the subdimensions within your leader–member exchange.

1 = strongly disagree
2 = disagree
3 = neither agree nor disagree
4 = agree
5 = strongly agree

1. I like my supervisor very much as a person.	1 — 2 — 3 — 4 — 5
2. My supervisor is the kind of person one would like to have as a friend.	1 — 2 — 3 — 4 — 5
3. My supervisor is a lot of fun to work with.	1 — 2 — 3 — 4 — 5
4. My supervisor defends my work actions to a superior, even without complete knowledge of the issue in question.	1 — 2 — 3 — 4 — 5
5. My supervisor would come to my defense if I were "attacked" by others.	1 — 2 — 3 — 4 — 5
6. My supervisor would defend me to others in the organization if I made an honest mistake.	1 — 2 — 3 — 4 — 5
7. I do work for my supervisor that goes beyond what is specified in my job description.	1 — 2 — 3 — 4 — 5
8. I am willing to apply extra efforts, beyond those normally required, to meet my supervisor's work goals.	1 — 2 — 3 — 4 — 5
9. I do not mind working my hardest for my supervisor.	1 — 2 — 3 — 4 — 5
10. I am impressed with my supervisor's knowledge of his/her job.	1 — 2 — 3 — 4 — 5
11. I respect my supervisor's knowledge of and competence on the job.	1 — 2 — 3 — 4 — 5
12. I admire my supervisor's professional skills.	1 — 2 — 3 — 4 — 5

Scoring Key

Mutual affection (add items 1–3) _____
Loyalty (add items 4–6) _____
Contribution to work activities (add items 7–9) _____
Professional respect (add items 10–12) _____
Overall score (add all 12 items) _____

Arbitrary Norms

Low mutual affection = 3–9
High mutual affection = 10–15
Low loyalty = 3–9
High loyalty = 10–15
Low contribution to work activities = 3–9
High contribution to work activities = 10–15
Low professional respect = 3–9
High professional respect = 10–15
Low overall leader–member exchange = 12–38
High overall leader–member exchange = 39–60

SOURCE: Survey items were taken from R C Liden and J M Maslyn, "Multidimensionality of Leader–Member Exchange: An Empirical Assessment through Scale Development," *Journal of Management*, 1998, p 56, copyright © 1998 by Sage Publications, Inc. Reprinted by permission of Sage Publications, Inc.

nurses and computer analysts but also career outcomes, such as promotability, salary level, and receipt of bonuses, over a seven-year period.[70] Finally, studies also have identified a variety of variables that influence the quality of an LMX. For example, LMX was related to personality similarity and demographic similarity.[71] Further, the quality of an LMX was positively related with the extent to which leaders and followers like each other, the leaders' positive expectations of their subordinates, and the frequency of communications between managers and their direct reports.[72]

Managerial Implications There are three important implications associated with the LMX model of leadership. First, leaders are encouraged to establish high-performance expectations for all of their direct reports because setting high-performance standards fosters high-quality LMXs. Second, because personality and demographic similarity between leaders and followers is associated with higher LMXs, managers need to be careful that they don't create a homogeneous work environment in the spirit of having positive relationships with their direct reports. Our discussion of diversity in Chapter 2 clearly documented that there are many positive benefits of having a diverse workforce. The third implication pertains to those of us who find ourselves in a poor LMX. Before providing advice about what to do in this situation, we would like you to assess the quality of your current leader–member exchange. The OB Exercise on page 529 contains a measure of leader–member exchange that segments an LMX into four subdimensions: mutual affection, loyalty, contribution to work activities, and professional respect.

What is the overall quality of your LMX? Do you agree with this assessment? Which subdimensions are high and low? If your overall LMX and associated subdimensions are all high, you should be in a very good situation with respect to the relationship between you and your manager. Having a low LMX overall score or a low dimensional score, however, reveals that part of the relationship with your manager may need improvement. A management consultant offers the following tips for improving the quality of leader–member exchanges.[73]

1. Stay focused on your department's goals and remain positive about your ability to accomplish your goals. An unsupportive boss is just another obstacle to be overcome.

2. Do not fall prey to feeling powerless, and empower yourself to get things done.

3. Exercise the power you have by focusing on circumstances you can control and avoid dwelling on circumstances you cannot control.

4. Work on improving your relationship with your manager. Begin by examining the level of trust between the two of you and then try to improve it by frequently and effectively communicating. You can also increase trust by following through on your commitments and achieving your goals.

5. Use an authentic, respectful, and assertive approach to resolve differences with your manager. It also is useful to use a problem-solving approach when disagreements arise.

Shared Leadership

A pair of OB scholars noted that "there is some speculation, and some preliminary evidence, to suggest that concentration of leadership in a single chain of command may be less optimal than shared leadership responsibility among two or more individuals in certain task environments."[74] This perspective is quite different from the previous theories and models discussed in this chapter, which assume that leadership is a vertical, downward-flowing process. In contrast, the notion of shared leadership is based on the idea that people need to share information and collaborate to get things done at work. This in turn underscores the need for employees to adopt a horizontal process of influence or leadership. **Shared leadership** entails a simultaneous, ongoing, mutual influence process in which individuals share responsibility for leading regardless of formal roles and titles. Mayo Clinic, which employs more than 42,000 employees in various hospitals and clinics around the United States, is an excellent example of an organization that relies on shared leadership to provide high-quality health care and customer service.[75] For Mayo, shared leadership is a matter of life or death (see Real World/Real People on page 531).

Shared leadership
Simultaneous, ongoing, mutual influence process in which people share responsibility for leading.

Shared Leadership Means Life or Death at Mayo Clinic

Not only does Mayo Clinic's core strategy of integrated, multispecialty medicine require teamwork; the complexity of the illnesses also compels the team approach. I asked one Mayo gastroenterologist how he copes with stress—after observing him on hospital service dealing with one complicated case after another. He replied: "I get a lot of input from my colleagues."

Mayo hires at the top of the talent pool, but it goes beyond talent and seeks team players. Its culture, strategy, and prestige require the right kind of talented people, people who view quality in medicine as a team endeavor. . . .

Mayo Clinic shuns the star system in favor of organizational achievement. Many excellent clinicians would not fit at Mayo, including those who prefer to work independently, covet personal acclaim, lack interpersonal competencies, or seek to maximize their income. Mayo is well known within the academic medicine community for what it is—and is not. Self-selection influences who works at Mayo. States a gastroenterologist:

> The Mayo culture attracts individuals who see the practice of medicine best delivered when there is an integration of medical specialties functioning as a team. It is what we do best, and most of us love to do it. What is most inspiring is when a case is successful because of the teamwork of a bunch of docs from different specialties; it has the same feeling as a homerun in baseball.

Medical professionals, such as those shown here, increasingly rely on shared leadership to provide high-quality care and service. Is shared leadership the best approach to providing better patient care?

SOURCE: Excerpted from L L Berry, "The Collaborative Organization: Leadership Lessons from Mayo Clinic," *Organizational Dynamics*, August 2004, pp 230–31, © 2004, with permission from Elsevier.

Shared leadership is most likely to be needed when people work in teams, when people are involved in complex projects, and when people are doing knowledge work—work that requires voluntary contributions of intellectual capital by skilled professionals. Shared leadership also is beneficial when people are working on tasks or projects that require interdependence and creativity.[76] Despite these recommendations, it is important to remember that people vary in the preference for shared leadership. Some of these differences are culturally based (recall our discussion in Chapter 4). For example, we conducted a consulting project with a manufacturing company in Portugal and realized that many employees preferred a directive rather than collaborative approach toward decision making and leadership. As exemplified by the doctors who work at Mayo Clinic, employees are more likely to enjoy and be satisfied by shared leadership when they prefer to work with others as opposed to working alone as single contributors.[77]

Researchers are just now beginning to explore the process of shared leadership, and results are promising. For example, shared leadership in teams was positively associated with group cohesion, group citizenship, and group effectiveness.[78] Table 16–6 contains a list of key questions and answers that managers should consider when determining how they can develop shared leadership.

Table 16–6   *Key Questions and Answers to Consider When Developing Shared Leadership*

Key Questions	Answers
What task characteristics call for shared leadership?	Tasks that are highly *interdependent.* Tasks that require a great deal of *creativity.* Tasks that are highly *complex.*
What is the role of the leader in developing shared leadership?	*Designing the team,* including clarifying purpose, securing resources, articulating vision, selecting members, and defining team processes. *Managing the boundaries* of the team.
How can organizational systems facilitate the development of shared leadership?	*Training and development systems* can be used to prepare both designated leaders and team members to engage in shared leadership. *Reward systems* can be used to promote and reward shared leadership. *Cultural systems* can be used to articulate and to demonstrate the value of shared leadership.
What vertical and shared leadership behaviors are important to team outcomes?	*Directive leadership* can provide task-focused directions. *Transactional leadership* can provide both personal and material rewards based on key performance metrics. *Transformational leadership* can stimulate commitment to a team vision, emotional engagement, and fulfillment of higher-order needs. *Empowering leadership* can reinforce the importance of self-motivation.
What are the ongoing responsibilities of the vertical leader?	The vertical leader needs to be able to step in and *fill voids* in the team. The vertical leader needs to continue to *emphasize the importance of the shared leadership approach,* given the task characteristics facing the team.

SOURCE: C L Pearce, "The Future of Leadership: Combining Vertical and Shared Leadership to Transform Knowledge Work," *Academy of Management Executive: The Thinking Manager's Source,* February 2004, p 48. Copyright 2004 by The Academy of Management. Reprinted by permission of The Academy of Management via The Copyright Clearance Center.

Level 5 Leadership

This model of leadership was not derived from any particular theory or model of leadership. Rather, it was developed from a longitudinal research study attempting to answer the following question: Can a good company become a great company and, if so, how? The study was conducted by a research team headed by Jim Collins, a former university professor who started his own research-based consulting company. He summarized his work in the best seller *Good to Great.*[79]

To answer the research question, Collins identified a set of companies that shifted from good performance to great performance. Great performance was defined as "cumulative stock returns at or below the general stock market for 15 years, punctuated by a transition point, then cumulative returns at least three times the market over the next 15 years."[80] Beginning with a sample of 1,435 companies on the *Fortune* 500 from 1965 to 1995, he identified 11 good-to-great companies: Abbot, Circuit City, Fannie Mae, Gillette, Kimberly-Clark, Kroger, Nucor, Philip Morris, Pitney Bowes, Walgreens, and Wells Fargo. His next step was to compare these 11 companies with a targeted set of direct-comparison companies. This comparison enabled him to uncover the drivers of good-to-great transformations. One of the key drivers was called Level 5 leadership (see Figure 16–5). In other words, every company that experienced good-to-great performance was led by an individual possessing the characteristics associated with Level 5 leadership. Let us consider this leadership hierarchy.

Figure 16–5   *The Level 5 Hierarchy*

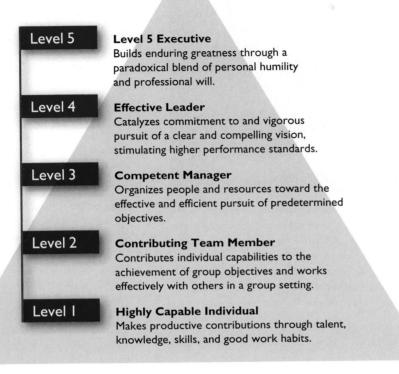

Level 5 Executive
Builds enduring greatness through a paradoxical blend of personal humility and professional will.

Level 4   Effective Leader
Catalyzes commitment to and vigorous pursuit of a clear and compelling vision, stimulating higher performance standards.

Level 3   Competent Manager
Organizes people and resources toward the effective and efficient pursuit of predetermined objectives.

Level 2   Contributing Team Member
Contributes individual capabilities to the achievement of group objectives and works effectively with others in a group setting.

Level 1   Highly Capable Individual
Makes productive contributions through talent, knowledge, skills, and good work habits.

SOURCE: Figure from J Collins, *Good to Great: Why Some Companies Make the Leap and Others Don't.* Copyright © 2001 by J Collins. Used by permission of the author.

Figure 16–5 reveals that a Level 5 leader possesses the characteristics of humility and a fearless will to succeed. American president Abraham Lincoln is an example of such an individual. Although he was soft-spoken and shy, he possessed great will to accomplish his goal of uniting his country during the Civil War in the 1860s. This determination resulted in the loss of 250,000 Confederates, 360,000 Union soldiers, and ultimately to a united country. Being humble and determined, however, was not enough for Lincoln to succeed at his quest. Rather, a Level 5 leader must also possess the capabilities associated with the other levels in the hierarchy. Although an individual does not move up the hierarchy in a stair-step fashion, a Level 5 leader must possess the capabilities contained in Levels 1–4 before he or she can use the Level 5 characteristics to transform an organization.

It is important to note the overlap between the capabilities represented in this model and the previous leadership theories discussed in this chapter. For example, Levels 1 and 2 are consistent with research on trait theory. Trait research tells us that leaders are intelligent, self-confident, determined, honest, sociable, emotionally intelligent, extroverted, and conscientious. Levels 3 and 4 also seem to contain behaviors associates with transactional and transformational leadership. Level 5 leadership thus appears to integrate components of trait theory and the full-range theory of leadership. The novel and unexpected component of this theory revolves around the conclusion that good-to-great leaders are not only transactional

Michael Dell (behind and to the left of the students) is a classic entrepreneur. He started his first computer company called PC's Limited in his dormitory room at the University of Texas at Austin with $1,000 and a new idea for assembling and selling computers. Dell's accomplishments include "Entrepreneur of the Year" from *Inc.* magazine, "Man of the Year" from *PC Magazine,* and "CEO of the Year" from *Financial World* and *Industry Week* magazines. Michael Dell still displays the humility associated with a Level 5 leader despite his vast achievements.

and transformational, but most important, they possess the traits of humility and determination. Michael Dell, chairman of Dell, is a good example of someone who is humble and driven. Here is what Dell had to say to a reporter from *Fortune* after being informed that his company was named America's Most Admired Company in 2005.

"I know my mom would be proud, but I certainly don't feel like we're the most admired company," he says. "I would be relatively dismissive of that kind of thing and say, 'Well that's really nice, thank you very much. I'm humbled by that, but we've got a lot of work to do.'"[81]

There are three points to keep in mind about Level 5 leadership. First, Collins notes that there are additional drivers for taking a company from good to great other than being a Level 5 leader.[82] Level 5 leadership enables the implementation of these additional drivers. Second, to date there has not been any additional research testing Collins's conclusions. Future research is clearly needed to confirm the Level 5 hierarchy. Finally, Collins believes that some people will never become Level 5 leaders because their narcissistic and boastful tendencies do not allow them to subdue their own ego and needs for the greater good of others.

Servant-Leadership

Servant-leadership

Focuses on increased service to others rather than to oneself.

Servant-leadership is more a philosophy of managing than a testable theory. The term *servant-leadership* was coined by Robert Greenleaf in 1970. Greenleaf believes that great leaders act as servants, putting the needs of others, including employees, customers, and community, as their first priority. **Servant-leadership** focuses on increased service to others rather than to oneself.[83] Because the focus of servant-leadership is serving others over self-interest, servant-leaders are less likely to engage in self-serving behaviors that hurt others (e.g., stockholders and employees).

More and more companies are trying to instill a philosophy of servant-leadership into their organizational cultures. Consider how TDI Industries is attempting to embed servant-leadership into its culture:

> A major player in the high-turnover construction industry, TDI's workforce is a loyal lot: 368 of the company's 1,413 employees have been with the Dallas-based company for more than five years, and more than 85 have been there for at least 20 years.
>
> Why? Because of TDI's commitment to the personal and professional development of each employee, which is best illustrated in the company's "People Objective." This objective promises to ensure that employees will succeed as a "total person," grow with the company, and feel important. Through extensive personal and professional training programs, TDI cultivates well-rounded employees, while simultaneously enhancing its bottom line.

For TDI, creating an environment that promotes longevity begins with the concept of servant leadership. Based on Robert Greenleaf's Servant as Leader theory, the philosophy—in which managers (servants) cultivate employees (leaders) by serving and meeting the needs of others—lies at the heart of nearly all business functions.

To keep servant-leadership central to TDI's corporate culture, new employees are assigned to servant-leadership discussion groups, which meet weekly for six weeks to discuss particular elements of servant-leadership and how to apply the concept to all areas of their particular job. Additionally, TDI's employees who supervise at least one person must go through more extensive servant-leadership training at TDI's Leadership Institute.[84]

This example illustrates that it takes more than words to embed servant-leadership into an organization's culture. Servant-leadership must be reinforced through organizational structure, systems, and rewards for it take hold. At the individual level, however, managers also need to commit to a set of behaviors underlying servant-leadership.

According to Jim Stuart, co-founder of the leadership circle in Tampa, Florida, "Leadership derives naturally from a commitment to service. You know that you're practicing servant-leadership if your followers become wiser, healthier, more autonomous—and more likely to become servant-leaders themselves."[85] Servant-leadership is not a quick-fix approach to leadership. Rather, it is a long-term, transformational approach to life and work. Table 16–7 presents 10 characteristics possessed by servant-leaders. One can hardly go wrong by trying to adopt these characteristics.

Table 16–7   *Characteristics of the Servant-Leader*

Servant-Leadership Characteristics	Description
1. Listening	Servant-leaders focus on listening to identify and clarify the needs and desires of a group.
2. Empathy	Servant-leaders try to empathize with others' feelings and emotions. An individual's good intentions are assumed even when he or she performs poorly.
3. Healing	Servant-leaders strive to make themselves and others whole in the face of failure or suffering.
4. Awareness	Servant-leaders are very self-aware of their strengths and limitations.
5. Persuasion	Servant-leaders rely more on persuasion than positional authority when making decisions and trying to influence others.
6. Conceptualization	Servant leaders take the time and effort to develop broader based conceptual thinking. Servant-leaders seek an appropriate balance between a short-term, day-to-day focus and a long-term, conceptual orientation.
7. Foresight	Servant-leaders have the ability to foresee future outcomes associated with a current course of action or situation.
8. Stewardship	Servant-leaders assume that they are stewards of the people and resources they manage.
9. Commitment to the growth of people	Servant-leaders are committed to people beyond their immediate work role. They commit to fostering an environment that encourages personal, professional, and spiritual growth.
10. Building community	Servant-leaders strive to create a sense of community both within and outside the work organization.

SOURCE: These characteristics and descriptions were derived from L C Spears, "Introduction: Servant-Leadership and the Greenleaf Legacy," in *Reflections on Leadership: How Robert K Greenleaf's Theory of Servant-Leadership Influenced Today's Top Management Thinkers*, ed L C Spears (New York: John Wiley & Sons, 1995), pp 1–14.

The Role of Followers in the Leadership Process

All of the previous theories discussed in this chapter have been leader-centric. That is, they focused on understanding leadership effectiveness from the leader's point of view. We conclude this chapter by discussing the role of followers in the leadership process. Although very little research has been devoted to this topic, it is an important issue to consider because the success of both leaders and followers is contingent on the dynamic relationship among the people involved.[86]

We begin our discussion by noting that both leaders and followers own the quality of their mutual relationship. If something is wrong with the relationship, one or the other needs to intervene. Poor relationships between leaders and followers are frequently caused by unmet expectations—recall our discussion of job satisfaction in Chapter 8. Let us thus consider the nature of leaders' and employees' expectations.

Leaders want followers to be productive, reliable, honest, cooperative, proactive, and flexible.[87] Leaders do not benefit from followers who hide the truth, withhold information, collude against them, or provide inaccurate feedback.[88] In contrast, research shows that followers seek, admire, and respect leaders who foster three emotional responses in others: Followers want organizational leaders to create feelings of *significance* (what one does at work is important and meaningful), *community* (a sense of unity encourages people to treat others with respect and dignity and to work together in pursuit of organizational goals), and *excitement* (people are engaged and feel energy at work).[89] What then can followers do to enhance the achievement of these mutual expectations?

A pair of OB experts developed a four step process for followers to use in managing the leader–follower relationship.[90] First, it is critical for followers to understand their boss. Followers should attempt to gain an appreciation for their manager's leadership style, interpersonal style, goals, expectations, pressures, and strengths and weaknesses. Second, followers need to understand their own style, needs, goals, expectations, and strengths and weaknesses.[91] The next step entails conducting a gap analysis between the understanding a follower has about his or her boss and the understanding the follower has about him- or herself. With this information in mind, followers are ready to proceed to the final step of developing and maintaining a relationship that fits both parties' needs and styles.

This final step requires followers to build on mutual strengths and to adjust or accommodate the leader's divergent style, goals, expectations, and weaknesses.[92] For example, a follower might adjust his or her style of communication in response to the boss's preferred method for receiving information. Other adjustments might be made in terms of decision making. If the boss prefers a participative approach, then followers should attempt to involve their manager in all decisions regardless of the follower's decision-making style—recall our discussion of decision-making styles in Chapter 12. Good use of time and resources is another issue for followers to consider. Most managers are pushed for time, energy, and resources and are more likely to appreciate followers who save rather than cost them time and energy. Followers should not use up their manager's time discussing trivial matters.

There are two final issues to consider. First, a follower may not be able to accommodate a leader's style, expectations, or weaknesses and may have to seek a transfer or quit his or her job to reconcile the discrepancy. We recognize that there are personal and ethical trade-offs that one may not be willing to make when managing the leader–follower relationship. Second, we can all enhance our boss's leadership effectiveness and our employer's success by becoming better followers. Remember, it is in an individual's best interest to be a good follower because leaders need and want competent employees.

Summary of Key Concepts

1. *Define the term* leadership, *and explain the difference between leading versus managing.* Leadership is defined as a process in which an individual influences a group of individuals to achieve a common goal. Although leadership and management overlap, each entails a unique set of activities or functions. Managers typically perform functions associated with planning, investigating, organizing, and control, and leaders deal with the interpersonal aspects of a manager's job. Table 16–2 summarizes the differences between leading and managing. All told, organizational success requires a combination of effective leadership and management.

2. *Review trait theory research and the takeaways from this theoretical perspective.* Historical leadership research did not support the notion that effective leaders possessed unique traits from followers. More recent research showed that effective leaders possessed the following traits: intelligence, self-confidence, determination, honesty/integrity, sociability, emotional intelligence, extraversion, and conscientiousness. In contrast, bad leaders displayed the following characteristics: incompetence, rigid, intemperate, callous, corrupt, insular, and evil. Research also demonstrated that men and women exhibited different styles of leadership. The takeaways from trait theory are that (*a*) we can no longer ignore the implications of leadership traits; traits influence leadership effectiveness; (*b*) organizations may want to include personality and trait assessments into their selection and promotion processes; and (*c*) management development programs can be used to enhance employees' leadership traits.

3. *Explain behavioral styles theory and its takeaways.* The thrust of behavioral styles theory is to identify the leader behaviors that directly affect work-group effectiveness. Researchers at Ohio State uncovered two key leadership behaviors: consideration and initiating structure. These behaviors are similar to the employee-centered and job-centered behaviors uncovered by researchers at the University of Michigan. The takeaways from this theoretical perspective are as follows: (*a*) leaders are made, not born; (*b*) there is no one best style of leadership; (*c*) the effectiveness of a particular style depends on the situation at hand; and (*d*) managers are encouraged to concentrate on improving the effective execution of their leader behaviors.

4. *Explain, according to Fiedler's contingency model, how leadership style interacts with situational control.* Fiedler believes leader effectiveness depends on an appropriate match between leadership style and situational control. Leaders are either task motivated or relationship motivated. Situation control is composed of leader–member relations, task structure, and position power. Task-motivated leaders are effective under situations of both high and low control. Relationship-motivated leaders are more effective when they have moderate situational control.

5. *Discuss House's revised path–goal theory.* There are three key changes in the revised path–goal theory. Leaders now are viewed as exhibiting eight categories of leader behavior (see Table 16–5) instead of four. In turn, the effectiveness of these styles depends on various employee characteristics and environmental factors. Second, leaders are expected to spend more effort fostering intrinsic motivation through empowerment. Third, leadership is not limited to people in managerial roles. Rather, leadership is shared among all employees within an organization.

6. *Describe the difference between laissez-fair, transactional, and transformational leadership.* Laissez-faire leadership is the absence of leadership. It represent a general failure to take responsibility for leading. Transactional leadership focuses on clarifying employees' role and task requirements and providing followers with positive and negative rewards contingent on performance. Transformational leaders motivate employees to pursue organizational goals above their own self-interests. Transactional and transformational leadership are both important for organizational success.

7. *Discuss how transformational leadership transforms followers and work groups.* Individual characteristics and organizational culture are key precursors of transformational leadership, which is comprised of four sets of leader behavior. These leader behaviors in turn positively affect followers' and work-group goals, values, beliefs, aspirations, and motivation. These positive effects are then associated with a host of preferred outcomes.

8. *Explain the leader–member exchange (LMX) model of leadership and the concept of shared leadership.* The LMX model revolves around the development of dyadic relationships between managers and their direct reports. These leader–member exchanges qualify as either in-group or out-group relationships. Research supports this model of leadership. Shared leadership involves a simultaneous, ongoing, mutual influence process in which individuals share responsibility for leading regardless of formal roles and titles. This type of leadership is most likely to be needed when people work in teams, when people are involved in complex projects, and when people are doing knowledge work. Shared leadership also is beneficial when people are working on tasks or projects that require interdependence and creativity.

9. *Review the Level 5 model of leadership and the principles of servant-leadership.* Level 5 leadership represents a hierarchy of leadership capabilities that are needed to lead companies in transforming from good to great. Servant-leadership is more a philosophy than a testable theory. It is based on the premise that great leaders act as servants, putting the needs of others, including employees, customers, and community, as their first priority.

10. *Describe the follower's role in the leadership process.* Followers can use a four-step process for managing the leader–follower relationship. Followers need to understand their boss and themselves. They then conduct a gap analysis between the understanding they have about their boss and themselves. The final step requires followers to build on mutual strengths and to adjust or accommodate the leader's divergent style, goals, expectations, and weaknesses.

Discussion Questions

1. Is everyone cut out to be a leader? Explain.

2. Has your college education helped you develop any of the traits that characterize leaders? Explain.

3. Should organizations change anything in response to research pertaining to gender and leadership? If yes, describe your recommendations.

4. What leadership traits and behavioral styles are possessed by the President of the United States?

5. Does it make more sense to change a person's leadership style or the situation? How would Fred Fiedler and Robert House answer this question?

6. Describe how a professional coach in any sport might use House's revised path–goal theory to clarify players' path–goal perceptions.

7. Identify three transformational leaders, and describe their leadership traits and behavioral styles.

8. Have you ever worked for a transformational leader? Describe how he or she transformed followers.

9. Have you ever been a member of an in-group or out-group? For either situation, describe the pattern of interaction between you and your manager.

10. In your view, which leadership theory has the greatest practical application? Why?

OB in Action Case Study

Leadership Lessons from CEOs at Hewlett-Packard, Procter & Gamble, United Technologies, and IBM[93]

Carleton S Fiorina faced a daunting task when she took over as CEO of Hewlett-Packard Co. in 1999. She was an outsider brought in to revive a troubled tech giant. Iconic though HP was, its deeply rooted engineering culture was badly in need of an overhaul. Her failure to achieve her goals was a fiasco that reflected the quirks of both Fiorina as an executive and HP's corporate milieu. So are there any lessons here about how to handle the job of shaking up a company or its business model? Certainly, it is difficult to generalize—every CEO has his or her own style, every company has its own culture. But Fiorina broke three key rules that most CEOs would do well to heed.

Make It about the Company, Not You

By the time CEOs rise to their post, most have a healthy ego, and Fiorina was no exception. She was also a sales whiz known for high-profile marketing events and a fondness for global gatherings packed with A-list politicians, celebs and

CEOs. Problem is, many who spent time around her came away with the impression that she was as interested in burnishing her own image as she was in turning the company around. As Jim Collins noted in his 2001 book, *Good to Great: Why Some Companies Make the Leap . . . and Others Don't,* the defining hallmark of market-beating long-term leadership is the exact opposite—CEOs who place their companies' well-being above all else, including themselves.

Nowhere has that difference been starker than at Procter & Gamble Co., which has seen both kinds of leaders over the last decade. Durk I Jager sought to shake up P&G's insular culture and jump-start innovation when he took over the helm in 1999, but his abrasive nature and insistence on rapid change alienated the troops. Under Alan G "AG" Lafley, who also has a broad agenda but a less contentious and more patient style, P&G has made a comeback. Lafley also has no qualms about letting others take credit for success—a critical trait for enlisting subordinates to your cause.

Know Your Company Inside and Out

As skilled an executive as she was, Fiorina focused on marketing and didn't fully comprehend the impact on operations of her vision to transform HP's structure and strategy. She also resisted board efforts to name a strong chief operations officer to compensate for that weakness. As difficult as it is, successful CEOs must immerse themselves in the details of their empires—or have a sidekick who does.

United Technologies Corp.'s George David is no backslapper and lacks Fiorina's marketing flair. But he is obsessed with the minutiae of production techniques that can make or break his company—and has quietly amassed an extraordinary record: 10 straight years of higher profits.

General Electric Co. under Jack Welch was likewise a study in total management immersion. Talent, in particular, was a Welch obsession. He participated in hundreds of executive evaluations each year. If one slipped, he was among the first to know it, not the last.

Hold People Accountable—Including Yourself

Fiorina's decision to fire three top executives after the company missed third-quarter earnings targets last year went down poorly. Many inside the company thought it looked more like scapegoating and a way to assuage Wall Street than good management.

Contrast that with the dismissals Louis V Gerstner Jr made after coming to IBM in 1993. The first item on his agenda was to learn everything he could about the troubled tech giant's business, staff, and customers. So when it came time to hand out pink slips, workers had confidence that the cuts were necessary and that the right people were being fired for the right reasons.

Much of this sounds obvious, the sort of thing any executive should know by the time he or she reaches the corner office. What's surprising is how many of them don't.

Questions for Discussion

1. Use Table 16–2 to evaluate the extent to which Carly Fiorina displayed the characteristics associated with being a good leader and good manager.

2. Which different positive and negative leadership traits and styles were displayed by Fiorina, Alan Lafley, George David, Jack Welch, and Louis Gerstner? Cite examples.

3. To what extent were Fiorina's problems a function of too little transactional or transformational leadership? Explain.

4. To what extent are the different styles of Fiorina, Lafley, David, and Gerstner consistent with research regarding gender and leadership? Discuss your rationale.

5. What did you learn about leadership from this case? Use examples to reinforce your conclusions.

Personal Awareness and Growth Exercise

How Ready Are You to Assume the Leadership Role?

Objectives

1. To assess your readiness for the leadership role.
2. To consider the implications of the gap between your career goals and your readiness to lead.

Introduction

Leaders assume multiple roles. Roles represent the expectations that others have of occupants of a position. It is important for potential leaders to consider whether they are ready for the leadership role because mismatches in expectations or skills can derail a leader's effectiveness. This exercise assesses your readiness to assume the leadership role.[94]

Instructions

For each statement, indicate the extent to which you agree or disagree with it by selecting one number from the scale provided. Circle your response for each statement. Remember, there are no right or wrong answers. After completing the survey, add your total score for the 20 items, and record it in the space provided.

1 = strongly disagree
2 = disagree
3 = neither agree nor disagree
4 = agree
5 = strongly agree

1. It is enjoyable having people count on me for ideas and suggestions.	1 — 2 — 3 — 4 — 5
2. It would be accurate to say that I have inspired other people.	1 — 2 — 3 — 4 — 5
3. It's a good practice to ask people provocative questions about their work.	1 — 2 — 3 — 4 — 5
4. It's easy for me to compliment others.	1 — 2 — 3 — 4 — 5
5. I like to cheer people up even when my own spirits are down.	1 — 2 — 3 — 4 — 5

6. What my team accomplishes is more important than my personal glory.   1 — 2 — 3 — 4 — 5
7. Many people imitate my ideas.   1 — 2 — 3 — 4 — 5
8. Building team spirit is important to me.   1 — 2 — 3 — 4 — 5
9. I would enjoy coaching other members of the team.   1 — 2 — 3 — 4 — 5
10. It is important to me to recognize others for their accomplishments.   1 — 2 — 3 — 4 — 5
11. I would enjoy entertaining visitors to my firm even if it interfered with my completing a report.   1 — 2 — 3 — 4 — 5
12. It would be fun for me to represent my team at gatherings outside our department.   1 — 2 — 3 — 4 — 5
13. The problems of my teammates are my problems too.   1 — 2 — 3 — 4 — 5
14. Resolving conflict is an activity I enjoy.   1 — 2 — 3 — 4 — 5
15. I would cooperate with another unit in the organization even if I disagreed with the position taken by its members.   1 — 2 — 3 — 4 — 5
16. I am an idea generator on the job.   1 — 2 — 3 — 4 — 5
17. It's fun for me to bargain whenever I have the opportunity.   1 — 2 — 3 — 4 — 5
18. Team members listen to me when I speak.   1 — 2 — 3 — 4 — 5
19. People have asked me to assume the leadership of an activity several times in my life.   1 — 2 — 3 — 4 — 5
20. I've always been a convincing person.   1 — 2 — 3 — 4 — 5
Total score: _____

Norms for Interpreting the Total Score[95]

90–100 = high readiness for the leadership role
60–89 = moderate readiness for the leadership role
40–59 = some uneasiness with the leadership role
39 or less = low readiness for the leadership role

Questions for Discussion

1. Do you agree with the interpretation of your readiness to assume the leadership role? Explain why or why not.

2. If you scored below 60 and desire to become a leader, what might you do to increase your readiness to lead? To answer this question, we suggest that you study the state-ments carefully—particularly those with low responses—to determine how you might change either an attitude or a behavior so that you can realistically answer more questions with a response of "agree" or "strongly agree."

3. How might this evaluation instrument help you to become a more effective leader?

Group Exercise

Exhibiting Leadership within the Context of Running a Meeting[96]

Objectives

1. To consider the types of problems that can occur when running a meeting.
2. To identify the leadership behaviors that can be used to handle problems that occur in meetings.

Introduction

Managers often find themselves playing the role of formal or informal leader when participating in a planned meeting (e.g., committees, work groups, task forces, etc.). As a leader, indi-viduals often must handle a number of interpersonal situations that have the potential of reducing the group's productivity. For example, if an individual has important information that is not shared with the group, the meeting will be less productive. Similarly, two or more individuals who engage in conversa-tional asides could disrupt the normal functioning of the group. Finally, the group's productivity will also be threatened by two or more individuals who argue or engage in personal attacks on one another during a meeting. This exercise is designed to help you practice some of the behaviors necessary to over-come these problems and at the same time share in the re-sponsibility of leading a productive group.[97]

Instructions

Your instructor will divide the class into groups of four to six. Once the group is assembled, briefly summarize the types of problems that can occur when running a meeting—start with the material presented in the preceding introduction. Write your final list on a piece of paper. Next, for each problem on the group's list, the group should brainstorm a list of appropriate leader behaviors that can be used to handle the problem. Use the guidelines for brainstorming discussed in Chapter 12. Try to arrive at a consensus list of leadership behaviors that can be used to handle the various problems encountered in meetings.

Questions for Discussion

1. What type of problems that occur during meetings are most difficult to handle? Explain.

2. Are there any particular leader behaviors that can be used to solve multiple problems during meetings? Discuss your rationale.

3. Was there a lot of agreement about which leader behaviors were useful for dealing with specific problems encountered in meetings? Explain.

Ethical Dilemma

Doug Durand's Staff Engages in Questionable Sales Activities[98]

In his 20 years as a pharmaceutical salesman, Douglas Durand thought he had seen it all. Then, in 1995, he signed on as vice president for sales at TAP Pharmaceutical Products Inc. in Lake Forest, Illinois. Several months later, in disbelief, he listened to a conference call among his sales staff: They were openly discussing how to bribe urologists. Worried about a competing drug coming to market, they wanted to give a 2% "administration fee" up front to any doctor who agreed to prescribe TAP's new prostate cancer drug, Lupron. When one of Durand's regional managers fretted about getting caught, another quipped: "How do you think Doug would look in stripes?" Durand didn't say a word. "That conversation scared the heck out of me," he recalls. "I felt very vulnerable." . . .

For years, TAP sales reps had encouraged doctors to charge government medical programs full price for Lupron they received at a discount or gratis. Doing so helped TAP establish Lupron as the prostrate treatment of choice, bringing in annual sales of $800 million, about a quarter of the company's revenues. . . .

Durand grew increasingly concerned. Colleagues told him he didn't understand TAP's culture. He was excluded from top marketing and sales meetings. Then came the crack about how he would look in stripes. Durand's stomach knotted in fear that he would become the company scapegoat. Yet he felt trapped: If he left within a year, he wouldn't be able to collect his bonus. He also doubted that anyone would hire him if he bolted so hastily.

What would you do if you were Doug Durand?

1. It's a tough market, and giving kickbacks is nothing more than a form of building product loyalty. I wouldn't make a big issue about this practice.

2. I wouldn't do anything because I would not receive my bonus and it wouldn't look good on my résumé to leave the job within one year.

3. I would gather information about TAP and send it to a federal prosecutor. After all, TAP is giving kickbacks and it is encouraging doctors to charge full price for a drug they receive on a discount.

4. I would go to TAP's president and get his or her blessing for our sales activities.

5. Invent other options. Discuss.

For the Chapter 16 Internet Exercise featuring an investigation of the leadership style possessed by historical leaders (www.leader-values.com), visit our Web site at **www.mhhe.com/kreitner.**

Creating Effective Organizations

Learning Objectives

When you finish studying the material in this chapter, you should be able to:

1   Describe the four characteristics common to all organizations, and explain the difference between closed and open systems.

2   Define the term *learning organization*.

3   Describe horizontal, hourglass, and virtual organizations.

4   Describe the four generic organizational effectiveness criteria, and discuss how managers can prevent organizational decline.

5   Explain what the contingency approach to organization design involves.

6   Describe the relationship between differentiation and integration in effective organizations.

7   Discuss Burns and Stalker's findings regarding mechanistic and organic organizations.

8   Define and briefly explain the practical significance of centralization and decentralization.

9   Discuss the effective management of organizational size.

There is an evil company in Arkansas, some say. It's a discount store—a very, very big discount store—and it will do just about anything to get bigger. You've seen the headlines. Illegal immigrants mopping its floors. Workers locked inside overnight. A big gender discrimination suit. Wages low enough to make *other* companies' workers go on strike. And we know what it does to weaker suppliers and competitors. Crushing the dream of the independent proprietor— an ideal as American as Thomas Jefferson—it is the enemy of all that's good and right in our nation.

There is another big discount store in Arkansas, yet this one couldn't be more different from the first. Founded by a folksy entrepreneur whose notions of thrift, industry, and the square deal were pure Ben Franklin, this company is not a tyrant but a servant. Passing along the gains of its brilliant distribution system to consumers, its farsighted managers have done nothing less than democratize the American dream. Its low prices are spurring productivity and helping win the fight against inflation. It is America's most admired company.

Weirdest part is, both these companies are named Wal-Mart Stores Inc.

The more America talks about Wal-Mart, it seems, the more polarized its image grows. Its executives are credited with the most expansive of visions and the meanest of intentions; its CEO is presumed to be in league with Lex Luthor *and* St Francis of Assisi. It's confusing. Which should we believe in: good Wal-Mart or evil Wal-Mart?

Some of the allegations—and Wal-Mart was sued more than 6,000 times in 2002—certainly seem damning. Yet there's an important piece of context: Wal-Mart employs 1.4 million people. That's three times as many as the nation's next biggest employer and 56 times as many as the average *Fortune* 500 company. Meaning that all things being equal, a bad event is 5,500% more likely to happen at Wal-Mart than at Borders.

One consistent refrain is that Wal-Mart squeezes its suppliers to death—

Is Wal-Mart an effective organization? It depends on your perspective.

and you don't have to do much digging to find horror stories. But while Wal-Mart's reputation for penny-pinching is well deserved, so is its reputation for straightforwardness—none of the slotting fees, rebates, or other game playing that many merchants engage in....

Another rap on Wal-Mart—that it stomps competitors to dust through sheer brute force—seems undeniable: Studies have indicated a decline in the life expectancy of local businesses after Wal-Mart moves in. But this morality play is missing some key characters—namely, you and me. The scene where we drop into Wal-Mart to pick up a case of Coke, for instance, has been conveniently cut. No small omission, since the main reason we can't shop at Ed's Variety Store anymore is that we stopped shopping at Ed's Variety Store.

Evil Wal-Mart's original sin, then, was to open stores that sold things for less. This was a powerful idea but hardly a new one....

Not surprisingly, that's how the people running Good Wal-Mart see their story. They cast their jobs in almost missionary terms—"to lower the world's cost of living"—and in this, they have succeeded spectacularly. One consultancy estimates that Wal-Mart saves consumers $20 billion a year. Its constant push for low prices, meanwhile, puts the heat on suppliers and competitors to offer better deals.

That's a good thing, right? If a company achieves its lower prices by finding better and smarter ways of doing things, then yes, everybody wins. But if it cuts costs by cutting pay and benefits—or by sending production to China—then not everybody wins. And here's where the story of Good Wal-Mart starts to falter. Just as its Everyday Low Prices benefit shoppers who've never

come near a Wal-Mart, there are mounting signs that its Everyday Low Pay (Wal-Mart's full-time hourly employees average $9.76 an hour) is hurting some workers who have never worked there....

Where you stand on Wal-Mart, then, seems to depend on where you sit. If you're a consumer, Wal-Mart is good for you. If you're a wage earner, there's a good chance it's bad. If you're a Wal-Mart shareholder, you want the company to grow. If you're a citizen, you probably don't want it growing in your backyard. So, which one are you?

And that's the point: Chances are, you're more than one. And you may think each role is important. Yet America has elevated one above the rest....

Wal-Mart swore fealty to the consumer and rode its coattails straight to the top. Now we have more than just a big retailer on our hands, though. We have a servant-king—one powerful enough to place everyone else in servitude to the consumer too. Gazing up at this new order, we wonder if our original choices made so much sense after all....

Now Wal-Mart has been brought face to face with its own contradiction: Its promises of the good life threaten to ring increasingly hollow if it doesn't pay its workers enough to have that good life.

It's important that this debate continue. But in holding the mirror up to Wal-Mart, we would do well to turn it back on ourselves. Sam Walton created Wal-Mart. But we created it, too.[1]

FOR DISCUSSION
Would you call Wal-Mart an effective organization? Explain.

Virtually every aspect of life is affected at least indirectly by some type of organization. We look to organizations to feed, clothe, house, educate, and employ us. Organizations attend to our needs for entertainment, police and fire protection, insurance, recreation, national security, transportation, news and information, legal assistance, and health care. Many of these organizations, such as Wal-Mart, seek a profit, others do not. Some are extremely large, others are tiny mom-and-pop operations. Despite this mind-boggling diversity, modern organizations have one basic thing in common. They are the primary context for organizational behavior. As mentioned in Chapter 1, organizations are the chessboard upon which the game of organizational behavior is played. Therefore, present and future organizational members need a working knowledge of modern organizations to improve their chances of making the right moves.

This chapter explores the changing shape, effectiveness, and design of today's organizations. Our overriding challenge is to build organizations capable of thriving in an environment characterized by rapid change and relentless global competition.

Organizations: Definition and Perspectives

As a necessary springboard for this chapter, we need to formally define the term *organization,* clarify the meaning of organization charts, and explore two open-system perspectives of organizations.

What Is an Organization?

According to Chester I Barnard's classic definition cited in Chapter 1, an **organization** is "a system of consciously coordinated activities or forces of two or more persons."[2] Embodied in the *conscious coordination* aspect of this definition are four common denominators of all organizations: coordination of effort, a common goal, division of labor, and a hierarchy of authority[3] (see Figure 17–1). Organization theorists refer to these factors as the organization's *structure.*[4]

Coordination of effort is achieved through formulation and enforcement of policies, rules, and regulations. Division of labor occurs when the common goal is pursued by individuals performing separate but related tasks. The hierarchy of authority, also called the chain of command, is a control mechanism dedicated to making sure the right people do the right things at the right time. Historically, managers have maintained the integrity of the hierarchy of authority by adhering to the unity of command principle. The **unity of command principle** specifies that each employee should report to only one manager. Otherwise, the argument goes, inefficiency would prevail because of conflicting orders and lack of personal accountability.[5] (Indeed, these are problems in today's more fluid and flexible organizations based on innovations such as cross-functional, self-managed, and virtual teams.) Managers in the hierarchy of authority also administer rewards and punishments. When the four factors in Figure 17–1 operate in concert, the dynamic entity called an organization exists.

Organization
System of consciously coordinated activities of two or more people.

Unity of command principle
Each employee should report to a single manager.

Figure 17–1   *Four Characteristics Common to All Organizations*

Organization Charts

Organization chart

Boxes-and-lines illustration showing chain of formal authority and division of labor.

An **organization chart** is a graphic representation of formal authority and division of labor relationships. To the casual observer, the term *organization chart* means the family tree–like pattern of boxes and lines posted on workplace walls. Within each box one usually finds the names and titles of current position holders.[6] To organization theorists, however, organization charts reveal much more. The partial organization chart in Figure 17–2 reveals four basic dimensions of organizational structure: (1) hierarchy of authority (who reports to whom), (2) division of labor, (3) spans of control, and (4) line and staff positions.

Hierarchy of Authority
As Figure 17–2 illustrates, there is an unmistakable hierarchy of authority.[7] Working from bottom to top, the 10 directors report to the two executive directors who report to the president who reports to the chief executive officer. Ultimately, the chief executive officer answers to the hospital's board of directors. The chart in Figure 17–2 shows strict unity of command up and down the line. A formal hierarchy of authority also delineates the official communication network.

Figure 17–2   *Sample Organization Chart for a Hospital (executive and director levels only)*

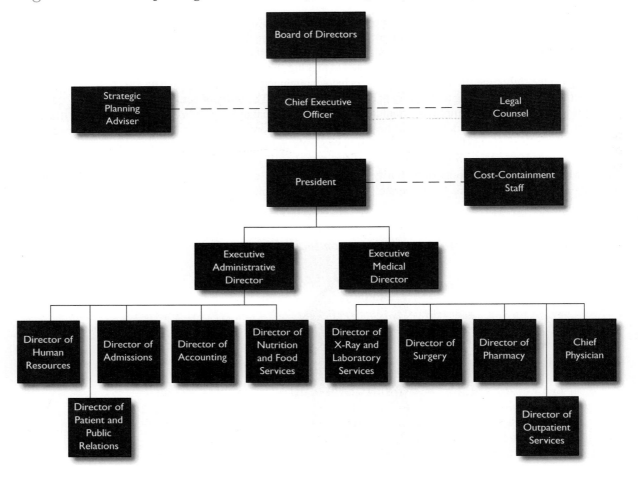

Division of Labor   In addition to showing the chain of command, the sample organization chart indicates extensive division of labor. Immediately below the hospital's president, one executive director is responsible for general administration while another is responsible for medical affairs. Each of these two specialities is further subdivided as indicated by the next layer of positions. At each successively lower level in the organization, jobs become more specialized.

Spans of Control   The **span of control** refers to the number of people reporting directly to a given manager.[8] Spans of control can range from narrow to wide. For example, the president in Figure 17–2 has a narrow span of control of two. (Staff assistants usually are not included in a manager's span of control.) The executive administrative director in Figure 17–2 has a wider span of control of five. Spans of control exceeding 30 can be found in assembly-line operations where machine-paced and repetitive work substitutes for close supervision. Historically, spans of five to six were considered best. Despite years of debate, organization theorists have not arrived at a consensus regarding the ideal span of control.

Generally, the narrower the span of control, the closer the supervision and the higher the administrative costs as a result of a higher manager-to-worker ratio. Recent emphasis on leanness and administrative efficiency dictates spans of control as wide as possible but guarding against inadequate supervision and lack of coordination. Wider spans also complement the trend toward greater worker autonomy and empowerment.[9]

Line and Staff Positions   The organization chart in Figure 17–2 also distinguishes between line and staff positions. Line managers such as the president, the two executive directors, and the various directors occupy formal decision-making positions within the chain of command. Line positions generally are connected by solid lines on organization charts. Dotted lines indicate staff relationships. **Staff personnel** do background research and provide technical advice and recommendations to their **line managers,** who have the authority to make decisions. For example, the cost-containment specialists in the sample organization chart merely advise the president on relevant matters. Apart from supervising the work of their own staff assistants, they have no line authority over other organizational members. Modern trends such as cross-functional teams and reengineering are blurring the distinction between line and staff.

According to a study of 207 police officers in Israel, line personnel exhibited greater job commitment than did their staff counterparts.[10] This result was anticipated because the line managers' decision-making authority empowered them and gave them comparatively more control over their work situations.

An Open-System Perspective of Organizations

To better understand how organizational models have evolved over the years, we need to know the difference between closed and open systems. A **closed system** is said to be a self-sufficient entity. It is "closed" to the surrounding environment. In contrast, an **open system** depends on constant interaction with the environment for survival. The distinction between closed and open systems is a matter of degree. Because every worldly system is partly closed and partly open, the key question is: How great a role does the environment play in the functioning of the system? For instance, a battery-powered clock is a relatively closed system. Once the battery is inserted, the clock performs its time-keeping function hour after hour until the battery goes dead. The human body, on the other hand, is a highly open system because it requires a constant supply of life-sustaining oxygen from the environment.

Span of control
The number of people reporting directly to a given manager.

Staff personnel
Provide research, advice, and recommendations to line managers.

Line managers
Have authority to make organizational decisions.

Closed system
A relatively self-sufficient entity.

Open system
Organism that must constantly interact with its environment to survive.

Figure 17–3   *The Organization as an Open System*

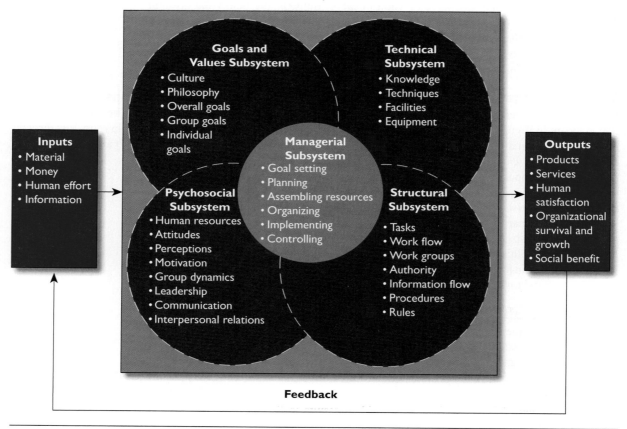

SOURCE: This model is a combination of Figures 5–2 and 5–3 in F E Kast and J E Rosenzweig, *Organization and Management: A Systems and Contingency Approach,* 4th ed (New York: McGraw-Hill, 1986), pp 112, 114. Copyright © 1986. Reprinted by permission of the McGraw-Hill Companies, Inc.

Nutrients also are imported from the environment. Open systems are capable of self-correction, adaptation, and growth, thanks to characteristics such as homeostasis and feedback control.

Historically, management theorists downplayed the environment as they used closed-system thinking to characterize organizations as either well-oiled machines or highly disciplined military units. They believed rigorous planning and control would eliminate environmental uncertainty. But that proved unrealistic. Drawing upon the field of general systems theory that emerged during the 1950s, organization theorists suggested a more dynamic model for organizations.[11] The resulting open-system model likened organizations to the human body.[12] Accordingly, the model in Figure 17–3 reveals the organization to be a living organism that transforms inputs into various outputs. The outer boundary of the organization is permeable. People, information, capital, and goods and services move back and forth across this boundary. Moreover, each of the five organizational subsystems—goals and values, technical, psychosocial, structural, and managerial—is dependent on the others. Feedback about such things as sales and customer satisfaction or dissatisfaction enables the organization to self-adjust and survive despite uncertainty and change.[13] In effect, the organization is alive (see Real World/Real People).

Switzerland's ABB Encourages Open-System Thinking at Its Tennessee Power Technologies Unit

ABB, along with its management consultancy, The Hayes Group, created "Learn or Burn: Making the Right Business Decisions," a one-day workshop required of all employees. Working in teams of four, employees participate in a simulation in which they must run a manufacturing business for three years. They purchase materials, move products through production, pay for overhead, complete profit and loss statements, and analyze financial ratios. The idea is that employees will be able to more clearly see the direct impact that their decisions have on an organization.

"It's everyone's responsibility to make decisions, not just management," says Eduardo Miller, ABB manager and workshop co-instructor. "If all of us are not learning to make the right decisions, we can burn the business."

SOURCE: H Johnson, "Learn or Burn," *Training*, April 2004, p 19.

Learning Organizations

In recent years, organization theorists have extended the open-system model by adding a "brain" to the "living body." Organizations are said to have human-like cognitive functions, such as the abilities to perceive and interpret, solve problems, and learn from experience. Today, managers read and hear a good deal about learning organizations and knowledge management (as discussed in Chapter 12).[14] Peter Senge, a professor at the Massachusetts Institute of Technology, popularized the term *learning organization* in his best-selling book *The Fifth Discipline*. He described a learning organization as "a group of people working together to collectively enhance their capacities to create results that they truly care about."[15] A practical interpretation of these ideas results in the following definition. A **learning organization** is one that proactively creates, acquires, and transfers knowledge and that changes its behavior on the basis of new knowledge and insights.[16]

Learning organizations actively try to infuse their organizations with new ideas and information. They do this by constantly scanning their external environments, hiring new talent and expertise when needed, and by devoting significant resources to train and develop their employees. Next, new knowledge must be transferred throughout the organization. Learning organizations strive to reduce structural, process, and interpersonal barriers to the sharing of information, ideas, and knowledge among organizational members. Finally, behavior must change as a result of new knowledge. Learning organizations are results oriented. They foster an environment in which employees are encouraged to use new behaviors and operational processes to achieve corporate goals. Consider Ernst & Young's approach, for example:

> Ernst & Young figures that its knowledge falls into three categories of "content." The first is benchmark data—studies, surveys, industry facts, and figures. "Each year we buy about $30 million of this stuff in the United States alone, so that's valuable right there," says [chief knowledge officer John] Peetz. "The second content is point-to-point knowledge, which is people sharing what they know. And finally, we've got expert knowledge, or the best people in a given area who know how to solve specific problems." To tie this together, Ernst & Young created "power packs," or databases on specific business areas that employees load into laptops. Those packs also contain contact information for the firm's network of subject matter experts. If a consultant runs into a glitch in a supply-chain

Learning organization
Proactively creates, acquires, and transfers knowledge throughout the organization.

549

management proposal, for example, he or she can instantly find and get help from Ernst & Young's most experienced supply-chain master.[17]

Now let us see how this evolution of ideas is reshaping organizations.

The Changing Shape of Organizations

Organizations are basically tools invented to get things done through collective action. As any carpenter or plumber knows, different jobs require different tools. So it is with organizations. When the situation changes significantly, according to contingency thinking, a different type of organization may be appropriate. The need for new organizations is greater than ever today because managers face revolutionary changes. *Fortune* magazine offered this perspective:

> We all sense that the changes surrounding us are not mere trends but the workings of large, unruly forces; the globalization of markets; the spread of information technology and computer networks; the dismantling of hierarchy, the structure that has essentially organized work since the mid-19th century. Growing up around these is a new, information-age economy, whose fundamental sources of wealth are knowledge and communication rather than natural resources and physical labor.[18]

What sorts of organizations will prosper in the age of the Internet and e-business? Will they be adaptations of the traditional pyramid-shaped organization? Or will they be radically different? Let us put our imaginations to work by envisioning the shape of tomorrow's organizations, the rough outlines of which are visible today.

New-Style versus Old-Style Organizations

Organization theorists Jay R Galbraith and Edward E Lawler III have called for a "new logic of organizing."[19] They recommend a whole new set of adjectives to describe organizations (see Table 17–1). Traditional pyramid-shaped organizations, conforming to the old-style pattern, tend to be too slow and inflexible today. Leaner, more flexible organizations

Table 17–1   *Profiles of the New-Style and Old-Style Organizations*

New	Old
Dynamic, learning	Stable
Information rich	Information is scarce
Global	Local
Small and large	Large
Product/customer oriented	Functional
Skills oriented	Job oriented
Team oriented	Individual oriented
Involvement oriented	Command/control oriented
Lateral/networked	Hierarchical
Customer oriented	Job requirements oriented

SOURCE: J R Galbraith and E E Lawler III, "Effective Organizations: Using the New Logic of Organizing," in *Organizing for the Future: The New Logic for Managing Complex Organizations,* eds J R Galbraith, E E Lawler III, and Associates, p 298. Copyright 1993, John Wiley & Sons, Inc. Reprinted with permission of John Wiley & Sons, Inc.

are needed to accommodate today's strategic balancing act between cost, quality, and speed. These new-style organizations are customer focused, dedicated to continuous improvement and learning, and structured around teams. These qualities, along with computerized information technology, should enable big organizations to mimic the speed and flexibility of small organizations.[20]

Three New Organizational Patterns

Figure 17–4 illustrates three radical departures from the traditional pyramid-shaped organization. Each is the logical result of various trends that are evident today. In other words, we have exaggerated these new organizations for instructional purposes. You will likely encounter various combinations of these pure types in the years ahead. Let us imagine life in the organizations of tomorrow. (Importantly, these characterizations are not intended to be final answers. We simply seek to stimulate thoughtful discussion.)

Horizontal Organizations   Despite the fact that *reengineering* became synonymous with huge layoffs and has been called a passing fad,[21] it will likely have a lasting effect on organization design. Namely, it helped refine the concept of a horizontally oriented organization. Unlike traditional vertically oriented organizations with functional units such as production, marketing, and finance, horizontal organizations are flat and built around core processes aimed at satisfying customers. *Fortune* magazine characterized horizontal organizations this way:

> The horizontal corporation includes these potent elements: Teams will provide the foundation of organizational design. They will not be set up inside departments, like marketing, but around core processes, such as new-product development. Process owners, not department heads, will be the top managers, and they may sport wonderfully weird titles; GE Medical Systems has a "vice president of global sourcing and order to remittance."

Figure 17–4   *The Shape of Tomorrow's Organizations*

The Horizontal Organization

The Hourglass Organization

The Virtual Organization

Rather than focusing single-mindedly on financial objectives or functional goals, the horizontal organization emphasizes customer satisfaction. Work is simplified and hierarchy flattened by combining related tasks—for example, an account-management process that subsumes the sales, billing, and service functions—and eliminating work that does not add value. Information zips along an internal superhighway: The knowledge worker analyzes it, and technology moves it quickly across the corporation instead of up and down, speeding up and improving decision making.[22]

What will it be like to work in a horizontal organization?[23] It will be a lot more interesting than traditional bureaucracies with their functional ghettos. Most employees will be *close to the customer* (both internal and external)—asking questions, getting feedback, and jointly solving problems. Constant challenge also will come from being on cross-functional teams where co-workers with different technical specialties work side-by-side on projects. Sometimes people will find themselves dividing their time among several projects. Blurred and conflicting lines of authority will break the traditional unity-of-command principle. Project goals and deadlines will tend to replace the traditional supervisor role. Training in both technical and teamwork skills will be a top priority. Multiskilled employees at all levels will find themselves working on different teams and various projects during the year. Paradoxically, self-starters and team players will thrive. Because of the flatness of the organization, lateral transfers will be more common than traditional vertical promotions. This will be a source of discontent for many of those who want to move upward. Constant change will take its toll in terms of interpersonal conflict, personal stress, and burnout. Skill-based pay will supplement pay-for-performance.

Hourglass Organizations

This pattern gets its name from the organization's pinched middle. Thanks to modern information technology, a relatively small executive group will be able to coordinate the efforts of numerous operating personnel who make goods or render services. Multiple and broad layers of middle managers who served as conduits for information in old-style organizations will be unnecessary in hourglass organizations. Competition for promotions among operating personnel will be intense because of the restricted hierarchy. Lateral transfers will be more common. Management will compensate for the lack of promotion opportunities with job rotation, skill training, and pay-for-performance. What few middle managers there are will be cross-functional problem solvers who also possess a number of technical skills. The potential for alienation between the executive elite and those at the base of the hourglass will be great, thus giving labor unions an excellent growth opportunity.

Virtual Organizations

Like virtual teams, discussed in Chapter 11, modern information technology allows people in virtual organizations to get something accomplished despite being geographically dispersed.[24] Instead of relying heavily on face-to-face meetings, as before, members of virtual organizations send e-mail and voicemail messages, exchange project information over the Internet, and convene videoconferences among far-flung participants. In addition, cellular phones and the wireless Internet have made the dream of doing business from the beach a reality! This disconnection between work and location is causing managers to question traditional assumptions about centralized offices and factories. Why have offices for people who are never there because they are out finding and helping customers? Why have a factory when it is less expensive to contract out the work? Indeed, many so-called virtual organizations are really a *network* of several independent contractors or organizations hooked together contractually and electronically (see Real World/ Real People).

When It Comes to Outsourcing, How Much Is Too Much?

BusinessWeek After spending years squeezing costs out of the factory floor, back office, and warehouse, CEOs are asking tough questions about their once-cloistered R&D operations: Why are so few hit products making it out of the labs into the market? How many of those pricey engineers are really creating game-changing products or technology breakthroughs? "R&D is the biggest single remaining controllable expense to work on," says Allen J Delattre, head of Accenture Ltd.'s high-tech consulting practice. "Companies either will have to cut costs or increase R&D productivity."

The result is a rethinking of the structure of the modern corporation. What, specifically, has to be done in-house anymore? At a minimum, most leading Western companies are turning toward a new model of innovation, one that employs global networks of partners. These can include US chipmakers, Taiwanese engineers, Indian software developers, and Chinese factories. IBM is even offering the smarts of its famed research labs and a new global team of 1,200 engineers to help customers develop future products using next-generation technologies. When the whole chain works in sync, there can be a dramatic leap in the speed and efficiency of product development.

The downside of getting the balance wrong, however, can be steep. Start with the danger of fostering new competitors. Motorola hired Taiwan's BenQ Corp. to design and manufacture millions of mobile phones. But then BenQ began selling phones last year in the prized China market under its own brand. That prompted Motorola to pull its contract. Another risk is that brand-name companies will lose the incentive to keep investing in new technology. "It is a slippery slope," says Boston Consulting Group senior vice president Jim Andrew. "If the innovation starts residing

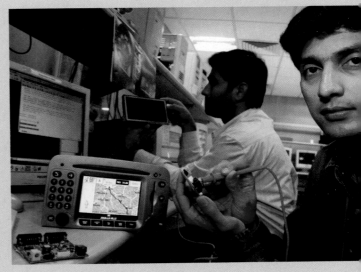

Wipro engineers in Bangalore, India, design a GPS system for European car makers.

in the suppliers, you could incrementalize yourself to the point where there isn't much left."

The key, execs say, is to guard some sustainable competitive advantage, whether it's control over the latest technologies, the look and feel of new products, or the customer relationship. "You have to draw a line," says Motorola CEO Edward J Zander. At Motorola, "core intellectual property is above it, and commodity technology is below."

SOURCE: Excerpted from P Engardio and Bruce Einhorn, "Outsourcing Innovation," *BusinessWeek,* March 21, 2005, pp 87–88. Reprinted by permission of The McGraw-Hill Companies, Inc.

Here is how we envision life in the emerging virtual organizations and organizational networks. Things will be very interesting and profitable for the elite core of entrepreneurs and engineers who hit on the right business formula. Turnover among the financial and information have-nots—data entry, customer service, and production employees—will be high because of glaring inequities and limited opportunities for personal fulfillment and growth. Telecommuters who work from home will feel liberated and empowered (and sometimes lonely). Commitment, trust, and loyalty could erode badly if managers do not heed this caution by Charles Handy, a British management expert. According to Handy: "A shared commitment still requires personal contact to make the commitment feel real.

Beth Williams is an inspiring role model for both personal and organizational effectiveness. After the sudden death of her father, the Boston-area single parent left her high-level post at Blue Cross & Blue Shield and pursued her father's dream of turning Roxbury Technology into a successful manufacturer of toner cartridges. By 2005, thanks in part to an assist from Staples' CEO Tom Stemberg, she had built an $8 million-a-year company employing 25 people in a depressed neighborhood.

Paradoxically, the more virtual an organization becomes the more its people need to meet in person."[25] Independent contractors, both individuals and organizations, will participate in many different organizational networks and thus have diluted loyalty to any single one. Substandard working conditions and low pay at some smaller contractors will make them little more than Internet-age sweatshops. Companies living from one contract to another will offer little in the way of job security and benefits. Opportunities to start new businesses will be numerous, but prolonged success could prove elusive at Internet speed.[26]

Be Prepared for Some Surprises   The only certainty about tomorrow's organizations is they are not a cure-all and will produce their fair share of surprises. For instance, consider what happened at Cisco Systems during the 2000–2002 recession.

> It turned out that Cisco's networked-manufacturing model was not nearly as accurate as [CEO John] Chambers had boasted. Only 40% of what Cisco sells is actually made by the company. Instead, a network of suppliers and contract manufacturers delivers an unusually large chunk of Cisco-branded merchandise direct to customers. This business model was supposed to keep fixed costs to a minimum, eliminate the need for inventory, and give management an instantaneous, real-time fix on orders, shipments, and demand.
>
> The highly hyped systems, however, failed to account for the double and triple ordering by customers tired of long waits for shipments. So Cisco began to stockpile parts and finished products. . . .
>
> When a weakening economy brought capital spending to a near halt, Chambers found himself stuck with billions of dollars of inventory he didn't expect to have. In April [2001] he wrote off $2.2 billion of excess inventory and cut 18% of Cisco's staff, or 8,500 employees.[27]

If you are a flexible and adaptable person who sees problems as opportunities, are a self-starter capable of teamwork, and are committed to life-long learning, don't worry. You will likely thrive in tomorrow's organizations.

Organizational Effectiveness (and the Threat of Decline)

How effective are you? If someone asked you this apparently simple question, you would likely ask for clarification before answering. For instance, you might want to know if they were referring to your grade point average, annual income, actual accomplishments, ability to get along with others, public service, or perhaps something else entirely. So it is with modern organizations. Effectiveness criteria abound. For example, see Real World/Real People for Starbucks' unique vision of effectiveness.

Starbucks' Founder and Chairman, Howard Schultz, Brewed Up a Grand Vision

I wanted to build a different kind of company—a company that had a conscience. So it wasn't only that I needed people with skills and discipline and business acumen that complemented my own qualities, but most important, I needed to attract and retain people with like-minded values. What tied us together was not our respective disciplines, and it was not chasing an exit strategy driven by money. What tied us together was the dream of building a company that would achieve the fragile balance of profitability, shareholder value, a sense of benevolence, and a social conscience.

SOURCE: As quoted in "The Best Advice I Ever Got," *Fortune,* March 21, 2005, p 98.

Assessing organizational effectiveness is an important topic for an array of people, including managers, stockholders, government agencies, and OB specialists. The purpose of this section is to introduce a widely applicable and useful model of organizational effectiveness; we will also deal with the related problem of organizational decline.

Generic Organizational-Effectiveness Criteria

A good way to better understand this complex subject is to consider four generic approaches to assessing an organization's effectiveness (see Figure 17–5). These effectiveness criteria apply equally well to large or small and profit or not-for-profit organizations. Moreover, as denoted by the overlapping circles in Figure 17–5, the four effectiveness criteria can be used in various combinations. The key thing to remember is "no single approach to the evaluation of effectiveness is appropriate in all circumstances or for all organization types."[28] What do Coca-Cola and France Télécom, for example, have in common, other than being large profit-seeking corporations? Because a multidimensional approach is required, we need to look more closely at each of the four generic effectiveness criteria.

Goal Accomplishment   Goal accomplishment is the most widely used effectiveness criterion for organizations. Key organizational results or outputs are compared with previously stated goals or objectives. Deviations, either plus or minus, require corrective action. This is simply an organizational variation of the personal goal-setting process discussed in Chapter 9. Effectiveness, relative to the criterion of goal accomplishment, is gauged by how well the organization meets or exceeds its goals.

Productivity improvement, involving the relationship between inputs and outputs, is a common organization-level goal.[29] Goals also may be set for organizational efforts such as minority recruiting, pollution prevention, and quality improvement. Given today's competitive pressures and e-business revolution, *innovation* and *speed* are very important organizational goals worthy of measurement and monitoring.[30] Toyota recently gave us a powerful indicator of where things are going in this regard. The Japanese automaker announced it could custom-build a car in just five days! A customer's new Toyota would roll off the Ontario, Canada, assembly line just five days after the order was placed. A 30-day lag was the industry standard at the time.[31]

Figure 17–5   *Four Ways to Assess Organizational Effectiveness*

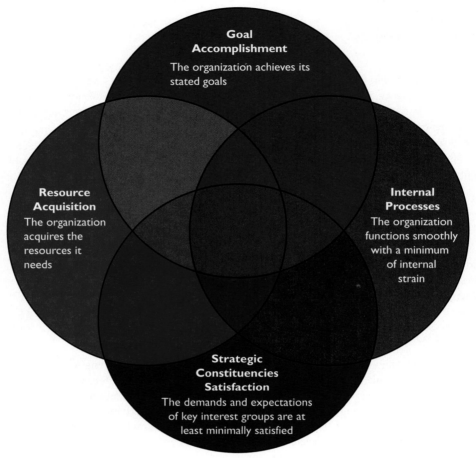

SOURCES: Adapted from discussion in K Cameron, "Critical Questions in Assessing Organizational Effectiveness," *Organizational Dynamics,* Autumn 1980, pp 66–80; and K S Cameron, "Effectiveness as Paradox: Consensus and Conflict in Conceptions of Organizational Effectiveness," *Management Science,* May 1986, pp 539–53.

Resource Acquisition   This second criterion relates to inputs rather than outputs. An organization is deemed effective in this regard if it acquires necessary factors of production such as raw materials, labor, capital, and managerial and technical expertise. Charitable organizations such as the Salvation Army judge their effectiveness in terms of how much money they raise from private and corporate donations.

Internal Processes   Some refer to this third effectiveness criterion as the "healthy systems" approach. An organization is said to be a healthy system if information flows smoothly and if employee loyalty, commitment, job satisfaction, and trust prevail.[32] Goals may be set for any of these internal processes. Healthy systems, from a behavioral standpoint, tend to have a minimum of dysfunctional conflict and destructive political maneuvering. M Scott Peck, the physician who wrote the highly regarded book *The Road Less Traveled,* characterizes healthy organizations in ethical terms:

> A healthy organization, Peck says, is one that has a genuine sense of community: It's a place where people are emotionally present with one another, and aren't afraid to talk about fears and disappointments—because that's what allows us to care for one another. It's a place where there is authentic communication, a willingness to be vulnerable, a commitment to speaking frankly and respectfully—and a commitment not to walk away when the going gets tough.[33]

Strategic Constituencies Satisfaction

Organizations both depend on people and affect the lives of people. Consequently, many consider the satisfaction of key interested parties to be an important criterion of organizational effectiveness.

A **strategic constituency** is any group of individuals who have some stake in the organization—for example, resource providers, users of the organization's products or services, producers of the organization's output, groups whose cooperation is essential for the organization's survival, or those whose lives are significantly affected by the organization.[34]

Strategic constituencies (or *stakeholders*) generally have competing or conflicting interests.[35] For instance, when the major oil companies were reaping record profits in 2004–2005, customers at the gas pumps weren't cheering. Strategic constituents or stakeholders can be identified systematically through a stakeholder audit.[36] A **stakeholder audit** enables management to identify all parties significantly impacted by the organization's performance (see Figure 17–6). Conflicting interests and relative satisfaction among the listed stakeholders can then be dealt with.

A never-ending challenge for management is to strike a workable balance among strategic constituencies so as to achieve at least minimal satisfaction on all fronts.

Strategic constituency
Any group of people with a stake in the organization's operation or success.

Stakeholder audit
Systemic identification of all parties likely to be affected by the organization.

Figure 17–6   *A Sample Stakeholder Audit Identifying Strategic Constituencies*

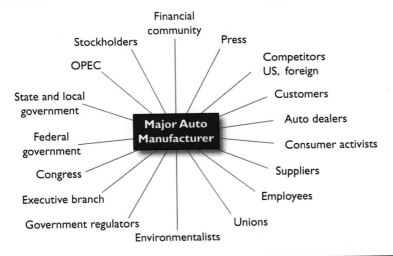

SOURCE: N C Roberts et al., "The Stakeholder Audit Goes Public," *Organizational Dynamics,* Winter 1989. © 1989. Reprinted with permission from Elsevier Science.

Multiple Effectiveness Criteria: Some Practical Guidelines

Experts on the subject recommend a multidimensional approach to assessing the effectiveness of modern organizations. This means no single criterion is appropriate for all stages of the organization's life cycle. Nor will a single criterion satisfy competing stakeholders. Well-managed organizations mix and match effectiveness criteria to fit the unique requirements of the situation.[37] Managers need to identify and seek input from strategic constituencies. This information, when merged with the organization's stated mission and philosophy, enables management to derive an appropriate *combination* of effectiveness criteria. The following guidelines are helpful in this regard:

- *The goal accomplishment approach* is appropriate when "goals are clear, consensual, time-bounded, measurable."[38]
- *The resource acquisition approach* is appropriate when inputs have a traceable effect on results or output. For example, the amount of money the American Red Cross receives through donations dictates the level of services provided.
- *The internal processes approach* is appropriate when organizational performance is strongly influenced by specific processes (e.g., cross-functional teamwork).
- *The strategic constituencies approach* is appropriate when powerful stakeholders can significantly benefit or harm the organization.[39]

Keeping these basic concepts of organizational effectiveness in mind, we turn our attention to preventing organizational decline.

The Ever-Present Threat of Organizational Decline

Sadly, there are many examples of organizational decline and failure in the wake of the recent corporate scandals and recession. Some failed because of illegal acts. Enron, for one, had the dubious honor of going from number seven on the 2001 *Fortune* 500 list to bankruptcy within a single year! During that time, Enron shareholders saw their shares plummet from $83 a share to 67 cents, when the stock was finally delisted. Thousands of Enron jobs evaporated and employee retirement plans and dreams were wiped out.[40] Other companies tripped over strategic blunders and bad luck (see Real World/Real People). Although the problems at these particular companies varied, both of them turned the corner from success to decline rather suddenly and dramatically.[41] Donald N Sull, a strategy professor at the London Business School, added this perspective:

> One of the most common business phenomena is also one of the most perplexing: when successful companies face big changes in their environment, they often fail to respond effectively. Unable to defend themselves against competitors armed with new products, technologies, or strategies, they watch their sales and profits erode, their best people leave, and their stock valuations tumble. Some ultimately manage to recover—usually after painful rounds of downsizing and restructuring—but many don't.[42]

Organizational decline

Decrease in organization's resource base (money, customers, talent, innovations).

Researchers call this downward spiral **organizational decline** and define it as "a decrease in an organization's resource base."[43] The term *resource* is used very broadly in this context, encompassing money, talent, customers, and innovative ideas and products. Managers seeking to maintain organizational effectiveness need to be alert to the problem because experts tell us "decline is almost unavoidable unless deliberate steps are taken to prevent it."[44] The first key step is to recognize the early warning signs of organizational decline.

How Coke Lost Its Fizz

As late as the 1990s, Coca-Cola Co. was one of the most respected companies in America, a master of brand-building and management in the dawning global era. Now the Coke machine is badly out of order. The spectacle of Coke's struggles has become almost painful to watch: the battles with its own bottlers; the aged, overbearing board; the failed CEOs and failed attempts to recruit a successor; the dearth of new products; the lackluster marketing. "They've been their own worst enemy, a casualty of their own success," says Emanuel Goldman, who has followed Coke as an analyst since the 1970s.

Yet as grave as those problems are, they only hint at the real dimensions of Coke's woes. The Coca-Cola organization is stuck in a mind-set formed during its heyday in the 1980s and '90s, when [former CEO Roberto C] Goizueta made Coke into a growth story that captivated the world. An unwillingness to tamper with the structures and beliefs formed during those glory years has left the company unable to adapt to consumer demands for new kinds of beverages, from New Age teas to gourmet coffees, that have eaten into the cola king's market share.

SOURCE: D Foust, "Gone Flat," *Business Week,* December 20, 2004, p 76. Reprinted by permission of The McGraw-Hill Companies, Inc.

Early Warning Signs of Decline

Short of illegal conduct, there are 14 early warning signs of organizational decline:

1. Excess personnel.
2. Tolerance of incompetence.
3. Cumbersome administrative procedures.
4. Disproportionate staff power (e.g., technical staff specialists politically overpower line managers, whom they view as unsophisticated and too conventional).
5. Replacement of substance with form (e.g., the planning process becomes more important than the results achieved).
6. Scarcity of clear goals and decision benchmarks.
7. Fear of embarrassment and conflict (e.g., formerly successful executives may resist new ideas for fear of revealing past mistakes).
8. Loss of effective communication.
9. Outdated organizational structure.[45]
10. Increased scapegoating by leaders.
11. Resistance to change.
12. Low morale.
13. Special interest groups are more vocal.
14. Decreased innovation.[46]

Managers who monitor these early warning signs of organizational decline are better able to reorganize in a timely and effective manner.[47] However, research has uncovered a troublesome perception tendency among entrenched top management teams. In companies where there had been little if any turnover among top executives, there was a tendency to attribute organizational problems to *external* causes (e.g., competition, the government, technology shifts). Oppositely, *internal* attributions tended to be made by top management

"Frankly, at this point in the flow chart, we don't know what happens to these people..."

SOURCE: Chris Wildt, *Harvard Business Review*, September 2004, p 86. © Chris Wildt. Used by permission.

teams with *many* new members. Thus, proverbial "new blood" at the top appears to be a good insurance policy against misperceiving the early-warning signs of organizational decline.[48]

Preventing Organizational Decline   The time to start doing something about organizational decline is when everything is going *right*. For it is during periods of high success that the seeds of decline are sown.[49] *Complacency* is the number one threat because it breeds overconfidence and inattentiveness. As one management writer recently explained,

> In organizations, complacency is a side effect of success. Growth brings bloat, and bloat slows the organization's response to competitive threats. It is after sustained periods of success that organizations run the highest risk of getting hurt. At the moment of a company's greatest triumph, senior management's most important duty is to make sure that the butterflies are still fluttering in everybody's belly.[50]

Judging from what has been written about Enron, complacency also can breed arrogance and unethical or illegal conduct.[51]

Total quality management advocates remind us that *continuous improvement* is the first line of defense against organizational decline. Japan's Toyota is a world leader in this regard.

> Of all the slogans kicked around Toyota City, the key one is *kaizen,* which means "continuous improvement" in Japanese. While many other companies strive for dramatic breakthroughs, Toyota keeps doing lots of little things better and better. . . .
>
> One consultant calls Toyota's strategy "rapid inch-up": Take enough tiny steps and pretty soon you outdistance the competition. . . .
>
> In short, Toyota is the best carmaker in the world. And it keeps getting better. Says Iwao Isomura, chief of personnel: "Our current success is the best reason to change things." Extensive interviews with Toyota executives in the United States and Japan demonstrate the company's total dedication to continuous improvement. What is often mistaken for excessive modesty is, in fact, an expression of permanent dissatisfaction—even with exemplary performance.[52]

General Motors, whose US market share dropped from more than 50% in the 1960s to less than 25% by 2005,[53] has worked hard to catch up with Toyota. But it is chasing a moving target. According to *BusinessWeek:* "In 1987, GM . . . had 180 problems per 100 cars in a JD Power quality study, versus 127 for Toyota. By 2002, in a redesigned survey, GM's quality had improved to 130 defects per 100 cars and trucks versus 107 for Toyota."[54] *Kaizen* works!

Contingency approach to organization design

Creating an effective organization–environment fit.

The Contingency Approach to Organization Design

According to the **contingency approach to organization design,** organizations tend to be more effective when they are structured to fit the demands of the situation.[55] A contingency approach can be put into practice by first assessing the degree of environmental uncertainty

Figure 17–7   *Assessing Environmental Uncertainty*

	Low	Moderate	High
1. How strong are social, political, and economic pressures on the organization?	Minimal	Moderate	Intense
2. How frequent are technological breakthroughs in the industry?	Infrequent	Occasional	Frequent
3. How reliable are resources and supplies?	Reliable	Occasional, predictable shortages	Unreliable
4. How stable is the demand for the organization's product or service?	Highly stable	Moderately stable	Unstable

SOURCE: R Kreitner, *Management,* 9th ed. Copyright © 2004 by Houghton Mifflin Company. Used with permission.

(see Figure 17–7).[56] Next, the contingency model calls for using various organization design configurations to achieve an effective organization–environment fit. Carol Bartz, the longtime CEO of Autodesk, captures the essence of the contingency approach with a sailboat metaphor. This is what she had to say in a recent *Fortune* magazine interview:

How do you explain your longevity as CEO?

I've turned this company around three times. It's like a sailboat. The weather changed, and I had to change. The economy changed, the technology changed, and luckily I had a patient board.

Autodesk started out making software for designers and architects. Where are your customers coming from these days?

About 35% of them are in manufacturing. . . . Another 30% is building and construction, 20% is infrastructure like roads and bridges, and 15% is media, like games and special effects. Our media division has software that layers the blood on Tom Cruise in *The Last Samurai.* Our customers have won the last nine Academy Awards for special effects—*Master and Commander, Titanic, Lord of the Rings*—you name it.[57]

Keeping this spirit of organizational flexibility and adaptability in mind,[58] let us review two classic contingency design studies.

Differentiation and Integration: The Lawrence and Lorsch Study

In their classic text *Organization and Environment,* Harvard researchers Paul Lawrence and Jay Lorsch explained how two structural forces simultaneously fragment the organization and bind it together. They cautioned that an imbalance between these two forces—labeled *differentiation* and *integration*—could hinder organizational effectiveness.

Figure 17–8   *Differentiation and Integration Are Opposing Structural Forces*

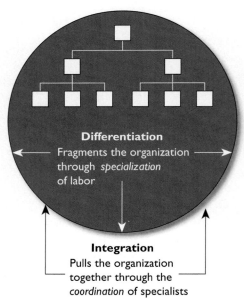

Differentiation
Division of labor and specialization that cause people to think and act differently.

Differentiation Splits the Organization Apart   **Differentiation** occurs through division of labor and technical specialization. A behavioral outcome of differentiation is that technical specialists such as computer programmers tend to think and act differently than specialists in, say, accounting or marketing. Excessive differentiation can cause the organization to bog down in inefficiency, miscommunication, conflict, and politics. Thus, differentiation needs to be offset by an opposing structural force to ensure needed *coordination*. This is where integration enters the picture (see Figure 17–8).

Integration
Cooperation among specialists to achieve a common goal.

Integration Binds the Organization Together   **Integration** occurs when specialists cooperate to achieve a common goal. According to the Lawrence and Lorsch model, integration can be achieved through various combinations of the following six mechanisms: (1) a formal hierarchy; (2) standardized policies, rules, and procedures; (3) departmentalization; (4) committees and cross-functional teams; (5) human relations training; and (6) individuals and groups acting as liaisons between specialists.

Achieving the Proper Balance   When Lawrence and Lorsch studied successful and unsuccessful companies in three industries, they concluded the following: *As environmental complexity increased, successful organizations exhibited higher degrees of both differentiation and integration.* In other words, an effective balance was achieved. Unsuccessful organizations, in contrast, tended to suffer from an imbalance of too much differentiation and not enough offsetting integration. Managers need to fight this tendency if their growing and increasingly differentiated organizations are to be coordinated.

Lawrence and Lorsch also discovered that "the more differentiated an organization, the more difficult it is to achieve integration."[59] Managers of today's complex organizations need to strive constantly and creatively to achieve greater integration.[60] For example, how does 3M Company, with its dozens of autonomous divisions and more than 60,000 products, successfully maintain its competitive edge in technology? Among other things, 3M makes sure its technical specialists frequently interact with one another so cross-fertilization of ideas takes place. Art Fry, credited with inventing the now ubiquitous Post-it Notes, actually owes much of his success to colleague Spencer Silver, an engineer down the hall who created an apparently useless semi-adhesive. If Fry and Silver had worked in a company without a strong commitment to integration, we probably would not have Post-it Notes. 3M does not leave this sort of cross-fertilization of ideas to chance. It organizes for integration with such things as a Technology Council that regularly convenes researchers from various divisions and an annual science fair at which 3M scientists enthusiastically hawk their new ideas, not to customers, but to each other![61]

Mechanistic versus Organic Organizations

A second landmark contingency design study was reported by a pair of British behavioral scientists, Tom Burns and G M Stalker. In the course of their research, they drew a very instructive distinction between what they called mechanistic and organic organizations. **Mechanistic organizations** are rigid bureaucracies with strict rules, narrowly defined tasks, and top-down communication. For example, when *BusinessWeek* correspondent Kathleen Deveny spent a day working in a McDonald's restaurant, she found a very mechanistic organization:

> Here every job is broken down into the smallest of steps, and the whole process is automated. . . .
>
> Anyone could do this, I think. But McDonald's restaurants operate like Swiss watches, and the minute I step behind the counter I am a loose part in the works. . . .
>
> I bag French fries for a few minutes, but I'm much too slow. Worse, I can't seem to keep my station clean enough. Failing at French fries is a fluke, I tell myself. . . .
>
> I try to move faster, but my co-workers are [leaving me behind].[62]

This sort of mechanistic structure is necessary at McDonald's because of the competitive need for uniform product quality, speedy service, and cleanliness. Oppositely, **organic organizations** are flexible networks of multitalented individuals who perform a variety of tasks.[63] W L Gore, maker of the popular Gore-Tex fabric found in outdoor gear, is the epitome of an organic organization. This is what Diane Davidson, a sales executive with 15 years of experience, encountered when she joined W L Gore:

> "I came from a very traditional male-dominated business—the men's shoe business," she recalls. "When I arrived at Gore, I didn't know who did what. I wondered how anything got done here. It was driving me crazy." Like all new hires, Davidson was given a "starting sponsor" at Gore—a mentor, not a boss. But she didn't know how to work without someone telling her what to do.
>
> "Who's my boss?" she kept asking.
>
> "Stop using the B-word," her sponsor replied. . . .
>
> "Secretly, there are bosses, right?" she asked.

Mechanistic organizations
Rigid, command-and-control bureaucracies.

Organic organizations
Fluid and flexible networks of multi-talented people.

W L Gore, the maker of many products including the unique Gore-Tex fabric found in popular sportswear, is a very unique organization itself. Hierarchy, titles, and rank have been cast aside in favor of a highly organic and entrepreneurial culture in which teams, creativity, initiative, flexibility, open communication, and long-term thinking prevail. Gore's employees even "celebrate" failures to encourage risk taking.

There weren't. She eventually figured out that "your team is your boss, because you don't want to let them down. Everyone's your boss, and no one's your boss."

What's more, Davidson saw that people didn't fit into standard job descriptions. They had all made different sets of "commitments" to their team, often combining roles that remained segregated in different fiefdoms at conventional companies.[64]

A Matter of Degree Importantly, as illustrated in Table 17–2, each of the mechanistic-organic characteristics is a matter of degree. Organizations tend to be *relatively* mechanistic or *relatively* organic. Pure types are rare because divisions, departments, or units in the same organization may be more or less mechanistic or organic. From an employee's standpoint, which organization structure would you prefer?

Different Approaches to Decision Making

Centralized decision making
Top managers make all key decisions.

Decentralized decision making
Lower-level managers are empowered to make important decisions.

Decision making tends to be centralized in mechanistic organizations and decentralized in organic organizations. **Centralized decision making** occurs when key decisions are made by top management. **Decentralized decision making** occurs when important decisions are made by middle- and lower-level managers. Generally, centralized organizations are more tightly controlled while decentralized organizations are more adaptive to changing situations.[65] Each has its appropriate use. For example, both Exxon and General Electric are very respected and successful companies, yet the former prefers centralization while the latter pushes decentralization.

Experts on the subject warn against extremes of centralization or decentralization. The challenge is to achieve a workable balance between the two extremes. A management consultant put it this way:

> The modern organization in transition will recognize the pull of two polarities: a need for greater centralization to create low-cost shared resources; and, a need to improve market responsiveness with greater decentralization. Today's winning organizations are the ones that can handle the paradox and tensions of both pulls. These are the firms that analyze the optimum organizational solution in each particular circumstance, without prejudice for one type of organization over another. The result is, almost invariably, a messy mixture of decentralized units sharing cost-effective centralized resources.[66]

Centralization and decentralization are not an either–or proposition; they are an *and–also* balancing act.

Table 17–2 *Characteristics of Mechanistic and Organic Organizations*

Characteristic	Mechanistic Organization		Organic Organization
1. Task definition and knowledge required	Narrow; technical	→	Broad; general
2. Linkage between individual's contribution and organization's purpose	Vague or indirect	→	Clear or direct
3. Task flexibility	Rigid; routine	→	Flexible; varied
4. Specification of techniques, obligations, and rights	Specific	→	General
5. Degree of hierarchical control	High	→	Low (self-control emphasized)
6. Primary communication pattern	Top-down	→	Lateral (between peers)
7. Primary decision-making style	Authoritarian	→	Democratic; participative
8. Emphasis on obedience and loyalty	High	→	Low

SOURCE: Adapted from discussion in T Burns and G M Stalker, *The Management of Innovation* (London: Tavistock, 1961), pp 119–25.

Relevant Research Findings   When they classified a sample of actual companies as either mechanistic or organic, Burns and Stalker discovered one type was not superior to the other. Each type had its appropriate place, depending on the environment. When the environment was relatively *stable and certain,* the successful organizations tended to be *mechanistic. Organic* organizations tended to be the successful ones when the environment was *unstable and uncertain.*[67]

In a study of 103 department managers from eight manufacturing firms and two aerospace organizations, managerial skill was found to have a greater impact on a global measure of department effectiveness in organic departments than in mechanistic departments. This led the researchers to recommend the following contingencies for management staffing and training:

> If we have two units, one organic and one mechanistic, and two potential applicants differing in overall managerial ability, we might want to assign the more competent to the organic unit since in that situation there are few structural aids available to the manager in performing required responsibilities. It is also possible that managerial training is especially needed by managers being groomed to take over units that are more organic in structure.[68]

Another interesting finding comes from a study of 42 voluntary church organizations. As the organizations became more mechanistic (more bureaucratic) the intrinsic motivation of their members decreased. Mechanistic organizations apparently undermined the volunteers' sense of freedom and self-determination. Additionally, the researchers believe their findings help explain why bureaucracy tends to feed on itself: "A mechanistic organizational structure may breed the need for a more extremely mechanistic system because of the reduction in intrinsically motivated behavior."[69] Thus, bureaucracy begets greater bureaucracy.

Most recently, field research in two factories, one mechanistic and the other organic, found expected communication patterns. Command-and-control (downward) communication characterized the mechanistic factory. Consultative or participative (two-way) communication prevailed in the organic factory.[70]

Both Mechanistic and Organic Structures Are Needed   Although achievement-oriented students of OB typically express a distaste for mechanistic organizations, not all organizations or subunits can or should be organic. For example, as mentioned earlier, McDonald's could not achieve its admired quality and service standards without extremely mechanistic restaurant operations. Imagine the food and service you would get if McDonald's employees used their own favorite ways of doing things and worked at their own pace! On the other hand, mechanistic structure alienates some employees because it erodes their sense of self-control.

Three Important Contingency Variables: Technology, Size, and Strategic Choice

Both contingency theories just discussed have one important thing in common. Each is based on an *environmental imperative,* meaning the environment is said to be the primary determinant of effective organizational structure. Other organization theorists disagree. They contend that factors such as the organization's core technology, size, and corporate strategy hold the key to organizational structure. This section examines the significance of these three additional contingency variables.

The Effect of Technology on Structure—Woodward and Beyond

Joan Woodward proposed a *technological imperative* in 1965 after studying 100 small manufacturing firms in southern England. She found distinctly different structural patterns for effective and ineffective companies based on technologies of low, medium, or high *complexity*. Effective organizations with either low- or high-complexity technology tended to have an organic structure. Effective organizations based on a technology of medium complexity tended to have a mechanistic structure. Woodward concluded that technology was the overriding determinant of organizational structure.[71]

Since Woodward's landmark work, many studies of the relationship between technology and structure have been conducted. Unfortunately, disagreement and confusion have prevailed. For example, a comprehensive review of 50 studies conducted between 1965 and 1980 found six technology concepts and 140 technology-structure relationships.[72] A statistical analysis of those studies prompted the following conclusions:

- The more the technology requires *interdependence* between individuals or groups, the greater the need for integration (coordination).
- "As technology moves from routine to nonroutine, subunits adopt less formalized and [less] centralized structures."[73]

Additional insights can be expected in this area as researchers coordinate their definitions of technology and refine their methodologies.[74]

Organizational Size and Performance

Size is an important structural variable subject to two schools of thought. According to the first school, economists have long extolled the virtues of economies of scale. This approach, often called the "bigger is better" model, assumes the per-unit cost of production decreases as the organization grows. In effect, bigger is said to be more efficient. For example, on an annual basis, Honda supposedly can produce its 100,000th car less expensively than its 10th car.

The second school of thought pivots on the law of diminishing returns. Called the "small is beautiful" model,[75] this approach contends that oversized organizations and subunits tend to be plagued by costly behavioral problems. Large and impersonal organizations are said to breed apathy and alienation, with resulting problems such as turnover and absenteeism. Two strong advocates of this second approach are the authors of the book *In Search of Excellence:*

> In the excellent companies, small in *almost every case* is beautiful. The small facility turns out to be the most efficient; its turned-on, motivated, highly productive worker, in communication (and competition) with his peers, outproduces the worker in the big facilities time and again. It holds for plants, for project teams, for divisions—for the entire company.[76]

Is Complexity the Issue? (A Case against Mergers?)   Recent research suggests that when designing their organizations, managers should follow a middle ground between "bigger is better" and "small is beautiful" because both models have been oversold. Indeed, a newer perspective says *complexity,* not size, is the central issue.[77] British management teacher and writer Charles Handy, cited earlier, offered this instructive perspective:

> Growth does not have to mean more of the same. It can mean better rather than bigger. It can mean leaner or deeper, both of which might improve rather than expand the current position. Businesses can grow more profitable by becoming better, or leaner, or deeper, more concentrated, without growing bigger. Bigness, in both business and life, can lead to a lack of focus, too much complexity and, in the end, too wide a spread to control. We have to know when big is big enough.[78]

We do not have a definite answer to the question of how big is too big, but the excessive complexity argument is compelling. This argument may also help explain why many mergers have been disappointing in recent years. According to *BusinessWeek,* the "historic surge of consolidations and combinations is occurring in the face of strong evidence that mergers and acquisitions, at least over the past 35 years or so, have hurt more than helped companies and shareholders."[79] A prime case in point is the Newell Rubbermaid merger. According to *Harvard Business Review,*

> When Newell's top managers approached their counterparts at Rubbermaid in 1999 about the possibility of a merger, it looked like a deal from heaven. . . .
>
> Because Newell and Rubbermaid both sold household products through essentially the same sales channels, the cost synergies from the combination loomed large. . . .
>
> Eager to seize the opportunity, Newell rushed to close the $5.8 billion megamerger—a deal ten times larger than any it had done before.
>
> But the deal from heaven turned out, to use *Business Week*'s phrase, to be the "merger from hell." Instead of lifting Newell to a new level of growth, the acquistion dragged the company down. In 2002, Newell wrote off $500 million in goodwill, leading its former CEO and chairman, Daniel Ferguson, to admit, "We paid too much." By that time, Newell shareholders had lost 50% of the value of their investment; Rubbermaid shareholders had lost 35%.[80]

Research Insights   Researchers measure the size of organizations and organizational subunits in different ways. Some focus on financial indicators such as total sales or total asset value. Others look at the number of employees, transactions (such as the number of students in a school district), or capacity (such as the number of beds in a hospital). A meta-analysis[81] of 31 studies conducted between 1931 and 1985 that related organizational size to performance found

- Larger organizations (in terms of assets) tended to be more productive (in terms of sales and profits).
- There were "no positive relationships between organizational size and efficiency, suggesting the absence of net economy of scale effects."[82]
- There were zero to slightly negative relationships between *subunit* size and productivity and efficiency.

A more recent study examined the relationship between organizational size and employee turnover over a period of 65 months. Turnover was unrelated to organizational size.[83]

Striving for Small Units in Big Organizations   In summary, bigger is not necessarily better and small is not necessarily beautiful.[84] Hard-and-fast numbers regarding exactly how big is too big or how small is too small are difficult to come by.

Table 17–3   *Organizational Size: Management Consultants Address the Question of How Big Is Too Big?*

Peter F Drucker, well-known management consultant:

   The real growth and innovation in this country has been in medium-size companies that employ between 200 and 4,000 workers. If you are in a small company, you are running all out. You have neither the time nor the energy to devote to anything but yesterday's crisis.

   A medium-sized company has the resources to devote to new products and markets, and it's still small enough to be flexible and move fast. And these companies now have what they once lacked—they've learned how to manage.

Thomas J Peters and Robert H Waterman Jr, best-selling authors and management consultants:

   A rule of thumb starts to emerge. We find that the lion's share of the top performers keep their division size between $50 and $100 million, with a maximum of 1,000 or so employees each. Moreover, they grant their divisions extraordinary independence—and give them the functions and resources to exploit.

SOURCES: Excerpted from J A Byrne, "Advice from the Dr Spock of Business," *BusinessWeek*, September 28, 1987, p 61; and T J Peters and R H Waterman Jr, *In Search of Excellence* (New York: Harper & Row, 1982), pp 272–73.

Management consultants offer some rough estimates (see Table 17–3). Until better evidence is available, the best that managers can do is monitor the productivity, quality, and efficiency of divisions, departments, and profit centers. Unwieldy and overly complex units need to be promptly broken into ones of more manageable size. The trick is to *create smallness within bigness.*[85] (See Real World/Real People for a *positive* merger outcome.)

Strategic Choice and Organizational Structure

In 1972, British sociologist John Child rejected the environmental imperative approach to organizational structure. He proposed a *strategic choice* model based on behavioral rather than rational economic principles.[86] Child believed structure resulted from a political process involving organizational power holders. According to the strategic choice model that has evolved from Child's work,[87] an organization's structure is determined largely by a dominant coalition of top-management strategists.[88]

A Strategic Choice Model   As Figure 17–9 on page 570 illustrates, specific strategic choices or decisions reflect how the dominant coalition perceives environmental constraints and the organization's objectives. These strategic choices are tempered by the decision makers' personal beliefs, attitudes, values, and ethics. For example, consider this unusual relationship between top management's ethics and corporate strategy, as reported by *Business Ethics* magazine:

   As a manufacturer and retailer of outdoor clothing and equipment, it's natural for Patagonia to be concerned about the environment. But as a for-profit business, it's also natural for the company to feel a need to look at its bottom line.

   Patagonia has found a way to do both, and to turn upside down traditional concepts of how companies grow in the bargain.

CEO Jean-Pierre Garnier Strives for Smallness within Bigness at Britain's GlaxoSmithKline

[W]e decided to use gene sequencing to make drug discovery more systematic. We were the first to sign with Human Genome Sciences to get access to its technology. We had also built a huge bureaucracy. I mean Big Pharma companies have pyramids of 15,000, 16,000, 20,000 scientists. I tried to change the structure at SmithKline, and all the top R&D guys rebelled against me. But the merger with Glaxo gave me the opportunity I needed. We don't have a big pyramid anymore. We have a head of R&D, and then we have seven small organizations—about 600 scientists each—that do the critical part of drug discovery. We are seeing phenomenal numbers. We have the largest pipeline of new drugs in the industry.

SOURCE: A Lustgarten, "Wisdom from Big Pharma's Dr Gloom," *Fortune*, March 21, 2005, p 38.

The company first warned its customers of the impending change in its [1992] fall/winter catalog.... "We are limiting Patagonia's growth in the United States with the eventual goal of halting growth altogether. We dropped 30% of our clothing line....

"What does this mean to you? Well, last fall you had a choice of five ski pants; now you may choose between two. This is, of course, unAmerican, but two styles of ski pants are all anyone needs."

And ... [the 1993] catalog featured the following message: "At Patagonia, as a company, and as individuals, we sometimes find the array of choices dizzying. But the choices must be faced, resolved soberly, and judicious action taken. To fully include environmental concerns in our ordinary work is to give something back to the planet that sustains us, and that we have taxed so heavily. It's a complex process, but the simplest of gifts."

To that end, say Patagonia spokespeople Lu Setnicksa and Mike Harrelson, the company has embarked on an aggressive effort to examine everything from the materials it uses to produce its products, to which products it actually makes, to what kind of paper it uses in its copying machines.[89]

A more efficient Patagonia enjoyed increased profits, despite an initial decrease in sales revenue. According to a recent search of Patagonia's Web site, the company still prefers "the human scale to the corporate."[90] Directing our attention once again to Figure 17–9, the organization is structured to accommodate its mix of strategies. Ultimately, corrective action is taken if organizational effectiveness criteria are not met.

Research and Practical Lessons   In a study of 97 small and mid-size companies in Quebec, Canada, strategy and organizational structure were found to be highly interdependent. Strategy influenced structure and structure influenced strategy. This was particularly true for larger, more innovative, and more successful firms.[91]

Strategic choice theory and research teaches managers at least two practical lessons. First, the environment is just one of many codeterminants of structure. Second, like any other administrative process, organization design is subject to the byplays of interpersonal power and politics.

569

Figure 17–9   *The Relationship between Strategic Choice and Organizational Structure*

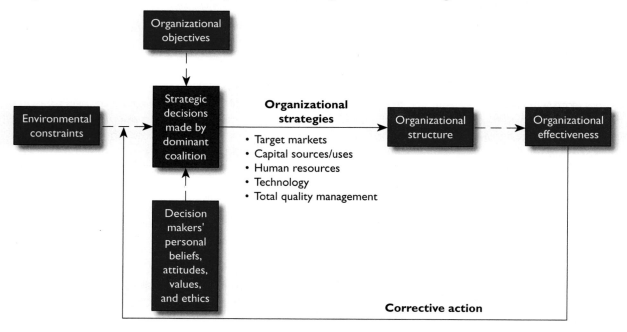

Summary of Key Concepts

1. *Describe the four characteristics common to all organizations, and explain the difference between closed and open systems.* They are coordination of effort (achieved through policies and rules), a common goal (a collective purpose), division of labor (people performing separate but related tasks), and a hierarchy of authority (the chain of command). Closed systems, such as a battery-powered clock, are relatively self-sufficient. Open systems, such as the human body, are highly dependent on the environment for survival. Organizations are said to be open systems.

2. *Define the term learning organization.* A learning organization is one that proactively creates, acquires, and transfers knowledge and changes its behavior on the basis of new knowledge and insights.

3. *Describe horizontal, hourglass, and virtual organizations.* Horizontal organizations are flat structures built around core processes aimed at identifying and satisfying customer needs. Cross-functional teams and empowerment are central to horizontal organizations. Hourglass organizations have a small executive level; a short and narrow middle-management level (because

information technology links the top and bottom levels), and a broad base of operating personnel. Virtual organizations typically are families of interdependent companies. They are contractual and fluid in nature.

4. *Describe the four generic organizational effectiveness criteria, and discuss how managers can prevent organizational decline.* They are goal accomplishment (satisfying stated objectives), resource acquisition (gathering the necessary productive inputs), internal processes (building and maintaining healthy organizational systems), and strategic constituencies satisfaction (achieving at least minimal satisfaction for all key stakeholders). Because complacency is the leading cause of organizational decline, managers need to create a culture of continuous improvement. Decline automatically follows periods of great success if preventive steps are not taken to avoid the erosion of organizational resources (money, customers, talent, and innovative ideas).

5. *Explain what the contingency approach to organization design involves.* The contingency approach to organization design calls for fitting the organization to the demands of the situation. Environmental uncertainty can be assessed in terms of social, political, economic, technological, resource, and demand factors.

6. *Describe the relationship between differentiation and integration in effective organizations.* Harvard researchers Lawrence and Lorsch found that successful organizations achieved a proper balance between the two opposing structural forces of differentiation and integration. Differentiation forces the organization apart. Through a variety of mechanisms—including hierarchy, rules, teams, and liaisons—integration draws the organization together.

7. *Discuss Burns and Stalker's findings regarding mechanistic and organic organizations.* British researchers Burns and Stalker found that mechanistic (bureaucratic, centralized) organizations tended to be effective in stable situations. In unstable situations, organic (flexible, decentralized) organizations were more effective. These findings underscored the need for a contingency approach to organization design.

8. *Define and briefly explain the practical significance of centralization and decentralization.* Because key decisions are made at the top of centralized organizations, they tend to be tightly controlled. In decentralized organizations, employees at lower levels are empowered to make important decisions. Contingency design calls for a proper balance.

9. *Discuss the effective management of organizational size.* Regarding the optimum size for organizations, the challenge for today's managers is to achieve smallness within bigness by keeping subunits at a manageable size.

Discussion Questions

1. How many organizations directly affect your life today? List as many as you can.

2. What would an organization chart of your current (or last) place of employment look like? Does the chart you have drawn reveal the hierarchy (chain of command), division of labor, span of control, and line–staff distinctions? Does it reveal anything else? Explain.

3. Why is it appropriate to view modern organizations as open systems?

4. Which of the three new organizational configurations probably will be most prevalent 10 to 15 years from now? Why?

5. How would you respond to a manager who claimed the only way to measure a business's effectiveness is in terms of how much profit it makes?

6. Why is it important to focus on the role of complacency in organizational decline?

7. In a nutshell, what does contingency organization design entail?

8. What is wrong with an organization having too much differentiation and too little integration?

9. If organic organizations are popular with most employees, why can't all organizations be structured in an organic fashion?

10. How can you tell if an organization (or subunit) is too big?

OB in Action Case Study

Shaking Up Intel's Insides[92]

BusinessWeek Long before announcing a sweeping reorganization of Intel Corp.'s operating divisions [in January 2005], CEO-designate Paul S Otellini had been telling the world about a major shift in the chipmaker's strategy. Gone were the days, he said, when the company could get by with a single-minded focus on microprocessor design. Intel would instead focus more on bringing together chips and software into so-called platforms designed to perform specific tasks, such as showing movies on home PCs or keeping corporate computers virus-free. "For the first three decades of the company, we made mostly discrete chips. But they weren't designed to be used together . . . and they weren't marketed together," Otellini told *BusinessWeek* in November [2005].

Now he's making it clear to employees that, under his leadership, Intel truly is entering a new era. Otellini, who officially [took over in May 2005], will be the first chief executive without an engineering degree at a company where gearheads have reigned supreme. He believes that to keep Intel growing, every idea and technical solution should be focused on meeting customers' needs from the outset. So rather than relying on its engineering prowess, Intel's reorganization will bring together engineers, software writers, and marketers into five market-focused units: corporate computing, the digital home, mobile computing, health care, and channel products—PCs for small manufacturers.

The reorganization is not without challenges, but if Otellini succeeds it will amount to a revolution. For years, Intel has built one-size-fits-all processors, then expected customers to adopt them in various markets. But tech companies increasingly are being asked to deliver solutions that respond to the end user's demands. Corporations, for instance, are looking to prevent their systems from crashing, but employees frequent sites that contain viruses or spyware. Intel has responded by developing chips and software that quarantine these PCs and limit the damage.

Tandem Approach

Otellini's reorganization is supposed to ensure that such product tailoring becomes part of Intel's DNA. How will it work? The company's Centrino wireless notebook platform provides some clues. Intel first determined consumers wanted a powerful notebook with decent battery life that connected wirelessly to the Net. Armed with this knowledge, engineers and software writers designed a package of chips that would do that. Later, engineers and marketing people joined forces to create advertising that would persuade consumers to pay a premium for Centrino-powered notebooks. It worked: As of December [2004], Intel had 87% of the notebook PC market, says Mercury Research.

But imposing such a management structure across the company won't be easy. For one thing, Otellini has taken the unusual step of putting two execs apiece in charge of the two biggest groups, mobility and corporate computing. Intel has used this "two-men-in-a-box" approach before, but it will be particularly tricky under the new structure. Each unit will be responsible for several market segments; for example, the mobility unit will build platforms for notebooks, handhelds, and cell phones. So divvying up each co-chief's duties will be a challenge. Getting that right is crucial or the rank and file won't know who to report to.

The new regime will cause a jolt to the culture. For decades, employees have been compensated for their own work. Now teams will be judged as a whole. Engineers, long the top dogs, may resist working with others. "It's like saying to a baseball player, 'Gee, we're deciding to play pro football,' " says Edward E Lawler, a professor at USC's Marshall School of Business. "All of a sudden, the rules of the game are very different."

Otellini has begun to put the pieces in place. Now he'll need the teamwork of his people to pull it off.

Questions for Discussion

1. What does Intel's two-in-a-box approach do to the traditional unity of command principle? What are the positives and negatives?

2. What evidence of new-style organizations (see Table 17–1) do you find in this case?

3. Is Otellini turning Intel into a horizontal organization (see Figure 17–4)? Explain.

4. How should Otellini measure Intel's effectiveness? Explain.

5. Does Otellini's reorganization make Intel more mechanistic or more organic? Explain.

Personal Awareness and Growth Exercise

Organization Design Field Study

Objectives

1. To get out into the field and talk to a practicing manager about organizational structure.

2. To increase your understanding of the important distinction between mechanistic and organic organizations.

3. To broaden your knowledge of contingency design, in terms of organization–environment fit.

Introduction

A good way to test the validity of what you have just read about organizational design is to interview a practicing manager. (*Note:* If you are a manager, simply complete the questionnaire yourself.)

Instructions

Your objective is to interview a manager about aspects of organizational structure, environmental uncertainty, and organizational effectiveness. A *manager* is defined as anyone who supervises other people in an organizational setting. The organization may be small or large and for-profit or not-for-profit. Higher-level managers are preferred, but middle managers and first-line supervisors are acceptable. If you interview a lower-level manager, be sure to remind him or her that you want a description of the overall organization, not just an isolated subunit. Your interview will center on the adaptation of Table 17–2, as discussed below.

When conducting your interview, be sure to explain to the manager what you are trying to accomplish. But assure the manager that his or her name will not be mentioned in class discussion or any written projects. Try to keep side notes during the interview for later reference.

Questionnaire

The following questionnaire, adapted from Table 17–2, will help you determine if the manager's organization is relatively mechanistic or relatively organic in structure. *Note:* For items 1 and 2 on the following questionnaire, have the manager respond in terms of the average nonmanagerial employee. (Circle one number for each item.)

Characteristics

1. Task definition and knowledge required	Narrow; technical	1—2—3—4—5—6—7	Broad; general
2. Linkage between individual's contribution and organization's purpose	Vague or indirect	1—2—3—4—5—6—7	Clear or direct
3. Task flexibility	Rigid; routine	1—2—3—4—5—6—7	Flexible; varied
4. Specification of techniques, obligations, and rights	Specific	1—2—3—4—5—6—7	General
5. Degree of hierarchical control	High	1—2—3—4—5—6—7	Low (self-control emphasized)
6. Primary communication pattern	Top-down	1—2—3—4—5—6—7	Lateral (between peers)
7. Primary decision-making style	Authoritarian	1—2—3—4—5—6—7	Democratic; participative
8. Emphasis on obedience and loyalty	High	1—2—3—4—5—6—7	Low

Total score = _____

Additional Question about the Organization's Environment
This organization faces an environment that is (circle one number):
Stable and certain   1—2—3—4—5—6—7—8—9—10   Unstable and uncertain

Additional Questions about the Organization's Effectiveness
1. Profitability (if a profit-seeking business):
   Low   1—2—3—4—5—6—7—8—9—10   High
2. Degree of organizational goal accomplishment:
   Low   1—2—3—4—5—6—7—8—9—10   High
3. Customer or client satisfaction:
   Low   1—2—3—4—5—6—7—8—9—10   High
4. Employee satisfaction:
   Low   1—2—3—4—5—6—7—8—9—10   High

Total effectiveness score = _____
(Add responses from above)

Questions for Discussion

1. Using the following norms, was the manager's organization relatively mechanistic or organic?

   8–24 = relatively mechanistic
   25–39 = mixed
   40–56 = relatively organic

2. In terms of Burns and Stalker's contingency theory, does the manager's organization seem to fit its environment? Explain.

3. Does the organization's degree of effectiveness reflect how well it fits its environment? Explain.

Group Exercise

Stakeholder Audit Team

Objectives

1. To continue developing your group interaction and team-work skills.
2. To engage in open-system thinking.
3. To conduct a stakeholder audit and thus more fully appreciate the competing demands placed on today's managers.
4. To establish priorities and consider trade-offs for modern managers.

Introduction

According to open-system models of organizations, environmental factors—social, political, legal, technological, and economic—greatly affect what managers can and cannot do. This exercise gives you an opportunity to engage in open-system thinking within a team setting. It requires a team meeting of about 20 to 25 minutes followed by a 10- to 15-minute general class discussion. Total time required for this exercise is about 30 to 40 minutes.

Instructions

Your instructor will randomly assign you to teams with five to eight members each. Choose one team member to act as recorder/spokesperson. Either at your instructor's prompting or as a team, choose one of these two options:

1. Identify an organization that is familiar to everyone on your team (it can be a local business, your college or university, or a well-known organization such as McDonald's, Wal-Mart, or Southwest Airlines).

2. Select an organization from any of the OB in Action Case Studies following each chapter in this book.

Next, using Figure 17–6 as a model, do a *stakeholder audit* for the organization in question. This will require a team brainstorming session followed by brief discussion. Your team will need to make reasonable assumptions about the circumstances surrounding your target organization.

Finally, your team should select the three (or more) *high-priority* stakeholders on your team's list. Rank them number

one, number two, and so on. (*Tip:* A top-priority stakeholder is one with the greatest short-term impact on the success or failure of your target organization.) Be prepared to explain to the entire class your rationale for selecting each high-priority stakeholder.

Questions for Discussion

1. How does this exercise foster open-system thinking? Give examples.

2. Did this exercise broaden your awareness of the complexity of modern organizational environments? Explain.

3. Why do managers need clear priorities when it comes to dealing with organizational stakeholders?

4. How many *trade-offs* (meaning one party gains at another's expense) can you detect in your team's list of stakeholders? Specify them.

5. How difficult was it for your team to complete this assignment? Explain.

Ethical Dilemma

Burger King Serves Up a High-Calorie Strategy

Background

Since Greg Brenneman was hired as CEO in August 2004, Burger King's same-store sales have steadily grown. In 2003, Burger King introduced a low-fat sandwich that proved unpopular.

A Really Big Idea[93]

Greg Brenneman starts his morning in the middle of the night. He's up at 4:15, then races his Porsche to the office in Miami. He hits the StairMaster for an hour in the corporate gym, lifts weights, showers and is at his desk before 7.... He drinks decaf: "I'm wound tight enough." Lunch is often a salad. To relax, he skis and trains for triathlons.

Brenneman could have easily looked smart just adopting the McStrategy. The industry leader was enjoying its own upswing, eliminating supersizes and pushing salads. Instead, Brenneman went after his antithesis: the guy who downs fast food up to five times a week and wants decadent items, like the 760-calorie Enormous Omelet Sandwich (two omelets and cheese slices, three strips of bacon and a sausage patty on a bun). The strategy is just about giving his best customers what they want.

Is Burger King an effective organization, and what are the ethical implications of its "give 'em what they want" strategy?

1. Burger King is effective because the new CEO has profitably refocused the company on satisfying its core customers (18- to 34-year-old men who want a lot of food at a low price). Explain.

2. A health-nut CEO who is selling heart attacks on a bun is contrary to any reasonable notion of organizational effectiveness. Explain.

3. The CEO's lifestyle preferences are irrelevant when determining Burger King's effectiveness. Explain.

4. Invent other options, Discuss.

For the Chapter 17 Internet Exercise on organizational effectiveness (www.fastcompany.com/backissues), visit our Web site at **www.mhhe.com/kreitner.**

Managing Change and Stress

Learning Objectives

When you finish studying the material in this chapter, you should be able to:

1 Discuss the external and internal forces that create the need for organizational change.

2 Describe Lewin's change model and the systems model of change.

3 Discuss Kotter's eight steps for leading organizational change.

4 Define *organization development* (OD), and demonstrate your familiarity with its four identifying characteristics.

5 Summarize the 10 reasons employees resist change.

6 Discuss the five personal characteristics related to resistance to change.

7 Identify alternative strategies for overcoming resistance to change.

8 Define the term *stress,* and describe the model of occupational stress.

9 Discuss the stress moderators of social support, hardiness, and Type A behavior.

10 Discuss employee assistance programs (EAPs) and a holistic approach toward stress reduction.

BusinessWeek During the recent *Sturm and Drang* at Hewlett-Packard Co., there has been little soul-searching in the tech giant's gold mine printer business. For almost two decades, this $24-billion-a-year division has sailed along on a river of ink-cartridge profits, dominating rivals with a market share of more than 50%—and remaining blissfully detached from the problems at HP's computer units.

But with overall growth in printer demand slowing and margins tightening in the face of an assault from Dell Inc. and others, HP has decided there's no room for complacency. *BusinessWeek* has learned that printer chief Vyomesh Joshi is knee-deep in a "transformation" to ensure HP's dominance in printing and imaging.

Originally started at the urging of ousted CEO Carleton S Fiorina but supported by new boss Mark V Hurd, the effort, "Operation Lead Dog," involves cutting the division's head count by 10% or more, while pruning HP's cluttered portfolio of businesses, say four HP managers and an outside consultant. While Joshi hasn't determined the exact savings goals, his aim is to refocus on the biggest opportunities while lowering costs to maintain profit margins amid falling printer prices. HP declined to comment on the restructuring, but one printer division manager, speaking on condition of anonymity, described it as a "Jack Welch kind of thing. If you can't be no. 1 or 2, why do it?"

Let's be clear: HP's printer division is still a heavyweight. It accounted for 73% of HP's $4.2 billion in earnings for fiscal 2004, despite delivering less than a third of its $80 billion in sales. But tough times loom. Revenue growth is expected to slow to 5.7% for the fiscal year ending in October, down from 7.2% in fiscal '04, says Goldman, Sachs & Co., which also predicts that operating margins will slip to 15% this year, down from 15.9%.

A cross-current of pressures is to blame. Now that most PC owners have printers, demand is expected to be nearly flat in coming years. Yet Dell and others are competing harder for HP's customers. HP's share of the US printer market, measured in unit sales, fell six points in 2004, to 47%, according to

IDC. HP is expected to grab some of that back this year by cutting prices, but that could hurt profits. Meanwhile, a host of cartridge refillers wants to horn in on HP's lucrative sales of ink. "They're getting whacked from all sides," says Marco Boer, a consulting partner at IT Strategies consultancy.

Severance Frenzy

All that explains the urgency to get the printer division firing on all cylinders. The cost-cutting phase of the restructuring is well under way. Many staffers have taken a voluntary severance program that ended on April 22, according to several managers in the printing unit. Once the total is tallied, these people say, management will turn to mandatory layoffs that could run higher than 25% for some units. Much of the focus is on slashing bureaucracy and revamping basics such as processing orders, developing products, and the like. Says one staffer: "I've never seen the frenzy that's going on right now, with people not knowing if they have a job or not." . . .

It's far from crisis time for HP's printer business. Yet it's also clear the division no longer has a license to print profits. As a result, Joshi has plenty of support inside the company to take drastic—even painful—measures. "Everyone realizes that someone with a pair of scissors could do a lot of snipping around here," says one staffer at HP's operation in Corvallis, Oregon. "This transformation is necessary." And, if executed well, probably not too late.[1]

FOR DISCUSSION

To what extent is Vyomesh Joshi likely to encounter resistance to change? Explain your rationale.

Vyomesh Joshi's experiences at Hewlett-Packard are not the exception. Increased global competition, startling breakthroughs in information technology, and calls for greater corporate ethics are forcing companies to change the way they do business. Employees want satisfactory work environments, customers are demanding greater value, and investors want more integrity in financial disclosures. The rate of organizational and societal change is clearly accelerating.

As exemplified by HP in the opening vignette, organizations must change in order to satisfy customers and shareholders. The HP case also illustrates a subtle and important aspect about any type of change, whether it is market driven, personal, or organizational. Change is more likely to succeed when it is proactive rather than reactive. Peter Senge, a well-known expert on the topic of organizational change, made the following comment about organizational change during an interview with *Fast Company* magazine:

> When I look at efforts to create change in big companies over the past 10 years, I have to say that there's enough evidence of success to say that change is possible—and enough evidence of failure to say that it isn't likely.[2]

If Senge is correct, then it is all the more important for current and future managers to learn how they can successfully implement organizational change. This final chapter was written to help managers navigate the journey of change.

Specifically, we discuss the forces that create the need for organization change, models of planned change, resistance to change, and how managers can better manage the stress associated with organizational change.

Forces of Change

How do organizations know when they should change? What cues should an organization look for? Although there are no clear-cut answers to these questions, cues signaling the need for change are found by monitoring the forces for change.

Organizations encounter many different forces for change. These forces come from external sources outside the organization and from internal sources. This section examines the

Figure 18–1   *The External and Internal Forces for Change*

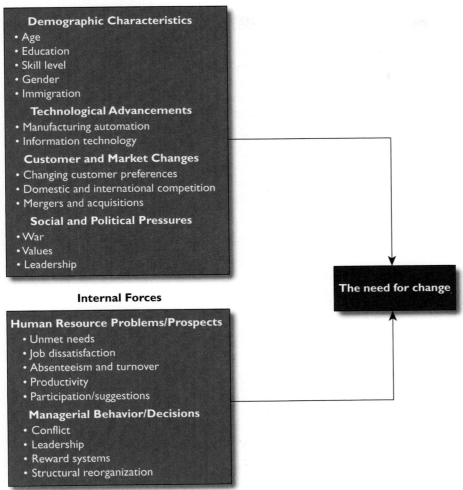

forces that create the need for change. Awareness of these forces can help managers determine when they should consider implementing an organizational change. The external and internal forces for change are presented in Figure 18–1.

External Forces

External forces for change originate outside the organization. Because these forces have global effects, they may cause an organization to question the essence of what business it is in and the process by which products and services are produced. Consider IBM for example. CEO Sam Palmisano wants to transform the very nature of IBM's core business from one that focuses on technology and technology services into one that offers a broad array of specialized services. The Real World/Real People feature on page 580 illustrates how Palmisano's new vision and strategy worked at Marathon Oil.[3] Let us now consider

External forces for change
Originate outside the organization.

Marathon Oil Experiences IBM's New Service Strategy

BusinessWeek Below is an example of how IBM's new business strategy was implemented with Marathon Oil.

A Push for Change In 2002, Marathon Oil's executives want to trim costs in the finance department and put in place monitoring tools so that managers can follow daily operations and make quick adjustments. They call in IBM consultants and researchers to talk it over.

IBM Responds Big Blue's consultants and software developers analyze Marathon's business processes. They suggest ways to reduce accounts payable and other processes from 18 days to eight. They build a "dashboard" on execs' PCs to help monitor the business.

The Path Forks While some clients keep control of their business processes and technology supplied by IBM, Marathon hands much of its finance operations directly to Big Blue. Other customers go further, having IBM manage human resources and customer service.

IBM Creates New Products IBM builds new businesses around the knowhow it develops for early customers such as Marathon. Already, IBM has sold the business-analysis dashboard it created for Marathon to more than a dozen other clients—and has installed it within IBM itself.

SOURCE: S Hamm, "Beyond Blue," *BusinessWeek*, April 18, 2005, p 72. Reprinted by permission of The McGraw-Hill Companies, Inc.

the four key external forces for change that influenced Palmisano's decision to transform IBM. They are demographic characteristics, technological advancements, market changes, and social and political pressures.

Demographic Characteristics

Chapter 2 provided a detailed discussion of demographic changes occurring in the US workforce. We concluded that organizations need to effectively manage diversity if they are to receive maximum contribution and commitment from employees. Consider the implications associated with hiring the 80 million people dubbed the Net or Echo-Boom Generation—people born between 1977 and 1997.

> Employers will have to face the new realities of the Net Generation's culture and values, and what it wants from work if they expect to attract and retain those talents and align them with corporate goals....The new wave of 80 million young people entering the workforce during the next 20 years are technologically equipped and, therefore, armed with the most powerful tools for business. That makes their place in history unique: No previous generation has grown up understanding, using, and expanding on such a pervasive instrument as the PC.[4]

Technological Advancements

Both manufacturing and service organizations are increasingly using technology as a means to improve productivity, competitiveness, and customer service while also cutting costs. The US Postal Service is a good example. Not only has information technology enhanced customer service by allowing customers to purchase services, track mail, and sign forms online, but it produced significant reductions in head count and supply-chain enhancements that resulted in $8.8 billion in savings. The Postal Service further estimates that Internet sales will generate $258 million in sales in 2005.[5] There is no question that the development and use of information technologies is probably one of the biggest forces for change. Organizations, large and small, private and public, for profit and not-for-profit, all must adapt to using a host of information technologies.

Customer and Market Changes Increasing customer sophistication is requiring organizations to deliver higher value in their products and services. Customers are simply demanding more now than they did in the past. Moreover, customers are more likely to shop elsewhere if they do not get what they want because of lower customer switching costs. For example, Verizon lost nearly 2 million lines in 2002 as customers switched to alternatives such as wireless and telephone service via cable-TV wires.[6]

With respect to market changes, service companies are experiencing increased pressure to obtain more productivity because competition is fierce and prices have remained relatively stable. Further, the emergence of a global economy is forcing companies to change the way they do business. US companies have been forging new partnerships and alliances with their suppliers and potential competitors in order to gain advantages in the global marketplace.[7]

Social and Political Pressures These forces are created by social and political events. For example, the collapse of Enron and major accounting scandals at companies like WorldCom, American International Group, and Fannie Mae has created increased focus on the process by which organizations conduct financial reporting. This in turn has fueled boards of directors to pay more attention to what CEOs are doing and to exert more power and control into the manner in which organizations are being operated.[8]

In general, social and political pressure is exerted through legislative bodies that represent the American populace. Political events also can create substantial change. For example, the war in Iraq created tremendous opportunities for defense contractors and organizations like Halliburton that are involved in rebuilding the country. Although it is difficult for organizations to predict changes in political forces, many organizations hire lobbyists and consultants to help them detect and respond to social and political changes.

Internal Forces

Internal forces for change come from inside the organization. These forces may be subtle, such as low job satisfaction, or can manifest in outward signs, such as low productivity and conflict. Internal forces for change come from both human resource problems and managerial behavior/decisions.

**Internal forces
for change**
Originate inside the
organization.

Human Resource Problems/Prospects These problems stem from employee perceptions about how they are treated at work and the match between individual and organization needs and desires. Chapter 6 highlighted the relationship between an employee's unmet needs and job dissatisfaction. Dissatisfaction is a symptom of an underlying employee problem that should be addressed. Dell, for example, instituted a process of semiannual employee surveys to determine employees' job satisfaction and to assess the quality of managers' leadership skills. A manager's effectiveness ratings are tied to compensation, promotions, and attendance at management training.[9] Unusual or high levels of absenteeism and turnover also represent forces for change. Organizations might respond to these problems by using the various approaches to job design discussed in Chapter 8, by reducing employees' role conflict, overload, and ambiguity (recall our discussion in Chapter 10), and by removing the different stressors discussed in the final section of this chapter. Prospects for positive change stem from employee participation and suggestions.

Managerial Behavior/Decisions Excessive interpersonal conflict between managers and their subordinates is a sign that change is needed. Both the manager and the employee may need interpersonal skills training, or the two individuals may simply need to be separated. For example, one of the parties might be transferred to a new department. Inappropriate leader behaviors such as inadequate direction or support may result in human resource problems requiring change. As discussed in Chapter 16, leadership training is one potential solution for this problem. Inequitable reward systems—recall our discussion in Chapters 8 and 9—and the type of structural reorganizations discussed in Chapter 17 are additional forces for change. Finally, managerial decisions are a powerful force for change. For example, Glenn Tilton, CEO of United Airlines, is creating much-needed change at the airline in order to help the company navigate through its 18-month stay in bankruptcy court. He has cut the workforce, asked employees for wage concessions, and instituted a bonus system that rewards the company's 63,000 employees for achieving the company's goals for on-time flight departures and for customer intent to fly United. These changes seem to be working as employees across the board have made concessions and United's customer service ratings have gone from nearly the worst to among the best in the industry.[10]

Models and Dynamics of Planned Change

American managers are criticized for emphasizing short-term, quick-fix solutions to organizational problems. When applied to organizational change, this approach is doomed from the start. Quick-fix solutions do not really solve underlying problems, and they have little staying power. Researchers and managers alike have thus tried to identify effective ways to manage the change process. This section sheds light on their insights. After discussing different types of organizational changes, we review Lewin's change model, a systems model of change, Kotter's eight steps for leading organizational change, and organizational development.

Types of Change

A useful three-way typology of change is displayed in Figure 18–2.[11] This typology is generic because it relates to all sorts of change, including both administrative and technological changes. Adaptive change is lowest in complexity, cost, and uncertainty. It involves

Figure 18–2   *A Generic Typology of Organizational Change*

Wal-Mart Created Competitive Advantage through Operational Innovations

Between 1972 and 1992, Wal-Mart went from $44 million in sales to $44 billion, powering past Sears and Kmart with faster growth, higher profits, and lower prices. How did it score that hat trick? Wal-Mart pioneered a great many innovations in how it purchased and distributed goods. One of the best known of these is cross-docking, in which goods trucked to a distribution center from suppliers are immediately transferred to trucks bound for stores—without ever being placed into storage. Cross-docking and companion innovations led to lower inventory levels and lower operating costs, which Wal-Mart translated into lower prices. The rest is history. Although operational innovation wasn't the sole ingredient in Wal-Mart's success—its culture, strategy, human resource policies, and a host of other elements (including operational excellence) were also critical—it was the foundation on which the company was built.

Wal-Mart has one of the most effective distribution networks in the world. This network enables the company to reduce its costs and sell products at lower costs than many competitors. Do you like to shop at Wal-Mart?

SOURCE: Excerpted from M Hammer, "Deep Change: How Operational Innovation Can Transform Your Company," *Harvard Business Review,* April 2004, p 86.

reimplementation of a change in the same organizational unit at a later time or imitation of a similar change by a different unit. For example, an adaptive change for a department store would be to rely on 12-hour days during the annual inventory week. The store's accounting department could imitate the same change in work hours during tax preparation time. Adaptive changes are not particularly threatening to employees because they are familiar.

Innovative changes fall midway on the continuum of complexity, cost, and uncertainty. An experiment with flexible work schedules by a farm supply warehouse company qualifies as an innovative change if it entails modifying the way other firms in the industry already use it. Unfamiliarity, and hence greater uncertainty, make fear of change a problem with innovative changes.

At the high end of the continuum of complexity, cost, and uncertainty are radically innovative changes. Changes of this sort are the most difficult to implement and tend to be the most threatening to managerial confidence and employee job security.[12] At the same time, however, radically innovative changes potentially realize the greatest benefits.[13] Wal-Mart is a good example of an organization that achieved competitive advantage from operational innovations (see Real World/Real People). As noted in the Wal-Mart example, radically innovative changes must be supported by an organization's culture. Organizational change is more likely to fail if it is inconsistent with any of the three levels of organizational culture: observable artifacts, espoused values, and basic assumptions (see the discussion in Chapter 3).[14]

Lewin's Change Model

Most theories of organizational change originated from the landmark work of social psychologist Kurt Lewin. Lewin developed a three-stage model of planned change which explained how to initiate, manage, and stabilize the change process.[15] The three stages are unfreezing, changing, and refreezing. Before reviewing each stage, it is important to highlight the assumptions underlying this model:[16]

1. The change process involves learning something new, as well as discontinuing current attitudes, behaviors, or organizational practices.

2. Change will not occur unless there is motivation to change. This is often the most difficult part of the change process.

3. People are the hub of all organizational changes. Any change, whether in terms of structure, group process, reward systems, or job design, requires individuals to change.

4. Resistance to change is found even when the goals of change are highly desirable.

5. Effective change requires reinforcing new behaviors, attitudes, and organizational practices.

Let us now consider the three stages of change.

Unfreezing   The focus of this stage is to create the motivation to change. In so doing, individuals are encouraged to replace old behaviors and attitudes with those desired by management. Managers can begin the unfreezing process by disconfirming the usefulness or appropriateness of employees' present behaviors or attitudes. In other words, employees need to become dissatisfied with the old way of doing things. Glenn Tilton attempted to unfreeze employees for change at United Airlines by traveling around the country and talking to employees about what was needed to help the company recover from bankruptcy. One of his goals in these talks was to get employees to think about solving problems rather than blaming others for what was wrong in the company. He wanted to eliminate a "blame" mentality. To do this, Tilton used one ground rule with employees:

> They could ask any question as long as they didn't blame their colleagues, supervisors, unions, or management for the airline's plight. In a meeting where a burly male ground worker started blaming other employees for the airline's woes, Mr Tilton stopped the man and told him to leave the room.[17]

Benchmarking
Process by which a company compares its performance with that of high-performing organizations.

Benchmarking is a technique that can be used to help unfreeze an organization. **Benchmarking** "describes the overall process by which a company compares its performance with that of other companies, then learns how the strongest-performing companies achieve their results."[18] For example, one company for which we consulted discovered through benchmarking that their costs to develop software were twice as high as the best companies in the industry, and the time it took to get a new product to market was four times longer than the benchmarked organizations. These data were ultimately used to unfreeze employees' attitudes and motivate people to change the organization's internal processes in order to remain competitive. Managers also need to devise ways to reduce the barriers to change during this stage.

Changing   Organizational change, whether large or small, is undertaken to improve some process, procedure, product, service, or outcome of interest to management. Because change involves learning and doing things differently, this stage entails providing employees with new information, new behavioral models, new processes or procedures, new equipment, new technology, or new ways of getting the job done. How does management know what to change?

There is no simple answer to this question. Organizational change can be aimed at improvement or growth, or it can focus on solving a problem such as poor customer service or low productivity. Change also can be targeted at different levels in an organization. For example, sending managers to leadership training programs can be a solution to improving individuals' job satisfaction and productivity. In contrast, installing new information technology may be the change required to increase work group productivity and overall corporate profits. The point to keep in mind is that change should be targeted at some type of desired end-result. The systems model of change, which is the next model to be discussed, provides managers with a framework to diagnose the target of change.

Refreezing   Change is stabilized during refreezing by helping employees integrate the changed behavior or attitude into their normal way of doing things. This is accomplished by first giving employees the chance to exhibit the new behaviors or attitudes. Once exhibited, positive reinforcement is used to reinforce the desired change. Additional coaching and modeling also are used at this point to reinforce the stability of the change. Returning to the example of United Airlines, the company used a new incentive system to refreeze employee behavior regarding productivity and customer service. United paid out $26 million under the bonus plan in the first quarter of 2004 after the company exceeded its goals. This example highlights the power of using monetary incentives to reinforce behavioral change.[19]

A Systems Model of Change

A systems approach takes a "big picture" perspective of organizational change. It is based on the notion that any change, no matter how large or small, has a cascading effect throughout an organization.[20] For example, promoting an individual to a new work group affects the group dynamics in both the old and new groups. Similarly, creating project or work teams may necessitate the need to revamp compensation practices. These examples illustrate that change creates additional change. Today's solutions are tomorrow's problems.

A systems model of change offers managers a framework or model to use for diagnosing *what* to change and for determining *how* to evaluate the success of a change effort. To further your understanding about this model, we first describe its components and then discuss a brief application. The four main components of a systems model of change are inputs, strategic plans, target elements of change, and outputs (see Figure 18–3).

Inputs   All organizational changes should be consistent with an organization's mission, vision, and resulting strategic plan. A **mission statement** represents the "reason" an organization exists, and an organization's *vision* is a long-term goal that describes "what" an organization wants to become. Consider how the difference between mission and vision affects organizational change. Your university probably has a mission to educate people. This mission does not necessarily imply anything about change. It simply defines the university's overall purpose. In contrast, the university may have a vision to be recognized as the "best" university in the country. This vision requires the organization to benchmark itself against other world-class universities and to create plans for achieving the vision. For example, the vision of the W P Carey School of Business at Arizona State University is to be among the top 25 business schools in the world. An assessment of an organization's internal strengths and weaknesses against its environmental opportunities and threats (SWOT) is another key input within the systems model. This SWOT analysis is a key component of the strategic planning process.

Mission statement
Summarizes "why" an organization exists.

Figure 18-3   *A Systems Model of Change*

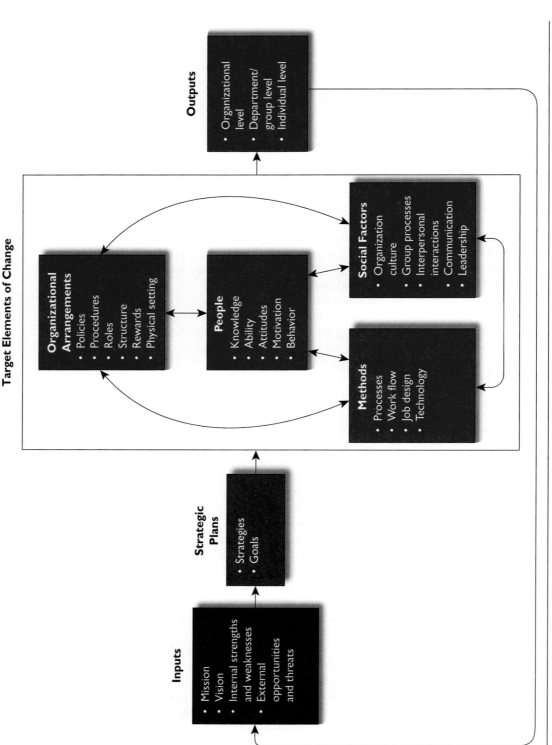

Target Elements of Change

Outputs
- Organizational level
- Department/group level
- Individual level

Organizational Arrangements
- Policies
- Procedures
- Roles
- Structure
- Rewards
- Physical setting

People
- Knowledge
- Ability
- Attitudes
- Motivation
- Behavior

Social Factors
- Organization culture
- Group processes
- Interpersonal interactions
- Communication
- Leadership

Methods
- Processes
- Work flow
- Job design
- Technology

Strategic Plans
- Strategies
- Goals

Inputs
- Mission
- Vision
- Internal strengths and weaknesses
- External opportunities and threats

SOURCES: Adapted from D R Fuqua and D J Kurpius, "Conceptual Models in Organizational Consultation," *Journal of Counseling and Development*, July–August 1993. pp 602–18; and D A Nadler and M L Tushman, "Organizational Frame Bending: Principles for Managing Reorientation," *Academy of Management Executive*, August 1989, pp 194–203.

Strategic Plans
A **strategic plan** outlines an organization's long-term direction and the actions necessary to achieve planned results. Among other things, strategic plans are based on results from a SWOT analysis. This analysis aids in developing an organizational strategy to attain desired goals such as profits, customer satisfaction, quality, adequate return on investment, and acceptable levels of turnover and employee satisfaction and commitment.

Strategic plan
A long-term plan outlining actions needed to achieve desired results.

Target Elements of Change
Target elements of change are the components of an organization that may be changed. They essentially represent change levers that managers can push and pull to influence various aspects of an organization. The choice of which lever to pull, however, is based on a diagnosis of a problem, or problems, or the actions needed to accomplish a goal: A problem exists when managers are not obtaining the results they desire. The target elements of change are used to diagnose problems and to identify change-related solutions.

As shown in Figure 18–3, there are four targeted elements of change: organizational arrangements, social factors, methods, and people.[21] Each target element of change contains a subset of more detailed organizational features. For instance, the "social factors" component includes consideration of an organization's culture, group processes, interpersonal interactions, communication, and leadership. There are two final issues to keep in mind about the target elements of change shown in Figure 18–3. First, the double-headed arrows connecting each target element of change convey the message that change ripples across an organization. For example, changing a reward system to reinforce team rather than individual performance (an organizational arrangement) is likely to impact organizational culture (a social factor). Second, the "people" component is placed in the center of the target elements of change box because all organizational change ultimately impacts employees. Organizational change is more likely to succeed when managers proactively consider the impact of change on its employees.

Target elements of change
Components of an organization that may be changed.

Outputs
Outputs represent the desired end-results of a change. Once again, these end-results should be consistent with an organization's strategic plan. Figure 18–3 indicates that change may be directed at the organizational level, department/group level, or individual level. Change efforts are more complicated and difficult to manage when they are targeted at the organizational level. This occurs because organizational-level changes are more likely to affect multiple target elements of change shown in the model.

Applying the Systems Model of Change
There are two different ways to apply the systems model of change. The first is as an aid during the strategic planning process. Once a group of managers have determined their vision and strategic goals, the target elements of change can be considered when developing action plans to support the accomplishment of goals. For example, the management team at JP Morgan Chase & Co. established goals to increase revenue and decrease costs. They decided to cut 12,000 jobs (a people factor), decrease executive perks like country club memberships and first-class airfare (an organizational arrangements factor), and to invest heavily in information technology in order to redesign the work flow (a method factor).[22] The second application involves using the model as a diagnostic framework to determine the causes of an organizational problem and to propose solutions. We highlight this application by considering a consulting project in which we used the model.

We were contacted by the CEO of a software company and asked to figure out why the presidents of three divisions were not collaborating with each other—the problem. It turned out that two of the presidents submitted a proposal for the same $4 million project from a potential customer. Our client did not get the work because the customer was appalled at having received two proposals from the same company; hence the CEO's call to us. We decided to interview employees by using a structured set of questions that pertained to each of the target elements of change. For instance, we asked employees to comment on the extent to which the reward system, organizational culture, work flow, and physical setting contributed to collaboration across divisions. The interviews taught us that the lack of collaboration among the division presidents was due to the reward system (an organizational arrangement), a competitive culture and poor communications (social factors), and poor work flow (a methods factor). Our recommendation was to change the reward systems, restructure the organization, and redesign the work flow.

Kotter's Eight Steps for Leading Organizational Change

John Kotter, an expert in leadership and change management, believes that organizational change typically fails because senior management commits one or more of the following errors:[23]

1. Failure to establish a sense of urgency about the need for change.
2. Failure to create a powerful-enough guiding coalition that is responsible for leading and managing the change process.
3. Failure to establish a vision that guides the change process.
4. Failure to effectively communicate the new vision.
5. Failure to remove obstacles that impede the accomplishment of the new vision.
6. Failure to systematically plan for and create short-term wins. Short-term wins represent the achievement of important results or goals.
7. Declaration of victory too soon. This derails the long-term changes in infrastructure that are frequently needed to achieve a vision.
8. Failure to anchor the changes into the organization's culture. It takes years for long-term changes to be embedded within an organization's culture.

Based on these errors, Kotter proposed an eight-step process for leading change (see Table 18–1). Unlike the systems model of change, this model is not diagnostic in orientation. Its application will not help managers to diagnose *what* needs to be changed. Rather, this model is more like Lewin's model of change in that it prescribes *how* managers should sequence or lead the change process.

Each of Kotter's eight steps shown in Table 18–1 is associated with the eight fundamental errors just discussed. These steps also subsume Lewin's model of change. The first four steps represent Lewin's "unfreezing" stage. Steps 5, 6, and 7 represent "changing," and step 8 corresponds to "refreezing." The value of Kotter's steps is that it provides specific recommendations about behaviors that managers need to exhibit to successfully lead organizational change. It is important to remember that Kotter's research reveals that it is ineffective to skip steps and that successful organizational change is 70 to 90% leadership and only 10 to 30% management. Senior managers are thus advised to focus on leading rather than managing change.[24]

Table 18–1   *Steps to Leading Organizational Change*

Step	Description
1. Establish a sense of urgency	Unfreeze the organization by creating a compelling reason for why change is needed.
2. Create the guiding coalition	Create a cross-functional, cross-level group of people with enough power to lead the change.
3. Develop a vision and strategy	Create a vision and strategic plan to guide the change process.
4. Communicate the change vision	Create and implement a communication strategy that consistently communicates the new vision and strategic plan.
5. Empower broad-based action	Eliminate barriers to change, and use target elements of change to transform the organization. Encourage risk taking and creative problem solving.
6. Generate short-term wins	Plan for and create short-term "wins" or improvements. Recognize and reward people who contribute to the wins.
7. Consolidate gains and produce more change	The guiding coalition uses credibility from short-term wins to create more change. Additional people are brought into the change process as change cascades throughout the organization. Attempts are made to reinvigorate the change process.
8. Anchor new approaches in the culture	Reinforce the changes by highlighting connections between new behaviors and processes and organizational success. Develop methods to ensure leadership development and succession.

SOURCE: The steps were developed by J P Kotter, *Leading Change* (Boston: Harvard Business School Press, 1996).

Creating Change through Organization Development

Organization development (OD) is different from the previously discussed models of change. OD does not entail a structured sequence as proposed by Lewin and Kotter, but it does possess the same diagnostic focus associated with the systems model of change. That said, OD is much broader in orientation than any of the previously discussed models. Specifically, a pair of experts in this field of study and practice defined **organization development** as follows:

> OD consists of planned efforts to help persons work and live together more effectively, over time, in their organizations. These goals are achieved by applying behavioral science principles, methods, and theories adapted from the fields of psychology, sociology, education, and management.[25]

Organization development
A set of techniques or tools used to implement planned organizational change.

As you can see from this definition, OD constitutes a set of techniques or interventions that are used to implement "planned" organizational change aimed at increasing "an organization's ability to improve itself as a humane and effective system."[26] OD techniques or interventions apply to each of the change models discussed in this section. For example OD is used during Lewin's "changing" stage. It also is used to identify and implement targeted elements of change within the systems model of change. Finally, OD might be used during Kotter's steps 1, 3, 5, 6, and 7. In this section, we briefly review the four identifying characteristics of OD and its research and practical implications.[27]

OD Involves Profound Change
Change agents using OD generally desire deep and long-lasting improvement. OD consultant Warner Burke, for example, who strives for fundamental *cultural* change, wrote: "By fundamental change, as opposed to fixing a

problem or improving a procedure, I mean that some significant aspect of an organization's culture will never be the same."[28]

OD Is Value-Loaded
Owing to the fact that OD is rooted partially in humanistic psychology, many OD consultants carry certain values or biases into the client organization. They prefer cooperation over conflict, self-control over institutional control, and democratic and participative management over autocratic management. In addition to OD being driven by a consultant's values, some OD practitioners now believe that there is a broader "value perspective" that should underlie any organizational change. Specifically, OD should always be customer focused. This approach implies that organizational interventions should be aimed at helping to satisfy customers' needs and thereby provide enhanced value of an organization's products and services.

OD Is a Diagnosis/Prescription Cycle
OD theorists and practitioners have long adhered to a medical model of organization. Like medical doctors, internal and external OD consultants approach the "sick" organization, "diagnose" its ills, "prescribe" and implement an intervention, and "monitor" progress.

OD Is Process-Oriented
Ideally, OD consultants focus on the form and not the content of behavioral and administrative dealings. For example, product design engineers and market researchers might be coached on how to communicate more effectively with one another without the consultant knowing the technical details of their conversations. In addition to communication, OD specialists focus on other processes, including problem solving, decision making, conflict handling, trust, power sharing, and career development.

OD Research and Practical Implications
Before discussing OD research, it is important to note that many of the topics contained in this book are used during OD interventions. For example, role analysis, which was discussed in Chapter 10, is used to enhance cooperation among work group members by getting them to discuss their mutual expectations. Team building also is commonly used as an OD technique. It is used to improve the functioning of work groups and was reviewed in Chapter 11. The point is that OD research has practical implications for a variety of OB applications previously discussed. OD-related interventions produced the following insights:

- A meta-analysis of 18 studies indicated that employee satisfaction with change was higher when top management was highly committed to the change effort.[29]

- A meta-analysis of 52 studies provided support for the systems model of organizational change. Specifically, varying one target element of change created changes in other target elements. Also, there was a positive relationship between individual behavior change and organizational-level change.[30]

- A meta-analysis of 126 studies demonstrated that multifaceted interventions using more than one OD technique were more effective in changing job attitudes and work attitudes than interventions that relied on only one human-process or technostructural approach.[31]

- A survey of 1,700 firms from China, Japan, the United States, and Europe revealed that (1) US and European firms used OD interventions more frequently than firms from China and Japan and (2) some OD interventions are culture free and some are not.[32]

There are four practical implications derived from this research. First, planned organizational change works. However, management and change agents are advised to rely on multifaceted interventions. As indicated elsewhere in this book, goal setting, feedback, recognition and rewards, training, participation, and challenging job design have good track records relative to improving performance and satisfaction. Second, change programs are more successful when they are geared toward meeting both short-term and long-term results. Managers should not engage in organizational change for the sake of change. Change efforts should produce positive results. Third, organizational change is more likely to succeed when top management is truly committed to the change process and the desired goals of the change program. This is particularly true when organizations pursue large-scale transformation. Finally, the effectiveness of OD interventions is affected by cross-cultural considerations. Managers and OD consultants should not blindly apply an OD intervention that worked in one country to a similar situation in another country.

Understanding and Managing Resistance to Change

Organizational change essentially represents a form of influence. That is, organizational change is management's attempt to get employees to behave, think, or perform differently. Viewing change from this perspective underscores what we discussed about influence techniques and outcomes in Chapter 15. You may recall that resistance is one of the three possible influence outcomes; the other two are commitment and compliance. Resistance to change thus represents a failed influence attempt. Let us consider one of the overriding causes of resistance to change.

We are all creatures of habit. It generally is difficult for people to try new ways of doing things. It is precisely because of this basic human characteristic that most employees do not have enthusiasm for change in the workplace. Rare is the manager who does not have several stories about carefully cultivated changes that died on the vine because of resistance to change. It is important for managers to learn to manage resistance because failed change efforts are costly. Costs include decreased employee loyalty, lowered probability of achieving corporate goals, a waste of money and resources, and difficulty in fixing the failed change effort. This section examines employee resistance to change, relevant research, and practical ways of dealing with the problem.

Why People Resist Change in the Workplace

No matter how technically or administratively perfect a proposed change may be, people make or break it. Individual and group behavior following an organizational change can take many forms (see Figure 18–4). The extremes range from acceptance to active resistance. **Resistance to change** is an emotional/behavioral response to real or imagined threats to an established work routine.

Figure 18–4 shows that resistance can be as subtle as passive resignation and as overt as deliberate sabotage. Managers need to learn to recognize the manifestations of resistance both in themselves and in others if they want to be more effective in creating and supporting change. For example, managers can use the list in Figure 18–4 to prepare answers and tactics to combat the various forms of resistance.

Resistance to change
Emotional/ behavioral response to real or imagined work changes.

Figure 18–4 *The Continuum of Responses to Change*

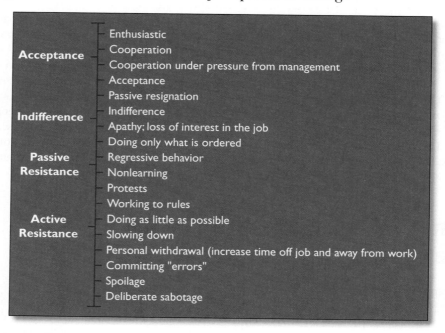

SOURCE: A S Judson, *Changing Behavior in Organizations: Minimizing Resistance to Change* (Cambridge, MA: Basil Blackwell Inc., 1991), p 48 Copyright © 1991. Used by permission of Blackwell Publishing.

Now that we have examined the manifestations of resistance to change, let us consider the reasons employees resist change in the first place. Ten of the leading reasons are listed here:[33]

1. *An individual's predisposition toward change.* This predisposition is highly personal and deeply ingrained. It is an outgrowth of how one learns to handle change and ambiguity as a child. Consider the hypothetical examples of Mary and Jim. Mary's parents were patient, flexible, and understanding. From the time Mary was weaned from a bottle, she was taught that there were positive compensations for the loss of immediate gratification. She learned that love and approval were associated with making changes. In contrast, Jim's parents were unreasonable, unyielding, and forced him to comply with their wishes. They forced him to take piano lessons even though he hated them. Changes were demands for compliance. This taught Jim to be distrustful and suspicious of change. These learned predispositions ultimately affect how Mary and Jim handle change as adults.[34]

2. *Surprise and fear of the unknown.* When innovative or radically different changes are introduced without warning, affected employees become fearful of the implications. Grapevine rumors fill the void created by a lack of official announcements. Harvard's Rosabeth Moss Kanter recommends appointing a transition manager charged with keeping all relevant parties adequately informed.[35]

3. *Climate of mistrust.* Trust, as discussed in Chapter 11, involves reciprocal faith in others' intentions and behavior. Mutual mistrust can doom to failure an otherwise well-conceived change. Mistrust encourages secrecy, which begets deeper

Can a Foreigner Successfully Run Sony?

Idei announced that he had asked six other corporate officers who were fellow "inside" directors to join him in resigning from the Sony board when he steps down officially as CEO this June, leaving the "outsiders" with a hefty eight-to-three majority.

The moves sent a shock wave through the electronics and media industries, and not just because Stringer, 63, is a Welsh-born American who doesn't speak Japanese. Stringer is not an engineer, nor much of a gadget freak, nor even a marketing whiz; his main claim to fame is overseeing the resurgence of Sony's movie and music business. But shock is clearly what Idei intended. "It's funny, 100% of the people around here agree we need to change, but 90% of them don't really want to change themselves," he says. "So I finally concluded that we needed our top management to quite literally speak another language."

SOURCE: Excerpted from B Schlender, "Inside the Shakeup at Sony," *Fortune* April 4, 2005, pp 94, 96.

mistrust. Managers who trust their employees make the change process an open, honest, and participative affair. Employees who, in turn, trust management are more willing to expend extra effort and take chances with something different.

4. *Fear of failure.* Intimidating changes on the job can cause employees to doubt their capabilities. Self-doubt erodes self-confidence and cripples personal growth and development. Recall our discussion about self-efficacy in Chapter 5.

5. *Loss of status or job security.* Administrative and technological changes that threaten to alter power bases or eliminate jobs generally trigger strong resistance. For example, most corporate restructuring involves the elimination of managerial jobs. One should not be surprised when middle managers resist restructuring and participative management programs that reduce their authority and status.

6. *Peer pressure.* Someone who is not directly affected by a change may actively resist it to protect the interests of his or her friends and co-workers.

7. *Disruption of cultural traditions or group relationships.* Whenever individuals are transferred, promoted, or reassigned, cultural and group dynamics are thrown into disequilibrium. For example, Nobuyuki Idei, former CEO of Sony Corp., was worried about employees' resistance to change in March 2005 when he named Sir Howard Stringer as the next chairman and CEO of Sony and asked six corporate officers to resign. Nobuyki's concern, rightfully so, stemmed from the fact that Stringer's appointment is inconsistent with Sony's tradition of promoting an insider with technical background (see Real World/Real People) and resignations will create a majority board of foreigners.[36] Time will tell whether or not Stringer's promotion was the right decision.

8. *Personality conflicts.* Just as a friend can get away with telling us something we would resent hearing from an adversary, the personalities of change agents can breed resistance.

9. *Lack of tact or poor timing.* Undue resistance can occur because changes are introduced in an insensitive manner or at an awkward time. Proposed organizational changes are more likely to be accepted by others when managers effectively explain or "sell" the value of their proposed changes. This can be done by explaining how a proposed change is strategically important to an organization's success.

10. *Nonreinforcing reward systems.* Individuals resist when they do not foresee positive rewards for changing. For example, an employee is unlikely to support a change effort that is perceived as requiring him or her to work longer with more pressure.

Research on Resistance to Change

People resist changes for a variety of reasons. These United Airlines employees are protesting outside a federal courthouse in Chicago prior to attending the company's bankruptcy hearing. A federal bankruptcy judge approved United's desire to terminate its employees' pension plan. This decision will adversely affect most employees while helping the company to reduce its costs. Do you think it is fair for a company to eliminate its pension plan once it has been promised?

The classic study of resistance to change was reported in 1948 by Lester Coch and John R P French. They observed the introduction of a new work procedure in a garment factory. The change was introduced in three different ways to separate groups of workers. In the "no participation" group, the garment makers were simply told about the new procedure. Members of a second group, called the "representative" group, were introduced to the change by a trained co-worker. Employees in the "total participation" group learned of the new work procedure through a graphic presentation of its cost-saving potential. Mixed results were recorded for the representative group. The no participation and total participation groups, meanwhile, went in opposite directions. Output dropped sharply for the no participation group, while grievances and turnover climbed.

After a small dip in performance, the total participation group achieved record-high output levels while experiencing no turnover.[37] Since the Coch and French study, participation has been the recommended approach for overcoming resistance to change.[38]

Commitment to change

A mind-set of doing whatever it takes to effectively implement change.

Empirical research uncovered five additional personal characteristics related to resistance to change. The first involves an employee's commitment to change. **Commitment to change** is defined as a mind-set "that binds an individual to a course of action deemed necessary for the successful implementation of a change initiative."[39] A series of studies showed that an employee's commitment to change was a significant and positive predictor of behavioral support for a change initiative.[40] In order to bring this concept to life, we would like you to complete a shortened version of a commitment to change instrument presented in the OB Exercise. Were you committed to the change? Did this level of commitment affect your behavioral support for what management was trying to accomplish?

Resilience to change

Composite personal characteristic reflecting high self-esteem, optimism, and an internal locus of control.

The second personal characteristic is resilience to change. **Resilience to change** is a composite characteristic reflecting high self-esteem, optimism, and an internal locus of control: Self-esteem and locus of control were discussed in Chapter 5. People with high resilience are expected to be more open and adaptable toward change.[41] In support of this prediction, a study of 130 individuals working in the areas of public housing and community development revealed that resilience to change was associated with respondents' willingness to accommodate or accept a specific organizational change. In turn, willingness to accept change was positively related to job satisfaction and negatively associated with work irritations and intentions to quit.[42]

Does Your Commitment to a Change Initiative Predict Your Behavioral Support for the Change?

Instructions

First, think of a time in which a previous or current employer was undergoing a change initiative that required you to learn something new or to discontinue an attitude, behavior, or organizational practice. Next, evaluate your commitment to this change effort by indicating the extent to which you agree with the following survey items. Use the rating scale shown below. Finally, assess your behavioral support for the change.

1 = strongly disagree
2 = disagree
3 = neither agree nor disagree
4 = agree
5 = strongly agree

1. I believe in the value of this change.	1—2—3—4—5
2. This change serves an important purpose.	1—2—3—4—5
3. This change is a good strategy for the organization.	1—2—3—4—5
4. I have no choice but to go along with this change.	1—2—3—4—5
5. It would be risky to speak out against this change.	1—2—3—4—5
6. It would be too costly for me to resist this change.	1—2—3—4—5
7. I feel a sense of duty to work toward this change.	1—2—3—4—5
8. It would be irresponsible of me to resist this change.	1—2—3—4—5
9. I feel obligated to support this change.	1—2—3—4—5

Total score = _____

Arbitrary Norms

9–18 = low commitment
19–35 = moderate commitment
36–45 = high commitment

Behavioral Support for the Change

Overall, I modified my attitudes and behavior in line with what management was trying to accomplish.

1—2—3—4—5

SOURCE: Survey items were obtained from L Herscovitch and J P Meyer, "Commitment to Organizational Change: Extension of a Three-Component Model," *Journal of Applied Psychology*, June 2002, p 477.

The third and fourth characteristics were identified in a study of 514 employees from six organizations headquartered in four different continents (North America, Europe, Asia, and Australia). Results revealed that personal dispositions pertaining to having a "positive self-concept" and "tolerance for risk" were positively related to coping with change. That is, people with a positive self-concept and a tolerance for risk handled organizational change better than those without these dispositions.[43]

Finally, high levels of self-efficacy (recall our discussion in Chapter 5) were negatively associated with resistance to change.[44]

The preceding research is based on the assumption that individuals directly or consciously resist change. Some experts contend that this is not the case. Rather, there is a growing belief that resistance to change really represents employees' responses to obstacles in the organization that prevent them from changing.[45] For example, John Kotter, the researcher who developed the eight steps for leading organizational change that were discussed earlier in this chapter, studied more than 100 companies and concluded that employees generally wanted to change but were unable to do so because of obstacles that prevented execution. He noted that obstacles in the organization's structure or in a "performance appraisal system [that] makes people choose between the new vision and their own self-interests" impeded change more than an individual's direct resistance.[46] This new perspective implies that a systems model such as that shown in Figure 18–3 should be used to determine the causes of failed change. Such an approach would likely reveal that ineffective organizational change is due to faulty organizational processes and systems as opposed to employees' direct resistance.[47] In conclusion, a systems perspective suggests that people do not resist change, per se, but rather that individuals' antichange attitudes and behaviors are caused by obstacles within the work environment.

Alternative Strategies for Overcoming Resistance to Change

We previously noted that participation historically has been the recommended approach for overcoming resistance to change. More recently, however, organizational change experts criticized the tendency to treat participation as a cure-all for resistance to change. They prefer a contingency approach because resistance can take many forms and, furthermore, be-

Table 18–2   *Six Strategies for Overcoming Resistance to Change*

Approach	Commonly Used in Situations	Advantages	Drawbacks
Education + communication	Where there is a lack of information or inaccurate information and analysis.	Once persuaded, people will often help with the implementation of the change.	Can be very time consuming if lots of people are involved.
Participation + involvement	Where the initiators do not have all the information they need to design the change and where others have considerable power to resist.	People who participate will be committed to implementing change, and any relevant information they have will be integrated into the change plan.	Can be very time consuming if participators design an inappropriate change.
Facilitation + support	Where people are resisting because of adjustment problems.	No other approach works as well with adjustment problems.	Can be time consuming, expensive, and still fail.
Negotiation + agreement	Where someone or some group will clearly lose out in a change and where that group has considerable power to resist.	Sometimes it is a relatively easy way to avoid major resistance.	Can be too expensive in many cases if it alerts others to negotiate for compliance.
Manipulation + co-optation	Where other tactics will not work or are too expensive.	It can be a relatively quick and inexpensive solution to resistance problems.	Can lead to future problems if people feel manipulated.
Explicit + implicit coercion	Where speed is essential and where the change initiators possess considerable power.	It is speedy and can overcome any kind of resistance.	Can be risky if it leaves people mad at the initiators.

SOURCE: Reprinted by permission of *Harvard Business School Press*. Exhibit from J P Kotter and L A Schlesinger, "Choosing Strategies for Change," March/April 1979. Copyright © 1979 by the Harvard Business School of Publishing Corporation; all rights reserved.

OB Exercise — Assessing an Organization's Readiness for Change

Instructions

Circle the number that best represents your opinions about the company being evaluated.

3 = yes
2 = somewhat
1 = no

1. Is the change effort being sponsored by a senior-level executive (CEO, COO)?	3—2—1
2. Are all levels of management committed to the change?	3—2—1
3. Does the organization culture encourage risk taking?	3—2—1
4. Does the organization culture encourage and reward continuous improvement?	3—2—1
5. Has senior management clearly articulated the need for change?	3—2—1
6. Has senior management presented a clear vision of a positive future?	3—2—1
7. Does the organization use specific measures to assess business performance?	3—2—1
8. Does the change effort support other major activities going on in the organization?	3—2—1
9. Has the organization benchmarked itself against world-class companies?	3—2—1
10. Do all employees understand the customers' needs?	3—2—1
11. Does the organization reward individuals and/or teams for being innovative and for looking for root causes of organizational problems?	3—2—1
12. Is the organization flexible and cooperative?	3—2—1
13. Does management effectively communicate with all levels of the organization?	3—2—1
14. Has the organization successfully implemented other change programs?	3—2—1
15. Do employees take personal responsibility for their behavior?	3—2—1
16. Does the organization make decisions quickly?	3—2—1

Total score: _____

Arbitrary Norms

40–48 = high readiness for change
24–39 = moderate readiness for change
16–23 = low readiness for change

SOURCE: Based on the discussion contained in T A Stewart, "Rate Your Readiness to Change," *Fortune,* February 7, 1994, pp 106–10.

---

cause situational factors vary (see Table 18–2). As shown in Table 18–2, participation + involvement does have its place, but it takes time that is not always available. Also as indicated in Table 18–2, each of the other five methods has its situational niche, advantages, and drawbacks. In short, there is no universal strategy for overcoming resistance to change. Managers need a complete repertoire of change strategies.

Moreover, there are four additional recommendations managers should consider when leading organizational change. First, an organization must be ready for change. Just as a table must be set before you can eat, so must an organization be ready for change before it can be effective.[48] The OB Exercise above contains a survey that assesses an organization's readiness for change. Use the survey to evaluate a company that you worked for or are familiar with that undertook a change effort. What was the company's readiness for change, and how did this evaluation relate to the success of the change effort?

Second, do not assume that people are consciously resisting change. Managers are encouraged to use a systems model of change to identify the obstacles that are affecting the implementation process. Third, radical innovative change is more likely to succeed when middle-level managers are highly involved in the change process. Hewlett-Packard successfully implemented change by following this recommendation.

> [W]hen new executives were charged with turning around Hewlett-Packard's Santa Rosa Systems division, which produces test and measurement equipment for electronic systems, they enlisted a task force of eight middle managers to collect employees' views about the current leadership (negative) and customers' views about the division's performance (also negative). The result was candid, detailed feedback that sometimes felt like "an icy bucket of water over the head," as one executive described it, but that also allowed executives to adjust their change proposals on the fly. Middle managers were consulted early and often about strategic and operational questions. As a result, they understood better what the senior team was trying to accomplish and felt more comfortable supporting executives' intentions. The end result was one of the speediest turnarounds ever of an HP division.[49]

Fourth, employees' perceptions or interpretations of a change significantly affect resistance. Employees are less likely to resist when they perceive that the benefits of a change overshadow the personal costs. At a minimum then, managers are advised to (1) provide as much information as possible to employees about the change, (2) inform employees about the reasons/rationale for the change, (3) conduct meetings to address employees' questions regarding the change, and (4) provide employees the opportunity to discuss how the proposed change might affect them.[50] These recommendations underscore the importance of communicating with employees throughout the process of change.

Dynamics of Stress

Fight-or-flight response
To either confront stressors or try to avoid them.

We all experience stress on a daily basis. Although stress is caused by many factors, researchers conclude that stress triggers one of two basic reactions: active fighting or passive flight (running away or acceptance), the so-called **fight-or-flight response**.[51] Physiologically, this stress response is a biochemical "passing gear" involving hormonal changes that mobilize the body for extraordinary demands. Imagine how our prehistoric ancestors responded to the stress associated with a charging saber-toothed tiger. To avoid being eaten, they could stand their ground and fight the beast or run away. In either case, their bodies would have been energized by an identical hormonal change, involving the release of adrenaline into the bloodstream.

In today's hectic urbanized and industrialized society, charging beasts have been replaced by problems such as deadlines, role conflict and ambiguity, financial responsibilities, information overload, technology, traffic congestion, noise and air pollution, family problems, and work overload. As with our ancestors, our response to stress may or may not trigger negative side effects, including headaches, ulcers, insomnia, heart attacks, high blood pressure, and strokes. The same

This lion has clearly created a flight response from its targeted prey. Have you ever run away from danger?

stress response that helped our prehistoric ancestors survive has too often become a factor that seriously impairs our daily lives.

Because stress and its consequences are manageable, it is important for managers to learn as much as they can about occupational stress. After defining stress, this section provides an overview of the dynamics associated with stress by presenting a model of occupational stress, discussing moderators of occupational stress, and reviewing the effectiveness of several stress-reduction techniques.

Defining Stress

To an orchestra violinist, stress may stem from giving a solo performance before a big audience. While heat, smoke, and flames may represent stress to a firefighter, delivering a speech or presenting a lecture may be stressful for those who are shy. In short, stress means different things to different people. Managers need a working definition.

Stress
Behavioral, physical, or psychological response to stressors.

Formally defined, **stress** is "an adaptive response, mediated by individual characteristics and/or psychological processes, that is a consequence of any external action, situation, or event that places special physical and/or psychological demands upon a person."[52] This definition is not as difficult as it seems when we reduce it to three inter-related dimensions of stress: (1) environmental demands, referred to as stressors, that produce (2) an adaptive response that is influenced by (3) individual differences.

Hans Selye, considered the father of the modern concept of stress, pioneered the distinction between stressors and the stress response. Moreover, Selye emphasized that both positive and negative events can trigger an identical stress response that can be beneficial or harmful. He referred to stress that is positive or produces a positive outcome as **eustress.** Receiving an award in front of a large crowd or successfully completing a difficult work assignment both are examples of stressors that produce eustress. He also noted that

Eustress
Stress that is good or produces a positive outcome.

- Stress is not merely nervous tension.
- Stress can have positive consequences.
- Stress is not something to be avoided.
- The complete absence of stress is death.[53]

These points make it clear that stress is inevitable. Efforts need to be directed at managing stress, not at somehow escaping it altogether.

A Model of Occupational Stress

Figure 18–5 presents an instructive model of occupational stress. The model shows that an individual initially appraises four types of stressors. This appraisal then motivates an individual to choose a coping strategy aimed at managing stressors, which, in turn, produces a variety of outcomes. The model also specifies several individual differences that moderate the stress process. A moderator is a variable that causes the relationship between two variables—such as stressors and cognitive appraisal—to be stronger for some people and weaker for others. Three key moderators are discussed in the next section. Let us now consider the remaining components of this model in detail.

Stressors   **Stressors** are environmental factors that produce stress. Stated differently, stressors are a prerequisite to experiencing the stress response. Figure 18–5 shows the four major types of stressors: individual, group, organizational, and extraorganizational.

Stressors
Environmental factors that produce stress.

Figure 18–5   *A Model of Occupational Stress*

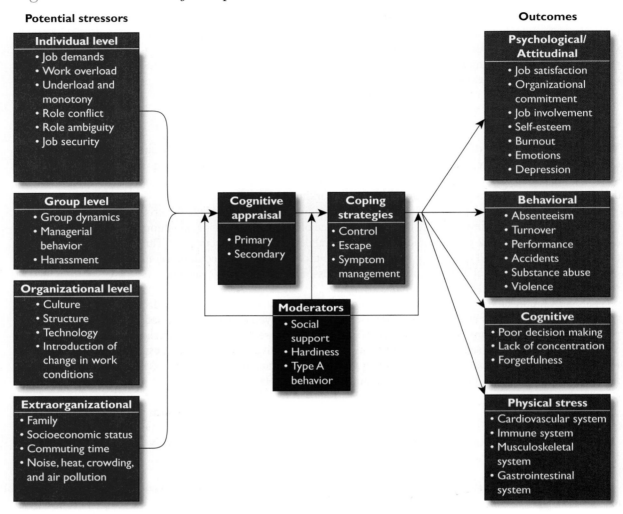

Individual-level stressors are those directly associated with a person's job duties. The most common examples of individual stressors are job demands, work overload, role conflict, role ambiguity, everyday hassles, perceived control over events occurring in the work environment, job characteristics, and work/family conflict (recall our discussion in Chapter 6).[54] Losing one's job is another important individual-level stressor. Job loss is a very stressful event that is associated with decreased psychological and physical well-being.[55] Finally, sleep-related issues are important stressors. Research shows that most people need about seven hours of sleep per night and that alertness, energy, performance, creativity, and thinking are related to how much we sleep.[56] Further, working nights creates sleep-related disorders that cost organizations "an estimated $28 billion in health-insurance costs nationwide."[57]

Group-level stressors are caused by group dynamics (recall our discussion in Chapter 10) and managerial behavior. Managers create stress for employees by (1) exhibiting inconsistent behaviors, (2) failing to provide support, (3) showing lack of concern, (4) providing inadequate direction, (5) creating a high-productivity environment, and (6) focusing on negatives while ignoring good performance. Sexual harassment experiences represent another group-level stressor. Studies show that harassing experiences are negatively associated with work, supervision, and promotion satisfaction and are positively related to ambiguity, conflict, and stress.[58]

Organizational stressors affect large numbers of employees. Organizational culture, which was discussed in Chapter 3, is a prime example. For instance, a high-pressure environment that fuels employee fear about performing up to standard increases the stress response.[59] The increased use of information technology is another source of organizational stress, as is the air quality and ventilation found throughout the organization. The World Health Organization, for instance, reports that roughly 30% of all new and remodeled buildings have problems related to air quality, and air quality is associated with a variety of conditions such as headaches, dizziness, and the ability to concentrate.[60]

Extraorganizational stressors are those caused by factors outside the organization. For instance, in Chapter 6 we discussed how conflicts associated with balancing one's career and family life are stressful. Socioeconomic status is another extraorganizational stressor. Stress is higher for people with lower socioeconomic status, which represents a combination of (1) economic status, as measured by income, (2) social status, assessed by education level, and (3) work status, as indexed by occupation. These stressors are likely to become more important in the future.

Cognitive Appraisal of Stressors

Cognitive appraisal reflects an individual's overall perception or evaluation of a situation or stressor. It is an important component within the stress process because people interpret the same stressors differently. For example, some individuals perceive unemployment as a positive liberating experience, whereas others perceive it as a negative debilitating one.

Figure 18–5 shows that people make two types of appraisals when evaluating the potential impact of stressors on their lives: primary and secondary appraisals.[61] A **primary appraisal** results in categorizing a situation or stressor as irrelevant, positive, or stressful. Stress appraisals are obviously the most important in terms of our current discussion because they imply that a situation or stressor is perceived as harmful, threatening, or challenging.

A **secondary appraisal** only occurs in response to a stressful primary appraisal and entails an assessment of what might and can be done to reduce the level of perceived stress. During this evaluation a person considers which coping strategies are available and which ones are most likely to help resolve the situation at hand. Ultimately, the combination of an individual's primary and secondary appraisal influences the choice of coping strategies used to reduce stress.

Coping Strategies

Coping strategies are characterized by the specific behaviors and cognitions used to cope with a situation. People use a combination of three approaches to cope with stressors and stress (see Figure 18–5). The first, called a **control strategy,** consists of using behaviors and cognitions to directly anticipate or solve problems. A control strategy has a take-charge tone. Consider the behavior of quitting a job in order to gain flexibility in your life. Kathy Dawson, for example, resigned from a six-figure job at Pinnacle Brands Inc., a trading-card company in Grand Prairie, Texas, because she wanted to spend more time with her two young daughters. She coped by starting a personnel consulting company.[62] In support of this example, a recent study of 29 hospital workers revealed that a control coping strategy was positively associated with indicators of well-being.[63]

Primary appraisal
Determining whether a stressor is irrelevant, positive, or stressful.

Secondary appraisal
Assessing what might and can be done to reduce stress.

Control strategy
Coping strategy that directly confronts or solves problems.

Escape strategy
Coping strategy that avoids or ignores stressors and problems.

Symptom management strategy
Coping strategy that focuses on reducing the symptoms of stress.

In contrast to tackling the problem head-on, an **escape strategy** amounts to avoiding the problem. Behaviors and cognitions are used to avoid or escape situations. Individuals use this strategy when they passively accept stressful situations or avoid them by failing to confront the cause of stress (an obnoxious co-worker, for instance). Finally, a **symptom management strategy** consists of using methods such as relaxation, meditation, medication, or exercise to manage the symptoms of occupational stress.

Stress Outcomes   Theorists contend stress has psychological/attitudinal, behavioral, cognitive, and physical health consequences or outcomes. A large body of research supports the negative effects of perceived stress on many aspects of our lives. Workplace stress is negatively related to job satisfaction, organizational commitment, positive emotions, performance, and turnover.[64] Research also shows that stress is associated with negative behaviors such as yelling and verbal abuse and violence toward others. These stress outcomes are very costly. The American Institute of Stress estimates that one million people miss work daily as a result of stress. All told, "the annual tab for all these lost hours due to absenteeism; reduced productivity; turnover; and medical, legal, and insurance costs comes to $300 billion or $7,500 per worker."[65] Finally, ample evidence supports the conclusion that stress negatively affects our physical health. Stress contributes to the following health problems: lessened ability to ward off illness and infection, high blood pressure, coronary artery disease, tension headaches, back pain, diarrhea, and constipation.[66] In fact, it's stressful to even think about all these problems!

Moderators of Occupational Stress

Moderators, once again, are variables that cause the relationships between stressors, perceived stress, and outcomes to be weaker for some people and stronger for others. Managers with a working knowledge of important stress moderators can confront employee stress in the following ways:

1. Awareness of moderators helps identify those most likely to experience stress and its negative outcomes. Stress-reduction programs then can be formulated for high-risk employees.

2. Moderators, in and of themselves, suggest possible solutions for reducing negative outcomes of occupational stress.

Keeping these objectives in mind, we will examine three important moderators: social support, hardiness, and Type A behavior.

Social support
Amount of helpfulness derived from social relationships.

Social Support   Talking with a friend or taking part in a bull session can be comforting during times of fear, stress, or loneliness. For a variety of reasons, meaningful social relationships help people do a better job of handling stress. **Social support** is the amount of perceived helpfulness derived from social relationships. Importantly, social support is determined by both the quantity and quality of an individual's social relationships. We receive four types of social support from others:

• *Esteem support.* Providing information that a person is accepted and respected despite any problems or inadequacies.

• *Informational support.* Providing help in defining, understanding, and coping with problems.

• *Social companionship.* Spending time with others in leisure and recreational activities.

• *Instrumental support.* Providing financial aid, material resources, or needed services.[67]

Social Support Helps Amanda Albertelli Cope with Divorce

When Amanda Albertelli was hired for her job at Home-Banc Mortgage Corp. in Atlanta, she was married. By the time she showed up for work a few weeks later, she was separated; six months after that, she was divorced.

Throughout those months, she was not only adapting to her new role as a single mother, but also learning the ropes at the company's fledgling nonprofit arm, the HomeBanc Foundation. No one would have been the least surprised if she had buckled under the pressure.

Instead, Albertelli thrived. . . .

While she credits her own hard work, she also values the unwavering support of her manager and the company's chief people officer.

For example, when Albertelli needed time off for court dates or to sign documents, she got it—without drawing down her personal or vacation time. When she began to feel overburdened and underconfident, she received one-on-one counseling from her company's corporate chaplain and a life/career coach. And when she was ready to buy a new home, she turned to the mortgage company's associate loan program.

Says Albertelli: "The support here has just been amazing every step of the way."

Without that support, it's easy to imagine Albertelli's story having a very different outcome—personally and professionally.

SOURCE: Excerpted from L W Andrews, "Help Maintain Your Employees' Workplace Productivity during a Personal Crisis," *HR Magazine*, pp 59–60. Reprinted with the permission of HR Magazine, published by the Society for Human Resource Management, Alexandria, VA.

Research shows that social support is negatively related to physiological processes and mortality. In other words, people with low social support tend to have poorer cardiovascular and immune system functioning and tend to die earlier than those with strong social support networks.[68] Further, social support protects against the perception of stress, depression, psychological problems, pregnancy complications, anxiety, loneliness, high blood pressure, and a variety of other ailments. In contrast, negative social support, which amounts to someone undermining another person, negatively affects one's mental health.[69] We are well advised to avoid people who try to undermine us.

Social support research highlights two practical recommendations. First, managers are advised to keep employees informed about external and internal social support systems. Internally, managers can use all four forms of social support when employees experience a personal crisis. Coping with a divorce is a good example (see Real World/Real People). Second, participative management programs and company-sponsored activities that make employees feel they are an important part of an extended family can be rich sources of social support. Employees need time and energy to adequately maintain their social relationships. If organizational demands are excessive, employees' social relationships and support networks will suffer, resulting in stress-related illness and decreased performance.

Hardiness   Suzanne Kobasa, a behavioral scientist, identified a collection of personality characteristics that neutralize occupational stress. This collection of characteristics, referred to as **hardiness,** involves the ability to perceptually or behaviorally transform negative stressors into positive challenges. Hardiness embraces the personality dimensions of commitment, locus of control, and challenge.[70]

Commitment reflects the extent to which an individual is involved in whatever he or she is doing. Committed people have a sense of purpose and do not give up under pressure because they tend to invest themselves in the situation. As discussed in Chapter 5, individuals

Hardiness
Personality characteristic that neutralizes stress.

with an *internal locus of control* believe they can influence the events that affect their lives. People possessing this trait are more likely to foresee stressful events, thereby reducing their exposure to anxiety-producing situations. Moreover, their perception of being in control leads "internals" to use proactive coping strategies. *Challenge* is represented by the belief that change is a normal part of life. Hence, change is seen as an opportunity for growth and development rather than a threat to security.

Research supports the moderating influence of hardiness on the stress process. For example, a five-year study of 259 managers from a public utility revealed that hardiness—commitment, locus of control, and challenge—reduced the probability of illness following exposure to stress.[71] The three components of hardiness also were found to directly influence how 276 members of the Israeli Defense Forces appraised stressors and ultimately coped with them. Hardy individuals interpreted stressors less negatively and were more likely to use control coping strategies than unhardy people.[72] Furthermore, additional research demonstrated that hardy individuals displayed lower stress, burnout, and psychological distress and higher job satisfaction than their less hardy counterparts.[73] Finally, a study of 73 pregnant women revealed that hardy women had fewer problems during labor and more positive perceptions about their infants than unhardy women.[74]

One practical offshoot of this research is organizational training and development programs that strengthen the characteristics of commitment, personal control, and challenge. For example, a team of researchers developed a hardiness training program based on this recommendation and tested it on a group of students and working adults. Results revealed that students' grade point average, retention, and health improved after the training. Training also resulted in increased performance, job satisfaction, and health for the working adults.[75] The hardiness concept also meshes nicely with job design. Enriched jobs are likely to fuel the hardiness components of commitment and challenge. A final application of the hardiness concept is as a diagnostic tool. Employees scoring low on hardiness would be good candidates for stress-reduction programs.

Type A Behavior Pattern   According to Meyer Friedman and Ray Rosenman (the cardiologists who isolated the Type A syndrome in the 1950s):

Type A behavior pattern
Aggressively involved in a chronic, determined struggle to accomplish more in less time.

Type A behavior pattern is an action-emotion complex that can be observed in any person who is aggressively involved in a chronic, incessant struggle to achieve more and more in less and less time, and if required to do so, against the opposing efforts of other things or persons. It is not psychosis or a complex of worries or fears or phobias or obsessions, but a socially acceptable—indeed often praised—form of conflict. Persons possessing this pattern also are quite prone to exhibit a free-floating but, extraordinarily well-rationalized hostility. As might be expected, there are degrees in the intensity of this behavior pattern.[76]

While labeling Type A behavior as "hurry sickness," Friedman and Rosenman noted that Type A individuals frequently tend to exhibit most of the behaviors listed in Table 18–3.

Because Type A behavior is a matter of degree, it is measured on a continuum. This continuum has the hurried, competitive Type A behavior pattern at one end and the more relaxed Type B behavior pattern at the other. Take a moment to complete the Type A survey contained in the OB Exercise on page 606. This exercise will help you better understand the characteristics of the Type A behavior pattern. Where did you fall on the Type A continuum?

Let us now consider the pros and cons of being Type A. OB research has demonstrated that Type A employees tend to be more productive than their Type B co-workers. For instance, Type A behavior yielded a significant and positive correlation with 766 students' grade point averages, the quantity and quality of 278 university professors' performance,

Table 18–3   *Type A Characteristics*

1. Hurried speech; explosive accentuation of key words.
2. Tendency to walk, move, and eat rapidly.
3. Constant impatience with the rate at which most events take place (e.g., irritation with slow-moving traffic and slow-talking and slow-to-act people).
4. Strong preference for thinking of or doing two or more things at once (e.g., reading this text and doing something else at the same time).
5. Tendency to turn conversations around to personally meaningful subjects or themes.
6. Tendency to interrupt while others are speaking to make your point or to complete their train of thought in your own words.
7. Guilt feelings during periods of relaxation or leisure time.
8. Tendency to be oblivious to surroundings during daily activities.
9. Greater concern for things worth *having* than with things worth being.
10. Tendency to schedule more and more in less and less time; a chronic sense of time urgency.
11. Feelings of competition rather than compassion when faced with another Type A person.
12. Development of nervous tics or characteristic gestures.
13. A firm belief that success is due to the ability to get things done faster than the other guy.
14. A tendency to view and evaluate personal activities and the activities of other people in terms of "numbers" (e.g., number of meetings attended, telephone calls made, visitors received).

SOURCE: Adapted from M Friedman and R H Rosenman, *Type A Behavior and Your Heart* (Greenwich, CT: Fawcett Publications, 1974), pp 100–2.

and sales performance of 222 life insurance brokers.[77] On the other hand, Type A behavior is associated with some negative consequences.

A meta-analysis of 99 studies revealed that Type A individuals had higher heart rates, diastolic blood pressure, and systolic blood pressure than Type B people. Type A people also showed greater cardiovascular activity when they encountered the following situations:

1. Receipt of positive or negative feedback.
2. Receipt of verbal harassment or criticism.
3. Tasks requiring mental as opposed to physical work.[78]

Unfortunately for Type A individuals, these situations are frequently experienced at work. A second meta-analysis of 83 studies further demonstrated that the hard-driving and competitive aspects of Type A are related to coronary heart disease, but the speed and impatience and job involvement aspects are not. This meta-analysis also showed that feelings of anger, hostility, and aggression were more strongly related to heart disease than was Type A behavior.[79]

Do these results signal the need for Type A individuals to quit working so hard? Not necessarily. First off, the research indicated that feelings of anger, hostility, and aggression were more detrimental to our health than being Type A. We should all attempt to reduce these negative emotions. Second, researchers have developed stress-reduction techniques to help Type A people pace themselves more realistically and achieve better balance in their lives; they are discussed in the next section. Management can help Type A people, however, by not overloading them with work despite their apparent eagerness to take an ever-increasing workload. Managers need to actively help rather than unthinkingly exploit Type A individuals.

Where Are You on the Type A–B Behavior Continuum?

Instructions
Indicate the extent to which each statement is true of you.

	Not at All True of Me	Neither Very True Nor Very Untrue of Me	Very True of Me
1. I hate giving up before I'm absolutely sure that I'm licked.	1 —— 2 —— 3 —— 4 —— 5		
2. Sometimes I feel that I shouldn't be working so hard, but something drives me on.	1 —— 2 —— 3 —— 4 —— 5		
3. I thrive on challenging situations. The more challenges I have, the better.	1 —— 2 —— 3 —— 4 —— 5		
4. In comparison to most people I know, I'm very involved in my work.	1 —— 2 —— 3 —— 4 —— 5		
5. It seems as if I need 30 hours a day to finish all the things I'm faced with.	1 —— 2 —— 3 —— 4 —— 5		
6. In general, I approach my work more seriously than most people I know.	1 —— 2 —— 3 —— 4 —— 5		
7. I guess there are some people who can be nonchalant about their work, but I'm not one of them.	1 —— 2 —— 3 —— 4 —— 5		
8. My achievements are considered to be significantly higher than those of most people I know.	1 —— 2 —— 3 —— 4 —— 5		
9. I've often been asked to be an officer of some group or groups.	1 —— 2 —— 3 —— 4 —— 5		

Total score = _____

Arbitrary Norms
9–22 = Type B
23–35 = Balanced Type A and Type B
36–45 = Type A

SOURCE: Taken from R D Caplan, S Cobb, J R P French Jr, R Van Harrison, and S R Pinneau Jr, *Job Demands and Worker Health* (HEW Publication No. [NIOSH] 75–160). (Washington, DC: US Department of Health, Education, and Welfare, 1975), pp 253–54.

Stress-Reduction Techniques

International data reveal that Americans are fatter, do less strenuous exercise, and eat less healthful foods than people from Australia, Britain, France, and Japan. Still, the number of obese people increased over the last decade in all of these countries.[80] All told, the National Council on Compensation Insurance estimates that stress-related medical and disability payments cost US companies $26 billion a year plus an additional $95 billion a year in lost productivity.[81] It is, therefore, not surprising that organizations are increasingly implementing a variety of stress-reduction programs to help employees cope with modern-day stress.

There are many different stress-reduction techniques available. The four most frequently used approaches are muscle relaxation, biofeedback, meditation, and cognitive restructuring. Each method involves somewhat different ways of coping with stress (see Table 18–4).

Two teams of OB researchers reviewed the research on stress management interventions. Although much of the published research is methodologically weak, results offer preliminary support for the conclusion that muscle relaxation, biofeedback, meditation, and cognitive restructuring all help employees cope with occupational stress.[82]

Table 18–4   *Stress-Reduction Techniques*

Technique	Description	Assessment
Muscle relaxation	Uses slow, deep breathing and systematic muscle tension reduction.	Inexpensive and easy to use; may require a trained professional to implement.
Biofeedback	A machine is used to train people to detect muscular tension; muscle relaxation is then used to alleviate this symptom of stress.	Expensive due to costs of equipment; however, equipment can be used to evaluate effectiveness of other stress-reduction programs.
Meditation	The relaxation response is activated by redirecting one's thoughts away from oneself; a four-step procedure is used to attain passive stress-free state of mind.	Least expensive, simple to implement, and can be practiced almost anywhere.
Cognitive restructuring	Irrational or maladaptive thoughts are identified and replaced with those that are rational or logical.	Expensive because it requires a trained psychologist or counselor.
Holistic wellness	A broad, interdisciplinary approach that goes beyond stress reduction by advocating that people strive for personal wellness in all aspects of their lives.	Involves inexpensive but often behaviorally difficult lifestyle changes.

Some researchers advise organizations not to implement these stress-reduction programs despite their positive outcomes. They rationalize that these techniques relieve *symptoms* of stress rather than eliminate stressors themselves.[83] Thus, they conclude that organizations are using a Band-Aid approach to stress reduction. This has led to the creation of much broader approaches toward stress reduction. The recommendation is for organizations to use employee assistance programs and for individuals to use a holistic wellness approach. Let us now consider each of these approaches toward stress reduction.

Employee Assistance Programs (EAPs)   **Employee assistance programs**
consist of a broad array of programs aimed at helping employees to deal with personal problems such as substance abuse, health-related problems, family and marital issues, and other problems that negatively affect their job performance.[84] EAPs are typically provided by employers or in combination with unions. Alternatively, referral-only EAPs simply provide managers with telephone numbers that they can distribute to employees in need of help. Employees then pay for these services themselves.

Employee assistance programs
Help employees to resolve personal problems that affect their productivity.

Holistic Wellness Approach   A **holistic wellness approach** encompasses and
goes beyond stress reduction by advocating that individuals strive for "a harmonious and productive balance of physical, mental, and social well-being brought about by the acceptance of one's personal responsibility for developing and adhering to a health promotion program."[85] Five dimensions of a holistic wellness approach are as follows:

Holistic wellness approach
Advocates personal responsibility for healthy living.

1. *Self-responsibility.* Take personal responsibility for your wellness (e.g., quit smoking, moderate your intake of alcohol, wear your seat belt, and eat less food). As a case in point, experts estimate that 50 to 70% of all diseases are caused by lifestyle choices under our control.[86]

Farcus

by David Waisglass
Gordon Coulthart

© 1991 Farcus Cartoons   WAISGLASS/COULTHART

www.farcus.com

When stress management works too well.

2. *Nutritional awareness.* Because we are what we eat, try to increase your consumption of foods high in fiber, vitamins, and nutrients—such as fresh fruits and vegetables, poultry, and fish—while decreasing those high in sugar and fat.

3. *Stress reduction and relaxation.* Use techniques to relax and reduce the symptoms of stress.

4. *Physical fitness.* Exercise regularly to maintain strength, flexibility, endurance, and a healthy body weight. A review of employee fitness programs indicated that they were a cost-effective way to reduce medical costs, absenteeism, turnover, and occupational injuries. Fitness programs also were positively linked with job performance and job satisfaction.[87]

5. *Environmental sensitivity.* Be aware of your environment and try to identify the stressors that are causing your stress. A control coping strategy might be useful to eliminate stressors.

Summary of Key Concepts

1. *Discuss the external and internal forces that create the need for organizational change.* Organizations encounter both external and internal forces for change. There are four key external forces for change: demographic characteristics, technological advancements, customer and market changes, and social and political pressures. Internal forces for change come from both human resource problems and managerial behavior/decisions.

2. *Describe Lewin's change model and the systems model of change.* Lewin developed a three-stage model of planned change that explained how to initiate, manage, and stabilize the change process. The three stages were unfreezing, which entails creating the motivation to change, changing, and stabilizing change through refreezing. A systems model of change takes a big picture perspective of change. It focuses on the interaction among the key components of change. The three main components of change are inputs, target elements of change, and outputs. The target elements of change represent the components of an organization that may be changed. They include organizational arrangements, social factors, methods, and people.

3. *Discuss Kotter's eight steps for leading organizational change.* John Kotter believes that organizational change fails for one or more of eight common errors. He proposed eight steps that organizations should follow to overcome these errors. The eight steps are (1) establish a sense of urgency, (2) create the guiding coalition, (3) develop a vision and strategy, (4) communicate the change vision, (5) empower broad-based action, (6) generate short-term wins, (7) consolidate gains and produce more change, and (8) anchor new approaches in the culture.

4. *Define organization development (OD), and demonstrate your familiarity with its four identifying characteristics.* Organization development is a set of tools or techniques that are used to implement planned organizational change. OD is broader in focus and has a diagnostic focus. The identifying characteristics of OD are that it involves profound change, is value loaded, is a diagnosis/prescription cycle, and is process oriented.

5. *Summarize the 10 reasons employees resist change.* Resistance to change is an emotional/behavioral response to real or imagined threats to an established work routine. Ten reasons employees resist change are

(1) an individual's predisposition toward change, (2) surprise and fear of the unknown, (3) climate of mistrust, (4) fear of failure, (5) loss of status or job security, (6) peer pressure, (7) disruption of cultural traditions or group relationships, (8) personality conflicts, (9) lack of tact or poor timing, and (10) nonreinforcing reward systems.

6. *Discuss the five personal characteristics related to resistance to change.* The first entails an employee's commitment to change, which reflects a mind-set of doing whatever it takes to effectively implement change. Resilience to change, a composite characteristic reflecting high self-esteem, optimism, and an internal locus of control, is the second personal characteristic. People with a positive self-concept and a tolerance for risk also handle change better than those without these two dispositions. High levels of self-efficacy also are negatively associated with resistance to change.

7. *Identify alternative strategies for overcoming resistance to change.* Organizations must be ready for change. Assuming an organization is ready for change, the alternative strategies for overcoming resistance to change are education + communication, participation + involvement, facilitation + support, negotiation + agreement, manipulation + co-optation, and explicit + implicit coercion. Each has its situational appropriateness and advantages and drawbacks.

8. *Define the term* stress *and describe the model of occupational stress.* Stress is an adaptive reaction to environmental demands or stressors that triggers a fight-or-flight response. This response creates hormonal changes that mobilize the body for extraordinary demands. According to the occupational model of stress, the stress process begins when an individual cognitively appraises stressors. This appraisal then motivates an individual to choose a coping strategy aimed at reducing stressors, which, in turn, results in a variety of stress outcomes.

9. *Discuss the stress moderators of social support, hardiness, and Type A behavior.* People use each of these moderators to help reduce the impact of stressors that are appraised as harmful, threatening, or challenging. Social support represents the amount of perceived helpfulness derived from social relationships. People use four types of support (esteem, informational, social, and instrumental) to reduce the impact of stress. Hardiness is a collection of personality characteristics that neutralize stress. It includes the characteristics of commitment, locus of control, and challenge. The Type A behavior pattern is characterized by someone who is aggressively involved in a chronic, determined struggle to accomplish more and more in less and less time. Management can help Type A individuals by not overloading them with work despite their apparent eagerness to take on an ever-increasing workload.

10. *Discuss employee assistance programs (EAPs) and a holistic approach toward stress reduction.* Employee assistance programs help employees to resolve personal problems that affect their productivity. EAPs are typically funded by organizations or in combination with unions. A holistic approach toward wellness goes beyond stress-reduction techniques by advocating that people strive for a harmonious balance among physical, mental, and social well-being. This approach to stress management has five key components: self-responsibility, nutritional awareness, stress reduction and relaxation, physical fitness, and environmental sensitivity.

Discussion Questions

1. Which of the external forces for change do you believe will prompt the greatest change between now and the year 2010?

2. Have you worked in an organization where internal forces created change? Describe the situation and the resulting change.

3. How would you respond to a manager who made the following statement? "Unfreezing is not important, employees will follow my directives."

4. What are some useful methods that can be used to refreeze an organizational change?

5. Have you ever observed the systems model of change in action? Explain what occurred.

6. Have you ever resisted a change at work? Explain the circumstances and your thinking at the time.

7. Which source of resistance to change do you think is the most common? Which is the most difficult for management to deal with?

8. Describe the behavioral and physiological symptoms you have observed in others when they are under stress.

9. How can someone increase their hardiness and reduce their Type A behavior?

10. Have you used any of the stress-reduction techniques? Evaluate their effectiveness.

GM Must Change to Survive[88]

BusinessWeek But GM, of course, is no ordinary company. With sales of $193 billion, it stands as an icon of fading American industrial might. Size and symbolism dictate that its fate has sweeping implications. After all, GM's payroll pumps $8.7 billion a year into its assembly workers pockets. Directly or indirectly, it supports nearly 900,000 jobs—everyone from auto-parts workers to advertising writers, car salespeople, and office-supply vendors. When GM shut down for 54 days during a 1998 labor action, it knocked a full percentage point off the US economic growth rate that quarter. So what's bad for General Motors is still, undeniably, bad for America.

And make no mistake, GM is in a horrible bind. That $1.1 billion loss in the first quarter doesn't begin to tell the whole story. The carmaker is saddled with a $1,600-per-vehicle handicap in so-called legacy costs, mostly retiree health and pension benefits. Any day now, GM is likely to get slapped with a junk-bond rating. GM has lost a breathtaking 74% of its market value—some $43 billion—since spring of 2000, giving it a valuation of $15 billion. What really scares investors is that GM keeps losing ground in its core business of selling cars. Underinvestment has left it struggling to catch up in technology and design. Sales fell 5.2% on GM's home turf last quarter as Toyota Motor Corp., Nissan Motor Co., and other more nimble competitors ate GM's lunch. Last month, CEO G Richard "Rick" Wagoner Jr and his team gave up even guessing where they'll stand financially at the end of this year.

Worst of all, GM reached a watershed in its four-decade decline in market share. After losing two percentage points of share over the past year to log in at 25.6%, GM has reached the point at which it actually consumes more cash than it brings in making cars, for the first time since the early '90s. GM, once the world's premier auto maker, is now cash-flow-negative. That's a game changer. Without growth, GM's strategy of simply trying to keep its factories humming and squeaking by until its legacy costs start to diminish is no longer tenable. If market share continues to slip, its losses will rapidly balloon.

Normally a company in such straits contracts until it reaches equilibrium. But for GM, shrinkage is not much of an option. Because of its union agreements, the auto maker can't close plants or lay off workers without paying a stiff penalty, no matter how far its sales or profits fall. It must run plants at 80% capacity, minimum, whether they make money or not. Even if it halts its assembly lines, GM must pay laid-off workers and foot their extraordinarily generous health care and pension costs. Unless GM scores major givebacks from the union, those costs are fixed, at least until the next round of contract talks in two years. The plan has been to run out the clock until actuarial tables tilt in GM's favor (a nice way of saying that older retirees eventually will die off). But with decreasing sales and a smaller slice of the market, that plan backfires—leaving GM open to an array of highly unattractive possibilities.

How Bad could It Get?

BusinessWeek's analysis is that within five years GM must become a much smaller company, with fewer brands, fewer models, and reduced legacy costs. It's undeniable that getting to that point will require a drastically different course from the one Wagoner has laid out so far. He is going to have to force a radical restructuring on his workers and the rest of the entrenched GM system, or have it forced on him by outsiders or a bankruptcy court. The only question is whether that reckoning comes in the next year, if models developed by vice chairman Robert A Lutz fall flat; in 2007, when the union contract comes up for negotiation; or perhaps in five years, when GM may have burned through its substantial cash cushion.

Why is it so hard for those inside GM to see the inevitable? Take a step into the Detroit mind-set. No active employee was even alive in 1930, the last time a rival sold more cars in the US than GM. The idea of being no. 1 is etched into the company's DNA—which makes it all but impossible for execs to embrace a strategy of getting smaller. And union leaders have never seen a problem that couldn't be ironed out at the bargaining table. "I think GM and the American auto industry are facing a lot of competition," says United Auto Workers president Ronald Gettelfinger. "But we've always had difficult times." . . .

Let's be clear: GM is not in danger of going bankrupt while it still has a cash hoard. It has a ton of liquidity—$19.8 billion in cash, marketable securities, and money it can tap from a prefunded retiree benefits fund. . . .

But all that cash just ensures that GM can continue its ways for a few extra years. Without a sharp course correction, GM is on a glide path to disaster. Things got downright embarrassing in April when Toyota chairman Hiroshi Okuda raised the possibility of hiking prices to give GM breathing space, saying, "I'm concerned about the current situation GM is in." (Toyota subsequently backed off.) Wagoner has ratcheted up the urgency level in recent weeks, signaling to unions that he needs relief from GM's $5.6 billion in annual health care costs and accelerating the delivery of new sport-utility vehicles and pickups by several months. And it now looks like he may bite the bullet and close at least a couple of auto plants to reduce GM's overcapacity. But he probably won't quickly enact a fundamental restructuring of GM's tired business model. And without that, he is relying on new car and truck models to stop the sales slide. That's a high-stakes bet that he probably can't win. . . .

Breakup or bankruptcy are the ghosts of GM's future. They become much more substantial threats if current management can't deliver on its promised turnaround over the next couple of years—or if the board doesn't find someone who has a better idea of how to deploy GM's $468 billion in assets. . . .

What would a healthy GM look like? It might have five fewer assembly plants, building around 4 million vehicles a year in North America instead of 5.1 million. That would slash US market share to around 20%, but factories would hum with real demand, stoked less by rebate giveaways and cheapo rental-car sales. Workers would have a cost-competitive health care plan but would fall back on government unemployment benefits when hard times demanded layoffs. Profitable auto sales and finance operations would fuel a richer research budget, tightly focused on four or five divisions instead of eight.

This new GM might make two-thirds as many models: Chevrolet, perhaps its most recognized global brand, handling trucks and mass-market cars; Saturn, behind its cool new Euro styling, selling more expensive cars with design flair. A resurgent Cadillac would parade advanced technology and luxury. Hummer would only last as long as brawny SUVs are hip. GMC, which is very profitable these days, would stick around if Chevy couldn't satisfy America's yen for trucks. Pontiac, Buick, and Saab would follow Oldsmobile to the scrap heap.

Maybe Wagoner will decide to bite the bullet and spend the billions needed to launch such a dramatic overhaul now, rather than waiting. And maybe the UAW leadership will get religion and offer more than token help. Where they decide to take GM will matter a great deal to the army of auto workers toiling away in its factories, the vast web of businesses that feed off of them, and legions of investors. As we learned a long time ago from outfits like AT&T, no company is too big to fail, or at least shrink dramatically. Not even mighty GM.

Questions for Discussion

1. What are the external and internal forces for change at GM?

2. Using Figure 18–2, how would you classify the changes occurring at GM? Explain.

3. Use the systems model of change to diagnose the problems that GM is facing and their associated causes. Based on this assessment, what would you recommend that Rick Wagoner do over the next two years? Discuss.

4. Based on GM's past organizational culture and business practices, do you expect employees to resist organizational change? Discuss your rationale. If you predict resistance, discuss what management can do to reduce it.

5. Based on everything you have learned about organizational behavior, what is your opinion about GM's approach to organizational change? Explain.

Personal Awareness and Growth Exercise

Applying the Systems Model of Change

Objectives

1. To help you understand the diagnosis step of planned organizational change.

2. To give you a practical diagnostic tool to assess which target elements of change in Figure 18–3 should be changed during a change process.

Introduction

Diagnosis is the first step in planned organizational change. It is used to identify past or current organizational problems that inhibit organizational effectiveness. As indicated in Figure 18–3, there are four organizational areas in which to look for problems: organizational arrangements, social factors, methods, and people. In this exercise, you will be asked to complete a brief survey assessing these four areas of an organization.

Instructions

If you currently have a full- or part-time job, think of your organization and describe it by circling an appropriate response for each of the following 14 statements. Calculate a total score for each diagnostic area. Then connect the set of points for your organization in a vertical profile. If you are not currently employed, describe the last organization you worked for. If you have never worked, use your current university or school as your frame of reference.

After completing the survey, think of an ideal organization: an organization that you believe would be most effective. How do you believe this organization would stand in terms of the four diagnostic areas? We would like you to assess this organization with the same diagnostic survey. Circle your responses with a different color or marking. Then vertically connect the set of points for your ideal organization. Calculate a total score for each diagnostic area.

Organizational Diagnostic Survey

1 = strongly disagree
2 = disagree
3 = neutral
4 = agree
5 = strongly agree

Organizing Arrangements

1. The company has the right recognition and rewards in place to support its vision and strategies.   1—2—3—4—5
2. The organizational structure facilitates goal accomplishment.   1—2—3—4—5
3. Organizational policies and procedures are administered fairly.   1—2—3—4—5

Total Organizing Arrangements score = _____   _____

Social Factors

4. The culture promotes adaptability and flexibility.   1—2—3—4—5
5. Interpersonal and group conflict are handled in a positive manner.   1—2—3—4—5
6. Horizontal and vertical communication is effective.   1—2—3—4—5
7. Leaders are good role models and decision makers.   1—2—3—4—5

Total Social Factors score = _____   _____

Methods

8. The work flow promotes higher quality and quantity of performance.   1—2—3—4—5
9. Technology is effectively utilized.   1—2—3—4—5
10. People focus on solving root cause problems rather than symptoms.   1—2—3—4—5

Total Methods score = _____   _____

People

11. This organization inspires the very best in me in the way of job performance.   1—2—3—4—5
12. I understand my job duties and responsibilities.   1—2—3—4—5
13. I like working in this company.   1—2—3—4—5
14. People are motivated to do the best job they can.   1—2—3—4—5

Total People score = _____   _____

Questions for Discussion

1. Based on your evaluation of your current organization, which diagnostic area(s) is most in need of change?

2. Based on a comparison of your current and ideal organizations, which diagnostic area(s) is most in need of change? If your answer is different from the first question, explain the difference.

3. What sort of intervention would be appropriate for your work group or organization? Give details.

Group Exercise

Creating Change at General Motors[89]

Objectives

1. To apply force-field analysis to the OB in Action Case Study involving General Motors (see case on pages 610–611).

Introduction

The theory of force-field analysis is based on the premise that people resist change because of counteracting positive and negative forces. Positive forces for change are called *thrusters*. They propel people to accept change and modify their behavior. In contrast, *counterthrusters* or *resistors* are negative forces that motivate an individual to maintain the status quo. People frequently fail to change because they experience equal amounts of positive and negative forces to change.

Force-field analysis is a technique used to facilitate change by first identifying the thrusters and resistors that exist in a specific situation. To minimize resistance to change, it is generally recommended to first reduce or remove the negative forces to change. Removing counterthrusters should create increased pressure for an individual to change in the desired direction. Managers can also further increase motivation to change by following up the reduction of resistors with an increase in the number of positive thrusters of change.

Instructions

Your instructor will divide the class into groups of four to six. Once the group is assembled, make sure that everyone has read the General Motors case. Next, complete the force-field analysis form presented after these instructions. Finally, answer the questions for discussion.

FORCE FIELD ANALYSIS FORM[90]

Step 1
As a group, brainstorm the major problems that GM's senior management is facing (see the guidelines for brainstorming in Chapter 12). Write the list on a piece of paper. Now select the most important problem from this list that requires organizational change. You can vote to select the most important problem. Write this problem in the space below.
Key problem facing GM: _____

Step 2
On the form following step 3, indicate existing forces that are pushing GM in the direction of creating change around the problem identified in step 1. Thrusters may be forces internal to the organization (e.g., employee concerns, organizational culture, legacy contracts, etc.) or they may be external to the organization (e.g., competition, interest rates, technological advancements, etc.). Next, list existing forces that are preventing GM from changing. Again, the counterthrusters may be internal to organization (e.g., organizational culture, union contracts) or external to the organization (e.g., union pressures).

Step 3
In the space to the right of your list of thrusters and counterthrusters indicate their relative strength. For consistency, use a scale of 1 to 10, with 1 indicating a weak force and 10 indicating a high force.

Thrusters	Strength
_____	_____
_____	_____
_____	_____
_____	_____
_____	_____

Counterthrusters	Strength
_____	_____
_____	_____
_____	_____
_____	_____
_____	_____

Step 4
Analyze your thrusters and counterthrusters, and develop a strategy for bringing about the desired change. Remember that it is possible to produce the desired results by strengthening existing thrusters, introducing new thrusters, weakening or removing counterthrusters, or some combination of the above. It is important to consider the organization's internal resources when you devise a change strategy. Write your recommendations in the space below.

_____

_____

_____

_____

_____

_____

Questions for Discussion

1. What was your reaction to doing a force-field analysis? Was it insightful and helpful?

2. How would you assess the probability of GM effectively implementing your recommendations? Explain.

3. Would this technique help you to plan for personal changes? Discuss.

Ethical Dilemma

What Would You Do if Your Boss Had a Serious Mental Illness?[91]

Paul Gottlieb was a 40-something rising star in the publishing world, sought after for top positions at major book publishers in New York City. In meetings with authors, business associates, and employees, he was a take-charge executive. No one realized that sometimes at the end of the day, Mr Gottlieb would sit at his desk, exhausted, and think about jumping out the window. . . .

Coping with employee depression is increasingly on the minds of workplace managers. But what happens when the boss is the one with a mental illness? The repercussions on a business, its employees and stockholders can be enormous if the illness interferes with a leader's performance. . . .

Securities laws require public companies to disclose anything that materially affects the company, and that can theoretically include serious health problems of key executives.

Assume that your boss suffers from a serious mental condition and he or she is trying to withhold this information from others? What would you do?

1. Nothing. The boss's mental condition is none of my business.

2. I would not say a word because I could be ignored or punished for saying anything. Identify the pros and cons of this option.

3. Discuss the issue only with my boss and encourage him or her to get help. Explain your rationale.

4. Discuss the issue with someone from the human resources department. Explain your rationale.

5. Invent other options. Discuss.

For the Chapter 18 Internet Exercise featuring a Type A behavior style assessment (www.queendom.com), visit our Web site at **www.mhhe.com/kreitner.**

Chapter 1 Video Case

Wild Oats

Wild Oats Market is a supermarket with a difference. Since its start in Boulder, Colorado, in 1987, Wild Oats has been committed to offering fresh, affordable natural and organic foods and providing knowledgeable customer service that goes beyond selling into consumer education. As it has grown, Wild Oats has reaped a reputation for being environmentally conscious, socially responsible, and people-oriented.

Wild Oats sprung up as strong consumer interest in healthy eating developed. Demand for natural foods grew during the 1990s and continues to rise amid concerns about pesticides, fertilizers, artificial ingredients, and genetically altered food. With sales topping $21 billion in 2004, natural and organic foods are moving from a niche category into the mainstream.[1] With more than 100 stores in 25 US states and Canada, Wild Oats is the second-largest retailer of natural and organic foods.

Since Perry Odak became CEO in 2001, Wild Oats has undergone massive restructuring to evolve from a company put together by various acquisitions to one with a consistent and profitable store base. Wild Oats planned to open 20 stores in 2005 and 40 the next year.[2] To increase profit margins, it has developed a private-label strategy. The company has rolled out hundreds of products under its own brand in its own stores and has tested the brand in a "store within a store" concept at a few outlets operated by other retailers. Wild Oats also has experimented with offering its private-label products online.[3]

Wild Oats stores are designed to offer a customer-friendly shopping experience. A new store in Superior, Colorado, stands as the model outlet. It uses color and attention-getting graphics for a fresh, dynamic feel. The center of the store is open and inviting with low shelves that allow customers an unobstructed view from any area. Educational opportunities abound, including a demonstration kitchen with seating and an information center in the health and beauty aids department.[4]

Focusing on the customer ranks at the top of Wild Oats' values. The service expectations are higher than at traditional supermarkets, explains Peter Williams. Customers at Wild Oats stores typically have questions, and employees must be able to answer them. The company is careful to hire people who are committed to providing service and to give them the expertise they need. Employee training begins with a full-day orientation centering on the company's mission and values and how to live up to them. Then employees take a month-long course (and written test) in natural foods and receive hands-on training. While some employees were customers first before joining the staff, others were unfamiliar with natural and organic foods but were eager to learn. Once on board, Wild Oats employees share the belief that they make a difference in the health and lives of customers.

Communicating information, ideas, and concerns helps build trust and teamwork at Wild Oats. Experienced employees help new ones learn about the products. The company has an open door policy that extends all the way to the top. Its Ethics Line is an online forum available for employees to give input—anonymously— on what they see as unethical behavior.

A recent Work Life Survey, available to all employees, provided managers with lots of useful feedback and insight into why staffers like or dislike working at Wild Oats. The number one reason employees cited for working there: the company's mission and values, which they share. Among the values is giving back to the community. Each Wild Oats store chooses small, local charities to support, and the company reimburses full-time employees for up to 52 hours of volunteer work a year. Carrying out its mission of service, Wild Oats was named one of "100 Best Corporate Citizens" by *Business Ethics* magazine and was the highest-ranking food retailer on the list.

Questions for Discussion

1. What principles of TQM are evident in the management of Wild Oats? How does Wild Oats apply them?

2. In what ways does Wild Oats build human and social capital?

3. Why are "21st century managers" essential to the success of an organization like Wild Oats?

[1] "Naturally, Consumer Trends Skew to Organic Foods," *DSN Retailing Today*, April 11, 2005, p 29.

[2] Heather Draper, "Wild Oats Still Awaits Harvest from Its Big Turnaround Effort," *The Wall Street Journal* (Eastern edition), August 18, 2004, p 1.

[3] Mike Duff, "Wild Oats Pushes PL Plan," *DSN Retailing Today*, November 22, 2004, p 5.

[4] "Wild Oats Markets," *Chain Store Age*, February 2005, p 98.

Learning Module A
Video Case

Enron

In August 2001, Sherron Watkins, vice president of corporate development for energy and telecommunications giant Enron, wrote an anonymous letter to her boss, CEO Kenneth Lay. The memo warned that the company might "implode in a wave of accounting scandals." Soon after, Watkins wrote a longer memo and met with Lay, who called for Enron's attorneys to look into partnership deals. In mid-October 2001, Enron announced a $618 million third-quarter loss and a write-off of $1.2 billion.[1] In December 2001, Enron—America's seventh largest company in 2000—filed for bankruptcy. Investment companies and individual investors lost billions; Enron employees lost jobs and retirement savings.

In January 2002, a congressional subcommittee looking into Enron's collapse released Watkins's memo. She subsequently testified—one session lasted five hours—about the financial schemes Enron officials used to hide billions of dollars of debt in questionable partnerships. Watkins said Jeffrey Skilling, Enron's previous CEO, misled Ken Lay about the firm's finances and that CFO Andy Fastow had improperly profited from partnership deals. Skilling, who had sold $66 million of his Enron stock in the previous three years while encouraging employees to buy company stock to fund their retirement, denied knowledge of any improprieties.

The Justice Department and the Securities and Exchange Commission began lengthy criminal proceedings. Suits charged Enron executives with fraudulently inflating the company's stock value. In 2004, a shocked public heard recordings of Enron traders' conversations that included cursing and derisive laughter about plans to cheat the public. By September 2004, Justice Department and SEC cases charged some 30 individuals,[2] among them Skilling and Lay, who each pleaded not guilty. Lay, who received around $325 million in salary, bonuses, stock-option gains, and stock sales over five years, claimed he did not know what Fastow was doing.[3] Fastow and other Enron executives pleaded guilty to criminal conduct and became government witnesses in hopes of receiving reduced prison sentences.

The Enron scandal brought down Arthur Andersen, the 89-year-old, Chicago-based accounting firm that earned $1 million a week from Enron. With a team inside Enron headquarters, Andersen had not only audited Enron's financial statements but also served as internal auditor to help Enron manage risk, a situation that critics called a conflict of interest. At Enron's collapse, David Duncan, the Andersen auditor who had certified Enron's false financial reports, ordered massive record shredding and computer deleting. Andersen was charged with obstructing the SEC's investigation of Enron. Duncan pleaded guilty to obstruction of justice and became a key prosecution witness.[4] After Andersen was convicted in 2002, clients took their business elsewhere, and the accounting firm, which once employed 85,000 people, had to surrender its licenses to practice in all 50 states.[5] Besides Andersen, banking and securities firms that had deals with Enron—JP Morgan Chase, Citigroup, Merrill Lynch—suffered consequences in the forms of fines, shareholder lawsuits, and criminal indictments of individuals. Enron itself collapsed.

Joining Watkins as whistle-blower was Maureen Castenada, a manager in Enron's foreign-investments section. She witnessed widespread document shredding at the company's Houston headquarters after the SEC investigation had begun in October 2001 and after Enron employees had been told to preserve all records. Castenada saw boxes of documents begin to accumulate on the 19th floor around Thanksgiving. Employees went through the contents page by page and removed documents; by the end of each day, trash bags and boxes of shredded papers were stacked up in the hallway. Castenada identified many of the papers as accounting documents because of the colors, yellow and pink. The shredding continued at least into mid-January 2002; Castenada was laid off then. She took a box of shredded paper away with her—one box of many—and eventually gave the box of paper scraps to lawyers representing Enron shareholders and investors who lost retirement savings when the company collapsed.[6] Castenada testified in the lawsuit and repeated her story to ABC News and other media outlets.

The media celebrated the women whistle-blowers as heroes standing firm against institutional impropriety and organizational misdeeds. *Time* magazine named Sherron Watkins Person of the Year in 2002, along with Coleen Rowley and Cynthia Cooper. Rowley, an FBI staff attorney, had claimed in a memo to FBI director Robert Mueller that the bureau ignored pleas from her Minneapolis field office to investigate Zacarias Moussaoui—later indicted as a 9/11 conspirator. Cooper informed the board of WorldCom that the company had used phony bookkeeping to hide $3.8 billion in losses.[7] *Time* said the three women were "of ordinary demeanor but exceptional guts and sense"; they were not seeking publicity but had tried to keep their criticisms inside their institutions and became public figures only because their memos were leaked.

The misdeeds at Enron and other giants such as Tyco and WorldCom focused attention on corporate governance and accountability and prompted legal changes. In 2002, Congress passed the Sarbanes-Oxley Act, which requires firms to put independent directors on their boards, adhere strictly to accounting rules, and have senior managers vouch for the accuracy of financial reports—at the risk of heavy penalties, including fines and criminal prosecution.[8]

The law also gives corporate whistle-blowers legal protection. They are not any more popular, however, according to Sherron Watkins. While Rowley and Cooper expressed dislike at the term *whistle-blower,* Watkins has used it to describe herself and has suggested that her gender may have played a role in her decision to act. She said her only regret is that she did not take her concerns to a higher authority than Enron's CEO. Watkins resigned from Enron, wrote a book about her experiences, and began speaking to groups. "I tell college students to be certain that ethics are at the top," says Watkins. "Don't stay with a company that isn't ethical, because something like an Enron could happen to you."[9]

Questions for Discussion

1. Which internal organizational influences may have affected the decisions of Enron and Andersen executives? Which individual characteristics probably influenced Sherron Watkins and other so-called whiste-blowers?

2. To what degree do you think that moral orientations vary by gender? Explain.

3. How effective do you think a code of ethics would be in preventing corporate wrongdoing, such as the fraud for which Enron and Arthur Andersen were investigated?

[1] Jodie Morse and Amanda Bower, "The Party Crasher," *Time,* December 30–January 6, 2003, p 53.
[2] John R Emshwiller, "Enron Ex-Chief of Telecom Unit Pleads Guilty," *The Wall Street Journal* (Eastern edition), September 1, 2004.
[3] Allan Sloan, "Lay's a Victim? Not a Chance," *Newsweek,* July 19, 2004, p 50.
[4] Cathy Booth Thomas, "Will Enron's Auditor Sing?" *Time,* May 20, 2002, p. 44.
[5] "Leaders: Reversed and Remanded—Arthur Andersen," *The Economist,* June 4, 2005, p 13.
[6] Peter Behr, "Manager Says Enron Shredded Documents," *Washington Post,* January 22, 2002; reprinted at www.shockandawe.us/archives/Enron/020122a.htm.
[7] Richard Lacayo and Amanda Ripley, "Persons of the Year," *Time,* December 30, 2002–January 6, 2003, p 32.
[8] Jackie Calmes and Deborah Solomon, "Snow Says 'Balance' Is Needed in Enforcing," *The Wall Street Journal* (Eastern edition), December 17, 2004.
[9] Alice Haythornthwaite and Lesley Bolton, "Analysis: Enron Whistle-Blower—Power Point," *Accountancy* 133, no. 1325 (January 2004), p 64.

Chapter 2 Video Case

Police Chief Annetta Nunn

In 1963, Birmingham, Alabama was at the center of the civil rights movement. Then–police chief Eugene "Bull" Connor grew infamous for his prejudicial views and public remarks. Forty years later, with Connor long dead and Kelly Ingram Park a memorial to those who protested there, Birmingham and one of its citizens made history again. On February 11, 2003, Annetta Nunn was appointed the city's first female African-American police chief; she assumed the office on March 7.[1] A Birmingham native, Nunn was educated in the public school system and graduated as valedictorian of Jackson–Olin High School. She received her BA in Criminal Justice from the University of Alabama and graduated Magna Cum Laude.[2]

As a ninth grader, Nunn knew she wanted to be a police officer. She grew up in a neighborhood where she witnessed illegal activities and police officers on the take; even as a youngster she knew their actions were wrong. Nunn liked to help people and wanted to make a difference in her community. Modest and soft-spoken, Nunn has a low-key style much different than other police chiefs, but after only a few years on the job she is already credited with inspiring community activism. She has earned tremendous respect from her 800 police officers and Mayor Bernard Kincaid, who tapped her for the job. Kincaid selected Nunn because of her reputation for being fair, thorough, and bright—highly desirable qualities in a police chief. In short, Kincaid says he chose Nunn because she was the best qualified person, who, incidentally, happened to be female and African-American.

Nunn was four years old during the days of Bull Connor. Her mother, who lived through segregation, says it is amazing that her daughter is police chief. The fact that she holds the top law enforcement job in Birmingham, Nunn points out, demonstrates that the city has changed and has become a progressive community. She realizes that more work needs to be done; for instance, not everyone accepts the idea of women in certain powerful positions. Despite that, Nunn knows the symbolism of an African-American woman in the job is critical.

Nunn especially values her relationship with Nolan Shivers, the most senior officer on the force, who wears badge #1. A rookie back in the days of Bull Connor, Shivers couldn't be more supportive of Annetta Nunn. He acknowledges that when he began on the force he could never have imagined a woman, much less an African-American woman, as police chief. Shivers now thinks Nunn has brought a welcome change and will go down in history as a great chief.

After a few years in the top cop position, Chief Nunn, who is married with two sons, says she is focusing on the future. She admits, however, that walking through Kelly Ingram Park makes her think about those people who laid their lives down so she could be where she is today. Civil rights demonstrators endured fire hoses and attack dogs so others could enjoy the freedoms they have. What would Bull Connor think? According to Nunn, some say he is probably turning over in his grave. But she is more hopeful that Connor and others like him would have progressed enough to realize that it's progress for her to have this job.

Questions for Discussion

1. Why do you think there been so few female police chiefs? How did Annetta Nunn manage to break this barrier?

2. What are the managerial implications of appointing a female, African-American police chief?

3. What are some of the barriers and challenges to diversify a police force? What are some practices that can be used to manage diversity?

[1] http://birminghamcrimestoppers.org/chief_nunn.htm.
[2] www.informationbirmingham.com/pressrele/nunn.htm.

Chapter 3 Video Case

Pike Place Fish

Pike Place Fish is located in Seattle's historic, open-air Pike Place Market. Visitors from many parts of the world come not only to buy high-quality seafood and have it shipped home but also to watch fishmongers throwing their wares and having fun. From a humble beginning as a small stand, Pike Place Fish has gained a big reputation. The change began when a young employee said, "Let's be world famous," and the owner responded, "Why not?"

John Yokoyama worked at Pike Place Fish when the owner offered to sell him the business in 1965. Only 25, Yokoyama was reluctant to buy the struggling market, but after much thought he decided to give it a try. He knew nothing about managing people, and his management style was that of a tyrant: You do what I tell you or else. Pike Place Fish did not do well, and Yokoyama was close to failing. That's when Jim Bergquist entered the scene.

A consultant whose wife worked at the fish market, Bergquist approached Yokoyama with a proposition: Give me three months and I'll improve your business or else I'll quit. They agreed. Then, when they were trying to decide their strategy, a young worker made his wild suggestion. At first the partners regarded the notion of becoming world famous as a joke, but the idea began to grow on them. They adopted the idea of becoming "world famous," added the words to the logo, and had them printed on shipping boxes.

What does it mean to be world famous? That's what Yokoyama, Bergquist, and their crew had to figure out. They decided it means making a difference in the lives of customers and others with whom they come into contact. "For us it means going beyond just providing outstanding service to people," explains Yokoyama. "We're out to discover how we can make their day. We've made a commitment to have our customers leave with the experience of having been served. They experience being . . . appreciated whether they buy fish or not."[1]

Providing such an experience for customers requires total commitment. At Pike Place Fish there are no jobs; rather, there are positions available for those who make the team. You have to commit to the purpose—being world famous—or you won't even want to be on the team. New employees sometimes take three months to understand the distinction—*being* world famous rather than merely wanting to be or believing you are—and become productive team members.

A big change for John Yokoyama was to share responsibility and power with workers. Yokoyama found that the best way to manage the type of team he needed was to stay out of employees' way and let them be creative and manage themselves. Inspirational management is the preferred style. Pike Place Fish creates a context for personal growth and development. For instance, someone who wants to master the art of filleting fish will be coached to reach that goal. Anyone can be a coach, and everyone is allowed to coach others. The intention is for the coach to empower the other person to achieve. When coaching is needed, everyone has the responsibility to step up and contribute.

A best-selling book, *Fish!*, has popularized the workplace philosophy at Pike Place Fish. The book identifies four principles for creating a fun-filled environment based on the fishmongers at the Seattle market: play, make their day, be there, and choose your attitude. The Coffee Bean & Tea Leaf, a specialty coffee retailer with 250 outlets in California and Asia uses these principles to create a fun culture where employees are creative and mix well with customers. Sales and customer and employee retention have increased steadily since the "fish" philosophy has been introduced. Other companies, including Sprint and Marriott, also have adopted the principles.[2]

Questions for Discussion

1. What does it mean at Pike Place Fish to be world famous? Why does it take some new employees months to understand this concept?

2. What role does organizational culture play in Pike Place Fish's quest to be world famous? Why are other firms such as Coffee Bean & Tea Leaf adopting the "fish" philosophy?

3. How does Pike Place Fish create the context for workers to reach their maximum potential? What roles do socialization and mentoring play in creating and nurturing this atmosphere?

[1] www.pikeplacefish.com/aboutus/aboutus.htm.
[2] Dina Berta, "Go 'Fish': Coffee Co. Takes a Cue from Seattle Seafood Market," *Nation's Restaurant News*, January 12, 2004, p 50.

Chapter 4 Video Case

Cirque du Soleil

In 1984, Guy Laliberté left his home in Canada to make his way across Europe as a circus performer. There he and other artists entertained in the street. The troupe was called Cirque du Soleil—circus of the sun. It started with a simple dream: a group of young artists getting together to entertain audiences, see the world, and have fun doing it.[1] Laliberté and company quickly found that their entertainment form without words—stilt-walking, juggling, music, and fire breathing—transcended all barriers of language and culture. Though he understood that an entertainer could bring the exotic to every corner of the world, Laliberté did not envision the scope to which his Cirque du Soleil would succeed. Today, Cirque performs five permanent shows—four in Las Vegas and one in Walt Disney World—and five traveling shows. Combined, they gross about $500 million annually.[2] In 20-plus years of live performances, 44 million people have seen a Cirque show.[3] Despite a long-term decline in the circus industry, Cirque has increased revenue 22-fold over the last 10 years.[4] Growth plans include additional tours in Asia and permanent shows in New York, Tokyo, and London.[5]

Cirque du Soleil is a family of more than 3,000 individuals—700 of whom are the shows' artists—from 40 different countries.[6] Each of Cirque's employees is encouraged to contribute to the group. This input has resulted in rich, deep performances and expansion into alternative media outlets such as music, books, television, film, Web sites, and merchandising. The company's diversity assures that every show reflects many different cultural influences. Different markets will have an exotic experience at a Cirque show, regardless of which show is playing where. Cirque does target specific markets with products designed to engage a particular audience. Yet Cirque has little need to adapt its product to new markets; the product is already a blend of global influences. The result is a presentation of acrobatic arts and traditional, live circus with an almost indescribable freshness and beauty.

Cirque du Soleil's commitment to excellence and innovation transcends cultural differences and the limits of many modern media. Its intense popularity has made Cirque both the global standard of live entertainment and the place for talented individuals from around the world to perfect their talents. The extent of the diversity, however, does pose a host of unique challenges. Every employee must be well-versed in various forms and styles. To foster cultural enrichment, Cirque purchases and shares a large collection of art with employees and gives them tickets to different events and shows.

The performers work in the most grueling and intimate situations, with their lives depending on one another. The astounding spectacles they achieve on stage result from hours of planning, practice, and painstaking attention to detail among artists from diverse cultures who speak 25 different languages. Sensitivity, compromise, and hunger for new experiences are prerequisites for success at Cirque. The organization has learned the art of sensitivity and compromise in its recruiting. Cirque du Soleil has had a presence in the Olympics for a decade. It works closely with coaches and teams to help athletes consider a career with Cirque *after* their competitive years are over, rather than luring talent away from countries that have made huge investments in athletes. This practice has given Cirque a huge advantage in the athletic community, a source of great talent from all over the globe.

Guy Laliberté has not forgotten his humble beginnings as a Canadian street performer. Now that Cirque du Soleil has achieved an international presence and incredible success—the group expects to be doing $1 billion in annual gross revenue by 2007—it has chosen to help at-risk youth, especially street kids. Cirque allocates 1% of its revenues to outreach programs targeting youth in difficulty, regardless of location in the world.[7] Laliberté understands that to be successful in a world market, one must be a committed and sensitive neighbor. Cirque's Montreal headquarters is the center of an urban revitalization project that the company sponsors. Community participation and outreach bring international goodwill and help Cirque du Soleil prevent many of the difficulties global brands often face when spanning cultures.

Questions for Discussion

1. Why is Cirque du Soleil successful throughout the world? Why does the product transcend culture differences between countries?

2. How do the cultural influences discussed in Figure 4–2 influence organizational behavior at Cirque du Soleil?

3. Why is it important for Cirque du Soleil to be a good corporate citizen? How does ethnocentrism relate to fulfilling this role?

[1] "Founder's Message," www.cirquedusoleil.com.

[2] Richard Corliss, "Bigger than Vegas," *Time*, February 14, 2005, p 52.

[3] Mario D'Amico and Vincent Gagné, "Big Top Television," *Marketing* 109, no. 26 (August 9–16, 2004), p 20.

[4] W. Chan Kim and Renée Mauborgne, "Blue Ocean Strategy," *Harvard Business Review*, October 2004, p 77.

[5] "Business: Lord of the Rings," *The Economist*, February 5, 2005, p 66.

[6] Cindy Waxer, "Life's a Balancing Act for Cirque du Soleil's Human Resources Troupe," *Workforce Management*, January 2005, p 52.

[7] "Social Action," www.cirquedusoleil.com.

Chapter 5 Video Case

Toying with Success:
The McFarlane Companies

Todd McFarlane, president and CEO of the McFarlane Companies, is an entrepreneur who understands the importance of product development. Comics, sports, toys, and rock-and-roll have all benefited from his creativity. When McFarlane's dream to play major league baseball didn't happen, he fell back on another interest he developed as a teenager—drawing superheroes. He faced the same question faced by all entrepreneurs: Could he make money pursuing his dream? He sent his sketches to prospective employers, and after 300 rejection letters McFarlane got a job freelancing for Marvel Comics. Working many hours for low pay, he made a name for himself and by 1990 was the highest-paid comic book artist in the industry.

Frustrated over creative differences and his desire to own the rights to his characters, McFarlane quit, took six other artists with him, and started his own company. He went from artist to entrepreneur overnight. While industry experts predicted he would last less than a year, McFarlane didn't even think about the future. *Spawn,* his first comic, sold 1.7 million copies.

Entrepreneurship rewards individuals willing to take risks. In Todd McFarlane's case, the need to control his destiny drove his aspirations. His path is similar to that taken by many: receiving training at a large company, then leaving when he decided he could provide a better product on his own.

Today's dynamic business environment has a tremendous effect on the success or failure of entrepreneurs like Todd McFarlane. Economics plays a key role at the McFarlane Companies. The firm must protect the many intellectual properties it creates and licenses. The business uses technology to support and spark creativity in developing new products. The competitive environment drives quality at McFarlane, which produces high-quality products even if they cost more and thus gains an edge over competitors. The CEO uses the Web to interact with his key demographic, or as he puts it, the freaks with long hair and cool tattoos. Spawn.com provides a place where fans can interact with each other and with the company. Finally, the global influence on business impacts all the other environments. Knowing he can't control the global environment, McFarlane focuses on managing what he can control.

Todd McFarlane's purchase of Mark McGwire's 70th home run ball for $3 million illustrates his willingness to take a risk and focus on what he controls. While many thought he was crazy, McFarlane saw an opportunity. He combined the ball with several others hit by McGwire and Sammy Sosa to create the McFarlane Collection, which was displayed in every major league stadium and garnered enormous publicity. A portion of the proceeds was donated to the Lou Gehrig Foundation. Most significant, McFarlane began a relationship with professional sports that led to his obtaining the exclusive rights to nearly every professional sports team toy license.

Questions for Discussion

1. What personality traits do entrepreneurs like Todd McFarlane possess that distinguish them from other individuals? Do you think McFarlane has an internal or external locus of control?

2. What cognitive abilities do you think contributed most to McFarlane's success?

3. Why is the development of new products such as sports figures critical to the McFarlane Companies? How important are self-efficacy beliefs and intelligence in the creative process that leads to new product concepts?

Chapter 6 Video Case

Patagonia

Yvon Chouinard began climbing as a 14-year-old member of the Southern California Falcony Club. At the time, the only available pitons (spikes used in mountain climbing) were made of soft iron, used once, and left in the rock. In 1957 Chouinard bought a used coal-fired forge to make reusable iron pitons; the word spread and soon he was in business.[1] From climbing equipment to apparel, his company, Patagonia, has evolved into a highly successful private firm with annual revenues of $250 million. Chouinard has kept it private so that he can continue to pursue his mission: earth first, profits second.[2]

According to CEO Michael Crooke, Patagonia is a very special company with a set of core values that is more than the bottom line. Because of the basic values, employees come to work every day with the attitude that they are making a difference. For each new hire, Patagonia receives 900 résumés. To understand the firm's success in satisfying employees, one needs only to look at a catalog. Not many companies place such significance on environmental and social issues. From the start, Yvon Chouinard advocated a purer, equipment-light approach to making climbing hardware in order to preserve the environment.[3] The philosophy has continued. A recent catalog featured an essay entitled, "Do You Need This Product?" The message? If you don't need another shirt or jacket, don't buy it. Patagonia's management believes that this honest approach, while rare, creates loyal customers and dedicated employees.

To many environmentalists, corporations are the enemy. Patagonia takes a different approach. The company's goal is to make a difference; to do so, it must use its power to work from within the system. Patagonia is a successful company socially, environmentally, and financially. The success starts with great products and great people. Product quality and guarantees assure that the products meet high expectations at any store no matter the location in the world.

In choosing employees, Patagonia looks for people passionate about an interest or cause. Over the years, many workers with similar causes and values have joined the company. The culture is based on commitment to environmental, moral, ethical, and philosophical causes. Patagonia employees derive true meaning from work, family, and health, rather than money and status. The goal is psychological success, achieved through a protean career.

Patagonia spends little on recruiting. The firm experiences very low turnover, about 4% annually. Each year, *Fortune* magazine rates the company as one of the best to work for. Why have workers found so much satisfaction with their jobs at Patagonia? Four reasons:

- *Let My People Surf.* The philosophy of Yvon Chouinard, not only an accomplished climber but also a passionate surfer, is that you have to surf when the surf's up. At Patagonia, workers set their own schedules; when they need to work, they get their jobs finished. To develop great products, you need to be users of the products. You can't develop great surfboards if you don't surf.

- *Enviro Internships.* After employees have completed a year, the company pays up to 60 days' salary for each individual to intern for an environmental group. The only requirement is that employees present a slide show when they return. Some employees have left Patagonia after the internships to become full-time activists. That's fine with the firm. Patagonia recently joined with several other apparel companies and six leading anti-sweatshop groups to devise a single set of labor standards with a common factory inspection system.[4]

- *Child Development Center.* Started in 1985, the child care facility is one of the first of its kind and an integral component of the company. Children are part of the campus all day, every day. The connection between work and family increases job satisfaction. Knowing their children are being well cared for onsite helps employees become fully committed.

- *One Percent for the Planet.* In 1985, Patagonia started an "earth tax" and donates 1% of sales to grassroots environmental activists worldwide. Each group has its own budget for local activism. Patagonia employees serve on grant committees that fund proposals. Because of employee involvement, this program also contributes to worker satisfaction.

Questions for Discussion

1. What values are important at Patagonia? How do values play an important role in attracting and retaining top employees?

2. How does Patagonia foster organizational commitment? How does the firm influence the work attitudes of job involvement and job satisfaction?

3. Using the values model of work/family conflict, (Figure 6–1), explain how programs at Patagonia reduce the conflict between work and family responsibilities.

[1] www.patagonia.com/culture/patagonia_history.shtml.

[2] Abraham Lustgarten et al., "14 Innovators," *Fortune*, November 15, 2004, p 193.

[3] www.patagonia.com/culture/clean_climb.shtml.

[4] Aaron Bernstein, "A Major Swipe at Sweatshops," *BusinessWeek*, May 23, 2005, p 98.

Chapter 7 Video Case

Wal-Mart Faces Discrimination Lawsuit

Among the ranks of retailers, Wal-Mart has no peer, no one even close. Wal-Mart sells about $300 billion of merchandise a year, more than four times as much as the world's next biggest retailer, Carrefour SA of France. In the last few years, the giant retailer has opened nearly 500 stores a year, bringing the total to more than 5,000 worldwide.[1] With 1.4 million people on the payroll, the Bentonville, Arkansas–based company is the world's biggest employer.[2] In June 2004, Wal-Mart reached another record—one it certainly was not seeking—when it was faced with the largest lawsuit ever filed against a private employer and the largest civil rights case ever against a US company.

The case began in 2001, when a group of female Wal-Mart employees sued, claiming that the company regularly pays women less than men in the same jobs and promotes men ahead of women with comparable skills. The suit burgeoned to massive proportions when a Northern California District Court judge granted the six plaintiffs class status, which allowed them to represent all women who have worked at Wal-Mart's US stores since December 1998. The class included about 1.6 million female employees across 3,400 stores. Wal-Mart faced damages of more than a billion dollars.

The lawsuit, and the statistics cited to justify it, echoed discrimination accusations leveled by others against Wal-Mart, where women hold a whopping 93% of the cashier jobs, the lowest-wage category.[3] The National Organization for Women has called Wal-Mart the "Merchant of Shame" to emphasize its belief that the retailer discriminates against female employees in both pay and promotions. The leader of a group called Women versus Wal-Mart offers statistics; she claims that women hold two-thirds of all hourly Wal-Mart store jobs and 80% of the hourly paid supervisory positions, but that only one-third of all salaried management jobs and less than 10% of the store manager jobs and above are given to women.[4]

Wal-Mart has maintained that it doesn't discriminate against women. In response to the charges of discrimination, the retailer started companywide computer postings of management openings, hired a director of diversity, and cut executive managers' bonuses for failing to achieve diversity targets. Even CEO Lee Scott personally stood to lose $600,000 of his bonus if the company fell short of diversity goals.[5] Scott began meeting more with investors, community groups, and the media. The company conducted a television ad campaign featuring women who'd moved up the ranks into management.

Wal-Mart has tried to stop the class-action lawsuit. The retailer engaged in settlement talks with the plaintiffs. Then in an ambitious defense, Wal-Mart filed a brief with the US Ninth Circuit Court of Appeals in California giving reasons why the sex-discrimination suit should lose its class-action status. It said the class size—exceeding the entire population of at least 12 US states—was too large for the company to address individual plaintiff's claims.[6] The retailer claimed that its constitutional rights would be violated because it would not be allowed to defend itself against each woman's claim. Wal-Mart asked the court to allow plaintiffs to file class actions only at individual Wal-Mart stores.[7]

The class-action discrimination suit followed a trail of controversies and negative publicity plaguing Wal-Mart. The company's well-publicized pursuit of low prices has been criticized for causing bankruptcies among competitors and the loss of US manufacturing jobs as the company and its suppliers turn to cheaper sources abroad. The retail giant has faced government investigations, immigration raids, boycotts, sweatshop allegations, accusations by animal rights groups and conservationists, and grassroots efforts to keep outlets from opening in small towns across America. Critics have accused Wal-Mart of using child labor, predatory pricing, false advertising, paying low wages, sending American jobs overseas, destroying historic and natural resources, being anti-union, and destroying small towns. There are even anti-Wal-Mart Web sites. According to Michael Bergdahl, who worked for Wal-Mart and is writing a book about his former employer, the company is loved by its millions of customers but often is despised by competitors and special interest groups. "It was a lot easier for Wal-Mart to run its business when it wasn't perceived as a threat by anyone," says Bergdahl. "But that all changed when it became perceived as a global retail predator."[8]

Questions for Discussion

1. How could sex-role stereotypes influence the hiring, evaluation, and promotion of employees at large retail stores such as Wal-Mart?

2. In what ways could a giant corporation like Wal-Mart, with 5,000-some outlets worldwide, prevent or at least minimize sex discrimination throughout the organization?

3. In Wal-Mart stores, women hold 93% of the cashier jobs, the lowest wage category. To what extent might the self-fulfilling prophecy affect female employees' performance in a corporation where the lowest-paid jobs are done mostly by women?

[1] Ann Zimmerman, "Boss Talk: Defending Wal-Mart," *The Wall Street Journal* (Eastern edition), October 6, 2004.

[2] Michael Bergdahl, "Being the World's Biggest Target," *Retail Merchandiser,* September 2004, p 44.

[3] Aaron Bernstein, "Wal-Mart vs. Class Actions," *Business Week,* March 21, 2005, p 73.

[4] Bergdahl, "Being the World's Biggest Target," p 44.

[5] Zimmerman, "Boss Talk."

[6] "Wal-Mart Seeks to Have Suit Reclassified," *The Wall Street Journal* (Eastern edition), November 30, 2004.

[7] Bernstein, "Wal-Mart vs. Class Actions," p 73.

[8] Bergdahl, "Being the World's Biggest Target," p 44.

Chapter 8 Video Case

Working for the Best: The Container Store

The Container Store managers hope that customers will immediately notice two things: great products and happy employees. The Container Store has received much recognition for many of its practices, including high levels of customer service, employee training programs, and an innovative culture.[1] A perennial top-five on lists of best companies, The Container Store twice has been selected by *Fortune* magazine as the number one company to work for in the United States. According to chairman and co-founder Garrett Boone, this recognition results directly from hiring great people—one of the six foundation principles that comprise the company's culture. The key is for employees to provide great customer service *when* it is needed, whether it be helping a customer organize a garage or closet or answering a simple question. Great service requires motivated employees who are empowered to exceed customer expectations. Since the first store opened in Dallas in 1978, the company has expanded into a 33-store nationwide chain with annual revenue exceeding $370 million. Much of this success is attributed to motivated, top-performing employees.[2]

How are employees at The Container Store motivated to provide great customer service? Managers have applied several theories of motivation to develop a culture in which jobs are interesting and employees are not afraid to take a chance—or even to fail. While Frederick W. Taylor and the Scientific Management proponents emphasized efficiency and proper programming, The Container Store takes a much more humanistic approach to motivating, by recognizing a wide range of employee needs.

In the 1940s, psychologist Abraham Maslow theorized that people are motivated to satisfy current needs in the categories of physiological, safety, social, esteem, and self-actualization. They form a hierarchy, with the most basic needs, physiological and safety, at the bottom. The higher-level needs—social, esteem, and self-actualization—are at the top of the hierarchy. The Container Store plays a role in meeting all these employee needs. Wages among the highest in the industry help individuals satisfy physiological needs and motivate employees to perform at higher levels of productivity. The environment helps people feel emotionally secure by stressing such values as integrity, honesty, and open communication. Social needs are met by The Container Store's family atmosphere, where people feel they belong to a group. By recognizing employees both formally and informally when they do something extra special, the company helps employees meet the need for esteem. Finally, the highest-level need of self-actualization is met by encouraging employees to reach their highest potential. Many part-time employees become full-time employees; many of the managers began their careers as part-timers. Customers recruited seasonally to fill temporary jobs apply hoping to find a career opportunity.[3] The turnover at The Container Store provides some evidence that employees' needs are being met. The company averages about 15–20% in an industry with turnover of 90–100% annually.

The Container Store seeks out managers who follow McGregor's Theory Y in their assumptions about employees. Theory Y assumes that workers are not lazy by nature, and when the opportunity arises, they will do what is best for the organization. Following this belief fosters a relaxed atmosphere and empowered workers. Employees are expected to think for themselves and are given the authority to make decisions without checking with a manager first.

Pride in the work itself is also obvious at The Container Store. Employees are cross-trained so they understand everyone else's job, a practice that makes jobs more interesting and prepares employees to make decisions should the need arise. Says Amy Carovillano, vice president of logistics and distribution, "We give employees all the tools they need. They understand the business and why they need to do different jobs."[4] Employees operate much like a store manager, capable of making decisions that generate better customer service.

The Container Store emphasizes daily coaching and learning. Managers work with employees on a daily and weekly basis to help them develop skills, work on weaknesses, and enhance strengths. Victor Vroom's expectancy theory states that the amount of effort employees put in depends on their expectations of the outcome. Similarly, equity theory deals with the question: If I do a good job, will it be worth it? What's fair? When it comes to employee expectations and equity, the key point is that organizations communicate effectively. Kip Tindell, The Container Store president and CEO, says communication is the number one factor when it comes to motivation. Open communication extends down to the team level where peers are encouraged to share their knowledge with each other regardless of position.

Questions for Discussion

1. Using Maslow's hierarchy of needs theory, explain how The Container Store satisfies the needs of its employees.

2. How are workers at The Container Store motivated? What theories can be used to explain motivation at The Container Store?

3. Why don't managers at The Container Store use just one approach in motivating employees? What issues must be considered in designing and implementing a motivational program?

[1] Janet Groeber, "How Close Is Too Far?" *Stores*, December 2004, p 60.
[2] Vicki Powers, "Finding Workers Who Fit The Container Store," *Business 2.0*, November 2004, p 74.
[3] Gary Forger, "Good Today, Better Tomorrow," *Modern Materials Handling*, October 2004, p 22.
[4] Karen Blumenthal, "Turning Buyers into Sellers," *The Wall Street Journal* (Eastern edition), November 22, 2004.

Chapter 9 Video Case

The Legacy of Jack Welch

As General Electric's chairman, Jack Welch was one of the world's most powerful corporate leaders. He was also viewed as one of America's toughest executives and an icon to be admired. The now-retired Welch, his famous management style, and his accomplishments have been the subjects of books and university business classes.

Under Welch, from 1981 to 2001, GE became the world's most valuable company with a market value of $406 billion. Welch spurred that dramatic growth by performing traditional management functions his own way. He chose not to follow the traditional strategy of sticking with what a company knows and instead accumulated diverse businesses. Originally a manufacturer of household appliances, lighting, and jet engines, GE bought NBC as well as companies offering medical products, financial services, and car leasing.

Welch restructured GE before restructuring became common among large corporations. Although his company was profitable, Welch sold some of GE's subsidiaries and reduced payroll. Some 118,000 jobs—about one in four—were slashed. The deep cuts earned Welch the nickname, "Neutron Jack," a moniker he is said to have detested. Welch endured the criticism and continued his practice of identifying, keeping, and rewarding high-performing employees at General Electric.

Welch is known for dismantling GE's large bureaucracy and opening up corporate communication. Some have said that Welch listened as much as he talked and that he always spoke in a straightforward manner. He excelled at personal interaction and motivation and as the top executive was highly visible in his company. Welch visited and taught at GE's famous Management Development Institute in Crotonville, New York. His leadership style centered on having strong employees and managers at all levels and empowering them to make decisions and engage in what he called "boundaryless thinking."[1]

Some people who worked with Welch have described the former chairman's interaction as more aggressive than egalitarian or cooperative. Others have said that Welch's oft-used motivational technique was the fear factor: perform or hit the road. Welch determined in the early 1980s that to be at the top, GE could not fill management positions with deadwood—people who felt comfortable, secure, and protected from competition in their jobs within the depths of a large corporation. Welch thought it was better for individuals performing at the lowest levels to move on in other directions when they are young. During his tenure at GE, Welch selected the best people he could find, then trained and promoted them. Many who learned from him took their leadership skills to other large firms. Some of Welch's "lieutenants" head up some of the world's major corporations, such as Home Depot, TRW, Boeing, and others.

Widely publicized and lauded, Welch's leadership techniques also surface in noncorporate environments. The head of the Junior League of London, a nonprofit organization of volunteers offering social services, has employed Welch-style principles to motivate her group's 400 members.

Of course, Jack Welch's years at GE included not only stunning corporate accomplishments but also setbacks and controversies. A proposed merger with Honeywell was rejected by European Union regulators. The Environmental Protection Agency under the Bush administration ordered GE, at a cost of $500 million, to clean up 40 miles of Hudson River bottom polluted by PCBs before the substances were banned. After Welch's exit from GE in September 2001, critics attacked his substantial benefit package, including an arrangement that provided more than $2 million a year for an array of perks, including air transportation and personal services. Welch promptly agreed to give back $2 million.

Even in retirement, Welch continues to be one of the most celebrated corporate leaders of his time. *Winning,* his autobiography written along with his new wife, Suzy Welch, was published in 2005 and immediately hit bestseller lists. In it he outlines his business philosophy, how to win within a company, how to win against the competition, and how to win over the course of a career.[2] Welch gives three steps in developing strategy. First, come up with a smart, realistic, fast way to gain a sustainable advantage; he calls this the "big aha." Second, put the right people in the jobs needed to move the big aha forward. Finally, find the best practices to move the big aha forward and focus on them.[3] In addition to writing, Welch spends time consulting for buyout firm Clayton Dubilier and for Barry Diller's growing Internet empire, and giving talks throughout the world for $150,000 per appearance.[4]

Questions for Discussion

1. How could learning goals and performance goals help an executive like Jack Welch be a more effective leader?

2. How important do you think instrinsic rewards were to Welch? How do you think he viewed money as a motivator for employees?

3. What form of behavior shaping did Jack Welch engage in?

[1]Russell H. Mouritsen, "Boundaryless Thinking," *American Salesman* 49, no. 8 (August 2004), p 12.
[2]Diane Brady, "Welch Has More to Say, Really," *Business Week*, April 18, 2005, p 22.
[3]Jack Welch, "Jack Welch: 'It's All in the Sauce'," *Fortune*, April 18, 2005, p 138.
[4]Daniel McGinn, "Jack on Jack: His Next Chapter," *Newsweek*, April 4, 2005, p 41.

Chapter 10 Video Case

Are Americans Overworked?

The image of the American worker, putting in long hours at the office and at home and rarely taking time off, is one popularized by television programs and magazine columns. Is the overworked American an urban legend or a reality? It's a fact that 26% of Americans take no vacations at all; 13% of American companies don't even offer them. Some firms require employees to perform extra tasks before getting a vacation. Unlike other countries, the United States has no laws mandating companies to offer vacations. On average, workers in America take about 10 days of vacation a year, compared with 25 days in France, 20 in Italy and Great Britain, and 15 in China.

In much of the world, time off is a time for renewal. In the United States, taking time off can put people on a guilt trip, says author Jo Robinson. Without it, however, workers are more inclined to experience what Robinson calls vacation deficit disorder, the negative consequences of being overworked. Vacations serve the valuable function of interrupting job stress, which Robinson says is rampant among American workers. The Families and Work Institute states that an environment where workers don't take all of their vacation results in high stress rates and employee burnout.[1]

Yet some experts believe that increased vacation for workers could bring more harm than good for the American workplace. Professor Brigitte Madison of the University of Chicago School of Business argues that more vacation time for Americans could mean lost jobs. "If employers can't pass the cost of vacation time onto workers in terms of lower wages," says Madison, "then we'll end up with reduced employment levels as well."

Besides foregoing vacations, many people never really leave their work on a day-to-day basis. Technology has linked people to their jobs even when they are out of their offices. E-mail, fax machines, cell phones, and laptop computers make workers more readily available day and night. Along with the time spent on the job, the nature of the work itself influences how employees feel. Demanding jobs that require a great degree of multitasking leave employees feeling more overwhelmed. Low-value work, which people complain about as a waste of time, increases the likelihood of feeling overworked.

One in three American employees is chronically overworked, according to Ellen Galinsky, the Families and Work Institute president who wrote a study called "Overworked in America." Galinsky looked at three different factors to determine whether someone is chronically overworked: Does a worker feel overworked? Is a worker overwhelmed by everything he or she has to do? Do workers have time to stop and think about what they are doing? The study showed that the percentage of overworked Americans goes up from 29 to 54 if you consider people who are overwhelmed by what they do. Only 29% of that study's respondents said they never feel overworked. Galinsky notes that while America's perspective on work and families is different than that of other countries, younger US workers are more likely to put an equal emphasis on work and family. She attributes this attitude in part to the downsizing and the demanding jobs they have seen their parents experience.

Feeling overworked can influence not only job performance but also personal and family relationships and health. Galinsky reported that 20% of those feeling overworked make more mistakes, 39% feel angry with the employer, and 34% indicate being resentful of co-workers. In terms of personal outcomes, 36% report high levels of stress and 21% have symptoms of clinical depression. Additionally, those feeling overworked experience more work/life conflict, feel less successful in their personal relationships, are more likely to lose sleep because of work, and are less likely to report they are in good health.[2]

Several strategies can be used to help prevent feeling overworked. On the job, workers can focus on the task at hand and the contribution they are making. Taking breaks during the day is also beneficial. Away from work, people are learning to create more boundaries between work and their personal lives. For instance, some workers simply refuse to work while on vacation. Finally, employees should take their full vacations and leave the job behind.

Questions for Discussion

1. Do you think Americans are overworked? Explain your opinion.
2. What are some of the negative consequences of feeling overworked? How could this feeling influence group dynamics?
3. What can be done to decrease the negative feelings associated with being overworked? How can reducing role overload, role conflict, and role ambiguity have a positive impact on individuals who feel overworked?

[1] Megan Santosus, "All Work and No Play," *CIO,* April 15, 2004, p 1.
[2] "When Work Becomes Too Much," *Worklife Report* 13, no. 3 (2001), p 7.

Chapter 11 Video Case

Two for the Price of One

Dana Meade and Paula Rivers are co–vice presidents and general managers of Zoomerang, the world's premier online survey software. Zoomerang, known for being simple to use, allows customers to design and send surveys via the Internet and analyze results in real time.[1] Meade and Rivers share responsibility for the bottom line, so they work in sync in all facets of running the business, whether it be marketing, finance, or product management.

Women in the workforce have struggled to find the delicate balance between career and home. Meade and Rivers pursued a unique approach in an effort to have it all. They each work 2.5 days a week. The two share one salary equally, but each receives full benefits. They proposed this arrangement after earning MBAs, working more than a decade in the industry, and facing the choice of career or motherhood. As Rivers puts it, sharing the position was a way to keep her career moving ahead while spending ample time with her daughter. For Meade, it was either part-time or nothing. She wanted to spend at least a few days a week watching her daughter grow up.

Meade and Rivers are not alone. A national trend suggests that more women are sacrificing pay for time at home with their children. A recent study conducted by the research group Catalyst found that one in three women with MBAs does not work full-time. Women often find that the juggling act between work and family is more difficult as they progress higher up the corporate ladder. According to Ellen Galinsky, president of the Families and Work Institute, the higher the level in the organization, the more restrictive the network and job expectations become. While the notion of total dedication to the job has eased somewhat, Galinsky says, rising to the top of a corporation often precludes having a full life outside of work.

It wasn't easy for Meade and Rivers to establish executive-level job sharing, but persistence paid off. When they presented the idea to Jon Finley, CEO of Zoomerang, he said no at first. Finley was concerned with the impact the job sharing would have on the business and how well it would work for their subordinates. Others on the senior leadership team shared concerns about the day-to-day operation. Nonetheless, Finley gave them a shot. After a three-month trial, he and his staff decided to make it permanent.

The job-sharing experiment at Zoomerang has succeeded in large part because of an open line of communication among Meade and Rivers, the staff, and the CEO. Employees can reach either of the women by cell phone and they both check e-mails regularly, so even when they are not in the office they are readily available. In fact, this availability may be the one downside of the arrangement—days off are not usually days off. Meade and Rivers talk every day; sometimes these calls require rearranging schedules concerning children.

According to Finley, the results speak for themselves. Since Meade and Rivers began sharing the vice president/general manager job, Zoomerang's revenues have doubled, and the company has expanded to include more than 200 countries. By taking a risk, Finley believes he was able to keep two great people that may have otherwise gotten away. For Meade and Rivers, the risk has produced huge rewards, not just in dollars but also in family time.

Questions for Discussion

1. Why are Dana Meade and Paula Rivers effective as a team? What type of team do they comprise?

2. Of the competencies necessary for team members to possess, which are most important when two people share the same job?

3. Why is it critical for Meade and Rivers to build trust with their boss and their subordinates? Have they been successful in building trust?

[1] http://info.zoomerang.com/products.htm.

Chapter 12 Video Case

Columbia Space Shuttle Disaster and the Future of NASA

Early on February 1, 2003, television viewers watched in disbelief and sadness as the space shuttle Columbia, returning from its mission, seemed simply to break apart. Later in a scathing report, investigators said that NASA's management practices were as much to blame for the accident that killed seven astronauts as the foam that broke away from the fuel tank and hit the left wing during blastoff. The report concluded that NASA had known of problems with the foam insulation over a long period but had never invested the time or energy to resolve the problem. Former astronaut and NBC analyst Sally Ride agreed with the findings. She noted that foam had been falling off the external tanks since the first shuttle launch and that it had fallen off on nearly every flight. Ride considered the foam problem an accident waiting to happen, which of course it did. NASA recognized the foam as a serious problem and tried to fix it; unfortunately, it didn't get as much attention as many other problems NASA faced during the past decade.

Columbia was a sad reminder of the Challenger disaster 17 years earlier. In the case of Challenger, engineers suspected problems with O-rings, but didn't fix them. It appeared that NASA didn't learn from its mistakes with Challenger and, more important, that a deeper problem existed: Safety concerns had not been given top priority. According to Ride, while NASA officials did not suppress dissenting views, they did not encourage them. Echoes of Challenger? Ride thought so. The further the Columbia investigation progressed, the more echoes were heard. The Columbia Accident Investigation Board cited several failures, chief among them a corporate culture at NASA that discouraged the communication of dissenting opinions or safety related information.[1] The lessons learned in the years after 1986 seemed to have been lost.

To ensure the vitality of the space program, NASA needed to change its culture, called "a broken safety culture" by Columbia accident investigators.[2] Failing to do so would have placed the organization in the unenviable position of relying on crisis management to protect its tarnished image.[3] The can-do spirit had to change to one of safety first. Changing the culture required strong leadership and personal investment at all levels within NASA. Budgets and schedules could no longer be emphasized at the cost of safety. Processes had to be put in place to make sure that anyone aware of a safety problem would come forward and would be heard effectively up through the chain of management.

Safety has not been the only issue putting pressure on the space program; NASA also has been scrutinized over its mission. For years NASA has been facing questions such as, What are we doing in space? What is the payoff? Since the Challenger explosion, the goal has been to conduct scientific experiments and to construct the International Space Station, where people can live and work for months. But some experts say the knowledge achieved is not beneficial enough. According to Professor Robert Park, the knowledge acquired from either the space shuttle or the space station may be good research, but it simply is not very important. For instance, the shuttle and space station fly the same orbit John Glenn achieved in 1963; much of what could be learned has been learned already. The idea that NASA has passed along useful products over the years, such as Teflon and Tang, has been questioned. According to Park, most of the products had been developed independently; manufacturers found it good business to say their offerings had been developed in the space program.

NASA has continued its program amid concerns over its mission, budgets, and safety. Aging equipment has been a concern. The basic shuttle design dates to 1969; NASA started building the three remaining shuttles in 1979, 1980, and 1982. NASA planned to use the three shuttles to take up additions to the International Space Station until it is completed, then retire the shuttles in 2010.

In the last few years, NASA has strived to design systems providing multiple opportunities to break any chain of events like the one leading to the Columbia disaster.[4] The Columbia Accident Investigation Board required extensive engineering oversight reforms before the Discovery shuttle return-to-flight mission in 2005. Set for July 13, the widely publicized Discovery launch was delayed because of a fuel-gauge problem. After making repairs, NASA launched Discovery nearly two weeks later with seven astronauts on board and quickly encountered a familiar complication. Video cameras positioned on the shuttle detected falling debris, including insulating tile and foam. A large piece of foam had broken off Discovery's external fuel tank during liftoff, but because it did not strike the shuttle, Discovery and its crew continued the mission to the International Space Station. One of its astronauts, restrained to a robotic arm, made an emergency repair during an unprecedented six-hour spacewalk in which he reached the shuttle's belly and pulled away dangling fiber strips.

At NASA, after two and a half years and millions of dollars spent to fix the foam problem, engineers expressed deep disappointment. Shuttle program deputy manager N Wayne Hale said that NASA was "in the business of flying in space—it's a very difficult business."[5] The agency considered grounding its shuttles, which it had planned to operate for five more years. Twenty-four more launches to complete the space station had been scheduled. NASA then planned to test-fly a new crew vehicle and start work on an ambitious plan, backed by President Bush, to take astronauts to the Moon again in 2020 and on to Mars in a new spaceship.[6]

Questions for Discussion

1. What has seemed to be the major problem facing NASA? Apply your knowledge of group dynamics and decision making to identify the problem.

2. What must NASA accomplish to ensure the vitality of the space program? Has groupthink accounted for some of NASA's problems? If so, what symptoms can you identify?

3. What group-decision making challenges has NASA faced in changing its culture?

[1] Linda B Johnson, "Report: Columbia Accident Investigation Board," *Library Journal* 130, no. 9 (May 15, 2005), p 58.
[2] John Schwartz, "NASA Grounds Shuttle Fleet," *Lexington Herald-Leader*, July 28, 2005.
[3] James Kaufman, "Lost in Space: A Critique of NASA's Crisis Communications in the Columbia Disaster," *Public Relations Review* 31, no. 2 (June 2005), p 263.
[4] Craig Covault, "Layered Defense," *Aviation Week and Space Technology*, May 9, 2005, p 50.
[5] Schwartz, "NASA Grounds Shuttle Fleet."
[6] Seth Borenstein, "Should Fleet Be Retired ASAP?" *Lexington Herald-Leader*, August 3, 2005.

Chapter 13 Video Case
Dealing with Office Bullies

Workplace bullying has been depicted in such movies as *Wall Street* and the comedy *Nine to Five,* but it's no laughing matter. According to a study published by the University of Manchester, during your working life there is a 50:50 chance you will be bullied.[1] Research conducted by *Personnel Today* and an antibullying charity the Andrea Adams Trust Fund found that more than three-quarters of human resource professionals have been bullied at work.[2] Like 20-year Navy veteran Bea Pearson, victims of bullying can experience physical symptoms including trouble sleeping, stress, headaches, and even long-term trauma.

Bea quit her job after six months; some victims of bullying fare even worse. After Dr Ruth Namie was bullied at her job, she and her husband, Dr Gary Namie, founded the Workplace Bullying and Trauma Institute to help victims of bullying who experience trauma. According to Gary Namie, adult bullies don't pick only on the weak; they pick on the well-liked, strong, and independent. Former office bully Ron Vid acknowledges that some companies create an atmosphere that encourages bullying by rewarding results regardless of the methods used to attain them. In fact, surveys ranking the best and worst bosses often rely on a composite measure of sales, profits, assets, and market value.[3]

Because workplace bullying is difficult to define, there are no laws against it. According to Lynne Witheridge, founder and CEO of the Andrea Adams Trust, "bullying is an abuse of power or position that usually manifests itself in persistently criticizing someone, openly condemning them, or humiliating them." Bullying doesn't readily fall under the legal definitions of harassment and discrimination. Therefore, it isn't subject to laws prohibiting those behaviors. In many instances, individuals don't even recognize they are being bullied, and if they do, they often see it as a sign of their own weakness.

Dr Gary Namie makes several suggestions for dealing with office bullies. First is to identify the bullying. Recognizing that bullying is taking place stops self-blame. Second, Namie suggests taking time off. The time can be used to collect data about turnover rate, absenteeism, and lost productivity. This information can be used to make a case about the bully's destructive impact on the workplace. Finally, he recommends exposing the bully. Though this may be risky, Namie says it is the only way for the situation to improve.[4]

Questions for Discussion

1. Can workplace bullying lead to conflict between managers and subordinates?

2. Why is bullying a concern to organizations? What are some of the adverse affects of bullying in the workplace?

3. How can office bullying be managed? Is there legal recourse for victims of bullying?

[1] www.hays.com/uk/index.jsp?Content=/uk/jobseekers/common/dealing-with-office-bullies.
[2] David Thomas, "HR the Victim as Bullying Takes Hold in UK Business," *Personnel Today,* September 28, 2004, p 1.
[3] Scott DeCarlo, "The Best and Worst Bosses," *Forbes,* May 9, 2005, p 109.
[4] Alexander Garrett, "How to Cure Bullying at Work," *Management Today,* May 2003, p 80.

Chapter 14 Video Case
Defensive and Supportive Communication

The Situation

Kerstin is a hospital nurse who is feeling job stress. Recently, she has forgotten to complete some Medicaid forms and has experienced some problems with a patient. His IV fell out, he wasn't fed dinner one evening, and he has been complaining that his pain medication is late. Charlie, Kerstin's supervisor, wishes to communicate with her about the situation.

Defensive Communication

Charlie interrupts Kerstin while she is on the telephone and asks her why she forgot to fill out the Medicaid form. With an aggressive tone, he reminds her that this paperwork is part of her job. Kerstin suggests she is very busy and the hospital is like a "nut house." Charlie calls this language inappropriate and proceeds to tell her that one of her patients lost his IV and wasn't fed dinner the previous evening. Kerstin then becomes defensive and blames a new intern for not feeding the patient. Sarcastically, Charlie compares Kerstin unfavorably to another nurse. He also mentions that the patient is complaining about his pain medication and disregards Kerstin's suggestion that the medication should perhaps be increased. Charlie closes the conversation by threatening Kerstin with a bad performance review if she doesn't do a better job.

Supportive Communication

Once Kerstin finishes her telephone conversation, Charlie expresses concern about the amount of work facing her. When he reminds her about the Medicaid form, she notes that she has been extremely busy as the wing has been like a "nut house." Charlie concurs, recognizing how tough double shifts can be and mentioning that a patient's IV fell out. As he tells Kerstin that the same patient wasn't fed dinner the previous evening, the nurse accepts responsibility and agrees to talk to a new intern who was to have fed the patient. Charlie also tells Kerstin that the patient has complained about not getting his pain medication on time. At Kerstin's suggestion, Charlie agrees to talk to the patient's doctor about increasing the medication. Charlie expresses concern for the amount of work Kerstin is responsible for and lets her know that her efforts are appreciated.

Questions for Discussion

1. Contrast the two communication styles, defensive and supportive, in terms of assertiveness, aggressiveness, and nonassertiveness.

2. What message did Charlie want to communicate with Kerstin? What style of communication do you think was more effective in communicating this message? Why?

3. Discuss some of the nonverbal communication that took place between Charlie and Kerstin. Do you think the gender difference had any impact on the communication process?

Chapter 15 Video Case

eBay

Recently, eBay changed merchant Karen Young's life. Young, a housewife, was selling used computer parts on eBay and spending a lot of money wrapping and packaging them when the light went on in her head. Now known as the "bubble wrap lady," Young sold about a half million dollars in shipping supplies last year. She is one of the millions of registered users of the huge online auction, where buyers and sellers can bargain over a huge variety of goods ranging from rare valuables to junk. According to Young, "If you can't find it on eBay, you can't find it." Someone searching for an item as specific as bronze bears, for example, can be connected with hundreds of users selling them in all descriptions and price ranges.

Many eBay users consider themselves part of a big, happy family. As many as 4,400 people have gathered in Anaheim, California, at eBay Live for a chance to meet other vendors face-to-face and link a user name with an actual person. Some discontentment has arisen, though, among smaller sellers concerned that large companies have set up shop on eBay. Adam Cohen, who wrote the book *The Perfect Store,* notes the difficulty eBay faces in achieving a delicate balance: attracting and satisfying investors by bringing in big sellers and high-priced items, while at the same time catering to small individual sellers—the moms and pops. CEO Meg Whitman understands that keeping people like the bubble wrap lady happy will keep her business prospering.

Whitman, who says she learned from her mother to never fear the future, left a terrific job and moved her family across the country to take over at the San Jose, California–based eBay. A graduate of Princeton University and Harvard Business School, she moved up the ranks at several blue chip companies such as FTD, Procter & Gamble, and the Walt Disney Company, then jumped into the upstart world of online business with little knowledge of the Internet. In two years, eBay's workforce grew from 5 to 800. The company's stock rose 2,400% since going public. It has about eight million customers. The number of registered users has grown sharply; in 2005 their ranks swelled to 157.3 million, a 38% increase in one year.[1] In that same period, 64.4 million people bid, bought, or listed an item. Each day, more than 3.3 million items go up for sale.

The mission at eBay, according to Whitman, is to create a global online marketplace where the next-door neighbor's chances of success are equal to those of a large corporation.[2] To accomplish this, almost anything can be sold on eBay. (There are limits to eBay offerings; the auction site won't allow trade in body parts, for example, or a person's soul.) Sellers and buyers can be almost anywhere. Although the company had no international operations five years ago, it now has 31 sites throughout the world. Management expected eBay's international trading revenue to surpass domestic revenue at the end of 2005. Approximately half of eBay's registered users are outside the United States.[3]

The future looks bright for eBay, which claimed $1.1 billion in revenue in July 2005.[4] Looking for growth, the company has acquired businesses to diversify its revenue from auctions by adding fixed-price listings such as classified ads and rental-property listings.[5] Much of eBay's success has been credited to CEO Whitman, who led the transformation from a little Internet auction site into a vast global marketplace that dominates its category. Board member Robert Kogle says that Whitman is into winning competitively and is one of the best strategists he has ever met. To handle eBay's rapid growth, she has restructured the organization several times, which she says keeps people excited and gives them new opportunities. Motivation comes from the eBay mission and empowerment. "We give people a chance to settle in," she says, "and then we make sure that they are well managed, that they are focused on high-impact projects, and that they understand the results they are going to be accountable for."[6]

The company's future may not include Whitman for long. In 2005, she was the top outside candidate for the CEO job at Disney, then withdrew her name, a move many considered a plus for eBay. "She loves this company and the employees," says eBay spokesman Henry Gomez.[7] Industry experts think the visibility of the Disney search will make her an even more attractive candidate for other CEO jobs. Whitman herself has said that 10 years is the longest any CEO should remain at a company; companies need a fresh perspective and an energized leader to tackle corporate challenges.[8] After seven years as CEO, Whitman has begun grooming several senior managers who may eventually be chosen to re-place her. Three senior executives have rotated jobs, a situation seen as Whitman's way to get each manager to learn about other corporate units and to share expertise.[9] Other executives have joined eBay in management and technical positions as Whitman continues to populate the company with strong managers.

Questions for Discussion

1. What do you think accounts for eBay's success?

2. How does the concept of mutuality of interest apply to eBay and its users?

3. Where does Meg Whitman derive her power? Using French and Raven's five bases, discuss which are most relevant to Whitman.

[1] Jon Swartz, "eBay Earnings Going, Going Up, Rising 53%," *USA Today,* July 21, 2005.

[2] Erik Schonfeld, "How to Manage Growth," *Business 2.0,* December 2004, p 98.

[3] Erik Schonfeld, "The World According to eBay," *Business 2.0,* January–February 2005, p 76.

[4] Swartz, "eBay Earnings Going, Going Up."

[5] Mylene Mangalindan and Joann S. Lublin, "After Disney Try, eBay's Whitman Sees Star Rise," *The Wall Street Journal* (Eastern edition), March 14, 2005.

[6] Schonfeld, "How to Manage Growth."

[7] Mangalindan and Lublin, "After Disney Try, eBay's Whitman Sees Star Rise."

[8] Ibid.

[9] Ibid.

Chapter 16 Video Case

Martha Stewart and Celebrity CEOs

In the healthy business climate and stock market boom of the 1990s, CEOs gained attention as the value of their companies soared. Growing stock portfolios and tremendous media focus on corporate leaders led investors, employees, and the public to view many executives as celebrities and even gurus.

Companies joined in the hero worship. CEOs became valued more for their charisma than their experience, says Rakesh Khurana of the Harvard Business School. Over 17 years he studied the selection process 850 firms used to find top executives and found a major change. Traditionally, companies chose promising executives and developed them for years to take over their top jobs. In the 1990s, however, boards often looked instead for a well-known executive outside their organization in the hopes that bringing on a dynamic, personable, media-savvy CEO would spur investors and stock prices.

To find such a CEO, companies often use head-hunters—and pay these middlemen well. For example, headhunter Gerry Roache receives a third of the executive's first year's pay, a cut that could be millions. Do firms get their money's worth by bringing in celebrity CEOs rather than developing managers the old-fashioned way? Executive recruiter Roache has commented candidly that "if management and directors worked harder at management development, we would be close to being out of business." Several companies, Kodak, Xerox, and AT&T among them, have found that having a celebrity CEO does not guarantee a better bottom line. AT&T hired high-profile Michael Armstrong as CEO in 1997. Known as outgoing and smooth, Armstrong had been a top salesperson for IBM and CEO of Hughes Electronics.[1] To supplement AT&T's core long-distance business, Armstrong invested $100 billion to buy cable companies and a high-speed Internet business. Within a few years, facing heavy debt, AT&T under Armstrong split into separate smaller companies and ended up losing its cable unit.[2] Armstrong left AT&T in 2002. The century-old company was sold to SBC Communications in 2005. Perhaps it's much better to have an executive who doesn't get publicity for his or her deal-making or personality, but who concentrates on the business. Under CEO Marsh Carter, for example, Boston's State Street Bank experienced 700% growth in stock value in the 1990s.

Probably the ultimate celebrity CEO has been Martha Stewart, whose company, Martha Stewart Omnimedia (MSO), has been tied closely to its founder from the start. Few executives have received as much media exposure as Stewart, who starred in her television program and infused her magazine with her point of view. After her conviction in an insider trading case brought by the Securities and Exchange Commission, Stewart resigned from her company's board of directors and stepped down as the chief creative officer. She assumed a new role as founding editorial director, giving input on new products.

Stewart's resignation furthered the attempt to separate Martha Stewart the person from the brand bearing her ubiquitous name. The company changed the *Martha Stewart Living* magazine logo by shrinking her name to a smaller box and enlarging the typeface for *Living*. It also made plans for a new nationwide PBS program called *Everyday Foods,* which would use the staff Stewart had assembled but not her name. The firm also planned to drop its catalog business, although it would keep its direct-to-consumer floral business and its Web site.[3]

Many industry analysts thought the move to distance Stewart from her company was the right one, since the brand was badly damaged in the enormous publicity surrounding her case. The magazine suffered huge losses—40%—in advertising revenue. Yet others said that removing Stewart's name left the company with very little, because it had no "diva" to replace her.[4] Some said that despite being tarnished in public opinion, the Stewart name was still good among millions of women. Even after her trial and conviction, the mass-market brand she founded, Martha Stewart Everyday, continued to sell well in retail stores. One retailer commented that the brand has always sold well because the quality is consistent and because Stewart and her company understand the tastes of "middle America."[5] Kmart extended its agreement with Martha Stewart Omnimedia and will hold the rights to the brand through 2009.[6]

In spite of legal troubles, Martha Stewart continued building her celebrity status as she wrote two books and conducted book signings. Convicted, she served her highly publicized five-month jail sentence and subsequent five-month home confinement before launching a comeback for her company and herself. In April 2005, a month after Stewart's media-saturated release from prison, two of her firm's magazines won National Magazine Awards. MSO announced a deal with Sirius Satellite to produce a 24-hour radio channel, a deal that offers a chance to introduce new talent and a guarantee of $30 million over four years. Stewart signed to star in a daytime lifestyle TV show and a home-improvement reality show, a spin-off of Donald Trump's *The Apprentice,* both to be broadcast by cable company Discovery Communications. In 2005, MSO saw its stock value more than triple from the previous year, and CEO Susan Lyne expected advertising sales to rise 35%.[7]

Questions for Discussion

1. Would you consider Martha Stewart a leader or a manager?

2. How does the success of Martha Stewart and her enterprise demonstrate the important role personality plays in leadership?

3. Why do you think Martha Stewart was able to retain and reclaim power and effectiveness after a conviction and prison sentence?

[1]Charles Gasparino, "Out of School," *Newsweek,* January 17, 2005, p 38.
[2]Rebecca Blumenstein, "The Bell Tolls," *The Wall Street Journal* (Eastern edition), February 10, 2005, p D10.
[3]Denise Lugo, "Martha: Will She Live On? Going Private, after Jail, May Be Better Solution than Dumping the Brand," *Investment Dealer's Digest (IDD),* August 9, 2004, p 1.
[4]Ibid., p 1.
[5]Mike Duff, "Note to Stewart Wannabes: Don't Count Martha Out," *DSN Retailing Today,* August 2, 2004, p 6.
[6]Ibid.
[7]"Some Stars Fall, Others Bounce Back—But Who Else Loses Out?" *Marketing Week,* May 26, 2005, p 32.

Chapter 17 Video Case

BP: Building a Global Brand

British Petroleum was a midsized international company before 1998. Then over four years the company doubled in size and expanded into new markets. A merger with Amoco gave BP an important position in the American market. BP then acquired Arco, another American firm, to gain a coast-to-coast presence in the United States. Acquiring the lubricant brand Castrol, the German company Aral, and several other firms resulted in a strong presence in the European market. Growing from 55,000 employees to 117,000, BP emerged as one of the world's largest energy companies and faced the challenge of reinventing itself as a global corporation.

The merging of nine companies made BP a company with no common past, but its leaders recognized the need for a common future. BP undertook a major initiative to rebrand itself so that everyone in the organization could identify with the large new company. The objective was to create a sense of belonging through a new set of values, with which all employees could align and relate in their everyday dealings with customers and other stakeholders.

To create the new brand, BP consulted employees from all of its component companies. Four core values were identified:

- *Performance,* about meeting goals, including financial performance.
- *Innovation,* about allowing your people to seek new solutions to new problems.
- *Progressive,* relating to an attitude that constantly challenges the organization and recognizes diversity.
- *Green,* representing the responsibility to society and the environment; for example, by searching for new types of fuels and engines.

BP looks at these four values as its corporate brand, what BP stands for, and how it operates. They influence the approach everyone at BP takes. These core values

move beyond cultural differences and business environments across the globe. Ways of doing business may differ, but the values remain the same. For instance, the operating guidelines BP has established in Columbia are stricter than those required by the local and national legislatures. BP applies its core values even if it means taking a more difficult route.

Employees were crucial to the successful implementation of the new brand. A major challenge was to unify, excite, and motivate the entire organization. To get employees to understand and commit to the core values, BP made the brand a major part of a training process that occurs throughout employees' careers. In "brand modules," employees discuss with team leaders the values and what they actually mean in their daily lives. Once employees internalize the firm's values, delivery across various cultures comes naturally.

After the new brand was developed, it had to be communicated externally. BP faced the first challenge of changing consumers' negative view of the oil industry. One strategy was to base marketing efforts on the core values to create a positive response in customers' minds and to establish a new type of relationship with society. BP put one group in charge of worldwide communication to develop a consistent message to the public and at the same time be responsive to local needs.

Questions for Discussion

1. Does a global organization's brand and the values it communicates to customers and employees have any impact on the organization's effectiveness? What implication does the concept of a learning organization have for brand management?

2. Why was it important for BP to change its brand? What was the objective of the rebranding initiative?

3. Could the new brand help prevent organizational decline? Can a brand contribute to complacency? Explain.

Chapter 18 Video Case

Louisville Slugger—Hillerich & Bradsby

What do Babe Ruth's 60th home run, Joe DiMaggio's 56-game hitting streak, Ted Williams' .406 season, and Hank Aaron's record-breaking 715th home run have in common? They all were accomplished with Louisville Slugger bats manufactured on the Ohio River at Hillerich & Bradsby.[1] The company makes about 300 models for major league baseball and has about 60% of the major league market.[2] Best known for its wooden bats, the Louisville, Kentucky–based firm also manufactures a variety of baseball, golf, and hockey equipment for amateur and professional athletes.

The company was founded in 1857 as J F Hillerich & Son to manufacture butter churns. It entered the baseball market when one of Hillerich's sons, Bud, promised a star player he could make a bat for him. H&B began producing aluminum bats in 1928 and today relies on the wooden and aluminum bat business for nearly three-quarters of annual revenues.

The company remains family-run; John Hillerich IV is the fourth-generation CEO, taking over the private company from his father. He feels the pressure heading a successful company more than 120 years old, as competition in the industry has intensified as never before. The Louisville Slugger bat now competes with bats made by a host of others ranging from carpenters to Amish craftsmen. To gain an advantage, H&B looked at its internal system in order to streamline operations. The company needed to address everything from order entry problems to production deficiencies to returns. The overview led to discussion of a new system to handle the flow of information.

H&B had a big decision to make; it could either reconfigure its information system or start over. A new system would need to streamline information flow in support of the sales operation and supply chain management, as well as accounting, finance, and marketing. Management realized it needed a new system to improve its dismal shipping record; about 40% of its orders were being shipped on time. They opted for the enterprise resource planning (ERP) system, designed to simplify all processes by storing all information in one common database and automatically updating the information in every stage of production.

Implementation of the new ERP system usually takes years, and the transition from the old system to the new one is difficult. Since the ERP system uses real-time information, the production department manufactures only the inventory that the sales department has requested, and the shipping department has the proper amount of inventory to send to customers. The benefits of ERP are bottom-line savings for the company and improved morale as frustration from repetitive tasks and missing information dissipates. H&B managers thought that the cost of implementing the new system was worth the potential savings. Communication between production and sales had been inefficient, as well as that with management. Getting an answer to one simple question could take a week.

The first step in streamlining production was to identify problems and devise the needs of the new ERP system. Then, the German company SAP was chosen to provide the software. SAP is a system in which a common server holds all the company's information. Every personal computer (PC) is connected to the server. Once data is entered, it is stored in the server where everyone can access it from a PC.

During the 18-month configuration process, morale sagged as longtime employees struggled to change the way they worked. Some employees left during training class, stress levels temporarily increased, and some production processes failed. H&B managers thought about halting the new system, but after struggling through implementation, the company began seeing benefits. It took five years to see quantifiable results. Now the company ships 85% of its orders complete and on time, compared to 40% before SAP. Top customers surveyed rate H&B in the 90–95% satisfaction category.

Questions for Discussion

1. What role do information systems play at H&B? What were the internal and external trade-offs between reconfiguring the old information system and designing a new one?

2. Why was the transition to the new system difficult? How could Kotter's eight steps be used to facilitate such a transition?

3. Why did some people resist change and experience stress? What strategies could H&B have used to overcome resistance to change?

[1] Monte Burke, "Carry a Big Stick," *Forbes*, April 14, 2003, p 220.
[2] Mark Yost, "Ballpark Figure: He's a Hit Pitching Bats to Major League Players," *The Wall Street Journal*, March 31, 2005.

Photo Credits

CHAPTER 1

Photo on page 3 AP/Wide World Photos.

Photo on page 7 Warren Brown, Cake Love.

Photo on page 8 property of AT&T Archives. Reprinted with permission of AT&T.

Photo on page 11 courtesy of Toyota Motor North America.

Photo on page 16 courtesy of Intel Corporation.

LEARNING MODULE A

Photo on page 32 © Marianna Day Massey/ZUMA/CORBIS.

Photo on page 35 AP/Wide World Photos.

Photo on page 39 AP/Wide World Photos.

CHAPTER 2

Photo on page 45 © Najlah Feanny/CORBIS.

Photo on page 51 courtesy of Wegmans.

Photo on page 56 © Tony Savino/The Image Works.

Photo on page 61 © Royalty-Free/CORBIS.

Photo on page 65 © Michael S. Yamashita/CORBIS.

CHAPTER 3

Photo on page 75 AP/Wide World Photos.

Photo on page 88 © Steven Georges/Press-Telegram/CORBIS.

Photo on page 89 © Jon Freilich/Bloomberg News/Landov.

Photo on page 95 © Ryan McVay/Getty Images.

CHAPTER 4

Photo on page 107 © Toshifumi Kitamura/AFP/Getty Images.

Photo on page 112 AP/Wide World Photos.

Photo on page 115 courtesy of Jennifer Chang.

Photo on page 128 © McGraw-Hill Companies/John Flournoy, photographer.

CHAPTER 5

Photo on page 144 © Amanda Marsalis Photography.

Photo on page 159 © McGraw-Hill Companies/Jill Braaten, photographer.

Photo on page 162 AP/Wide World Photos.

Photo on page 164 AP/Wide World Photos.

CHAPTER 6

Photo on page 173 © Jack Hollingsworth/Getty Images.

Photo on page 175 © Landon Nordeman/Getty Images.

Photo on page 177 © Kent Knudson/PhotoLink/Getty Images.

Photo on page 191 courtesy of Vinton Studios.

Photo on page 195 courtesy of Great Harvest Bread Company.

CHAPTER 7

Photo on page 205 © McGraw-Hill Companies/Lars A. Niki, photographer.

Photo on page 208 © Chris McGrath/Getty Images.

Photo on page 217 © Dominique Nabokov/Getty Images.

Photo on page 219 © Harry How/Getty Images.

Photo on page 222 © Thomas Cooper/Getty Images.

CHAPTER 8

Photo on page 235 © Greg Pease/Getty Images/Stone.

Photo on page 241 © Owen Franken/CORBIS.

Photo on page 249 © Geostock/Getty Images.

Photo on page 255 © James H. Pickerell/The Image Works.

Photo on page 260 © Elsa/Getty Images.

CHAPTER 9

Photo on page 269 © Ed Quinn/CORBIS.

Photo on page 276 © Journal-Courier/Steve Warmowski/The Image Works.

Photo on page 285 courtesy of Giftcard.com.

Photo on page 286 Michael A. Foley/©2002 Rycus Associates Photography, LLC.

Photo on page 290 courtesy of Margaret A. Sova.

CHAPTER 10

Photo on page 303 © Ryan McVay/Getty Images.

Photo on page 311 © George Shelly/CORBIS.

CHAPTER 11

CHAPTER 12

CHAPTER 13

CHAPTER 14

CHAPTER 15

CHAPTER 16

CHAPTER 17

CHAPTER 18

Endnotes

CHAPTER 1

[1]P Burrows, "Architects of the Info Age," *BusinessWeek,* March 29, 2004, p 22.

[2]Based on Jeffrey Pfeffer, *The Human Equation: Building Profits by Putting People First* (Boston: Harvard Business School Press, 1998); and Jeffrey Pfeffer and John F. Veiga, "Putting People First for Organizational Success," *Academy of Management Executive,* May 1999, pp 37–48.

[3]Data from Pfeffer and Veiga, "Putting People First for Organizational Success," p 47. Also see C A O'Reilly and Pfeffer, *Hidden Value: How Great Companies Achieve Extraordinary Results with Ordinary People* (Boston: Harvard Business School Press, 2000); and J P Guthrie, "High-Involvement Work Practices, Turnover, and Productivity: Evidence from New Zealand," *Academy of Management Journal,* February 2001, pp 180–90.

[4]As quoted in P B Brown, "What I Know Now," *Fast Company,* February 2005, p 96.

[5]See T Butler and J Waldroop, "Understanding 'People' People," *Harvard Business Review,* June 2004, pp 78–86; R Levering and M Moskowitz, "The 100 Best Companies to Work For," *Fortune,* January 24, 2005, pp 72–90; A Harrington, "Hall of Fame," *Fortune,* January 24, 2005, p 994; A Pomeroy, "How HR Can Affect the Bottom Line," *HR Magazine,* February 2005, pp 14, 16; D K Datta, J P Guthrie, and P M Wright, "Human Resource Management and Labor Productivity: Does Industry Matter?" *Academy of Management Journal,* February 2005, pp 135–45; and P Babcock, "Find What Workers Want," *HR Magazine,* April 2005, pp 50–56.

[6]C I Barnard, *The Functions of the Executive* (Cambridge, MA: Harvard University Press, 1938), p 73.

[7]F Zakaria, "The Education of Paul Wolfowitz," *Newsweek,* March 28, 2005, p 37.

[8]See J B Miner, "The Rated Importance, Scientific Validity, and Practical Usefulness of Organizational Behavior Theories: A Quantitative Review," *Academy of Management Learning and Education,* September 2003, pp 250–68.

[9]Edward E Lawler III, *Treat People Right! How Organizations and Individuals Can Propel Each Other into a Virtuous Spiral of Success* (San Francisco: Jossey-Bass, 2003), p 19. Also see D Rosato, "21 Ways to Jump Start Your Career," *Money,* April 2005, pp 162–66.

[10]B S Lawrence, "Historical Perspective: Using the Past to Study the Present," *Academy of Management Review,* April 1984, p 307.

[11]Evidence indicating that the original conclusions of the famous Hawthorne studies were unjustified may be found in R G Greenwood, A A Bolton, and R A Greenwood, "Hawthorne a Half Century Later: Relay Assembly Participants Remember," *Journal of Management,* Fall–Winter 1983, pp 217–31; and R H Franke and J D Kaul, "The Hawthorne Experiments: First Statistical Interpretation," *American Sociological Review,* October 1978, pp 623–43. For a positive interpretation of the Hawthorne studies, see J A Sonnenfeld, "Shedding Light on the Hawthorne Studies," *Journal of Occupational Behaviour,* April 1985, pp 111–30.

[12]See M Parker Follett, *Freedom and Coordination* (London: Management Publications Trust, 1949).

[13]See D McGregor, *The Human Side of Enterprise* (New York: McGraw-Hill, 1960).

[14]For a story of a manager's switch from Theory X to Theory Y, see D Dorsey, "Andy Pearson Finds Love," *Fast Company,* August 2001, pp 78–86. Also see J S Nielsen, *The Myth of Leadership: Creating Leaderless Organizations* (Palo Alto, CA: Davies-Black, 2004).

[15]S Bates, "Getting Engaged," *HR Magazine,* February 2004, pp 44, 46.

[16]See D W Organ, "Elusive Phenomena," *Business Horizons,* March–April 2002, pp 1–2.

[17]See, for example, R Zemke, "TQM: Fatally Flawed or Simply Unfocused?" *Training,* October 1992, p 8.

[18]J McGregor, "The Performance Paradox," *Fast Company,* April 2005, pp 29–30. Also see A Levin, "Fewer Crashes Caused by Pilots," *USA Today,* March 2, 2004, p 1A.

[19]Instructive background articles on TQM are R Zemke, "A Bluffer's Guide to TQM," *Training,* April 1993, pp 48–55; R R Gehani, "Quality Value-Chain: A Meta-Synthesis of Frontiers of Quality Movement," *Academy of Management Executive,* May 1993, pp 29–42; P Mears, "How to Stop Talking about, and Begin Progress toward, Total Quality Management," *Business Horizons,* May–June 1993, pp 11–14; and the Total Quality Special Issue of *Academy of Management Review,* July 1994.

[20]M Sashkin and K J Kiser, *Putting Total Quality Management to Work* (San Francisco: Berrett-Koehler, 1993), p 39.

[21]R J Schonberger, "Total Quality Management Cuts a Broad Swath—Through Manufacturing and Beyond," *Organizational Dynamics,* Spring 1992, p 18. Also see R Gulati and J B Oldroyd, "The Quest for Customer Focus," *Harvard Business Review,* April 2005, pp 92–101; and A Tilin, "Vespa Goes Back to School," *Business 2.0,* April 2005, p 24.

[22]Based on C Hui, S S K Lam, and J Schaubroeck, "Can Good Citizens Lead the Way in Providing Quality Service? A Field Quasi Experiment," *Academy of Management Journal,* October 2001, pp 988–95. Also See J Pfeffer, "How Companies Get Smart," *Business 2.0,* January–February 2005, p 74.

[23]Deming's landmark work is W E Deming. *Out of the Crisis* (Cambridge, MA: MIT, 1986).

[24]See M Trumbull, "What Is Total Quality Management?" *The Christian Science Monitor,* May 3, 1993, p 12; J Hillkirk, "World-Famous Quality Expert Dead at 93," *USA Today,* December 21, 1993, pp 1B–2B; and O Port, "The Kings of Quality," *BusinessWeek,* August 30, 2004, p 20.

[25]Based on discussion in M Walton, *Deming Management at Work* (New York: Putnam/Perigee, 1990).

[26]Ibid., p 20.

[27]Adapted from D E Bowen and E E Lawler III, "Total Quality-Oriented Human Resources Management," *Organizational Dynamics,* Spring 1992, pp 29–41.

[28]See T F Rienzo, "Planning Deming Management for Service Organizations," *Business Horizons,* May–June 1993, pp 19–29. Also see M R Yilmaz and S Chatterjee, "Deming and the Quality of Software Development," *Business Horizons,* November–December 1997, pp 51–58.

[29]For details, see T J Douglas and W Q Judge Jr, "Total Quality Management Implementation and Competitive Advantage: The Role of Structural Control and Exploration," *Academy of Management Journal,* February 2001, pp 158–69; and K B Hendricks and V R Singhal, "The Long-Run Stock Price Performance of Firms with Effective TQM Programs," *Management Science,* March 2001, pp 359–68.

[30]For example, see J R Dew, "Learning from Baldrige Winners at the University of Alabama," *Journal of Organizational Excellence,* Spring 2001, pp 49–56; R B Chase and S Dasu, "Want to Perfect Your Company's Service? Use Behavioral Science," *Harvard Business Review,* June 2001, pp 79–84; A W Ulwick, "Turn Customer Input into Innovation," *Harvard Business Review,* January 2002, pp 91–97; and S Thomke and E von Hippel, "Customers as Innovators: A New Way to Create Value," *Harvard Business Review,* April 2002, pp 74–81.

[31]See G Hamel, "Is This All You Can Build with the Net? Think Bigger," *Fortune,* April 30, 2001, 134–38; and B Rosenbloom, "The Ten Deadly Myths of E-Commerce," *Business Horizons,* March–April 2002, pp 61–66. Internet and Web pioneers are profiled in O Port, "He Made the Net Work," *BusinessWeek,* September 27, 2004, p 20; and O Port, "Spinning the World's Web," *BusinessWeek,* November 8, 2004, p 16.

[32]M J Mandel and R D Hof, "Rethinking the Internet," *BusinessWeek,* March 26, 2001, p 118. Also see G T Lumpkin and G G Dess, "E-Business Strategies and Internet Business Models: How the Internet Adds Value," *Organizational Dynamics,* no. 2, 2004, pp 161–73; and T J Mullaney, "E-Biz Strikes Again!" *BusinessWeek,* May 10, 2004, pp 80–82.

[33]A Bernasek, "Buried in Tech," *Fortune,* April 16, 2001, p 52.

[34]T J Mullaney and A Weintraub, "The Digital Hospital," *BusinessWeek,* March 28, 2005, p 77.

[35]See S Boehle, "Simulations: The Next Generation of E-Learning," *Training,* January 2005, pp 22–31; and A Fisher, "Find Online Training That Pays Off," *Fortune,* February 7, 2005, p 34.

[36]See R J Grossman, "Blind Investment," *HR Magazine,* January 2005, pp 40–47; and A Pomeroy, "People Are Our Greatest Asset," *HR Magazine,* April 2005, p 20.

[37]For details on these trends, see S Hamm, "Tech's Future," *BusinessWeek,* September 27, 2004, pp 82–89; J Puliyenthuruthel and M Kripalani, "Good Help Is Hard to Find," *BusinessWeek,* February 14, 2005, p 52; J Pfeffer, "A Blueprint for Success," *Business 2.0,* April 2005, p 66; S Clifford, "Employers Tackle a Tricky Math Problem," *Inc.,* March 2005, p 28; S Ladika, "Unwelcome Changes," *HR Magazine,* February 2005, pp 83–90; E E Gordon, "The 2010 Crossroad," *Training,* January 2005, pp 33–35; R J Grossman, "The Truth about the Coming Labor Shortage," *HR Magazine,* March 2005, pp 46–53; A Fisher, "How to Battle the Coming Brain Drain," *Fortune,* March 21, 2005, pp 121–28; and J Puliyenthuruthel, "The Soft Underbelly of Offshoring," *BusinessWeek,* April 25, 2005, p 52.

[38]B E Becker, M A Huselid, and D Ulrich, *The HR Scorecard: Linking People, Strategy, and Performance* (Boston: Harvard Business School Press, 2001), p 4.

[39]See D Stamps, "Measuring Minds," *Training,* May 2000, pp 76–85; C A Bartlett and S Ghoshal, "Building Competitive Advantage through People," *MIT Sloan Management Review,* Winter 2002, pp 34–41; and R Rodriguez, "Meet the New Learning Executive," *HR Magazine,* April 2005, pp 64–69.

[40]See "Top High School Scientists Selected," *USA Today,* March 16, 2005, p 5D; and O Port, "Meet the Best and Brightest," *BusinessWeek,* March 28, 2005, pp 88–91.

[41]Data from "The 100 Best Companies to Work For," *Fortune,* February 4, 2002, p 84.

[42]Inspired by P S Adler and S Kwon, "Social Capital: Prospects for a New Concept," *Academy of Management Review,* January 2002, pp 17–40. Also see D Lidsky, "Winning the Relationship Game," *Fast Company,* October 2004, pp 113–15; J Steinberg, "One Heart at a Time," *Fast Company,* November 2004, p 49; K H Hammonds, "A Lever Long Enough to Move the World," *Fast Company,* January 2005, pp 60–63; and A C Inkpen and E W K Tsang, "Social Capital, Networks, and Knowledge Transfer," *Academy of Management Review,* January 2005, pp 146–65.

[43]L Prusak and D Cohen, "How to Invest in Social Capital," *Harvard Business Review,* June 2001, p 93.

[44]Data from "What Makes a Job OK," *USA Today,* May 15, 2000, p 1B.

[45]See W L Garner and J R Schermerhorn Jr, "Unleashing Individual Potential: Performance Gains through Positive Organizational Behavior and Authentic Leadership," *Organizational Dynamics,* no. 3, 2004, pp 270–81; T A Wright and R Cropanzano, "The Role of Psychological Well-Being in Job Performance: A Fresh Look at an Age-Old Quest," *Organizational Dynamics,* no. 4, 2004, pp 338–51; and J H Gavin and R O Mason, "The Virtuous Organization: The

Value of Happiness in the Workplace," *Organizational Dynamics,* no. 4, 2004, pp 379–92.

[46]M E P Seligman and M Csikszentmihalyi, "Positive Psychology: An Introduction," *American Psychologist,* January 2000, p 5. Also see the other 15 articles in the January 2000 issue of *American Psychologist;* and M Elias, "What Makes People Happy: Psychologists Now Know," *USA Today,* December 9, 2002, pp 1A–2A.

[47]See F Luthans, K W Luthans, and B C Luthans, "Positive Psychological Capital: Beyond Human and Social Capital," *Business Horizons,* January–February 2004, pp 45–50; and F Luthans and C M Youssef, "Human, Social, and Now Positive Psychological Capital Management: Investing in People for Competitive Advantage," *Organizational Dynamics,* no. 2, 2004, pp 143–60.

[48]F Luthans, "The Need for and Meaning of Positive Organizational Behavior," *Journal of Organizational Behavior,* September 2002, p 698. Also see T A Wright, "Positive Organizational Behavior: An Idea Whose Time Has Truly Come," *Journal of Organizational Behavior,* June 2003, pp 437–42.

[49]R Levering and M Moskowitz, "2004 Special Report: The 100 Best Companies to Work For," *Fortune,* January 12, 2004, p 78.

[50]A Harrington, "Hall of Fame," *Fortune,* January 24, 2005, p 94. Also see S Zuboff, "The Case for Optimism," *Fast Company,* April 2005, p 101.

[51]Levering and Moskowitz, "2004 Special Report: The 100 Best Companies to Work For," p 76.

[52]See P F Drucker, "What Makes an Effective Executive," *Harvard Business Review,* June 2004, pp 58–63; M E Porter, J W Lorsch, and N Nohria, "Seven Surprises for New CEOs," *Harvard Business Review,* October 2004, pp 62–72; D McGinn, "Building a Better CEO," *Newsweek,* March 28, 2005, pp 38–39; and J Welch and S Welch, "How to Be a Good Leader," *Newsweek,* April 4, 2005, pp 45–48.

[53]H Mintzberg, "The Manager's Job: Folklore and Fact," *Harvard Business Review,* July–August 1975, p 61. Also see J Gosling and H Mintzberg, "The Five Minds of a Manager," *Harvard Business Review,* November 2003, pp 54–63; and H Mintzberg, "Third-Generation Management Development," *Training and Development,* March 2004, pp 28–38.

[54]See, for example, H Mintzberg, "Managerial Work: Analysis from Observation," *Management Science,* October 1971, pp B97–B110; and F Luthans, "Successful vs. Effective Real Managers," *Academy of Management Executive,* May 1988, pp 127–32. For an instructive critique of the structured observation method, see M J Martinko and W L Gardner, "Beyond Structured Observation: Methodological Issues and New Directions," *Academy of Management Review,* October 1985, pp 676–95. Also see N Fondas, "A Behavioral Job Description for Managers," *Organizational Dynamics,* Summer 1992, pp 47–58.

[55]See L B Kurke and H E Aldrich, "Mintzberg Was Right!: A Replication and Extension of *The Nature of Managerial Work,*" *Management Science,* August 1983, pp 975–84.

[56]For example, see H Bruch and S Ghoshal, "Beware the Busy Manager," *Harvard Business Review,* February 2002, pp 62–69.

[57]Validation studies can be found in E Van Velsor and J B Leslie, *Feedback to Managers, Volume II: A Review and Comparison of Sixteen Multi-Rater Feedback Instruments* (Greensboro, NC: Center for Creative Leadership, 1991); F Shipper, "A Study of the Psychometric Properties of the Managerial Skill Scales of the Survey of Management Practices," *Educational and Psychological Measurement,* June 1995, pp 468–79; and C L Wilson, *How and Why Effective Managers Balance Their Skills: Technical, Teambuilding, Drive* (Columbia, MD: Rockatech Multimedia Publishing, 2003).

[58]For example, see S B Parry, "Just What Is a Competency? (And Why Should You Care?)" *Training,* June 1998, pp 58–64.

[59]See F Shipper, "Mastery and Frequency of Managerial Behaviors Relative to Sub-Unit Effectiveness," *Human Relations,* April 1991, pp 371–88.

[60]Ibid.

[61]Data from F Shipper, "A Study of Managerial Skills of Women and Men and Their Impact on Employees' Attitudes and Career Success in a Nontraditional Organization," paper presented at the Academy of Management Meeting, August 1994, Dallas, Texas. The same outcome for on-the-job studies is reported in A H Eagly and B T Johnson, "Gender and Leadership Style: A Meta-Analysis," *Psychological Bulletin,* September 1990, pp 233–56.

[62]For instance, see J B Rosener, "Ways Women Lead," *Harvard Business Review,* November–December 1990, pp 119–25; and C Lee, "The Feminization of Management," *Training,* November 1994, pp 25–31.

[63]Based on F Shipper and J E Dillard Jr, "A Study of Impending Derailment and Recovery of Middle Managers across Career Stages," *Human Resource Management,* Winter 2000, pp 331–45. Also see S Finkelstein, *Why Smart Executives Fail: and What You Can Learn from Their Mistakes* (New York: Portfolio, 2003); and B Stone, "The Music Stops for a Rock Star," *Newsweek,* February 21, 2005, pp 38–40.

[64]See S Cummings and D Angwin, "The Future Shape of Strategy: Lemmings or Chimeras?" *Academy of Management Executive,* May 2004, pp 21–36; and M C Mankins, "Stop Wasting Valuable Time," *Harvard Business Review,* September 2004, pp 58–65.

[65]Essential sources on reengineering are M Hammer and J Champy, *Reengineering the Corporation: A Manifesto for Business Revolution* (New York: HarperCollins, 1993); and J Champy, *Reengineering Management: The Mandate for New Leadership* (New York: HarperCollins, 1995). Also see "Anything Worth Doing Is Worth Doing from Scratch," *Inc.,* May 18, 1999 (20th Anniversary Issue), pp 51–52.

[66]See C A Beatty and B A Barker Scott, *Building Smart Teams: A Roadmap to High Performance* (Thousand Oaks, CA: Sage, 2004).

[67]See, for example, W A Randolph and M Sashkin, "Can Organizational Empowerment Work in Multinational Settings?" *Academy of Management Executive,* February 2002, pp 102–15; S E Seibert, S R Silver, and W A Randolph, "Taking

Empowerment to the Next Level: A Multiple-Level Model of Empowerment, Performance, and Satisfaction," *Academy of Management Journal,* June 2004, pp 332–49; J L Kerr, "The Limits of Organizational Democracy," *Academy of Management Executive,* August 2004, pp 81–97; and J Janove, "A 3,500-Year-Old Lesson in Delegating," *HR Magazine,* March 2005, pp 109–22.

[68]M Buckingham, "What Great Managers Do," *Harvard Business Review,* March 2005, pp 70–79. Also see M Buckingham, *One Thing You Need to Know: . . . About Great Managing, Great Leading, and Sustained Individual Success* (New York: Free Press, 2005).

[69]H L Tosi Jr and J W Slocum Jr, "Contingency Theory: Some Suggested Directions," *Journal of Management,* Spring 1984, p 9.

[70]For empirical evidence in a cross-cultural study, see D I Jung and B J Avolio, "Effects of Leadership Style and Followers' Cultural Orientation on Performance in Groups and Individual Task Conditions," *Academy of Management Journal,* April 1999, pp 208–18.

[71]See Ann Crittenden, *If You've Raised Kids, You Can Manage Anything: Leadership Begins at Home* (New York: Gotham Books, 2004).

[72]See S L Rynes, J M Bartunek, and R L Daft, "Across the Great Divide: Knowledge Creation and Transfer between Practitioners and Academics," *Academy of Management Journal,* April 2001, pp 340–55.

[73]See R L Daft, "Learning the Craft of Organizational Research," *Academy of Management Review,* October 1983, pp 539–46.

[74]See K E Weick, "Theory Construction as Disciplined Imagination," *Academy of Management Review,* October 1989, pp 516–31. Also see C C Lundberg, "Is There Really Nothing So Practical as a Good Theory?" *Business Horizons,* September–October 2004, pp 7–14.

[75]Theory-focused versus problem-focused research is discussed in K E Weick, "Agenda Setting in Organizational Behavior: A Theory-Focused Approach," *Journal of Management Inquiry,* September 1992, pp 171–82. Also see the collection of articles about theory in the March 2005 issue of *Academy of Management Learning and Education,* pp 74–113.

[76]For instance, see M R Buckley, G R Ferris, H J Bernardin, and M G Harvey, "The Disconnect between the Science and Practice of Management," *Business Horizons,* March–April 1998, pp 31–38. Also see D Cohen, "Research: Food for Future Thought," *HR Magazine,* May 2001, p 184.

[77]Complete discussion of this technique can be found in J E Hunter, F L Schmidt, and G B Jackson, *Meta-Analysis: Cumulating Research Findings across Studies* (Beverly Hills, CA: Sage Publications, 1982); and J E Hunter and F L Schmidt, *Methods of Meta-Analysis: Correcting Error and Bias in Research Findings* (Newbury Park, CA: Sage Publications, 1990). Also see J Merritt and L Lavelle, "A Different Kind of Governance Guru," *BusinessWeek,* August 9, 2004, pp 46–47.

[78]Limitations of meta-analysis technique are discussed in P Bobko and E F Stone-Romero, "Meta-Analysis May Be Another Useful Tool, but It Is Not a Panacea," in *Research in Personnel and Human Resources Management,* vol. 16, ed G R Ferris (Stamford, CT: JAI Press, 1998), pp 359–97. Also see R A Peterson and S P Brown, "On the Use of Beta Coefficients in Meta-Analysis," *Journal of Applied Psychology,* January 2005, pp 175–81.

[79]For an interesting debate about the use of students as subjects, see J Greenberg, "The College Sophomore as Guinea Pig: Setting the Record Straight," *Academy of Management Review,* January 1987, pp 157–59; and M E Gordon, L A Slade, and N Schmitt, "Student Guinea Pigs: Porcine Predictors and Particularistic Phenomena," *Academy of Management Review,* January 1987, pp 160–63.

[80]Good discussions of case studies can be found in A S Lee, "Case Studies as Natural Experiments," *Human Relations,* February 1989, pp 117–37; and K M Eisenhardt, "Building Theories from Case Study Research," *Academy of Management Review,* October 1989, pp 532–50. The case survey technique is discussed in R Larsson, "Case Survey Methodology: Analysis of Patterns across Case Studies," *Academy of Management Journal,* December 1993, pp 1515–46.

[81]Based on discussion found in J M Beyer and H M Trice, "The Utilization Process: A Conceptual Framework and Synthesis of Empirical Findings," *Administrative Science Quarterly,* December 1982, pp 591–622. Also see S Albers Mohrman, C B Gibson, and A M Mohrman Jr, "Doing Research That Is Useful to Practice: A Model and Empirical Exploration," *Academy of Management Journal,* April 2001, pp 357–75.

[82]See J J Martocchio, "Age-Related Differences in Employee Absenteeism: A Meta-Analysis," *Psychology & Aging,* December 1989, pp 409–14.

[83]See J Beeson, "Building Bench Strength: A Tool Kit for Executive Development," *Business Horizons,* November–December 2004, pp 3–9.

[84]L Tischler, "IBM's Management Makeover," *Fast Company,* November 2004, pp 112–13. For more on IBM, see S Hamm, "Beyond Blue," *BusinessWeek,* April 18, 2005, pp 68–76. By Linda Tischler, © 2005 Gruner & Jahr USA Publishing. First published in *Fast Company* Magazine. Reprinted with permission.

[85]These research results are discussed in detail in J B Miner and N R Smith, "Decline and Stabilization of Managerial Motivation over a 20-Year Period," *Journal of Applied Psychology,* June 1982, pp 297–305.

[86]See J B Miner, J M Wachtel, and B Ebrahimi, "The Managerial Motivation of Potential Managers in the United States and Other Countries of the World: Implications for National Competitiveness and the Productivity Problem," in *Advances in International Comparative Management,* vol. 4, ed B Prasad (Greenwich, CT: JAI Press, 1989), pp 147–70; and J B Miner, C C Chen, and K C Yu, "Theory Testing under Adverse Conditions: Motivation to Manage in the People's Republic of China," *Journal of Applied Psychology,* June 1991, pp 343–49.

[87]See J B Miner, B Ebrahimi, and J M Wachtel, "How Deficiencies in Motivation to Manage Contribute to the United States' Competitiveness Problem (and What Can Be Done about It)," *Human Resource Management,* Fall 1995, pp 363–87.

[88]Based on K M Bartol and D C Martin, "Managerial Motivation among MBA Students: A Longitudinal Assessment," *Journal of Occupational Psychology,* March 1987, pp 1–12.

[89]Excerpted from K Gurchiek, "I Can't Make It to Work Today, Boss . . . Gotta Round Up My Ostriches," *HR Magazine,* March 2005, p 30.

LEARNING MODULE A

[1]Excerpted from Ellen E Schultz and Theo Francis, "Financial Surgery: How Cuts in Retiree Benefits Fatten Companies' Bottom Lines," *The Wall Street Journal,* March 1, 2004, p A1. Copyright 2004 by Dow Jones & Co. Inc. Reproduced with permission of Dow Jones & Co. Inc. via The Copyright Clearance Center.

[2]Results can be found in "HR Poll Results," http://hr2.blr.com/index.cfm/Nav/11.0.0.0/Action/Poll_Question/qid/170, accessed April 8, 2005.

[3]Results can be found in Matthew Boyle, "By the Numbers: Liarliar!" *Fortune,* May 26, 2003, p 44.

[4]See www.josephsoninstitute.org/pdf/workplace-flier_0604.pdf, accessed April 8, 2005.

[5]A discussion of ethics and financial performance is provided by R M Fulmer, "The Challenge of Ethical Leadership," *Organizational Dynamics,* August 2004, pp 307–17.

[6]Results can be found in "Tarnished Employment Brands Affect Recruiting," *HR Magazine,* November 2004, pp 16, 20.

[7]A W Mathews and B Martinez, "Painful Drug: E-Mails Suggest Merck Knew Vioxx's Dangers at Early Stage," *The Wall Street Journal,* November 1, 2004, p A1.

[8]See C Gilligan, "In a Different Voice: Women's Conceptions of Self and Morality," *Harvard Educational Review,* November 1977, pp 481–517.

[9]The following discussion is based on A J Daboub, A M A Rasheed, R L Priem, and D A Gray, "Top Management Team Characteristics and Corporate Illegal Activity," *Academy of Management Review,* January 1995, pp 138–70.

[10]L Simpson, "Taking the High Road," *Training,* January 2002, p 38.

[11]Supporting results can be found in M E Schweitzer, L Ordóñez, and B Douma, "Goal Setting as a Motivator of Unethical Behavior," *Academy of Management Journal,* June 2004, pp 422–32.

[12]These statistics, and counterfeiting in general, are discussed in F Balfour, "The Global Counterfeit Business Is Out of Control, Targeting Everything from Computer Chips to Life-Saving Medicines. It's So Bad That Even China May Need to Crack Down," *BusinessWeek,* February 7, 2005, pp 54–64.

[13]Supporting research can be found in J B Cullen, K P Parboteeah, and M Hoegl, "Cross-National Differences in Managers' Willingness to Justify Ethically Suspect Behaviors: A Test of Institutional Anomie Theory," *Academy of Management Journal,* June 2004, pp 411–21.

[14]Results can be found in T Jackson, "Cultural Values and Management Ethics: A 10-Nation Study," *Human Relations,* October 2001, pp 1267–302.

[15]The following discussion is based on Daboub et al., "Top Management Team Characteristics and Corporate Illegal Activity."

[16]This discussion is based on Constance E Bagley, "The Ethical Leader's Decision Tree," *Harvard Business Review,* February 2003, pp 18–19.

[17]For a thorough discussion of this issue, see Schultz and Francis, "Financial Surgery: How Cuts in Retiree Benefits Fatten Companies' Bottom Lines."

[18]T Gutner, "Blowing Whistles—and Being Ignored," *BusinessWeek,* March 18, 2002, p 107.

[19]Results are discussed in ibid.

[20]C Gilligan and J Attanucci, "Two Moral Orientations: Gender Differences and Similarities," *Merril-Palmer Quarterly,* July 1988, pp 224–25.

[21]Results can be found in S Jaffee and J Hyde, "Gender Differences in Moral Orientation: A Meta-Analysis," *Psychological Bulletin,* September 2000, pp 703–26.

[22]Ibid, p 719.

[23]See Ch 6 in K Hodgson, *A Rock and a Hard Place: How to Make Ethical Business Decisions When the Choices Are Tough* (New York: AMACOM, 1992), pp 66–77.

[24]D Matten and A Crane, "Corporate Citizenship: Toward an Extended Theoretical Conceptualization," *Academy of Management Review,* January 2005, p 167.

[25]Adapted from W E Stead, D L Worrell, and J Garner Stead, "An Integrative Model for Understanding and Managing Ethical Behavior in Business Organizations," *Journal of Business Ethics,* March 1990, pp 233–42.

[26]For an excellent review of integrity testing, see D S Ones and C Viswesvaran, "Integrity Testing in Organizations," in *Dysfunctional Behavior in Organizations: Violent and Deviant Behavior,* eds R W Griffin et al. (Stamford, CT: JAI Press, 1998), pp 243–76.

[27]Guidelines for conducting ethics training are discussed by K Tyler, "Do the Right Thing," *HR Magazine,* February 2005, pp 99–101.

[28]For details regarding Boeing, see "Boeing Hires Outsider to Monitor Its Ethics," *Arizona Republic,* May 5, 2004, p D5.

[29]These scenarios were excerpted from L M Dawson, "Women and Men, Morality, and Ethics," *Business Horizons,* July–August 1995, pp 62, 65.

[30]Comparative norms were obtained from Dawson, "Women and Men, Morality and Ethics." Scenario 1: would sell (28% males, 57% females); would not sell (66% males, 28%

females); unsure (6% males, 15% females). Scenario 2: would consult (84% males, 32% females); would not consult (12% males, 62% females); unsure (4% males, 6% females).

[31]The following trends were taken from Dawson, "Women and Men, Morality and Ethics." Women were likely to primarily respect feelings, ask "who will be hurt?", avoid being judgmental, search for compromise, seek solutions that minimize hurt, rely on communication, believe in contextual relativism, be guided by emotion, and challenge authority. Men were likely to primarily respect rights, ask "who is right?", value decisiveness, make unambiguous decisions, seek solutions that are objectively fair, rely on rules, believe in blind impartiality, be guided by logic, and accept authority.

CHAPTER 2

[1]Excerpted from D Thomas, "Diversity as Strategy," *Harvard Business Review,* September 2004, p 98.

[2]See ibid.

[3]L Wasmer Andrews, "Hard-Core Offenders," *HR Magazine,* December 2004, p 44.

[4]This distinction is made by D A Harrison, K H Price, and M P Bell, "Beyond Relational Demography: Time and the Effects of Surface- and Deep-Level Diversity on Work Group Cohesion," *Academy of Management Journal,* February 1998, pp 96–107.

[5]H Collingwood, "Who Handles a Diverse Work Force Best?" *Working Women,* February 1996, p 25.

[6]A description of Ford's program can be found in E Garsten, "Ford Muslim Workers Organize 'Islam,' " *Arizona Republic,* December 13, 2001, p D2.

[7]Excerpted from "Workforce Optimas Awards 2003," *Workforce,* March 2003, p 47.

[8]R Thomas Jr, "From Affirmative Action to Affirming Diversity," *Harvard Business Review,* March–April 1990, pp 107–17.

[9]Opposition to affirmative action was investigated by E H James, A P Brief, J Dietz, and R R Cohen, "Prejudice Matters: Understanding the Reactions of Whites to Affirmative Action Programs Targeted to Benefit Blacks," *Journal of Applied Psychology,* December 2001, pp 1120–28.

[10]For a thorough review of relevant research, see M E Heilman, "Affirmative Action: Some Unintended Consequences for Working Women," in *Research in Organizational Behavior,* vol. 16, eds B M Staw and L L Cummings (Greenwich, CT: JAI Press, 1994), pp 125–69.

[11]Results from this study can be found in M E Heilman, W S Battle, C E Keller, and R A Lee, "Type of Affirmative Action Policy: A Determinant of Reactions to Sex-Based Preferential Selection?" *Journal of Applied Psychology,* April 1998, pp 190–205.

[12]A complete description of Wegmans' progressive managerial practices can be found in M Boyle, "The Wegmans Way," *Fortune,* January 24, 2005, pp 62–71.

[13]A M Morrison, *The New Leaders: Guidelines on Leadership Diversity in America* (San Francisco: Jossey-Bass, 1992), p 78.

[14]Results can be found in N London-Vargas, *Faces of Diversity* (New York: Vantage Press, 1999).

[15]V J Weaver, "What These CEOs and Their Companies Know about Diversity," *BusinessWeek,* September 10, 2001, special advertising section.

[16]These statistics were derived from E E Gordon, "The 2010," *Training,* January 2005, pp 33–35.

[17]The glass ceiling is discussed by P L Perrewé and D L Nelson, "Gender and Career Success: The Facilitative Role of Political Skill," *Organizational Dynamics,* December 2004, pp 366–78.

[18]See K Blanton, "More Women in Top-Tier Jobs Earn 6 Figures," *Arizona Republic,* March 11, 2004, pp D1, D5.

[19]Results can be found in K S Lyness and D E Thompson, "Above the Glass Ceiling: A Comparison of Matched Samples of Female and Male Executives," *Journal of Applied Psychology,* June 1997, pp 359–75.

[20]This study was conducted by K S Lyness and M K Judiesch, "Are Women More Likely to Be Hired or Promoted into Management Positions?" *Journal of Vocational Behavior,* February 1999, pp 158–73.

[21]See D Jones, "Female CEOs Struggle in '04' but over Two Years, They're Topping Firms Led by Men," *USA Today,* January 4, 2005, retrieved March 29, 2005, from www.usatoday.com/educate/college/careers/hottopic35.htm, January 4, 2005; and C. Hymowitz, "Women Put Noses to the Grindstone, and Miss Opportunities," *The Wall Street Journal,* February 3, 2004, p B1.

[22]Details of this study can be found in B R Ragins, B Townsend, and M Mattis, "Gender Gap in the Executive Suite: CEOs and Female Executives Report on Breaking the Glass Ceiling," *Academy of Management Review,* February 1998, pp 28–42.

[23]Here are the ranks for each career strategy: Strategy 1 = 12; Strategy 2 = 6; Strategy 3 = 5; Strategy 4 = 11; Strategy 5 = 9; Strategy 6 = 3; Strategy 7 = 10; Strategy 8 = 1; Strategy 9 = 7; Strategy 10 = 8; Strategy 11 = 4; Strategy 12 = 2; and Strategy 13 = 13.

[24]"Sara Lee Cleans Out Its Cupboards," *Fortune,* March 7, 2005, p 38.

[25]For details regarding these statistics, see G C Armas, "Almost Half of US Likely to be Minorities by 2050," *Arizona Republic,* March 18, 2004, p A5.

[26]These statistics were obtained from "Race-Based Charges FY 1992–FY 2004," The US Equal Employment Opportunity Commission, www.eeoc/stats/race.html, last modified January 27, 2005.

[27]See D Weinberg, "Real Median Household Income by Race and Hispanic Origin: 2003," www.census.gov/hhes/www/img/incpov03/fig07.jpg, August 24, 2004.

[28]Results can be found in R J Contrada, R D Ashmore, M L Gary, E Coups, J D Egeth, A Sewell, K Ewell, T M Goyal, and V Chasse, "Measures of Ethnicity-Related Stress: Psychometric Properties, Ethnic Group Differences, and Associations with Well-Being," *Journal of Applied Social Psychology,* 2001, pp 1775–820.

[29]Results can be found in E H James, "Race-Related Differences in Promotions and Support: Underlying Effects of Human and Social Capital," *Organization Science,* September–October 2000, pp 493–508.

[30]Results are reported in C Daniels, "Young, Gifted, Black—and Out of Here," *Fortune,* May 3, 2004, p 48.

[31]This statistic was reported in B Grow, "Labor Notes: Hispanics Learn to Cry Foul," *BusinessWeek,* September 20, 2004, p 14.

[32]See "USA Statistics in Brief—Law, Education, Communications, Transportation, Housing," www.census.gov, last revised March 16, 2004.

[33]See D Dooley and J Prause, "Underemployment and Alcohol Misuse in the National Longitudinal Survey of Youth," *Journal of Studies on Alcohol,* November 1998, pp 669–80; and D C Feldman, "The Nature, Antecedents and Consequences of Underemployment," *Journal of Management,* 1966, pp 385–407.

[34]The survey is discussed in "Underemployment Affects 18 Percent of Entry Level Job Seekers," www.collegrad.com/press/underemployed.shtml, September 9, 2004.

[35]Statistics are reported in "Earnings Increase with Educational Attainment," http://factfinder.census.gov/jsp/saff/SAFFInfo.jsp?_pageId=tp5_education, last revised January 19, 2005.

[36]Literacy statistics can be found in D Baynton, "America's $60 Billion Problem," *Training,* May 2001, pp 51–56.

[37]"Facts on Literacy," *National Literacy Facts,* August 27, 1998, www.svs.net/wpci/Litfacts.htm.

[38]See Baynton, "America's $60 Billion Problem."

[39]See A R Karr, "Work Week: A Special News Report about Life on the Job—and Trends Taking Shape There," *The Wall Street Journal,* May 18, 1999, p A1.

[40]See H London, "The Workforce, Education, and the Nation's Future," Summer 1998, www.hudson.org/american_outlook/articles_sm 98/london.htm.

[41]See P Engardio, C Matlack, G Edmondson, I Rowley, C Barraclough, and G Smith, "Now the Geezer Glut," *BusinessWeek,* January 31, 2005, pp 44–47.

[42]This point was made by K Dychtwald, T Erickson, and B Morison, "It's Time to Retire Retirement," *Harvard Business Review,* March 2004, pp 48–57.

[43]The survey results can be found in "Are Executives Entering the Age of Paranoia?" *HR Magazine,* March 2005, pp 16, 18.

[44]Examples are provided by K Gurchiek, "Survey: Exodus Follows an Improving Economy," *HR Magazine,* March 2005, pp 28, 34; and N Cossack, R R Hastings, and A Maingault, "Day Care, Pay Raises, Rules on Part-Timers," *HR Magazine,* February 2005, pp 43–44.

[45]See R Levering and M Moskowitz, "The 100 Best Companies to Work For," *Fortune,* January 24, 2005, p 76.

[46]Details of this program can be found in S A Hewlett and C Buck Luce, "Off-Ramps and On-Ramps: Keeping Talented Women on the Road to Success," *Harvard Business Review,* March 2005, pp 43–54.

[47]S Armour, "Welcome Mat Rolls Out for Hispanic Workers: Corporate America Cultivates Talent as Ethnic Population Booms," *USA Today,* April 12, 2001, pp 1B, 2B.

[48]D A Thomas, "The Truth about Mentoring Minorities: Race Matters," *Harvard Business Review,* April 2001, p 107.

[49]This statistic was reported by H Dolezalek, "Training Magazine's 23rd Annual Comprehensive Analysis of Employer-Sponsored Training in the United States," *Training,* October 2004, p 20.

[50]Results from international achievement tests are discussed by M Dittmann, "US Students Continue to Lag Behind Their International Counterparts in Math," *Monitor on Psychology,* March 2005, p 11; and R J Grossman, "The Truth about the Coming Labor Shortage," *HR Magazine,* March 2005, pp 47–53.

[51]These examples are discussed by J Barbian, "Get 'Em While They're Young," *Training,* January 2004, pp 44–46.

[52]P M Elsass and D A Ralston, "Individual Responses to the Stress of Career Plateauing," *Journal of Management,* Spring 1989, p 35.

[53]Supportive findings can be found in D R Ettington, "Successful Career Plateauing," *Journal of Vocational Behavior,* February 1998, pp 72–88.

[54]Approaches for handling elder care are discussed by T F Shea, "Help with Elder Care," *HR Magazine,* September 2003, pp 113–14, 116, 118.

[55]Managerial issues and solutions for an aging workforce are discussed by M M Greller and L K Stroh, "Making the Most of 'Late-Career' for Employers and Workers Themselves: Become Elders Not Relics," *Organizational Dynamics,* May 2004, pp 202–14.

[56]The cost of health care is reviewed by L A Weatherly, "The Rising Cost of Health Care: Strategic and Societal Considerations for Employees," *2004 SHRM Research Quarterly,* 2004, pp 1–11.

[57]See Levering and Moskowitz, "The 100 Best Companies to Work For," pp 80, 86.

[58]The cost of smoking and smoking cessation programs are discussed by K Gurchiek, "Study: Smoking Ban Improved Air," *HR Magazine,* January 2005, p 34; and S Bates, "Where There Is Smoke, There Are Terminations," *HR Magazine,* March 2005, pp 28, 34.

[59]D van Knippenberg, C K W De Dreu, and A C Homan, "Work Group Diversity and Group Performance: An Integrative Model and Research Agenda," *Journal of Applied Psychology,* December 2004, p 1009.

[60]See ibid., pp 1008–22; and S E Jackson and A Joshi, "Diversity in Social Context: A Multi-Attribute, Multilevel Analysis of Team Diversity and Sales Performance," *Journal of Organizational Behavior,* September 2004, pp 675–702.

[61]See R J Ely and D A Thomas, "Cultural Diversity at Work: The Effects of Diversity Perspectives on Work Group Processes and Outcomes," *Administrative Science Quarterly,* June 2001, pp 229–73.

[62]See Jackson and Joshi, "Diversity in Social Context."

[63]Results can be found in J M Sacco and N Schmitt, "A Dynamic Multilevel Model of Demographic Diversity and Misfit Effects," *Journal of Applied Psychology,* March 2005, pp 203–31; and H Liao, A Joshi, "Sticking Out Like a Sore Thumb: Employee Dissimilarity and Deviance at Work," *Personnel Psychology,* Winter 2004, pp 969–1000.

[64]van Knippenberg, De Dreu, and Homan, "Work Group Diversity and Group Performance," p 1009.

[65]These conclusions were derived from Jackson and Joshi, "Diversity in Social Context."

[66]Ibid.

[67]For research on TMT demographics, see K Y Williams, "Demography and Diversity in Organizations: A Review of 100 Years of Research," in *Research in Organizational Behavior,* vol. 20, eds B M Staw and L L Cummings (Greenwich, CT: JAI Press, 1998), pp 77–140.

[68]See R Moss-Kanter, *The Change Masters* (New York: Simon and Schuster, 1983); and L K Larkey, "Toward a Theory of Communicative Interactions in Culturally Diverse Workgroups," *Academy of Management Review,* April 1996, pp 463–91.

[69]See Williams, "Demography and Diversity in Organizations."

[70]This example was discussed by H Johnson, "Daring to Be Diverse," *Training,* March 2004, pp 34–35.

[71]This recommendation was proposed by J A Chatman and C A O'Reilly, "Asymmetric Reactions to Work Group Sex and Diversity among Men and Women," *Academy of Management Journal,* April 2004, pp 193–208.

[72]These barriers were taken from discussions in M Loden, *Implementing Diversity* (Chicago: Irwin, 1996); E E Spragins, "Benchmark: The Diverse Work Force," *Inc.,* January 1993, p 33; and Morrison, *The New Leaders.*

[73]M G Danaher, "Prompt Response Avoids Liability for Hostile Work Environment," *HR Magazine,* June 2004, p 181.

[74]See the related discussion in Perrewé and Nelson, "Gender and Career Success."

[75]For complete details and results from this study, see Morrison, *The New Leaders.*

[76]Excerpted from "The Diversity Factor," *Fortune,* October 13, 2003, p S4.

[77]Excerpted from R Koonce, "Redefining Diversity," *Training & Development,* December 2001, pp 24, 26.

[78]Excerpted from M Gardner, "Younger Bosses, Older Employees Learn New Ropes: Workplace Generation Gap," *Arizona Republic,* January 22, 2005, p D3. By Marilyn Gardner. Reproduced with permission from the January 3, 2005 issue of *The Christian Science Monitor* (http://www.csmonitor.com). © 2005 *The Christian Science Monitor.* All rights reserved.

[79]This exercise was modified from Gardenswartz and Rowe, *Diverse Teams at Work* (New York: McGraw-Hill, 1994), pp 60–61 1994. Reproduced with permission of The McGraw-Hill Companies.

[80]D A Blackmon and N Harris, "Racial Bind: Black Utility Workers in Georgia See Nooses as Sign of Harassment," *The Wall Street Journal,* April 2, 2001. Reprinted by permission of Dow Jones & Co. Inc. via The Copyright Clearance Center.

CHAPTER 3

[1]Excerpted from L Conley, "Cultural Phenomenon: How Do You Build a Fast-Growing Bank? Try Ice-Cream Sandwiches, Dog Bowls, and Yoga Lessons," *Fast Company,* April 2005, p 76. By Lucas Conley, © 2005 Gruner & Jahr USA Publishing. First published in *Fast Company* Magazine. Reprinted with permission.

[2]Ibid., pp 76–77.

[3]J E Garten, "Andy Grove Made the Elephant Dance," *BusinessWeek,* April 11, 2005, p 26.

[4]Ibid.

[5]E H Schein, "Culture: The Missing Concept in Organization Studies," *Administrative Science Quarterly,* June 1996, p 236.

[6]This example was taken from "Seen and Heard: Kramer Conferences . . . Short Timer . . . Asian Aid," *Arizona Republic,* January 7, 2005, p D2.

[7]S H Schwartz, "Universals in the Content and Structure of Values: Theoretical Advances and Empirical Tests in 20 Countries," in *Advances in Experimental Social Psychology,* ed M P Zanna (New York: Academic Press, 1992), p 4.

[8]P Babcock, "Is Your Company Two-Faced?" *HR Magazine,* January 2004, p 43.

[9]Results can be found in S Clarke, "Perceptions of Organizational Safety: Implications for the Development of Safety Culture," *Journal of Organizational Behavior,* March 1999, pp 185–98.

[10]"Time to Take Action," *Training,* September 2004, p 18.

[11]For an example of identifying organizational values, see S Maitlis, "The Social Processes of Organizational Sensemaking," *Academy of Management Journal,* February 2005, pp 21–49.

[12]See the discussion in J R Detert, R G Schroeder, and J J Mauriel, "A Framework for Linking Culture and Improvement Initiatives in Organizations," *Academy of Management Review,* October 2000, pp 850–63.

[13]Details of this model can be found in V Sathe, "Implications of Corporate Culture: A Manager's Guide to Action," *Organizational Dynamics,* Autumn 1983, pp 4–23.

[14]Statistics and data contained in the Southwest Airlines example can be found in the "Southwest Airlines Fact Sheet," February 2005, www.southwest.com.

[15]K D Godsey, "Slow Climb to New Heights," *Success,* October 1996, p 21.

[16]Southwest's mission statement can be found in "Customer Service Commitment," April 2005, www.southwest.com.

[17]See C Ostroff, A Kinicki, and M Tamkins, "Organizational Culture and Climate," in *Handbook of Psychology,* vol. 12, eds W C Borman, D R Ilgen, and R J Klimoski (New York: Wiley and Sons, 2003), pp 565–93.

[18]The validity of these cultural types was summarized and supported by R A Cooke and J L Szumal, "Using the Organizational Culture Inventory to Understand the Operating Cultures of Organizations," in *Handbook of Organizational Culture and Climate,* eds N M Ashkanasy, C P M Wilderom, and M F Peterson (Thousand Oaks, CA: Sage Publications, 2000), pp 147–62.

[19]C Garvey, "Philophizing Compensation," *HR Magazine,* January 2005, p 74.

[20]B Bremner and G Edmondson, "Japan: A Tale of Two Mergers." *BusinessWeek,* May 10, 2004, p 42.

[21]Subcultures were examined by G Hofstede, "Identifying Organizational Subcultures: An Empirical Approach," *Journal of Management Studies,* January 1998, pp 1–2.

[22]Results can be found in R Cooke and J Szumal, "Measuring Normative Beliefs and Shared Behavioral Expectations in Organizations: The Reliability and Validity of the Organizational Culture Inventory," *Psychological Reports,* June 1993, pp 1299–330.

[23]Supportive results can be found in C Ostroff, Y Shin, and A Kinicki, "Multiple Perspectives of Congruence: Relationships between Value Congruence and Employee Attitudes," *Journal of Organizational Behavior,* in press; and D M Cable and J R Edwards, "Complementary and Supplementary Fit: A Theoretical and Empirical Integration," *Journal of Applied Psychology,* October 2004, pp 822–34.

[24]See C Wilderom, U Glunk, and R Maslowski, "Organizational Culture as a Predictor of Organizational Performance," in *Handbook of Organizational Culture & Climate,* eds N Ashkanasy, C Wilderom, and M Peterson (Thousand Oaks, CA: Sage, 2000), pp 193–210.

[25]Results can be found in J P Kotter and J L Heskett, *Corporate Culture and Performance* (New York: Free Press, 1992).

[26]The success rate of mergers is discussed in M J Epstein, "The Drivers of Success in Post-Merger Integration," *Organizational Dynamics,* May 2004, pp 174–89.

[27]This perspective was promoted by T E Deal and A A Kennedy, *Corporate Cultures: The Rites and Rituals of Corporate Life* (Reading, MA: Addison-Wesley Publishing, 1982).

[28]"About Us: Corporate Objectives," www.hp.com/cgi-bin/hpinfo/oovpf_hpinfo.pl, accessed April 2005.

[29]The HP Way is thoroughly discussed by J Dong, "The Rise and Fall of the HP Way," *Palo Alto Weekly Online Edition,* www.paloaltoonline.com/weekly/morgue/2002/2002_04_10.hpway10.html, accessed April 10, 2005.

[30]P Burrows and B Elgin, "Memo to: Mark Hurd," *BusinessWeek,* April 11, 2005, p 39.

[31]R H Kilman, M J Saxton, and R Serpa, *Gaining Control of the Corporate Culture* (San Francisco: Jossey-Bass, 1986), p 356.

[32]These results can be found in Kotter and Heskett, *Corporate Culture and Performance.*

[33]W Disney, quoted in B Nanus, *Visionary Leadership: Creating a Compelling Sense of Direction for Your Organization* (San Francisco: Jossey-Bass, 1992), p 28; reprinted from B Thomas, *Walt Disney: An American Tradition* (New York: Simon & Schuster, 1976), p 247.

[34]C A O'Reilly III and M L Tushman, "A Clear Eye for Innovation," *Harvard Business School Working Knowledge,* April 26, 2004; excerpted from "The Ambidextrous Organization," *Harvard Business Review,* April 2004, http://hbswk.hbs.edu/item.jhtml? id=4097&t=leadership&nl=y, accessed April 2005.

[35]S McCartney, "Airline Industry's Top-Ranked Woman Keeps Southwest's Small-Fry Spirit Alive," *The Wall Street Journal,* November 30, 1996, pp B1, B11.

[36]The mechanisms were based on material contained in E H Schein, "The Role of the Founder in Creating Organizational Culture," *Organizational Dynamics,* Summer 1983, pp 13–28.

[37]Wal-Mart's values can be found in "About Wal-Mart," www.walmart.com, accessed April 10, 2005.

[38]Excerpted from D F Kuratko, R D Ireland, and J S Hornsby, "Improving Firm Performance through Entrepreneurial Actions: Acordia's Corporate Entrepreneurship Strategy," *Academy of Management Executive,* November 2001, p 67.

[39]See W Zellner, "Dressed to Kill . . . Competitors," *BusinessWeek,* February 21, 2005, pp 60–61.

[40]Excerpted from F Arner and L Young, "Can This Man Save Putnam?" *BusinessWeek,* April 19, 2004, p 103.

[41]C Hymowitz, "Does Rank Have Too Much Privilege?" *The Wall Street Journal,* February 26, 2002, p B1.

[42]J Ball, "Mighty Profit Maker," *The Wall Street Journal,* April 8, 2005, p B1.

[43]M France and W Zellner, "Enron's Fish Story," *BusinessWeek,* February 25, 2002, p 40.

[44]Excerpted from T Galvin, "Birds of a Feather," *Training,* March 2001, p 60.

[45]J Van Maanen, "Breaking In: Socialization to Work," in *Handbook of Work, Organization, and Society,* ed R Dubin (Chicago: Rand-McNally, 1976), p 67.

[46]This example was described in J Stearns, "Sedona Company Wants Happy Employees," *Arizona Republic,* April 10, 2005, p D2.

[47]Supportive evidence is provided by R W Griffeth and P W Hom, *Retaining Valued Employees* (Thousand Oaks, CA: Sage Publications, 2001), pp 46–65.

[48]See J M Phillips, "Effects of Realistic Job Previews on Multiple Organizational Outcomes: A Meta-Analysis," *Academy of Management Journal,* December 1998, pp 673–90.

[49]Onboarding programs are discussed by D Moscato, "Using Technology to Get Employees on Board," *HR Magazine,* March 2005, pp 107–09.

[50]S J Wells, "Diving In," *HR Magazine,* March 2005, p 56.

[51]Reprinted by permission of *Harvard Business Review.* Excerpt from N M Tichy, "No Ordinary Boot Camp," April 2001. Copyright © 2001 by the Harvard Business School Publishing Corporation; all rights reserved.

[52]Results can be found in T-Y Kim, D M Cable, and S-P Kim, "Socialization Tactics, Employee Proactivity, and Person-Organization Fit," *Journal of Applied Psychology,* March 2005, pp 232–41.

[53]See D Cable and C Parsons, "Socialization Tactics and Person-Organization Fit," *Personnel Psychology,* Spring 2001, pp 1–23.

[54]A review of stage model research can be found in B E Ashforth, *Role Transitions in Organizational Life: An Identity-Based Perspective* (Mahwah, NJ: Lawrence Erlbaum Associates, 2001).

[55]See A M Saks and B E Ashforth, "Proactive Socialization and Behavioral Self-Management," *Journal of Vocational Behavior,* June 1996, pp 301–23.

[56]For a thorough review of research on the socialization of diverse employees with disabilities, see A Colella, "Organizational Socialization of Newcomers with Disabilities: A Framework for Future Research," in *Research in Personnel and Human Resources Management,* ed G R Ferris (Greenwich, CT: JAI Press, 1996), pp 351–417.

[57]This definition is based on the network perspective of mentoring proposed by M Higgins and K Kram, "Reconceptualizing Mentoring at Work: A Developmental Network Perspective," *Academy of Management Review,* April 2001, pp 264–88.

[58]Results can be found in T D Allen, L T Eby, M L Poteet, and E Lentz, "Career Benefits Associated with Mentoring for Protégés: A Meta-Analysis," *Journal of Applied Psychology,* February 2004, pp 127–36; and S C Payne and A H Huffman, "A Longitudinal Examination of the Influence of Mentoring on Organizational Commitment and Turnover," *Academy of Management Journal,* February 2005, pp 158–68.

[59]Career functions are discussed in detail in K Kram, *Mentoring of Work: Developmental Relationships in Organizational Life* (Glenview, IL: Scott, Foresman, 1985).

[60]Excerpted from K Maher, "The Jungle: Focus on Retirement, Pay and Getting Ahead," *The Wall Street Journal,* February 24, 2004, p B8.

[61]This discussion is based on Higgins and Kram, "Reconceptualizing Mentoring at Work."

[62]Ibid.

[63]Supportive results can be found in T Allen, M Poteet, and J Russell, "Protégé Selection by Mentors: What Makes the Difference?" *Journal of Organizational Behavior,* May 2000, pp 271–82.

[64]Recommendations for how to improve your networking skills can be found in A Fisher, "How to Network—and Enjoy It," *Fortune,* April 4, 2005, p 38; and J C Berkshire, " 'Social Network' Recruiting," *HR Magazine,* April 2005, pp 95–98.

[65]Excerpted from D Brady, "The Immelt Revolution," *BusinessWeek,* March 28, 2005, pp 64, 66, 71.

[66]The survey items were adapted from D Cable and C Parsons, "Socialization Tactics and Person-Organization Fit," *Personnel Psychology,* Spring 2001, pp 1–23.

[67]See E H Schein, *The Corporate Culture Survival Guide* (San Francisco: Jossey-Bass, 1999).

[68]K Brown and J Weil, "How Andersen's Embrace of Consulting Altered the Culture of the Auditing Firm," *The Wall Street Journal,* March 12, 2002, pp C1, C16.

ANSWERS TO OB EXERCISE

[1]The whiteboard is a shared object at Setpoint. There are two shared sayings. Employees talk about monitoring GP—gross profit—during their "weekly huddles." Employees at Setpoint like to ride dirt bikes together, and they put photos of their experiences on the bulletin board. This is a shared doing. Controlling cash and conducting the weekly huddles to review the budget are two additional shared behaviors among employees at Setpoint. Finally, the management system at Setpoint seems to fuel employee motivation, a component of shared feelings.

[2]The artifacts include the whiteboard and its financial information, the bulletin board with pictures of employees on motorcycles, the weekly huddle, and discussions about GP. The case would suggest that Setpoint espouses the value of making profit, monitoring projects, and rational decision making. The value or importance of controlling appears to represent a basic assumption.

[3]While the management system at Setpoint is a mechanism for controlling employee behavior, the implementation of the system allows employees much freedom to determine how they can control costs and increase gross profit.

CHAPTER 4

[1]B Bremner, G Edmondson, and C Dawson, "Nissan's Boss," *BusinessWeek,* October 4, 2004, p 52. Also see C Dawson, "The Wild, Wild East," *BusinessWeek,* March 21, 2005, p 33; and E Edmondson, "What Ghosn Will Do with Renault," *BusinessWeek,* April 25, 2005, p 54.

[2]A Taylor, "Advice from a Fellow Outsider," *Fortune,* April 4, 2005, p 104.

[3]See A Bernstein, "Shaking up Trade Theory," *BusinessWeek,* December 6, 2004, pp 116–20; E Wasserman, "Happy Birthday, WTO?" *Inc.,* January 2005, pp 21–23; T C Fishman, "How China Will Change Your Business," *Inc.,* March 2005, pp 70–84; R B Reich, "Plenty of Knowledge Work to Go Around," *Harvard Business Review,* April 2005, p 17; P Magnusson, "Globalization Is Great—Sort of," *BusinessWeek,* April 25, 2005, p 25; and J Puliyenthuruthel, "The Soft Underbelly of Offshoring," *BusinessWeek,* April 25, 2005, p 52.

[4]P Wiseman, "Chinese Factories Struggle to Hire," *USA Today,* April 12, 2005, p 1B.

[5]E Schonfeld, "The World According to eBay," *Business 2.0,* January–February 2005, p 78.

[6]D Fenn, "John Stollenwerk: For His Commitment to US Workers. We Also Love the Shoes," *Inc.,* April 2004, p 129.

[7]S Kirchhoff, "Fed Imposes Fine of $100 Million on Swiss Bank," *USA Today,* May 11, 2004, p 2B.

[8]Data from L Dobbs, "Dangerously Dependent," *US News & World Report,* February 9, 2004, p 40.

[9]Data from M A Carpenter, W G Sanders, and H B Gregersen, "Bundling Human Capital with Organizational Context: The Impact of International Assignment Experience on Multinational Firm Performance and CEO Pay," *Academy of Management Journal,* June 2001, pp 493–511. Also see "International Experience Aids Career," *USA Today,* January 28, 2002, p. 1B.

[10]G Dutton, "Building a Global Brain," *Management Review,* May 1999, p 35.

[11]M Mabry, "Pin a Label on a Manager—and Watch What Happens," *Newsweek,* May 14, 1990, p 43.

[12]Ibid.

[13]M Javidan and R J House, "Cultural Acumen for the Global Manager: Lessons from Project GLOBE," *Organizational Dynamics,* Spring 2001, p 292. (Emphasis added.)

[14]For instructive discussion, see J S Black, H B Gregersen, and M E Mendenhall, *Global Assignments: Successfully Expatriating and Repatriating International Managers* (San Francisco: Jossey-Bass, 1992), Ch 2.

[15]F Trompenaars and C Hampden-Turner, *Riding the Waves of Culture: Understanding Cultural Diversity in Global Business,* 2nd ed (New York: McGraw-Hill, 1998), pp 6–7.

[16]See G Strauss, "Catastrophe Suspends Business as Usual in USA," *USA Today,* September 12, 2001, pp 1B–2B; and B Powell, "Battered but Unbroken," *Fortune,* October 1, 2001, pp 68–80.

[17]"How Cultures Collide," *Psychology Today,* July 1976, p 69.

[18]See C L Sharma, "Ethnicity, National Integration, and Education in the Union of Soviet Socialist Republics," *Journal of East and West Studies,* October 1989, pp 75–93; and R Brady and P Galuszka, "Shattered Dreams," *BusinessWeek,* February 11, 1991, pp 38–42.

[19]As quoted in D Jones, "American CEO in Europe Blends Leadership Styles," *USA Today,* June 21, 2004, 4B. Also see Y Paik and J D Sohn, "Expatriate Managers and MNC's Ability to Control International Subsidiaries: The Case of Japanese MNCs," *Journal of World Business,* February 2004, pp 61–71; and G Hawawini, V Subramanian, and P Verdin, "The Home Country in the Age of Globalization: How Much Does It Matter for Firm Performance?" *Journal of World Business,* May 2004, pp 121–35.

[20]See R Inglehart and W E Baker, "Modernization's Challenge to Traditional Values: Who's Afraid of Ronald McDonald?" *The Futurist,* March–April 2001, pp 16–21.

[21]G Farrell, "Capitalism Comes to German Town," *USA Today,* December 11, 2001, p 6B.

[22]See S Kirchhoff, "Different Cultures Value Different Features," *USA Today,* August 5, 2004, p 2B; and W Gong, Z G Li, T Li, "Marketing to China's Youth: A Cultural Transformation Perspective," *Business Horizons,* November–December 2004, pp 41–50.

[23]J Main, "How to Go Global—and Why," *Fortune,* August 28, 1989, p. 73.

[24]For another cross-cultural GE example, see D Brady and K Capell, "GE Breaks the Mold to Spur Innovation," *BusinessWeek,* April 26, 2004, pp 88–89.

[25]W D Marbach, "Quality: What Motivates American Workers?" *BusinessWeek,* April 12, 1993, p 93.

[26]See G A Sumner, *Folkways* (New York: Ginn, 1906). Also see J G Weber, "The Nature of Ethnocentric Attribution Bias: Ingroup Protection or Enhancement?" *Journal of Experimental Social Psychology,* September 1994, pp 482–504.

[27]"House English-Only Bill Aims at Federal Agencies," *USA Today,* July 25, 1996, p 3A. Also see G M Combs and S Nadkarni, "The Tale of Two Cultures: Attitudes towards Affirmative Action in the United States and India," *Journal of World Business,* May 2005, pp 158–71.

[28]D A Heenan and H V Perlmutter, *Multinational Organization Development* (Reading, MA: Addison-Wesley, 1979), p 17.

[29]Data from R Kopp, "International Human Resource Policies and Practices in Japanese, European, and United States Multinationals," *Human Resource Management,* Winter 1994, pp 581–99. Also see G Balabanis, A Diamantopoulos, R D Mueller, and T C Melewar, "The Impact of Nationalism, Patriotism and Internationalism on Consumer Ethnocentric Tendencies," *Journal of International Business Studies,* First Quarter 2001, pp 157–75.

[30]J S Osland and A Bird, "Beyond Sophisticated Stereotyping: Cultural Sensemaking in Context," *Academy of Management Executive,* February 2000, p 67.

[31]"Fujio Mitarai: Canon," *BusinessWeek,* January 14, 2002. p 55.

[32]P C Earley and E Mosakowski, "Cultural Intelligence," *Harvard Business Review,* October 2004, p 140. Also see P C Earley and E Mosakowski, "Toward Culture Intelligence: Turning Cultural Differences into a Workplace Advantage," *Academy of Management Executive,* August 2004, pp 151–57.

33See "How Cultures Collide," pp 66–74, 97; and M Munter, "Cross-Cultural Communication for Managers," *Business Horizons,* May–June 1993, pp 69–78.

34The German management style is discussed in R Stewart, "German Management: A Challenge to Anglo-American Managerial Assumptions," *Business Horizons,* May–June 1996, pp 52–54.

35I Adler, "Between the Lines," *Business Mexico,* October 2000, p 24.

36The tips were excerpted from R Drew, "Working with Foreigners," *Management Review,* September 1999, p 6.

37For background, see Javidan and House, "Cultural Acumen for the Global Manager," pp 289–305; the entire Spring 2002 issue of *Journal of World Business;* and R J House, P J Hanges, M Javidan, P W Dorfman, and V Gupta, eds *Culture, Leadership, and Organizations: The GLOBE Study of 62 Societies* (Thousand Oaks, CA: Sage, 2004).

38R House, M Javidan, P Hanges, and P Dorfman, "Understanding Cultures and Implicit Leadership Theories across the Globe: An Introduction to Project GLOBE," *Journal of World Business,* Spring 2002, p 4.

39Adapted from the list in ibid., pp 5–6. Also see M Javidan, G K Stahl, F Brodbeck, and C P M Wilderom, "Cross-Border Transfer of Knowledge: Cultural Lessons from Project GLOBE," *Academy of Management Executive,* May 2005, pp 59–76.

40See D Oyserman, H M Coon, and M Kemmelmeier, "Rethinking Individualism and Collectivism: Evaluation of Theoretical Assumptions and Meta-Analyses," *Psychological Bulletin,* January 2002, pp 3–72; S Soh and F T L Leong, "Validity of Vertical and Horizontal Individualism and Collectivism in Singapore: Relationships with Values and Interests," *Journal of Cross-Cultural Psychology,* January 2002, pp 3–15; and J Kurman and N Sriram, "Interrelationships among Vertical and Horizontal Collectivism, Modesty, and Self-Enhancement," *Journal of Cross-Cultural Psychology,* January 2002, pp 71–86.

41M Edwards, "As Good as It Gets," *AARP: The Magazine,* November–December 2004, p 48.

42See table in ibid., p 49.

43Data from Trompenaars and Hampden-Turner, *Riding the Waves of Culture,* Ch 5. For recent research, see J Allik and A Realo, "Individualism–Collectivism and Social Capital," *Journal of Cross-Cultural Psychology,* January 2004, pp 29–49; K H Lim, K Leung, C L Sia, and M K Lee, "Is eCommerce Boundary-less? Effects of Individualism–Collectivism and Uncertainty Avoidance on Internet Shopping," *Journal of International Business Studies,* November 2004, pp 545–59; and E G T Green and J Deschamps, "Variation of Individualism and Collectivism within and between 20 Countries," *Journal of Cross-Cultural Psychology,* May 2005, pp 321–39.

44As quoted in E E Schultz, "Scudder Brings Lessons to Navajo, Gets Some of Its Own," *The Wall Street Journal,* April 29, 1999, p C12.

45Trompenaars and Hampden-Turner, *Riding the Waves of Culture,* p 56.

46For related readings, see E Mosakowski and P C Earley, "A Selective Review of Time Assumptions in Strategy Research," *Academy of Management Review,* October 2000, pp 796–812; M J Waller, J M Conte, C B Gibson, and M A Carpenter, "The Effect of Individual Perceptions of Deadlines on Team Performance," *Academy of Management Review,* October 2001, pp 586–600; and M Crossan, M P E Cunha, D Vera, and J Cunha, "Time and Organizational Improvisation," *Academy of Management Review,* January 2005, pp 129–45.

47For a comprehensive treatment of time, see J E McGrath and J R Kelly, *Time and Human Interaction: Toward a Social Psychology of Time* (New York: Guilford Press, 1986). Also see L A Manrai and A K Manrai, "Effects of Cultural-Context, Gender, and Acculturation on Perceptions of Work versus Social/Leisure Time Usage," *Journal of Business Research,* February 1995, pp 115–28.

48A good discussion of doing business in Mexico is G K Stephens and C R Greer, "Doing Business in Mexico: Understanding Cultural Differences," *Organizational Dynamics,* Summer 1995, pp 39–55. Also see P Seldon, *The Business Traveler's World Guide* (New York: McGraw-Hill, 1998), pp 311–17.

49R W Moore, "Time, Culture, and Comparative Management: A Review and Future Direction," in *Advances in International Comparative Management,* vol. 5, ed S B Prasad (Greenwich, CT: JAI Press, 1990), pp 7–8.

50See A C Bluedorn, C F Kaufman, and P M Lane, "How Many Things Do You Like to Do at Once? An Introduction to Monochronic and Polychronic Time," *Academy of Management Executive,* November 1992, pp 17–26.

51See N Hellmich, "Most People Multitask, So Most People Don't Sit Down to Eat," *USA Today,* September 30, 2004, p 8D.

52O Port, "You May Have to Reset This Watch—in a Million Years," *BusinessWeek,* August 30, 1993, p 65.

53See E T Hall, *The Hidden Dimension* (Garden City, NY: Doubleday, 1966).

54"How Cultures Collide," p 72.

55See A B Cohen and A Rankin, "Religion and the Morality of Positive Mentality," *Basic and Applied Social Psychology,* March 2004, pp 45–57; T W Rice and B J Steele, "Subjective Well-Being and Culture across Time and Space," *Journal of Cross-Cultural Psychology,* November 2004, pp 633–47; and J Ginsburg, "Koran-Friendly Lenders," *BusinessWeek,* February 14, 2005, p 12.

56Results adapted from and value definitions quoted from S R Safranski and I-W Kwon, "Religious Groups and Management Value Systems," in *Advances in International Comparative Management,* vol. 3, eds R N Farner and E G McGoun (Greenwich, CT: JAI Press, 1988), pp 171–83.

57Ibid., p 180.

58N J Adler, *International Dimensions of Organizational Behavior,* 4th ed (Cincinnati: South-Western, 2002), p 11. (Emphasis added.)

59See D Matsumoto, R J Grissom, and D L Dinnel, "Do Between-Culture Differences Really Mean That People Are

Different? A Look at Some Measures of Cultural Effect Size," *Journal of Cross-Cultural Psychology,* July 2001, pp 478–90.

60M Javidan and R J House, "Leadership and Cultures around the World: Findings from GLOBE—An Introduction to the Special Issue," *Journal of World Business,* Spring 2002, p 1.

61For complete details, see G Hofstede, *Culture's Consequences: International Differences in Work-Related Values,* abridged ed (Newbury Park, CA: Sage, 1984); G Hofstede, "The Interaction between National and Organizational Value Systems," *Journal of Management Studies,* July 1985, pp 347–57; and G Hofstede, "Management Scientists Are Human," *Management Science,* January 1994, pp 4–13. Also see M H Hoppe, "Introduction: Geert Hofstede's *Culture's Consequences: International Differences in Work-Related Values,*" *Academy of Management Executive,* February 2004, pp 73–74; M H Hoppe, "An Interview with Geert Hofstede," *Academy of Management Executive,* February 2004, pp 75–79; J W Bing, "Hofstede's Consequences: The Impact of His Work on Consulting and Business Practices," *Academy of Management Executive,* February 2004, pp 80–87; and H C Triandis, "The Many Dimensions of Culture," *Academy of Management Executive,* February 2004, pp 88–93.

62A similar conclusion is presented in the following replication of Hofstede's work: A Merritt, "Culture in the Cockpit: Do Hofstede's Dimensions Replicate?" *Journal of Cross-Cultural Psychology,* May 2000, pp 283–301. Another extension of Hofstede's work can be found in S M Lee and S J Peterson, "Culture, Entrepreneurial Orientation, and Global Competitiveness," *Journal of World Business,* Winter 2000, pp 401–16.

63J Guyon, "David Whitwam," *Fortune,* July 26, 2004, p 174.

64M Vande Berg, "Siemens: Betting That Big Is Once again Beautiful," *Milken Institute Review,* Second Quarter 2002, p 47.

65Data from D Beck, "What Negotiating Tactics Reveal about Executives," February 11–17, 2002, www.careerjournal.com.

66J S Black and H B Gregersen, "The Right Way to Manage Expats," *Harvard Business Review,* March–April 1999, p 53. A more optimistic picture is presented in R L Tung, "American Expatriates Abroad: From Neophytes to Cosmopolitans," *Journal of World Business,* Summer 1998, pp 125–44. For interesting expatriate metaphors, see A Harzing, "Of Bears, Bumble-Bees, and Spiders: The Role of Expatriates in Controlling Foreign Subsidiaries," *Journal of World Business,* Winter 2001, pp 366–79.

67Data from G S Insch and J D Daniels, "Causes and Consequences of Declining Early Departures from Foreign Assignments," *Business Horizons,* November–December 2002, pp 39–48. Also see J P Shay and S A Baack, "Expatriate Assignment, Adjustment and Effectiveness: An Empirical Examination of the Big Picture," *Journal of International Business Studies,* May 2004, pp 216–32; and A E M Van Vianen, I E De Pater, A L Kristof-Brown, and E C Johnson, "Fitting In: Surface- and Deep-Level Cultural Differences and Expatriates' Adjustment," *Academy of Management Journal,* October 2004, pp 697–709.

68S Dallas, "Rule No. 1: Don't Diss the Locals," *BusinessWeek,* May 15, 1995, p 8. Also see S M Toh and A S DeNisi, "A Local

Perspective to Expatriate Success," *Academy of Management Executive,* February 2005, pp 132–46.

69P Capell, "Employers Seek to Trim Pay for US Expatriates," April 16, 2005, www.careerjournal.com. Also see E Krell, "Evaluating Returns on Expatriates," *HR Magazine,* March 2005, pp 60–65; and S P Nurney, "The Long and Short of It," *HR Magazine,* March 2005, pp 91–94.

70These insights come from Tung, "American Expatriates Abroad"; P M Caligiuri and W F Cascio, "*Can We Send Her There?* Maximizing the Success of Western Women on Global Assignments," *Journal of World Business,* Winter 1998, pp 394–416; L K Stroh, A Varma, and S J Valy-Durbin, "Why Are Women Left Home: Are They Unwilling to Go on International Assignments?" *Journal of World Business,* Fall 2000, pp 241–55; A Varma, L K Stroh, and L B Schmitt, "Women and International Assignments: The Impact of Supervisor-Subordinate Relationships," *Journal of World Business,* Winter 2001, pp 380–88; and R L Tung, "Female Expatriates: The Model Global Manager?" *Organizational Dynamics,* no. 3, 2004, pp 243–53.

71A good resource book is M W McCall Jr and G P Hollenbeck, *Developing Global Executives: The Lessons of International Experience* (Boston: Harvard Business School Press, 2002). Also see Y Baruch, "No Such Thing as a Global Manager," *Business Horizons,* January–February 2002, pp 36–42; and A K Gupta and V Govindarajan, "Cultivating a Global Mindset," *Academy of Management Executive,* February 2002, pp 116–26.

72See A Fisher, "Offshoring Could Boost Your Career," *Fortune,* January 24, 2005, p 36.

73See J I Sanchez, P E Spector, and C L Cooper, "Adapting to a Boundaryless World: A Developmental Expatriate Model," *Academy of Management Executive,* May 2000, pp 96–106; M Janssens, "Developing a Culturally Synergistic Approach to International Human Resource Management," *Journal of World Business,* Winter 2001, pp 429–50; and, S Jun and J W Gentry, "An Exploratory Investigation of the Relative Importance of Cultural Similarity and Personal Fit in the Selection and Performance of Expatriates," *Journal of World Business,* February 2005, pp 1–8.

74Data from "E-Pulse," *Training,* January 2002, p 60.

75J S Lublin, "Younger Managers Learn Global Skills," *The Wall Street Journal,* March 31, 1992, p B1.

76See P C Earley, "Intercultural Training for Managers: A Comparison of Documentary and Interpersonal Methods," *Academy of Management Journal,* December 1987, pp 685–98; J S Black and M Mendenhall, "Cross-Cultural Training Effectiveness: A Review and a Theoretical Framework for Future Research," *Academy of Management Review,* January 1990, pp 113–36; D Landis, J M Bennett, and M J Bennett, eds *Handbook of Intercultural Training,* 3rd ed (Thousand Oaks, CA: Sage, 2004); and M M L Wong, "Organizational Learning via Expatriate Managers: Collective Myopia as Blocking Mechanism," *Organization Studies,* 2005, pp 325–50.

77See E Marx, *Breaking through Culture Shock: What You Need to Succeed in International Business* (London: Nicholas Brealey Publishing, 2001).

78See M Janssens, J Lambert, and C Steyaert, "Developing Language Strategies for International Companies: The Contribution of Translation Studies," *Journal of World Business,* November 2004, pp 414–30; D Doke, "Perfect Strangers," *HR Magazine,* December 2004, pp 62–68; R Rosmarin, "Text Messaging Gets a Translator," *Business 2.0,* March 2005, p 32; J Alsever, "English to Go," *Business 2.0,* March 2005, p 56; T Price, "Talk Is Cheap," *Business 2.0,* March 2005, pp 110, 112; and "Online Conversations Build Language Skills," *Training,* April 2005, p 9.

79See H H Nguyen, L A Messe, and G E Stollak, "Toward a More Complex Understanding of Acculturation and Adjustment," *Journal of Cross-Cultural Psychology,* January 1999, pp 5–31; S Jun, J W Gentry, and Y J Hyun, "Cultural Adaptation of Business Expatriates in the Host Marketplace," *Journal of International Business Studies,* Second Quarter 2001, pp 369–77; M Lazarova and P Caligiuri, "Retaining Repatriates: The Role of Organizational Support Practices," *Journal of World Business,* Winter 2001, pp 389–401; and S Overman, "Mentors without Borders," *HR Magazine,* March 2004, pp 83–85.

80K L Miller, "How a Team of Buckeyes Helped Honda Save a Bundle," *BusinessWeek,* September 13, 1993, p 68.

81B Newman, "For Ira Caplan, Re-Entry Has Been Strange," *The Wall Street Journal,* December 12, 1995, p A12.

82See Black, Gregersen, and Mendenhall, *Global Assignments,* p 227.

83Ibid., pp 226–27.

84See A C Poe, "Welcome Back," *HR Magazine,* March 2000, pp 94–105; J Barbian, "Return to Sender," *Training,* January 2002, pp 40–43; and A B Bossard and R B Peterson, "The Repatriate Experience as Seen by American Expatriates," *Journal of World Business,* February 2005, pp 9–28.

85J Hempel, "It Takes a Village—and a Consultant," *BusinessWeek,* September 6, 2004, pp 76–77.

86This list of work goals is quoted from I Harpaz, "The Importance of Work Goals: An International Perspective," *Journal of International Business Studies,* First Quarter 1990, p 79. Reproduced with permission of Palgrave Macmillan.

87Adapted from a seven-country summary in ibid., Table 2, p 81.

88See A Nimgade, "American Management as Viewed by International Professionals," *Business Horizons,* November–December 1989, pp 98–105; W A Hubiak and S J O'Donnell, "Do Americans Have Their Minds Set against TQM?" *National Productivity Review,* Summer 1996, pp 19–32; and Adler, *International Dimensions of Organizational Behavior,* pp 84–91.

89Excerpted from M V Gratchev, "Making the Most of Cultural Differences," *Harvard Business Review,* October 2001, pp 28, 30. For relevant background information, see C J Robertson, K M Gilley, and M D Street, "The Relationship between Ethics and Firm Practices in Russia and the United States," *Journal of World Business,* November 2003, pp 375–84; A Kolk and R Van Tulder, "Ethics in International Business: Multinational Approaches to Child Labor," *Journal of World Business,*

February 2004, pp 49–60; and J Singh, E Carasco, G Svensson, G Wood, and M Callaghan, "A Comparative Study of the Contents of Corporate Codes of Ethics in Australia, Canada, and Sweden," *Journal of World Business,* February 2005, pp 91–109.

CHAPTER 5

1Excerpted from M Conlin, "I'm a Bad Boss? Blame My Dad," *BusinessWeek,* May 10, 2004. Reprinted by permission of The McGraw-Hill Companies, Inc.

2Data from www.census.gov/main/www/popclock.html.

3B Horovitz, "You Want It Your Way," *USA Today,* March 5, 2004, p 2A.

4D Seligman, "The Trouble with Buyouts," *Fortune,* November 30, 1992, p 125.

5S I Cheldelin and L A Foritano, "Psychometrics: Their Use in Organisation Development," *Journal of Managerial Psychology,* no. 4, 1989, p 21.

6See P Babcock, "Diversity: Down to the Letter," *HR Magazine,* June 2004, pp 90–94; C Daniels, "50 Best Companies for Minorities," *Fortune,* June 28, 2004, pp 136–146; D A Thomas, "Diversity as Strategy," *Harvard Business Review,* September 2004, pp 98–108; and *Journal of Organizational Behavior,* "Special Issue: Diversity and the Workplace," September 2004, pp 675–785.

7Data from "If We Could Do It Over Again," *USA Today,* February 19, 2001, p 4D.

8J Gosling and H Mintzberg, "Reflect Yourself," *HR Magazine,* September 2004, p 152. Other dimensions of self and self-concept are covered in R W Tafarodi, C Lo, S Yamaguchi, W W S Lee, and H Katsura, "The Inner Self in Three Countries," *Journal of Cross-Cultural Psychology,* January 2004, pp 97–117; D K Sherman and H S Kim, "Is There an 'I' in 'Team'? The Role of the Self in Group-Serving Judgments," *Journal of Personality and Social Psychology,* January 2005, pp 108–20; J A Clair, J E Beatty, and T L Maclean, "Out of Sight but Not Out of Mind: Managing Invisible Social Identities in the Workplace," *Academy of Management Review,* January 2005, pp 78–95; and J M Howell and B Shamir, "The Role of Followers in the Charismatic Leadership Process: Relationships and Their Consequences," *Academy of Management Review,* January 2005, pp 96–112.

9V Gecas, "The Self-Concept," in *Annual Review of Sociology,* eds R H Turner and J F Short Jr (Palo Alto, CA: Annual Reviews Inc., 1982), vol. 8, p 3. Also see T A Judge and J E Bono, "Relationship of Core Self-Evaluations Traits—Self-Esteem, Generalized Self-Efficacy, Locus of Control, and Emotional Stability—with Job Satisfaction and Job Performance: A Meta-Analysis," *Journal of Applied Psychology,* February 2001, pp 80–92; and A Erez and T A Judge, "Relationship of Core Self-Evaluations to Goal Setting, Motivation, and Performance," *Journal of Applied Psychology,* December 2001, pp 1270–79.

[10]L Festinger, *A Theory of Cognitive Dissonance* (Stanford, CA: Stanford University Press, 1957), p 3.

[11]Based in part on a definition found in Gecas, "The Self-Concept." Also see N Branden, *Self-Esteem at Work: How Confident People Make Powerful Companies* (San Francisco: Jossey-Bass, 1998). Two types of self-esteem—explicit and implicit—are discussed in A Dijksterhuis, "I Like Myself but I Don't Know Why: Enhancing Implicit Self-Esteem by Subliminal Evaluative Conditioning," *Journal of Personality and Social Psychology,* February 2004, pp 345–55.

[12]H W Marsh, "Positive and Negative Global Self-Esteem: A Substantively Meaningful Distinction or Artifacts?" *Journal of Personality and Social Psychology,* April 1996, p 819.

[13]Ibid.

[14]For more on self-esteem, see M D Seery, J Blascovich, M Weisbuch, and S B Vick, "The Relationship between Self-Esteem Level, Self-Esteem Stability, and Cardiovascular Reactions to Performance Feedback," *Journal of Personality and Social Psychology,* July 2004, pp 133–45; C Sedikides, E A Rudich, A P Gregg, M Kumashiro, and C Rusbult, "Are Normal Narcissists Psychologically Healthy? Self-Esteem Matters," *Journal of Personality and Social Psychology,* September 2004, pp 400–16; and D De Cremer, D van Knippenberg, D van Knippenberg, D Mullenders, and F Stinglhamber, "Rewarding Leadership and Fair Procedures as Determinants of Self-Esteem," *Journal of Applied Psychology,* January 2005, pp 3–12.

[15]See D G Gardner, L Van Dyne, and J L Pierce, "The Effects of Pay Level on Organization-Based Self-Esteem and Performance: A Field Study," *Journal of Occupational and Organizational Psychology,* September 2004, pp 307–22.

[16]A J Fiacco, "Over 50? Keep Foot in Door," *Arizona Republic,* June 20, 2004, p D4.

[17]Ibid.

[18]E Diener and M Diener, "Cross-Cultural Correlates of Life Satisfaction and Self-Esteem," *Journal of Personality and Social Psychology,* April 1995, p 662. Also see D H Silvera and C R Seger, "Feeling Good about Ourselves," *Journal of Cross-Cultural Psychology,* September 2004, pp 571–85.

[19]Based on data in F L Smoll, R E Smith, N P Barnett, and J J Everett, "Enhancement of Children's Self-Esteem through Social Support Training for Youth Sports Coaches," *Journal of Applied Psychology,* August 1993, pp 602–10.

[20]K Bland, "Purple Reigns: Teachers Spare Feelings by Rejecting Red Ink," *Arizona Republic,* February 19, 2005, p A19. Also see S Hofius, "A Spiritually Inclined Student Is a Happier Student," *USA Today,* October 27, 2004, p 7D.

[21]W J McGuire and C V McGuire. "Enhancing Self-Esteem by Directed-Thinking Tasks: Cognitive and Affective Positivity Asymmetries," *Journal of Personality and Social Psychology,* June 1996, p 1124.

[22]See G Chen, S M Gully, and D Eden, "General Self-Efficacy and Self-Esteem: Toward Theoretical and Empirical Distinction between Correlated Self-Evaluations," *Journal of Organizational Behavior,* May 2004, pp 375–95.

[23]M E Gist, "Self-Efficacy: Implications for Organizational Behavior and Human Resource Management," *Academy of Management Review,* July 1987, p 472. Also see A Bandura, "Self-Efficacy: Toward a Unifying Theory of Behavioral Change," *Psychological Review,* March 1977, pp 191–215; T J Maurer and K D Andrews, "Traditional, Likert, and Simplified Measures of Self-Efficacy," *Educational and Psychological Measurement,* December 2000, pp 965–73; and S L Anderson and N E Betz, "Sources of Social Self-Efficacy Expectations: Their Measurement and Relation to Career Development," *Journal of Vocational Behavior,* February 2001, pp 98–117.

[24]Based on D H Lindsley, D A Brass, and J B Thomas, "Efficacy-Performance Spirals: A Multilevel Perspective," *Academy of Management Review,* July 1995, pp 645–78. Also see G L S C Oates, "The Color of the Undergraduate Experience and the Black Self-Concept: Evidence from Longitudinal Data," *Social Psychology Quarterly,* March 2004, pp 16–32; G D Markman, R A Baron, and D B Balkin, "Are Perseverance and Self-Efficacy Costless? Assessing Entrepreneurs' Regretful Thinking," *Journal of Organizational Behavior,* February 2005, pp 1–19; and J C Lang and C H Lee, "Identity Accumulation, Others' Acceptance, Job-Search Self-Efficacy, and Stress," *Journal of Organizational Behavior,* May 2005, pp 293–312.

[25]See, for example, V Gecas, "The Social Psychology of Self-Efficacy," in *Annual Review of Sociology,* eds W R Scott and J Blake (Palo Alto, CA: Annual Reviews, Inc., 1989), vol. 15, pp 291–316; C K Stevens, A G Bavetta, and M E Gist, "Gender Differences in the Acquisition of Salary Negotiation Skills: The Role of Goals, Self-Efficacy, and Perceived Control," *Journal of Applied Psychology,* October 1993, pp 723–35; D Eden and Y Zuk, "Seasickness as a Self-Fulfilling Prophecy: Raising Self-Efficacy to Boost Performance at Sea," *Journal of Applied Psychology,* October 1995, pp 628–35; and S M Jex, P D Bliese, S Buzzell, and J Primeau, "The Impact of Self-Efficacy on Stressor-Strain Relations: Coping Style as an Explanatory Mechanism," *Journal of Applied Psychology,* June 2001, pp 401–9.

[26]For more on learned helplessness, see Gecas, "The Social Psychology of Self-Efficacy"; M J Martinko and W L Gardner, "Learned Helplessness: An Alternative Explanation for Performance Deficits," *Academy of Management Review,* April 1982, pp 195–204; C R Campbell and M J Martinko, "An Integrative Attributional Perspective of Empowerment and Learned Helplessness: A Multimethod Field Study," *Journal of Management,* 1998, pp 173–200; and A Dickerson and M A Taylor, "Self-Limiting Behavior in Women: Self-Esteem and Self-Efficacy as Predictors," *Group and Organization Management,* June 2000, pp 191–210.

[27]Research on this connection is reported in R B Rubin, M M Martin, S S Bruning, and D E Powers, "Test of a Self-Efficacy Model of Interpersonal Communication Competence," *Communication Quarterly,* Spring 1993, pp 210–20.

[28]T Petzinger Jr, "Bob Schmonsees Has a Tool for Better Sales, and It Ignores Excuses," *The Wall Street Journal,* March 26, 1999, p B1.

[29]Data from A D Stajkovie and F Luthans, "Self-Efficacy and Work-Related Performance: A Meta-Analysis," *Psychological Bulletin,* September 1998, pp 240–61.

[30]Based in part on discussion in Gecas, "The Social Psychology of Self-Efficacy."

[31]See S K Parker, "Enhancing Role Breadth Self-Efficacy: The Roles of Job Enrichment and Other Organizational Interventions," *Journal of Applied Psychology,* December 1998, pp 835–52.

[32]The positive relationship between self-efficacy and readiness for retraining is documented in L A Hill and J Elias, "Retraining Midcareer Managers: Career History and Self-Efficacy Beliefs," *Human Resource Management,* Summer 1990, pp 197–217. Also see A M Saks, "Longitudinal Field Investigation of the Moderating and Mediating Effects of Self-Efficacy on the Relationship between Training and Newcomer Adjustment," *Journal of Applied Psychology,* April 1995, pp 211–25; and S P Brown, S Ganesan, and G Challagalla, "Self-Efficacy as a Moderator of Information-Seeking Effectiveness," *Journal of Applied Psychology,* October 2001, pp 1043–51.

[33]See A D Stajkovic and Fred Luthans, "Social Cognitive Theory and Self-Efficacy: Going beyond Traditional Motivational and Behavioral Approaches," *Organizational Dynamics,* Spring 1998, pp 62–74.

[34]See P C Earley and T R Lituchy, "Delineating Goal and Efficacy Effects: A Test of Three Models," *Journal of Applied Psychology,* February 1991, pp 81–98; and J B Vancouver, C M Thompson, and A A Williams, "The Changing Signs in the Relationships among Self-Efficacy, Personal Goals, and Performance," *Journal of Applied Psychology,* August 2001, pp 605–20.

[35]See W S Silver, T R Mitchell, and M E Gist, "Response to Successful and Unsuccessful Performance: The Moderating Effect of Self-Efficacy on the Relationship between Performance and Attributions," *Organizational Behavior and Human Decision Processes,* June 1995, pp 286–99; and S Berglas, "The Very Real Dangers of Executive Coaching," *Harvard Business Review,* June 2002, pp 89–92.

[36]For a model of "leadership self-efficacy," see L L Paglis and S G Green, "Leadership Self-Efficacy and Managers' Motivation for Leading Change," *Journal of Organizational Behavior,* March 2002, pp 215–35.

[37]M Snyder and S Gangestad, "On the Nature of Self-Monitoring: Matters of Assessment, Matters of Validity," *Journal of Personality and Social Psychology,* July 1986, p 125.

[38]T Morganthau, "Throwing Long," *Newsweek,* August 19, 1996, p 29.

[39]Data from D V Day, D J Schleicher, A L Unckless, and N J Hiller, "Self-Monitoring Personality at Work: A Meta-Analytic Investigation of Construct Validity," *Journal of Applied Psychology,* April 2002, pp 390–401. Also see S W Gangestad and M Snyder, "Self-Monitoring: Appraisal and Reappraisal," *Psychological Bulletin,* July 2000, pp 530–55; and I M Jawahar, "Attitudes, Self-Monitoring, and Appraisal Behaviors," *Journal of Applied Psychology,* October 2001, pp 875–83.

[40]Data from M Kilduff and D V Day, "Do Chameleons Get Ahead? The Effects of Self-Monitoring on Managerial Careers," *Academy of Management Journal,* August 1994, pp 1047–60.

[41]Data from D B Turban and T W Dougherty, "Role of Protege Personality in Receipt of Mentoring and Career Success," *Academy of Management Journal,* June 1994, pp 688–702.

[42]See F Luthans, "Successful vs. Effective Managers," *Academy of Management Executive,* May 1988, pp 127–32. Also see W H Turnley and M C Bolino, "Achieving Desired Images while Avoiding Undesired Images: Exploring the Role of Self-Monitoring in Impression Management," *Journal of Applied Psychology,* April 2001, pp 351–60; and "Defanging the Drainers," *Training,* January 2005, p 12.

[43]M G Pratt, "To Be or Not to Be? Central Questions in Organizational Identification," in *Identity in Organizations,* eds D A Whetten and P C Godfrey (Thousand Oaks, CA: Sage Publications, 1998), p 172. Also see S Albert, B E Ashforth, and J E Dutton, "Organizational Identity and Identification: Charting New Waters and Building New Bridges," *Academy of Management Review,* January 2000, pp 13–17; J L Pierce, T Kostova, and K T Dirks, "Toward a Theory of Psychological Ownership in Organizations," *Academy of Management Review,* April 2001, pp 298–310; A Smidts, A T H Pruyn, and C B M van Riel, "The Impact of Employee Communication and Perceived External Prestige on Organizational Identification," *Academy of Management Journal,* October 2001, 1051–62; G E Kreiner and B E Ashforth, "Evidence toward an Expanded Model of Organizational Identification," *Journal of Organizational Behavior,* February 2004, pp 1–27; B Shamir and R Kark, "A Single-Item Graphic Scale for the Measurement of Organizational Identification," *Journal of Occupational and Organizational Psychology,* March 2004, pp 115–23; and R van Dick, U Wagner, J Stellmacher, and O Christ, "The Utility of a Broader Conceptualization of Organizational Identification: Which Aspects Really Matter?" *Journal of Occupational and Organizational Psychology,* June 2004, pp 171–91.

[44]See G Dessler, "How to Earn Your Employees' Commitment," *Academy of Management Executive,* May 1999, pp 58–67.

[45]Based on C Sertoglu and A Berkowitch, "Cultivating Ex-Employees," *Harvard Business Review,* June 2002, pp 20–21.

[46]For more, see B Filipezak, "The Soul of the Hog," *Training,* February 1996, pp 38–42.

[47]For a good overview, see L R James and M D Mazerolle, *Personality in Work Organizations* (Thousand Oaks, CA: Sage Publications, 2002). Also see D S Moskowitz and D C Zuroff, "Flux, Pulse, and Spin: Dynamic Additions to the Personality Lexicon," *Journal of Personality and Social Psychology,* June 2004, pp 880–93; D J Ozer, "Personality out of Proportion?" *Journal of Personality Assessment,* October 2004, pp 131–35; and K E Markon, R F Krueger, and D Watson, "Delineating the Structure of Normal and Abnormal Personality: An Integrative Hierarchical Approach," *Journal of Personality and Social Psychology,* January 2005, pp 139–57.

[48]Data from M C Ashton, K Lee, and L R Goldberg, "A Historical Analysis of 1,710 English Personality-Descriptive

Adjectives," *Journal of Personality and Social Psychology,* November 2004, pp 707–21.

49The landmark report is J M Digman, "Personality Structure: Emergence of the Five-Factor Model," *Annual Review of Psychology,* vol. 41, 1990, pp 417–40. Also see M R Barrick and M K Mount, "Autonomy as a Moderator of the Relationships between the Big Five Personality Dimensions and Job Performance," *Journal of Applied Psychology,* February 1993, pp 111–18; C Viswesvaran and D S Ones, "Measurement Error in 'Big Five Factors' Personality Assessment: Reliability Generalization across Studies and Measures," *Educational and Psychological Measurement,* April 2000, pp 224–35; S J T Branje, C F M van Lieshout, and M A G van Aken, "Relations between Big Five Personality Characteristics and Perceived Support in Adolescents' Families," *Journal of Personality and Social Psychology,* April 2004, pp 615–28; and C J Thoresen, J C Bradley, P D Bliese, and J D Thoresen, "The Big Five Personality Traits and Individual Job Performance Growth Trajectories in Maintenance and Transitional Job Stages," *Journal of Applied Psychology,* October 2004, pp 835–53.

50Data from S V Paunonen et al., "The Structure of Personality in Six Cultures," *Journal of Cross-Cultural Psychology,* May 1996, pp 339–53; and K Yoon, F Schmidt, and R Ilies, "Cross-Cultural Construct Validity of the Five-Factor Model of Personality among Korean Employees," *Journal of Cross-Cultural Psychology,* May 2002, pp 217–35. Also see J Allik and R R McCrae, "Toward a Geography of Personality Traits," *Journal of Cross-Cultural Psychology,* January 2004, pp 13–28; M C Ashton, K Lee, M Perugini, P Szarota, R E de Vries, L D Blas, K Boies, and B De Raad, "A Six-Factor Structure of Personality-Descriptive Adjectives: Solutions from Psycholexical Studies in Seven Languages," *Journal of Personality and Social Psychology,* February 2004, pp 356–66; and R R McCrae, A Terracciano, and 78 members of the Personality Profiles of Cultures Project, "Universal Features of Personality Traits from the Observer's Perspective: Data from 50 Cultures," *Journal of Personality and Social Psychology,* March 2005, pp 547–61.

51J Allik and R R McCrae, "Escapable Conclusions: Toomela (2003) and the Universality of Trait Structure," *Journal of Personality and Social Psychology,* August 2004, p 261.

52See M R Barrick and M K Mount, "The Big Five Personality Dimensions and Job Performance: A Meta-Analysis," *Personnel Psychology,* Spring 1991, pp 1–26. Also see R P Tett, D N Jackson, and M Rothstein, "Personality Measures as Predictors of Job Performance: A Meta-Analytic Review," *Personnel Psychology,* Winter 1991, pp 703–42.

53Barrick and Mount, "The Big Five Personality Dimensions and Job Performance," p 18. Also see H Moon, "The Two Faces of Conscientiousness: Duty and Achievement Striving in Escalation of Commitment Dilemmas," *Journal of Applied Psychology,* June 2001, pp 533–40; M R Barrick, G L Stewart, and M Piotrowski, "Personality and Job Performance: Test of the Mediating Effects of Motivation among Sales Representatives," *Journal of Applied Psychology,* February 2002, pp 43–51; L A Witt, L A Burke, M R Barrick, and M K Mount, "The Interactive Effects of Conscientiousness and Agreeableness on

Job Performance," *Journal of Applied Psychology,* February 2002, pp 164–69; G B Yeo and A Neal, "A Multilevel Analysis of Effort, Practice, and Performance: Effects of Ability, Conscientiousness, and Goal Orientation," *Journal of Applied Psychology,* April 2004, pp 231–47; and B W Roberts, O S Chernyshenko, S Stark, and L R Goldberg, "The Structure of Conscientiousness: An Empirical Investigation Based on Seven Major Personality Questionnaires," *Personnel Psychology,* Spring 2005, pp 103–39.

54Based on S E Seibert and M L Kraimer, "The Five-Factor Model of Personality and Career Success," *Journal of Vocational Behavior,* February 2001, pp 1–21.

55J M Crant, "Proactive Behavior in Organizations," *Journal of Management,* 2000, p 439.

56Ibid., pp 439–41. Problems with excessive proactive personality traits are discussed in K Ludeman and E Erlandson, "Coaching the Alpha Male," *Harvard Business Review,* May 2004, pp 58–67. Also see R W Hill, T J Huelsman, R M Furr, J Kibler, B B Vicente, and C Kennedy, "A New Measure of Perfectionism: The Perfection Inventory," *Journal of Personality Assessment,* February 2004, pp 80–91.

57See H Johnson, "Strength of Heart," *Training,* July 2004, p 16; D Lidsky, "Test Your Courage: How Do You Rate?" *Fast Company,* September 2004, pp 107–9; G P Hollenbeck and D T Hall, "Self-Confidence and Leader Performance," *Organizational Dynamics,* 2004, pp 254–69; and "Measuring Character," *Training,* October 2004, p 16.

58R Kurtz, "Testing, Testing," *Inc.,* June 2004, p 36. Also see A Overholt, "Personality Tests: Back with a Vengeance," *Fast Company,* November 2004, pp 115–17.

59See discussion in Barrick and Mount, "The Big Five Personality Dimensions and Job Performance: A Meta-Analysis," pp 21–22. Also see J M Cortina, M L Doherty, N Schmitt, G Kaufman, and R G Smith, "The 'Big Five' Personality Factors in the IPI and MMPI: Predictors of Police Performance," *Personnel Psychology,* Spring 1992, pp 119–40; M J Schmit and A M Ryan, "The Big Five in Personnel Selection: Factor Structure in Applicant and Nonapplicant Populations," *Journal of Applied Psychology,* December 1993, pp 966–74; and C Caggiano, "Psychopath," *Inc.,* July 1998, pp 77–85.

60M K Mount and M R Barrick, "The Big Five Personality Dimensions: Implications for Research and Practice in Human Resources Management," in *Research in Personnel and Human Resources Management,* ed G R Ferris (Greenwich, CT: JAI Press, 1995), vol. 13, p 189. See J M Collins and D H Gleaves, "Race, Job Applicants, and the Five-Factor Model of Personality: Implications for Black Psychology, Industrial/ Organizational Psychology, and the Five-Factor Theory," *Journal of Applied Psychology,* August 1998, pp 531–44.

61See M Hofman, "Doesn't Work Well with Others," *Inc.,* January 2000, p 95; S Bates, "Personality Counts," *HR Magazine,* February 2002, pp 28–34; and D Patel, "Testing, Testing, Testing," *HR Magazine,* February 2002, p 112.

62W Lambert, "Psychological Tests Designed to Weed Out Rogue Cops Get a 'D,' " *The Wall Street Journal,* September

1995, p A1. Also see A M Ryan, R E Ployhart, and L A Friedel, "Using Personality Testing to Reduce Adverse Impact: A Cautionary Note," *Journal of Applied Psychology,* April 1998, pp 298–307.

[63]For more, see S Stark, O S Chernyshenko, K Chan, W C Lee, and F Drasgow, "Effects of the Testing Situation on Item Responding: Cause for Concern," *Journal of Applied Psychology,* October 2001, pp 943–53. Also see G M Alliger and S A Dwight, "A Meta-Analytic Investigation of the Susceptibility of Integrity Tests to Faking and Coaching," *Educational and Psychological Measurement,* February 2000, pp 59–72; and K Frieswick, "Casting to Type," *CFO,* July 2004, pp 71–72.

[64]See A Murphy Paul, *The Cult of Personality: How Personality Tests Are Leading Us to Miseducate Our Children, Mismanage Our Companies, and Misunderstand Ourselves* (New York: Free Press, 2004).

[65]H Dolezalek, "Tests on Trial," *Training,* April 2005, p 34. Also see A Fisher, "Can I Refuse to Take a Personality Test?" *Fortune,* May 3, 2004, p 70.

[66]R Lieber, "Wired for Hiring: Microsoft's Slick Recruiting Machine," *Fortune,* February 5, 1996, p 124.

[67]For an instructive update, see J B Rotter, "Internal versus External Control of Reinforcement: A Case History of a Variable," *American Psychologist,* April 1990, pp 489–93. For relevant research updates, see M Zuckerman, C R Knee, S C Kieffer, and M Gagne, "What Individuals Believe They Can and Cannot Do: Explorations of Realistic and Unrealistic Control Beliefs," *Journal of Personality Assessment,* April 2004, pp 215–32; R Shirazi and A Biel, "Internal-External Causal Attributions and Perceived Government Responsibility for Need Provision: A 14-Culture Study," *Journal of Cross-Cultural Psychology,* January 2005, pp 96–116; W Johnson and R F Krueger, "Higher Perceived Life Control Decreases Genetic Variance in Physical Health: Evidence from a National Twin Study," *Journal of Personality and Social Psychology,* January 2005, pp 165–73; and J Rossier, D Dahourou, and R R McCrae, "Structural and Mean-Level Analyses of the Five-Factor Model and Locus of Control: Further Evidence from Africa," *Journal of Cross-Cultural Psychology,* March 2005, pp 227–46.

[68]See A S Wellner, "Everyone's a Critic," *Inc.,* July 2004, pp 38, 41.

[69]J Fierman, "What's Luck Got to Do with It?" *Fortune,* October 16, 1995, p 149.

[70]For an overall review of research on locus of control, see P E Spector, "Behavior in Organizations as a Function of Employee's Locus of Control," *Psychological Bulletin,* May 1982, pp 482–97; the relationship between locus of control and performance and satisfaction is examined in D R Norris and R E Niebuhr, "Attributional Influences on the Job Performance–Job Satisfaction Relationship," *Academy of Management Journal,* June 1984, pp 424–31; salary differences between internals and externals were examined by P C Nystrom, "Managers' Salaries and Their Beliefs about Reinforcement Control," *Journal of Social Psychology,* August 1983, pp 291–92.

[71]Robert Solomon, as quoted in D Vera and A Rodriguez-Lopez, "Strategic Virtues: Humility as a Source of Competitive Advantage," *Organizational Dynamics,* no. 4, 2004, pp 394–95.

[72]Ibid., p 395.

[73]S B Parry, "The Quest for Competencies," *Training,* July 1996, p 48. Also see S Meisinger, "Shortage of Skilled Workers Threatens Economy," *HR Magazine,* November 2004, p 12; and S Holt, "More Job Simulations," *Arizona Republic,* February 26, 2005, p D3.

[74]See D L Coutu, "How Resilience Works," *Harvard Business Review,* May 2002, pp 46–55; and M M Tugade and B L Fredrickson, "Resilient Individuals Use Positive Emotions to Bounce Back from Negative Emotional Experiences," *Journal of Personality and Social Psychology,* February 2004, pp 320–33.

[75]See "Nappers of the World, Lie Down and Be Counted!" *Training,* May 2000, p 24; K Fackelmann, "Deep Sleep Beats All-Nighter for Retaining What You Learn," *USA Today,* November 27, 2000, p 10D; D M Osborne, "Sleep: The Final Frontier," *Inc.,* September 2001, p 68; and A Pomeroy, "The Doctor Is Still In," *HR Magazine,* February 2002, pp 36–42.

[76]Data from "People Rate How They Sleep," *USA Today,* April 12, 2005, p 1A.

[77]A Pomeroy, "Sleep Deprivation and Medical Errors," *HR Magazine,* February 2002, p 42.

[78]For interesting reading on intelligence, see M Elias, "Mom's IQ, Not Family Size, Key to Kids' Smarts," *USA Today,* June 12, 2000, p 1D; R Sapolsky, "Score One for Nature—or Is It Nurture?" *USA Today,* June 21, 2000, p 17A; D Lubinski, R M Webb, M J Morelock, and C P Benbow, "Top 1 in 10,000: A 10-Year Follow-Up of the Profoundly Gifted," *Journal of Applied Psychology,* August 2001, pp 718–29; and T A Judge, A E Colbert, and R Ilies, "Intelligence and Leadership: A Quantitative Review and Test of Theoretical Propositions," *Journal of Applied Psychology,* June 2004, pp 542–52.

[79]For an excellent update on intelligence, including definitional distinctions and a historical perspective of the IQ controversy, see R A Weinberg, "Intelligence and IQ," *American Psychologist,* February 1989, pp 98–104. Also see R Plomin and F M Spinath, "Intelligence: Genetics, Genes, and Genomics," *Journal of Personality and Social Psychology,* January 2004, pp 112–29; and C Arnst, "Getting Girls to the Lab Bench," *BusinessWeek,* February 7, 2005, p 42.

[80]Weinberg, "Intelligence and IQ."

[81]S L Wilk, L Burris Desmarais, and P R Sackett, "Gravitation to Jobs Commensurate with Ability: Longitudinal and Cross-Sectional Tests," *Journal of Applied Psychology,* February 1995, p 79.

[82]B Azar, "People Are Becoming Smarter—Why?" *APA Monitor,* June 1996, p 20. Also see " 'Average' Intelligence Higher than It Used to Be," *USA Today,* February 18, 1997, p 6D.

[83]See D Lubinski, "Introduction to the Special Section on Cognitive Abilities: 100 Years after Spearman's (1904) 'General Intelligence, Objectively Determined and Measured,' " *Journal of Personality and Social Psychology,* January 2004, pp 96–111; and N L Vasilopoulos, J M Cucina, and J M McElreath, "Do Warnings of Response Verification Moderate the Relationship between Personality and Cognitive Ability?" *Journal of Applied Psychology,* March 2005, pp 306–22.

[84]See F L Schmidt and J E Hunter, "Employment Testing: Old Theories and New Research Findings," *American Psychologist,* October 1981, p 1128. Also see Y Ganzach, "Intelligence and Job Satisfaction," *Academy of Management Journal,* October 1998, pp 526–39.

[85]See H Gardner, *Frames of Mind: The Theory of Multiple Intelligences,* 10th anniversary ed (New York: Basic Books, 1993); and H Gardner, *Intelligence Reframed: Multiple Intelligences for the 21st Century* (New York: Basic Books, 2000).

[86]For a good overview of Gardner's life and work, see M K Smith, "Howard Gardner and Multiple Intelligences," *Encyclopedia of Informal Education,* 2002, www.infed.org/thinkers/gardner.htm.

[87]R J Sternberg, "WICS: A Model of Leadership in Organizations," *Academy of Management Learning and Education,* December 2003, p 388.

[88]See K Albrecht, "Social Intelligence: Beyond IQ," *Training,* December 2004, pp 26–31; and A A Loort, "Multiple Intelligences: A Comparative Study Between the Preferences of Males and Females," *Social Behavior and Personality,* no.1, 2005, pp 77–88.

[89]See C D Fisher and N M Ashkanasy, "The Emerging Role of Emotions in Work Life: an Introduction," *Journal of Organizational Behavior,* March 2000, pp 123–29; P M Muchinsky, "Emotions in the Workplace: The Neglect of Organizational Behavior," *Journal of Organizational Behavior,* November 2000, pp 801–5; N M Ashkanasy and C S Daus, "Emotion in the Workplace: The New Challenge for Managers," *Academy of Management Executive,* February 2002, pp 76–86; D A Shepherd, "Educating Entrepreneurship Students about Emotion and Learning from Failure," *Academy of Management Learning and Education,* September 2004, pp 274–87; J E Stets, "Examining Emotions in Identity Theory," *Social Psychology Quarterly,* March 2005, pp 39–74; and M G Beaupre and U Hess, "Cross-Cultural Emotion Recognition among Canadian Ethnic Groups," *Journal of Cross-Cultural Psychology,* May 2005, pp 355–70.

[90]S Hamm, "Bill's Co-Pilot," *BusinessWeek,* September 14, 1998, pp 85, 87.

[91]G Anders, "John Chambers after the Deluge," *Fast Company,* July 2001, p 108.

[92]R S Lazarus, *Emotion and Adaptation* (New York: Oxford University Press, 1991), p 6. Also see C Scott and K Myers, "The Socialization of Emotion: Learning Emotion Management at the Fire Station," *Journal of Applied Communication Research,* February 2005, pp 67–92.

[93]Based on discussion in R D Arvey, G L Renz, and T W Watson, "Emotionality and Job Performance: Implications for Personnel Selection," in *Research in Personnel and Human Resources Management,* vol. 16, ed G R Ferris (Stamford, CT: JAI Press, 1998), pp 103–47. Also see L F Barrett, "Feelings or Words? Understanding the Content in Self-Report Ratings of Experienced Emotion," *Journal of Personality and Social Psychology,* August 2004, pp 266–81; and P A Simpson and L K Stroh, "Gender Differences: Emotional Expression and Feelings of Personal Inauthenticity," *Journal of Applied Psychology,* August 2004, pp 715–21.

[94]See D L Coutu, "Managing Emotional Fallout: Parting Remarks from America's Top Psychiatrist," *Harvard Business Review,* February 2002, pp 55–59.

[95]See S Sturmer, M Snyder, and A M Omoto, "Prosocial Emotions and Helping: The Moderating Role of Group Membership," *Journal of Personality and Social Psychology,* March 2005, pp 532–46.

[96]J A Byrne and H Timmons, "Tough Times," *BusinessWeek,* October 29, 2001, p 66. Also see J E Dutton, P J Frost, M C Worline, J M Lilius, and J M Kanov, "Leading in Times of Trauma," *Harvard Business Review,* January 2002, pp 54–61; and J Creswell, "Ken Chenault Reshuffles His Cards," *Fortune,* April 18, 2005, pp 180–86.

[97]J McGregor, "#1 Taryn Rose," *Fast Company,* May 2005, p 69.

[98]D Goleman, *Emotional Intelligence* (New York: Bantam Books, 1995), p 34. For more, see Q N Huy, "Emotional Capability, Intelligence, and Radical Change," *Academy of Management Review,* April 1999, pp 325–45; K S Law, C Wong, and L J Song, "The Construct and Criterion Validity of Emotional Intelligence and Its Potential Utility for Management Studies," *Journal of Applied Psychology,* June 2004, pp 483–96; and J Yang and K W Mossholder, "Decoupling Task and Relationship Conflict: The Role of Intragroup Emotional Processing," *Journal of Organizational Behavior,* August 2004, pp 589–605.

[99]See "What's Your EQ at Work," *Fortune,* October 26, 1998, p 298; V U Druskat and S B Wolff, "Building the Emotional Intelligence of Groups," *Harvard Business Review,* March 2001, pp 80–90; D Goleman, R Boyatzis, and A McKee, "Primal Leadership: The Hidden Driver of Great Performance," *Harvard Business Review,* "Special Issue: Breakthrough Leadership," December 2001, pp 43–51; J J Salopek, "Social Intelligence," *Training & Development,* September 2004, pp 17–19; J Rossi, "Growing Strong Leaders," *Training & Development,* February 2005, pp 53–55; and T Estep, "In Search of the Secrets of Peak Performers," *Training and Development,* February 2005, pp 78–80. Also see L W Andrews, "When It's Time for Anger Management," *HR Magazine,* June 2005, pp 131–136.

[100]Data from S D Pugh, "Service with a Smile: Emotional Contagion in the Service Encounter," *Academy of Management Journal,* October 2001, pp 1018–27.

[101]Drawn from P Totterdell, S Kellett, K Teuchmann, and R B Briner, "Evidence of Mood Linkage in Work Groups," *Journal of Personality and Social Psychology,* June 1998, pp 1504–15. Also see A Singh-Manoux and C Finkenauer, "Cultural Variations in Social Sharing of Emotions: An Intercultural Perspective," *Journal of Cross-Cultural Psychology,* November 2001, pp 647–61; H H Tan, M D Foo, and M H Kwek, "The Effects of Customer Personality Traits on the Display of Positive Emotions," *Academy of Management Journal,* April 2004, pp 287–96; and T Sy, S Cote, and R Saavedra, "The Contagious Leader: Impact of the Leader's Mood on the Mood of Group Members, Group Affective Tone, and Group Processes," *Journal of Applied Psychology,* March 2005, pp 295–305.

[102]"Ulrich Schumacher," *BusinessWeek,* June 11, 2001, p 82.

[103]N M Ashkanasy and C S Daus, "Emotion in the Workplace: The New Challenge for Managers," *Academy of Management Executive,* February 2002, p 79. Also see A A Grandey, D N Dickter, and H Sin, "The Customer is *Not* Always Right: Customer Aggression and Emotion Regulation of Service Employees," *Journal of Organizational Behavior,* May 2004, pp 397–418; T M Glomb, J D Kammeyer-Mueller, and M Rotundo, "Emotional Labor Demands and Compensating Wage Differentials," *Journal of Applied Psychology,* August 2004, pp 700–14; A A Grandey, G M Fisk, A S Mattila, K J Jansen, and L A Sideman, "Is 'Service with a Smile' Enough? Authenticity of Positive Displays during Service Encounters," *Organizational Behavior and Human Decision Processes,* January 2005, pp 38–55; and J M Diefendorff, M H Croyle, and R H Gosserand, "The Dimensionality and Antecedents of Emotional Labor Strategies," *Journal of Vocational Behavior,* April 2005, pp 339–57.

[104]Data from A M Kring and A H Gordon, "Sex Differences in Emotions: Expressions, Experience, and Physiology," *Journal of Personality and Social Psychology,* March 1998, pp 686–703.

[105]See P J Frost, "Handling Toxic Emotions: New Challenges for Leaders and Their Organizations," *Organizational Dynamics,* no. 2, 2004, pp 111–27.

[106]C Salter, "Driving Ambition," *Fast Company,* May 2005, pp 78, 80. By Chuck Salter, © 2005 Gruner & Jahr USA Publishing. First published in *Fast Company* Magazine. Reprinted with permission.

[107]Adapted in part from James and Mazerolle, *Personality in Work Organizations,* p 89.

[108]Excerpted from J Macht, "To Get Ahead, Get Mad," *Business 2.0,* May 2002, p 94. © Time, Inc. All rights reserved.

CHAPTER 6

[1]Excerpted from N Byrnes, "Green Eyeshades Never Looked So Sexy," *BusinessWeek,* January 10, 2005, p 44.

[2]These results are presented in D E Lewis, "US Workers Making Plans to Job-Hop This Year," *Arizona Republic,* January 2, 2005, p D1.

[3]Research on turnover is summarized by P W Hom and R W Griffeth, *Employee Turnover* (Cincinnati, OH: Southwestern, 1995).

[4]Examples are provided by R Levering and M Moskowitz, "The 100 Best Companies to Work For," *Fortune,* January 24, 2005, pp 72–90; K Gurchiek, "Survey: Exodus Follows an Improving Economy," *HR Magazine,* March 2005, pp 28, 34; and N Cossack, R R Hastings, and A Maingault, "Day Care, Pay Raises, Rules on Part-Timers," *HR Magazine,* February 2005, pp 43–44.

[5]M Rokeach, *The Nature of Values* (New York: Free Press, 1973), p 5.

[6]See the related discussion in D N Sull and D Houlder, "Do Your Commitments Match Your Convictions?" *Harvard Business Review,* January 2005, pp 82–91.

[7]See S H Schwartz and W Bilsky, "Toward a Theory of the Universal Content and Structure of Values: Extensions and Cross-Cultural Replications," *Journal of Personality and Social Psychology,* May 1990, pp 878–91. For other values-related research, see G R Maio and J M Olson, "Values as Truisms: Evidence and Implications," *Journal of Personality and Social Psychology,* February 1998, pp 294–311.

[8]See M Rokeach, *Beliefs, Attitudes, and Values* (San Francisco: Jossey-Bass, 1968).

[9]This example was taken from D Jones, "Sara Lee Biggest Company (for Now) with Female CEO," *USA Today,* February 11, 2005, p 43.

[10]P B Brown, "What I Know Now," *Fast Company,* February 2005, p 96.

[11]W Shapiro, "Peace Corp Inexpensive, Yet Priceless," *USA Today,* May 5, 1999, p 15A.

[12]For a thorough discussion of person–culture fit, see A L Kristof, "Person–Organization Fit: An Integrative Review of Its Conceptualizations, Measurements, and Implications," *Personnel Psychology,* Spring 1996, pp 1–49.

[13]Supportive results can be found in C Ostroff, Y Shin, and A Kinicki, "Multiple Perspectives of Congruence: Relationships between Value Congruence and Employee Attitudes," *Journal of Organizational Behavior,* in press; and D M Cable and J R Edwards, "Complementary and Supplementary Fit: A Theoretical and Empirical Integration," *Journal of Applied Psychology,* October 2004, pp 822–34.

[14]B Moses, "The Busyness Trap," *Training,* November 1998.

[15]See P Engardio, C Matlack, G Edmondson, I Rowley, C Barraclough, and G Smith, "Now the Geezer Glut," *BusinessWeek,* January 31, 2005, pp 44–47; and A Park, "Between a Rocker and a High Chair," *BusinessWeek,* February 21, 2005, pp 86–88.

[16]K W Smola and C D Sutton, "Generational Differences: Revisiting Generational Work Values for the New Millennium," *Journal of Organizational Behavior,* June 2002, p 379.

[17]M Conlin and T J Mullaney, "Far from the Madding Crowd," *BusinessWeek,* January 31, 2005, p 70.

[18]P L Perrewé and W A Hochwarter, "Can We Really Have It All? The Attainment of Work and Family Values," *Current Directions in Psychological Science,* February 2001, p 31.

[19]Based on T D Allen, "Family-Supportive Work Environments: The Role of Organizational Perceptions," *Journal of Vocational Behavior,* June 2001, pp 414–35.

[20]F Haley, "Mutual Benefit," *Fast Company,* October 2004, p 98.

[21]Based on S C Clark, "Work Cultures and Work/Family Balance," *Journal of Vocational Behavior,* June 2001, pp 348–65.

[22]T R Nielson, D S Carlson, and M J Lankau, "The Supportive Mentor as a Means of Reducing Work-Family Conflict," *Journal of Vocational Behavior,* December 2001, pp 374–75.

[23]Supportive results can be found in S Aryee, E S Srinvas, and H H Tan, "Rhythms of Life: Antecedents and Outcomes of

Work-Family Balance in Employed Parents," *Journal of Applied Psychology,* January 2005, pp 132–46; and L T Eby, W J Casper, A Lockwood, C Bordeaux, and A Brinley, "Work and Family Research in IO/OB: Content Analysis and Review of the Literature (1980–2002)," *Journal of Vocational Behavior,* February 2005, pp 124–97.

24C Hymowitz, "In the Lead: More Managers Allow Workers to Multitask as Jobs and Home Blur," *The Wall Street Journal,* October 28, 2003, p B1.

25Based on S Parasuraman and C A Simmers, "Type of Employment, Work-Family Conflict and Well-Being: A Comparative Study," *Journal of Organizational Behavior,* August 2001, pp 551–68.

26The benefits of family-friendly programs are discussed by N Cossack, R R Hastings, and A Maingault, "Day Care, Pay Raises, Rules on Part-Timers," *HR Magazine,* February 2005, p 43; and J D Quick, A B Henley, and J C Quick, "The Balancing Act: At Work and at Home," *Organizational Dynamics,* November 2004, pp 426–37.

27R Rapoport, L Bailyn, J K Fletcher, and B H Pruitt, *Beyond Work-Family Balance: Advancing Gender Equity and Workplace Performance* (San Francisco: Jossey-Bass, 2002), p 36.

28M Fishbein and I Ajzen, *Belief, Attitude, Intention and Behavior: An Introduction to Theory and Research* (Reading, MA: Addison-Wesley Publishing, 1975), p 6.

29For a discussion of the difference between values and attitudes, see B W Becker and P E Connor, "Changing American Values—Debunking the Myth," *Business,* January–March 1985, pp 56–59.

30The components or structure of attitudes is thoroughly discussed by A P Brief, *Attitudes in and around Organizations* (Thousand Oaks, CA: Sage, 1998), pp 49–84.

31For details about this theory, see L Festinger, *A Theory of Cognitive Dissonance* (Stanford, CA: Stanford University Press, 1957). A recent test of this theory in a group context was conducted by D C Matz and W Wood, "Cognitive Dissonance in Groups: The Consequences of Disagreement," *Journal of Personality and Social Psychology,* January 2005, pp 22–37.

32See B M Staw and J Ross, "Stability in the Midst of Change: A Dispositional Approach to Job Attitudes," *Journal of Applied Psychology,* August 1985, pp 469–80. Also see J Schaubroeck, D C Ganster, and B Kemmerer, "Does Trait Affect Promote Job Attitude Stability?" *Journal of Organizational Behavior,* March 1996, pp 191–96.

33Data from P S Visser and J A Krosnick, "Development of Attitude Strength over the Life Cycle: Surge and Decline," *Journal of Personality and Social Psychology,* December 1998, pp 389–410.

34I Ajzen, "The Theory of Planned Behavior," *Organizational Behavior and Human Decision Processes,* vol. 50 (1991), p 188.

35See R P Steel and N K Ovalle II, "A Review and Meta-Analysis of Research on the Relationship between Behavioral Intentions and Employee Turnover," *Journal of Applied Psychology,* November 1984, pp 673–86. Also see

W V Breukelen, R V D Vklist, and H Steensma, "Voluntary Employee Turnover: Combining Variables from the 'Traditional' Turnover Literature with the Theory of Planned Behavior," *Journal of Organizational Behavior,* November 2004, pp 893–914.

36Results can be found in M R Barrick and R D Zimmerman, "Reducing Voluntary Turnover through Selection," *Journal of Applied Psychology,* January 2005, pp 159–66.

37Drawn from I Ajzen and M Fishbein, *Understanding Attitudes and Predicting Social Behavior* (Englewood Cliffs, NJ: Prentice Hall, 1980); and K I van der Zee, A B Bakker, and P Bakker, "Why Are Structured Interviews So Rarely Used in Personnel Selection?" *Journal of Applied Psychology,* February 2002, pp 176–84. Also see D Albarracín, B T Johnson, M Fishbein, and P A Muellerleile, "Theories of Reasoned Action and Planned Behavior as Models of Condom Use: A Meta-Analysis," *Psychological Bulletin,* January 2001, pp 142–61; K A Finlay, D Trafimow, and A Villarreal, "Predicting Exercise and Health Behavioral Intentions: Attitudes, Subjective Norms, and Other Behavioral Determinants," *Journal of Applied Social Psychology,* February 2002, pp 342–58; and M Riketta, "Attitudinal Organizational Commitment and Job Performance: A Meta-Analysis," *Journal of Organizational Behavior,* May 2002, pp 257–66.

38See P W Hom and C L Hulin, "A Competitive Test of the Prediction of Reenlistment by Several Models," *Journal of Applied Psychology,* February 1981, pp 23–39.

39Results can be found in M L Kraimer, S J Wayne, R C Liden, and R T Sparrowe, "The Role of Job Security in Understanding the Relationship between Employees' Perceptions of Temporary Workers and Employees' Performance," *Journal of Applied Psychology,* March 2005, pp 389–98.

40Based on evidence in C J Thomsen, A M Basu, and M Tippens Reinitz, "Effects of Women's Studies Courses on Gender-Related Attitudes of Women and Men," *Psychology of Women Quarterly,* September 1995, pp 419–26.

41L Yerkes, *Fun Works: Creating Places Where People Love to Work* (San Francisco: Berrett-Koehler, 2001), p 73.

42The concept of commitment and its relationship to motivated behavior is thoroughly discussed by J P Meyer, T E Becker, and C Vandenberghe, "Employee Commitment and Motivation: A Conceptual Analysis and Integrative Model," *Journal of Applied Psychology,* December 2004, pp 991–1007.

43J P Meyer and L Herscovitch, "Commitment in the Workplace: Toward a General Model," *Human Resource Management Review,* Autumn 2001, p 301.

44J P Meyer and N J Allen, "A Three-Component Conceptualization of Organizational Commitment," *Human Resource Management Review,* Spring 1991, p 67.

45Supportive results can be found in C Hult, "Organizational Commitment and Person–Environment Fit in Six Western Countries," *Organization Studies,* 2005, pp 249–70.

46This definition was provided by D M Rousseau, "Psychological and Implied Contracts in Organizations," *Employee Responsibilities and Rights Journal,* June 1989, 121–39.

[47]A thorough review of research on psychological contracts is provided by L M Shore, L E Tetrick, M S Taylor, J Coyle Shapiro, R C Liden, J McLean Parks, E Wolf Morrison, L W Porter, S L Robinson, M V Roehling, D M Rousseau, R Schalk, A S Tsui, and L Van Dyne, "The Employee-Organization Relationship: A Timely Concept in a Period of Transition," in *Research in Personnel and Human Resources Management,* ed J Martocchio (Boston: Elsevier, 2004), vol. 23, pp 291–370.

[48]See R P Tett and J P Meyer, "Job Satisfaction, Organizational Commitment, Turnover Intention, and Turnover: Path Analysis Based on Meta-Analytic Findings," *Personnel Psychology,* Summer 1993, pp 259–93.

[49]Results can be found in M Riketta, "Attitudinal Organizational Commitment and Job Performance: A Meta-Analysis," *Journal of Organizational Behavior,* March 2002, pp 257–66.

[50]Results can be found in R W Griffeth, P W Hom, and S Gaertner, "A Meta-Analysis of Antecedents and Correlates of Employee Turnover: Update, Moderator Tests, and Research Implications for the Next Millennium," *Journal of Management,* 2000, pp 463–88.

[51]W Zeller, C Palmeri, M France, J Weber, and D Carney, "Jeff Skilling: Enron's Missing Man," *BusinessWeek,* February 11, 2002, p 39.

[52]D Wessel, "How Loyalty Comes by Degrees," *The Wall Street Journal,* May 17, 2001, p A1.

[53]Ibid.

[54]Levering and Moskowitz, "The 100 Best Companies to Work For," p 84.

[55]Ibid, pp 80, 82.

[56]I M Paullay, G M Alliger, and E F Stone-Romero, "Construct Validation of Two Instruments Designed to Measure Job Involvement and Work Centrality," *Journal of Applied Psychology,* April 1994, p 224.

[57]Yerkes, *Fun Works,* p 126.

[58]Ibid.

[59]Results can be found in S P Brown, "A Meta-Analysis and Review of Organizational Research on Job Involvement," *Psychological Bulletin,* September 1996, pp 235–55.

[60]Results can be found in J M Diefendorff, D J Brown, A M Kamin, and R G Lord, "Examining the Roles of Job Involvement and Work Centrality in Predicting Organizational Citizenship Behaviors and Job Performance," *Journal of Organizational Behavior,* February 2002, pp 93–108.

[61]For a review of the development of the JDI, see P C Smith, L M Kendall, and C L Hulin, *The Measurement of Satisfaction in Work and Retirement* (Skokie, IL: Rand McNally, 1969).

[62]For norms on the MSQ, see D J Weiss, R V Dawis, G W England, and L H Lofquist, *Manual for the Minnesota Satisfaction Questionnaire* (Minneapolis: Industrial Relations Center, University of Minnesota, 1967).

[63]Results are reported in M Boyle, "Happiness Index: Nothing Is Rotten in Denmark," *Fortune,* February 19, 2001, p 242.

[64]See A J Kinicki, F M McKee-Ryan, C A Schriesheim, and K P Carson, "Assessing the Construct Validity of the Job Descriptive Index: A Review and Meta-Analysis," *Journal of Applied Psychology,* February 2002, pp 14–32.

[65]For a review of these models, see Brief, *Attitudes in and around Organizations.*

[66]See A R Karr, "Work Week: A Special News Report about Life on the Job—and Trends Taking Shape There," *The Wall Street Journal,* June 29, 1999, p A1.

[67]The survey was conducted by Hewitt and Associates, and results were presented in J Saranow, "Anybody Want to Take a Nap?" *The Wall Street Journal,* January 24, 2005, p R5.

[68]For a review of need satisfaction models, see E F Stone, "A Critical Analysis of Social Information Processing Models of Job Perceptions and Job Attitudes," *Job Satisfaction: How People Feel about Their Jobs and How It Affects Their Performance,* eds C J Cranny, P Cain Smith, and E F Stone (New York: Lexington Books, 1992), pp 21–52.

[69]See J P Wanous, T D Poland, S L Premack, and K S Davis, "The Effects of Met Expectations on Newcomer Attitudes and Behaviors: A Review and Meta-Analysis," *Journal of Applied Psychology,* June 1992, pp 288–97.

[70]A complete description of this model is provided by E A Locke, "Job Satisfaction," in *Social Psychology and Organizational Behavior,* eds M Gruneberg and T Wall (New York: John Wiley & Sons, 1984).

[71]The results and recommendations can be found in J Chatzky, "Making Time for Time Off," *Money,* April 2005, pp 48, 50.

[72]For a test of the value fulfillment value, see W A Hochwarter, P L Perrewé, G R Ferris, and R A Brymer, "Job Satisfaction and Performance: The Moderating Effects of Value Attainment and Affective Disposition," *Journal of Vocational Behavior,* April 1999, pp 296–313.

[73]Results can be found in J Cohen-Charash and P E Spector, "The Role of Justice in Organizations: A Meta-Analysis," *Organizational Behavior and Human Decision Processes,* November 2001, pp 278–321.

[74]A thorough discussion of this model is provided by C L Hulin, and T A Judge, "Job Attitudes," in *Handbook of Psychology,* vol. 12, eds W C Borman, D R Ilgen, and R J Klimoski (Hoboken, NJ: John Wiley & Sons, Inc., 2003), pp 255–76.

[75]A summary and interpretation of this research is provided by B M Staw and Y Choen-Charash, "The Dispositional Approach to Job Satisfaction: More than a Mirage, but Not Yet an Oasis," *Journal of Organizational Behavior,* February 2005, pp 59–78; and B Gerhart, "The (Affective) Dispositional Approach to Job Satisfaction: Sorting Out the Policy Implications," *Journal of Organizational Behavior,* February 2005, pp 79–97.

[76]See R D Arvey, T J Bouchard Jr, N L Segal, and L M Abraham, "Job Satisfaction: Environmental and Genetic Components," *Journal of Applied Psychology,* April 1989, pp 187–92.

[77]See C Dormann and D Zapf, "Job Satisfaction: A Meta-Analysis of Stabilities," *Journal of Organizational Behavior,* August 2001, pp 483–504.

[78]P Wakeman, "The Good Life and How to Get It," *Inc.,* February 2001, p 50.

[79]See Kinicki, McKee-Ryan, Schriesheim, and Carson, "Assessing the Construct Validity of the Job Descriptive Index."

[80]See Brown, "A Meta-Analysis and Review of Organizational Research on Job Involvement."

[81]D W Organ, "The Motivational Basis of Organizational Citizenship Behavior," in *Research in Organizational Behavior,* eds B M Staw and L L Cummings (Greenwich, CT: JAI Press, 1990), p 46.

[82]Results can be found in J A LePine, A Erez, and D E Johnson, "The Nature and Dimensionality of Organizational Citizenship Behavior: A Critical Review and Meta-Analysis," *Journal of Applied Psychology,* February 2002, pp 52–65.

[83]Supportive results can be found in B J Tepper, M K Duffy, J Hoobler, and M D Ensley, "Moderators of the Relationship between Coworkers' Organizational Citizenship Behavior and Fellow Employees' Attitudes," *Journal of Applied Psychology,* June 2004, pp 455–65; and P M Podsakoff, S B MacKenzie, J B Paine, and D G Bachrach, "Organizational Citizenship Behaviors: A Critical Review of the Theoretical and Empirical Literature and Suggestions for Future Research," *Journal of Management,* 2000, pp 513–63.

[84]Supportive findings are presented in T W Lee, T R Mitchell, C J Sablynski, J P Burton, and B C Holtom, "The Effects of Job Embeddedness on Organizational Citizenship, Job Performance, Volitional Absences, and Voluntary Turnover," *Academy of Management Journal,* October 2004, pp 711–22; and L Van Dyne and J L Pierce, "Psychological Ownership and Feelings of Possession: Three Field Studies Predicting Employee Attitudes and Organizational Behavior," *Journal of Organizational Behavior,* June 2004, pp 439–59.

[85]Results can be found in D J Koys, "The Effects of Employee Satisfaction, Organizational Citizenship Behavior, and Turnover on Organizational Effectiveness: A Unit-Level, Longitudinal Study," *Personnel Psychology,* Spring 2001, pp 101–14.

[86]These results can be found in K Gurchiek, "'I Can't Make It to Work Today, Boss . . . Gotta Round Up My Ostriches," *HR Magazine,* March 2005, p 30.

[87]These cost estimates are provided in E Robertson Demby, "Do Your Family-Friendly Programs Make Cents?" *HR Magazine,* January 2004, pp 74–78.

[88]See R D Hackett, "Work Attitudes and Employee Absenteeism: A Synthesis of the Literature," *Journal of Occupational Psychology,* 1989, pp 235–48.

[89]A thorough review of the cognitive process associated with quitting is provided in C P Maertz Jr and M A Campion, "Profiles in Quitting: Integrating Process and Content Turnover Theory," *Academy of Management Journal,* August 2004, pp 566–82.

[90]Results can be found in P W Hom and A J Kinicki, "Toward a Greater Understanding of How Dissatisfaction Drives Employee Turnover," *Academy of Management Journal,* October 2001, pp 975–87.

[91]Y Lermusiaux, "Calculating the High Cost of Employee Turnover," www.ilogos.com/en/expertviews/articles/strategic/200331007_YL.html, accessed April 15, 2005, p 1. The various costs of employee turnover are also discussed by W G Bliss, "Cost of Employee Turnover," www.isquare.com/turnover.cfm, accessed April 15, 2005.

[92]See Lermusiaux, "Calculating the High Cost of Employee Turnover." An automated program for calculating the cost of turnover can be found at "Calculate Your Turnover Costs," www.keepemployees.com/turnovercalc.htm, accessed April 15, 2005.

[93]Techniques for reducing employee turnover are discussed by R W Griffeth and P W Hom, *Retaining Valued Employees* (Thousand Oaks, CA: Sage Publications, 2001).

[94]Results can be found in Griffeth, Hom, and Gaertner, "A Meta-Analysis of Antecedents and Correlates of Employee Turnover."

[95]See P W Hom and R W Griffeth, *Employee Turnover* (Cincinnati: South-Western, 1995), pp 35–50.

[96]Results can be found in M A Blegen, "Nurses' Job Satisfaction: Meta-Analysis of Related Variables," *Nursing Research,* January–February 1993, pp 36–41.

[97]The various models are discussed in T A Judge, C J Thoresen, J E Bono, and G K Patton, "The Job Satisfaction–Job Performance Relationship: A Qualitative and Quantitative Review," *Psychological Bulletin,* May 2001, pp 376–407.

[98]Results can be found in ibid.

[99]One example is provided by D J Schleicher, J D Watt, and G J Greguras, "Reexamining the Job Satisfaction–Performance Relationship: The Complexity of Attitudes," *Journal of Applied Psychology,* February 2004, pp 165–77.

[100]These issues are discussed by C Ostroff, "The Relationship between Satisfaction, Attitudes, and Performance: An Organizational Level Analysis," *Journal of Applied Psychology,* December 1992, pp 963–74.

[101]Results can be found in J K Harter, F L Schmidt, and T L Hayes, "Business-Unit-Level Relationship between Employee Satisfaction, Employee Engagement, and Business Outcomes: A Meta-Analysis," *Journal of Applied Psychology,* April 2002, pp 268–79.

[102]Excerpted from E White, "New Recipe: To Keep Employees, Domino's Decides It's Not All about Pay," *The Wall Street Journal,* February 17, 2005. Reprinted by permission of Dow Jones & Co Inc. via The Copyright Clearance Center.

[103]This exercise was based on material contained in D N Sull and D Houlder, "Do Your Commitments Match Your Convictions?" *Harvard Business Review,* January 2005, pp 82–91.

[104]The matrix was developed by ibid.

[105]This exercise was based on S M Dunphy and K E Aupperle, "Flight Plan: Motivation," *Training & Development,* October 2001, pp 18–19.

[106]Excerpted from M Schneider, "How an MBA Can Bend Your Mind," *BusinessWeek,* April 1, 2002, p 12.

CHAPTER 7

[1]Excerpted from C Bush, "Image Is Everything in Workplace," *Arizona Republic,* January 30, 2005, p EC1. Copyright © 2005. Reprinted by permission of the author.

[2]Excerpted from C Daniels, "Women vs. Wal-Mart," *Fortune,* July 21, 2003, p 80.

[3]S T Fiske and S E Taylor, *Social Cognition,* 2nd ed (Reading, MA: Addison-Wesley Publishing, 1991), pp 1–2.

[4]The negativity bias was examined and supported by O Ybarra and W G Stephan, "Misanthropic Person Memory," *Journal of Personality and Social Psychology,* April 1996, pp 691–700.

[5]E Rosch, C B Mervis, W D Gray, D M Johnson, and P Boyes-Braem, "Basic Objects in Natural Categories," *Cognitive Psychology,* July 1976, p 383.

[6]Washing clothes.

[7]Results can be found in M Rotundo, D-H Nguyen, and P R Sackett, "A Meta-Analytic Review of Gender Differences in Perceptions of Sexual Harassment," *Journal of Applied Psychology,* October 2001, pp 914–22.

[8]See J Halberstadt, "Featural Shift in Explanation-Biased Memory for Emotional Faces," *Journal of Personality and Social Psychology,* January 2005, pp 38–49.

[9]See A J Kinicki, P W Hom, M R Trost, and K J Wade, "Effects of Category Prototypes on Performance-Rating Accuracy," *Journal of Applied Psychology,* June 1995, pp 354–70.

[10]The relationship between depression and information processing is discussed by A Zelli and K A Dodge, "Personality Development from the Bottom Up," in *The Coherence of Personality,* eds D Cervone and Y Shoda (New York: Guilford Press, 1999), pp 94–126.

[11]For a thorough discussion about the structure and organization of memory, see L R Squire, B Knowlton, and G Musen, "The Structure and Organization of Memory," in *Annual Review of Psychology,* eds L W Porter and M R Rosenzweig (Palo Alto, CA: Annual Reviews Inc., 1993), vol. 44, pp 453–95.

[12]A study of the retrieval process was conducted by L K Libby, R P Eibach, and T Gilovich, "Here's Looking at Me: The Effect of Memory Perspectives on Assessments of Personal Change," *Journal of Personality and Social Psychology,* January 2005, pp 50–62.

[13]This statistic was provided by L G Otting, "Don't Rush to Judgment," *HR Magazine,* January 2004, pp 95–97.

[14]Results can be found in C M Marlowe, S L Schneider, and C E Nelson, "Gender and Attractiveness Biases in Hiring Decisions: Are More Experienced Managers Less Biased?" *Journal of Applied Psychology,* February 1996, pp 11–21.

[15]Details of this study can be found in C K Stevens, "Antecedents of Interview Interactions, Interviewers' Ratings, and Applicants' Reactions," *Personnel Psychology,* Spring 1998, pp 55–85.

[16]See R C Mayer and J H Davis, "The Effect of the Performance Appraisal System on Trust for Management: A Field Quasi-Experiment," *Journal of Applied Psychology,* February 1999, pp 123–36. Also see R P Wright, "Mapping Cognitions to Better Understand Attitudinal and Behavioral Responses in Appraisal Research," *Journal of Organizational Behavior,* May 2004, pp 339–74.

[17]Results can be found in W H Bommer, J L Johnson, G A Rich, P M Podsakoff, and S B Mackenzie, "On the Interchangeability of Objective and Subjective Measures of Employee Performance: A Meta-Analysis," *Personnel Psychology,* Autumn 1995, pp 587–605.

[18]See J I Sanchez and P D L Torre, "A Second Look at the Relationship between Rating and Behavioral Accuracy in Performance Appraisal," *Journal of Applied Psychology,* February 1996, pp 3–10.

[19]The effectiveness of rater training was supported by D V Day and L M Sulsky, "Effects of Frame-of-Reference Training and Information Configuration on Memory Organization and Rating Accuracy," *Journal of Applied Psychology,* February 1995, pp 158–67.

[20]Leadership schema are discussed by B V Knippenberg and D V Knippenberg, "Leader Self-Sacrifice and Leadership Effectiveness: The Moderating Role of Leader Prototypicality," *Journal of Applied Psychology,* January 2005, pp 25–37; and O Epitropaki and R Martin, "Implicit Leadership Theories in Applied Settings: Factor Structure, Generalizability, and Stability over Time," *Journal of Applied Psychology,* April 2004, pp 239–310.

[21]Results can be found in J S Phillips and R G Lord, "Schematic Information Processing and Perceptions of Leadership in Problem-Solving Groups," *Journal of Applied Psychology,* August 1982, pp 486–92.

[22]J Ewing, "Wal-Mart: Local Pipsqueak," *BusinessWeek,* April 11, 2005, p 54.

[23]S Power, "Mickey Mouse, Nike Give Advice on Air Security," *The Wall Street Journal,* January 24, 2002, p B4.

[24]C M Judd and B Park, "Definition and Assessment of Accuracy in Social Stereotypes," *Psychological Review,* January 1993, p 110.

[25]For a thorough discussion of stereotype accuracy, see M C Ashton and V M Esses, "Stereotype Accuracy: Estimating the Academic Performance of Ethnic Groups," *Personality and Social Psychology Bulletin,* February 1999, pp 225–36.

[26]Results can be found in E H James, "Race-Related Differences in Promotions and Support: Underlying Effects of Human and Social Capital," *Organization Science,* September–October 2000, pp 493–508.

[27]The study was conducted by K S Lyness and D E Thompson, "Climbing the Corporate Ladder: Do Female and Male Executives Follow the Same Route?" *Journal of Applied Psychology,* February 2000, pp 86–101.

[28]The process of stereotype formation and maintenance is discussed by S T Fiske, M Lin, and S L Neuberg, "The Continuum Model: Ten Years Later," in *Dual-Process Theories in Social Psychology,* eds S Chaiken and Y Trope (New York: Guilford Press, 1999) pp 231–54.

[29]This discussion is based on material presented in G V Bodenhausen, C N Macrae, and J W Sherman, "On the Dialectics of Discrimination," in *Dual-Process Theories in Social Psychology,* eds S Chaiken and Y Trope (New York: Guilford Press, 1999) pp 271–90.

[30]Results are reported in "USA Today Snapshots®," *USA Today,* March 14, 2001, p 5D.

[31]Supportive results can be found in J T Jost and A C Kay, "Exposure to Benevolent Sexism and Complementary Gender Stereotypes: Consequences for Specific and Diffuse Forms of System Justification," *Journal of Personality and Social Psychology,* March 2005, pp 498–509.

[32]M Barrier, "Should Looks Count?" *HR Magazine,* September 2004, p 68.

[33]See J D Olian, D P Schwab, and Y Haberfeld, "The Impact of Applicant Gender Compared to Qualifications on Hiring Recommendations: A Meta-Analysis of Experimental Studies," *Organizational Behavior and Human Decision Processes,* April 1988, pp 180–95.

[34]Results from the meta-analyses are discussed in K P Carson, C L Sutton, and P D Corner, "Gender Bias in Performance Appraisals: A Meta-Analysis," paper presented at the 49th Annual Academy of Management Meeting, Washington, DC: 1989. Results from the field study can be found in T J Maurer and M A Taylor, "Is Sex by Itself Enough? An Exploration of Gender Bias Issues in Performance Appraisal," *Organizational Behavior and Human Decision Processes,* November 1994, pp 231–51.

[35]See J Landau, "The Relationship of Race and Gender to Managers' Ratings of Promotion Potential," *Journal of Organizational Behavior,* July 1995, pp 391–400.

[36]Results from this study can be found in M Biernat, C S Crandall, L V Young, D Kobrynowicz, and S M Halpin, "All That You Can Be: Stereotyping of Self and Others in a Military Context," *Journal of Personality and Social Psychology,* August 1998, pp 301–17.

[37]The negative effects of sex-role stereotypes were also uncovered by T K Vescio, S J Gervais, M Snyder, and A Hoover, "Power and the Creation of Patronizing Environments: The Stereotype-Based Behaviors of the Powerful and Their Effects on Female Performance in Masculine Domains," *Journal of Personality and Social Psychology,* April 2005, pp 658–72; and P G Davies, S J Spencer, and C M Steele, "Clearing the Air: Identity Safety Moderates the Effects of Stereotype Threat on Women's Leadership Aspirations," *Journal of Personality and Social Psychology,* February 2005, pp 276–87.

[38]For a complete review, see S R Rhodes, "Age-Related Differences in Work Attitudes and Behavior: A Review and Conceptual Analysis," *Psychological Bulletin,* March 1983, pp 328–67.

[39]Results were reported in E Kaplan-Leiserson, "Aged to Perfection," *Training & Development,* October 2001, pp 16–17.

[40]See G M McEvoy, "Cumulative Evidence of the Relationship between Employee Age and Job Performance," *Journal of Applied Psychology,* February 1989, pp 11–17.

[41]A thorough discussion of the relationship between age and performance is contained in D A Waldman and B J Avolio, "Aging and Work Performance in Perspective: Contextual and Developmental Considerations," in *Research in Personnel and Human Resources Management,* ed G R Ferris (Greenwich, CT: JAI Press, 1993), vol. 11, pp 133–62.

[42]For details, see B J Avolio, D A Waldman, and M A McDaniel, "Age and Work Performance in Nonmanagerial Jobs: The Effects of Experience and Occupational Type," *Academy of Management Journal,* June 1990, pp 407–22.

[43]D H Powell, "Aging Baby Boomers: Stretching Your Workforce Options," *HR Magazine,* July 1998, p 83.

[44]K Helliker, "The Doctor Is Still in: Secrets of Health from a Famed 96-Year-Old Physician," *The Wall Street Journal,* March 8, 2005, p D1.

[45]Results can be found in R W Griffeth, P W Hom, and S Gaertner, "A Meta-Analysis of Antecedents and Correlates of Employee Turnover: Update, Moderator Tests, and Research Implications for the Next Millennium," *Journal of Management,* 2000, pp 463–88.

[46]See J J Martocchio, "Age-Related Differences in Employee Absenteeism: A Meta-Analysis," *Psychology and Aging,* December 1989, pp 409–14.

[47]Racial stereotypes are studied and discussed by J K Maner, D T Kenrick, V D Becker, T E Robertson, B Hofer, and S Neuberg, "Functional Projection: How Fundamental Social Motives Can Bias Interpersonal Perception," *Journal of Personality and Social Psychology,* January 2005, pp 63–78; and N London-Vargas, *Faces of Diversity* (New York: Vantage Press, 1999).

[48]See J L Eberhardt, "Imaging Race," *American Psychologist,* February 2005, pp 181–90.

[49]Summaries of this research can be found in M Greer, "Automatic Racial Stereotyping Appears Based on Facial Features in Addition to Race," *Monitor on Psychology,* January 2005, p 14; and L Winerman, "Racial Stereotypes Can Speed Visual Processing," *Monitor on Psychology,* January 2005, p 15.

[50]This information was obtained from the official Web site of Tiger Woods, www.tigerwoods.com/home_custom/default,sps?itype=6596, accessed March 18, 2005.

[51]Details of the study on race and attitudes may be found in J H Greenhaus, S Parasuraman, and W M Wormley, "Effects of Race on Organizational Experiences, Job Performance Evaluations, and Career Outcomes," *Academy of Management Journal,* March 1990, pp 64–86.

[52]Results from these studies can be found in A I Huffcutt and P L Roth, "Racial Group Differences in Employment Interview Evaluations," *Journal of Applied Psychology,* April 1998, pp 179–89; and T-R Lin, G H Dobbins, and J-L Farh, "A Field

Study of Race and Age Similarity Effects on Interview Ratings in Conventional and Situational Interviews," *Journal of Applied Psychology*, June 1992, pp 363–71.

[53]See D A Waldman and B J Avolio, "Race Effects in Performance Evaluations: Controlling for Ability, Education, and Experience," *Journal of Applied Psychology*, December 1991, pp 897–901; and E D Pulakos, L A White, S H Oppler, and W C Borman, "Examination of Race and Sex Effects on Performance Ratings," *Journal of Applied Psychology*, October 1989, pp 770–80.

[54]Results can be found in Landau, "The Relationship of Race and Gender to Managers' Ratings of Promotion Potential."

[55]C M Schall, "The Americans with Disabilities Act—Are We Keeping Our Promise? An Analysis of the Effect of the ADA on the Employment of Persons with Disabilities," *Journal of Vocational Rehabilitation*, June 1998, p 191.

[56]Statistics on disabilities can be found in "Table 2. Labor Force Status—Work Disability Status of Civilians 16 to 74 Years Old, by Educational Attainment and Sex: 2001," March 2001, www.census.gov/hhes/www/disable/cps/cps201.html.

[57]Disability stereotypes are discussed by A Colella, "Organizational Socialization of Newcomers with Disabilities: A Framework for Future Research," in *Research in Personnel and Human Resources Management*, ed G R Ferris (Greenwich, CT: JAI Press, 1996), vol. 14, pp 351–417.

[58]The ADA and its associated accommodation requirements are discussed by D Cadrain, "Advocates for the Disabled Seek Overhaul of ADA," *HR Magazine*, February 2005, pp 27–31; and M G Danaher, "Accommodation Does Not Prove 'Regarded as' Claim," *HR Magazine*, February 2005, p 115.

[59]The discussion about the performance of disabled employees and the costs of their employment was based on P Digh, "People with Disabilities Show What They Can Do," *HR Magazine*, June 1998, pp 141–45.

[60]See Day and Sulsky, "Effects of Frame-of-Reference Training and Information Configuration on Memory Organization and Rating Accuracy."

[61]The background and results for this study are presented in R Rosenthal and L Jacobson, *Pygmalion in the Classroom: Teacher Expectation and Pupils' Intellectual Development* (New York: Holt, Rinchart & Winston, 1968).

[62]D B McNatt, "Ancient Pygmalion Joins Contemporary Management: A Meta-Analysis of the Result," *Journal of Applied Psychology*, April 2000, pp 314–22. Also see L Aaronson, "Two Beliefs Are Stronger than One," *Psychology Today*, April 2005, p 30; and P Tierney and S M Farmer, "The Pygmalion Process and Employee Creativity," *Journal of Management*, 2004, pp 413–32.

[63]A summary of the samples used in past research is contained in N M Kierein and M A Gold, "Pygmalion in Work Organizations: A Meta-Analysis," *Journal of Organizational Behavior*, December 2000, pp 913–28.

[64]The Golem effect is defined and investigated by O B Davidson and D Eden, "Remedial Self-Fulfilling Prophecy: Two Field Experiments to Prevent Golem Effects among Disadvantaged Women," *Journal of Applied Psychology*, June 2000, pp 386–98.

[65]The role of self-expectations in this process are discussed and tested by D B McNatt and T A Judge, "Boundary Conditions of the Galatea Effect: A Field Experiment and Constructive Replication," *Academy of Management Journal*, August 2004, pp 550–65.

[66]The role of positive expectations at Microsoft is discussed by S Hamm and O Port, "The Mother of All Software Projects," *BusinessWeek*, February 22, 1999, pp 69, 72.

[67]Pygmalion leadership training is discussed by D Eden, D Geller, A Gewirtz, R Gordon-Terner, I Inbar, M Liberman, Y Pass, I Salomon-Segev, and M Shalit, "Implanting Pygmalion Leadership Style through Workshop Training: Seven Field Experiments," *Leadership Quarterly*, Summer 2000, pp 171–210.

[68]Kelley's model is discussed in detail in H H Kelley, "The Processes of Causal Attribution," *American Psychologist*, February 1973, pp 107–28.

[69]See A Valenzuela, J Srivastava, and S Lee, "The Role of Cultural Orientation in Bargaining under Incomplete Information: Differences in Causal Attributions," *Organizational Behavior and Human Decision Processes*, January 2005, pp 72–88; and S Taggar and M Neubert, "The Impact of Poor Performers on Team Outcomes: An Empirical Examination of Attribution Theory," *Personnel Psychology*, Winter 2004, pp 935–68.

[70]Examples can be found in A C Morales, "Giving Firms an 'E' for Effort: Consumer Responses to High-Effort Firms," *Journal of Consumer Research*, March 2005, pp 806–12; and J Cotte, R A Coulter, and M Moore, "Enhancing or Disrupting Guilt: The Role of Ad Credibility and Perceived Manipulation Intent," *Journal of Business Research*, March 2005, pp 361–68.

[71]Results from these studies can be found in D A Hofmann and A Stetzer, "The Role of Safety Climate and Communication in Accident Interpretation: Implications for Learning from Negative Events," *Academy of Management Journal*, December 1998, pp 644–57; and I Choi, R E Nisbett, and A Norenzayan, "Causal Attribution across Cultures: Variation and Universality," *Psychological Bulletin*, January 1999, pp 47–63.

[72]Results can be found in E Cowley, "Views from Consumers Next in Line: The Fundamental Attribution Error in a Service Setting," *Academy of Marketing Science Journal*, Spring 2005, pp 139–52.

[73]D Bickley, "Russians Won't Stop Whining," *Arizona Republic*, February 23, 2002, p C1.

[74]Results can be found in E W K Tsang, "Self-Serving Attributions in Corporate Annual Reports: A Replicated Study." *Journal of Management Studies*, January 2002, pp 51–65.

[75]This research is summarized by T S Duval and P J Silvia, "Self-Awareness, Probability of Improvement, and the Self-Serving Bias," *Journal of Personality and Social Psychology*, January 2002, pp 49–61.

[76]Ibid., p 58.

[77]Details may be found in S E Moss and M J Martinko, "The Effects of Performance Attributions and Outcome Dependence on Leader Feedback Behavior following Poor Subordinate Performance," *Journal of Organizational Behavior,* May 1998, pp 259–74; and E C Pence, W C Pendelton, G H Dobbins, and J A Sgro, "Effects of Causal Explanations and Sex Variables on Recommendations for Corrective Actions following Employee Failure," *Organizational Behavior and Human Performance,* April 1982, pp 227–40.

[78]See D Konst, R Vonk, and R V D Vlist, "Inferences about Causes and Consequences of Behavior of Leaders and Subordinates," *Journal of Organizational Behavior,* March 1999, pp 261–71.

[79]See M Miserandino, "Attributional Retraining as a Method of Improving Athletic Performance," *Journal of Sport Behavior,* August 1998, pp 286–97.

[80]Excerpted from C Hymowitz, "Top Executives Chase Youthful Appearance, but Miss Real Issue," *The Wall Street Journal,* February 17, 2004, p B1. Reprinted by permission of Dow Jones & Co. Inc. via The Copyright Clearance Center.

[81]This exercise was modified and reprinted with permission from one contained in L Gardenwartz and A Rowe, *Diverse Teams at Work: Capitalizing on the Power of Diversity,* published by the Society for Human Resource Management, Alexandria, VA.

[82]The worksheet was adapted from ibid, p 169.

[83]Excerpted from Jason Leopold, "En-Ruse? Workers at Enron Say They Posed as Busy Traders to Impress Visiting Analysts," *The Wall Street Journal,* February 17, 2002, p C1. Reprinted by permission of Dow Jones & Co. Inc. via The Copyright Clearance Center.

CHAPTER 8

[1]Excerpted from S Bates, "Getting Engaged," *HR Magazine,* February 2004, pp 49–50. Copyright 2004 by Society for Human Resource Management. Reprinted with permission of HR Magazine published by the Society for Human Resource Management, Alexandria, VA.

[2]T R Mitchell, "Motivation: New Direction for Theory, Research, and Practice," *Academy of Management Review,* January 1982, p 81.

[3]A review of content and process theories of motivation is provided by R M Steers, R T Mowday, and D L Shapiro, "The Future of Work Motivation Theory," *Academy of Management Review,* July 2004, pp 379–87.

[4]For a complete description of Maslow's theory, see A H Maslow, "A Theory of Human Motivation," *Psychological Review,* July 1943, pp 370–96.

[5]See A Fisher, "Wipro Plays Cupid for Lonely Workers," *Fortune,* May 2, 2005, p 26; and K Maher, "Popular . . . but Cheap," *The Wall Street Journal,* January 24, 2005, p R4.

[6]For a complete review of ERG theory, see C P Alderfer, *Existence, Relatedness, and Growth: Human Needs in Organizational Settings* (New York: Free Press, 1972).

[7]See ibid., and J P Wanous and A Zwany, "A Cross-Sectional Test of Need Hierarchy Theory," *Organizational Behavior and Human Performance,* February 1977, pp 78–97.

[8]See S Glazer, "Past, Present and Future of Cross-Cultural Studies in Industrial and Organizational Psychology," in *International Review of Industrial and Organizational Psychology,* vol. 17, eds C L Cooper and I T Robertson (West Sussex, England: John Wiley, 2002), pp 145–86.

[9]L Buchanan, "Managing One-to-One," *Inc.,* October 2001, p 87.

[10]H A Murray, *Explorations in Personality* (New York: John Wiley & Sons, 1938), p 164.

[11]See K G Shaver, "The Entrepreneurial Personality Myth," *Business and Economic Review,* April/June 1995, pp 20–23.

[12]See the discussion in "Can't We All Just Get Along?" *HR Magazine,* April 2005, p 16.

[13]See the following series of research reports: D K McNeese-Smith, "The Relationship between Managerial Motivation, Leadership, Nurse Outcomes and Patient Satisfaction," *Journal of Organizational Behavior,* March 1999, pp 243–59; A M Harrell and M J Stahl, "A Behavioral Decision Theory Approach for Measuring McClelland's Trichotomy of Needs," *Journal of Applied Psychology,* April 1981, pp 242–47; and M J Stahl, "Achievement, Power and Managerial Motivation: Selecting Managerial Talent with the Job Choice Exercise," *Personnel Psychology,* Winter 1983, pp 775–89.

[14]For a review of the foundation of achievement motivation training, see D C McClelland, "Toward a Theory of Motive Acquisition," *American Psychologist,* May 1965, pp 321–33. Evidence for the validity of motivation training can be found in H Heckhausen and S Krug, "Motive Modification," in *Motivation and Society,* ed A J Stewart (San Francisco: Jossey-Bass, 1982).

[15]Results can be found in D B Turban and T L Keon, "Organizational Attractiveness: An Interactionist Perspective," *Journal of Applied Psychology,* April 1993, pp 184–93.

[16]See D Steele Johnson and R Perlow, "The Impact of Need for Achievement Components on Goal Commitment and Performance," *Journal of Applied Social Psychology,* November 1992, pp 1711–20.

[17]See F Herzberg, B Mausner, and B B Snyderman, *The Motivation to Work* (New York: John Wiley & Sons, 1959).

[18]For an application, see D Lacy, "Recordkeeping, Social Security, Recognition," *HR Magazine,* March 2005, pp 43–44.

[19]Excerpted from M Conlin and A Bernstein, "Working . . . and Poor," *BusinessWeek,* May 31, 2004, p 60.

[20]F Herzberg, "One More Time: How Do You Motivate Employees?" *Harvard Business Review,* January–February 1968, p 56.

[21] For a thorough review of research on Herzberg's theory, see C C Pinder, *Work Motivation: Theory, Issues, and Applications* (Glenview, IL: Scott, Foresman, 1984).

[22] Results can be found in P Babcock, "Find What Workers Want," *HR Magazine,* April 2005, pp 51–56.

[23] The generalizability of the equity norm was examined by L K Scheer, N A Kumar, J-B E M Steenkamp, "Reactions to Perceived Inequity in US and Dutch Interorganizational Relationships," *Academy of Management Journal,* June 2003, pp 303–16.

[24] The choice of a comparison person is discussed by E E Umphress, G Labianca, D J Brass, E Kass, and L Scholten, "The Role of Instrumental and Expressive Social Ties in Employees' Perceptions of Organizational Justice," *Organization Science,* November–December 2003, pp 738–53.

[25] These data were obtained from L Lavelle, "A Payday for Performance," *BusinessWeek,* April 18, 2005, pp 78–80.

[26] M N Bing and S M Burroughs, "The Predictive and Interactive Effects of Equity Sensitivity in Teamwork-Oriented Organizations," *Journal of Organizational Behavior,* May 2001, p 271.

[27] Types of equity sensitivity are discussed by ibid., pp 271–90; and K S Sauley and A G Bedeian, "Equity Sensitivity: Construction of a Measure and Examination of Its Psychometric Properties," *Journal of Management,* 2000, pp 885–910.

[28] For a thorough review of organizational justice theory and research, see R Cropanzano, D E Rupp, C J Mohler, and M Schminke, "Three Roads to Organizational Justice," in *Research in Personnel and Human Resources Management,* vol. 20, eds G R Ferris (New York: JAI Press, 2001), pp 269–329.

[29] J A Colquitt, D E Conlon, M J Wesson, C O L H Porter, and K Y Ng, "Justice at the Millennium: A Meta-Analytic Review of 25 Years of Organizational Justice Research," *Journal of Applied Psychology,* June 2001, p 426.

[30] E Tahmincioglu, "Electronic Workplace Vulnerable to Revenge," *Arizona Republic,* August 6, 2001, p D1.

[31] Results from these two studies can be found in Y Cohen-Charash and P E Spector, "The Role of Justice in Organizations: A Meta-Analysis," *Organizational Behavior and Human Decision Processes,* November 2001, pp 278–321; and Colquitt, Conlon, Wesson, Porter, and Ng, "Justice at the Millennium."

[32] For recent studies that support the impact of justice on employee attitudes see A G Tekleab, R Takeuchi, and M S Taylor, "Extending the Chain of Relationships among Organizational Justice, Social Exchange, and Employee Reactions: The Role of Contract Violations," *Academy of Management Journal,* February 2005, pp 146–57; and D D Cremer, B van Knippenberg, D van Knippenberg, D Mullenders, and F Stinglhamber, "Rewarding Leadership and Fair Procedures as Determinants of Self-Esteem," *Journal of Applied Psychology,* January 2005, pp 3–12.

[33] R C Ford, "Darden Restaurants CEO Joe Lee on the Impact of Core Values: Integrity and Fairness," *Academy of Management Executive,* February 2002, p 35.

[34] Results from this study are discussed in K Mollica, "Perceptions of Fairness," *HR Magazine,* June 2004, pp 169–78.

[35] The role of voice in justice perceptions was investigated by D R Avery and M A Quiñones, "Disentangling the Effects of Voice: The Incremental Roles of Opportunity, Behavior, and Instrumentality in Predicting Procedural Fairness," *Journal of Applied Psychology,* February 2002, pp 81–86.

[36] Supporting studies were conducted by D P Skarlicki, R Folger, and P Tesluk, "Personality as a Moderator in the Relationship between Fairness and Retaliation," *Academy of Management Journal,* February 1999, pp 100–8.

[37] Supportive results can be found in P A Siegel, C Post, J Brockner, A Y Fishman, and C Garden, "The Moderating Influence of Procedural Fairness on the Relationship between Work-Life Conflict and Organizational Commitment," *Journal of Applied Psychology,* January 2005, 13–24; and T A Judge and J A Colquitt, "Organizational Justice and Stress: The Mediating Role of Work-Family Conflict," *Journal of Applied Psychology,* June 2004, pp 395–404.

[38] The impact of groups on justice perceptions was investigated by D A Jones and D P Skarlicki, "The Effects of Overhearing Peers to Discuss an Authority's Fairness Reputation on Reactions to Subsequent Treatment," *Journal of Applied Psychology,* March 2005, pp 363–72; and J A Colquitt, "Does the Justice of the One Interact with the Justice of the Many? Reactions to Procedural Justice in Teams," *Journal of Applied Psychology,* August 2004, pp 633–46.

[39] Climate for justice was studied by H Liao and D E Rupp, "The Impact of Justice Climate and Justice Orientation on Work Outcomes: A Cross-Level Multifoci Framework," *Journal of Applied Psychology,* March 2005, pp 242–56.

[40] The relationship between organizational justice and customer service is discussed by D E Bowen, S W Gilliland, and R Folger, "HRM Service Fairness: How Being Fair with Employees Spills over to Customers," *Organizational Dynamics,* Winter 1999, pp 7–23.

[41] For a complete discussion of Vroom's theory, see V H Vroom, *Work and Motivation* (New York: John Wiley & Sons, 1964).

[42] E E Lawler III, *Motivation in Work Organizations* (Belmont, CA: Wadsworth, 1973), p 45.

[43] See J Chowdhury, "The Motivational Impact of Sales Quotas on Effort," *Journal of Marketing Research,* February 1993, pp 28–41; and C C Pinder, *Work Motivation* (Glenview, IL: Scott, Foresman, 1984), Ch 7.

[44] This issue is discussed by R Grover and A Bernstein, "Arnold Gets Strict with the Teachers," *BusinessWeek,* May 2, 2005, pp 84–85; and A Bernstein, "Up the Down Staircase—Warily," *BusinessWeek,* April 25, 2005, p 14.

[45] The measurement and importance of valence was investigated by N T Feather, "Values, Valences, and Choice: The Influence of Values on the Perceived Attractiveness and Choice of Alternatives," *Journal of Personality and Social Psychology,* June 1995, pp 1135–51; and A Pecotich and G A Churchill Jr, "An Examination of the Anticipated-Satisfaction Importance

Valence Controversy," *Organizational Behavior and Human Performance,* April 1981, pp 213–26.

[46]"Federal Express's Fred Smith," *Inc.,* October 1986, p 38.

[47]Results can be found in W van Eerde and H Thierry, "Vroom's Expectancy Models and Work-Related Criteria: A Meta-Analysis," *Journal of Applied Psychology,* October 1996, pp 575–86.

[48]See J P Wanous, T L Keon, and J C Latack, "Expectancy Theory and Occupational/Organizational Choices: A Review and Test," *Organizational Behavior and Human Performance,* August 1983, pp 66–86.

[49]See the discussion in T R Mitchell and D Daniels, "Motivation," in *Handbook of Psychology,* vol. 12, eds W C Borman, D R Ilgen, and R J Klimoski (Hoboken, NJ: John Wiley & Sons, Inc., 2003), pp 225–54.

[50]The pros and cons of pay for performance systems are discussed by "Many Companies Don't Do Enough to Benefit from Performance-Based Pay Plans," http://was4.hewitt.com/hewitt/resource/newsroom/pressrel/2004/05-05-04.htm, accessed April 15, 2005; and "Many Companies Fail to Achieve Success with Pay-for-Performance Programs," http://was4.hewitt.com/hewitt/resource/newsroom/pressrel/2004/06-09-04.htm, accessed April 15, 2005.

[51]Excerpted from E Tahmincioglu, "Gifts That Gall," *Workforce Management,* April 2004, p 44.

[52]E A Locke, K N Shaw, L M Saari, and G P Latham, "Goal Setting and Task Performance: 1969–1980," *Psychological Bulletin,* July 1981, p 126.

[53]See "100 Best Companies to Work For," *Fortune,* January 12, 2004, p 70.

[54]Annika Sorenstam's biography can be found at www.lpga.com/player-career.aspx?id=29, accessed April 27, 2005.

[55]J Davis, "For Now, Sorenstam Feels She Still Has Peaks to Scale," *Arizona Republic,* March 18, 2004, p C14.

[56]Results can be found in P M Wright, "Operationalization of Goal Difficulty as a Moderator of the Goal Difficulty-Performance Relationship," *Journal of Applied Psychology,* June 1990, pp 227–34. Also see G Seijts and G P Latham, "Learning versus Performance Goals: When Should Each Be Used?" *Academy of Management Executive,* February 2005, pp 124–31.

[57]Results from the meta-analysis can be found in R E Wood, A J Mento, and E A Locke, "Task Complexity as a Moderator of Goal Effects: A Meta-Analysis," *Journal of Applied Psychology,* August 1987, pp 416–25. The impact of time on goal specificity was discussed by Y Fried and L H Slowik, "Enriching Goal-Setting Theory with Time: An Integrated Approach," *Academy of Management Executive,* July 2004, pp 404–22.

[58]Supportive results can be found in K L Langeland, C M Johnson, and T C Mawhinney, "Improving Staff Performance in a Community Mental Health Setting: Job Analysis, Training, Goal Setting, Feedback, and Years of Data," *Journal of Organizational Behavior Management,* 1998, pp 21–43.

[59]See E A Locke and G P Latham, *A Theory of Goal Setting and Task Performance* (Englewood Cliffs, NJ: Prentice Hall, 1990).

[60]See J J Donovan and D J Radosevich, "The Moderating Role of Goal Commitment on the Goal Difficulty-Performance Relationship: A Meta-Analytic Review and Critical Reanalysis," *Journal of Applied Psychology,* April 1998, pp 308–15.

[61]Results can be found in G H Seijts and G P Latham, "The Effect of Distal Learning, Outcome, and Proximal Goals on a Moderately Complex Task," *Journal of Organizational Behavior,* May 2001, pp 291–307.

[62]See P M Wright, J M George, S R Farnsworth, and G C McMahan, "Productivity and Extra-Role Behavior: The Effects of Goals and Incentives on Spontaneous Helping," *Journal of Applied Psychology,* June 1993, pp 374–81.

[63]J L Bowditch and A F Buono, *A Primer on Organizational Behavior* (New York: John Wiley & Sons, 1985), p 210.

[64]This framework was proposed by M A Campion and P W Thayer, "Development and Field Evaluation of an Interdisciplinary Measure of Job Design," *Journal of Applied Psychology,* February 1985, pp 29–43.

[65]These outcomes are discussed by J R Edwards, J A Scully, and M D Brtek, "The Nature and Outcomes of Work: A Replication and Extension of Interdisciplinary Work-Design Research," *Journal of Applied Psychology,* December 2000, pp 860–68.

[66]G D Babcock, *The Taylor System in Franklin Management,* 2nd ed (New York: Engineering Magazine Company, 1917), p 31.

[67]For a thorough discussion, see F B Copley, *Frederick W Taylor: The Principles of Scientific Management* (New York: Harper & Brothers, 1911).

[68]Supporting results can be found in B Melin, U Lundberg, J Söderlund, and M Granqvist, "Psychological and Physiological Stress Reactions of Male and Female Assembly Workers: A Comparison between Two Different Forms of Work Organization," *Journal of Organizational Behavior,* January 1999, pp 47–61.

[69]For an example, see M Workman and W Bommer, "Redesigning Computer Call Center Work: A Longitudinal Field Experiment," *Journal of Organizational Behavior,* May 2004, pp 317–37.

[70]This type of program was developed and tested by M A Campion and C L McClelland, "Follow-Up and Extension of the Interdisciplinary Costs and Benefits of Enlarged Jobs," *Journal of Applied Psychology,* June 1993, pp 339–51.

[71]Excerpted from R J Grossman, "Putting HR in Rotation," *HR Magazine,* March 2003, p 53.

[72]J R Hackman, G R Oldham, R Janson, and K Purdy, "A New Strategy for Job Enrichment," *California Management Review,* Summer 1975, p 58.

[73]Definitions of the job characteristics were adapted from J R Hackman and G R Oldham, "Motivation through the Design of Work: Test of a Theory," *Organizational Behavior and Human Performance,* August 1976, pp 250–79.

[74]A review of this research can be found in M L Ambrose and C T Kulik, "Old Friends, New Faces: Motivation Research in the 1990s," *Journal of Management,* 1999, pp 231–92.

[75]This example was taken from R Levering and M Moskowitz, "The 100 Best Companies to Work For," *Fortune,* January 24, 2005, p 76.

[76]Research on autonomy was conducted by F P Morgeson, K Delaney-Klinger, and M A Hemingway, "The Importance of Job Autonomy, Cognitive Ability, and Job-Related Skill for Predicting Role Breadth and Job Performance," *Journal of Applied Psychology,* March 2005, pp 399–406; and C W Langfred and N A Moye, "Effects of Task Autonomy on Performance: An Extended Model Considering Motivational, Informational, and Structural Mechanisms," *Journal of Applied Psychology,* December 2004, pp 934–45.

[77]Results can be found in M R Kelley, "New Process Technology, Job Design, and Work Organization: A Contingency Model," *American Sociological Review,* April 1990, pp 191–208.

[78]Productivity studies are reviewed in R E Kopelman, *Managing Productivity in Organizations* (New York: McGraw-Hill, 1986).

[79]The turnover meta-analysis was conducted by R W Griffeth, P W Hom, and S Gaertner, "A Meta-Analysis of Antecedents and Correlates of Employee Turnover: Update, Moderator Tests, and Research Implications for the Next Millennium," *Journal of Management,* 2000, pp 463–88. Absenteeism results are discussed in Y Fried and G R Ferris, "The Validity of the Job Characteristics Model: A Review and Meta-Analysis," *Personnel Psychology,* Summer 1987, pp 287–322.

[80]See K Dobbs, "Knowing How to Keep Your Best and Brightest," *Workforce,* April 2001, pp 557–60.

[81]This description was taken from Edwards, Scully, and Britek, "The Nature and Outcomes of Work."

[82]S Armour, "Young Tech Workers Face Crippling Injuries," *USA Today,* February 9, 2001, p 2B.

[83]See R Malkin, S D Hudock, C Hayden, T J Lentz, J Topmiller, and R W Niemeier, "An Assessment of Occupational Safety and Health Hazards in Selected Small Business Manufacturing Wood Pallets—Part 1. Noise and Physical Hazards," *Journal of Occupational and Environmental Hygiene,* April 2005, pp D18–D21.

[84]These descriptions were excerpted from J Prichard, "Reinventing the Office," *Arizona Republic,* January 16, 2002, p D1.

[85]Armour, "Young Tech Workers Face Crippling Injuries," p 2B. A description of various repetitive motion injuries is presented by "What Is a Repetitive Motion Injury and Carpal Tunnel Syndrome?" www.gag.org/resources/rmi.php, accessed April 27, 2005.

[86]T R Mitchell, "Motivation: New Directions for Theory, Research, and Practice," *Academy of Management Review,* January 1982, p 81.

[87]Excerpted from D Patrick, "Summit Still Driven to Be Best," *USA Today,* March 15, 2005, p 2C.

[88]An example is provided by "Contented Employees Mean Satisfied Customers at Baptist Health Care," *Training,* January 2005, p 11.

[89]Elements of an effective appraisal system are discussed by C Joinson, "Making Sure Employees Measure Up," *HR Magazine,* March 2001, pp 36–41.

[90]C Hymowitz, "Ranking Systems Gain Popularity but Have Many Staffers Riled," *The Wall Street Journal,* May 15, 2001, p B1.

[91]See D J Burrough, "More Firms Rank Employees," *Arizona Republic,* May 20, 2001, p E1.

[92]"HMO Clerks Who Pare Doctor Visits Rewarded," *Arizona Republic,* May 18, 2002, p A10.

[93]See J Appleby, "HMO to Pay Bonuses for Good Care," *USA Today,* July 11, 2001, p 3B.

[94]The motivational effects of feedback are discussed by J W Smither, M London, and R R Reilly, "Does Performance Improve following Multisource Feedback? A Theoretical Model, Meta-Analysis, and Review of Empirical Findings," *Personnel Psychology,* Spring 2005, pp 33–66.

[95]Excerpted from P-W Tam and N Wingfield, "Silicon Volley: As Tech Matures, Workers File a Spate of Salary Complaints," *The Wall Street Journal,* February 24, 2005, pp A1, A11. Reprinted by permission of Dow Jones & Co. Inc. via The Copyright Clearance Center.

[96]Actual survey rankings are as follows: (1) interesting work, (2) full appreciation of work done, (3) feeling of being in on things, (4) job security, (5) good wages, (6) promotion and growth in the organization, (7) good working conditions, (8) personal loyalty to employees, (9) tactful discipline, and (10) sympathetic help with personal problems.

[97]The complete JDS can be found in J R Hackman and G R Oldham, *Work Redesign* (Reading, MA: Addison-Wesley, 1980).

[98]The JDS and its norms were adapted from Hackman and Oldham, *Work Redesign,* pp 280, 281, 317.

[99]Excerpted from M Whitehouse, "Closing the Deal: As Banks Bid for City Bond Work, 'Pay to Play' Tradition Endures," *The Wall Street Journal,* March 25, 2005, p A1. Reprinted by permission of Dow Jones & Co. Inc. via The Copyright Clearance Center.

CHAPTER 9

[1]L Buchanan, "For Knowing the Power of Respect," *Inc.,* April 2004, p 143. By Leigh Buchanan, © 2005 Gruner & Jahr USA Publishing. First published in *Inc.* Magazine. Reprinted with permission.

[2]B Tulgan, "The Under-Management Epidemic," *HR Magazine,* October 2004, p 119. Also see B Marcus and H Schuler, "Antecedents of Counterproductive Behavior at Work: A General Perspective," *Journal of Applied Psychology,* August 2004, pp 647–60; and J Malanowski, "Soul Assassins," *Fast Company,* May 2005, pp 85–89.

3See E E Lawler III, *Treat People Right! How Organizations and Individuals Can Propel Each Other into a Virtuous Spiral of Success* (San Francisco: Jossey-Bass, 2003); A Rossett and E Mohr, "Performance Support Tools: Where Learning, Work, and Results Converge," *Training & Development,* February 2004, pp 34–39; L A Weatherly, "Performance Management: Getting It Right from the Start," 2004 Research Quarterly, *HR Magazine,* March 2004, pp 1–11; D Robb, "Building a Better Workforce," *HR Magazine,* October 2004, pp 86–94; and A Kleingeld, H Van Tuijl, and J A Algera, "Participation in the Design of Performance Management Systems: A Quasi-Experimental Field Study," *Journal of Organizational Behavior,* November 2004, pp 831–51.

4This distinction is drawn from G P Latham, J Almost, S Mann, and C Moore, "New Developments in Performance Management," *Organizational Dynamics,* no. 1, 2005, pp 77–87.

5See G Johnson, "Room for Improvement," *Training,* December 2003, pp 18–19; P Falcone, "Watch What You Write," *HR Magazine,* November 2004, pp 125–28; K Ellis, "Individual Development Plans: The Building Blocks of Development," *Training,* December 2004, pp 20–25.

6As quoted in P B Brown, "What I Know Now," *Fast Company,* April 2005, p 104. Also see C Garvey, "The Next Generation of Hiring Metrics," *HR Magazine,* April 2005, 71–76.

7See B Cooper, "Training as an Operational Necessity," *Training,* April 2005, p 42; and K Tyler, "Training Revs Up," *HR Magazine,* April 2005, pp 58–63.

8Adapted and quoted from "ThermoSTAT," *Training,* July–August 2003, p 16.

9G H Seijts and G P Latham, "Learning versus Performance Goals: When Should Each Be Used?" *Academy of Management Executive,* February 2005, pp 126–27.

10A thorough discussion of MBO is provided by P F Drucker, *The Practice of Management* (New York: Harper, 1954); and P F Drucker, "What Results Should You Expect? A User's Guide to MBO," *Public Administration Review,* January–February 1976, pp 12–19.

11Results from both studies can be found in R Rodgers and J E Hunter, "Impact of Management by Objectives on Organizational Productivity," *Journal of Applied Psychology,* April 1991, pp 322–36; and R Rodgers, J E Hunter, and D L Rogers, "Influence of Top Management Commitment on Management Program Success," *Journal of Applied Psychology,* February 1993, pp 151–55.

12See J A Colquitt and M J Simmering, "Conscientiousness, Goal Orientation, and Motivation to Learn During the Learning Process: A Longitudinal Study," *Journal of Applied Psychology,* August 1998, pp 654–65.

13D VandeWalle, S P Brown, W L Cron, and J W Slocum Jr, "The Influence of Goal Orientation and Self-Regulated Tactics on Sales Performance: A Longitudinal Field Test," *Journal of Applied Psychology,* April 1999, p 250. Also see G H Seijts, G P Latham, K Tasa, and B W Latham, "Goal Setting and Goal Orientation: An Integration of Two Different yet Related Literatures," *Academy of Management Journal,* April 2004, pp 227–39.

14See D VandeWalle, "Goal Orientation: Why Wanting to Look Successful Doesn't Always Lead to Success," *Organizational Dynamics,* 2001, pp 162–71; and D VandeWalle, W L Cron, and J W Slocum Jr, "The Role of Goal Orientation Following Performance Feedback," *Journal of Applied Psychology,* August 2001, pp 629–40.

15See S Kerr and S Landauer, "Using Stretch Goals to Promote Organizational Effectiveness and Personal Growth: General Electric and Goldman Sachs," *Academy of Management Executive,* November 2004, pp 134–38.

16See E A Locke, "Linking Goals to Monetary Incentives," *Academy of Management Executive,* November 2004, pp 130–33.

17E A Locke and G P Latham, *Goal Setting: A Motivational Technique That Works!* (Englewood Cliffs, NJ: Prentice Hall, 1984), p 79.

18For more on goal setting, see G B Yeo and A Neal, "A Multilevel Analysis of Effort, Practice, and Performance: Effects of Ability, Conscientiousness, and Goal Orientation," *Journal of Applied Psychology,* April 2004, pp 231–47; Y Fried and L H Slowik, "Enriching Goal-Setting Theory with Time: An Integrated Approach," *Academy of Management Review,* July 2004, pp 404–22; E A Locke, "Guest Editor's Introduction: Goal-Setting Theory and Its Applications to the World of Business," *Academy of Management Executive,* November 2004, pp 124–25; G P Latham, "The Motivational Benefits of Goal-Setting," *Academy of Management Executive,* November 2004, pp 126–29; and K N Shaw, "Changing the Goal-Setting Process at Microsoft," *Academy of Management Executive,* November 2004, pp 139–42.

19K Tyler, "One Bad Apple," *HR Magazine,* December 2004, p 85.

20Data from "Fortune 500 Largest US Corporations," *Fortune,* April 18, 2005, p F58.

21As quoted in C Fishman, "Fred Smith," *Fast Company,* June 2001, p 66.

22C Bell and R Zemke, "On-Target Feedback," *Training,* June 1992, p 36. Also see R Zemke, "The Feather Factor: You Gotta Believe," *Training,* May 2002, p 10.

23Both the definition of feedback and the functions of feedback are based on discussion in D R Ilgen, C D Fisher, and M S Taylor, "Consequences of Individual Feedback on Behavior in Organizations," *Journal of Applied Psychology,* August 1979, pp 349–71; and R E Kopelman, *Managing Productivity in Organizations: A Practical People-Oriented Perspective* (New York: McGraw-Hill, 1986), p 175.

24See P C Earley, G B Northcraft, C Lee, and T R Lituchy, "Impact of Process and Outcome Feedback on the Relation of Goal Setting to Task Performance," *Academy of Management Journal,* March 1990, pp 87–105. Also see D VandeWalle, W L Cron, and J W Slocum Jr, "The Role of Goal Orientation following Performance Feedback," *Journal of Applied Psychology,* August 2001, pp 629–40; J S Goodman, R E Wood, and M Hendrickx, "Feedback Specificity, Exploration, and Learning," *Journal of Applied Psychology,* April 2004, pp 248–62; and J S Goodman and R E Wood, "Feedback

Specificity, Learning Opportunities, and Learning," *Journal of Applied Psychology,* October 2004, pp 809–21.

[25]Data from A N Kluger and A DeNisi, "The Effects of Feedback Interventions on Performance: A Historical Review, a Meta-Analysis, and a Preliminary Feedback Intervention Theory," *Psychological Bulletin,* March 1996, pp 254–84. Also see G Morse, "Feedback Backlash," *Harvard Business Review,* October 2004, p 28.

[26]Data from K D Harber, "Feedback to Minorities: Evidence of a Positive Bias," *Journal of Personality and Social Psychology,* March 1998, pp 622–28.

[27]See D M Herold and D B Fedor. "Individuals' Interaction with Their Feedback Environment: The Role of Domain-Specific Individual Differences," in *Research in Personnel and Human Resources Management,* vol. 16, ed G R Ferris (Stamford, CT: JAI Press, 1998), pp 215–54.

[28]See P E Levy, M D Albright, B D Cawley, and J R Williams, "Situational and Individual Determinants of Feedback Seeking: A Closer Look at the Process," *Organizational Behavior and Human Decision Processes,* April 1995, pp 23–37; M R Leary, E S Tambor, S K Terdal, and D L Downs, "Self-Esteem as an Interpersonal Monitor: The Sociometer Hypothesis," *Journal of Personality and Social Psychology,* June 1995, pp 518–30; and M A Quinones, "Pretraining Context Effects: Training Assignment as Feedback," *Journal of Applied Psychology,* April 1995, pp 226–38.

[29]See T Matsui, A Okkada, and T Kakuyama, "Influence of Achievement Need on Goal Setting, Performance, and Feedback Effectiveness," *Journal of Applied Psychology,* October 1982, pp 645–48.

[30]S J Ashford, "Feedback-Seeking in Individual Adaptation: A Resource Perspective," *Academy of Management Journal,* September 1986, pp 465–87. Also see D B Fedor, R B Rensvold, and S M Adams, "An Investigation of Factors Expected to Affect Feedback Seeking: A Longitudinal Field Study," *Personnel Psychology,* Winter 1992, pp 779–805; and M F Sully De Luque and S M Sommer, "The Impact of Culture on Feedback-Seeking Behavior: An Integrated Model and Propositions," *Academy of Management Review,* October 2000, pp 829–49.

[31]See D B Turban and T W Dougherty, "Role of Protege Personality in Receipt of Mentoring and Career Success," *Academy of Management Journal,* June 1994, pp 688–702. Also see M E Burkhardt, "Social Interaction Effects Following a Technological Change: A Longitudinal Investigation," *Academy of Management Journal,* August 1994, pp 869–98.

[32]See D M Herold, C K Parsons, and R B Rensvold, "Individual Differences in the Generation and Processing of Performance Feedback," *Educational and Psychological Measurement,* February 1996, pp 5–25.

[33]See B D Bannister, "Performance Outcome Feedback and Attributional Feedback: Interactive Effects on Recipient Responses," *Journal of Applied Psychology,* May 1986, pp 203–10; and J B Vancouver and E C Tischner, "The Effect of Feedback Sign on Task Performance Depends on Self-Concept Discrepancies," *Journal of Applied Psychology,* December 2004, pp 1092–98.

[34]For complete details, see P M Podsakoff and J-L Farh, "Effects of Feedback Sign and Credibility on Goal Setting and Task Performance," *Organizational Behavior and Human Decision Processes,* August 1989, pp 45–67. Also see S J Ashford and A S Tsui, "Self-Regulation for Managerial Effectiveness: The Role of Active Feedback Seeking," *Academy of Management Journal,* June 1991, pp 251–80.

[35]W S Silver, T R Mitchell, and M E Gist, "Responses to Successful and Unsuccessful Performance: The Moderating Effect of Self-Efficacy on the Relationship between Performance and Attributions," *Organizational Behavior and Human Decision Processes,* June 1995, p 297. Also see T A Louie, "Decision Makers' Hindsight Bias after Receiving Favorable and Unfavorable Feedback," *Journal of Applied Psychology,* February 1999, pp 29–41.

[36]J M Kouzes and B Z Posner, *Credibility: How Leaders Gain and Lose It, Why People Demand It* (San Francisco: Jossey-Bass, 1993), p 25. For recent research support, see A J Kinicki, G E Prussia, B Wu, and F M McKee-Ryan, "A Covariance Structure Analysis of Employees' Response to Performance Feedback," *Journal of Applied Psychology,* December 2004, pp 1057–69.

[37]See R B Jelley and R D Goffin, "Can Performance-Feedback Accuracy Be Improved? Effects of Rater Priming and Rating-Scale Format on Rating Accuracy," *Journal of Applied Psychology,* February 2001, pp 134–44; G L Graham, "If You Want Honesty, Break Some Rules," *Harvard Business Review,* April 2002, pp 42–47; S Aryee, P S Budhwar, and Z X Chen, "Trust as a Mediator of the Relationship between Organizational Justice and Work Outcomes: Test of a Social Exchange Model," *Journal of Organizational Behavior,* May 2002, pp 267–85.

[38]See S E Moss and M J Martinko, "The Effects of Performance Attributions and Outcome Dependence on Leader Feedback Behavior Following Poor Subordinate Performance," *Journal of Organizational Behavior,* May 1998, pp 259–74; and K Leung, S Su, and M W Morris, "When Is Criticism *Not* Constructive? The Roles of Fairness Perceptions and Dispositional Attributions in Employee Acceptance of Critical Supervisory Feedback," *Human Relations,* September 2001, pp 1123–54.

[39]Based on discussion in Ilgen, Fisher, and Taylor, "Consequences of Individual Feedback on Behavior in Organizations," pp 367–68. Also see A M O'Leary-Kelly, "The Influence of Group Feedback on Individual Group Member Response," in *Research in Personnel and Human Resources Management,* vol. 16, ed G R Ferris (Stamford, CT: JAI Press, 1998), pp 255–94.

[40]See P C Earley, "Computer-Generated Performance Feedback in the Magazine-Subscription Industry," *Organizational Behavior and Human Decision Processes,* February 1988, pp 50–64.

[41]See M De Gregorio and C D Fisher, "Providing Performance Feedback: Reactions to Alternate Methods," *Journal of Management,* December 1988, pp 605–16.

[42]For details, see R A Baron, "Countering the Effects of Destructive Criticism: The Relative Efficacy of Four Interventions," *Journal of Applied Psychology,* June 1990,

pp 235–45. Also see M L Smith, "Give Feedback, Not Criticism." *Supervisory Management,* February 1993, p 4.

43C O Longenecker and D A Gioia, "The Executive Appraisal Paradox," *Academy of Management Executive,* May 1992, p 18. Also see M D Cannon and R Witherspoon, "Actionable Feedback: Unlocking the Power of Learning and Performance Improvement," *Academy of Management Executive,* May 2005, pp 120–134; and S B Silverman, C E Pogson, and A B Cober, "When Employees at Work Don't Get It: A Model for Enhancing Individual Employee Change in Response to Performance Feedback," *Academy of Management Executive,* May 2005, pp 135–147.

44A Serwer, "The Education of Michael Dell," *Fortune,* March 7, 2005, p 76.

45H J Bernardin, S A Dahmus, and G Redmon, "Attitudes of First-Line Supervisors toward Subordinate Appraisals," *Human Resource Management,* Summer–Fall 1993, p 315.

46See L Atwater, P Roush, and A Fischthal, "The Influence of Upward Feedback on Self- and Follower Ratings of Leadership," *Personnel Psychology,* Spring 1995, pp 35–59; and J W Smither, M London, N L Vasilopoulos, R R Reilly, R E Millsap, and N Salvemini, "An Examination of the Effects of an Upward Feedback Program over Time," *Personnel Psychology,* Spring 1995, pp 1–34.

47See J J Salopek, "Rethinking Likert," *Training & Development,* September 2004, pp 26–29.

48J W Smither, M London, and R R Reilly, "Does Performance Improve following Multisource Feedback? A Theoretical Model, Meta-Analysis, and Review of Empirical Findings," *Personnel Psychology,* Spring 2005, p 33. Also see J W Smither and A G Walker, "Are the Characteristics of Narrative Comments Related to Improvements in Multirater Feedback Ratings over Time?" *Journal of Applied Psychology,* June 2004, pp 575–81; M A Korsgaard, B M Meglino, and S W Lester, "The Effect of Other Orientation on Self-Supervisor Rating Agreement," *Journal of Organizational Behavior,* November 2004, pp 873–91; and J E Bono and A E Colbert, "Understanding Responses to Multi-Source Feedback: The Role of Core Self-Evaluations," *Personnel Psychology,* Spring 2005, pp 171–203.

49D E Coates, "Don't Tie 360 Feedback to Pay," *Training,* September 1998, pp 68–78. Also see A S Wellner, "Everyone's a Critic," *Inc.,* July 2004, pp 38, 41; and W C Byham, "Fixing the Instrument," *Training,* July 2004, p 50.

50Data from "Fortune 500 Largest US Corporations," *Fortune,* April 18, 2005, pp F3, F48.

51For more, see Latham et al., "New Developments in Performance Management," p 83; M Goldsmith, "It's Not about the Coach," *Fast Company,* October 2004, p 120; T Estep, "Taming the Feedback Nightmare," *Training & Development,* November 2004, pp 71–72; S Sherman and A Freas, "The Wild West of Executive Coaching," *Harvard Business Review,* November 2004, pp 82–90; A Fisher, "Turn Star Employees into Superstars," *Fortune,* December 13, 2004, p 70; and R Underwood, "Are You Being Coached?" *Fast Company,* February 2005, pp 83–85.

52See L Grensing-Pophal, "Money Talks," *HR Magazine,* September 2004, pp 125–32; G Colvin, "Outraged over CEO Exit Packages? You're Too Late," *Fortune,* March 7, 2005, p 62; and G Strauss and B Hansen, "CEO Pay Packages 'Business as Usual,' " *USA Today,* March 31, 2005, pp 1B–2B.

53"The Stat," *BusinessWeek,* October 4, 2004, p 16.

54For example, see "Flatliners," *Training,* February 2005, p 12; B Schaefer, S Lau, and D Lacy, "Recordkeeping, Social Security, Recognition," *HR Magazine,* March 2005, pp 43–44; and D Cadrain, "Just Desserts," *HR Magazine,* March 2005, pp 97–100.

55See P Babcock, "Find What Workers Want," *HR Magazine,* April 2005, pp 50–56.

56List adapted from J L Pearce and R H Peters, "A Contradictory Norms View of Employer–Employee Exchange," *Journal of Management,* Spring 1985, pp 19–30. Also see C Garvey, "Philosophizing Compensation," *HR Magazine,* January 2005, pp 73–76.

57D Brady, "The Immelt Revolution," *BusinessWeek,* March 28, 2005, p 66.

58"The 100 Best Companies to Work For," *Fortune,* February 4, 2002, p 90.

59See E L Deci, R Koestner, and R M Ryan, "A Meta-Analytic Review of Experiments Examining the Effects of Extrinsic Rewards on Intrinsic Motivation," *Psychological Bulletin,* November 1999, pp 627–68; and R Eisenberger, W D Pierce, and J Cameron, "Effects of Reward on Intrinsic Motivation—Negative, Neutral, and Positive: Comment on Deci, Koestner, and Ryan (1999)." *Psychological Bulletin,* November 1999, pp 677–91.

60See K W Thomas, *Intrinsic Motivation at Work: Building Energy and Commitment* (San Francisco: Berrett-Koehler Publishers, 2000).

61See E L Deci and R M Ryan, "The 'What' and 'Why' of Goal Pursuits: Human Needs and Self-Determination of Behavior," *Psychological Inquiry,* December 2000, pp 227–68.

62This study is summarized by S Ellingwood, "On a Mission," *Gallup Management Journal,* Winter 2001, pp 6–7.

63M Littman, "Best Bosses Tell All," *Working Woman,* October 2000, p 55.

64Ibid., p 54.

65D R Spitzer, "Power Rewards: Rewards That Really Motivate," *Management Review,* May 1996, p 47. Also see S Kerr, "An Academy Classic: On the Folly of Rewarding A, while Hoping for B," *Academy of Management Executive,* February 1995, pp 7–14.

66List adapted from discussion in Spitzer, "Power Rewards," pp 45–50. Also see L Lavelle, "Thinking beyond the One-Size-Fits-All Pay Cut," *BusinessWeek,* December 3, 2001, p 45; and A Fox, "The Right Rewards?" *HR Magazine,* May 2002, p 8.

67See T B Wilson, *Innovative Reward Systems for the Changing Workplace,* 2nd (New York: McGraw-Hill, 2002); and

"Acculturate, Educate, and Motivate," *Training,* December 2004, pp 10–11.

[68]"Performance-Based Pay Plans," *HR Magazine,* June 2004, p 22. Also see C Taylor, "On-the-Spot Incentives," *HR Magazine,* May 2004, pp 80–84; N Heintz, "All in the Family," *Inc.,* September 2004, p 34; K Kroll, "Paying for Performance," *Inc.,* November 2004, p 46; M Sisk, "Taking Stock," *Inc.,* April 2005, p 34; L Lavelle, "A Payday for Performance," *BusinessWeek,* April 18, 2005, pp 78–80; and S J Wells, "No Results, No Raise," *HR Magazine,* May 2005, pp 76–80.

[69]For both sides of the "Does money motivate?" debate, see N Gupta and J D Shaw, "Let the Evidence Speak: Financial Incentives *Are* Effective!!" *Compensation & Benefits Review,* March–April 1998, pp 26, 28–32; A Kohn, "Challenging Behaviorist Dogma: Myths about Money and Motivation," *Compensation & Benefits Review,* March–April 1998, pp 27, 33–37; and B Ettorre, "Is Salary a Motivator?" *Management Review,* January 1999, p 8. Also see W J Duncan, "Stock Ownership and Work Motivation," *Organizational Dynamics,* Summer 2001, pp 1–11.

[70]Data from D Kiley, "Crafty Basket Makers Cut Downtime, Waste," *USA Today,* May 10, 2001, p 3B.

[71]Data from N J Perry, "Here Come Richer, Riskier Pay Plans," *Fortune,* December 19, 1988, p 51. Also see W Zellner, "Trickle-Down Is Trickling Down at Work," *BusinessWeek,* March 18, 1996, p 34.

[72]Data from M Bloom and G T Milkovich, "Relationships among Risk, Incentive Pay, and Organizational Performance," *Academy of Management Journal,* June 1998, pp 283–97.

[73]For details, see G D Jenkins Jr, N Gupta, A Mitra, and J D Shaw, "Are Financial Incentives Related to Performance? A Meta-Analytic Review of Empirical Research," *Journal of Applied Psychology,* October 1998, pp 777–87.

[74]See M J Mandel, "Those Fat Bonuses Don't Seem to Boost Performance," *BusinessWeek,* January 8, 1990, p 26.

[75]Based on discussion in R Ricklefs, "Whither the Payoff on Sales Commissions?" *The Wall Street Journal,* June 6, 1990, p B1.

[76]G Koretz, "Bad Marks for Pay-by-Results," *BusinessWeek,* September 4, 1995, p 28. Also see S Bates, "Now, the Downside of Pay for Performance," *HR Magazine,* March 2002, p 10; and R Grover and A Bernstein, "Arnold Gets Strict with the Teachers," *BusinessWeek,* May 2, 2005, pp 84–85.

[77]"Performance-Based Pay Plans," p 22.

[78]Ranking based on research evidence in F Trompenaars, *Riding the Waves of Culture: Understanding Diversity in Global Business* (Chicago: Irwin Professional Publishing, 1994), p 52.

[79]See J E Beatty, "Grades as Money and the Role of the Market Metaphor in Management Education," *Academy of Management Learning and Education,"* June 2004, pp 187–96.

[80]P V LeBlanc and P W Mulvey, "Research Study: How American Workers See the Rewards of Work," *Compensation & Benefits Review,* January–February 1998, pp 24–28.

[81]J S Dematteo, L T Eby, and E Sundstrom, "Team-Based Rewards: Current Empirical Evidence and Directions for Future Research," in *Research in Organizational Behavior,* vol. 20, eds B M Staw and L L Cummings (Greenwich, CT: JAI Press, 1998), p 152. Also see T R Zenger and C R Marshall, "Determinants of Incentive Intensity in Group-Based Rewards," *Academy of Management Journal,* April 2000, pp 149–63; and M Natter, A Mild, M Feurstein, G Dorffner, and A Taudes, "The Effect of Incentive Schemes and Organizational Arrangements on the New Product Development Process," *Management Science,* August 2001, pp 1029–45.

[82]For example, see R L Heneman and C von Hippel, "Balancing Group and Individual Rewards: Rewarding Individual Contributions to the Team," *Compensation & Benefits Review,* July–August 1995, pp 63–68; A Muoio, "At SEI, Teamwork Pays," *Fast Company,* April 1999, p 186; L N McClurg, "Team Rewards: How Far Have We Come?" *Human Resource Management,* Spring 2001, pp 73–86; and C Garvey, "Steer Teams with the Right Pay," *HR Magazine,* May 2002, pp 71–78.

[83]See C Ginther, "Incentive Programs That Really Work," *HR Magazine,* August 2000, pp 117–20; and E A Locke, "Linking Goals to Monetary Incentives," *Academy of Management Executive,* November 2004, pp 130–33.

[84]For a recent unconventional perspective, see R J DeGrandpre, "A Science of Meaning? Can Behaviorism Bring Meaning to Psychological Science?" *American Psychologist,* July 2000. pp 721–38.

[85]See E L Thorndike, *Educational Psychology: The Psychology of Learning, Vol. II* (New York: Columbia University Teachers College, 1913).

[86]Discussion of an early behaviorist who influenced Skinner's work can be found in P J Kreshel, "John B Watson at J Walter Thompson: The Legitimation of 'Science' in Advertising," *Journal of Advertising,* no. 2, 1990, pp 49–59. Recent discussions involving behaviorism include M R Ruiz, "B F Skinner's Radical Behaviorism: Historical Misconstructions and Grounds for Feminist Reconstructions." *Psychology of Women Quarterly,* June 1995, pp 161–79; J A Nevin, "Behavioral Economics and Behavioral Momentum," *Journal of the Experimental Analysis of Behavior,* November 1995, pp 385–95; and H Rachlin, "Can We Leave Cognition to Cognitive Psychologists? Comments on an Article by George Loewenstein," *Organizational Behavior and Human Decision Processes,* March 1996, pp 296–99.

[87]For recent discussion, see J W Donahoe, "The Unconventional Wisdom of B F Skinner: The Analysis-Interpretation Distinction," *Journal of the Experimental Analysis of Behavior,* September 1993, pp 453–56.

[88]See B F Skinner, *The Behavior of Organisms* (New York: Appleton-Century-Crofts, 1938).

[89]For modern approaches to respondent behavior, see B Azar, "Classical Conditioning Could Link Disorders and Brain Dysfunction, Researchers Suggest," *APA Monitor,* March 1999, p 17.

[90]For interesting discussions of Skinner and one of his students, see M B Gilbert and T F Gilbert. "What Skinner Gave Us," *Training,* September 1991, pp 42–48; and "HRD Pioneer Gilbert Leaves a Pervasive Legacy," *Training,* January 1996, p 14. Also see F Luthans and R Kreitner, *Organizational Behavior Modification and Beyond: An Operant and Social Learning Approach* (Glenview, IL: Scott, Foresman, 1985).

[91]The effect of praise is explored in C M Mueller and C S Dweck, "Praise for Intelligence Can Undermine Children's Motivation and Performance," *Journal of Personality and Social Psychology,* July 1998, pp 33–52. Also see C Garvey, "Meaningful Tokens of Appreciation," *HR Magazine,* August 2004, pp 101–6; K Hannon, "Praise Cranks Up Productivity," *USA Today,* August 30, 2004, p 6B; B Hindo, "Drive Green and Get Some Green," *BusinessWeek,* December 13, 2004, p 14; and D Jones, "Coach Says Honey Gets Better Results than Vinegar," *USA Today,* February 21, 2005, p 4B.

[92]C Salter, "Customer Service," *Fast Company,* May 2002, p 86. Also see R Kegan and L L Lahey, "More Powerful Communication: From the Language of Prizes and Praising to the Language of Ongoing Regard," *Journal of Organizational Excellence,* Summer 2001, pp 11–17.

[93]Research on punishment is reported in B P Niehoff, R J Paul, and J F S Bunch, "The Social Effects of Punishment Events: The Influence of Violator Past Performance Record and Severity of the Punishment on Observers' Justice Perceptions and Attitudes," *Journal of Organizational Behavior,* November 1998, pp 589–602; and L E Atwater, D A Waldman, J A Carey, and P Cartier, "Recipient and Observer Reactions to Discipline: Are Managers Experiencing Wishful Thinking?" *Journal of Organizational Behavior,* May 2001, pp 249–70.

[94]See C B Ferster and B F Skinner, *Schedules of Reinforcement* (New York: Appleton-Century-Crofts, 1957).

[95]See L M Saari and G P Latham, "Employee Reactions to Continuous and Variable Ratio Reinforcement Schedules Involving a Monetary Incentive," *Journal of Applied Psychology,* August 1982, pp 506–8.

[96]P Brinkley-Rogers and R Collier, "Along the Colorado, the Money's Flowing," *Arizona Republic,* March 4, 1990, p A12.

[97]M Schrage, "Actually, I'd Rather Have That Favor than a Raise," *Fortune,* April 16, 2001, p 412.

[98]For a circus lion tamer in action, see R Underwood, "A Day in the Life of Work," *Fast Company,* October 2004, p 124.

[99]Data from K L Alexander, "Continental Airlines Soars to New Heights," *USA Today,* January 23, 1996, p 4B; and M Knez and D Simester, "Making Across-the-Board Incentives Work," *Harvard Business Review,* February 2002, pp 16–17.

[100]C Cannella, "Kill the Commissions," *Inc.,* August 2004, p 38. By Cara Cannella, © 2005 Gruner & Jahr USA Publishing. First published in *Inc.* Magazine. Reprinted with permission.

[101]This exercise is adapted from material in D M Herold and C K Parsons, "Assessing the Feedback Environment in Work Organizations: Development of the Job Feedback Survey," *Journal of Applied Psychology,* May 1985, pp 290–305.

[102]Excerpted from J A Byrne, "How to Fix Corporate Governance," *Business Week,* May 6, 2002, p 72. For additional background material, see J Hempel, "A $140 Million Payday for Frank Raines," *BusinessWeek,* January 10, 2005, p 13; "CEO Pay at 100 of the Largest Companies," *USA Today,* March 31, 2005, p 3B; and P Burrows, "Nice Work if You Can Get It," *BusinessWeek,* April 18, 2005, p 9.

CHAPTER 10

[1]Excerpted from N Heintz, "Why Can't We Be Friends?" *Inc.,* January 2004, pp 31–32. By N Heintz, © 2004 Gruner & Jahr USA Publishing. First published in *Inc.* Magazine. Reprinted with permission.

[2]E Van Velsor and J Brittain Leslie, "Why Executives Derail: Perspectives across Time and Cultures," *Academy of Management Executive,* November 1995, p 62.

[3]Ibid., p 63. For the social side of a "tough guy" CEO, see M Gunther, "The Sumner of Love," *Fortune,* May 2, 2005, pp 90–99.

[4]See P S Adler and S Kwon, "Social Capital: Prospects for a New Concept," *Academy of Management Review,* January 2002, pp 17–40; and J Savage and S Kanazawa, "Social Capital and the Human Psyche: Why Is Social Life 'Capital'?" *Sociological Theory,* September 2004, pp 504–24.

[5]See C W Struthers, J Eaton, A Ratajczak, and M Perunovic, "Social Conduct toward Organizations," *Basic and Applied Social Psychology,* December 2004, pp 277–88; and G Lindemann, "The Analysis of the Borders of the Social World: A Challenge for Sociological Theory," *Journal for the Theory of Social Behaviour,* March 2005, pp 69–98.

[6]This definition is based in part on one found in D Horton Smith, "A Parsimonious Definition of 'Group': Toward Conceptual Clarity and Scientific Utility," *Sociological Inquiry,* Spring 1967, pp 141–67. Also see M S Poole, A B Hollingshead, J E McGrath, R L Moreland, and J Rohrbaugh, "Interdisciplinary Perspectives on Small Groups," *Small Group Research,* February 2004, pp 3–16; G M Wittenbaum, A B Hollingshead, P B Paulus, R Y Hirokawa, D G Ancona, R S Peterson, K A Jehn, and K Yoon, "The Functional Perspective as a Lens for Understanding Groups," *Small Group Research,* February 2004, pp 17–43; and G A Fine and B Harrington, "Tiny Publics: Small Groups and Civil Society," *Sociological Theory,* September 2004, pp 341–46.

[7]E H Schein, *Organizational Psychology,* 3rd ed (Englewood Cliffs, NJ: Prentice Hall, 1980), p 145. For more, see L R Weingart, "How Did They Do That? The Ways and Means of Studying Group Process," in *Research in Organizational Behavior,* vol. 19, eds L L Cummings and B M Staw (Greenwich, CT: JAI Press, 1997), pp 189–239.

[8]See E Bonabeau, "Predicting the Unpredictable," *Harvard Business Review,* March 2002, pp 109–16; R Cross and L Prusak, "The People Who Make Organizations Go—or Stop," *Harvard Business Review,* June 2002, pp 105–12; J Labianca,

"The Ties That Blind," *Harvard Business Review,* October 2004, p 19; and J J Anove, "FOB: Friend of Boss," *HR Magazine,* June 2005, pp 153–56.

[9]J Castro, "Mazda U.," *Time,* October 20, 1986, p 65.

[10]For more, see M S Cole, W S Schaninger Jr, and S G Harris, "The Workplace Social Exchange Network: A Multilevel, Conceptual Examination," *Group & Organization Management,* March 2002, pp 142–67. Also see P Brandes, R Dharwadkar, and K Wheatley, "Social Exchanges within Organizations and Work," *Group & Organization Management,* June 2004, pp 276–301; N Katz, D Lazer, H Arrow, and N Contractor, "Network Theory and Small Groups," *Small Group Research,* June 2004, pp 307–32; D J Brass, J Galaskiewicz, H R Greve, and W Tsai, "Taking Stock of Networks and Organizations: A Multilevel Perspective," *Academy of Management Journal,* December 2004, pp 795–817; and N A Doherty and J A Feeney, "The Composition of Attachment Networks throughout the Adult Years," *Personal Relationships,* December 2004, pp 469–88.

[11]See P Cardona, B S Lawrence, and P M Bentler, "The Influence of Social and Work Exchange Relationships on Organizational Citizenship Behavior," *Group & Organization Management,* April 2004, pp 219–47.

[12]For an instructive overview of five different theories of group development, see J P Wanous, A E Reichers, and S D Malik, "Organizational Socialization and Group Development: Toward an Integrative Perspective," *Academy of Management Review,* October 1984, pp 670–83.

[13]See B W Tuckman, "Developmental Sequence in Small Groups," *Psychological Bulletin,* June 1965, pp 384–99; and B W Tuckman and M A C Jensen, "Stages of Small-Group Development Revisited," *Group & Organization Studies,* December 1977, pp 419–27. An instructive adaptation of the Tuckman model can be found in L Holpp, "If Empowerment Is So Good, Why Does It Hurt?" *Training,* March 1995, p 56. Also see S A Furst, M Reeves, B Rosen, and R S Blackburn, "Managing the Life Cycle of Virtual Teams," *Academy of Management Executive,* May 2004, pp 6–20.

[14]Alternative group development models are discussed in L N Jewell and H J Reitz, *Group Effectiveness in Organizations* (Glenview, IL: Scott, Foresman, 1981), pp 15–20; and R S Wellins, W C Byham, and J M Wilson, *Empowered Teams: Creating Self-Directed Work Groups That Improve Quality, Productivity and Participation* (San Francisco: Jossey-Bass, 1991). Also see H Arrow, M S Poole, K B Henry, S Wheelan, and R Moreland, "Time, Change, and Development," *Small Group Research,* February 2004, pp 73–105; K J Klein, B Lim, J L Saltz, and D M Mayer, "How Do They Get There? An Examination of the Antecedents of Centrality in Team Networks," *Academy of Management Journal,* December 2004, pp 952–63; and L A Erbert, G M Mearns, and S Dena, "Perceptions of Turning Points and Dialectical Interpretations in Organizational Team Development," *Small Group Research,* February 2005, pp 21–58.

[15]For related research, see C Kampmeier and B Simon, "Individuality and Group Formation: The Role of Independence and Differentiation," *Journal of Personality and Social Psychology,* September 2001, pp 448–62.

[16]B L Riddle, C M Anderson, and M M Martin, "Small Group Socialization Scale: Development and Validity," *Small Group Research,* October 2000, pp 554–72; and M Van Vugt and C M Hart, "Social Identity as Social Glue: The Origins of Group Loyalty," *Journal of Personality and Social Psychology,* April 2004, pp 585–98.

[17]Jewell and Reitz, *Group Effectiveness in Organizations,* p 19. Also see C B Gibson, A E Randel, and P C Earley, "Understanding Group Efficacy: An Empirical Test of Multiple Assessment Methods," *Group & Organization Management,* March 2000, pp 67–97; V U Druskat and S B Wolff, "Building the Emotional Intelligence of Groups," *Harvard Business Review,* March 2001, pp 80–90; S W Lester, B M Meglino, and M A Korsgaard, "The Antecedents and Consequences of Group Potency: A Longitudinal Investigation of Newly Formed Work Groups," *Academy of Management Journal,* April 2002, pp 352–68; and A Edmondson, R Bohmer, and G Pisano, "Speeding Up Team Learning," *Harvard Business Review,* October 2001, pp 125–32.

[18]Based on J F McGrew, J G Bilotta, and J M Deeney, "Software Team Formation and Decay: Extending the Standard Model for Small Groups," *Small Group Research,* April 1999, pp 209–34.

[19]Ibid., p 232.

[20]Ibid., p 231.

[21]D Davies and B C Kuypers, "Group Development and Interpersonal Feedback," *Group & Organizational Studies,* June 1985, p 194.

[22]Ibid., pp 184–208.

[23]C J G Gersick, "Marking Time: Predictable Transitions in Task Groups," *Academy of Management Journal,* June 1989, pp 274–309.

[24]D K Carew, E Parisi-Carew, and K H Blanchard, "Group Development and Situational Leadership: A Model for Managing Groups," *Training and Development Journal,* June 1986, pp 48–49. For evidence linking leadership and group effectiveness, see G R Bushe and A L Johnson, "Contextual and Internal Variables Affecting Task Group Outcomes in Organizations," *Group & Organization Studies,* December 1989, pp 462–82.

[25]See C Huxham and S Vangen, "Leadership in the Shaping and Implementation of Collaboration Agendas: How Things Happen in a (Not Quite) Joined-Up World," *Academy of Management Journal,* December 2000, pp 1159–75; N Sivasubramaniam, W D Murry, B J Avolio, and D I Jung, "A Longitudinal Model of the Effects of Team Leadership and Group Potency on Group Performance," *Group & Organization Management,* March 2002, pp 66–96; and J Sell, M J Lovaglia, E A Mannix, C D Samuelson, and R K Wilson, "Investigating Conflict, Power, and Status within and among Groups," *Small Group Research,* February 2004, pp 44–72.

[26]See K K Smith and D N Berg, *Paradoxes of Group Life: Understanding Conflict, Paralysis, and Movement in Group Dynamics* (San Francisco: Jossey-Bass, 1997).

[27]G Graen, "Role-Making Processes within Complex Organizations," in *Handbook of Industrial and Organizational*

Psychology, ed M D Dunnette (Chicago: Rand McNally, 1976), p 1201. Also see L Van Dyne and J A LePine, "Helping and Voice Extra-Role Behaviors: Evidence of Construct and Predictive Validity," *Academy of Management Journal,* February 1998, pp 108–19.

[28]Role modeling applications are covered in J Barbian, "A Little Help from Your Friends," *Training,* March 2002, pp 38–41. Also see A D Cast, "Role-Taking and Interaction," *Social Psychology Quarterly,* September 2004, pp 296–309.

[29]G L Miles, "Doug Danforth's Plan to Put Westinghouse in the 'Winner's Circle,' " *BusinessWeek,* July 28, 1986, p 75.

[30]For a review of research on the role episode model, see L A King and D W King, "Role Conflict and Role Ambiguity: A Critical Assessment of Construct Validity," *Psychological Bulletin,* January 1990, pp 48–64. Consequences of role perceptions are discussed in R C Netemeyer, S Burton, and M W Johnston, "A Nested Comparison of Four Models of the Consequences of Role Perception Variables," *Organizational Behavior and Human Decision Processes,* January 1995, pp 77–93.

[31]Schein, *Organizational Psychology,* p 198.

[32]Ibid. The relationship between interrole conflict and turnover is explored in P W Hom and A J Kinicki, "Toward a Greater Understanding of How Dissatisfaction Drives Employee Turnover," *Academy of Management Journal,* October 2001, pp 975–87.

[33]See A Park, "Between a Rocker and a High Chair," *BusinessWeek,* February 21, 2005, pp 86, 88; M Goldsmith, "Do You Love What You Do?" *Fast Company,* March 2005, p 88; and J Merritt, "MBA Family Values," *BusinessWeek,* March 14, 2005, pp 104–6.

[34]See D J Brass, K D Butterfield, and B C Skaggs, "Relationships and Unethical Behavior: A Social Network Perspective," *Academy of Management Review,* January 1998, pp 14–31.

[35]Schein, *Organizational Psychology,* p 198. Four types of role ambiguity are discussed in M A Eys and A V Carron, "Role Ambiguity, Task Cohesion, and Task Self-Efficacy," *Small Group Research,* June 2001, pp 356–73.

[36]Drawn from M Peterson et al., "Role Conflict, Ambiguity, and Overload: A 21-Nation Study," *Academy of Management Journal,* April 1995, pp 429–52.

[37]Based on Y Fried, H A Ben-David, R B Tiegs, N Avital, and U Yeverechyahu, "The Interactive Effect of Role Conflict and Role Ambiguity on Job Performance," *Journal of Occupational and Organizational Psychology,* March 1998, pp 19–27. Also see A Risberg, "Employee Experiences of Acquisition Processes," *Journal of World Business,* Spring 2001, pp 58–84; M R Beauchamp and S R Bray, "Role Ambiguity and Role Conflict within Interdependent Teams," *Small Group Research,* April 2001, pp 133–57; S R Bray and L R Brawley, "Role Efficacy, Role Clarity, and Role Performance Effectiveness," *Small Group Research,* April 2002, pp 233–53; and M R Beauchamp, S R Bray, M A Eys, and A V Carron, "Leadership Behaviors and Multidimensional Role Ambiguity Perceptions in Team Sports," *Small Group Research,* February 2005, pp 5–20.

[38]R R Blake and J Srygley Mouton, "Don't Let Group Norms Stifle Creativity," *Personnel,* August 1985, p 28.

[39]See K Montgomery, K Kane, and C M Vance, "Accounting for Differences in Norms of Respect: A Study of Assessments of Incivility through the Lenses of Race and Gender," *Group & Organization Management,* April 2004, pp 248–68; A Spicer, T W Dunfee, and W J Bailey, "Does National Context Matter in Ethical Decision Making? An Empirical Test of Integrative Social Contracts Theory," *Academy of Management Journal,* August 2004, pp 610–20; and K S Cook, "Networks, Norms, and Trust: The Social Psychology of Social Capital," *Social Psychology Quarterly,* March 2005, pp 4–14.

[40]A Dunkin, "Pepsi's Marketing Magic: Why Nobody Does It Better," *BusinessWeek,* February 10, 1986, p 52.

[41]1 = A; 2 = C; 3 = A; 4 = A; 5 = C; 6 = A; 7 = C; 8 = A; 9 = C; 10 = C.

[42]For related reading, see A J Towler and D J Schneider, "Distinctions among Stigmatized Groups," *Journal of Applied Social Psychology,* January 2005, pp 1–14.

[43]D C Feldman, "The Development and Enforcement of Group Norms," *Academy of Management Review,* January 1984, pp 50–52.

[44]See D M Casperson, "Mastering the Business Meal," *Training & Development,* March 2001, pp 68–69; J M Marques, D Abrams, and R G Serodio, "Being Better by Being Right: Subjective Group Dynamics and Derogation of In-Group Deviants When Generic Norms Are Undermined," *Journal of Personality and Social Psychology,* September 2001, pp 436–47; and T Wildschut, C A Insko, and L Gaertner, "Intragroup Social Influence and Intergroup Competition," *Journal of Personality and Social Psychology,* June 2002, pp 975–92.

[45]Feldman, "The Development and Enforcement of Group Norms."

[46]See R G Netemeyer, M W Johnston, and S Burton, "Analysis of Role Conflict and Role Ambiguity in a Structural Equations Framework," *Journal of Applied Psychology,* April 1990, pp 148–57; and G W McGee, C E Ferguson Jr, and A Seers, "Role Conflict and Role Ambiguity: Do the Scales Measure These Two Constructs?" *Journal of Applied Psychology,* October 1989, pp 815–18.

[47]See S E Jackson and R S Schuler, "A Meta-Analysis and Conceptual Critique of Research on Role Ambiguity and Role Conflict in Work Settings," *Organizational Behavior and Human Decision Processes,* August 1985, pp 16–78.

[48]Based on C S Crandall, A Eshleman, and L O'Brien, "Social Norms and the Expression and Suppression of Prejudice: The Struggle for Internalization," *Journal of Personality and Social Psychology,* March 2002, pp 359–78. Also see J A Chatman and F J Flynn, "The Influence of Demographic Heterogeneity on the Emergence and Consequences of Cooperative Norms in Work Teams," *Academy of Management Journal,* October 2001, pp 956–74.

[49]See T Halfhill, E Sundstrom, J Lahner, W Calderone, and T M Nielsen, "Group Personality Composition and Group

Effectiveness: An Integrative Review of Empirical Research," *Small Group Research,* February 2005, pp 83–105.

[50]See K D Benne and P Sheats, "Functional Roles of Group Members," *Journal of Social Issues,* Spring 1948, pp 41–49. Also see J Strijbos, R L Martens, W M G Jochems, and N J Broers, "The Effect of Functional Roles on Group Efficiency," *Small Group Research,* April 2004, pp 195–229.

[51]See H J Klein and P W Mulvey, "Two Investigations of the Relationships among Group Goals, Goal Commitment, Cohesion, and Performance," *Organizational Behavior and Human Decision Processes,* January 1995, pp 44–53; D F Crown and J G Rosse, "Yours, Mine, and Ours: Facilitating Group Productivity through the Integration of Individual and Group Goals," *Organizational Behavior and Human Decision Processes,* November 1995, pp 138–50; and A Chirumbolo, L Mannetti, A Pierro, A Areni, and A W Kruglanski, "Motivated Closed-Mindedness and Creativity in Small Groups," *Small Group Research,* February 2005, pp 59–82.

[52]A Zander, "The Value of Belonging to a Group in Japan," *Small Group Behavior,* February 1983, pp 7–8. Also see P R Harris and R T Moran, *Managing Cultural Differences,* 4th ed (Houston: Gulf Publishing, 1996), pp 267–76.

[53]For example, see B Grofman, S L Feld, and G Owen, "Group Size and the Performance of a Composite Group Majority: Statistical Truths and Empirical Results," *Organizational Behavior and Human Performance,* June 1984, pp 350–59.

[54]See P Yetton and P Bottger, "The Relationships among Group Size, Member Ability, Social Decision Schemes, and Performance," *Organizational Behavior and Human Performance,* October 1983, pp 145–59.

[55]This copyrighted exercise may be found in J Hall, "Decisions, Decisions, Decisions," *Psychology Today,* November 1971, pp 51–54, 86, 88.

[56]Yetton and Bottger, "The Relationships among Group Size, Member Ability, Social Decision Schemes, and Performance," p 158.

[57]Based on R B Gallupe, A R Dennis, W H Cooper, J S Valacich, L M Bastianutti, and J F Nunamaker Jr, "Electronic Brainstorming and Group Size," *Academy of Management Journal,* June 1992, pp 350–69. Also see H Barki and A Pinsonneault, "Small Group Brainstorming and Idea Quality: Is Electronic Brainstorming the Most Effective Approach?" *Small Group Research,* April 2001, pp 158–205; and T J Kramer, G P Fleming, and S M Mannis, "Improving Face-to-Face Brainstorming through Modeling and Facilitation." *Small Group Research,* October 2001, pp 533–57.

[58]Data from E Salas, D Rozell, B Mullen, and J E Driskell, "The Effect of Team Building on Performance: An Integration," *Small Group Research,* June 1999, pp 309–29.

[59]Drawn from B Mullen, C Symons, L-T Hu, and E Salas, "Group Size, Leadership Behavior, and Subordinate Satisfaction," *Journal of General Psychology,* April 1989, pp 155–69. Also see P Oliver and G Marwell, "The Paradox of Group Size in Collective Action: A Theory of the Critical Mass, II.," *American Sociological Review,* February 1988, pp 1–8.

[60]T Howard, "FTC Impasse Allows Pepsi, Quaker Deal," *USA Today,* August 2, 2001, p 1B.

[61]See J A Bonito and B L Lambert, "Information Similarity as a Moderator of the Effect of Gender on Participation in Small Groups: A Multilevel Analysis," *Small Group Research,* April 2005, pp 139–65; and H F M Lodewijkx, M van Zomeren, and J E M M Syroit, "The Anticipation of a Severe Initiation: Gender Differences in Effects on Affiliation Tendency and Group," *Small Group Research,* April 2005, pp 237–62.

[62]See L Smith-Lovin and C Brody, "Interruptions in Group Discussions: The Effects of Gender and Group Composition," *American Sociological Review,* June 1989, pp 424–35.

[63]L Karakowsky, K McBey, and D L Miller, "Gender, Perceived Competence, and Power Displays: Examining Verbal Interruptions in a Group Context," *Small Group Research,* August 2004, p 407.

[64]E M Ott, "Effects of the Male-Female Ratio at Work," *Psychology of Women Quarterly,* March 1989, p 53.

[65]"Daily Downer," *Training,* April 2005, p 12. Also see S Armour, "More Men Say They Are Sexually Harassed at Work," *USA Today,* September 17, 2004, p 1B; and L W Andrews, "Hardcore Offenders," *HR Magazine,* December 2004, pp 42–48.

[66]Data from B A Gutek, A Groff Cohen, and A M Konrad, "Predicting Social-Sexual Behavior at Work: A Contact Hypothesis," *Academy of Management Journal,* September 1990, pp 560–77. Also see C A Pierce and H Aguinis, "A Framework for Investigating the Link between Workplace Romance and Sexual Harassment," *Group & Organization Management,* June 2001, pp 206–29; K Gurchiek, "Be Ready for Slings, Arrows of Cupid in the Cubicles," *HR Magazine,* March 2005, pp 27, 36–37; and S Shellenbarger, "Employers Often Ignore Office Affairs, Leaving Co-Workers in Difficult Spot," *The Wall Street Journal,* March 10, 2005, p D1.

[67]Data from M Rotundo, D Nguyen, and P R Sackett, "A Meta-Analytic Review of Gender Differences in Perceptions of Sexual Harassment," *Journal of Applied Psychology,* October 2001, pp 914–22. Also see K E Smirles, "Attributions of Responsibility in Cases of Sexual Harassment: The Person and the Situation," *Journal of Applied Social Psychology,* February 2004, pp 342–65; J A Chatman and C A O'Reilly, "Asymmetric Reactions to Work Group Sex Diversity among Men and Women," *Academy of Management Journal,* April 2004, pp 193–208; L M Cortina and S A Wasti, "Profiles in Coping: Responses to Sexual Harassment across Persons, Organizations, and Cultures," *Journal of Applied Psychology,* January 2005, pp 182–92; M Barreto and N Ellemers, "The Perils of Political Correctness: Men's and Women's Responses to Old-Fashioned and Modern Sexist Views," *Social Psychology Quarterly,* March 2005, pp 75–88; and L Bowes-Sperry and A M O'Leary-Kelly, "To Act or Not to Act: The Dilemma Faced by Sexual Harassment Observers," *Academy of Management Review,* April 2005, pp 288–306.

[68]S J South, C M Bonjean, W T Markham, and J Corder, "Female Labor Force Participation and the Organizational Experiences of Male Workers," *Sociological Quarterly,* Summer 1983, p 378.

69B T Thornton, "Sexual Harassment, 1: Discouraging It in the Work Place," *Personnel,* April 1986, p 18. Also see R K Robinson, G M Franklin, and W J Davis, "Sexual Harassment Redux," *Business Horizons,* July–August 2004, pp 3–5; J W Janove, "Conclude and Communicate," *HR Magazine,* August 2004, pp 131–34; and T O McCarthy, "Sexual Conduct: Equal Abuse Unequal Harm," *HR Magazine,* January 2005, pp 93–94.

70Data from T Galvin, "2001 Industry Report," *Training,* October 2001, pp 41, 54.

71I Pave, "A Woman's Place Is at GE, Federal Express, P&G . . . ," *BusinessWeek,* June 23, 1986, p 78. Also see S K Willman, "The New Law of Training: Training on Harassment and Discrimination Is Not a Luxury Anymore," *HR Magazine,* May 2004, pp 115–18; and J I Sanchez and N Medkik, "The Effects of Diversity Awareness Training on Differential Treatment," *Group & Organization Management,* August 2004, pp 517–36.

72Diversity and group effectiveness are examined in D C Lau and J K Murnighan, "Demographic Diversity and Faultlines: The Compositional Dynamics of Organizational Groups," *Academy of Management Review,* April 1998, pp 325–40; B L Kelsey, "The Dynamics of Multicultural Groups: Ethnicity as a Determinant of Leadership," *Small Group Research,* October 1998, pp 602–23; D C Thomas, "Cultural Diversity and Work Group Effectiveness: An Experimental Study," *Journal of Cross-Cultural Psychology,* March 1999, pp 242–63; and L M Millhous, "The Experience of Culture in Multicultural Groups: Case Studies of Russian-American Collaboration in Business," *Small Group Research,* June 1999, pp 280–308.

73For details, see R A Rodriguez, "Challenging Demographic Reductionism: A Pilot Study Investigating Diversity in Group Composition," *Small Group Research,* December 1998, pp 744–59.

74See Blake and Mouton, "Don't Let Group Norms Stifle Creativity."

75For additional information, see S E Asch, *Social Psychology* (Englewood Cliffs, NJ: Prentice Hall, 1952), Ch. 16.

76See T P Williams and S Sogon, "Group Composition and Conforming Behavior in Japanese Students," *Japanese Psychological Research,* no. 4, 1984, pp 231–34; and T Amir, "The Asch Conformity Effect: A Study in Kuwait," *Social Behavior and Personality,* no. 2, 1984, pp 187–90.

77Data from R Bond and P B Smith, "Culture and Conformity: A Meta-Analysis of Studies Using Asch's (1952b, 1956) Line Judgment Task," *Psychological Bulletin,* January 1996, pp 111–37. Also see H Liao, A Joshi, and A Chuang, "Sticking Out Like a Sore Thumb: Employee Dissimilarity and Deviance at Work," *Personnel Psychology,* Winter 2004, pp 969–1000.

78J L Roberts and E Thomas, "Enron's Dirty Laundry," *Newsweek,* March 11, 2002, p 26. Also see G Farrell and J O'Donnell, "Watkins Testifies Skilling, Fastow Duped Lay, Board," *USA Today,* February 15, 2002, pp 1B–2B; and M Schminke, D Wells, J Peyrefitte, and T C Sebora, "Leadership and Ethics in Work Groups: A Longitudinal Assessment," *Group & Organization Management,* June 2002, pp 272–93.

79For a comprehensive update on groupthink, see the entire February–March 1998 issue of *Organizational Behavior and Human Decision Processes* (12 articles).

80I L Janis, *Groupthink,* 2nd ed (Boston: Houghton Mifflin, 1982), p 9. Alternative models are discussed in K Granstrom and D Stiwne, "A Bipolar Model of Groupthink: An Expansion of Janis's Concept," *Small Group Research,* February 1998, pp 32–56; and A R Flippen, "Understanding Groupthink From a Self-Regulatory Perspective," *Small Group Research,* April 1999, pp 139–65.

81Ibid. For an alternative model, see R J Aldag and S Riggs Fuller, "Beyond Fiasco: A Reappraisal of the Groupthink Phenomenon and a New Model of Group Decision Processes," *Psychological Bulletin,* May 1993, pp 533–52. Also see A A Mohamed and F A Wiebe, "Toward a Process Theory of Groupthink," *Small Group Research,* August 1996, pp 416–30.

82L Baum, "The Job Nobody Wants," *BusinessWeek,* September 8, 1986, p 60. Also see J G Koretz, "Friendly Boards Are Not All Bad," *BusinessWeek,* June 14, 1999, p 34; W Shapiro, "Groupthink a Danger for White House War Planners," *USA Today,* October 3, 2001, p 7A; and K Brooker, "Trouble in the Boardroom," *Fortune,* May 13, 2002, pp 113–16.

83Details of this study may be found in M R Callaway and J K Esser, "Groupthink: Effects of Cohesiveness and Problem-Solving Procedures on Group Decision Making," *Social Behavior and Personality,* no. 2, 1984, pp 157–64. Also see C R Leana, "A Partial Test of Janis's Groupthink Model: Effects of Group Cohesiveness and Leader-Behavior on Defective Decision Making," *Journal of Management,* Spring 1985, pp 5–17; and G Moorhead and J R Montanari, "An Empirical Investigation of the Groupthink Phenomenon," *Human Relations,* May 1986, pp 399–410. A more modest indirect effect is reported in J N Choi and M U Kim, "The Organizational Application of Groupthink and Its Limitations in Organizations," *Journal of Applied Psychology,* April 1999, pp 297–306.

84Adapted from discussion in Janis, *Groupthink,* Ch. 11.

85J A Byrne, "How to Fix Corporate Governance," *BusinessWeek,* May 6, 2002, p 78. Also see J A Byrne, "Restoring Trust in Corporate America," *BusinessWeek,* June 24, 2002, pp 30–35; and D A Nadler, "Building Better Boards," *Harvard Business Review,* May 2004, pp 102–11.

86See S Mohammed and L C Angell, "Surface- and Deep-Level Diversity in Workgroups: Examining the Moderating Effects of Team Orientation and Team Process on Relationship Conflict," *Journal of Organizational Behavior,* December 2004, pp 1015–39; and L C Chandler, "Beyond Political Correctness: Discover the Benefits of Board Diversity," *Association Management,* January 2005, pp 29–32.

87Based on discussion in B Latane, K Williams, and S Harkins, "Many Hands Make Light the Work: The Causes and Consequences of Social Loafing," *Journal of Personality and Social Psychology,* June 1979, pp 822–32; and D A Kravitz and B Martin, "Ringelmann Rediscovered: The Original Article," *Journal of Personality and Social Psychology,* May 1986, pp 936–41. Also see D Moyer, "First among Equals," *Harvard Business Review,* December 2004, p 152.

[88]See J A Shepperd, "Productivity Loss in Performance Groups: A Motivation Analysis," *Psychological Bulletin,* no. 1, 1993, pp 67–81; R E Kidwell Jr, and N Bennett, "Employee Propensity to Withhold Effort: A Conceptual Model to Intersect Three Avenues of Research," *Academy of Management Review,* July 1993, pp 429–56; S J Karau and K D Williams, "Social Loafing: Meta-Analytic Review and Theoretical Integration," *Journal of Personality and Social Psychology,* October 1993, pp 681–706; and S G Scott and W O Einstein, "Strategic Performance Appraisal in Team-Based Organizations: One Size Does Not Fit All," *Academy of Management Executive,* May 2001, pp 107–16.

[89]See S J Zaccaro, "Social Loafing: The Role of Task Attractiveness," *Personality and Social Psychology Bulletin,* March 1984, pp 99–106; J M Jackson and K D Williams, "Social Loafing on Difficult Tasks: Working Collectively Can Improve Performance," *Journal of Personality and Social Psychology,* October 1985, pp 937–42; and J M George, "Extrinsic and Intrinsic Origins of Perceived Social Loafing in Organizations," *Academy of Management Journal,* March 1992, pp 191–202.

[90]For complete details, see K Williams, S Harkins, and B Latane, "Identifiability as a Deterrent to Social Loafing: Two Cheering Experiments," *Journal of Personality and Social Psychology,* February 1981, pp 303–11.

[91]See J M Jackson and S G Harkins, "Equity in Effort: an Explanation of the Social Loafing Effect," *Journal of Personality and Social Psychology,* November 1985, pp 1199–206.

[92] Both studies are reported in S G Harkins and K Szymanski, "Social Loafing and Group Evaluation," *Journal of Personality and Social Psychology,* June 1989, pp 934–41.

[93] Data from J A Wagner III, "Studies of Individualism-Collectivism: Effects on Cooperation in Groups," *Academy of Management Journal,* February 1995, pp 152–72. Also see P W Mulvey and H J Klein, "The Impact of Perceived Loafing and Collective Efficacy on Group Goal Processes and Group Performance," *Organizational Behavior and Human Decision Processes,* April 1998, pp 62–87; P W Mulvey, L Bowes-Sperry, and H J Klein, "The Effects of Perceived Loafing and Defensive Impression Management on Group Effectiveness," *Small Group Research,* June 1998, pp 394–415; L Karakowsky and K McBey, "Do My Contributions Matter? The Influence of Imputed Expertise on Member Involvement and Self-Evaluations in the Work Group," *Group & Organization Management,* March 2001, pp 70–92; and R C Liden, S J Wayne, R A Jaworski, and N Bennett, "Social Loafing: A Field Investigation," *Journal of Management,* no. 2, 2004, pp 285–304.

[94]S G Rogelberg, J L Barnes-Farrell, and C A Lowe, "The Stepladder Technique: An Alternative Group Structure Facilitating Effective Group Decision Making," *Journal of Applied Psychology,* October 1992, p 730.

[95]Case up to the end of this paragraph was excerpted from P Hoversten, "Thiokol Wavers, Then Decides to Launch," *USA Today,* January 22, 1996, p 2A. Copyright 1996, *USA Today.* Reprinted with permission.

[96]This paragraph and the balance of the case are excerpted from P Hoversten, P Edmonds, and H El Nasser, "Debate Raged before Doomed Launch," *USA Today,* January 22, 1996, pp 1A–2A. Copyright 1996, *USA Today.* Reprinted with permission.

[97]Twenty items excerpted from S A Wheelan and J M Hochberger, "Validation Studies of the Group Development Questionnaire," *Small Group Research,* February 1996, pp 143–70.

[98]From D A Whetten and K S Cameron, *Developing Management Skills.* Copyright © 1984 by Scott, Foresman and Company. Reprinted by permission of Addison Wesley Educational Publishers, Inc.

[99]K J Sulkowicz, "The Corporate Shrink," *Fast Company,* May 2004, p 54.

CHAPTER 11

[1]Excerpted from G Gloeckler, "This Is Not Your Father's MBA," *BusinessWeek,* May 16, 2005, pp 74–75. Reprinted by permission of The McGraw-Hill Companies, Inc.

[2]As quoted in Z Olijnyk, "The Home Depot Boss on Small Wins," *Canadian Business,* November 8, 2004, www.canadianbusiness.com. For a scholarly debate on teams, see N J Allen and T D Hecht, "The 'Romance of Teams': Toward an Understanding of Its Psychological Underpinnings and Implications," *Journal of Occupational and Organizational Psychology,* December 2004, pp 439–61; and J R Meindl, "The Romance of Teams: Is the Honeymoon Over?" *Journal of Occupational and Organizational Psychology,* December 2004, pp 463–66.

[3]See N Enbar, "What Do Women Want? Ask 'Em," *BusinessWeek,* March 29, 1999, p 8; M Hickins. "Duh! Gen Xers Are Cool with Teamwork," *Management Review,* March 1999, p 7; T D Green and S Holeman, "Athletes' Attributions for Team Performance: A Theoretical Test across Sports and Genders," *Social Behavior and Personality,* no. 2, 2004, pp 199–206; and "You and Your Posse: Headhunter Kelvin Thompson Talks about How—and Why—to Sell Yourself as a Team Player," *Fast Company,* January 2005, p 88.

[4]J R Katzenbach, and D K Smith, *The Wisdom of Teams: Creating the High-Performance Organization* (New York: HarperBusiness, 1999), p 45. Sports teams are discussed in N Katz, "Sports Teams as a Model for Workplace Teams: Lessons and Liabilities," *Academy of Management Executive,* August 2001, pp 56–67; R Fusaro, "The Big Comeback," *Harvard Business Review,* January 2002, p 20; and G Colvin, "Think You Can Bobsled? Ha!" *Fortune,* March 18, 2002, p 50.

[5]For an interesting case study, see P F Levy. "The Nut Island Effect: When Good Teams Go Wrong," *Harvard Business Review,* March 2001, pp 51–59.

[6]J R Katzenbach and D K Smith, "The Discipline of Teams," *Harvard Business Review,* March–April 1993, p 112.

[7]"A Team's-Eye View of Teams." *Training,* November 1995, p 16.

[8]See E Sundstrom, K P DeMeuse, and D Futrell, "Work Teams," *American Psychologist,* February 1990, pp 120–33.

[9]For an alternative typology of teams, see S G Scott and Walter O Einstien, "Strategic Performance Appraisal in Team-Based Organizations: One Size Does Not Fit All," *Academy of Management Executive,* May 2001, pp 107–16. Also see C L Pearce and M D Ensley, "A Reciprocal and Longitudinal Investigation of the Innovation Process: The Central Role of Shared Vision in Product and Process Innovation Teams (PPITs)," *Journal of Organizational Behavior,* March 2004, pp 259–78.

[10]See G Van der Vegt, B Emans, and E Van de Vliert, "Effects of Interdependencies in Project Teams," *Journal of Social Psychology,* April 1999, pp 202–14; and A L Kristof-Brown and C K Stevens, "Goal Congruence in Project Teams: Does the Fit between Members' Personal Mastery and Performance Goals Matter?" *Journal of Applied Psychology,* December 2001, pp 1083–95.

[11]For a description of medical teams in action, see J Appleby and R Davis, "Teamwork Used to Be a Money Saver: Now It's a Lifesaver," *USA Today,* March 1, 2001, pp 1B–2B. Also see M A Prospero, "In Indy's Pits, It's More than Speed," *Fast Company,* August 2004, p 26.

[12]P King, "What Makes Teamwork Work?" *Psychology Today,* December 1989, p 16.

[13]See C A Beatty and Brenda A Barker Scott, *Building Smart Teams: A Roadmap to High Performance* (Thousand Oaks, CA: Sage, 2004); J W Whitcoak, L Chalip, and L K Hort, "Assessing Group Efficacy: Comparing Three Methods of Measurement," *Small Group Research,* April 2004, pp 158–73; S Taggar and M Neubert, "The Impact of Poor Performers on Team Outcomes: An Empirical Examination of Attribution Theory," *Personnel Psychology,* Winter 2004, pp 935–68; T A Timmerman, "Missing Persons in the Study of Groups," *Journal of Organizational Behavior,* February 2005, pp 21–36; J Vilaga, "The Teamster," *Fast Company,* April 2005, p 94; and M Cardinal and T O'Leary, "For Rewriting the Rules for Husband-and-Wife Teams," *Inc.,* April 2005, p 83.

[14]For more on team-member satisfaction, see M A Griffin, M G Patterson, and M A West, "Job Satisfaction and Teamwork: The Role of Supervisor Support," *Journal of Organizational Behavior,* August 2001, pp 537–50; and C M Mason and M A Griffin, "Group Task Satisfaction: Applying the Construct of Job Satisfaction to Groups," *Small Group Research,* June 2002, pp 271–312.

[15]"Collaboration Provides Edge," *Arizona Republic,* April 10, 2005, p 2. Also see L L Berry, "The Collaborative Organization: Leadership Lessons from Mayo Clinic," *Organizational Dynamics,* no. 3, 2004, pp 228–42.

[16]P Burrows, "Cisco's Comeback," *BusinessWeek,* November 24, 2003, p 124.

[17]For more on the intersection between individuals and teams, see D K Sherman and H S Kim, "Is There an 'I' in 'Team'? The Role of the Self in Group-Serving Judgments," *Journal of Personality and Social Psychology,* January 2005, pp 108–20; T Halfhill, E Sundstrom, J Lahner, W Calderone, and T M Nielsen, "Group Personality Composition and Group Effectiveness," *Small Group Research,* February 2005, pp 83–105; N Bacon, "Worker Responses to Teamworking: Exploring Employee Attributions of Managerial Motives," *International Journal of Human Resource Management,* February 2005, pp 238–55; J E Mathieu, T S Heffner, G F Goodwin, J A Cannon-Bowers, and E Salas, "Scaling the Quality of Teammates' Mental Models: Equifinality and Normative Comparisons," *Journal of Organizational Behavior,* February 2005, pp 37–56; and G Chen, "Newcomer Adaptation in Teams: Multilevel Antecedents and Outcomes," *Academy of Management Journal,* February 2005, pp 101–16.

[18]As quoted in P B Brown, "What I Know Now," *Fast Company,* January 2005, p 96.

[19]For example, see C O Longenecker and M Neubert, "Barriers and Gateways to Management Cooperation and Teamwork," *Business Horizons,* September–October 2000, pp 37–44; and M D Cannon and A C Edmondson, "Confronting Failure: Antecedents and Consequences of Shared Beliefs about Failure in Organizational Work Groups," *Journal of Organizational Behavior,* March 2001, pp 161–77.

[20]P Raeburn, "Whoops! Wrong Patient," *BusinessWeek,* June 17, 2002, p 85.

[21]See J D Knottnerus, "The Need for Theory and the Value of Cooperation: Disruption and Deritualization," *Sociological Spectrum,* January–February 2005, pp 5–19; and Z Simsek, J F Veiga, M H Lubatkin, and R N Dino, "Modeling the Multilevel Determinants of Top Management Team Behavioral Integration," *Academy of Management Journal,* February 2005, pp 69–84.

[22]See M E Haskins, J Liedtka, and J Rosenblum, "Beyond Teams: Toward an Ethic of Collaboration," *Organizational Dynamics,* Spring 1998, pp 34–50; C C Chen, X P Chen, and J R Meindl, "How Can Cooperation Be Fostered? The Cultural Effects of Individualism-Collectivism," *Academy of Management Review,* April 1998, pp 285–304; and A Pomeroy, "Can't We All Just Get Along?" *HR Magazine,* April 2005, p 16.

[23]A Kohn, "How to Succeed without Even Vying," *Psychology Today,* September 1986, pp 27–28. Sports psychologists discuss "cooperative competition" in S Sleek, "Competition: Who's the Real Opponent?" *APA Monitor,* July 1996, p 8.

[24]D W Johnson, G Maruyama, R Johnson, D Nelson, and L Skon, "Effects of Cooperative, Competitive, and Individualistic Goal Structures on Achievement: A Meta-Analysis," *Psychological Bulletin,* January 1981, pp 56–57. An alternative interpretation of the foregoing study that emphasizes the influence of situational factors can be found in J L Cotton and M S Cook, "Meta-Analysis and the Effects of Various Reward Systems: Some Different Conclusions from Johnson et al.," *Psychological Bulletin,* July 1982, pp 176–83. Also see A E Ortiz, D W Johnson, and R T Johnson, "The Effect of Positive Goal and Resource Interdependence on Individual Performance," *Journal of Social Psychology,* April 1996, pp 243–49; and S L Gaertner, J F Dovidio, M C Rust, J A Nier, B S Banker, C M Ward, G R Mottola, and M Houlette, "Reducing Intergroup Bias: Elements of Intergroup

Cooperation," *Journal of Personality and Social Psychology,* March 1999, pp 388–402.

[25]R Zemke, "Office Spaces," *Training,* May 2002, p 24.

[26]R Lieber, "Timex Resets Its Watch," *Fast Company,* November 2001, p 48; F Warner, "He Builds Company Towns," *Fast Company,* January 2002, pp 46, 48; and L Tischler, "Death to the Cubicle!" *Fast Company,* June 2005, pp 29–30.

[27]S W Cook and M Pelfrey, "Reactions to Being Helped in Cooperating Interracial Groups: A Context Effect," *Journal of Personality and Social Psychology,* November 1985, p 1243. Also see W E Watson, L Johnson, and D Merritt, "Team Orientation, Self-Orientation, and Diversity in Task Groups," *Group & Organization Management,* June 1998, pp 161–88.

[28]See A J Stahelski and R A Tsukuda, "Predictors of Cooperation in Health Care Teams," *Small Group Research,* May 1990, pp 220–33. Also see K Aquino and A Reed II, "A Social Dilemma Perspective on Cooperative Behavior in Organizations," *Group & Organization Management,* December 1998, pp 390–413.

[29]See R Zemke, "The Confidence Crisis," *Training,* June 2004, pp 22–30; A S Wellner, "Who Can You Trust?" *Inc.,* October 2004, pp 39–40; and D N Sull and D Houlder, "Do Your Commitments Match Your Convictions?" *Harvard Business Review,* January 2005, pp 82–91.

[30]Data from "US CEOs Rank Low in Trust," *USA Today,* March 22, 2005, p 1B.

[31]J Barbian, "Short Shelf Life," *Training,* June 2002, p 52.

[32]See R Zemke, "Trust Inspires Trust," *Training,* January 2002, p 10; Y Schul, R Mayo, and E Burnstein, "Encoding under Trust and Distrust: The Spontaneous Activation of Incongruent Cognitions," *Journal of Personality and Social Psychology,* May 2004, pp 668–79; M D Spector and G E Jones, "Trust in the Workplace: Factors Affecting Trust Formation between Team Members," *Journal of Social Psychology,* June 2004, pp 311–21; and K S Cook, "Networks, Norms, and Trust: The Social Psychology of Social Capital," *Social Psychology Quarterly,* March 2005, pp 4–14.

[33]J D Lewis and A Weigert, "Trust as a Social Reality," *Social Forces,* June 1985, p 971. Trust is examined as an *indirect* factor in K T Dirks, "The Effects of Interpersonal Trust on Work Group Performance," *Journal of Applied Psychology,* June 1999, pp 445–55.

[34]R C Mayer, J H Davis, and F D Schoorman, "An Integrative Model of Organizational Trust," *Academy of Management Review,* July 1995, p 715.

[35]Lewis and Weigert, "Trust as a Social Reality," p 970. Also see C A Insko, J L Kirchner, B Pinter, J Efaw, and T Wildschut, "Interindividual–Intergroup Discontinuity as a Function of Trust and Categorization: The Paradox of Expected Cooperation," *Journal of Personality and Social Psychology,* February 2005, pp 365–85.

[36]For an interesting trust exercise, see G Thompson and P F Pearce. "The Team-Trust Game," *Training & Development Journal,* May 1992, pp 42–43. Also see E C Tomlinson,

B R Dineen, and R J Lewicki, "The Road to Reconciliation: Antecedents of Victim Willingness to Reconcile following a Broken Promise," *Journal of Management,* no. 2, 2004, pp 165–87.

[37]M Powell, "Betrayal," *Inc.,* April 1996, p 24. Also see L Prusak and D Cohen, "How to Invest in Social Capital," *Harvard Business Review,* June 2001, pp 86–93; and G Colvin, "Tapping the Trust Fund," *Fortune,* April 29, 2002, p 44.

[38]See G L Graham, "If You Want Honesty, Break Some Rules," *Harvard Business Review,* April 2002, pp 42–47.

[39]For support, see G M Spreitzer and A K Mishra, "Giving Up Control without Losing Control: Trust and Its Substitutes' Effects on Managers' Involving Employees in Decision Making," *Group & Organization Management,* June 1999, pp 155–87. Also see K Ayers, "Creating a Responsible Workplace," *HR Magazine,* February 2005, pp 111–13; and "Hector Ruiz, CEO of AMD," *Fortune,* March 21, 2005, p 114.

[40]Adapted from F Bartolomé, "Nobody Trusts the Boss Completely—Now What?" *Harvard Business Review,* March–April 1989, pp 135–42. Also see R Zemke, "Can You Manage Trust?" *Training,* February 2000, pp 76–83; D Seidman, "The Case for Ethical Leadership," *Academy of Management Executive,* May 2004, pp 134–38; and P Cairo, D L Dotlich, and S H Rhinesmith, "The Unnatural Leader," *Training & Development,* March 2005, pp 26–31.

[41]W Foster Owen, "Metaphor Analysis of Cohesiveness in Small Discussion Groups," *Small Group Behavior,* August 1985, p 416. Also see M D Michalisin, S J Karau, and C Tangpong, "Top Management Team Cohesion and Superior Industry Returns: An Empirical Study of the Resource-Based View," *Group & Organization Management,* February 2004, pp 125–40; K Sanders and A Nauta, "Social Cohesiveness and Absenteeism: The Relationship between Characteristics of Employees and Short-Term Absenteeism within an Organization," *Small Group Research,* December 2004, pp 724–41; J Hardy, M A Eys, and A V Carron, "Exploring the Potential Disadvantages of High Cohesion in Sports Teams," *Small Group Research,* April 2005, pp 166–87; and S M Burke et al., "Cohesion as Shared Beliefs in Exercise Classes," *Small Group Research,* June 2005, pp 267–88.

[42]This distinction is based on discussion in A Tziner, "Differential Effects of Group Cohesiveness Types: A Clarifying Overview," *Social Behavior and Personality,* no. 2, 1982 pp 227–39.

[43]B Mullen and C Copper, "The Relation between Group Cohesiveness and Performance: An Integration," *Psychological Bulletin,* March 1994, p 224.

[44]Ibid. Additional research evidence is reported in P J Sullivan and D L Feltz, "The Relationship between Intrateam Conflict and Cohesion within Hockey Teams," *Small Group Research,* June 2001, pp 342–55; and A Chang and P Bordia, "A Multidimensional Approach to the Group Cohesion–Group Performance Relationship," *Small Group Research,* August 2001, pp 379–405.

[45]Based on B Mullen, T Anthony, E Salas, and J E Driskell, "Group Cohesiveness and Quality of Decision Making: An

Integration of Tests of the Groupthink Hypothesis," *Small Group Research,* May 1994, pp 189–204. Also see A V Carron et al., "Using Consensus as a Criterion for Groupness: Implications for the Cohesion–Group Success Relationship," *Small Group Research,* August 2004, pp 466–91.

46G L Miles, "The Plant of Tomorrow Is in Texas Today," *Business Week,* July 28, 1986, p 76.

47See, for example, P Jin, "Work Motivation and Productivity in Voluntarily Formed Work Teams: A Field Study in China," *Organizational Behavior and Human Decision Processes,* 1993, pp 133–55. Also see S Reysen, "Construction of a New Scale: The Reysen Likability Scale," *Social Behavior and Personality,* no. 2, 2005, pp 201–8.

48Based on discussion in E E Lawler III and S A Mohrman, "Quality Circles: After the Honeymoon," *Organizational Dynamics,* Spring 1987, pp 42–54.

49For a report on 8,000 quality circles in Mexico, see R Carvajal, "Its Own Reward," *Business Mexico,* special edition 1996, pp 26–28.

50The historical development of quality circles is discussed by C Stohl, "Bridging the Parallel Organization: A Study of Quality Circle Effectiveness," in *Organizational Communication,* ed M L McLaughlin (Beverly Hills, CA: Sage Publications, 1987), pp 416–30; T Li-Ping Tang, P Smith Tollison, and H D Whiteside, "The Effect of Quality Circle Initiation on Motivation to Attend Quality Circle Meetings and on Task Performance," *Personnel Psychology,* Winter 1987, pp 799–814; and N Kano, "A Perspective on Quality Activities in American Firms," *California Management Review,* Spring 1993, pp 12–31. Also see the discussion of quality circles in J B Keys, L T Denton, and T R Miller, "The Japanese Management Theory Jungle—Revisited," *Journal of Management,* Summer 1994, pp 373–402.

51Based on discussion in K Buch and R Spangler, "The Effects of Quality Circles on Performance and Promotions," *Human Relations,* June 1990, pp 573–82.

52See G R Ferris and J A Wagner III, "Quality Circles in the United States: A Conceptual Reevaluation," *Journal of Applied Behavioral Science,* no. 2, 1985, pp 155–67.

53Lawler and Mohrman, "Quality Circles: After the Honeymoon," p 43. Also see E E Lawler III, "Total Quality Management and Employee Involvement: Are They Compatible?" *Academy of Management Executive,* February 1994, pp 68–76.

54See M L Marks, "The Question of Quality Circles," *Psychology Today,* March 1986, pp 36–38, 42, 44, 46.

55See A K Naj, "Some Manufacturers Drop Effort to Adopt Japanese Techniques," *The Wall Street Journal,* May 7, 1993, p A1.

56See E E Adam, Jr, "Quality Circle Performance," *Journal of Management,* March 1991, pp 25–39.

57See R P Steel and R F Lloyd, "Cognitive, Affective, and Behavioral Outcomes of Participation in Quality Circles: Conceptual and Empirical Findings," *Journal of Applied Behavioral Science,* no. 1, 1988, pp 1–17; M L Marks, P H Mirvis, E J Hackett, and J F Grady Jr, "Employee Participation in a Quality Circle Program: Impact on Quality of Work Life, Productivity, and Absenteeism," *Journal of Applied Psychology,* February 1986, pp 61–69; and Buch and Spangler, "The Effects of Quality Circles on Performance and Promotions." Additional research is reported in T Li-Ping Tang, P Smith Tollison, and H D Whiteside, "Differences between Active and Inactive Quality Circles in Attendance and Performance," *Public Personnel Management,* Winter 1993, pp 579–90; and C Doucouliagos, "Worker Participation and Productivity in Labor-Managed and Participatory Capitalist Firms: A Meta-Analysis," *Industrial and Labor Relations Review,* October 1995, pp 58–77.

58See D D Davis, "The Tao of Leadership in Virtual Teams," *Organizational Dynamics,* no. 1, 2004, pp 47–62; S A Furst, M Reeves, B Rosen, and R S Blackburn, "Managing the Life Cycle of Virtual Teams," *Academy of Management Executive,* May 2004, pp 6–20; L L Martins, L L Gilson, and M T Maynard, "Virtual Teams: What Do We Know and Where Do We Go from Here?" *Journal of Management,* no. 6, 2004, pp 805–36; and L M Maruping and R Agarwal, "Managing Team Interpersonal Processes through Technology: A Task-Technology Fit Perspective," *Journal of Applied Psychology,* December 2004, pp 975–990.

59See W F Cascio, "Managing a Virtual Workplace," *Academy of Management Executive,* August 2000, pp 81–90; C Joinson, "Managing Virtual Teams," *HR Magazine,* June 2002, pp 69–73; and D Robb, "Virtual Workplace," *HR Magazine,* June 2002, pp 105–13.

60Based on P Bordia, N DiFonzo, and A Chang, "Rumor as Group Problem Solving: Development Patterns in Informal Computer-Mediated Groups," *Small Group Research,* February 1999, pp 8–28. Also see M L Baba, J Gluesing, H Ratner, and K H Wagner, "The Contexts of Knowing: Natural History of a Globally Distributed Team," *Journal of Organizational Behavior,* August 2004, pp 547–87.

61See K A Graetz, E S Boyle, C E Kimble, P Thompson, and J L Garloch, "Information Sharing in Face-to-Face, Teleconferencing, and Electronic Chat Groups," *Small Group Research,* December 1998, pp 714–43.

62Based on F Niederman and R J Volkema, "The Effects of Facilitator Characteristics on Meeting Preparation, Set Up, and Implementation," *Small Group Research,* June 1999, pp 330–60; and B Whitworth, B Gallupe, and R McQueen, "Generating Agreement in Computer-Mediated Groups," *Small Group Research,* October 2001, pp 625–65.

63Based on J J Sosik, B J Avolio, and S S Kahai, "Inspiring Group Creativity: Comparing Anonymous and Identified Electronic Brainstorming," *Small Group Research,* February 1998, pp 3–31. For practical advice on brainstorming, see C Caggiano, "The Right Way to Brainstorm," *Inc.,* July 1999, p 94. Also see S S Kahai, J J Sosik, and B J Avolio, "Effects of Participative and Directive Leadership in Electronic Groups," *Group and Organization Management,* February 2004, pp 67–105.

[64]Based on M M Montoya-Weiss, A P Massey, and M Song, "Getting It Together: Temporal Coordination and Conflict Management in Global Virtual Teams," *Academy of Management Journal,* December 2001, pp 1251–62.

[65]Data from C Joinson, "Teams at Work," *HR Magazine,* May 1999, pp 30–36.

[66]B Dumaine, "Who Needs a Boss?" *Fortune,* May 7, 1990, p 52. Also see D Vredenburgh and I Y He, "Leadership Lessons from a Conductorless Orchestra," *Business Horizons,* September–October 2003. pp 19–24; and C A O'Reilly III and M L Tushman, "The Ambidextrous Organization," *Harvard Business Review,* April 2004, pp 74–81.

[67]Adapted from Table 1 in V U Druskat and J V Wheeler, "Managing from the Boundary: The Effective Leadership of Self-Managing Work Teams," *Academy of Management Journal,* August 2003, pp 435–57.

[68]See A E Randal and K S Jaussi, "Functional Background Identity, Diversity, and Individual Performance in Cross-Functional Teams," *Academy of Management Journal,* December 2003, pp 763–74; and L Fleming, "Perfecting Cross-Pollination," *Harvard Business Review,* September 2004, pp 22–24.

[69]Excerpted from "Fast Talk," *Fast Company,* February 2004, p 50.

[70]See "1996 Industry Report: What Self-Managing Teams Manage," *Training,* October 1996, p 69.

[71]See L L Thompson, *Making the Team: A Guide for Managers* (Upper Saddle River, NJ: Prentice Hall, 2000).

[72]See P S Goodman, R Devadas, and T L Griffith Hughson, "Groups and Productivity: Analyzing the Effectiveness of Self-Managing Teams," in *Productivity in Organizations,* eds J P Campbell, R J Campbell, and Associates (San Francisco: Jossey-Bass, 1998), pp 295–327. Also see R C Liden, S J Wayne, and M L Kraimer, "Managing Individual Performance in Work Groups," *Human Resource Management,* Spring 2001, pp 63–72; R Batt, "Who Benefits from Teams? Comparing Workers, Supervisors, and Managers," *Industrial Relations,* January 2004, pp 183–209; and H van Mierlo, C G Rutte, M A J Kompier, and H A C M Doorewaard, "Self-Managing Teamwork and Psychological Well-Being: Review of a Multilevel Research Domain," *Group & Organization Management,* April 2005, pp 211–35.

[73]See C Douglas and W L Gardner, "Transition to Self-Directed Work Teams: Implications of Transition Time and Self-Monitoring for Managers' Use of Influence Tactics," *Journal of Organizational Behavior,* February 2004, pp 47–65; and R G Perry and A Zender, "Let's Get Together," *Association Management,* July 2004, pp 28–33, 84.

[74]Based on K Lowry Miller, "GM's German Lessons," *BusinessWeek,* December 20, 1993, pp 67–68.

[75]See E Brown, "War Games to Make You Better at Business," *Fortune,* September 28, 1998, pp 291–96; C Dahle, "Can This Off-Site Be Saved?" *Fast Company,* October 2001, pp 118–27; J Merritt, "Welcome to Ethics 101," *BusinessWeek,* October 18, 2004, p 90; "Leadership Tanks," *Training,* December 2004,

p 18; and M R della Cava, "Corporate Teams, Built by a Tank," *USA Today,* December 21, 2004, pp 1D–2D.

[76]R Henkoff, "Companies that Train Best," *Fortune,* March 22, 1993, p 73.

[77]See M J McCarthy, "A Management Rage: Beating the Drums for the Company," *The Wall Street Journal,* August 13, 1996, pp A1, A6.

[78]An excellent resource is W G Dyer, *Team Building: Current Issues and New Alternatives,* 3rd ed (Reading, MA: Addison-Wesley, 1995). Also see J R Hackman and R Wageman, "A Theory of Team Coaching," *Academy of Management Review,* April 2005, pp 269–87.

[79]S Bucholz and T Roth, *Creating the High-Performance Team* (New York: John Wiley & Sons, 1987), p xi. Also see L L Gilson and C E Shalley, "A Little Creativity Goes a Long Way: An Examination of Teams' Engagement in Creative Processes," *Journal of Management,* no. 4, 2004, pp 453–70; and M F R Kets de Vries, "Leadership Group Coaching in Action: The Zen of Creating High-Performance Teams," *Academy of Management Executive,* February 2005, pp 61–76.

[80]Bucholz and Roth, *Creating the High-Performance Team,* p 14. Also see V U Druskat and S B Wolff, "Building the Emotional Intelligence of Groups," *Harvard Business Review,* March 2001, pp 80–90; and A Edmondson, R Bohmer, and G Pisano, "Speeding Up Team Learning," *Harvard Business Review,* October 2001, pp 125–32.

[81]P King, "What Makes Teamwork Work?" *Psychology Today,* December 1989, p 17. A critical view of teams is presented in C Casey, " 'Come, Join Our Family': Discipline and Integration in Corporate Organizational Culture," *Human Relations,* February 1999, pp 155–78.

[82]J Raelin, "Preparing for Leaderful Practice," *Training & Development,* March 2004, pp 65–70.

[83]Adapted from C C Manz and H P Sims Jr, "Leading Workers to Lead Themselves: The External Leadership of Self-Managing Work Teams," *Administrative Science Quarterly,* March 1987, pp 106–29. Also see C C Manz, *Mastering Self-Leadership: Empowering Yourself for Personal Excellence* (Englewood Cliffs, NJ: Prentice Hall, 1992); M Uhl-Bien and G B Graen, "Individual Self-Management: Analysis of 'Professional' Self-Managing Activities in Functional and Cross-Functional Work Teams," *Academy of Management Journal,* June 1998, pp 340–50; G E Prussia, J S Anderson, and C C Manz, "Self-Leadership and Performance Outcomes: The Mediating Influence of Self-Efficacy," *Journal of Organizational Behavior,* September 1998, pp 523–38; and P Troiano, "Nice Guys Finish First," *Management Review,* December 1998, p 8.

[84]D Brady, "Reaping the Wind," *BusinessWeek,* October 11, 2004, pp 201–2. Reprinted by permission of The McGraw-Hill Companies, Inc.

[85]Questionnaire items adapted from C Johnson-George and W C Swap, "Measurement of Specific Interpersonal Trust: Construction and Validation of a Scale to Assess Trust in a Specific Other," *Journal of Personality and Social Psychology,* December 1982, pp 1306–17; and D J McAllister, "Affect- and

Cognition-Based Trust as Foundations for Interpersonal Cooperation in Organizations," *Academy of Management Journal,* February 1995, pp 24–59.

[86]Ten questionnaire items excerpted from W G Dyer, *Team Building: Current Issues and New Alternatives,* 3rd ed (Reading, MA: Addison-Wesley, 1995), pp 96–99. © 1995. Used by permission of the Estate of William G Dyer.

[87]S Williams, "All Smoke, No Fire," *Fast Company,* April 1996, p 134. Also in *Fast Company's* online archives at www.fastcompany.com/backissues.

CHAPTER 12

[1]Excerpted from K Tyler, "Training Revs Up," *HR Magazine,* April 2005, pp 60–61. Reprinted with the permission of HR Magazine published by the Society for Human Resource Management, Alexandria, VA.

[2]Problems with rational decision making are discussed by P Coy, "Why Logic Often Takes a Backseat," *BusinessWeek,* March 28, 2005, pp 94–95.

[3]Excerpted from "Contented Employees Mean Satisfied Customers at Baptist Health Care," *Training,* January 2005, p 11.

[4]See K Gruber, "Scenario Technique: Scenarios Europe 2010," www.dbresearch.com/servlet/reweb2.ReWEB?rwkey=u436490, accessed March 28, 2005.

[5]The steps for conducting scenario planning are outlined by "Scenario Technique: Addressing Key Drivers in the Future," http://innovation.im-boot.org/modules.php?name=Content&pa=showpage&pid=153, accessed March 28, 2005.

[6]This study was conducted by P C Nutt, "Expanding the Search for Alternatives during Strategic Decision-Making," *Academy of Management Executive,* November 2004, pp 13–28.

[7]Results can be found in J P Bymes, D C Miller, and W D Schafer, "Gender Differences in Risk Taking: A Meta-Analysis," *Psychological Bulletin,* May 1999, pp 367–83.

[8]The implementation process and its relationship to decision outcomes is discussed by S J Miller, D J Hickson, and D C Wilson, "Decision-Making in Organizations," in *Handbook of Organization Studies,* eds S R Clegg, C Hardy and W R Nord (London: Sage Publications, 1996), pp 293–312.

[9]H A Simon, "Rational Decision Making in Business Organizations," *American Economic Review,* September 1979, p 510.

[10]For a complete discussion of bounded rationality, see H A Simon, *Administrative Behavior,* 2nd ed (New York: Free Press, 1957); J G March and H A Simon, *Organizations* (New York: John Wiley, 1958): H A Simon, "Altruism and Economics," *American Economic Review,* May 1993, pp 156–61; and R Nagel, "A Survey on Experimental Beauty Contest Games: Bounded Rationality and Learning," in *Games and Human Behavior,* eds D V Budescu, I Erev, and R Zwick (Mahwah, NJ: 1999), pp 105–42.

[11]Biases associated with using shortcuts in decision making are discussed by A Tversky and D Kahneman, "Judgment under Uncertainty: Heuristics and Biases," *Science,* September 1974, pp 1124–31; and E Hölzl and E Kirchler, "Causal Attribution and Hindsight Bias for Economic Developments," *Journal of Applied Psychology,* January 2005, pp 167–74.

[12]M D Hovanesian, "Don't Just Analyze the Market, Analyze the Investor," *BusinessWeek,* May 21, 2001, pp 124–25.

[13]Results can be found in "The Big Picture: 'Hurry Up and Decide!' " *BusinessWeek,* May 14, 2001, p 16.

[14]See the related discussion in J Cross and T O'Driscoll, "Welcome to an Era in Which Learning Fuses with Real-Time Work. The Convergence Is Ushering in a Whole New Era," *Training,* February 2005, pp 31–35.

[15]D W De Long and P Seemann, "Confronting Conceptual Confusion and Conflict in Knowledge Management," *Organizational Dynamics,* Summer 2000, p 33.

[16]Supportive research is reviewed by A C Inkpen and E W K Tsang, "Social Capital, Networks, and Knowledge Transfer," *Academy of Management Review,* January 2005, pp 146–65.

[17]These statistics can be found in P Babcock, "Shedding Light on Knowledge Management," *HR Magazine,* May 2004, pp 47–50.

[18]R Lubit, "Tacit Knowledge and Knowledge Management: The Keys to Sustainable Competitive Advantage," *Organizational Dynamics,* 2001, p 166.

[19]See M A McFadyen and A A Cannella Jr, "Social Capital and Knowledge Creation: Diminishing Returns of the Number and Strength of Exchange Relationships," *Academy of Management Journal,* October 2004, pp 735–46.

[20]Details of the application of KM to hospital settings can be found in T J Mullaney and A Weintraub, "The Digital Hospital," *BusinessWeek,* March 28, 2005, pp 77–84.

[21]Excerpted from R Cross, A Parker, L Prusak, and S P Borgatti, "Knowing What We Know: Supporting Knowledge Creation and Sharing in Social Networks," *Organizational Dynamics,* Fall 2001, p 109.

[22]Ibid.

[23]Results can be found in W H Stewart Jr and P L Roth, "Risk Propensity Differences between Entrepreneurs and Managers: A Meta-Analytic Review," *Journal of Applied Psychology,* February 2001, pp 145–53.

[24]This definition was derived from A J Rowe and R O Mason, *Managing with Style: A Guide to Understanding, Assessing and Improving Decision Making* (San Francisco: Jossey-Bass, 1987).

[25]The discussion of styles was based on material contained in ibid.

[26]See Z Stambor, "Older Consumers Factor More Positives, Specifics into Product Choices," *Monitor on Psychology,* April 2005, p 10; and Rowe and Mason, *Managing with Style.*

[27]The details of this case are discussed in J Ross and B M Staw, "Organizational Escalation and Exit: Lessons from the

Shoreham Nuclear Power Plant," *Academy of Management Journal,* August 1993, pp 701–32.

[28]Ibid.

[29]Results can be found in S L Kirby and M A Davis, "A Study of Escalating Commitment in Principal-Agent Relationships: Effects of Monitoring and Personal Responsibility," *Journal of Applied Psychology,* April 1998, pp 206–17.

[30]Supportive results can be found in H Moon, "Looking Forward and Looking Back: Integrating Completion and Sunk-Cost Effects within an Escalation-of-Commitment Progress Decision," *Journal of Applied Psychology,* February 2001, pp 104–13.

[31]See D A Hantula and J L D Bragger, "The Effects of Feedback Equivocality on Escalation of Commitment: An Empirical Investigation of Decision Dilemma Theory," *Journal of Applied Social Psychology,* February 1999, pp 424–44.

[32]Results can be found in C R Greer and G K Stephens, "Escalation of Commitment: A Comparison of Differences between Mexican and US Decision Makers," *Journal of Management,* 2001, pp 51–78.

[33]See Ross and Staw, "Organizational Escalation and Exit."

[34]Supportive results are provided by G McNamara, H Moon, and P Bromiley, "Banking on Commitment: Intended and Unintended Consequences of an Organization's Attempt to Attenuate Escalation of Commitment," *Academy of Management Journal,* April 2002, pp 443–52; and J B Schmidt and R J Calantone, "Escalation of Commitment during New Product Development," *Journal of the Academy of Marketing Science,* April 2002, pp 103–18.

[35]See K Shimizu and M A Hitt, "Strategic Flexibility: Organizational Preparedness to Reverse Ineffective Strategic Decisions," *Academy of Management Executive,* November 2004, pp 44–59; and B M Staw and J Ross, "Behavior in Escalation Situations: Antecedents, Prototypes, and Solutions," in *Research in Organizational Behavior,* vol. 9, eds L L Cummings and B M Staw (Greenwich, CT: JAI Press, 1987), pp 39–78.

[36]E Sadler-Smith and E Shefy, "The Intuitive Executive: Understanding and Applying 'Gut Feel' in Decision-Making," *Academy of Management Executive,* November 2004, p 77.

[37]Ibid., pp 76–91,

[38]Excerpted from C C Miller and R D Ireland, "Intuition in Strategic Decision Making: Friend or Foe in the Fast-Paced 21st Century," *Academy of Management Executive,* February 2005, p 20.

[39]Ibid., pp 19–30.

[40]This discussion was based on material in Sadler-Smith and Shefy, "The Intuitive Executive"; and Miller and Ireland, "Intuition in Strategic Decision Making."

[41]A summary of research on the hindsight bias is provided by R L Guilbault, F B Bryant, J H Brockway, and E J Posavac,

"A Meta-Analysis of Research on Hindsight Bias," *Basic and Applied Social Psychology,* vol. 26, no. 2, 2004, pp 103–17.

[42]Results can be found in C K W De Dreu and M A West, "Minority Dissent and Team Innovation: The Importance of Participation in Decision Making," *Journal of Applied Psychology,* December 2001, pp 1191–201.

[43]These recommendations were derived from R Y Hirokawa, "Group Communication and Decision-Making Performance: A Continued Test of the Functional Perspective," *Human Communication Research,* October 1988, pp 487–515.

[44]See the related discussion in B B Baltes, M W Dickson, M P Sherman, C C Bauer, and J S LaGanke, "Computer-Mediated Communication and Group Decision Making: A Meta-Analysis," *Organizational Behavior and Human Decision Processes,* January 2002, pp 156–79.

[45]These guidelines were derived from G P Huber, *Managerial Decision Making* (Glenview, IL: Scott, Foresman, 1980), p 149.

[46]G W Hill, "Group versus Individual Performance: Are N + 1 Heads Better than One?" *Psychological Bulletin,* May 1982, p 535.

[47]D Pringle, "Finnish Line: Facing Big Threat from Microsoft, Nokia Places a Bet," *The Wall Street Journal,* May 22, 2002, p A16.

[48]J H Davis, "Some Compelling Intuitions about Group Consensus Decisions, Theoretical and Empirical Research, and Interpersonal Aggregation Phenomena: Selected Examples, 1950–1990," *Organizational Behavior and Human Decision Processes,* June 1992, pp 3–38.

[49]Supporting results can be found in J Hedlund, D R Ilgen, and J R Hollenbeck, "Decision Accuracy in Computer-Mediated versus Face-to-Face Decision-Making Teams," *Organizational Behavior and Human Decision Processes.* October 1998, pp 30–47.

[50]See J R Winquist and J R Larson Jr, "Information Pooling: When It Impacts Group Decision Making," *Journal of Personality and Social Psychology,* February 1998, pp 371–77.

[51]G M Parker, *Team Players and Teamwork: The New Competitive Business Strategy* (San Francisco, CA: Jossey-Bass, 1990).

[52]These recommendations were obtained from ibid.

[53]See A F Osborn, *Applied Imagination: Principles and Procedures of Creative Thinking,* 3rd ed (New York: Scribners, 1979).

[54]See W H Cooper, R Brent Gallupe, S Pollard, and J Cadsby, "Some Liberating Effects of Anonymous Electronic Brainstorming," *Small Group Research,* April 1998, pp 147–78;

[55]These recommendations and descriptions were derived from B Nussbaum, "The Power of Design," *BusinessWeek,* May 17, 2004, pp 86–94.

[56]An application of the NGT can be found in C Y Yiu, H K Ho, S M Lo, and B Q Hu, "Performance Evaluation for Cost

Estimators by Reliability Interval Method," *Journal of Construction Engineering and Management,* January 2005, pp 108–16.

[57]See L Thompson, "Improving the Creativity of Organizational Work Groups," *Academy of Management Executive,* February 2003, pp 96–109.

[58]See N C Dalkey, D L Rourke, R Lewis, and D Snyder, *Studies in the Quality of Life: Delphi and Decision Making* (Lexington, MA: Lexington Books: D C Heath and Co., 1972).

[59]Applications of the Delphi technique can be found in A Alahlafi and S Burge, "What Should Undergraduate Medical Students Know about Psoriasis? Involving Patients in Curriculum Development: Modified Delphi Technique," *British Medical Journal,* March 19, 2005, pp 633–36; and A M Deshpande, R N Shiffman, and P M Nadkarni, "Metadata-Driven Delphi Rating on the Internet," *Computer Methods and Programs in Biomedicine,* January 2005, pp 49–56.

[60]A thorough description of computer-aided decision-making systems is provided by M C Er and A C Ng, "The Anonymity and Proximity Factors in Group Decision Support Systems," *Decision Support Systems,* May 1995, pp 75–83.

[61]See J Greene, "Combat over Collaboration," *BusinessWeek,* April 18, 2005, pp 64, 66.

[62]Supportive results can be found in S S Lam and J Schaubroeck, "Improving Group Decisions by Better Polling Information: A Comparative Advantage of Group Decision Support Systems," *Journal of Applied Psychology,* August 2000, pp 565–73; and I Benbasat and J Lim, "Information Technology Support for Debiasing Group Judgments: An Empirical Evaluation," *Organizational Behavior and Human Decision Processes,* September 2000, pp 167–83.

[63]Results can be found in Baltes et al., "Computer-Medicated Communication and Group Decision Making."

[64]See "B-Schools for the 21st Century," *BusinessWeek,* April 18, 2005, p 112.

[65]This definition was adapted from one provided by R K Scott, "Creative Employees: A Challenge to Managers," *Journal of Creative Behavior,* First Quarter, 1995, pp 64–71.

[66]R Langreth and Z Moukheiber, "Medical Merlins," *Forbes,* June 2003, p 115.

[67]See the discussion in O Janssen, E V De Vliert, and M West, "The Bright and Dark Sides of Individual and Group Innovation: A Special Issue Introduction," *Journal of Organizational Behavior,* March 2004, pp 129–45.

[68]Excerpted from T M Burton, "By Learning from Failures, Lilly Keeps Drug Pipeline Full," *The Wall Street Journal,* April 21, 2004, p A1.

[69]Results can be found in E Tahmincioglu, "Gifts that Gall," *Workforce Management,* April 2004, p 45.

[70]Details of this study can be found in M Basadur, "Managing Creativity: A Japanese Model," *Academy of Management Executive,* May 1992, pp 29–42.

[71]This recommendation is supported by R M Kanter, "The Middle Manager as Innovator," *Harvard Business Review,* July–August 2004, pp 150–61.

[72]A review of innovation research is provided by N Anderson, C K W De Dreu, and B A Nijstad, "The Rountinization of Innovation Research: A Constructively Critical Review of the State-of-the-Science," *Journal of Organizational Behavior,* March 2004, pp 147–73.

[73]See E Ferlie, L Fitzgerald, M Wood, and C Hawkins, "The Nonspread of Innovations: The Mediating Role of Professionals," *Academy of Management Journal,* February 2005, pp 117–34; and A Pirola-Merlo and L Mann, "The Relationship between Individual Creativity and Team Creativity: Aggregating across People and Time," *Journal of Organizational Behavior,* March 2004, pp 235–57.

[74]P Magnusson, "Small Biz vs. the Terrorists," *BusinessWeek,* March 4, 2002, p 68.

[75]T A Matherly and R E Goldsmith, "The Two Faces of Creativity," *Business Horizons,* September–October 1985, p 9.

[76]This discussion is based on research reviewed in M A Collins and T M Amabile, "Motivation and Creativity," in *Handbook of Creativity,* eds R J Sternberg (Cambridge, UK: Cambridge University Press, 1999), pp 297–311; and G J Feist, "A Meta-Analysis of Personality in Scientific and Artistic Creativity," *Personality and Social Psychology Review,* 1998, pp 290–309.

[77]Personality and creativity were investigated by S Taggar, "Individual Creativity and Group Ability to Utilize Individual Creative Resources: A Multilevel Model," *Academy of Management Journal,* April 2002, pp 315–30; and J M George and J Zhou, "When Openness to Experience and Conscientiousness Are Related to Creative Behavior: An Interactional Approach," *Journal of Applied Psychology,* June 2001, pp 513–24.

[78]J M Higgins, "Innovate or Evaporate: Seven Secrets of Innovative Corporations," *The Futurist,* September–October 1995, p 46.

[79]See the related discussion in T M Amabile, "How to Kill Creativity," *Harvard Business Review,* September–October 1998, pp 77–87.

[80]R P Weiss, "How to Foster Creativity at Work," *Training & Development,* February 2001, pp 64–65.

[81]Excerpted from Nussbaum, "The Power of Design," pp 88, 90–92, 94. Reprinted by permission of The McGraw-Hill Companies, Inc.

[82]The survey and detailed norms can be found in A J Rowe and R O Mason, *Managing with Style: A Guide to Understanding, Assessing, and Improving Decision Making* (San Francisco: Jossey-Bass, 1987).

[83]Excerpted from E J Pollock, "Limited Partners: Lawyers for Enron Faulted Its Deals, Didn't Force Issue," *The Wall Street Journal,* May 22, 2002, pp A1, A18. Reprinted by permission of Dow Jones & Co. Inc. via The Copyright Clearance Center.

CHAPTER 13

[1]Excerpted from A S Wellner, "Let's Be Friends," *Inc.,* March 2005, pp 33–34. By A S Wellner, © 2005 Gruner & Jahr USA Publishing. First published in *Inc.* Magazine. Reprinted with permission.

[2]D Tjosvold, *Learning to Manage Conflict: Getting People to Work Together Productively* (New York: Lexington Books, 1993), p xi.

[3]Ibid., pp xi–xii. Also see " 'Peaceful' Ancient Humans Had a Dark Side," *USA Today,* August 9, 2004, p 6D.

[4]J A Wall Jr and R Robert Callister, "Conflict and Its Management," *Journal of Management,* no. 3 (1995), p 517.

[5]Ibid., p 544.

[6]See M A von Glinow, D L Shapiro, and J M Brett, "Can We Talk, and Should We? Managing Emotional Conflict in Multicultural Teams," *Academy of Management Review,* October 2004, pp 578–92; C Palmeri, "Hair-Pulling in the Dollhouse," *BusinessWeek,* May 2, 2005, pp 76–77; and G Colvin, "CEO Knockdown," *Fortune,* April 4, 2005, pp 19–20.

[7]K Cloke and J Goldsmith, *Resolving Conflicts at Work: A Complete Guide for Everyone on the Job* (San Francisco: Jossey-Bass, 2000), pp 25, 27, 29.

[8]See P J Sauer, "Are You Ready for Some Football Clichés?" *Inc.,* October 2003, pp 97–100; and V P Rindova, M Becerra, and I Contardo, "Enacting Competitive Wars: Competitive Activity, Language Games, and Market Consequences," *Academy of Management Review,* October 2004, pp 670–86.

[9]Cloke and Goldsmith, *Resolving Conflicts at Work,* pp 31–32. Also see M Delahoussaye, "Don't Get Mad, Get Promoted," *Training,* June 2002, p 20; and R E Shea, "Break the Retaliation Cycle," *HR Magazine,* July 2002, pp 89–96.

[10]See "Dying from Work-Related Incidents," *USA Today,* August 10, 2004, p 1A; T Maxon, "Violence in Workplace," *Arizona Republic,* November 13, 2004, p D3; A Fisher, "How to Prevent Violence at Work," *Fortune,* February 21, 2005, p 42; K Gurchiek, "Study: Domestic Violence Spills over into Workplace," *HR Magazine,* March 2005, pp 32, 38; and H Mohr, "Lockheed Sued after Slayings at Plant," *Arizona Republic,* March 20, 2005, pp D1, D3.

[11]See S Alper, D Tjosvold, and K S Law, "Interdependence and Controversy in Group Decision Making: Antecedents to Effective Self-Managing Teams," *Organizational Behavior and Human Decision Processes,* April 1998, pp 33–52.

[12]S P Robbins, " 'Conflict Management' and 'Conflict Resolution' Are Not Synonymous Terms," *California Management Review,* Winter 1978, p 70. For examples of functional and dysfunctional conflict, see A Lashinsky, "At Motorola, a Vet Answers the Call," *Fortune,* September 20, 2004, p 48; C Edwards, "Supercharging Silicon Valley," *BusinessWeek,* October 4, 2004, p 18; and G Farrell, "Witness: Ebbers Pushed Rosy Numbers," *USA Today,* February 23, 2005, p 5B.

[13]Cooperative conflict is discussed in Tjosvold, *Learning to Manage Conflict: Getting People to Work Together Productively.*

Also see A C Amason, "Distinguishing the Effects of Functional and Dysfunctional Conflict on Strategic Decision Making: Resolving a Paradox for Top Management Teams," *Academy of Management Journal,* February 1996, pp 123–48.

[14]Excerpted from T Ursiny, *The Coward's Guide to Conflict: Empowering Solutions for Those Who Would Rather Run than Fight* (Naperville, IL: Sourcebooks, 2003), p 27.

[15]Adapted in part from discussion in A C Filley, *Interpersonal Conflict Resolution* (Glenview, IL: Scott, Foresman, 1975), pp 9–12; and B Fortado, "The Accumulation of Grievance Conflict," *Journal of Management Inquiry,* December 1992, pp 288–303. For related research on the antecedents of marital conflict, see P R Amato and A Booth, "The Legacy of Parents' Marital Discord: Consequences for Children's Marital Quality," *Journal of Personality and Social Psychology,* October 2001, pp 627–38.

[16]Adapted from discussion in Tjosvold, *Learning to Manage Conflict,* pp 12–13.

[17]L Gardenswartz and A Rowe, *Diverse Teams at Work: Capitalizing on the Power of Diversity* (New York: McGraw-Hill, 1994), p 32.

[18]F Keenan, "EMC: Turmoil at the Top?" *BusinessWeek,* March 11, 2002, pp 58–60. Reprinted by permission of The McGraw-Hill Companies, Inc.

[19]Based on "Joseph Tucci, EMC," *BusinessWeek,* January 10, 2005, p 60.

[20]C M Pearson and C L Porath, "On the Nature, Consequences and Remedies of Workplace Incivility: No Time for 'Nice'? Think Again," *Academy of Management Executive,* February 2005, p 7. Also see K Montgomery, K Kane, and C M Vance, "Accounting for Differences in Norms of Respect: A Study of Assessments of Incivility through the Lenses of Race and Gender," *Group and Organization Management,* April 2004, pp 248–68; M Elias, "Bullying Crosses the Line into Workplace," *USA Today,* July 28, 2004, p 7D; S Jayson, "On or off the Field, It's a 'Civility' War out There," *USA Today,* November 30, 2004, p 9D; L W Andrews, "Hard-Core Offenders," *HR Magazine,* December 2004, pp 42–48; "When Bosses Attack," *Training,* May 2005, p 10; and K Gurchiek, "Bullying: It's Not Just on The Playground," *HR Magazine,* June 2005, p 40.

[21]See R Kurtz, "Is Etiquette a Core Value?" *Inc.,* May 2004, p 22; and D Weinstein, "Grace in Small Space: Cubicles Encourage New Era of Etiquette," *Arizona Republic,* March 12, 2005, p D3.

[22]Data from D Stamps, "Yes, Your Boss Is Crazy," *Training,* July 1998, pp 35–39. Also see K Robinson, "Stigma Prevents Depressed Workers from Seeking Treatment, Study Shows," *HR Magazine,* June 2004, p 50; G Morse, "Executive Psychopaths," *Harvard Business Review,* October 2004, pp 20, 22; "Weirdos in the Workplace," *Training,* January 2005, p 14; M Elias, "On the Couch: Mental Health," *USA Today,* April 27, 2005, p 6D; and M Elias, "Mental Illness: Surprising, Disturbing Findings," *USA Today,* June 7, 2005, p 8D.

[23]See S H Milne and T C Blum, "Organizational Characteristics and Employer Responses to Employee Substance Abuse,"

Journal of Management, no. 6, 1998, pp 693–715; J Kline Jr and L Sussman, "An Executive Guide to Workplace Depression," *Academy of Management Executive,* August 2000, pp 103–14; J A Segal, "I'm Depressed—Accommodate Me!" *HR Magazine,* February 2001, pp 139–48; L Tanner, "With Less Stigma, More Drugs, Treatment for Depression Soars," *USA Today,* January 9, 2002, p 9D; K Tyler, "Happiness from a Bottle?" *HR Magazine,* May 2002, pp 30–37; and S Berfield, "A CEO and His Son," *BusinessWeek,* May 27, 2002, pp 72–80.

[24]Also see H Weeks, "Taking the Stress out of Stressful Conversations," *Harvard Business Review,* July–August 2001, pp 112–19; M Delahoussaye, "I'm Not OK, You're Not OK," *Training,* February 2002, p 70; and "Defanging the Drainers," *Training,* January 2005, p 12.

[25]Drawn from J C McCune, "The Change Makers," *Management Review,* May 1999, pp 16–22.

[26]Based on discussion in G Labianca, D J Brass, and B Gray, "Social Networks and Perceptions of Intergroup Conflict: The Role of Negative Relationships and Third Parties," *Academy of Management Journal,* February 1998, pp 55–67. Also see A Bizman and Y Yinon, "Intergroup Conflict Management Strategies as Related to Perceptions of Dual Identity and Separate Groups," *Journal of Social Psychology,* April 2004, pp 115–26; and R J Crisp and J K Nicel, "Disconfirming Intergroup Evaluations: Asymmetric Effects for In-Groups and Out-Groups," *Journal of Social Psychology,* June 2004, pp 247–71.

[27]See C L Aberson, C Shoemaker, and C Tomolillo, "Implicit Bias and Contact: The Role of Interethnic Friendships," *Journal of Social Psychology,* June 2004, pp 335–47; D A Rabuzzi, "The Duh Factor: Understanding Intergenerational Differences in Association Life," *Association Management,* July 2004, pp 24–27, 83; L A Rudman and S A Goodwin, "Gender Differences in Automatic In-Group Bias: Why Do Women Like Women More than Men Like Men?" *Journal of Personality and Social Psychology,* October 2004, pp 494–509; and G Cowan, "Interracial Interactions at Racially Diverse University Campuses," *Journal of Social Psychology,* February 2005, pp 49–63.

[28]Labianca, Brass, and Gray, "Social Networks and Perceptions of Intergroup Conflict," p 63 (emphasis added).

[29]For example, see S C Wright, A Aron, T McLaughlin-Volpe, and S A Ropp, "The Extended Contact Effect: Knowledge of Cross-Group Friendships and Prejudice," *Journal of Personality and Social Psychology,* July 1997, pp 73–90.

[30]See C D Batson, M P Polycarpou, E Harmon-Jones, H J Imhoff, E C Mitchener, L L Bednar, T R Klein, and L Highberger, "Empathy and Attitudes: Can Feeling for a Member of a Stigmatized Group Improve Feelings toward the Group?" *Journal of Personality and Social Psychology,* January 1997, pp 105–18. Also see R van Dick et al., "Role of Perceived Importance in Intergroup Contact," *Journal of Personality and Social Psychology,* August 2004, pp 211–27; D R Avery and K M Thomas, "Blending Content and Contact: The Roles of Diversity Curriculum and Campus Heterogeneity in Fostering Diversity Management Competency," *Academy of Management Learning and Education,* December 2004, pp 380–96; and J N Shelton and J A Richeson, "Intergroup Contact and

Pluralistic Ignorance," *Journal of Personality and Social Psychology,* January 2005, pp 91–107.

[31]Evidence that it pays to ignore interpersonal conflicts in teams is reported in C K W De Dreu, and A E M Van Vianen, "Managing Relationship Conflict and the Effectiveness of Organizational Teams," *Journal of Organizational Behavior,* May 2001, pp 309–28.

[32]For a good overview, see N J Adler, *International Dimensions of Organizational Behavior,* 4th ed (Cincinnati: South-Western, 2002).

[33]See J Duckitt and C Parra, "Dimensions of Group Identification and Out-Group Attitudes in Four Ethnic Groups in New Zealand," *Basic and Applied Social Psychology,* December 2004, pp 237–47; and A L Molinsky, M A Krabbenhoft, N Ambady, and Y S Choi, "Cracking the Nonverbal Code: Intercultural Competence and Gesture Recognition across Cultures," *Journal of Cross-Cultural Psychology,* May 2005, pp 380–95.

[34]"Negotiating South of the Border," *Harvard Management Communication Letter,* August 1999, p 12.

[35]A Rosenbaum, "Testing Cultural Waters," *Management Review,* July–August 1999, p 43 © 1999 American Management Association International. Reprinted by permission of American Management Association International, New York, NY. All rights reserved. (www.amanet.org)

[36]See R L Tung, "American Expatriates Abroad: From Neophytes to Cosmopolitans," *Journal of World Business,* Summer 1998, pp 125–44.

[37]See J Weiss and J Hughes, "What Collaboration? Accept—and Actively Manage—Conflict," *Harvard Business Review,* March 2005, pp 92–101; and G Colvin, "The Wisdom of Dumb Questions," *Fortune,* June 27, 2005, p 157.

[38]R A Cosier and C R Schwenk, "Agreement and Thinking Alike: Ingredients for Poor Decisions," *Academy of Management Executive,* February 1990, p 71. Also see J P Kotter, "Kill Complacency," *Fortune,* August 5, 1996, pp 168–70; and S Caudron, "Keeping Team Conflict Alive," *Training & Development,* September 1998, pp 48–52.

[39]For example, see "Facilitators as Devil's Advocates," *Training,* September 1993, p 10. Also see K L Woodward, "Sainthood for a Pope?" *Newsweek,* June 21, 1999, p 65.

[40]Good background reading on devil's advocacy can be found in C R Schwenk, "Devil's Advocacy in Managerial Decision Making," *Journal of Management Studies,* April 1984, pp 153–68.

[41]See G Katzenstein, "The Debate on Structured Debate: Toward a Unified Theory," *Organizational Behavior and Human Decision Processes,* June 1996, pp 316–32.

[42]W Kiechel III, "How to Escape the Echo Chamber," *Fortune,* June 18, 1990, p 130.

[43]See D M Schweiger, W R Sandberg, and P L Rechner, "Experiential Effects of Dialectical Inquiry, Devil's Advocacy, and Consensus Approaches to Strategic Decision Making," *Academy of Management Journal,* December 1989, pp 745–72.

[44]See J S Valacich and C Schwenk, "Devil's Advocacy and Dialectical Inquiry Effects on Face-to-Face and Computer-Mediated Group Decision Making," *Organizational Behavior and Human Decision Processes,* August 1995, pp 158–73.

[45]Other techniques are presented in Cloke and Goldsmith, *Resolving Conflicts at Work,* pp 229–35.

[46]As quoted in D Jones, "CEOs Need X-Ray Vision in Transition," *USA Today,* April 23, 2001, p 4B. Also see K Daley, "How to Disagree," *Training & Development,* April 2004, pp 82–84; M Silberman and F Hansburg, "Are You People-Smart? It's Good Business," *Training & Development,* September 2004, pp 74–76; and F Haley, "Tough-Love Leadership," *Fast Company,* September 2004, p 110.

[47]Based on C K W De Dreu and M A West, "Minority Dissent and Team Innovation: The Importance of Participation in Decision Making," *Journal of Applied Psychology,* December 2001, pp 119–201.

[48]A statistical validation for this model can be found in M A Rahim and N R Magner, "Confirmatory Factor Analysis of the Styles of Handling Interpersonal Conflict: First-Order Factor Model and Its Invariance across Groups," *Journal of Applied Psychology,* February 1995, pp 122–32. Also see C K W De Dreu, A Evers, B Beersma, E S Kluwer, and A Nauta, "A Theory-Based Measure of Conflict Management Strategies in the Workplace," *Journal of Organizational Behavior,* September 2001, pp 645–68; and M A Rahim, *Managing Conflict in Organizations* (Westport, CT: Greenwood Publishing Group, 2001).

[49]M A Rahim, "A Strategy for Managing Conflict in Complex Organizations," *Human Relations,* January 1985, p 84.

[50]"Female Officers Draw Fewer Brutality Suits," *USA Today,* May 2, 2002, p 3A. Also see L W Andrews, "When It's Time for Anger Management," *HR Magazine,* June 2005, pp 131–36.

[51]P Ruzich, "Triangles: Tools for Untangling Interpersonal Messes," *HR Magazine,* July 1999, p 129.

[52]See K Mollica, "Stay above the Fray," *HR Magazine,* April 2005, pp 111–15; And G Roper, "Managing Employee Relations," *HR Magazine,* May 2005, pp 101–4.

[53]For background, see D L Jacobs, "First, Fire All the Lawyers," *Inc.,* January 1999, pp 84–85; P S Nugent, "Managing Conflict: Third-Party Interventions for Managers," *Academy of Management Executive,* February 2002, pp 139–54; and F P Phillips, "Ten Ways to Sabotage Dispute Management," *HR Magazine,* September 2004, pp 163–68.

[54]See M Bordwin, "Do-It-Yourself Justice," *Management Review,* January 1999, pp 56–58.

[55]B Morrow and L M Bernardi. "Resolving Workplace Disputes," *Canadian Manager,* Spring 1999, p 17. For related research, see R Friedman, C Anderson, J Brett, M Olekalns, N Goates, and C C Lisco, "The Positive and Negative Effects of Anger on Dispute Resolution: Evidence from Electronically Mediated Disputes," *Journal of Applied Psychology,* April 2004, pp 369–76; and C B Gibson and T Saxton, "Thinking Outside the Black Box: Outcomes of Team Decisions with Third-Party Intervention," *Small Group Research,* April 2005, pp 208–36.

[56]Adapted from discussion in K O Wilburn, "Employment Disputes: Solving Them Out of Court," *Management Review,* March 1998, pp 17–21; and Morrow and Bernardi, "Resolving Workplace Disputes," pp 17–19, 27. Also see W H Ross and D E Conlon, "Hybrid Forms of Third-Party Dispute Resolution: Theoretical Implications of Combining Mediation and Arbitration," *Academy of Management Review,* April 2000, pp 416–27.

[57]Wilburn, "Employment Disputes," p 19. Also see B P Sunoo, "Hot Disputes Cool Down in Online Mediation," *Workforce,* January 2001, pp 48–52.

[58]For background on this contentious issue, see S Armour, "Arbitration's Rise Raises Fairness Issue," *USA Today,* June 12, 2001, pp 1B–2B; T J Heinsz, "The Revised Uniform Arbitration Act: An Overview," *Dispute Resolution Journal,* May–July 2001, pp 28–39; C Hirschman, "Order in the Hearing!" *HR Magazine,* July 2001, pp 58–64; J D Wetchler, "Agreements to Arbitrate," *HR Magazine,* August 2001, pp 127–34; and J Biskupic, "Supreme Court Ruling Defends Power of EEOC," *USA Today,* January 16, 2002, p 2B.

[59]See R E Jones and B H Melcher, "Personality and the Preference for Modes of Conflict Resolution," *Human Relations,* August 1982, pp 649–58.

[60]See R A Baron, "Reducing Organizational Conflict: An Incompatible Response Approach," *Journal of Applied Psychology,* May 1984, pp 272–79.

[61]See G A Youngs Jr, "Patterns of Threat and Punishment Reciprocity in a Conflict Setting," *Journal of Personality and Social Psychology,* September 1986, pp 541–46.

[62]For more details, see V D Wall Jr and L L Nolan, "Small Group Conflict: A Look at Equity, Satisfaction, and Styles of Conflict Management," *Small Group Behavior,* May 1987, pp 188–211. Also see S M Farmer and J Roth, "Conflict-Handling Behavior in Work Groups: Effects of Group Structure, Decision Processes, and Time," *Small Group Research,* December 1998, pp 669–713.

[63]Based on B Richey, H J Bernardin, C L Tyler, and N McKinney, "The Effects of Arbitration Program Characteristics on Applicants' Intentions toward Potential Employers," *Journal of Applied Psychology,* October 2001, pp 1006–13.

[64]See M E Schnake and D S Cochran, "Effect of Two Goal-Setting Dimensions on Perceived Intraorganizational Conflict," *Group & Organization Studies,* June 1985, pp 168–83. Also see O Janssen, E Van De Vliert, and C Veenstra, "How Task and Person Conflict Shape the Role of Positive Interdependence in Management Teams," *Journal of Management,* no. 2, 1999, pp 117–42.

[65]Drawn from L H Chusmir and J Mills, "Gender Differences in Conflict Resolution Styles of Managers: At Work and at Home," *Sex Roles,* February 1989, pp 149–63.

[66]See K K Smith, "The Movement of Conflict in Organizations: The Joint Dynamics of Splitting and Triangulation," *Administrative Science Quarterly,* March 1989, pp 1–20. Also see J B Olson-Buchanan, F Drasgow, P J Moberg, A D Mead,

P A Keenan, and M A Donovan, "Interactive Video Assessment of Conflict Resolution Skills." *Personnel Psychology,* Spring 1998, pp 1–24; and D E Conlon and D P Sullivan, "Examining the Actions of Organizations in Conflict: Evidence from the Delaware Court of Chancery," *Academy of Management Journal,* June 1999, pp 319–29.

[67]Based on C Tinsley, "Models of Conflict Resolution in Japanese, German, and American Cultures," *Journal of Applied Psychology,* April 1998, pp 316–23; and S M Adams, "Settling Cross-Cultural Disagreements Begins with 'Where' Not 'How,' " *Academy of Management Executive,* February 1999, pp 109–10. Also see K Ohbuchi, O Fukushima, and J T Tedeschi, "Cultural Values in Conflict Management: Goal Orientation, Goal Attainment, and Tactical Decision," *Journal of Cross-Cultural Psychology,* January 1999, pp 51–71; and R Cropanzano, H Aguinis, M Schminke, and D L Denham, "Disputant Reactions to Managerial Conflict Resolution Tactics: A Comparison among Argentina, the Dominican Republic, Mexico, and the United States," *Group & Organization Management,* June 1999, pp 124–54.

[68]Based on a definition in M A Neale and M H Bazerman, "Negotiating Rationally: The Power and Impact of the Negotiator's Frame," *Academy of Management Executive,* August 1992, pp 42–51.

[69]See A Fisher, "How to Ask for—and Get—a Raise Now," *Fortune,* December 27, 2004, p 47; K Tyler, "Good-Faith Bargaining," *HR Magazine,* January 2005, pp 48–53; and S Clifford, "Something for Nothing," *Inc.,* May 2005, pp 54, 56.

[70]M H Bazerman and M A Neale, *Negotiating Rationally* (New York: Free Press, 1992), p 16. Also see G Cullinan, J Le Roux, and R Weddigen, "When to Walk Away from a Deal," *Harvard Business Review,* April 2004, pp 96–104; P B Stark and J Flaherty, "How to Negotiate," *Training & Development,* June 2004, pp 52–54; K Tyler, "The Art of Give-and-Take," *HR Magazine,* November 2004, pp 107–16; D Ertel, "Getting Past Yes: Negotiating as if Implementation Mattered," *Harvard Business Review,* November 2004, pp 60–68; and M Kaplan, "How to Negotiate Anything," *Money,* May 2005, pp 117–19.

[71]Good win–win negotiation strategies can be found in R R Reck and B G Long, *The Win–Win Negotiator: How to Negotiate Favorable Agreements That Last* (New York: Pocket Books, 1987); R Fisher and W Ury, *Getting to YES: Negotiating Agreement without Giving In* (Boston: Houghton Mifflin, 1981); and R Fisher and D Ertel, *Getting Ready to Negotiate: The Getting to YES Workbook* (New York: Penguin Books, 1995). Also see B Spector, "An Interview with Roger Fisher and William Ury," *Academy of Management Executive,* August 2004, pp 101–8; B Booth and M McCredie, "Taking Steps toward 'Getting to Yes' at Blue Cross and Blue Shield of Florida," *Academy of Management Executive,* August 2004, pp 109–12; and L Thompson and G J Leonardelli, "The Big Bang: The Evolution of Negotiation Research," *Academy of Management Executive,* August 2004, pp 113–17.

[72]See L R Weingart, E B Hyder, and M J Prietula, "Knowledge Matters: The Effect of Tactical Descriptions on Negotiation Behavior and Outcome." *Journal of Personality and Social Psychology,* June 1996, pp 1205–17.

[73]For more, see C H Tinsley, "How Negotiators Get to Yes: Predicting the Constellation of Strategies Used across Cultures to Negotiate Conflict," *Journal of Applied Psychology,* August 2001, pp 583–93; P Ghauri and T Fang, "Negotiating with the Chinese: A Socio-Cultural Analysis." *Journal of World Business,* Fall 2001, pp 303–25; and A Valenzuela, J Srivastava, and S Lee, "The Role of Cultural Orientation in Bargaining under Incomplete Information: Differences in Causal Attributions," *Organizational Behavior and Human Decision Processes,* January 2005, pp 72–88.

[74]For supporting evidence, see J K Butler Jr, "Trust Expectations, Information Sharing, Climate of Trust, and Negotiation Effectiveness and Efficiency," *Group & Organization Management,* June 1999, pp 217–38.

[75]See H J Reitz, J A Wall Jr, and M S Love, "Ethics in Negotiation: Oil and Water or Good Lubrication?" *Business Horizons,* May–June 1998, pp 5–14; M E Schweitzer and Jeffrey L Kerr, "Bargaining under the Influence: The Role of Alcohol in Negotiations," *Academy of Management Executive,* May 2000, pp 47–57; and A M Burr, "Ethics in Negotiation: Does Getting to Yes Require Candor?" *Dispute Resolution Journal,* May–July 2001, pp 8–15.

[76]For related research, see A E Tenbrunsel, "Misrepresentation and Expectations of Misrepresentation in an Ethical Dilemma: The Role of Incentives and Temptation," *Academy of Management Journal,* June 1998, pp 330–39.

[77]Based on R L Pinkley, T L Griffith, and G B Northcraft, " 'Fixed Pie' a la Mode: Information Availability, Information Processing, and the Negotiation of Suboptimal Agreements," *Organizational Behavior and Human Decision Processes,* April 1995, pp 101–12.

[78]Based on A E Walters, A F Stuhlmacher, and L L Meyer, "Gender and Negotiator Competitiveness: A Meta-Analysis," *Organizational Behavior and Human Decision Processes,* October 1998, pp 1–29.

[79]Based on B Barry and R A Friedman, "Bargainer Characteristics in Distributive and Integrative Negotiation," *Journal of Personality and Social Psychology,* February 1998, pp 345–59. Also see C K W De Dreu, E Giebels, and E Van de Vliert, "Social Motives and Trust in Integrative Negotiation: The Disruptive Effects of Punitive Capability," *Journal of Applied Psychology,* June 1998, pp 408–22.

[80]For more, see J P Forgas, "On Feeling Good and Getting Your Way: Mood Effects on Negotiator Cognition and Bargaining Strategies," *Journal of Personality and Social Psychology,* March 1998, pp 565–77. Also see G A van Kleef, C K W De Dreu, and A S R Manstead, "The Interpersonal Effects of Anger and Happiness in Negotiations," *Journal of Personality and Social Psychology,* January 2004, pp 57–76; and G A van Kleef, C K W De Dreu, and A S R Manstead, "The Interpersonal Effects of Emotions in Negotiations: A Motivated Information Processing Approach," *Journal of Personality and Social Psychology,* October 2004, pp 510–28.

[81]Drawn from J M Brett and T Okumura, "Inter- and Intracultural Negotiation: US and Japanese Negotiators," *Academy of Management Journal,* October 1998, pp 495–510.

Also see W L Adair, T Okumura, and J M Brett, "Negotiation Behavior when Cultures Collide: The United States and Japan," *Journal of Applied Psychology,* June 2001, pp 37–85. More negotiation research is reported in S Kwon and L R Weingart, "Unilateral Concessions from the Other Party: Concession Behavior, Attributions, and Negotiation Judgments," *Journal of Applied Psychology,* April 2004, pp 263–78; K M O'Connor, J A Arnold, and E R Burris, "Negotiators' Bargaining Histories and Their Effects on Future Negotiation Performance," *Journal of Applied Psychology,* March 2005, pp 350–62; and P H Kim and A R Fragale, "Choosing the Path to Bargaining Power: An Empirical Comparison of BATNAs and Contributions in Negotiation," *Journal of Applied Psychology,* March 2005, pp 373–81.

[82]Excerpted from S Holmes, "Pulp Friction at Weyerhaeuser," *BusinessWeek,* March 11, 2002, pp 66, 68. Reprinted by permission of The McGraw-Hill Companies, Inc.

[83]The complete instrument may be found in M A Rahim, "A Measure of Styles of Handling Interpersonal Conflict," *Academy of Management Journal,* June 1983, pp 368–76. A validation study of Rahim's instrument may be found in E Van De Vliert and B Kabanoff, "Toward Theory-Based Measures of Conflict Management," *Academy of Management Journal,* March 1990, pp 199–209.

[84]This case is quoted from D A Whetten and K S Cameron, *Developing Management Skills,* 6th edition, © 2005, pp 385–86. Reprinted by permission of Pearson Education, Inc., Upper Saddle River, NJ.

[85]Excerpted from A Cortese, "Where Fight Club Meets the Office," *Business 2.0,* May 2005, p 129.

CHAPTER 14

[1]Excerpted from J Mintz, "When Bloggers Make News," *The Wall Street Journal,* January 21, 2005, pp B1, B4. Reprinted by permission of Dow Jones & Co. Inc., via The Copyright Clearance Center.

[2]C Hymowitz, "In the Lead: What Adecco Can Do to Improve Its Image after Bad News Bungle," *The Wall Street Journal,* January 20, 2004, p B1.

[3]See M A Jaasma and R J Koper, "The Relationship of Student–Faculty Out-of-Class Communication to Instructor Immediacy and Trust and to Student Motivation," *Communication Education,* January 1999, pp 41–47; and P G Clampitt and C W Downs, "Employee Perceptions of the Relationship between Communication and Productivity: A Field Study," *Journal of Business Communication,* 1993, pp 5–28.

[4]J L Bowditch and A F Buono, *A Primer on Organizational Behavior,* 4th ed (New York: John Wiley & Sons, 1997), p 120.

[5]For a review of these criticisms see L L Putnam, N Phillips, and P Chapman, "Metaphors of Communication and Organization," in *Handbook of Organization Studies,* eds S R Clegg, C Hardy, and W R Nord (London: Sage Publications, 1996), pp 375–408.

[6]Results of this study can be found in C M Fiol, "Corporate Communications: Comparing Executives' Private and Public Statements," *Academy of Management Journal,* April 1995, pp 522–36.

[7]M Orey, "Lawyer's Firing Signals Turmoil in Legal Circles," *The Wall Street Journal,* May 21, 2001, p B1.

[8]Cross-cultural communication and decoding are discussed by A Fisher, "Offshoring Could Boost Your Career," *Fortune,* January 24, 2005, p 36; and M L Smith, G W Cottrell, F Gosselin, and P G Schyns, "Transmitting and Decoding Facial Expressions," *Psychological Science,* no. 3, 2005, pp 184–89.

[9]J Weil, "Two Andersen Employees Believed Enron Shredding Was Firm's Policy," *The Wall Street Journal,* March 13, 2002, p C1.

[10]Ibid.

[11]Noise associated with conference calls is discussed by J Sandberg, "Funny Things Happen as Conference Callers Attempt to Multitask," *The Wall Street Journal,* January 26, 2005, p B1.

[12]Excerpted from J Sandberg, "Cookies, Gossip, Cubes: It's a Wonder Any Work Gets Done at the Office," *The Wall Street Journal,* April 28, 2004, p B1.

[13]A discussion of the impact of communication barriers between medical doctors and patients is provided by A Underwood and J Adler, "When Cultures Clash," *Newsweek,* April 25, 2005, pp 68–70.

[14]For a thorough discussion of these barriers, see C R Rogers and F J Roethlisberger, "Barriers and Gateways to Communication," *Harvard Business Review,* July–August 1952, pp 46–52.

[15]Ibid., p 47.

[16]M Rich, "Shut Up So We Can Do Our Jobs!" *The Wall Street Journal,* August 29, 2001, p B1.

[17]Results can be found in J D Johnson, W A Donohue, C K Atkin, and S Johnson, "Communication, Involvement, and Perceived Innovativeness," *Group & Organization Management,* March 2001, pp 24–52; and B Davenport Sypher and T E Zorn Jr, "Communication-Related Abilities and Upward Mobility: A Longitudinal Investigation," *Human Communication Research,* Spring 1986, pp 420–31.

[18]Communication competence is discussed by J S Hinton and M W Kramer, "The Impact of Self-Directed Videotape Feedback on Students' Self-Reported Levels of Communication Competence and Apprehension," *Communication Education,* April 1998, pp 151–61; and L J Carrell and S C Willmington, "The Relationship between Self-Report Measures of Communication Apprehension and Trained Observers' Ratings of Communication Competence," *Communication Reports,* Winter 1998, pp 87–95.

[19]1. *False.* Clients always take precedence, and people with the greatest authority or importance should be introduced first.

2. *False.* You should introduce yourself. Say something like "My name is _____. I don't believe we've met."

3. *False.* It's OK to admit you can't remember. Say something like "My mind just went blank, your name is?" Or offer your name and wait for the other person to respond with his or hers.

4. *False.* Business etiquette has become gender neutral.

5. *a. Host.* This enables him or her to lead their guest to the meeting place.

6. *False.* Not only is it rude to invade public areas with your conversation, but you never know who might hear details of your business transaction or personal life.

7. *b. 3 feet.* Closer than this is an invasion of personal space. Farther away forces people to raise their voices. Because communication varies from country to country, you should also inform yourself about cultural differences.

8. *True.* An exception to this would be if your company holds an event at the beach or the pool.

9. *False.* Just wave your hand over it when asked, or say "No thank you."

10. *True.* The person who initiated the call should redial if the connection is broken.

11. *True.* If you must use a speakerphone, you should inform all parties who are present.

12. *True.* You should record a greeting such as "I'm out of the office today, March 12. If you need help, please dial _____ at extension . . ."

[20]Cross-cultural communication is discussed by M A Von Glinow, D L Shapiro, and J M Brett, "Can We Talk, and Should We? Managing Emotional Conflict in Multicultural Teams," *Academy of Management Review,* October 2004, pp 578–92; and P C Earley and E Mosakowski, "Cultural Intelligence," *Harvard Business Review,* October 2004, pp 139–46.

[21]See F Timmins and C McCabe, "How Assertive Are Nurses in the Workplace? A Preliminary Pilot Study," *Journal of Nursing Management,* January 2005, pp 61–67.

[22]J A Waters, "Managerial Assertiveness," *Business Horizons,* September–October 1982, p 25.

[23]W D St. John, "You Are What You Communicate," *Personnel Journal,* October 1985, p 40.

[24]This statistic was reported in A Fisher, "How Can I Survive a Phone Interview?" *Fortune,* April 19, 2004, p 54.

[25]A study of decoding nonverbal cues was conducted by E L Cooley, "Attachment Style and Decoding of Nonverbal Cues," *North American Journal of Psychology,* 2005, pp 25–33.

[26]Results can be found in S D Kelly, D J Barr, R B Church, and K Lynch, "Offering a Hand to Pragmatic Understanding: The Role of Speech and Gesture in Comprehension and Memory," *Journal of Memory and Language,* May 1999, pp 577–92.

[27]Related research is summarized by J A Hall, "Male and Female Nonverbal Behavior," in *Multichannel Integrations of Nonverbal Behavior,* eds A W Siegman and S Feldstein (Hillsdale, NJ: Lawrence Erlbaum, 1985), pp 195–226.

[28]Results can be found in ibid.

[29]See J A Russell, "Facial Expressions of Emotion: What Lies beyond Minimal Universality?" *Psychological Bulletin,* November 1995, pp 379–91; and Z Stambor, "Women's Facial Expressions Interpreted as Angrier, Less Happy than Men's," *Monitor on Psychology,* January 2005, p 21.

[30]Norms for cross-cultural eye contact are discussed by C Engholm, *When Business East Meets Business West: The Guide to Practice and Protocol in the Pacific Rim* (New York: John Wiley & Sons, 1991).

[31]These recommendations were adapted from those in P Preston, "Nonverbal Communication: Do You Really Say What You Mean?" *Journal of Healthcare Management,* March–April 2005, pp 83–86.

[32]See D Knight, "Perks Keeping Workers out of Revolving Door," *The Wall Street Journal,* April 30, 2005, p D3; and G Roper, "Managing Employee Relations," *HR Magazine,* May 2005, pp 101–4.

[33]The discussion of listening styles is based on "5 Listening Styles," www.crossroadsinstitute.org/listyle.html, accessed May 5, 2005; and "Listening and Thinking: What's Your Style?" www.pediatricservices.com/prof/prof-10.htm, last modified August 10, 2002, accessed May 5, 2005.

[34]These recommendations were excerpted from J Jay, "On Communicating Well," *HR Magazine,* January 2005, pp 87–88.

[35]D Tannen, "The Power of Talk: Who Gets Heard and Why," *Harvard Business Review,* September–October 1995, p 139.

[36]For a thorough review of the evolutionary explanation of sex differences in communication, see A H Eagly and W Wood, "The Origins of Sex Differences in Human Behavior," *American Psychologist,* June 1999, pp 408–23. A recent critique of evolutionary psychology was also provided by S Begley, "Evolutionary Psych May Not Help Explain Our Behavior after All," *The Wall Street Journal,* April 29, 2005, p B1.

[37]See Tannen, "The Power of Talk," pp 160–73; and D Tannen, *You Just Don't Understand: Women and Men in Conversation* (New York: Ballantine Books, 1990).

[38]See P A Simpson and L K Stroh, "Gender Differences: Emotional Expression and Feelings of Personal Inauthenticity," *Journal of Applied Psychology,* August 2004, pp 715–21; and E L MacGeorge, A R Graves, B Feng, S J Gillihan, and B R Burleson, "The Myth of Gender Cultures: Similarities Outweigh Differences in Men's and Women's Provision of and Responses to Supportive Communication," *Sex Roles,* 2004, pp 143–75.

[39]This definition was taken from J C Tingley, *Genderflex: Men and Women Speaking Each Other's Language at Work* (New York: American Management Association, 1994), p 16.

[40]Tannen, "The Power of Talk," pp 147–48.

[41]The pros and cons of exit interviews are discussed by E White, "The Jungle: Focus on Retirement, Pay and Getting Ahead," *The Wall Street Journal,* May 3, 2005, p B6. Characteristics of effective and ineffective suggestion systems are reviewed by S J Wells, "From Ideas to Results," *HR Magazine,* February 2005, pp 55–58.

[42]Organizational benefits of the grapevine are discussed by T Galpin, "Pruning the Grapevine," *Training & Development,* April 1995, pp 28–32; and J Smythe, "Harvesting the Office Grapevine," *People Management,* September 1995, pp 24–27.

[43]Results can be found in S J Modic, "Grapevine Rated Most Believable," *Industry Week,* May 15, 1989, pp 11, 14.

[44] H B Vickery III, "Tapping into the Employee Grapevine," *Association Management,* January 1984, pp 59–60.

[45] The most recent research is discussed by S M Crampton, J W Hodge, and J M Mishra, "The Informal Communication Network: Factors Influencing Grapevine Activity," *Public Personnel Management,* Winter 1998, pp 569–84, "Pruning the Company Grapevine," *Supervision,* September 1986, p 11; and R Half, "Managing Your Career: 'How Can I Stop the Gossip?' " *Management Accounting,* September 1987, p 27.

[46] L Grensing-Pophal, "Got the Message?" *HR Magazine,* April 2001, pp 75–76.

[47] A C Poe, "Don't Touch That 'Send' Button!" *HR Magazine,* July 2001, pp 74–75.

[48] R L Daft and R H Lengel, "Information Richness: A New Approach to Managerial Behavior and Organizational Design," in *Research in Organizational Behavior,* eds B M Staw and L L Cummings (Greenwich, CT: JAI Press, 1984), p 196.

[49] Details of this example are provided in L Grensing-Pophal, "Spread the Word—Correctly," *HR Magazine,* March 2005, pp 83–88.

[50] See B Barry and I S Fulmer, "The Medium and the Message: The Adaptive Use of Communication Media in Dyadic Influence," *Academy of Management Review,* April 2004, pp 272–92; and T J Andersen, "The Performance Effect of Computer-Mediated Communication and Decentralized Strategic Decision Making," *Journal of Business Research,* August 2005, pp 1059–111.

[51] See R E Rice and D E Shook, "Relationships of Job Categories and Organizational Levels to Use of Communication Channels, Including Electronic Mail: A Meta-Analysis and Extension," *Journal of Management Studies,* March 1990, pp 195–229.

[52] See J Sandberg, "Bosses Often Sugarcoat Their Worst News, but Staffers Don't Bite," *The Wall Street Journal,* April 21, 2004, p B1; and E W Larson and J B King, "The Systematic Distortion of Information: An Ongoing Challenge to Management," *Organizational Dynamics,* Winter 1996, pp 49–61.

[53] J Fulk and S Mani, "Distortion of Communication in Hierarchical Relationships," in *Communication Yearbook 9,* ed M L McLaughlin (Beverly Hills, CA: Sage Publications, 1986), p 483.

[54] For a review of this research, see ibid., pp 483–510.

[55] M Frase-Blunt, "Boss: Understanding and Improve Communications," *HR Magazine,* June 2003, p 96.

[56] These statistics were obtained from "Kids' Lives 'Saturated' by Media, Study Says," *Arizona Republic,* March 10, 2005, p A7.

[57] These statistics were obtained from "Internet Usage Statistics—The Big Picture: World Internet Users and Population Stats," www.internetworldstats.com/stats.htm, last updated on March 31, 2005, accessed May 6, 2005.

[58] Results can be found in D Smith, "One-Tenth of College Students Are Dependent on the Internet, Research Finds," *Monitor on Psychology,* May 2001, p 10.

[59] These examples were discussed in D Caterinicchia, "University HR's Self-Service Solution," *HR Magazine,* February 2005, pp 105–9.

[60] See "Nearly Eight in Ten US Employees Register for Benefits Online," http://was4.hewitt/resource/newsroom/pressrel/2004/01-27-04.htm, accessed April 15, 2005.

[61] This statistic was reported in H Green, S Rosenbush, R O Crockett, and S Holmes, "Wi-Fi Means Business," *BusinessWeek,* April 28, 2003, pp 86–92.

[62] Online training is discussed by S Overman, "Dow, Hewlett-Packard Put E-Learning to Work to Save Time and Money," *HR Magazine,* February 2004, pp 33; and S Bates, "Study: Older Workers Are Good Students," *HR Magazine,* May 2005, pp 32, 38.

[63] See M E Medland, "Time Squeeze," *HR Magazine,* November 2004, pp 66–70; and "X-Rated," *Training,* p 10.

[64] See D Buss, "Spies Like Us," *Training,* December 2001, pp 44–48.

[65] Results of the survey are presented in "Electronic Monitoring," www.nolo.com/lawcenter/ency/article.cfm/ObjectID/C1066E74-A5CA-4EE3-Acd2, accessed June 20, 2004.

[66] See "Making E-Mail Work Again—ClearContext 2005 E-mail Usage Survey Analysis," http://blog.clearcontext.com/2005/04/making_email_wo.html, posted April 5, 2005, accessed May 6, 2005.

[67] See B Hemphill, "File, Act, or Toss?" *Training & Development,* February 2001, pp 38–41.

[68] See "Making E-Mail Work Again."

[69] M Rose and M Peers, "AOL's Latest Internal Woe: 'You've Got Mail'—'Oops, No You Don't,' " *The Wall Street Journal,* March 22, 2002, p B1.

[70] This statistic was reported in E Chambers, "Web Watch: The Lid on Spam Is Still Loose," *BusinessWeek,* February 7, 2005, p 10.

[71] Results can be found in M S Thompson and M S Feldman, "Electronic Mail and Organizational Communication: Does Saying 'Hi' Really Matter?" *Organization Science,* November–December 1998, pp 685–98.

[72] See the related discussion in A Pomeroy, "Business 'Fast and Loose' with E-Mail, IMs—Study," *HR Magazine,* November 2004, pp 32, 34.

[73] See descriptions in S H Wildstrom, "The New Bluetooth: More on the Beam," *BusinessWeek,* April 18, 2005, p 24; and M Heinzl, "With Its Blackberry a Big Hit, RIM Is Squeezed by All Comers," *The Wall Street Journal,* April 25, 2005, pp A1, A6.

[74] Excerpted from M Conlin, "Take a Vacation from Your BlackBerry," *BusinessWeek,* December 20, 2004, p 56.

[75] See ibid.

[76] Background on blogs is provided by S Baker and H Green, "Blogs Will Change Your Business," *BusinessWeek,* May 2, 2005, pp 57–67; and "Businesses, Blogs Colliding in Courts," *Arizona Republic,* May 1, 2005, p D3.

[77]Cell phone blogging is discussed by "The Son Rises at Qualcomm," *Fortune,* April 18, 2005, p 45.

[78]See D Kirkpatrick, "Sun Microsystems: It's Hard to Manage if You Don't Blog," *Fortune,* Ocotober 4, 2004, p 46; and A Lashinsky, "Is This the Right Man for Intel?" *Fortune,* April 18, 2005, pp 110–20.

[79]See Kirkpatrick, "Sun Microsystems."

[80]This example is discussed in "Firms Taking Action against Worker Blogs," *MSNBC News,* www.msnbc.msn.com/id/7116338, posted March 7, 2005, accessed March 7, 2005.

[81]E Krell, "Videoconferencing Gets the Call," *Training,* December 2001, p 38.

[82]Results can be found in S A Rains, "Leveling the Organizational Playing Field—Virtually: A Meta-Analysis of Experimental Research Assessing the Impact of Group Support System Use on Member Influence Behaviors," *Communication Research,* April 2005, pp 193–234.

[83]Challenges associated with virtual operations are discussed by S O'Mahony and S R Barley, "Do Digital Telecommunications Affect Work and Organization? The State of Our Knowledge," in *Research in Organizational Behavior,* vol. 21, eds R I Sutton and B M Staw (Stamford, CT: JAI Press, 1999), pp 125–61.

[84]S Shellenbarger, "Work and Family: 'Telework' Is on the Rise, But It Isn't Just Done from Home Anymore," *The Wall Street Journal,* January 23, 2002, p B1.

[85]This statistic was obtained from "Work at Home Continues to Grow," *International Telework Association & Council,* www.telecommute.org, accessed May 7, 2005.

[86]Supporting evidence can be found in B Hemphill, "Telecommuting Productively," *Occupational Health & Safety,* March 2004, pp 16, 18; R Konrad, "Sun's 'iWork' Shuns Desks for Flexibility," *Arizona Republic,* May 28, 2003, p D4; and C Hymowitz, "Remote Managers Find Ways to Narrow the Distance Gap," *The Wall Street Journal,* April 6, 1999, p B1.

[87]Excerpted from C Hymowitz, "In the Lead: Missing from Work: The Chance to Think, Even to Dream a Little," *The Wall Street Journal,* Eastern Edition, March 23, 2004, p B1. Copyright 2004 by Dow Jones & Co. Inc. Reprinted by permission of Dow Jones & Co. Inc. via The Copyright Clearance Center.

[88]Excerpted from Yuri Kageyama, "Cellphones with Cameras Creating Trouble: Concerns Include Voyeurism," *Arizona Republic,* July 10, 2003, pp A18.

CHAPTER 15

[1]Excerpted from P Sellers, "eBay's Secret," *Fortune,* October 18, 2004, pp 161–62 © 2004 Time Inc. Reprinted by permission. All rights reserved. Also see P Sellers, "A G Lafley: Procter & Gamble," *Fortune,* August 9, 2004, p 98.

[2]H Malcolm and C Sokoloff, "Values, Human Relations, and Organization Development," in *The Emerging Practice of Organizational Development,* eds W Sikes, A Drexler, and J Gant (San Diego: University Associates, 1989), p 64.

[3]See D Kipnis, S M Schmidt, and I Wilkinson, "Intraorganizational Influence Tactics: Explorations in Getting One's Way," *Journal of Applied Psychology,* August 1980, pp 440–52. Also see C A Schriesheim and T R Hinkin, "Influence Tactics Used by Subordinates: A Theoretical and Empirical Analysis and Refinement of the Kipnis, Schmidt, and Wilkinson Subscales," *Journal of Applied Psychology,* June 1990, pp 246–57; G Yukl and C M Falbe, "Influence Tactics and Objectives in Upward, Downward, and Lateral Influence Attempts," *Journal of Applied Psychology,* April 1990, pp 132–40; and G Yukl and B Tracey, "Consequences of Influence Tactics Used with Subordinates, Peers, and the Boss," in *Organizational Influence Processes,* eds L W Porter, H L Angle, and R W Allen (Armonk, NY: M E Sharpe, 2003), 2nd ed, pp 96–116.

[4]Based on Table 1 in G Yukl, C M Falbe, and J Y Youn, "Patterns of Influence Behavior for Managers," *Group & Organization Management,* March 1993, pp 5–28. An additional influence tactic is presented in B P Davis and E S Knowles, "A Disrupt-then-Reframe Technique of Social Influence," *Journal of Personality and Social Psychology,* February 1999, pp 192–99.

[5]For comprehensive coverage, see L W Porter, H L Angle, and R W Allen, eds *Organizational Influence Processes,* 2nd ed (Armonk, NY: M E Sharpe, 2003).

[6]Based on discussion in G Yukl, H Kim, and C M Falbe, "Antecedents of Influence Outcomes," *Journal of Applied Psychology,* June 1996, pp 309–17.

[7]Data from ibid.

[8]Data from G Yukl and J B Tracey, "Consequences of Influence Tactics Used with Subordinates, Peers, and the Boss," *Journal of Applied Psychology,* August 1992, pp 525–35. Also see C M Falbe and G Yukl, "Consequences for Managers of Using Single Influence Tactics and Combinations of Tactics," *Academy of Management Journal,* August 1992, pp 638–52.

[9]Data from R A Gordon, "Impact of Ingratiation on Judgments and Evaluations: A Meta-Analytic Investigation," *Journal of Personality and Social Psychology,* July 1996, pp 54–70. Also see S J Wayne, R C Liden, and R T Sparrowe, "Developing Leader-Member Exchanges," *American Behavioral Scientist,* March 1994, pp 697–714; A Oldenburg, "These Days, Hostile Is Fitting for Takeovers Only," *USA Today,* July 22, 1996, pp 8B, 10B; and J H Dulebohn and G R Ferris, "The Role of Influence Tactics in Perceptions of Performance Evaluations' Fairness," *Academy of Management Journal,* June 1999, pp 288–303.

[10]Data from Yukl, Kim, and Falbe, "Antecedents of Influence Outcomes."

[11]Data from B J Tepper, R J Eisenbach, S L Kirby, and P W Potter, "Test of a Justice-Based Model of Subordinates' Resistance to Downward Influence Attempts," *Group & Organization Management,* June 1998, pp 144–60. Also see M W Firmin, J M Helmick, B A Iezzi, and A Vaughn, "Say Please: The Effect of the Word 'Please' in Compliance-Seeking Requests," *Social Behavior and Personality,* no. 1, 2004, pp 67–72.

[12]J E Driskell, B Olmstead, and E Salas, "Task Cues, Dominance Cues, and Influence in Task Groups," *Journal of Applied Psychology,* February 1993, p 51. No gender bias was found in H Aguinis and S K R Adams, "Social-Role versus Structural Models of Gender and Influence Use in Organizations: A Strong Inference Approach," *Group & Organization Management,* December 1998, pp 414–46. Also see R J Green, J C Sandall, and C Phelps, "Effect of Experimenter Attire and Sex on Participant Productivity," *Social Behavior and Personality,* no. 2, 2005, pp 125–32.

[13]See P P Fu et al., "The Impact of Societal Cultural Values and Individual Social Beliefs on the Perceived Effectiveness of Managerial Influence Strategies: A Meso Approach," *Journal of International Business Studies,* July 2004, pp 284–305.

[14]B Moses, "You Can't Make Change; You Have to Sell It," *Fast Company,* April 1999, p 101. Also see D Jones, "Debating Skills Come in Handy in Business," *USA Today,* September 30, 2004, p 3B; and J Reingold, "Suck Up and Move Up," *Fast Company,* January 2005, p 34.

[15]S Bates, "Poll: Employees Skeptical about Management Actions," *HR Magazine,* June 2002, p 12.

[16]See M J Mandel, "A New Economy Needs a New Morality," *BusinessWeek,* February 25, 2002, pp 114–15; and M A Barnett, F W Sanborn, and A C Shane, "Factors Associated with Individuals' Likelihood of Engaging in Various Minor Moral and Legal Violations," *Basic and Applied Social Psychology,* March 2005, pp 77–84.

[17]Adapted from R B Cialdini, "Harnessing the Science of Persuasion," *Harvard Business Review,* October 2001, pp 72–79. Also see C Decker, "The 5 Paths to Persuasion," *Fast Company,* July 2004, p 92; D A Garvin and M A Roberto, "Change through Persuasion," *Harvard Business Review,* February 2005, pp 104–12; J Pfeffer, "Executive-in-Chief," *Business 2.0,* March 2005, p 62; I Mount, "The Great Persuader," *Inc.,* March 2005, pp 92–97; and J Pfeffer, "Breaking through Excuses," *Business 2.0,* May 2005, p 76.

[18]Cialdini, "Harnessing the Science of Persuasion," p 77. Also see K M Douglas and R M Sutton, "Right about Others, Wrong about Ourselves? Actual and Perceived Self–Other Differences in Resistance to Persuasion," *British Journal of Social Psychology,* December 2004, pp 585–603.

[19]For example, see H Ma, R Karri, and K Chittipeddi, "The Paradox of Managerial Tyranny," *Business Horizons,* July–August 2004, pp 33–40; D Henry, M France, and L Lavelle, "The Boss on the Sidelines," *BusinessWeek,* April 25, 2005, pp 86–96; and S Bing, "A Righteous Development," *Fortune,* May 30, 2005, p 152.

[20]D Tjosvold, "The Dynamics of Positive Power," *Training and Development Journal,* June 1984, p 72. Also see "The Exercise of Power," *Harvard Business Review,* May 2002, p 136; G Colvin, "Power 25: The Most Powerful People in Business," *Fortune,* August 9, 2004, pp 90–106; and Ann Harrington and P Bartosiewicz, "50 Most Powerful Women: Who's Up? Who's Down?" *Fortune,* October 18, 2004, pp 181–98.

[21]M W McCall, Jr *Power, Influence, and Authority: The Hazards of Carrying a Sword,* Technical Report No. 10 (Greensboro, NC: Center for Creative Leadership, 1978), p 5. For an excellent discussion, see J O Hagberg, *Real Power: Stages of Personal Power in Organizations,* 3rd ed (Salem, WI: Sheffield Publishing, 2003).

[22]D Weimer, "Daughter Knows Best," *BusinessWeek,* April 19, 1999, pp 132, 134. Also see "How to Stage a Coup," *Inc.,* March 2005, p 52.

[23]For an update, see C L Bernick, "When Your Culture Needs a Makeover," *Harvard Business Review,* June 2001, pp 53–61.

[24]L H Chusmir, "Personalized versus Socialized Power Needs among Working Women and Men," *Human Relations,* February 1986, p 149.

[25]See A Pomeroy, "Thanks, but No Thanks," *HR Magazine,* December 2004, p 18; and A Molinsky and J Margolis, "Necessary Evils and Interpersonal Sensitivity in Organizations," *Academy of Management Review,* April 2005, pp 245–68.

[26]For example, see "It's Trump's World," *BusinessWeek,* January 10, 2005, p 86.

[27]D W Cantor and T Bernay, *Women in Power: The Secrets of Leadership* (Boston: Houghton Mifflin, 1992), p 40; and K Morris, "Trouble in Toyland," *BusinessWeek,* March 15, 1999, p 40.

[28]See J R P French and B Raven, "The Bases of Social Power," in *Studies in Social Power,* ed D Cartwright (Ann Arbor: University of Michigan Press, 1959), pp 150–67. Also see J M Whitmeyer, "Interest-Network Structures in Exchange Networks," *Sociological Perspectives,* Spring 1999, pp 23–47; and C M Fiol, E J O'Connor, and H Aguinis, "All for One and One for All? The Development and Transfer of Power across Organizational Levels," *Academy of Management Review,* April 2001, pp 224–42.

[29]Examples can be found in "Greenberg & Sons," *Fortune,* February 21, 2005, pp 104–14.

[30]See M Goldsmith, "It's Not a Fair Fight if You're the CEO," *Fast Company,* December 2004, p 99; and E Thornton, "Maybe Low-Key Is the Answer," *BusinessWeek,* February 7, 2005, pp 70–71.

[31]Data from J R Larson Jr, C Christensen, A S Abbott, and T M Franz, "Diagnosing Groups: Charting the Flow of Information in Medical Decision-Making Teams," *Journal of Personality and Social Psychology,* August 1996, pp 315–30.

[32]See M Maccoby, "Why People Follow the Leader: The Power of Transference," *Harvard Business Review,* September 2004, pp 76–85.

[33]Details may be found in Chusmir, "Personalized versus Socialized Power Needs among Working Women and Men," pp 149–59. For a review of research on individual differences in the need for power, see R J House, "Power and Personality in Complex Organizations," in *Research in Organizational Behavior,* ed B M Staw and L L Cummings (Greenwich, CT: JAI Press, 1988), pp 305–57.

[34]B Filipczak, "Is It Getting Chilly in Here?" *Training,* February 1994, p 27.

[35]Data from J Onyx, R Leonard, and K Vivekananda, "Social Perception of Power: A Gender Analysis," *Perceptual and Motor Skills,* February 1995, pp 291–96.

[36]P M Podsakoff and C A Schriesheim, "Field Studies of French and Raven's Bases of Power: Critique, Reanalysis, and Suggestions for Future Research," *Psychological Bulletin,* May 1985, p 388. Also see M A Rahim and G F Buntzman, "Supervisory Power Bases, Styles of Handling Conflict with Subordinates, and Subordinate Compliance and Satisfaction," *Journal of Psychology,* March 1989, pp 195–210; D Tjosvold, "Power and Social Context in Superior-Subordinate Interaction," *Organizational Behavior and Human Decision Processes,* June 1985, pp 281–93; and C A Schriesheim, T R Hinkin, and P M Podsakoff, "Can Ipsative and Single-Item Measures Produce Erroneous Results in Field Studies of French and Raven's (1950) Five Bases of Power? An Empirical Investigation," *Journal of Applied Psychology,* February 1991, pp 106–14.

[37]See T R Hinkin and C A Schriesheim, "Relationships between Subordinate Perceptions and Supervisor Influence Tactics and Attributed Bases of Supervisory Power," *Human Relations,* March 1990, pp 221–37. Also see D J Brass and M E Burkhardt, "Potential Power and Power Use: An Investigation of Structure and Behavior," *Academy of Management Journal,* June 1993, pp 441–70; K W Mossholder, N Bennett, E R Kemery, and M A Wesolowski, "Relationships between Bases of Power and Work Reactions: The Mediational Role of Procedural Justice," *Journal of Management,* no. 4, 1998, pp 533–52; and J Sell, M J Lovaglia, E A Mannix, C D Samuelson, and R K Wilson, "Investigating Conflict, Power, and Status within and among Groups," *Small Group Research,* February 2004, pp 44–72.

[38]See H E Baker III," 'Wax On—Wax Off:' French and Raven at the Movies," *Journal of Management Education,* November 1993, pp 517–19.

[39]Based on P A Wilson, "The Effects of Politics and Power on the Organizational Commitment of Federal Executives," *Journal of Management,* Spring 1995, pp 101–18. For related research, see J B Arthur, "Effects of Human Resource Systems on Manufacturing Performance and Turnover," *Academy of Management Journal,* June 1994, pp 670–87.

[40]For related research, see L G Pelletier and R J Vallerand, "Supervisors' Beliefs and Subordinates' Intrinsic Motivation: A Behavioral Confirmation Analysis," *Journal of Personality and Social Psychology,* August 1996, pp 331–40.

[41]As quoted in G Smith, "Here Comes Abby," *BusinessWeek,* July 8, 2002, p 62.

[42]As quoted in W A Randolph and M Sashkin, "Can Organizational Empowerment Work in Multinational Settings?" *Academy of Management Executive,* February 2002, p 104. (Emphasis added.) Also see J S Harrison and R E Freeman, "Special Topic: Democracy in and around Organizations: Is Organizational Democracy Worth the Effort?" *Academy of Management Executive,* August 2004, pp 49–53; and J L Kerr, "The Limits of Organizational Democracy," *Academy of Management Executive,* August 2004, pp 81–97.

[43]R M Hodgetts, "A Conversation with Steve Kerr," *Organizational Dynamics,* Spring 1996, p 71. Also see S E Seibert, S R Silver, and W Alan Randolph, "Taking Empowerment to the Next Level: A Multiple-Level Model of Empowerment, Performance, and Satisfaction," *Academy of Management Journal,* June 2004, pp 332–49; B Roberts, "Empowerment or Imposition?" *HR Magazine,* June 2004, pp 157–66; H Mintzberg, "Enough Leadership," *Harvard Business Review,* November 2004, p 22; and K Ayers, "Creating a Responsible Workplace," *HR Magazine,* February 2005, pp 111–13.

[44]L Shaper Walters, "A Leader Redefines Management," *Christian Science Monitor,* September 22, 1992, p 14.

[45]See S Zuboff, "Ranking Ourselves to Death," *Fast Company,* November 2004, p 125; and "Managing a Micromanager," *Inc.,* April 2005, p 50.

[46]For a 15-item empowerment scale, see Table 1 on p 103 of B P Niehoff, R H Moorman, G Blakely, and J Fuller, "The Influence of Empowerment and Job Enrichment on Employee Loyalty in a Downsizing Environment," *Group & Organization Management,* March 2001, pp 93–113.

[47]M Gunther, "The Sumner of Love," *Fortune,* May 2, 2005, p 99.

[48]For an extended discussion of this model, see M Sashkin, "Participative Management Is an Ethical Imperative," *Organizational Dynamics,* Spring 1984, pp 4–22.

[49]S Carey, "The Thrifty Get Thriftier," *The Wall Street Journal,* May 10, 2004, p R7.

[50]For more on delegation, see L Bossidy, "The Job No CEO Should Delegate," *Harvard Business Review,* March 2001, pp 46–49; F Dalton, "Delegation Pitfalls," *Association Management,* February 2005, pp 65–72; T Estep, "Devilish Delegation at the Department of Ominous Mechanical Mishaps," *Training & Development,* March 2005, pp 68–70; and J Janove, "A 3,500-Year-Old Lesson in Delegating," *HR Magazine,* March 2005, pp 109–12.

[51]See S Gazda, "The Art of Delegating," *HR Magazine,* January 2002, pp 75–78.

[52]M Memmott, "Managing Government Inc.," *USA Today,* June 28, 1993, p 2B. Also see R C Ford and C P Heaton, "Lessons from Hospitality That Can Serve Anyone," *Organizational Dynamics,* Summer 2001, pp 30–47.

[53]R Kreitner, *Management,* 9th ed (Boston: Houghton Mifflin, 2004), p 339. Also see C A Walker, "Saving Your Rookie Managers from Themselves," *Harvard Business Review,* April 2002, pp 97–102.

[54]Drawn from G Yukl and P P Fu, "Determinants of Delegation and Consultation by Managers," *Journal of Organizational Behavior,* March 1999, pp 219–32. Also see C A Schriesheim, L L Neider, and T A Scandura, "Delegation and Leader-Member Exchange: Main Effects, Moderators, and Measurement Issues," *Academy of Management Journal,* June 1998, pp 298–318.

[55]See R Zemke, "The Confidence Crisis," *Training,* June 2004, pp 22–30; and D N Sull and D Houlder, "Do Your Commitments Match Your Convictions?" *Harvard Business Review,* January 2005, pp 82–91.

56M Frese, W Kring, A Soose, and J Zempel, "Personal Initiative at Work: Differences between East and West Germany," *Academy of Management Journal,* February 1996, p 38. (Emphasis added.) For comprehensive updates, see D J Campbell, "The Proactive Employee: Managing Workplace Initiative," *Academy of Management Executive,* August 2000, pp 52–66; and M Frese and D Fay, "Personal Initiative: An Active Performance Concept for Work in the 21st Century," in *Research in Organizational Behavior,* vol. 23, eds B M Staw and R I Sutton (New York: JAI, 2001), pp 133–87.

57See J A Belasco and R C Stayer, "Why Empowerment Doesn't Empower: The Bankruptcy of Current Paradigms," *Business Horizons,* March–April 1994, pp 29–41; and W A Randolph, "Re-thinking Empowerment: Why Is It So Hard to Achieve?" *Organizational Dynamics,* Fall 2000, pp 94–107.

58Results can be found in B D Cawley, L M Keeping, and P E Levy, "Participation in the Performance Appraisal Process and Employee Reactions: A Meta-Analytic Review of Field Investigations," *Journal of Applied Psychology,* August 1998, pp 615–33.

59Results are contained in J A Wagner III, C R Leana, E A Locke, and D M Schweiger, "Cognitive and Motivational Frameworks in US Research on Participation: A Meta-Analysis of Primary Effects," *Journal of Organizational Behavior,* 1997, pp 49–65.

60Based on B L Kirkman and B Rosen, "Beyond Self-Management: Antecedents and Consequences of Team Empowerment," *Academy of Management Journal,* February 1999, pp 58–74. Also see W J Burpitt and W J Bigoness, "Leadership and Innovation among Teams: The Impact of Empowerment," *Small Group Research,* August 1997, pp 414–23.

61Based on J P Guthrie, "High-Involvement Work Practices, Turnover, and Productivity: Evidence from New Zealand," *Academy of Management Journal,* February 2001, pp 180–90.

62Based on M Workman and W Bommer, "Redesigning Computer Call Center Work: A Longitudinal Field Experiment," *Journal of Organizational Behavior,* May 2004, pp 317–37. Also see M K Hui, K Au, and H Fock, "Empowerment Effects across Cultures," *Journal of International Business Studies,* January 2004, pp 46–60; H K S Laschinger, J E Finegan, J Shamian, and P Wilk, "A Longitudinal Analysis of the Impact of Workplace Empowerment on Work Satisfaction," *Journal of Organizational Behavior,* June 2004, pp 527–45; M G Patterson, M A West, and T D Wall, "Integrated Manufacturing, Empowerment, and Company Performance," *Journal of Organizational Behavior,* August 2004, pp 641–65; and A Kleingeld, H van Tuijl, and J A Algera, "Participation in the Design of Performance Management Systems: A Quasi-Experimental Field Study," *Journal of Organizational Behavior,* November 2004, pp 831–51.

63W A Randolph, "Navigating the Journey to Empowerment," *Organizational Dynamics,* Spring 1995, p 31.

64See D Jones, "America Loves to Hate Dastardly CEOs," *USA Today,* September 15, 2004, pp 1B–2B; D Jones and B Keveney, "10 Lessons of 'The Apprentice,'" *USA Today,* April 15, 2004, pp 1A, 5A; A Pomeroy, "Business Reality TV?" *HR Magazine,* January 2005, p 14; and R Underwood, "Fast Talk: What I Learned on *The Apprentice,*" *Fast Company,* May 2005, pp 45–50.

65D J Burrough, "Office Politics Mirror Popular TV Program," *Arizona Republic,* February 4, 2001, p EC1.

66L B MacGregor Serven, *The End of Office Politics as Usual* (New York: American Management Association, 2002), p 5. Also see K J Sulkowitz, "The Corporate Shrink," *Fast Company,* May 2005, p 96.

67R Bhasin, "On Playing Corporate Politics," *Pulp & Paper,* October 1985, p 175. Also see G R Ferris, P L Perrewé, W P Anthony, and D C Gilmore, "Political Skill at Work," *Organizational Dynamics,* Spring 2000, pp 25–37; R M Kramer, "When Paranoia Makes Sense," *Harvard Business Review,* July 2002, pp 62–69; J Barbian, "Office Politics: Swinging with the Sharks," *Training,* July 2002, p 16; L P Frankel, *Nice Girls Don't Get the Corner Office: Unconscious Mistakes Women Make That Sabotage Their Career* (New York: Warner, 2004); T Estep, "Winning the Rat Race," *Training & Development,* January 2005, pp 71–72; and S B Bacharach, "Politically Proactive," *Fast Company,* May 2005, p 93.

68R W Allen, D L Madison, L W Porter, P A Renwick, and B T Mayes, "Organizational Politics: Tactics and Characteristics of Its Actors," *California Management Review,* Fall 1979, p 77. A comprehensive update can be found in K M Kacmar and R A Baron, "Organizational Politics: The State of the Field, Links to Related Processes, and an Agenda for Future Research," in *Research in Personnel and Human Resources Management,* vol. 17, ed G R Ferris (Stamford, CT: JAI Press, 1999), pp 1–39. Also see K A Ahearn, G R Ferris, W A Hochwarter, C Douglas, and A P Ammeter, "Leader Political Skill and Team Performance," *Journal of Management,* no. 3, 2004, pp 309–27; P L Perrewé and D L Nelson, "Gender and Career Success: The Facilitative Role of Political Skill," *Organizational Dynamics,* no. 4, 2004, pp 366–78; G R Ferris, D C Treadway, R W Kolodinsky, W A Hochwarter, C J Kacmar, C Douglas, and D D Frink, "Development and Validation of the Political Skill Inventory," *Journal of Management,* no. 1, 2005, pp 126–52; and T B Lawrence, M K Mauws, B Dyck, and R F Kleysen, "The Politics of Organizational Learning: Integrating Power into the 4I Framework," *Academy of Management Review,* January 2005, pp 180–91.

69See P M Fandt and G R Ferris, "The Management of Information and Impressions: When Employees Behave Opportunistically," *Organizational Behavior and Human Decision Processes,* February 1990, pp 140–58.

70First four based on discussion in D R Beeman and T W Sharkey, "The Use and Abuse of Corporate Politics," *Business Horizons,* March–April 1987, pp 26–30.

71A Raia, "Power, Politics, and the Human Resource Professional," *Human Resource Planning,* no. 4, 1985, p 203.

72A J DuBrin, "Career Maturity, Organizational Rank, and Political Behavioral Tendencies: A Correlational Analysis of Organizational Politics and Career Experience," *Psychological Reports,* October 1988, p 535.

73This three-level distinction comes from A T Cobb, "Political Diagnosis: Applications in Organizational Development," *Academy of Management Review,* July 1986, pp 482–96.

[74]An excellent historical and theoretical perspective of coalitions can be found in W B Stevenson, J L Pearce, and L W Porter, "The Concept of 'Coalition' in Organization Theory and Research," *Academy of Management Review*, April 1985, pp 256–68.

[75]L Baum, "The Day Charlie Bradshaw Kissed off Transworld," *BusinessWeek*, September 29, 1986, p 68. Also see C J Loomis, "How the HP Board KO'd Carly," *Fortune*, March 7, 2005, pp 99–102.

[76]See M L Forret and T W Dougherty, "Networking Behaviors and Career Outcomes: Differences for Men and Women," *Journal of Organizational Behavior*, May 2004, pp 419–37; R Cross and S Colella, "Building Vibrant Employee Networks," *HR Magazine*, December 2004, pp 101–4; A S Wellner, "Playing Well with Others," *Inc.*, January 2005, pp 29–31; A Fisher, "How to Network—and Enjoy It," *Fortune*, April 4, 2005, p 38; and A Fisher, "Wipro Plays Cupid for Lonely Workers," *Fortune*, May 2, 2005, p 26.

[77]Allen et al., "Organizational Politics," p 77. Also see D C Treadway, W A Hochwarter, C J Kacmar, and G R Ferris, "Political Will, Political Skill, and Political Behavior," *Journal of Organizational Behavior*, May 2005, pp 229–45.

[78]See J Pfeffer, "The Whole Truth and Nothing But," *Business 2.0*, October 2004, p 78; and M Seldman and E Betof, "An Illuminated Path," *Training & Development*, December 2004, pp 34–39.

[79]A Rao, S M Schmidt, and L H Murray, "Upward Impression Management: Goals, Influence Strategies, and Consequences," *Human Relations*, February 1995, p 147. Also see J A Clair, J E Beatty, and T L Maclean, "Out of Sight but Not out of Mind: Managing Invisible Social Identities in the Workplace," *Academy of Management Review*, January 2005, pp 78–95; and S L Grover, "The Truth, the Whole Truth, and Nothing but the Truth: The Causes and Management of Workplace Lying," *Academy of Management Executive*, May 2005, pp 148–157.

[80]See W L Gardner and B J Avolio, "The Charismatic Relationship: A Dramaturgical Perspective," *Academy of Management Review*, January 1998, pp 32–58; L Wah, "Managing—Manipulating?—Your Reputation," *Management Review*, October 1998, pp 46–50; M C Bolino, "Citizenship and Impression Management: Good Soldiers or Good Actors?" *Academy of Management Review*, January 1999, pp 82–98; and W H Turnley and M C Bolino, "Achieving Desired Images while Avoiding Undesired Images: Exploring the Role of Self-Monitoring in Impression Management," *Journal of Applied Psychology*, April 2001, pp 351–60.

[81]See A Wheat, "Work That Room," *Fortune*, May 27, 2002, 187–90; A Heller, "How to Give Your Career a Lift," *BusinessWeek*, July 8, 2002, p 10; W Tsai and S Chien-Cheng Chiu, "Exploring Boundaries of the Effects of Applicant Impression Management Tactics in Job Interviews," *Journal of Management*, no. 1, 2005, pp 108–25; H Ibarra and K Lineback, "What's Your Story?" *Harvard Business Review*, January 2005, pp 64–71; and Z I Barsness, K A Diekmann, and M L Seidel, "Motivation and Opportunity: The Role of Remote Work, Demographic Dissimilarity, and Social Network Centrality in Impression Management," *Academy of Management Journal*, June 2005, in press.

[82]S Friedman, "What Do You Really Care About? What Are You Most Interested In?" *Fast Company*, March 1999, p 90. Also see B M DePaulo and D A Kashy, "Everyday Lies in Close and Casual Relationships," *Journal of Personality and Social Psychology*, January 1998, pp 63–79; B M DePaulo, M E Ansfield, S E Kirkendol, and J M Boden, "Serious Lies," *Basic and Applied Social Psychology*, nos. 2 and 3, 2004, pp 147–67; and J Alsever, "The Ethics Monitor," *Fast Company*, May 2005, p 33.

[83]See S J Wayne and G R Ferris, "Influence Tactics, Affect, and Exchange Quality in Supervisor-Subordinate Interactions: A Laboratory Experiment and Field Study," *Journal of Applied Psychology*, October 1990, pp 487–99. For another version, see Table 1 (p 246) in S J Wayne and R C Liden, "Effects of Impression Management on Performance Ratings: A Longitudinal Study," *Academy of Management Journal*, February 1995, pp 232–60.

[84]See R Vonk, "The Slime Effect: Suspicion and Dislike of Likeable Behavior toward Superiors," *Journal of Personality and Social Psychology*, April 1998, pp 849–64; and M Wells, "How to Schmooze Like the Best of Them," *USA Today*, May 18, 1999, p 14E.

[85]See A Montagliani and R A Giacalone, "Impression Management and Cross-Cultural Adaptation," *Journal of Social Psychology*, October 1998, pp 598–608.

[86]M E Mendenhall and C Wiley, "Strangers in a Strange Land: The Relationship between Expatriate Adjustment and Impression Management," *American Behavioral Scientist*, March 1994, pp 605–20.

[87]T E Becker and S L Martin, "Trying to Look Bad at Work: Methods and Motives for Managing Poor Impressions in Organizations," *Academy of Management Journal*, February 1995, p 191.

[88]Ibid., p 181. Also see M K Duffy, D C Ganster, and M Pagon, "Social Undermining in the Workplace," *Academy of Management Journal*, April 2002, pp 331–51.

[89]Adapted from ibid., pp 180–81.

[90]Data from G R Ferris, D D Frink, D P S Bhawuk, J Zhou, and D C Gilmore, "Reactions of Diverse Groups to Politics in the Workplace," *Journal of Management*, no. 1, 1996, pp 23–44. For other findings from the same database, see G R Ferris, D D Frink, M C Galang, J Zhou, K M Kacmar, and J L Howard, "Perceptions of Organizational Politics: Prediction, Stress-Related Implications, and Outcomes," *Human Relations*, February 1996, pp 233–66. Also see M L Inman, N McDonald, and A Ruch, "Boasting and Firsthand and Secondhand Impressions: A New Explanation for the Positive Teller-Listener Extremity Effect," *Basic and Applied Social Psychology*, no. 1, 2004, pp 59–75; and S Zivnuska, K M Kacmar, L A Witt, D S Carlson, and V K Bratton, "Interactive Effects of Impression Management and Organizational Politics on Job Performance," *Journal of Organizational Behavior*, August 2004, pp 627–40.

[91] A Drory and D Beaty, "Gender Differences in the Perception of Organizational Influence Tactics," *Journal of Organizational Behavior,* May 1991, pp 256–57. Also see L A Rudman, "Self-Promotion as a Risk Factor for Women: The Costs and Benefits of Counterstereotypical Impression Management," *Journal of Personality and Social Psychology,* March 1998, pp 629–45; and J Tata, "The Influence of Gender on the Use and Effectiveness of Managerial Accounts," *Group & Organization Management,* September 1998, pp 267–88.

[92] Based on L A Witt, T F Hilton, and W A Hochwarter, "Addressing Politics in Matrix Teams," *Group & Organization Management,* June 2001, pp 230–47.

[93] S A Akimoto and D M Sanbonmatsu, "Differences in Self-Effacing Behavior between European and Japanese Americans," *Journal of Cross-Cultural Psychology,* March 1999, pp 172–73.

[94] A Zaleznik, "Real Work," *Harvard Business Review,* January–February 1989, p 60. Also see G P Zachary, "How Intel Grooms Its Leaders," *Business 2.0,* July 2004, pp 43–45; B Dumaine, "I'd Rather Be Inventing," *Fortune,* November 15, 2004, p 194; and D Lidsky, "Similarity Breeds Success," *Fast Company,* February 2005, p 43.

[95] C M Koen, Jr, and S M Crow, "Human Relations and Political Skills," *HR Focus,* December 1995, p 11.

[96] See L A Witt, "Enhancing Organizational Goal Congruence: A Solution to Organizational Politics," *Journal of Applied Psychology,* August 1998, pp 666–74.

[97] Excerpted from J Weber, "Waging War on Hunger," *BusinessWeek,* May 16, 2005, pp 94, 96. Reprinted by permission of The McGraw-Hill Companies, Inc.

[98] Ten quiz items quoted from J F Byrnes, "Connecting Organizational Politics and Conflict Resolution," *Personnel Administrator,* June 1986, p 49. Reprinted with the permission of *Personnel Administrator* published by the Society for Human Resource Management, Alexandria, VA.

[99] Scoring system quoted from ibid.

[100] B R Schlenker and T W Britt, "Beneficial Impression Management: Strategically Controlling Information to Help Friends," *Journal of Personality and Social Psychology,* April 1999, p 559.

[101] Excerpted from K Tse and D Foust, "At Risk from Smoking: Your Job," *BusinessWeek,* April 15, 2002, p 12. Reprinted by permission of The McGraw-Hill Companies, Inc. For additional background information, see K Gurchiek, "Study: Smoking Ban Improved Air," *HR Magazine,* January 2005, p 34; K Springer, "Smoking: Light Up and You May Be Let Go," *Newsweek,* February 7, 2005, p 10; and S Bates, "Where There Is Smoke, There Is Terminations," *HR Magazine,* March 2005, pp 28, 40.

CHAPTER 16

[1] Excerpted from C Hymowitz, "The Perils of Picking CEOs," *The Wall Street Journal,* March 15, 2005, pp B1, B4. Reprinted by permission of Dow Jones & Co. via The Copyright Clearance Center.

[2] A summary of leadership research is provided by B J Avolio, J J Sosik, D I Jung, and Y Berson, "Leadership, Models, Methods, and Applications," in *Handbook of Psychology,* eds W C Borman, D R Ilgen, and R J Klimoski (Hoboken, NJ: John Wiley & Sons, 2003), vol. 12, pp 277–307.

[3] See S Lieberson and J F O'Connor, "Leadership and Organizational Performance: A Study of Large Corporations," *American Sociological Review,* April 1972, pp 117–30. The impact of leadership on financial performance was also supported by "How HR Can Affect the Bottom Line," *HR Magazine,* February 2005, pp 14, 16.

[4] Results can be found in K T Dirks, "Trust in Leadership and Team Performance: Evidence from NCAA Basketball," *Journal of Applied Psychology,* December 2000, pp 1004–12; and D Jacobs and L Singell, "Leadership and Organizational Performance: Isolating Links between Managers and Collective Success," *Social Science Research,* June 1993, pp 165–89.

[5] The multiple levels of leadership are discussed by F J Yammarino, F Dansereau, and C J Kennedy, "A Multiple-Level Multidimensional Approach to Leadership: Viewing Leadership through an Elephant's Eye," *Organizational Dynamics,* 2001, pp 149–63.

[6] The four commonalities were identified by P G Northouse, *Leadership: Theory and Practice,* 3rd ed (Thousand Oaks, CA: Sage Publications, 2004), p 3.

[7] Ibid.

[8] B M Bass, *Bass & Stogdill's Handbook of Leadership: Theory, Research, and Managerial Applications,* 3rd ed. (New York: Free Press, 1990), p 383.

[9] For a thorough discussion about the differences between leading and managing, see P Lorenzi, "Managing for the Common Good: Prosocial Leadership," *Organizational Dynamics,* August 2004, pp 282–90; and A Zalesnik, "Managers and Leaders: Are They Different?" *Harvard Business Review,* May–June 1977, pp 67–78.

[10] See L V Gerstner Jr, *Who Says Elephants Can't Dance?* (New York: HarperBusiness, 2002); and L Bossidy and R Charan, *Execution: The Discipline of Getting Things Done* (New York: Crown Business, 2002).

[11] Leadership development programs are discussed by B J Avolio, *Leadership Development in Balance* (Mahwah, NJ: Lawrence Erlbaum Associates, 2005); and B Hall, "The Top Training Priorities for 2005," *Training,* February 2005, pp 22–29.

[12] For complete details, see R M Stogdill, *Handbook of Leadership* (New York: Free Press, 1974); and R D Mann, "A Review of the Relationships between Personality and Performance in Small Groups," *Psychological Bulletin,* July 1959, pp 241–70.

[13] See O Epitropaki and R Martin, "Implicit Leadership Theories in Applied Settings: Factor Structure, Generalizability, and Stability over Time," *Journal of Applied Psychology,* April 2004, pp 293–310.

[14] Results can be found in R G Lord, C L De Vader, and G M Alliger, "A Meta-Analysis of the Relation between

Personality Traits and Leadership Perceptions: An Application of Validity Generalization Procedures," *Journal of Applied Psychology,* August 1986, pp 402–10.

[15]Results from this study can be found in F C Brodbeck et al., "Cultural Variation of Leadership Prototypes across 22 European Countries," *Journal of Occupational and Organizational Psychology,* March 2000, pp 1–29.

[16]Results can be found in J M Kouzes and B Z Posner, *The Leadership Challenge* (San Francisco: Jossey-Bass, 1995).

[17]See "The Best and Worst Managers of the Year," *BusinessWeek,* January 10, 2005, pp 55–83.

[18]D Goleman, "What Makes a Leader?" *Harvard Business Review,* November–December 1998, pp 93–102.

[19]D Goleman, R Goyatzis, and A McKee, "Primal Leadership: The Hidden Driver of Great Performance," *Harvard Business Review,* December 2001, p 44.

[20]Results can be found in T A Judge, J E Hono, R Ilies, and M W Gerhardt, "Personality and Leadership: A Qualitative and Quantitative Review," *Journal of Applied Psychology,* August 2002, pp 765–80.

[21]See T A Judge, A E Colbert, and R Ilies, "Intelligence and Leadership: A Quantitative Review and Test of Theoretical Propositions," *Journal of Applied Psychology,* June 2004, pp 542–52.

[22]Kellerman's research can be found in B Kellerman, *Bad Leadership* (Boston: Harvard Business School Press, 2004).

[23]The trait definitions were quoted from ibid. pp 40–46.

[24]Gender and the emergence of leaders was examined by A H Eagly and S J Karau, "Gender and the Emergence of Leaders: A Meta-Analysis," *Journal of Personality and Social Psychology,* May 1991, pp 685–710; and R K Shelly and P T Munroe, "Do Women Engage in Less Task Behavior than Men?" *Sociological Perspectives,* Spring 1999, pp 49–67.

[25]See A H Eagly, S J Karau, and B T Johnson, "Gender and Leadership Style among School Principals: A Meta-Analysis," *Educational Administration Quarterly,* February 1992, pp 76–102.

[26]Supportive findings are contained in J M Twenge, "Changes in Women's Assertiveness in Response to Status and Roles: A Cross-Temporal Meta-Analysis, 1931–1993," *Journal of Personality and Social Psychology,* July 2001, pp 133–45.

[27]For a summary of this research, see R Sharpe, "As Leaders, Women Rule," *BusinessWeek,* November 20, 2000, pp 74–84.

[28]The process of preparing a development plan is discussed by L Morgan, G Spreitzer, J Dutton, R Quinn, E Heaphy, and B Barker, "How to Play to Your Strengths," *Harvard Business Review,* January 2005, pp 75–80.

[29]Executive coaching is discussed by M F R Kets de Vries, "Leadership Group Coaching in Action: The Zen of Creating High-Performance Teams," *Academy of Management Executive,* February 2005, pp 61–76; and H Johnson, "The Ins and Outs of Executive Coaching," *Training,* May 2004, pp 36–41.

[30]Details on Hasbro's program can be found in A Pomeroy, "Head of the Class," *HR Magazine,* January 2005, pp 54–58.

[31]This research is summarized and critiqued by E A Fleishman, "Consideration and Structure: Another Look at Their Role in Leadership Research," in *Leadership: The Multiple-Level Approaches,* eds F Dansereau and F J Yammarino (Stamford, CT: JAI Press, 1998), pp 51–60.

[32]Results can be found in T A Judge, R F Piccolo, and R Ilies, "The Forgotten Ones? The Validity of Consideration and Initiating Structure in Leadership Research," *Journal of Applied Psychology,* February 2004, pp 36–51.

[33]See V H Vroom, "Leadership," in *Handbook of Industrial and Organizational Psychology,* ed M D Dunnette (Chicago: Rand McNally, 1976).

[34]See Bass, *Bass & Stogdill's Handbook of Leadership,* Chs. 20–25.

[35]The relationships between the frequency and mastery of leader behavior and various outcomes were investigated by F Shipper and C S White, "Mastery, Frequency, and Interaction of Managerial Behaviors Relative to Subunit Effectiveness," *Human Relations,* January 1999, pp 49–66.

[36]For more on this theory, see F E Fiedler, "A Contingency Model of Leadership Effectiveness," in *Advances in Experimental Social Psychology,* vol. 1, ed L Berkowitz (New York: Academic Press, 1964); and F E Fiedler, *A Theory of Leadership Effectiveness* (New York: McGraw-Hill, 1967).

[37]Additional information on situational control is contained in F E Fiedler, "The Leadership Situation and the Black Box in Contingency Theories," in *Leadership Theory and Research: Perspectives and Directions,* eds M M Chemers and R Ayman (New York: Academic Press, 1993), pp 2–28.

[38]See the discussion in Chapter 6 from Northouse, *Leadership.*

[39]See L H Peters, D D Hartke, and J T Pohlmann, "Fiedler's Contingency Theory of Leadership: An Application of the Meta-Analyses Procedures of Schmidt and Hunter," *Psychological Bulletin,* March 1985, pp 274–85. The meta-analysis was conducted by C A Schriesheim, B J Tepper, and L A Tetrault, "Least Preferred Co-Worker Score, Situational Control, and Leadership Effectiveness: A Meta-Analysis of Contingency Model Performance Predictions," *Journal of Applied Psychology,* August 1994, pp 561–73.

[40]A recent review of the contingency theory and suggestions for future theoretical development is provided by R Ayman, M M Chemers, and F Fiedler, "The Contingency Model of Leadership Effectiveness: Its Levels of Analysis," in *Leadership: The Multiple-Level Approaches,* eds Dansereau and Yammarino, pp 73–94.

[41]Excerpted from D Kirkpatrick, "Inside Sam's $100 Billion Growth Machine," *Fortune,* June 14, 2004, pp 86, 88.

[42]For more detail on this theory, see R J House, "A Path–Goal Theory of Leader Effectiveness," *Administrative Science Quarterly,* September 1971, pp 321–38.

[43]This research is summarized by R J House, "Path–Goal Theory of Leadership: Lessons, Legacy, and a Reformulated Theory," *Leadership Quarterly,* Autumn 1996, pp 323–52.

[44]See ibid.

[45]Supportive results can be found in "Hewitt Associates Study Shows More Engaged Employees Drive Improved Business Peformance and Return," http://was4.hewitt.com/hewitt/resource/newsroom/pressrel/2004/05-18-04.htm, posted May 18, 2004, accessed April 15, 2005.

[46]Results can be found in P M Podsakoff, S B MacKenzie, M Ahearne, and W H Bommer, "Searching for a Needle in a Haystack: Trying to Identify the Illusive Moderators of Leadership Behaviors," *Journal of Management,* 1995, pp 422–70.

[47]For a complete description of this theory, see B J Avolio and B M Bass, *A Manual for Full-Range Leadership Development* (Binghamton, NY: Center for Leadership Studies, 1991). The manual is now published by www.mindgarden.com.

[48]Results can be found in A H Eagly, M C Johannesen-Schmidt, and M L van Engen, "Transformational, Transactional, and Laissez-Faire Leadership Styles: A Meta-Analysis Comparing Women and Men," *Psychological Bulletin,* June 2003, pp 569–91.

[49]A definition and description of transactional leadership is provided by J Antonakis and R J House, "The Full-Range Leadership Theory: The Way Forward," in *Transformational and Charismatic Leadership: The Road Ahead,* eds B J Avolio and F J Yammarino (New York: JAI Press, 2002), pp 3–34.

[50]M Arndt, "3M's Rising Star," *BusinessWeek,* April 12, 2004, p 65.

[51]U R Dumdum, K B Lowe, and B J Avolio, "A Meta-Analysis of Transformational and Transactional Leadership Correlates of Effectiveness and Satisfaction: An Update and Extension," in *Transformational and Charismatic Leadership: The Road Ahead,* eds B J Avolio and F J Yammarino (New York: JAI Press, 2002), p 38.

[52]Supportive research is summarized by Antonakis and House, "The Full-Range Leadership Theory."

[53]Arndt, "3M's Rising Star," pp 65, 68.

[54]Supportive results can be found in K S Groves, "Linking Leader Skills, Follower Attitudes, and Contextual Variables via an Integrated Model of Charismatic Leadership," *Journal of Management,* 2005, pp 255–77; J E Bono and T A Judge, "Personality and Transformational and Transactional Leadership: A Meta-Analysis," *Journal of Applied Psychology,* October 2004, pp 901–10; and B-C Lim and R E Ployhart, "Transformational Leadership: Relations to the Five-Factor Model and Team Performance in Typical and Maximum Contexts," *Journal of Applied Psychology,* August 2004, pp 610–21.

[55]See Eagly, Johannesen-Schmidt, and van Engen, "Transformational, Transactional, and Laissez-Faire Leadership Style."

[56]See M Greer, "The Science of Savoir Faire," *Monitor on Psychology,* January 2005, pp 28–30; and T Divir, D Eden, B J Avolio, and B Shamir, "Impact of Transformational Leadership on Follower Development and Performance: A Field Experiment," *Academy of Management Journal,* August 2002, pp 735–44.

[57]These definitions are derived from R Kark, B Shamir, and C Chen, "The Two Faces of Transformational Leadership: Empowerment and Dependency," *Journal of Applied Psychology,* April 2003, pp 246–55.

[58]B Nanus, *Visionary Leadership* (San Francisco: Jossey-Bass, 1992), p 8.

[59]A Lashinsky, "Can Moto Find Its Mojo?" *Fortune,* April 5, 2004, p 132.

[60]Results from this study are discussed in "Calling All Visionary Leaders," *HR Magazine,* March 2005, p 16.

[61]See R Kark, B Shamir, and G Chen, "The Two Faces of Transformational Leadership," *Journal of Applied Psychology,* April 2003, pp 246–55.

[62]Supportive results can be found in B van Knippenberg and D Van Knippenberg, "Leader Self-Sacrifice and Leadership Effectiveness: The Moderating Role of Leader Prototypicality," *Journal of Applied Psychology,* January 2005, pp 25–37; Y Beson and B J Avolio, "Transformational Leadership and the Dissemination of Organizational Goals: A Case Study of a Telecommunication Firm," *Leadership Quarterly,* October 2004, pp 625–46; and B J Avolio, W Zhu, W Koh, and P Bhatia, "Transformational Leadership and Organizational Commitment: Mediating Role of Psychological Empowerment and Moderating Role of Structural Distance," *Journal of Organizational Behavior,* December 2004, pp 951–68.

[63]Results can be found in T A Judge and R F Piccolo, "Transformational and Transactional Leadership: A Meta-Analytic Test of Their Relative Validity," *Journal of Applied Psychology,* October 2004, pp 755–68.

[64]See ibid.

[65]See A J Towler, "Effects of Charismatic Influence Training on Attitudes, Behavior, and Performance," *Personnel Psychology,* Summer 2003, pp 363–81; and M Frese and S Beimel, "Action Training for Charismatic Leadership: Two Evaluations of Studies of a Commercial Training Module on Inspirational Communication of a Vision," *Personnel Psychology,* Autumn 2003, pp 671–97.

[66]These recommendations were derived from J M Howell and B J Avolio, "The Ethics of Charismatic Leadership: Submission or Liberation?" *Academy of Management Executive,* May 1992, pp 43–54.

[67]See F Dansereau Jr, G Graen, and W Haga, "A Vertical Dyad Linkage Approach to Leadership within Formal Organizations," *Organizational Behavior and Human Performance,* February 1975, pp 46–78; and R M Dienesch and R C Liden, "Leader–Member Exchange Model of Leadership: A Critique and Further Development," *Academy of Management Review,* July 1986, pp 618–34.

[68]These descriptions were taken from D Duchon, S G Green, and T D Taber, "Vertical Dyad Linkage: A Longitudinal Assessment of Antecedents, Measures, and Consequences," *Journal of Applied Psychology,* February 1986, pp 56–60.

[69]Supportive results can be found in O Janssen and N W V Yperen, "Employees' Goal Orientations, the Quality of Leader–Member Exchange, and the Outcomes of Job Performance and Job Satisfaction," *Academy of Management Journal*, June 2004, pp 368–84; B Erdogan, M L Kraimer, and R C Liden, "Work Value Congruence and Intrinsic Career Success: The Compensatory Roles of Leader–Member Exchange and Perceived Organizational Support," *Personnel Psychology*, Summer 2004, pp 305–32; and C A Schriesheim, S L Castro, and F J Yammarino, "Investigating Contingencies: An Examination of the Impact of Span of Supervision and Upward Controllingness on Leader–Member Exchange Using Traditional and Multivariate within—and between—Entities Analysis," *Journal of Applied Psychology*, October 2000, pp 659–77.

[70]A turnover study was conducted by G B Graen, R C Liden, and W Hoel, "Role of Leadership in the Employee Withdrawal Process," *Journal of Applied Psychology*, December 1982, pp 868–72. The career progress study was conducted by M Wakabayashi and G B Graen, "The Japanese Career Progress Study: A 7-Year Follow-Up," *Journal of Applied Psychology*, November 1984, pp 603–14.

[71]See D O Adebayo and I B Udegbe, "Gender in the Boss–Subordinate Relationship: A Nigerian Study," *Journal of Organizational Behavior*, June 2004, pp 515–25.

[72]Supportive results can be found in K M Kacmar, L A Witt, S Zivnuska, and S M Gully, "The Interactive-Effect of Leader–Member Exchange and Communication Frequency on Performance Ratings," *Journal of Applied Psychology*, August 2003, pp 764–72; and S J Wayne, L M Shore, and R C Liden, "Perceived Organizational Support and Leader–Member Exchange: A Social Exchange Perspective," *Academy of Management Journal*, February 1997, pp 82–111.

[73]These recommendations were derived from G C Mage, "Leading Despite Your Boss," *HR Magazine*, September 2003, pp 139–44.

[74]R J House and R N Aditya, "The Social Scientific Study of Leadership Ouo Vadis?" *Journal of Management*, 1997, p 457.

[75]For information about Mayo Clinc's use of shared leadership, see L L Berry, "The Collaborative Organization: Leadership Lessons from Mayo Clinic," *Organizational Dynamics*, August 2004, pp 228–41.

[76]A thorough discussion of shared leadership is provided by C L Pearce "The Future of Leadership: Combining Vertical and Shared Leadership Transform Knowledge Work," *Academy of Management Executive*, February 2004, pp 47–59.

[77]See the related discussion in T Butler and J Waldroop, "Understanding 'People' People," *Harvard Business Review*, June 2004, pp 78–86.

[78]This research is summarized in B J Avolio et al., "Leadership Models, Methods, and Application." Also see S J Zaccaro, A L Rittman, and M A Marks, "Team Leadership," *Leadership Quarterly*, 2001, pp 451–83.

[79]See J Collins, *Good to Great: Why Some Companies Make the Leap and Others Don't* (New York: Harper Business, 2001).

[80]J Collins, "Level 5 Leadership: The Triumph of Humility and Fierce Resolve," *Harvard Business Review*, January 2001, p 68.

[81]A Serwer, "The Education of Michael Dell," *Fortune*, March 7, 2005, p 73.

[82]See Collins, *Good to Great*.

[83]An overall summary of servant-leadership is provided by L C Spears, *Reflections on Leadership: How Robert K Greenleaf's Theory of Servant-Leadership Influenced Today's Top Management Thinkers* (New York: John Wiley & Sons, 1995).

[84]T Galvin, "Birds of a Feather," *Training*, March 2001, p 84.

[85]J Stuart, *Fast Company*, September 1999, p 114.

[86]The role of followers is discussed by J M Howell and B Shamir, "The Role of Followers in the Charismatic Leadership Process: Relationships and Their Consequences," *Academy of Management Review*, January 2005, pp 96–112.

[87]This point was made by J J Gabarro and J P Kotter, "Managing Your Boss," *Harvard Business Review*, January 2005, pp 92–99.

[88]See the related discussion in L R Offermann, "When Followers Become Toxic," *Harvard Business Review*, January 2004, pp 54–60.

[89]See R Goffee and G Jones, "Followership: It's Personal, Too," *Harvard Business Review*, December 2001, p 148.

[90]This checklist was proposed by Gabarro and Kotter, "Managing Your Boss."

[91]A process for conducting self-awareness is discussed by P F Drucker, "Managing Oneself," *Harvard Business Review*, January 2005, pp 100–9.

[92]The following suggestions were discussed by Gabarro and Kotter, "Managing Your Boss."

[93]L Lavelle, "Three Simple Rules Carly Ignored: Why Things Went Wrong at HP—and Went Right at P&G, UTC, and IBM," *BusinessWeek*, February 28, 2005, p 46. Reprinted by permission of The McGraw-Hill Companies, Inc.

[94]The scale used to assess readiness to assume the leadership role was taken from A J DuBrin, *Leadership: Research Findings, Practice, and Skills* (Boston: Houghton Mifflin Company, 1995), pp 10–11.

[95]The norms were taken from ibid.

[96]This exercise was based on one contained in L W Mealiea, *Skills for Managers in Organizations* (Burr Ridge, IL: Irwin, 1994), pp 96–97.

[97]The introduction was excerpted from ibid., p 96.

[98]Excerpted from C Haddad and A Barrett, "A Whistle-Blower Rocks an Industry," *BusinessWeek*, June 24, 2002, pp 126, 128.

CHAPTER 17

[1]Excerpted from J Useem, "Should We Admire Wal-Mart?" *Fortune*, March 8, 2004, pp 118, 120. © 2004 Time Inc. Reprinted by permission. All rights reserved. Also see G Colvin, "Wal-Mart's Growth Will Slow Down—Eventually," *Fortune*,

February 7, 2005, p 48; C Salter, "Pulling Punches," *Fast Company*, April 2005, p 31; A Serwer, "Bruised in Bentonville," *Fortune*, April 18, 2005, pp 84–89; and M Maier, "How to Beat Wal-Mart," *Business 2.0*, May 2005, pp 108–14.

2C I Barnard, *The Functions of the Executive* (Cambridge, MA: Harvard University Press, 1938), p 73. Also see C Vibert, *Theories of Macro Organizational Behavior: A Handbook of Ideas and Explanations* (Armonk, NY: M E Sharpe, 2004); D Robichaud, H Giroux, and J R Taylor, "The Metaconversation: The Recursive Property of Language as a Key to Organizing," *Academy of Management Review*, October 2004, pp 617–34; and M Kets de Vries and K Balazs, "Organizations as Optical Illusions: A Clinical Perspective on Organizational Consultation," *Organizational Dynamics*, no. 1, 2005, pp 1–17.

3Drawn from E H Schein, *Organizational Psychology*, 3rd ed (Englewood Cliffs, NJ: Prentice Hall, 1980), pp 12–15.

4For interesting and instructive insights about organization structure and theory, see J G March, "Continuity and Change in Theories of Organizational Action," *Administrative Science Quarterly*, June 1996, pp 278–87; and J Ofori-Dankwa and S D Julian, "Complexifying Organizational Theory: Illustrations Using Time Research," *Academy of Management Review*, July 2001, pp 415–30.

5For related research, see S Finkelstein and R A D'Aveni, "CEO Duality as a Double-Edged Sword: How Boards of Directors Balance Entrenchment Avoidance and Unity of Command," *Academy of Management Journal*, October 1994, pp 1079–108.

6See M Cecere, "Drawing the Lines," *Harvard Business Review*, November 2001, p 24.

7See H J Leavitt, "Why Hierarchies Thrive," *Harvard Business Review*, March 2003, pp 96–102.

8For an excellent overview of the span of control concept, see D D Van Fleet and A G Bedeian, "A History of the Span of Management," *Academy of Management Review*, July 1977, pp 356–72. Also see E E Lawler III and J R Galbraith, "New Roles for the Staff: Strategic Support and Service," in *Organizing for the Future: The New Logic for Managing Complex Organizations*, eds J R Galbraith, E E Lawler III, and Associates (San Francisco: Jossey-Bass, 1993), pp 65–83.

9A contrary example involving Southwest Airlines can be found in J Pfeffer, "How Companies Get Smart," *Business 2.0*, January–February 2005, p 74.

10M Koslowsky, "Staff/Line Distinctions in Job and Organizational Commitment," *Journal of Occupational Psychology*, June 1990, pp 167–73.

11A management-oriented discussion of general systems theory—an interdisciplinary attempt to integrate the various fragmented sciences—may be found in K E Boulding, "General Systems Theory—The Skeleton of Science," *Management Science*, April 1956, pp 197–208. For more recent systems-related ideas, see A M Webber, "How Business Is a Lot like Life," *Fast Company*, April 2001, pp 130–36; E Bonabeau and C Meyer, "Swarm Intelligence: A Whole New Way to Think about Business," *Harvard Business Review*, May 2001,

pp 106–14; S Godin, "Survival Is Not Enough," *Fast Company*, January 2002, pp 90–94; E K Clemons and J A Santamaria, "Maneuver Warfare: Can Modern Military Strategy Lead You to Victory?" *Harvard Business Review*, April 2002, pp 56–65; C Oswick, T Keenoy, and D Grant, "Metaphor and Analogical Reasoning in Organization Theory: Beyond Orthodoxy," *Academy of Management Review*, April 2002, pp 294–303; and D Ticoll, "Get Self-Organized," *Harvard Business Review*, September 2004, pp 18–19.

12See L Buchanan, "No More Metaphors," *Harvard Business Review*, March 2005, p 19; and L Prusak, "The Madness of Individuals," *Harvard Business Review*, June 2005, p 22.

13For more on this subject, see V-W Mitchell, "Organizational Homoeostasis: A Role for Internal Marketing," *Management Decision*, no. 2, 1992, pp 3–7. Biological metaphors are explored in T Petzinger Jr. "A New Model for the Nature of Business: It's Alive!" *The Wall Street Journal*, February 26, 1999, pp B1, B4: and T Petzinger Jr, "Two Doctors Give New Meaning to Taking Your Business to Heart," *The Wall Street Journal*, April 30, 1999, p B1.

14For updates, see J J Salopek, "Targeting the Learning Organization," *Training & Development*, March 2004, pp 46–51; T B Lawrence, M K Mauws, B Dyck, and R F Kleysen, "The Politics of Organizational Learning: Integrating Power into the 4I Framework," *Academy of Management Review*, January 2005, pp 180–91; and J Gordon, "CLO: A Strategic Player?" *Training*, April 2005, pp 15–19.

15R M Fulmer and J B Keys, "A Conversation with Peter Senge: New Development in Organizational Learning," *Organizational Dynamics*, Autumn 1998, p 35.

16This definition was based on D A Garvin, "Building a Learning Organization," *Harvard Business Review*, July–August 1993, pp 78–91.

17J Stuller, "Chief of Corporate Smarts," *Training*, April 1998, p 32. For more on learning organizations, see R S Snell, "Moral Foundations of the Learning Organization," *Human Relations*, March 2001, pp 319–42; A Edmondson, R Bohmer, and G Pisano, "Speeding Up Team Learning," *Harvard Business Review*, October 2001, pp 125–32; B Breen, "Lilly's R&D Prescription," *Fast Company*, April 2002, pp 44, 46; and K Ellis, "The Mindset that Matters: Linking Learning to the Business," *Training*, May 2005, pp 38–43.

18T A Stewart, "Welcome to the Revolution," *Fortune*, December 13, 1993, p 66. Also see J A Byrne, "Management by Web," *BusinessWeek*, August 28, 2000, pp 84–96; and J Child and R G McGrath, "Organizations Unfettered: Organizational Form in an Information-Intensive Economy," *Academy of Management Journal*, December 2001, pp 1135–48.

19See J R Galbraith and E E Lawler III, "Effective Organizations: Using the New Logic of Organizing," in *Organizing for the Future: The New Logic for Managing Complex Organizations*, eds J R Galbraith, E E Lawler III, and Associates (San Francisco: Jossey-Bass, 1993).

20See N Nohria, W Joyce, and B Roberson, "What Really Works," *Harvard Business Review*, July 2003, pp 42–52; and S M Puffer, "Changing Organizational Structures: An Interview with Rosabeth Moss Kanter," *Academy of Management Executive,* May 2004, pp 96–105.

[21]See D McGinn, "Re-engineering 2.0," *Newsweek,* November 22, 2004, p 59.

[22]R Jacob, "The Struggle to Create an Organization for the 21st Century," *Fortune,* April 3, 1995, pp 91–92.

[23]See S Sonnesyn Brooks, "Managing a Horizontal Revolution," *HR Magazine,* June 1995, pp 52–58; and M Hequet, "Flat and Happy," *Training,* April 1995, pp 29–34.

[24]See Y Shin, "A Person–Environment Fit Model for Virtual Organizations," *Journal of Management,* no. 5, 2004, pp 725–43; D Roth, "The Amazing Rise of the Do-It-Yourself Economy," *Fortune,* May 30, 2005, pp 43, 46; and M V Copeland and A Tilin, "The New Instant Companies," *Business 2.0,* June 2005, pp 82–94.

[25]C Handy, *The Hungry Spirit* (New York: Broadway Books, 1998), p 186. (Emphasis added.)

[26]See S Hamm, "Linux Inc.," *BusinessWeek,* January 31, 2005, pp 60–68; A R Winger, "Face-to-Face Communication: Is It Really Necessary in a Digitizing World?" *Business Horizons,* May–June 2005, pp 247–53; and D Ernst and J Bamford, "Your Alliances Are Too Stable," *Harvard Business Review,* June 2005, pp 133–41.

[27]J A Byrne and B Elgin, "Cisco: Behind the Hype," *BusinessWeek,* January 21, 2002, p 58.

[28]K Cameron, "Critical Questions in Assessing Organizational Effectiveness," *Organizational Dynamics,* Autumn 1980, p 70. Also see K Gawande and T Wheeler, "Measures of Effectiveness for Governmental Organizations," *Management Science,* January 1999, pp 42–58; E J Walton and S Dawson, "Managers' Perceptions of Criteria of Organizational Effectiveness," *Journal of Management Studies,* March 2001, pp 173–200; M Beer, "How to Develop an Organization Capable of Sustained High Performance: Embrace the Drive for Results-Capability Development Paradox," *Organizational Dynamics,* Spring 2001, pp 233–47; and K H Roberts and R Bea, "Must Accidents Happen? Lessons from High-Reliability Organizations," *Academy of Management Executive,* August 2001, pp 70–78.

[29]See, for example, R O Brinkerhoff and D E Dressler, *Productivity Measurement: A Guide for Managers and Evaluators* (Newbury Park, CA: Sage Publications, 1990); and J McCune, "The Productivity Paradox," *Management Review,* March 1998, pp 38–40.

[30]See W E Halal, "The Intelligent Internet: The Promise of Smart Computers and E-Commerce," *The Futurist,* March–April 2004, pp 27–32; and N Koiso-Kanttila, "Time, Attention, Authenticity and Consumer Benefits of the Web," *Business Horizons,* January–February 2005, pp 63–70.

[31]Data from M Maynard, "Toyota Promises Custom Order in 5 Days," *USA Today,* August 6, 1999, p 1B.

[32]See M G Wilson, D M DeJoy, R J Vandenberg, H A Richardson, and A L McGrath, "Work Characteristics and Employee Health and Well-Being: Test of a Model of Healthy Work Organization," *Journal of Occupational and Organizational Psychology,* December 2004, pp 565–88.

[33]"Interview: M Scott Peck," *Business Ethics,* March–April 1994, p 17.

[34]Cameron, "Critical Questions in Assessing Organizational Effectiveness," p 67. Also see C Fishman, "The Wal-Mart You Don't Know," *Fast Company,* December 2003, pp 68–80; and A Reinhardt, "Will Rewiring Nokia Spark Growth?" *BusinessWeek,* February 14, 2005, pp 46–47.

[35]See S L Hart and S Sharma, "Engaging Fringe Stakeholders for Competitive Imagination," *Academy of Management Executive,* February 2004, pp 7–18; O C Ferrell, "Business Ethics and Customer Stakeholders," *Academy of Management Executive,* May 2004, pp 126–29; and R J Martinez and P M Norman, "Whither Reputation? The Effects of Different Stakeholders," *Business Horizons,* September–October 2004, pp 25–32.

[36]See N C Roberts and P J King, "The Stakeholder Audit Goes Public," *Organizational Dynamics,* Winter 1989, pp 63–79; and I Henriques and P Sadorsky, "The Relationship between Environmental Commitment and Managerial Perceptions of Stakeholder Importance," *Academy of Management Journal,* February 1999, pp 87–99.

[37]See C Ostroff and N Schmitt, "Configurations of Organizational Effectiveness and Efficiency," *Academy of Management Journal,* December 1993, pp 1345–61; M Boyle, "The Right Stuff," *Fortune,* March 4, 2002, pp 85–86; and J Useem, "America's Most Admired Companies," *Fortune,* March 7, 2005, pp 66–70.

[38]K S Cameron, "Effectiveness as Paradox: Consensus and Conflict in Conceptions of Organizational Effectiveness," *Management Science,* May 1986, p 542.

[39]Alternative effectiveness criteria are discussed in ibid.; A G Bedeian, "Organization Theory: Current Controversies, Issues, and Directions," in *International Review of Industrial and Organizational Psychology,* eds C L Cooper and I T Robertson (New York: John Wiley & Sons, 1987), pp 1–33; and M Keeley, "Impartiality and Participant-Interest Theories of Organizational Effectiveness," *Administrative Science Quarterly,* March 1984, pp 1–25.

[40]For details, see A Sloan, "Lights Out for Enron," *Newsweek,* December 10, 2001, pp 50–51; W Zellner and S A Forest, "The Fall of Enron," *BusinessWeek,* December 17, 2001, pp 30–36; B McLean, "Why Enron Went Bust," *Fortune,* December 24, 2001, pp 58–68; and G Farrell and D Jones, "How Did Enron Come Unplugged?" *USA Today,* January 14, 2002, pp 1B–2B.

[41]See M Goldsmith, "Learning from the Jurassic Office Park," *Fast Company,* May 2005, p 98.

[42]D N Sull, "Why Good Companies Go Bad," *Harvard Business Review,* July–August 1999, pp 42–52. Also see H B Cohen, "The Performance Paradox," *Academy of Management Executive,* August 1998, pp 30–40.

[43]M A Mone, W McKinley, and V L Barker III, "Organizational Decline and Innovation: A Contingency Framework," *Academy of Management Review,* January 1998, p 117.

44P Lorange and R T Nelson, "How to Recognize—and Avoid—Organizational Decline," *Sloan Management Review,* Spring 1987, p 47. Also see M L Marks and K P De Meuse, "Resizing the Organization: Maximizing the Gain while Minimizing the Pain of Layoffs, Divestitures, and Closings," *Organizational Dynamics,* no. 1, 2005, pp 19–35.

45Excerpted from ibid., pp 43–45. Also see E E Lawler III and J R Galbraith, "Avoiding the Corporate Dinosaur Syndrome," *Organizational Dynamics,* Autumn 1994, pp 5–17; and K Labich, "Why Companies Fail," *Fortune,* November 14, 1994, pp 52–68.

46For details, see K S Cameron, M U Kim, and D A Whetten, "Organizational Effects of Decline and Turbulence," *Administrative Science Quarterly,* June 1987, pp 222–40. Also see, G Probst and S Raisch, "Organizational Crisis: The Logic of Failure," *Academy of Management Executive,* February 2005, pp 90–105.

47For a success story, see B Stone, "Motorola's Good Call," *Newsweek,* March 14, 2005, pp 42–43.

48Data from V L Barker III and P W Patterson Jr. "Top Management Team Tenure and Top Manager Causal Attributions at Declining Firms Attempting Turnarounds," *Group & Organization Management,* September 1996, pp 304–36. Related research is reported in V L Barker III, P W Patterson Jr, and G C Mueller, "Organizational Causes and Strategic Consequences of the Extent of Top Management Team Replacement during Turnaround Attempts," *Journal of Management Studies,* March 2001, pp 235–70.

49See H Ma and R Karri, "Leaders Beware: Some Sure Ways to Lose Your Competitive Advantage," *Organizational Dynamics,* no. 1, 2005, pp 63–76.

50B Treasurer, "How Risk-Taking Really Works," *Training,* January 2000, p 43.

51See J L Roberts and E Thomas, "Enron's Dirty Laundry," *Newsweek,* March 11, 2002, pp 22–28.

52A Taylor III, "Why Toyota Keeps Getting Better and Better and Better," *Fortune,* November 19, 1990, pp 66–67.

532005 data from D Welch, "Running out of Gas," *BusinessWeek,* March 28, 2005, pp 28–31. Also see A Taylor III, "GM Hits the Skids," *Fortune,* April 4, 2005, pp 71–74; D Welch and D Beucke, "Why GM's Plan Won't Work . . . and the Ugly Road Ahead," *BusinessWeek,* May 9, 2005, pp 84–93; and D Welch, "Just What GM Needs," *BusinessWeek,* May 16, 2005, pp 36–37.

54J Muller, "Autos: A New Industry," *BusinessWeek,* July 15, 2002, p 106.

55For updates, see J M Pennings, "Structural Contingency Theory: A Reappraisal," *Research in Organizational Behavior* vol. 14 (Greenwich, CT: JAI Press, 1992), pp 267–309; and M Goold and A Campbell, "Do You Have a Well-Designed Organization?" *Harvard Business Review,* March 2002, pp 117–24.

56See G J Lewis and B Harvey, "Perceived Environmental Uncertainty: The Extension of Miller's Scale to the Natural Environment," *Journal of Management Studies,* March 2001, pp 201–34.

57D Kirkpatrick, "The Reigning Queen of Tech," *Fortune,* May 16, 2005, p 40.

58See C B Gibson and J Birkinshaw, "The Antecedents, Consequences, and Mediating Role of Organizational Ambidexterity," *Academy of Management Journal,* April 2004, pp 209–26; and C A O'Reilly III and M L Tushman, "The Ambidextrous Organization," *Harvard Business Review,* April 2004, pp 74–81.

59P R Lawrence and J W Lorsch, *Organization and Environment* (Homewood, IL: Richard D Irwin, 1967), p 157.

60A good example can be found on p 85 in F Arner, "J&J: Toughing out the Drought," *BusinessWeek,* January 26, 2004, pp 84–85.

61For more on 3M, see M Arndt, "3M's Rising Star," *BusinessWeek,* April 12, 2004, pp 62–74.

62K Deveny, "Bag Those Fries, Squirt That Ketchup, Fry That Fish," *BusinessWeek,* October 13, 1986, p 86.

63See D A Morand, "The Role of Behavioral Formality and Informality in the Enactment of Bureaucratic versus Organic Organizations," *Academy of Management Review,* October 1995, pp 831–72.

64A Deutschman, "The Fabric of Creativity," *Fast Company,* December 2004, p 59.

65See G P Huber, C C Miller, and W H Glick, "Developing More Encompassing Theories about Organizations: The Centralization-Effectiveness Relationship as an Example," *Organization Science,* no. 1, 1990, pp 11–40; and C Handy, "Balancing Corporate Power: A New Federalist Paper," *Harvard Business Review,* November–December 1992, pp 59–72. For a case study of decentralization, see K Maney, "CEO Helps Microsoft Enter Its 30s Gracefully," *USA Today,* January 25, 2005, pp 1B–2B.

66P Kaestle, "A New Rationale for Organizational Structure," *Planning Review,* July–August 1990, p 22. Also see M E Raynor and J L Bower, "Lead from the Center: How to Manage Divisions Dynamically," *Harvard Business Review,* May 2001, pp 92–100; and R F Freeland, "When Organizational Messiness Works," *Harvard Business Review,* May 2002, pp 24–25.

67Details of this study can be found in T Burns and G M Stalker, *The Management of Innovation* (London: Tavistock, 1961).

68D J Gillen and S J Carroll, "Relationship of Managerial Ability to Unit Effectiveness in More Organic versus More Mechanistic Departments," *Journal of Management Studies,* November 1985, pp 674–75.

69J D Sherman and H L Smith, "The Influence of Organizational Structure on Intrinsic versus Extrinsic Motivation," *Academy of Management Journal,* December 1984, p 883.

70See J A Courtright, G T Fairhurst, and L E Rogers, "Interaction Patterns in Organic and Mechanistic Systems," *Academy of Management Journal,* December 1989, pp 773–802.

71See J Woodward, *Industrial Organization: Theory and Practice* (London: Oxford University Press, 1965); and P D Collins and F Hull, "Technology and Span of Control:

Woodward Revisited," *Journal of Management Studies,* March 1986, pp 143–64.

[72]See L W Fry, "Technology-Structure Research: Three Critical Issues," *Academy of Management Journal,* September 1982, pp 532–52.

[73]Ibid., p 548. Also see R Reese, "Redesigning for Dial Tone: A Socio-Technical Systems Case Study," *Organizational Dynamics,* Autumn 1995, pp 80–90.

[74]For example, see C C Miller, W H Glick, Y-D Wang, and G P Huber, "Understanding Technology-Structure Relationships: Theory Development and Meta-Analytic Theory Testing," *Academy of Management Journal,* June 1991, pp 370–99; and K H Roberts and M Grabowski, "Organizations, Technology and Structuring," in *Handbook of Organization Studies,* eds S R Clegg, C Hardy, and W R Nord (Thousand Oaks, CA: Sage Publications, 1996), pp 409–23.

[75]The phrase "small is beautiful" was coined by the late British economist E F Schumacher. See E F Schumacher, *Small Is Beautiful: Economics as if People Mattered* (New York: Harper & Row, 1973).

[76]T J Peters and R H Waterman Jr, *In Search of Excellence* (New York: Harper & Row, 1982), p 321. Also see T Peters, "Rethinking Scale," *California Management Review,* Fall 1992, pp 7–29; P Ghemawat, "The Growth Boosters," *Harvard Business Review,* July–August 2004, pp 35–40; N J Mass, "The Relative Value of Growth," *Harvard Business Review,* April 2005, pp 102–12.

[77]See, for example, W McKinley, "Decreasing Organizational Size: To Untangle or Not to Untangle?" *Academy of Management Review,* January 1992, pp 112–23; W Zellner, "Go-Go Goliaths," *BusinessWeek,* February 13, 1995, pp 64–70; T Brown, "Manage 'BIG!' " *Management Review,* May 1996, pp 12–17; and E Shapiro, "Power, Not Size, Counts," *Management Review,* September 1996, p 61.

[78]Handy, *The Hungry Spirit,* pp 107–8. Also see C Handy, "The Doctrine of Enough," *Management Review,* June 1998, pp 52–54.

[79]P L Zweig, "The Case against Mergers," *BusinessWeek,* October 30, 1995, p 122. Also see S Tully, "What Went Wrong at WaMu," *Fortune,* August 9, 2004, pp 127–32; E Thornton, "Why Consumers Hate Mergers," *BusinessWeek,* December 6, 2004, pp 58–63; M J Epstein, "The Determinants and Evaluation of Merger Success," *Business Horizons,* January–February 2005, pp 37–46; S Tully, "The Urge to Merge," *Fortune,* February 21, 2005, pp 21–22, 26; and J C Linder, "Outsourcing Integration," *Harvard Business Review,* June 2005, p 19.

[80]D Harding and S Rovit, "Building Deals on Bedrock," *Harvard Business Review,* September 2004, pp 121–28.

[81]R Z Gooding and J A Wagner III, "A Meta-Analytic Review of the Relationship between Size and Performance: The Productivity and Efficiency of Organizations and Their Subunits," *Administrative Science Quarterly,* December 1985, pp 462–81.

[82]Ibid., p 477.

[83]Results are presented in P G Benson, T L Dickinson, and C O Neidt, "The Relationship between Organizational Size and

Turnover: A Longitudinal Investigation," *Human Relations,* January 1987, pp 15–30. Also see M Yasai-Ardekani, "Effects of Environmental Scarcity and Munificence on the Relationship of Context to Organizational Structure," *Academy of Management Journal,* March 1989, pp 131–56.

[84]See E E Lawler III, "Rethinking Organization Size," *Organizational Dynamics,* Autumn 1997, pp 24–35; O Harari, "Honey, I Shrunk the Company!" *Management Review,* December 1998, pp 39–41; and J C McCune, "Stuck in the Middle?" *Management Review,* February 1999, pp 44–49.

[85]See D McGinn, "Honey, I Shrunk the Store," *Newsweek,* June 3, 2002, pp 36–37.

[86]See J Child, "Organizational Structure, Environment and Performance: The Role of Strategic Choice," *Sociology,* January 1972, pp 1–22.

[87]See J Galbraith, *Organization Design* (Reading, MA: Addison-Wesley Publishing, 1977); J R Montanari, "Managerial Discretion: An Expanded Model of Organization Choice," *Academy of Management Review,* April 1978, pp 231–41; and H R Bobbitt, Jr, and J D Ford, "Decision-Maker Choice as a Determinant of Organizational Structure," *Academy of Management Review,* January 1980, pp 13–23.

[88]For an alternative model of strategy making, see S L Hart, "An Integrative Framework for Strategy-Making Processes," *Academy of Management Review,* April 1992, pp 327–51. Also see M Iansiti and R Levien, "Strategy as Ecology," *Harvard Business Review,* March 2004, pp 68–78; and J J Sosik, D I Jung, Y Berson, S D Dionne, and K S Jaussi, "Making All the Right Connections: The Strategic Leadership of Top Executives in High-Tech Organizations," *Organizational Dynamics,* no. 1, 2005, pp 47–61.

[89]S Perlstein, "Less Is More," *Business Ethics.* September–October 1993, p 15.
Business Ethics
P.O. Box 8439
Minneapolis, MN 55408
Reprinted with permission from *Business Ethics,* P.O. Box 8439, Minneapolis, MN 55408. www.business-ethics.com/612/879-0695.

[90]From "Our Culture" in www.patagonia.com, May 29, 2005.

[91]Details may be found in D Miller, "Strategy Making and Structure: Analysis and Implications for Performance," *Academy of Management Journal,* March 1987, pp 7–32. For more, see T L Amburgey and T Dacin, "As the Left Foot Follows the Right? The Dynamics of Strategic and Structural Change," *Academy of Management Journal,* December 1994, pp 1427–52; and M W Peng and P S Heath, "The Growth of the Firm in Planned Economies in Transition: Institutions, Organizations, and Strategic Choice," *Academy of Management Review,* April 1996, pp 492–528.

[92]C Edwards, "Shaking Up Intel's Insides," *BusinessWeek,* January 31, 2005, p 35. Reprinted by permission of The McGraw-Hill Companies, Inc. Also see J E Garten, "Andy Grove Made the Elephant Dance," *BusinessWeek,* April 11, 2005, p 26.

[93]Excerpted from B Begun, "A Really Big Idea," *Newsweek,* May 23, 2005, pp 48–49.

CHAPTER 18

[1]Excerpted from P Burrows and B Elgin, "Why HP Is Pruning the Printers," *BusinessWeek,* May 9, 2005, pp 38–39. Reprinted by permission of The McGraw-Hill Companies, Inc.

[2]A M Webber, "Learning for a Change," *Fast Company,* May 1999, p 180.

[3]Details of IBM's transformation are discussed in S Hamm, "Beyond Blue," *BusinessWeek,* April 18, 2005, pp 68–76.

[4]M L Alch, "Get Ready for the Net Generation," *Training & Development,* February 2000, pp 32, 34.

[5]The example of the US Postal Service is discussed in A Aston, "A First-Class Crisis in the Making?" *BusinessWeek,* April 11, 2005, Manufacturing, Technology & Logistics, pp 7–8.

[6]This statistic was reported in A Latour, "Defensive Linemen: After 20 Years, Baby Bells Face Some Grown-Up Competition," *The Wall Street Journal,* May 28, 2004, pp A1, A5.

[7]The link between corporate strategy and market changes is discussed by D Lei and J W Slocum Jr, "Strategic and Organizational Requirements for Competitive Advantage," *Academy of Management Executive,* February 2005 pp 31–45.

[8]The new role of boards of directors is discussed by D Henry, M France, and L Lavelle, "The Boss on the Sidelines," *BusinessWeek,* April 25, 2005, pp 86–96.

[9]This example was discussed in A Pomeroy, "Agent of Change," *HR Magazine,* May 2005, pp 52–56.

[10]The United example is derived from S Carey, "Friendlier Skies: In Bankruptcy, United Airlines Forges a Path to Better Service," *The Wall Street Journal,* June 15, 2004, pp A1, A12.

[11]This three-way typology of change was adapted from discussion in P C Nutt, "Tactics of Implementation," *Academy of Management Journal,* June 1986, pp 230–61.

[12]Types of organizational change are discussed by K E Weick and R E Quinn, "Organizational Change and Development," in *Annual Review of Psychology,* vol. 50, eds J T Spence, J M Darley, and D J Foss (Palo Alto, CA: Annual Reviews, 1999), pp 361–86.

[13]See M Hammer, "Deep Change: How Operational Innovation Can Transform Your Company," *Harvard Business Review,* April 2004, pp 85–93.

[14]The relationship between organizational culture and change is thoroughly discussed by C Ostroff, A Kinicki, and M Tomkins, "Organizational Culture and Climate," in *Handbook of Psychology, Vol. 12: Industrial and Organizational Psychology,* eds W C Borman, D R Ilgen, & R J Klimoski (New York: John Wiley & Sons, 2003), pp 565–93.

[15]For a thorough discussion of the model, see K Lewin, *Field Theory in Social Science* (New York: Harper & Row, 1951).

[16]These assumptions are discussed in E H Schein, *Organizational Psychology,* 3rd ed (Englewood Cliffs, NJ: Prentice Hall, 1980).

[17]Carey, "Friendlier Skies," p A12.

[18]C Goldwasser, "Benchmarking: People Make the Process," *Management Review,* June 1995, p 40.

[19]The sequencing of organizational change was investigated by J Amis, T Slack, and C R Hinings, "The Pace, Sequence, and Linearity of Radical Change," *Academy of Management Journal,* February 2004, pp 15–39.

[20]A cascading model of organizational change is discussed by P S Goodman and D M Rousseau, "Organizational Change That Produces Results: The Linkage Approach," *Academy of Management Executive,* August 2004, pp 7–19.

[21]A thorough discussion of the target elements of change can be found in M Beer and B Spector, "Organizational Diagnosis: Its Role in Organizational Learning," *Journal of Counseling and Development,* July–August 1993, pp 642–50.

[22]Details of this example can be found in M D Hovanesian, "Dimon's Grand Design," *BusinessWeek,* March 28, 2005, pp 96–99.

[23]These errors are discussed by J P Kotter, "Leading Change: The Eight Steps to Transformation," in *The Leader's Change Handbook,* eds J A Conger, G M Spreitzer, and E E Lawler III (San Francisco: Jossey-Bass, 1999) pp 87–99.

[24]The type of leadership needed during organizational change is discussed by J P Kotter, *Leading Change* (Boston: Harvard Business School Press, 1996); and B Ettorre, "Making Change," *Management Review,* January 1996, pp 13–18.

[25]P G Hanson and B Lubin, "Answers to Questions Frequently Asked about Organization Development," in *The Emerging Practice of Organization Development,* ed W Sikes, A Drexler, and J Grant (Alexandria, VA: NTL Institute, 1989), p 16.

[26]Different stage-based models of OD are discussed by R A Gallagher, "What Is OD?" www.orgdct.com/what_is_od.htm, accessed May 12, 2005.

[27]The stages of OD are discussed by R Cacioppe and M Edwards, "Seeking the Holy Grail of Organizational Development: A Synthesis of Integral Theory, Spiral Dynamics, Corporate Transformation and Action Inquiry," *Leadership and Organization Development Journal,* no. 2, 2005, pp 86–105.

[28]W W Burke, *Organization Development: A Normative View* (Reading, MA: Addison-Wesley Publishing, 1987), p 9.

[29]See R Rodgers, J E Hunter, and D L Rogers, "Influence of Top Management Commitment on Management Program Success," *Journal of Applied Psychology,* February 1993, pp 151–55.

[30]Results can be found in P J Robertson, D R Roberts, and J I Porras, "Dynamics of Planned Organizational Change: Assessing Empirical Support for a Theoretical Model," *Academy of Management Journal,* June 1993, pp 619–34. Also see A Cusick, "Organizational Development Facilitates Effective Regulation Compliance," *Leadership and Organization Development Journal,* no. 2, 2005, pp 106–19.

[31]Results from the meta-analysis can be found in G A Neuman, J E Edwards, and N S Raju, "Organizational Development Interventions: A Meta-Analysis of Their Effects on Satisfaction and Other Attitudes," *Personnel Psychology,* Autumn 1989, pp 461–90.

[32]Results can be found in C-M Lau and H-Y Ngo, "Organization Development and Firm Performance: A Comparison of Multinational and Local Firms," *Journal of International Business Studies,* First Quarter 2001, pp 95–114.

[33]Adapted in part from B W Armentrout, "Have Your Plans for Change Had a Change of Plan?" *HR Focus,* January 1996, p 19; and A S Judson, *Changing Behavior in Organizations: Minimizing Resistance to Change* (Cambridge, MA: Blackwell, Inc., 1991).

[34]See "Vulnerability and Resilience," *American Psychologist,* January 1996, pp 22–28.

[35]See R Moss Kanter, "Managing Traumatic Change: Avoiding the 'Unlucky 13,' " *Management Review,* May 1987, pp 23–24.

[36]Details of this example are provided by B Schlender, "Inside the Shakeup at Sony," *Fortune* April 4, 2005, pp 94–104.

[37]See L Coch and J R P French Jr, "Overcoming Resistance to Change," *Human Relations,* 1948, pp 512–32.

[38]For a thorough review of the role of participation in organizational change, see W A Pasmore and M R Fagans, "Participation, Individual Development, and Organizational Change: A Review and Synthesis," *Journal of Management,* June 1992, pp 375–97.

[39]L Herscovitch and J P Meyer, "Commitment to Organizational Change: Extension of a Three-Component Model," *Journal of Applied Psychology,* June 2002, p 475.

[40]Ibid., pp 474–87.

[41]Research regarding resilience is discussed by K Kersting, "Resilience: The Mental Muscle Everyone Has," *Monitor on Psychology,* April 2005, pp 32–33; and S R Maddi, "On Hardiness and Other Pathways to Resilience," *American Psychologist,* April 2005, pp 261–63.

[42]Results can be found in C R Wanberg and J T Banas, "Predictors and Outcomes of Openness to Changes in a Reorganizing Workplace," *Journal of Applied Psychology,* February 2000, pp 132–42.

[43]Results from this study can be found in T A Judge, C J Thoresen, V Pucik, and T W Welbourne, "Managerial Coping with Organizational Change: A Dispositional Perspective," *Journal of Applied Psychology,* February 1999, pp 107–22.

[44]See Wanberg and Banas, "Predictors and Outcomes of Openness to Changes in a Reorganizing Workplace," pp 132–42.

[45]See the related discussion in E B Dent and S G Goldberg, "Challenging 'Resistance to Change,' " *Journal of Applied Behavioral Science,* March 1999, pp 25–41.

[46]J P Kotter, "Leading Change: Why Transformation Efforts Fail," *Harvard Business Review,* 1995, p 64.

[47]See the related discussion in S J Wall, "The Protean Organization: Learning to Love Change," *Organizational Dynamics,* February 2005, pp 37–46.

[48]Readiness for change is examined by L T Eby, D M Adams, J E A Russell, and S H Gaby, "Perceptions of Organizational Readiness for Change: Factors Related to Employees' Reactions to the Implementation of Team-Based Selling," *Human Relations,* March 2000, pp 419–42.

[49]See Q N Huy, "In Praise of Middle Managers," *Harvard Business Review,* September 2001, p 76.

[50]For a discussion of how managers can reduce resistance to change by providing different explanations for an organizational change, see D M Rousseau and S A Tijoriwala, "What's a Good Reason to Change? Motivated Reasoning and Social Accounts in Promoting Organizational Change," *Journal of Applied Psychology,* August 1999, pp 514–28.

[51]The stress response is thoroughly discussed by H Selye, *Stress without Distress* (New York: J B Lippincott, 1974).

[52]J M Ivancevich and M T Matteson, *Stress and Work: A Managerial Perspective* (Glenview, IL: Scott, Foresman, 1980), pp 8–9.

[53]See Selye, *Stress without Distress.*

[54]See T A Judge and J A Colquitt, "Organizational Justice and Stress: The Mediating Role of Work-Family Conflict," *Journal of Applied Psychology,* June 2004, pp 395–404; and P E Spector, C L Cooper, S Poelmans, T D Allen, M O'Driscoll, J I Sanchez, O L Siu, P Dewe, P Hart, and L Lu, "A Cross-National Comparative Study of Work-Family Stressors, Working Hours, and Well-Being: China and Latin America versus the Anglo World," *Personnel Psychology,* Spring 2004, pp 119–42.

[55]Supportive results can be found in F M McKee-Ryan, Z Song, C R Wanberg, and A J Kinicki, "Psychological and Physical Well-Being during Unemployment: A Meta-Analytic Study," *Journal of Applied Psychology,* January 2005, pp 53–76.

[56]This research is discussed in M Greer, "Strengthen Your Brain by Resting It," *Monitor on Psychology,* July–August 2004, pp 60–62.

[57]K Dybis, "Time-Tested Humans Reset Clocks in Dark," *Arizona Republic,* January 8, 2005, p D3.

[58]Supportive results can be found in V J Magley, C L Hulin, L F Fitzgerald, and M DeNardo, "Outcomes of Self-Labeling Sexual Harassment," *Journal of Applied Psychology,* June 1999, pp 390–402.

[59]See the related discussion in E M Hallowell, "Smart People Underperform," *Harvard Business Review,* January 2005, pp 55–62.

[60]The issue of environmental conditions is discussed by A Bruzzese, "Is Building Making You 'Sick' of Work?" *Arizona Republic,* January 29, 2005, p D3.

[61]The discussion of appraisal is based on R S Lazarus and S Folkman, *Stress, Appraisal, and Coping* (New York: Springer Publishing, 1984).

[62]This example was taken from S N Mehta, "Hear Them Roar: More Women Quit Lucrative Jobs to Start Their Own Businesses," *The Wall Street Journal,* November 11, 1996, pp A1, A4.

[63]See K Daniels and C Harris, "A Daily Dairy Study of Coping in the Context of the Job Demands-Control-Support Model," *Journal of Vocational Behavior,* April 2005, pp 199–218. Coping strategies were also investigated by L M Cortina and S A Wasti, "Profiles in Coping: Responses to Sexual Harassment across Persons, Organizations, and Cultures," *Journal of Applied Psychology,* January 2005, pp 182–92.

[64]Supportive results can be found in A Barsky, C J Thoresen, C R Warren, and S A Kaplan, "Modeling Negative Affectivity and Job Stress: A Contingency-Based Approach," *Journal of Organizational Behavior,* December 2004, pp 915–36; E M de Croon, J K Sluiter, R W B Blonk, J P J Broersen, and M H W Frings-Dresen, "Stressful Work, Psychological Job Strain, and Turnover: A 2-Year Prospective Cohort Study of Truck Drivers," *Journal of Applied Psychology,* June 2004, pp 442–54; and A J Kinicki, F M McKee-Ryan, C A Schriesheim, and K P Carson, "Assessing the Construct Validity of the Job Descriptive Index: A Review and Meta-Analysis," *Journal of Applied Psychology,* February 2002, pp 14–32.

[65]S Caminiti, "A New Health Care Prescription," *Fortune,* January 24, 2005, special advertising section, p S3.

[66]Supportive results can be found in P L Perrewé, K L Zellars, G R Ferris, A M Rossi, C J Kacmar, and D A Ralston, "Neutralizing Job Stressors: Political Skill as an Antidote to the Dysfunctional Consequences of Role Conflict," *Academy of Management Journal,* February 2004, pp 141–52; and D C Ganster, M L Fox, and D J Dwyer, "Explaining Employees' Health Care Costs: A Prospective Examination of Stressful Job Demands, Personal Control, and Physiological Reactivity," *Journal of Applied Psychology,* October 2001, pp 954–64.

[67]Types of support are discussed by S Cohen and T A Wills, "Stress, Social Support, and the Buffering Hypothesis," *Psychological Bulletin,* September 1985, pp 310–57.

[68]See the discussion in R A Clay, "Research to the Heart of the Matter," *Monitor on Psychology,* January 2001, pp 42–45.

[69]Supportive results can be found in L L Schirmer and F G Lopez, "Probing the Social Support and Work Strain Relationship among Adult Workers: Contributions of Adult Attachment Orientations," *Journal of Vocational Behavior,* August 2001, pp 17–33.

[70]This pioneering research is presented in S C Kobasa, "Stressful Life Events, Personality, and Health: An Inquiry into Hardiness," *Journal of Personality and Social Psychology,* January 1979, pp 1–11.

[71]See S C Kobasa, S R Maddi, and S Kahn, "Hardiness and Health: A Prospective Study," *Journal of Personality and Social Psychology,* January 1982, pp 168–77.

[72]Results can be found in V Florian, M Mikulincer, and O Taubman, "Does Hardiness Contribute to Mental Health during a Stressful Real Life Situation? The Roles of Appraisal and Coping," *Journal of Personality and Social Psychology,* April 1995, pp 687–95; and K L Horner, "Individuality in Vulnerability: Influences on Physical Health," *Journal of Health Psychology,* January 1998, pp 71–85.

[73]See C Robitschek and S Kashubeck, "A Structural Model of Parental Alcoholism, Family Functioning, and Psychological Health: The Mediating Effects of Hardiness and Personal Growth Orientation," *Journal of Counseling Psychology,* April 1999, pp 159–72.

[74]B Priel, N Gonik, and B Rabinowitz, "Appraisals of Childbirth Experience and Newborn Characteristics: The Role of Hardiness and Affect," *Journal of Personality,* September, 1993, pp 299–315.

[75]Results from this study are discussed in S R Maddi, "On Hardiness and Other Pathways to Resilience." *American Psychologist,* April 2005, pp 261–262.

[76]M Friedman and R H Rosenman, *Type A Behavior and Your Heart* (Greenwich, CT: Fawcett Publications, 1974), p 84. (Boldface added.)

[77]See C Lee, L F Jamieson, and P C Earley, "Beliefs and Fears and Type A Behavior: Implications for Academic Performance and Psychiatric Health Disorder Symptoms," *Journal of Organizational Behavior,* March 1996, pp 151–77; S D Bluen, J Barling, and W Burns, "Predicting Sales Performance, Job Satisfaction, and Depression by Using the Achievement Strivings and Impatience–Irritability Dimensions of Type A Behavior," *Journal of Applied Psychology,* April 1990, pp 212–16; and M S Taylor, E A Locke, C Lee and M E Gist, "Type A Behavior and Faculty Research Productivity: What Are the Mechanisms?" *Organizational Behavior and Human Performance,* December 1984, pp 402–18.

[78]Results from the meta-analysis are contained in S A Lyness, "Predictors of Differences between Type A and B Individuals in Heart Rate and Blood Pressure Reactivity," *Psychological Bulletin,* September 1993, pp 266–95.

[79]See S Booth-Kewley and H S Friedman, "Psychological Predictors of Heart Disease: A Quantitative Review" *Psychological Bulletin,* May 1987, pp 343–62. More recent results can be found in T Q Miller, T W Smith, C W Turner, M L Guijarro, A J Hallet, "A Meta-Analytic Review of Research on Hostility and Physical Health," *Psychological Bulletin,* March 1996, pp 322–48.

[80]Results from this study were reported in R Winslow and P Landers, "Obesity: A World-Wide Woe," *The Wall Street Journal,* July 1, 2002, pp B1, B4.

[81]These statistics were derived from J Norman, "Stress Relief Is Good Business," *Arizona Republic,* March 25, 2002, pp D1, D5.

[82]See S Reynolds, E Taylor, and D A Shapiro, "Session Impact in Stress Management Training," *Journal of Occupational Psychology,* June 1993, pp 99–113; and J M Ivancevich, M T Matteson, S M Freedman, and J S Phillips, "Worksite Stress Management Interventions," *American Psychologist,* February 1990, pp 252–61.

[83]An evaluation of stress-reduction programs is conducted by P A Landsbergis and E Vivona-Vaughan, "Evaluation of an Occupational Stress Intervention in a Public Agency," *Journal of Organizational Behavior,* January 1996, pp 29–48; and D C Ganster, B T Mayes, W E Sime, and G D Tharp, "Managing Organizational Stress: A Field Experiment," *Journal of Applied Psychology,* October 1982, pp 533–42.

[84]Descriptions of EAPs are provided by "Employee Assistance Programs," www.health.org/workplace/fedagencies/employee_assistance_programs.aspx, accessed May 18, 2005; and "Employee Assistance Programs," www.foh.dhhs.gov/Public/WhatWeDo/EAP/eap.asp, accessed May 18, 2005.

[85]R Kreitner, "Personal Wellness: It's Just Good Business," *Business Horizons,* May–June 1982, p 28.

[86]This statistic was reported in "Meeting the Challenge of Motivating Employees to Embrace Wellness," *HR Magazine,* May 2005, pp 15–17.

[87]A thorough review of this research is provided by D L Gebhardt and C E Crump, "Employee Fitness and Wellness Programs in the Workplace," *American Psychologist,* February 1990, pp 262–72.

[88]Excerpted from D Welch and D Beucke, "Why GM'S Plan Won't Work: And the Ugly Road Ahead," *BusinessWeek,* May 9, 2005, pp 85–87, 93. Reprinted by permission of The McGraw-Hill Companies, Inc.

[89]Based on a group exercise in L W Mealiea, *Skills for Managers in Organizations* (Burr Ridge, IL: Irwin, 1994), pp 198–201. © 1994. Reprinted by permission of the McGraw-Hill Companies, Inc.

[90]Parts of the force-field analysis form was quoted directly from ibid., pp 199, 201.

[91]Excerpted from E Tanouye, "What Happens When It's the Boss Who's Suffering?" *The Wall Street Journal,* June 13, 2001, pp B1, B6.

Glossary

ability Stable characteristic responsible for a person's maximum physical or mental performance.

accountability practices Focus on treating diverse employees fairly.

adaptive perspective Assumes that adaptive cultures enhance a firm's financial performance.

affective component The feelings or emotions one has about an object or situation.

affirmative action Focuses on achieving equality of opportunity in an organization.

aggressive style Expressive and self-enhancing, but takes unfair advantage of others.

alternative dispute resolution Avoiding costly lawsuits by resolving conflicts informally or through mediation or arbitration.

Americans with Disabilities Act Prohibits discrimination against the disabled.

anticipatory socialization Occurs before an individual joins an organization, and involves the information people learn about different careers, occupations, professions, and organizations.

Asch effect Giving in to a unanimous but wrong opposition.

assertive style Expressive and self-enhancing, but does not take advantage of others.

attention Being consciously aware of something or someone.

attitude Learned predisposition toward a given object.

availability heuristic Tendency to base decisions on information readily available in memory.

benchmarking Process by which a company compares its performance with that of high-performing organizations.

blog Online journal in which people comment on any topic.

bounded rationality Constraints that restrict rational decision making.

brainstorming Process to generate a quantity of ideas.

care perspective Involves compassion and an ideal of attention and response to need.

career plateauing The end result when the probability of being promoted is very small.

case study In-depth study of a single person, group, or organization.

causal attributions Suspected or inferred causes of behavior.

centralized decision making Top managers make all key decisions.

change and acquisition Requires employees to master tasks and roles and to adjust to work group values and norms.

closed system A relatively self-sufficient entity.

coalition Temporary groupings of people who actively pursue a single issue.

coercive power Obtaining compliance through threatened or actual punishment.

cognitions A person's knowledge, opinions, or beliefs.

cognitive categories Mental depositories for storing information.

cognitive dissonance Psychological discomfort experienced when attitudes and behavior are inconsistent.

cohesiveness A sense of "we-ness" helps group stick together.

collectivist culture Personal goals less important than community goals and interests.

commitment to change A mind-set of doing whatever it takes to effectively implement change.

communication Interpersonal exchange of information and understanding.

communication competence Ability to effectively use communication behaviors in a given context.

conflict One party perceives its interests are being opposed or set back by another party.

conflict triangle Conflicting parties involve a third person rather than dealing directly with each other.

consensus Presenting opinions and gaining agreement to support a decision.

consideration Creating mutual respect and trust with followers.

content theories of motivation Identify internal factors influencing motivation.

contingency approach Using management tools and techniques in a situationally appropriate manner; avoiding the one-best-way mentality.

contingency approach to organization design Creating an effective organization–environment fit.

contingency factors Variables that influence the appropriateness of a leadership style.

continuous reinforcement Reinforcing every instance of a behavior.

control strategy Coping strategy that directly confronts or solves problems.

core job dimensions Job characteristics found to various degrees in all jobs.

creativity Process of developing something new or unique.

cross-cultural management Understanding and teaching behavioral patterns in different cultures.

cross-cultural training Structured experiences to help people adjust to a new culture/country.

cross-functionalism Team made up of technical specialists from different areas.

cultural intelligence The ability to interpret ambiguous cross-cultural situations accurately.

culture Beliefs and values about how a community of people should and do act.

culture shock Anxiety and doubt caused by an overload of new expectations and cues.

decentralized decision making Lower-level managers are empowered to make important decisions.

decision making Identifying and choosing solutions that lead to a desired end result.

decision-making style A combination of how individuals perceive and respond to information.

delegation Granting decision-making authority to people at lower levels.

Delphi technique Process to generate ideas from physically dispersed experts.

development practices Focus on preparing diverse employees for greater responsibility and advancement.

developmental relationship strength The quality of relationships among people in a network.

devil's advocacy Assigning someone the role of critic.

dialectic method Fostering a debate of opposing viewpoints to better understand an issue.

differentiation Division of labor and specialization that causes people to think and act differently.

discrimination Occurs when employment decisions are based on factors that are not job related.

distributive justice The perceived fairness of how resources and rewards are distributed.

diversity The host of individual differences that make people different from and similar to each other.

diversity of developmental relationships The variety of people in a network used for developmental assistance.

dysfunctional conflict Threatens organization's interests.

e-business Running the *entire* business via the Internet.

electronic mail Uses the Internet/intranet to send computer-generated text and documents.

emotional intelligence Ability to manage oneself and interact with others in mature and constructive ways.

emotions Complex human reactions to personal achievements and setbacks that may be felt and displayed.

employee assistance programs Help employees to resolve personal problems that affect their productivity.

empowerment Sharing varying degrees of power with lower-level employees to tap their full potential.

enacted values The values and norms that are exhibited by employees.

encounter phase Employees learn what the organization is really like and reconcile unmet expectations.

equity sensitivity An individual's tolerance for negative and positive equity.

equity theory Holds that motivation is a function of fairness in social exchanges.

ERG theory Three basic needs—existence, relatedness, and growth—influence behavior.

escalation of commitment Sticking to an ineffective course of action too long.

escape strategy Coping strategy that avoids or ignores stressors and problems.

espoused values The stated values and norms that are preferred by an organization.

ethics Study of moral issues and choices.

ethnocentrism Belief that one's native country, culture, language, and behavior are superior.

eustress Stress that is good or produces a positive outcome.

expatriate Anyone living or working in a foreign country.

expectancy Belief that effort leads to a specific level of performance.

expectancy theory Holds that people are motivated to behave in ways that produce valued outcomes.

expert power Obtaining compliance through one's knowledge or information.

explicit knowledge Information that can be easily put into words and shared with others.

external factors Environmental characteristics that cause behavior.

external forces for change Originate outside the organization.

external locus of control Attributing outcomes to circumstances beyond one's control.

extinction Making behavior occur less often by ignoring or not reinforcing it.

extranet Connects internal employees with selected customers, suppliers, and strategic partners.

extrinsic motivation Motivation caused by the desire to attain specific outcomes.

extrinsic rewards Financial, material, or social rewards from the environment.

feedback Objective information about performance.

field study Examination of variables in real-life settings.

fight-or-flight response To either confront stressors or try to avoid them.

fit perspective Assumes that culture must align with its business or strategic context.

formal communication channels Follow the chain of command or organizational structure.

formal group Formed by the organization.

functional conflict Serves organization's interests.

fundamental attribution bias
Ignoring environmental factors that affect behavior.

Galatea effect   An individual's high self-expectations lead to high performance.

genderflex   Temporarily using communication behaviors typical of the other gender.

glass ceiling   Invisible barrier blocking women and minorities from top management positions.

goal   What an individual is trying to accomplish.

goal commitment   Amount of commitment to achieving a goal.

goal difficulty   The amount of effort required to meet a goal.

goal specificity   Quantifiability of a goal.

Golem effect   Loss in performance due to low leader expectations.

grapevine   Unofficial communication system of the informal organization.

group   Two or more freely interacting people with shared norms and goals and a common identity.

group cohesiveness   A "we feeling" binding group members together.

group support systems   Using computer software and hardware to help people work better together.

groupthink   Janis's term for a cohesive in-group's unwillingness to realistically view alternatives.

hardiness   Personality characteristic that neutralizes stress.

high-context cultures   Primary meaning derived from nonverbal situational cues.

holistic wellness approach
Advocates personal responsibility for healthy living.

human capital   The productive potential of one's knowledge and actions.

humility   Considering the contributions of others and good fortune when gauging one's success.

hygiene factors   Job characteristics associated with job dissatisfaction.

impression management   Getting others to see us in a certain manner.

individualistic culture   Primary emphasis on personal freedom and choice.

informal communication channels
Do not follow chain of command or organizational structure.

informal group   Formed by friends or those with common interests.

information/decision making theory   Diversity leads to better task-relevant processes and decision making.

information richness   Information-carrying capacity of data.

in-group exchange   A partnership characterized by mutual trust, respect, and liking.

initiating structure   Organizing and defining what group members should be doing.

instrumental cohesiveness   Sense of togetherness based on mutual dependency needed to get the job done.

instrumental values   Personally preferred ways of behaving.

instrumentality   A performance→ outcome perception.

integration   Cooperation among specialists to achieve a common goal.

intelligence   Capacity for constructive thinking, reasoning, problem solving.

interactional justice   Extent to which people feel fairly treated when procedures are implemented.

intermittent reinforcement
Reinforcing some but not all instances of behavior.

internal factors   Personal characteristics that cause behavior.

internal forces for change
Originate inside the organization.

internal locus of control
Attributing outcomes to one's own actions.

Internet   A global system of computer networks.

intranet   An organization's private Internet.

intrinsic motivation   Motivation caused by positive internal feelings.

intrinsic rewards   Self-granted, psychic rewards.

intuition   Making a choice without the use of conscious thought or logical inference.

job design   Changing the content or process of a specific job to increase job satisfaction and performance.

job enlargement   Putting more variety into a job.

job enrichment   Building achievement, recognition, stimulating work, responsibility, and advancement into a job.

job involvement   Extent to which an individual is immersed in his or her present job.

job rotation   Moving employees from one specialized job to another.

job satisfaction   An affective or emotional response to one's job.

judgmental heuristics   Rules of thumb or shortcuts that people use to reduce information-processing demands.

justice perspective   Based on the ideal of reciprocal rights and driven by rules and regulations.

knowledge management
Implementing systems and practices that increase the sharing of knowledge and information throughout an organization.

laboratory study   Manipulation and measurement of variables in contrived situations.

law of effect   Behavior with favorable consequences is repeated; behavior with unfavorable consequences disappears.

leader–member relations   Extent that leader has the support, loyalty, and trust of work group.

leader trait   Personal characteristics that differentiate leaders from followers.

leadership   Process whereby an individual influences others to achieve a common goal.

leadership prototype Mental representation of the traits and behaviors possessed by leaders.

learned helplessness Debilitating lack in one's ability to control the situation.

learning goal Encourages learning, creativity, and skill development.

learning organization Proactively creates, acquires, and transfers knowledge throughout the organization.

legitimate power Obtaining compliance through formal authority.

liaison individuals Those who consistently pass along grapevine information to others.

line managers Have authority to make organizational decisions.

linguistic style A person's typical speaking pattern.

listening Actively decoding and interpreting verbal messages.

low-context cultures Primary meaning derived from written and spoken words.

maintenance roles Relationship-building group behavior.

management Process of working with and through others to achieve organizational objectives efficiently and ethically.

management by objectives Management system incorporating participation in decision making, goal setting, and feedback.

managing diversity Creating organizational changes that enable all people to perform up to their maximum potential.

mechanistic organizations Rigid, command-and-control bureaucracies.

mentoring Process of forming and maintaining developmental relationships between a mentor and a junior person.

met expectations The extent to which one receives what he or she expects from a job.

meta-analysis Pools the results of many studies through statistical procedure.

mission statement Summarizes "why" an organization exists.

monochronic time Preference for doing one thing at a time because time is limited, precisely segmented, and schedule driven.

motivation Psychological processes that arouse and direct goal-directed behavior.

motivators Job characteristics associated with job satisfaction.

mutuality of interest Balancing individual and organizational interests through win-win cooperation.

need for achievement Desire to accomplish something difficult.

need for affiliation Desire to spend time in social relationships and activities.

need for power Desire to influence, coach, teach, or encourage others to achieve.

need hierarchy theory Five basic needs—physiological, safety, love, esteem, and self-actualization—influence behavior.

needs Physiological or psychological deficiencies that arouse behavior.

negative inequity Comparison in which another person receives greater outcomes for similar inputs.

negative reinforcement Making behavior occur more often by contingently withdrawing something negative.

negotiation Give-and-take process between conflicting interdependent parties.

noise Interference with the transmission and understanding of a message.

nominal group technique Process to generate ideas and evaluate solutions.

nonassertive style Timid and self-denying behavior.

nonverbal communication Messages sent outside of the written or spoken word.

norm Shared attitudes, opinions, feelings, or actions that guide social behavior.

normative beliefs Thoughts and beliefs about expected behavior and modes of conduct.

onboarding Programs aimed at helping employees integrate, assimilate, and transition to new jobs.

open system Organism that must constantly interact with its environment to survive.

operant behavior Skinner's term for learned, consequence-shaped behavior.

optimizing Choosing the best possible solution.

organic organizations Fluid and flexible networks of multitalented people.

organization System of consciously coordinated activities of two or more people.

organization chart Boxes-and-lines illustration showing chain of formal authority and division of labor.

organization development A set of techniques or tools used to implement organizational change.

organizational behavior Interdisciplinary field dedicated to better understanding and managing people at work.

organizational citizenship behaviors (OCBs) Employee behaviors that exceed work-role requirements.

organizational commitment Extent to which an individual identifies with an organization and its goals.

organizational culture Shared values and beliefs that underlie a company's identity.

organizational decline Decrease in organization's resource base (money, customers, talent, innovations).

organizational identification Organizational values or beliefs become part of one's self-identity.

organizational moles Those who use the grapevine to enhance their power and status.

organizational politics Intentional enhancement of self-interest.

organizational socialization Process by which employees learn an organization's values, norms, and required behaviors.

ostracism Rejection by other group members.

out-group exchange A partnership characterized by a lack of mutual trust, respect, and liking.

participative management Involving employees in various aspects of decision making.

pay for performance Monetary incentives tied to one's results or accomplishments.

perception Process of interpreting one's environment.

perceptual model of communication Process in which receivers create their own meaning.

performance management Continuous cycle of improving job performance with goal setting, feedback and coaching, and rewards and positive reinforcement.

performance outcome goal Targets a specific end-result.

persistence Extent to which effort is expended on a task over time.

personal initiative Going beyond formal job requirements and being an active self-starter.

personality Stable physical and mental characteristics responsible for a person's identity.

personality conflict Interpersonal opposition driven by personal dislike or disagreement.

personalized power Directed at helping oneself.

polychronic time Preference for doing more than one thing at a time because time is flexible and multidimensional.

position power Degree to which leader has formal power.

positive inequity Comparison in which another person receives lesser outcomes for similar inputs.

positive organizational behavior (POB) The study and improvement of employees' positive attributes and capabilities.

positive reinforcement Making behavior occur more often by contingently presenting something positive.

primary appraisal Determining whether a stressor is irrelevant, positive, or stressful.

proactive personality Action-oriented person who shows initiative and perseveres to change things.

problem Gap between an actual and desired situation.

procedural justice The perceived fairness of the process and procedures used to make allocation decisions.

process theories of motivation Identify the process by which internal factors and cognitions influence motivation.

programmed conflict Encourages different opinions without protecting management's personal feelings.

propensity to trust A personality trait involving one's general willingness to trust others.

proxemics Hall's term for the study of cultural expectations about interpersonal space.

psychological contract An individual's perception about the terms and conditions of a reciprocal exchange with another party.

punishment Making behavior occur less often by contingently presenting something negative or withdrawing something positive.

purposeful communication distortion Purposely modifying the content of a message.

quality circles Small groups of volunteers who strive to solve quality-related problems.

rational model Logical four-step approach to decision making.

realistic job preview Presents both positive and negative aspects of a job.

recruitment practices Attempts to attract qualified, diverse employees at all levels.

referent power Obtaining compliance through charisma or personal attraction.

representativeness heuristic Tendency to assess the likelihood of an

event occurring based on impressions about similar occurrences.

resilience to change Composite personal characteristic reflecting high self-esteem, optimism, and an internal locus of control.

resistance to change Emotional/behavioral response to real or imagined work changes.

respondent behavior Skinner's term for unlearned stimulus–response reflexes.

reward power Obtaining compliance with promised or actual rewards.

role ambiguity Others' expectations are unknown.

role conflict Others have conflicting or inconsistent expectations.

role overload Others' expectations exceed one's ability.

roles Expected behaviors for a given position.

sample survey Questionnaire responses from a sample of people.

satisficing Choosing a solution that meets a minimum standard of acceptance.

scenario technique Speculative forecasting method.

schema Mental picture of an event or object.

scientific management Using research and experimentation to find the most efficient way to perform a job.

secondary appraisal Assessing what might and can be done to reduce stress.

self-concept Person's self-perception as a physical, social, spiritual being.

self-efficacy Belief in one's ability to do a task.

self-esteem One's overall self-evaluation.

self-fulfilling prophecy Someone's high expectations for another person result in high performance.

self-managed teams Groups of employees granted administrative oversight for their work.

self-management leadership
Process of leading others to lead
themselves.

self-monitoring   Observing one's
own behavior and adapting it to the
situation.

self-serving bias   Taking more
personal responsibility for success than
failure.

servant-leadership   Focuses on
increased service to others rather than to
oneself.

sex-role stereotype   Beliefs about
appropriate roles for men and women.

shaping   Reinforcing closer and closer
approximations to a target behavior.

shared leadership   Simultaneous,
ongoing, mutual influence process in
which people share responsibility for
leading.

situational theories   Propose that
leader styles should match the situation
at hand.

skill   Specific capacity to manipulate
objects.

social capital   The productive
potential of strong, trusting, and
cooperative relationships.

social categorization theory
Similarity leads to liking and attraction.

social loafing   Decrease in individual
effort as group size increases.

social power   Ability to get things
done with human, informational, and
material resources.

social support   Amount of helpfulness derived from social relationships.

socialized power   Directed at helping
others.

socio-emotional cohesiveness
Sense of togetherness based on
emotional satisfaction.

span of control   The number of
people reporting directly to a given
manager.

staff personnel   Provide research,
advice, and recommendations to line
managers.

stakeholder audit   Systematic
identification of all parties likely to be
affected by the organization.

stereotype   Beliefs about the
characteristics of a group.

strategic constituency   Any group
of people with a stake in the
organization's operation or success.

strategic plan   A long-term plan
outlining actions needed to achieve
desired results.

strength perspective   Assumes that
the strength of corporate culture is
related to a firm's financial performance.

stress   Behavioral, physical, or
psychological response to stressors.

stressors   Environmental factors that
produce stress.

symptom management strategy
Coping strategy that focuses on reducing
the symptoms of stress.

tacit knowledge   Information gained
through experience that is difficult to
express and formalize.

target elements of change
Components of an organization that may
be changed.

task roles   Task-oriented group
behavior.

task structure   Amount of structure
contained within work tasks.

team   Small group with
complementary skills who hold
themselves mutually accountable for
common purpose, goals, and approach.

team-based pay   Linking pay to
teamwork behavior and/or team results.

team building   Experiential learning
aimed at better internal functioning of
groups.

team viability   Team members
satisfied and willing to contribute.

telecommuting   Doing work that is
generally performed in the office away
from the office using different
information technologies.

terminal values   Personally preferred
end-states of existence.

theory   A story defining key terms,
providing a conceptual framework, and
explaining why something occurs.

Theory Y   McGregor's modern and
positive assumptions about employees
being responsible and creative.

360-degree feedback   Comparison
of anonymous feedback from one's
superior, subordinates, and peers with
self-perceptions.

total quality management   An
organizational culture dedicated to
training, continuous improvement, and
customer satisfaction.

transactional leadership   Focuses
on interpersonal interactions between
managers and employees.

transformational leadership
Transforms employees to pursue
organizational goals over self-interests.

trust   Reciprocal faith in others'
intentions and behavior.

Type A behavior pattern
Aggressively involved in a chronic,
determined struggle to accomplish more
in less time.

underemployment   The result of
taking a job that requires less education,
training, or skills than possessed by a
worker.

unity of command principle   Each
employee should report to a single
manager.

upward feedback   Subordinates
evaluate their boss.

valence   The value of a reward or
outcome.

value attainment   The extent to
which a job allows fulfillment of one's
work values.

value system   The organization of
one's beliefs about preferred ways of
behaving and desired end-states.

**value congruence or person–
culture fit**   The similarity between
personal values and organizational
values.

values   Enduring belief in a mode of
conduct or end-state.

virtual team   Information technology
allows group members in different
locations to conduct business.

vision   Long-term goal describing
"what" an organization wants to
become.

withdrawal cognitions   Overall
thoughts and feelings about quitting a
job.

workforce demographics
Statistical profiles of adult workers.

Name Index

Subject Index